P9-CCI-400

"No other guide has as much to offer . . . these books are a pleasure to read."   Gene Shalit on the *Today Show*

". . . Excellently organized for the casual traveler who is looking for a mix of recreation and cultural insight."
Washington Post

★ ★ ★ ★ ★ (5-star rating) "Crisply written and remarkably personable. Cleverly organized so you can pluck out the minutest fact in a moment. Satisfyingly thorough."
Réalités

"The information they offer is up-to-date, crisply presented but far from exhaustive, the judgments knowledgeable but not opinionated."   *New York Times*

"The individual volumes are compact, the prose succinct, and the coverage up-to-date and knowledgeable . . . The format is portable and the index admirably detailed."
John Barkham Syndicate

". . . An abundance of excellent directions, diversions, and facts, including perspectives and getting-ready-to-go advice — succinct, detailed, and well organized in an easy-to-follow style."   *Los Angeles Times*

"They contain an amount of information that is truly staggering, besides being surprisingly current."
Detroit News

"These guides address themselves to the needs of the modern traveler demanding precise, qualitative information . . . Upbeat, slick, and well put together."
Dallas Morning News

". . . Attractive to look at, refreshingly easy to read, and generously packed with information."   *Miami Herald*

"These guides are as good as any published, and much better than most."   *Louisville* (Kentucky) *Times*

Stephen Birnbaum Travel Guides

Canada
Caribbean, Bermuda, and the Bahamas
Disneyland
Europe
Europe for Business Travelers
Florida for Free
France
Great Britain
Hawaii
Ireland
Italy
Mexico
South America
Spain and Portugal
United States
USA for Business Travelers
Walt Disney World

CONTRIBUTING EDITORS

Andrew Allentuck
Diana Barkley
Libby Barlow
Susan Baumgartner
Cathy Beason
Cristine Bye Beaty
Janet Bennett
Kevin Causey
Elizabeth Chambers
Stacey Chanin
Suzanne Chicoine
Mike Cramond
Richard Daignault
Rebecca Day
Linda Drouin
Sean Fine
Ted Folke
Joan Fulcher

Louise Gagnon
Margot Gibb-Clark
Jurgen Göthe
Horward Horwood
Sam Jannarone
Geoff Johnson
Mark Kalish
David Katz
Jerome Knap
Andrea Lang
Bruce Little
Patricia Lowe
Anne Millman
Marilyn Mirabelli
Gordon Morash
Brigit Paradis
Michael Perreca
Kevin Pittman

John Porteous
New Powers
Alan Rach
Allan Rocach
Len Russo
Roland Semjanovs
Jonathan Siskin
Gillian Steward
Joan Sullivan
Jennifer Taylor
Colleen Thompson
Ian Thompson
Michael Trembly
Sally Warren
Loralee Wenger
Leslie Westbrook
Amy Zierler
Kristin Zimmerman

COVER   Robert Anthony

MAPS   B. Andrew Mudryk   SYMBOLS   Gloria McKeown

A Stephen Birnbaum Travel Guide

Birnbaum's
CANADA
1991

Stephen Birnbaum
Alexandra Mayes Birnbaum
EDITORS

Lois Spritzer
EXECUTIVE EDITOR

Laura L. Brengelman
Managing Editor

Kristin Moehlmann
Senior Editor

Ann-Rebecca Laschever
Julie Quick
Beth Schlau
Associate Editors

Julie Hassinger Marks
Assistant Editor

HOUGHTON MIFFLIN COMPANY / BOSTON 1990

Copyright © 1990 by Houghton Mifflin Company

All rights reserved.

For information about permission to reproduce selections from this book, write to Permissions, Houghton Mifflin Company, 2 Park Street, Boston, Massachusetts 02108.

ISBN: 0-395-55735-6
ISSN: 0749-2561 (Stephen Birnbaum Travel Guides)
ISSN: 0884-1039 (Canada)

Printed in the United States of America

WP 10 9 8 7 6 5 4 3 2 1

Contents

GETTING READY TO GO

A mini-encyclopedia of all the practical travel data you need to plan your vacation down to the final detail.

When and How to Go

Preparing

On the Road

PERSPECTIVES

A cultural and historical survey of Canada's past and present, its people, politics, and heritage.

THE CITIES

Thorough, qualitative guides to each of the nine cities most often visited by vacationers and businesspeople. Each section, a comprehensive report of the city's most compelling attractions and amenities, is designed to be used on the spot. Directions and recommendations are immediately accessible because each guide is presented in a consistent form.

DIVERSIONS

A selective guide to 15 active and cerebral vacations, including the places to pursue them where your quality of experience is likely to be highest.

For the Experience

DIRECTIONS

Canada's most spectacular routes and roads, most arresting natural wonders, most magnificent parks and forests, all organized into 45 specific driving tours.

Newfoundland

The Northwest Territories

Nova Scotia

Ontario

Prince Edward Island

Quebec

Saskatchewan

The Yukon Territory

A Word from the Editor

Most veteran transatlantic air travelers had a less than auspicious introduction to Canada, since the old propeller plane route to and from Europe usually included a stop in Gander (Newfoundland), hardly the Confederation's most scenic spot. A broader recognition of Canada's abundant attractions came somewhat later, and it is really only in recent years — with the coming of a couple of Expos and a pair of Olympic extravaganzas — that Canada's travel bounty has even begun to be understood by the rest of the world.

Part of the problem of comprehending all that Canada has to offer is the sheer size of the undertaking. Few countries offer as vast a panorama or as diverse a spectrum of landscapes — to say nothing of the variety of ethnic and cultural influences. To even the most cursory observer, Canada seems at least three countries: the marvelously austere Maritimes of the east, the fiercely French Quebecois nearer the center of the continent, and the vast sweep of the pioneer west that stretches from the province of Ontario (just above the Great Lakes) to the Pacific Ocean. And that doesn't even begin to consider the trackless wilderness of the Yukon and the Northwest Territories.

Canada is one of my own favorite travel destinations, so creating and revising this book has been more joy than toil; even my least pleasant experiences in Canada have enhanced my appreciation of Canadian kindness and the hospitality that is regularly offered to visitors. I recall with some embarrassment the occasion of being stopped by an unmarked patrol car of the Royal Canadian Mounted Police — they call them "ghost" cars in Canada — and getting myself set for the sort of dressing down that my speed would have earned me in any other country. Instead, the RCMP officer was almost apologetic in warning me that driving too fast might well endanger my safety, and I was sent on my way with just that warning — and a very pleasant one at that. It not only made me observe the speed limit thereafter, but also made me feel particularly welcome and well cared for in what was, after all, a foreign land.

For visitors from the US, the foreign quality of Canada can take on quite a different cast from place to place. The dour demeanor of the Atlantic provinces is an extension (and occasionally an exaggeration) of the inscrutable mien that is regularly encountered in Maine. In contrast, the Canadian west — from the flat prairies of Saskatchewan and Manitoba to the islands of Vancouver Harbour — are almost unfailingly and heartily friendly; this is the segment of Canada where it is most difficult to realize that you have crossed a national border.

French Canada has come to be a somewhat different matter, and Montreal's advertisement of itself as "the second-largest French-speaking city in the world" has lately taken on new meaning. (We won't tell them that they've lately dropped to fourth place, behind Paris, Nice, and Kinshasa.) As a vacation alternative to Paris, Montreal has substantial appeal both in its ambience and in the fact that the US dollar currently fares far better in Canada than in Europe. But the newly revitalized separatist spirit has shown its face in a myriad of ways, including the frequent reluctance of Montreal cabdrivers to speak English to US visitors. For the visitor, however, this slight inconvenience may prove oddly welcome; it means that the Montreal taxi ranks now more closely approximate the indifference regularly shown foreign visitors in France.

In creating this guide, we've tried as much as possible to offer some insights into a country that we consider vastly underrated as a tourist destination. The genesis of this book was clearly our own increasing interest in the Canadian countryside and urban experience, and our perception that more and more of our sophisticated and knowledgeable traveling acquaintances were reporting extremely pleasant experiences just north of the US border.

But I should, I think, apologize for at least one indulgence in this text that is baldly chauvinistic, and that is our constant reference to citizens of the US as "Americans." Strictly speaking, Canadian citizens are just as much residents of the North American continent as US citizens, and we apologize for any slight our Canadian readers may feel about our having appropriated this terminology. It was done strictly in an effort to simplify the narrative, rather than an attempt to appropriate a common continental distinction.

As I've indicated, part of Canada's appeal is its extremely wide variety of terrain and cultural influence. And although Canada is often referred to as a single destination, it is actually a dazzling blend of ethnic and historic diversity. While this diversity often spawns internal political confrontations, a visitor is more likely to notice environments and atmospheres that are almost always intriguing and often unique. So in preparing this guide, we have tried to produce a book that accurately reflects the variety of the appeal of this vast country.

In the same way, the increasing and broadening sophistication of US travelers — no matter where they are headed — has made it essential that any Canadian guidebook reflect and keep pace with the real needs of its prospective readers. That's why we've tried to create a guide that's specifically organized, written, and edited for today's more demanding modern audience, travelers for whom qualitative information is infinitely more desirable than mere quantities of unappraised data. We think that this book — as well as the other guides in our series — represents a new generation of travel guides, ones that are especially responsive to contemporary needs and nuances.

For years, dating back as far as Herr Baedeker, travel guides have tended to be encyclopedic, seemingly much more concerned with demonstrating expertise in geography and history than in any analysis of the sorts of things that more naturally concern a typical modern tourist. But today, when it is hardly necessary to tell a traveler where Vancouver is located, it is hard to justify devoting endless pages to historical perspectives. In many cases, the traveler has been to Canada nearly as often as the guidebook editor, so it becomes the responsibility of that editor to provide new perspectives and to suggest new directions in order to make his guide genuinely valuable.

That's exactly what we've tried to do in this series. I think you'll notice a different, more contemporary tone to the text, as well as an organization and focus that are distinctive and more functional. And even a random reading of what follows will demonstrate a substantial departure from the standard guidebook orientation, for we've not only attempted to provide information of a more compelling sort, but we also have tried to present the data in a format that makes it particularly accessible.

Needless to say, it's difficult to decide what to include in a guide of this size — and what to omit. Early on, we realized that giving up the encyclopedic approach precluded listing every single route and restaurant, a realization that helped define our overall editorial focus. Similarly, when we discussed ways of presenting certain information in other than strict geographic order, we found that the new format enabled us to arrange data in a way we feel best answers the questions travelers typically ask.

Large numbers of specific questions have provided the real editorial skeleton for this book. The volume of mail I regularly receive seems to emphasize that modern travelers want very precise information, so we've tried to address these needs and have organized our material in the most responsive way possible. Readers who want to know about the best restaurant in Montreal, the steepest peak in British Columbia, or the best beach on Prince Edward Island will have no trouble extracting that data from this guide.

Travel guides are, above all, reflections of personal taste, and putting one's name on a title page obviously puts one's preferences on the line. But I think I ought to amplify just what "personal" means. I don't believe in the sort of personal guidebook that's a palpable misrepresentation on its face. It is, for example, hardly possible for any single travel writer to visit thousands of restaurants (and nearly that many hotels) in any given year and provide accurate appraisals of each one. And even if it were physically possible for one human being to survive such an itinerary, it would of necessity have to be done at a dead sprint, and the perceptions derived therefrom would probably be less valid than those of any other intelligent individual visiting the same establishments. It is, therefore, impossible (especially in a large, annually revised guidebook *series* such as we offer) to have only one person provide all the data on the entire world.

I also happen to think that such individual orientation is of substantially less value to readers. Visiting a single hotel for just one night or eating one hasty meal in a random restaurant hardly equips anyone to provide appraisals that are of more than passing interest. No amount of doggedly alliterative or oppressively onomatopoeic text can camouflage a technique that is essentially specious on its face. We have, therefore, chosen what I like to describe as the "thee and me" approach to restaurant and hotel appraisal and, to a somewhat more limited degree, to the sites and sights we have included in the other sections of our text. What this really reflects is personal sampling tempered by intelligent counsel from informed local sources; these additional friends-of-the-editors are almost always residents of the city and/or area about which they have been consulted.

Despite the presence of several editors, a considerable number of writers, researchers, and local correspondents, very precise editing and tailoring keep our text fiercely subjective. So what follows is purposely designed to be the gospel according to the Birnbaums, and it represents as much of our own tastes and preferences as we can manage. It is probable, therefore, that if you like your cities stylish and your mountains uncrowded, prefer small hotels with personality to huge high-rise anonymities, and can't tolerate vegetables or fresh fish that have been relentlessly overcooked, we're likely to have a long and meaningful relationship. Readers with dissimilar tastes may be less enraptured.

I also should point out something about the person to whom this guidebook is directed. Above all, he or she is a "visitor." This means that such elements as restaurants have been specifically picked to provide the visitor with a representative, illuminating, stimulating, and above all pleasant experience. Since so many extraneous considerations can affect the reception and service accorded a regular restaurant patron, our choices can in no way be construed as an exhaustive guide to resident dining. We think we've listed all the best places in various price ranges, but they were chosen with a visitor's perspective in mind.

Other evidence of how we've tried to tailor our text to reflect changing travel habits is most apparent in the section we call DIVERSIONS. Where once it was common for travelers to spend a Canadian visit nailed to a single spot, the emphasis today is more on pursuing some athletic enterprise or special interest while seeing the surrounding countryside. So we've selected every activity we could reasonably evaluate and have organized the material in a way that is especially accessible to activists of either an athletic or cerebral bent. It is no longer necessary, therefore, to wade through a pound or two of extraneous prose just to find the best golf course or quaintest country inn within a reasonable radius of your destination.

If there is a single thing that best characterizes the revolution and evolution of current travel habits, it is that most travelers now consider travel a right rather than a privilege. Travel today translates as the enthusiastic desire to sample all of the world's opportunities, to find that elusive quality of experience that is not only enriching but comfortable. For that reason, we've tried to make what follows not only helpful and enlightening, but also the sort of welcome companion of which every traveler dreams.

I also should point out that every good travel guide is a living enterprise; that is, no part of this text is carved in stone. In our annual revisions, we expect to refine, expand, and further hone all our material to serve your travel needs even better. To this end, no contribution is of greater value to us than your personal reaction to what we have written, as well as information reflecting your own experiences while using our book. We earnestly and enthusiastically solicit your comments about this guide *and* your opinions and perceptions about places you have recently visited. In this way, we will be able to provide the most current information — including the actual experiences of recent travelers — to make those experiences more readily available to others. Please write to us at 60 E. 42nd St., New York, NY 10165.

We sincerely hope to hear from you.

STEPHEN BIRNBAUM

How to Use This Guide

A great deal of care has gone into the organization of this guide-book, and we believe it represents a real breakthrough in the presentation of travel information. Our aim is to create a new, more modern generation of travel books, and to make this guide the most useful and practical travel tool available today.

Our text is divided into five basic sections in order to present information in the most useful way on every possible aspect of a Canadian trip. This organization itself should alert you to the vast and varied opportunities available, as well as indicate all the specific data necessary to plan a successful visit. You won't find much of the conventional "swaying palms and shimmering sands" text in this guide; we've chosen instead to deliver more useful and practical information. Prospective Canadian itineraries tend to speak for themselves, and with so many diverse travel opportunities, we feel our main job is to highlight what's where and to provide basic details — how, when, where, how much, and what's best — to assist you in making the most intelligent choices possible.

Here is a brief summary of the five basic sections of this book and what you can expect to find in each. We believe that you will find both your travel planning and en route enjoyment enhanced considerably by having this book at your side.

GETTING READY TO GO

This mini-encyclopedia of practical travel facts is a sort of know-it-all companion with all the precise information necessary to create a successful trip through Canada. There are entries on more than 2 dozen separate topics, including how to travel, what preparations to make before leaving, what to expect in the different regions of Canada, what your trip is likely to cost, and how to avoid prospective problems. The individual entries are specific, realistic, and, where appropriate, cost-oriented. Except where noted, all prices in this book are in US dollars.

We expect you to use this section most in the course of planning your trip, for its ideas and suggestions are intended to simplify this often confusing period. Entries are intentionally concise in an effort to get to the meat of the matter, with the least extraneous prose. These entries are augmented by extensive lists of specific sources from which to obtain even more detailed data, plus some suggestions for obtaining travel information on your own.

PERSPECTIVES

A cultural and historical survey of Canada's past and present, its people, politics, and heritage, this section provides a glimpse of the cultural diversity that characterizes Canadian life, and the current conflicts that permeate contemporary economic and social activity.

THE CITIES

Individual reports are presented on the 9 Canadian cities most visited by travelers, prepared with the aid of researchers, contributors, professional journalists, and other experts on the spot. Each report offers a short-stay guide within a consistent format: An essay introduces the city as a contemporary place to live and visit; *At-a-Glance* material is actually a site-by-site survey of the most important, interesting, and sometimes most eclectic sights to see and things to do; *Sources and Resources* is a concise listing of pertinent tourism information, meant to answer a broad range of potentially pressing questions as they arise — from simple things like the address of the local tourist office, how to get around, which sightseeing tours to take, and when special events occur to something more difficult like where to find the best nightspot or hail a taxi, which are the chic places to shop, and where the best local skiing, golf, tennis, fishing, and swimming are to be found; and *Best in Town* is our collection of cost-and-quality choices of the best places to eat and sleep on a variety of budgets.

DIVERSIONS

This section is designed to help travelers find the very best locations at which to pursue a wide range of athletic and cerebral activities, without having to wade through endless pages of unrelated text. This very selective guide lists the broadest possible range of activities, including all the best places to pursue them.

We start with a list of possibilities that offer various places to stay and eat, and move to those that require some perspiration — sports preferences and other rigorous pursuits — and go on to report on a number of more cerebral and spiritual vacation opportunities. In every case, our suggestion of a particular location — and often our recommendation of a specific resort — is intended to guide you to that special place where the quality of experience is likely to be highest. Whether you opt for golf or tennis, fishing or canoeing, visiting battle sites or climbing mountain peaks, each entry is the equivalent of a comprehensive checklist of the absolute best in Canada.

DIRECTIONS

This series of 46 Canadian driving itineraries, from Prince Edward Island to British Columbia's Vancouver Island, traverses Canada's most beautiful routes and roads, past its most spectacular natural wonders, through its most magnificent national parks and forests. DIRECTIONS is the only section of the book that is organized geographically, and its itineraries cover Canada in short, independent segments that each describe journeys of 1 to 3 days' duration. Itineraries can be "connected" for longer trips, or used individually for short, intensive explorations.

Each entry includes a guide to sightseeing highlights; a qualitative guide to accommodations and food along the road (small inns, clean and comfortable motels, country hotels, campgrounds, and off-the-main-road discoveries); and suggestions for activities.

Although each of this book's sections has a distinct format and a special function, they have been designed to be used together to provide a complete inventory of travel information. To use this book to full advantage, take a few minutes to read the table of contents and random entries in each section to get a feel of how it all fits together.

Pick and choose needed information. Assume, for example, that you always have been interested in an outdoor vacation walking through one of Canada's wilderness areas, but you never knew exactly how to organize it or where to go. You might well begin by reading the short, informative section on hiking in GETTING READY TO GO. This would provide plenty of ideas on how to organize the trip, where to go for more information, and what to take along. But where to go? Turn to *Hiking and Backpacking,* DIVERSIONS, for a list of the best hiking trails in Canada, or to *National Parks,* DIVERSIONS, for a survey of every Canadian national park; a look through the selections will direct you to a trail equal to your expertise. Perhaps you will choose as your destination one of the Lake Louise trails in Banff National Park. Turn next to DIRECTIONS for suggestions on what else to see while in Alberta, including the Dinosaur Provincial Park and Blackfoot Indian Preserve. In fact, you may even decide to take a break from hiking in the wilds and visit Alberta's two major cities, Calgary and Edmonton; each is fully covered in THE CITIES.

In other words, the sections of this book are building blocks to help you put together the best possible trip. Use them selectively as tools, sources of ideas, a reference work for accurate facts, and a guide to the best buys, the most exciting sights and sites, the most pleasant accommodations, the tastiest food, *the best travel experiences* that you can have in Canada.

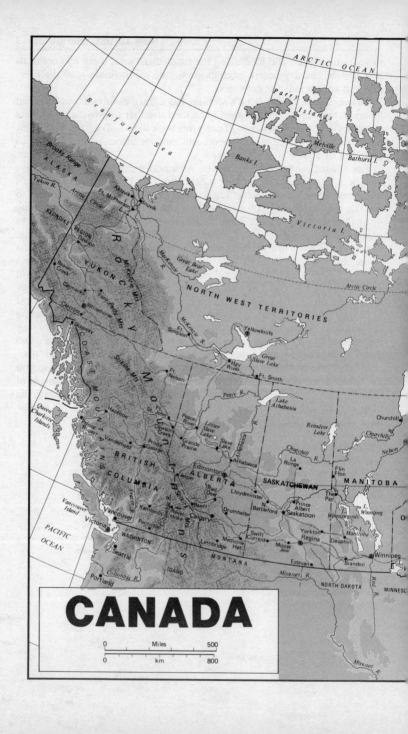

CANADA

| 0 | Miles | 500 |
| 0 | km | 800 |

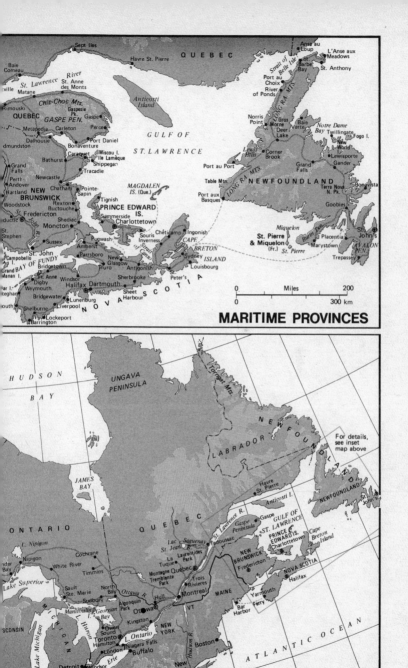

MARITIME PROVINCES

GETTING READY TO GO

When and How to Go

What's Where: Canada East to West

 Canada, the second-largest country in the world, sprawls across the Northern Hemisphere like a silent giant, flinging mountains and plains, tundra, and Arctic islands over 3.8 million square miles. Only the Soviet Union, with a total area of 8.65 million square miles, is larger; yet Canada has only 25 million people, just one-tenth the population of the US. Because of Canada's exceptional geography — the proximity of the Arctic Ocean and vast expanses of virtually uninhabited northern territories where the soil never fully thaws and agriculture is impossible — the huge majority of Canadians live in a temperate belt 200 miles deep that runs just north of the 4,000-mile US-Canada border like an artful seam.

Canada's formidable magnitude is divided into 12 separate political entities. These include ten provinces (east to west: Newfoundland — including Labrador — Nova Scotia, Prince Edward Island, New Brunswick, Quebec, Ontario, Manitoba, Saskatchewan, Alberta, and British Columbia) and two territories (the Northwest Territories and the Yukon Territory). The territories account for 38% of Canada's area but for only a minute fraction of the population.

TERRAIN: The Canadian landmass is shaped roughly like a ship, its bow pointed bravely into the Atlantic, its stern rising high along the country's long Pacific coast and the Yukon Territory. Ontario's southernmost toehold in Lake Erie provides an anchor for this ship, and the ragged sail of islands 2,850 miles to the north — Ellesmere, Axel Heiberg, Perry, Queen Elizabeth — flutters in the Arctic Ocean, the country's northernmost point, facing the permanent polar ice that announces the North Pole. Some 5,780 miles separate Canada's easternmost point, Newfoundland's Cape Spear, from Mt. St. Elias on the Yukon's border with Alaska. If Canada resembles a ship, it is a ship not only surrounded by, but nearly aswamp with, water. Hudson Bay, a vast inland arm of the Arctic Ocean, dips into the landmass like a giant puncture, and more than one-third of the world's known freshwater sources are held within the country's huge, interlocking system of natural inland waterways.

The country forms five distinct geographical regions, each characterized by a dominating physical feature.

Appalachian Region – The finger of land that extends along Canada's eastern shore, like an extension of New England, includes the provinces of Nova Scotia, Newfoundland, New Brunswick, and Prince Edward Island, bounded on the east by the sea and on the west by the St. Lawrence River. The area derives its name from the mountain system that originates in Quebec and runs south all the way to Alabama. In Canada, this ancient range of folded mountains has eroded to summits less than 5,000 feet high. Most of the mountains have been submerged by the sea, and what remains are predominantly islands and peninsulas: Newfoundland, Anticosti Island, Prince Edward Island, Cape Breton Island, the Gaspé Peninsula, Nova Scotia, and New Brunswick.

The land consists of two parallel highlands of hard, ancient rock separated by lower land. One of the upland areas is in northwest New Brunswick; the other extends through Nova Scotia and Cape Breton Island. In between these two ridges lies a lower area that once was covered with water; eons ago, the area was filled in with sediment rich in carbon, and now coal is mined there.

The sea has been instrumental in shaping the geography of this region. In fact, the provinces are known collectively as the Maritime Provinces, indicating their close relation to the sea. Land comes into crashing contact with sea in the Bay of Fundy between New Brunswick and Nova Scotia where massive waves beat against rugged sandstone cliffs. The Gulf of St. Lawrence, from which the St. Lawrence River flows to the Great Lakes, is a large body of water separating Newfoundland, Nova Scotia, and the southeast mainland. Northumberland Strait, in the gulf, lies between Prince Edward Island and the northern coasts of New Brunswick and Nova Scotia. These waters are rich with fish, because the cold waters of the Labrador current from the Arctic Ocean meet the warmer Gulf Stream current and support a wide variety of marine life. Lobsters, clams, oysters, scallops, cod, mackerel, tuna, herring, haddock, and swordfish are among the species found here. Fishermen living in small villages up and down the white or red sand coasts fish in the same waters as did their fathers and grandfathers. The principal cities in the area all are seaports: Halifax, Nova Scotia; Saint John, New Brunswick; and St. John's, Newfoundland.

Inland, the land becomes a series of gently rolling hills and plains, much of which is forest or farmland. Red spruce, balsam, yellow birch, sugar maple, and beech are common in the forest zones. The upland areas, once covered with glacier deposits, now offer no fertile soils. But the lower areas support agriculture, particularly potato fields in New Brunswick and Prince Edward Island and the apple and cherry orchards and cranberry bogs of Nova Scotia.

Canadian Shield – The Canadian (or Precambrian) Shield is Canada's largest geographic region, encompassing 1.6 million square miles, almost half of the country. This shield-shaped region stretches from the coast of Labrador in the northeast through northern Quebec, northern Ontario, northern Manitoba, northern Saskatchewan, and the Northwest Territories to the Arctic Ocean. It surrounds and includes the Hudson Bay. This huge embayment of the Arctic Ocean, 650 miles wide and 850 miles long, was explored and named (none too modestly) by Henry Hudson in 1610 during his search for the Northwest Passage.

Hudson's expedition opened the way to English and French traders and merchants who were attracted by the rich profits of fur trading with the Indians. Two large rival companies, the Hudson's Bay Company and the Northwest Company, were formed to exploit the wealth of the region. Today the area still survives by its rich natural resources, particularly gold, uranium, iron ore, radium, timber, and waterfalls and rapids with potential hydroelectric power. Most of the towns located in the shield revolve around these commercial concerns, and generally are centers of lumbering, pulp and paper, or mining.

The terrain itself, one of the oldest sections of the earth's crust, is rough and wild. Ancient Precambrian (prior to Paleozoic) rocks with crystalline form line the surface. During the Ice Age, glaciers rubbed away the top soil; as they retreated, they left the surface strewn with rocks and boulders, which still characterize the area. Forested hills and numerous lakes and streams are also found here. Though you will not encounter too many people, you probably will see some of the shield's other inhabitants: lynx, snowshoe rabbit, wolf, beaver, wolverine, mink, river otter, bobcat, weasel, and, in the far north, the arctic fox.

Most of the shield is agriculturally poor because of the lack of soil and preponderance of rocks. An exception is the area south of James Bay, the southernmost section of Hudson Bay, known as the Clay Belt. A layer of sediment that once was the floor of a lake remains around the bay and supports agriculture. The vegetation in the rest of the shield is restricted to forest and woodland and occurs in three major zones. Just north of the Clay Belt is a stretch of forest where spruce, fir, larch, hemlock, and pine grow. The northern woodland prevails above this zone and looks like open parkland, where widely separate candelabra spruce stand on a deep lichen floor. The northernmost zone of the shield is the forest tundra with permafrost. Strips of white and black spruce dominate the southern edge of this zone.

The shield offers great opportunities for fishermen, hunters, trekkers, and people seeking a rugged solitude. Wilderness camps from which woodspeople launch various expeditions are located in many small towns (see *Where They Bite, Hiking and Backpacking,* and *Hunting,* DIVERSIONS).

St. Lawrence Lowland and Lakes Region – Below the Canadian Shield and to the west of the Appalachian region is the St. Lawrence Lowland, the center of Canada's population and industry. In its two provinces, Quebec and Ontario, live 62% of all Canadians. The lifeline of the area is the St. Lawrence River, which traverses southern Ontario and Quebec through a series of fertile valleys.

The geography of the region itself has spawned development. Eons ago there were many more lakes in the area than there are today. As they dried and contracted, they left deposits of fertile sediments. Consequently, the lands along the St. Lawrence River and between Lakes Huron, Erie, and Ontario are excellent for farming. With the St. Lawrence Seaway providing access from the Atlantic Ocean to the heartland of North America 2,000 miles away, the development of agricultural business, industry, and commerce was inevitable. In these lowlands rose the greatest cities of Canada, Montreal and Toronto, each with populations nearing 3 million; Ottawa, the nation's capital, with a population of 750,000; and the other major urban-industrial centers of Hamilton, Kitchener, London, Sarnia, and Windsor.

On the map, Ontario resembles a bulky leg with the toes pointing southwest. The thigh and upper leg are part of the Canadian Shield, while the lower portion, with footholds in the St. Lawrence River and Lakes Ontario, Huron, and Erie, is the center of population. The climate here is mild, ranging from January temperatures of 25F to July highs in the 80s F. Ontario is Canada's most productive province; the north is a major source of minerals, and the south, of farm and dairy products and tobacco. Toronto, the largest city in Canada, is clean and cosmopolitan, with a significant French-speaking population, a diverse ethnic composition, and the avant-garde architecture of Mies van der Rohe and Viljo Revell. In Ottawa, the nation's capital, the government offices create an interesting juxtaposition of geometric modern and older Gothic architecture. (For complete descriptions of these cities, including their points of interest and best restaurants and hotels, see THE CITIES.)

Quebec is the largest province in Canada and also the largest region in North America where the language, culture, and people are French. The province covers 594,860 square miles, from the temperate south, where the St. Lawrence flows through Quebec City, to the cold Ungava and James bays, where Eskimos live and hunt over vast regions of scrubby bush. Quebec is only slightly less productive than Ontario. Its mines yield iron, copper, and asbestos; its farms fill the dairy needs of Quebec and some of the other provinces.

Quebec City is the heart of Quebec and French Canada. The 17th-century city is the center of French culture in Canada. Its abundance of churches and old ecclesiastical structures emphasizes Quebec's importance as a stronghold of the Roman Catholic Church. But the traditional character of the city belies the fact that it is a fast-growing urban and industrial center. Indeed, it is here in Quebec that the St. Lawrence River meets one of its tributaries, the St. Charles, and narrows to a mere three-quarters of a mile; as a result, the St. Lawrence harbor can accommodate huge tankers.

Farther down the St. Lawrence, 1,000 miles from the Atlantic, lies Montreal, Canada's second-largest city and the world's biggest inland seaport. The metropolitan area sprawls over Montreal Island, one of a group of islands near the confluence of the St. Lawrence and the Ottawa River, which flows in from the west. Montreal is Canada's major industrial and commercial center and the terminus of international airlines, major rail systems, and several shipping lines. Its port is the most important grain-shipping station in the world. Like Quebec City, the city is predominantly French Canadian, although there is a significant Anglo-Saxon minority; the two cultures have a history of conflict. In many ways, Montreal is the flagship city of Canada. It has been the point of entry for most overseas visitors and the major destination of many others.

Great Plains and Prairies – To the west of the St. Lawrence Lowlands and the Canadian Shield, extending from the US border northwest to the Arctic Ocean, lies a vast stretch of Canada composed of wide prairies and sweeping plains. This region encompasses the provinces of Manitoba, Saskatchewan, and Alberta, as well as a large chunk of the Northwest Territories. Most of the people here live on the prairie in the southern part of these provinces. The countryside is flat, and grass covers the rich, dark soil laid down by the rivers that run into Hudson Bay. The only trees are thin screens of oak, poplar, and birch surrounding the many farmhouses. When the railway opened up these lands at the end of the 19th century, it was used primarily to transport wheat crops at harvest time. Today much of this region still is a calm, gold sea, but erosion due to single-crop farming and the removal of the grass cover have reduced its fertility and hurt farming. Farther west, out of the reach of the Saskatchewan rivers, the climate and terrain are too dry for wheat; these lands are used primarily for cattle ranching. The recent discovery of oil in this area has stimulated additional commercial development. New businesses and industries have located in the larger prairie cities of Winnipeg, Regina, Saskatoon, Calgary, and Edmonton.

In the north the land is mostly wild. Moose, elk, bear, timber wolves, and deer roam this region, similar to the Canadian Shield. Too cold for agriculture and covered with coniferous forest, lake, and swamp, the north is rich in oil and minerals, including nickel, copper, and zinc. Mining settlements have sprung up on the shores of the three major lakes: Great Bear Lake, Great Slave Lake, and Lake Athabasca. Except for these, the region is desolate; in the far north the soil is permanently frozen and the forest gives way to tundra.

Province by province, the geography of the prairies changes from east to west. In Manitoba the prairie begins at the edge of the Canadian Shield; most of the population lives in the south in a fertile triangle that is the dry bed of a glacial lake that drained into Hudson Bay 15,000 years ago, leaving rich, black earth in its place. The soil yields great quantities of wheat while the myriad lakes in the north produce millions of pounds of fish. Winnipeg, the capital of Manitoba and the sixth-largest city in Canada, is the center of the grain market and home to over 620,000 inhabitants of the province — a blend of British, Indian, Ukrainian, German, Dutch, Icelandic, Polish, and French (concentrated primarily in St. Boniface, across the Red River from the capital).

Saskatchewan is the heart of the prairie provinces. Most of it is farmland, though many of the farms now are owned by agribusinesses rather than families. Regina is the administrative, financial, and commercial center of the province.

In Alberta the wheat fields of the east give way to ranch country in the west. Underneath the surface is a wealth of oil and gas. Edmonton, the northernmost city in North America, is one of Canada's major petrochemical centers and the retail trade center of the province. Large numbers of Ukrainians, French, Germans, and Poles populate this province. Calgary, Alberta's second city, sits at the point where the Rockies meet the prairie flatlands. This old cattle town now is a communications and transportation center, but it recalls its heritage for a few days every summer when several hundred thousand would-be cowboys and cowgirls descend on the city for the *Calgary Stampede,* an orgy of bronco busting, branding, and pony racing.

Western Mountains – Canada's westernmost region begins where the Great Plains merge into the Rocky Mountains and extends across British Columbia to the Coast Range. It is one of the world's finest fishing, hunting, canoeing, and wilderness camping areas. The region is geographically the most diverse in Canada, encompassing the rugged Rocky peaks, the rain forests of the Coast Range, the great boreal forests and rivers of the interior plains, mild Vancouver, and the frozen tundra of the Yukon Territory. The region stretches north to south from the US border to Alaska.

The northern Rockies march down the eastern side of the region, forming the border between British Columbia and Alberta. Like the Andes in South America, the Alps of Europe, and the Himalayas of Asia, the Rockies were created by a relatively recent upfolding and, therefore, are very high. The tallest Canadian peaks approach 20,000 feet: Mt. Logan is 19,850 feet and Mt. St. Elias is 18,000 feet. It is an area of alpine lakes, meadows, glacier-studded peaks, and big game. The Rocky Mountain Valley runs from Flathead Lake in Montana to about 1,000 miles up into the Yukon; it varies greatly in terrain, from flatlands to rugged cliffs with steep, sheer walls. Except at great altitudes, the mountains and valleys are forested and provide commercial lumber.

Between the Rocky Mountain Valley on the east and the Coast Mountains on the west lies the Interior Plateau, with boreal forests, a plethora of rivers, and deep, blue lakes (including Babine, Chilko, Morice, Francois, Stuart, and Tatla) inhabited by giant lake trout, rainbow trout, and Dolly Varden trout. On the west the plateau runs into the snow-capped Coast Range, which stretches from the mainland opposite Vancouver to the Yukon Territory. The peaks here are lower than the Rocky summits but are noted for their rain forests, streams stocked with steelhead, and, in the northern reaches, the juxtaposition of glaciers and forests. Beyond the Coast Range lies the shore of the Pacific Ocean, warmed by the mild Japan Current and studded with the numerous islands, bays, and inlets of the archipelago better known as the Inside Passage, through which 19th-century prospectors made their way to the Yukon and Alaska in search of gold.

Most of the population is concentrated around Vancouver and Victoria in the southwest, close to the US border. Winter temperatures seldom drop below freezing, summers are cool, and it rains all year. Vancouver is a modern city with a spectacular island setting, the Pacific to the west and the Coast Range to the north and east, and is the lumbering, mining, industrial, and commercial center of British Columbia. Across the Strait of Juan de Fuca to the southeast lies Victoria, the capital of British Columbia. An extensive network of ferries connects points on the mainland with Vancouver Island.

Compared with the mild climate of southwestern Canada, the Yukon Territory makes a strong contrast. These 200,000 square miles are very mountainous and abound in alpine meadows, lakes, wild rivers (the Yukon River is navigable in summertime from Whitehorse to the Bering Sea), tundra, and snow. In fact, the only time it doesn't snow in the Yukon is during June, July, and August. Most of the year is winter, with average temperatures dropping well below 0 degrees F. People are scarce in these parts, and over half of the territory's 50,000 inhabitants (a mix of Caucasians, Eskimos, and Indians) live in Whitehorse, the largest town. However, there's plenty of big game, including grizzlies, and if you're interested in hunting, camping, backpacking, or mountain climbing, the Yukon is a true frontier, still beckoning with the call of the wild.

When to Go

 The decision of exactly when to travel may be imposed by the requirements of a rigid schedule; more likely there will be some choice, and the decision will be made on the basis of precisely what you want to see and do, the activities in which you'd like to participate, or events you'd like to attend, and what suits your mood.

There really isn't a "best" time to visit Canada. Due to the vast range of topography and climate across this nation, Canada provides year-round travel opportunities. Summer generally is best for touring and sightseeing; winter, obviously, best for snow and ice sports. But even such broad distinctions don't recognize that Canada's major cities — Montreal, Toronto, Vancouver — make wonderful long-weekend winter destinations, even when the snow is piled high and the wind is whistling. And the Canadian climate deals out some significant surprises — for instance, spring in the far north is late, but exquisite. Timing a visit to Canada depends far more on your own interests and expectations than on anything inherent in the Canadian weather or tourist facilities.

It is important to emphasize that more and more vacationers who have a choice are enjoying the substantial advantages of off-season travel. As discussed below, this period varies substantially throughout the country. Though many of the lesser tourist attractions in an area may close during the slower seasons, the major ones remain open and tend to be less crowded with tourists — as is Canada in general. During the off-season, people relax and life proceeds at a more natural pace. What's more, travel generally is less expensive.

For some, the most convincing argument in favor of off-season travel is the economic one. Airfares drop and hotel rates go down during less popular travel periods. Canada is not like the Caribbean, however, where high and low season are precisely defined and rates drop automatically on a particular date. It generally will be less expensive to fly to and stay in any area where the primary attraction is winter sports — areas in Ottawa, Quebec, and Toronto — during the summer than the height of winter, and popular summer destinations — such as the Maritime Provinces — reduce rates after sun-seeking, boating, and touring vacationers depart. But special packages and promotional rates can be offered in any season.

Although many smaller guesthouses, inns, and other establishments in some areas may close during the off-season in response to reduced demand, there still are plenty of alternatives, and cut-rate "mini-break" packages — for stays of more than 1 night, especially over a weekend (when business travelers traditionally go home) — are more common. Even during the off-season, however, high-season rates may prevail because of an important local event. Particularly in the larger cities, major trade shows or conferences held at the time of your visit also are sure to affect not only the availability of discounts on accommodations, but the basic availability of a place to stay.

It should be noted that what the travel industry refers to as the shoulder season — the months immediately before and after the peak months in any area — often are sought out because they offer reasonably good weather and smaller crowds. But be aware that near high-season prices still can prevail for many popular destinations during these periods.

CLIMATE: The travel plans of most visitors to Canada are affected by the availability of vacation time and a desire to visit when the weather is likely to be best — or most appropriate for a particular sport or other activity. The most common concerns about travel have to do with questions of temperature, rain, and snow. It's difficult to generalize about Canadian weather. Changes are frequent, but the whole country does experience four distinct seasons, and each season has something different to offer travelers. Below is a brief description of the climate in various Canadian regions to help in planning. (*Please note that although temperatures most often are recorded on the Celsius scale in Canada, for purposes of clarity we use the more familiar Fahrenheit scale.*)

The Maritimes: New Brunswick, Newfoundland, Nova Scotia, Prince Edward Island – The seasons are quite distinct: cold, snowy winters with temperatures in the 20s or lower (much lower inland in Newfoundland, New Brunswick, and Prince Edward Island); short, temperate springs; warm summers, in the 60s and 70s (which are, however, briefer and often cooler in inland and northern regions); mostly clear, crisp autumns with beautiful red, yellow, and orange foliage, especially in New Brunswick. Prime tourist seasons are summer, for coastal resorts; autumn (especially the last 2 weeks in September and the first 2 weeks in October) throughout the region for foliage. Since the Maritime Provinces are relatively flat, winter sports are limited to cross-country skiing and snowmobiling (see DIVERSIONS). The best foliage route is the Trans-Canada Highway through New Brunswick.

Central Canada: Ontario, Quebec – Again, seasons are distinct; temperatures range from below freezing in winter to the 80s in summer. Winters are cold, damp, and overcast in southern Ontario, drier but colder in Quebec. In the summer, humidity tends to be high throughout Ontario and Quebec — Toronto also often is hotter than Miami. Fall is pleasant, with moderate temperatures, and is the region's best season. A temperate spring begins in April and continues into June. Visitors to the metropolitan areas usually come in summer, when many urbanites spend their weekends in the country, and the cities are, consequently, pleasantly uncrowded.

The Prairies: Alberta, Manitoba, Saskatchewan – Very cold and dry winters and moderate summers are characteristic of this region. Manitoba suffers the harshest winters, with heavy snowfalls and temperatures in the -10 to -15 range. In the more westerly areas, such as southern Alberta, winter temperatures average in the 20s. Summers across the region are comfortable, in the high 60s and 70s, and can be quite dry. With the exception of winter skiing in the Canadian Rockies, summer is the most popular tourist season, when the prairies are at their most attractive. Trees are few and far between due to the weather extremes. Consequently, the short autumn is not as dramatic as in other areas of the country. The most extraordinary weather phenomena are the chinooks in southern Alberta, sudden breaths of warm weather from the west which in the middle of winter can raise the temperature as much as 30 degrees in a few hours. Though short-lived (no more than a few days, and most last only a day or less), chinooks are a looked-for part of winter in cities like Calgary.

British Columbia – This region is a delight year-round, especially in the southwestern corner around Vancouver. The coastal regions get a high rainfall in the winter. The range of temperature is not as great as in other regions, varying between the 30s in the winter and the high 60s and 70s in summer. In general, this region is best seen in late spring, summer, or early fall when the weather is warm. The winters can be damp and therefore colder than temperatures indicate, particularly in the interior of British Columbia. Vancouver and Victoria almost always are warmer than New York or Chicago in winter: Spring and autumn are pleasant, but again quite damp in coastal areas.

The North: Northwest Territories, Yukon Territory – This region, the coldest in Canada, includes the great expanses of the Northwest Territories and the Yukon Territory in the Arctic Circle. Winter is bitterly cold, with temperatures of -25 quite common even in the region's southernmost city, Yellowknife. Summer heat is quite welcome in the North — though you may have to contend with mosquitoes instead of the cold. The tundra has a beautiful brief, late spring; in summer temperatures reach the 70s and the sun shines late into the night.

For a city-by-city review of weather, also see the *Climate* entry in each city report in THE CITIES, and for basic wardrobe information, see *How to Pack,* in this section.

Travelers also can get current readings and 3-day Accu-Weather forecasts through *American Express Travel Related Services*' Worldwide Weather Report number. By dialing 900-WEATHER and punching in either the area code for any city in the US or an access code for any one of 225 major travel destinations around the world, an up-to-date recording will provide current temperature, sky conditions, wind speed and direction, heat index, relative humidity, local time, beach and boating reports or ski conditions (where appropriate), and highway reports. For locations in Canada, punch in the first three letters of the city: By entering CAL you will hear the weather report for Calgary (Alberta) — EDM will give you Edmonton (Alberta); HAL, Halifax (Nova Scotia); MON, Montreal (Quebec); OTT, Ottawa (Ontario); QUE, Quebec City (Quebec); THU, Thunder Bay (Ontario); TOR, Toronto (Ontario); VAN, Vancouver (British Columbia); and WIN, Windsor (Nova Scotia) or Winnipeg (Manitoba). This 24-hour service can be accessed from any Touch-Tone phone in the US and costs 75¢ per minute. The charge will show up on your phone bill. For a free list of the cities covered, send a self-addressed, stamped envelope to *1-900-WEATHER*, 261 Central Ave., Farmingdale, NY 11735.

SPORTS: In Vancouver and lower British Columbia, virtually any season is a warm-weather sports season — although it is possible for snow to fall anywhere in Canada. For the rest of the country, the weather dictates the types of sports played.

In most parts of the country, golf and tennis play generally begins in May and lasts well into October. For detailed information on when and where to play Canada's best greens and courts, see *Golf in Canada: A Land of Links* and *The Best Tennis Vacations*, both in DIVERSIONS.

Backpacking, canoeing, mountain climbing, and wilderness trips usually are pursued in the summer, since this is when lakes and the mountain air are warmer and less equipment is required. All sections of Canada, except the prairies, are popular for these sports. For information on exploring Canada's great outdoors, see *Camping and RVs, Hiking and Biking*, in this section, as well as the applicable sections of DIVERSIONS.

Water sports, like yachting and water skiing, begin in the coastal waters and large lakes of eastern Canada in the late spring and continue through fall. Most regattas and other events are scheduled in July and August. On British Columbia's coast, the season lasts longer, with regattas starting in June and finishing in September.

The country has a full range of winter sports, such as ice skating, snowmobiling, dogsledding, and curling, but skiing — both downhill and cross-country — is the most popular. There are slopes in every province, but those in Alberta, British Columbia, and Quebec are the best. The season usually starts in earnest around *Christmas* (although snowfalls as early as *late October* are common), and lasts through early April. Naturally, skiing conditions depend upon snow, so the determined skier should be prepared to make plans around the weather. Newspapers and radio stations in ski areas carry daily ski-condition reports, often updated several times a day. If you are uncertain of the conditions at your destination call the management of the resort to get a complete report; *American Express' Travel Related Services'* Worldwide Weather Report number (see above) also will provide information on current conditions. Further information on skiing is included in a number of publications available from the provincial tourist offices listed in *Tourist Information Offices*, in this section. For further information on the best places to pursue winter sports, see the appropriate sections of DIVERSIONS.

PARKS: Canada's national parks are open year-round, though some are in such remote areas they are difficult to get to in winter months. All provide camping facilities year-round, too. As parks are most crowded in the summer, during high season — July and August — there may be as many as 17 different campgrounds open in popular parks such as Banff and Jasper, but during winter, only one or two may be open. A list of campgrounds in national parks can be found in the *National Parks* brochure, available from the Canadian Parks Service, Ottawa, Ontario K1A 0H3 (phone: 819-997-2800). There also are numerous provincial parks, many of which allow camping. Information on these parks generally is contained in travel literature put out by the individual provinces. For further information, see *Camping and RVs, Hiking and Biking*, in this section, as well as *National Parks* and other sections of DIVERSIONS.

CULTURAL EVENTS: Many travelers may want to schedule a trip to Canada to coincide with some special cultural event. For music lovers and theatergoers, a concert or play set in a splendid natural setting may be a thrilling experience and much more memorable than seeing the same place on an ordinary sightseeing itnerary. For history buffs, not to mention dedicated photographers, there are numerous folkloric happenings which bring part of Canada's rich heritage alive for visitors.

As in the US, the height of the Canadian cultural season for concerts, plays, art exhibits, dance, and other events is November through April, but if you're visiting at another time of the year, don't despair — there is plenty going on year-round. Montreal and Toronto still are the two great cultural centers, and the *Montreal Symphony* and the *Toronto Symphony* are Canada's two major orchestras. Toronto is the major theatrical center, with over 25 theaters. Schedules of events are available in local magazines and from the tourism bureaus in most cities (addresses are given in THE CITIES).

Summer activities are less formal, and often held outdoors. The major cities offer full schedules of concerts, exhibits, and theater, as well as entertainment for children. Of national (and often international) interest are the *Shakespeare Festival* in Stratford, Ontario; the *Shaw Drama Festival,* Niagara-on-the-Lake, Ontario; *Folklorama,* Winnipeg, Manitoba; and the *Charlottetown Summer Festival,* Charlottetown, Prince Edward Island. (See also "Special Events" in THE CITIES and *Festivals, Fairs, and Fancy Acts,* DIVERSIONS.)

Turtle derbies, bathtub races, blossom festivals, provincial fairs, rodeos and stampedes, horse shows, ethnic festivals, and numerous similar events — from the *Chocolate Fest* in New Brunswick to the Yukon's *Sourdough Rendezvous* — bring people together throughout the country. To find out what events are taking place along your itinerary or to get a list so that you can plan your trip around them, write the provincial tourist boards, most of which publish a calendar of events.

Traveling by Plane

 Flying usually is the most efficient way to get to Canada, and, given its size, it is the quickest, most convenient means of travel between different parts of the country once you are there. Although touring by car, bus, or train certainly is the most scenic way to see the countryside, most travelers only have time to explore one area. Air travel is far faster and more direct — the less time spent in transit, the more time spent at your vacation destinations. It also can be one of the least expensive ways to travel if you have a great distance to cover.

If you do decide to fly, you probably will spend more for your airfare than for any other single item in your Canadian travel budget, so try to take advantage of the lowest fares offered by either scheduled airlines or charter companies. You should know what kinds of flights are available, the rules and regulations pertaining to air travel, and all the special package options.

SCHEDULED FLIGHTS: Air service to Canada is provided by two Canadian airlines — *Air Canada* and *Canadian Airlines International* — and a number of US carriers — *American, Continental, Delta, Eastern, Northwest, United,* and *US Air.* Flights to major Canadian cities depart from a number of US cities, including Atlanta, Baltimore, Boston, Buffalo, Chicago, Dallas, Denver, Detroit, Ft. Lauderdale, Hartford, Houston, Los Angeles, Miami, Minneapolis, Newark, New York, Orlando, Philadelphia, Pittsburgh, Portland, Salt Lake City, San Francisco, Seattle, Tampa, and Washington, DC.

Tickets – When traveling on one of the many regularly scheduled flights, a full-fare ticket provides maximum travel flexibility (although at considerable expense), because there are no advance booking requirements: A prospective passenger can buy a ticket for a flight right up to the minute of takeoff — if a seat is available. If your ticket is for a round trip, you can make the return reservation any time you wish, months before you leave, or the day before you return. You can stay at your destination for as long as you like. (Tickets generally are good for a year, but can be renewed if not used.) You also can cancel your flight at any time without penalty. However, while it is true that this category of ticket can be purchased at the last minute, it is advisable to reserve well in advance during popular vacation periods and around holiday times.

No matter what kind of ticket you buy, it is wise to reconfirm that you will be using your return reservations. For instance, if you do not call the airline to let them know you will be using the return leg of your reservation, they (or their computer) may assume you are not coming and automatically cancel your seat. For further information, see "Reservations," below.

Fares – Airfares continue to change so rapidly that even experts find it difficult to keep up with them. This ever-changing situation is due to a number of factors, including airline deregulation, volatile labor and fuel costs, and vastly increased competition. Before the Airline Deregulation Act of 1978, US airlines had no choice but to set their rates and routes within the guidelines of the Civil Aeronautics Board (CAB), and they could compete for passengers only by offering better service than their competitors. With the loosening of controls (and the elimination of the CAB), airlines now are engaged in a far more intense competition relating to price and schedule, which has opened the door to a wide range of discount fares and promotional offers. Intensifying the competitive atmosphere has been the creation of several new carriers offering fewer frills and far lower prices. These carriers seem to appear and disappear with dismaying regularity. They have, however, served to drive down fares from time to time and make the older, more entrenched carriers aware that they are in a genuine competition for travelers' dollars.

Now that fares for flights within Canada also have been deregulated, the situation is similar in the Canadian airline industry. Both Canadian and American airlines still are required to file their proposed fares for international flights between the US and Canada — the former with Canada's Air Transport Committee, the latter with the US Department of Transportation.

Perhaps the most common misconception about fares on scheduled airlines is that the cost of the ticket determines how much service will be provided on the flight. This is true only to a certain extent. A far more realistic rule of thumb is that the less you pay for your ticket, the more restrictions and qualifications are likely to come into play before you board the plane (as well as after you get off). These qualifying aspects relate to the months during which you must travel, how far in advance you must purchase your ticket, the minimum and maximum amount of time you may or must remain abroad, your willingness to make up your mind concerning a return date at the time of booking — and your ability to stick to that decision. It is not uncommon for passengers sitting side by side on the same wide-body jet to have paid fares varying by hundreds of dollars, and all too often the traveler paying more would have been equally willing to accept the terms regulating the far less expensive ticket. The ticket you buy will fall into one of several fare categories currently being offered by scheduled carriers flying between the US and Canada, and within Canada.

In general, the great variety of US domestic fares, Canadian domestic fares, and fares between the two countries can be reduced to four basic categories, including first class, coach (also called economy or tourist class), and excursion or discount fares. The fourth category, called business class (an intermediate class between first class and coach, with many of the amenities of first class and more legroom than coach), has been added by many airlines in recent years. In addition, Advance Purchase Excursion (APEX) fares offer savings under certain conditions.

A first class ticket is your admission to the special section of the aircraft with larger seats, more legroom, sleeperette seating on some wide-body aircraft, better (or more elaborately served) food, free drinks and headsets for movies and music channels, and, above all personal attention. First class fares are about double those of full-fare economy, although both first class passengers and people paying economy fares are entitled to reserve seats and are sold tickets on an open reservation system.

Not too long ago, there were only two classes of air travel, first class and all the rest, usually called economy or tourist. But because passengers paying full economy fares traveled in the same compartment as passengers flying for considerably less on various promotional or discount fares, the airlines introduced special services to compensate those paying the full price. Thus, business class came into being — one of the most successful recent airline innovations. At first, business class passengers merely were curtained off from the other economy passengers. Now a separate cabin or cabins — usually toward the front of the plane — is the norm. While standards of comfort and service are not as high as in first class, they represent a considerable improvement over conditions in the rear of the plane, with roomier seats, more leg and shoulder space between passengers, and fewer seats abreast. Free liquor and headphones, a choice of meal entrées, and a separate counter for speedier check-in are other inducements. As in first class, a business class passenger may travel on any scheduled flight he or she wishes, may buy a one-way or round-trip ticket, and have the ticket remain valid for a year. There are no minimum or maximum stay requirements, no advance booking requirements, and no cancellation penalties. Airlines often have their own names for their business class service, however, the only two airlines currently offering business class to Canada — *Air Canada* and *Canadian Airlines International* — simply refer to it as business class.

The terms of the coach or economy fare may vary slightly from airline to airline, and, in fact, from time to time airlines may be selling more than one type of economy fare. Economy fares sell for substantially less than business fares, the savings effected by limited frills and stopovers. Coach or economy passengers sit more snugly, as many as 10 in a single row on a wide-body jet, behind the first class section and receive standard meal service. Alcoholic drinks are not free, nor are the headsets. If there are two economy fares on the books, one (often called "regular economy") still may offer unlimited stopovers. The other, less expensive fare (often called "special economy") may limit stopovers to one or two, with a charge (typically $25) for each one. Like first class passengers, however, passengers paying the full coach fare are subject to none of the restrictions that usually are attached to less expensive discount fares. There are no advance booking requirements, no minimum stay requirements, and no cancellation penalties. Tickets are sold on an open reservation system: They can be bought for a flight up to the minute of takeoff (if seats are available), and if the ticket is round-trip, the return reservation can be made any time you wish — months before you leave or the day before you return. Both first class and coach tickets generally are good for a year, after which they can be renewed if not used, and if you ultimately decide not to fly at all, your money will be refunded. The cost of economy and business class tickets does not vary much in the course of the year between the US and Canada, though on some routes they vary in price from a basic (low-season) price in effect most of the year to a peak (high-season) price — these seasonal variations vary according to the destination.

Excursions and other discount fares are the airlines' equivalent of a special sale, and usually apply to round-trip bookings. These fares generally differ according to the season and the number of travel days permitted. They are only a bit less flexible than full-fare economy tickets and are, therefore, useful for both business travelers and tourists. Most round-trip excursion tickets include strict minimum and maximum stay requirements, and reservations can be changed only within the prescribed time limits. So don't count on extending a ticket beyond the prescribed time of return or staying less time than required. Different airlines may have different regulations concerning the number of stopovers permitted, and sometimes excursion fares are less expensive during midweek. Needless to say, these reduced-rate seats are most limited at busy times such as holidays, when full-fare coach seats sell more quickly than usual. Passengers fortunate enough to get a discount or excursion fare ticket sit with the coach passengers, and for all intents and purposes are indistinguishable from them. They receive all the same basic services, even though they have paid anywhere between 30% and 55% less for the trip. Obviously, it's wise to make plans early enough to qualify for this less expensive transportation.

These discount or excursion fares may masquerade under a variety of names, and they may vary from city to city (from the East Coast to the West Coast, especially), but they invariably have strings attached. A common requirement is that the ticket be purchased a certain number of days — usually no fewer than 7, 14, or 21 days — in advance of departure, though it may be booked weeks or months in advance (it has to be "ticketed," or paid for, shortly after booking, however). The return reservation usually has to be made at the time of the original ticketing and cannot be changed later than a certain number of days (again, usually 7, 14, or 21 days) before the return flight. If events force a passenger to change the return reservation after the date allowed, the difference between the round-trip excursion rate and the round-trip coach rate probably will have to be paid, though most airlines allow passengers to use their discounted fares by standing by for an empty seat, even if they don't otherwise have standby fares. Another common condition is a minimum and maximum stay requirement: for example 6 to 14 days, or 1 to 6 days, and including at least a Saturday night. Last, cancellation penalties of up to 50% of the full price of the ticket have been assessed — check the specific penalty in effect when you purchase your discount/excursion ticket — so careful planning is imperative.

Of even greater risk — and bearing the lowest price of all the current discount fares — is the ticket where no change at all in departure and/or return flights is permitted, and where the ticket price is totally nonrefundable. If you do buy a nonrefundable ticket, you should be aware of a new policy followed by many airlines, regarding international flights, that may make it easier to change your plans if necessary. For a fee — set by each airline and payable at the airport when checking in — you *may* be able to change the time or date of a return flight on a nonrefundable ticket. However, if the nonrefundable ticket price for the replacement flight is higher than that of the original (as generally is the case when trading in a weekday for a weekend flight), you will have to pay the difference. Any such change must be made a certain number of days in advance — in some cases as little as 2 days — of either the original or the replacement flight, whichever is earlier; restrictions are set by the individual carrier.

A newer and less expensive type of excursion fare, the APEX, or Advance Purchase Excursion also is offered by some airlines flying between the US and Canada. As with traditional excursion fares, passengers paying an APEX fare sit with and receive the same basic services as any other coach or economy passengers, even though they may have paid up to 50% less for their seats. In return, they are subject to certain restrictions. In the case of flights to Canada, the ticket usually is good for a minimum of approximately 7 days abroad (spanning at least 1 weekend), and a maximum, currently, of 1 month to 1 year (depending on the destination); and as its name implies, it must be "ticketed," or paid for in its entirety, a certain period of time before departure — usually 21 days. The drawback to an APEX fare is that it penalizes travelers who change their minds — and travel plans. The return reservation must be made at the time of the original ticketing, and if for some reason you change your schedule while abroad, you pay a penalty of $100 or 10% of the ticket value, whichever is greater, as long as you travel within the validity period of your ticket. But if you change your return to a date less than the minimum stay or more than the maximum stay, the difference between the round-trip APEX fare and the full round-trip coach rate will have to be paid. There also is a penalty of $125 or more for canceling or changing a reservation *before* travel begins — check the specific penalty in effect when you purchase your ticket. No stopovers are allowed on an APEX ticket, but it is possible to create an open-jaw effect by buying an APEX on a split-ticket basis; for example, flying to Toronto and returning from Quebec City (or some other city). The total price would be half the price of an APEX to Toronto plus half the price of an APEX to Quebec City. APEX tickets to Canada are sold at basic and peak rates — again, depending on the destination — and may include surcharges for weekend flights.

Standby fares, at one time the rock-bottom price at which a traveler could fly to Canada, have become elusive. At the time of this writing, most major scheduled airlines did not regularly offer standby fares on most direct flights to Canada. Because airline fares and their conditions constantly change, however, bargain hunters should not hesitate to ask if such a fare exists at the time they plan to travel.

While the definition of standby varies somewhat from airline to airline, it generally means that you make yourself available to buy a ticket for a flight (usually no sooner than the day of departure), then literally stand by on the chance that a seat will be empty. Once aboard, however, a standby passenger has the same meal service and frills (or lack of them) enjoyed by others in the economy class compartment.

Something else to check is the possibility of qualifying for a GIT (group inclusive travel) fare, which requires that a specific dollar amount of ground arrangements be purchased, in advance, along with the ticket. The requirements vary as to number of travel days and stopovers permitted, and the number of passengers required for a group. The actual fares also vary, but the cost will be spelled out in brochures distributed by the tour operators handling the ground arrangements. In the past, GIT fares were among the least expensive available from the established carriers, but the prevalence of discount fares has caused group fares to all but disappear from some air routes. Travelers reading brochures on group package tours to Canada will find that, in almost all cases, the applicable airfare given as a sample (to be added to the price of the land package to obtain the total tour price) is an APEX fare, the same discount fare available to the independent traveler.

The major airlines serving Canada from the US also may offer individual fare excursion rates similar to GIT fares, which are sold in conjunction with ground accommodation packages. Previously called ITX, these fares generally are offered as part of "air/hotel/car/transfer packages" and can reduce the cost of an economy fare by more than a third. The packages are booked for a specific amount of time, with return dates specified; rescheduling and cancellation restrictions and penalties vary from carrier to carrier. These fares are offered to popular destinations throughout Canada. At the time of this writing, this type of fare was offered by *American, Delta,* and *Northwest,* however, only *American*'s and *Northwest*'s offers represented substantial savings over the standard economy fare. (For further information on package options, see *Package Tours,* in this section.)

Finally, travelers looking for the least expensive possible airfares should scan the pages of their local newspapers for announcements of special promotional fares. Most major airlines traditionally have offered their most attractive special fares to encourage travel during slow seasons and to inaugurate and publicize new routes. Even if none of the above factors apply, prospective passengers can be fairly sure that the number of discount seats per flight at this lowest price is strictly limited, or that the fare offering includes a set expiration date — which means it's absolutely necessary to move fast to obtain the lowest possible prices. Unfortunately, special fare offers come and go quickly, and may not be available precisely when you want to travel.

Among other special airline promotional deals for which you should be on the lookout are discount or upgrade coupons, sometimes offered by the major carriers and found in mail-order merchandise catalogues. For instance, airlines sometimes issue coupons which typically cost around $25 and are good for a percentage discount or an upgrade on an international airline ticket — including flights to Canada. The only requirement beyond the fee generally is that a coupon purchaser is required to buy at least one item from the catalogue. There usually are some minimum airfare restrictions before the coupon is redeemable, but in general these are worthwhile offers. Restrictions often include certain blackout days (when the coupon cannot be used at all), usually imposed during peak travel periods. These coupons are particularly valuable to business travelers who tend to buy full-fare tickets, and while the coupons are issued in the buyer's name, they can be used by others who are traveling on the same itinerary.

Given the frequency with which the airfare picture changes, it is more than possible that by the time you are ready to fly, the foregoing discussion may be somewhat out of date. That's why it always is wise to comparison shop, and that requires reading the business and travel sections of your newspaper regularly, and making calls to all the airlines that serve your destination from your most convenient gateway. The potential savings are well worth the effort.

Ask about discount or promotional fares and about any conditions that might restrict booking, payment, cancellation, and changes in plans. Check the prices from other cities. A special rate may be offered in a nearby city but not in yours, and it may be enough of a bargain to warrant your leaving from that city. If you have a flexible schedule, investigate standby fares. But remember that, depending on your departure point, these may not work out to be the rock-bottom price. Ask if there is a difference in price for midweek versus weekend travel, or if there is a further discount for traveling early in the morning or late at night. Also be sure to investigate package deals, which are offered by virtually every airline. These may include a car rental, accommodations, and dining and/or sightseeing features, in addition to the basic airfare, and the combined cost of packaged elements usually is considerably less than the cost of the exact same elements when purchased separately.

If in your research you come across a deal that seems too good to be true, keep in mind that logic may not be a component of deeply discounted airfares — there's not always any sane relationship between miles to be flown and the price to get there. More often than not, the level of competition on a given route dictates the degree of discount, and don't be dissuaded from accepting an offer that sounds irresistible just because it also sounds illogical. Better to buy that inexpensive fare while it's being offered and worry about the sense — or absence thereof — while you're flying to your desired destination.

When you're satisfied that you've found the lowest possible price for which you can conveniently qualify (you may have to call the airline more than once, because different clerks have been known to quote different prices), make your booking. Then, to protect yourself against fare increases, purchase and pay for your ticket as soon as possible after you've received a confirmed reservation. Airlines generally will honor their tickets, even if the operative price at the time of your flight is higher than the price you paid; if fares go up between the time you *reserve* a flight and the time you *pay* for it, you likely will be out of luck. Finally, with excursion or discount fares, it is important to remember that when a reservation clerk says that you must purchase a ticket by a specific date, this is an absolute deadline. Miss the deadline and the airline automatically may cancel your reservation without telling you.

■ **Note:** Another wrinkle on the airfare scene is that if the fares go *down* after you purchase your ticket, you *may* be entitled to a refund of the difference. However, this is only possible in certain situations — availability and advance purchase restrictions pertaining to the lower rate are set by the airline. If you suspect that you may be able to qualify for such a refund, check with your travel agent or the airline (although some airline clerks may not be aware of this policy).

Frequent Flyers – Most of the leading US carriers serving Canada — including *American, Continental, Delta, Eastern, Northwest,* and *United* — now also offer a bonus system to frequent travelers. After the first 10,000 miles, for example, a passenger might be eligible for a first class seat for the coach fare; after another 10,000 miles, he or she might receive a discount on his or her next ticket purchase. The value of the bonuses continues to increase as more miles are logged.

Bonus miles also may be earned by patronizing affiliated car rental companies or hotel chains, or by using one of the credit cards that now offers this reward. In deciding whether to accept one of the many offers of a credit card from one of the issuing organizations that tempt you by offering frequent flyer mileage bonuses on a specific airline, first determine whether the interest rate charged on the unpaid balance is the same as (or less than) possible alternate credit cards, and whether the annual "membership" fee also is equal or lower. If these charges are slightly higher than those of competing cards, weigh the difference against the potential value in airfare savings. Also ask about any bonus miles awarded just for signing up — 1,000 is common, 5,000 generally the maximum. (For further information on credit cards, see *Credit and Currency,* in this section.)

For the most up-to-date information on frequent flyer bonus options, you may want to send for the monthly *Frequent* newsletter. Issued by Frequent Publications, it provides current information about frequent flyer plans in general, as well as specific data about promotions, awards, and combination deals to help you keep track of the profusion — and confusion — of current and upcoming availabilities. For a year's subscription, send $28 to Frequent Publications, 4715-C Town Center Dr., Colorado Springs, CO 80916 (phone: 800-333-5937).

There also is a monthly magazine called *Frequent Flyer,* but unlike the newsletter mentioned above, its focus is primarily on newsy articles of interest to business travelers and other frequent flyers. Published by Official Airline Guides (PO Box 58543, Boulder, CO 80322-8543; phone: 800-323-3537), *Frequent Flyer* is available for $24 for a 1-year subscription.

Low-Fare Airlines – In today's economic climate, the stimulus for special fares increasingly is the appearance of new airlines along popular routes. These tend to be smaller carriers that offer low fares because of lower overhead, non-union staffs, uncomplicated route networks, and other limitations in their service. On these airlines, all seats on any given flight generally sell for the same price, which is somewhat below the lowest discount fare offered by the larger, more established airlines. It is important to note that tickets offered by the smaller airlines specializing in low-cost travel frequently are not subject to the same restrictions as the lowest-priced ticket offered by the more established carriers. They may not require advance purchase or minimum and maximum stays, may involve no cancellation penalties, may be available one way or round-trip, and may, for all intents and purposes, resemble the competition's high-priced full-fare coach. But never assume this until you know it's so. A disadvantage to many of the low-fare airlines, however, is that when something goes wrong, such as delayed baggage or a flight cancellation due to equipment breakdown, their smaller fleets and fewer flights mean that passengers may have to wait longer for a solution than they would on one of the equipment-rich major carriers.

Taxes and Other Fees – Travelers who have shopped for the best possible flight at the lowest possible price should be warned that a number of extras will be added to that price and collected by the airline or travel agent who issues the ticket. In addition to the $6 International Air Transportation Tax — a departure tax paid by all passengers flying from the US to a foreign destination — the 8% federal US Transportation Tax applies to travel within the US or US territories. It does not apply to passengers flying between US cities en route to a foreign destination, unless the trip includes a stopover of more than 12 hours at a US point. Someone flying from Los Angeles to New York and stopping in New York for more than 12 hours before boarding a flight to Canada, for instance, would pay the 8% tax on the domestic portion of the trip. When flying from Canada back to the US, a Canadian Departure tax also is charged; this amounts to 5% of the ticket cost, plus CN$4, the total of which may not exceed CN$19. Note that all of these taxes *usually* are included in advertised fares and in the prices quoted by airlines reservation clerks.

Reservations – For those who don't have the time and patience to investigate personally all possible air departures and connections for a proposed trip, a travel agent can be of inestimable help. A good agent should have all the information on which flights go where and when, and which categories of tickets are available on each. Most have computerized reservation links with the major carriers, so that a seat can be reserved and confirmed in minutes. An increasing number of agents also possess fare-comparison computer programs, so they often are very reliable sources of detailed competitive price data. (For more information, see *How to Use a Travel Agent,* in this section.)

When making reservations through a travel agent, ask the agent to give the airline your home phone number, as well as your daytime business phone number. All too often the agent uses the agency number as the official contact for changes in flight plans. Especially during the winter, weather conditions hundreds or even thousands of miles away can wreak havoc with flight schedules. Aircraft are constantly in use, and a plane delayed in the Orient or on the West Coast can miss its scheduled flight from the East Coast the next morning. The airlines are fairly reliable about getting this sort of information to passengers if they can reach them; diligence does little good at 10 PM if the airline has only the agency or an office number.

Reconfirmation is strongly recommended for all international flights (though generally it is not required on US domestic flights). Some (though increasingly fewer) reservations to and from international destinations automatically are canceled after a required reconfirmation period (typically 72 hours) has passed — even if you have a confirmed, fully paid ticket in hand. It always is a good idea to call ahead to make sure that the airline did not slip up in entering your original reservation, or in registering any changes you may have made since, and that it has your seat reservation and/or special meal request in the computer. Although policies vary from carrier to carrier, some recommend that you reconfirm your return flight 48 to 72 hours in advance. If you look at the back of your ticket, you'll see the airline's reconfirmation policy stated explicitly. If in doubt — call.

Every travel agent or airline ticket office should give each passenger a reminder to reconfirm flights, but this seldom happens, so the responsibility rests with the traveler. Don't be lulled into a false sense of security by the "OK" on your ticket next to the number and time of the flight. That only means that a reservation has been entered; a reconfirmation still may be necessary.

If you plan not to take a flight on which you hold a confirmed reservation, by all means inform the airline. Because the problem of "no-shows" is a constant expense for airlines, they are allowed to overbook flights, a practice that often contributes to the threat of denied boarding for a certain number of passengers (see "Getting Bumped," below). Let the airline know you're not coming and you'll spare everyone some inconvenience and confusion. Bear in mind that only certain kinds of tickets allow the luxury of last minute changes in flight plans: Those sold on an open reservation system (first class and full-fare coach) do, while excursions and other discount fares often are restricted in some way. Even first class and coach passengers should remember that if they do not show up for a flight that is the first of several connecting ones, the airline very likely will cancel all of their ongoing reservations unless informed not to do so.

Seating – For most types of tickets, airline seats usually are assigned on a first-come, first-served basis at check-in, although some airlines make it possible to reserve a seat at the time of ticket purchase. Always check in early for your flight, even with advance seat assignments. A good rule of thumb for international flights is to arrive at the airport *at least* 2 hours before the scheduled departure to give yourself plenty of time in case there are long lines.

Most airlines furnish seating charts, which make choosing a seat much easier, but there are a few basics to consider. You must decide whether you prefer a window, aisle, or middle seat. On flights where smoking is permitted, you also should specify if you prefer the smoking or nonsmoking section.

The amount of legroom provided (as well as chest room, especially when the seat in front of you is in a reclining position) is determined by something called "pitch," a measure of the distance between the back of the seat in front of you and the front of the back of your seat. The amount of pitch is a matter of individual airline policy, not a function of the type of plane you fly. First class and business class seats have the greatest pitch, a fact that figures prominently in airline advertising. In economy class or coach, the standard pitch ranges from 33 to as little as 31 inches — downright cramped.

The number of seats abreast, another factor determining comfort, depends on a combination of airline policy and airplane dimensions. First and business classes have the fewest seats per row. Economy generally has 9 seats per row on a DC-10 or an L-1011, making either one slightly more comfortable than a 747, on which there normally are 10 seats per row. Charter flights on DC-10s and L-1011s, however, often have 10 seats per row and can be noticeably more cramped than 747 charters, on which the seating normally remains at 10 per row.

Airline representatives claim that most aircraft are more stable toward the front and midsection, while seats farthest away from the engines are quietest. Passengers who have long legs and are traveling on a wide-body aircraft might request a seat directly behind a door or emergency exit, since these seats often have greater than average pitch, or a seat in the first row of a given section, since these seats have extra legroom. It often is impossible, however, to see the movie from these seats, which are directly behind the plane's exits. Be aware that the first row of the economy section (called a "bulkhead" seat) on a conventional aircraft (not a widebody) does *not* offer extra legroom, since the fixed partition will not permit passengers to slide their feet under it, and that watching a movie from this first-row seat can be difficult and uncomfortable. A window seat protects you from aisle traffic and clumsy serving carts, and also allows you a view, while an aisle seat enables you to get up and stretch your legs without disturbing your fellow travelers. Middle seats are the least desirable, and seats in the last row are the worst of all, since they seldom recline fully. If you wish to avoid children on your flight or if you find that you are sitting in an especially noisy section, you usually are free to move to any unoccupied seat — if there is one.

If you are overweight, you may face the prospect of a long flight with special trepidation. Center seats in the alignments of wide-body 747s, L-1011s, and DC-10s are about 1½ inches wider than those on either side, so larger travelers tend to be more comfortable there.

Despite all these rules of thumb, finding out which specific rows are near emergency exits or at the front of a wide-body cabin can be difficult because seating arrangements on two otherwise identical planes vary from airline to airline. There is, however, a quarterly publication called the *Airline Seating Guide* that publishes seating charts for most major US airlines and many foreign carriers as well. Your travel agent should have a copy, or you can buy the US edition for $39.95 per year and the overseas edition for $44.95. Order from Carlson Publishing Co., Box 888, Los Alamitos, CA 90720 (phone: 213-493-4877).

Simply reserving an airline seat in advance, however, actually may guarantee very little. Most airlines require that passengers arrive at the departure gate at least 45 minutes (sometimes more) ahead of time to hold a seat reservation. *Air Canada,* for example, may cancel seat assignments and may not honor reservations of passengers who have not checked in some period of time — usually around 20 to 30 minutes, depending on the airport — before the scheduled departure time, and they *ask* travelers to check in at least 1 hour before all domestic flights and 2 hours before international flights. As this is only one airline's policy, it pays to read the fine print on the back of your ticket carefully and plan ahead.

A far better strategy is to visit an airline ticket office (or one of a select group of travel agents) to secure an actual boarding pass for your specific flight. Once this has been issued, airline computers show you as checked in, and you effectively own the seat you have selected (although some carriers may not honor boarding passes of passengers arriving at the gate less than 10 minutes before departure). This also is good — but not foolproof — insurance against getting bumped from an overbooked flight and is, therefore, an especially valuable tactic at peak travel times.

Smoking – One decision regarding choosing a seat has been taken out of the hands of many travelers who smoke. Effective February 25, 1990, the US government adopted a ban that prohibits smoking on all flights scheduled for 6 hours or less within the US and its territories. The new regulation applies to both domestic and international carriers serving these routes.

In the case of flights to Canada, by law these rules do not apply to nonstop flights going directly from the US to Canada, or those flying with a continuous flight time of over 6 hours between stops in the US or its territories. As we went to press, however, all major carriers flying from the US to Canada included such flights in their "domestic" category in terms of nonsmoking rules, and no smoking was allowed on flights between the US and Canada with a continuous flight time of under 6 hours. (Note that there is no smoking on any North American *Canadian Airlines International* or *Air Canada* flight.)

On those few remaining flights that do permit smoking, the US Department of Transportation has determined that nonsmoking sections must be enlarged to accommodate all passengers who wish to sit in one. The airline does not, however, have to shift seating to accommodate nonsmokers who arrive late for a flight or travelers flying standby, and in general not all airlines can guarantee a seat in the nonsmoking section on international flights. Cigar and pipe smoking are prohibited on all flights, even in the smoking sections.

For a wallet-size guide, which notes in detail the rights of nonsmokers according to these regulations, send a self-addressed, stamped envelope to ASH (Action on Smoking and Health), Airline Card, 2013 H St. NW, Washington, DC 20006 (phone: 202-659-4310).

Flying with Children – On longer flights, the bulkhead seats usually are reserved for families traveling with small children. As a general rule, infants under 2 years of age travel free on most flights to Canada, provided they do not occupy a seat (a second infant without a second adult would pay the fare applicable to children ages 2 through 11, generally 75% of the adult fare). On *Canadian Airlines International* and *Air Canada,* this applies only to adults paying full economy fares; if the adult is traveling on a discounted fare, the 25% discount for the child does not apply.

Although airlines will, on request, supply bassinets for infants, most carriers encourage parents to bring their own infant safety seat on board, which then is strapped into the airline seat with a regular seat belt. This is much safer — and certainly more comfortable — than holding the child in your lap. If you do not purchase a seat for your baby, you have the option of bringing the infant restraint along on the off-chance that there might be an empty seat next to yours — in which case many airlines will let you have that seat free for your baby and infant seat. However, if there is no empty seat available, the infant seat no doubt will have to be checked as baggage (and most likely you will have to pay an additional charge), since it generally does not fit under the seat or in the overhead racks.

The safest bet is to pay for a seat — this usually will be the same as fares applicable to children ages 2 through 11. You might have to do some number-juggling to determine the cheapest fare for the infant. Excursion fares, which usually are the least expensive, often do not have children's rates, whereas the higher-priced fares usually are the ones that offer discounts for children.

Be forewarned: Some safety seats designed primarily for use in cars do not fit properly into plane seats. Although nearly all seats manufactured since 1985 carry labels indicating whether they meet federal standards for use aboard planes, actual seat sizes may vary from carrier to carrier. At the time of this writing, the FAA was in the process of reviewing and revising airline policies with regard to infant travel and safety devices — it was still to be determined if children should be *required* to sit in safety seats and whether the airlines will have to provide them. Canada's aviation regulatory authority, Transport Canada, recently participated with the FAA in a joint dynamic testing project of various methods of restraining infants. Transport Canada also is examining designs for seats specifically for aircraft use, and moving toward a policy similar to that being discussed by the FAA.

When checking in, and using either a bassinet or infant seat, request a bulkhead or other seat that has enough room in front to use it. On some planes, bassinets hook into a bulkhead wall; on others it is placed on the floor in front of you. Even if you do use a bassinet, babies must be held during takeoff and landing.

The entire subject of flying with children — including a discussion of car seats — is covered in a special supplementary issue of a newsletter called *Family Travel Times,* published by *Travel With Your Children (TWYCH).* An annual subscription (10 issues) is $35, and the "Airline Guide" supplement is available separately for $10, or it will be included free with a subscription. Contact *TWYCH* at 80 Eighth Ave., New York, NY 10011 (phone: 212-206-0688). (For more information on flying with children, see *Hints for Traveling with Children,* in this section.)

Meals – If you have specific diet requirements, be sure to let the airline know well before departure time. The available meals include vegetarian, seafood, kosher, Muslim, Hindu, high-protein, low-calorie, low-cholesterol, low-fat, low-sodium, diabetic, bland, and children's menus. There is no extra charge for this option. It usually is necessary to request special meals when you make your reservations — check-in time is too late. It's also wise to reconfirm that your request for a special meal has made its way into the airline's computer — the time to do this is 24 hours before departure. (Note that special meals generally are not available on intra-Canadian flights on small local carriers. If this poses a problem, try to eat before you board, or bring food with you.)

Baggage – Travelers from the US face two different kinds of rules. When you fly in on a US airline or on a major international carrier, US baggage regulations will be in effect. Though airline baggage allowances vary slightly, in general all passengers are allowed to carry on board, without charge, one piece of luggage that will fit easily under a seat of the plane or in an overhead bin and whose combined dimensions (length, width, and depth) do not exceed 45 inches. (If you prefer not to carry it with you, most airlines will allow you to check this bag in the hold.) A reasonable amount of reading material, camera equipment, and a handbag also are allowed. In addition, all passengers are allowed to check two bags in the cargo hold: one usually not to exceed 62 inches when length, width, and depth are combined, the other not to exceed 55 inches in combined dimensions. Generally no single bag may weigh more than 70 pounds.

In general, baggage allowances follow these guidelines in Canada, but care should be exercised on regional and local airlines. If you are flying from the US to Canada and connecting to a domestic flight, you generally will be allowed the same amount of baggage as on the international flight; if you break your trip and then take a domestic flight, the local carrier's weight restrictions will apply. The smaller aircraft of domestic carriers, however, often don't have the same luggage capacity and also may have to carry mail and freight to outpost destinations. When booking flights off the routes of major trunk carriers, verify baggage allowances.

Charges for additional, oversize, or overweight bags usually are made at a flat rate — the actual dollar amount varying from carrier to carrier. If you plan to travel with a bike, skis, golf clubs, or other sports gear, be sure to check with the airline beforehand. Most have procedures for handling such baggage, but you probably will have to pay for transport regardless of how much other baggage you have checked.

Airline policies regarding baggage allowances for children vary and usually are based on the percentage of full adult fare paid. Children paying 50% or more of an adult fare on most US carriers are entitled to the same baggage allowances as a full-fare passenger, whereas infants traveling at 10% of the adult fare are entitled to only one piece of baggage, the combined dimensions of which may not exceed 45 inches. Particularly for international carriers, it's wise to check ahead. Often there is no luggage allowance for a child traveling on an adult's lap or in a bassinet.

To reduce the chances of your luggage going astray, remove all airline tags from previous trips, label each bag inside and out — with your business address rather than your home address on the outside, to prevent thieves from knowing whose house might be unguarded. Lock everything and double-check the tag that the airline attaches to make sure that it is coded correctly for your destination: YOW for Ottawa International Airport, YUL for Dorval Airport in Montreal, or YYZ for Lester B. Pearson Airport in Toronto, for instance.

If your bags are not in the baggage claim area after your flight, or if they're damaged, report the problem to airline personnel immediately. Keep in mind that policies regarding the specific time limit in which you have to make your claim vary from carrier to carrier. Fill out a report form on your lost or damaged luggage and hold on to a copy of it and your original baggage claim check. If you must surrender the check to claim a damaged bag, get a receipt for it to prove that you did, indeed, check your baggage on the flight. If luggage is missing, be sure to give the airline your destination and/or a telephone number where you can be reached. Also take the name and number of the person in charge of recovering lost luggage.

Most airlines have emergency funds for passengers stranded away from home without their luggage, but if it turns out your bags are truly lost and not simply delayed, do not then and there sign anything indicating you'll accept an offered settlement. Since the airline is responsible for the value of your bags within certain statuary limits ($1,250 per passenger for lost baggage on a US domestic flight; $9.07 per pound or $20 per kilo for checked baggage, and up to $400 per passenger for unchecked baggage on an international flight), you should take some time to assess the extent of your loss (see *Insurance,* in this section). It's a good idea to keep records indicating the value of the contents of your luggage. A wise idea is to take a Polaroid picture of the most valuable of your packed items just after putting them in your suitcase.

Considering the increased incidence of damage to baggage, it's now more than ever a good idea to keep the sales slips that confirm how much you paid for your bags. These are invaluable in establishing the value of damaged baggage and eliminate any arguments. A better way to protect your precious baggage from the luggage-eating conveyers is to try to carry your gear on board wherever possible.

Airline Clubs – US carriers often have clubs for travelers who pay for membership. These clubs are not solely for first class passengers, although a first class ticket *may* entitle a passenger to lounge privileges. Membership (which, by law, now requires a fee) entitles the traveler to use the private lounges at airports along their route, to refreshments served in those lounges, and to check-cashing privileges at most of their counters. Extras include special telephone numbers for individual reservations, embossed luggage tags, and a membership card for identification. Two airlines that fly to

Canada and offer membership in such clubs are: *American* — the *Admiral's Club,* single yearly membership is $150 for the first year, $100 yearly thereafter, spouse an additional $70, and lifetime memberships also available — and *Continental* — the *President's Club,* single yearly membership is $140 for the first year, $90 yearly thereafter, lifetime membership including spouse also available. And frequent travelers who have flown over 60,000 miles on *Air Canada* can join the *Maple Leaf Club,* single yearly membership is $150 and holders of the club's Elite Card can share lounge facilities with one guest. However, such companies do not have club facilities in all airports; other airlines also offer a variety of special services in many airports.

Getting Bumped – A special air travel problem is the possibility that an airline will accept more reservations (and sell more tickets) than there are seats on a given flight. This is entirely legal and is done to make up for "no-shows," passengers who don't show up for a flight for which they have made reservations and bought tickets. If the airline has oversold the flight and everyone does show up, there simply aren't enough seats. When this happens, the airline is subject to stringent rules designed to protect travelers.

In such cases, the airline first seeks ticketholders willing to give up their seats voluntarily in return for a negotiable sum of money, or some other inducement such as an offer of upgraded seating on the next flight or a voucher for a free trip at some other time. If there are not enough volunteers, the airline may bump passengers against their wishes.

Anyone inconvenienced in this way, however, is entitled to an explanation of the criteria used to determine who does and does not get on the flight, as well as compensation if the resulting delay exceeds certain limits. If the airline can put the bumped passengers on an alternate flight that is *scheduled to arrive* at their original destination within 1 hour of their originally scheduled arrival time, no compensation is owed. If the delay is more than an hour but less than 2 hours on a domestic US flight or less than 4 hours on an international flight, they must be paid denied-boarding compensation equivalent to the one-way fare to their destination (but not more than $200). If the delay is more than 2 hours beyond the original arrival time on a domestic flight or more than 4 hours on an international flight, the compensation must be doubled (but not more than $400). The airline also may offer bumped travelers a voucher for a free flight instead of the denied-boarding compensation. The passenger can choose either the money or the voucher, the dollar value of which may be no less than the monetary compensation to which the passenger would be entitled. The voucher is not a substitute for the bumped passenger's original ticket; the airline continues to honor that as well. Keep in mind that the above regulations and policies are for flights leaving the US only, and do *not* apply to charters or to inbound flights originating abroad, even on US carriers.

In Canada, each airline is free to determine what compensation it will pay to passengers who are bumped because of overbooking. However, they generally spell out their policies on airline tickets. *Air Canada*'s policy, for example, is similar to US policy. Passengers involuntarily bumped usually are paid the price of a one-way ticket (up to $200) if the airline can get them to their destination within 4 hours of the original arrival time, and twice that amount (up to $400) if they reach their destination 4 or more hours late. Keep in mind that this is one airline's policy only. Don't assume all carriers will be as generous.

To protect yourself as best you can against getting bumped, arrive at the airport early, allowing plenty of time to check in and get to the gate. If the flight is oversold, ask immediately for the written statement explaining the airline's policy on denied-boarding compensation and its boarding priorities. If the airline refuses to give you this information, or if you feel they have not handled the situation properly, file a complaint with both the airline and the appropriate government agency (see "Consumer Protection," below).

Delays and Cancellations – The above compensation rules also do not apply if the flight is canceled or delayed, or if a smaller aircraft is substituted due to mechanical problems. Each airline has its own policy for assisting passengers whose flights are delayed or canceled or who must wait for another flight because their original one was overbooked. Most airline personnel will make new travel arrangements if necessary. If the delay is longer than 4 hours, the airline may pay for a phone call or telegram, a meal, and, in some cases, a hotel room and transportation to it.

■ **Caution:** If you are bumped or miss a flight, be sure to ask the airline to notify other airlines on which you have reservations or connecting flights. When your name is taken off the passenger list of your initial flight, the computer usually cancels all of your reservations automatically, unless *you* take steps to preserve them.

CHARTER FLIGHTS: By booking a block of seats on a specially arranged flight, charter operators offer travelers air transportation, often coupled with a hotel room, meals, and other travel services, for a substantial reduction over the full coach or economy fare.

Charters once were the best bargains around, but this is no longer necessarily the case. As a result, charter flights have been discontinued in many areas, but they still can be a good buy to some popular travel destinations, including Canada. Charters are especially attractive to people living in smaller cities or out-of-the-way places, because they frequently take off from nearby airports, saving travelers the inconvenience and expense of getting to a major gateway to begin their Canadian trip.

Where demand persists, charter operators will continue to rent planes or seats from scheduled airlines (or from special charter airlines) and offer flights to the public directly through advertisements or travel agents. You buy the ticket from the operator or the agent, not from the airline owning the plane. With the advent of APEX and various promotional fares on the major airlines and the appearance of low-fare airlines, however, charter flights lost some of their budget-conscious clientele and suffered some lean years, especially on highly competitive routes with a choice of other bargains. At the same time, many of the larger companies running charter programs began to offer both charter flights and discounted scheduled flights (see below). Nevertheless, among the current offerings, charter flights to Canadian cities are common, a sign that they still represent a good value.

Charter travel once required that an individual be a member of a club or other "affinity" group whose main purpose was not travel. But since the approval of "public charters" years ago, operators have had some of the flexibility of scheduled airlines, making charters more competitive. Public charters are open to anyone, whether part of a group or not, and have no advance booking requirements or minimum stay requirements. Operators can offer air-only charters, selling transportation alone, or they can offer charter packages — the flight plus a combination of land arrangements such as accommodations, meals, tours, or car rental.

From the consumer's standpoint, charters differ from scheduled airlines in two main respects: You generally need to book and pay in advance, and you can't change the itinerary or the departure and return dates once you've booked the flight. In practice, however, these restrictions don't always apply. Though charters almost always are round-trip, and it is unlikely that you would be sold a one-way seat on a round-trip flight, it may be possible to book a one-way charter in the US, giving you more flexibility in scheduling your return. Although most charters still require advance reservations, some permit last-minute bookings (when there are unsold seats available), and some even offer seats on a standby basis. And if you take a charter within Canada, you can buy a ticket up to the day of departure — if a seat is available.

The savings provided by charters varies, depending on their point of departure in the US and their destination in Canada. As a rule, a charter to any given destination can cost anywhere from $50 to $200 less than an economy fare on a major carrier.

Some things to keep in mind about the charter game are:

1. It cannot be repeated often enough that if you are forced to cancel your trip, you can lose much (and possibly all) of your money unless you have cancellation insurance, which is a *must* (see *Insurance*, in this section). Frequently, if the cancellation is made sufficiently far in advance (often 6 weeks or more), you may forfeit only a $25 or $50 penalty. If you cancel only 2 or 3 weeks before the flight, there may be no refund at all unless you or the operator can provide a substitute passenger.
2. Charter flights may be canceled by the operator up to 10 days before departure for any reason, usually underbooking. Your money is returned in this event, but there may be too little time to make new arrangements.
3. Most charters have little of the flexibility of regularly scheduled flights regarding refunds and the changing of flight dates; if you book a return flight, you must be on it or lose your money.
4. Charter operators are permitted to assess a surcharge, if fuel or other costs warrant it, of up to 10% of the airfare up to 10 days before departure.
5. Because of the economics of charter flights, your plane almost always will be full, so you will be crowded, though not necessarily uncomfortable.

Booking – If you do take a charter, read the contract's fine print carefully and pay particular attention to the following:

1. Instructions concerning the payment of the deposit and its balance and to whom the check is to be made payable. Ordinarily, checks are made out to an escrow account, which means the charter company can't spend your money until your flight has safely returned. This provides some protection for you. To ensure the safe handling of your money, make out your check to the escrow account, the number of which must appear by law on the brochure, though all too often it is on the back in fine print. Write the details of the charter, including the destination and dates, on the face of the check; on the back, print "For Deposit Only." Your travel agent may prefer that you make out your check to the agency, saying that it will then pay the tour operator the fee minus commission. It is perfectly legal to write the check as we suggest, however, and if your agent objects too vociferously (he or she should trust the tour operator to send the proper commission), consider taking your business elsewhere. If you don't make your check out to the escrow account, you lose the protection of escrow should the trip be canceled. Furthermore, recent bankruptcies in the travel industry have served to point out that even the protection of escrow may not be enough to safeguard a traveler's investment. More and more, insurance is becoming a necessity. The charter company should be bonded (usually by an insurance company), and if you want to file a claim against it, the claim should be sent to the bonding agent. The contract will set a time limit within which a claim must be filed.
2. Specific stipulations and penalties for cancellations. Most charters allow you to cancel up to 45 days in advance without major penalty, but some cancellation dates are 50 to 60 days before departure.
3. Stipulations regarding cancellation and major changes made by the charterer. US rules say that charter flights may not be canceled within 10 days of departure except when circumstances — such as natural disasters or political upheavals — make it physically impossible to fly. Charterers may make "major changes," however, such as in the date or place of departure or return, but you are entitled

to cancel and receive a full refund if you don't accept these changes. A price increase of more than 10% at any time up to 10 days before departure is considered a major change; no price increase is allowed during the last 10 days immediately before departure.

Canadian Airlines International offers charter flights through its subsidiary *Canadian Holidays,* both within Canada and to foreign destinations. Bookings can be made through *Canadian Airlines International* or through a travel agent. If you're interested in charter flights within Canada, particularly to more remote destinations, it's best to bear in mind that US travel agents may be unaware of the full range of possibilities. The Sunday travel section of a major Canadian city newspaper is the best source of intra-Canadian charter flight opportunities. Provincial tourist offices also may be able to provide information on reliable local charter companies.

DISCOUNTS ON SCHEDULED FLIGHTS: The APEX fare is an example of a promotional fare offered on regularly scheduled transatlantic flights by most major airlines. Promotional fares often are called discount fares because they cost less than what used to be the standard airline fare — full-fare economy. Nevertheless, they cost the traveler the same whether they are bought through a travel agent or directly from the airline. Tickets that cost less if bought from some outlet other than the airline do exist, however. While it is likely that the vast majority of travelers flying to Canada in the near future will be doing so on a promotional fare or charter rather than on a "discount" air ticket of this sort, it still is a good idea for cost-conscious consumers to be aware of the latest developments in the budget airfare scene. Note that the following discussion makes clear distinctions among the types of discounts available based on how they reach the consumer; in actual practice, the distinctions are not nearly so precise. One organization may operate part of its business in one fashion and the remainder in another; a second organization may operate all of its business in the same fashion, but outsiders — and sometimes the organization itself — would have difficulty classifying it.

Courier Travel – There was a time when traveling as a courier was a sort of underground way to save money and visit otherwise unaffordable destinations, but more and more the once exotic idea of traveling as a courier is becoming a very "establishment" exercise. Courier means no more than a traveler who accompanies freight of one sort or another, and typically that freight replaces what otherwise would be the traveler's checked baggage. Be prepared, therefore, to carry all your own personal travel gear in a bag that fits under the seat in front of you. In addition, the so-called courier usually pays only a portion of the total airfare — the freight company pays the remainder — and the courier also may be assessed a small registration fee.

There are over 4 dozen courier companies operating actively around the globe, and there are at least two travel newsletters that have sprung up for the purpose of publishing courier opportunities. One of these, called *Travel Secrets* (PO Box 2325, New York, NY 10108), lists more than 20 US and Canadian courier companies. The other, *Travel Unlimited* (PO Box 1058, Allston, MA 02135), lists 30 to 40 courier companies and agents worldwide. In addition, courier companies are listed in the yellow pages and, in general, are best used by folks with *very* flexible travel schedules.

Net Fare Sources – The newest notion for reducing the costs of travel services comes from travel agents who offer individual travelers "net" fares. Defined simply, a net fare is the bare minimum amount at which an airline or tour operator will carry a prospective traveler. It doesn't include the amount that normally would be paid to the travel agent as a commission. Traditionally, such travel agent commissions amount to about 10% on domestic fares and from 8% to 20% on international tickets — not counting significant additions to these commission levels that are payable retroactively when agents sell more than a specific volume of tickets or trips for a single supplier. At press time, at least one travel agency in the US was offering travelers the opportunity to purchase tickets and/or tours for a net price. Instead of making its income from individual commissions, this agency assesses a fixed fee that may or may not provide a bargain for travelers; it requires a little arithmetic to determine whether to use the services of a net travel agent or those of one who accepts conventional commissions. One of the potential drawbacks of buying from agencies selling travel services at net fares is that some airlines refuse to do business with them, thus possibly limiting your flight options.

Travel Avenue (formerly *McTravel Travel Services*) is a formula fee-based agency that rebates its ordinary agency commission to the customer. For domestic flights, an agent will find the lowest retail fare, then rebate 8% to 11% (depending on the airline selected) of that price minus an $8 ticket-writing charge. The rebate percentage for international flights varies from 8% to 25% (again depending on the airline), and the ticket-writing fee is $20. The ticket-writing charge is imposed per ticket; if the ticket includes more than eight separate flights, an additional $8 or $20 fee is added.

Travel Avenue will rebate on all tickets including Max Savers, Super Savers, and senior citizen passes; if the customer is using a free flight coupon, an additional $5 coupon processing fee also is added. Available 7 days a week, reservations should be made far enough in advance to allow the tickets to be sent by first class mail, since extra charges accrue for special handling. It's possible to economize further by making your own airline reservation, then asking *Travel Avenue* only to write/issue your ticket. For travelers who live outside the Chicago area, business may be transacted by phone, and purchases may be charged to a credit card.

And for travelers seeking discounts on other travel services, *Travel Avenue* offers a similar net cost service, through which travelers can collect rebates on the cost of hotel accommodations and car rentals if the booking is made through *Travel Avenue*. Upon returning home, you simply send *Travel Avenue* a copy of your receipt and they will send you a check for 5% of the total bill — returning part of their agency commission to the consumer. For further information, contact *Travel Avenue* at 641 W. Lake St., Suite 201, Chicago, IL 60606-1012 (phone: 312-876-1116 in Illinois; 800-333-3335 elsewhere in the US).

Consolidators and Bucket Shops – Other vendors of travel services can afford to sell tickets to their customers at an even greater discount because the airline has sold the tickets to them at a substantial discount, a practice in which many airlines indulge, albeit discreetly, preferring that the general public not know they are undercutting their own "list" prices. Airlines anticipating a slow period on a particular route sometimes sell off a certain portion of their capacity to a wholesaler or consolidator at a deep discount. The wholesaler sometimes is a charter operator who resells the seats to the public as though they were charter seats, which is why prospective travelers perusing the brochures of charter operators with large programs frequently see a number of flights designated as "scheduled service." As often as not, however, the consolidator, in turn, sells the seats to a travel agency specializing in discounting. Airlines also can sell seats directly to such an agency, which thus acts as its own consolidator. The airline offers the seats either at a net wholesale price, but without the volume-purchase requirement that would be difficult for a retail travel agency to fulfill, or at the standard price, but with a commission override large enough (as high as 50%) to allow both a profit and a price reduction to the public.

Travel agencies specializing in discounting are sometimes called "bucket shops," a term fraught with connotations of unreliability in this country. But in today's highly competitive travel marketplace, more and more conventional travel agencies are selling consolidator-supplied tickets, and the old bucket shops' image is becoming more respectable. Agencies that specialize in discounted tickets exist in most large cities, and usually can be found by studying the smaller ads in the travel sections of the Sunday newspapers. They deal mostly in transatlantic and other international tickets.

Before buying a discounted ticket, whether from a bucket shop or a conventional, full-service travel agency, keep the following considerations in mind: To be in a position to judge how much you'll be saving, first find out the "list" prices of tickets to your destination. Then do some comparison shopping among agencies, always bearing in mind that the lowest-priced ticket may not provide the most convenient or most comfortable flight. Also bear in mind that a ticket that may not differ much in price from one available directly from the airline may, however, allow the circumvention of such things as the advance-purchase requirement. If your plans are less than final, be sure to find out about any other restrictions, such as penalties for canceling a flight or changing a reservation. Most discount tickets are non-endorsable, meaning they can be used only on the airline that issued them, and they usually are marked "nonrefundable" to prevent their being cashed in for a list price refund. (A refund of the price paid for the ticket often is possible, but it must be obtained from the outlet from which it was purchased rather than from the airline.)

A great many bucket shops are small businesses operating on a thin margin, so it's a good idea to check the local Better Business Bureau for any complaints registered against the one with which you're dealing — before parting with any money. If you still do not feel reassured, consider buying discounted tickets only through a conventional travel agency, which can be expected to have found its own reliable source of consolidator tickets — some of the largest consolidators, in fact, sell only to travel agencies.

A few bucket shops require payment in cash or by certified check or money order, but if credit cards are accepted, use that option, which allows purchasers to refuse to pay charges for services they haven't received. Note, however, if buying from a charter operator selling seats for both scheduled and charter flights, that the scheduled seats are not protected by the regulations — including the use of escrow accounts — governing the charter seats. Well-established charter operators, nevertheless, may extend the same protection to their scheduled flights. When this is the case, consumers should be sure that the payment option selected directs their money into the escrow account.

Among the consolidators offering discount fares to Canada are *25 West Tours* (2490 Coral Way, Miami, FL 33145; phone: 305-856-0810; 800-423-6954 in Florida; 800-252-5052 elsewhere in the US) and *TFI Tours International* (34 W. 37th St., 12th Floor, New York, NY 10001; phone: 212-736-1140).

■ **Note:** Although rebating and discounting are becoming increasingly common, there is some legal ambiguity concerning them. Strictly speaking, it is legal to discount domestic tickets, but not international tickets. On the other hand, the law that prohibits discounting, the Federal Aviation Act of 1958, consistently is ignored these days, in part because consumers benefit from the practice and in part because many illegal arrangements are indistinguishable from legal ones. Since the line separating the two is so fine that even the authorities can't always tell the difference, it is unlikely that most consumers would be able to do so, and in fact it is not illegal to *buy* a discounted ticket. If the issue of legality bothers you, ask the agency whether any ticket you're about to buy would be permissible under the above-mentioned act.

OTHER DISCOUNT TRAVEL SOURCES: An excellent source of information on economical travel opportunities is the *Consumer Reports Travel Letter,* published monthly by Consumers Union. It keeps abreast of the scene on a wide variety of fronts, including package tours, rental cars, insurance, and more, but it is especially helpful for its comprehensive coverage of airfares, offering guidance on all the options from scheduled flights on major or low-fare airlines to charters and discount sources. For a year's subscription, send $37 to *Consumer Reports Travel Letter* (PO Box 2886, Boulder, CO 80322; phone: 800-525-0643). Another source is *Travel Smart,* a monthly newsletter offering information on a wide variety of trips with additional discount travel services available to subscribers. For a year's subscription, send $37 to Communications House (40 Beechdale Rd., Dobbs Ferry, NY 10522; phone: 914-693-8300 in New York; 800-327-3633 elsewhere in the US).

Still another way to take advantage of bargain airfares is open to those who have a flexible schedule. A number of organizations, usually set up as last-minute travel clubs and functioning on a membership basis, routinely keep in touch with travel suppliers to help them dispose of unsold inventory at discounts of between 15% and 60%. A great deal of the inventory consists of complete tour packages and cruises, but some clubs offer air-only charter seats and, occasionally, seats on scheduled flights. Members pay an annual fee and get a toll-free hot line number to call for information on imminent trips. In some cases, they also receive periodic mailings with information on bargain travel opportunities for which there is more advance notice.

Despite the suggestive names of the clubs providing these services, last-minute travel does not necessarily mean than you cannot make plans until literally the last minute. Trips can be announced as little as a few days or as much as 2 months before departure, but the average is from 1 to 4 weeks' notice. It does mean that your choice at any given time is limited to what is offered and if your heart is set on a particular destination, you might not find what you want, no matter how attractive the bargains. Among these organizations are the following:

> *Discount Club of America,* 61-33 Woodhaven Blvd., Rego Park, NY, 11374; (phone: 800-321-9587 or 718-335-9612). Annual fee: $39 per family.
>
> *Discount Travel International,* Ives Building, 114 Forrest Ave., Suite 205, Narberth, PA 19072 (phone: 800-334-9294). Annual fee: $45 per household.
>
> *Encore Short Notice,* 4501 Forbes Blvd., Lanham, MD 20706 (phone: 301-459-8020 or 800-638-0930 for customer service). Annual fee: $48 per family.
>
> *Last-Minute Travel Club,* 132 Brookline Ave., Boston, MA 02215 (phone: 800-LAST-MIN or 617-267-9800). As of this year, no fee.
>
> *Moment's Notice,* 425 Madison Ave., New York, NY 10017 (phone: 212-486-0503). Annual fee: $45 per family.
>
> *Spur-of-the-Moment Tours and Cruises,* 10780 Jefferson Blvd., Culver City, CA 90230 (phone: 213-839-2418 in California; 800-343-1991 elsewhere in the US). No fee.
>
> *Traveler's Advantage,* 3033 S. Parker Rd., Suite 1000, Aurora, CO 80014 (phone: 800-548-1116). Annual fee: $49 per family.
>
> *Worldwide Discount Travel Club,* 1674 Meridian Ave., Miami Beach, FL 33139 (phone: 305-534-2082). Annual fee: $40 per person; $50 per family.

Bartered Travel Sources – Say a company buys advertising space for a hotel in a newspaper. As payment, the hotel gives the publishing company a number of hotel rooms in lieu of cash. This is barter, a common means of exchange among hotels, airlines, car rental companies, cruise lines, tour operators, restaurants, and other travel service companies. When a bartering company finds itself with excess hotel rooms (or empty airline seats or cruise ship cabin space, and so on) and offers them to the public, considerable savings can be enjoyed.

Bartered-travel clubs often offer discounts of up to 50% to members, who pay an annual fee (approximately $50 at press time) that entitles them to select from the flights, cruises, or hotels which the company obtained by barter. Members usually present a voucher, club credit card, or scrip (a dollar-denomination voucher negotiable only for the bartered product) to the hotel, which in turn subtracts the dollar amount from the bartering company's account.

Selling bartered travel is a perfectly legitimate means of retailing. One advantage to club members is that they don't have to wait until the last minute to obtain room or flight reservations. However, hotel rooms and airline seats usually are offered to members on a space-available basis. Ticket vouchers are good only for a particular hotel and cannot be used elsewhere. The same applies to car rentals, cruises, package tours, and restaurants. The following clubs offer bartered travel at a discount to members:

IGT (In Good Taste) Services, 1111 Lincoln Rd., 4th Floor, Miami Beach, FL 33139 (phone: 800-444-8872 or 305-534-7900). Annual membership fee: $48 per person.

Travel Guild, 18210 Redmond Way, Redmond, WA 98052 (phone: 206-885-1213). Annual membership fee: $48 per family.

Travel World Leisure Club, 225 W. 34th St., Suite 2203, New York, NY 10122 (phone: 800-444-TWLC or 212-239-4855). Annual membership fee: $50 per family.

CONSUMER PROTECTION: Consumers who feel that they have not been dealt with fairly by an airline should make their complaints known. Begin with the customer service representative at the airport where the problem occurs. If he or she cannot resolve your complaint to your satisfaction, write to the airline's consumer office. In a businesslike, typed letter, explain what reservations you held, what happened, the names of the employees involved, and what you expect the airline to do to remedy the situation. Send copies (never the originals) of the tickets, receipts, and other documents that support your claims. Ideally, all correspondence should be sent via certified mail, return receipt requested. This provides proof that your complaint was received.

If you still receive no satisfaction and your complaint is against a US carrier, contact the US Department of Transportation. Passengers with consumer complaints — lost baggage, compensation for getting bumped, smoking and nonsmoking rules, deceptive practices by an airline, charter regulations — should contact the Consumer Affairs Division, US Department of Transportation (400 Seventh St. SW, Room 10405, Washington, DC 20590; phone: 202-366-2220). DOT personnel stress, however, that consumers initially should direct their complaints to the airline that provoked them.

If your complaint involves a Canadian airline, you can enlist the aid of the Canadian government. Write a formal letter requesting assistance (attaching copies of your correspondence with the airline, if you think it helps explain your case), and address the letter to the Director, Air and Marine Complains Investigations (15 80th St., 17th Floor, Jules Leger Bldg., Hull, Quebec K1A 0N9, Canada). For further information call 613-997-6567.

The deregulation of US airlines has meant that a traveler must find out for himself or herself what he or she is entitled to receive. The Department of Transportation's informative consumer booklet *Fly Rights* is a good place to start. To receive a copy, send $1 to the Superintendent of Documents, US Government Printing Office (Washington, DC 20402-9325; phone: 202-783-3238). Specify its stock number, 050-000-000513-5, and allow 3 to 4 weeks for delivery.

To avoid more serious problems, *always* choose charter flights and tour packages with care. When you consider a charter, ask your travel agent who runs it and carefully check out the company. The Better Business Bureau in the company's home city can report on how many complaints, if any, have been lodged against it in the past. As emphasized above, protect yourself with trip cancellation and interruption insurance, which can help safeguard your investment if you or a traveling companion is unable to make the trip and must cancel too late to receive a full refund from the company providing your travel services. (This is advisable whether you're buying a charter flight alone or a tour package for which the airfare is provided by charter or scheduled flight.)

Some travel insurance policies have an additional feature, covering the possibility of default or bankruptcy on the part of the tour operator or airline, charter or scheduled.

Should this type of coverage not be available to you (state insurance regulations vary, there is a wide difference in price, and so on), your best bet is to pay for airline tickets and tour packages with a credit card. The federal Fair Credit Billing Act permits purchasers to refuse payment for credit card charges where services have not been delivered, so the onus of dealing with the receiver for a bankrupt airline falls on the credit card company. Do not rely on another airline to honor the ticket you're holding, since the days when virtually all major carriers subscribed to a default protection program that bound them to do so are long gone. Some airlines may voluntarily step forward to accommodate the stranded passengers of a fellow carrier, but this now is an entirely altruistic act.

Traveling by Train

Perhaps the most economical, and often the most pleasant way to see a lot of a foreign country in a relatively short time is by rail. It certainly is the quickest way to travel between two city centers up to 300 miles apart (beyond that, a flight normally would be quicker, even counting the time it takes to get to and from the airport). But time isn't always the only consideration. Traveling by train is a way to keep moving and to keep seeing at the same time, and with the special discounts available to visitors, it can be an almost irresistible bargain. You only need to get to a station on time; after that, put your watch in your pocket and relax. You may not get to your destination exactly at the appointed hour (although Canadian trains are quite punctual for the most part), but you'll have a marvelous time looking out the window and enjoying the ride.

Despite recent cutbacks in Canadian rail service, transcontinental service still exists. If you have the time — the 3,000-mile trip takes about 4 days and 3 nights — there is no better way to grasp the vastness of Canada than to cross the nation aboard connecting trains from Halifax to Montreal to Toronto to Vancouver (or vice versa). In the course of the journey you'll see the variety of geography that shapes the lives of Canadians from the East Coast to the West Coast, from the St. Lawrence to the Pacific. Prospective train travelers with less time should note that the route segment between Calgary and Vancouver, through the Canadian Rockies, is by far the most beautiful.

Canada's two transcontinental passenger services — the *Canadian National Railway* and the *Canadian Pacific* — were reorganized in 1977 into one overall managing system, *VIA Rail Canada.* The reorganization integrated the two railways and provided more coordinated and economical service. In addition to transcontinental routes, *VIA* runs shorter lines between the major eastern cities, and between Winnipeg, Manitoba, and Churchill on the Hudson Bay. Also note that, *Amtrak* offers overnight *Montrealer* service between Washington, DC, New York, and Montreal.

Information on rail service between the US and Canada is available from *Amtrak* (phone: 800-USA-RAIL). Information on routes, schedules, fares, and special tours and packages within Canada can be obtained from *VIA Rail* (2 Place Ville Marie, Suite 400, Montreal, Quebec H3C 3N3; phone: 514-871-1331). Details regarding *VIA Rail* service also is available at any railway station in Canada.

ACCOMMODATIONS AND FARES: *VIA Rail* fares are based on the quality of accommodation the passenger enjoys on the journey. Least expensive is the basic transportation fare, called coach. It guarantees that the passengers have a right to seats, which are allocated on a first-come, first-served basis. A first class ticket entitles a passenger to a seat in the somewhat more comfortable "club cars."

The "daynighter" is even more luxurious, offering complimentary pillow and blanket, and reclining lounging seats with footrests. Sleeping berths, called "section accommodations," cost a bit more and provide an upper or lower sleeping berth that folds into a seat during the day; washroom facilities are shared. Roomettes are small rooms with one bed and a private washroom. Most comfortable are double-occupancy bedroom accommodations, with two beds and a private washroom. Roomettes and bedrooms are scarce on transcontinental trains, and especially for summer travel they should be booked well in advance.

The cost of a coach seat — basic transportation fare — on a train generally will be something more than the cost of a bus ticket to the same destination, and something less than coach fare on a plane — except on particularly competitive routes — such as Montreal to Toronto or Vancouver — where very inexpensive flights may be available. While the plane makes the trip in a few hours, however, the train can take several days, and it is likely that anyone making the trip by train will want some kind of sleeping accommodation rather than just a coach seat — and the cost of a train compared with that of a plane is very much relative to the level of comfort. When calculating costs, however, take into account that the extra expense of accommodations on the train are offset by the comparable expense of a hotel room at your destination.

Note that *VIA Rail* recently adjusted the fare structure on many routes to correspond with ridership (instead of distance traveled), therefore, the price of a ticket may vary according to peak travel times and season. The effect of this change is a substantial ticket price increase on popular routes. Off-peak discounts may be available, and if you have a somewhat flexible schedule it may pay to travel at these times. Ask when you are buying your ticket about applicable restrictions.

VIA also has introduced a number of incentive fares to encourage off-peak, excursion, and group travel. The Canrail Pass, for example, like the Eurailpass and USA Rail Pass, allows unlimited travel in selected areas for specified periods at extremely low rates. (Note that as we went to press, the Canrail Pass was not being offered. *VIA Rail* had plans, however, to reinstate this pass this year — call and check at the time you are planning to travel.) Other special fares are available to passengers over 60, and children between 2 and 11 travel at half-fare; children under 2 travel free in coach.

BOOKING: Tickets may be obtained from *VIA Rail* offices and stations, from *Amtrak* offices, or from travel agents. Payment can be made in cash or by major credit card. Remember to ask about group, senior citizen, and youth discounts, as well as any special incentive fares. Reservations are advised for all club cars (*VIA*'s first class), section accommodations, roomettes, and bedrooms, and on a number of regular short runs. For information on scheduled departures and the routes offering these special services, contact *VIA Rail* (address above).

Passengers usually can stop anywhere along their route for as long as they like if they reach their final destination before their ticket expires (tickets are good for a year). If you have a round-trip excursion fare, you must return to your departure point before the ticket expires. Meals or snacks are served on board most trains, and on longer routes, full dining facilities may be available. No reservations for meals are required — passengers are accommodated in these dining cars on a first-come, first-served basis. Sleeping car attendants should be tipped at least $1 a night, assuming you're pleased with the service.

Always allow extra time to make connections in case the train is running late. If you have confirmed reservations and miss a connection because of a delayed train, *VIA Rail* will provide alternate arrangements if necessary.

BAGGAGE: On long-distance trains (ones with baggage cars), bags can be checked through to your destination up to 30 minutes before departure (and should be claimed within 30 minutes after arrival). You are allowed to check free of charge up to 150 pounds for each adult and 75 pounds for each child traveling at half fare. (There is no baggage allocation for children under 2 traveling for free.) Attendants on the train, or

Red Caps in most stations, will help you with your luggage (tip about $1 per bag). (For further information on recommended gratuities, see *Tipping*, in this section.)

SPECIAL TRAINS AND TOURS: Two special train treks will appeal to hikers and backpackers. The *Algoma Central Railway* runs from Sault Ste.-Marie, Ontario, to the gorgeous wilderness Agawa Canyon, 114 miles (183 km) north of the city. (A complete description of the trip can be found in *Ontario, The Western Lakeshores*, DIRECTIONS.) For information, contact *Algoma Central Railway* (129 Bay St., Sault Ste.-Marie, Ontario P6A 1W7; phone: 705-254-4331/2/3/4). The other, the *Polar Bear Express*, ventures into the Arctic watershed from Cochrane to Moosonee in northern Ontario. The express is run by *Ontario Northland Transportation Commission* (555 Oak St. E., North Bay, Ontario P1B 8L3; phone: 705-472-4500).

For those interested in a more luxurious rail experience, the *Royal Canadian Railway* offers a 3-day trip between Toronto and Vancouver aboard plush passenger cars. The one-way fare ranges from $1,865 to $2,975, and includes lavish meals, all drinks, and a variety of comfortable accommodations — ranging from single berths to deluxe suites. For information, contact their US representative, *Blyth & Company* (1 Rockefeller Plaza, Suite 1712, New York, NY 10020; phone: 212-265-9600).

Finally, although any travel agent can assist you in making arrangements to tour Canada by rail, you may want to consult a train travel specialist, such as *Accent on Travel* (1030 Curtis St., Suite 201, Menlo Park, CA 94025; phone: 415-326-7330 in California; 800-347-0645 elsewhere in the US). And for further information, pick up a copy of *Rail Ventures: Complete Guide to Train Travel in North America* by Jack Swansen and Jeff Karsh, which is available in bookstores or can be ordered from the publisher, Wayfinder Press (PO Box 1877, Ouray, CO 81427; phone: 303-325-4797) for $12.95, plus $2 for shipping and handling.

Traveling by Bus

Going from place to place by bus may not be the fastest way to get from here to there, but that (and, in some cases, a little less comfort) may be the only drawback to bus travel. Bus companies comprise Canada's most comprehensive transport system. Except for the far north, you can get virtually anywhere you want by bus. The system covers almost every populated area of the country and serves many towns without airports or railway connections. Buses are, however, somewhat slower than trains, planes, or private cars, and there clearly is a trade-off of money saved for time spent en route.

Gray Coach, Greyhound Lines of Canada, and *Voyageur* are the three largest bus lines. None is truly national: *Voyageur* operates only in Ontario and Quebec; *Gray Coach,* only in Ontario; while *Greyhound Lines of Canada* runs some 415 buses over 14,000 miles, but does not operate east of Toronto. (*Eastern Greyhound* — one of the four companies that once were part of *Greyhound* in the US — has service from New York to Montreal.) With its head office in Calgary, *Greyhound* is the main operator in western Canada. For further information on *Gray Coach* or *Voyageur* service, call 416-393-7911; for information on *Greyhound Lines of Canada,* call 416-367-8747.

These three companies, with many smaller lines around the country, offer the most frequent transportation in Canada. Among the smaller regional lines are the following:

Alberta: *Pacific West Trains* provides service throughout the province; call 800-661-1668.

British Columbia: *Island Coach Lines* provides service on Vancouver Island; call 604-385-4411. *Maverick Coach Lines* provides service throughout the rest of British Columbia; call 604-662-3222.

Manitoba: *Grey Goose Lines* provides service throughout the province; call 204-786-8891.

New Brunswick: *SMT (Eastern) Limited* provides service throughout the province; call 506-458-8350.

Newfoundland and Labrador: *CN Road Cruiser* provides service throughout the province; call 709-737-5916.

Nova Scotia: *Acadian Lines Limited* provides service throughout the province; call 902-454-9321.

Ontario: *Travelways* provides service throughout the province; call 416-393-7911.

Prince Edward Island: *Island Transit* provides island-wide service; call 902-892-6167.

Quebec: *Orleans Bus Line* provides service throughout the province; call 514-842-2281.

Saskatchewan: *Saskatchewan Transit Company* provides service throughout the province; 306-787-3340.

FARES: Long-distance, round-trip bus journeys once were by far the most economical way to go, though deregulation and lessening competition have caused the cost of bus travel to inch up. Still, in general, the cost of a bus trip in Canada is less than half that of a journey by plane and in some cases — such as long-distance, return excursion trips — the savings are even greater. Rail clearly offers some competition for the bus lines, but it really can't compete with the buses' unlimited travel tickets, which represent considerable savings over normal fares. *Greyhound*'s unlimited travel program, called Ameripass, allows the ticket holder to travel anywhere in mainland Canada and the US (on both company and non-company routes) within specified time periods (7 days, 15 days, and 30 days). The competitive atmosphere affecting all modes of transportation makes it worthwhile to ask about other special and promotional fares.

BOOKING: Reservations are not necessary on most bus routes; companies usually send as many buses as are needed to handle all passengers. Most companies allow passengers to make free stopovers along the route, though some limit the stopovers to cities where passengers must make a change of bus. Tickets usually are bought at bus stations or from a central office, although on very rural and some city routes they may be bought from the bus driver. (Note that exact change often is required.) Sightseeing tours and special programs generally require reservations, and are subject to slightly different stopover rules. Tickets issued by some bus lines have no expiration date. (However, a company might not honor a ticket that they consider too old.) *Greyhound* one-way tickets are good for 30 days; round-trip tickets, for 1 year.

SERVICES: Most buses are not equipped for food service. On long trips they make meal stops, and most bus terminals also provide food service of one kind or another. It is not a bad idea to bring some food aboard, although you may be better off waiting until you reach a stop in a town or city where you can eat more comfortably at a restaurant. Most companies provide air conditioned, heated buses, with toilets, even on short runs. Most seats have reading lamps, and are both upholstered and adjustable.

FOR COMFORTABLE TRAVEL: Dress casually with loose-fitting clothes. Be sure you have a sweater or jacket (even in the summer, air conditioning can make buses quite cool). Passengers are allowed to listen to radios or cassette players, but must use earphones. Choose a seat in the front near the driver for the best view or in the middle between the front and rear wheels for the smoothest ride. Smokers (on those lines that permit on-board smoking) usually are restricted to the last rows of any bus; often pipes and cigars are forbidden. (If you don't smoke, avoid the back near the toilet.)

TOURS: In addition to its regular service, *Gray Coach* offers a wide variety of bus tours that include transportation, hotels, and escorted sightseeing. These tours go to such popular destinations as Agawa Canyon, Montreal, Quebec, and Ottawa, as well as to Atlantic and western Canada. *Gray Coach* also offers sightseeing tours of Toronto. Information on the tour program can be obtained from any local *Gray Coach* office and most travel agents, or call 416-979-3511.

Traveling by Car

DRIVING YOUR OWN CAR: Automobile travel is the most popular mode of transportation to and in Canada, just as it is in the US. Driving certainly is the most flexible way to explore out-of-the-way regions of Canada. Trains often whiz much too fast past too many enticing landscapes, pass between hills and mountains rather than climb up and around them for a better view, frequently deposit passengers in an unappealing part of town, and skirt some areas of the country altogether. Buses have a greater range, but they still don't permit many spur-of-the-moment stops and starts. In a car you go where you want when you want, and can stop along the way as often as you like for a meal, a photograph, or a particularly appealing view.

Canada is ideally suited for driving tours. Although distances between major Canadian cities vary from area to area, a traveler can cover large amounts of territory visiting major sites or spend the same amount of time motoring from small town to town. (See DIRECTIONS for our choices of the most interesting driving routes.) Travelers who wish to cover the country from coast to coast can count on a good system of highways to help them make time, while those exploring only one region will find even the most out-of-the-way roads generally are in reasonably good condition (except in the depths of winter, when only major and secondary roads may be plowed). Canadian roads generally are better, speed limits are higher, and there are fewer toll roads than in the US. And there is plenty of satisfying scenery en route.

While driving is not necessarily the least expensive way to travel, it does, however, become more economical with more passengers. Rather than just the means to an end, a well-planned driving route also can be an important part of the adventure.

Before setting out, make certain that everything you need is in order. Read about the places you intend to visit and study relevant maps. If at all possible, discuss your intended trip with someone who already has driven the route to find out about road conditions and available services. If you can't speak to someone personally, try to read about others' experiences. Automobile clubs (see below) and provincial tourist offices (see *Tourist Information Offices,* in this section, for addresses) can be good sources of travel information, although when requesting brochures and maps, be sure to specify your interests and the areas you are planning to visit. (Also see "Maps," below.)

Driving – A valid driver's license from his or her state of residence enables a US citizen to drive throughout Canada. American, British, and most other European drivers' licenses also are recognized by Canadian officials. US motorists should obtain a Canadian Non-Resident Inter-Provincial Motor Vehicle Liability Insurance Card, which proves the holder has a valid automobile liability insurance policy. This will be required as proof of financial responsibility should you be involved in an accident in Canadian territory. You can get this card only in the US through a US insurance agent.

Canadians drive on the right, as in the US, and obey similar traffic rules. Canada uses the metric system, so distances are expressed in kilometers (km) and speed limits are posted in kilometers per hour (kmh). Common speed limits are 100 kmh on freeways, 80 kmh on highways, and 50 kmh on city streets. The "Rule of Six" is a convenient rule of thumb for converting kilometers to miles: Take the figure in kilometers and multiply by .6 (six-tenths). Thus, 100 kmh is approximately equivalent to 60 mph; 80 kmh equals approximately 50 mph; 50 kmh, about 30 mph. Road signs and traffic symbols are standardized under the International Roadsign System and their meanings are indicated by their shapes — triangular signs indicate danger; circular signs give instructions; and rectangular signs are informative. So even when you're driving through Quebec where French is spoken, you should have no problem understanding the rules of the road.

Keep in mind when touring along Canada's scenic roadways that it is all too easy to inch up over the speed limit. And use alchohol sparingly prior to getting behind the wheel. Canadian officials are most zealous in prosecuting offenders of driving laws, especially in the matter of drinking and driving. Breathalyzer tests are routinely administered and fines and even jail sentences are rigorously imposed. If you've been drinking, do as the natives do and walk home, take a cab, or make sure that a licensed member of your party sticks strictly to seltzer water or soft drinks.

Canadian law specifies that all motor vehicle drivers and passengers must wear safety belts at all times. (Even when wearing safety belts is not compulsory, both front and back seat passengers *always* should wear one.)

Maps – Consult road maps. Many automobile clubs offer their members free maps and precise routings. Other travelers can get road maps free by writing to the provincial tourist offices (see *Tourist Information Offices* in this section). Maps are available at Canadian service stations, but due to budget cutbacks in the oil industry, most companies now charge for them (usually about $1 each).

The *Rand McNally Road Atlas: US, Canada and Mexico* ($7.95 paperback; $11.95 hardcover) is excellent. Rand McNally atlases and maps are available in most bookstores or can be bought directly from the following Rand McNally retail stores: 444 N. Michigan Ave., Chicago, IL 60611 (phone: 312-332-4628); 150 E. 52nd St., New York, NY 10022 (phone: 212-758-7488); 595 Market St., San Francisco, CA 94105-2803 (phone: 415-777-3131). Other detailed road maps available at general and travel bookstores include the *Hammond Road Atlas of North America* (Hammond; $5.95).

Michelin's *Green Guide to Canada* is primarily a guide to hotels, restaurants, and attractions, but does provide some useful regional and city maps to help you find your way. It is readily available in bookstores and map shops around the US, and also can be ordered from the company's US headquarters, Michelin Guides and Maps (PO Box 3305, Spartanburg, SC 29304-3305; phone: 803-599-0850 in South Carolina; 800-423-0485 elsewhere in the US). A new edition of each map appears every year; if you're not buying directly from the publisher, make sure that the edition you buy is no more than 2 years old by opening one fold and checking the publication date, given just under the black circle with the map number.

Another good source for these and just about any other map available is *Map Link* (25 E. Mason St., Santa Barbara, CA 93101; phone: 805-965-4402). You may want to order their excellent guide to maps worldwide, *The World Map Directory* ($29.95). If they don't have the map you want in stock — although it is likely that you'll find what you want as they have over 1,000 maps of Canada — they will order it for you.

If touring through a number of provinces, in addition to provincial maps, it helps to have at least one national map to help plan your overall route. Use this broader reference to plot your general course, choosing the portions you will drive on major highways to make the best time. Then refer to the detailed provincial or regional maps for information on local roads that will provide the more scenic and leisurely legs of your journey, covering the areas you are most interested in touring. By cross-referencing between the global and specific sources, you will be best prepared to adjust your route as you go along. And if you decide to veer off on a course that even your regional maps don't cover, pick up a local map along the way. Gas stations, truck stops, and tourist information centers throughout Canada are well stocked with a variety of area maps, as well as interesting pamphlets on local attractions well worth a detour if you have time.

Automobile Clubs – To protect yourself in case of on-the-road breakdowns, you should consider joining a reputable national automobile club, preferably one that has reciprocal service with affiliates in Canada. Any club should offer three basic services:

1. On-the-road insurance, covering accidents, personal injury, arrest and bail bond, and lawyer's fees for defense of contested traffic cases. For example, *AAA* (described below) offers a $100,000 travel insurance package for auto accidents and personal injury.) Check with your auto club before you go.
2. Around-the-clock (24-hour) emergency breakdown service, including reduced rates on (or free) towing to the nearest garage. For instance, *AAA* has a toll-free number for emergency road service: 800-336-HELP (throughout the US and Canada). Members are referred to the nearest service facility. Other clubs allow members to call any local mechanic — they will be reimbursed at a later date for expenses incurred.
3. Vacation planning and routing services, including advice and maps. The *AAA* and most of the other clubs listed below offer these services for itineraries throughout both the US and Canada.

These are the basic types of services; specific policies and programs vary widely from club to club. Before joining any one, get information and brochures from several national clubs, and compare benefits and costs to find the services that best match your travel needs. Most clubs cost between $17 and $60 a year and include your spouse in membership.

The largest automobile club in North America is the *American Automobile Association (AAA),* with over 31 million members in chapters throughout the US and Canada. The *AAA* has branch offices throughout Canada and is affiliated with the *Canadian Automobile Association* (a federation of provincial Canadian auto clubs). Through its US and Canadian affiliates, the *AAA* provides a variety of services to members traveling in either country, including a travel agency, trip planning, free traveler's checks at some locations, and roadside assistance. They will help plan an itinerary, send a map with clear routing directions, and even make hotel reservations. *AAA* publishes a pamphlet called *AAA Offices to Serve You Abroad,* which lists offices in Canada and the US. Although *AAA* members receive maps and other brochures for no charge or at a discount, non-members also can order from an extensive selection of highway and topographical maps. You can join the *AAA* through local chapters (listed in the telephone books under *AAA*) or contact the national office at 1000 AAA Dr., Heathrow, FL 32746-5063 (phone: 407-444-8544).

Other clubs offer similar services, but their domain generally is more limited to the US. Some will reimburse you for towing charges incurred in Canada upon receiving a receipt, but the difference between having *AAA* officers on hand to advise at the time of the trouble and being paid several weeks after your return is substantial. Keep this in mind when choosing a club. If paying for car service in US dollars, be sure that this is clearly indicated on your receipt. Also, when filing a claim, be sure to keep a copy of the claim form and all receipts.

Listed below are the major Canadian and several of the largest US auto and travel clubs:

Allstate Motor Club: A member of the *Sears* family, run by *Allstate Insurance.* Will reimburse up to $50 for emergency road service in Canada and the national office provides trip routing services for Canadian trips. Join through any *Allstate* agency or contact Customer Service, PO Box 3093, Arlington Heights, IL 60006 (phone: 800-323-6282).

Amoco Motor Club: Although the organization has no branches in Canada, it is affiliated with *Canadian Tires* which provides service to *Amoco* club members.

The US national office provides maps and does routings for Canadian driving tours. Will reimburse for up to $40 on any service call in Canada upon receipt of a claim form. Join at any *Amoco* dealer or contact the national office, PO Box 9014, Des Moines, IA 50306 (phone: 800-334-3300, for information and assistance in the US; 800-263-1023, for roadside service in Canada).

Canadian Automobile Association: Provides full membership services to *AAA* members. Affiliated visiting members are entitled to travel information, itineraries, maps, tourbooks, bulletins on road and weather conditions, and accommodation reservations, emergency road, and travel agency services upon presentation of an *AAA* membership card. Contact *CAA* at 1775 Courtwood Crescent, Ottawa, Ontario K2C 3J2, Canada (phone: 613-226-7631; for emergency road service, both *AAA* and *CAA* members can call 800-336-HELP).

Exxon Travel Club: Provides a wide range of services throughout the US and Canada including trip routing, maps and atlases, reimbursement for towing, discounts on car rentals and accommodations, and a variety of insurance packages. Ask for information from the national office, PO Box 3633, Houston, TX 77253 (phone: 713-680-5723).

Ford Auto Club: Provides trip routing services through the national office and reimbursement for emergency towing service up to $50. Contact the Membership Services Division, PO Box 224688, Dallas, TX 75222 (phone: 800-348-5220).

Montgomery Ward Auto Club: Open to (but not limited to) people with a *Montgomery Ward* charge account. Although the organization has no offices in Canada, it does chart driving routes through Canada and will reimburse members up to $80 for Canadian road service upon receipt of a claim. Join through the credit manager at any *Montgomery Ward* store, or contact the national office, 200 N. Martingale Rd., Schaumburg, IL 60173 (phone: 708-605-3000 in Illinois; 800-621-5151 elsewhere in the US).

Motor Club of America: No offices in Canada, but provides routings for Canadian trips. Reimburses members for the amount of a local tow upon receipt of the bill. Ask for information from the national office, 484 Central Ave., Newark, NJ 07107 (phone: 201-733-1234; 800-222-6288 in New York; 800-435-7622 in New Jersey).

United States Auto Club Motoring Division: No Canadian offices, but US branches do trip routings. Reimburses members up to $70 for Canadian road service. Ask for information from the national office, PO Box 660460, Dallas, TX 75266-0460 (phone: 800-348-2761 or 215-541-4246).

Oil Company Credit Cards – Most oil companies offer credit cards that can be used to pay for gas, repairs, and most car parts at their respective service stations throughout the US and Canada. Particularly if you are driving a long distance, a credit card will reduce the amount of cash you must carry on your trip. Applications for cards are available at the respective service stations (*Sunoco* stations have applications for *Sunoco* cards only, and so on), and you will be granted a card if you can establish creditworthiness — another credit card of any kind or an established credit rating. These cards are issued free, and usually take about a month for processing after application.

Charges are handled in two ways, and it is important to know under which system your card is operated. A few companies — *Amoco,* for example — allow some cardholders (depending on the kind of account) to carry charges from month to month. The cardholder pays only a minimum amount each month, and the balance is carried over. For this privilege the cardholder is charged an interest rate (usually about 1½% a month, 18% a year — this varies for different cards and from state to state) on the balance carried over. If you spent $300 on gasoline during a 2-week trip, you could spread the payment of this $300 over several months — virtually a "travel now, pay later" system — but you will end up paying more than the basic $300 when interest charges are included.

Other companies — an example is *Gulf* — insist that the cardholder pay the full balance due at the end of each billing period (usually a month) if it's under $50. On any balance over $50, if only partial payment is made, revolving credit is then extended to the unpaid balance, but interest charges will be added. There are advantages to both systems; when you consider a credit card, know which way it works and decide which is best for you.

When you buy gas or pay for car repairs in Canada with a credit card, make sure you are paying in Canadian dollars, and be sure to check the bill you receive at home. There have been cases of people being charged, say, CN$10 in Manitoba, and when they return home being billed US$10 and, depending on the current exchange rate, such an overcharge can be 15% or more.

Preparing Your Car – Before heading off on the road, always make certain that your car is in the best possible mechanical condition. Have it inspected very carefully, paying special attention to brakes and tires, and be sure that your spare tire is in good shape. If you have room, a full-size spare is preferable to the small, solid rubber spares provided with many new cars. (If driving on one of these small lightweight spares, *drive slowly and carefully.*) The days when every gas station had a mechanic on the premises have given way to self-service gas "stops" with convenience stores or, in Canada, road-side diners — so if you need a tire repaired, ask at your hotel or refer to the local yellow pages to find a service station that provides this service. Always carry liability insurance. Other suggestions include the following:

1. In addition to the spare tire, bring the following equipment: a first-aid kit; a white towel (useful for signaling for help, as well as for wiping the car windows); gloves; wrench; jack; and two wooden blocks; jumper cables; flares and/or reflectors; winshield washer fluid; a container of water or coolant for the radiator; and a steel container of gasoline (also see "Saving on Gas," below). For driving during the winter in Canada, the well-prepared traveler also should carry an ice scraper, anti-freeze, and snow chains.

   If traveling in an isolated area, you also may want to carry a couple of extra fan belts, distributor points, a fuel pump replacement kit, condensers, and spark plugs. When driving a foreign car through rural areas it is advisable to carry a basic selection of spare parts (ask your local mechanic for a list of essentials), as service stations in small towns are not likely to stock them. This can prevent a wait of up to several days for parts to be sent from a foreign parts distributor in a distant metropolitan area.

2. Make the first days of your trip the shortest, and plan to drive no more than 300 to 400 miles per day (6 to 7 hours of driving time); this is a comfortable pace for most travelers. When traveling with children, plan on 200 to 250 miles a day (4 to 5 hours) at the most. Stop to rest when you are tired.

3. For current information on weather and road conditions, call the *AAA* at 800-336-HELP. Another useful number to call is *American Express Travel Related Services'* nationwide weather report service; call 900-WEATHER. You also can call the National Weather Service at 416-676-3066 for weather reports in the Toronto (Ontario) area, and 416-676-4567 for information on weather throughout the rest of Canada. In some areas, you also will see local AM radio or CB (Citizen's Band) channels posted for area weather and road condition information — tuning into these special reports can be particularly helpful if there is a blizzard or other storm developing in the area.

Breakdowns – If you break down on the road, the first emergency procedure is to get the car off the highway. If the road has a narrow shoulder, try to get all the way off, even if you have to hang off the shoulder a bit. Better yet, try to make it to an area where the shoulder is wider — if you are crawling along well below the speed limit, use your emergency flashers to warn other drivers. Once you've pulled off, raise the hood as a signal that help is needed, and tie a white handkerchief or rag to the door handle or radio antenna. Don't leave the car unattended, and don't try any major repairs on the road.

Those who break down or are involved in an accident on major highways and require assistance should look for highway mile-markers which measure the number of miles from the provincial border. When calling for roadside assistance from the next public pay phone en route, identifying the closest mile-marker to your broken-down vehicle will help the police and/or service station truck reach you as quickly as possible.

■ **Note:** If planning a trip in very remote areas, you might want to add a CB (Citizen's Band) radio to your vehicle. In addition to giving you access to information on weather and road conditions ahead, it will enable you to call for help in the event of a breakdown or other emergency.

Mechanics and Car Care – For any but the most simple malfunctions, you probably will need a mechanic. If you are a member of the *AAA* or another automobile club, a call to the toll-free assistance number provided by these organizations may provide information on recommended service stations. (Note that some automobile clubs will reimburse members for towing service and other on-the-road repairs only if they use an affiliated service company.)

It helps to have some idea of what might be wrong with your car and to know something about standard maintenance. An excellent series of booklets on car care, mileage, and mechanical problems and their sources is published by *Shell Oil Company* in its *Experience the Difference* series, available from some *Shell* dealers or directly from the company at 3484 11th St., Houston, TX 77008 (phone: 713-241-6161).

Other suggestions for breakdowns and on-the-road car care include the following:

1. Look for mechanics with certification. The *Canadian Automobile Association* certifies individual mechanics and repair shops, which fulfill a variety of requirements — ranging from training and expertise to equipment and facilities — and have demonstrated fair business practices. These shops display certificates of accreditation; to find the nearest *CAA*-certified mechanic in an area contact the nearest *CAA* office, or call 613-226-7631.
2. Have some idea of what needs to be done. Oil needs to be changed approximately every 3,000 miles; a tune-up is needed every 12,000 miles (every 24,000 miles for transistorized ignition cars); spark plugs need to be changed every 25,000 miles; fan and air conditioning belts every 5,000 miles.
3. Get an estimate in writing on major repairs, and make sure there is a firm understanding that the mechanic will call if any other problems arise. The average cost for labor varies substantially between rural and metropolitan areas, as well as from station to station.
4. Be aware of dishonest practices. Some mechanics will cheat you. While checking oil they can "short stick" the dipper so the full amount of oil in your engine doesn't register; be sure to watch while oil is being checked. When buying gas, make sure the attendant resets the pump, moving the counter back to zero. The best way to avoid being cheated is to know your car's oil and gas consumption.
5. Recognize the warning signals.
   • Fluid leaks: Spread paper and look for brown or black fluid, which usually means an *oil leak;* straw-colored fluid near wheel is likely to be *leaking brake fluid;* pink or reddish fluid means an *automatic transmission leak;* colorless or greenish fluid near the front, a *radiator or hose leak.*

- Car has trouble starting: May be a vapor lock caused by hot weather; a cold, wet rag on the fuel line and pump may help.
- Engine missing after quick acceleration: Could be a fleck of carbon lodged between electrodes of a spark plug. Clean plugs. (If you are driving at a high altitude, change cold spark plugs for hot, and advance the spark to prevent the engine from stalling.)
- Rattle in rear: Loose muffler or tail pipe.
- Rattling noise: Bent fan blade or loose pulley.
- Loud squealing noise when wheel turns: Low power-steering fluid.

5. If your car needs to be towed, agree in advance on the price and on the station to which it will be towed. If you ask *AAA, CAA,* or other clubs, they often will name stations they consider reliable.

SPEED: Watch the speedometer closely, especially in small towns, where speed limits, designed to protect pedestrians and local residents pulling out of driveways and side streets, may seem agonizingly slow. And remember that Canada's speed limits are in kilometers per hour *not* miles per hour.

It is all too easy when touring along Canada's open and well-maintained and de-signed roadways to inch up in speed. Speed traps (or radar traps) mean expensive tickets that may also affect your insurance rates. As in the US, police lie in wait for motorists to zoom by on major highways and may issue tickets to those driving even a few miles over the speed limit. Especially on major holiday weekends, these speed traps can consist of a number of separate police vehicles converging on the same area.

Also, when traveling at dawn and dusk in forested areas, keep in mind the high incident of fatal accidents due to animals (particularly deer and massive moose) cross-ing the roads. It pays to exercise extra care and drive more slowly at these times; many Canadian drivers prefer to limit highway driving in such areas to prime daylight hours.

■ **Note:** Particularly if you will be doing a lot of driving in heavily wooded areas, you may want to pick up a "deer whistle." This simple and inexpensive device, which is available from sporting goods stores and auto parts shops in rural areas, attaches to the front of your vehicle. The wind whistling through it makes a sound that scares off any deer and moose that may have strayed onto the road ahead.

GASOLINE: The major oil companies have stations in Canada: *Chevron, Exxon, Gulf, Shell, Sunoco,* and *Texaco.* Even more common are Canadian companies, like *Petro-Canada.* Gas is sold in liters in Canada. (A liter is slightly more than 1 quart; approximately 3.8 liters equals 1 gallon.) As in the US, regular, leaded, and diesel gas generally is available in several grades, and self-service (where you do the pumping) often is less expensive than full service. Similarly, gas paid for in cash often costs less than when paid for with a credit card.

Gas prices everywhere rise and fall depending on the world supply of oil, and the US traveler in Canada is further affected by the prevailing rate of exchange, so it is difficult to say exactly how much fuel will cost when you travel. It is not difficult to predict, however, that gas prices will be substantially higher than in the US — at press time, the cost of gas was as much as 50% to 60% more expensive than in the US.

In the more remote reaches of Canada, gas stations are not very numerous, so fill up whenever you come to a station. (Touring routes described in DIRECTIONS note where gas stations are scarce.) Even in more populated areas, it may be difficult to find an open station after standard business hours or on Sundays or holidays.) You don't want to get stranded on an isolated stretch — so it is a good idea to bring along an extra few gallons in a steel container. (Plastic containers tend to break when a car is bouncing over rocky roads. This, in turn, creates the danger of fire should the gasoline ignite from a static electricity spark. Plastic containers also may burst at high altitudes.)

Considering the cost of gas in Canada relative to US prices at the time of this writing, gas economy is of particular concern. The prudent traveler should plan an itinerary and make as many reservations as possible in advance, in order to not waste gas figuring out where to go, stay, or eat. Drive early in the day, when there is less traffic. Then leave your car at the hotel and use local transportation whenever possible after you arrive at your destination.

Make sure that your tires are properly inflated and your engine is tuned correctly to cut gas consumption. Although it may be as dangerous to drive at a speed much below the posted limit as it is to drive above it (particularly on freeways — where the speed limit generally is 100 kph or about 60 mph), at 88 kph (55 mph) a car gets 25% better mileage than at 112 kph (70 mph). The number of miles per liter or gallon also is increased by driving smoothly. Accelerate gently, anticipate stops, get into high gear quickly, and maintain a steady speed.

RENTING A CAR: Unless planning a round-trip driving route from home, most travelers who want to drive while in Canada simply rent a car. Travelers to Canada can reserve a rental car through a travel agent or international rental firm before leaving home, or from a local company once they are in Canada. And although you can rent a car in the US for a driving tour to and through Canada, you may well find that flying to Canada and renting there will cost no more than the total cost of renting in the US, particularly if you rent the car as part of a larger travel package (see "Fly/Drive," below, as well as *Package Tours,* in this section).

Renting is not inexpensive, but it is possible to economize by determining your own needs and then shopping around among car rental companies until you find the best deal. As you comparison shop, keep in mind that rates vary considerably, not only from city to city, but also from location to location within the same city. It might be less expensive to rent a car in the center of a city rather than at the airport. Ask about special rates or promotional deals, such as weekend or weekly rates, bonus coupons for airline tickets, or 24-hour rates that include gas and unlimited mileage.

Rental car companies operating in the US and Canada can be divided into large international companies, national or regional companies, and small local companies. *Avis, Budget, Hertz,* and other international firms maintain offices in cities throughout North America. Because of aggressive local competition, the cost of renting a car can be less expensive once a traveler arrives in Canada, as compared to the price quoted in advance from the US. Local companies usually are less expensive than international giants.

Given this situation, it's tempting to wait until arriving to scout out the lowest-priced rental from the company located the farthest from the airport high-rent district and offering no pick-up services. But if your arrival coincides with a holiday or a peak travel period, you may be disappointed to find that even the most expensive car in town was spoken for months ago. Whenever possible, it is best to reserve in advance, anywhere from a few days in slack periods to a month or more during the busier seasons.

There are legitimate bargains in car rentals if you shop for them. Begin your comparison shopping early, because the best deals may be booked to capacity quickly and may require payment 14 to 21 days or more before picking up the car.

Renting from the US – Travel agents can arrange foreign rentals for clients, but it is just as easy to do it yourself by calling the internationl divisions of the following US companies with branches in Canada and major Canadian rental firms:

> *American International Rent-A-Car:* 800-225-2529 in Boston, MA, and Portland, ME; 800-527-0202 elsewhere in the US and throughout Canada.
>
> *Avis:* 800-331-1212 throughout the US; 800-268-0303 in Ontario and Quebec; 800-268-2310 elsewhere in Canada.
>
> *Budget Rent-A-Car:* 800-527-0700 in the US; 416-622-1000 in Canada.

Dollar Rent-A-Car System: 800-421-6878 throughout the US and Canada.

Hertz: 800-654-3001 in the US; 800-620-9620 in Toronto; 800-263-0600 elsewhere in Canada.

National: 800-CAR-RENT throughout the US and Canada.

Sears Rent-A-Car: 800-527-0770 or 800-268-8900 throughout the US and Canada.

Thrifty Rent-A-Car: 800-367-2277 in the US and Canada.

Tilden Rent-A-Car System: Largest Canadian firm, affiliated with *National* in the States; for *National,* or reservations through them with *Tilden* in Canada: 800-328-4567 in the continental US; 800-CAR-RENT in Alaska, Hawaii, and throughout Canada.

All of these companies publish directories listing their locations in Canada, and all quote weekly flat rates based on unlimited mileage with the renter paying for gas. Some also offer time and mileage rates (i.e., a basic per-day or per-week charge, plus a charge for each mile, or kilometer, driven), which generally are only to the advantage of those who plan to do very little driving — the basic time and mileage charge for a given period of time is lower than the unlimited mileage charge for a comparable period, but the kilometers add up more quickly than most people expect.

It also is possible to rent a car before you go by contacting any of a number of smaller or less well known US companies that do not operate worldwide but specialize in North American auto travel, including leasing and car purchase in addition to car rental, or actually are tour operators with a well-established Canadian car rental program. These firms, whose names and addresses are listed below, act as agents for a variety of Canadian suppliers, offer unlimited mileage almost exclusively, and frequently manage to undersell their larger competitors by a significant margin.

Comparison shopping always is advisable, however, because the company that has the least expensive rentals in one city may not have the least expensive in another, and even the international giants offer discount plans whose conditions are easy for most travelers to fulfill. For instance, *Budget* and *National* offer discounts of anywhere from 15% to 30% off their usual rates (according to the size of the car and the duration of the rental), provided that the car is reserved a certain number of days before departure (usually 7, but it can be less), is rented for a minimum period (5 days or, more often, a week), and in most cases, is returned to the same location that supplied it or to another in the same country. Similar discount plans include *Hertz*'s Affordable Canada and *Avis*'s Supervalue Rates Canada.

Local Rentals – It has long been common wisdom that the least expensive way to rent a car is to make arrangements upon arrival. This is less true today than it used to be. Many medium to large Canadian car rental companies have become the foreign suppliers of stateside companies, such as those mentioned previously, and often the stateside agency, by dint of sheer volume, has been able to negotiate more favorable rates for its US customers than the Canadian firm offers its own. Still, lower rates may be found by searching out small, strictly local rental companies in Canada, whether at less-than-prime addresses in major cities or in more remote areas. But to find them you must be willing to invest a sufficient amount of vacation time comparing prices on the scene. You also must be prepared to return the car to the location that rented it; drop-off possibilities are likely to be limited.

The brochures of some of the smaller car rental companies, often available from provincial tourist board offices, can serve as a useful basis for comparison. On arrival, the local telephone book is a good place to begin. (For further information on local rental companies, see the individual reports in THE CITIES.)

Requirements – Whether you decide to rent a car in advance from a large international rental company with Canadian branches or wait to rent from a local company, you should know that renting a car is rarely as simple as signing on the dotted line and roaring off into the night. If you are renting for personal use, you must have a valid drivers license and will have to convince the renting agency that (1) you are personally credit-worthy, and (2) you will bring the car back at the stated time. This will be easy if you have a major credit card; most rental companies accept credit cards in lieu of a cash deposit, as well as for payment of your final bill. If you prefer to pay in cash, leave your credit card imprint as a "deposit," then pay your bill in cash when you return the car.

If you don't have a major credit card, renting a car for personal use becomes more complicated. If you are planning to rent from an agency near your home, the best thing to do is to call the company several days in advance and give them your name, home address, and information on your business or employer; the agency then runs its own credit check on you. This can be time consuming, so you should try to have it done before you leave home. If you plan to pay for your rental car in Canada, it is best to make arrangements in advance — otherwise you must bring along a letter of employment and go to the agency during business hours so that it can call your employer for verification (don't forget to take any time difference into account).

In addition to paying the rental fee up front, you also will have to leave a hefty deposit when you pick up the car — either a substantial flat fee or a percentage of the total rental cost. (Each company has a different deposit policy; look around for the best deal.) If you return the car on time, the full deposit will be refunded; otherwise, additional charges will be deducted and any unused portion of the deposit will be returned.

If you are planning to rent a car once in Canada, *Avis, Hertz,* and other US rental companies usually *will* rent to travelers paying in cash and leaving either a credit card imprint or a substantial amount of cash as a deposit. This is not necessarily standard policy, however, as *Budget,* some of the other international chains, and many Canadian companies *will not* rent to an individual who doesn't have a valid credit card. In this case, you may have to call around to find a company that accepts cash.

Also keep in mind that although the minimum age to drive a car in the US or Canada is 16 to 18 years (this varies from state to state and province to province), the minimum age to rent a car varies with the company. Many firms have a minimum age requirement of 21 years, some raise that to 23 or 25 years, and for some models of cars it rises to 30 years. The upper age limit at many companies is between 69 and 75; others have no upper limit or may make drivers above a certain age subject to special conditions.

Costs – Given all the competition, the price charged for a rental car changes continuously, rising and falling according to the level of renter traffic. The rate your friend paid last December may have been higher than the one you'll pay in May, and a super-bargain rate may be withdrawn as soon as the advertiser moves some cars off the lot and onto the road again. Nevertheless, there are some constants governing pricing in the international car rental market.

Finding the most economical car rental will require some telephone shopping on your part. As a *general* rule, expect to hear lower prices quoted by the smaller, strictly local companies than by the well-known international names, with those of the national Canadian companies falling somewhere between the two.

If you are driving short distances for only a day or two, the best deal may be a per-day, per-mile (or per-kilometer) rate: You pay a flat fee for each day you keep the car (which can be as low as $25), plus a per-mile charge of 12¢ to 40¢ — or 7¢ to 25¢ per kilometer — or more.

It used to be that cars were rented *only* on a per-day, per-mile basis. Now most US-based car rental companies — including the giants — offer flat rates including unlimited mileage. This certainly is the most economical rate if you plan to drive over 100 miles (160 km) a day. Make sure that the low, flat daily rate that catches your eye, however, is indeed a per-day rate: Often the lowest price advertised by a company turns out to be available only with a minimum 3-day rental — fine if you want the car that long, but not the bargain it appears if you really intend to use it no more than 1 or 2 days for short distances. Flat weekly rates and some flat monthly rates that represent a further saving over the daily rate also are available.

Canadian companies, however, seem to prefer a combination of the two rental schemes. Most rent cars for a per-day rate that usually includes a certain number of free kilometers (generally 100) per day; customers then are charged on a per-kilometer basis for distances driven over that number. (Note: When renting a car in Canada, the term "mileage" may refer either to miles or kilometers.) Most Canadian companies also have weekly rates that offer a substantial savings over the daily rate. These, too, come with free kilometers (usually 1,000 or 1,500). Unlike car rental companies in the US, Canadian firms generally don't offer unlimited free kilometers. If you intend to cover a lot of ground, consider renting a car in the US, where deals offering unlimited free mileage can be found.

Other factors influencing cost include the type of car you rent. Rentals are based on a tiered price system, with different sizes of cars — variations of budget, economy, regular, and luxury — often listed as A (the smallest and least expensive) through F, G, or H, and sometimes even higher. The typical A car available in Canada is a two-door subcompact or compact, often a hatchback, seating two or three adults, while the typical F, G, or H luxury car is a four-door sedan seating four or five adults. The larger the car, the more it costs to rent in the first place and the more gas it consumes, but for some people the greater comfort and extra luggage space of a larger car (in which bags can be safely locked out of sight) may make it worth the additional expense, especially on a long trip.

Electing to pay for collision damage waiver (CDW) protection will add considerably to the cost of renting a car. The renter may be responsible for the *full value* of the vehicle being rented, but you can dispense with the possible obligation by buying the offered waiver at a cost of about $13 a day. Before making any decisions about optional collision damage waivers, check with your own insurance agent and determine whether your personal automobile insurance policy covers rented vehicles; if it does, you probably won't need to pay for the waiver. Be aware, too, that increasing numbers of credit cards automatically provide CDW coverage if the car rental is charged to the appropriate credit card. However, the specific terms of such coverage differ sharply among individual credit card companies, so check with the company for information on the nature and amount of coverage provided (also see *Credit and Currency,* in this section). Considering that repair costs for a rental car have become a real headache of late, and car rental companies are getting away with steep fees (up to the full retail price of the car) for damage to their property, if you are not otherwise covered it is wise to pay for the insurance offered by the car rental company rather than risk traveling without any coverage.

In Canada, the amount for which renters may be liable should damage occur has not risen to the heights it has in the US. In addition, some Canadian car rental agreements include collision damage coverage. In this case, the CDW supplement frees the renter from liability for the *deductible* amount — as opposed to the standard CDW coverage, described above, which releases the driver from liability for the full value of the car. In Canada, this deductible typically ranges from $2,000 to $2,500 at present, but can be more for some luxury car groups. As with the full liability waiver, the cost of waiving this liability — anywhere from $10 to $20 a day — is far from negligible, however. Drivers who rent cars in the US often are able to decline the CDW because many personal car insurance policies (subject to their own deductibles) extend to rental cars. Although this coverage usually includes cars rented for use in both the US and Canada, some policies may not cover driving in Canada. Similarly, CDW coverage provided by some credit cards if the rental is charged to the card may be limited to cars rented for use only in the US.

When inquiring about CDW coverage and costs, you should be aware that a number of the major international car rental companies now are automatically including the cost of this waiver in their quoted prices. This does not mean that they are absorbing this cost and you are receiving free coverage — total rental prices have increased to include the former CDW charge. The disadvantage of this inclusion is that you probably will not have the option to refuse this coverage, and will end up paying the added charge — even if you already are adequately covered by your own insurance policy or through a credit card company.

Additional costs to be added to the price tag include drop-off charges or one-way service fees. The lowest price quoted by any given company may apply only to a car that is returned to the same location from which it was rented. A slightly higher rate may be charged if the car is to be returned to a different city, and a considerably higher rate may prevail if the rental begins in one country and ends in another (for instance, if you rent in the US and drop off the car in Canada and fly home).

A further consideration: In addition to provincial sales tax (which varies from province to province), Canada recently adopted a 7% Goods and Services Tax (GST) similar to the European Value Added Tax (VAT), and all car rentals are subject to this tax. This tax rarely is included in the rental price that's advertised or quoted, but it always must be paid — whether you pay in advance in the US or pay it when you drop off the car. One-way rentals between the US and Canada are not exempt from this tax. The only way to avoid paying it is to get a round-trip rental from the US, picking up and dropping the car off on the US side of the border.

Though the cost of gasoline is higher in Canada than in the US, it's something motorists often forget to budget into their car rental expenses. Rental cars usually are delivered with a full tank of gas. (This is not always the case, however, so check the gas gauge when picking up the car, and have the amount of gas noted on your rental agreement if the tank is not full.) Also, when picking up a rental car, be sure to confirm the policy regarding the gas tank level on return. Some agencies include a charge for the initial tank of gas in the rental fee and suggest that you return the car with a close to empty tank. In other cases, if you do not return the car with a full tank, you will have to pay to refill it, and gasoline at the car rental company's pump always is much more expensive than gasoline bought at a service station.

Finally, if renting a car in Canada, currency fluctuation is another factor to consider. Most brochures quote rental prices in US dollars, but these amounts frequently are only guides; that is, they represent the prevailing rate of exchange at the time the brochure was printed. The rate may be very different when you call to make a reservation and different again when the time comes to pay the bill (when the amount owed may be paid in cash in Canadian currency or as a charge to a credit card, which is recalculated at a still later date's rate of exchange). Some companies guarantee rates in US dollars (often for a slight surcharge), but this is an advantage only when the value of the US dollar is steadily declining abroad. If the US dollar is growing stronger in Canada, you may be better off with rates in Canadian dollars.

Before you leave the lot, check to be sure the rental car has a spare tire and jack in the trunk. In addition, particularly for extensive touring, you may want to pick up the following equipment: a first-aid kit; a flashlight with an extra set of batteries; a white towel (useful for signaling for help, as well as for wiping the car windows); jumper cables; flares and/or reflectors; a container of water or coolant for the radiator; snow chains for winter travel; and a steel container for extra gasoline.

Fly/Drive Packages – Airlines, charter companies, car rental companies, and tour operators have been offering fly/drive packages for years, and even though the basic components of the package have changed somewhat — return airfare, a car waiting at the airport, and perhaps a night's lodging in the gateway city all for one price used to be the rule — the idea remains the same. You rent a car *here* for use *there* by booking it along with other arrangements for the trip. These days, the very minimum arrangement possible is the result of a tie-in between a car rental company and an airline, which entitles customers to a rental car for less than the company's usual rates, provided they show proof of having booked a flight on that airline.

Slightly more elaborate fly/drive packages are listed under various names (go-as-you-please, self-drive, or, simply, car tours) in the independent vacations sections of tour catalogues. Their most common ingredients are the rental car plus some sort of hotel voucher plan, with the applicable airfare listed separately. You set off on your trip with a block of prepaid accommodations vouchers, a list of hotels that accept them (usually members of a hotel chain or association), and a reservation for the first night's stay, after which the staff of each hotel books the next one for you or you make your own reservations. Naturally, the greater the number of establishments participating in the scheme, the more freedom you have to range at will during the day's driving and still be near a place to stay for the night. The cost of these combination packages generally varies according to the size of the car and the quality of the hotels; there usually is an additional drop-off charge if the car is picked up in one city and dropped off in another. Most packages are offered at several different price levels, ranging from a standard plan covering stays in hotels to a budget plan using acccommodations such as small inns, bed and breakfast establishments, or farmhouses.

Airlines — such as *Air Canada* and *Canadian Airlines International* — also have special rental car rates available when you book their flights, often with a flexible hotel voucher program. Several Canadian tour wholesalers also offer fly/drive packages that include airfare and car rental. For further information on available packages, check with the airline or your travel agent.

Package Tours

 If the mere thought of buying a package for travel to and through Canada conjures up visions of a race through the twelve provinces in as many days in lockstep with a horde of frazzled fellow travelers, remember that packages have come a long way. For one thing, not all packages necessarily are escorted tours, and the one you buy does not have to include any organized touring at all — nor will it necessarily include traveling companions. If it does, however, you'll find that people of all sorts — many just like yourself — are taking advantage of packages today because they are economical and convenient, save you an immense amount of planning time, and exist in such variety that it's virtually impossible not to find one that suits at least the majority of your travel preferences. Given the high cost of travel these days, packages have emerged as a particularly wise buy.

Aside from the cost-saving advantages of package arrangements, Canada itself is ideally suited to package travel. The reason is that, essentially, Canada is a roam-and-do destination distinct from, say, the Caribbean, where most visitors go to a single island for a week or two and unpack everything until they're ready to return home. To be sure, many visitors to Canada do seek out a single city or province for a concentrated visit, booking themselves into a hotel, country inn, bed and breakfast establishment, apartment, cottage, or house that serves as a base from which they make regional tours and visits. But the bulk of travelers to Canada want to explore as much of the country as possible within the restrictions of time and travel funds available. Hence the popularity — and practicality — of package arrangements.

There are hundreds of package programs on the market today. In the US, numerous packages to Canada are offered by tour operators or wholesalers, some retail travel agencies, airlines, charter companies, hotels, and even special-interest organizations, and what goes into them depends on who is organizing them. The most common type, assembled by tour wholesalers and sold through travel agents, runs the gamut from deluxe everything to simple tourist class amenities or even bare necessities. Fly/drive packages usually are the joint planning efforts of airlines and car rental companies. Charter flight programs may range from little more than airfare and a minimum of ground arrangements to full-scale escorted tours or special-interest vacations. There also are hotel packages, organized by hotel chains or associations of independent hotels and applicable to stays at any combination of member establishments; resort packages, covering arrangements at a specific hotel; and special-interest tours, which can be once-only programs organized by particular groups through a retail agency or regular offerings packaged by a tour operator. They can feature food, festivals, a commemorative occasion, nature study, or scientific exploration. Many of these are sports packages, especially ski packages, and one good reason to use a package is to ensure good accommodations where it is difficult to book hotels on your own, such as in wilderness spots.

In essence, a package is an amalgam of travel services that can be purchased in a single transaction. A package tour to and through Canada may include any or all of the following: round-trip transportation, local transportation (and/or car rentals), accommodations, some or all meals, sightseeing, entertainment, transfers to and from the hotel at each destination, taxes, tips, escort service, and a variety of incidental features that might be offered as options at additional cost. In other words, a package can be any combination of travel elements, from a fully escorted tour offered at an all-inclusive price to a simple fly/drive booking allowing you to move about totally on your own. Its principal advantage is that it saves money: The cost of the combined arrangements invariably is well below the price that would be paid for all of the same elements if bought separately, and particularly if transportation is provided by charter or discount flight, it could even be less than a round-trip economy airline ticket on a regularly scheduled flight. A package tour provides more than economy and convenience: It releases the traveler from having to make individual arrangements for each separate element of a trip.

Lower prices are possible through package travel as a result of high-volume purchasing. The tour packager negotiates for services in wholesale quantities — blocks of airline seats or hotel rooms, group meals, dozens of rental cars, busloads of ground transport, and so on — and they are made available at a lower per-person price because of the quantities purchased for use during a given time period. Most packages, however, are subject to restrictions governing the duration of the trip and require total payment by a given time before departure.

Tour programs generally can be divided into two categories — escorted (or locally hosted) and independent — depending on the arrangements offered. An escorted tour means that a guide will accompany the group from the beginning of the tour through to return; a locally hosted tour means that the group will be met upon arrival in each city by a different local host. On independent tours, there generally is a choice of hotels, meal plans, and sightseeing trips in each city, as well as a variety of special excursions. The independent plan is for people who do not want a set itinerary, but who prefer confirmed reservations. Whether you choose an escorted or independent tour, always bring along complete contact information for your tour operator in case problems arise, although US tour operators often have Canadian affiliates who are available to give additional assistance or make other arrangements on the spot.

To determine whether a package — or more specifically, which package — fits your travel plans, start by evaluating your interests and needs, deciding how much and what you want to spend, see, and do. Gather whatever package tour information is available for your schedule. Be sure that you take the time to read the brochure *carefully* to determine precisely what is included. Keep in mind that travel brochures are written to entice you into signing up for a package tour. Often the language is deceptive and devious. For example, a brochure may quote the lowest prices for a package tour based on facilities that are unavailable during the off-season, undesirable at any season, or just plain nonexistent. Information such as "breakfast included" (as it often is in packages to Canada) or "plus tax" (which can add up) should be taken into account. Note, too, that the prices quoted almost always are based on double occupancy: The rate listed is for each of two people sharing a double room, and if you travel alone, the supplement for single accommodations can raise the price considerably (see *Hints for Single Travelers,* in this section).

In this age of rapidly rising airfares, the brochure most often will *not* include the price of an airline ticket in the price of the package, though sample applicable fares from various gateway cities usually will be listed separately as extras to be added to the price of the ground arrangements. Before doing this, check the latest fares with the airline, because the samples invariably are out of date by the time you read them. If the brochure gives more than one category of sample fares per gateway city — such as an individual tour-basing fare, a group fare, an excursion or other discount ticket, or in the case of flights to Canada, an APEX fare — your travel agent or airline tour desk will be able to tell you which one applies to the package you choose, depending on when you travel, how far in advance you book, and other factors. (An individual tour-basing fare is a fare computed as part of a package that includes land arrangements, thereby entitling a carrier to reduce the air portion almost to the absolute minimum. Though it always represents a saving over full-fare coach or economy, lately it has not been as inexpensive as the excursion and other discount fares that also are available to individuals. The group fare usually is the least expensive fare, and it is the tour operator, not you, who makes up the group.) When the brochure does include round-trip transportation in the package price, don't forget to add the round-trip transportation cost from your home city to the departure city to come up with the total cost of the package.

Finally, read the general information regarding terms and conditions and the responsibility clause (usually in fine print at the end of the descriptive literature) to determine the precise elements for which the tour operator is — and is not — liable. Here the tour operator frequently expresses the right to change services or schedules as long as equivalent arrangements are offered. This clause also absolves the operator of responsibility for circumstances beyond human control, such as floods or forest fires, or injury to you or your property. In reading, ask the following questions:

1. Does the tour include airfare or other transportation, sightseeing, meals, transfers, taxes, baggage handling, tips, or any other services? Do you want all these services?
2. If the brochure indicates that "some meals" are included, does this mean a welcoming and farewell dinner, two breakfasts, or every evening meal?
3. What classes of hotels are offered? If you will be traveling alone, what is the single supplement?
4. Does the tour itinerary or price vary according to the season?
5. Are the prices guaranteed; that is, if costs increase between the time you book and the time you depart, can surcharges unilaterally be added?
6. Do you get a full refund if you cancel? If not, be sure to obtain cancellation insurance.
7. Can the operator cancel if too few people join? At what point?

One of the consumer's biggest problems is finding enough information to judge the reliability of a tour packager, since individual travelers seldom have direct contact with the firm putting the package together. Usually, a retail travel agent is interposed between customer and tour operator, and much depends on his or her candor and cooperation. So ask a number of questions about the tour you are considering. For example: Has the agent ever used the package provided by this tour operator? How long has the tour operator been in business? Is the tour operator a member of the *United States Tour Operators Association (USTOA)?* (The *USTOA* will provide a list of its members upon request; it also offers a useful brochure, *How to Select a Package Tour.* Contact the *USTOA,* 211 E. 51st St., Suite 12B, New York, NY 10022; phone: 212-944-5727. Also check the Better Business Bureau in the area where the tour operator is based to see if any complaints have been filed against it.) Which and how many companies are involved in the package? If air travel is by charter flight, is there an escrow account in which deposits will be held; if so, what is the name of the bank?

This last question is very important. US law requires that tour operators deposit every charter passenger's deposit and subsequent payment in a proper escrow account. Money paid into such an account cannot legally be used except to pay for the costs of a particular package or as a refund if the trip is canceled. To ensure the safe handling of your money, make your check payable to the escrow account — by law, the name of the depository bank must appear in the operator-participant contract and usually is found in that mass of minuscule type on the back of the brochure. Write the details of the charter, including the destination and dates, on the face of the check; on the back, print "For Deposit Only." Your travel agent may prefer that you make your check out to the agency, saying that it will then pay the tour operator the fee minus commission. But it is perfectly legal to write your check as we suggest, and if your agent objects too strongly (the agent should have sufficient faith in the tour operator to trust him or her to send the proper commission), consider taking your business elsewhere. If you don't make your check out to the escrow account, you lose the protection of that escrow should the trip be canceled or the tour operator or travel agent fail. Furthermore, recent bankruptcies in the travel industry have served to point out that even the protection of escrow may not be enough to safeguard your investment. Increasingly, insurance is becoming a necessity (see *Insurance,* in this section), and payment by credit card has become popular since it offers some additional safeguards if the tour operator defaults.

Be aware that US laws don't apply if you book a tour in Canada. The Canadian federal government has no jurisdiction over tour operators, and provincial laws vary. British Columbia, Ontario, and Quebec have consumer legislation that will protect a traveler's funds if a tour operator goes bankrupt. However, the other provinces have no such laws, and just what you should do if the operator fails and you're out a trip is distressingly unclear. To protect yourself as much as possible, book a tour only through an established, reputable agent. And remember that tours run in conjunction with the large airlines — *Air Canada* and *Canadian Airlines International* for instance — or *VIA Rail Canada* are among the safest bets.

■ **A word of advice:** Purchasers of vacation packages who feel they're not getting their money's worth are more likely to get a refund if they complain in writing to the operator — and bail out of the whole package immediately. Alert the tour operator or resort manager to the fact that you are dissatisfied, that you will be leaving for home as soon as transportation can be arranged, and that you expect a refund. They may have forms to fill out detailing your complaint; otherwise, state your case in a letter. Even if the availability of transportation home detains you, your dated, written complaint should help in procuring a refund from the operator.

Camping and RVs, Hiking and Biking

CAMPING: One of the major attractions of Canada is its size — vast wilderness areas from east to west. Camping is probably the best way to see the outdoors, and that can mean anything from backpacking with a small tent to living in comfort in a plush recreational vehicle. Canadians welcome campers, and, fortunately, campgrounds in Canada number in the thousands, some privately run, but most in national or provincial parks.

Where to Camp – The national and provincial park system has preserved some of Canada's most beautiful areas for the enjoyment of visitors. There are also some 80 historic parks and sites, administered by Parks Canada, in which Canada's cultural heritage can be experienced firsthand. Campsites are located in or near all these parks.

Camping facilities also are located along the Trans-Canada Highway, which stretches from St. John's, Newfoundland, to Victoria, British Columbia. There's a campground approximately every 100 miles and a picnic ground every 50 miles.

National and provincial parks have a variety of camping facilities, distinguished by the kind of camping experience they cater to and divided into five categories:

1. *Tents and RVs:* Most of the campgrounds do not have trailer hook-ups, although many have sewage disposal stations. Particularly in provincial parks "comfort stations" with toilet, shower, and laundry facilities are common.
2. *Tents:* For tent campers only. Most campsites have level tent pads, picnic tables, firepits or grills, parking places for cars, nearby potable water sources, and pit privies.
3. *Primitive:* Pit privies, firepits, and, in some cases, communal shelters. These sites generally do not have potable water (even if it is marked as drinkable, the Canadian Park Service still recommends that you boil it). Often these sites must be reached by a good hike or by boat.
4. *Group Tenting:* Campgrounds for organized groups which must be reserved in advance.
5. *Winter Camping:* Those campgrounds open for winter use, some with heated toilet facilities and enclosed kitchen shelters.

For general information on Canada's national parks, see *National Parks,* DIVERSIONS. Campgrounds are also listed in the *Best en Route* sections of DIVERSIONS.

Campsites in most Canadian parks are all assigned on a first-come, first-served basis with no advance reservations except for group tenting areas. No one may camp longer than 2 weeks in a national park; the maximum allowed at provincial campgrounds varies with the province. All campgrounds in national parks are open from May to September, and because of the increasing popularity of winter camping, there's at least one campground open all winter long in most national parks. Fees range from CN$6 to CN$15, depending on location, services offered, and time of year.

Park rangers and directors of campgrounds often have a great deal of information about their region, and some even will arrange local tours or recommend sports facilities or attractions in the immediate area. Also ask about special programs such as fireside talks and/or slide shows which are offered at many public facilities. These often are informative and interesting, covering topics as diverse as local history, folklore, native flora and fauna, and the Canadians' preservation and commercial use of natural resources. Other interpretative nature programs held at national and provincial parks include walks or car tours and exhibits.

Campgrounds also provide the atmosphere and opportunity to meet other travelers and exchange useful information. Too much so, sometimes — the popularity of the Canadian campgrounds causes them to be quite crowded during the summer, and campsites sometimes are so close together that any attempt at privacy or getting away from it all is sabotaged. As campgrounds fill quickly at the height of the season, and the more isolated sites always go first, it's a good idea to arrive early in the day and reserve your chosen spot — which leaves you free to explore the area for the rest of the day. (Note that as a general rule, government run — national and provincial — campgrounds tend to offer more appealing and isolated sites, particularly for tent campers, than private facilities.)

In rural areas, it often is possible to obtain permission from a local landowner to camp on private property. Using private property, however, means that you must assume the responsibility of leaving the land exactly as it was found in return for the hospitality.

Canadian campgrounds are well marked — signs indicating nearby camping facilities are posted on most major roads. Still, it's best to have a map or check the information available in one of the numerous comprehensive guides to sites across the nation. It's also not always easy to find camping facilities open before May or after September, so a guide that gives this information comes in particularly handy off-season.

Camping maps, brochures, and lists of sites are available free from the the the tourist office of each province or from national tourist offices. (See *Tourist Information Offices* later in this section for addresses of provincial and national tourist offices.) A particularly good guide to help you locate campgrounds along your route is the *National Parks* brochure, which, in addition to providing a wealth of other information, details the parks' many and varied campgrounds. It's available free from the Canadian Parks Service, Ottawa, Ontario K1A 0H3, Canada (phone: 819-997-2800).

Other publications that include detailed information on camping facilities throughout Canada include the following:

> *Allstate Motor Club: RV Park and Campground Directory:* Issued as three large, comprehensive guides to all camping facilities throughout North America, including Canada, ($14.95), the East ($9.95), and the West ($9.95). Available from the publisher, Prentice-Hall (200 Old Tappan Rd., Old Tappan, NJ 07675; phone: 201-767-5937), they also may be found in bookstores.
>
> *Campground and Trailer Park Directory:* Information on campgrounds throughout North America, including Canada ($14.95). Also available from Prentice-Hall (address above) or from bookstores.
>
> *Woodalls' North American Campground Directory: Woodall's Eastern Campground Directory;* and *Woodall's Western Campground Directory* (Simon & Schuster; $10.95, $8.95, and $8.95, respectively) both include information on Canada and are available in bookstores. And new this year is *Woodall's Canadian Campground Directory,* which is available only from Simon & Schuster's mail-order department (28167 N. Keith Dr., Lake Forest, IL 60045; phone: 708-295-7799) for $4.95, plus $2 shipping and handling.

Necessities – Remember, first, that mosquitoes and blackflies are at their worst from early June to July in Canada, so be sure to bring along *plenty* of insect repellent, as well as something for treating the inevitable bites. (For our suggestions, see *Staying Healthy,* later in this section.) The farther into the wilderness you camp, the more annoying the bugs become.

For outdoor camping, necessities include a tent with flyscreens (the lighter and easier to carry and assemble the better); a sleeping bag; a foam pad, air mattress, or one of the new combination self-inflatable foam mattresses; a waterproof ground cloth; a rain poncho (which, in a pinch, can double as a ground cloth); a first-aid kit (including insect repellent, sunscreen, and a snakebite kit); sewing and toilet kits (including a roll of toilet paper in a plastic bag); a backpack stove; matches; nested cooking pots and cooking utensils; a three-quarter ax (well-sharpened and sheath-protected); a jackknife; and a flashlight with extra batteries. If you want a campfire, you may want to pick up some supplies (and wood or charcoal) en route to the campground (though some campgrounds do sell bundles of firewood) — particularly if going to where there is little wood, as in the open plains of the west and northwest. Be aware, however, that fires are prohibited in many areas, especially during dry periods.

If you have room, bring (or pick up on arrival) a compact Coleman lantern (with extra mantles, fuel, and a funnel) or battery-powered light (with extra batteries); if not, candles will do. You can make a simple windscreen that also will reflect and amplify candlelight using aluminium foil, which also is useful for campfire cooking. Small Coleman-type lanterns that will take either candle inserts or lamp oil are another alternative; these are more practical than the standard lanterns, as they are designed for backpackers and the glass is protected by a metel sheath for safe transport.

For the backpack stove, consider a Mountain Safety Research (MSR) — unlike most stoves that run only on white gas (which is hard to find in some parts of Canada), it also works with kerosene or alcohol. No matter what kind of camp stove you choose, however, it is still a good idea to bring along extra fuel. A stove helps out when you're knee-deep in the mud of a rainy day, and in-camp cooking is a great way to help stretch your travel funds.

Also include a canteen and/or plastic containers for water. Unless you are told that the campground where you are staying provides purified water, you should use it only for washing (don't even brush your teeth with it). In such cases, use only bottled, purified, or boiled water for drinking. To purify tap water, either use a water purification kit (available at most camping supply stores) or bring the water to a full, rolling boil over a camp stove. Unless deep in the wilderness, it is inadvisable to use water from streams, rivers, or lakes — even purified.

Keep food simple. Unless backpacking deep in the wilds, you probably will be close enough to a store to stock up on perishables; staples such as sugar, coffee, powdered milk, rice and other grains, and a basic assortment of spices can be carried along. Dehydrated food has become quite popular among both hikers and campers, but it can be expensive. An economical option for the more enterprising camper is to dry a variety of food at home; camping supply stores and bookstores carry cookbooks covering this simple process.

Keep in mind that many forest rangers warn about the dangers of leaving food in an area accessible to animals, repeating countless stories of scavenging bears and other wildlife invading tents and vehicles. (Bears have been known to rip open cars to reach food.) As a basic safety precaution, it is advisable to hang *all* foodstuffs from a tree some distance from your sleeping area. Bring along an extra waterproof stuff sack (available in a variety of sizes in camping supply stores) and some rope for this purpose.

RECREATIONAL VEHICLES: The term *recreational vehicle*s — RVs — is applied to all manner of camping vehicles, whether towed or self-propelled. RVs will appeal most to the kind of person who prefers the flexibilty of accommodation — there are countless private, provincial, and national campgrounds throughout the country that provide RV hookups — and enjoys camping with a little extra comfort. The level of comfort in an RV is limited only by the amount of money you choose to spend. At their simplest, they are fold-down campers, tents on wheels that unfold into sleeping quarters for several people when unhitched. The most luxurious RV is a fully equipped home on wheels, requiring electrical hookups at night to run the TV set, air conditioning, and kitchen appliances.

An RV undoubtedly saves a traveler a great deal of money on accommodations and, if cooking appliances are part of the unit, on food as well. However, it is important to remember that buying or renting an RV is a major expense; also, any kind of RV increases gas consumption considerably.

Be aware that there are limits on the size of towed RVs (trailers) allowed on Canadian roads, so before you go, it is wise to check the regulations for the provinces you plan to visit. For instance, in Ontario, the maximum length allowed for a trailer is 48 feet (75 feet for trailer plus car). Should your combination of vehicles and load exceed this limit, you must secure an Oversize Permit from the Oversize/Overweight Permit Office of the Ministry of Transportation and Communication (2680 Keele St.,

Main Fl., East Building, Downsview, Ontario M3M 1J8; phone: 416-750-3407). For other provinces, contact the same department in the provincial capital.

US citizens generally need no permit to bring a car or trailer into Canada. You must carry motor vehicle registration forms and, if the vehicle is rented, a copy of the rental contract stipulating permission for use in Canada. If you are driving a car not registered in your name, carry a letter from the registered owner authorizing you to use it. When towing a camper, note that nothing towed is covered automatically by the liability insurance of the primary vehicle, so the driver must carry a specific endorsement for the towed vehicle.

Vehicles from all countries other than the US, transported directly to Canada by air or sea, must be thoroughly washed or otherwise treated to remove all soil, and an affidavit or declaration to that effect must accompany the vehicle. This mandate includes vehicles (even those of US origin) arriving by ferry from Newfoundland, in which case this is done at ferry departure points. (Vehicles arriving in the US must meet the same requirements on arrival and are similarly inspected by US officials.)

Whether driving a camper or towing, it is essential to have some idea of the terrain you'll be encountering en route. Not only are numerous mountain passes closed in winter, but grades often are too steep for certain vehicles to negotiate, and some roads are off limits to towed caravans. Car tunnels, or "piggyback" services on trains can help bypass those summits too difficult to climb, but they also impose dimension limitations (cars or mini-vans generally are accepted onto trains, but not the larger types of RVs) and often charge high fees. Local tourist offices and police are the best sources of information about existing conditions and whether or not a particular pass is closed.

Towable RVs – Tow vehicles are hitched to cars or trucks and pulled. At their simplest, they are fold-down campers — tents on wheels that unfold into sleeping spaces. Fold-down camping trailers weigh about 1,100 pounds and cost between $1,500 and $8,000, with an average price of $4,000. More elaborate are travel trailers, 10 to 30 feet long (average is about 22 feet), weighing up to 10,000 pounds and costing from $5,000 to $37,000, with an average price of about $12,500. Fifth-wheel models, built to be towed by a pickup truck, range in price from $9,000 to $36,000, with an average price of $18,000. The park trailer, designed for seasonal or temporary living, sleeps up to 8 people and costs $14,000 to $26,000, with an average price of $17,500. The trailer should be equipped with brakes unless you expect that the combined weight of the trailer and its load will never exceed 3,000 pounds.

The *Canadian Recreational Vehicle Association* (670 Bloor St. W., Toronto, Ontario M6G 1L2; phone: 416-533-7800) represents manufacturers of all types of Canadian Standards Association-certified RVs. *AAA* and its Canadian equivalents can provide good booklets on trailers.

Motorized RVs – There are three styles of motorized recreational vehicles:

1. The motor home is a recreational vehicle built on or as part of a motorized vehicle chassis. It usually has kitchen, dining, bathroom, and sleeping facilities, all accessible from the driver's area. Electricity, heat, air conditioning, water, and propane-gas systems generally are included. Prices for compact models average $30,000; larger, more luxurious models cost an average of $55,300.

2. Van conversions are vans manufactured by auto makers and modified for recreation by customization specialists. Among the custom features are side windows, carpeting, paneling, and sofas. These vehicles, which usually sleep 2 to 4 but have no cooking facilities, sell for an average of $20,700.

3. Also in this category are truck-campers — camping units that are loaded onto the bed of a pickup. They sleep 2 to 6, often have kitchen facilities, and range in price from $2,000 to $10,000. This may seem like the most economical option of the three, however, keep in mind that this cost is in addition to the initial investment

in the pickup truck. Simple shells or covers for pickup truck beds are even less expensive — these leave the furnishings up to you.

Gas Consumption – Although an RV does save the traveler a great deal of money on on food and accommodations, the major expense in operating any RV is its high gas consumption. At the time of this writing, this substantial expense is of particular concern when budgeting for travel in Canada, as recent Canadian gas prices have sky-rocketed to as much as 50% to 60% over US prices.

It is most expensive to tow a large trailer camper, which decreases auto mileage by 50%. More economical, because it's smaller, is the fold-down tow camper, which will reduce normal car mileage by only about 10% to 15%. Self-propelled RVs have no better mileage records. A truck camper gets about 20% less mileage than the same truck without a camper, and an average Class A motorhome gets only 7 to 12 miles per gallon of gas. (Remember that gas in Canada generally is sold in liters, and you must adjust calculations accordingly.) Only in a converted van or a pickup truck with a lightweight cover (with minimal interior furnishings) will you find that your gas consumption does not change too drastically.

To reduce gas consumption, travel lightly (for every 100 pounds of weight, you use about 1% more gas). Carry only the water you need on the road. Put everything inside your RV to reduce wind resistance and thereby save on gas.

Renting – RVs are a poor choice for people who do not like to drive. They also are not for people who want to leave housekeeping chores behind when they set off on vacation. They are sure to sour a person who cannot stand to do any maintenance or simple handyman chores, nor are they for people who need lots of privacy. (RV sites generally are set in relatively open areas where the vehicles easily can be driven into position; the more secluded spots usually are designated for tent campers.) The best way to introduce yourself to traveling by RV is to rent one.

Rental rates vary depending on the size and complexity of the RV and the number of days rented, and often include customer pick-up and drop-off services at the airport. Although a common source of vans and towable campers (as well as the larger types of RVs) are the car rental companies listed in *Traveling by Car* in this section, you are likely to find a greater choice of models and range of prices offered by a dealer specializing in RV sales, rentals, and leases. Some dealers will apply rental fees to the eventual price of purchase (check the yellow pages, then shop around for the best terms). Although you can rent an RV in the US and drive it into Canada, there are numerous dealers throughout Canada, and some provincial tourist offices, such as Ontario Travel and Tourism British Columbia, publish guides listing these dealers.

When renting in Canada, bear the following in mind: Companies often require several months' notice in peak periods, so make inquiries as early as possible. Insurance, mileage costs, and the provincial sales tax should be discussed at the time of booking. Advance deposits and rental costs vary and usually are based on a weekly rate with an additional cost per kilometer, depending on the season and the lavishness of the motorhome. A truck-camper rental may be as much as 50% less per week than a luxury motorhome rental.

For information on how to operate, choose, and use a recreational vehicle, see *Living on Wheels* by Richard A. Wholters (Dutton; currently out of print; check your library or bookstore). You also might want to subscribe to *Trailer Life*, published by *TL Enterprises* (29901 Agoura Rd., Agoura, CA 91301; phone: 800-234-3450 or 818-991-4980). A 1-year subscription costs $12; $9 for members of the Good Sam Club, which provides discounts on a variety of services for RV owners and which also is run by *TL Enterprises.*

Another useful resource is the complimentary package of information on RVs offered by the *Recreational Vehicle Industry Association (RVIA)*. It includes a catalogue of RV sources and consumer information; write to the *Recreational Vehicle Industry Association* (Dept. RK, PO Box 2999, Reston, VA 22090; phone: 703-620-6003). The *Recreational Vehicle Rental Association (RVRA)*, an RV dealers group, publishes an annual rental directory, *Who's Who in RV Rentals;* send $5 to the *Recreational Vehicle Rental Association* (3251 Old Lee Hwy., Suite 500, Fairfax, VA 22030; phone: 703-591-7130).

Finally, you may want to subscribe to *Trailblazer,* a recreational vehicle and motor-home magazine. A year's subscription costs $24; write to *Trailblazer* (1000 124th Ave. NE, Bellevue, WA 98005).

Organized Camping Trips – A packaged camping tour is a good way to have your cake and eat it, too. The problems of advance planning and day-to-day organizing are left to someone else, yet you still reap the savings that shoestring travel affords. Be aware, however, that these packages often are geared to the young, with ages 18 to 35 a common age group. Transfer from place to place generally is by bus or van (as on other sightseeing tours) — although on some trips participants may hike, bike, canoe, raft, snowshoe, cross-country ski (and so on) from camp to camp. Overnights are in tents or shelters (depending on the season), and meal arrangements vary. Often there is a food fund that covers meals in restaurants or in the camp; sometimes there is a chef, and sometimes the cooking is done by the participants themselves.

If you want to go farther afield with an experienced guide and other campers, camping trips are available through a number of organizations including the following:

American Wilderness Experience, PO Box 1486, Boulder, CO 80306 (phone: 303-494-2992). Offers 5- to 6-day horseback riding/camping trips in Banff National Park in Alberta.

American Wildlands, 7500 E. Arapahoe Rd., Suite 355, Englewood, CO 80112 (phone: 800-332-WILD or 303-771-0380). Offers a 6-day sea kyaking/camping trip on Vancouver Island and a 6-day whale watching/camping trip in British Columbia.

Federation of Ontario Naturalists, 355 Lesmill Rd., Don Mills, Ontario M3B 2W8 (phone: 416-444-8419). Offers year-round nature tours, many of which include camping.

Pacific Rim Paddling Company, PO Box 1840, Station E, Victoria, British Columbia V8W 2Y3, Canada (phone: 604-384-6103). Offers camping and kayaking excursions throughout coastal British Columbia.

REI Adventures, PO Box 8090, Berkeley, CA 94707 (phone: 800-622-2236 nationwide except California; 800-624-2236 in California; 415-526-4005 in Canada). Offers camping trips to the Yukon.

Sierra Club, 730 Polk St., San Francisco, CA 94109 (phone: 415-766-2211). Offers a variety of base-camp and backpacking camping trips throughout Canada, which include biking, canoeing, hiking, kayaking, and rafting.

Sobek Canada, 159½ Main St., Unionville, Ontario L3R 2G8, Canada (phone: 416-479-2600). This Canadian branch of the adventure packager *Sobek Expeditions* offers camping/canoeing/kayaking trips throughout Canada.

In addition, a number of packagers listed under "Hiking" and "Biking" (below) also may offer these pursuits in combination with camping — it pays to call and ask when planning your trip.

The *Specialty Travel Index* is a directory to special-interest travel and an invaluable resource. Listings include tour operators specializing in camping, not to mention myriad other interests that combine nicely with a camping trip, such as biking, ballooning, diving, horseback riding, canoeing, motorcycling, and river rafting. It costs $5 per copy, $8 for a year's subscription of two issues. Contact *Specialty Travel Index,* 305 San Anselmo Ave., Suite 217, San Anselmo, CA 94960 (phone: 415-459-4900).

HIKING: If you would rather eliminate all the gear and planning and take to the outdoors unencumbered, park the car and go for a day's hike. Canada is blessed with fabulous trails (some of the very best are included in our park-by-park discussion of trails in *Hiking and Backpacking,* DIVERSIONS).

There are numerous sources for information on hiking, ranging from large national guidebooks and series to small retional guides. One good guide to them is *The Canadian Rockies Trail Guide: A Hiker's Manual to the National Parks,* by Bart Robinson and Brian Patton (Summerthought Publishing, PO Box 1420, Banff, Alberta T0L 0C0; $11). The *Canadian Rockies Access Guide* by Gayle Helgason and John Dodd (Hunter Publishing, 300 Raritan Center Parkway, Eddison, NJ 08818; $14.95) also provides detailed information on hiking and other outdoor adventures in the Rockies. Also useful is a series of recreation maps detailing hiking, as well as cross-country and downhill skiing trails, put out by the Outdoor Recreation Council of British Columbia, Suite 334, 1367 W. Broadway, Vancouver, British Columbia V6H 4A9, Canada. Probably the best maps for hikers are the maps of the detailed (1:250,000 and 1:50,000) *Canadian Topographical Series* available from *Map Link* (25 E. Mason St., Santa Barbara, CA 93101; phone: 805-965-4402) for $15 each, plus postage and handling.

And for those who want to drop a line, the detailed *Fishing Canada's Mountain Parks* by James R. Butler and Roland R. Maw (Falcon Press; $8.95, paperback) will tell you the type of waterways it's worth hiking to in Canada's national park's (where they're bound to be biting), tell you what kind of bait to use, the kind (and size) of fish to expect to bring to your griddle, and how to make sure that the big one doesn't get away (or the little one does). It can be ordered from the publisher, Falcon Press (PO Box 1718, Helena, MT 59624; phone: 800-582-2665) for $8.95, plus $1.75 postage and handling.

Mountaineering and hiking clubs also are a particularly good source of trail information for the average hiker. Among such Canadian clubs are the following:

Alpine Club of Canada, PO Box 519, Indian Flats Rd., Canmore, Alberta T0L 0M0, Canada (phone: 403-678-5855). This mountaineering club organizes hiking and skiing excursions throughout western Canada.

Fédération Québécoise de la Marche, 4545 Pierre de Coubertin, PO Box 1000, Montreal, Quebec H1V 3R2, Canada (phone: 514-252-3004). This is a hiking club; for those seeking the heights, a mountaineering club, *Fèdèration Quèbècoise de la Montagne,* is located at the same address.

Manitoba Sports Federation, 1700 Ellice Ave., Winnipeg, Manitoba, R3H 0B1, Canada (phone: 204-985-4000). A multi-sport association which also offers information on exploring Manitoba afoot.

Waskahegan Trail Association, PO Box 131, Edmonton, Alberta T5J 2G9, Canada (phone: 403-483-4838 or 403-434-2341). A hiking club which offers guidance to those interested in exploring central Alberta's Waskahegan trails.

Skyline Hikers of the Canadian Rockies, PO Box 3514, Postal Station B, Calgary, Alberta T2M 4M2, Canada (phone: 403-244-9179). Once a year this independent group of mountain enthusiasts sets up a base camp in the Rocky Mountains and organizes a variety of day hikes in the area from mid-July to mid-August.

For further information on mountaneering associations and climbing schools, see *Mountain Climbing,* in DIVERSIONS.

For those who are hiking on their own, without benefit of a guide or group, a map of the trail is a must. Most provincial and national parks provide maps of the trails in their domains. Even those tourist offices that do not have detailed enough literature on hand can direct you to associations in their province that supply maps, guides, and further information. For long visits, membership in a local club such as those listed above is suggested.

To make outings safe and pleasant, find out in advance about the trails you plan to hike and be realistic about your own physical limitations. If hiking at high altitudes — such as in the Canadian Rockies — keep in mind that it is easy to underestimate the challenge of the grade combined with the thinner air. Choose an easy route if you are out of shape. Stick to defined trails unless you are an experience hiker or know the area well. Whether heading out for a short jaunt or a longer trek, particularly in more remote areas, let someone know where you are going and when you expect to be back. If the hike is impromptu, leave a note in or on your car.

All you need to set out are a pair of sturdy shoes and socks; jeans or long pants to keep branches, thorns, thistles, and bugs off your legs; a canteen of water; a hat to protect you from the sun; and, if you like, a picnic lunch. It is a good idea to dress in layers, so that you can add or remove clothing according to the elevation and weather. Make sure, too, to wear clothes with pockets or bring a pack to keep your hands free. Some useful and important pocket or pack stuffers include trail mix, a jackknife, waterproof matches, a small first-aid kit (including insect repellent — it wears off when you sweat), a map, a compass, and sunglasses. You also may want to tuck in a lightweight waterproof poncho (available in camping supply stores) in case of unexpected showers. In areas where snakes are common, include a snakebite kit.

■ **A word of warning:** It is particularly important to wear socks, long pants, and long-sleeve shirts when hiking in heavily wooded areas due to the danger of Neuro Borreliosis, which is spread through the bite of the deer tick and other ticks. This disease recently has become familiar to Americans as Lyme Borreliosis (also known as "Lyme Tick Disease"). A strong insect repellent designed to repel ticks also may be helpful. The initial symptoms of this disease often are a swelling and/or a rash, generally accompanied by flu-like symptoms — such as fever and aching muscles. Readily curable in the early stages through antibiotics, if left untreated it can lead to serious complications. For information on precautions and treatment, contact the *Lyme Borreliosis Foundation,* PO Box 462, Tolland, CT 06084 (phone: 203-871-2900).

An increasingly popular pastime with hikers is trail riding. Even if you've never ridden a horse before, you can enjoy the outdoor experience of trail riding in the Canadian Rockies. When you book an organized tour from any of the several operators specializing in foothill and mountain trail rides, they'll take your riding experience into account. On a typical trail ride, an experienced guide takes the group along trails opened up by early explorers. You'll see mountain majesty as you've never seen it from the highway or campsite. These trips average about 5 days and are available as packages. Contact the Alberta or British Columbia provincial tourist offices for more information and the names of the tour operators.

Organized Hiking Trips – Those who prefer to travel as part of an organized group should refer to the January/February issue of *Sierra* magazine for the *Sierra Club*'s annual list of foreign outings. The *Sierra Club* offers a selection of trips each year, usually about 2 weeks in length. Some are backpacking trips, moving to a new camp each day; others make day hikes from a base camp. Overnights can be in small hotels, inns, farmhouses, guesthouses, or campgrounds and mountain cabins. Last year, among a number of outdoor explorations afoot was a base-camp hiking trip in the Northwest Territories and British Columbia. For information, contact the *Sierra Club,* Outing Department, 730 Polk St., San Francisco, CA 94109 (phone: 415-776-2211).

American Youth Hostels (see address below) also sponsors foreign hiking trips, though fewer than its foreign biking trips. As with the *Sierra Club,* the itineraries offered vary from year to year, usually ranging from around 15 to 52 days. *AYH*'s 1990 roster included a 16-day hiking tour of the Great Divide in Alberta. For information on upcoming offerings, contact the *American Youth Hostels* (address below; see *Hints for Single Travelers,* in this section, for membership information.)

Other companies that offer hiking tours in Canada include the following:

Black Feather Wilderness Adventures, 1341 Wellington St., Ottawa, Ontario K1Y 3B8, Canada (phone: 613-722-9717); or 40 Wellington St. E., Toronto, Ontario M5E 1C1, Canada (phone: 416-862-0881). Guided hikes and canoe trips in many areas of Canada.

Butterfield & Robinson, 70 Bond St., Suite 300, Toronto, Ontario M5B 1X3, Canada (phone: 800-387-1147 or 416-864-1354). This company offers several hiking tours, although fewer than it's biking tours (see below). Recent itineraries included a hiking/biking/horseback riding trip in the Canadian Rockies. (Also see "Biking," below.)

Yamnuska, Inc., PO Box 1920, Canmore, Alberta T0L 0M0, Canada (phone: 403-678-4164). Offers two different 7-day hiking itineraries in the Canadian Rockies, as well as 1-day to 3-month rock-climbing and mountaineering courses in the Rockies.

An alternative to dealing directly with the above companies is to contact *All Adventure Travel,* a specialist in hiking and biking trips worldwide. This company, which acts as a representative for numerous special tour packagers offering such outdoor adventures, can provide a wealth of detailed information about each packager and programs offered. They also will help you design and arrange all aspects of a personalized itinerary. This company operates much like a travel agency, collecting commissions from the packagers. Therefore, there is no additional charge for these services. For information, contact *All Adventure Travel,* PO Box 4307, Boulder, CO 80306 (phone: 800-537-4025 or 303-939-8885.)

BIKING: In recent years, the North American cycling scene has expanded considerably to include everything from competition rallies to 3-week guided tours of Nova Scotia or the mountains of western Canada. For young or energetic travelers, the bicycle offers a marvelous way of seeing Canada, especially where the terrain is conducive to easy cycling. And even where the hills and dales prove more challenging, successfully completing a biking itinerary can be truly rewarding. Biking does have its drawbacks: Little baggage can be carried, travel is slow, and cyclists are exposed to the elements. However, should a cyclist need a rest or refuge from the weather, unless peddling along Canada's more remote and vast wild stretches, there generally is a welcoming diner or comfortable hotel around the next bend. And besides being a viable way to tour Canada — and to burn calories to make room for unlimited portions of hearty Canadian food — biking is a great way to meet people.

In choosing bike routes, long or short, look for ways to escape the omnipresent automobile and its fumes and noise. Stick to back roads; use provincial highway maps which list secondary roads that the gasoline company maps often ignore.

Road Safety – While the car may be the bane of cyclists, cyclists who do not follow the rules of the road strike terror into the hearts of drivers. Follow the same rules and regulations as motor vehicle drivers. Stay to the right side of the road. Ride no more than two abreast — single file where traffic is heavy. Keep three bicycle lengths behind the cycle in front of you. Stay alert to sand, gravel, potholes, and wet or oily surfaces, all of which can make you lose control. Wear bright clothes and use lights or wear reflective material at dusk or at night, and, above all — even though Canadian cyclists often don't — always wear a helmet.

Choosing and Renting a Bike – Although many bicycling enthusiasts choose to take along their own bikes, bicycles can be rented throughout Canada. There are five basic types of bicycle available for rent: the children's fun bike, the domestic one-gear bike, the three-gear bike with caliper brakes, the touring bike with dropped handlebars and 5, 10, or even 15 gears, and the lightweight competition bike. A newer type of bike particularly suited to Canada's more mountainous terrain is the specially designed mountain bike.

As an alternative to renting, you might consider buying a bicycle in Canada. However, the bicycle may take some getting used to — seats especially need breaking in at first — and if you bring it home, it will be subject to an import duty by US Customs if its price (or the total of all purchases made in Canada) exceeds $400. When evaluating this cost, take into account additional charges for shipping. Bike shops in major cities that rent bikes sometimes also sell used ones — a particularly economical option that may be even less expensive than a long-term rental.

A bicycle is the correct size for you if you can straddle its center bar with feet flat on the ground and still have an inch or so between your crotch and the bar. (Nowadays, because women's old-fashioned barless bikes are not as strong as men's, most women use men's bicycles.) The seat height is right if your leg is just short of completely extended when you push the pedal to the bottom of its arc.

To be completely comfortable, divide your weight; put about 50% on your saddle and about 25% each on your arms and legs. To stop sliding in your seat and for better support, set your saddle level. A firm saddle is better than a soft springy one for a long ride. Experienced cyclists keep the tires fully inflated (pressure requirements vary widely, but always are imprinted on the side of the tire; stay within 5 pounds of the recommended pressure). Do not use top, or tenth, gear all the way; for most riding the middle gears are best. On long rides remember that until you are very fit, short efforts with rests in between are better than one long haul, and pedal at an an even pace.

The happiest biker in a foreign country is the one who arrives best prepared. Bring saddlebags, a handlebar bag, a tool kit that contains a bike wrench, screwdriver, pliers, tire repair kit, cycle oil, and work gloves, a bike repair book, a helmet, a rain suit, a water bottle, a flashlight with an extra set of batteries, a small first-aid kit, and muscles that have been limbered up in advance.

Even the smallest towns usually have a bike shop, so it's not difficult to replace or add to gear; however, because tires and tubes are sized to metric dimensions in Canada, when riding your own bike, bring extras from home. Seasoned bikers swear that the second day of any trip always is the worst, so keep this in mind and be ready to meet the mental and physical challenges ahead.

If you are planning to travel by plane to Canada with your bicycle, be sure to check with the airline beforehand. Airlines going from the US (or elsewhere) to Canada generally allow bicycles to be checked as baggage; they require that the pedals be removed, handlebars be turned sideways, and the bike be in a shipping carton, which some airlines provide, subject to availability — call ahead to make sure. If buying a shipping carton from a bicycle shop, check the airline's specifications and also ask about storing the carton at the destination airport so you can use it again for the return flight. Although some airlines charge only a nominal fee, if the traveler already has checked two pieces of baggage there may be an additional excess baggage charge of $70 to $80 for the bicycle. As regulations vary from carrier to carrier, be sure to call well before departure to find out your airline's specific regulations. As with other baggage, make sure that the bike is thoroughly labeled with your name, a business address and phone number, and the correct airport destination code.

An excellent resource is the *Canadian Cycling Association (CCA),* an umbrella organization of provincial cycling groups. The *CCA* is the distributor of *The Great Canadian Bicycle Trail* (available as three regional trail guides for $5.35 each or as a three-volume set for $15). Other useful books published by the association are *The Complete Guide to Bicycling in Canada* ($12.65), *The Canadian Rockies Bicycling Guide* ($8.75), *The British Columbia Bicycling Guide* ($7.80), and *Backcountry Biking in the Canadian Rockies* ($11.70) — these prices all include postage and handling. To order these books or for a copy of *CAA*'s free brochure listing its publications as well as those of its member groups, contact *CCA* (1600 James Naismith Dr., Gloucester, Ontario K1B 5N4, Canada; phone: 613-748-5629). For general biking information, try

The Complete Book of Bicycling by Eugene A. Sloane (Simon & Schuster; $15.95 paperback) and *Anybody's Bike Book* by Tom Cuthbertson (Ten Speed Press; $8.95 paperback).

Good maps will infinitely improve a biking tour (or any kind of outdoor exploration), and detailed maps show the scenic byways, as well as the route that goes around the mountain, not up it. Such maps are available from a number of sources, and one of the best sources for detailed topographical maps and just about any other type of map (of just about anywhere in the world) is *Map Link* (25 E. Mason St., Santa Barbara, CA 93101; phone: 805-965-4402). Their comprehensive guide *The World Map Directory* ($29.95) includes a wealth of sources for travelers afoot, and if they don't stock a map of the area in which you are interested (or the type of map best suited to your outdoor adventure), they will order it for you. It is likely that they'll have something to suit your needs — they carry over 1,000 maps on Canada.

Biking Tours – A number of organizations offer bike tours in Canada. Linking up with a bike tour is more expensive than traveling alone, but with experienced leaders, an organized tour often becomes an educational as well as a very social experience that may lead to long-term friendships.

One of the attractions of a bike tour is that shipment of equipment — the bike — is handled by organizers, and the shipping fee is included in the total tour package. If flying to Canada, travelers simply deliver the bike to the airport, already disassembled and boxed; shipping boxes can be obtained from most bicycle shops with little difficulty. Bikers not with a tour must make their own arrangements with the airline, and there are no standard procedures (see above). Although some tour organizers will rent bikes, most prefer that participants show up with a bike with which they are already familiar. Another attraction of *some* tours is the existence of a "sag wagon" to carry extra luggage, fatigued cyclists, and their bikes, too, when pedaling another mile is impossible.

Most bike tours are scheduled from May to September, last 1 or 2 weeks, are limited to 20 or 25 people, and provide lodging in inns or hotels, though some use hostels or even tents. Tours vary considerably in style and ambience, so request brochures from several operators in order to make the best decision. When contacting groups, be sure to ask about the maximum number of people on the trip, the maximum number of miles to be traveled each day, and the degree of difficulty of the biking; these details should determine which tour you join and can greatly affect your enjoyment of the experience. Planning ahead is essential because trips often fill up 6 months or more in advance.

Among the companies specializing in biking tours to Canada are the following:

Backroads Bicycle Touring, 1516 Fifth St., Berkeley, CA 94710-1713 (phone: 415-527-1555 in California; 800-533-2573 elsewhere in the US). Offers superior food and accommodations on its tours. Recent itineraries in Canada included a 6-day biking trip in Alberta, from Banff to Jasper, and a 5-day trip in the Gulf Islands off the coast of British Columbia. Tours are geared to beginning and intermediate riders.

Breakaway Vacations, 164 E. 90th St., #2Y, New York, NY 10128 (phone: 212-722-4221). Offers 6-day inn-to-inn biking tours of Quebec.

Butterfield & Robinson, 70 Bond St., Suite 300, Toronto, Ont. M5B 1X3, Canada (phone: 416-864-1354). Offers a number of first class, sophisticated bike trips in Canada, including an 8-day leisurely biking trip in Quebec, and an 8-day biking/ hiking/horseback riding trip in the Canadian Rockies. Bikes are provided, though you can take your own, and there are many departure dates for each itinerary. This company also offers trips designed for riders ages 17 or older; tours are rated at four levels of difficulty. (Also see "Hiking," above.)

On the Loose Bicycle Vacations, 1020 Merced St., Berkeley, CA 94707 (phone:

800-346-6712 or 415-527-4005). Offers a variety of biking trips. Recent itineraries in Canada included a 6-day trip between Banff and Jasper in Alberta.

Progressive Travel Ltd., 1932 First Ave., Seattle, WA 98101 (phone: 800-245-
2229). Offers a 6-day biking trip in British Columbia.

Rocky Mountain Cycle Tours, PO Box 1978, Canmore, Alberta T0L 0M0, Canada
(phone: 403-678-6770). Offers high-country bikers a full range of tours lasting
1, 6, and 14 days. Their 6-day biking/camping tour from Banff to Jasper passes
through some of the most spectacular scenery in the Canadian Rockies. Also
offered is a 6-day biking trip in the Rocky Mountain lakes, and a 6-day hike and
bike tour in Alberta from Banff to the Columbia ice fields.

Vermont Bicycle Touring, Box 711, Bristol, VT 05443 (phone: 802-453-4811).
Offers 10-day a biking tour of Nova Scotia.

Vermont Country Cyclers, PO Box 145, Waterbury Center, Vermont 05677
(phone: 802-244-5135). Offers 6-day biking tours of Nova Scotia, and a 5-day
biking/rafting trip in Ottawa.

Hundreds of other organizations sponsoring biking tours have sprung up across
North America in response to the explosion of interest in this form of travel.

The *American Youth Hostels (AYH)* and its local chapters or councils also sponsor
a variety of biking tours to Canada each year. You don't have to be a youngster to take
an *AYH* trip; membership is open to all ages. The catalogue includes trips for teens
and explains the custom adult trips offered (groups design their own itineraries). *AYH*
tours are for small groups of 9 or 10 participants and tend to be longer than average
(up to 5 weeks). Departures are geared to various age groups and levels of skill and
frequently feature accommodations in hostels — along with hotels for adult groups and
campgrounds for younger groups. Recent Canadian itineraries included a 21-day biking
trip in New Brunswick, Newfoundland, Nova Scotia, and Prince Edward Island, and
a 22-day trip from Seattle to British Columbia. The *Metropolitan New York Council
of American Youth Hostels* is an affiliate with a particularly broad tour program of its
own, and is a good source of camping, hiking, and cycling equipment. For information
on current offerings, contact your local council, the national organization (PO Box
37613, Washington, DC 20013-7613; phone: 202-783-6161), or The *Metropolitan New
York Council of American Youth Hostels* (891 Amsterdam Ave., New York, NY 10025;
phone: 212-932-2300).

The *International Bicycle Touring Society (IBTS)* is another nonprofit organization
that regularly sponsors low-cost bicycle tours overseas led by member volunteers.
Participants must be over 21. A sag wagon accompanies the tour group, accommodations are in inns and hotels, and breakfast is included. For information, send $2 plus
a self-addressed, stamped envelope to *IBTS* (PO Box 6979, San Diego, CA 92106-0979;
phone: 619-226-TOUR). The *Sierra Club* also occasionally includes a bike tour in its
Canadian offerings. For news about upcoming freewheeling events, contact the club's
Outing Department (address above).

You also may want to investigate the tours of Canada offered by the *Cyclists' Touring
Club (CTC),* Britain's largest cycling association. In addition to offering organized
tours (including Canada), *CTC* has a number of planned routes available in pamphlet
form for bikers on their own and helps members plan their own tours. The club also
publishes a yearly handbook, as well as magazines. For information contact the *CTC*
at Cotterell House, 69 Meadrow, Godalming, Surrey GU7 3HS, England (phone:
44-4868-7217).

The *League of American Wheelmen* (6707 Whitestone Rd., Suite 209, Baltimore,
MD 21207; phone: 301-944-3399) publishes *Tourfinder,* a list of organizations, nonprofit and commercial, that sponsor bicycle tours of the US and abroad; the list is free
with membership ($25 individual, $30 family) and can be obtained by non-members

who send $5. The *League* also can put you in touch with biking groups in your area. Once you are in Canada, also look under "Associations" or "Clubs" in major city yellow pages for addresses, or contact the *Canadian Cycling Association* (1600 James Naismith Dr., Gloucester, Ontario K1B 5N4; phone: 613-748-5629), which can direct you to provincial groups sponsoring trips.

Preparing

Calculating Costs

$ The value of the Canadian dollar relative to the US dollar has made Canada an attractive destination for Americans in recent years. Toronto and Montreal, Canada's most expensive cities, have prices approaching, but still less than, those of major US cities; generally speaking, prices in Canada's medium-size cities and small towns also compare favorably to US prices in equivalent places.

A Canadian vacation becomes an even more appealing bargain if you take advantage of discount fares and charter flights which can greatly reduce travel costs; package tours can even further reduce the price. Canada always has been one of the most popular destinations for both first-time and seasoned travelers, and it certainly is one where the competition for visitors from the US works to inspire suprisingly affordable travel opportunities. Nevertheless, most travelers still have to plan carefully and manage their travel funds prudently.

In Canada, estimating the cost of travel expenses depends on the mode of transportation you choose, the part or parts of the country you plan to visit, how long you will stay there, the level of luxury to which you aspire, and in some cases, what time of the year you plan to travel. In addition to the basics of transportation, hotels, meals, and sightseeing, you have to take into account seasonal price changes that apply on certain air routings and at popular vacation destinations, as well as inflation, price fluctuations, and the vagaries of currency exchange. So, while the guidelines in this book will remain useful, costs for both facilities and services may have changed somewhat in the months since publication.

DETERMINING A BUDGET: A realistic appraisal of your travel expenses is the most crucial bit of planning you will undertake before any trip. It also is, unfortunately, one for which it is most difficult to give precise, practical advice. Travel styles are intensely personal, and personal taste determines cost to a great extent. Will you stay in a hotel every night and eat every meal in a restaurant, or are you planning to camp or picnic amidst Canada's often spectacular wilderness, thus reducing your daily expenditures? Base your calculations on your own travel style, and make estimates of expenses from that. If published figures on the cost of travel always were taken as gospel, many trips would not be taken. But in reality, it's possible to economize. On the other hand, don't be lulled into feeling that it is not necessary to do some arithmetic before you go. No matter how generous your travel budget, without careful planning beforehand — and strict accounting along the way — you will spend more than you anticipated.

When calculating costs, start with the basics, the major expenses being transportation, accommodations, and food. However, don't forget such extras as local transportation, shopping, and such miscellaneous items as laundry and tips. The reasonable cost of these items usually is a positive surprise to your budget; such extras as drinks served with imported liquours and airport departure taxes are definite negatives.

Package programs can reduce the price of a vacation in Canada, because the group rates obtained by the tour packager usually are lower than the tariffs for someone traveling on a freelance basis, that is, paying for each element — airfare, hotel, meals, car rental — separately. And keep in mind, particularly when calculating the major expenses, that costs vary according to fluctuations in the exchange rate — that is, how much Canadian currency a US dollar will buy.

Other expenses, such as the cost of local sightseeing tours, will vary from city to city. Official tourist information offices are plentiful throughout Canada, and most of the better hotels will have someone at the front desk who can provide a rundown on the cost of local tours and full-day excursions in and out of the city. Travel agents also can provide this information. Special discount passes that provide tourists with unlimited travel by the day or the week on regular city transportation are available in some cities. Provincial tourist offices, as well as railway offices, can provide information on current discount offerings (for offices in the US, see *Tourist Information Offices* and *Traveling by Train,* both in this section). Entries in the individual city reports in THE CITIES also give helpful information on local transportation options.

There are regional differences in prices in Canada, although they tend to be between rural and urban areas. Based on a national average, which is nonetheless somewhat arbitrary, you can get an indication of the regional differences. Remember that Canada is not a country of averages, since its population is so small relative to that of the US. Also, 90% of the Canadian population lives within 200 miles of the US.

For purposes of a rough estimate — if you spend every night in a hotel or motel and eat every meal in a modestly priced restaurant, you can expect to spend around $125 to $150 for two people per day. This figure does not include transportation costs, but it does include accommodations (based on two people sharing a room), three meals, some sightseeing, and other modest entertainment costs. The accommodations take into consideration the differences between relatively inexpensive lodgings in rural areas (about $40 to $50 per night for two) and moderate hotels in urban areas (about $60 to $80 per night for two). With the exception of major cities, these averages should be about right for a room for two throughout most of Canada. You can find places that are much less expensive, or places at which you spend more for a commensurate increase in quality of service and comfort.

Meals are calculated for inexpensive to moderate restaurants. The entertainment calculated in this daily expense figure includes one sightseeing tour and admission to one museum or historic site and/or one recreation — such as greens fees for a round of golf or a lift ticket for an afternoon of skiing.

Adjusted for regional price differences, the estimate above — which breaks down to an average of $70-per-person-per-day — can be useful. For instance, overall prices in rural areas such as the British Columbia interior, the Maritimes, southern Ontario, the prairies, and southern Quebec are the lowest in the country — about 10% less than the national figure. Travel in major cities such as Calgary and Edmonton (Alberta), Montreal (Quebec), Toronto (Ontario), and Vancouver (British Columbia) costs about 20% more. The travel cost for medium-size cities such as Halifax (Nova Scotia), Hamilton and London (Ontario), Quebec City (Quebec), Regina and Saskatoon (Saskatchewan), and Winnipeg (Manitoba) runs about 10% more than average. In remote areas (more than 250 miles north of the US border) such as the Northwest Territories, northern Ontario, northern Quebec, and the Yukon, expect to pay as much as 15% more.

As noted in *When to Go,* slightly lower hotel rates can be expected in Canada during the off-season — which varies from area to area. Many hotels offer "mini-break" packages, that is, a discount for a stay of 2 or more nights, usually over a weekend; though these discounts may be in effect any time of the year, they are most common when demand is lowest. In large cities, seasonal price variations may be negligible — with the exception of a dramatic rise in the cost of accommodations and services during holidays. During the shoulder season months (which vary), prices generally are somewhat more reasonable even for luxury hotels, although, again, high-season prices may prevail in large cities and popular tourist areas.

You should be able to use these averages to forecast a reasonably accurate picture of your daily travel costs, based on exactly how you want to travel. Savings on the daily allowance can occur while motoring in rural areas; budget-minded families also can take advantage of very inexpensive guesthouse accommodations in the Maritime Provinces and elsewhere in the countryside. Campgrounds in national and provincial parks and on private land are particularly inexpensive and they are located throughout Canada (see *Camping and RVs, Hiking and Biking,* in this section). For information on other economical accommodations alternatives, such as renting an apartment, house, or cottage, home exchanges, and bed and breakfast accommodations, see the discussion of accommodations in *On the Road,* in this section.

Picnicking is another excellent way to cut costs. Most provinces have major scenic highways with well-maintained rest areas equipped with log tables and benches, trash cans, and sometimes fireplaces, running water, and toilets. A stop at a local store or market can provide a feast at a suprisingly economical price — especially when compared to the cost of a restaurant lunch.

In planning any travel budget, it also is wise to allow a realistic amount for both entertainment and recreation. Are you planning to spend time sightseeing and visiting local museums? Do you intend to spend your days skiing at a popular resort? Is daily golf or tennis a part of your plan? Will your children be disappointed if they don't take a whale watching cruise or explore the midway and displays of the *Canadian National Exhibition* in Toronto? If so, charges for these attractions and recreations must be taken into account. Information (and where to write or call for more) on these and other activities can be found in our DIVERSIONS chapters, as well as in the *Sources and Resources* sections of the individual city reports in THE CITIES. Finally, don't forget that if haunting clubs, discotheques, or other nightspots every night is an essential part of your vacation, or you feel that one performance of the city's top ballet troupe, orchestra, or theater company may not be enough, allow for the extra cost of nightlife. This one item alone can add a great deal to your daily expenditures, particularly in the large cities and major tourist and resort areas.

When estimating costs for eating out, also don't forget to include 15% on your total restaurant bill for tipping. Additionally, most provinces (the Northwest Territories and the Yukon are two exceptions) have sales tax on most items, including food and lodging. Quebec, however, doesn't impose a separate tax on accommodations. If you spend over CN$100 on goods in Ontario, you will be eligible for a refund of provincial sales tax. Forms to use when applying for the refund are available at retail shops throughout the province.

In addition, don't forget to factor in the new Canada-wide 7% Goods and Services Tax (GST), which is similar to the Value Added Tax imposed in many European countries. This new tax replaces a 13.5% federal sales tax on goods manufactured in Canada — the difference is that it also applies to services, which were not taxed before. The taxed items include travel services such as package tours, car rentals, accommodations, meals, and most purchases. Note, however, that foreign visitors to Canada are able to get a rebate of the tax on any goods purchased in Canada but later sent or taken out of the country, and the rebate — unlike most VAT — also will apply to up to 30 nights of lodging per visit. Restaurant meals, sightseeing, gasoline, and alcholic beverages are taxable but not rebatable. The amount of the tax rebate claimed must be for a minimum of $20 — which means your expenditures in Canada for accommodations and other applicable purchases must be at least CN$286 — CN$306 including the tax. Visitors are entitled to make up to four rebate claims per year, or purchases can be accumulated on any number of visits and one claim made for the calendar year. Visitors can mail the rebate forms back after returning home. As we went to press, in addition to the mail-back program, there were tentative plans to establish instant-rebate centers at points of departure from Canada — i.e., duty-free shops and border crossing areas. If you have any questions about the tax while you're in Canada, you can call the information hot line that has been set up: 800-267-6620.

If at any point in the planning process it appears impossible to estimate expenses, consider this suggestion: The easiest way to put a ceiling on the price of all of these elements is to buy a package tour. A totally planned and escorted one, with almost all transportation, rooms, meals, sightseeing, local travel, tips, and a dinner show or two included and prepaid, provides an exact total of what the trip will cost beforehand, and the only surprise will be the one you spring on yourself by succumbing to some irresistible, expensive souvenir.

The various types of packages available are discussed under *Package Tours* in this section, but a few points bear repeating here. Not all packages are package *tours.* They often are no more than loosely organized arrangements including a stay at a hotel, transfers between hotel and airport, baggage handling, taxes, and tips, which leave the entire matter of how you spend your time and where you eat your meals — and with whom — up to you. Equally common are the hotel-plus-car packages, which take care of accommodations and local transportation. On such independent or hosted "tours," there may be a tour company representative or affiliated travel agent available at a nearby office to answer questions, or a host may be stationed at a desk in the hotel to arrange optional excursions, but you will never have to travel in a group unless you wish to.

More and more, even experienced travelers are being won over to the idea of package travel, not only for the convenience and planning time saved, but above all for the money that can be saved. Whatever elements you include in your package, the organizer has gotten them for you wholesale — and they are paid for in advance, thus eliminating the dismal prospect of returning to your hotel room each night to subtract the day's disbursements from your remaining cash, when you should be enjoying a cold Canadian beer in peace.

The possibility of prepaying certain elements of your trip is an important point to consider even if you intend to be strictly independent, with arrangements entirely of your own making, all bought separately. You may not be able to match the price of the wholesale tour package, but at least you will have introduced an element of predictability into your accounting, thus reducing the risk that some budget-busting expense along the way might put a damper on the rest of your plans.

Those who want to travel independently — but also want to eliminate the element of surprise from their accommodations budget — can take advantage of the hotel voucher schemes that frequently come as part of a fly/drive package. Travelers receive a block of prepaid vouchers and a list of hotels that accept them as total payment for a night's stay, and for those who may want to upgrade their lodgings from time to time, there often is another set of hotels that accepts the same vouchers with payment of a supplement.

With the independent traveler in mind, what follows are some suggestions of how to pin down the cost of a trip beforehand. But there are two more variables that will influence the cost of your holiday whether you buy a package or do it all yourself. One is timing. If you are willing to travel during the off-season months, when airfares are lower, you'll find many hotel rates lower also. Keep in mind those periods between the high and low season in any area, generally referred to as the shoulder months. Although costs are only a little lower than in high season and the weather may not be as predictable, you won't be bucking the crowds that in peak months can force a traveler without a hotel reservation into the most expensive hostelry in town. Don't forget, however, to find out what is going on in any place where you plan to spend a good deal of your vacation. The availability and possible economy gained by off-season travel often are negated if a major conference or other special event is scheduled when you plan to visit.

Another factor influencing the cost of your trip is whether you will be traveling alone or as a couple. The prices quoted for package tours almost always are based on double occupancy of hotel rooms, and the surcharge — or single supplement — for a room by yourself can be quite hefty. When shopping for a hotel room, you'll find that there are many more double rooms than singles. Don't expect a discount if you occupy a double room as a single, and don't expect single rooms to cost less than two-thirds the price of doubles.

■**Note:** Although the value of US and Canadian currencies doesn't vary as much as in other countries during the course of the year, the volatility of exchange rates may mean that between the time you originally make your hotel reservations and the day you arrive, the price in US dollars may vary substantially from the price originally quoted. To avoid paying more than you expected, it's wise to investigate rates that are guaranteed in US dollars. Remember that you also can determine whether it's more economical to pay for services in US dollars before departure or in Canadian dollars once you're there.

TRANSPORTATION COSTS: In earlier sections of GETTING READY TO GO we have discussed the comparative costs of different modes of transportation and the myriad special rates available through package tours, charter flights, car rental packages, and train and bus and other budget deals. See each of the relevant sections for specific information. Transportation is likely to represent the largest item in your travel budget in a country as vast as Canada (cummulatively, only food and accommodations are likely to be higher), but the encouraging aspect of this is that you will be able to determine most of these costs before you leave. Most fares will have to be paid in advance, particularly if you take advantage of charter air travel or other special offerings.

Airfare is really the easiest cost to pin down precisely, though the range and variety of flights available may be confusing initially. The possibilities were outlined fully in *Traveling by Plane,* earlier in this section. Essentially you can choose from various types of tickets on scheduled flights, ranging in expense from first class and excursion fares to APEX and discount tickets and charters.

The most important factors in determining which mode of transportation to choose to tour around Canada are the amount of traveling you plan to do and the length of time you will be abroad. If you intend to move about a great deal among cities, train or bus travel is likely to be the most economical approach.

Driving provides maximum flexibility. If driving your own car, except for breakdowns or repairs (for which you should budget something), car costs can be calculated by figuring mileage, based upon your own experience, and average gas prices.

Renting a car can be a substantial expense, although car rental costs vary from city to city, as well as according to season, the type of car you choose, and whether the car is rented independently or as part of a package deal. Look carefully into fly/drive arrangements versus straight rentals and also compare the rates offered by some of the smaller firms specializing in North American car travel with the rates offered by the larger, more familiar car rental companies. (For specific information on local car rental companies, see *Sources and Resources* in the individual THE CITIES chapters.) The latter all have discount plans, provided the car is booked a certain number of days before pick-up and the rental is for a minimum period of time. Look for a flat rate that also offers unlimited mileage — usually the best deal. Also, when estimating driving costs, don't forget that the price of gas in Canada averages 50% to 60% more than the price you're accustomed to paying in the US, so be sure to take this substantial expense into account. This cost also provides a significant incentive to rent a car that delivers the highest possible mileage per gallon — or liter — of gas.

FOOD: Meals are a more difficult expense to estimate. If you rent an apartment, house, or cottage, or are camping out, you will be able to prepare some meals yourself. Depending on where you're staying, groceries can be more expensive than they are at home, but they certainly will be less expensive than eating out. Restaurant dining — particularly in the better establishments of major cities and prime tourist areas — is going to hit your purse, wallet, or credit card hardest.

In general, you can expect to pay somewhat less at most Canadian restaurants than at US restaurants of equal quality. Independent travelers eating all their meals in restaurants should allow roughly $60 to $80 a day per couple for food. This amount includes breakfast (about $10 to $15 for two), lunch (about $15 to $20 for two), and an average dinner. The estimate for dinner is based on a fixed menu (at a fixed price) in a moderate, neither-scrimp-nor-splurge restaurant, which at least can include a tasty and occasionally imaginative food selection, but no cocktails before dinner. You easily could add a beer and a glass of house wine to the dinner tab without wreaking havoc with these figures, but you won't be splurging. If ordering an à la carte dinner and the pick of the wine list, expect the tab, even in a moderate establishment, to rise much higher. And if you're addicted to *haute gastronomie,* the sky is the limit.

All of this is no reason to forgo your trip, however — remember, it's *dining* that is going to hit your wallet hard. Those who are up to a steady diet of fast food can get by on a lot less. And there is some relief out in the countryside where the breakfast that comes with the bed in the typical bed and breakfast establishments and small country inns still can be a filling one, apt to hold most folks straight through midday, though even travelers on a severe budget are advised not to skip lunch. As in the US, diners throughout Canada — suprisingly, some of the best are located along major highways — offer hearty fare, the menus often are suprisingly varied, and they're among the best food buys encountered. Picnic lunches, with ingredients purchased at shops and markets along the route, are less expensive (and, weather permitting, more fun) still. Finish off the day with a carefully chosen meal in a tavern or inn and you will sacrifice nothing in experience and still hold down costs. Our restaurant selections, chosen to give the best value for money — whether expensive or dirt cheap — are listed in the *Best in Town* sections of THE CITIES.

ACCOMMODATIONS: There is a wide range of choice and a substantial difference in degrees of luxury provided among the expensive, moderate, and inexpensive Canadian hotels. Although room costs in Canada cover a very broad spectrum, for purposes of making an estimate, expect to pay slightly less than you would pay in a major US city for equivalent accommodations. And figure on the high side if you're visiting tourism centers during high season. Slightly lower rates can be expected in an areas' off-season.

Generally, the member hotels of international chains in any given city are priced roughly equally. In the larger cities, such as Quebec and Toronto, this ranges from around $150 and up for a double, although similar hotels elsewhere range from about $80 to $120. There is a big step down from these international class hotels to those in the moderate category in the same cities, and accommodations generally will cost about $20 to as much as $50 less per night.

There is no sacred edict stating that travelers must stay at deluxe hotels, and, in fact, you might be missing a good deal of the Canadian experience by insisting on international standards and skipping over smaller establishments that often are older and full of charm. Other less expensive alternatives, which many will find perfectly adequate, include the hotels of less expensive chains. These do not offer the same extensive business services as deluxe hotels, but do provide clean and comfortable accommodations. Such less expensive yet acceptable hotels in major cities charge about $50 to $75 for a double room. In small towns and rural areas, these price ranges will be substantially lower. Also watch for budget motels designed to offer basic accommodations at especially economical prices, where a double room may cost as little as $20 to $25 (for a list of some nationwide chains see *On the Road,* in this section).

When inquiring about hotel rates, be certain to ask if they include local taxes and service charges. It also is wise to note that rates will likely be quoted in Canadian dollars, so it will be necessary to convert costs to US dollars to budget accurately. For specific information on accommodations throughout Canada, see *Best in Town,* THE CITIES, and *Best en Route,* DIRECTIONS.

In addition to standard hotel accommodations, there is a wide range of alternatives available throughout the country. Bed and breakfast accommodations are springing up all over, and although the night can be spent in surroundings that are steeped in history, homey, or spartan, these almost always are clean and adequate. Camping facilities are available in every corner of Canada (see *Camping and RVs, Hiking and Biking,* in this section). Country inns and package options, including resorts catering to a variety of special interests and vacations on farms and ranches, abound. (For information on these and other adventures across Canada, see DIVERSIONS.)

Should you require more advance information on accommodations options, contact the provincial tourist offices. Each provincial tourist office provides a comprehensive accommodations guide describing all licensed establishments in its territory. The most reliable restaurant listings (detailing costs, menus, and so on) usually are found in the weekly and monthly city magazines that are published in most major Canadian cities. Again, provincial tourist offices can be of some assistance. (For a list of provincial tourist offices, see *Tourist Information Offices,* in this section.)

■ **A note on our hotel/restaurant cost categories:** There are a great many moderate and inexpensive hotels and restaurants which we have not included in this book. Our *Best in Town* and *Best en Route* listings include only those places we think are best in their price range. We have rated our listings by general price categories: expensive, moderate, and inexpensive. The introductory paragraph of each listing explains just what those categories mean within the context of local prices.

Planning a Trip

123 Travelers fall into two categories: those who make lists and those who do not. Some people prefer to plot the course of their trip to the finest detail, with contingency plans and alternatives at the ready. For others, the joy of a voyage is its spontaneity; exhaustive planning only lessens the thrill of anticipation and the sense of freedom.

For most travelers, however, a week-plus trip to Canada can be too expensive for an "I'll take my chances" attitude. Even perennial gypsies and anarchistic wanderers have to take into account the time-consuming logistics of getting around, and even with minimal baggage, they need to think about packing. Hence, at least some planning is crucial. This is not to suggest that you work out every hour of your itinerary in minute detail before you go, but it's still wise to decide certain basics at the very start: where to go, what to do, and how much to spend. These decisions require a certain amount of consideration. So before rigorously planning specific details, you might want to establish your general travel objectives:

1. How much time do you have for the entire trip and how much of it are you willing to spend getting where you're going?

2. What interests and/or activities do you want to pursue on vacation? Do you want to visit one, a few, or many different places?
3. At what time of year do you want to go?
4. What kind of topography or climate do you prefer?
5. Do you want peace and privacy or lots of activity and company?
6. How much money can you afford to spend for the entire vacation?

Obviously, your answers will be determined by your personal tastes and lifestyle. These will dictate the degree of comfort you require; whether you select a tour or opt for total independence; and how much responsibility you want to take for your own arrangements (or whether you want everything arranged for you, with the kinds of services provided in a comprehensive package trip).

With firm answers to these major questions, start reviewing literature on the areas in which you're most interested. Good sources of information are airlines, hotel representatives, and travel agents. Also consult such other sources of general travel information as reliable, annually updated guidebooks and maps. Motor clubs (see *Traveling by Car,* in this section) often can be a good source for brochures and other information on Canada. There also are lots of useful little city guides available at newsstands and bookstores on the spot throughout Canada.

Government departments and affinity clubs focusing on individual outdoor activities — golf, fishing, hunting, boating, mountain-climbing, skiing, hiking, biking, nature study, and other such special interests — also may be able to provide information on these sports. For information on wilderness trips, hiking, and biking, see *Camping and RVs, Hiking and Biking,* in this section, and for information on these and other activities, see the various sections of DIVERSIONS, as well as the individual city reports in THE CITIES.

In addition, city and provincial tourist offices all are ready sources for brochures, maps, and other information on Canadian cities and the countryside, which are of inestimable value. For a complete list of provincial tourism offices see *Tourist Information Offices* in this section; city tourist offices are listed in the individual city reports of THE CITIES.

Up-to-date information on Canada is plentiful, and you should be able to accumulate everything you want to know, not only about the places you plan to visit, but also about the relevant tour and package options. And if you're visiting Canada for the first time, make a special effort to read about your destinations' food, history, and culture. A good place to start is the section in this guide called PERSPECTIVES, but if you're planning an extended stay in a particular city or region, you'll probably want to do even more extensive reading.

You now can make almost all of your own travel arrangements if you have the time to follow through with hotels, airlines, tour operators, and so on. But you'll probably save considerable time and energy if you have a travel agent make the reservations and arrangements for you. The agent also should be able to advise you of alternate arrangements of which you may not be aware. Only rarely will a travel agent's services cost you any money, and they may even save you some (see *How to Use a Travel Agent,* in this section). Well before departure (depending on how far in advance you make your reservations), the agent will deliver a packet that includes all your tickets and hotel confirmations and often a day-by-day outline of where you'll be when, along with a detailed list of all your flights.

If it applies to your schedule and destination, pay particular attention to the dates when off-season rates go into effect. In major tourism areas, accommodations costs may be lower during the off-season (and the weather often is perfectly acceptable at this time). Off-season rates frequently are lower for other facilities, too, although don't expect to save much on car rental costs during any season. In general, it is a good idea to beware of holiday weeks, as rates at hotels generally are higher during these periods and rooms are heavily booked. (In addition, service is apt to be under par unless more staff people are employed for the holidays, since the regular bellhops, maids, dining room personnel, and others will be trying to cope with a full house instead of being able to provide personal attention to individual guests.)

Make plans early. During the summer season and other American holiday periods, make hotel reservations at least a month in advance in all major cities. If you are flying at these times, and want to benefit from savings offered through discount fares or charter programs, purchase tickets as far ahead as possible. Ski season — from November to April — is another busy time, especially in the Canadian Rockies and in the mountains north and south of Montreal.The less flexible your schedule requirements, the earlier you should book. Many hotels require deposits before they will guarantee reservations, and this most often is the case during peak travel periods. (Be sure you have a receipt for any deposit, or better yet, charge the deposit to a credit card.)

While arranging a vacation is fun and exciting, don't forget to prepare for your absence from home. Before you leave, attend to these household matters:

1. Arrange for your mail to be forwarded, held by the post office, or picked up daily at your house. Someone should check your door occasionally to pick up any unexpected deliveries. Piles of mail or packages announce to thieves that no one is home.
2. Cancel all deliveries (newspapers, milk, and so on).
3. Arrange for the lawn to be mowed and plants to be watered at regular intervals.
4. Arrange for the care of pets.
5. Etch your social security number in a prominent place on all appliances (television sets, radios, cameras, kitchen appliances). This considerably reduces their appeal to thieves and facilitates identification.
6. Leave a house key, your itinerary, and your automobile license number (if you are driving your own car) with a relative or friend. Notify the police, the building manager, or a neighbor that you are leaving, and tell them who has the key and itinerary.
7. Empty the refrigerator and lower the thermostat.
8. If you use a computer with a hard disk, back up all your files onto diskettes and store them in a safe place away from the equipment.
9. Immediately before leaving, check that all doors, windows, and garage doors are securely locked.

To discourage thieves further, it is wise to set up several variable timers around the house so that lights and even the television set go on and off several times in different rooms each night.

Make a list of any valuable items you are carrying with you, including credit card numbers and the serial numbers of your traveler's checks. Put copies in your purse, or pocket, and leave copies at home. Put a label with your name and home address on the inside of your luggage to facilitate identification in case of loss. Put your name and business address — *never your home address* — on a label on the outside of your luggage.

Review your travel documents. If you are traveling by air, check to see that your ticket has been filled in correctly. The left side of the ticket should have a list of each stop you will make (even if you are only stopping to change planes), beginning with your departure point. Be sure that the list is correct, and count the number of carbons to see that you have one for each plane you will take. If you have confirmed reservations, be sure that the column marked "status" says "OK" beside each flight. Have in hand vouchers or proof of payment for any reservations for which you've paid in advance; this includes hotels, transfers to and from the airport, sightseeing tours, car rentals, and tickets to special events.

If you are traveling by plane, reconfirmation is strongly recommended for all international flights. Although policies vary from carrier to carrier, it's still smart to reconfirm your flight 48 to 72 hours before departure, both going and returning. This will not, however, prevent you from getting bumped in case the flight is overbooked. Reconfirmation is particularly recommended for point-to-point flights within Canada.

If you are traveling by car, bring your driver's license, automobile registration, proof of insurance, gasoline credit cards and auto service card (if you have them), extra car keys, sunglasses, maps, guidebooks, a flashlight with an extra set of batteries, emergency flasher, jack and spare tire, a container of water or coolant for the radiator, and a steel container for extra gas. A small first-aid kit also is a good idea.

Finally, you always should bear in mind that despite the most careful plans, things do not always occur on schedule. If you maintain a flexible attitude at all times, shrug as cheerfully as possible in the face of postponements and cancellations, you will enjoy yourself a lot more.

How to Use a Travel Agent

 A reliable travel agent remains your best source of service and information for planning a trip, whether you have a specific itinerary and require an agent only to make reservations, or need extensive help in sorting through the maze of airfares, tour offerings, hotel packages, and the score of other elements that may be involved in a trip to Canada.

You should know what you want from a travel agent so that you can evaluate what you are getting. It is perfectly reasonable to expect your travel agent to be a thoroughly knowledgeable travel specialist, with information about your destination and, even more crucial, a command of current airfares, ground arrangements, and other wrinkles in the travel scene. Most travel agents work through computer reservations systems (CRS) to assess the availability and rates of flights, hotels, and car rentals, and they can book reservations through the CRS. Despite reports of "computer bias," in which a computer may favor one airline over another, the CRS should provide agents with the entire spectrum of flights available to a given destination and the complete range of fares in considerably less time than it takes to telephone the airlines individually — and at no extra charge to the client.

To make the most intelligent use of a travel agent's time and expertise, you should know something of the economics of the industry. As a client, traditionally you pay nothing for the agent's services; with few exceptions, it's all free, from hotel bookings to advice on package tours and the best hunting lodges. Any money the travel agent makes on the time spent arranging your itinerary — booking hotels or flights, or suggesting activities — comes from commissions paid by the suppliers of these services — the airlines, hotels, and so on. These commissions generally run from about 8% to 20% of the total cost of the service, although suppliers often reward agencies that sell their services in volume with an increased commission called an override.

Among the few exceptions to the general rule of free service by a travel agent are the agencies beginning to practice *net pricing*. In essence, such agencies return all of their commissions and overrides to their customers and make their income by charging a flat fee per transaction instead (thus adding a charge after a reduction for the commissions has been made). Sometimes the rebate from the agent arrives later, in the form of a check. For further information, see "Net Fare Sources" in *Traveling by Plane*, in this section.

Net fares and fees are a very recent and not very widespread practice, but even a conventional travel agent sometimes may charge a fee for such special services as long-distance telephone or cable costs incurred in making a booking, for reserving a room in a place that does not pay a commission (such as a small, out-of-the-way hotel), or for special attention such as planning a highly personalized itinerary. A fee also may be assessed in instances of deeply discounted airfares. In most instances, however, you'll find that travel agents make their time and experience available to you at no charge, and you do not pay more for an airline ticket, package tour, or other product bought from a travel agent than you would for the same product bought directly from the supplier.

This system implies two things about your relationship with an agent:

1. You will get better service if you arrive at the agent's desk with your basic itinerary already planned. Know roughly where you want to go, what you want to do, and how much you want to spend. Use the agent to make bookings (which pay commissions) and to advise you on facilities, activities, and alternatives within the limits of your itinerary. You get the best service when you are requesting commissionable items. Since there are few commissions on camping or driving/camping tours, an agent is unlikely to be very enthusiastic about helping to plan one. (If you have this type of trip in mind, see *Camping and RVs, Hiking and Biking,* in this section, for other sources of information on camping throughout Canada.) The more vague your plans, the less direction you can expect from most agents. If you walk into an agency and say, "I have 2 weeks in June; what shall I do?" you most likely will walk out with nothing more than a handful of brochures. So do a little preliminary homework.

2. Be wary. There always is the danger that an incompetent or unethical agent will send you to places offering the best commissions rather than the best facilities for your enjoyment. The only way to be sure you are getting the best service is to pick a good, reliable travel agent, one who knows where to go for information if he or she is unfamiliar with an area — although most agents are familiar with major destinations throughout Canada.

You should choose a travel agent with the same care with which you would choose a doctor or lawyer. You will be spending a good deal of money on the basis of the agent's judgment, so you have a right to expect that judgment to be mature, informed, and interested. At the moment, unfortunately, there aren't many standards within the travel agent industry to help you gauge competence, and the quality of individual agents varies enormously.

At present, only nine states have registration, licensing, or other form of travel agent-related legislation on their books. Rhode Island licenses travel agents; Florida, Hawaii, Iowa, and Ohio register them; and California, Illinois, Oregon, and Washington have laws governing the sale of transportation or related services. While state licensing of agents cannot absolutely guarantee competence, it at least can ensure that an agent has met some minimum requirements.

Perhaps the best-prepared agents are those who have completed the CTC Travel Management program offered by the *Institute of Certified Travel Agents* and carry the initials CTC (Certified Travel Counselor) after their names. This indicates a relatively high level of expertise. For a free list of CTCs in your area, send a self-addressed, stamped, #10 envelope to *ICTA,* 148 Linden St., Box 82-56, Wellesley, MA 02181 (phone: 617-237-0280 in Massachusetts; 800-542-4282 elsewhere in the US).

An agent's membership in the *American Society of Travel Agents (ASTA)* can be a useful guideline in making a selection. But keep in mind that *ASTA* is an industry organization, requiring only that its members be licensed in those states where required; be accredited to represent the suppliers whose products they sell, including airline and cruise tickets; and adhere to its Principles of Professional Conduct and Ethics code.

ASTA does not guarantee the competence, ethics, or financial soundness of its members, but it does offer some recourse if you feel you have been dealt with unfairly. Complaints may be registered with *ASTA* (Consumer Affairs Department, PO Box 23992, Washington, DC 20026-3992; phone: 703-739-2782). First try to resolve the complaint directly with the supplier. For a list of *ASTA* members in your area, send a self-addressed, stamped, #10 envelope to *ASTA,* Public Relations Dept., at the address above.

There also is the *Association of Retail Travel Agents (ARTA),* a smaller but highly respected trade organization similar to *ASTA.* Its member agencies and agents similarly agree to abide by a code of ethics, and complaints about a member can be made to *ARTA*'s Grievance Committee, 1745 Jeff Davis Hwy., Arlington, VA 22202-3402 (phone: 800-969-6069 or 703-553-7777).

Agencies that are members of the *National Association of Cruise Only Agencies (NACOA)* have demonstrated special knowledge in the selling of cruises. For a list of cruise-only agencies in your area (requests are limited to three states), send a self-addressed, stamped envelope to *NACOA* (PO Box 7209, Freeport, NY 11520) or call 516-378-8006. Agencies that belong to a travel consortium, such as *Travel Trust International* (phone: 800-522-2700 in New York; 800-223-8953 elsewhere in the US), have access to preferred rates, as do the huge networks of *American Express* (phone: 800-YES-AMEX) and *Carlson Travel Network* (formerly *Ask Mr. Foster;* phone: 818-788-4118) travel agencies.

A number of banks own travel agencies, too. These provide the same services as other accredited commercial travel bureaus. Anyone can become a client, not only the bank's customers. You can find out more about these agencies, which belong to the *Association of Bank Travel Bureaus,* by inquiring at your bank or looking in the yellow pages.

Perhaps the best way to find a travel agent is by word of mouth. If the agent (or agency) has done a good job for your friends over a period of time, it probably indicates a certain level of commitment and competence. Always ask not only for the name of the company, but for the name of the specific agent with whom your friends dealt, for it is that individual who will serve you, and quality can vary widely within a single agency. There are some superb travel agents in the business, and they can facilitate vacation or business arrangements.

Once you've made an initial selection, be entirely frank and candid with the agent. Budget considerations rank at the top of the candor list, and there's no sense in wasting the agent's (or your) time poring over itineraries that you know you can't afford. Similarly, if you like a fair degree of comfort, that fact should not be kept secret from your travel agent, who may assume that you wish to travel on a tight budget even when that's not the case.

Border Crossings

 ENTRY REQUIREMENTS: The only requirement for citizens and legal residents of the US crossing the US-Canada border in either direction is that they present two forms of identification. For native US citizens, these include a current passport, and a driver's license, original or certified birth certificate, baptismal certificate, voter's certificate, or other identification that officially verifies their US citizenship. In some instances, however, a passport may not be required. Proof of current residency also may be required. Naturalized US citizens should carry their naturalization certificate or some other evidence of citizenship. Permanent residents of the US who are not American citizens should have Alien Registration Receipt cards (US Form I-151 or Form I-551). Visitors under 18 years of age not accompanied by an adult should carry a letter from a parent or guardian giving them permission to travel to Canada.

Any visitor to Canada who is not a US citizen or a permanent resident of the US must have a valid passport from some other nation. In addition, a visa may be required of visitors other than British citizens. Generally speaking, the Canadian government doesn't require visas of citizens of most Commonwealth countries or Common Market members. But the situation changes frequently, and citizens of countries other than the US and Great Britain would do well to contact the nearest Canadian consulate to find out whether or not a visa is required. These travelers also should be aware that visas are issued in the *home* country of the applicant. Thus, someone planning to travel to both the US and Canada shouldn't wait until arriving in the US to apply for a visa. Citizens of countries with no official Canadian representative in residence should contact the Canadian consulate in a neighboring country. Questions about entering Canada should be addressed to the Employment and Immigration Commission, Phase IV, Place du Portage, Ottawa-Hull, Ontario K1A 0J9, Canada (phone: 613-994-7141).

Visitors to the US who cross into Canada and then return to the US should check with the US Immigration and Naturalization Service to make sure that they have all the papers they need for reentry into the US.

PASSPORTS: If you lose your passport while abroad, report the loss to the nearest US consulate or embassy immediately. You can get a 3-month temporary passport directly from the consulate, but you must fill out a "loss of passport" form and follow the same application procedure — and pay the same fees — as you did for the original (see below). It's likely to speed things up if you have a record of your passport number and the place and date of its issue (a photocopy of the first page of your passport is perfect); keep this information separate from your passport — you might want to give it to a traveling companion to hold or put it in the bottom of your suitcase. (For a complete list of US consulates and embassies in Canada, see *Medical and Legal Aid and Consular Services,* in this section.)

US passports now are valid for 10 years from the date of issue (5 years for those under age 16). The expired passport itself is not renewable, but must be turned in along with your application for a new and valid one (you will get it back, voided, when you receive the new one). Delivery can take as little as 2 weeks or as long as a month, and anyone applying for a passport for the first time should allow at least 4 weeks for delivery — even 6 weeks during the busiest season — from approximately mid-March to mid-September.

Normal passports contain 24 pages, but frequent travelers can request a 48-page passport at no extra cost. Every individual, regardless of age, must have his or her own passport. Family passports no longer are issued.

Passport renewal can be done by mail, but anyone applying for the first time or anyone under 16 renewing a passport must do so in person at one of the following places:

1. The State Department passport agencies in Boston, Chicago, Honolulu, Houston, Los Angeles, Miami, New Orleans, New York City, Philadelphia, San Francisco, Seattle, Stamford, CT, and Washington, DC.
2. A federal or state courthouse.
3. Any of the 1,000 post offices across the country with designated acceptance facilities.

Application blanks are available at all these offices and must be presented with the following:

1. Proof of US citizenship. This can be a previous passport or one in which you were included. If you are applying for your first passport and you were born in the United States, an original or certified birth certificate is the required proof. If you were born abroad, a Certificate of Naturalization, a Certificate of Citizenship, a Report of Birth Abroad of a Citizen of the United States, or a Certification of Birth is necessary.
2. Two 2-by-2-inch, front-view photographs in color or black and white, with a light, plain background, taken within the previous 6 months. These must be taken by a photographer rather than by a machine.
3. A $42 passport fee ($27 for travelers under 16), which includes a $7 execution fee. *Note:* Your best bet is to bring the exact amount in cash (no change is given), or a separate check or money order for each passport.
4. Proof of identity. Again, this can be a previous passport, a Certificate of Naturalization or of Citizenship, a driver's license, or a government ID card with a physical description or a photograph. Failing any of these, you should be accompanied by a blood relative or a friend of at least 2 years' standing who will testify to your identity. Credit cards or social security cards do not suffice as proof of identity — but note that since 1988, US citizens *must* supply their social security numbers.

Passports can be renewed by mail with forms obtained at designated locations only if the expired passport was issued no more than 8 years before the date of application for renewal and if it was not issued before the applicant's 16th birthday. Send the completed form with the expired passport, two photos, and $35 (no execution fee required) to the nearest passport agency office.

As getting a passport — or international visa — through the mail can mean waiting as much as 6 weeks or more, a new mini-industry has cropped up in those cities where there is a US passport office. The yellow pages currently list quite a few organizations willing to wait on line to expedite obtaining a visa or passport renewal; there's even one alternative for those who live nowhere near the cities mentioned above. In the nation's capital there's an organization called the *Washington Passport and Visa Service.* It may be the answer for folks in need of special rapid action, since this organization can get a passport application or renewal turned around in a single day. What's more, their proximity to an embassy or consulate of every foreign country represented in the US helps to speed the processing of visa applications as well. *Washington Passport and Visa*'s fee for a 3- to 5-day turnaround is $25; for next-day service the charge is $50; for same-day service they charge $75. For information, application forms, and other prices, call 800-272-7776.

If you need an emergency passport, it also is possible to be issued a passport in a matter of hours by going directly to your nearest passport office (there is no way, however, to avoid waiting in line). Explain the nature of the emergency, usually as serious as a death in the family; a ticket in hand for a flight the following day also will suffice. Should the emergency occur outside of business hours, all is not lost. There's a 24-hour telephone number in Washington, DC (phone: 202-634-3600), that can put you in touch with a State Department duty officer who may be able to expedite your application.

DUTY AND CUSTOMS: Vehicles and trailers can be taken into Canada for tours of up to 12 months without duty; permits, when necessary, are issued at the point of entry. Rental vehicles or trailers of the *U-Haul* variety are also admissible with authorization from the rental company for use in Canada. All driver's licenses, including international licenses, are valid in Canada.

Sporting equipment, including fishing tackle, boats, outboard motors, motorized toboggans, snowmobiles, skis, and camping equipment, can be brought into Canada duty-free. Occasionally a deposit is requested to ensure that items are being brought into the country for pleasure, not to be sold. Hunting rifles and shotguns can be brought into Canada duty-free, and no permits are required to enter, although a hunting license authorizing use of these firearms is required. Handguns *cannot* be brought into the country, nor can automatic weapons, which are illegal. No permit is required to bring tackle for sport fishing into Canada.

Every visitor is allowed to bring, duty-free, a reasonable amount of food for the length of the stay; otherwise, all food is subject to duty of 17.5%. Up to 22 pounds (10 kilograms) of meat per person can be imported without duty.

Each visitor is allowed to bring into Canada up to 50 cigars, 200 cigarettes, and 2 pounds (0.9 kilograms) of manufactured tobacco. Each visitor over legal drinking age (which varies from province to province and territory to territory; see *Drinking and Drugs,* in this section) may import 40 ounces (1.1 liters) of liquor or wine, or 24 12-ounce cans or bottles of beer or ale into Canada duty-free as personal baggage.

All plants and plant material must be declared at the border. House plants from the continental US generally are permitted entry, but bonsai and all outdoor plants, including bulbs, require permits. Plants from other countries are only permitted under the authority of the Plant Quarantine Act. Visitors planning to bring plants should write in advance for specific regulations to Plant Protection Division, Food Production and Inspection Branch, Agriculture Canada, Ottawa, Ontario K1A 0L5, Canada.

Direct any further inquiries concerning Canadian customs regulations to Revenue Canada, Customs and Excise, Public Relations Branch, Ottawa, Ontario K1A OL5, Canada (phone: 613-993-0534).

If you are bringing along a computer, camera, or other electronic equipment for your own use, which you will be taking back to the US, you should register the item with the US Customs Service in order to avoid being asked to pay duty both entering and returning from Canada. For information on this procedure, as well as for a variety of pamphlets on US customs regulations, contact the local office of the US Customs Service or the central office, PO Box 7407, Washington, DC 20044 (phone: 202-566-8195).

REENTERING THE US: US residents who have spent 48 hours or less in Canada can bring into the US duty-free merchandise worth a total of $25, including any of the following: 10 cigars (not Cuban), 50 cigarettes, 4 ounces (150 milliliters) of alcoholic beverages, or perfume.

American residents who have spent more than 48 hours in Canada may return with up to $400 worth of merchandise for personal or household use once every 30 days without paying any duty. Up to 1 liter of an alcoholic beverage (depending on the laws of the state to which you return), 100 cigars, and 200 cigarettes may be imported into the US for personal use. Members of the same family traveling together may combine their duty-free exemptions. Gifts valued at $50 or less may be sent to people in the US duty- and tax-free. The package should be clearly marked "Unsolicited Gift."

US residents are prohibited from bringing certain goods into the US from Canada, including items made from whalebone and sealskin, any Cuban-made goods, items from North Korea, Vietnam, or Cambodia. Tourists who want to bring Canadian plants into the US must have a plant certificate from an office of the Canadian Plant Health Division. (For more information, contact the Permit Officer, Food Production and Inspection Branch, Agriculture Canada, Ottawa, Ontario K1A 0L5, Canada.) To check on the regulations governing the importation of a wildlife product (for example, furs and leathers), contact the US Fish and Wildlife Service, Department of the Interior, Washington, DC 20240 (phone: 202-343-9242).

■**One rule to follow:** When passing through customs, it is illegal not to declare dutiable items; penalties range from stiff fines and seizure of the goods to prison terms. So don't try to sneak anything through — it just isn't worth it.

Insurance

 It is unfortunate that most decisions to buy travel insurance are impulsive and usually are made without any real consideration of the traveler's existing policies. Too often the result is the purchase of needlessly expensive, short-term policies that duplicate existing coverage and reinforce the tendency to buy coverage on a trip-by-trip basis rather than to work out a total and continuing travel insurance package that might well be more effective and economical.

Therefore, the first person with whom you should discuss travel insurance is your own insurance broker, not a travel agent or the clerk behind the airport insurance counter. You may discover that the insurance you already carry — homeowner's policies and/or accident, health, and life insurance — protects you adequately while you travel and that your real needs are in the more mundane areas of excess value insurance for baggage or trip cancellation insurance.

TYPES OF INSURANCE: To make insurance decisions intelligently, however, you first should understand the basic categories of travel insurance and what they cover. Then you can decide what you should have in the broader context of your personal insurance needs, and you can choose the most economical way of getting the desired protection: through riders on existing policies; with one-time short-term policies; through a special program put together for the frequent traveler; through coverage that's part of a travel club's benefits; or with a combination policy sold by insurance companies through brokers, automobile clubs, tour operators, and travel agents.

There are seven basic categories of travel insurance:

1. Baggage and personal effects insurance
2. Personal accident and sickness insurance
3. Trip cancellation and interruption insurance
4. Default and/or bankruptcy insurance
5. Flight insurance (to cover injury or death)
6. Automobile insurance (for driving your own or a rented car)
7. Combination policies

Baggage and Personal Effects Insurance – Ask your agent if baggage and personal effects are included in your current homeowner's policy, or if you will need a special floater to cover you for the duration of a trip. The object is to protect your bags and their contents in case of damage or theft any time during your travels, not just while you're in flight and covered by the airline's policy. Furthermore, only limited protection is provided by the airline. Baggage liability varies from carrier to carrier, but generally speaking, for domestic flights, luggage usually is insured to $1,250 — that's per passenger, not per bag. For most international flights, including domestic portions of international flights, the airline's liability limit is approximately $9.07 per pound or $20 per kilo (which comes to about $360 per 40-pound suitcase) for checked baggage and up to $400 per passenger for unchecked baggage. Canadian airlines insure baggage for up to a maximum of CN$750 on domestic flights and CN$640 on flights originating in the US that cross the Canadian border only. These limits should be specified on your airline ticket, but to be awarded the specified amount, you'll have to provide an itemized list of lost property, and if you're including new and/or expensive items, be prepared for a request that you back up your claim with sales receipts or other proofs of purchase.

If you are driving your own car or a rental, check the protection necessary from damage or theft with your insurance agent. If traveling by bus or train, you may need more protection than automatically is included in the ticket as *VIA Rail* and Canadian bus companies provide only limited protection. *VIA Rail* takes responsibility for a maximum of CN$100 per passenger, as do some bus companies — check the fine print on every ticket.

If you are carrying goods worth more than the maximum protection offered by the airline, bus, or train company, you should consider excess value insurance. Additional coverage is available from the airlines at an average, currently, of $1 per $100 worth of coverage, up to a maximum value of $5,000. This insurance can be purchased at the airline counter when you check in, though you should arrive early enough to fill out the necessary forms and avoid holding up other passengers. You also can buy excess value insurance from *VIA Rail* and some bus lines. But either the cost may be too high — as with *VIA Rail,* which bases cost on the value of the bags and their contents, as well as the number of days traveling in Canada — or the maximum protection too low, as with *Greyhound Lines of Canada,* which will accept only liability for up to CN$50. So, you would be wise to buy coverage elsewhere. Excess value insurance also is included in some of the combination travel insurance policies discussed below.

■ **A note of warning:** Be sure to read the fine print of any excess value insurance policy; there often are specific exclusions, such as cash, tickets, furs, gold and silver objects, art, and antiques. And remember that insurance companies ordinarily will pay only the depreciated value of the goods rather than their replacement value. The best way to protect the items you're carrying in your luggage is to take photos of your valuables, and keep a record of the serial numbers of such items as cameras, typewriters, radios, and so on. This will establish that you do, indeed, own the objects. If your luggage disappears or is damage en route, deal with the situation immediately. If an airline loses your luggage, you will be asked to fill out a Property Irregularity Report before you leave the airport. If your property disappears at other transportation centers, tell the local company, but also report it to the police (since the insurance company will check with the police when processing the claim). When traveling by train, if you are sending excess luggage as registered baggage, remember that some trains may not have provisions for extra cargo; if your baggage does not arrive when you do, it may not be lost, just on the next train!

Personal Accident and Sickness Insurance – This covers you in case of illness during your trip or death in an accident. Most policies insure you for hospital and doctors' expenses, lost income, and so on. In most cases, it is a standard part of existing health insurance policies, though you should check with your broker to be sure that your policy will pay for any medical expenses incurred abroad. If not, take out a separate vacation accident policy or an entire vacation insurance policy that includes health and life coverage.

Trip Cancellation and Interruption Insurance – Although modern public charters have eliminated many of the old advance booking requirements, most charter and package tour passengers still pay for their travel well before departure. The disappointment of having to miss a vacation because of illness or any other reason pales before the awful prospect that not all (and sometimes none) of the money paid in advance might be returned. So cancellation insurance for any package tour is a must. Although cancellation penalties vary (they are listed in the fine print in every tour brochure, and before you purchase a package tour you should know exactly what they are), rarely will a passenger get more than 50% of this money back if forced to cancel within a few weeks of leaving. Therefore, if you book a package tour or charter flight, you should have trip cancellation insurance to guarantee full reimbursement or refund should you, a traveling companion, or a member of your immediate family get sick, forcing you to cancel your trip or *return home early.* The key here is *not* to buy just enough insurance to guarantee full reimbursement for the cost of the package or charter in case of cancellation. The proper amount of coverage should be sufficient to reimburse you for the cost of having to catch up with a tour after its departure or having to travel home at the full economy airfare if you have to forgo the return flight of your charter. There usually is quite a discrepancy between the charter fare and the amount charged to travel the same distance on a regularly scheduled flight at full economy fare.

Trip cancellation insurance is available from travel agents and tour operators in two forms: as part of a short-term, all-purpose travel insurance package (sold by the travel agent); or as specific cancellation insurance designed by the tour operator for a specific charter tour. Generally, tour operators' policies are less expensive, but also less inclusive. Cancellation insurance also is available directly from insurance companies or their agents as part of a short-term, all-inclusive travel insurance policy.

Before you decide on a policy, read each one carefully. (Either type can be purchased from a travel agent when you book the charter or package tour.) Be certain that your policy includes coverage to pay your fare from the farthest destination on your itinerary should you have to miss the charter flight. Also, be sure to check the fine print for stipulations concerning "family members" and "pre-existing medical conditions," as well as allowance for living expenses if you must delay your return due to bodily injury or illness.

Default and/or Bankruptcy Insurance – Although trip cancellation insurance usually protects you if *you* are unable to complete — or begin — your trip, a fairly recent innovation is coverage in the event of default and/or bankruptcy on the part of the tour operator, airline, or other travel supplier. In some travel insurance packages, this contingency is included in the trip cancellation portion of the coverage; in others, it is a separate feature. Either way, it is becoming increasingly important. Whereas sophisticated travelers have long known to beware of the possibility of default or bankruptcy when buying a charter flight or tour package, in recent years more than a few respected airlines unexpectedly have revealed their shaky financial condition, sometimes leaving hordes of stranded ticketholders in their wake. Moreover, the value of escrow protection of a charter passenger's funds lately has been unreliable. While default/bankruptcy insurance will not ordinarily result in reimbursement in time to pay for new arrangements, it can ensure that eventually you will get your money back, and even independent travelers buying no more than an airplane ticket may want to consider it.

Should this type of coverage be unavailable to you (state insurance regulations vary, there is a wide variation in price, and so on), the best bet is to pay for airline tickets and tour packages with a credit card. The federal Fair Credit Billing Act permits purchasers to refuse payment for credit card charges where services have not been delivered, so the potential onus of dealing with a receiver for a bankrupt airline falls on the credit card company. You must, however, make your claim within 60 days of receiving your bill from the credit card company. What's more, do not assume that another airline automatically will honor the ticket you're holding if it was written by a bankrupt airline, since the days when virtually all major carriers subscribed to a default protection program are long gone. Some airlines may voluntarily step forward to accommodate stranded passengers, but this is now an entirely altruistic act.

Flight Insurance – US airlines have carefully established limits of liability for the death or injury of passengers. For international flights, they are printed right on the ticket: a maximum of $75,000 in case of death or injury. Although these limitations once were established by state law for domestic flights, each case currently is decided in court on its own merits — this means potentially unlimited liability. But remember, these limits of liability are not the same thing as insurance policies; every penny that an airline must pay in the case of injury or death may be subject to a legal battle.

This may make you feel that you are not adequately protected, but before you buy last-minute flight insurance from an airport vending machine, consider the purchase in light of your total existing insurance coverage. A careful review of your current policies may reveal that you already are amply covered for accidental death, sometimes up to three times the amount provided for by the flight insurance you're buying in the airport.

Be aware that airport insurance, the kind typically bought at a counter or from a vending machine, is among the most expensive forms of life insurance coverage, and that even within a single airport, rates for approximately the same coverage vary widely. Often policies sold in vending machines are more expensive than those sold over the counter, even when they are with the same national company.

If you buy your plane ticket with an American Express, Carte Blanche, or Diners Club credit card, you automatically are issued life and accident insurance at no extra cost. American Express automatically provides $100,000 in insurance to its Green and Gold cardholders, and $500,000 to Platinum cardholders; Carte Blanche provides $150,000, and Diners Club provides $350,000. Additional coverage can be obtained at extremely reasonable prices, but a cardholder must sign up for it in advance. With American Express, $4 per ticket buys an additional $250,000 worth of flight insurance; $7.50 buys $500,000 worth; and $14 provides an added $1 million worth of coverage. (Rates vary slightly for New York residents.) Both Carte Blanche and Diners Club also offer an additional $250,000 worth of insurance for $4; $500,000 for $6.50. Both also provide $1,250 free insurance — over and above what the airline will pay — for checked baggage that's lost or damaged. American Express provides $500 coverage for checked baggage; $500 for carry-on baggage; and $250 for valuables, such as cameras and jewelry.

Automobile Insurance – All drivers in Canada are required by law to have automobile insurance for their car. The minimum coverage is determined by provincial law, but this minimum usually is too low for adequate protection. Your insurance agents can advise you on the proper amount of insurance necessary. There are several kinds of coverage you should have in Canada:

1. *Liability Insurance:* This provides protection if you are sued for injuring someone or his or her property. US motorists driving in Canada should carry a Canadian Non-Resident Inter-Province Motor Vehicle Liability Insurance Card, which provides evidence of financial responsibility by a valid automobile liability insurance policy. This card only is available through insurance agents in the US. (There should be no charge for this card.) All provinces in Canada require visiting motorists to produce evidence of financial responsibility should they be involved in an accident. Minimum liability requirements vary from CN$50,000 to CN$200,000 depending upon the province or territory. Information and advice regarding auto insurance may be obtained from the *Insurance Bureau of Canada,* 181 University Avenue, Toronto, Ontario M5H 3M7, Canada (phone: 416-362-2031).

2. *Accident Insurance:* This protects against payments for death or bodily injury and includes loss of pay, medical expenses, and so on. These policies also include coverage against uninsured motorists. Note that Ontario and Quebec have no-fault insurance laws.

3. *Comprehensive and Collision Insurance:* This protects against loss of or damage to your car. There usually is a deductible amount indicated for this coverage; it either is paid by the policyholder toward the cost of repairs or deducted from the loss settlement.

When you rent a car, the rental company is required to provide collision protection. In your car rental contract, you'll see that for about $13 a day, you may buy optional collision damage waiver (CDW) protection. (If partial coverage with a deductible is included in the rental contract, the CDW will cover the deductible in the event of an accident, and will cost from $10 to $20 per day.) If the contract does not include collision damage coverage, you may be liable for as much as the full retail value of the car, and by paying for the CDW you are relieved of all responsibility for any damage to the rental car. Before agreeing to this coverage, however, check your own auto insurance policy with your own broker. It very well may cover your entire liability exposure without any additional cost, or you automatically may be covered by the credit card company to which you are charging the cost of your rental.

You also should know that an increasing number of the major international car rental companies are automatically including the cost of the CDW in their basic rates. Car rental prices have increased to include this coverage, although rental company ad campaigns may promote this as a new, improved rental package "benefit." The disadvantage of this inclusion is that you may not have the option to turn down the CDW — even if you already are adequately covered by your own insurance policy or through a credit card company. For more information on this confusing issue, see *Traveling by Car,* in this section.

Combination Packages – Short-term insurance policies, which may include a combination of any or all of the types of insurance discussed above, are available through retail insurance agencies, automobile clubs, and many travel agents. These combination policies are designed to cover you for the duration of a single trip.

Two examples of standard combination policies, providing comprehensive coverage for travelers, are offered by *Wallach & Co.* The first, *HealthCare Global,* is available to men and women up to age 84. The medical insurance, which may be purchased for periods of 10 to 180 days, provides $25,000 medical insurance and $50,000 accidental death benefit. The cost for 10 days is $25; for 76 days and over, it is $1.50 a day. Combination policies may include additional accidental death coverage and baggage and trip cancellation insurance options. For $3 per day (minimum 10 days, maximum 90 days), another program, *HealthCare Abroad,* offers significantly better coverage in terms of dollar limits, although the age limit is 75. Its basic policy includes $100,000 medical insurance and $25,000 accidental death benefit. As in the first policy, trip cancellation and baggage insurance also are available. For further information, write to *Wallach & Co.,* 243 Church St. NW, Suite 100D, Vienna, VA 22180 (phone: 703-281-9500 in Virginia, 800-237-6615 elsewhere in the US).

Other policies of this type include the following:

Access America International: A subsidiary of the Blue Cross/Blue Shield plans of New York and Washington, DC, now available nationwide. Contact *Access America,* 600 Third Ave., PO Box 807, New York, NY 10163 (phone: 800-284-8300 or 212-490-5345).

Carefree: Underwritten by The Hartford. Contact *Carefree Travel Insurance,* Arm Coverage, PO Box 310, Mineola, NY 11501 (phone: 800-645-2424 or 516-294-0220).

NEAR Services: Part of a benefits package offered by a travel service organization. An added feature is coverage for lost or stolen airline tickets. Contact *NEAR Services,* 450 Prairie Ave., Calumet City, IL 60409 (phone: 800-654-6700 or 708-868-6700).

Tele-Trip: Underwritten by the Mutual of Omaha Companies. Contact *Tele-Trip Co.,* PO Box 31685, 3201 Farnam St., Omaha, NE 68131 (phone: 402-345-2400 in Nebraska; 800-228-9792 elsewhere in the US).

Travel Assistance International: Provided by Europ Assistance Worldwide Services, and underwritten by Transamerica Occidental Life Insurance. Contact *Travel Assistance International,* 1333 15th St. NW, Suite 400, Washington, DC 20005 (phone: 202-347-2025 in Washington, DC; 800-821-1828 elsewhere in the US).

Travel Guard International: Underwritten by the Insurance Company of North America, it is available through authorized travel agents, or contact *Travel*

Guard International, 1145 Clark St., Stevens Point, WI 54481 (phone: 715-345-0505 in Wisconsin; 800-826-1300 elsewhere in the US).

Travel Insurance PAK: Underwritten by The Travelers. Contact *The Travelers Companies,* Ticket and Travel Plans, One Tower Sq., Hartford, CT 06183-5040 (phone: 203-277-2319 in Connecticut; 800-243-3174 elsewhere in the US).

WorldCare Travel Assistance Association: This organization offers insurance packages underwritten by Transamerica Premier Insurance Company and Transamerica Occidental Life Insurance. Contact *WorldCare Travel Assistance Association,* 605 Market St., Suite 1300, San Francisco, CA 94105 (phone: 800-666-4993 or 415-541-4991).

How to Pack

No one can provide a completely foolproof list of precisely what to pack, so it's best to let common sense, space, and comfort guide you. Keep one maxim in mind: Less is more. You simply won't need as much clothing as you think, and al though there is nothing more frustrating than arriving at your destination without the very item that in its absence becomes crucial, you are far more likely to need a forgotten accessory — or a needle and thread or scissors — than a particular piece of clothing.

As with almost anything relating to travel, a little advance planning can go a long way. There are specific things to consider before you open the first drawer or fold the first pair of underwear:

1. Where are you going — city, country, or both?
2. How many total days will you be gone?
3. What's the average temperature likely to be during your stay?

The goal is to remain perfectly comfortable, neat, clean, and adequately fashionable wherever you go, but actually to pack as little as possible. The main obstacle to achieving this end is habit: Most of us wake up each morning with an entire wardrobe in our closets, and we assume that our suitcase should offer the same variety and selection. Not so — only our anxiety about being caught short makes us treat a suitcase like a mobile closet. This worry can be eliminated by learning to travel light and by following two firm packing principles:

1. Organize your travel wardrobe around a single color — blue or brown, for example — that allows you to mix, match, and layer clothes. Holding firm to one color scheme will make it easy to eliminate items of clothing that don't harmonize; and by picking clothes for their adaptability and compatibility with your basic color, you will put together the widest selection with the fewest pieces of clothing.
2. Use laundries to replenish your wardrobe. Never overpack to ensure a supply of fresh clothing — shirts, blouses, underwear — for each day of a long trip. Businesspeople routinely use hotel laundries or dry-cleaning services to wash and clean clothes. If these are too expensive, there are self-service laundries in most towns of any size.

CLIMATE AND CLOTHES: Exactly what you pack for your trip will be a function of where you are going and when, and the kinds of things you intend to do. A few degrees can make all the difference between being comfortably attired and very real suffering, so your initial step should be to find out what the general weather conditions — temperature, rainfall, seasonal variations — are likely to be in the areas you will visit.

Information about the climate in Canada, is given in *When to Go,* in this section; as well as in the individual city reports of THE CITIES. Other sources of information are airlines and travel agents. The Canadian Government Office of Tourism publishes *Canada Travel Information,* a brochure with a chart of general weather information and suggested clothing (available from the Canadian tourist offices listed under *Tourist Information Offices,* in this section).

Keeping temperature and climate in mind, consider the problem of luggage. Plan on one suitcase per person (and in a pinch, remember that it's always easier to carry two small suitcases than to schlepp one that's roughly the size of the *QE2*). Standard 26- to 28-inch suitcases can be made to work for 1 week or 1 month, and unless you are going for no more than a weekend, never cram wardrobes for two people into one suitcase.

Attire is quite casual throughout Canada; only at the most elegant hotels and restaurants are dressy clothes required. A blazer or sport jacket, trousers, and tie will get a man into the finest restaurant anywhere, and sometimes even the tie is not *de rigueur.* For women, a dress or a suit will do in the same situations. Other diners may be more formally dressed, but you won't be turned away or made to feel self-conscious if you do not mirror them. By the same token, you won't feel you've overdone it if you choose to turn an evening at an elegant restaurant into something special and dress accordingly. If you're planning a number of more formal evenings during your trip, bring two or three changes of clothes. Bear in mind that coordinates also are a good way of providing a number of dressier options without adding to your luggage content.

Women should figure on a maximum of five daytime and three late afternoon–evening changes. Whether you are going to be gone for a week or a month, this number should be enough. For daytime activities, women might pack jeans or light slacks, blouses, one or two swimsuits (depending on where you're going), and a pair of comfortable shoes or sneakers. In warmer weather, include T-shirts and a pair of shorts; skirts and summer dresses are a cool choice for touring. Also pack lightweight sandals for beach and evening wear. As the weather can be damp and chilly even during the summer, also include a lightweight sweater or jacket. In colder weather, corduroy or wool slacks, a longer skirt which can be worn with turtlenecks, blouses, and sweaters, and a pair of boots will provide a number of comfortable alternatives. Low-heel pumps are appropriate for both dressier daytime and evening wear. For travel in the depths of the Canadian winter, include a set of silk or wool-cotton-blend long underwear and your warmest coat or jacket. And don't forget warm socks and gloves and a wool hat and scarf. Again, before packing, lay out every piece of clothing you think you might want to take. Select clothing on the basis of what can serve several functions, and accessorize everything beforehand so you know exactly what you will be wearing with what. Eliminate items that don't mix, match, or interchange within your chosen color scheme. If you can't wear it in at least two distinct incarnations, leave it home.

Men also will find that color coordination is crucial. Solid colors coordinate best, and a sport jacket that goes with a pair of pants from a suit and several pairs of slacks provides added options. For travel in warmer weather, lightweight cotton shirts and a coordinating cotton sweater paired with casual slacks or chinos (and the sport jacket on damp, chilly days) will suffice for many occasions; also bring along shorts and one or two bathing suits (again, depending on your destination). Include several shirts that can be used for both daytime and evening wear, and sneakers and/or loafers (include at least one pair of double-duty shoes that go with both casual and dressier attire). For touring in colder weather, bring heavier slacks or corduroys, long-sleeve shirts or turtlenecks, a wool sweater, and a warm jacket or coat. Again, a set of long underwear will provide a welcome additional insulating layer in the coldest weather; also bring warm socks, gloves, a hat, and a scarf. Hanging bags are best for packing suits and jackets.

For both men and women, layering is the key to comfort — particularly when touring in parts of the countryside where mornings and evenings can be chilly even when the days are mild. No matter when and where you are traveling in Canada, however, layering is a good way to prepare for atypical temperatures or changes in the weather. For unexpectedly cold days or for outings in the countryside, a recommended basic is a lightweight wool or heavy cotton turtleneck, which can be worn under a shirt and perhaps a third layer, such as a pullover sweater, jacket, or windbreaker. In warmer weather, substitute a T-shirt and lightweight cotton shirts or sweaters for the turtleneck and wool layers. As the weather changes, you can add or remove clothes as required, and layering adapts well to the ruling principle of dressing according to a single color scheme. Individual items in layers can mix and match, be used together or independently.

If you are planning to be on the move — either in a car, bus, train, or plane — consider loose-fitting clothes that do not wrinkle, although the recent trend toward fabrics with a deliberately wrinkled look is a boon to travelers. Despite the tendency of designers to use more 100% natural fabrics, synthetics — particularly the new washable rayon blends — are immensely practical for a trip, and they have improved immeasurably in appearance lately. As a general rule, clothes in pure cotton and linen are the most perishable and hardest to keep fresh-looking. Lightweight wools, man-made fabrics — such as jerseys and knits, and drip-dry fabrics that can be rinsed in Woolite or a similar cold-water detergent — travel best (although in very hot weather, cotton clothing may be the most comfortable), and prints look fresher longer than solids.

Pack clothes that have a lot of pockets for traveler's checks, documents, and tickets. Then if your bag gets lost or stolen, you will retain possession of the essentials. Men who prefer to keep their pockets free of coins, papers, and keys might consider a shoulder bag, useful for carrying camera equipment, as well as daily necessities.

A versatile item of clothing that travelers in Canada will find indispensable is a raincoat. Particularly when traveling in the fall or spring, a raincoat with a zip-out lining — and maybe even a hood — is a wise choice. The removable lining allows you to adapt to temperature changes, and the hood is better suited (and less cumbersome) than an umbrella for fine, misty rain, although a practical alternative is a rain hat that can be rolled up in a pocket or carry-on bag. (If you do decide to take an umbrella, a compact telescoping model is best.) However, as mentioned above, if you are traveling during the harsh Canadian winter, you probably will want an even warmer outer garment. And finally — since the best touring of Canadian cities and countryside is done on foot — pack a comfortable pair of walking shoes.

Your carry-on luggage should contain a survival kit with the basic things you will need in case your luggage gets lost or stolen: a toothbrush, toothpaste, all medications, a sweater, nightclothes, and a change of underwear. With these essential items at hand, you will be prepared for any unexpected occurrence that separates you from your suitcase. If you have many 1- or 2-night stops, you can live out of your survival case without having to unpack completely at each hotel.

Other items you might consider packing are a flashlight with extra batteries, small sewing and first-aid kits (including insect repellent), binoculars, and a camera or camcorder (see *Cameras and Equipment,* in this section).

Sundries – If you are traveling in the heat of summer and will be spending a lot of time outdoors, pack special items so you won't spend your entire vacation horizontal in a hotel room (or hospital) because of sunburn. Be sure to take a sun hat (to protect hair as well as skin), sunscreen, and tanning lotion, which is available in graduated degrees of sunblock corresponding to the level of your skin's sensitivity. (The quantity of sunscreen is indicated by number: the higher the number, the greater the protection.) A good moisturizer is necessary to help keep your skin from drying out and peeling.

The best advice is to take the sun's rays in small doses — no more than 20 minutes at a stretch — increasing your sunbathing time gradually as your vacation progresses. Also, if you are heading for a holiday on skis, do not underestimate the effect of the sun's glare off snowy slopes, especially in higher altitudes — the exposed areas of your face and neck are particularly susceptible to a burning.

PACKING: The basic idea of packing is to get everything into the suitcase and out again with as few wrinkles as possible. Simple, casual clothes — shirts, jeans and slacks, permanent press skirts — can be rolled into neat, tight sausages that keep other packed items in place and leave the clothes themselves amazingly unwrinkled. The rolled clothes can be retrieved, shaken out, and hung up at your destination. However, for items that are too bulky or delicate for even careful rolling, a suitcase should be packed with the heaviest items on the bottom so that they will not wrinkle more perishable clothes. Candidates for the bottom layer include shoes (stuff them with small items to save space), a toilet kit, handbags (stuff them to help keep their shape), and an alarm clock. Fill out this layer with things that will not wrinkle or will not matter if they do, such as sweaters, socks, a bathing suit, gloves, and underwear.

If you get this first, heavy layer as smooth as possible with the fill-ins, you will have a shelf for the next layer — the most easily wrinkled items, like slacks, jackets, shirts, dresses, and skirts. These should be buttoned and zipped and laid along the whole length of the suitcase with as little folding as possible. When you do need to make a fold, do it on a crease (as with pants), along a seam in the fabric, or where it will not show (such as shirttails). Alternate each piece of clothing, using one side of the suitcase, then the other, to make the layers as flat as possible. Make the layers even and the total contents of your bag as full and firm as possible to keep things from shifting around during transit. On the top layer put the things you will want at once: nightclothes, an umbrella or raincoat, a sweater.

With men's two-suiter suitcases, follow the same procedure. Then place jackets on hangers, straighten them out, and leave them unbuttoned. If they are too wide for the suitcase, fold them lengthwise down the middle, straighten the shoulders, and fold the sleeves in along the seam.

While packing, it is a good idea to separate each layer of clothes with plastic cleaning bags, which will help preserve pressed clothes while they are in the suitcase. Unpack your bags as soon as you get to your hotel. Nothing so thoroughly destroys freshly cleaned and pressed clothes as sitting for days in a suitcase. Finally, if something is badly wrinkled and can't be professionally pressed before you must wear it, hang it overnight in a bathroom where the tub has been filled with very hot water; keep the bathroom door closed so that the room becomes something of a steamroom. It really works miracles.

LUGGAGE: If you already own serviceable luggage, do not feel compelled to buy new bags. If, however, you have been looking for an excuse to throw out that old suitcase that saw you through 4 years of college and innumerable weekends, this trip to Canada can be the perfect occasion.

Luggage falls into three categories — hard, soft-sided, and soft — and each has advantages and disadvantages. Hard suitcases have a rigid frame and sides. They provide the most protection from rough handling, but they also are the heaviest. Wheels and pull straps can rectify this problem, but they should be removed before the luggage is turned over at check-in or they may be wrenched off in transit. In addition, hard bags sometimes will pop open, even when locked, so a strap around the suitcase is advised.

Soft-sided suitcases have a rigid frame that has been covered with leather, fabric, or a synthetic material. The weight of the suitcase is greatly reduced, but many of the coverings (except leather, which also is heavy) are vulnerable to rips and tears from conveyor machinery. Not surprisingly, the materials that wear best generally are found on more expensive luggage.

The third category, seen more and more frequently, is soft luggage. Lacking any rigid structural element, it comes in a wide variety of shapes and sizes and is easy to carry, especially since it often has a shoulder strap. Most carry-on bags are of this type because they can be squeezed under the plane seat. They are even more vulnerable to damage on conveyor equipment than soft-sided bags, and as the weak point on these bags is the zipper, be sure to tie some cord or put several straps around the bag for extra insurance. Also be prepared to find a brand-new set of wrinkles pressed into everything that was carefully ironed before packing.

Whatever type of luggage you choose, remember that it should last for many years. Shop carefully, but be prepared to make a sizable investment.

It always is a good idea to add an empty, flattened airline bag or similarly light carrying case to your suitcase; you'll find it indispensable as a beach bag or to carry a few items for a day's outing. Keep in mind, too, that you're likely to do some shopping, so save room for those items. If you're planning on any extensive shopping, you might consider packing one of those soft, parachute-cloth suitcases that fold into a small envelope when not in use.

For more information on packing and luggage, send your request with a self-addressed, stamped, #10 envelope to *Samsonite Travel Advisory Service* (PO Box 39609, Dept. 80, Denver, CO 80239) for its free booklet, *Lightening the Travel Load: Travel Tips & Tricks.*

SOME PACKING HINTS: Apart from the items you pack as carry-on luggage (see above), always keep all necessary medicine, valuable jewelry, and travel or business documents in your purse, briefcase, or carry-on bag — *not in the luggage you will check.* Tuck a bathing suit into your handbag or briefcase, too; in the event of lost baggage, it's frustrating to be without one. And whether in your overnight bag or checked luggage, cosmetics and any liquids should be packed in plastic bottles or at least wrapped in plastic bags and tied.

If you are flying to Canada, golf clubs and skis may be checked through as luggage (most airlines are accustomed to handling them), but tennis rackets should be carried onto the plane. Some airlines require that bicycles be partially dismantled and packaged (see *Camping and RVs, Hiking and Biking,* in this section). Check with the airline before departure to see if there is a specific regulation regarding any special equipment or sporting gear you plan to take.

Hints for Handicapped Travelers

From 35 to 50 million people in the US alone have some sort of disability, and at least half this number are physically handicapped. Like everyone else today, they — and the uncounted disabled millions around the world — are on the move. More than ever before, they are demanding facilities they can use comfortably, and they are being heard. The disabled traveler will find that services for the handicapped have improved considerably over the last few years, both in the US and abroad, and though accessibility is far from universal, it is being brought up to more acceptable standards every day.

PLANNING: Good planning is essential: Collect as much information as you can about your specific disability and facilities for the disabled in the area you're visiting, make your travel arrangements well in advance, and specify to all services involved the exact nature of your condition or restricted mobility, as your trip will be much more comfortable if you know that there are accommodations and facilities to suit your needs. The best way to find out if your intended destination can accommodate a handicapped traveler is to write or phone the local tourist association or hotel and ask specific questions. If you require a corridor of a certain width to maneuver a wheelchair or if you need handles on the bathroom walls for support, ask the hotel manager. A travel agent or the local chapter or national office of the organization that deals with your particular disability — for example, the *American Foundation for the Blind* or the *American Heart Association* — will supply the most up-to-date information on the subject. The following sources offer general information on access:

Access to the World, by Louise Weiss, offers sound tips for the disabled traveler abroad. Published by Facts on File (460 Park Ave. S., New York, NY 10016; phone: 212-683-2244), it costs $16.95. Check with your local bookstore; it also can be ordered by phone with a credit card.

Access Travel: A Guide to the Accessibility of Airport Terminals, published by the Airport Operators Council International, provides information on more than 500 airports worldwide — including airports in Canada — with ratings according to 70 features, including accessibility to bathrooms, corridor width, and parking spaces. For a free copy, write to the Consumer Information Center, Access America (Dept. 563W, Pueblo, CO 81009), or call 202-293-8500 and ask for "Item 563W-Access Travel." To help travel agents plan trips for the handicapped, this material is reprinted with additional information on tourist boards, city information offices, and tour operators specializing in travel for the handicapped (see "Tours," below) in the *Worldwide Edition* of the *Official Airline Guides Travel Planner,* issued quarterly by Official Airline Guides (2000 Clearwater Dr., Oak Brook, IL 60521; phone: 708-574-6000).

Air Transportation of Handicapped Persons is a booklet published by the US Department of Transportation, and will be sent at no charge upon written request. Ask for "Free Advisory Circular #AC-120-32" from the Distribution Unit, US Dept. of Transportation, Publications Section, M-443-2, Washington, DC 20590.

Handicapped Travel Newsletter is regarded as one of the best sources of information for the disabled traveler. It is edited by wheelchair-bound Vietnam veteran Michael Quigley, who has traveled to 93 countries around the world. Issued every 2 months (plus special issues), a subscription is $10 per year. Write to *Handicapped Travel Newsletter,* PO Box 269, Athens, TX 75751 (phone: 214-677-1260).

Information Center for Individuals with Disabilities (ICID), Fort Point Pl., 1st Floor, 27-43 Wormwood St., Boston, MA 02210; phone: 617-727-5540/1 or 800-462-5015 in Massachusetts only; both numbers offer voice and TDD (telecommunications device for the deaf) service. *ICID* provides information and referral services on disability-related issues and will help you research your trip. The center publishes fact sheets on vacation planning, tour operators, travel agents, and travel resources.

The Itinerary is a travel magazine for people with disabilities. Published bimonthly, it includes information on accessibility, listings of tours, news of adaptive devices, travel aids, and special services, as well as numerous general travel hints. A subscription is $10 a year; write to *The Itinerary,* PO Box 2012, Bayonne, NJ 07002-2012 (phone: 201-858-3400).

Mobility International/USA (MIUSA), the US branch of *Mobility International,* a nonprofit British organization with affiliates in some 35 countries, offers advice and assistance to disabled travelers — including information on accommodations, access guides, and study tours. Among its publications are a quarterly newsletter and a comprehensive sourcebook, *World of Options for the '90s: A*

Guide to International Educational Exchange, Community Service, and Travel for Persons with Disabilities. Individual membership is $20 a year; subscription to the newsletter alone is $10 annually. For more information, contact *MIUSA,* PO Box 3551, Eugene, OR 97403 (phone: 503-343-1284, voice and TDD — telecommunications device for the deaf).

National Rehabilitation Information Center, 8455 Colesville Rd., Suite 935, Silver Spring, MD 20910 (phone: 301-588-9284). A general information, resource, research, and referral service.

Paralyzed Veterans of America (PVA) is a national veterans service organization. Its members all are veterans who have suffered spinal cord injuries, but it offers advocacy services and information to all persons with a disability. *PVA* also sponsors *Access to the Skies,* a program that coordinates the efforts of the national and international air travel industry in providing airport and airplane access for the disabled. Members receive several helpful publications, as well as regular notification of conferences on subjects of interest to the disabled traveler. For information, contact *PVA/ATTS Program,* 801 18th St. NW, Washington, DC 20006 (phone: 202-USA-1300).

Society for the Advancement of Travel for the Handicapped (SATH), 26 Court St., Penthouse, Brooklyn, NY 11242 (phone: 718-858-5483). To keep abreast of developments in travel for the handicapped as they occur, you may want to join *SATH,* a nonprofit organization whose members include travel agents, tour operators, and other travel suppliers, as well as consumers. Membership costs $40 ($25 for students and travelers who are 65 and older) and the fee is tax deductible. *SATH* publishes a quarterly newsletter, an excellent booklet, *Travel Tips for the Handicapped,* and provides information on travel agents or tour operators who have experience (or an interest) in travel for the handicapped. *SATH* also offers a free 48-page guide, *The United States Welcomes Handicapped Visitors,* that covers transportation and accommodations, as well as travel insurance and other useful hints for the handicapped traveler abroad. Send a self-addressed, #10 envelope to *SATH* at the address above, and include $1 for postage.

TravelAbility, by Lois Reamy, is a vast database with information on locating tours for the handicapped, coping with public transport, and finding accommodations, special equipment, and travel agents, and includes a helpful step-by-step planning guide. Although geared mainly to travel in the US, it is full of information useful to handicapped travelers anywhere. Previously published by Macmillan, *TravelAbility* is currently out of print, but may be available at your library.

Travel Information Service at Moss Rehabilitation Hospital is a service designed to help physically handicapped people plan trips. It cannot make travel arrangements, but it will supply information on travel accessibility for a nominal fee. Contact the *Travel Information Service,* Moss Rehabilitation Hospital, 12th St. and Tabor Rd., Philadelphia, PA 19141 (phone: 215-456-9600).

The *Canadian Rehabilitation Council for the Disabled* publishes a useful book by Cinnie Noble, *Handi-Travel: A Resource Book for Disabled and Elderly Travelers* ($12.95, plus $2 for shipping and handling, 50¢ each additional copy). This comprehensive travel guide is full of practical tips for those with disabilities affecting mobility, hearing, or sight. To order this book and for other useful information, contact the *Canadian Rehabilitation Council for the Disabled,* 45 Sheppard Ave. E., Suite 801, Toronto, Ontario M2N 5W9, Canada (phone: 416-250-7490).

A few more basic resources to look for are *Travel for the Disabled,* by Helen Hecker ($9.95), and by the same author, *The Directory of Travel Agencies for the Disabled* ($12.95). *Wheelchair Vagabond,* by John G. Nelson, is another useful guide for travelers confined to a wheelchair (softcover, $9.95; hardcover, $14.95). All three are published by Twin Peaks Press (PO Box 129, Vancouver, WA 98666; to order call 800-637-CALM). Additionally, *The Physically Disabled Traveler's Guide,* by Rod W. Durgin and Norene Lindsay, is helpful and informative. It is available from Resource Directories (3361 Executive Pkwy., Suite 302, Toledo, OH 43606; phone: 419-536-5353) for $9.95, plus $2 for postage and handling.

The library of the *Canadian Paraplegic Association* (520 Sutherland Dr., Toronto, Ontario M4G 3V9, Canada; phone: 416-422-5644) is another good source of information on travel for the mobility disabled. The association also offers accessibility information, travel advice, and referral services.

It should be noted that almost all of the material published with disabled travelers in mind deals with the wheelchair-bound traveler, for whom architectural barriers are of prime concern. For travelers with diabetes, a pamphlet entitled *Ticket to Safe Travel* is available for 50¢ from the New York chapter of the *American Diabetes Association* (505 Eighth Ave., 21st Floor, New York, NY 10018; phone: 212-947-9707). For those with heart-related ailments, *Travel for the Patient with Chronic Obstructive Pulmonary Disease,* is available for $2 from Dr. Harold Silver (1601 18th St. NW, Washington, DC 20009; phone: 202-667-0134); the *American Heart Association* (7320 Greenville Ave., Dallas, TX 75231; phone: 214-373-6300) also provides a number of useful publications. For blind travelers, a wealth of additional information is available from the *American Foundation for the Blind* (15 W. 16th St., New York, NY 10011; phone: 212-620-2147 in New York State; 800-232-5463 elsewhere in the US).

Travelers who depend on Seeing Eye dogs should check with the airline they plan to fly and the authorities of the countries they plan to visit well before they leave. Canada requires veterinary health certificates for dogs entering the country. These certificates must include a statement of rabies inoculation administered within the preceding 3 years.

The American Society for the Prevention of Cruelty to Animals (ASPCA) offers a very useful book, *Traveling With Your Pet,* which includes inoculation and quarantine requirements by country and territory. It is available for $5 (which includes postage and handling). Send check or money order to the *ASPCA,* Education Dept., 441 E. 92nd St., New York, NY 10128 (phone: 212-876-7700). For helpful information and a general discussion of travel with Seeing Eye dogs, *Seeing Eye Dogs as Air Travelers* can be obtained free from *Seeing Eye* (Box 375, Morristown, NJ 07963-0375; phone: 201-539-4425).

PLANE: Advise the airline that you are handicapped when you book your flight. The Federal Aviation Administration (FAA) has ruled that US airlines must accept disabled and handicapped passengers as long as the airline has advance notice and the passenger represents no potentially insurmountable problem in the event that emergency evacuation becomes necessary. As a matter of course, US airlines were pretty good about helping handicapped passengers even before the ruling, although each airline has somewhat different procedures. Canadian airlines also are good about accommodating the disabled traveler, but, again, policies vary from carrier to carrier. Ask for specifics when you book your flight.

Disabled passengers always should make reservations well in advance, and should provide the airline with all relevant details of their condition at that time. These details include information on mobility, toilet and special oxygen needs, and requirements for equipment that must be supplied by the airline, such as a wheelchair or portable oxygen. Be sure that the person to whom you speak understands fully the degree of your disability — the more details provided, the more effective the help the airline can give you. On the day before the flight, call back to make sure that all arrangements have been prepared, and arrive early on the day of the flight so that you can board before the rest of the passengers. Carry a medical certificate with you, stating your specific disability or the need to carry particular medicine. (Some airlines require the certificate; you should find out the regulations of the airline you'll be flying well beforehand.)

Because most airports have jetways (corridors connecting the terminal with the door of the plane), a disabled passenger usually can be taken as far as the plane, and sometimes right on it, in a wheelchair. If not, a narrow boarding chair may be used to take you to your seat. Your own wheelchair, which will be folded and put in the baggage compartment, should be tagged as escort luggage to assure that it's available at planeside upon landing rather than in the baggage claim area. Travel is not quite as simple if your wheelchair is battery-operated: Unless it has non-spillable batteries, it might not be accepted on board, and you will have to check with the airline ahead of time to find out how the batteries and the chair should be packaged for the flight. Usually people in wheelchairs are asked to wait until other passengers have disembarked. If you are making a tight connection, be sure to tell the attendant.

Passengers who use oxygen may not use their personal supply in the cabin, though it may be carried on the plane as cargo when properly packed and labeled. If you will need oxygen during the flight, the airline will supply it to you (there is a charge) provided you have given advance notice — 24 hours to a few days, depending on the carrier.

Several airlines now have booklets describing procedures for accommodating the handicapped on their flights. For example, *United* has a list of travel tips for the handicapped; contact *United Airlines,* Consumer Affairs Department, PO Box 66100, Chicago, IL 60666 (phone: 708-952-6796).

Useful information on every stage of air travel, from planning to arrival, is provided in the booklet *Incapacitated Passengers Air Travel Guide.* To receive a free copy, write to Senior Manager, Passenger Services, International Air Transport Association, 2000 Peel St., Montreal, Quebec H3A 2R4, Canada (phone: 514-844-6311).

For an access guide to hundreds of airports worldwide, write for *Access Travel: A Guide to the Accessibility of Airport Terminals,* a free publication of the *Airport Operators Council International,* which includes detailed information on airports in Calgary and Edmonton (Alberta); Sidney, Vancouver, and Victoria (British Columbia); Fredricton and Moncton (New Brunswick); Gander and St. John's (Newfoundland); Halifax (Nova Scotia); London, Ottawa, Thunder Bay, Toronto, and Windsor (Ontario); Charlottetown (Prince Edward Island); Montreal, Quebec City, and Sept Isles (Quebec); and Saskatoon (Saskatchewan). The US Department of Transportation's *Air Transportation of Handicapped Persons* explains the general guidelines that govern air carrier policies. It is available free when requested in writing. For information on obtaining both of these publications, see the source list above.

The following airlines serving Canada have TDD toll-free lines in the US for the hearing-impaired: *American* (phone: 800-582-1573 in Ohio; 800-543-1586 elsewhere in the US); *Continental* (phone: 800-343-9195 from 8 AM to 1 AM, Eastern Standard Time); and *United* (phone: 800-942-8819 in Illinois; 800-323-0170 elsewhere in the US).

GROUND TRANSPORTATION: Perhaps the simplest solution to getting around is to travel with an able-bodied companion who can drive. If you are accustomed to driving your own hand-controlled car and want to rent one, you are in luck. Some rental companies offer cars with hand controls. *Avis* (phone: 800-331-1212) can convert a car to hand controls with as little as 24 hours' notice, though it's a good idea to arrange for one a day in advance. *Hertz* (phone: 800-654-3131) requires a minimum of 2 days to install the controls, and makes the additional stipulation that the car be returned to the office from which it was rented. Neither company charges extra for hand controls, but *Avis* will fit them only on a full-size car, and both request that you bring your handicapped driver's permit with you. Other car rental companies provide hand-control cars at some locations; however, as there usually are only a limited number available, call well in advance.

The *American Automobile Association* (*AAA*) publishes the booklet *The Handicapped Driver's Mobility Guide,* available free to members and for $3 to non-members. Contact your local *AAA* office, or send a self-addressed, stamped, 6-by-9-inch envelope to *AAA* Traffic Safety Department, 1000 AAA Dr., Heathrow, FL 32746-5063.

Taking taxis or hiring a chauffeur-driven car are other solutions to the mobility problem. Contact local transportation authorities for information on special van or bus services for disabled travelers.

TRAIN: On most routes *VIA Rail* accepts wheelchair passengers, although 24-hour advance notice is required. However, on some shorter runs trains do not have baggage cars, thus no place to store the wheelchair. As *VIA Rail* personnel aren't required to carry a disabled passenger on or off the train and some of the older equipment may present barriers, it's wise to have a companion along. Disabled persons who can't travel by themselves can apply for a two-for-one fare certificate, which allows a companion to travel free on the Canadian railway. The certificate is issued by the *Canadian Rehabilitation Council for the Disabled* (45 Sheppard Ave. E., Suite 801, Toronto, Ontario M2N 5W9, Canada; phone: 416-250-7490) on receipt of an application signed by a doctor. Blind passengers and their companions also are eligible for the two-for-one fare. (Seeing Eye dogs ride in the passenger cars at no extra charge.) On long distance journeys it's a good idea to reserve a bedroom or a roomette, which have private washrooms and room service.

BY BUS: Bus companies do not have consistent written policies on carrying handicapped people. For wheelchair-bound passengers, the rule essentially is that if the wheelchair can be folded to fit in the baggage compartment, the bus will take you. Make sure to ask about the bus company's regulations when making reservations. Like *VIA Rail, Gray Coach, Greyhound Lines of Canada, Voyageur,* and many smaller lines also honor the two-for-one fare certificates.

TOURS: Programs designed for the physically impaired are run by specialists who have researched hotels, restaurants, and sites to be sure they present no insurmountable obstacles. The following travel agencies and tour operators specialize in making group or individual arrangements for travelers with physical or other disabilities. Because of the requirements of handicapped travel, however, the same packages may not be offered regularly.

Access: The Foundation for Accessibility by the Disabled, PO Box 356, Malvern, NY 11565 (phone: 516-887-5798). Travelers referral service that acts as an intermediary with tour operators and agents worldwide, and provides information on accessibility at various locations. The firm also offers access to its audio/video travel library.

Accessible Tours/Directions Unlimited, 720 N. Bedford Rd., Bedford Hills, NY 10507 (phone: 914-241-1700 in New York State; 800-533-5343 elsewhere in the US). Arranges group or individual tours for disabled persons traveling in the company of able-bodied friends or family members. Accepts the unaccompanied traveler if completely self-sufficient.

Evergreen Travel Service/Wings on Wheels Tours, 19505L 44th Ave. W., Lynnwood, WA 98036-5658 (phone: 206-776-1184 or 800-435-2288 throughout the US). The oldest company in the world offering worldwide tours and cruises for the disabled (Wings on Wheels) and sight impaired/blind (White Cane Tours). Most programs are first class or deluxe, and include a trained escort. *Evergreen* also offers a service called Evergreen Flying Fingers, for the deaf.

Flying Wheels Travel, 143 W. Bridge St., Box 382, Owatonna, MN 55060 (phone: 507-451-5005 or 800-535-6790 throughout the US). Handles both tours and individual arrangements.

The Guided Tour, 555 Ashbourne Rd., Elkins Park, PA 19117 (phone: 215-782-1370). Arranges tours for people with developmental and learning disabilities and sponsors separate tours for members of the same population who also are physically disabled or who simply need a slower pace.

Sprout, 893 Amsterdam Ave., New York, NY 10025 (phone: 212-222-9575). Arranges travel programs for mildly and moderately disabled teens and adults.

Travel Horizons Unlimited, 11 E. 44th St., New York, NY 10017 (phone: 212-687-5121 in New York; 800-343-5032 elsewhere in the US). Travel agent and registered nurse Mary Ann Hamm designs trips for individual travelers requiring all types of kidney dialysis and handles arrangements for the dialysis.

Whole Person Tours, PO Box 1084, Bayonne, NJ 07002-1084 (phone: 800-462-2237 or 201-858-3400). Handicapped owner Bob Zywicki travels the world with his wheelchair and offers a lineup of escorted tours (many by himself) for the disabled. Send a self-addressed, stamped envelope for a general tour brochure of foreign and domestic programs. *Whole Person Tours* also publishes *The Itinerary,* a bimonthly newsletter for disabled travelers (a 1-year subscription costs $10).

Hints for Single Travelers

Just about the last trip in human history on which the participants were neatly paired was the voyage of Noah's Ark. Ever since, passenger lists and tour groups have reflected the same kind of asymmetry that occurs in real life, as countless individuals set forth to see the world unaccompanied (or unencumbered, depending on your outlook) by spouse, lover, friend, or relative.

There are some things to be said for traveling alone. There is the pleasure of privacy, though a solitary traveler must be self-reliant, independent, and responsible. Unfortunately, traveling alone also can turn a traveler into a second class citizen.

The truth is that the travel industry is not very fair to people who vacation by themselves. People traveling alone almost invariably end up paying more than individuals traveling in pairs. Most travel bargains, including package tours, accommodations, resort packages, and cruises, are based on *double occupancy* rates. This means that the per-person price is offered on the basis of two people traveling together and sharing a double room (which means they each will spend a good deal more on meals and extras). The single traveler will have to pay a surcharge, called a single supplement, for exactly the same package. In extreme cases, this can add as much as 30% to 50% to the basic per-person rate. As far as the travel industry is concerned, single travel has not yet come into its own.

Don't despair, however. There are, after all, countless thousands of indivuduals who *do* travel alone. Inevitably, their greatest obstacle is the single supplement charge, which prevents them from cashing in on travel bargains available to anyone traveling as part of a pair.

The obvious, most effective alternative is to find a traveling companion. Even special "singles' tours" that promise no supplements usually are based on people sharing double rooms. Perhaps the most recent innovation along these lines is the creation of organizations that "introduce" the single traveler to other single travelers, somewhat like a dating service. If you are interested in finding another single traveler to help share the cost, consider contacting the agencies listed below. Some charge fees, others are free, but the basic service offered by all is the same: to match the unattached person with a compatible travel mate, often as part of the company's own package tours. Among the better established of these agencies are the following:

Classic Singles Network: Offers tours catering to the mature single client — the majority of its members are over 45 years old. For information, contact

Classic Singles Network, 100 N. Sepulveda Blvd., Suite 1010, El Segundo, CA 90245 (phone: 800-421-5785 in California; 800-421-2255 elsewhere in the US).

Cosmos: This agency, specializing in budget motorcoach tours, offers a guaranteed-share plan whereby singles who wish to share rooms (and avoid paying the single supplement) are matched by the tour escort with like-minded individuals of the same sex and charged the basic double-occupancy tour price. Contact the firm at any one of its three North American branches: 95-25 Queens Blvd., Rego Park, NY 11374 (phone: 800-221-0090 from the eastern US); 150 S. Los Robles Ave., Pasadena, CA 91101 (phone 818-449-0919; 800-556-5454 from the western US); 1801 Eglinton Ave. W., Suite 104, Toronto, Ontario M6E 2H8, Canada (phone: 416-787-1281).

Grand Circle Travel: Arranges extended vacations, escorted tours, and cruises for retired Americans, including singles. Membership, which is automatic when you book a trip through *Grand Circle,* includes discount certificates on future trips and other extras. Contact *Grand Circle Travel,* 347 Congress St., Boston, MA 02210 (phone: 800-248-3737 or 617-350-7500).

Insight International Tours: Offers a matching service for single travelers. Several tours are geared for travelers in the 18 to 35 age group. Contact *Insight International Tours,* 745 Atlantic Ave., Boston, MA 02111 (phone: 800-582-8380 or 617-482-2000).

Jane's International: This service puts potential traveling companions in touch with one another. No age limit, no fee. Contact *Jane's International,* 2603 Bath Ave., Brooklyn, NY 11214 (phone: 718-266-2045).

Saga International Holidays: A subsidiary of a British company specializing in older travelers, many of them single, *Saga* offers a broad selection of escorted coach tours, cruises, and apartment-stay holidays, including packages, for people age 60 and over or those 50 to 59 traveling with someone 60 or older. Members of the *Saga Holiday Club* receive the club magazine, which contains a column aimed at helping lone travelers find suitable traveling companions. A 1-year club membership costs $5. Contact *Saga International Holidays,* 120 Boylston St., Boston, MA 02116 (phone: 800-343-0273 or 617-451-6808).

Singleworld, which organizes its own packages and also books singles on the cruises and tours of other operators, arranges shared accommodations if requested, charging a one-time surcharge that is much less than the single supplement would be. *Singleworld* actually is a club joined through travel agents for a yearly fee of $20, paid at the time of booking. About two-thirds of this agency's clientele are under 35, and about half this number are women. *Singleworld* organizes tours and cruises with departures categorized by age group. Contact *Singleworld,* 401 Theodore Fremd Ave., Rye, NY 10580 (phone: 914-967-3334 or 800-223-6490 in the continental US).

Travel Companion Exchange: Every 8 weeks, this group publishes a directory of singles looking for travel companions and provides members with full-page profiles of likely partners. Members fill out a lengthy questionnaire to establish a personal profile and write a small listing, much like an ad in a personal column. This listing is circulated to other members who can request a copy of the complete questionnaire and then go on to make contact to plan a joint vacation. It is wise to join as far ahead of your scheduled vacation as possible so that there's enough time to determine the suitability of prospective traveling companions. Membership fees range from $6 to $11 per month (with a 6-month minimum enrollment), depending on the level of service required. The membership package includes a travel newsletter for singles. A sample issue costs $4. Contact *Travel Companion Exchange,* PO Box 833, Amityville, NY 11701 (phone: 516-454-0880).

A special guidebook for solo travelers, prepared by Eleanor Adams Baxel, offers information on how to avoid paying supplementary charges, how to pick the right travel agent, how to calculate costs, and much more. Entitled *A Guide for Solo Travel Abroad* (Berkshire Traveller Press), it's out of print, so check your library. A new book for single travelers is *Traveling on Your Own* by Eleanor Berman; available in bookstores, it also can be ordered by sending $12.95, plus $2 postage and handling (per book), to Random House, Customer Service Dept., 400 Hahn Rd., Westminster, MD 21157 (phone: 800-726-0600).

WOMEN AND STUDENTS: Two specific groups of single travelers deserve special mention: women and students. Countless women travel by themselves, and such an adventure need not be feared. You normally will find people very courteous and welcoming, but remember that crime is a worldwide problem. Keep a careful eye on your belongings while on the beach, or lounging in a park, or traveling on a bus or train; lock your car and hotel doors; deposit your valuables in the hotel's safe; and never hitchhike.

One lingering inhibition many female travelers still harbor is that of eating alone in public places. The trick here is to relax and enjoy your meal and surroundings; while you may run across the occasional unenlightened waiter, a female dining solo is no longer uncommon. A book offering lively, helpful advice on female solo travel is *The Traveling Woman,* by Dena Kaye. Though out of print, it may be found in your local library.

Students traveling on a strict budget have a few accommodation options. They can stay at one of the many *YMCA* or *YWCA* residences in Montreal, Toronto, and other major cities. For information and locations, you may contact the national office of *YMCA Canada* at 416-485-9447. Note that membership often is required if you plan to stay more than a day or two.

Students and singles in general should keep in mind that youth hostels exist in many cities throughout Canada. They always are inexpensive, generally clean and well situated, and they are a sure place to meet other people traveling alone. Hostels are run by the hosteling associations of some 60-plus countries that make up the *International Youth Hostel Federation* (*IYHF*); membership in one of the national associations affords access to the hostels of the rest. To join the American affiliate, *American Youth Hostels* (*AYH*), contact the national office (PO Box 37613, Washington, DC 20013-7613; phone: 202-783-6161), or contact the local *AYH* council nearest you. As we went to press, new membership rules and rates were in effect: Membership in *AYH* currently costs $25 for people between the ages of 18 and 54; $10 for youths under 18, $15 for seniors, $35 for family membership. The *AYH Handbook,* which lists hostels in the US, comes with your *AYH* card (non-members can purchase the handbook for $5, plus $2 for postage and handling); the *International Youth Hostel Handbooks,* which list hostels worldwide, must be purchased ($10.95 each, plus $2 for postage).

You also may want to contact the *Canadian Hostelling Association* (1600 James Naismith Dr., Suite 608, Gloucester, Ottawa, Ontario K1B 5N4, Canada; phone: 613-748-5638), which publishes a free handbook listing Canadian hostels.

Another option is *Campus Holidays USA,* which offers accommodations in universities throughout the US and Canada. It includes single, twin, and even triple rooms for friends or families traveling together. Contact *Campus Holidays USA,* 242 Bellevue Ave., Upper Montclair, NJ 07043 (phone: 201-744-8724 in New Jersey; 800-526-2915 elsewhere in the US).

Those interested in campus stays also should know about the *U.S. and Worldwide Travel Accommodations Guide,* which lists several hundred colleges and universities in the US and Canada that offer simple, but comfortable, accommodations in their residence halls, primarily during the summer season. The accommodations vary from single and double rooms to full apartments and suites with kitchens, and the rooms can be booked by the day, week, or month. Prices range from $12 to $24 per night, with an average of about $18. An added bonus of this type of arrangement is that visitors usually are free to utilize various campus sport and recreation facilities. For a copy of the guide, which describes services and facilities in detail, send $11.95 to *Campus Travel Service,* PO Box 5007, Laguna Beach, CA 92652 (phone: 714-497-3044).

Elderhostel is a network of schools, colleges, and universities that sponsors week-long study programs for people over 60 years of age on campuses throughout the US and Canada. Contact *Elderhostel* (80 Boylston St., Suite 400, Boston, MA 02116; phone: 617-426-7788 or 617-426-8056). An informational videotape describing *Elderhostel's* programs is available for $5.

Hints for Older Travelers

Special package deals and more free time are just two factors that have given Americans over age 65 a chance to see the world at affordable prices. Senior citizens make up an ever-growing segment of the travel population, and the trend among them is to travel more frequently and for longer periods of time. No longer limited by 3-week vacations or the business week, older travelers can take advantage of off-season, off-peak travel, which is both less expensive and more pleasant than traveling in high season. October to mid-November and May and June are good times of the year to travel in Canada to avoid the crowds and still enjoy relatively moderate temperatures for touring and outdoor activities.

PLANNING: When planning a vacation, prepare your itinerary with one eye on your own physical condition and the other on a topographical map. Keep in mind variations in climate, terrain, and altitudes, which may pose some danger for anyone with heart or breathing problems.

An excellent book to read before embarking on any trip, domestic or foreign, is Rosalind Massow's *Travel Easy: The Practical Guide for People Over 50,* available for $6.50 to members of the *American Association of Retired Persons (AARP),* $8.95 for non-members (add $1.75 postage and handling per order, not per book). Order from AARP Books (c/o Scott, Foresman, 1865 Miner St., Des Plaines, IL 60016; phone: 800-238-2300). It discusses a host of subjects, from choosing a destination to getting set for departure, with chapters on transportation options, tours, cruises, avoiding health problems, and handling dental emergencies en route. Another book, *The International Health Guide for Senior Citizens,* covers such topics as trip preparations, food and water precautions, adjusting to weather and climate conditions, finding a doctor, motion sickness, and jet lag. The book also discusses specific health and travel problems, and includes a list of resource organizations that provide medical assistance for travelers; it is available for $4.95 postpaid from Pilot Books (103 Cooper St., Babylon, NY 11702; phone: 516-422-2225). A third book on health for older travelers, Rosalind Massow's excellent *Now It's Your Turn to Travel* (Collier Books), has a chapter on medical problems; it is out of print but may be available in your library. (Also, see *Staying Healthy,* in this section.) *Travel Tips for Senior Citizens* (State Department publication 8970), a useful booklet with general advice, also is currently out of print but may be found in libraries.

An ideal book for budget-conscious older travelers is *The Discount Guide for Travelers Over 55* by Caroline and Walter Weintz (Dutton; $7.95). Another useful discount guide is *Senior Citizen's Guide to Budget Travel in the US and Canada* by Paige Palmer; available from Pilot Books (address above) for $3.95, plus $1 for postage and handling. You also may want to send for *101 Tips for the Mature Traveler* a free publication available from *Grand Circle Travel,* 347 Congress St., Suite 3A, Boston, MA 02210 (phone: 617-350-7500, 800-221-2610, or 800-831-8880).

Bear in mind also that even in summer you will need something warm for the evening in many areas of Canada, and rainwear year-round is a good idea, too. However, remember that one secret to happy traveling is to *pack lightly.* (For further hints on what to bring, see *How to Pack,* in this section.)

HEALTH: Health facilities generally are maintained by individual Canadian provinces, but Blue Cross usually is honored throughout Canada. Be sure to take along any prescription medication you need, enough to last *without a new prescription* for the duration of your trip; pack all medications with a note from your doctor for the benefit of airport and other authorities. It also is wise to bring a few common non-prescription over-the-counter medications with you: Aspirin or a non-aspirin pain reliever and something for stomach upset may come in handy. If you have specific medical problems, bring prescriptions and a "medical file" composed of the following:

1. A summary of medical history and current diagnosis.
2. A list of drugs to which you are allergic.
3. Your most recent electrocardiogram, if you have heart problems.
4. Your doctor's name, address, and telephone number.

■**A word of caution:** Don't overdo it. Allow time for some relaxation each day to refresh yourself for the next scheduled sightseeing event. Traveling across time zones can be exhausting, and adjusting to major climatic changes can make you feel dizzy and drained. Plan on spending at least 1 full day resting before you start touring. If you're part of a group tour, be sure to check the itinerary thoroughly. Some package deals sound wonderful because they include all the places you've ever dreamed of visiting. In fact, visiting all of them can become so hectic and tiring that you'll be reaching for a pillow instead of a camera.

DISCOUNTS AND PACKAGES: Senior citizens with identification are eligible for a large variety of discounts across Canada. Some discounts are only available to Canadians, but many others are available to anyone over 65. Although the rules change from place to place and from city to city, acceptable proof of eligibility (or age) is, for Canadians, a special card issued by the province; for older people from the US and other countries, a driver's license, passport, birth certificate, a membership card in a recognized senior citizens' organization such as the *American Association of Retired Persons* (see below), or a Medicare card. Because senior citizen discounts are common, but by no means standard, always ask about them before you pay — whether it's for a movie in Toronto or a hotel in Vancouver. Discounts often are available for transportation, museums, cultural and sports events, and dozens of other activities. Depending on the local management, discounts of 10% to 25% often are available at a variety of hotel chains, including *Holiday Inn, Howard Johnson, Marriott, Rodeway Inns,* and *Sheraton.* The following are some standard reductions available to all senior citizens in Canada:

Bus: Voyageur offers senior citizens one-third off regular one-way or round-trip fares, while *Greyhound* and *Gray Coach* each offer a 10% reduction on regular fares. Many of the smaller Canadian lines also give discounts to older travelers.

Train: VIA Rail offers older travelers 10% to 50% discounts on regular coach fares. Discount varies according to the destination and the time of travel.

Plane: Air Canada offers reductions on confirmed reservations for flights from the US. *Canadian Airlines International* also offers special senior citizen rates, as do most smaller regional airlines. Check with the airline or your travel agent for current discounted rates.

Many other travel suppliers offer discounts to older travelers. Some of these discounts, however, are extended only to bona fide members of certain senior citizens organizations. Because the same organizations frequently offer package tours to both domestic and international destinations, the benefits of membership are twofold: Those who join can take advantage of discounts as individual travelers and also reap the savings that group travel affords. In addition, because the age requirements for some of these organizations are quite low (or nonexistent), the benefits can begin to accrue early. Among the organizations dedicated to helping you see the world are the following:

American Association of Retired Persons (AARP): The largest and best known of these organizations. Membership is open to anyone 50 or over, whether retired or not. AARP offers travel programs, designed exclusively for older travelers, that cover the globe; they include a broad range of escorted tours, hosted tours, and cruises, including tours and resort packages. Dues are $5 per year or $12.50 for 3 years, and include spouse. For membership information, contact AARP Travel Service, 100 N. Sepulveda Blvd., Suite 1010, El Segundo, CA 90245 (phone: 800-227-7737 or 213-322-7323).

Mature Outlook: Through its Travel Alert, last-minute tours, cruises, and other vacation packages are available to members at special savings. Hotel and car rental discounts and travel accident insurance also are available. Membership is open to anyone 50 years of age or older, costs $9.95 a year, and includes its bimonthly newsletter and magazine, as well as information on package tours. Contact the Customer Service Center, 6001 N. Clark St., Chicago, IL 60660 (phone: 800-336-6330).

National Council of Senior Citizens: Here, too, the emphasis always is on keeping costs low. This group offers a different roster of tours each year, and its travel service also will book individual tours for members. Although most members are over 50, membership is open to anyone, regardless of age, for an annual fee of $12 per person or $16 per couple. Lifetime membership costs $150. For information, contact the National Council for Senior Citizens, 925 15th St. NW, Washington, DC 20005 (phone: 202-347-8800).

Certain travel agencies and tour operators specialize in group travel for older travelers, among them the following:

Gadabout Tours: Operated by Lois Anderson, this organization offers escorted tours to a number of destinations worldwide, including Canada. See a travel agent or contact Gadabout Tours, 700 E. Tahquitz, Palm Springs, CA 92262 (phone: 619-325-5556 or 800-521-7309 in California; 800-952-5068 elsewhere in the US).

Grand Circle Travel: Caters exclusively to the over-50 traveler and packages a large variety of escorted tours, cruises, and extended vacations. Grand Circle also publishes a quarterly magazine (with a column for the single traveler) and a helpful free booklet, 101 Tips for the Mature Traveler Abroad. Contact Grand Circle Travel, 347 Congress St., Suite 3A, Boston, MA 02210 (phone: 617-350-7500, 800-221-2610, or 800-831-8880).

Insight International Tours: Offers a matching service for single travelers. Several tours are geared for mature travelers. Contact Insight International Tours, 745 Atlantic Ave., Boston, MA 02111 (phone: 617-482-2000 or 800-582-8380 throughout the US).

Saga International Holidays: A subsidiary of a British company specializing in the older traveler, Saga offers a broad selection of escorted coach tours, cruises, and apartment-stay holidays, including packages, for people age 60 and over or those 50 to 59 traveling with someone 60 or older. Members of the Saga Holiday Club receive the club magazine, which contains a column aimed at helping lone travelers find suitable traveling companions (see *Hints for Single Travelers*). A 1-year club membership costs $5. Contact *Saga International Holidays,* 120 Boylston St., Boston, MA 02116 (phone: 800-343-0273 or 617-451-6808).

Many travel agencies, particularly the larger ones, are delighted to make presentations to help a group select destinations. A local chamber of commerce should be able to provide the names of such agencies. Once a time and place are determined, an organization member or travel agent can obtain group quotations for transportation, accommodations, meal plans, and sightseeing. Groups of 40 or more usually get the best breaks.

Another choice open to older travelers is a trip that includes an educational element. *Elderhostel* is a network of schools, colleges, and universities that sponsors weeklong study programs for people over 60 years of age on campuses worldwide, including Canada. An informational videotape describing *Elderhostel*'s programs is available for $5. Accommodations are in residence halls, and meals are taken in student cafeterias. Travel to the programs usually is by designated scheduled flights, and participants can arrange to extend their stay at the end of the program. Elderhostelers must be at least 60 years old (younger if a spouse or companion qualifies), in good health, and not in need of special diets. For information, contact *Elderhostel,* 80 Boylston St., Suite 400, Boston, MA 02116 (phone: 617-426-7788 or 617-426-8056).

Hints for Traveling with Children

 What better way to be receptive to the experiences you will encounter than to take along the young, wide-eyed members of your family? Their company does not have to be a burden or their presence an excessive expense. The current generation of discounts for children and family package deals can make a trip together quite reasonable.

A family trip will be an investment in your children's future, making geography and history come alive to them and leaving a sure memory that will be among the fondest you will share with them someday. Their insights will be refreshing to you; their impulses may take you to unexpected places with unexpected dividends. The experience will be invaluable to them at any age.

PLANNING: It is necessary to take some extra time beforehand to prepare children for travel. Here are several hints for making a trip with them easy and fun.

1. Children, like everyone else, will derive more pleasure from a trip if they know something about the country before they arrive. Begin their education about a month before you leave. Using maps, travel magazines, and books, give children a clear idea of where you are going and how far away it is. Part of the excitement of the journey will be associating the tiny dots on the map with the very real places they soon will visit. You can show them pictures of streets and scenes in which they will stand. Don't shirk history lessons, but don't burden them with dates. Make history light, anecdotal, pertinent, but most of all, fun. If you simply make materials available and keep your destination and your plans a topic of everyday conversation, your children will absorb more than you realize.

2. Children should help to plan the itinerary, and where you go and what you do should reflect some of their ideas. If they already know something about the sites they'll visit, they'll have the excitement of recognition when they arrive and the illumination of seeing how something is or is not the way they expected it to be.

3. If you are traveling in parts of Canada where French is spoken, it is helpful to learn

the language with your children — a few basics like *bonjour* ("good morning"), *au revoir* ("good-bye"), and *merci bien* ("thanks a lot"). You need no other motive than a perfectly selfish one: Thus armed, your children will delight the Canadians and help break the ice wherever you go.

4. Familiarize the children with Canadian dollars (see *Credit and Currency*). Give them an allowance for the trip and be sure they understand just how far it will or won't go.

5. Give children specific responsibilities: The job of carrying their own flight bags and looking after their personal things, along with some other light chores, will give them a stake in the journey. Tell them how they can be helpful when you are checking in or out of hotels.

6. Give each child a diary or scrapbook to take along. Filling these with impressions, observations, and mementos will pass the time on trains and planes and help them assimilate their experiences.

If you will be spending much time in Quebec and want to familiarize your children with French words and phrases, one useful resource to which you may want to refer is the *Berlitz Jr.* instructional series, which includes a French edition. The series combines an illustrated storybook with a lively 60-minute audiocassette. Each book features a character, Teddy, who goes to school and learns to count and spell and speak French phrases. The book/cassette package is available from the Aladdin Books division of Macmillan Publishing for $19.95, plus shipping and handling. To order, contact Aladdin Books, Front and Brown Sts., Riverside, NJ 08075 (phone: 800-257-5755 or 212-702-9039).

PACKING: Choose your children's clothes much as you would your own. Select a basic color (perhaps different for each child) and coordinate everything with it. Plan their wardrobes with layering in mind — shirts and sweaters that can be taken off and put back on as the temperature varies. Take only drip-dry, wrinkle-resistant items that they can manage themselves and comfortable shoes — sneakers and sandals. Younger children will need more changes, but keep it to a minimum. No one likes to carry added luggage (remember that *you* will have to manage most of it!)

Take as many handy snacks as you can squeeze into the corners of your suitcases — things like dried fruit and nut mixes, hard candies, peanut butter, and crackers — and moist towelettes for cleaning. Don't worry if your supply of nibbles is quickly depleted. Airports and bus and train stations are well stocked with such items.

Pack a special medical kit, including children's aspirin or acetaminophen, an antihistamine or decongestant, Dramamine, and diarrhea medication. Do not feel you must pack a vacation's worth of Pampers. Diapers are available at drugstores and supermarkets. A selection of baby foods also is available in most supermarkets, but in case you cannot find the instant formula to which your child is accustomed, bring along a supply in the 8-ounce "ready-to-feed" cans. Disposable nursers are expensive but handy. If you breast-feed your baby, there is no reason you can't enjoy your trip; just be sure you get enough rest and liquids.

Good toys to take for infants are the same sorts of things they like at home — well-made, bright huggables and chewables; for small children, a favorite doll or stuffed animal for comfort, spelling and counting games, and tying, braiding, and lacing activities; for older children, playing cards, travel board games with magnetic pieces, and hand-held electronic games. Softcover books and art materials (crayons, markers, paper, scissors, glue sticks, and stickers) ward off boredom for children of most ages, as do radio-cassette players with headphones. Take along a variety of musical and storytelling cassettes, extra batteries, and maybe even an extra set of headphones so two children can listen. *Advice:* Avoid toys that are noisy, breakable, or spillable, those that require a large play area, and those that have lots of little pieces that can be scattered and lost. When traveling, coordinate activities with attention spans; dole out playthings one at a time so you don't run out of diversions before you get where you're going. Children become restless during long waiting periods, and a game plus a small snack — such as a box of raisins or crackers — will help keep them quiet. It is also a good idea to carry tissues, Band-Aids, a pocket medicine kit (described above), and moistened washcloths.

GETTING THERE AND GETTING AROUND: Begin early to investigate all available discount and charter flights, as well as any package deals and special rates offered by the major airlines. Booking sometimes is required up to 2 months in advance. You may find that charter plans offer no reductions for children, or not enough to offset the risk of last-minute delays or other inconveniences to which charters are subject. The major scheduled airlines, on the other hand, almost invariably provide hefty discounts for children (for specific information on fares and in-flight accommodations for children, also see *Traveling by Plane,* in this section).

PLANE: When you make your reservations, tell the airline that you are traveling with a child. As a general rule, children under 2 travel free in a plane if they sit on an adult's lap — although on some carriers you will have to pay 10% of the adult fare. But it's much safer — and certainly more comfortable — to purchase an adjacent seat for a baby and bring an infant restraint which is then strapped into the airline seat with a regular seat belt. (The airlines do not provide infant seats, so you will have to bring your own. If you do not purchase a seat for your baby and bring the infant restraint along on the off chance that there may be an empty seat next to yours, if an additional seat is not available, you will have to pay to check it as baggage.) There is no special fare for an infant, although discounts for children sometimes are in effect, and you can inquire about this when making a reservation — between the ages of 2 and 12, children generally travel at 75% of the adult fare — if the adult is traveling on a full economy. (There may be no discount for children if the accompany adult is traveling on a discounted ticket.)

If using one of these infant restraints, you should try to get bulkhead seats which will provide extra room to care for your child during the flight. You also should request a bulkhead seat when using a bassinet (some airlines do provide bassinets) — again, this is not as safe as strapping a child in. On some planes, bassinets may hook into a bulkhead wall; on others it is placed on the floor in front of you. Even if you do use a bassinet, babies must be held during takeoff and landing. Request seats on the aisle if you have a toddler or if you think you will need to use the bathroom frequently. (Try to discourage children from being in the aisle when meals are served.)

Carry onto the plane all you will need to care for and occupy your children during the flight — formula, diapers, a sweater, books, favorite stuffed animals, and so on. (Never check as baggage any item essential to a child's well-being, such as prescription medicine.) Dress your baby simply, with a minimum of buttons and snaps, because the only place you may have to change a diaper is at your seat. The flight attendant can warm a bottle for you.

Just as you would request a vegetarian or kosher meal, you are entitled to ask for a hot dog or hamburger instead of the airline's regular dinner if you give at least 24 hours' notice. Some, but not all, airlines have baby food aboard. While you should bring along toys from home, you also can ask about children's diversions. Some carriers have terrific free packages of games, coloring books, and puzzles.

When the plane takes off and lands, make sure your baby is nursing or has a bottle, pacifier, or thumb in its mouth. This sucking will make the child swallow and help to clear stopped ears. A piece of hard candy will do the same thing for an older child.

Avoid night flights. Since you probably won't sleep nearly as well as your kids, you risk an impossible first day at your destination, groggily taking care of your rested, energetic children. Nap time is, however, a good time to travel, especially for babies, and try to travel during off-hours, when there are apt to be extra seats. If you do have to take a long night flight, keep in mind that when you disembark, you probably will be tired and not really ready for sightseeing. The best thing to do is to head for your hotel, shower, have a snack, and take a nap. If your children are too excited to sleep, give them some toys to play with while you rest.

■**Note:** Newborn babies, whose lungs may not be able to adjust to the altitude, should not be taken aboard an airplane. And some airlines may refuse to allow a pregnant woman in her 8th or 9th month aboard, for fear that something could go wrong with an in-flight birth. Check with the airline well ahead of departure and carry a letter from your doctor stating that you are fit to travel — and indicating the estimated date of birth.

CAR: Traveling by car, you can be flexible — making any number of stops at roadside shops or in small towns, and meeting moods and emergencies as they arise. You also can take more with you, including items like ice chests and charcoal grills for picnics. Keep your car supplied with dried fruits, crackers, candy bars, bottled water, and facial tissue and/or toilet paper. Games and simple toys, such as magnetic checkerboards or drawing pencils and pads also can provide a welcome diversion. Frequent stops for children to run around make car travel much easier. Along most major highways, there are well-spaced rest areas where you can pull over and have a meal. If a break is in order between these facilities, the next best alternative is to get off at a local exit and follow the signs to a nearby park or town.

TRAIN: *VIA Rail,* Canada's train network, offers special arrangements for children and families. Children under 2 (accompanied by an adult) are allowed to travel free anytime; a second child under 2 travels at half-fare (half the full adult fare). Children 2 to 11 travel at half-fare at all times.

Amtrak, which connects major US East Coast cities with Montreal and Toronto, also offers discounts for families. Children under 2 (accompanied by an adult) are allowed to travel free at any time; children 2 to 12 who accompany an adult traveling on an excursion fare are charged half the adult fare. All long-distance trains with dining car service offer children's dishes.

BUS: Major Canadian bus companies offer special discounts for children. For example, children 5 to 11 traveling on *Gray Coach, Greyhound Lines of Canada,* or *Voyageur* coach lines travel at half-fare, although on some *Greyhound* routes they must be accompanied by an adult. Children under 5 who sit on an adult's lap travel free. Particularly on long trips, if traveling with small children be sure your bus has a bathroom.

FAMILY TRIPS: An alternative to long car trips are holidays specifically planned for the family that are based on some adventure or activity exciting for all. A few examples are the following:

Ice skating on the largest indoor or outdoor rinks in the world — on Ottawa's *Rideau Canal Skating Rink* (open October through March), 14 million square feet of ice, 5.3 miles, accommodating some 50,000 skaters at once; or in *Columbian Four Rinks,* the year-round facilities in Burnaby, Vancouver, with 68,000 square feet of enclosed ice.

Skiing in the Quebec Laurentians. All the major ski areas have ski schools that offer lessons for all ages. (See *Downhill Skiing,* DIVERSIONS.)

Any one of Canada's many vibrant summer festivals, ranging from the *Shediac Lobster Festival* in New Brunswick (featuring lobster-eating contests and stage shows), to the *Calgary Stampede,* in which the city celebrates its Old West bronco-busting heritage. (See *Festivals, Fairs, and Fancy Acts,* DIVERSIONS.)

Theme parks are rapidly expanding family vacation places. They offer entertainment, rides, and games for the whole family. Good examples are *Canada's Wonderland,* about

20 miles (32 km) northwest of Toronto, and *Storyland,* outside Renfrew, Ontario, where over 150 storybook characters come to life to tell their own stories.

These are just a few of the literally hundreds of Canadian vacation possibilities for families. For other ideas, see DIVERSIONS and the individual city reports in THE CITIES.

One book of ideas, with the names and addresses of the companies that feature such adventures, is *Adventure Travel North America* by Pat Dickerman (Holt). It's currently out of print, but check your local library. Also see *What to Do with the Kids This Year: One Hundred Family Vacation Places with Time Off for You!* by Jane Wilford and Janet Tice (Globe Pequot Press; $8.95).

Eeyore's Books For Children (2212 Broadway, New York, NY 10024; phone 212-362-0634; and 25 E. 83rd St., New York, NY 10028; phone 212-988-3404) also features a number of publications ideal for children and parents. Among the books offered are *Super Family Vacations* (Harper & Row; $12.95) and *How to Take Great Trips with Your Kids* (Harvard Common Press; $8.95).

And, for parents, *Travel With Your Children* publishes a newsletter, *Family Travel Times,* that focuses on the young traveler and offers helpful hints. Membership is $35 a year. For a sample copy of the newsletter, send $1 to *Travel With Your Children,* 80 Eighth Ave., New York, NY 10011 (phone: 212-206-0688).

Travel With Your Children also publishes two helpful guides, *Cruising With Children* ($20, plus $1.65 tax for New York residents) and *Skiing With Children* ($29, plus $2.06 tax for New York residents). Contact the company at the address above.

Libraries, museums, and various organizations like the *YMCA* in major cities have special programs for children; these run the gamut from movies and puppet shows to storytelling hours in city parks. Listings of these events, many of which are free, usually can be found in the Friday and Sunday editions of local newspapers or at the city's tourism bureau or information center. Local or provincial festivals, fairs, rodeos, parades, and other special events capture children's imaginations. For a list of these events, write to the city or provincial tourist bureau where you plan to visit; also, see *Festivals, Fairs, and Fancy Acts* in DIVERSIONS. And ask about discounts; children often get discounts on everything from movies to monuments.

ACCOMMODATIONS AND MEALS: Often a cot for a child will be placed in a hotel room at little or no extra charge. If you wish to sleep in separate rooms, special rates sometimes are available for families; some places do not charge for children under a certain age. In many of the larger chain hotels, the staffs are more used to noisy or slightly misbehaving children. These hotels also are likely to have swimming pools or gamerooms — both popular with most young travelers. Write to the hotel in advance to discuss how old your children are, how long you plan to stay, and to ask for suggestions on sleeping arrangements.

As is happening in the US, Canadian colleges and universities are opening campuses to travelers during traditional academic vacations and summers. These facilities generally are very modestly priced, an advantage for families on the road. Some offer accommodations only (usually in dormitory rooms); others open recreational facilities and sports centers to visitors. (See listings in *Hints for Single Travelers,* in this section.)

Guest farms and dude ranches are popular Canadian destinations; lists of them can be obtained from Canadian tourist offices in US cities or Canadian provinces. In the eastern provinces, guest farms generally are under 200 acres and specialize in dairy or mixed farming; in Alberta and Manitoba there are working ranches where visitors are a sideline; also out west are the dude or guest ranches, where guests contribute substantially to the property's income. (For more information see *Farm and Ranch Vacations,* DIVERSIONS.)

■ **A final word of advice:** If you are spending your vacation traveling, rather than visiting one spot or engaging in one activity, pace the days with children in mind; break the trip into half-day segments, with running around or "doing" time built in; keep travel time on the road to a maximum of 4 or 5 hours a day. First and foremost, don't forget that a child's attention span is far shorter than an adult's. Children don't have to see every museum or all of any museum to learn something from their trip; watching, playing with, and talking to other children can be equally enlightening experiences. Also, remember the places that children the world over love to visit: zoos, country fairs, amusement parks, beaches, and nature trails. Let your children lead the way sometimes — their perspective is different than yours, and they may lead you to things you never would have noticed on your own.

Hints for Traveling with Pets

 You may wish to bring your pet along on your vacation. Although all animals are subject to inspection by the Animal Health inspectors at the border, there are no substantial obstacles in traveling with your pet throughout Canada. Your pet should be fully vaccinated, however, and you will have to bring along the paperwork described below.

DOGS AND CATS: Dogs and cats from the US may be brought into Canada if the owner has a certificate, signed by a licensed veterinarian of Canada or the US, that clearly identifies the animal and certifies that it has been vaccinated against rabies during the preceding 36 months. Puppies or kittens under 3 months old may be imported into Canada without certification or further restriction.

Pet dogs and cats entering Newfoundland by car or bus must be certified with the paperwork above. If a dog or cat is entering Newfoundland by plane, an entry permit also is required. Entry permits should be obtained in advance from: Provincial Veterinary Service, Government of Newfoundland, PO Box 7400, St. John's West, Newfoundland A1E 3Y5, Canada (phone: 709-576-6886).

BIRDS AND OTHER ANIMALS: Other pets from the US, including monkeys, fish, and reptiles, are allowed to enter without restriction. Turtles and tortoises require a Canadian import permit before admission. Up to two pet birds (of the parrot family and songbirds) per family may be imported provided: 1) the owner accompanies the birds to Canada; 2) the owner makes a declaration on arrival in Canada that certifies that, for the 90 days preceding the date of entry, the birds have not been in contact with any other birds and have been in the visitor's personal possession for this period. Send requests for permits to the Chief of Imports, Animal Health Division, Food Production and Inspection Branch, Agriculture Canada, Ottawa, Ontario K1A 0Y9 Canada (phone: 613-995-5433).

The American Society for the Prevention of Cruelty to Animals (ASPCA) offers a very useful book, *Traveling With Your Pet,* which includes innoculation requirement by country and territory. It is available for $5 (which includes postage and handling). Send check or money order to the *ASPCA,* Education Dept., 441 E. 92nd St., New York, NY 10128 (phone: 212-876-7700).

BY PLANE AND CAR: Many US airlines require a health certificate for your pet. *United,* for example, requires a US Interstate Health Certificate, signed by an accredited veterinarian and dated no more than 30 days before travel. Canadian airlines do not require a certificate, but travelers should follow the procedures listed above to pass the customs inspection upon arrival. As do many US carriers, both *Air Canada* and *Canadian Airlines International* require a leak-proof kennel for a dog or cat. Policies and restrictions vary among other carriers — so check with the airline well before your departure.

It's a good idea to buy a traveling kennel if your dog is being transported by plane or car. Most airlines sell them, as do pet stores. Any animal must be boxed for the plane trip; in a car, a kennel is a good safety measure. The most important features of a kennel are size, comfort, and cleanliness. Your kennel should be large enough to permit room for your pet to turn around and lie down; it should be constructed completely of non-chewable materials — metal or high-grade plastic. Chewable materials such as cardboard or fiberboard can be toxic. The kennel should have a sanitized pad on the bottom with a wire mesh floor that is raised at least an inch above the pad. The box should lock, be thoroughly ventilated, and be easy to handle and transport.

If your pet is traveling by plane, label the kennel with your name, address, destination, pet's name, and special handling instructions. Remove the animal's collar before putting it in the kennel. Dogs should not be muzzled. Put a few toys and familiar objects in the kennel to acquaint the animal with its box before the start of the trip.

Airlines usually will allow one kenneled pet to fly in the passenger compartment for a standard fee, if the kennel fits underneath the seat. This space should be reserved when you reserve your own seat. If there is no space in the passenger compartment, or the animal is too large to be brought in, it must fly as cargo, in a special area reserved for live cargo. Charges are established on the basis of the weight and size of the animal and the kennel.

Don't ship your pet during very hot or very cold weather; animals are sometimes left on the runway during the loading and unloading of the hold. Afternoon and evening flights are best in hot weather. Fly at off-peak times, when the cargo hold has less baggage and more ventilation and the personnel have more time to watch your pet. Pets should be the last cargo loaded, and the boxed pet should be given to the cargo officer, not to the ticket-counter person, who will place the kennel on a conveyor belt. Avoid flights with stopovers and transfers lest your pet be misplaced.

When you land, retrieve your pet as soon as possible. Return it to its normal feeding schedule slowly.

If you decide to drive with an animal, be aware that animals can suffer motion sickness. You can ascertain if your pet is susceptible by taking it for short trips before you undertake the real journey. Here are a few tips to make your trip with your pet as much fun as possible:

1. Bring along a kennel or sleeping box for a dog or cat.
2. Make plenty of exercise and feeding stops. *You* may want to set a new record for the distance — your pet does not.
3. Take along some of your pet's toys or most adored objects.
4. Don't let your dog ride with its head out of the window. Cinders, dirt, and rocks can injure its eyes and head, and the wind can irritate its nasal and respiratory passages. Keep the windows almost closed, allowing enough ventilation for comfort.
5. If you have to leave your pet alone in the car, park in the shade and leave the windows down an inch or two for air. But don't leave the car unlocked. Canadians like dogs, too.

But it is best to leave your pet at home. That way you won't miss the thrill of finding out how glad it is to see you when you get back.

Staying Healthy

The surest way to return home in good health is to be prepared for medical problems that might occur on vacation. Below we've outlined everything you need to think about before you go.

Obviously, your state of health is crucial to the success of a vacation.

There's nothing like an injury or illness, whether serious or relatively minor, to dampen or destroy a holiday. And health problems always seem more debilitating when you are away. Most problems, however, can be prevented or greatly alleviated with intelligent foresight and attention to precautionary details.

Older travelers or anyone suffering from a chronic medical condition, such as diabetes, high blood pressure, cardiopulmonary disease, asthma, or ear, eye, or sinus trouble, should consult a physician before leaving home. A checkup is advisable. A pre-trip dental checkup is not a bad idea, either.

People with conditions requiring special consideration when traveling should consider seeing, in addition to their regular physician, a specialist in travel medicine. For a referral in a particular community, contact the nearest medical school or ask a local doctor to recommend such a specialist. The *American Society of Tropical Medicine and Hygiene* publishes a directory of more than 70 travel doctors across the country. Send a 9-by-12-inch self-addressed, stamped envelope ($1.05 postage) to Dr. Leonard Marcus, Tufts University, 200 W. Boro Rd., North Grafton, MA 01536.

FIRST AID: Put together a compact, personal medical kit including Band-Aids, first-aid cream, antiseptic, nose drops, insect repellent, aspirin, an extra pair of prescription glasses or contact lenses (and a copy of your prescription for glasses or lenses); sunglasses; over-the-counter remedies for diarrhea, indigestion, and motion sickness, a thermometer, and a supply of those prescription medicines you take regularly. In a corner of your kit, keep a list of all the drugs you have brought and their purpose, as well as duplicate copies of your doctor's prescriptions (or a note from your doctor). These copies could come in handy if you are ever questioned by police or airport authorities about any drugs you are carrying, and also will be necessary to refill any prescriptions in the event of loss. Considering the essential contents of this kit, keep it with you, rather than in your luggage.

SUNBURN: Depending on when and where you're traveling, the burning power of the sun can be phenomenal and quickly can cause severe sunburn or sunstroke. To protect yourself against these ills, wear sunglasses, take along a broad-brimmed hat and cover-up, and use a sunscreen lotion. When choosing a sunscreen, look for one that has a PABA (para-amino-benzoic acid) base. PABA blocks out most of the harmful ultraviolet rays of the sun.

Some tips on tanning:

1. Allow only 20 minutes or so the first day; increase your exposure gradually.
2. You are most likely to get a painful burn when the sun is the strongest, between 10 AM and 2 PM.
3. When judging if you've had enough sun, remember that time in the water (in terms of exposure to ultraviolet rays) is the same as time lying on the beach.
4. A beach umbrella or other cover doesn't keep all the rays of the sun from reaching you. If you are sensitive to light, be especially careful.
5. As many ultraviolet rays reach you on cloudy days as on sunny days. Even if you don't feel hot, you still are exposed to rays. And remember the sun is particularly strong when reflected off snowy slopes.

If, despite these precautions, you find yourself with a painful sunburn, take a cooling bath, apply a first-aid spray, and stay out of the sun. If you develop a more serious burn and experience chills, dizziness, fever, headaches, or nausea, consult a doctor at once.

WATER SAFETY: Canada, particularly in the Maritime Provinces, boasts some beautiful beaches, but it's important to remember that they also can be treacherous. A few precautions are necessary. Beware of the undertow, that current of water running back down the beach after a wave has washed ashore; it can knock you off your feet and into the surf. Even more dangerous is the riptide, a strong current of water running against the tide, which can pull you out toward sea. If this happens, don't panic or try to fight the current, because it will only exhaust you; instead, ride it out while waiting for it to subside, which usually happens not too far from shore, or try swimming away parallel to the beach.

INSECTS AND OTHER PESTS: Blackflies, horse flies, mosquitoes, and other biting insects can be troublesome. We recommend using some form of repellent against bug bites, especially for campers. Vitamin B-1 or thiamine tablets may alter your body chemistry to help repel mosquitoes — which can be a terrific nuisance in some areas. If you are at all susceptible to mosquito bites, you will be amazed at how quickly the vitamins work — although they do not work for everyone. Discuss this strategy with your doctor before trying it. It still *always* is a good idea to use some form of topical insect repellent. As many of the stronger, effective insect repellents have a pungent odor, you may want to try a relatively new alternative, Skin-So-Soft hand lotion, made by *Avon.* This orderless skin softener actually has been approved by the FDA as an effective insect repellent. Burning mosquito coils containing pyrethrin or citronella candles is another effective precaution.

If you do get bitten — by mosquitoes or other bugs — the itching can be relieved with baking soda or antihistamine tablets. Should a bite become infected, treat it with a disinfectant or antibiotic cream. *Note:* Antihistamines should not be combined with alcohol or cortisone cream, or taken when driving.

If you are bitten and the area becomes painful or swollen and you develop flu-type symptoms, you may have been bitten by a tick carrying what is known as Lyme Borreliosis disease (or "Lyme Tick Disease") in the US. Many Americans believe that this disease is unique to the US, however, it was first diagnosed in Europe and has made its way to many countries, including Canada. Caution should be taken in all wooded areas.

Though rarer than insect bites, bites from poisonous centipedes, venomous snakes, spiders, or sea creatures can be serious. If possible, always try to catch the villain for identification purposes. In most cases, particularly if spasms, numbness, convulsions, or hemorrhaging occurs, consult a doctor at once. The best course of action may be to head directly to the nearest emergency ward or outpatient clinic of a hospital. Cockroaches, termites, and waterbugs thrive in warm weather, but pose no serious health threat.

WATER: The tap water in Canada generally is quite pure. However, when traveling in rural areas, be aware that the local water supply may not be purified and local residents either have developed immunities to the natural bacteria or boil the water for drinking. You also should avoid drinking water from streams or freshwater pools. In campgrounds, water usually is indicated as drinkable or for washing only — if you're not sure, ask.

Following all these precautions will not guarantee an illness-free trip, but it should minimize the risk. As a final hedge against economic if not physical problems, make sure your health insurance will cover all eventualities while you are away. If not, there are policies designed specifically for travel. Many are worth investigating. As with all insurance, they seem like a waste of money until you need them. For further information, also see *Insurance* and *Medical and Legal Help on the Road,* both in this section.

HELPFUL PUBLICATIONS: Practically every phase of health care — before, during, and after a trip — is covered in *The New Traveler's Health Guide* by Drs. Patrick J. Doyle and James E. Banta. It is available for $4.95, plus $2 postage and handling, from Acropolis Books Ltd., 80 S. Early, Alexandria, VA 22304 (phone: 800-451-7771 or 703-709-0006).

The *Traveling Healthy Newsletter,* which is published six times a year, also is brimming with healthful travel tips. For a subscription, which costs $24, contact Dr. Karl Neumann, MD, 108-48 70th Rd., Forest Hills, NY 11375, (phone: 718-268-7290).

For more information regarding preventive health care for travelers, contact the

International Association for Medical Assistance to Travelers (IMAT; at 417 Center St., Lewiston, NY 14092; phone: 716-754-4883), or write to the US Government Printing Office (Washington, DC 20402) and ask for the US Public Health Service's booklet *Health Information for International Travel* (HEW Publication CDC-86-8280; enclose a check or money order for $4.75 payable to the Superintendent of Documents).

On the Road

Credit and Currency

 FOREIGN EXCHANGE: It may seem hard to believe, but one of the greatest (and least understood) costs of travel is money itself. If that sounds simplistic, consider the fact that you can lose as much as 30% of your dollars' value simply by changing money at the wrong place or in the wrong form. So your one single objective in relation to the care and retention of your travel funds is to make them stretch as far as possible. When you do spend money, it should be on things that expand and enhance your travel experience, with no buying power lost due to carelessness or lack of knowledge. This requires more than merely ferreting out the best airfare or the most charming budget hotel. It means being canny about the management of money itself. Herewith, a primer on making money go as far as possible in Canada.

CURRENCY: Travelers from the US should have little difficulty with matters of exchange in Canada. Both countries have money systems based on 100 cents to the dollar, although the US dollar and the Canadian dollar are not equal in value. The value of Canadian currency in relation to the US dollar fluctuates daily, affected by a wide variety of phenomena. As we went to press, the Canadian dollar was worth around US.85¢, or US$1 was worth CN$1.15 — providing Americans in Canada with a bonus of 15% in buying power.

Although US dollars usually are accepted in Canada, you certainly will lose a percentage of your dollar's buying power if you do not take the time to convert it into the local legal tender. By paying for goods and services in local currency, you save money by not negotiating invariably unfavorable exchange rates for every small purchase, and avoid difficulty where US currency is not readily — or happily — accepted. *Throughout this book, unless specifically stated otherwise, prices are given in US dollars.*

FOREIGN EXCHANGE: Although the relative value of US and Canadian dollars generally has been stable during the past few years, because of the frequent volatility of exchange rates, be sure to check the current exchange rate before finalizing any travel budget. And before you actually depart on your trip, be aware of the most advantageous exchange rates offered by various financial institutions — US banks, currency exchange firms (at home and in Canada), or foreign banks. Almost invariably, the best exchange rate offered for US dollars will be found in Canadian banks.

For the best sense of current trends, follow the rates posted in the financial section of your local newspaper or in such international newspapers as the *International Herald Tribune.* It also is possible to check with your own bank. *Harold Reuter and Company,* a currency exchange service in New York City (200 Park Ave., Suite 332 E., New York, NY 10166; phone: 212-661-0826) also is particularly helpful in determining current trends in exchange rates, or check with *Deak International Ltd.* (for the nearest location, call 800-972-2192 in Illinois; 800-621-0666 elsewhere in the US). *Ruesch International* also offers up-to-date foreign currency information and currency-related services (such as converting foreign currency VAT refund checks into US dollars; see *Shopping,* in this section). *Ruesch* also offers a pocket-size *Foreign Currency Guide* (good for estimating general equivalents while planning) and a helpful brochure, *6 Foreign Exchange Tips for the Traveler*. Contact *Ruesch International* at one of the following addresses: 3 First National Plaza, Suite 2020, Chicago, IL 60602 (phone: 312-332-5900); 1925 Century Park E., Suite 240, Los Angeles, CA 90067 (phone: 213-277-7800); 608 Fifth Ave., "Swiss Center," New York, NY 10020 (phone: 212-977-2700); or 1350 Eye St. NW, 10th Floor and street level, Washington, DC 20005 (phone: 800-424-2923 or 202-408-1200).

In Canada, you will find the official rate of exchange posted in banks, airports, money exchange houses, and some hotels. The difference between the exchange rates offered in banks and in hotels varies from country to country — although generally you will get more local currency for your US dollar at banks than at any other commercial establishment. The convenience of exchanging money in your hotel (sometimes on a 24-hour basis) *may* make up for some of the difference in the exchange rate. Don't try to bargain in banks or hotels — no one will alter the rates for you.

Money exchange houses are financial institutions that charge a fee for the service of exchanging dollars into local currency. When considering alternatives, be aware that although the rate again varies among these establishments, the rates of exchange offered are bound to be slightly less favorable than the terms offered at nearby banks — again, don't be surprised if you get less Canadian currency for your US dollar than the rate published in the papers.

Money and all types of negotiable instruments, in any amount, may be brought into or taken out of the US. Citizens of any country importing or exporting $10,000 or more between Canada and the US are required to file a report of the transaction with US Customs (US Customs Form 4790; available at US Customs counters). If you have any questions about this regulation, contact the US Customs Service in your city, or at 1301 Constitution Ave. NW, Washington, DC 20229 (phone: 202-566-8005).

That said, however, the following rules of thumb are worth remembering.

Rule number one is as simple as it is inflexible: Never (repeat: *never*) willingly exchange dollars for foreign currency at hotels, restaurants, or retail shops, where you are sure to lose a significant amount of your dollars' buying power. If you do come across a storefront exchange counter offering what appears to be an incredible bargain, there's just too much counterfeit specie in circulation to take the chance (see Rule Number Three, below).

Rule number two: Estimate your needs carefully; if you overbuy, you lose twice — buying and selling back. Every time you exchange money, someone is making a profit, and rest assured, it isn't you. Use up foreign notes before leaving, saving just enough for last-minute incidentals, and tips.

Rule number three: Learn the local currency quickly and keep abreast of daily fluctuations in the exchange rate. These are listed in the *International Herald Tribune* daily for the preceding day, as well as in every major newspaper in Canada. Banks post their daily exchange rates, which might vary by only a few cents — or even tenths of a cent — from bank to bank. Rates change to some degree every day. For rough calculations, it is quick and safe to use round figures, but for purchases and actual currency exchanges, carry a small pocket calculator that helps you compute the exact rate. Inexpensive calculators specifically designed to quickly convert currency amounts for travelers are widely available.

When changing money, don't be afraid to ask how much commission you're being charged, and the exact amount of the prevailing exchange rate. In fact, in any exchange of money for goods or services, you should work out the rate before making any payment.

TIP PACKS: It's not a bad idea to buy a *small* amount in Canadian coins and banknotes before your departure. But note the emphasis on "small," because, for the most part, you are better off carrying the bulk of your travel funds to Canada in US dollar traveler's checks (see below). Still, the advantages of tip packs are threefold: You become familiar with the currency (really the only way to guard against making mistakes or being cheated during your first few hours in a new country); you are guaranteed some money should you arrive when a bank or exchange counter isn't open or available; and you don't have to depend on hotel desks, porters, or taxi drivers to change your money. A "tip pack" is the only foreign currency you should buy before you leave.

If you do run short upon arrival, US dollars are accepted throughout most of Canada and at most establishments. Where US dollars are not accepted someone may accommodate you by changing a small amount — though invariably at a less than advantageous rate.

TRAVELER'S CHECKS: It's wise to carry traveler's checks on the road instead of (or in addition to) cash, since it's possible to replace traveler's checks if they are stolen or lost; travelers usually can receive partial or full replacement funds the same day if they have their purchase receipt and proper identification. Issued in various denominations and available in both US and Canadian dollars, with adequate proof of identification (credit cards, driver's license, passport) traveler's checks are as good as cash in most hotels, restaurants, stores, and banks.

You will be able to cash traveler's checks fairly easily in Canada, but don't expect to meander into a small town and be able to get instant cash. Also, even in metropolitan areas, don't assume that restaurants, small shops, and other establishments are going to be able to change checks of large denominations. Worldwide, more and more establishments are beginning to restrict the amount of traveler's checks they will accept or cash, so it is wise to purchase at least some of your checks in small denominations — say, $10 and $20 or the current equivalent in Canadian dollars. Also, don't expect to change them into US currency except at banks and international airports.

When deciding whether to buy your travel funds in US or Canadian denomination traveler's checks, keep in mind that the exchange rates offered by the issuing companies in the US generally are far less favorable than those available from banks both in the US and abroad. Therefore, it usually is better to carry the bulk of your travel funds abroad in US dollar denomination traveler's checks.

Every type of traveler's check is legal tender in banks around the world and each company guarantees full replacement if checks are lost or stolen. After that the similarity ends. Some charge a fee for purchase, others are free; you can buy traveler's checks at almost any bank, and some are available by mail. Most important, each traveler's check issuer differs slightly in its refund policy — the amount refunded immediately, the accessibility of refund locations, the availability of a 24-hour refund service, and the time it will take for you to receive replacement checks. For instance, American Express offers a 3-hour replacement of lost or stolen traveler's checks at any American Express office — other companies may not be as prompt. (Note that American Express's 3-hour policy is based on the traveler's being able to provide the serial numbers of the lost checks — without these numbers, refunds can take up to 3 business days.)

We cannot overemphasize the importance of knowing how to replace lost or stolen checks. All of the traveler's check companies have agents around the world, both in their own name and at associated agencies (usually, but not necessarily, banks), where refunds can be obtained during business hours. Most of them also have 24-hour toll-free telephone lines, and some will even provide emergency funds to tide you over on a Sunday.

Be sure to make a photocopy of the refund instructions that will be given to you by the issuing institution at the time of purchase. To avoid complications should you need to redeem lost checks (and to speed up the replacement process), keep the purchase receipt and an accurate list, by serial number, of the checks that have been spent or cashed. You may want to incorporate this information in an "emergency packet," also including your passport number and date of issue, the numbers of the credit cards you are carrying, and any other bits of information you can't bear to be without. Always keep these records separate from the checks and original records themselves (you may want to give them to a traveling companion to hold).

Although most people understand the desirability of carrying travel funds in the form of traveler's checks as protection against loss or theft, an equally good reason is that US dollar traveler's checks invariably get a better rate of exchange than cash — usually by at least 1% (although the discrepancy has been known to be substantially higher). The reasons are technical, but it is a fact of travel life that should not be ignored.

That 1% won't do you much good, however, if you already have spent it buying your traveler's checks. Several of the major traveler's check companies charge 1% for the privilege of using their checks; others don't, but the issuing institution (i.e., the particular bank at which you purchase them) may itself charge a fee. Thomas Cook checks issued in US currency are free if you make your travel arrangements through its travel agency, for example; and if you purchase traveler's checks at a bank in which you or your company maintains significant accounts (especially commercial accounts of some size), you also might find that the bank will absorb the 1% fee as a courtesy. American Express traveler's checks are available without charge to members of the *Automobile Association of America (AAA)* at some *AAA* offices in the US (the policy varies from state to state).

American Express, Citicorp, Thomas Cook, MasterCard, and Visa all offer traveler's checks, but not at all locations. Call the service numbers listed below to find a participating branch near you. Here is a list of the major companies issuing traveler's checks that are accepted widely in Canada and the numbers to call in case loss or theft makes replacement necessary:

> *American Express:* To report lost or stolen checks in the US and Canada, call 800-221-7282.
>
> *Bank of America:* To report lost or stolen checks in the US, call 800-227-3460; in Canada, call collect, 24 hours, 415-624-5400.
>
> *Citicorp:* To report lost or stolen checks in the US, call 800-645-6556; in Canada, call 813-623-1709, collect.
>
> *MasterCard:* To report lost or stolen checks in the US, call 800-223-9920; in Canada, call 212-974-5696, collect.
>
> *Thomas Cook MasterCard:* To report lost or stolen checks in the US, call 800-223-7373; in Canada, call 609-987-7300, collect.
>
> *Visa:* To report lost or stolen checks in the continental US and Canada, call 800-227-6811.

CREDIT CARDS: There are two different kinds of credit cards available to consumers in the United States, and travelers must decide which kind best serves their needs — although many travelers elect to carry both types. "Convenience" or "charge" or "travel and entertainment" cards — American Express, Diners Club, and Carte Blanche — are widely accepted. They cost the cardholder a basic annual membership fee ($40 to $65 is typical for these three), but put no strict limit on the amount that may be charged on the card in any month. However, the entire amount charged must be paid in full at the end of each billing period (usually a month), so the cardholder is not actually extended any long-term credit.

"Bank cards" also are rarely issued free these days (with the exception of Sears Discover Card), and certain services they provide (check cashing, for example) can carry an extra charge. But this category comprises *real* credit cards, in the sense that the cardholder has the privilege of paying a small amount (1/36 is typical) of the total outstanding balance in each billing period. For the privilege, the cardholder is charged a high annual interest rate (currently three to four times the going bank passbook savings rate) on the balance owed. Many banks now charge interest from the purchase date, not from the first billing date (as they used to do); consider this when you are calculating the actual cost of a purchase. In addition, a maximum is set on the total amount the cardholder can charge, which represents the limit of credit the card company is willing to extend. The major bank cards are Visa and MasterCard, with Discover growing rapidly.

Unless you have established a firm credit history, getting any credit card will involve a fairly extensive credit check. To pass, you will need a job (at which you have worked for at least a year), a certain minimum salary, and a good credit rating.

Note that some establishments you may encounter during the course of your travels may not honor any credit cards and some may not honor all cards, so there is a practical reason to carry more than one. Most US credit cards, including the principal bank cards, are honored in Canada. The following is a list of credit cards that enjoy wide domestic and international acceptance:

American Express: Emergency personal check cashing at American Express or representatives' offices (up to $500 in cash for all cardholders; traveler's check limits depend on the type of card: up to $500 for Green cardholders; up to $1,000 for Optima cardholders; up to $4,500 for Gold cardholders; and up to $9,500 for Platinum cardholders); emergency personal check cashing for guests at participating hotels in the US and Canada (up to $100), and, for holders of airline tickets, at participating airlines in the US (up to $50). Extended payment plan for cruises, tours, railway and airline tickets, as well as other prepaid travel arrangements. $100,000 to $500,000 travel accident insurance (depending on the type of card) if ticket was charged to card; up to $1 million additional low-cost flight insurance available. Contact *American Express,* PO Box 39, Church St. Station, New York, NY 10008 (phone: 212-477-5700 in New York; 800-528-4800 elsewhere in the US; 800-268-9805 in Ontario; 800-361-4343 in Quebec; 416-474-9380, collect, in the Yukon and Northwest Territories; 800-387-9700 elsewhere in Canada.).

Carte Blanche: Extended payment plan for air travel (from $2,000 to $5,000, depending on credit line). $150,000 free travel accident insurance on plane, train, and ship if ticket was charged to card, plus $1,250 checked or carry-on baggage insurance, and $25,000 rental car insurance. Medical, legal, and travel assistance available worldwide (phone: 800-356-3448 in the US; 214-680-6480, collect, in Canada). Contact *Carte Blanche,* PO Box 17326, Denver, CO 80217 (phone: 800-525-9135 in the US; 303-790-2433 in Canada — cardholders may call collect).

Diners Club: Emergency personal check cashing for guests at participating hotels and motels (up to $250 per stay). Qualified card members are eligible for extended payment plan. $350,000 free travel accident insurance on plane, train, and ship if ticket was charged to your card, plus $1,250 checked and carry-on baggage insurance and $25,000 rental car insurance. Medical, legal, and travel assistance available worldwide (phone: 800-356-3448 in the US; 214-680-6480, collect, from Canada). Contact *Diners Club,* PO Box 17326, Denver, CO 80217 (phone: 800-525-9135 throughout the US for customer service; for lost or stolen cards, call one of the following 24-hour service numbers: 800-525-9341 in the US; 303-790-2433, collect, from Canada).

Discover Card: Created by Sears, Roebuck and Co., it provides the holder with cash advances at more than 500 locations in the US, and offers a revolving credit line for purchases at a wide range of service establishments. Other deposit, lending, and investment services also are available. For information, call 800-

858-5588 in the US (if you can't reach this number by dialing directly, dial an operator, who will be able to place the call).

MasterCard: Cash advances are available at participating banks worldwide, and a revolving credit line can be set up for purchases at a wide range of service establishments. Interest charges on unpaid balance and other details are set by each individual issuing bank. Check with your bank for information. Master-Card also offers a 24-hour emergency lost card service; call 800-336-8472 in the US; 314-275-6690, collect, from Canada.

Visa: Cash advances are available at participating banks worldwide, and a revolving credit line can be set up for purchases at a wide range of service establishments provided by issuer. Interest charges on unpaid balance and other details are set by issuing bank. Check with your bank for information. Visa also offers a 24-hour emergency lost card service; call 800-336-8472 in the US; 415-574-7700, collect, from abroad.

In addition to the credit card services discussed above, a number of other benefits and/or details are set by the issuing institutions. For instance, some credit cards now offer the added incentive of "bonus" programs. Each time the card is used, the cardholder may gather either points with a monetary equivalent, which can be applied toward the total cost of selected purchases or travel arrangements, or a credit with a specific travel supplier, such as frequent flyer mileage bonuses with an airline. When deciding on whether one of these cards provides the best deal, you should compare the potential value of these and other special programs with the variations in interest rates charged on unpaid balances and annual membership fees.

One of the thorniest problems relating to the use of credit cards abroad concerns the rate of exchange at which a purchase is charged. Be aware that the exchange rate in effect on the date that you make a foreign purchase or pay for a foreign service has nothing at all to do with the rate of exchange at which your purchase is billed to you when you get the invoice (sometimes months later) in the US. The amount American Express (and other convenience cards) charges is ultimately a function of the exchange rate in effect on the day your charge is received at an American Express service center, and there is a 1-year limit on the time a shop or hotel can take to forward its charge slips. The rate at which Visa and other bank cards process an item is a function of the rate at which the hotel's or shop's bank processed it.

The principle at work in this credit card–exchange rate roulette is simple, but very hard to predict. You make a purchase at a particular dollar versus local currency exchange rate. If the US dollar gets stronger in the time between purchase and billing, your purchase actually costs you less than you anticipated. If the dollar drops in value during the interim, you pay more than you thought you would. There isn't much you can do about these vagaries except to follow one very broad, very clumsy rule of thumb: If the US dollar is doing well at the time of purchase, its value increasing against the Canadian dollar, use your credit card on the assumption it still will be doing well when billing takes place. If the US dollar is doing badly, assume it will continue to do badly and pay with traveler's checks or cash. If you get too badly stuck, the best recourse is to complain, loudly. Be aware, too, that most credit card companies charge an unannounced, un-itemized 1% fee for converting foreign currency charges to US dollars.

No matter what you are using — traveler's checks, credit cards, or cash — plan ahead. That way you won't live through the nightmare of arriving in a small Canadian village on a Friday afternoon without any local currency. If you do get caught in this situation, you may have to settle for a poor exchange rate at a hotel or a restaurant. In this case, exchange just enough dollars to get you through the weekend.

Also, carry your travel funds carefully. You might consider carrying them (cash and traveler's checks) in more than one place. Never put money in a back pocket or an open purse. Money should be kept in a buttoned front pocket, in a money purse pinned inside your shirt or blouse, or in one of the convenient money belts or leg pouches sold by many travel shops. It may be quaint and old-fashioned, but it's safe.

SENDING MONEY ABROAD: If you have used up your traveler's checks, cashed as many emergency personal checks as your credit card allows, drawn on your cash advance line to the fullest extent, and still need money, have it sent abroad via the *Western Union Telegraph Company.* A friend or relative can go, cash in hand, to any of *Western Union*'s 9,000 offices in the US, where, for a *minimum* charge of $12 (it rises with the amount of the transaction) plus a $9 to $22 transfer fee, the funds will be transferred to *Western Union*'s correspondent bank or the main post office branch in the nearest major city of the province you're visiting. When the money arrives in Canada, you will not be notified — you must go to the nearest *Western Union* office (there are over 100 Canadian branches) to inquire. The transfer may take as little as 15 minutes. The funds will be turned over in Canadian currency, based on the rate of exchange in effect on the day of receipt. For a higher fee, the US party to this transaction may use his or her MasterCard or Visa card to send up to $2,000 by phone by dialing *Western Union*'s toll-free number (800-325-4176) anywhere in the US.

American Express offers a similar service in Canada called "Moneygram," completing money transfers in as little as 10 minutes. The sender — who must be an American Express cardholder — must go to an American Express office in the US and can use cash, a personal check, money order, or an American Express Optima, Gold, or Platinum card for the transfer. Optima cardholders also can arrange for this transfer over the phone. The minimum transfer charge is $10, which rises with the amount of the transaction; the sender can forward funds of up to $10,000 (credit card users are limited to the amount of pre-established credit line). To collect at the other end, the receiver must go to an American Express office in Canada (there are over 3,000) and present proof of identification (any official picture ID). For further information on this service, call 800-543-4080.

If you are literally down to your last cent, the nearest US consulate (see *Medical and Legal Aid and Consular Services,* in this section) will let you call home to set these matters in motion.

Accommodations

 As everywhere else in the world, tourism to Canada has increased, with a concomitant explosion in the Canadian motel and hotel industry. In Vancouver, planners were spurred into action by *EXPO '86* and Calgary responded to hosting the *1988 Winter Olympics* in much the same way that Montreal reacted to *Expo '67* and the *1976 Summer Olympics.* Reverberations of the recent international boom also have been felt everywhere in Canada, as virtually every major hotel chain built new hostelries across the country. In this respect, the accommodations situation in Canada is not so different from that in the US. Though there are many independently owned places to stay in varying price ranges — including some fine old hotels and lovely country inns (you will find our pick of them listed in THE CITIES, DIVERSIONS, and DIRECTIONS) — the majority of the hotels in Canada are relatively new establishments that are part of national or international chains, and they are to a great extent standardized in price and quality.

There is at least one benefit to this standardization: The overall level of accommodations is quite high. The traveler in Canada, arriving in an unfamiliar area, can assume that there will be safe, clean, and comfortable accommodations nearby in an acceptable price range. Admittedly there are numerous deluxe establishments providing expensive services to people with money to burn, but fortunately, affordable alternatives always have been available, particularly in the countryside. On the whole, however, deluxe and first class accommodations in Canada are somewhat less expensive than the same types of accommodations in the US (see *Calculating Costs,* in this section).

HOTELS: Hotels may be large or small, part of a chain or independent, new and of the "international standard" type or well established and traditional. There are built-for-the-purposes premises and converted stately homes, resort hotels offering plenty of opportunities for recreation, and smaller tourist hotels offering virtually none.

Each of the provincial tourist offices publishes a comprehensive accommodations booklet that gives a complete rundown on all licensed establishments in its territory. Listings include prices, amenities, and, sometimes, nearby attractions. Some provinces, such as Manitoba, Quebec, and Ontario, go a step further and use a star system to rate the standards of comfort found at each hotel; Quebec also rates restaurants in the various establishments.

You can choose for yourself just what price range is acceptable. Some chains — like the *Four Seasons, Hilton International,* and *Westin* — offer accommodations with a broad range of facilities and amenities. The hotels are modern and comfortable, the service is competent, and the facilities complete; and the prices, as you would expect, are relatively high — anywhere from $150 to $200 and up for a double room in major metropolitan or resort areas. More and more, the trend in such top-ranking Canadian hotels is toward year-round convenience: They are built in conjunction with business-residential-shopping complexes, clustered together within short, weatherproof walking distance. Also on the expensive side are Canada's big resort hotels, with extensive first class sports facilities, amenities, and locations — the *Banff Springs* hotel in Alberta and the *Gray Rocks Inn* in Quebec, for example.

As in the US, hotels in the more moderate price category — which may or may not be members of chains — also are located throughout Canada. These establishments generally do not offer the extensive business services provided by the top-ranking hotels but do provide adequate and comfortable accommodations. Often the older hostelries in this category are particularly charming and welcome travelers with a strong dose of Canadian warmth and hospitality.

A great many hotels in Canada are members of chains or hotel associations. Among the well-known, internationl names with properties throughout Canada, particularly in major cities, are the following:

> *Best Western:* Has over 75 properties throughout Canada. Call 800-528-1234.
>
> *Four Seasons:* Has 5 properties in Canada: 2 in Toronto (Ontario), and 1 each in Vancouver (British Columbia), Ottawa (Ontario), and Montreal (Quebec). Call 800-332-3442.
>
> *Hilton International:* Owned by the Ladbroke's gambling group of Great Britain, there is no proprietary connection with the US *Hilton* chain. Has 9 Canadian properties: 1 in Edmonton (Alberta), 1 each in Halifax and Windsor (Nova Scotia), 1 in St. John (New Brunswick), 2 in Toronto (Ontario), 2 in Montreal and 1 Quebec City (Quebec). Call 800-445-8667.
>
> *Holiday Inn:* Has 45 properties throughout Canada. Call 800-465-4329.
>
> *Inter-Continental:* Has 2 Canadian properties: 1 in Toronto (Ontario) and 1 in Montreal (Quebec). Call 800-327-0200.
>
> *Marriott:* Has 1 Canadian property in Toronto (Ontario). Call 800-228-9290.
>
> *Trusthouse Forte:* Also has 1 property in Toronto. Call 800-225-5843.
>
> *Westin:* Has 5 Canadian properties: 1 each in Edmonton (Alberta), Vancouver (British Columbia), Winnipeg (Manitoba), and Ottawa and Toronto (Ontario). Call 800-228-3000.

Note that while Canadian hotels do not observe well-defined high and low seasons as far as room rates are concerned, visitors can expect to pay a premium for travel during the peak summer months at warm weather destinations and at popular ski resorts during the winter and to encounter more advantageous terms during the off-season in these areas. Special offers — such as a discount for stays of 3 nights or longer (particularly over weekends, when business travelers traditionally go home) — also are more common during the off-season, though they may be found at any time of year.

BUDGET ACCOMMODATIONS: The budget hotel is designed to offer basic accommodations (a comfortable bed, clean bathroom, central heating and air conditioning) without frills or ancillary services, bar or restaurant, or elaborate lobby. Among the budget chains with properties in Canada are the following:

Bugdet Host Inns: Has 5 Canadia properties in Alberta, British Columbia, and Ontario. Call 817-626-7064.

Chimo and *Welcome Inn:* These affiliated chains have 6 Canadian properties: 1 in Quebec and 5 in Ontario. Call 800-387-9779.

Days Inn: Has 8 Canadian properties in Ontario. Call 800-325-2525.

Econo-Lodge: Has 2 Canadian properties in Ontario. Call 800-446-6900.

Journey's End: This Canadian chain has over 100 properties across the country. Call 800-668-4200 in the US and Canada.

Relax Inns: This Canadian chain has 26 properties across the country. Call 800-661-9563 throughout Canada.

Many other pleasant, clean, and inexpensive independents — motels and guest-houses — can be found throughout the country. At hotels and motels in all price ranges, ask about minimum rates, weekend discounts, weekly rates, commercial discounts for business travelers, special promotions, and special rates for children staying in the same room as their parents.

During the summer, major universities and colleges throughout Canada put up travelers in their dormitories for modest prices. There's no one guide that lists all the accommodations offered, but provincial tourist offices should be able to tell you what's available in campus housing. (See *Tourist Information Offices* in this section.) Hostels are another inexpensive choice. The *Canadian Hostelling Association* (1600 James Naismith Dr., 6th Fl., Gloucester, Ottawa, Ontario K1B 5N4; phone: 613-748-5638) publishes a free handbook listing Canadian hostels. For additional information on campus housing and hostels, see *Hints for Single Travelers* in this section.

BED AND BREAKFAST ESTABLISHMENTS AND OTHER ACCOMMODATIONS: Bed and breakfast establishments are a relatively new phenomena in North America; however, travelers who have become devotees of this type of accommodation through trips to Europe will be happy to hear that, as in the US, in Canada bed and breakfasts properties are increasingly common, and not only in rural areas. Bed and breakfast establishments are becoming a staple of the lower-cost lodging scene, and are cropping up wherever there are extra rooms to let in a private home and a host or hostess willing to attend to the details of this homespun form of hospitality.

Bed and breakfast establishments (commonly known as B&Bs) provide exactly what the name implies. Though any hotel or guesthouse does the same, it is unusual for a bed and breakfast establishment to offer the extra services found in other hostelries, and consequently the bed and breakfast route often is the least expensive way to go.

Beyond these two fundamentals, nothing else is predictable about going the bed and breakfast route. The bed may be in an extra room in a family home, in an apartment with a separate entrance, or in a free-standing cottage elsewhere on the host's property. A private bath isn't always offered; so check before you reserve. You may have a patio, garden, or pool at your door, or only the bare necessities. The breakfast generally is a version of the continental breakfast: fruit plus juice, toast or roll or homemade bread and jam, and coffee or tea, although, particularly in rural areas, the breakfast may be a hearty one, and, as often as not, served along with some helpful hints on what to see and do and a bit of family history to add to the local lore. If you're in a studio with a kitchenette, you may be furnished with the makings of a breakfast you'll have to prepare for yourself.

Some hosts enjoy helping guests with tips on what to see and do and even serve as informal tour guides, while in other places your privacy won't be disturbed. Whichever the case, the beauty of bed and breakfast establishments is that you'll always have a warm reception and the opportunity to meet many more inhabitants of the region than you otherwise would, which means that you'll experience their hospitality in a special fashion.

Bed and breakfast accommodations range from private homes and lovely mansions to small inns and guesthouses. Prices average from $15 to $35 per person per night, breakfast included — with establishments offering luxurious surroundings running somewhat higher. Despite their name, some bed and breakfast establishments offer an evening meal as well — by prior arrangement and at extra cost.

Although most Canadian hosts may be contacted directly, others prefer that arrangements be made through a reservations organization. The general procedure for making reservations through bed and breakfast services is that you contact them with your requirements, they help find the right place, and confirm your reservations upon receipt of a deposit. Any further information needed will be provided by either the service or by the owner of the bed and breakfast establishment.

In Canada, there can be a fine line between "bed and breakfast establishment" and "boarding house," so find out as much as you can before you book to avoid disappointment. The big-city version of this type of accommodation are guesthouses, common in Montreal. These usually are well-maintained brownstones that rent rooms on a daily or weekly basis. Both bed and breakfast establishments and guesthouses are listed in local newspapers. Other sources of information include the local Chamber of Commerce and provincial or local tourist information offices.

The Canadian Bed & Breakfast Guide by Gerda Pantel is a well-organized and comprehensive guide to a wide range of bed and breakfast establishments throughout Canada — from an old sea captain's cabin to mountain chalets and prairie ranches. Organized by province, it provides detailed information on the accommodations and breakfast served, as well as nearby recreations and attractions. Available in bookstores, it also can be ordered from Independent Publishers Group (814 N. Franklin St., Chicago, IL 60610; phone: 800-888-4741) for $12.95, plus $3 for shipping and handling. Another useful directory, *The Complete Guide to Bed & Breakfast, Inns, and Guesthouses in the U.S. and Canada* by Pamela Lanier, covers over 5,000 bed and breakfast establishments (over 300 in Canada), as well as over 250 bed and breakfast reservations services; available for $14.95 from John Muir Publications (Box 613, Santa Fe, NM 87505; phone: 505-982-4078).

Another source of information on bed and breakfast establishments is the *Bed & Breakfast Reservations Services Worldwide* (a trade association), which provides a list of its members for $3. To order the most recent edition, contact them at PO Box 39000, Washington, DC 20016 (phone: 800-842-1486).

For the true bed and breakfast aficionados, there is even a monthly magazine, *Country Inns: Bed & Breakfast.* Issued bimonthly, every issue includes feature articles on special bed and breakfast and similar inn-type establishments throughout Canada sure to tempt many a visitor, as well as advertisements placed by organizations and individual properties. To subscribe, send $15 to *The Inn Traveler's Magazine,* PO Box 182, S. Orange, NJ 07079 (phone: 201-762-7090).

Finally, you may want to subscribe to *Gracious Stays & Special Places,* a publication focusing on guesthouses and bed and breakfast establishments set in historic and architecturally significant buildings. Published by a nonprofit organization, *Person to Person Travel Productions, Inc.* (2856 Hundred Oaks, Baton Rouge, LA 70808; phone:

504-346-1928), the annual membership fee, which starts at $20, includes four issues of the newsletter.

Farmhouses – In the country, city people rediscover the sounds of songbirds and the smell of grass. Suburbanites get the chance to poke around an area where the nearest neighbor lives miles away. Parents can say to their children, "No, milk does not originate in a cardboard carton," and prove it. Youngsters can meet people who live differently, think differently, and have different values. But even if there were no lessons to be learned, a stay at a farm would be a decidedly pleasant way to pass a couple of weeks, so it's no wonder that all over Canada there are numerous farms welcoming guests.

Farm families in Canada often put up guests on a bed and breakfast basis — for a night or two or by the week, with weekly half-board plans often available. Travelers can pick a traditional or a modern farm, a dairy farm over a sheep farm, one with ponies to ride, or one near a river or coastline for fishing. If the peace and quiet and the coziness of the welcome are appealing, a farmhouse can be an ideal base from which to explore a region by car or by foot and an especially good idea for those traveling with children.

Farm, seashore, or ranch vacations, offer excellent vacation value in a comfortable Canadian home environment. Provincial and city tourist authorities have lists of participating farms (see also *Farm and Ranch Vacations*, DIVERSIONS). Or contact *Canadian Country Vacations Association* (525 Kylemore Ave., Winnipeg, Manitoba R3L 1B5, Canada; phone: 204-475-6624), which offers "Meet the People" tours, including a variety of locally hosted vacations in Manitoba and eastern Canada.

Apartments, Homes, and Cottages – Another alternative to hotels for the visitor content to stay in one spot for a week or more is to rent a house or an apartment. A vacation in a furnished rental has both the advantages and disadvantages of living "at home" abroad. It certainly is less expensive than staying in a first class hotel for the same period of time (although very luxurious and expensive rentals are available, too). It has the comforts of home, including a kitchen, which means saving on food costs. Furthermore, it gives a sense of the country being visited that a large hotel often cannot. On the other hand, a certain amount of housework is involved because if you don't eat out, you have to cook, and though some holiday rentals (especially the luxury ones) include a cleaning person, most don't. (If the rental doesn't include daily cleaning, arrangements often can be made with a nearby service.)

Many tour operators regularly include a few rental packages among their more conventional offerings; these generally are available through a travel agent. In addition, certain companies in the US specialize in rentals of apartments, houses, cottages, and other properties. They handle the booking and confirmation paperwork, generally for a fee included in the rental price, and can be expected to provide more information about the properties they handle than that which might ordinarily be gleaned from a listing in an accommodations guide. Among such agencies that represent properties in Canada are the following:

Coast to Coast Resorts, 860 Solar Bldg., 1000 16th St. NW, Washington, DC 20036 (phone: 800-368-5721 or 202-293-8000). Rents cabins and trailerhomes in resort areas of Alberta, British Columbia, and Ontario.

Hideaways International, PO Box 1270, Littleton, MA 01460 (phone: 800-843-4433 or 508-486-8955). Rents apartments, cottages, and houses in Nova Scotia, Prince Edward Island, and Quebec.

International Lodging Corp., 89-27 182nd Pl., Hollis, NY 11423 (phone: 718-291-1342). Although this company generally does not list Canadian properties, rentals can be arranged in Canada upon request.

Rent a Vacation Everwhere (RAVE), 328 Main St. E., Suite 526, Rochester, NY

14604 (phone: 716-454-6440). Rents apartments and cottages on Prince Edward Island and most major cities throughout Canada.

HOME EXCHANGES: Still another alternative for travelers who are content to stay in one place is a home exchange: The Smith family from Atlanta moves into the home of the Coutran family in Quebec, while the Coutran family enjoys a stay in the Smiths' home. The home exchange is an exceptionally inexpensive way to ensure comfortable, reasonable living quarters with amenities that no hotel possibly could offer; often the trade includes a car. Moreover, it allows you to live in a new community in a way that few tourists ever do: For a little while, at least, you will become something of a local resident.

Several companies publish directories of individuals and families willing to trade homes with others for a specific period of time. In some cases, you must be willing to list your own home in the directory; in others, you can subscribe without appearing in it. Most listings are for straight exchanges only, but each of the directories also has a number of listings placed by people interested in either exchanging or renting (for instance, if they own a second home). Other types of arrangements include exchanges of hospitality while owners are in residence, or youth exchanges, where your teenager is put up as a guest in return for your putting up their teenager at a later date. A few house-sitting opportunities also are available. In most cases, arrangements for the actual exchange take place directly between you and the foreign host. There is no guarantee that you will find a listing in the area you are interested in, but each of the organizations given below includes Canadian homes among its hundreds or even thousands of foreign listings.

International Home Exchange Service/Intervac US: The $35 fee includes copies of the three directories published yearly and an option to list your home in one of them; a black-and-white photo may be included with the listing for an additional $8.50. A 10% discount is given to travelers over 65. Box 190070, San Francisco, CA 94119 (call collect: 415-435-3497).

InterService Home Exchange, Inc.: An affiliate of *Intervac International,* this service publishes three directories annually which include more than 7,000 exchanges in over 300 countries worldwide. For $35, interested home-swappers are listed in and receive a copy of the February, March, and May directories; a black-and-white photo of your home may be included with the listing for an additional $10. Box 387, Glen Echo, MD 20812 (phone: 301-229-7567).

Loan-A-Home: Specializes in long-term (4 months or more — excluding July and August) housing arrangements worldwide for students and professors, business-people, and retirees, although its two annual directories (with supplements) carry a small list of short-term rentals and/or exchanges. $35 for a copy of one directory and one supplement; $45 for a copy of two directories and two supplements. 2 Park La., Apt. 6E, Mt. Vernon, NY 10552 (phone: 914-664-7640).

Vacation Exchange Club: Some 6,000 listings, about half of which are foreign. For $24.70 a year, the subscriber receives two directories — one in late winter and one in the spring — and is listed in one. For $16, subscribers receive both directories but no listing. 12006 111th Ave., Suite 12, Youngtown, AZ 85363 (phone: 602-972-2186).

World Wide Exchange: The $45 annual membership fee includes one listing (for house, yacht, or motorhome) and three guides. 1344 Pacific Ave., Suite 103, Santa Cruz, CA 95060 (phone: 408-476-4206).

Home Exchange International, with offices in New York, Los Angeles, London, Paris, and Milan, functions differently in that it publishes no directory and shepherds the exchange process most of the way. Interested parties supply *HEI* with photographs of themselves and their homes, information on the type of home they want and where, and a registration fee of $50. The company then works with its other offices to propose a few possibilities, and only when a match is made do the parties exchange names, addresses, and phone numbers. For this service, *HEI* charges a closing fee, which ranges from $150 to $450 for domestic or international switches from 2 weeks to 3 months in duration, and from $275 to $525 for switches longer than 3 months. Contact *Home Exchange International,* 185 Park Row, PO Box 878, New York, NY 10038-0272 (phone: 212-349-5340), or 22458 Ventura Blvd., Woodland Hills, CA 91364 (phone: 818-992-8990).

HOME STAYS: If the idea of actually staying in a private home as the guest of a foreign family appeals to you, check with the United States Servas Committee, which maintains a list of hosts throughout the world willing to throw open their doors to foreigners, entirely free of charge. The aim of this nonprofit cultural program is to promote international understanding and peace, and every effort is made to discourage freeloaders. Servas will send you an application form and the name of the nearest of some 200 interviewers around the US for you to contact. After the interview, if you're approved, you'll receive documentation certifying you as a Servas traveler. There is a membership fee of $45 for an individual and there also is a deposit of $15 to receive the host list, refunded on its return. The list gives the name, address, age, occupation, and other particulars of the hosts, including languages spoken. From then on, it is up to you to write to them directly, and Servas makes no guarantee that you will be accommodated. If you are, you'll normally stay 2 nights.

Servas stresses that you should choose only people you really want to meet and that for this brief period you should be interested mainly in your hosts, not in sightseeing. It also suggests that one way to show your appreciation once you've returned home is to become a host yourself. The minimum age of a Servas traveler is 18 (however, children under 18 may accompany their parents), and though quite a few are young people who've just finished college, there are travelers (and hosts) in all age ranges and occupations. Contact Servas at 11 John St., Room 706, New York, NY 10038 (phone: 212-267-0252).

You also might be interested in a publication called *International Meet-the-People Directory,* published by the *International Visitor Information Service.* It lists several agencies in a number of foreign countries (37 worldwide, including Canada) that arrange home visits for Americans, either for dinner or overnight stays. To order a copy, send $4.95 to the *International Visitor Information Service* (733 15th St. NW, Suite 300, Washington, DC 20005; phone: 202-783-6540). For other local organizations and services offering home exchanges, contact the local tourist authority.

RESERVATIONS: To the extent that you are able to settle on a precise itinerary beforehand, it is best to make advance reservations for accommodations in any major Canadian city, even if you are traveling during the off-season. To be sure of finding space in the hotel of your choice, booking several months before arrival is not too soon. Hotel rooms in the larger provincial cities also should be reserved ahead year-round. Because some of them also are important meeting centers, even off-season travelers may find hotel space scarce and "full" signs everywhere if a large convention is being hosted. Also keep in mind that larger hotels are the ones most frequently booked as 2- and 3-day stopover centers for tour groups ranging the country, and major cities may be busiest during off- or shoulder season months due to the simultaneous presence of business and convention travelers and tourists.

During the peak season in any area, visitors should expect to pay a premium for traveling in Canada. However, not even a willingness to pay for top accommodations will guarantee a room if you don't have reservations. It is wise to make reservations as far in advance as possible for popular tourist destinations throughout Canada, as well as for hotel, farm, and other accommodations near major summer destinations such as Banff and the Maritime Provinces, where the number of rooms and limited facilities, not the price, is likely to be the qualifying factor.

The simplest way to make a reservation is to leave it all to a travel agent, who will provide this service at no charge if the hotel or guesthouse in question pays agents a commission. The larger and more expensive establishments invariably do, and more and more budget hotels are beginning to follow suit. If the one selected doesn't, the travel agent may charge a fee to cover costs or you may have to make the reservation yourself.

Reserving a room yourself is not difficult if you intend to stay mainly in hotels that are members of chains or associations, whether Canadian ones with US representatives or US chains with hotels in Canada. Most international hotel chains list their toll-free (800) reservation numbers in the white pages of the telephone directory, and any hotel in a chain can secure reservations for you at sister facilities. Naturally, the more links in the chain, the more likely that an entire stay can be booked with a minimum number of letters or phone calls to one central reservations system. If booking with primarily Canadian establishments, either a travel agent or the particular provincial tourist office should be able to tell you who in the US represents the chain or a particular hotel. (The US phone numbers of some of these chains and associations in Canada are given in the discussion of hotels above.)

Hotels that are not represented in the US will have to be contacted directly. All the hotel entries in the *Best in Town* sections of THE CITIES chapters include phone numbers for reservations; where they exist, phone numbers also are included in the *Best en Route* sections of DIRECTIONS. If you choose to write rather than telephone, it's a good idea to enclose at least two International Reply Coupons (sold at post offices and banks) to facilitate a response, and leave *plenty* of time for the answer. Give full details of your requirements and several alternate dates, if possible. You probably will be asked to send a deposit for at least 1 night's lodging, payable by check or credit card; in return, be sure to get written confirmation of your reservation and a receipt for any deposit.

Nevertheless, if the hotel you want to visit has no rooms available on your chosen dates, take heart. The advice to make reservations early always is woven into every travel article; making a *late* reservation may be almost as good advice. It's not at all unusual for hotel rooms, totally unavailable as far as 6 months ahead, suddenly to become available a week to a day before your desired arrival. Cancellations tend to occur closer to, rather than farther from, a designated date. One possible strategy is to make reservations at another hotel so you won't be left high and dry, determine the cancellation penalties, if any, and check back with your first choice closer to your date of arrival. It also is true that hotels that report SRO status to travel agents may remarkably discover a room if you call directly (FAX is even better) close to your proposed arrival date.

There also is reason to believe that hotels increasingly are offering one rate to travelers working through travel agents and less expensive rates to clients who book directly. Even if you do use a travel agent, it sounds like a prudent course to double-check hotel rates if saving money is one of your prime travel concerns.

■**Note:** Though not all travelers would face the prospect of arriving in a strange city without a reservation with equal sangfroid, in Canada there are services that help book empty rooms for those who risk it. Generally, information on these services is available at the airport information desk or from the local tourist board office. One such service is *Accommodations Toronto,* which can book rooms at over 100 hotels in the Toronto (Ontario) area, free of charge; for information or reservations, call 416-369-9200.

OVERBOOKING: Although the problem is not unique to Canada, the worldwide travel boom has brought with it some abuses that are pretty much standard operating procedure in any industry facing a demand that frequently outstrips supply. Anticipating a certain percentage of no-shows, hotels routinely overbook rooms. When cancellations don't occur and everybody with a confirmed reservation arrives as promised, it's not impossible to find yourself with a valid reservation for which no room exists.

There's no sure way to avoid all the pitfalls of overbooking, but you can minimize the risks. Always carry evidence of your confirmed reservation. This should be a direct communication from the hotel — to you or your travel agent — and should specify the exact dates and duration of yur accommodations and the price. The weakest form of confirmation is the voucher slip a travel agent routinely issues, since it carries no official indication that the hotel itself has verified your reservation.

Even better is the increasing opportunity to guarantee hotel reservations by giving the hotel (or its reservation system) your credit card number and agreeing that the hotel is authorized to charge you for that room no matter what. It's still possible to cancel if you do so before 6 PM of the day of your reservations (before 4 PM in some areas), but when you do cancel under this arrangement, make sure you get a cancellation number to protect you from being billed erroneously.

If all these precautions fail and you are left standing at the reservation desk with a reservation the hotel clerk won't honor, you have a last resort: Complain as long and as loudly as necessary to get satisfaction! The person who makes the most noise usually gets the last room in the house. It might as well be you.

What if you can't get reservations in the first place? This is a problem that often confronts businesspeople who can't plan months ahead. The word from savvy travelers is that a bit of currency (perhaps attached discreetly to a business card) often increases your chances with recalcitrant desk clerks. There are less venal ways of improving your odds, however. If you are traveling on business, ask an associate at your destination to make reservations for you.

There is a good reason to do this above and beyond the very real point that a resident has the broadest knowledge of local hotels. Often a hotel will appear sold out on its computer when in fact a few rooms are available. The proliferation of computerized reservations has made it unwise for a hotel to indicate that it suddenly has five rooms available (from cancellations) when there might be 30 or 40 travel agents lined up in the computer waiting for them. That small a number of vacancies is much more likely to be held by the hotel for its own sale, so a local associate is an invaluable conduit to these otherwise inaccessible rooms. Another efficient alternative is communication with the hotel via a FAX machine, which can prove useful in arranging and confirming reservations.

Dining Out

In the past 15 years, Canadian cities have been experiencing something of a restaurant boom. Part of this is due to the larger change of medium-size cities becoming conscious of their distinctive qualities as urban communities. Another factor that affects these areas, as well as the large cities is the recent establishment of training programs for cooks, chefs, and restaurateurs in colleges across the country. Although most of these programs are less than 15 years old, they already are having an impact on the dining-out scene.

The change is reflected in a proliferation of restaurants that serve everything from traditional French food with rich sauces to nouvelle cuisine, in which the emphasis is on basic ingredients, carefully and creatively prepared. It also is evident in the international reputation Canadian chefs have earned in recent years, starting in 1983 when Canadian chefs took five first places in the six international culinary competitions they entered, and continuing the next year at the *World Culinary Olympics,* where *Team Canada* won a total of 15 gold medals (including one Grand Gold and the title of World Champion of the Nations). In November 1987, the Canadian team picked up seven gold medals at an international culinary competition in Basel, Switzerland. So now travelers have even greater reason to discover the regional specialties reponsible for Canada's gastronomic success.

The four Atlantic provinces — Newfoundland, Prince Edward Island, New Brunswick, and Nova Scotia — specialize in fresh seafood. Lobsters turn up everywhere from traditional country inn lobster suppers to summer beach parties and in various shapes and forms — boiled, broiled, steamed, in casseroles, and in salads. Atlantic salmon and oyster stews are New Brunswick's main dishes, served with baked beans and steamed brown bread. Prince Edward Island's juicy Malpeque oysters are very popular, and large sea scallops, clam chowder, and herring dishes are specialties of Nova Scotia. In Newfoundland cod is king, but the Great Banks also brings salmon, trout, halibut, and hake to the table, served fresh, dried, salted, or in a thick fish stew — due to Newfoundland's often bone-chilling climate, even in summer meals tend to be hot and hearty. Throughout the provinces, the abundant native fruits and berries find their way into rich desserts — apple, bakeapple (a kind of bog berry), blueberry, cranberry, blackberry, and strawberry pies, puddings, jams, and jellies.

Farther inland lies the traditional gastronomic capital of Canada, Montreal. Like all of Quebec, Montreal is renowned for its French dishes; in Montreal it's done with a special panache. Restaurants here run the gamut from classic haute cuisine served in austere settings to the provincial French fare of Brittany and Normandy. French Canadians have developed a distinct cuisine similar to the food of Normandy, where many French Canadians originated. Typical dishes include thick pea or cabbage soups; for the main course, meat pies filled with pork (known as *tourtière*) or *cipâte,* a beef pie, and for dessert, fruit pies stuffed with a triple layer of blueberries. Another Quebec specialty served after meals is *trempette,* home-baked bread soaked in maple syrup and topped with whipped cream.

Also special in Montreal is Brome Lake duckling, prepared with a specimen from the famous duck-raising area of Quebec near the Vermont border. The duckling is filled with apple stuffing and cooked in calvados (apple brandy). It's a highly touted delicacy, available in any number of Montreal's rustic French Canadian restaurants. Montreal also has a good selection of ethnic restaurants — Chinese, Vietnamese, Italian, Spanish, and Greek. Quebec City's restaurants are dominated by provincial French kitchens, the pervasive style of cooking in its elegant restaurants, as well as in the city's many bistros and crêperies.

Toronto is Canada's third East Coast food center. There is a strong French influence here, as well as a substantial number of ethnic restaurants which reflect the cosmopolitan atmosphere of the city. In addition to Greek, Chinese, and Italian restaurants, you can sample various Eastern European specialties in the Hungarian, Czechoslovakian, and Polish shops and restaurants of *Kensington Market.*

Across the prairies and cattle country of Manitoba, Saskatchewan, and Alberta, restaurants serve hearty fare. Thick, tender steaks and freshly baked breads made with Canada's high-quality grains are a mainstay. The myriad lakes yield freshwater fish such as whitefish and pickerel. Menus are enriched by the heritage of the Ukrainian immigrants who populate the prairie cities; stuffed cabbage, potato dumplings, spicy sausage, and borscht are routinely served.

West Coast cuisine is dominated by the sea; the Pacific provides a bounty of seafood — king crab, oysters, shrimp, cod, haddock, and salmon — usually served up with produce grown in British Columbia. Apples, peaches, plums, pears, Bing cherries, and a variety of berries (if they're in season, try cloudberries) grow here and appear on the table — fresh and unadorned, in fancy desserts, and sometimes as locally produced fruit cordials or wines. Vancouver and Victoria are the best food cities on the West Coast and offer an innovative selection of regional specialties and international cuisine.

A good countrywide guide to Canadian restaurants is *Where to Eat in Canada,* by Anne Hardy (Oberon Press, Ottawa; $11.95). Though it leaves a little to be desired in the way of organization, it does provide useful descriptions and informed opinions on the places it covers and is updated annually.

RESERVATIONS: Restaurants vary widely on reservation policies. At some, it is absolutely required (especially at more expensive and popular places in larger cities); other equally fine restaurants refuse to take reservations at all — the patron simply arrives and waits until a table is free. If you are planning a big night out, it certainly is advisable to call the restaurant early in the day (or a few days in advance) to find out its policy. Every restaurant listing in *Best in Town* gives its reservation policy and a telephone number (if the restaurant has a phone).

■ **Note:** Canada recently adopted a 7% Goods and Services Tax (GST), similar to the Value Added Tax imposed in many European countries. Although foreigners visiting Canada are able to obtain a rebate of the tax on some goods and services, restaurant meals are taxable but not rebatable. (For further information on the GST, see "Calculating Costs," in *Preparing,* earlier in this section.)

Time Zones, Business Hours, and Holidays

 TIME ZONES: Canada is divided into seven time zones, but because the two most northeasterly zones — Newfoundland Standard Time and Atlantic Standard Time — are only a half-hour apart, there is no more than a 5½-hour difference between its east and west coasts. Traveling west from Atlantic Standard Time, the zones get earlier by hour intervals.

Greenwich Mean Time — measured from Greenwich, England, at longitude 0°0′ — is the base from which all other time zones are measured. Areas in zones west of Greenwich have earlier times and are called Greenwich Minus; those to the east have later times and are called Greenwich Plus. For example, New York City — which falls into the Greenwich Minus 5 time zone — is 5 hours earlier, than Greenwich, England; when it is noon in Greenwich, it is 7 AM in New York. In an approximately clockwise direction, the Canadian time zones encompass the following time differences and areas:

Newfoundland Standard Time: The time is 3½ hours earlier than in Greenwich, England, in Newfoundland and Labrador.

Atlantic Standard Time: The time is 4 hours earlier than in Greenwich, England, in the Maritime Provinces, Gaspé Peninsula, Anticosti Island, Quebec Province east of Comeau Bay, most of Baffin Island, and Melville Peninsula.

Eastern Standard Time: The time is 5 hours earlier than in Greenwich, England, in Quebec province west of Comeau Bay and all of Ontario east of 90° longitude.

Central Standard Time: The time is 6 hours earlier than in Greenwich, England, in Ontario west of 90° longitude, Manitoba, and the Keewatin district of Saskatchewan in the southeastern section of the province.

Mountain Standard Time: The time is 7 hours earlier than in Greenwich, England, in the remainder of Saskatchewan including Regina, Alberta, those parts of the Northwest Territories directly north of Saskatchewan and Alberta, and the northeastern section of British Columbia.

Pacific Standard Time: The time is 8 hours earlier than Greenwich, England, in the remainder of British Columbia.

Yukon Standard Time: The time is 8 hours earlier than Greenwich, England, in the Yukon Territory.

Daylight Savings Time in Canada corresponds to the same changes made in the US and begins across the country on the last Sunday in April and extends to the last Saturday in October. It is not observed, however, in most parts of Saskatchewan.

Canadian timetables use a 24-hour clock to denote arrival and departure times, which means that hours are denoted sequentially from 1 AM. By this method, 9 AM is recorded as 0900, noon as 1200, 1 PM as 1300, 6 PM as 1800, midnight as 2400, and so on. For example, the departure of a train at 7 AM will be announced as "0700"; one leaving at 7 PM will be announced as "1900."

BUSINESS HOURS: Business hours throughout Canada are fairly standard and very similar to those in the US: 9 AM to 5 PM, Mondays through Fridays. While an hour lunch break is customary, employees often take it in shifts so that it rarely interrupts service, especially at banks and other public service operations.

Banks traditionally are open from 10 AM to 3 PM, Mondays through Thursdays, and until 6 PM on Fridays, but as in the US, the trend is toward longer hours. Banks generally are closed on Saturdays and Sundays, although in major cities some banks offer services on Saturday mornings.

Retail stores usually are open from 9 or 9:30 AM to 5 or 5:30 PM. They often are open until 9 PM on Thursday or Friday nights. Most major stores are open on Saturdays, closed on Sundays. Blue laws, which close some bars and restaurants on Sundays or stipulate that you can only be served an alcoholic drink with a meal, vary from place to place. Delicatessens and supermarkets are open from 9:30 AM to 5:30 PM, although some stay open later. In major cities, you usually can find a drugstore that is open until midnight, or all night, and on Sundays; check the local yellow pages.

HOLIDAYS: National holidays, when banks, post offices, libraries, most stores, and many museums are closed, include: *New Year's Day,* January 1; *Good Friday,* the Friday before *Easter; Easter Monday,* the Monday following *Easter; Victoria Day,* a Monday in late May; *Canada Day,* July 1; *Labour Day,* the first Monday in September; *Thanksgiving,* the second Monday in October; *Remembrance Day,* November 11; *Christmas Day,* December 25; and *Boxing Day,* December 26.

There also are several provincial holidays, which may vary by a day or so from year to year. This year, Newfoundland residents are celebrating *St. Patrick's Day* on March 18; *St. George's Day* on April 22; *Discovery Day* on June 24; *Memorial Day* on July 1; and *Orangeman's Day* on July 15. In Quebec, *Saint-Jean Baptiste Day* will be celebrated on June 24; in the Yukon, *Discovery Days* will be celebrated from around August 16 through August 19. Alberta celebrates *Heritage Day,* which this year falls on August 5, and this date also is observed as *British Columbia Day* in British Columbia and as a civic holiday in Manitoba, New Brunswick, the Northwest Territories, Ontario, and Saskatchewan.

Mail, Telephone, and Electricity

MAIL: Before you leave home, fill in a "change of address card" (available at post offices), which is the form you need to get the post office to hold your mail until your return. If you are planning an extended stay abroad, you can have your first class mail forwarded to your vacation address. There generally is no charge for this service. (Note that many post offices will need 2 to 3 weeks' notice to put this change of address into effect.)

There are several places that will receive and hold mail for travelers in Canada. Mail sent to you at a hotel and clearly marked "tourist mail, hold for arrival" is one safe approach. Canadian post offices also will extend this service to you if the mail is sent to "General Delivery" by using the following: (Name), c/o General Office, Main Post Office, (City, Province, Postal Code), Canada. This probably is the best way for travelers to have mail sent if they do not have a definite address. Note that in large cities there may be several post offices, and travelers should be sure to call at the correct office (generally the main branch) when inquiring after mail. Also, note that most post offices require formal identification before they will release anything; there is no charge for this service. Letters sent to General Delivery in Canada must be picked up within approximately 15 days of receipt (this varies from one branch office to another), after which it will be returned to the sender.

As in the US, when sending mail to Canada, the postal code always should be specified. Sometimes this will merely speed delivery, but sometimes — because small towns in Canada may have similar names — delivery of a letter may depend on it. If you do not have the correct postal code, you can call the following number: 613-998-1296; once you are in Canada, you also can consult lists of codes available at all post offices. Alternatively, you could call the addressee directly — if you have the telephone number — and although this will be costly, it may be worth it to ensure delivery of your correspondence.

Main offices and postal stations in Canada are open from 9 AM to 5:30 PM, Mondays through Fridays. Some offices have Saturday hours. Stamps also are available at most hotel desks. Vending machines for stamps are outside post offices and in shopping centers. As we went to press, the rate for a regular letter or postcard mailed in Canada to be sent to the US was CN$.45. All but local or nearby deliveries are air mailed.

If you are an American Express customer (a cardholder, carrier of American Express traveler's checks, or traveling on an *American Express Travel Service* tour) you can have mail sent to their offices in cities along your route; letters are held free of charge — registered mail and packages are not accepted. You must be able to show an American Express card, traveler's checks, or a voucher proving you are on one of the company's tours to avoid paying for mail privileges. Those who aren't clients must pay a nominal charge each time they inquire if they have received mail, whether or not they actually have a letter. There also is a forwarding fee, for clients and non-clients alike. Mail should be addressed to you, care of American Express, and should be marked "Client Mail Service." Additional information on its mail service and addresses of American Express offices in Canada are contained in the pamphlet *Services and Offices,* available from any US branch of American Express.

US embassies and consulates abroad do not accept mail for tourists. They will, however, help out in emergencies — if you need to receive important business documents or personal papers, for example. It is best to inform them either by separate letter or cable, or by phone, that you will be using their address for this purpose.

Letters between Canada and the US have been known to arrive in as short a time as 5 days, but it is a good idea to allow at least 10 days for delivery in either direction. If your correspondence is important, you may want to send it via one of the special courier services: *Federal Express, DHL,* and other international services are available throughout Canada. The cost is considerably higher than sending something via the postal service — but the assurance of its timely arrival is worth it.

TELEPHONE: If you are planning to be away for more than a month, you may be able to save money by asking the telephone company to temporarily suspend your home telephone service. You also can arrange to have your calls forwarded to another number.

The procedure for calling any number in Canada is the same as when calling within the US: dial the area code + the local number. The reverse procedure — dialing a number in the US from Canada — is the same.

Long-distance rates are charged according to when the call is placed: weekdays daytime; weekdays evenings; and nights, weekends, and holidays. Least expensive are the calls you dial yourself from a private phone at night, and on weekends and holidays. It generally is more expensive to call from a pay phone than it is to call from a private phone (you must pay for a minimum 3-minute call). If the operator assists you, calls are more expensive. This includes credit card, bill-to-a-third-number, collect, and time-and-charge calls, as well as person-to-person calls, which are the most expensive. Check the phone directory of the city you are in for exact rates and reductions.

Public telephones are on hand just about everywhere if you are in a city or town. This includes transportation centers (airports, train stations, and so on), post offices, hotels, restaurants, drugstores, commercial centers, and booths on the street. The average price of a local call is CN25¢. US coins cannot be used in pay phones. The majority of Canadian pay phones still take coins, but phones that take telephone company or major credit cards (see *Credit and Currency,* in this section) are increasingly common, particularly in metropolitan areas and at major tourist destinations.

Hotel Surcharges – Avoiding operator-assisted calls can cut costs considerably and bring rates into a reasonable range — except for calls made through hotel switchboards. One of the most unpleasant surprises travelers encounter is the amount that they find tacked onto their hotel bill for telephone calls, because hotels routinely add on astronomical surcharges. A practice initially begun to cover the expense of installing phone equipment and maintaining personnel to run it around the clock, it now is firmly entrenched as a profit making operation for many hotels.

It's wise to ask the surcharge rate *before* calling from a hotel. If the rate is high, it's best to use a telephone credit card, make a collect call, or place the call and ask the party to call right back. If none of these choices is possible, to avoid surcharges make international calls from a public pay phone. Another way to keep down the cost of telephoning from Canada is to leave a copy of your itinerary and telephone numbers in the US so that people can call you instead.

Emergencies – Dial "O" for the operator, who will connect you directly with the emergency service you need.

■**Note:** For quick reference, you might want to get a copy of a helpful pamphlet *The Phone Booklet,* which lists the nationwide, toll-free (800) numbers of travel information sources and suppliers — such as major airlines, hotel and motel chains, car rental companies, and tourist information offices. Send $2 for postage and handling to *Scott American Corporation,* Box 88, West Redding, CT 06896.

ELECTRICITY: Canada has the same electrical current system as that in the US: 110 volts, 60-cycle alternating current (AC). US appliances running on standard current can be used throughout Canada without adapters or convertors.

Medical and Legal Aid and Consular Services

MEDICAL AID: Nothing ruins a vacation or business trip more effectively than sudden injury or illness. You will discover, in the event of an emergency, that most tourist facilities — transportation companies, hotels, and resorts — are equipped to handle the situation quickly and efficiently. Most towns and cities of any size have a public hospital, and even the tiniest of Canadian towns has a medical clinic or private physician nearby. All hospitals are prepared for emergency cases, and many hospitals also have walk-in clinics designed to serve people who do not really need emergency service, but who have no place to go for immediate medical attention. The level of medical care available in Canada generally is excellent, providing the same basic specialties and services that are available in the US. The cost of Canadian medical service also is comparable to what you might pay at home.

Before you go, be sure to check with your insurance company about the applicability of your policy while you're abroad; many policies do not apply, and others are not accepted in Canada. Older travelers should know that Medicare does not make payments outside the US. If your medical policy does not protect you while you're traveling, there are comprehensive combination policies specifically designed to fill the gap. (For a discussion of medical insurance and a list of inclusive combination policies, see *Insurance,* in this section.)

If a bona fide emergency occurs, the fastest way to receive attention may be to go directly to the emergency room of the nearest hospital. You also can get emergency help by dialing "0" for an Operator, who will connect you to the appropriate emergency service you require.

If a doctor is needed for something less than an emergency, there are several ways to find one. Ask at the hotel or check the local post office, where neighborhood physicians may be listed (though they often aren't). Calling the local hospital also may be of help; some hospitals actually have referral services for this purpose. Callers often will be given the name of a general practitioner, since private doctors (usually specialists) may see patients upon referral only. For the seriously ill or injured traveler, the attention of a specialist may be in order. If you are already at the hospital, you may see the specialist there, or you may make an appointment to be seen at his or her office.

In addition, though general practitioners deliver primary care, as in the US, there is no violation of protocol in approaching a specialist directly. The medical society in most provinces will refer you to a member physician in the specialty you need (listed in the telephone book under the city or provincial medical society). You also can call the appropriate department of a teaching hospital or the nearest US consulate or embassy (see "Legal Aid and Consular Services," below), which should maintain a list of doctors. Remember that if you are hospitalized, you will have to pay, even in an emergency.

If you are staying in a hotel or motel, ask for help in reaching a doctor or other emergency services, or for the house physician, who may visit you in your room or ask you to visit an office. (This service is apt to be expensive, especially if the doctor makes a "house" call to your room.) When you register at a hotel, it's not a bad idea to include your home address and telephone number; this will facilitate the process of notifying friends, relatives, or your own doctor in case of an emergency.

Emergency dental care also is available throughout Canada (again, consult the local telephone directory), although travelers are strongly advised to have a dental checkup some weeks before the trip to allow time for any necessary work to be done. Again, any US consul should be able to provide a list of dentists in the area the consulate serves.

There should be no problem finding a 24-hour drugstore in any major city. In many areas, pharmacists who close often list in the window the addresses of the nearest all-night drugstore. Sometimes all-night duty may rotate among pharmacies in an area; hospital emergency room should be able to give you the address of the evening's on call pharmacy. In small towns, where none many be officially open or on-call after normal business hours, you may be able to have one open in an emergency situation — such as a diabetic needing insulin — although you may be charged a fee for this off-hour service.

Bring along a copy of any prescription you may have from your doctor in case you should need a refill. In the case of minor complaints, Canadian pharmacists *may* agree to fill a foreign prescription; however, do not count on this. In most cases, you probably will need a local doctor to rewrite the prescription. Even in an emergency, a traveler will more than likely be given only enough of a drug to last until a local prescription can be obtained. As "brand" names vary in different countries, it's a good idea to ask your doctor for the generic names of any drugs you use so that you can ask for their equivalents should you need a refill. US visitors also will notice that some drugs sold only by prescription in the US are sold over the counter in Canada. Though this can be very handy, be aware that common cold medicines and aspirin that contain codeine or other controlled substances will not be allowed back into the US.

Emergency assistance also is available from the various medical programs designed for travelers who have chronic ailments or whose illness requires them to return home. The *Medic Alert Foundation* sells identification emblems which specify that the wearer has a health condition that may not be readily apparent to a casual observer. A heart condition, diabetes, epilepsy, or severe allergy are the sorts of things that these emblems were developed to communicate — conditions that can result in tragic errors if not recognized when emergency treatment is necessary and when you may be unable to speak for yourself. In addition to the identification emblems, the foundation maintains a computerized central file from which your complete medical history is available 24 hours a day by telephone (the phone number is clearly inscribed on the ID badge). The one-time membership fee is tax deductible, and is based on the type of metal from which the emblem is made — the choices range from stainless steel to 10K gold-filled. For information, contact the *Medic Alert Foundation,* Turlock, CA 95381-1009 (phone: 800-ID-ALERT or 209-668-3333).

International SOS Assistance also offers a program to cover medical emergencies while traveling. Members are provided with telephone access — 24 hours a day, 365 days a year — to a worldwide, monitored, multilingual network of medical centers. A phone call brings assistance ranging from a telephone consultation to transportation home by ambulance or aircraft, and in some cases transportation of a family member to wherever you are hospitalized. The service can be purchased for 2 weeks ($25), 2 weeks plus additional days ($25, plus $2.50 for each additional day), 1 month ($50), or 1 year ($195). These rates are for individual travelers; couple and family rates also are available. For information, contact *International SOS Assistance,* PO Box 11568, Philadelphia, PA 19116 (phone: 800-523-8930 or 215-244-1500).

The *International Association of Medical Assistance to Travellers (IAMAT)* provides its members with a directory of affiliated medical centers in more than 140 countries (including centers in Quebec, Toronto, and Vancouver) to call for a list of participating doctors. Participating physicians agree to adhere to a basic charge of around $30 to see a patient referred by *IAMAT.* A nonprofit organization, *IAMAT* appreciates donations; for $25, you will receive a set of worldwide climate charts detailing weather and sanitary conditions. Delivery of this material can take up to 5 weeks, so plan ahead. Contact *IAMAT,* 417 Center St., Lewiston, NY 14092 (phone: 716-754-4883).

The *International Health Care Service* provides information about health conditions in various foreign countries, as well as a variety of travel-related health services. A pre-travel counseling and immunization package costs $185 for the first family member and $165 for each additional member; a post-travel screening is $75 to $135, plus lab work. Appointments are required for all services. Contact the *International Health Care Service* (New York Hospital–Cornell Medical Center, 440 E. 69th St., New York, NY 10021; phone: 212-472-4284). *The International Health Care Travelers Guide,* a compendium of facts and advice on health care and diseases around the world, can be obtained by sending $4.50 and a self-addressed, stamped envelope to PO Box 210 at the address above.

Those who return home ill with a condition they suspect is travel-related and beyond the experience of their regular physician should consider seeing a specialist in travel medicine. For information on locating such a specialist in your area, see *Staying Healthy* in this section.

For a thorough description of the medical services in seven of Italy's larger cities, see *Traveling Healthy* by Sheilah M. Hillman and Robert S. Hillman, MD. Unfortunately out of print, it may be found in the library.

Practically every phase of health care — before, during, and after a trip — is covered in *The New Traveler's Health Guide* by Drs. Patrick J. Doyle and James E. Banta. It is available for $4.95, plus $2.50 postage and handling, from Acropolis Books Ltd., 80 S. Early St., Alexandria, VA 22304 (phone: 800-451-7771 or 703-709-0006).

LEGAL AID AND CONSULAR SERVICES: There is one crucial place to keep in mind when outside the US, namely, the American Services section of the US Consulate. If you are injured or become seriously ill, the consulate will direct you to medical assistance and notify your relatives. If, while abroad, you become involved in a dispute that could lead to legal action, the consulate, once again, is the place to turn.

It usually is far more alarming to be arrested abroad than at home. Not only are you alone among strangers, but the punishment can be worse. Granted, the US Consulate can advise you of your rights and provide a list of lawyers, but it cannot interfere with local legal process. Except for minor infractions of the local traffic code, there is no reason for any law-abiding traveler to run afoul of immigration, customs, or any other law enforcement authority.

The best advice is to be honest and law-abiding. If you get a traffic ticket, pay it. If you are approached by drug hawkers, ignore them. The penalties for possession of hashish, marijuana, cocaine, and other narcotics are are even more severe abroad than in the US. (If you are picked up for any drug-related offense, do not expect US foreign service officials to be sympathetic. Chances are they will notify a lawyer and your family and that's about all. See "Drugs," below.)

In the case of minor traffic accidents, it often is most expedient to settle the matter before the police get involved. If, however, you are involved in a serious accident, where an injury or fatality results, the first step is to contact the nearest US consulate (addresses below) and ask the consul to locate a lawyer to assist you. If you have a traveling companion, ask him or her to call the consulate (unless either of you has a local contact who can help you quickly). Competent lawyers practice throughout Canada, and it is possible to obtain good legal counsel on short notice.

Once you have found a lawyer, ask how many cases of this type the lawyer has worked on, and the arrangements to be made regarding fees and additional costs such as medical or ballistics experts, transcripts, or court fees. For most violations, you will receive a citation at most. There are, however, the rare occasions when travelers find themselves in jail. Since obtaining a bond can be difficult away from home, the bail bonds offered by *AAA* and other automobile clubs are extremely useful. If you do not have this protection, ask to see a copy of the local bail procedures, which differ from province to province. A lawyer will be able to advise you on the alternatives you have in the province in which you are incarcerated.

The US Department of State in Washington, DC, insists that any US citizen who is arrested abroad has the right to contact the US embassy or consulate "immediately," but it may be a while before you are given permission to use a phone. Do not labor under the illusion, however, that in a scrape with foreign officialdom, the consulate can act as an arbitrator or ombudsman on an American citizen's behalf. Nothing could be farther from the truth. Consuls have no power, authorized or otherwise, to subvert, alter, or contravene the legal processes, however unfair, of the foreign country in which they serve. Nor can a consul oil the machinery of a foreign bureaucracy or provide legal advice. The consul's responsibilities do encompass "welfare duties" including providing a list of lawyers and information on local sources of legal aid, informing relatives in the US, and organizing and administrating any defense monies sent from home. If a case is tried unfairly or the punishment seems unusually severe, the consul can make a formal complaint to the authorities. For questions about Americans arrested abroad, how to get money to them, and other useful information, call the *Citizens Emergency Center* of the Office of Special Consular Services in Washington, DC: phone: 202-647-5225. (For further information about this invaluable hot line, see below.)

Other. welfare duties, not involving legal hassles, cover cases of both illness and destitution. If you should get sick, the US consul can provide names of doctors and dentists as well as the names of all local hospitals and clinics; the consul also will contact family members in the US and help arrange special ambulance service for a flight home. In a situation involving "legitimate and proven poverty" — of an US citizen stranded abroad without funds — the consul will contact sources of money (such as family or friends in the US), apply for aid to agencies in foreign countries, and in a last resort — which is *rarely* — arrange for repatriation at government expense, although this is a loan that must be repaid. And in case of natural disasters or civil unrest, consulates around the world handle the evacuation of US citizens if it becomes necessary.

The consulate is not occupied solely with emergencies and is certainly not there to aid in trivial situations, such as canceled reservations or lost baggage, no matter how important these matters may seem to the victimized tourist. The main duties of any consulate are administrating statutory services, such as the issuance of passports and visas; providing notarial services; the distribution of VA, social security, and civil service benefits to US citizens; depositions; extradition cases; and reporting to Washington the births, deaths, and marriages of US citizens living within the consulate's domain.

We hope that none of the information in this section will be necessary during your stay in Canada. If you can avoid legal hassles altogether, you will have a much more pleasant trip. If you become involved in an imbroglio, the local authorities may spare you legal complications if you make clear your tourist status. And if you run into a confrontation that might lead to legal complications developing with a citizen or with local authorities, the best tactic is to apologize and try to leave as gracefully as possible. Do not get into fights with residents, no matter how belligerent or provocative they are in a given situation.

A list of US embassies and consulates in Canada (by province) follows. Note that mailing addresses may be different — so call before sending anything to these offices.

> *Alberta:* US Consulate, 615 McCleod Trail SE, Calgary, Alberta T2G 4T8, Canada (phone: 403-266-8962).
>
> *British Columbia:* US Consulate, 1075 W. George St., Vancouver, British Columbia V6E 4E9, Canada (phone: 604-685-4311).
>
> *Nova Scotia:* US Consulate, Cogswell Tower, Suite 910, Scotia Square, Halifax, Nova Scotia B3J 3K1, Canada (phone: 902-429-2480).
>
> *Ontario:* US Embassy, 100 Willington St., Ottawa, Ontario K1P 5T1, Canada (phone: 613-238-5335); US Consulate, 360 University Ave., Toronto, Ontario N5G 1S4, Canada (phone: 416-595-1700).
>
> *Quebec:* US Consulate, 1155 St. Alexander, Montreal, Quebec H2Z 1Z2, Canada (phone: 514-398-9695); US Consulate, 2 Terrace Duffrin, Quebec City, Quebec G1R 4TR, Canada (phone: 418-692-2095).

You also can obtain a booklet with addresses of most US embassies and consulates around the world by writing the Superintendent of Documents, US Government Printing Office, Washington, DC 20402, and asking for publication #78-77, *Key Offices of Foreign Service Posts.*

As mentioned above, the US State Department operates a *Citizens Emergency Center,* which offers a number of services to US travelers abroad and their families at home.

In addition to giving callers up-to-date information on trouble spots, the center will contact authorities abroad in an attempt to locate a traveler or deliver an urgent message. In case of illness, death, arrest, destitution, or repatriation of a US citizen on foreign soil, it will relay information to relatives at home if the consulate is unable to do so. Travel advisory information is available 24 hours a day to people with Touch-Tone phones (phone: 202-647-5225). Callers with rotary phones can get information at this number from 8:15 AM to 10 PM (Eastern Standard Time) on weekdays; 9 AM to 3 PM on Saturdays. For emergency calls, from 8:15 AM to 10 PM weekdays, and 9 AM to 3 PM Saturdays, call 202-647-5225. For emergency calls only, at all other times, call 202-634-3600 and ask for the duty officer.

Drinking and Drugs

Drinking: The legal drinking age is 19 in Newfoundland, Prince Edward Island, British Columbia, New Brunswick, the Northwest Territories, Nova Scotia, Ontario, Saskatchewan, and the Yukon territory. Only in Alberta, Manitoba, and Quebec is the legal age 18.

Although Canadian liquor laws have become more uniform across the country during the last decade, it still is difficult to generalize about what kinds of alcoholic drinks may be sold, at what hours, and to whom. Except in Quebec, which has the most liberal drinking laws in the country, liquor by the bottle usually is sold only through provincial government liquor stores, located in larger cities and most towns. In Quebec, beer and wine are sold at retail grocery stores; hard liquor is available at government liquor stores. In Ontario, domestic beer is sold through large outlets called Brewers' Retail; wine is sold through liquor control stores.

It is possible to find dry towns in all corners of Canada. Usually, however, you will find a community just a few minutes away where the sale of liquor is legal.

Licensed restaurants, hotels, lounges, and bars are found across the country, though some may sell only wine or beer (called beverage rooms). Again, hours during which bars and restaurants may serve liquor vary, though traditionally bar closing time is between midnight and 3 AM. Most provinces require liquor stores to close on Sundays and holidays. Some alcoholic beverages may be purchased on Sundays, usually only with meals at authorized dining rooms, restaurants, and private clubs.

Every visitor to Canada may import 40 ounces of liquor or wine, or 288 ounces of beer or ale (twenty-four 12-ounce cans, eighteen 16-ounce cans) as personal baggage, duty-free. Anything in excess of this amount is subject to duties and taxes and requires a provincial permit. If excess liquor is declared, it will be held by Canada Customs at the point of entry for 30 days. A receipt will be issued, and the owner can claim it upon return. People leaving Canada from a point other than their point of entry can make arrangements to have their property returned at the point of departure.

No provinces forbid the import of liquor from one province to another as long as it is for personal use. This is useful to know, since liquor and wine prices vary quite considerably throughout Canada. If you are visiting Alberta and British Columbia, for instance, you will notice an appreciable difference in liquor prices, Alberta being much less expensive. It is worth adding that the prices of beer do not vary as greatly (and domestic beer usually is among the best bargains), although it tends to be slightly more expensive in eastern Canada.

A warning: When setting off for an evening that will include some serious drinking, leave your car behind and make alternative plans for getting back to the hotel; otherwise choose a "designated driver" in your party who will stick strictly to soft drinks. Aside from the obvious danger in which you place yourself and others on the road, drivers who commit an offense while intoxicated will be severely penalized for their infraction — confiscation of the driver's license, high fines, and even imprisonment are common penalties.

DRUGS: Illegal narcotics are as prevalent in Canada as in the US, but the moderate legal penalties and vague social acceptance that marijuana has gained in the US has no equivalent in Canada. Due to the international war on drugs, enforcement of drug laws is becoming increasingly strict throughout the world. Local narcotics officers and customs officials are renowned for their absence of understanding and lack of a sense of humor — especially where non-Canadians are involved.

Opiates and barbiturates, and other increasingly popular drugs — "white powder" substances like heroin and cocaine — are as pervasive a problem in Canada as in the US. The main drawback to buying any illegal drug (besides the obvious health hazards) is the inherent risk of getting locked up. Like other countries worldwide, Canada has toughened laws regarding illegal drugs and narcotics, and these laws do not distinguish between types of drugs — possession of marijuana, cocaine, heroin, and other narcotics are treated with equal severity. Don't assume that you're safe in carrying even small amounts of controlled substances for "personal use." According to a sergeant with the narcotics division of the Royal Canadian Mounted Police, stiff penalties have been imposed on drug offenders convicted of possessing mere *traces* of illegal drugs.

The best advice we can offer is: Don't carry, use, buy, or sell illegal drugs. The dangers are clear enough when you are indulging in your own home; if taking drugs while traveling, you may not only endanger your own life but also put your fellow travelers in jeopardy. And if you get caught, you may end up spending your hard-earned travel funds on bail and attorney's fees — and still wind up in jail. There isn't much that the American consulate can do for drug offenders beyond providing a list of lawyers. Having broken a local law, an offender puts his or her fate in the hands of the local authorities.

Those who carry medicines that contain a controlled drug should be sure to have a current doctor's prescription with them. Ironically, travelers can get into almost as much trouble returning to the US with over-the-counter drugs picked up abroad that contain substances that are controlled in the US. Foreign cold medicines, pain relievers, and the like often have codeine or codeine derivatives that are illegal, except by prescription, in the US. Throw them out before leaving for home.

■ **Be forewarned:** US narcotics agents warn travelers of the increasingly common ploy of drug dealers asking travelers to transport a "gift" or other package back to the US. Don't be fooled into thinking that the protection of US law applies abroad — accused of illegal drug trafficking, you will be considered guilty until you prove your innocence. In other words, do not, under any circumstances, agree to take anything across the border for a stranger.

Tipping

 While tipping is done at the discretion of the person receiving the service, CN$.50 should be the rock-bottom tip for anything, and CN$1 is the current customary minimum for small services. *(Please note that the gratuities suggested below are given in Canadian dollars.)*

In restaurants, tip between 10% and 20% of the bill. For average service in an average restaurant, a 15% tip to the waiter is reasonable, although one should never hesitate to penalize poor service or reward excellent and efficient attention by leaving less or more. In bars, where you simply pay the bartender the price of drinks, tipping is not necessary, but it is customary to leave some change to a few dollars (depending on how many drinks you've had) on the bar when you leave. Where a "tab" is run up and a bill presented — in bars, cocktail lounges, nightclubs, and so on — tipping is similar to restaurants. If you serve yourself, as in a cafeteria, no tip is expected.

Although it's not necessary to tip the maître d' of most restaurants — unless he or she has been especially helpful in arranging a special party or providing a table (slipping him something in a crowded restaurant *may* get you seated sooner) — when tipping is desirable or appropriate, the least amount should be CN$5. The sommelier (wine waiter) is entitled to a gratuity of approximately CN$2 per bottle of wine. In the finest restaurants, where a multiplicity of servers are present, plan to tip 5% to the captain in addition to the standard 15% to the waiter.

In allocating gratuities at a restaurant, pay particular attention to what has become the standard credit card charge form, which now includes separate places for gratuities for waiters and/or captains. If these separate boxes are not on the charge slip presented, simply ask the waiter or captain how these separate tips should be indicated.

In a large hotel, where it's difficult to determine just who out of a horde of attendants actually performed particular services, it is perfectly proper for guests to ask to have an extra 10% to 15% added to their bill, to be distributed among those who served them. For those who prefer to distribute tips themselves, a chambermaid generally is tipped at the rate of CN$1 per day. Tip the concierge for specific services only, with the amount of such gratuities dependent on the level of service provided. If you leave your shoes outside the room at night for a shine, give the hall porter about CN$1 to CN$2 when you next see him. If you order from room service, again, CN$1 to CN$2 for each delivery is sufficient. For other special services, such as personal deliveries, the tip depends on the service rendered, but in most cases a few dollars is more than sufficient.

Train personnel usually do not expect tips, but the exceptions are dining car waiters (who expect 15% of the bill), sleeping car attendants (who should get CN$2 to CN$5, depending on the service you require), and porters (who expect CN$1 or more). Bellhops, doormen, and porters at hotels and other transportation centers generally are tipped at the rate of CN$1 per bag for carrying luggage, along with a small additional amount if a doorman helps with a cab or car. Taxi drivers should get about 10% to 15% of the total fare (the lesser amount for longer rides). And if you arrive without any Canadian currency, go ahead and tip in US dollars. (When in doubt, it is preferable to tip — in any denomination or currency — than not to tip.)

Some miscellaneous tips: Sightseeing tour guides usually are tipped. If you are traveling in a group, decide together what you feel like giving and present it from the group at the end of the tour. If you have been individually escorted, the amount will depend on your degree of satisfaction, but it should not be less than 10% and easily could be as high as 50% of the total tour fee. Museum and monument guides also usually are tipped, and it is a nice touch to tip a caretaker who unlocks a country church or other building for viewing.

In barbershops and beauty salons, tip as you would at home, keeping in mind that the percentages should vary according to the type of establishment. Since the prices usually are quite a bit higher in expensive salons (particularly in metropolitan areas), no more than 10% is common; in less expensive establishments, a 15% to 20% tip is in order. (As a general rule the woman who washes your hair should get an additional small tip.) Coat checks are worth about CN$.50 to CN$1 per coat, and washroom attendants, should get a small tip; often there is a coin in a dish indicating the suggested denomination.

Tipping always is a matter of personal preference. In the situations covered above, as well as in any others that arise where you feel a tip is expected, feel free to express your pleasure or displeasure. Again, never hesitate to reward excellent and efficient attention and to penalize poor service. Give an extra word of thanks when someone has gone out of his or her way for you. Either way, the more personal the act of tipping, the more appropriate it seems. And, if you didn't like the service — or the attitude — don't tip.

Religion on the Road

 The surest source of information on religious services in an unfamiliar town is the desk clerk of your hotel or motel. You also can check the yellow pages of the phone book under "Churches" and call for more information. Church listings also often are printed as part of general tourist guides provided locally. The local tourist council certainly can provide the information you need on services in the town. Some newspapers also print a listing of religious services in their area in weekend editions.

You may want to use your vacation to broaden your religious experience by joining an unfamiliar faith in its service. This can be a moving experience, especially if the service is held in a church, synagogue, or temple that is historically significant or architecturally notable. You almost always will find yourself made welcome and comfortable.

Certain kinds of services are prevalent in specific areas, depending upon the concentration of religious groups in that area. The Roman Catholic, United Church of Canada, and Anglican churches have the largest followings in Canada, and you will find their services in every province. Since 77% of the Jews in Canada are based in Toronto and Montreal, the largest number of synagogues are found in these two cities. The Presbyterian church is centered in Ontario; Canadian Baptists live primarily in the Maritime Provinces.

Sources and Resources

Tourist Information Offices

The Canadian tourism authorities generally are the best sources of travel information, and most publications are free for the asking. For the best result, request general information on specific provinces or cities in which you are interested (several areas have travel kits that include tourist attractions, maps, and so on), as well as your particular areas of interest: accommodations, restaurants, special events, guided tours, and facilities for specific sports. Because most of the material you receive will be oversize brochures, there is little point in sending a self-addressed, stamped envelope with your request, unless this requirement is specified. Offices generally are open on weekdays, during normal business hours.

The best places for tourist information in each Canadian city are listed in the *Sources and Resources* section of the individual city reports in THE CITIES. The following is a list of the provincial tourism offices. With the exception of the Yukon, all these offices can be called toll-free from the US (except Alaska). Where noted, the toll-free number is good for the eastern US only.

PROVINCIAL TOURIST OFFICES

Travel Alberta: 102nd St., City Center Bldg., Main Floor, Edmonton, Alberta P5J 4L6, Canada (phone: 403-427-4321 or 800-222-6501 from Alberta; 800-661-8888 from elsewhere in Canada and the US).

Tourism British Columbia: Parliament Buildings, Victoria, British Columbia V8V 1X4, Canada (phone: 604-387-1642, or 800-663-6000).

Labrador: See Newfoundland.

Travel Manitoba: 155 Carlton St., 7th Floor, Dept. 7020, Winnipeg, Manitoba R3C 3H8, Canada (phone: 204-945-3777, or 800-665-0040, ext. 20).

Tourism, Recreation, and Heritage New Brunswick: PO Box 12345, Fredericton, New Brunswick E3B 5C3, Canada (phone: 506-453-8745 or 800-442-4442 from New Brunswick; 800-561-0123 from elsewhere in Canada and the US).

Newfoundland and Labrador Tourism Branch: Department of Development and Tourism, PO Box 8730, St. John's, Newfoundland A1B 4K2, Canada (phone: 709-576-2830 or 800-563-6353 in Canada and the continental US).

TravelArctic: Yellowknife, Northwest Territories X1A 2L9, Canada (phone: 403-873-7200 or 800-661-0788).

Nova Scotia Department of Tourism: PO Box 456, Halifax, Nova Scotia B3J 2R5, Canada (phone: 902-425-5781 or 800-565-7105 from Nova Scotia, Prince Edward Island, and New Brunswick; 800-565-7180 from Newfoundland and Quebec; 800-565-0000 throughout Canada); *Nova Scotia Tourist Information Office,* 1601 Lower Water St., 4th Floor, Halifax, Nova Scotia B3J 3C6, Canada (phone: 902-424-5000). Note that the Nova Scotia tourist board offers a special "Check-Inns" accommodations reservations service for travelers calling these numbers.

Ontario Travel: Queen's Park, Toronto, Ontario M7A 2E5, Canada (phone: 800-668-2746 or 416-965-4008).

Department of Tourism and Parks (Prince Edward Island): PO Box 940, Charlottetown, Prince Edward Island C1A 7M5, Canada (phone: 902-368-4444; 800-565-9060 in the US east of the Mississippi; 800-565-0266 throughout the rest of North America).

Tourisme Quebec: PO Box 20,000, Quebec City, Quebec G1K 7X2, Canada (phone: 514-873-2015 or 800-363-7777 throughout North America).

Tourism Saskatchewan: 1919 Saskatchewan Dr., Regina, Saskatchewan S4P 3V7, Canada (phone: 306-787-2300 or 800-667-7538 from Saskatchewan; 800-667-7191 from elsewhere in Canada and the US).

Tourism Yukon: PO Box 2703, Whitehorse, Yukon Y1A 2C6, Canada (phone: 403-667-5340).

The Canadian Embassy and Consulates in the US

The Canadian government maintains one embassy and several consulates in the US. These are empowered to sign official documents and to notarize copies of US documents, which may be necessary for those papers to be considered legal abroad.

Listed below are the Canadian embassies and consulates in the US.

Atlanta: Canadian Consulate, 1 CNN Center, Suite 400, South Tower, Atlanta, GA 30303 (phone: 404-577-6810).

Dallas: Canadian Consulate, 750 N. St. Paul, Suite 1700, Dallas, TX 75201 (phone: 214-922-9806).

Los Angeles: Canadian Consulate, 300 S. Grand Ave., Los Angeles, CA 90071 (phone: 213-687-7432).

San Francisco: Canadian Consulate, 50 Freemont St., Suite 2100, San Francisco, CA 94105 (phone: 415-494-6021).

Washington, DC: Canadian Embassy, 501 Pennsylvania Ave. NW, Washington, DC 20001 (phone: 202-682-1740).

Theater and Special Event Tickets

 The various tourism authorities also can supply information on the many special events and festivals that take place in their respective provinces, though they cannot in all cases provide the actual program or detailed information on ticket prices. In more than one section of this book you will read about events that spark your interest — everything from music festivals and special theater seasons to sporting championships — along with telephone numbers and addresses for requesting descriptive brochures, reservations, or tickets. Since many of these occasions often are fully booked well in advance, you should think about having your reservation in hand before you go. If you do write, remember that any request from the US should be accompanied by an International Reply Coupon to ensure a response. Tickets usually can be paid for by an international money order or by foreign draft. These international coupons, money orders, and drafts are available at US post offices and banks.

Notes on Sports

 Both spectator and participatory sports are major activities in Canada. You can take in major seasonal sporting events during your travels whether you're inclined toward skiing in the Quebec Laurentians, watching a hockey game in Montreal, or summer snowmobiling on a huge glacier in the Canadian Rockies. See the individual city reports in THE CITIES for ticket information and the entries on specific sports in DIVERSIONS for more detailed information.

CURLING: This Canadian game has Scottish origins and is somewhat related to shuffleboard. The big difference is that it is played on a 46-yard long ice rink with 40-pound stones (also known as "granites"). Two players or "curlers" slide eight stones toward a circular target, while assistants vigorously brush the ice with brooms along the path of the stone in an attempt to place a stone nearest the center. Curling is a major winter sport in Canada, and the season extends from October to April. The *Labatt Brier* tournament highlights the curling season and features, in addition to curling, an opening day parade with Scottish bands. There are many teams throughout Canada; for ticket information, contact the tourist office of the province you visit.

FISHING: Canada is a fisherman's paradise. The hundreds of thousands of lakes and streams teem with all the major freshwater species: all families of trout, Arctic char, maskinonge (muskellunge), walleye, large- and small-mouth bass, Atlantic and Pacific salmon, northern pike, whitefish, Arctic grayling, inconnu, goldeye, perch, and a variety of panfish. On the Atlantic and Pacific coasts, you can go after a variety of saltwater fish: striped bass, bluefin tuna, sharks, and deep-sea fish.

Most of the best fishing spots are accessible by car, rail, or air and are located near comfortable lodges, resorts, hotels, or campgrounds. For the best of Canada's prime places to drop a line, see *Where They Bite* in DIVERSIONS.

FOOTBALL: This popular sport is under the aegis of the Canadian Football League. Though some 50% of the professional players are from the US, the rules are 100% Canadian: The game is played on a 110-yard field (larger than a US regulation field) with 12 players (1 more than US teams) and 3 downs (1 less than in US football). Toronto, Ottawa, Hamilton, Edmonton, Winnipeg, Calgary, Regina, and Vancouver all field professional teams that compete from late August to the end of November. The season culminates in the *Grey Cup National Championship.* For ticket information, see the *Sports* section of the individual city reports in THE CITIES.

GOLF: Part and parcel with the Canadians' British heritage is their love of golf and a corresponding abundance of first class golf courses. Golf is played at nearly 1,000 courses around the country. The largest number are concentrated in Ontario and Quebec, where the season extends from the end of April to the beginning of November, and in British Columbia, where people play golf all year, but there are even courses in the Northwest Territories. Canada hosts several tournaments on the PGA circuit, including the *Canadian Open* and the *Canadian PGA Championship* for male pros. Top female pros compete in the annual *Du Maurier Classic,* which is held alternately in Toronto and Montreal. For further information on men's tournaments, contact the *Royal Canadian Golf Association* (1333 Dorval Dr., Oakville, Ontario L6J 4Z3, Canada; phone: 416-844-1800); for the women's competitions, the *Canadian Ladies' Golf Association* (1600 James Naismith Dr., Suite 701, Gloucester, Ontario K1B 5N4, Canada; phone: 613-748-5642). For complete details on the best courses in Canada, see *Golf* in DIVERSIONS.

HOCKEY: Hockey is king in Canada and reigns over a broad domain encompassing professional, college, community, and school teams. With its long winters and the preponderance of frozen lakes and rinks, Canada is real hockey country; in fact, many of its citizens learn to skate about the same time they learn to walk. So the ice is hotly contested on all levels, from October through May by professionals in the long-established National Hockey League. The NHL is composed of seven Canadian teams, including the Calgary *Flames,* Edmonton *Oilers* (the *1990 Stanley Cup Champions*), Montreal *Canadiens,* Quebec *Nordiques,* Toronto *Maple Leafs,* Vancouver *Canucks,* Winnipeg *Jets,* and American teams in Boston, Buffalo, Chicago, Detroit, Hartford, Los Angeles, Minnesota, New Jersey, New York (the *Islanders* and the *Rangers*), Philadelphia, Pittsburgh, St. Louis, and Washington. The NHL's best teams compete for the *Stanley Cup* in May. The best way to get tickets for hockey games is to get a season schedule from the *National Hockey League* (960 Sun Life Bldg., 1155 Metcalfe, Montreal, Quebec H3B 2W2, Canada; phone: 514-871-9220), and then contact the team's home arena box office (see the individual city reports in THE CITIES for addresses for tickets). Tickets also may be bought in advance at various ticket offices in the host city.

College hockey competition takes place throughout the country from October to March. The leading teams are affiliated with the University of Toronto and York in Toronto, Concordia in Montreal, St. Mary's in Halifax, and the University of Alberta in Edmonton. For tickets to inter-collegiate hockey games, contact the universities. The *Canadian Inter-Athletic Championship Tournament* is the big game at the end of the season.

HORSE RACING: Thoroughbred racing and pari-mutuel betting take place in British Columbia, Alberta, Saskatchewan, Manitoba, and Ontario during the spring, summer, and fall. The oldest continuously run stake event in North America, the 129-year-old *Queen's Plate* takes place at *Woodbine Race Track* in Toronto each summer. For specifics, check the local newspapers.

LACROSSE: Though lacrosse is officially Canada's national sport, the two attempts to organize professional leagues in the past few years have failed. But the game is played widely on an amateur, minor league, and semi-pro level, particularly in western Canada and Ontario, during the late winter and the summer. At the end of the season, the best teams compete for the *Mann Cup.*

SKIING: Canadians love to ski and, between ideal snowy climate and extensive mountainous terrain, Canada has some of the finest ski areas in the world for both recreational and competitive skiing. Even near major metropolitan centers, a skier in Canada is seldom very far from a good run. The major regions are Mont Tremblant and Mont-Ste.-Anne in eastern Quebec, Lake Louise and Jasper in Alberta, and western British Columbia, all with breathtaking vertical drops for alpine skiing and extensive cross-country trails as well. The province of Ontario also has a myriad of popular ski slopes. Canada is on the *World Cup Circuit,* the most prestigious competition for amateur and Olympic-ranked skiers. Big events take place every few years, including the giant slalom and slalom at Whistler Mountain (north of Vancouver) and the *World Cup Downhill Championship.* For complete information on the best places to ski in Canada, see *Downhill* and *Cross-Country Skiing* in DIVERSIONS.

SNOWMOBILING: Once used primarily for winter transportation in rural areas, snowmobiles now are used mainly for recreation. Located in the heart of the snow belt, Canada has thousands of miles of groomed trails — 38,000 miles in the province of Quebec alone. Ontario is another major snowmobiling region, but snowmobiling tours and concessions are springing up across the country. In the Canadian Rockies, a variation on the snowmobiling tour is offered via large-track vehicle on 5-mile-long and ¾-mile-wide Athabasca Glacier. Canada has a professional snowmobiling circuit known as *Sno Pro,* where factory team racing pros whiz around the track at speeds greater than 100 mph for cash and prizes. These events generally are held in January at tracks in Beausejour, Manitoba, and Waldheim, Saskatchewan. In order to drive a snowmobile that can exceed 50 mph, one needs a driver's license; children must obtain a special permit.

TENNIS: There's a tennis boom in Canada, as many more people take up the sport and courts spring up to accommodate them. It is played a great deal in Ontario and Quebec from April to October and in British Columbia year-round. Facilities range from public, municipally maintained courts to indoor and outdoor private clubs and tennis cooperatives. The biggest events in tennis are two professionally sanctioned tournaments: the men's *Player's International* and the women's *Player's Challenge.* Both are held annually in August, with one played in Montreal, the other in Toronto, on an alternating basis; this year, the men's competition will be in Montreal, and the woman's in Toronto. For information, contact *Tennis Canada* (3111 Steeles Ave. W., Downsview, Ontario M3J 3H2, Canada; phone: 416-665-9777). For complete descriptions of the best courts in Canada, see *The Best Tennis Vacations* in DIVERSIONS.

For More Information

Throughout GETTING READY TO GO, numerous books and brochures have been recommended as good sources of further information on a variety of topics. In many cases these are publications of the various tourism authorities and are available at any of their offices both here and abroad. Others may be found in the travel section of any good, general bookstore. If you still can't find something, the following bookstores and/or mail-order houses specialize in travel, though not in travel to any particular country or continent. They offer books on Canada along with guides to the rest of the world, and in some cases even an old Baedeker or two.

Book Passage, 51 Tamal Vista, Corte Madera, CA 94925 (phone: 415-927-0960 in California; 800-321-9785 elsewhere in the US). Travel guides and maps to all areas of the world. A free catalogue is available.

Complete Traveller, 199 Madison Ave., New York, NY 10016 (phone: 212-685-9007). Travel guides and maps. A catalogue is available for $2.

Forsyth Travel Library, PO Box 2975, Shawnee Mission, KS 66201-1375 (phone: 800-367-7984 or 913-384-0496). Travel guides and maps, old and new, to all parts of the world. Ask for the "Worldwide Travel Books and Maps" catalogue.

Gourmet Guides, 2801 Leavenworth St., San Francisco, CA 94133 (phone: 415-771-3671). Travel guides and maps, along with cookbooks. Mail order lists available on request.

Phileas Fogg's Books and Maps, 87 Stanford Shopping Center, Palo Alto, CA 94304 (phone: 800-533-FOGG or 415-327-1754). Travel guides, maps, and language aids.

Tattered Cover, 2955 East First Ave., Denver, CO 80206 (phone: 800-833-9327 or 303-322-7727). The travel department alone of this enormous bookstore carries over 7,000 books, as well as maps and atlases. No catalogue is offered (the list is too extensive), but a newsletter, issued three times a year, is available on request.

Thomas Brothers Maps & Travel Books, 603 W. Seventh Street, Los Angeles, CA 90017 (phone: 213-627-4018). Maps (including road atlases, street guides, and wall maps), guidebooks, and travel accessories.

Traveller's Bookstore, 22 W. 52nd St. (lobby), New York, NY 10019 (phone: 212-664-0995). Travel guides, maps, literature, and accessories. A catalogue is available for $2.

Travel Suppliers, 16735 Lake Forest La., Yorba Linda, CA 93686 (phone: 714-528-2502). Mail order suppliers of books, maps, language aids, and travel paraphenalia from money belts and pouches to voltage and currency converters. A catalogue is available.

Weights and Measures

When traveling in Canada, you'll find that just about every quantity, whether it is distance, length, weight, or capacity, will be expressed in unfamiliar terms. In fact, this is true for travel almost everywhere in the world, since the US is one of the last countries to make its way to the metric system. It may happen soon in the US, and your trip to Canada will serve to familiarize you with what one day may be the weights and measures at your grocery store.

There are some specific things to keep in mind during your trip. Fruits and vegetables at a market generally are recorded in kilos (kilograms), as is your luggage at the airport and your body weight. (This latter is particularly pleasing to people of significant size, who instead of weighing 220 pounds hit the scales at a mere 100 kilos.) A kilo equals 2.2 pounds and 1 pound is .45 kilo.

APPROXIMATE EQUIVALENTS		
Metric Unit	**Abbreviation**	**US Equivalent**
LENGTH		
millimeter	mm	.04 inch
meter	m	39.37 inches
kilometer	km	.62 mile
AREA		
square centimeter	sq cm	.155 square inch
square meter	sq m	10.7 square feet
hectare	ha	2.47 acres
square kilometer	sq km	.3861 square mile
CAPACITY		
liter	l	1.057 quarts
WEIGHT		
gram	g	.035 ounce
kilogram	kg	2.2 pounds
metric ton	MT	1.1 tons
ENERGY		
kilowatt	kw	1.34 horsepower

CONVERSION TABLES METRIC TO US MEASUREMENTS

Multiply	by	to convert to
LENGTH		
millimeters	.04	inches
meters	3.3	feet
meters	1.1	yards
kilometers	.6	miles
CAPACITY		
liters	2.11	pints (liquid)
liters	1.06	quarts (liquid)
liters	.26	gallons (liquid)
WEIGHT		
grams	.04	ounces (avoir.)
kilograms	2.2	pounds (avoir.)

US TO METRIC MEASUREMENTS

LENGTH		
inches	25.	millimeters
feet	.3	meters
yards	.9	meters
miles	1.6	kilometers
CAPACITY		
pints	.47	liters
quarts	.95	liters
gallons	3.8	liters
WEIGHT		
ounces	28.	grams
pounds	.45	kilograms

TEMPERATURE

$$°F = (°C \times 9/5) + 32 \qquad °C = (°F - 32) \times 5/9$$

Body temperature usually is measured in degrees centigrade or Celsius rather than on the Fahrenheit scale — a normal body temperature is 37C, not 98.6F, and freezing is 0 degrees C rather than 32F. Gasoline is sold by the liter (approximately 4 liters to 1 gallon). Tire pressure gauges are in kilograms per square centimeter rather than pounds per square inch. Highway signs are written in kilometers rather than miles (1 mile equals 1.6 kilometers; 1 kilometer equals .62 mile). And speed limits are in kilometers per hour, so think twice before hitting the gas when you see a speed limit of 100. That means 62 miles per hour.

The tables and conversion factors listed above should give you all the information you will need to understand any transaction, road sign, or map you encounter during your travels.

Cameras and Equipment

Vacations are everybody's favorite time for taking pictures and home movies. After all, most of us want to remember the places we visit — and show them off to others. Here are a few suggestions to help you get the best results from your travel photography or videography.

BEFORE THE TRIP

If you're taking your camera or camcorder out after a long period in mothballs — or have just bought a new one — check it thoroughly before you leave to prevent unexpected breakdowns or disappointing pictures.

STILL CAMERAS

1. Shoot at least one test roll, using the kind of film you plan to take along with you. Use all the shutter speeds and f-stops on the camera, and vary the focus to make sure everything is in order. Do this well before your departure so there will be time to have the film developed and to make repairs, if necessary. If you're in a rush, most large cities have shops that can process film in as little as an hour. Repairs, unfortunately, take longer.

2. Clean your camera thoroughly, inside and out. Dust and dirt can jam mechanisms, scratch film, and mar photographs. Remove surface dust from lenses and camera body with a soft camel's hair brush. Next, use at least two layers of crumpled lens tissue and your breath to clean lenses and filters, but as they are easily scratched, don't rub hard and don't use water, saliva, or compressed air. Persistent stains can be removed by using a cotton swab moistened with liquid lens cleaner. Anything that doesn't come off easily needs professional attention; a periodic professional cleaning also is advisable. Once your lenses are clean, protect them from dirt and damage with skylight or ultraviolet filters.

3. Check the lithium batteries for your camera's light meter, and take along extras just in case yours wear out during the trip.

VIDEO CAMCORDERS

1. If you haven't used your camcorder lately, use a "practice" videocassette to reacquaint yourself with the various shooting techniques — such as panning, zooming, and segueing (that is, transitioning without pause) from one scene to another. Practice fully before you leave; don't save it for the plane.

2. Clean and maintain your camcorder lenses with a soft, dry cloth. Don't use solvents such as paint thinner or chemically treated cloths. Once your camcorder lenses are clean, protect them from dirt and damage with inexpensive skylight or ultraviolet filters. If your camcorder's heads need cleaning, a recorded tape will tell you. A "snowy" tape is a sign that a head cleaning is needed. If a head cleaning doesn't improve the picture, the problem may lie elsewhere. In that case, take the camcorder to a professional for a check-up. Check the operation of each component on your camcorder, making sure that each feature performs correctly. If there's an internal problem, don't try to fix it yourself. You could void the manufacturer's warranty or, even worse, cause further damage. Even if all appears well at home, take a head cleaner along on your trip to make sure your videos remain clear and sharp.

3. Check the lithium batteries for your camcorder's light indicators, and take along

extras just in case yours wear out during the trip. If you took along all your camcorder accessories, your carrying bag would get heavy and cumbersome, but there are a few "musts." Take extra nickel-cadmium (Ni-Cd) batteries so that you always have one or two power sources ready while another is recharging back at the hotel. You never know when a once-in-a-lifetime opportunity will present itself, and if you just used up your 45-minute allotment of power on a local festival, you'll have none left to shoot anything else. Remember that the more features you use, including reviewing what you've taped in the electronic viewfinder, the more battery power you will consume.

EQUIPMENT TO TAKE ALONG

Keep your gear light and compact. Items that are too heavy or bulky to be carried comfortably on a full-day excursion will likely remain in your hotel room, so leave them home.

1. Invest in a broad camera or camcorder strap if you now have a thin one. It will make carrying the camera much more comfortable.
2. A sturdy canvas or leather camera or camcorder bag, preferably with padded pockets (not an airline bag), will keep your equipment organized and easy to find.
3. For cleaning, bring along a camel's hair brush that retracts into a rubber squeeze bulb. Also take plenty of lens tissue, soft cloths, and plastic bags to protect equipment from dust and moisture.

STILL CAMERAS: Lenses and Other Equipment – Most single-lens-reflex (SLR) cameras come with a 50mm, or "normal," lens — a general-purpose lens that frames subjects within an approximately average angle of view. This is good for street scenes taken at a distance of 25 feet or more, and for full-length portraits shot at 8 to 12 feet.

Any lens from 35mm on down offers wide-angle capabilities, which in effect pull segments of the peripheral scene into the picture, and are especially handy for panoramas and landscapes. A wide-angle lens in the 20–28mm range is perfect for palace gardens. Where the normal perspective of a 50mm lens provides only a partial view of Toronto's massive *SkyDome* and CN Tower, a 20mm incorporates the striking modern design of these two structures and the surrounding buildings of downtown Toronto in one flowing scene. While a 50mm lens only provides a partial view of Niagra Falls, taken from the proper perspective a 20mm lens can encompass the breadth of this monumental cascade and geological wonder. The wide-angle lens also is excellent for linking people with their surroundings because of its great depth of field — that is, sharp focus from foreground to background — that can focus pictures between 3½ feet and infinity. And it also can be valuable when there's very little space between you and your subject.

Wide-angle lenses are especially handy for panoramas, for cityscapes, and for large buildings or statuary from which you can't step back. For extreme closeups, a macro lens is best, but a screw-on magnifying lens is an inexpensive alternative. Keep in mind that wide-angle lenses have a tendency to distort when used very close to a subject, or when dealing with vertical lines. Tall trees or a high-rise hotel may seem to converge toward the top of the frame, for example. Once you're aware of these effects, you can use them to creative advantage.

Where a wide-angle lens extends normal perspective, a telephoto lens focuses on a portion of the overview, providing perspective in detail. Telephoto lenses, 125mm to 1,000mm, are good for shooting details from a distance and permit dramatic silhouettes of sailboats against a setting sun, detailed portraits, floral design, and candids — although when choosing a lens, keep in mind that the weight of the higher ranges may prove difficult to support without a tripod (see below).

In addition to individual telephotos, a number of telephoto zoom lenses have become popular with travel photographers. Zooms offer the most versatility as they incorporate a range of focal lengths. A typical telephoto zoom — ranging from 70mm to 210mm, for example — allows you to frame a picture as you want it by choosing the most appropriate lens setting for the situation. That means carrying one lens with millimeter-to-millimeter variations from 70mm to 210mm. Also try a 35mm to 80mm. In general, beware of inexpensive models which can result in poor photographs.

The drawbacks of a zoom lens are its weight and a potential loss of clarity when compared with individual telephotos. This is less of a problem with the better lenses; and both problems are being eliminated by technological advances.

A 2X Teleconverter is a simple addition to a camera kit. Lightweight and easy to carry, the 2X doubles the focal length of various lenses, converting a 20mm into a 40mm, a 50mm into a 100mm, a 70mm to 210mm zoom into a 140mm to 420mm, and so forth. Though there is again a potential loss of clarity, and in low-lighting situations focusing may be somewhat more difficult due to the extra thickness of lens glass, the 2X is a versatile accessory that's easy to use.

While it may seem excessive, a small, lightweight tripod is a real asset in assuring picture quality. This is particularly true when the heavier telephoto lenses are used, or in situations where the available light is limited and shots will be made at speeds slower than 1/60 of a second. For sharp detail, closeups, night, or limited-light pictures while in Canada, a tripod is a must.

A small battery-powered electronic flash unit, or "strobe," is handy for very dim light or night use, but only if the subject is at a distance of 15 feet or less. Flash units cannot illuminate an entire scene (they're only effective up to about a dozen feet), and many museums and other establishments do not permit flash photography, so take such a unit only if you know you will need — and be able to use — it. (If you do violate these rules and take a picture in such a restricted area your film, and even your camera, may be confiscated.)

Subjects as varied as the interiors of churches, caves, and wine cellars all become photographable with a flash. It also can provide frontal light for a backlit subject and additional light in a variety of dim situations, as it is often overcast in many parts of Canada. If your camera does not have a hot-shoe, you will need a PC cord to synchronize the flash with your shutter. Be sure to take along extra batteries for the flash.

Film – Travel photographs are normally best in color. Good slide films are Kodachrome 64 and Kodachrome 50, both moderate- to slow-speed films that provide saturated colors and work well in most outdoor light. For very bright conditions, try slower film, like Kodachrome 25. If the weather is cloudy, or you're indoors with only natural light, use a faster film, such as Kodachrome 200 or 400. There are now even faster films on the market for low-light situations. The result may be pictures with whiter, colder tones and a grainier image, but high-speed films open up picture possibilities that slower films cannot.

Films tend to render color in slightly different ways. For instance, while Kodachrome results in "warmer" tones and brings out reds and oranges, Ektachrome, a similar film, is "colder" and produces crisp, clear colors — particularly blues and greens. (It is also worth noting that Ektachrome generally can be processed at more photolabs than Kodachrome.) Fujichrome is noted for its yellows, greens, and whites. You might test films as you test your camera (see above) to determine your preference.

If you prefer film that develops into prints rather than slides, try Kodacolor 100 or 400 for most lighting situations. Vericolor is a professional film which comes in speeds of 160 and 400 and gives excellent results, especially for skin tones, but is particularly sensitive to temperature extremes which may cause color alteration. Bring it along for taking shots of people *if* you're sure you can protect it from extreme heat and cold. A newer all-purpose film with similar properties to Vericolor in terms of quality results is Ektar. It is not as sensitive to temperature changes as Vericolor, and comes in three speeds: 25, 125, and 1000. All lens and filter information applies equally to print and slide films.

If you are concerned about airport security X-rays damaging undeveloped film (X-rays do not affect processed film), store it in one of the lead-lined bags sold in camera shops. This possibility is not as much of a threat as it used to be, however. In the US, incidents of X-ray damage to unprocessed film (exposed or unexposed) are few because low-dosage X-ray equipment is used virtually everywhere. However, when crossing international borders, travelers may find that foreign X-ray equipment may deliver higher levels of radiation and damage film.

As a rule of thumb, photo industry sources say that film with speeds up to ASA 400 can go through security machinery in the US five times without any noticeable effect. Nevertheless, if you're traveling without a protective bag, ask to have your photo equipment inspected by hand. (Naturally, this is possible only if you're carrying your film and camera on board with you — a good idea, because it helps to preclude loss or theft or the possibility at some airports that checked baggage will be X-rayed with equipment more powerful than normally used for hand baggage.)

In the US, Federal Aviation Administration regulations require that if you request a hand inspection, you get it, but in Canada the response may depend on the humor of the inspector. One type of film that never should be subjected to X-rays is the new, very high-speed ASA 1000 film; there are lead-lined bags made especially for it — and, in the event that you are refused a hand inspection, this is the only way to save your film. Finally, the walk-through metal detector devices at airports do not affect film, though film cartridges may set them off.

How much film should you take? If you are serious about photography, pack at least one roll of film (36 exposures) for each day of your trip. Film is more expensive in Canada than the US, and any extra can be bartered away or brought home and safely stored in your refrigerator. (Processing also is more expensive abroad and not as safe as at home.) Nevertheless, if you don't bring enough, you should have no trouble getting any standard film in most places in Canada; it's sold everywhere.

VIDEO CAMCORDERS: In general, camcorders are self-contained, automated, point-and-shoot devices, though for the more ambitious film-making traveler, 8mm video or movie cameras allow the operator a greater degree of control over the images recorded and superior image quality. What follows is a brief roundup of tips and suggestions for the beginning home moviemaker, and those travelers who need to brush up on their videotaping technique.

Your camcorder has some type of zoom feature, whether it's 4:1, 6:1, or all the way up to 12:1. For most people, that's enough. Although some models have a fixed lens, others, like 8mm video, provide you the option of adding a telephoto for close-up shooting or a wide-angle lens if you often find yourself not being able to fit all of what you want to shoot into the viewfinder. If you do decide to add a lens, check that the one you buy will fit your camcorder. You may be able to double up on your filters, though. As long as it's the same size, your camera filter should be able to fit on your camcorder lens. (See the discussion of filters below.)

Although the lux ratings of camcorders now are low enough to achieve some impressive videos in low-light situations, for good clarity and color saturation, you should have an additional light (10 watts or higher) to brighten indoor shooting. Generally, the lights easily can be attached to the camcorder and come with the necessary accessories such as battery charger, battery pack, and light diffuser. All that can get fairly heavy, however, so you might want to leave your light at home. Most museums and churches prohibit the use of video lights — both for security reasons and because they can be harmful to paintings and stained glass, not to mention annoying to other visitors.

Tapes – It usually is best to buy tapes before leaving home, as they probably will be lots more expensive near major tourist and resort areas. It also will be less confusing, since different countries have their own ways of labeling tape. If you do run out of tape while on your trip, you shouldn't have a hard time finding what you need. Most of the major tape brands — TDK, Sony, Memorex, Maxell, BASF, Fuji, and Scotch — are available throughout the US, but when buying tapes in Canada, you're bound to run into some unfamiliar names. Stick to what you know, if possible. When choosing, especially among unfamiliar brands, be sure that it is indeed the correct tape format — 8mm, VHS, Super-VHS, Beta, and so on — for your camcorder.

Also, if an unknown brand is priced substantially below the rest, there's probably a reason. First of all, the image quality may be poor. Secondly, the few dollars you save in buying the least expensive videocassettes will mean nothing a few years from now when the tape is showing signs of wear. You also should be aware of the potential problem of low-quality tapes damaging the heads of camcorders.

Because you'll want to keep your accessories to a manageable number — especially if you're using a full-size camcorder — you should use the longest-length tape possible for recording your trip. Depending on the tape speed of your equipment, the longest 8mm and VHS tapes generally run for 2 hours and VHS-C cassettes run for 20 minutes. VHS and VHS-C cassettes can record in the extended-play mode for 6-hour and 60-minute recordings, respectively, but extending the recording time reduces the picture quality substantially. It's best to record in the standard-play mode, because you'll get the best picture quality.

With the wide variety of grades and types of videocassettes on the market, it's easy to get confused about what kind of tape to buy for a particular application. Certain camcorders can record in stereo, so for those you'll want a hi-fi videocassette for better sound quality. If you have a Super VHS, Super VHS-C, or Hi Band 8mm camcorder, you'll want to buy the corresponding tapes for those high-end machines to achieve the best possible picture quality. A Super VHS-C videocassette will not improve your regular VHS-C video picture, however. Get a high-grade or professional quality tape for the once-in-a-lifetime videos that you plan to watch a lot. Before loading up on videocassettes for your trip, think about how much time you'll actually spend shooting, and about how many tapes you'll really want to view later. Plan on a tape for every other day of your vacation, or, if you intend to use your camcorder heavily, a tape for each day. Remember that you always can edit a tape, and even reuse it if you decide you don't want to keep it.

Your videocassettes generally are safe from the X-rays in airport detector devices, but the electromagnetic fields generated by those devices could cause dropouts in your tapes, which are recorded by an electromagnetic process. The lead-lined bags that protect against X-rays unfortunately don't protect against an electromagnetic field, so your best bet is to take your tapes along for a hand inspection. Because cassettes have been favorite carriers for terrorist explosives over the years, however, airport officials may insist that you put everything through the X-ray machine. If you don't have a choice, put them through and hope for the best.

FILTERS: For both Camcorders and SLR cameras, filters are important considerations. Take a skylight filter (1A or 1B) for each lens. There's no need to remove it, except to replace it with a different filter. Not only will it provide the filtration needed to combat atmospheric haze and ultraviolet light, but it also will protect the lens surface.

A polarizering filter goes one step beyond the skylight variety, cutting out reflections from non-metallic surfaces (water and glass, for instance) and penetrating haze for extra clarity and rich color saturation. It also will add impact to greens and blues in a landscape. While its effects are dramatic, it can be a difficult filter to use as it cuts back on light (it's a dark filter) and creates deep shadows. It will work well only under certain lighting conditions. In spite of these drawbacks, it remains an excellent filter for certain effects.

Unless you plan to experiment with the increasingly diverse range of specialty filters now available (diffraction, multiple image, and closeup, for instance), skylights and a polarizer are just about all you'll need. Stick to the high- to medium-priced glass filters (Hoya, Tiffen, or Vivitar, for example) to assure picture quality.

SOME FINAL TIPS

Get organized. A small, lightweight canvas camera bag with cushioning and Velcro dividers is perfect for carrying lenses, lens tissue, filters, rolls of film or tapes, and a strobe. It's amazing how compact camera equipment is when packed properly. For better pictures, remember the following pointers:

1. Get close. Move in to get your subject to fill the frame.
2. Vary your angle. Shoot from above or below; look for unusual perspectives.
3. Pay attention to backgrounds. Keep it simple or blur it out.
4. Look for details: not just a whole building, but a decorative element; not an entire street scene, but a single remarkable face.
5. Don't be lazy. Always carry your camera gear with you, loaded and ready for unexpected opportunities.

For Better Videos — Try to plan your movie with an introduction, a development, and a conclusion. Sometimes you can't help but get a video collage, but shoot with an eye — and an ear — toward how it's going to look and sound on a TV set. You're not just capturing a moment, as you do with still photography; you're telling a story.

1. To divide the tapes by city or province, use the camcorder's titling feature, if it has one, or shoot museum signs or some other kind of markers that indicate where you are. Use your fade in/fade out feature to provide smooth transitions.
2. Suppress your impulse to point and shoot and then find another object to shoot. Your viewers will need several seconds to focus on a subject and orient themselves to what they're seeing. Stay on each subject for at least 5 or 6 seconds — longer if the situation warrants.
3. Try not to shoot directly into strong, bright light, as this may damage your camcorder. Your subject also is likely to appear as a silhouette because the camcorder will adjust for the brightest source. Some camcorders, however, do have backlight compensating features.
4. Vary your shooting techniques. Using the various buttons available at your fingertips, zoom in and out and pan from side to side to view your subject. If your subject is stationary, walk around (but hold the camera steady) to get a different angle. Your objective should be to create a smooth flow.
5. Your camcorder won't be welcome everywhere, although as they become more popular, they are increasingly accepted. In any event, before lugging your gear with you, check with the places you plan to visit.
   ■ **A note about courtesy and caution:** When photographing in Canada (and anywhere else in the world), ask first. It's common courtesy. Furthermore, government security regulations regarding the use of cameras will not permit the photographing of certain subjects, such as some government and military installations. When in doubt, ask.

PERSPECTIVES

The Canadian Past: A Short History of a Huge Country

 For 2 million years, a land bridge between Asia and North America appeared and disappeared as great sheets of ice retreated and advanced across the North American continent. For the last 10,000 to 15,000 years these ice sheets — the word "glacier" hardly conveys their continent-spanning immensity — have been in retreat, and that land bridge, the Bering Strait, has been covered by the icy waters of the Bering Sea. But when the ice moved forward, as it did intermittently for millennia, sculpting the earth with implacable force as it crept south from the Arctic, whole seas were drawn into the frozen advance, and a bridge of some 50 to 60 miles of dry land appeared between Asia and North America.

It was during such a period of advance that the first Asian peoples crossed the land bridge and entered North America about 25,000 years ago. Their progression south is an epic — one that will never be told and never really known — that moved through corridors of thaw in the huge masses of ice. They and the peoples who followed were the antecedents of the spectacular Indian cultures of North America. At the time of the earliest crossings, more than three-quarters of the earth's surface was covered by ice, but by 8000 BC the great glaciers were in abeyance and native American cultures — from the Arctic to Mexico — were developing in astounding profusion and diversity.

The main Indian tribes of the Canadian northwest were the Tlinglit in what is now Alaska, the Tsimshian, Salish, and Kwakiutl along the coast, and the Chinook and Nootka on Vancouver Island and along the Columbia River. Their cultures were hierarchical; chiefs were rich and powerful men who could command the attention of both slaves and commoners. In return, they were expected to finance the great whale hunts and to provide both fishing and war canoes for the men of the tribe. The chief and his wife played a large part in the religious rituals that ensured good whaling. Life along the coast centered on the incredibly rich waters — fresh water, in the streams running to the sea, and the sea itself — that dominated every aspect of existence. The salmon and whale were treated like respected brothers of the sea, and seal, beaver, and otter provided food, clothing, and fur for trade.

The Indians of the Canadian plains — stretching from the eastern edge of the Rockies across what is now Alberta, Saskatchewan, and Manitoba — had nowhere near as comfortable an existence. The Blackfoot, Plains, Cree, and Assiniboine were hunters and foragers who spent their lives following the great buffalo herds. It was for only a relatively short time — from the 17th century — that they had horses, the "big dogs" that totally changed their lives. Before that, every move was made by human strength, and the only pack animals were dogs.

Though most of the East Coast Indians also were hunters and gatherers, their lives were far richer and more comfortable than that of their plains brothers. The Montagnais and Naskapi roamed northeastern Canada; the Algonquin, Abnaki, Maliseet, and Iroquois ranged through lower Canada, the Great Lakes district, and what became the northeastern US. The Huron and other tribes of the Iroquois Confederacy actually farmed portions of their land in addition to hunting; almost all the other northeastern tribes hunted in the huge, rich forests of the area.

As the Huron became increasingly agricultural and established themselves in lower Canada (Ontario), a schism developed that separated the Huron tribes from the more mobile tribes of the Iroquois Nation. By the early 1600s, this had resulted in open hostility between the two groups, and the Hurons not only defended the area we called Huronia from Iroquois raids, but forced the Five Nations Confederacy (as the Iroquois Nation also was called) to remain south of the St. Lawrence River.

On the eastern seaboard, across the Great Plains, up and down the Pacific Northwest Coast, groups of Indian tribes crafted lifestyles and practiced religions adapted to the realities of the life they found. By the time the Europeans arrived in North America, these peoples had for eons maintained stable and successful societies, as distinct from one another as the courts of the Renaissance were different from communities of Vikings. Into these delicate cultures stormed the realities of European history.

THE COMING OF EUROPEANS

At the northernmost tip of the huge island of Newfoundland is the tiny fishing village of L'Anse-au-Meadow. It is located in a desolate and remote part of the province, where the European history of Canada and the New World began.

Close to 1,000 years ago, about 500 years before Columbus planted the flag of imperial Spain on the sands of a Bahamian isle, the Vikings from Scandinavia, some of the most intrepid travelers of all time, established a settlement at L'Anse-au-Meadow and called it Vinland. The Vikings, in their longboats, reached this part of Canada by using the Faeroes, Iceland, and Greenland as stepping-stones. Although they attempted to maintain a colony here (the foundation of some of their buildings, unearthed by archaeologist Helge Ingstad and others, are still visible), their life in the New World was doomed. Viking families suffered from long, bitter winters and deadly Indian attacks. Many perished. The survivors fled back to the more congenial and familiar lands of Iceland, Denmark, and Sweden.

Scholars speculate that while the Vikings were in the New World they roamed far to the south, sailing down the coast of eastern North America, possibly establishing other settlements. In Yarmouth, Nova Scotia, for example, there is a strange runic stone that local folklore claims was left by the

Norsemen. But conclusive proof of their presence in other parts of Canada's eastern seaboard is yet to be found, except the very tangible remains at L'Anse-au-Meadow. And even much of what can be seen there today is shrouded in mystery.

It was not until 500 years after the Viking period that a more enduring exploration of Canada took place. John Cabot (Giovanni Caboto, a Venetian adventurer, using an English name) landed on a desolate Cape Breton Island beach in the summer of 1497. He claimed this "new-found land" for England, where he had moved, some historians say, in the 1480s to live in Bristol, then a major departure point for explorers headed for the New World. His English backers had financed his sail west in hopes of finding a new route to the East Indies. Cabot failed in this quest, but he did make a discovery that would, in due time, provide countless men and several nations with riches beyond expectation. He found one of the most fertile commercial fishing grounds in the world, the Grand Banks off the coast of Newfoundland.

At the time, Cabot's investors considered his voyage largely a loss. However, it was not long before other investors in France and Portugal heard about Cabot's exciting Grand Banks find, and began to send expeditions to exploit the cod fishing there.

The French and the Portuguese were the first to develop the cod fisheries of Newfoundland and to make handsome profits from them. Eventually England sent ships in great enough numbers to compete with the French and Portuguese. And in a relatively short period of time, England became master of the rich fisheries of this region, in part by exerting its sovereignty over Newfoundland — Britain's earliest colony. Cod was not only "king" in its own right, it was the lure that brought more adventurous explorers to open the doors of a vast, unknown continent.

One of these seekers was Jacques Cartier, a Frenchman from St.-Malo. In 1534, Cartier sailed into the Gulf of St. Lawrence, earning the right to name it. He landed on what is now the province of Prince Edward Island, which he called "Ile St. Jean," and on the Gaspé Peninsula, the eastern gateway via the St. Lawrence River into the heartland of Canada. Cartier sailed down the St. Lawrence as far as Montreal, following what he thought was the Northwest Passage. He claimed all he saw for France, and he called his discovery Kannata, an Algonquin word meaning "a settlement."

With England and France entrenched in Canada, the stage was set for an epic conflict between two old rivals. For several decades, the French neither explored nor exploited Cartier's rich discoveries. It wasn't until a craze for beaver hats — started by Francis II — overtook the royal court and forced ambitious hatters to press for a new source of beaver that the French sent expeditions into the St. Lawrence River to trade with the Indians. But they were unaware of the hostility between the tribes of lower Canada and those farther south. Unwittingly they became allies of the Huron tribes against the Iroquois Nation by supplying weapons and other goods to the nearby tribes.

French explorer Samuel de Champlain, the most honored of Canada's early explorers, charted the St. Lawrence River as far as Montreal Island and pushed up the Ottawa River to the point at which the city of Ottawa is presently located. In 1604, Champlain led an expedition to Acadia, the area that today includes Maine, Nova Scotia, and New Brunswick, in order to establish a trading colony. Sieur de Monts, a Huguenot aristocrat, sailed with Champlain as lieutenant governor of the new colony. The expedition spent its first winter on an island in the St. Croix River, losing many of its party to the climate and disease. Champlain moved the group to a more habitable site on Nova Scotia's Bay of Fundy. Here at Port Royal, in 1605, Champlain's Habitation started its life as the first permanent European settlement in Canada.

Three years later, in 1608, Champlain founded what became the most important city in New France and, later, the capital of one of Canada's provinces. On an apron of land below a massive rock mesa overlooking the St. Lawrence River, Champlain established the French village of Quebec. This historic event took place 1 year after the founding of Jamestown, Virginia, and 12 years before the Pilgrims landed at Plymouth, Massachusetts.

During the 17th century, Quebec not only became the locus of the fur trade in New France, but also a center of the Roman Catholic church in North America. The fur traders, *les coureurs de bois,* ranged into the interior as far as the Rocky Mountains and the Gulf of Mexico; only a step behind were the "black robe" priests. In many instances they blazed trails ahead of the traders. In the United States, Detroit, St. Louis, Pittsburgh, and New Orleans were discovered and originally settled by French pioneers from Quebec. It was Louis Joliet and Father Marquette who first reached the "Father of Waters," the Mississippi River. Cavelier de La Salle claimed Louisiana for the French. Among the different religious orders that came to New France, three stand out as exceptional in Canadian history: the Jesuits, who brought culture, scholarship, and missionary zeal combined with humane tolerance, courage, and inquiring minds; the Ursuline sisters, with their grace, compassion, knowledge, and medical skill; and the Société de Notre Dame, largely a lay group. In 1642, they founded the city of Montreal as a utopia of peace and prayer, and it soon replaced Quebec as the center for the fur trade — in spite of its purely inspirational origins. (Montreal retained its primacy as Canada's commercial center until the final third of this century, when Toronto assumed the dominant position.) As cod enriched the English off the foggy coast of Newfoundland, beaver and other animal pelts earned profits for France and created a new, politically powerful aristocracy in the North American colony.

THE FRENCH AND ENGLISH WARS

During the 17th century, England established colonies along the American eastern seaboard from Maine to Georgia. In addition, in 1610 Henry Hudson discovered the huge bay in the Canadian north that bears his name. Here, in 1670, the English established a fur trading company (the Hudson's Bay Company, still a very active concern on the Canadian retailing and trading scene), which brought them into open conflict with French interests.

From 1689 to 1815, England and France waged intermittent war in a struggle for commercial and military hegemony over much of the world. This conflict is often referred to as the Second Hundred Years' War. Canada was one of several areas at stake. The English fought the French in the Caribbean, in India, in the Pacific, in Belgium and Bavaria, and in Quebec. It is easiest to conceptualize the North American war as one aspect of a much larger global struggle. King William's War in America (1689–1697) was the War of the League of Augsburg in Europe; Queen Anne's War (1702–1713) was the War of the Spanish Succession; America's French and Indian War, which brought about the complete expulsion of the French from Canada, was Europe's Seven Years' War; and the War of 1812 was only a minor episode in the overwhelmingly long conflict known as the Wars of the French Revolution and Napoleon.

Amid this wide-ranging war, a smaller — but equally crucial — conflict was taking place. An offensive by the Iroquois Nation (Mohawk, Oneida, Onondaga, Cayuga, and Seneca) against the Huron Nation began with a series of raids against both the Huron and the French fur traders. The English, who had supplied the Iroquois with guns in exchange for furs, supported this action. Open warfare began in the 1640s and lasted until 1667, creating an environment of terror for all the European settlers caught in its wake. Both Indian nations wanted to control the fur trade with the tribes of the interior, because that was the only way to gain the valued goods of the Europeans. And the two European nations wanted control of the continent.

Nevertheless, the North American war of the mid-18th century, while nearly always related to European conflicts, displayed an increasingly indigenous character. During the War of the Spanish Succession, the French renewed their border raids, but the shape of the future was foretold when the British sent six men-of-war and a regiment of marines to Boston in 1710. Supplemented by militia raised in New England, this force captured Port Royal in Acadia. By the Treaty of Utrecht, the French recognized the English possession of Hudson Bay, Newfoundland, and Acadia (which the English promptly renamed Nova Scotia).

When the War of the Austrian Succession broke out in Europe in 1739, the challenge was readily accepted in North America. Led by Massachusetts's Governor William Shirley, ambitious Calvinist merchants sponsored an expedition against Louisbourg, in Nova Scotia. Lacking French support, the town fell to the New Englanders. A combination of New England militiamen and British seapower held the town against a French attempt to recapture it the following year. But on the European continent the French had done relatively well, and at the Peace of Aix-la-Chapelle (1748), Louisburg was returned to France — to the dismay and disgust of the men who had taken it.

At the advent of the French and Indian War in the middle of the century, the population of the English colonies was roughly 2 million, whereas in all of North America there were no more than 80,000 French. Even without English superiority on the sea, the struggle would have called for an amazing effort on the part of the French. In the first years of the war the French did quite well. In 1756 they sent substantial reinforcements to the St. Lawrence under a brilliant, well-read general, the Marquis de Montcalm. At first Montcalm overcame his heavy numerical disadvantages by a series of bold strikes. Aided by the disunity of the English colonies and by the inexperience of British leadership in the ways of wilderness warfare, he captured Fort Oswego, destroyed the English outposts in northern New York, and kept the British colonial forces on guard and off balance along the entire frontier. But Montcalm was unable to maintain these advantages.

The corruption and petty intrigue that riddled Quebec society had its effect on Montcalm's campaign. From the outset of his command, Montcalm had been suspicious of his colleagues in the government of Quebec, and they repaid his lack of confidence with hostility. The governor, the Marquis of Vaudreuil, a native of the colony, symbolized an interest that increasingly resented both overseas control and inadequate French support. Vaudreuil and Montcalm never resolved their differences, and the result took its toll on the French effort. Pure avarice further undermined the war effort. Some French merchants were intent on making a private fortune while the colony floundered in a sea of inflation, corrupt influences, and fraud.

In addition, a growing determination on the part of the English to clear the French from their path of expansion crystallized under the new leadership of William Pitt. His government waged a swift and brilliant campaign. In 1758, Pitt dispatched a fresh sea and land force and began a gigantic pincer movement. Fort Frontenac, guardian of the Lake Ontario approaches to the St. Lawrence Valley, fell in the summer of 1758 while a combined force under Generals Wolfe and Amherst smashed its way into the fortress of Louisburg and thereby secured the sea approaches to the St. Lawrence. In June 1759, an even larger assault force sailed up the river to just below Quebec. From July until early September the British played cat and mouse with Quebec, making feints above and below the citadel. As autumn approached, both Montcalm and Vaudreuil became convinced that Wolfe planned a direct attack; the British obviously could not risk an extended campaign during the winter, as the river would be sealed by ice.

During the siege, Quebec's Lower Town was repeatedly shelled by Wolfe's artillery at Lévis, on the south shore of the St. Lawrence. The Lower Town's buildings were either reduced to rubble or left barely standing. Montcalm had the strategic advantage of Quebec's Upper Town, which was protected by high, steep cliffs, but the hard siege took its toll. The French were running out of ammunition and food. Montcalm's previous efforts to protect New France had been undermined by corruption, and the weaknesses were now growing into bleeding wounds as he desperately tried to keep Quebec — and thus New France — from slipping out of his fingers. In the middle of September, Wolfe had a stroke of good luck. On the dark night of September 12, he led a force of British and Scottish infantry past French river patrols to a point west of Lower Town. Here they bluffed their way past French sentries and climbed up the steep cliffs, where they assembled on the Plains of Abraham on the morning of September 13. An astonished Montcalm rushed his forces out of the fortified walls of Upper Town to confront the British. Within moments the battle was over, won by the British. Both Wolfe and Montcalm were shot. Wolfe died in the midst of the smoke and slaughter on the Plains of Abraham. Montcalm succumbed to his wounds a few hours later inside the walls of Quebec. Although the Battle of Quebec was not the last between the French and British in this campaign, it proved decisive. New France ceased to exist.

According to legend, as New France faded away on the bloody ground of the Plains of Abraham, the cry "*Je me souviens*" ("I remember") was heard. The aristocracy and the affluent bourgeoisie abandoned Quebec and fled back to France, but the farmers, craftsmen, trappers, fishermen, and nuns and priests who stayed never forgot what they had lost on the Plains. They taught "Je me souviens" to the next generation, and it was passed on, generation by generation, down to the present day. "*Je me souviens*" is Quebec's motto, and can be seen everywhere in the province.

After the defeat of the French, there was a brief lull before an even more serious storm. The campaign in North America had been costly for the British, and the coffers of the national treasury needed replenishing. Since the American colonists had benefited from the war — they could now go about their business with a far greater sense of security — London felt it was only fair for them to bear part of the great cost of the war and of maintaining a standing army. The bitterness over "taxation without representation" was one of the well-known causes of the American Revolution, but few realize that it was far from a one-sided injustice.

Another major issue that exacerbated the problem was the Quebec Act of 1774. The act set aside the policy of uniform colonial growth and placed full authority in Quebec in the hands of the governor and an appointed council. In addition, it provided a string of benefits for the French-Canadian upper class: Roman Catholics were allowed to hold civil office; the seignorial land-holding system was confirmed, as was French civil law; and the Roman Catholic church was allowed to collect tithes. The province's boundaries were extended to include much of the old French empire — the region between the Ohio and the Mississippi rivers in which Montreal fur traders were still the dominant economic force.

To the staunchly Protestant "American" colonists, the Quebec Act was a bitter pill to swallow, especially because it closed off the Ohio and Mississippi valleys to expansion, protecting them for the French. On the part of the British, the Quebec Act was simply a graceful acknowledgment that over 60,000 white inhabitants of conquered Canada were French and Roman Catholic. And Britain felt it had a perfect right to control commercial activity in the western territories.

THE AMERICAN REVOLUTION

At the convening of the first Continental Congress in 1774, there was no United States and no Canada as such, only 15 British colonies (Nova Scotia the 14th and Quebec the 15th). Both Nova Scotia and Quebec were invited to attend; both declined. The Bishops of Quebec felt threatened by the Protestantism of the English colonies and by the new, revolutionary ideas that were sweeping the western world. There was strong pro-American sentiment in Nova Scotia, but the colony's geographical remoteness and the presence of the British navy, headquartered in Halifax, prevented any action. Thus, 13 English colonies declared their independence while two remained in the imperial fold. The US and Canada came into being as distinct entities.

Whether one thought of suppressing the rebellion or simply of retaining

British control of the northern half of the continent, Quebec remained a key. As was also to be the case in the struggle of 1812, the "Americans" moved first. Congress dispatched two hastily organized armies to capture Montreal and Quebec. In November 1775, General Richard Montgomery took Montreal and Trois-Rivières and moved on to Quebec, the keystone to this 15th British colony. Benedict Arnold, who later joined the British side and lived in Saint John, New Brunswick, led a force of men through the wilderness of Maine to join Montgomery at Quebec. It was a classic pincer that might have won Quebec and the rest of Canada for America. Unfortunately, in 1775 Montgomery was killed in an attack on Quebec, and Arnold had to withdraw the American forces south into New York State.

What went wrong with the American plan that almost worked? Although many of the French sided with the Americans and considered them liberators, it was the Americans themselves who, by their conduct in Montreal, soured their potential allies. While occupying Montreal, American troops insulted the Catholic clergy, took over private homes and buildings by force, and tried to buy goods and services with worthless paper money. An American delegation, under the leadership of Benjamin Franklin, went to Montreal to soothe the feelings of the people. But the damage had been done. At Quebec the French fought beside the British against the forces of Montgomery and Arnold. What could have been a relatively short war became a protracted one.

With the British in control of Quebec and Nova Scotia, the English-speaking population on the Canadian mainland and in the Maritimes increased dramatically and in a most unexpected way. Those Americans who remained loyal to the British monarchy fled from the 13 colonies for their personal safety. While many returned to England, over 40,000 went to Canada. Some 35,000 went to Nova Scotia and 7,000 to what is now Ontario. In every sense of the word they were war refugees. A significant portion of these people were well educated (at Harvard and Yale, especially) and had been the affluent ruling elite in the colonies. They fled with only minimal necessities, at best to what was essentially a hostile wilderness, and many did not survive. Some gave up and went to the West Indies and other less severe climates in the British Empire. Others waited out the war, returning to the American states when the new government granted them amnesty. Those who stayed in Canada, however, cut back the thick forests and established cities, towns, farms, and industries. Loyalists living on the north shore of the Bay of Fundy and in that area's interior developed the region and formed their own colony, New Brunswick.

At the conclusion of the war, many other Americans went to Canada, claiming to have been Loyalists. Some were, in truth; others pretended to be so only because they wanted the free land offered to Loyalists. The availability of land attracted many apolitical Americans in general. In 1791, Quebec, which had been extended west of Lake Erie, was divided into Upper Canada (present-day Ontario) and Lower Canada (present-day Quebec). Seventeen years later Upper Canada had a population of around 80,000; 80% were American. Lower Canada had the larger population: 250,000 in 1806, of whom 100,000 were American in origin. Both Nova Scotia and New Brunswick experienced dramatic population increases in the years immediately following what many called a civil war between Englishmen. In addition to the indigenous French and Indian populations, the Scottish who sought refuge in the Maritimes after the "clearances" of the highlands, the Acadians of the *Evangeline* saga who came back to Nova Scotia, and those British and Hessian soldiers who opted for a freer life in the New World, Canada's population in the early 19th century burgeoned with Americans who either felt more comfortable with a monarchy than with a republican democracy or simply wanted land on their own terms.

The fate of the British Loyalists is a historic footnote to the War of Independence. Those Americans who could prove their loyalty to the Crown were decreed by George III "United Empire Loyalists." They were entitled to add the initials *UEL* after their signature and could pass on this honor to future generations. This royal benediction created a new elite in Canada and strengthened its standing with the military, aristocratic, political, and commercial elites that began to pour into Canada from Great Britain. Both as a distinct class and by marriage into the British upper class, the Loyalists not only prospered but came to dominate much of Canada's social and commercial life. Saint John, New Brunswick, Halifax, Nova Scotia, Montreal, and Toronto became their centers of influence. Their power, and that of their descendants, continued well into the 20th century. In today's Canada, however, it is considerably diminished except in certain social circles and a few communities in Ontario and New Brunswick, where the initials *UEL* after one's name still carry some clout.

BRITISH CANADA

Between the signing of the Treaty of Versailles in 1783 and the War of 1812, the people of Canada developed farms, industries, communities, and cultural and political institutions. In Lower Canada, for example, the French professional class gained control of the elected assembly. Great Britain was a good customer for Canadian fur, fish, timber, and grain. However, the Jay Treaty of 1749 initiated a new era of trade between Great Britain and the US, and Canada was faced with serious competition for its chief market. Still, Canadian goods were allowed to enter Great Britain under the system of "imperial preference" duty free — and the US became Canada's second-best market.

The first 15 years of the 19th century saw Great Britain leading the opposition to Napoleonic expansion in Europe. It is doubtful that the English were looking for another fight with the Americans; they had their hands full with France. But interference with American shipping on the high seas and a number of confrontations between the US and Canada precipitated the War of 1812.

In 1813, American forces succeeded in capturing Toronto, then known as York, and burned and sacked it. The British retaliated in 1814 by capturing and burning Washington, DC. The war had reached its nadir.

A number of other battles took place along the border and on Lakes Erie, Ontario, and Champlain. In 1814 the Treaty of Ghent ended the war, but border disputes continued. And it was not until 1842 that the US-Canadian border at Maine, Quebec, and New Brunswick finally was determined after difficult negotiations and sporadic armed clashes. The Treaty of Ghent did not eliminate the strong British belief that the US would not be content until it finally took Canada, either by force or by seduction. The British were so concerned about the continuing American threat that they built an interlocking waterway of lakes and canals between Kingston and the Ottawa River to the northeast. This — the Rideau Waterway — was an alternate route to move people and goods to the safety of Montreal if the St. Lawrence River, easily accessible from northern New York State, came under American control. The Rideau was never used for the defense of Canada; today it is one of the country's finest recreational boating waterways. And contrary to past expectations, the border between Canada and the US is the longest and oldest *undefended* border in the world, a rare memorial to what is possible between nations when there is mutual goodwill and respect.

With the direct threat of American intervention becoming ever less urgent in 1837 and 1838, the Canadians experienced severe internal struggles, which, had they been successful, might have radically changed the course of Canadian history.

In Lower (French-speaking) Canada an increasing number of French intellectuals and politicians were convinced that English interests in both London and British North America were using their economic power to keep French Canadians in a state of perpetual inferiority (an opinion that is often just as passionately expressed today). Louis Joseph Papineau, a leading French political figure, and his colleagues pressed for a reform of Lower Canada's political system. They wanted to form an independent republic with separate executive and legislative branches of government, patterned after those of the US. Papineau was not only denounced by English-speaking Canadians, which was only to be expected, but also by French Canadian bishops and conservative professionals. Papineau, in effect, preached the same democratic liberalism that had produced radical change in the governments of America and France. The Roman Catholic clergy felt so threatened that anyone who openly declared himself to be a "liberal" was automatically excommunicated from the Church (a form of political control that persisted long after Papineau). Papineau and his "patriots," as they are remembered in Quebec, launched their rebellion in 1837. It was crushed in 1838, without excessive loss of life. Though Papineau failed, he did set in motion the desire of many to separate French Quebec from British Canada.

Around the same time that Papineau was active in Lower Canada, another rebellion, with somewhat similar goals, was taking place in English-speaking Upper Canada. A fiery, vociferous Scot, William Lyon Mackenzie, editor of the *Colonial Advocate,* sought to reform his government by taking it out of the hands of the conservative power elite and remaking it on the American model. Failing to achieve his goals in the legislative assembly, Mackenzie and his reformers felt that an independent, democratic state could only be forged by the force of arms. In December 1837, the quixotic Mackenzie and a poorly armed, poorly trained band of a few hundred followers marched to capture the capital of Toronto. Within a few hours, the lackluster assault ran out of steam, and Mackenzie had to flee for his life across the American border.

The Papineau and Mackenzie rebellions, although failures in their own right, did enable more moderate reformers, such as Robert Baldwin, to present a stronger case to the British Parliament for the doctrine of responsible government for Canada. The Canadians wanted a greater say in the running of their own political affairs. This doctrine led to the Union Act of 1840, which joined Upper and Lower Canada under a single government with the name of the Province of Canada. It was a big step toward self-rule, but as the bickering between the French and English continued, the union proved to be inadequate to its task.

A COUNTRY EMERGES

Canada in the mid-19th century was maturing and developing in other ways. The Maritime Provinces were prosperous as centers of fishing, lumber, shipbuilding, and trade. The Oregon Territory boundary was fixed on the 49th parallel in 1846 and became one of the longest sections of the border between Canada and the US. In 1856 gold was discovered in the Fraser River in British Columbia, unleashing a stampede of prospectors to the west coast.

Captain James Cook, the English explorer, is reputed to have been the first white man to set foot in British Columbia. He landed at Nootka, west of Vancouver Island, in 1778. Fourteen years later Captain George Vancouver explored the landscape and inlets where the city bearing his name is located. In 1858, its growth due mainly to the gold discovery, British Columbia became a colony of the English Crown. The territories between British Columbia and the western fringe of the Province of Canada were controlled by the great fur trading companies, such as Hudson's Bay. Between 1850 and 1867, Canada increased its railroads from a mere 66 miles of track (6,000 in the US at the same time) to 2,000 miles. This also was the period when slavery was legal in the US. For many black slaves, Canada was the Promised Land — the last stop on the Underground Railroad.

In the east, the population of Canada and the Maritimes continued to grow, in part through immigration. Though the vast majority of immigrants during this period came from the United Kingdom, many arrived from Germany, Switzerland, and other European countries. A large percentage of these new Canadians were Protestant, but there also were many Catholics, primarily Irish fleeing the potato famine, and an increasing number of Jews. Through hard work, good sense, and shrewd investment they built successful businesses and created outstanding cultural institutions. This effort eventually loosened the grip of the old upper classes and pushed Canada on the road to becoming a genuinely pluralistic society.

The French continued to build their community and increase in numbers. Many children were needed to work the farms, to counter the growing number of English-speaking peoples, and to preserve the French language and the Catholic religion in Canada. To English-speaking Canadians, the average French Canadian was considered inferior, no more than a "hewer of wood and a drawer of water." French Canadians, however, were products of a highly insular society that had survived against great odds and that viewed the outside world and new ideas with profound suspicion.

Without the Church, the French Canadians, as a distinct ethnic group, might have disappeared, making Canada more like the English-speaking melting pot of the US. But the Church did its job exceedingly well, and as a result the community became powerful. Huge churches with richly decorated interiors could be found even in small, rural hamlets. Thousands of men and women took religious vows and labored in seminaries, convents, schools, and hospitals owned by the Church. Those laypeople who aspired to be professionals received a "classical education," concentrating on the humanities, theology, and philosophy. Well-educated French Canadian males went into law, medicine, religion, or politics. The fields of industry, finance, and engineering were left to the English. Thus, French Canadians ensured their cultural survival and gained a large measure of control over their political life.

THE DOMINION OF CANADA

By the middle of the 19th century, political leaders in both British North America and England were talking about the need to establish a stronger union between the provinces. Their concern was based on population growth, westward expansion, political problems between the French and the English, and a possible threat from the US, which by the conclusion of its Civil War had amassed a huge army capable of invasion.

In October 1864, delegates met in Charlottetown, on Prince Edward Island, and drafted plans for a union. In Canadian history, these delegates are called the Fathers of Confederation. On July 1, 1867, the Dominion of Canada was born, with the British North America Act as its constitution. Sir John A. Macdonald, chief architect of confederation and leader of the Conservative party, became Canada's first prime minister. Confederation created a federal union under a parliamentary system of government in the provinces of Ontario, Quebec, Nova Scotia, and New Brunswick. Ironically, Prince Edward Island, the host of the Charlottetown conference, did not join the union until 1873. Newfoundland, the first land in North America to be inhabited by Europeans, did not become part of Canada until 1949. Manitoba joined the confederation in 1870; British Columbia, in 1871; Alberta and Saskatchewan, in 1905; Nova Scotia, not until 1949.

Sir John A. Macdonald, considered by many the greatest Canadian prime minister, launched the new Dominion of Canada with a national policy that promoted western settlement, encouraged the building of a transcontinental railroad, and established high tariffs on foreign goods.

Western settlement presented the new dominion with urgent problems. Over half the 40,000 inhabitants between the Great Lakes and the Rockies were Indians who lived off the seemingly endless herds of buffalo. The rest were French Canadian trappers, English-speaking traders, and Métis (half French and half Indian). In 1869 the government paid $1.5 million to the Hudson's Bay Company for territory from the Great Lakes to the Red River (in Manitoba). About 6,000 Métis lived along the banks of the Red River, and they felt threatened by the government's policy of expansion. Under the charismatic leadership of Louis Riel, the Métis took Fort Garry, a trading post where the city of Winnipeg eventually rose. Their price for cooperating with the federal government was the protection of their language, religion, and lands, and the establishment of a self-governing province on the pattern of the others in the confederation. Macdonald agreed to negotiate with Riel. Unhappily, just then Riel executed an arrogant white troublemaker from Ontario, which outraged English-speaking Canada. While accepting the Métis' terms, Macdonald also sent an army to the Red River to keep the peace and maintain control of the new lands. (Riel escaped before the troops took Fort Garry.)

The Canadian federal government, seeing how the Indian wars were inhibiting the development of the American West, was quick to sign treaties with its own native people. Its efforts were successful, and most of the Indians surrendered their lands to the government by the end of the 1870s. In 1873 the Northwest Mounted Police (now called the Royal Canadian Mounted Police) began kicking out whiskey traders from the new lands and building forts that later became western cities such as Calgary.

As the transcontinental railroad pushed west across the prairies, bringing hordes of new settlers hungry for land, the Métis again felt that their way of life and very survival were threatened. Riel, who had been living in Montana, came back to Canada to lead the Métis in a new uprising. In addition, the Indians, suffering from starvation resulting from broken treaty promises, took to the warpath against the whites. In 1885 Riel took the Mountie post at Duck Lake (on the southern Saskatchewan River, in what was then the Northwest Territories), killing and wounding policemen in the battle. This success sent the Indians against the town of Battleford, the trading post and mission at Frog Lake, and Fort Pitt. During May 1885, Canadian forces attacked Riel at Batoche, defeating his army of determined Métis.

Riel surrendered. The Métis went home to their destroyed settlements and the Indians to their pitiful reservations, and Riel was hanged. Though the west was secured for continued development, Riel's death stirred up a hornet's nest in eastern Canada. Many people believed that the man was insane (he had spent time in a Quebec asylum) and that his life should have been spared for that reason alone. Most of French Canada was against the execution. They felt that Riel was killed because he was French and a Roman Catholic. Riel became a legend, and his death continues to be a sore point between English and French Canadians.

APPROACHING THE TWENTIETH CENTURY

In 1885, the same year as the Battle of Batoche, the main line of the transcontinental *Canadian Pacific Railway* was completed. In terms of human effort, engineering skill, and private financing, it was a great accomplishment. It is fair to say that the transcontinental railroad was the link that joined the provinces of Canada into one nation.

Between 1885 and 1914, when Canada entered World War I, new resources were discovered, new lands were settled and made productive, new industries were developed, and new people arrived on the scene. In 1898, for example, gold was discovered in the Yukon, and the Klondike Gold Rush brought miners by the thousands. More significant were the continuing numbers of settlers who arrived. As all of the good, free land was taken up in the US, thousands of Europeans and Americans looked to western Canada. The prairie provinces of Manitoba, Saskatchewan, and Alberta not only produced enough grain to feed Canada, but also earned the nation the title the Granary of Great Britain. In time, Canada and the US were known as the breadbaskets of the world. Manufacturing, mining, lumbering, pulp and paper, fishing, and hydroelectric power continued to grow and add to the prosperity of the nation. Although Canada had a strong financial community (banks, insurance companies, and trading firms headquartered mainly in Montreal), much of the capital to fund the development of resources and the building of manufacturing plants came from Great Britain and the US. In time, the US dominated much of the nation's economic life. This became — and remains — a source of bitter anti-American feeling on the part of many Canadians.

THE FIRST WORLD WAR AND ITS AFTERMATH

On July 11, 1896, Sir Wilfrid Laurier, leader of the Liberal party, became prime minister of Canada. Laurier was Canada's first French Canadian, Roman Catholic prime minister, yet he spoke out against the meddling of the Church in Canadian politics. One of Laurier's ideas, which cost him his job in the election of 1911, was to create a Canadian navy rather than give money to Great Britain for the defense of Canada. English Canadians pilloried Laurier as the author of a naval policy designed to isolate Canada from Britain. In Quebec and French Canada, he was portrayed as the fool of British imperialism. French Canadians condemned Laurier because they feared being drawn into a war of Britain's making. They remembered Britain's desire to enlist Canadians to help fight the Boers in South Africa. (Though a volunteer force of French Canadians did join the combat, the majority resisted conscription.) Sir Robert Borden followed Laurier and was prime minister when World War I broke out in Europe. Parliament passed the War Measures Act in order to mobilize the nation to assist the Allies — the prime ally being Great Britain. During the early years of the war, enough Canadians were slaughtered in Europe to cause a serious shortage in the number of additional men the government had promised to send overseas. Conscription was the solution, but many French Canadians would have nothing to do with it. In a climate of hatred and bitterness on both sides of the issue, close to 122,000 men were drafted, only 47,000 of whom were sent to Europe before the war ended. It should be noted that while much of Quebec was against aiding Great Britain, many French Canadians served their country in Europe with exceptional valor and distinction.

World War I greatly increased Canada's capacity to produce. And land and jobs attracted people from all over Europe to Canada after the war. So many Ukrainians emigrated that in time their culture became second only to that of the English in many places on the Canadian prairie. Many Jews also came into the country, settling in Montreal and Toronto as tradespeople and storekeepers or moving west to farm land, which had been denied them by law in Europe.

By the 1920s McGill University in Montreal, Dalhousie University in Halifax, and Trinity College of the University of Toronto were considered among the finest academic institutions in the world. At the University of Toronto, for example, Frederick G. Banting and Charles Best isolated insulin in 1922. Canadian art reached new heights during this time with the Group of Seven landscape painters. Canadian music, drama, and literature were also gaining the respect of international audiences. But by end of the 1920s, the economic prosperity that provided the backbone of all these achievements was quickly evaporating. On the eve of the Great Depression, severe droughts decimated the rich, grain-producing prairie, and the 1930s were ushered in with the chill prospect of hunger and despair.

In September 1939, Hitler attacked Poland, Great Britain declared war on Germany, and 7 days later, Canada was once again embroiled in war. Before World War I, Prime Minister Laurier could not sell the concept of a Canadian navy to the people. At the start of World War II, however, Canada entered battle with a rather respectable armed force, including the famous Royal Canadian Air Force of 11 squadrons. Many Americans who wanted to fight joined the RCAF. President Franklin D. Roosevelt allowed American manufacturers to build aircraft on Canadian soil so that he could help Winston Churchill prior to America's official entry into the war. Roosevelt and Churchill had their famous Atlantic Conference off the coast of Newfoundland. Later, they met again at the Citadel, on the heights of Quebec City, to work on the invasion of France. This conference was held on Canadian soil as a gesture to Prime Minister William Lyon Mackenzie King, who insisted that Canada be made a full partner in the war effort.

In the deepwater ports of Halifax, Nova Scotia, and St. John's, Newfoundland, the great convoys formed to bring desperately needed supplies to England and Russia, sailing through Nazi U-boat wolf packs over the North Atlantic route.

In Quebec, conscription was again a passionate issue, and for the same reasons cited during World War I. While many avoided the war, other French Canadians joined Quebec regiments and fought bravely for Canada and the free world. Still other French Canadians — for example, Réné Lévesque, who later became premier of Quebec — joined the US Army and saw action throughout Europe.

THE CONTEMPORARY CHALLENGE

By the end of the war, 41,814 Canadians had died. Canada had more than paid its dues as a nation and could no longer be seen as a mere child of the British colonial system. As a result, the country was one of the founding nations of the UN and became an important part of NATO. As a member of the UN, Canada also fought in the Korean War, its soldiers suffering 1,557 casualties. In 1956, through the diplomatic efforts of Lester B. Pearson, the nation's chief delegate to the UN, Canada won the Nobel Peace Prize for a proposal for ending British and French intervention in Egypt.

In 1952 the Right Honourable Vincent Massey was the first native Canadian to be appointed governor-general of the country. In 1959 the St. Lawrence Seaway, a Canadian-American project, opened for shipping from the Great Lakes to the Atlantic. Also during this period, Canada was a strong advocate for establishing the multi-racial Commonwealth of Nations out of the old British Commonwealth, and it helped to organize the Colombo Plan to provide aid to underdeveloped nations. Between 1945 and 1957, Canada received over 1.5 million immigrants. These people, mostly skilled and educated, radically changed the complexion of many Canadian cities. Toronto, for example, has been transformed by immigrants from Italy, Greece, Poland, the West Indies, Uganda, Pakistan, and China; it is one of the most exciting multi-racial, multi-cultural cities in North America.

Canada also expanded its government social programs to better the quality of life for its people, such as providing comprehensive health care for all. Its national and provincial health care systems continue to be studied in Washington as models for a US national health care system. The policy of bilingualism was strengthened by the federal government, and French became the second official language of the country. Federal business must now be conducted in both French and English, and bilingualism is encouraged in all sectors of Canadian life, including the printing of labels on every kind of product. Canada adopted a new flag and the theme of "unity through diversity." By its 100th anniversary, in 1967, Canadian industries were booming, its cities were becoming showplaces, and its people were enjoying one of the highest standards of living in the world. There was an air of general complacency and self-congratulation in centennial celebrations around the country, a spirit only made stronger by the huge success of the *World's Fair* — *EXPO '67* — in Montreal.

It was at this international celebration, however, that France's president, Charles de Gaulle, dropped a verbal bomb that shook Canada to its foundation and set the course of political dialogue for the rest of the century. During a state visit, de Gaulle called for a free Quebec. His words shocked Canadians across the country, but they gave new legitimacy to a Quebec separatist movement that had begun to decay into terrorist tactics and hooliganism.

In 1968, inflated by de Gaulle's proclamation, separatists gathered around Réné Lévesque, a popular journalist, and formed the Parti Québecois. That same year Pierre Elliott Trudeau, a French Canadian whose style reminded voters of John F. Kennedy's, became prime minister. Trudeau advocated a better deal for French Canadians, but within the federal system. Canadians all over the country looked to Trudeau as the one person who might be able to save the country from being Balkanized or absorbed into the United States. In the Quebec provincial elections of 1970, Lévesque's Parti Quebecois won only seven seats in the legislature but received 23% of the popular vote.

During the same year, the FLQ, a terrorist organization, kidnapped James Cross, the British trade commissioner, and Pierre Laporte, a Quebec cabinet minister. Marxist elements in the FLQ hoped for a revolution in Quebec. Student and worker groups protested in support of the FLQ. Prime Minister Trudeau proclaimed the War Measures Act, giving the federal government virtually unlimited power, and in the process voided the civil liberties of a number of innocent people arrested or held during the period. The FLQ killed Laporte, a man with known links to organized crime. The invocation of the War Measures Act proved a double-edged sword for the government; many

Canadians applauded its use, but it created an aftermath of bitterness and anger in Quebec that remains today.

To the shock of many Canadians, Lévesque and his Parti Québecois won the provincial election of 1976, the same year the *Summer Olympics* were held in Montreal. As soon as Lévesque assumed power, he was on the road selling Quebec separatism, both inside and outside Canada. His party also passed strict language laws that abandoned the concept of bilingualism and established French as the only official language in Quebec.

There was an immediate effect on Canadian consciousness. Most visible among these changes was the flight, mainly of English-dominated businesses and commercial enterprises, from Quebec to more friendly locations elsewhere in Canada. During this period, the competition between Montreal and Toronto for preeminence as the most important municipality in Canada was won by Toronto, and today it is headquarters of the largest banks in Canada, has the more active and prosperous stock exchange, and it is the home base of many more important corporations than Montreal.

Canada's politics took on a rather volatile cast during 1979, and the 1980s did not see any easing of national tensions. The Conservative government of Joe Clark replaced Pierre Trudeau's Liberals in the spring of 1979, but lasted in office only a scant 8 months. In February 1980, Trudeau was returned to power with a significant national mandate — a more than interesting irony since Trudeau had personally announced his retirement from politics only 3 weeks before then-Prime Minister Clark's government fell. In May 1980, all Canada watched as Quebecois voted a resounding *"non"* to a specific separatism proposal that would have given Lévesque the right to negotiate sovereignty for Quebec. This long-debated question of separation — rejected by 60% of Quebec's population at that time — was viewed by some as a personal defeat for Réné Lévesque, then premier of the province. M. Lévesque's declining status was unceremoniously confirmed when his party lost the next provincial election to the far more conservative Liberals, making separatism a less contentious issue for most of the rest of the decade.

The overwhelming Quebec support for Prime Minister Brian Mulroney's Conservative party in the 1984 and 1988 national elections, and the triumph of the Liberal party in the 1985 provincial races signaled a further decline in separatist preoccupation. In addition, Mulroney has championed the Canada-US Free Trade Agreement, and in the November 1988 federal elections his Progressive Conservative Party and the Free Trade Agreement were supported by the majority; Quebecers led the way, electing 40% of the 171 Conservatives in the 295-member House of Commons.

The election results seemed to indicate that the people of Quebec were more concerned with improving their flagging economy than with insisting upon independence, echoing the economic concerns that seemed to preoccupy all of the rest of Canada. But widespread disagreement across Canada on the "specialness" of Quebec, as described in the Meech Lake Accord (of 1987), threatens to revive the separatist zeal — and may threaten the entire Canadian confederation. Failure to ratify the Meech Lake agreement in the prescribed time has put all Canada on edge, and all Canada anxiously awaits the resolution of the simmering dispute.

In the meantime, declining oil prices have deflated the oil-fueled boom of Canada's West, and the US/Canada free trade pact has spawned an uncertain period of opportunity and competitive pressure. Canadians remain strongly divided on the advantages and disadvantages of the Free Trade Agreement, and while the first year of free trade has gone better than expected, at this point no one can predict who will benefit most from the new trade relationship between the twin giants of North America. Everyone does agree, however, that the decade to come is to see changes that are likely to be far-reaching.

Contemporary Canada and the Storm of Separatism

 The 1980 Canadian national election brought the debate on provincial independence — especially in relation to Quebec — to an international audience. And despite the ebb and flow of the strength of the Parti Québécois — which zealously clings to the principle of separatism — US observers still ask: How can a province even attempt to secede? The recent voting patterns of the Quebec electorate, as indicated in both the 1984 and 1988 national elections (which went heavily for Conservative Prime Minister Brian Mulroney's party), and the controversy that continues over the failure of the 1987 Meech Lake Accord, only compounds this confusion.

If US citizens fail to comprehend the true divisiveness and passion of the separatist issue, it is because one of the gravest mistakes we make is to misunderstand — or worse still, simply miss — the profound difference between Canadians and ourselves. To be candid, these differences are not always so readily apparent. Where they are — as in Quebec City and certain other pockets of the province — they are unmistakable, and no one would suggest that Quebecois and New Yorkers are alike. But elsewhere, similarities are more striking than differences, and this is deceptive. But, a first-time visitor might argue, the Canadian people are made up of just about the same mixture of races and ethnic groups as Americans. And the landscape is much the same; we share the Rockies and the Appalachians, the Great Lakes and massive midwestern prairies. So what's deceptive?

Canadians do not have the same monolithic sense of national identity that characterizes the United States. (If you doubt that this is an American trait, just remember that we have appropriated the very word "American" to refer to ourselves, effectively disenfranchising every Canadian and Mexican, not to mention millions of South Americans.) Except for French Canadians, this is not true of many of Canada's citizens. Canadian culture is a curious contradiction, a manifestation of several conflicting forces. Not the least of these is that, until relatively recently, Canadians were British subjects. Their allegiances and alliances were directed across the Atlantic, and the confederation of provinces was less than a binding psychological reality. And Canada has always been under the economic domination of one or another industrial nation — first Britain and then the US.

The building of a national identity has required unceasing effort —

the rejection of foreign economic domination, at least in principle, even when in fact it has been impossible; the struggle to establish and maintain a cohesive national political unity that functions effectively in all parts of this huge country. But it also has meant finding a bridge across an even deeper schism in Canadian life. Canadians are keen observers of life in the United States, and early on they rejected the melting pot idea of culture that until a generation or so ago was so dear to us. They saw the price that arriving immigrants had to pay to melt into the American pot, and they foresaw the movement currently under way in the US to regain lost national and racial heritages in the third, fourth, and fifth generations. The Canadian national government adopted a policy of multi-culturalism to encourage Canadians to be proud of their ethnic roots, and established the Multi-culturalism Directorate of the Department of the Secretary of State.

Multi-culturalism has meant, however, that regional and ethnic identity vies with national identity in the Canadian heart. And that means that the threat of separatism is far more real in Canada than it probably could be in the US. A Canadian would not necessarily find the idea of an independent province, joined in an economic agreement with the other Canadian provinces, an unthinkable idea, especially if that Canadian region was populated by of a strong-minded minority with a powerful tradition of its own, or lived in a province endowed with abundant natural resources.

THE PEOPLE AND THE PROVINCES

Like the people of Western Europe and the US, the majority of Canadians — about 90% — dwell in urban centers settled, for the most part, within 200 miles of the US border. A huge portion of Canada's enormous land mass — the second-largest in the world — is uninhabited. The Yukon and Northwest Territories, comprising over 40% of the nation's land, have around 75,000 inhabitants (mostly Inuit and other native Canadian Indians), so the Canada most of us think of is southern, urban Canada, economically modern and socially advanced. Of Canada's 25 million people, over 15 million (nearly two-thirds) inhabit two provinces: Ontario, historically English-speaking Upper Canada; and Quebec, French-speaking Lower Canada. Over 40% of all Canadians are of British origin; 30% are French. The roots of provincial rivalry and separatism lie in this simple yet significant demographic fact.

Canada's modern history has witnessed a persistent effort on the part of its people to establish some kind of distinct identity. In contemporary times, this has crystallized both as a struggle for provincial autonomy and independence at the regional level and as the policy of multi-culturalism at the national level. The result is Canada's growing unwillingness to allow foreign influences to dominate its cultural life and to blur its national character.

But how successful has Canada been in resisting cultural and economic manipulation from abroad? During the 19th century, the dominant cultural and economic factor in Canadian life was British; in our century the US has replaced the UK and has come to symbolize foreign influence. It is hard to alter this picture. American investors control large percentages of Canadian industry, and what is more, Canada is still primarily a producer and exporter of raw materials. The US remains its chief supplier of finished products. Nor is this true in the industrial world alone. During the mid-1960s, when Ottawa expanded its university system and created thousands of academic positions, most of the professors and instructors were recruited from the US. When Canadians turn on television, what do they watch? "Dallas" and "Roseanne," and reruns of "Family Ties," starring native son Michael J. Fox. The Canadian Broadcasting Company has yet to find a national substitute (it is ironic that super-star anchorman Peter Jennings began his career here). And with the possible exception of *Maclean's,* there still are no weekly magazines to challenge the stature of *Newsweek* and *Time.* The impact of America — from popular music to fast-food chains — tends to lessen the reality of the political border separating the two countries.

In response to Americanization, the federal government has developed policies to regulate foreign investment. Federal programs encourage the development of resources and industries by Canadians, and try to create new markets for Canadian goods with countries other than the traditional trading partners. On a cultural level, the government's policies also are designed to limit foreign influence. For example, several years ago *Time* ceased publishing its Canadian edition when certain tax advantages were rescinded by the government and Canadian majority ownership was required. Most notably, large grants to artists, writers, filmmakers, and publishers have subsidized Canadian contributions to the international arts scene. Still, no government can legislate cultural values, and today's Canada remains a mixture of foreign influences and purely Canadian qualities. The new Free Trade Agreement between Canada and the US may blur national sovereignties in time.

Canadians live in ten self-governing provinces: Newfoundland-Labrador, Nova Scotia, New Brunswick, Prince Edward Island, Quebec, Ontario, Manitoba, Saskatchewan, Alberta, and British Columbia. The Yukon and Northwest territories are under federal jurisdiction.

Ethnically, the majority of groups in the Atlantic area are of English, Irish, Scottish, and German descent. Large numbers of Scots settled in Nova Scotia and Prince Edward Island. The port of Halifax, significant since the 18th century, has long attracted English immigrants. There is a large population of Irish in the Maritimes, and the Irish brogue is strong in Newfoundland. There are significant numbers of blacks in Nova Scotia, descendants of settlers who originally came to Canada on the Underground Railroad — and those who more recently have come from the West Indies. Pockets of Germans, Swiss, and Scandinavians also can be found in Nova Scotia and New Brunswick. And both provinces have sizable populations of Micmac Indians. Of all the peoples of the Atlantic provinces, the Scots are perhaps the most apparent, with their *Highland Games* in the summer and their concerts that feature bagpiping, sword dancing, and Celtic songs.

By contrast, the majority of Quebec's population is French and is undergoing rapid change. Prior to World War II, the prevailing image of the Quebec French was unquestionably conservative: a people dominated by their tradition and church, subject to high population growth and low economic status, unwilling to assimilate into the English-speaking mainstream. The postwar years witnessed a profound shift. The power of the Church has declined rapidly, and it now serves mainly in a pastoral capacity. The Church in Quebec, once one of the most conservative in the Roman Catholic world, today is considered one of the most progressive. Quebec families, once the largest in Canada, now have one of the lowest birth rates in the nation. More and more Quebec men and women are entering business and technical careers, areas previously reserved for the English-speaking minority in the province. Montreal has become a world center of fashion, filmmaking, recording, painting, and publishing.

Not long ago, the English in Quebec controlled most of its financial institutions, but with the dynamic growth of the credit union movement, the French have created huge pools of capital under their own control. This economic power is a very real factor in the controversy over French-speaking autonomy, an issue that divides the Quebecois as much as the rest of the country. It continues to be a hotly debated issue.

For example, new immigrants living in Quebec must send their children to French schools. This policy has caused great anguish among the large Italian and Greek segments of the population, who see their future in the larger context of English-speaking North America. An underlying racism is causing concern in the substantial Jewish community, which has made immense contributions to the economic and cultural life of the province. English-speaking shopkeepers in predominantly English-speaking neighborhoods have been forced by provincial law to change their signs to French.

Many of those who could afford to move left for Ontario and other provinces. A severe decline in property values detained others, who waited for better days. On the positive side, there is an increasing number of both French and English Quebecois who reject cultural extremes and the racism of the few and they have worked hard to retain a just society for all the people of the province. Recent elections — both national and provincial — suggested that sanity and self-preservation had triumphed, but the recent collapse of the Meech Lake Accord, which formally acknowledged the "specialness" of French Canada, may open old wounds.

The predominantly English-speaking Protestant province of Ontario has, in recent years, undergone rapid developments as well. For most of its history, Ontario's population has consisted mainly of people from Britain and America; its leading Protestant denominations — particularly the Anglicans — exerted enormous influence on political and social life. Strong family and business ties with the powerful elites of Britain greatly affected the economic development of not only Ontario but all of Canada.

Toronto and Montreal became centers of commercial and financial activity. There also was the influence of the fraternal orders, such as the Masons and the Orangemen. It used to be said in Ontario that a person couldn't get a political office unless he was either a Mason or an Orangeman. Torontonians of today look back on their own past with amusement when they recall what a straight-laced, WASPish society it was in which their forebears lived. It was a time of highly exclusive and restricted WASP neighborhoods, where even Jews or Catholics who had the money to buy homes were denied the opportunity on the basis of religion. The blue laws were so strict that a storekeeper could be fined for selling an ice cream cone on Sunday. Even as late as the

1950s, travelers were warned: "Don't get caught overnight in Toronto; you'll die of boredom."

The three prairie provinces — Manitoba, Saskatchewan, and Alberta — have a combined population of about 4.5 million people. The majority of these are descendants of the pioneers who came west in search of large tracts of inexpensive land for farming and ranching. These early settlers not only survived, but they also turned the prairie into one of the major grain- and meat-producing areas of the world, with usually enough surplus for export to other countries. The original inhabitants were the nomadic Plains Indians, such as the Sioux and the Blackfoot. Their descendants either live on reservations or have become assimilated into the white communities.

The first whites in the area were the French trappers, many of whom married Indian women. The Métis were the offspring of these unions. These descendants of the French have either become assimilated or live in a number of communities that are fairly homogeneous and where the language, religion, and culture of their forebears is kept alive. They consider themselves French Canadians, and they have mixed feelings about the separatist fuss their cousins in Quebec have made. The federal bilingual laws were promulgated just as much for them as for the people in Quebec. Because being a Métis means being part in the Indian's world and part in the white man's world — and not necessarily being accepted in either — this group has formed its own activist organizations and has pressed the provincial and federal governments to recognize its unique status and to provide legal, economic, and cultural services. Many Métis have blended into the population and have done very well for themselves, but for some it has been quite difficult.

Others who have settled in the prairie were Americans, English, Scots, Irish, Scandinavians, Jews, and Germans. One of the largest ethnic groups to flourish in the prairie provinces have been the Ukrainians. Travelers are surprised to suddenly see the onion domes of an Orthodox church sticking up over a broad field of golden wheat. And one of the most unusual groups in this area are the Hutterites, a communal religious society, originally from Germany, that bases its way of life on farming, hard work, strict discipline, and prayer.

For the first few years of this decade, the fastest-growing and most prosperous province in this region was Alberta. Its rapid growth was due to big finds of oil and natural gas. But the worldwide oil glut has slowed Alberta's boom, and many local companies and communities have felt unfamiliar bad times. Provincial officials are trying hard to regulate these domestic pendulum swings so the province can proceed at a more stable pace.

On Canada's Pacific coast is British Columbia, where 1.5 of the province's 2.8 million people live in the Greater Vancouver–Victoria urban area. By contrast, the people of rural British Columbia work in mining, lumbering, agriculture, and tourism. The mountainous interior of British Columbia is probably one of Canada's most beautiful regions. The Okanagan Valley is one of the most productive fruit-growing areas in the country. And though the majority of the province's population is of British origin, there are also unusual groups such as the Dukhobors, who can appropriately be called Russian Quakers.

As mentioned, the Yukon and Northwest Territories together comprise roughly 40% of the total Canadian land mass, but only 75,000 people live here. In recent years, oil and gas production has reached up into the Arctic, where it threatens to transform the traditional Inuit, or Eskimo, way of life. Ever since man can remember, the Inuit have lived in harmony with their often brutal natural habitat; now their transition into our contemporary world is painful and difficult.

In virtually every province some ethnic group is threatened by external forces, and every province boasts its own variety of multi-culturalism.

THE STORM OF SEPARATISM

The constitutionality of separatism has been an extremely subtle bit of business, since Canada is an independent sovereign state and a member of the Commonwealth of Nations. Constitutionally, the Queen of England also is the Queen of Canada and the head of state, although she exercises about as much influence on policy here as she does in Britain — which is to say, she is powerless. The foundations of modern Canadian government are based upon the British North America Act of 1867, and it is to this act that all debates on the legality of separatism must inevitably be traced.

The creators of the act closely examined the US federal system, but used it more as a warning than as a model (remember, the US Civil War had just ended!). To avoid issues like states' rights and the problems that might ensue, the central government was made very strong and was given the key role of legislation. The act also established quite explicitly that any unnamed or "residual" powers ought to reside in the central government as well. The provinces then were awarded jurisdiction over roads, direct taxation, municipal affairs, education, and the like.

In the years since then, the provinces began to question the very legality of Canada's constitution. In 1867, the provinces were not considered sovereign entities — as the states, prior to the Constitutional Convention of 1787, considered themselves — nor were "the Canadian people" directly consulted. Clearly the act flowed legally from London's imperial prerogative; it was a gift of the mother country. After much discussion and negotiation, a compromise was finally reached and a constitution of Canada's own making drafted. Despite disagreement and dissent from Quebec (which insisted on a greater degree of provincial autonomy) and arguments over the constitution's new Charter of Rights and Freedom, the constitution was sent to Great Britain, where it was approved by Parliament. In April 1982, Queen Elizabeth flew to Ottawa to sign the proclamation formally transferring constitutional power from Britain to Canada, the result of which was that Canada could amend its constitution without first seeking approval from Great Britain.

The major addition to the redrafted constitution has been the Canadian Charter of Rights and Freedom, which is based on the US Bill of Rights and guarantees certain rights and privileges to every Canadian citizen. The charter stirred much controversy in the Canadian Parliament, and was passed only after a compromise clause was negotiated, allowing the Canadian Parliament and the provincial legislatures to pass their own laws overriding the provisions of the charter. Despite this addition, Quebec never officially approved the repatriation of Canada's Constitution.

After much storm and debate, the spectre of a confrontation on the matter of separatism largely dematerialized after the Quebec provincial election of 1985. The defeat of the Parti Québecois at the polls brought a new feeling of accommodation into office. The Meech Lake Accord of 1987 sought, among other issues, to address the fact that Quebec had not approved the Constitution in 1982; one provision of the accord recognizes "that Quebec constitutes within Canada a distinct society." Yet, as we went to press, the accord — which also addresses issues revolving around immigration, the senate, conferences and amendments, and national programs — still had not officially been enacted into law, since Manitoba and Newfoundland have withheld their necessary ratifications. Quebec's desire to be a legally "distinct society" remains strong and separatism from the rest of Canada has become a very contentious issue once again. It also should be noted that a lingering — though seldom publicized — element in the Meech Lake dispute is the desire of Canada's native population to be recognized as "distinct" along with the Quebecers.

CANADIAN CULTURE TODAY

One of the most enjoyable aspects of a visit to Canada is the rich panorama of its culture. Only decades ago, both Canadians and foreigners viewed Canada as a cultural wasteland. What culture there was had usually been imported from Great Britain, France, or the US. It was the rule that talented Canadians had to flee the country to achieve fame. But the cultural scene in Canada has changed so since World War II that Canadian talent finds sufficient reward and acclaim working at home, and Canadian cultural offerings have become sought after abroad.

In dance, Canada has received international praise for the *National Ballet of Canada* in Toronto (with which Rudolph Nureyev was associated), for the *Grands Ballets Canadiens* in Montreal, and for the *Royal Winnipeg Ballet.* Original Canadian and international drama can be seen in playhouses across the country. The plays of Shakespeare and Shaw are beautifully performed at Stratford, Ontario, and Molière is popular in Montreal. The federal government sponsors touring companies that perform in even the most remote settlements in the land. There are opera companies in most of the major cities; the *Canadian Opera Company* in Toronto is one of the best. Canadian-born Jon Vickers and Theresa Strata have achieved international success as two of the great dramatic singers of our day. Almost every city has its own orchestra and smaller musical ensembles. Toronto, Montreal, and Winnipeg boast symphony orchestras of international status.

In the field of broadcasting, the Canadian Broadcasting Company (CBC) provides news, entertainment, and educational programs over radio and television. In the north the CBC broadcasts in English, French, Indian, and Inuktitut, the language of the Inuit. Radio Canada, the CBC's French-language service, produces and broadcasts programs to the French-speaking people of Quebec and other provinces; it is known for producing elaborate melodramas and musical shows. Radio Canada International, the CBC's shortwave service, broadcasts every day in 11 languages from transmitters in New Brunswick. The CBC also has an armed forces broadcasting service, which provides shortwave programming to Canadian troops around the world.

Canada has come a long way in the visual arts. At one level, an intensive search for identity was clearly seen in the extraordinarily influential group of artists known as the Group of Seven: Tom Thomson, Lawren Harris, J. E. H. MacDonald, A. Y. Jackson, Arthur Lismer, Franz Johnston, Frank Carmichael, and Frederick Varley. These painters went straight to the land, to the magnificent colors of Canadian autumns, to the cool darkness of northern lakes, to a vibrant sense of national image.

Today, painters and sculptors working in all media are exhibiting their work in private galleries and public museums throughout Canada. Some of the outstanding museums include the *Art Gallery of Ontario,* the *Royal Ontario Museum,* and the *McMichael Museum* in Ontario; the *National Gallery of Canada* in Ottawa; and the *Montreal Museum of Fine Arts.* The Royal Canadian Academy serves as a professional organization for visual artists, and the federally funded Canada Council supports many individual artists, galleries, and museums as well as activities in other cultural fields.

In addition to the visual arts, Canada boasts many excellent writers. Along with Lucy Maud Montgomery, who made Prince Edward Island's Cavendish area famous in her children's book, *Anne of Green Gables,* there are Margaret Atwood, Mordecai Richler, Robertson Davies, and the late economist-humorist Stephen Leacock.

Canada's other exceptional museums and restorations that depict the history of the country include the *National Museum of Natural Sciences,* the *National Museum of Civilization,* the *National Museum of Science and Technology,* and the *Canadian War Museum* (all in Ottawa); the *Alexander Graham Bell Museum* in Nova Scotia; the *Glenbow Museum of Calgary; Kings Landing Historic Settlement* and *Village Historique Acadien* (both in New Brunswick); *Fort Louisbourg* and *Champlain's Habitation* restorations (both in Nova Scotia); *Upper Canada Village* and *Black Creek Village* (both in Ontario); *Place Royale* in Quebec City; and *Vieux Montréal* in Montreal.

Canada boasts an excellent national library system, with the Metropolitan Research Library in Toronto being one of the most comprehensive and stunning facilities of its kind in North America. And, similar in nature to the Library of Congress in the US, the Library of Parliament in Ottawa maintains one of the most complete collections of books in Canada.

Culturally, contemporary Canada offers a wide spectrum of choices.

THE CITIES

CALGARY

For a very long time, Calgary was Canada's best kept secret. Oh, folks in the cattle business knew it as a railhead, and oil drillers came into town to change clothes on their way to or from the big drilling fields, but for the rest of the world Calgary was known mostly as a town out near the Rockies where they had a hell of a rodeo once a year.

Then, in just 2 weeks during the winter of 1988, Calgary came of age for the entire planet. As tens of millions of sports enthusiasts watched the pageantry and competition of the *Winter Olympics,* they could not escape noticing that the surroundings were something very special, and that the Calgarians were pretty good at putting on an international party. Suddenly, lots of folks from all over the world wanted to see Calgary for themselves.

What they found was a warm, welcoming metropolis sitting on the vast Canadian prairie, with the jagged, snow-capped peaks of the Canadian Rockies jutting up to the west, and fields of golden grain extending to the east. It was these vast, grassy plains in southern and central Alberta that spawned the development of a huge ranching industry, of which Calgary — then a brash, bustling prairie city — was the center.

Once a year Calgary still puts on the world-famous *Calgary Stampede* — that Rolls-Royce of rodeos — in an effort to fool itself and everyone else into believing that it remains the simple cowtown of earlier days. Don't believe it for a minute. The *Stampede* no more represents contemporary Calgary than Will Rogers's deceptively slow-talking stage persona mirrored his rapier wit. Certainly there is historical truth to the cowtown image, but nowadays this prairie city of 670,000 is heavily into oil — and oil money — and the ten-gallon hat, cowboy boots, and saddle have been shed for a business suit and a pocket calculator. More than 600 major Canadian oil and gas companies have their head offices here, with ancillary services provided by hundreds of drilling companies. Even the recent stagnation of oil demand and the loss of more than a few get-rich-quick fortunes have hardly dampened local enthusiasm.

Much of how modern-day Calgary looks is the result of the oil boom. This era of prosperity saw the city swell by more than 20,000 newcomers a year and city boundaries expand at a phenomenal rate. Those heady days produced an almost entirely new city core of steel and glass, which led one Canadian author to comment that the city looked as though it had just been uncrated. Many worried that the city's rapid growth would destroy traces of its tradition and history. Happily, public concern has led to the preservation of many examples of pioneer Calgary architecture. While its population has stabilized and construction slowed, the city continues to benefit from several ambitious projects launched during the boom. The impressive *Calgary Olympic Saddledome,* the major facility used during Calgary's stint as host of the *1988*

Winter Olympics; a spacious downtown performing arts center that incorporates the historic Burns Building; a mirrored-glass municipal building, next door to the quaint sandstone City Hall; and an ultramodern light rail transit system.

This city has literally risen from the prairies. Situated at the western end of the Great Plains that sweep westward across Manitoba, Saskatchewan, and Alberta to wash against the eastern face of the Rocky Mountains, Calgary sits in the foothills of the Rockies at an altitude of 3,440 feet. Though high, the city is a traditional plains city, very flat and spread out. Two small rivers, the Bow and the Elbow, flow through the city to meet near the downtown area. Its altitude assures that Calgary gets lots of sun, and on clear days — that is, most every day — the rugged snow-capped peaks of the Rockies are visible some 50 miles to the west.

Calgary was founded in the late summer of 1875 by a contingent of the Northwest Mounted Police (now called the Royal Canadian Mounted Police) who set up camp near the confluence of the Bow and Elbow rivers. The police had come west to control the whiskey traders, who were creating havoc among the Indians, and to prepare the way for the thousands of eastern Canadians and immigrants who wanted to homestead. Here they subsequently built a fort, named after Calgary Bay in Scotland.

For 8 years after it was established, Calgary was no more than a minor post, overshadowed by Fort Walsh and Fort Macleod to the south and by Rocky Mountain House and Edmonton to the north.

In 1877 the five Indian tribes that roamed and hunted in southern Alberta agreed to sign a treaty ceding all rights to the land except for areas designated by the government. In return, the government agreed to provide the Blackfoot, Stoney, Sarcee, Blood, and Peigan Indians with education, medical care, hunting rights, ammunition money, farm implements, and suits of clothing for the chiefs. The controversy over the terms, and whether the government ever actually fulfilled its end of the bargain, still rages. Nevertheless, the agreement was reached without bloodshed, and the government gained complete access to the lands of southern Alberta for agriculture and for the railroad, which rolled into Calgary in 1883. The young settlement suddenly took on a whole new importance. By the end of the year, its population reached 600, and by 1889 it had risen to 2,000. In the coming years, thousands of people making their way west stopped in Calgary, and many stayed.

The abundance of grassy plains in southern and central Alberta spawned the development of a huge ranching industry, of which Calgary was the center. When the lush grazing lands encouraged US cattle owners to move their tremendous herds north from overgrazed ranges in the American plains, the city's meat packing industry was an inevitable result.

By 1893 enough pioneers had homesteaded in Calgary to allow the city to be granted a charter. Farming and ranching formed the foundation of a thriving but unrepentantly agricultural economy. In 1914, when oil was discovered at Turner Valley, just south of Calgary, an era of new prosperity began. However, not until the big discovery in the Leduc fields, near Edmonton, years later did Calgary really start to make its mark as a focal point of Canada's oil and gas industry.

Calgary became a brash, bustling, prairie city — an atmosphere still apparent today. The city has always attracted a confident, entrepreneurial breed of individual. Many people are drawn here because one needn't belong to an entrenched establishment to get ahead.

During the recent surge of expansion, which resulted in millions of square feet of high-rise office space downtown, city planners managed to maintain a comfortable urban environment. For example, the Stephen Avenue pedestrian mall was created so pedestrians would have priority over traffic. These 4 blocks of open space, trees, benches, shops, restaurants, and sidewalk cafés are prime territory for just sitting back and watching the world go by (this activity is restricted to spring, summer, and fall, since Calgary winters often send the mercury down to −30F/−34C). Downtown Calgary is also the site of several interconnected shopping complexes, bracketed by the city's two largest department stores — *Eaton's* and *The Bay*. This arrangement allows residents to shop in a variety of stores without ever stepping outside. Calgary also has a number of enclosed overhead walkways that link stores and office buildings — another boon during the cold winters. Devonian Gardens at the top of *Toronto-Dominion Square* (one of the largest downtown shopping centers) is a completely enclosed garden with 2½ acres of lush tropical plants and fountains. On balmy summer days, workers head to Prince's Island, a park full of trees and running water only 3 blocks from downtown.

Hardly surprising in a city whose prosperity is based on natural resources, the hand of nature is writ large around Calgary. Just 81 miles (130 km) away is Banff National Park in the Canadian Rockies, gateway to some of the best skiing in the world. To the east are the endless plains, and over the western ridge of Rockies, the Pacific Ocean. Should residents be inclined to forget where they are and to what they owe their living, there are the incredible Canadian prairie winters, with temperatures dropping to an average of 0 degrees F (−18C) to remind them of nature's power. And should they come to think of nature as nothing but a harsh winter mistress, they also have the chinooks, the amazingly warm winds that sweep in from the Pacific on even the most bitterly cold days, bringing the temperature up 30 or 40 degrees in a matter of hours and leaving breathless Calgary residents with a brief, nearly supernatural spring respite.

This phenomenon culminates in a dramatic chinook arch, a layer of white clouds covered by an arch of brilliant blue sky. At sunset, the chinook produces astonishing contrasts of light and dark — lines of long, flat, absolutely black clouds topped by startlingly clear skies. It's a sight to set even the most jaded spirits wandering.

CALGARY AT-A-GLANCE

SEEING THE CITY: The best view of the city is from the top of the 626-foot Calgary Tower. On a clear day, the Rocky Mountains are visible to the west. You can have a meal or drinks in the revolving dining room and cocktail lounge or just admire the scenery from the observation deck (there's a snack bar, should you get hungry). Open daily from 7:30 AM to 11:30 PM weekdays, 8 AM to 11:30 PM Saturdays, and 8 AM to 10:30 PM Sundays; Ninth Ave. and Centre St. S. (phone: 266-7171).

SPECIAL PLACES: It's easy to get around downtown Calgary because there is no traffic on the downtown mall, and the overhead walkways allow you to cross streets above traffic, where it exists. The streets are numbered and laid out in a north-south, east-west grid pattern. Calgary Transit buses shuttle around downtown and connect it with all other sections. A light-rail transit line (a modern, high-speed version of the old cable-car system) links downtown with the southern, northeast, and northwest reaches of the city.

Olympic Plaza – A $5.6 million downtown park which was the setting for the presentation of the medals during the *1988 Winter Olympics.* Just 2 blocks from City Hall on Macleod Trail, between Seventh and Eighth Aves. Musicians and other entertainers often perform here in summer, and the Plaza is turned into an outdoor skating rink in winter.

Glenbow Museum – The art gallery has permanent and changing exhibits, with carvings and ceramics from all over the world. The highlight is the floor devoted to Indian artifacts from all over Canada and the US, with a strong emphasis on the Indian tribes of southern Alberta. Open daily, 10 AM to 6 PM. Admission charge, except on Saturdays. 130 Ninth Ave. SE (phone: 264-8300).

Alberta Science Centre and Planetarium – In the star chamber, the wonders of the universe are revealed by 100 special effects projectors and a sophisticated sound system. Or the moon and the planets can be viewed directly through the telescopes and slide-open roof at the observatory. The aerospace museum has displays of vintage aircraft and their engines, model rockets, and a weather station. Open Wednesdays through Sundays. Admission charge. 11th St. and Seventh Ave. SW (phone: 221-3700).

Fort Calgary – On the site of the original North West Mounted Police Fort built in 1875, this 40-acre park at the confluence of the Bow and Elbow rivers contains an interpretive center with exhibits and audiovisual presentations recounting Calgary's early days. The Deane House, built in 1906 by NWMP Captain Richard Deane, offers lunch and afternoon tea and charming views of the Elbow River; guided tours are provided (no admission charge). Interpretive center open daily in summer, Wednesdays through Sundays in winter (9 AM to 5 PM.) Deane House is open year-round; park is open daily. Closed Mondays from January 1 to April 1. Reservations advised (phone: 269-7747). No admission charge. 750 Ninth Ave. SE (phone: 290-1875).

Calgary Zoo – Animals live in their natural habitats; no barred cages at this large zoo. There are some innovative exhibit designs, too, which allow viewers to watch polar bears and seals swim from an underwater perspective. There are also expanded North American and Eurasian exhibits, a children's zoo, and interpretive programs for kids. Open daily. Admission charge. 1300 Zoo Rd. SE (phone: 232-9372).

Calgary Prehistoric Park – The Calgary Zoo's multimillion-dollar project transports visitors back to when southern Alberta was a land of swamps and volcanoes and hoodoos — those queer, toadstool-like rock formations that still exist in parts of the province. These manmade reproductions are painstakingly realistic, as are the fiberglass-skinned dinosaurs that populate the fern-filled swamps. The park, which is included in the zoo admission fee, is beside its main entrance, on the south side of Memorial Dr. SE. Closed in winter (phone: 232-9372).

Inglewood Bird Sanctuary – Just 1½ miles downstream from the zoo, this patch of nature offers visitors a chance to observe some 230 varieties of birds year-round. In summer, wildlife experts give guided tours and visitors bicycle along the riverpath. Ninth Ave. and Sanctuary Rd. SE (phone: 269-6688).

Stephen Avenue Mall – A 4-block, traffic-free pedestrian mall lined with outdoor cafés, trees, fountains, and benches; in summer, especially around noon, it is full of workers taking breaks, shoppers, and street musicians and performers. Many of the city's original sandstone buildings stand on the block between First and Second Streets. The second floor of the Lancaster Building, 304 Eighth Ave. SW, has many restaurants offering international fare.

Downtown Connection – This huge indoor shopping complex consists of three large malls (*Toronto-Dominion Square, Scotia Fashion Centre,* and *Bankers Hall*), two major department stores (*The Bay,* and *Eaton's*) and hundreds of smaller stores, all connected by a series of skywalks. *Bankers Hall* is a striking new office tower with 4 levels of shops found nowhere else in Calgary. They include *Laura Ashley, Rocky Mountain Chocolate,* a tea house, a cappuccino bar, and numerous restaurants. A 2½-acre park, the Devonian Gardens, on top of *Toronto-Dominion Square* is a popular gathering place, with stores carrying everything from souvenirs to clothing. There also are restaurants (*Earl's,* on the third level of *Toronto-Dominion Square,* the *Dilettante,* in *Scotia Centre*) and several fast-food outlets. Three blocks between First and Fourth Sts. SW, and Seventh and Eighth Aves.

Kensington-Louise Crossing – A revitalized, older neighborhood that today is thick with trendy restaurants, pubs, boutiques, bookstores, craft shops, and tiny stores scooping first-rate ice cream. The area stretches west along Kensington Road for several blocks from Tenth Street NW. *Victorian Rose* (1142 Kensington Rd.) sells beautiful lace, embroidered clothing, and linen. Explore *Through the Looking Glass's* treasure of children's literature (102 Tenth St. NW), and sample well-brewed coffee and sherbets at *Higher Ground* (1126 Kensington Rd. NW). A lovely Bow River pathway follows Memorial Drive, 1 block south of Kensington Road.

SUBURBS

Heritage Park – A pioneer village re-created with buildings transplanted from their original locations in small Alberta towns. Among the structures are a working blacksmith's shop, a bakery where you can buy fresh bread, a small log church still used for services and weddings, and a newspaper office distributing the park's official newspaper. The houses are furnished with period pieces, and the occupants even dress in early-1900s styles. For a journey back in time, the means of transportation are diverse: an old steam train, an electrical streetcar, a carousel, a horse-drawn bus, or the SS *Moyie,* a paddlewheeler that plies the waters of the Glenmore Reservoir. Available refreshments range from ice cream and snack bar fare to great Alberta beef and homemade apple pie served up in the dining room of the *Wainwright* hotel. Open from May to October. The hotel serves breakfast on Sundays during the winter. Admission charge. West of 14th St. and Heritage Dr. SW (phone: 252-1858).

Fish Creek Provincial Park – These 2,800 acres on the city's southern edge shelter a mixture of grassland, poplar and spruce groves, and native shrubs; a wildlife refuge is also located here. Park interpreters present slide shows and lead nature walks to acquaint visitors with the human and natural history of the area. There's also a small, manmade lake where people swim in the summer. Open daily. No admission charge. More than 5 miles (8 km) long from Canyon Meadows Drive and Bow Bottom Trail SE to Canyon Meadows Drive and 24th St. SW (phone: 297-5293).

■ **EXTRA SPECIAL:** High River, 30 miles (48 km) south of Calgary, has the atmosphere of an authentic small Western town. Several stores carry handicrafts made by local artisans, including ceramics, leatherwork, and wooden carvings. If you're in Alberta during July, check the dates for High River's annual *North American Chuckwagon Championship.* You'll see the same names and rigs that appear at the *Calgary Stampede.* For more information write to the High River Chamber of Commerce, Box 1258, High River, Alberta TOL 1B0.

Calgary is a major stopover for travelers bound for Banff National Park. Only 75 miles (120 km) west of Calgary along the Trans-Canada Highway, Banff has spectacular Rocky Mountain scenery and some of the best skiing areas in Canada (see *Skiing,* below, and *Skiing* in DIVERSIONS). For complete information on Banff, see *National Parks* in DIVERSIONS.

SOURCES AND RESOURCES

TOURIST INFORMATION: The Calgary Tourist and Convention Bureau, located in the historic Burne Building (237 Eighth Ave. SE, Calgary, Alberta T2G 0K8; phone: 263-8510), supplies maps, brochures, free accommodation assistance, and general information, and publishes an annual visitor's guide that lists city attractions and services (closed weekends).

Local Coverage – The *Calgary Sun* and the *Calgary Herald,* morning dailies; *Alberta Report,* weekly news magazine.

Food – See *My Favorite Restaurants in Calgary and Banff* by John Gilchrist.

Telephone – The area code for Calgary is 403.

Sales Tax – Neither the city of Calgary nor the province of Alberta has sales tax.

Currency – All prices are quoted in US dollars unless otherwise indicated.

TIPPING: At restaurants generally leave 15% of the bill. Taxi drivers should be given 10% to 15% of the fare. Airport porters and bellboys are given about CN$1 per bag, and hotel maids should receive about CN$1 per day, per person.

CLIMATE: Calgary tends to be sunny and dry during most of the year. Temperatures range from an average of 10F (−12C) in January to an average of 58F (16C) in July. From May to the middle of September, expect warm days and cool nights. During the winter, the city gets about 50 inches of snow and unpredictable chinooks — warm westerly winds that can boost the temperature 20 to 30 degrees in an hour. Anyone who ventures to Calgary in the winter should bring along boots, a heavy coat, gloves, and a hat.

GETTING AROUND: Bus – *Calgary Transit* serves all parts of the city. For detailed route information, call 276-7801, or stop in at the transit information booth (206 7th Ave. SW). *Brewster Transportation and Tours* (808 Centre St., SE; phone: 221-8242 or 800-332-1419 in Canada), *White Stetson Tours* (6312 Travois Crescent NW; phone: 274-2281), and *Cardinal Coach Lines* (732 41st Ave., NE; phone: 230-1491) are among those available for charter bus tours.

Car Rental – All major firms are represented at Calgary International Airport as well as downtown: *Avis* (240 Ninth Ave. SW; phone: 269-6166); *Hertz* (227 Sixth Ave. SW; phone: 221-1300); *Tilden* (First St. and Fifth Ave. S.; phone: 263-6386).

Taxi – Taxis generally cannot be hailed on the streets, but are available at hotels, or one can be called. Major companies are *Yellow Cab* (phone: 250-8311), *Prestige Cabs* (phone: 250-5911), and *Checker Cab* (phone: 272-1111).

SPECIAL EVENTS: During the famous *Calgary Exhibition and Stampede,* the first or second week of July, the city reclaims its Western heritage with rodeos, chuckwagon races, grandstand shows, exhibitions, displays, and general carryings-on. *Stampede* dates vary slightly every year; check with the CTCB before coming and make reservations for grandstand events well in advance (phone: 269-9822 or 800-661-1260). Most of the action takes place within walking distance of downtown, at *Stampede Park,* but the mall, suburban shopping centers, and parks are also filled with cowboys in wagons, Indians in traditional dress, and Western bands. If you can't make the *Stampede, Rodeo Royale* is held inside the *Stampede Corral* in March. For information on all events at *Stampede Park,* call 261-0101.

MUSEUMS: The *Glenbow Museum,* Fort Calgary, the *Planetarium,* and Heritage Park are described in *Special Places.* Other museums worth a visit include the following:

The Energeum – Oilfield memorabilia and video games tell the tale of energy in Alberta. No admission charge. 640 Fifth Ave. SW (phone: 297-4293).

Museum of the Regiments – The largest military museum in western Canada was completed in June 1990. Hands-on displays simulate life at the front line with an actual trench plus clothing and equipment that visitors can try on for size. Crowchild Trail and Flanders Ave. (phone: 240-7674).

Olympic Hall of Fame – The premier site of the *1988 Winter Olympic Games* is now a year-round attraction. View the serpentine bobsled and luge track, and gaze down from the top of the ski jumps into the landing basin that seated 50,000 spectators. The museum offers a film, displays, and a panoramic view of Canada Olympic Park. Rte. 1 at the city's western limits (phone: 286-2632).

Stockmen's Memorial Foundation – A museum, small gallery of Western art, and library illustrating the province's ranching history. 2116 27th Ave. NE (phone: 250-7529).

SHOPPING: The Downtown Connection (between First and Fourth Sts. SW, and Seventh and Eighth Aves.), is the site of three large shopping malls: *Toronto-Dominion Square, Scotia Fashion Centre,* and *Bankers Hall.* Special goods found in Calgary are mostly furs, Western wear, and Indian crafts. *Western Outfitters* (128 8th Ave. SE; phone: 266-3656) is a good place for cowboy hats, boots, and jeans. *Alberta Boots* (614 Tenth Ave. SW; phone: 263-4623) is the province's only cowboy boot manufacturer. For native crafts, try *Cottage Craft Gifts* (6503 Elbow Dr. SW; phone: 252-3797), which specializes in Eskimo sculptures but also carries everything from moccasins to prints by native artists. The *Glenbow Museum* (130 Ninth Ave. SE; phone: 264-8300) has an excellent gift shop for authentic native-made crafts from western and northern Canada, including soapstone carvings and beadwork. The Mount Royal Village area (on 17th Avenue SW) features trendy clothing shops, antiques stores, art galleries, and bookstores; similar shopping opportunities will be found in the Kensington district (Kensington Rd. and 10th St. NW).

SPORTS: Though Calgary is only 80 miles (128 km) away from the Rocky Mountain skiing areas, it has a fair share of its own diversions.

Auto Racing – The 160-acre *Race City Speedway* hosts major national and international stock car, motorcycle, hot rod, and formula Grand Prix–style competitions throughout the summer. 114 Ave. and 68th St. SE (phone: 236-7223).

Baseball – The Calgary *Cannons,* a farm team for the Seattle *Mariners* and part of the Pacific Coast League, play at *Foothills Baseball Stadium* from April through August. 24th Ave. and Crowchild Trail (phone: 284-1111).

Boating – There's sailing on the Glenmore Reservoir in the southwest section of the city. The City of Calgary Parks and Recreation Department rents sailboats Friday evenings and weekends (90th Ave. and 24th St. SW; phone: 268-5256). During the spring and summer many people canoe and kayak on the Bow and Elbow rivers;

University of Calgary *Campus Recreation Rentals* supplies equipment (2500 University Dr. NW; phone: 220-5038).

Fishing and Hunting – The area around Calgary supports upland birds, big game, waterfowl, and freshwater fish. For full information, contact Alberta Fish and Wildlife (Rm. 200, Sloane Square Bldg., 5920 1A St. SW; phone: 297-6423). The Bow River, downstream from Calgary, is reputed to be one of the finest fishing grounds in the world for brown and rainbow trout. Consult the "Float Trips" section of the *Adventure Guide* published by Travel Alberta (10025 Jasper Ave., 15th Fl., Edmonton, Alberta T5J 3Z3; phone: 403-427-4321 in Edmonton; 800-222-6501 elsewhere in Alberta; 800-661-8888 elsewhere in Canada or in the US). The Alberta Tourism office in Calgary is in the provincial government building at McDougall Centre (455 Sixth St. SW; phone: 800-222-6501 from Canada or 800-661-8888 from the US).

Football – The professional *Stampeders* play from June through November at *McMahon Stadium* in northwest Calgary. 1817 Crowchild Trail NW (phone: 289-0258).

Golf – Six municipal courses and numerous private courses will accept transient players. *Shaganappi Golf Course* is the closest municipal course to downtown. Bow Trail and 26th St. SW (phone: 249-1212).

Hockey – The Calgary *Flames* compete in the National Hockey League and play at the *Calgary Olympic Saddledome,* from October to May in Stampede Park, 12th Ave. and Olympic Way (phone: 261-0455).

Horseback Riding – Lessons, group trail rides, hayrides, and mountain trips in the summer are available at *Fish Creek Trail Rides,* southwest of Calgary in Fish Creek Provincial Park (phone: 251-6955). *Spruce Meadows Stables,* just southwest of the city (phone: 254-3200), is the site of several annual international equestrian competitions.

Horse Racing – Harness and thoroughbred racing can be enjoyed year-round at Stampede Park, 12th Ave. and Olympic Way (phone: 261-0214).

Skating – The *Olympic Oval* on the University of Calgary campus is the first covered 400-meter speed skating track in North America, and the first ever used in *Olympic* competition. This $40-million facility is not just for the use of the world's elite speed skaters, however. So, bring your own blades, or rent them here (288 Collegiate Blvd.; phone: 220-7890). The *Olympic Plaza* also becomes an outdoor skating rink during the winter months (MacLeod Trail between 7th and 8th Aves.).

Skiing – One of the newest ski destinations in the Canadian Rockies is Nakiska at Mount Allen, about 60 miles (96 km) west of Calgary, where the *1988 Olympic* alpine competition was held. Three big areas near Banff are Sunshine Village, Skiing Louise, and Mt. Norquay. For the novice or the experienced downhill skier who just wants a little practice, there's Canada *Olympic Park* (Route 1 west at Bowfort Rd.; phone: 286-2632). They also rent equipment and offer a wide range of lessons for skiers of all ages and abilities (see DIVERSIONS).

Swimming – The city-owned *Lindsay Park Sports Centre* (2225 Macleod Trail SE; phone: 233-8619), has three pools and numerous other facilities, including squash courts, running track, sauna, and weight room.

Tennis – There are private and public courts in the city. For information on the public courts, call 268-5218.

 THEATER: For complete listings, check the publications cited above. Two of the city's professional companies, *Theatre Calgary* and *Alberta Theatre Projects,* stage plays at the *Calgary Centre for the Performing Arts* (205 Eighth Ave. SE; phone: 266-8888 for tickets; 294-7444 for information). The *Lunchbox Theatre* (Bow Valley Square, downtown; phone: 265-4292) also presents short, noontime productions on Mondays through Saturdays. The *Stage West* (727 42 Ave. SE; phone: 243-6642) dinner-theater presents popular Broadway shows starring celebrity actors.

MUSIC: The *Calgary Philharmonic* presents concerts from fall through the spring at the *Jack Singer Concert Hall* in the *Calgary Centre for the Performing Arts.* 205 8th Ave. SE (phone: 294-7420).

NIGHTCLUBS AND NIGHTLIFE: *Electric Avenue* is the name Calgarians have given to a neon-lit strip of bistros and dance clubs along Eleventh Avenue SW between Fourth and Eighth Sts. It's heaven for bar-hoppers, and a muscular young rickshaw puller can even be hired to transport revelers from one watering hole to the next. Downtown, along the *Stephen Street Mall,* is the *Unicorn* (304 8th Ave. SW; phone: 233-2666); offering good food and a cozy pub where locals extend a hearty welcome to newcomers. If you want to listen or dance to western music in the company of real cowboys and cowgirls, head to *Ranchman's* in southern Calgary (9615 Macleod Trail; phone: 253-1100), just one of a number of country and western dance hall bars.

BEST IN TOWN

CHECKING IN: Calgary has several first class hotels downtown and a spate of motels on the two primary approaches to the city — along the southern end of Macleod Trail from the south and along 16th Avenue north from the Trans-Canada Highway. Accommodations are often booked solid during the *Stampede;* the city also hosts many conventions, so reserve rooms in advance. Expect to pay about $100 and up for a double room in the places listed as expensive and $35 to $80 in the moderate range. There are no inexpensive hotels worth recommending in Calgary, though bed and breakfast establishments provide a low-cost option. Contact the *Bed and Breakfast Bureau* (Box 7094, Station E., Calgary, Alberta T3C 3L8; phone: 403-242-5555). All telephone numbers are in the 403 area code unless otherwise indicated.

Delta Bow Valley Inn – Along with 398 rooms, including some that are for non-smokers, this place has exercise facilities, a dining room, tavern, pool, sauna, and a Jacuzzi. 209 Fourth Ave. SE (phone: 266-1980). Expensive.

Palliser – A gracious old hotel constructed in 1914 by the *Canadian Pacific Rail Company* and still a link in the company chain. The 11-story sandstone structure contains 400 rooms, all of which have been restored. Solid brass doors, original marble pillars and staircases, and a large chandelier decorate the elegant lobby. The *Rimrock* dining room has an Old West flavor in its decor and menu. There are also 2 coffee shops; covered walkways lead to the Calgary Tower complex of 80 shops, movie theaters, and offices. 133 Ninth Ave. SW (phone: 262-1234). Expensive.

Skyline – Located in the *Convention Centre* complex, it has 237 rooms and features an indoor garden and a pool. The *Traders* dining room has a fine menu (see *Eating Out*), and guests can catch a quick bite at the *Wheat Sheaf* coffee shop. Children under 18 can stay free in the same room as their parents, and rooms for non-smokers are available. Ninth Ave. and Centre St. SE (phone: 266-7331). Expensive.

Westin Calgary – This 525-room establishment is another of the city's best known. Its *Owl's Nest* restaurant is among the city's finest (see *Eating Out*), and there's also an informal dining room and cocktail lounge. Facilities include a swimming pool, shops in the lobby, underground parking; the rooms are air conditioned. Fourth Ave. and Third St. SW (phone: 266-1611). Expensive.

Prince Royal Inn Apartment Hotel – Great for families, it has a dining room, lounge, hot tub, and fully equipped kitchens. 618 Fifth Ave., SW (phone: 263-0520). Moderate.

Relax Inn–North – This family-style hostelry offers 200 rooms, a pool, hot tub, a restaurant, a gift shop, and game rooms. 2750 Sunridge Blvd. NE (phone: 291-1260). Moderate.

Relax Inn–South – A 265-unit motel with air conditioned rooms, it offers some of the most reasonably priced accommodations in the city. Rooms for non-smokers are available. 9206 Macleod Trail S. (phone: 253-7070). Moderate.

Stampeder Inn – In south Calgary, this modern hostelry has 140 rooms, air conditioning, a dining room, and a cocktail lounge. Children under 12 may stay in the room with their parents at no charge; rooms for non-smokers are available. 3828 Macleod Trail (phone: 243-5531). Moderate.

Sun Bow Inn – Built around an indoor courtyard with a swimming pool, the hotel has a poolside dining room. Rooms for non-smokers are available. 2359 Banff Trail NW (phone: 289-1973). Moderate.

EATING OUT: At the crossroads of the prairies, Calgary should — and does — have some of the best beef in North America. The city is no longer a traditional steak and lobster town; now visitors can sample a broad range of international dishes. Expect to pay about $50 and up for a dinner for two in the places we've listed as expensive; $20 to $40 in the moderate range; and under $20, inexpensive. Prices do not include drinks, wine, or tips. All telephone numbers are in the 403 area code unless otherwise indicated.

La Chaumière – Authentic French food and fine service are this Gallic restaurant's hallmarks. Specialties include breast of duck in brandy, rack of lamb, and scampi Parod. Closed Sundays. Reservations advised. Major credit cards accepted. 121 17th Ave. SE (phone: 228-5690). Expensive.

La Dolce Vita – Lovingly prepared Italian food (veal, seafood, pasta) presented in an elegant yet comfortable setting. The owner makes his own *cassata* — Sicilian ice cream with candied fruit — that is a must. Closed Sundays. Reservations advised. Major credit cards accepted. 916 1st Ave. NE (phone: 263-3445). Expensive.

Owl's Nest – Renowned for its beef entrées, British Columbia salmon, Beluga malossol caviar, medallions of venison, and quail, this plush place in the *Westin Calgary* is a Calgary institution. Open daily for dinner, lunch served weekdays only. Reservations essential. Major credit cards accepted. 320 Fourth Ave. SW (phone: 267-2823/4). Expensive.

Traders – Dark paneling, elegant table settings, and fine food distinguish this restaurant in the *Skyline* hotel. Open daily. Reservations advised. Major credit cards accepted. Ninth Ave. and Centre St. SW (phone: 266-7331). Expensive.

Le Flamboyant – Tiny and unassuming, but the Mauritian-style creole and curry dishes are exquisite. The bouillabaise, heaped with crab legs and mussels, is a specialty. Open Tuesdays through Saturdays. Reservations advised. Major credit cards accepted. 4018 16th St. SW (phone: 287-0060). Moderate.

Green Street Café – In the heart of downtown, this place has a quiet atmosphere with a pleasant view of the nearby park. The menu features everything from Cajun spiced entrées to steaks. Open Mondays through Fridays for lunch and dinner, Saturdays for dinner only, and Sundays for brunch only. Reservations advised. Major credit cards accepted. 815 Seventh Ave. SW (phone: 266-1551). Moderate to inexpensive.

Silver Inn – Though this family-run eatery is located outside Calgary's Chinatown, it offers the best Peking-style fare in town. The menu is extensive, service is efficient and friendly, and the restaurant is fully licensed. Closed Mondays and holidays. Reservations advised. Major credit cards accepted. 2702 Centre St. NE (phone: 276-6711). Moderate to inexpensive.

Café Danois – On the mezzanine floor of the Chevron Plaza, this tiny spot serves beautifully presented open-face Danish sandwiches, soup, and entrées such as homemade sausage or sole. Reservations unnecessary. Major credit cards accepted. 500 Fifth Ave. SW (phone: 263-1114). Inexpensive.

4 St. Rose – Centrally located, this eatery serves an eclectic menu including soup, salads, sandwiches, pizza, omelettes, and tempting desserts. The decor makes for a cozy atmosphere, and the offbeat clientele is great for people watching. No reservations. Major credit cards accepted. 2116 Fourth St. SW (phone: 228-5377). Inexpensive.

EDMONTON

Boom towns are a familiar western phenomenon, well anchored in North American folklore and mythology. The very term evokes dramatic images of towns materializing overnight in the midst of the untamed and uncharted wilderness, of hardy men engaged in a lonely struggle with the elements driven on by the dream of the mother lode, of dingy saloons and dance halls festering with crooked gambling and drunken brawls, and of incredible fortunes made over years and lost in a matter of hours.

From Charlie Chaplin's epic tale of Alaskan misadventure *The Gold Rush,* to Robert Altman's popular classic *McCabe and Mrs. Miller,* the boom town is embedded in our culture as an arena where both the brave and the foolish try to strike it rich — and where they most often fail. And when they fail and the mine or well runs dry, the boom town suddenly finds itself a ghost town.

Consider Edmonton, the capital of the province of Alberta, the largest northerly city in the Americas (with a metropolitan area population of 785,-500) and the wiliest boom town in the Northern Hemisphere. Three times it has experienced the frenetic explosion of a boom — in the days of the Hudson's Bay Company and "King Fur," during the Gold Rush of '98, and in the late 1970s to early 1980s with excessive oil and gas development. Each time the tide has passed, the boom dissipated, the prospectors giving up in despair, yet Edmonton has emerged stronger, richer, more stable, and more beautiful than before.

An example is the way the city handled its oil boom. (Just about 25 miles/40 km south of Edmonton, at Leduc, are a slew of very lucrative wells.) With more money flowing though provincial coffers than was imaginable 40 years before, it might have been easy for a city to lose its perspective. But not Edmonton. Shortly after the Progressive Conservatives came to power in the early 1970s, they decided it was time to establish a special fund for the wealth the province was amassing from its oil and gas royalties. It's called the Alberta Heritage Savings Trust Fund, and the politicians who sit under the dome in the Legislature Building in Edmonton make the final decisions on how to spend the surplus revenue. And they are very judicious.

Fort Edmonton was established as a fur trading post in 1795 on the mighty North Saskatchewan River, the banks of which rise some 200 feet near the original site. Chief Factor John Rowand was the first commander of the fort in the early 19th century, and as such he was regent of a realm known as Rupert's Land, which consisted of the southern half of Alberta and the southeastern quarter of Saskatchewan. From the very beginning, Edmonton was the seat of power and commerce in north-central Canada.

While Hudson's Bay fur traders roamed the north in search of beaver, muskrat, and mink pelts, a number of missionaries traveled around southern

Alberta, attempting to make Christian converts of the local Wood, Cree, and Blackfoot Indians. The missionaries built schools and churches, but their efforts were subverted when Rupert's Land became part of Canada in 1869, and whiskey traders and other unscrupulous characters moved up from the Montana Territory, founding Fort Whoop-Up and bedeviling the population. Most God-fearing citizens in the new province had to wait 5 years before the Royal Canadian Mounted Police arrived to restore order.

It was in 1871, in the midst of this lawless era, that Edmonton was incorporated as a town with a population of about 600. Soon after, when Canada's first transcontinental railway was laid, Edmonton became an important stop — the crossroads between east and west as well as north and south. The railroad has in many ways been the true source of Edmonton's wealth, and it is the reason Edmonton became known as Canada's "gateway to the north."

When gold was discovered in the Klondike in 1898, prospectors and other would-be millionaires prepared for the ordeal in Edmonton; the tiny town of 700 suddenly mushroomed into a respectably sized town of 4,000. A disaster for most of the unfortunate prospectors, the Gold Rush is remembered fondly by Edmonton folks, and their warm nostalgia takes yearly expression in a colorful bacchanalia known as *Klondike Days.* During this giant masquerade, which occurs during the last 2 weeks of July, they take a break from fortune hunting to traipse about town in "Gay Nineties" dress, occasionally panning for gold, often stopping for a drink, and generally attempting to celebrate as long as they can still stand. Unsuspecting tourists who are inappropriately attired are subjected to surprising citizens' arrests and may find themselves in a Klondike clink. Bail is a Klondike dollar that has been specially minted for the occasion.

The oil boom was particularly kind to Edmonton, and perhaps someday in the not too distant future Edmontonians will declare a local holiday to celebrate the invention of the internal combustion engine. The discovery of oil in Alberta early in this century, and the subsequent gusher at Leduc, spurred fantastic local industrial growth. An indication of just how much growth is involved is the fact that Edmonton's population quadrupled between 1939 and 1965.

While wallowing in the profitable wake of this boom, Edmontonians further benefited from the discovery of natural gas reserves at Viking and the development of the Alberta tar sands at Fort McMurray. Hence, the entire province of Alberta has no sales tax.

What may be a pleasant surprise, however, is seeing how intelligently the Edmontonians have used their wealth in city planning and development. Far from being the amorphous hodgepodge of slums and mansions one might expect in a boom town, Edmonton is an extremely well-designed modern city that has made a valiant effort to retain and even reconstruct valuable artifacts of its past while confronting its future.

For example, a replica of Fort Edmonton now stands on a 158-acre park in the suburbs, and replicas of the city in its various stages of development are being constructed in the same park. Other efforts at making the city a pleasant habitat include the recent establishment of Capital City Recreation Park. Set along the spectacular banks of the North Saskatchewan River, this

2,100-acre park now separates the downtown area of the city from the suburbs. The recreation area is a verdant complement to the already dramatic scenery, and it's a tribute to inspired city planning, as is the fact that Edmonton now has a total of 10,000 acres of city parks. In summer months, when it's often light until 10 or 11 PM, these green acres are filled with people cycling, riding horses, playing baseball, picnicking, and enjoying the outdoors.

In the winter, Edmontonians venture outdoors to use these same parks for skating and cross-country skiing. The winters are very cold, but rather than struggle through unplowed streets and icy sidewalks, Edmontonians can take advantage of an extensive system of underground and overhead walkways that crisscross the downtown area.

Today, a visitor to Edmonton will inevitably be struck by the dynamic high-rise skyline that stands starkly silhouetted against the deep blue western sky; he or she may well marvel at the sleek lines of the massive *Commonwealth Stadium,* built in 1978, or at the ultramodern technological grace of the Muttart Conservatory, a series of four huge glass pyramids near downtown Edmonton.

In spite of its economic enterprises and unabashed emphasis on capital gains, Edmonton has managed to save its abundance of sunlight and space for its most important natural resource — its people. As a result, Edmonton is more than just a boom town — it's the boom town that won.

EDMONTON AT-A-GLANCE

SEEING THE CITY: One of the best ways to get a bird's-eye view of Edmonton is from Vista 33, on the 33rd floor of the Alberta Telephone Tower. From an elevation of 388 feet you have a view of 2,500 square miles; you'll see everything from the International Airport to the refinery-petrochemical area to the university. Just as the viewing gallery gives guests an overview of Edmonton, the *Man and Telecommunications Museum,* an integral part of Vista 33, gives them an overview of telecommunications, from the primitive switchboard to modern technology. Vista 33 is open daily year-round, except *Christmas* and *New Year's Day,* from 10 AM to 8 PM. Elevation charge. 10020 100 St. (phone: 493-3333).

SPECIAL PLACES: You can walk around downtown Edmonton quite easily, although in the winter the under- and aboveground "pedways" make more sense. Like Manhattan, the streets are laid out in an urban geometric grid and, except for the major routes, are numbered. A public bus system operates from downtown to all the outlying areas of the city; and the *Light Rail Transit* tramway has a mile of track downtown and extends more than 6 miles (10 km) to the northeast tip of Edmonton's city limits.

DOWNTOWN

Alberta's Legislature Building – Constructed in 1912 on the site of the original trading post, Fort Edmonton, the elegant domed building lies nestled amid manicured lawns and formal gardens overlooking the North Saskatchewan River valley. You can take a guided tour of the building at any time of year, and if you're in town during

November or from February to late May, you can watch the Canadian politicians lobby and legislate. 109th St. and 97th Ave. (phone: 427-7362).

Edmonton Civic Centre – One of Edmonton's showcases is a 6-block area containing the *Edmonton Art Gallery,* Churchill Square, City Hall, the Law Courts Building, the Canada Place complex, the *Convention Centre,* the Centennial Library, and Edmonton's pride and joy, the spectacular *Citadel Theatre.* The *Citadel's* five-theater complex is one of Canada's major centers for the performing arts. 100th St. and 102nd Ave.

Muttart Conservatory – A controlled botanical incubator unique in North America, the Muttart is a collection of graceful, pyramid-shaped greenhouses. The small central pyramid is the reception foyer; each of the others contains the flora of a specific climatic zone, with one exception, which is used as a showcase for changing seasonal displays. The Muttart is open daily and has an admission charge. 98th Ave. and 96 St., south side (phone: 428-5226).

SUBURBS

Fort Edmonton – An authentic reconstruction of the early trading post from which the city grew, this is a nucleus for an entire park that allows visitors to step into the past and reexperience history. You can take a look at the fur press, the stockade, and a clay bake oven. The park also features "1885 Street" — urban Edmonton a century ago — with such highlights as *McDougall's General Store* and the Northwest Mounted Police Jail, and "1905 Street," with Ernest Brown's Photography Studio and the Masonic Temple. Near the park, which runs along the river, is the *John Janzen Nature Centre,* an interpretive museum that illustrates the geological eras preceding man's recorded history. From the *Janzen Centre* (phone: 428-7900) you can take a nature walk accompanied by a skilled guide and get a firsthand view of the North Saskatchewan River valley around which Edmonton grew. Fort Edmonton is closed in winter, except for some special programs and events; the *Janzen Centre* is open year-round. South bank of the North Saskatchewan off Whitemud Drive (phone: 428-2992).

Provincial Museum of Alberta – An important center for the preservation of Alberta's natural and human history, the museum was completed in 1967 to mark Canada's centennial. Exhibits depict early Indian life, pioneer settlement, and geological and ecological zones of the province. The museum presents regular film festivals and cultural performances and has a bookstore that features the works of Alberta authors. Open daily during summer; closed Mondays, *Labor Day* to *Victoria Day* (May 21). No admission charge. 12845 102nd Ave. (phone: 458-9100).

Valley Zoo – Expanded from the Storyland theme (fairy tale displays, farm animals, and a miniature train), the zoo now also features buildings for reptiles and nocturnal animals, and winter quarters for tropical birds and animals. Open year-round, daily in the summer and weekends in the winter. Admission charge. 13315 Buena Vista Rd. at 87th Ave. and 134th St. (phone: 483-5511).

Edmonton Space Sciences Centre – One of Edmonton's major attractions, the center houses a planetarium star theater, western Canada's first IMAX theater (projecting large-format films onto a 60-by-40-foot screen), a science exhibit galleries, a public observatory, science shop, and a café. Open daily; shows on Tuesdays through Sundays. Admission charge. 111th Ave. and 142nd St. (phone: 451-7722).

West Edmonton Mall – A shopper's *Disneyland,* this 5-million-plus-square-foot mall/amusement park (*Canada Fantasyland*) is listed in the *Guinness Book of World Records* as the largest in the world. It features more than 800 shops and services, the *Fantasyland* hotel, reasonable facsimiles of Bourbon Street and a Parisian boulevard, animal displays, aviaries, aquariums, a 20-ride *Fantasyland,* an ice palace, a water park with slides, deep-sea adventure submarine rides, and a miniature replica of California's *Pebble Beach* golf course. Open daily. Shuttle bus service operates from many downtown hotels for a small charge. Admission charge for most attractions. 87th Ave. and 170th St. (phone: 444-5200).

■**EXTRA SPECIAL:** If you're in Edmonton during the last 2 weeks of July, plan on celebrating *Klondike Days,* a remembrance of Edmonton's heritage as the starting point for prospectors heading northward to seek their fortunes. The city regresses to the wild era of the "Gay Nineties" and the Yukon Gold Rush as everyone dresses in the Victorian manner and enjoys the festivities, which include the *World Championship Sourdough Raft Race* on the North Saskatchewan River, parades, garden parties, sporting events, and more.

SOURCES AND RESOURCES

TOURIST INFORMATION: For general information, brochures, and maps, contact the Edmonton Tourism Visitor Information Centre, No. 104, 9797 Jasper Ave. (phone: 422-5505).

    Local Coverage – *The Edmonton Sun,* a morning daily, except Saturday; *The Edmonton Journal,* morning daily; *Alberta Report,* a weekly news magazine; *Western Living,* a monthly lifestyle magazine.

Food – For details on restaurants in the Edmonton area, the Edmonton Tourism Visitor Information Centre has two publications available — the *International Guide* and *Billy's Guide.* Restaurant reviews also are in the *Edmonton Journal* (Fridays), the *Edmonton Sun* (Sundays), and *Western Living* (monthly).

Telephone – The area code for Edmonton is 403.

Sales Tax – Neither the city of Edmonton nor the province of Alberta has a sales tax.

Currency – All prices are quoted in US dollars unless otherwise indicated.

TIPPING: At restaurants add 15% to 20% to your bill for service. At hotels, bellboys should receive CN$1 per bag and hotel maids, CN$1 per day, per person. Airport porters are tipped CN$1 per bag. Taxi drivers should be tipped 10% to 15% of the fare.

CLIMATE: At an altitude of 2,182 feet, the city averages 6.25 hours of sunshine a day. This is the result of Edmonton's extreme northerly position, which gives it daylight past 11 PM and average temperatures of 75F (24C) during the summer. Edmonton's location also accounts for very cold winters, with the mean January temperature averaging 5F (−15C).

GETTING AROUND: Bus – *Edmonton Transit* offers bus service around Edmonton and environs. For detailed information on routes, dial 421-4636.

    Car Rental – Most major North American firms are represented.

    Tramway – The *Light Rail Transit (LRT),* operated by *Edmonton Transit,* offers tram service in the downtown area and northeastern section of the city. For detailed route information, dial 421-4636.

Taxi – Taxis can be hailed on street corners and at taxi stands in front of major hotels. In the middle of the winter, however, you may want to call instead of venturing outside. Try *Yellow Cab* (phone: 462-3456) or *Co-Op Taxi* (phone: 425-8310).

Sightseeing Tours – *Royal Tours* offers guided tours to various attractions. Your hotel front desk can handle reservations, or call 424-8687.

SPECIAL EVENTS: In order to avoid being one-upped by the notorious *Calgary Stampede*, Edmontonians have come up with *Klondike Days* (phone: 426-4055), which they celebrate annually during the last 2 weeks of July (right after the *Stampede;* see *Extra Special*). In June, Edmonton hosts *Jazz City* (phone: 432-7166), a week-long, world class jazz festival. August brings the *Edmonton Folk Festival* (phone: 429-1899), 3 days on a sunny hill with some of the country's best folk artists. For the *Fringe Theatre Event* (phone: 448-9000), which runs for 9 days in August, 650 performances are staged in 12 theaters in the Old Strathcona district. Then there's the *Heritage Festival* (phone: 433-3378), a 2-day celebration in Hawrelak Park that celebrates Edmonton's multi-culturalism. It's only a few years old, but thousands come to partake of the food and cultures of more than 44 nations.

MUSEUMS: The *Provincial Museum* and Fort Edmonton are described in *Special Places.* Other Edmonton museums of note include the following:

Edmonton Art Gallery – Traditional and contemporary Canadian art. 2 Sir Winston Churchill Sq. (phone: 422-6223).

Father Lacombe Chapel – The original log cabin built in 1861 by Father Albert Lacombe, a prairie priest who translated the New Testament into Cree. St. Albert, 12 miles (19 km) north of Edmonton off Highway 2 (no phone).

Rutherford House – Alberta's first restored historical home. 11153 Saskatchewan Dr. (phone: 427-3995).

Ukrainian-Canadian Archives and Museum – Artifacts and costumes from the Ukrainian pioneers and settlers, starting from 1900; library. 9543 110th Ave. (phone: 424-7580).

Ukrainian Cultural Heritage Village – Exhibits displaying the history of the Ukrainian pioneers including a railway town, farmstead area, and rural community. Yellowhead Highway 16, 30 miles (48 km) east of Edmonton (phone: 662-3640).

SHOPPING: The Greater Edmonton area boasts some 25 shopping malls, all offering a wide variety of clothing and national chain stores from which to choose. Among them are *Edmonton Centre* (100th St. and 102nd Ave.) and *Eaton Centre* (101st St. and 102nd Ave.), both in the heart of downtown; *Londonderry Shopping Mall* (137th Ave. and 66th St.) and *Heritage Mall* (23rd Ave. and 111th St.), in the southwest section of the city; and *West Edmonton Mall* (87th Ave. and 170th St.). The city also has a number of specialty stores featuring local arts and crafts, books, and custom-made clothes, a selection of which follows:

Audrey's Books – New and back-list books. 10702 Jasper Ave. (phone: 423-3487).

Bearclaw Gallery – Contemporary crafts and paintings from the Inuits and Indians across the continent. 9724 111th Ave. (phone: 479-8502).

Birks Jewelers – A wide selection of sterling goods. *West Edmonton Mall* (phone: 444-1656) and *Edmonton Centre* (phone: 426-7290).

Canadiana Galleries – For Eskimo crafts and carvings. 12306 Jasper Ave. (phone: 482-5471).

Chocolaterie Bernard Callebaut – For some of the best chocolate in Canada. At several locations: 12516 102nd Ave. (phone: 452-3795); ManuLife Place, 10180 101st St. (phone: 423-3083); and 11004 51st Ave. (phone: 436-0908) — for French Canadian foods.

Dennis Miller Wine Merchant Ltd. – A wide variety of wines. 5708 111th St. (phone: 436-9463).

Fireweed Gallery – Handmade jewelry, pottery, and paintings. 8118 103rd St. (phone: 433-9551).

Frenchy's Deli – Sandwiches and other deli specialties. 6512 118th Ave.; phone: 477-5958).

Greenwood's Bookshoppe – New and out-of-print books plus a separate children's bookshop in the rear. 10355 Whyte Ave. (phone: 439-2005).

Henry Singer – High fashion, imported men's wear; fussy and extremely personalized service. 10360 Jasper Ave. (phone: 423-6868) and 2452 *West Edmonton Mall* (phone: 444-3444).

Holt Renfrew – An elegant selection of clothing, perfume, and more. ManuLife Place, 10180 101st St. (phone: 425-5300).

Pat Henning Custom Tailor & Shirt Maker – Clothes for men. In the *Hilton International,* 526-10235 101st St. (phone: 424-5679).

Silversmith Jewelry Designs Co. – Imported silver goods, including jewelry, from other parts of the country. 201 *Edmonton Centre* (phone: 424-8539).

Urban Renewal Men's Wear – Fashions from Europe and Japan. 220 *Edmonton Centre* (phone: 424-7031). Also try *Urban Renewal for Women,* 309 *Edmonton Centre* (phone: 429-0087) and *Urban Kids Clothier,* 216 *Edmonton Centre* (phone: 423-3283).

The Village Bookshop – Children's books, plus adult books at its parent shop, *Volume II,* both at the same address. 12433 102nd Ave. (phone: 488-4597).

Wine Cellar – A wide selection of vintages plus a tasting bar. 12421 102nd Ave. (phone: 488-9463).

Zenari's – Fancy foodstuffs, some of the best espresso in town, and a surprisingly eclectic selection of pizza, soup, and salads. ManuLife Place (phone: 423-5409).

SPORTS: Baseball – The Edmonton *Trappers* of the Pacific Coast League play in John Ducey Park (10233 96th Ave.), minutes from downtown. Call 429-2934 for schedule information.

   Football – Edmonton's professional football team, the *Eskimos,* plays from late July until the middle of November at *Commonwealth Stadium* (Stadium Rd.). Ticket information can be obtained from the *Eskimos'* box office (phone: 429-2881).

   Golf – There are both municipal and private golf courses. Two good municipal ones are *Riverside Golf Course,* (Rowland Rd. and 86th St.; phone: 428-5330); and *Victoria Golf Course and Driving Range* (99th Ave. and 121st St.; phone: 428-5343, clubhouse).

   Hockey – The *Stanley Cup* champion Edmonton *Oilers* belong to the National Hockey League and play from October to May. When at home, the team plays at *Northlands Coliseum,* 7424 118th Ave. (phone: 474-8561 for dates of games; 471-2191 for tickets).

   Horseback Riding – *Whitemud Equine Centre,* 12505 Keillor Rd. (phone: 435-3597).

   Skiing – *Rainbow Valley Ski Hill,* 132nd St. and 45th Ave. (phone: 434-4314).

   Swimming – There are indoor and outdoor pools. For information, call 428-7946.

   Tennis – Edmonton has a number of municipal and private courts. For more information about the municipal courts, call 428-3573.

THEATER: Edmonton caters to theatergoers; it has more theaters per capita than any other Canadian city. A few of them include the *Citadel Theatre* (9828 101 A Ave.; phone: 425-1820), Edmonton's largest with five stages; the *Phoenix Theatre* (phone: 429-4015 for information on what and where they're performing); *Stage West* at the *Mayfield Inn* has a dinner-theater (Mayfield Rd. and 109th Ave.; phone: 483-4051); *Studio Theatre* (82nd Ave. between 112th and 114th Sts.; phone: 492-2495), for the University of Alberta's drama department productions; the prominent *Northern Light Theatre* (phone: 471-1586), which performs at the *Jubilee Auditorium;* and *Walterdale Playhouse* (10322 83rd Ave.; phone: 439-2845), Edmonton's oldest community theater. *Mayfair Dinner Theatre* (10815 Jasper Ave.; phone: 428-8900) presents theater and cabaret productions in an intimate setting.

MUSIC: The *Edmonton Symphony Orchestra* presents concerts throughout the year (except in the summer) at the *Jubilee Auditorium* (10322 83rd Ave.; phone: 428-1414 for information. The *Jubilee Auditorium* is also home to the *Edmonton Opera,* one of North America's most financially stable opera associations. For more information, call 482-7030.

 NIGHTCLUBS AND NIGHTLIFE: There's live jazz at the *Yardbird Suite* (102nd St. and 86th Ave.; phone: 432-0428). For a singles bar with dancing, try *Barry T's On Location* (6111 104th St.; phone: 438-2582), or the very lively *Goose Loonie's Party & Playhouse* (99th St. and Argyll Rd.; phone: 438-5573), where the 18–25 set goes to be seen. *The Rose and Crown Pub* (in the *Hilton* hotel; phone: 428-7111) has a piano bar with sing-alongs and attracts a more sophisticated, professional crowd.

Gambling is a favorite pastime of Edmontonians, and as a result there's usually a casino with a temporary government permit operating somewhere in the city. For time and place, consult the local papers.

BEST IN TOWN

 CHECKING IN: Edmonton has several first class hotels as well as dozens of more moderately priced and serviceable establishments. Expect to pay about $64 or more for a double room in the hotels listed as expensive; between $42 and $64 in those categorized as moderate; and inexpensive, under $42. All telephone numbers are in the 403 area code unless otherwise indicated.

Fantasyland – Part of the *West Edmonton Mall* complex, this place features fantasy motifs (Polynesian, Arabian, Victorian, and even Western, where the bed is in the flat-bed of a pickup truck) in a third of its 360 deluxe rooms — most have a Jacuzzi. Amenities include rooms for non-smokers; a cocktail lounge and a dining room; and no charge for children under 12. There is a water slide and a wave pool in the adjoining mall. 87th Ave. and 170th St. (phone: 444-3000). Expensive.

Hilton International – Connected by a pedestrian walkway to the *Edmonton Centre* shopping mall, it has 314 rooms (27 of which are suites), nonsmoking floors, a concierge, exercise equipment, an indoor pool, a sauna, and a whirlpool bath. There are lounges, a café, and an old English-style pub, the *Rose and Crown.* Weekend rates are available. 10235 101st St. (phone: 428-7111). Expensive.

Macdonald – Reopening later this year after a $20-million, 7-year restoration, this 76-year-old establishment has been returned to its original 1915 grandeur. The exterior façade, lobby, Confederation Lounge, Wedgewood Room, and Empire Ballroom are designated Municipal Historic Resources. There are 172 rooms, 6 two-bedroom suites, 2 mini-suites, and a deluxe presidential suite. Facilities include tennis and squash courts, a swimming pool, sauna, steambaths, plus exercise and gamerooms. Located in the Saskatchewan River Valley. Jasper Ave. and 100th St. (phone: 424-5181). Expensive.

Westin – This handsome hostelry has become the place where royalty stops: the Queen of England visited in 1978; Prince Charles and Diana, in 1983. There are 413 rooms and suites, a swimming pool, sauna, whirlpool bath, and one of the finest dining rooms in the city (see *Eating Out*). A family plan and special weekend rates are available year-round. 10135 100th St. at 101 A Ave. (phone: 426-3636). Expensive.

Mayfair – This newly refurbished 123-room property has suites for business travelers requiring an office on the road. There are 3 restaurants, as well as a dinner-theater on the lower level. Seven blocks from the town center. 10815 Jasper Ave. (phone: 423-1650). Moderate.

Mayfield Inn – Located in the west end of the city, the 432-room property has a Rec Centre with a swimming pool, squash and racquetball courts, a gym, the *Stage West* dinner-theater, a dining room, 3 lounges, and a nightclub. 166th St. and 109th Ave. (phone: 484-0821). Moderate.

Renford Inn at Fifth – Between downtown Edmonton and the legislature grounds, this hotel has 107 rooms with telephones and color TV sets. There is an indoor swimming pool, dining room, cocktail lounge, and British-style pub. No charge for children under 12. 104th St. and 100th Ave. (phone: 423-5611). Moderate.

Kingsway Inn – Five minutes from downtown and just blocks from the midtown municipal airport, this place has 70 rooms with cable TV and phones, banquet and meeting facilities, a gift shop, free parking, a restaurant, and pubs. 10812 Kingsway Ave. (phone: 479-4266). Inexpensive.

Klondike Valley Tent & Trailer Park – This comfortable campground has 148 camping sites, 64 with sewage, electricity, and water, and 84 with electricity and water. There are flush toilets, showers, a playground, laundry facilities, a barbecue facility, and a small grocery store. 1660 Calgary Trail Southbound (phone: 988-5067). Inexpensive.

Relax Inn – Two very reasonably priced motels on the southern and western edges of the city, one just off the highway to Calgary and the International Airport, the other on the highway to Jasper. Each has an indoor pool and whirlpool bath, and all 220 rooms have a color TV set and a telephone. 10320 45th Ave. (phone: 436-9770) and 18320 Stony Plain Rd. (phone: 483-6031). Inexpensive.

EATING OUT: Besides making the city rich, those booms brought folks into Edmonton — all kinds of folks who cook all kinds of food. The result has been to augment regular prairie fare — which centers on Alberta beef, some of the best in the country — with a potpourri of cuisines that is truly delightful. Expect to pay about $40 and up for a meal for two at any of the restaurants listed as expensive; between $20 and $35 in the moderate range; and under $20, inexpensive. Prices don't include drinks, wine, or tips. All telephone numbers are in the 403 area code unless otherwise indicated.

Carvery – Known for its mammoth servings, this fine establishment with a woodsy, hunting hall atmosphere serves some of the best beef that Alberta produces, along with wild game such as buffalo. The chicken dishes are also good. Reservations advised. Major credit cards accepted. At the *Westin Hotel,* 10135 100th St. (phone: 426-3636). Expensive.

Chef's Table – One of Edmonton's most creative restaurants, in marked contrast to its industrial area location. Hong Kong-born, Edmonton-trained chef Peter Lai prepares delicious California-style dishes. The menu includes a wide variety of seafood, fowl, pasta, and veal — all prepared with unexpected touches; the appetizer of oysters comes stuffed with fresh ginger and chives, lightly breaded and pan-fried; the lobster and pasta entrée has undercooked seafood and crisp asparagus; and the honeydew melon balls are topped with a Tahitian vanilla-riesling sauce. Open daily. Reservations necessary. Major credit cards accepted. 11121 156th St. (phone: 453-3532). Expensive.

Hy's Steak Loft – The premier steakhouse in Edmonton, complete with a well-appointed dining room and tuxedoed waiters. Though seafood, fowl, and lamb fill out the menu, steaks are what this place does best, and considering that Alberta beef is among the best in the world, it would be a shame to order anything else. Closed Sundays. Reservations necessary. Major credit cards accepted. 10013-101 A Ave. (phone: 424-4444). Expensive.

Trumps – Owned by Peter Lai, the proprietor of *Chef's Table,* this California-style grill has an eclectic menu. Open daily. Reservations necessary. Major credit cards accepted. 3975 Calgary Trail South (phone: 438-8833). Expensive.

Un-Heard-Of – The intercom at the entrance gives this small restaurant a speakeasy feel, but the standards are much higher. The six-course prix fixe menu runs from a light pâté that changes with the best ingredients available, through a main course of lamb, beef, or game hen in a maple glaze. Light, delicious desserts. Open Tuesdays through Saturdays. Reservations, as far in advance as possible, are necessary. Major credit cards accepted. 9602 82nd Ave. (phone: 432-0480). Expensive.

La Suisse – This restaurant goes a long way to prove that there's much more to Swiss cuisine than fondue. Rich pâtés, garlic-steamed mussels, freshly made soups, fork-tender veal with local wild mushrooms, and pork tenderloin in a dark, brandy-laden sauce all receive eye-opening presentations. Service is top-notch and never cloying. Open daily. Reservations advised. Major credit cards accepted. 10304 111th St. (phone: 420-6005). Expensive to moderate.

Sushi Tomi – Sushi in a landlocked town can often be iffy, but Edmonton's premier sushi bar has garnered the praise of seafood connoisseurs from both coasts. Traditional cooked Japanese dishes also are available. Open daily. Reservations advised. Major credit cards accepted. 10126 100th St. (phone: 422-6083). Expensive to moderate.

Harbin – Named after Edmonton's northern-Chinese sister city, this place is known for the creativity in the kitchen and its light touch on the pocketbook. Particularly good are the Szechuan dishes that appear as benign as grandmother's oatmeal. Those green beans cut on the bias are hot chilies, and woe to the diner who mistakes them for anything else. Of the menu's 84 dishes, 23 are spicy. Diners with less flaming palates should try the sesame chicken (batter-fried, then drizzled with honey and rolled in sesame seeds), the cinnamon-salt prawns (exactly as they sound), or the *king-tu* chicken, which comes to your table sizzling, smothered in hoisin and soy, and seasoned with five-spice powder. Servings are more than ample. Open daily. Reservations advised. Major credit cards accepted. 10401 Mayfield Rd. (phone: 484-9452) and 10179 105th St. Moderate.

Jack's Grill – Chef-owner Peter Jackson, schooled in the wine valleys of California, prepares intriguing California-influenced dishes. The menu changes monthly, using seasonal fresh produce from the Edmonton markets. Excellent wine list. Open Wednesdays through Sundays. Reservations necessary. Major credit cards accepted. 290 Saddleback Rd. (phone: 434-1113). Moderate.

Smokey Joe's Hickory Smokehouse – Likely the most ethnically American restaurant to be found in this Canadian city, this is a small, family operation that's big on servings and heart, and relatively low on cost. The Goldfeder family smokes chicken, turkey, pork ribs, ham, sausage, beef ribs, and brisket Oklahoma-pit-barbecue-style: unseasoned over whole hickory logs for 24 to 30 hours. The result is moist, tender meat and fowl, which can be helped along with the devilish homemade hot sauce (served on the side) and jalapeños pickled in a Cajun brine spiked with a dose of cayenne. Also good are the pecan pies. Open daily. Reservations unnecessary. Major credit cards accepted. Two locations: 156th St. and 87th Ave. (phone: 448-0333) and 8006 103rd St. (phone: 448-0335). Moderate.

Vi's – A refurbished house within view of the North Saskatchewan River, this restaurant is known throughout town for its thick homemade soup, good sandwiches, fresher-than-fresh salads, and chocolate-glazed pecan pie. The supper menu changes weekly. Open daily. No reservations. Major credit cards accepted. 9712 111th St. (phone: 482-6402). Moderate.

Mongolian Food Experience – An eclectic mix of cuisines from China, India, and Malaysia makes the experience memorable. Most interesting (and most inexpensive) is the Mongolian barbecue, a serve-yourself buffet groaning with mushrooms, bean sprouts, green onions, cabbage, green pepper, turkey, lamb, and beef, all anointed with hoisin, oyster, curry, or hot sauces, stir-fried on a teppan grill and served with steamed rice. Other notable dishes include *mu shu* pork, B-4 duck (moist chunks of barbecued duck sautéed with bamboo shoots and black mushrooms), incendiary Szechuan beef strips, and delicate lemon chicken. Open daily. Reservations necessary. Major credit cards accepted. 10160 100 A St. (phone: 426-6806) and 12520 102nd Ave. (phone: 452-7367). Moderate to inexpensive.

Bul-Go-Gi House – One of several Korean restaurants in town, it started up as a small café, but has undergone steady expansion. Tops on the menu is the Bul-Go-Gi, a mélange of vegetables and marinated beef cooked at your table; the accompanying side dish of hot pickle *kim chee;* and Bee-Bim-Bab, a bowl of vegetables capped by a fried egg. Unlicensed. Closed Sundays. Reservations advised. Visa accepted. 8813 92nd St. (phone: 466-2330). Inexpensive.

HALIFAX

The largest city on Canada's eastern seaboard (with 115,000 people), Halifax has a long and rich military and naval heritage. It is known as both a garrison town and naval base, thanks to its strategic location overlooking the mouth of one of the world's great natural harbors. Halifax has always been a center of maritime activity. In its earliest days, it was a tiny Indian summer fishing settlement known as Chebucto, or "at the biggest harbor," smack in the middle of the southern Nova Scotia coast. During World War II, it became a major British naval base.

Today, Halifax is the provincial capital of Nova Scotia and the commercial, administrative, and military center of Atlantic Canada. Still, Halifax retains the feel of a small city. Ask a cross section of Haligonians (that's what they're called) why they like their town, and most will reply that they enjoy all the cultural amenities of bigger metropolises without the disadvantages of size and impersonality. The streets are lined with trees; there are beautiful, relaxing parks; fine old buildings; and the downtown area is a nicely balanced mixture of modern office towers and older restored shops.

Centuries before the city was founded in 1749 by Colonel Edward Cornwallis, Micmac Indians launched hunting, fishing, and war missions from the harbor. Early French and British explorers failed to convince authorities at home of the strategic importance of the harbor, and for many years the Micmac regularly massacred New England fishermen who had stopped along the coast to dry fish, gather firewood, or take on water. Eventually it became apparent to the British that the Micmac hostility was French-inspired and that there was a constant market for English scalps in the French settlement of Fort Louisbourg, located on the southeastern shore of Cape Breton Island, north of Nova Scotia. A rag-tag group of New England farmers, hunters, and townspeople shocked the world by invading and capturing Louisbourg. The French prepared a counterattack designed to recover Louisbourg, take control of all of Nova Scotia, and go on to destroy Boston. However, the attack ended in disaster without a shot being fired; storms, scurvy, typhus, and dissension verging on mutiny destroyed the mission.

When the Treaty of Aix-la-Chapelle returned Louisbourg to France, the need to establish an English fortress on mainland Nova Scotia was finally recognized, and in 1749 Colonel Edward Cornwallis, with 3,000 others in some 20 ships, landed and founded Halifax. The settlement was successful, and with few exceptions the French settlers were deported. When British control over all of Canada was finally established in 1763, Halifax became the chief station of His Majesty's Army and Navy on the Atlantic seaboard.

Before the fledgling town ever got a chance to establish its civilian identity, it was teeming with British military personnel. Army and navy men outnumbered civilians, and the American Revolution and the War of 1812 left the city with an indelibly military (and predominantly British) complexion. From the first, Halifax has been a port city, with emphasis clearly on the first word. But the superiority of its harbor and the wisdom of building there have been proven in every war Britain has had the misfortune to fight.

From the open ocean to the city, the harbor narrows gradually, a feature that made it easy to defend. The city was built on a shoe-shaped peninsula — the toe facing south to the sea, the heel north into Bedford Basin, and the sole opposite the mile-wide strip of water separating the city from neighboring Dartmouth.

The American Revolution and the 1812 war affected Halifax in other ways as well. The city enjoyed all the benefits of war — military spending, employment, and excitement — and none of the horror. The city thrived and its population grew. In the wake of the Revolutionary War, 25,000 Loyalists fled to Nova Scotia, and after the War of 1812, thousands of Blacks escaped from slavery to settle in the Halifax-Dartmouth region.

Wartime prosperity is notoriously ephemeral, but when peace came the Haligonians experienced a severe and sudden depression. However, the gradual development of a civilian shipbuilding industry, alongside the traditional military economy, led to increased affluence here until the outbreak of World War I, when it again became a military base — a vital link in the North American lifeline to the embattled countries of Europe.

Halifax suffered its worst maritime disaster late in the war. In fact, it was the worst recorded manmade explosion before the atomic bombing of Hiroshima in 1945. In December 1917, the munitions ship *Mont Blanc,* laden with 2,500 tons of explosives, collided with the Belgian relief ship *Imo* in Halifax Harbour. The explosion, felt 52 miles away, flattened the north end of the city, leaving 2,000 dead, 2,000 injured, 6,000 homeless, and 199 blinded. Known simply as "the Explosion," this tragic event is commemorated yearly. A monument to those who died is located at Fort Needham.

After swift reconstruction, Halifax assumed its position as a center of Canada's maritime industry. The city played an important role in the early days of World War II, when the German U-boat wolf packs sought to isolate England by cutting it off from Canadian or American supply ships. With its 10 square miles of deepwater anchorage, the Bedford Basin of Halifax Harbour was the natural staging area for the North Atlantic convoys. Some 17,500 ships sailed from here. When the war ended, soldiers and sailors (and more than a few Haligonians) released their pent-up frustrations in the *V-E Day* riots, a rampage of looting, drinking, and carousing that left the downtown area a shambles.

Superficially, Halifax has changed a great deal in the last decade. Shiny new office towers have sprung up on both sides of the harbor, vast shopping centers have followed the burgeoning population to the suburbs, and new restaurants reflect a far more cosmopolitan taste than before. Yet underneath, the city is much as it has always been: largely dependent on the military branches of government for its income; optimistic about the future (especially since the discovery of natural gas offshore); and still strongly English and Irish in temperament, culture, and tradition.

Fortunately, like many Canadian cities, Halifax has been blessed with cogent and restrained city planning. Newfound wealth has not caused residents to ignore their cultural and architectural heritage, and the city's 19th-century waterfront area reeks of brine, barnacles, and Her Majesty's Royal Navy. Halifax is a paradise for anyone who loves great seaports, the accompanying nautical lore and traditions, the ships, and most of all — the sea.

HALIFAX AT-A-GLANCE

 SEEING THE CITY: One of the abiding reminders of Halifax's British origin must be its policy of restoration and protection of historic buildings. The Haligonian passion for preservation even extends to the traditional viewing point of the city. As Halifax expanded, it became apparent that high-rise construction might block out the best view of the city and harbor, as seen from the roadway surrounding Citadel Hill. In 1973 Halifax passed an ordinance prohibiting the construction of any building that threatens certain "view planes." And so today you can see some of the same views that the Loyalists did when they arrived here 200 years ago — downtown Halifax, the harbor, and the Atlantic beyond. At noon every day a cannon is fired from Citadel Hill, as it has been for 150 years, and at the top of the hill, for a small entrance fee, the Citadel — a fort built in 1828 — and its museums can be visited.

 SPECIAL PLACES: Downtown Halifax easily can be seen on foot, although there is a steep grade from the harbor to Citadel Hill. Ferries link downtown Halifax with her sister city of Dartmouth, across the harbor. Motorists are cautioned about the large number of one-way streets.

DOWNTOWN

Historic Properties – On the Halifax waterfront, virtually at the foot of Citadel Hill, is the retail development that has brought life back to the 18th-century buildings. In those days the buildings were the center of activity. After coming within a vote or two of being demolished, the 3-acre site was saved by a private Halifax company, with assistance from the government, and is now known as the Historic Properties. The area has been expanded to include buildings on two other streets. During the summer, Historic Properties is the dock site for *Bluenose II,* a replica of the original *Bluenose,* the fishing schooner that dominated international racing for close to 2 decades and is depicted on the Canadian dime. The schooner cruises the harbor three times daily in summer, occasionally under full sail. (Information can be obtained on the site or by calling 422-2678.) The modern vessel, *Haligonian III,* with full bar and cafeteria, has regular tours leaving from the Historic Properties dock. In addition, the *Mar II,* a 75-foot Danish ship, offers 1- and 2-hour sailing tours of the harbor, both in the morning and the afternoon (phone: 423-8471). Charters are available on all three craft. Call *Halifax Water Tours* (phone: 423-1271) for more information.

Province House – The Nova Scotia legislature meets here. Built between 1811 and 1818, Province House was described as a "gem of Georgian architecture" by none other than Charles Dickens. It is one of the finest examples of the style on the Continent. If the legislature is in session, visitors can hear debates from the Public Gallery. The Legislative Library is handsome, with tall windows, two curving staircases leading to a mezzanine balcony, and alcoves adorned with fine wood carvings and metal tracings. Province House is also the location of the office of the Premier of Nova Scotia. The building is generally open to visitors year-round; the staff usually provides tours on request. 1690 Hollis St. (phone: 425-6300).

St. Paul's Church – Built in 1750, St. Paul's is the oldest existing building in Halifax and the oldest Protestant church in Canada. It welcomes visitors daily from June to September. The oak frame and pine timbers for St. Paul's were brought by sea from Boston and Portsmouth, New Hampshire. St. Paul's Cemetery, 3 blocks south, has a unique memorial to two Nova Scotians killed in the Crimean War. General Ross, who burned Washington, DC in the War of 1812, is buried here. Barrington St. (phone: 429-2240).

Citadel Hill – The key to the defense of Halifax, Citadel Hill today contains two museums inside the star-shaped fort built of granite and ironstone quarried at Purcell's Cove, a community on the outskirts of the city. The Citadel is a national historic park. One of the museums is part of the *Nova Scotia Museum;* the other is devoted to military artifacts. A 50-minute sound-and-light show, called *Tides of History,* reviews 300 years of life in the harbor. See it before exploring the ramparts. Summertime events include candlelight tours and dinners featuring hosts in historic costumes. Check with staff for times and dates. The Old Town Clock, which stands on the eastern slope of the hill and has clock faces on all four sides, was commissioned by the Duke of Kent, father of Queen Victoria, head of the garrison at Halifax from 1794 to 1800. Guided tours are available. Admission charge.

Halifax Public Gardens – Covering close to 18 acres, these grounds are among the finest in the country and are the oldest formal Victorian gardens in North America. Created in 1867, they were enlarged in 1874 to their present size. Tree-shaded gravel walks wind among the many flower beds, fountains, and a large pond. A bandstand commemorating Queen Victoria's *Golden Jubilee* in 1887 stands near the center of the gardens and, during summer, acts as a stage for concerts. At Spring Garden Rd., Summer St., Sackville St., and S. Park St.

Point Pleasant Park – The 186-acre wooded park at the extreme southerly end of peninsular Halifax, out of bounds to private automobiles, provides countless trails, picnic areas, a supervised saltwater beach on the harbor side, and several fortresses that are national historic sites, including, most notably, Martello tower.

Halifax Container Pier – Halterm, Halifax's container pier, one of the busiest in Canada, can be seen closely from the breakwater off the Point Pleasant Park parking lot. You can stand literally within a stone's throw of huge ocean vessels unloading cargoes day and night. Off Hollis St. just before Point Pleasant Park.

Nova Scotia Museum – Near the Citadel and Public Gardens, the museum contains countless displays and exhibits on all aspects of life in Nova Scotia — from its geological formation to the arrival of the first inhabitants 11,000 years ago through European settlement and up to the present day. The spacious foyer is dominated by a 10-foot-high lens from the old Sambro Lighthouse and a stagecoach that operated between Yarmouth and Tusket in the late 19th century. 1747 Summer St. (phone: 429-4610).

SUBURBS

Fleming Park – On the western shore of the North West Arm of Halifax Harbour, Fleming Park is the site of Memorial Tower, or the Dingle, as it is called locally. Built in 1912, the 10-story tower commemorates the 1758 establishment of representative government in Nova Scotia, the first in Canada. The top of the tower can be reached by walking up steps inside; those who do are rewarded by a remarkable view of the North West Arm, its yacht clubs, beautiful homes, Dalhousie University and other sections of the city, and the harbor mouth. The park is open during daylight hours.

York Redoubt – Just outside Halifax, on the Herring Cove Road, you can visit York Redoubt, a 200-year-old fort overlooking the harbor. A national historic site, the park features old muzzle-loaders, a photographic display, a viewing tower, and picnic facilities. From the park, there is a good view of Mauger's (pronounced Major's) Beach Lighthouse, on a sandspit projecting into the harbor from McNab's Island. The round trip from downtown Halifax to York Redoubt is about 20 miles (32 km). A longer trip on the same road leads to small fishing communities typical of those around the province — Herring Cove, Portuguese Cove, Ketch Harbour, and Sambro. The shops in Sambro usually have lobsters for sale, a good idea for a delightful seaside picnic. Sandy Cove Road affords a good view of Sambro Lighthouse on Sambro Island. Built in 1759, the 82-foot lighthouse was originally operated by three men with seal oil for fuel. The round trip from Halifax to Sambro is about 50 miles (80 km).

■ **EXTRA SPECIAL:** Peggy's Cove is a photographers' and artists' colony that is well-nigh legendary in Canada, thanks to its status as one of the best-preserved rustic fishing villages in North America. Named for one of its original inhabitants, Peggy's Cove has a number of quaint gift shops, as well as two spectacular murals in St. John's Anglican Church. About 35 miles (56 km) west of Halifax on Route 333.

SOURCES AND RESOURCES

TOURIST INFORMATION: For general information, brochures, and maps, contact the Nova Scotia Tourist Bureau (Old Red Store, Historic Properties; phone: 424-4247) or the Nova Scotia Department of Tourism (PO Box 130, Halifax; phone: 424-5000). US residents should write to Nova Scotia Tourism (136 Commercial St., Portland, ME 04101; phone: 800-341-6096 outside Maine; 800-492-0643 from Maine). The city of Halifax operates a tourist bureau in City Hall, with an entrance off Duke Street.

Metro Guide is one of the best guides to the city. Published by Metro Guide Publishing Ltd. (phone: 420-9943), it is distributed free in hotels, restaurants, some stores, the Halifax Visitors and Convention Bureau, bureaus of information around the province, the Dartmouth Tourist Bureau, and in *Air Canada* ticket offices. The book describes a walking tour of historic downtown Halifax and Dartmouth, and outlines the driving tour of Halifax known as the Kingfisher (the official city symbol) Motor Tour and marked by street signs. The book also describes a number of hotels, restaurants, lounges, and other tourist-related services. The *Halifax Visitor's Guide* is published by Art East & Company Ltd. (1652 Barrington St.). This magazine-format publication is a good source of up-to-date information on tours of all types, museums and libraries, parks and recreation, dining out, and shopping. A city and district map produced by the Royal Bank of Canada also is widely available.

Local Coverage – The *Chronicle-Herald,* morning daily tabloid; the *Mail-Star,* afternoon daily (same entertainment listings in both papers); the *Daily News,* morning daily.

Food – The tourist bureau has a list of restaurants, or you can check the *Metro Guide.*
Telephone – The area code for Halifax is 902.
Sales Tax – Meals over CN$4 and most purchased goods have a 10% sales tax.
Currency – All prices are quoted in US dollars unless otherwise indicated.

TIPPING: At restaurants generally leave 15% of the bill. Taxi drivers receive about CN$1. At hotels bellboys are usually given CN$1 per bag, but it usually is not customary to tip maids.

CLIMATE: Compared with the rest of Canada, Nova Scotia has relatively moderate temperatures, and, thanks to the Gulf Stream, Halifax is a bit more temperate than that. In February, the coldest month of the year, the average low is 16F (−9C) and the average high is 31F (−1C); in July and August, the average daytime high is 74F (23C) and the average nighttime low is 57F (14C); water temperature is rarely above 70F (22C). The climate is not particularly humid; in summer months the rainfall is usually less than 4 inches, although in the rainiest month, December, precipitation can be as much as 7 inches. For weather information, call 835-7277.

 GETTING AROUND: Bus – Regular transit service is operated by a metropolitan transit authority. Exact fare is required. For schedule and route information, call 426-6600.

Car Rental – All major national firms are represented.

Taxi – Cabs are hailed in the streets or found at taxi stands at major hotels, shopping areas, and around the city. To call a cab, try *Yellow Taxi* (phone: 422-1551) or the *Y Taxi* (phone: 422-4433). Meters are used on all trips except for some outside the city (to the airport, for example), during which flat rates apply.

Tours – In addition to water tours available at Historic Properties and the ferry across Halifax Harbour (see *Halifax At-a-Glance*), the best way to see the city is from a city bus tour offered by either the *Gray Line of Halifax* (phone: 454-9321) or *Halifax Transit* (phone: 426-6600). For those who prefer a more offbeat approach to seeing the city, rickshaws are available for both tour and taxi service (phone: 421-8736), or the energetic visitor can join a bicycle tour organized by the *Velo Bicycle Club* (phone: 423-4697). Tours are available during summer months only.

 SPECIAL EVENTS: *Halifax Natal Day* is celebrated the first weekend in August. The festivities include a parade, concerts, picnics, and fireworks. *Nova Scotia Festival of the Arts* is held in mid-August and includes a large display of local arts and crafts. The *Nova Scotia International Tattoo* is in late June. The *Tattoo* — a military pageant featuring marching bands, dancing, singing, and athletic displays — is an event worth seeing. It is rated among the top three in the world and is staged indoors at the *Metro Centre.* For information: Nova Scotia Dept. of Tourism, PO Box 130, Halifax (phone: 424-4247).

MUSEUMS: The *Nova Scotia Museum* and the *Citadel Museum* are described in *Special Places.* Other notable Halifax museums include the following:

Art Gallery of Nova Scotia – Paintings and sculptures from the area. 6152 Coburg Rd. (phone: 424-7542).

Maritime Museum of the Atlantic – Several exhibits chronicling the history of sailing and steam vessels, the Canadian Navy, plus a shipwreck gallery, and an exhibit about the Halifax explosion in 1917. Lower Water St. (phone: 429-8210).

Public Archives of Nova Scotia – On University Ave. at Robie St. (phone: 423-9115).

SHOPPING: Halifax is blessed with a number of native craftspeople who produce a wide range of goods, including pottery, jewelry, ceramics, rugs, quilts, woodwork, and all manner of dolls. If you have the time, it may be worth your while to visit the craftspeople at their shop, which more often than not doubles as their home. Handmade stained glass creations are sold at the *Glass Garden Studio* (1528½ Queen St.; phone: 422-9172); *Wayne Kelly* (1378 Robie St.; phone: 422-5652); and the *Stowe/Terris Studio* (2182 Gottingen St.; phone: 423-0681). Local weaver *V. Louise Whitton* (5798 South St.; phone: 422-6085) will fashion items from her loom. A list of other weavers is available from the *Atlantic Spinners and Handweavers Association,* through the *Nova Scotia Museum.* While some of the artisans keep shop hours, others are available by appointment only; it is best to call in advance. For more extensive information, call the Nova Scotia Department of Tourism and

Culture, (phone: 424-4062), or write to the department (Box 864, Halifax B3J 2V2) and ask for a copy of its *Buyer's Guide to Arts and Crafts in Nova Scotia,* a free publication which is also available at tourist bureaus and crafts outlets. For more conventional shopping, head to Historic Properties (see *Special Places*).

SPORTS: Halifax's only professional sports franchise is the Halifax *Citadels,* the farm team of the Quebec *Nordiques* of the National Hockey League. *Halifax Metro Centre* (phone: 426-8726).

Cycling – *Velo Halifax* is a non-competitive touring and recreational bicycle club whose members ride together for fun and friendship. Visitors to the city with access to a bicycle are welcome to join club members for Sunday or weekend rides. Weather permitting, members ride 30 to 50 miles (48 to 80 km). For those not up to tackling such an excursion, the club produces a pamphlet suggesting a couple of routes. It is available at the Halifax Tourist Bureau at Historic Properties. *Down East Bicycle Tours* (RR No.2, Kingston, Nova Scotia) organizes weekend, and 6- and 12-day tours that originate in Halifax. Guides and van support are provided, and accommodations are in bed and breakfast establishments along the way. Brochures are available at Historic Properties, or call George Dagley (phone: 765-8923).

Fishing – Trout fishing in stocked lakes is available within the Dartmouth city limits. For the true anglers, however, real trout and salmon fishing is available in the lakes and streams along Marine Drive on the road between Halifax and Sherbrooke to the east. Excellent Atlantic salmon fishing can be had in the St. Mary's River near Sherbrooke, which is about 120 miles (192 km) from Halifax.

Golf – Golfers have their choice of five 18-hole courses, all 10 miles (16 km) or less from downtown hotels. There are two *Ashburn* golf courses, the newer one in Fall River (phone: 861-2978), and the older in Halifax (phone: 443-8260). Both allow non-members to play weekdays. *Brightwood Golf and Country Club* in Dartmouth (phone: 466-7688) has a similar policy. *Hartlen Point Forces Golf Course* in Eastern Passage (phone: 465-6353), and *Oakfield Country Club* in Grand Lake (phone: 861-2777) are both open to the public. Four 9-hole courses are also within easy reach.

Jogging – Halifax is a city of joggers, and those looking for companionship should have no trouble finding some. Point Pleasant Park, the 186-acre wooded park in the city's south end, is frequented by joggers throughout daylight hours. The *YMCA* (1565 South Park St.; phone: 422-6437) is also a good spot to meet joggers, particularly at noon and shortly after 5 PM, when businesspeople leave the "Y" to jog around the city.

Tennis – Public courts are available on the Halifax Common, near the Halifax *Holiday Inn* and *Château Halifax* hotels. For serious players, the *Nova Scotia Open Tennis Tournament* is held in late August at the *Waegwoltic Club* (phone: 429-2822).

THEATER: *Neptune Theatre* (5216 Sackville St.; phone: 429-7070) offers live professional theater in an intimate setting. Check newspapers for performances. Lunchtime shows are sometimes offered. Summer dinner theater is featured around town; check local newspaper listings.

MUSIC: Dalhousie University's *Rebecca Cohn Auditorium* is the center for many visiting performers. It is located in the *Dalhousie Arts Centre;* call 424-2298 for the box office. Other concerts regularly are held at the *Neptune Theatre* and at *Metro Centre.*

NIGHTCLUBS AND NIGHTLIFE: Visitors to the city, particularly during the summer, are often surprised to discover how much of a party town Halifax is. The festive atmosphere is particularly noticeable on Friday and Saturday nights along Argyle Street, where pubs seem to be everywhere

— as do the patrons. This isn't a rowdy crowd, just one that knows how to have fun. In recent years, there have been so many bars and lounges popping up in the downtown core — and often closing just as quickly — that the scene has become a very fluid one. (To keep up with it, check the *Metro Guide.*) For pub crawlers, it's perfect: Most of the bars and lounges are within walking distance of one another. *Secretary's* (5184 Sackville St.) attracts a young crowd with live bands and rock videos filling out the entertainment schedule when the jive and lip-synch contests aren't happening. The *Thirsty Duck* (upstairs at 5472 Spring Garden Rd.) features traditional pub music, with live entertainment on weekends; the good food served here from 11 AM to 10 PM is an added enticement, and the shuffleboard or darts enthusiast won't be disappointed either. Dance to live rock music 6 days a week at *My Apartment* (1740 Argyle St.). It's usually loud and packed. The *Seahorse* (1665 Argyle St.) attracts the young and artsy set. Watch the revelers from the glassed-in patio at *Lawrence of Oregano* (1726 Argyle) while enjoying something from its menu of standard pasta fare. At the *Lower Deck* in Historic Properties along the waterfront, the entertainment usually features single acts ranging from comedy to Nova Scotia folk music; upstairs, at the *Middle Deck,* listen to live music that can be anything from R&B to contemporary. If you lose interest, cross the street to *O'Carroll's Oyster Bar* (1860 Upper Water St.) and enjoy their piano bar; if that doesn't suit you, try the *Up Here Bar* (1662 Barrington St.) where you can gaze at art for sale while having a drink and something to eat (waffles are a big item on this menu). Crave cabaret entertainment? Check out the *Misty Moon* (1595 Barrington St.) where Canadian and American bands are regularly featured; it's open nightly from 7 PM to 3 AM and there's a cover charge. Alternatively there is the *Palace* (1721 Brunswick St.). Other popular nightspots include *Thackeray's Pub* (5435 Spring Garden Rd.) and *Maxwell's Plum* (Sackville and Grafton Sts.). And to find plenty more possibilities — just follow the crowd.

BEST IN TOWN

CHECKING IN: There was a time not too many years ago when Halifax only had two hotels of distinction, the *Lord Nelson* and the *Nova Scotian.* But as the city began to grow into a major metropolitan area, hotels began to appear. More than 600 first class rooms have been added downtown, all with the basic amenities (phones, color TV sets, and so on). Expect to pay $75 or more for a double at those places classified as expensive and between $40 and $75 for those described as moderate. A toll-free number (phone: 800-565-7105) is available for reservations throughout the province. All telephone numbers are in the 902 area code unless otherwise indicated.

Château Halifax – Operated by Canadian Pacific Hotels, it is ideally situated in the city's downtown Scotia Square complex. The hotel has an enclosed patio garden and a tower with views of the harbor, Citadel Hill, and Bedford Basin; 305 rooms; a heated indoor-outdoor swimming pool; a sauna; and air conditioning. It has a special weekend rate. 1990 Barrington St. (phone: 425-6700). Expensive.

Citadel Halifax – Near Scotia Square and *Metro Centre,* it is not quite as posh as *Château Halifax* but is slightly less expensive. Some of its 278 air conditioned rooms are in a high-rise tower overlooking the harbor. 1960 Brunswick St. (phone: 422-1391). Expensive.

Delta Barrington Inn – One of the city's newer properties, belonging to the respected Delta chain, it is part of yet another restoration of the Old Town. The façade on the Granville Street side, dating back to the mid-19th century, was carefully dismantled and all the stones replaced once the hotel was built. It is situated between the Scotia Square complex and Historic Properties on the water-front and has 200 rooms, a restaurant, piano bar, heated indoor swimming pool, sauna, and whirlpool bath. Corner of Duke and Barrington Sts. (phone: 429-7410). Expensive.

Halifax Sheraton – A classy low-rise hostelry that blends well with the Historic Properties development next door on the waterfront. Great location, lovely sur-roundings, and tasteful decoration are its hallmarks. 1919 Upper Water St. (phone: 421-1700). Expensive.

Holiday Inn – Don't confuse this with the one in Dartmouth. This member of the chain overlooks Halifax Common, where hundreds of amateur athletes engage in softball, football, tennis, baseball, field hockey, soccer, and even cricket. There's a heated indoor swimming pool. Quinpool and Robie Sts. (phone: 423-1161). Expensive.

Nova Scotian Hilton – Adjoining the *Canadian National Railway* station, this venerable old property has been lovingly and tastefully refurbished. Much of its grandeur is back, along with some new touches, such as a pool and tennis court. Although located several blocks from downtown, it provides free shuttle service. Some of the 316 rooms overlook the harbor, and about half have air conditioning. 1181 Hollis St. (phone: 423-7231). Expensive.

Prince George – This place enjoys a convenient, city-center location, a block from the Grand Parade at City Hall. A handy underground walkway connects it with the World Trade and *Convention Centre* and the adjacent *Metro Centre,* the 10,000-seat entertainment-sports arena. Guests can enjoy the hotel pool, whirlpool bath, sauna, and exercise room; dine in the restaurant or café; or socialize in its popular lounge. Underground parking. 1725 Market St. (phone: 425-1986). Ex-pensive.

Chebucto Inn – Although removed from downtown, this 32-room air-conditioned property is situated near the main roads in and out of the city. 6151 Lady Ham-mond Rd. (phone: 453-4330). Moderate.

Lord Nelson – One of Halifax's oldies, a little rundown, but still well used, it is across the street from the Public Gardens. It has 320 rooms and free guest parking. At the corner of Spring Garden Rd. and South Park St. (phone: 423-6331). Moderate.

EATING OUT: Halifax's restaurants have improved dramatically over the last 2 decades. There was a time when those wishing to dine out were restricted to only two or three hotel dining rooms. Today things are better, but complaints are still heard that, given the city's proximity to some of the world's best fishing grounds, there is not enough high-quality fish available. Expect to pay more than $35 for two in those restaurants we've categorized as expensive; between $15 and $35 in the moderate range; under $17 at those places listed as inexpensive. Prices don't include wine, drinks, or tip. All telephone numbers are in the 902 area code unless otherwise indicated.

Clipper Cay – With an unsurpassed location on the harborfront in the Historic Properties area, this is probably one of the city's best seafood restaurants. Of particular note is the smoked salmon. Downstairs, at *The Cay Side,* inexpensive lunches and suppers are available. Open daily. Reservations advised. Major credit cards accepted. At the end of Water St. (phone: 423-6818). Expensive.

Scanway – Tucked away in a 2-story boutique complex, the menu features Scandina-vian fare. Closed Sundays. Reservations advised. Major credit cards accepted. 1569 Dresden Row, off Spring Garden Rd. (phone: 422-3733). Expensive.

Mother Tucker's – Close to Historic Properties and the business district, it is a popular spot for seafood and prime ribs, featuring a huge salad bar. During busy periods, patrons wait in an adjoining bar until their table is ready. Open daily. Reservations advised. Major credit cards accepted. 1668 Lower Water St. (phone: 422-4436). Expensive to moderate.

La Perla – This unpretentious pearl of a restaurant has wonderful food plus Old World charm. It's situated almost directly opposite the Dartmouth ferry terminal, and a ferry ride across the harbor is the quickest and most fun way to arrive. Outside the terminal, look for the small canopy over the entryway to a tiny house. Dine downstairs or up; the atmosphere is quiet and intimate, the music low and classical. The menu is primarily orthern Italian, though not limited to mounds of pasta. Salads are especially good here, and the main courses a delight. Open Mondays through Fridays for lunch and dinner, Saturdays and Sundays for dinner only. Reservations necessary. Major credit cards accepted. 71 Alderney Dr. (phone: 469-3241). Expensive to moderate.

McKelvie's – The decor is nautical, dress is informal, and the specialty is fish. The building is a grand old firehall that's been converted; there's also a terrace for summer dining. Conveniently opposite the *Maritime Museum of the Atlantic* on the waterfront, next to Historic Properties. Open daily. Reservations advised. Major credit cards accepted. 1680 Lower Water St. (phone: 421-6161). Moderate.

Old Man Morias – Here Greek food is served up in an original Halifax townhouse. Proprietors Vasilios and Panagiota Migas arrived in Canada without knowing any English and have worked hard to assimilate and become established. Closed Sundays. Reservations advised. Major credit cards accepted. 1150 Barrington St. (phone: 422-7960). Moderate.

Privateer's Warehouse – Made up of three entities: The *Lower Deck* is a pub, the *Middle Deck* is a lounge, and the *Upper Deck* is one of the best places to eat in town. There, seafood and steaks are served by a staff that is friendly and efficient. The Shrimps Lady Wentworth are especially good. The dining room's stone walls and wooden beams are decorated with things nautical, as befits the building's history. Closed Sundays. Reservations advised. Major credit cards accepted. At Historic Properties (phone: 422-1289). Moderate.

Sanremo – Seafood is the specialty here, northern Italian style. A sister restaurant to *La Perla*, patrons are finding it to be every bit as good as its elder sibling. The small dining room is situated in such a way as to present a lovely view of Halifax to every table. Open daily for dinner. Reservations advised. Major credit cards accepted. 67 Alderney Drive, Dartmouth, just across the street from the Dartmouth ferry terminal (phone: 469-3241). Moderate.

Silver Spoon – Its quaint coffeehouse/tearoom has satisfied many a sweet tooth, and its restaurant has delighted patrons with more substantial delicacies. Coffee, tea, and desserts are quite special. Closed Sundays. Reservations necessary. Most major credit cards accepted. The premises are back-to-back: dessert shop, 1866 Water St.; restaurant, 1865 Hollis St. (phone: 422-1519, for both). Moderate.

Suisha Gardens – One sign of the growing variety of cooking available in Halifax is evident at this Oriental eatery, which features *teppan* cooking, where the meal is prepared at your table, and other Japanese dishes. The cooking has been Westernized from its stricter Japanese roots, but the service is fast and the food good. Weekdays, lunches are a good bet for someone who wants to eat well but quickly. Open daily. Reservations advised. Major credit cards accepted. On the main floor of the *Maritime Centre* at the corner of Barrington St. and Spring Garden Rd. (phone: 422-1576). Moderate.

Thackeray's – At this pleasant and sophisticated dining spot, located on one of Halifax's most popular streets, the kitchen specializes in meat and poultry dishes, and also produces very good desserts. Open daily. Reservations advised. Major credit cards accepted. 5435 Spring Garden Rd. (phone: 423-5995). Moderate.

Lawrence of Oregano – Across the street from the Grand Parade, at City Hall, it caters to a youthful clientele of office workers and university students. A good spot to grab a pizza and a beer in a lively, pleasant ambience. Major credit cards accepted. 726 Argyle Street (phone: 422-6907). Moderate to inexpensive.

Midtown Tavern – This is a place for those not concerned about surroundings and who like to drink draft beer at a student hangout. The food is surprisingly good, particularly the fish and chips and the corned beef and cabbage. Closed Sundays. No credit cards accepted. Prince St. at Grafton St. (no phone). Inexpensive.

Soup'er Sandwich – An unpretentious place, popular with office workers looking to grab a quick bite. Homemade soup and chowder made with fresh ingredients have made this fast-food eatery a winner. The fish is always fresh, and there's a daily luncheon special and a quiche of the day. Closed Sundays. Visa accepted. 1820 Hollis St. (phone: 425-3474). Inexpensive.

■ **Note:** Halifax residents have a penchant for fast-food fish and chips. *Camille's, Fries and Company,* and *Wilman's* all are local favorites. Wrapped in brown paper, the deep-fried fish (clams and scallops usually are available) are great for a picnic in one of the city parks or along the waterfront. *Camille's:* Open daily. No credit cards accepted (2654 Barrington St.; phone: 423-8869). *Fries and Company:* Closed Sundays. No credit cards accepted (Chebucto Rd. at Connolly St.; phone: 455-5250). *Wilman's:* Closed Sundays. No credit cards accepted (5644 Kane St.; phone: 454-0929). All inexpensive.

Or sample some of the best French fries in town, alfresco, from *Bud the Spud's* popular chip wagon, usually parked at noon outside the Halifax Regional Public Library at Spring Garden Rd. and Grafton St.

MONTREAL

Since 1535 — when Jacques Cartier first laid eyes on the St. Lawrence River village of Hochelaga, climbed with its Indian residents to the top of its 764-foot mountain, took a look at the 50-mile view, and exclaimed "What a royal mount" — the spot has emerged as Canada's second-largest city, and just behind Paris, Nice, and Kinshasha, Zaire, as one of the world's largest French-speaking cities.

Yet some of the most dramatic changes on the face of Montreal have been etched in the past 30 years, with the construction of luxury hotels; a vast underground network of shops and services linked by a clean, efficient *Métro* system; an accretion of fashionable boutiques and excellent restaurants; and careful restorations in the historic quarter. Montreal's new look was sparked by a complete midtown facelift during the 1960s, a renovation that gained momentum during *EXPO '67,* when over 50 million people visited the *World's Fair* and brought Montreal to international attention. The increase in tourism continued throughout the early 1970s, and reached a peak in 1976, when Montreal hosted the *Summer Olympic Games.*

A second building boom transformed the downtown area with the completion of 12 major construction projects worth $1 million or more. They include the conversions of the former *Mount Royal* and *Windsor* hotels, both on Peel Street, into chic shopping, condo, and office complexes, along with several showy office towers.

The transformation has been so complete that some residents now claim they can't remember what Montreal looked like before. They exaggerate for effect. One of the first priorities when construction began was the preservation of Vieux Montréal (Old Montreal). No one considered destroying the historic city a reasonable way of effecting change, and as a result preservation and progress proceeded apace. The protection of special buildings extends to modern Montreal as well: The city's *Olympic Stadium* has become a spectacular sports facility open to the public, and the *EXPO '67* grounds on Ile Notre Dame (also part of the world's fair acreage) are now the site of the *Palais de la Civilisation,* the former French pavilion, which features one major cultural event each summer.

Compelling and cosmopolitan, Montreal sits on an anvil-shaped island 32 miles long and 10 miles wide in the middle of the St. Lawrence River, some 170 miles (274 km) northeast of Lake Ontario. The river borders the city on the south and east and provides the crucial navigable link between the inland Great Lakes and the Atlantic Ocean. (The other great French city on the St. Lawrence, Quebec City, is 153 miles/245 km north of Montreal.) A narrow branch of the St. Lawrence, known as Rivière des Prairies, borders the city on the west and the north. From the top of Mount Royal residents can see all the surrounding river country. Except for Mount Royal, the island is flat.

The most appealing fact about Montreal, especially for Americans, is its Frenchness. Without jet lag and with a minimum of cost and bother, Americans have easy access to what is essentially a European city, providing the very best of the traditional French experience. Two-thirds of Montreal's 2.8 million inhabitants are of French origin. It only takes about two steps into the city to discover that you are truly in a foreign country. Montreal — indeed, all of the surrounding province of Quebec — is proudly French, and it is the French Canadian patois that is heard all around. Nearly everyone is bilingual, but there is no question of the primary tongue.

What makes a visit to Montreal such a different experience from a visit to Quebec City is its size and sophistication: Montreal is simply more cosmopolitan. In part this is because Montreal benefits from its large minorities representation — from more than 100 ethnic groups. Sixteen percent of the non-French population is Anglo-Saxon; the remainder have far-flung roots in Central Europe, Greece, Italy, Hungary, or China. Montreal has the country's largest Jewish population and a Chinese community of more than 50,000. Groups of Italians (the third-largest group), Hungarians, Greeks, Germans, and West Indians also have brought their traditions to Montreal.

And yet Montreal's special character has to be accounted for by more than just the diversity of its population. When large numbers of European settlers moved into Toronto, they managed to break the English-only monopoly on politics, money, and culture that had held the city in thrall since its founding. They made Toronto more livable and changed the nature of life in the city. Not so in Montreal. There is no mistaking that its population is predominantly and profoundly French. Perhaps because Montreal was never the headquarters of the Catholic Church (as was Quebec City), or because it passed some part of this century as a "sin city," it seems to live easier with itself. The reasons for this subtle flavor of life — everywhere palpable but rarely tangible — must lie in its history.

When explorer-entrepreneur Samuel de Champlain reached Montreal's shores in 1603, he foresaw the great value of this natural transportation crossroad as an inland port and returned in 1611 to erect a trading post near the foot of the Lachine Rapids. (The ravages of warring tribes had left no trace of the Indian village of Hochelaga, first seen by Cartier.) The spot was christened Place Royale and is still a nucleus of commercial activity.

Champlain was followed by a succession of missionaries determined to convert the Indians to Christianity. In 1642 the permanent community of Ville Marie was founded at Place Royale (in what is now known as Vieux Montréal) by a small group led by the French career soldier Paul de Chomedey, Sieur de Maisonneuve. Shortly after their arrival, the colonists narrowly escaped being swept away in a disastrous flood. As a token of gratitude for their survival, they climbed Mount Royal's eastern slope and planted a wooden cross at the top. Today, the illuminated 100-foot steel cross that stands in its stead — and on a different site — can be seen for miles on clear nights.

While the flood did not obliterate Ville Marie, the Indians very nearly did. During the next 60 years, the rapidly growing colony of traders, explorers, and missionaries was besieged by numerous attacks; an open state of war existed with the Iroquois until an Indian treaty was signed in 1701.

In the 18th century, Montreal (the name Ville Marie was dropped during this period) prospered through its burgeoning fur trade, though not without difficulties. The Indians were quieted, but trouble with the English and Americans took its toll on the French settlement. In 1759, when Quebec City fell to the British as a result of the battle on the Plains of Abraham, the capital of New France moved briefly to Montreal. A year later Montreal, too, fell to the British.

After the Revolution, Americans eyed Montreal and Quebec City as potential extensions of the original 13 colonies. In November 1775, General Richard Montgomery marched on Montreal and occupied it without firing a shot. The American occupation lasted only 7 months, however, until June 1776, when Montgomery failed to capture Quebec City and Montreal returned to British rule.

Montreal's expansion under the British gained momentum during the early 19th century, when fur trading, shipbuilding, and railroading reached a crescendo. In 1832 Montreal was incorporated as a city, and by 1843 it was the capital of the Province of Canada (an 1841 union of Upper and Lower Canada, encompassing today's provinces of Ontario and Quebec).

The city's expansion during the early 1900s began a period when Montreal justifiably bore the reputation of being a "wicked city"; prostitution, illegal gambling, and other vices flourished, mostly under the well-paid protection of the authorities.

By the end of the 1940s, the central section of Montreal was a dreary core of slums and rundown buildings (since completely vanished). A war on corruption, mounted during the 1950s by city official Jean Drapeau, wiped out the modern blot on the face of Montreal.

Called to act as public prosecutor in the city's police inquiry in 1950, Drapeau earned a reputation as an uncompromising foe of vice; this reputation got him elected Mayor of Montreal for the first time in 1954. Drapeau's administration initiated a time of change in both the face and feeling of Montreal. He remained the city's most famous civic leader until he retired. Jean Doré was elected to a 4-year term as mayor in November 1986; he was up for re-election as we went to press.

The first renovation in Montreal was *Place Ville Marie,* an underground complex of shops, restaurants, and services in the heart of downtown, built to hide the ugly pityards of the *Canadian National Railway.* Place Ville Marie was only the first of six underground complexes in Montreal, each of which provides weatherproof access to hotels, office buildings, banks, stores, and two railway stations in different parts of the city, and is linked by the city's modern, quiet *Métro* system.

It was no sooner than the *Métro* began operation in 1966 that more than 50 million visitors flooded the city for *EXPO '67,* the *1967 World Exposition.*

The success of *EXPO '67* was part of an explosion of daring construction undertaken by the city. During the 1960s and 1970s Montreal put up a stunning cultural and performing arts center, *Place des Arts* (home of the *Montreal Symphony Orchestra*); became one of the two Canadian cities with a major league baseball team, the Montreal *Expos* (Toronto has the *Blue Jays*); and hosted the *1976 Summer Olympics.*

At the same time that the city was acquiring its new look, municipal and provincial ordinances wisely assured the preservation of Vieux Montréal, designating the 95-acre waterfront sector a historical site.

The city spreads out in all directions from the peaks on Mount Royal, and probably the best way to appreciate the mountain and its surrounding Mount Royal Park is to hire one of the omnipresent *calèches.* These horse-drawn carriages seem to be stationed at every important tourist area around the city, and they can't be beaten as a means of sightseeing locomotion. (In winter, in Mount Royal Park, the carriages give way to sleighs, and you can huddle down in a furry lap robe and see the city.)

In the course of meandering through Mount Royal Park, it's possible to assimilate a little local sociology along with an appreciation of the scenic beauty and arboreal pleasures. It is certainly no secret that there is no love lost between the descendants of the original French founders and the progeny of the British conquerers. They live a fairly cordial coexistence, although former antipathies are still evident in Montreal's neighborhood patterns. To the west is Westmount, the "bedroom" for Montreal's prosperous English community. On the other side of the mountain is Outremont, the turf of the wealthy French inhabitants. Each community is equally affluent, but entirely separate, and it is easy to distinguish the lines of demarcation. As you ride along, just note the names of the passing apartment buildings. When the names cease being such Anglophilic gems as "The Trafalgar" and begin to take on the markedly Gallic cast of "Le Trianon," you'll know that you have "crossed the channel."

While England and France enhance their connections with the channel tunnel and the European Economic Community, Montreal and the province of Quebec seem to get farther and farther away from unity with the rest of English-speaking Canada. At presstime, Quebec's separatist movement had received new momentum after Manitoba and Newfoundland refused to ratify the Meech Lake Accord, which (among other things) formally acknowledged the distinctiveness of French Canada. It remains to be seen just how much sentiment exists for secession.

Whichever course the province follows, it's safe to say that the city of Montreal always will offer a wide spectrum of sites and sounds. It would probably take about a week's conscientious effort to see just the most important sights, so you may have to be a bit selective your first time around. But no one ever visits Montreal just once, so console yourself with the inevitability of there being a next time.

MONTREAL AT-A-GLANCE

SEEING THE CITY: Montreal has several vantage points from which to capture the sweep of the city, its mountain — 764-foot Mount Royal — the St. Lawrence River, and, on a clear day, beyond to the mountains of New York and Vermont. Two lookout points on Mount Royal itself offer spectacular views. To reach the Mount Royal Chalet Lookout, follow the path up from the Mount Royal Park parking lot; in the summertime, you can mount the summit by horse-drawn *calèche* or a mini-train ride that begins at Beaver Lake. If driving, you have access to an impressive view of the north and east at the lookout on the eastern slope of Camillien Houde Parkway, the only road over the mountain on which automobiles are permitted.

The Westmount Lookout, also accessible by car, opens up an excellent view of the southwestern section of the city and surroundings. Arrows on the lookout's ledge indicate 22 points of interest, extending to the Green Mountains of Vermont and New York's Adirondacks. Ile Ste.-Hélène offers a magnificent view of downtown with a mountain backdrop.

The old clock tower, refurbished and now an interpretative center tracing the Old Port's past, yields a vista of the harbor from its top story. From St. Joseph's Oratory (3800 Queen Mary Road) there is an excellent view of the northern part of the city.

Still other panoramas of Montreal can be seen while having lunch, cocktails, or dinner at the *Château Champlain*'s *L'Escapade* (1050 de la Gauchetière St. W; phone: 878-1688), or at *Le Grand* hotel's *Tour de Ville* (777 University St.; phone: 879-1370).

SPECIAL PLACES: The best way to get a feel for Montreal is by walking through its streets and parks. Because of its layout, Montreal is easy to cope with on foot. Though not exactly true in direction, Montreal's street plan is laid out on a north-south, east-west axis. Each block covers approximately 100 numbers. The east-west numbering starts at St. Lawrence Boulevard, so the street number 900 West, for example, is 9 blocks west of St. Lawrence. The north-south numbers start at the river and run north, following the same formula. Most interesting to the visitor is the area wedged between the river on the south and east and Mount Royal on the north and west.

Anyone who wearies quickly or would like to visit places farther afield should head for the nearest *Métro* station and hop aboard a soundless, rubber-tired train. The city's four subway lines put visitors within proximity of the most important attractions.

UNDERGROUND MONTREAL

Also called *la ville souterraine,* this below-street-level network of commercial-business-residential complexes is for many as vital a part of the city as that aboveground. Conceived by architect I. M. Pei and developer William Zeckendorf during the 1950s, Montreal's first subterranean complex, *Place Ville Marie,* opened in 1962. Montrealers took to it immediately, moving underground to shop, socialize, and seek refuge from inclement weather and city traffic. Its successful reception prompted a gradual expansion into other sections of the city, and today the network extends some 9 pedestrian miles. All the centers, known as *"places,"* are linked by the *Métro* system. Plans exist for further development in the next decade.

Because of access to such a wide variety of attractions and services, it's possible to spend days in Montreal without ever going outside. Many Montrealers do just that — especially when winter dumps 100 inches of snow on the city. The complex network gives access to the city's main sports facilities, exhibits, and performing arts centers, about 1,500 shops, 150 restaurants, and apartments, 8 major hotels, the 2 main rail and bus terminals, numerous banks and 25 cinemas and theaters, some 11,000 indoor parking spaces, and even a municipal library branch at the McGill *Métro* station. Reasonably priced tours of Underground Montreal are conducted by *Les Montrealistes* (phone: 744-3009), *Guidatour* (phone: 844-4021), *Visites de Montréal* (phone: 843-3308), *Gray Line* (phone: 280-5327), and *Hertz Tourist Guide* (phone: 937-6690).

Place Ville Marie – The city's first underground complex has had a facelift and now houses over 85 boutiques and stores as well as an elegant marble and brass fast-food market, *Les Cours de la Place,* with everything from Baskin-Robbins ice cream to Oriental snacks. Interconnecting promenades link *Place Ville Marie* with *Place Bonaventure* and *Place du Canada,* forming an underground core of some 200 shops, 20 restaurants and bars, and entrances to three major hotels — the *Queen Elizabeth,* Hilton's *Bonaventure International* hotel, and *Château Champlain.* Enter *Place Ville Marie* through the *Queen Elizabeth,* 900 René-Lévesque Blvd. or on Cathcart St. at the foot of McGill College Ave.

Place Bonaventure – Linked to *Place Ville Marie* by walkways leading through Central Station, this 6-acre arcade houses about 100 shops that carry fashions, handicrafts, and furniture from around the world. Above the shopping concourse are a merchandise market, an exhibition hall, and the *Bonaventure International* hotel. Enter the *Bonaventure International* hotel through *Place Bonaventure,* corner of Lagauchetière and Mansfield Streets, or through *Château Champlain,* 1050 de la Gauchetière W.

Bell-Banque Nationale Towers – Joined to the pedestrian passageway between Place Victoria and the Beaver Hall Hill building, these two office towers have increased the underground city's shopping and dining potential with a 2-tiered mall of boutiques and a large restaurant complex on the lower level.

Place Victoria – Facing Victoria Square, this massive office tower is the tallest building in Montreal (47 stories) and home to the Montreal Stock Exchange and yet another underground shopping mall. Stock Exchange tours are given by reservation only. Admission charge (phone: 871-2424). The complex is connected to *Le Grand* hotel.

Place Alexis Nihon – A short subway ride away from the central core, this plaza offers more weatherproofed shopping. Some 80,000 people pass through the complex each day en route to the office building, apartment tower, 3-floor shopping mall, and covered parking levels. 1500 Atwater; take the *Métro* to Atwater.

Faubourg Ste.-Catherine – Near the Guy-Concordia *Métro* station is Montreal's answer to Boston's *Quincy Market,* a vast and colorful complex stretching one long city block on St. Catherine Street between Guy and St. Mathieu. Rows of boutiques and counters display a tempting array of delicious edibles, and there are a number of specialty stores as well.

Westmount Square – French high-fashion designers are represented in this poshest of Montreal's underground plazas, just a stroll away from Plaza Alexis Nihon. Situated directly beneath three gleaming office towers designed by Mies van der Rohe are a deli, restaurants, cinemas, and china and jewelry shops. But the main attractions are the salons of *Guy Laroche,* and *Cacharel.* Take the *Métro* to Atwater.

Place des Arts – The heart of Montreal's cultural life is its lavish performing arts center, which contains a stunning and acoustically superb concert hall and theater accommodating over 5,000 people. Home of the *Montreal Symphony Orchestra, Les Grands Ballets Canadiens,* and the *Montreal Opera,* it is also the setting for chamber music concerts, ballet recitals, and plays. On Sunday mornings, the lobby of the center hosts *"Sons et Brioche,"* informal concerts served up with a continental breakfast. (Tickets — very reasonably priced ones, at that — are available at *Place des Arts* half an hour prior to performance.) 175 St. Catherine St. W.; take the *Métro* to *Place des Arts.* (Call 842-2112 for program and ticket information.)

Complexe Desjardins – This impressive complex contains meeting halls, offices, and an enclosed shopping center with some 100 boutiques and specialty stores and 20 restaurants. Sculptures, fountains, plants, and a regular series of entertainment events and special exhibits make it a popular gathering place. It's linked by an underground walkway to *Place des Arts.*

Complexe Guy Favreau – A complex housing offices, apartments, and boutiques, as well as the *National Film Board*'s movie theater, connects to the *Complexe Desjar-*

dins and the city's convention center, *Palais des Congrès*. The latter is a favorite with visitors, who enjoy playing with its Telidon computers, which list all of Montreal's attractions, complete with tourist information and helpful graphics. (These computers also are found in most major hotel lobbies.) The convention center mall also melds with the Chinatown pedestrian plaza, lined with Oriental shops and restaurants.

Alcan Building – The Canadian aluminum company's international headquarters, Maison Alcan, is an award-winning blend of old and new architecture. Noontime concerts are presented and periodic exhibitions held in its marble atrium, which is ringed with various eateries, shops, and an art gallery. Just a few steps from the Peel *Métro* station, at the corner of Sherbrooke and Stanley Sts.

OLD MONTREAL

Both private enterprise and government funds are contributing to the restoration of important buildings in Vieux Montréal, the city's historic waterfront section. You can drive around it or see it by horse-drawn *calèche*, but the best way to get a feel for it is by strolling through the narrow streets. Arm yourself with a detailed guidebook to the area — get a free copy of *A Walking Tour of Vieux Montréal* from *Infotouriste*, in the Dominion Square Building (Dorchester Square at Peel St.; phone: 871-1595), or its satellite center (on the corner of Place Jacques Cartier and Notre Dame St. in Old Montreal). If you are visiting in July or August, join the weekly guided walking tour conducted by *Les Montréalistes* (phone: 744-3009), a professional guide company. Highlights include the following:

Notre Dame Basilica – Opened in 1829, this building was designed in neo-Gothic style by New York architect James O'Donnell, whose grave lies in the church basement. In addition to its monumental altar and exquisite wood carvings and paintings, the church houses an organ with 5,772 pipes and a small museum in the sacristy, open on weekends only from 9 AM to 5 PM for a small admission fee. Adjacent to the main church is the restored Sacred Heart Chapel (Sacré-Coeur). The stained glass windows depict the early history of Montreal. As you leave, step into the Place d'Armes to glance up at the twin spires and get a true perspective of the church's scale. Open daily. Place d'Armes (phone: 849-1070).

Place Jacques Cartier – This cobblestoned square, the largest in Old Montreal, was once the main marketplace. Now it's the hub of Old Montreal activity and is lined with attractive restaurants and restored houses. Dominating the square is a statue of Horatio Nelson atop a 35-foot column (erected in 1809). In warm weather, there is a flower market at the base of the column, offering blossoms of every conceivable size and hue; in autumn, apples and pumpkins are the fare. Alfresco cafés line both sides of the square, perfect for relaxing and drinking in the flavor of the early 19th century. Between St. Paul and Notre Dame.

Vieux Port – Developed as a government project a decade ago, it's now a summer-time entertainment center. The port itself has undergone extensive renovation of late with the addition of parkland, flowers, and fountains along the length of the federally owned dock area. Now strollers may rest on a bench and take in the waterfront as it was some 100 years ago. Encouraged by this government move to bring back the once-neglected harbor, nearby companies and property owners have refurbished their buildings with charming courtyards and outdoor cafés. The *Vieux Port Festival* kicks off the season on *Saint-Jean Baptiste Day* (June 24), and events continue until *Labor Day*. Daily activities include puppet shows, clowns, movies, dancing, and theater (all free); at night, the large outdoor stage facing the harbor might host the *Montreal Symphony Orchestra* or various rock groups. There also are summer exhibitions in the Vieux Port at the *Expotec* (phone: 397-6832) and *Image du Futur* (phone: 849-1612). The *IMAX Cinema* has a giant 7-story-high screen (phone: 496-IMAX). An immense flea market with piles of second-hand bargains is here, too. The former Louis-Joliet passenger ship terminal hosts exhibitions every summer. A favorite summer stop is the garden restaurant at *Gibby's* in the Youville courtyard (near the waterfront, at the foot of Place d'Youville; phone: 282-1837).

Château Ramezay – The manor, built in 1705, originally served as the residence of French governors in Montreal. It later housed the offices of the West India Company and, still later, was the residence of English governors. During the American occupation between 1775 and 1776, the Continental Army, under Generals Richard Montgomery and Benedict Arnold, established its headquarters here. Today the château is a fine historical museum, with exhibits reflecting its own past as well as that of Montreal. Closed Mondays except from June through August. Admission charge. 280 Notre Dame St. E. (phone: 861-7182 or 861-3708).

Notre Dame de Bonsecours Chapel – The city's oldest church is also called the Sailors' Chapel because of the large number of sailors who worship here. Built originally in 1657, it was destroyed by fire and twice rebuilt and modified. The present chapel dates from 1771, the façade from 1895. Inside, you'll see votive lamps in the shape of model ships, placed there by mariners as tokens of their faith. A series of dolls and miniatures in a small museum upstairs depicts the life of Ste.-Marguerite Bourgeoys, foundress of the Congregation of Notre Dame order of nuns and Canada's first saint. More energetic visitors may hike to the spire's summit for an uplifting view of the harbor and historic quarter. Church open daily; museum closed Mondays. Admission charge for the museum. 400 St. Paul St. E. (phone: 845-9991).

Place d'Youville – One of the first civic centers built in Montreal, Place d'Youville is now surrounded by monuments and historic sites. An interesting landmark is Fire Station 1, which has been restored and now houses the *Montreal History Centre*, where a synchronized audio-visual presentation leads visitors through 11 display rooms and 400 years of history. Permanent exhibits include an old streetcar, a "talking" telephone booth, and a simulated shoe factory. Periodic expositions feature Quebec's past. Closed Mondays, holidays, and from mid-September to mid-May. Admission charge. For information, call 872-3207.

ELSEWHERE IN THE CITY

Angrignon Park – A 262-acre recreational oasis summer and winter, this park is at its busiest from mid-December to late March, when it is the site of Winter Wonderland. Surrounding the Children's Zoo building, Wonderland offers all kinds of free outdoor fun, from cross-country skiing and snowshoeing, and skating on the decorated rink to thrilling slides down the icy toboggan run. Zoo open daily from 10 AM to 5 PM; park open daily from 10 AM to 10 PM. Admission charge for zoo. 3400 Trinitaires Blvd. Get off at Angrinon *Métro* Station.

Olympic Park – Having hosted the *1976 Summer Olympic Games,* Montreal is now using these spectacular facilities for all types of sports events and exhibits. The Montreal *Expos* play at the stadium which was topped with its long-awaited tower and retractable roof in 1987. A restaurant and observation deck offer panoramic views of the city. Meets, classes, and public swimming periods are held regularly in the 50-meter pool and 50-foot diving pool. The guided tour that offers a behind-the-scenes look at the facilities is 45 minutes well spent. You'll get an explanation of some impressive, technologically advanced features — like the ripple and bubble machines that diving coaches can use to create air bubbles instantly on the surface of the pool to mitigate the physical impact of an athlete's bad dive. Tours in English are conducted daily, except holidays. Admission charge. 4545 Pierre de Coubertin Ave.; take the *Métro* to Viau (phone: 252-8687 or 252-4737).

Botanical Garden – Across from the Olympic Park, this noted horticultural showplace was founded by naturalist Brother Marie Victorin. Actually a complex of some 30 specialized gardens and 9 greenhouses, there are more than 25,000 different species and varieties of plants on display, grouped according to use (economical, medicinal, ornamental) and habitat. It also claims to have North America's most complete collection of bonsai trees and the country's largest and grandest exhibition greenhouse. In the midst of expansion, the highly acclaimed Japanese gardens opened during the summer of 1988, and the Insectarium and Chinese gardens were completed last year, making Montreal's botanical gardens the second-largest in the world (after London's Kew Gardens). The visitors' reception center presents video, art, and photographic displays on the world of botany. A mini-train tour is conducted by bilingual guides. Open daily. Admission charge for greenhouses. 4101 Sherbrooke St. E. (phone: 872-1400).

Mount Royal – Because it dominates the city scene, you can't avoid seeing Mount Royal from one angle or another (the mountain has two major peaks: Mount Royal and Westmount). But lovely Mount Royal Park, planned by the renowned landscape architect Frederick Law Olmsted, of New York City's Central Park fame, is worth a closer look. Not only is it a fine vantage point from which to view the St. Lawrence River, Montreal, and the mountains beyond, it is also a good spot from which to observe Montrealers at their leisure. They use the 500-acre park year-round — especially in winter, for skiing, skating, or horse-drawn sleigh rides (you can hire them in the park). In summer, Beaver Lake is the site of twice-weekly folk dancing, and the audience is invited to participate. The Université de Montréal, the second-largest French-speaking university in the world, is located on the north side of Mount Royal; and St. Joseph's Oratory, described below, is on Westmount's north slope. The park is bounded by Avenue du Parc on the east and, continuing counterclockwise, Avenue du Mont Royal, Camillien Houde Parkway, Chemin Remembrance, Côte des Neiges, and Avenue des Pins.

St. Joseph's Oratory – For more than 2 million people each year, a visit to this shrine is reason enough for a trip to Montreal. Even if you don't make a pilgrimage up the 99 steps to the basilica of this church founded 75 years ago by Brother André of the Congregation de Ste.-Croix for the glorification of St. Joseph, the patron saint of Canada, you will notice the oratory's monumental dome as a distinctive landmark on the city's skyline. Brother André is said to have had great healing power; he is entombed here. Organ recitals are given on Wednesdays during the summer at 8 PM (admission charge), and the children's choir *Les Petits Chanteurs du Mont-Royal* performs Sundays at 11 AM. Crèches from around the world are featured every *Christmas*. The building is open daily from 6:30 AM to 9:30 PM; the museum is open daily from 10 AM to 5 PM. 3800 Queen Mary Rd. (phone: 733-8211).

St. Denis Street – This area, known as Montreal's Latin Quarter, is the site of the Université du Québec à Montréal campus. It features a pleasant square with an agora, fountains, and an art gallery. The façade of historic St.-Jacques Cathedral has been integrated into the institution's main building. St. Denis Street and its theater (*Théâtre St.-Denis*) were the original hosts to the city's annual *Jazz Festival* in early July, and they still provide the sites for many events in this now much expanded 10-day musicfest (see *Special Events*). The street is also popular for its restaurants and attracts an academic crowd to its bookshops, art galleries, and coffeehouses. St. Denis, above Sherbrooke Street, has gained a reputation as a fashion hub due to the many up-and-coming Quebec designers who have showrooms and boutiques here.

Westmount – This mountainside "city within a city" was traditionally the enclave of Montreal's wealthy English-speaking population. Today, the residents of this high-rent district must still be wealthy to maintain themselves in Westmount fashion, but the "English only" requisite has eased somewhat as the city's cultures have blended. This is the section of town for house-staring — or, more appropriately, mansion-staring. The palatial stone house West Mount, which gave the area its name and was owned by *Beaver Steamship Line*'s William Murray, has been torn down, but there are a number of other impressive examples of 19th- and early-20th-century homes (and a few even earlier landmarks) to fill the gap. The sturdy of limb can take the *Métro* to Atwater station, which is linked to elegant Westmount Square, and start a walking tour of the area from there. But because of Westmount's hills, the less hearty may prefer to see it by car. The most interesting sights fall between St. Catherine St. and Edgehill, from Greene Ave. to Victoria Ave.

Outremont – The traditional French-speaking counterpart to English-speaking Westmount is the "ville" of Outremont, hidden on the northeast slope of Mount Royal. Incorporated in 1875, the village was principally made up of large tracts of farmland owned and cultivated by elite residents. While the farms have long since been divided into smaller building lots, some of the original old farmhouses still exist. Outremont's terrain is easily as rugged as Westmount's, so it is best explored by car. The section's main thoroughfare, Côte Ste.-Catherine, and the parallel Maplewood Avenue display the best of Outremont's marvelous mansions, and Laurier Avenue is lined with smart boutiques and cafés. Try *Café Laurier* (394 Laurier W.; phone: 273-2484) for a relaxing coffee break. Bounded north and south by Glendale Ave. and Mont Royal Blvd., east and west by Hutchinson and Canterbury Aves.

Museum of Fine Arts – Galleries in this neo-classic building house an impressive permanent collection of European, Canadian, and Eastern art as well as frequent special exhibits. Canada's oldest fine arts museum (1860), it has staged a string of highly regarded international exhibitions, including Picasso, Miró, the Vatican Collection, Leonardo da Vinci, and Chagall. Free guided tours of permanent and temporary exhibitions. Closed Mondays. Admission charge. 1379 Sherbrooke W. (phone: 285-1600).

McGill University – Chartered in 1821, this prestigious school was built with funds from the estate of Scottish immigrant James McGill, who amassed a fortune as a fur trader and served in Lower Canada's Parliament. The campus is close to the site of the 16th-century Indian town of Hochelaga, discovered by Cartier in 1535. A stroll around the campus and down fashionable Sherbrooke Street reveals a number of interesting architectural façades, including some fine old mansions that now belong to the university. Guided tours of the university grounds can be arranged by calling 398-3770. The university's *McCord Museum,* which has a collection of Indian artifacts, Eskimo carvings, paintings, furnishings, and photographs that focus on the ethnology of Canada, is closed until 1992 for major renovations. Current museum activities and exhibits are held at other places in the city. During the summer, McGill provides inexpensive accommodations in its dormitories, with cafeteria service and sports facilities available to guests. Call 398-6367 for information.

Mackay to de la Montagne – A concentration of restaurants, pubs, discos, trendy fashion boutiques, and art galleries ensconced in brownstone and gray stone Victorian houses is centered in this 9-square-block downtown area that visitors are bound to discover sooner or later. Whether you choose to browse, shop, or bar-hop, you'll know that this is where the action is, and in good weather much of the action is out on the street. *Thursdays* (1449 Crescent St.) is a nice place to eat or have a drink. Mackay, Bishop, Crescent, and de la Montagne (also known as Mountain) Sts. between Sherbrooke St. and René-Lévesque Blvd.

Prince Arthur Pedestrian Mall – Once a quiet residential street, part of McGill's low-cost student ghetto from the 1950s to the early 1970s, today the stretch of Prince Arthur from St. Laurent Boulevard to St. Louis Square has been transformed into an attractive mall. Enhanced by a fountain, overflowing tubs of flowers, and streetlamps, it is currently home to an array of moderately priced restaurants that run the gamut of ethnicities from Greek and Italian to Vietnamese, Polish, and Quebecoise. People watchers will find summer a great time to take advantage of one of the many outdoor cafés that line this lovely street. Most of the restaurants are BYOW (bring your own wine). Summer is also the season for outdoor performances by local musicians, magicians, and acrobats.

Dow Planetarium – Outer space is highlighted in this giant theater of the stars, Canada's first major planetarium, a gift to the city from Dow Brewery Ltd. in the mid-1960s. Its special programs change at various times of year and are narrated in French and English on alternate hours (call for times). Closed Mondays, holidays, and for 3 weeks after *Labor Day*. Admission charge. 1000 St. Jacques W. (phone: 872-4530).

Maison Radio–Canada – One of the world's largest and most modern radio and television centers, the Canadian Broadcasting Company's (CBC's) headquarters of French and English broadcasting sprawls over 25 acres in downtown Montreal. The 23-story hexagonal building that houses the studios also has galleries and an extensive art collection of paintings, sculptures, and graphics done mostly by artists of Quebec and the Atlantic provinces. Visitors are allowed only at a limited number of shows. Call ahead for more information. 1400 René-Lévesque Blvd. (phone: 728-1122).

St. Lawrence Seaway – Montreal is the starting point of this modern engineering miracle, which makes it possible for oceanbound ships to travel all the way through the Great Lakes. Often missed by the average visitor, the observatory at the St. Lambert Lock offers a close look at the intricate locking procedures. Ships from the ocean must be raised and lowered some 15 feet as they pass through the lock. The observation tower also commands a fine view of Montreal's skyline across the St. Lawrence River. A scenic bicycle path runs along the lock. Open May to mid-October; weekends only September and October. No admission charge. Take the Victoria Bridge from downtown across to St. Lambert Lock on Route 15 on the south shore of the river (phone: 672-4110).

■**EXTRA SPECIAL:** Montreal's largest satellite among its St. Lawrence River islands is Ile Ste.-Hélène, which Samuel de Champlain named after his wife, Hélène Boulé. It was once the site of a military installation and, more recently, part of the extensive grounds of *EXPO '67,* which also included its neighboring island, Ile Notre Dame. (When the fair was over, these facilities were renamed Man and His World, after the *EXPO*'s main theme.) There's plenty to do on these two islands, which are linked to the city proper by two bridges — Pont de la Concorde and Pont Jacques Cartier — as well as by the *Métro* system. Get off at the Ile Ste.-Hélène stop on the *Métro.*

Ile Notre Dame – Its annual *Floralies* flower show has been so successful that the island has become a popular year-round park. Pedal boat rentals are an ideal way to explore the island's canals in summer while, in winter, the frozen canals become huge ice skating rinks. Snowshoeing, cross-country skiing, and horse-drawn sleigh rides can also be enjoyed. Other sites here include the Olympic rowing basin, which is transformed into a skating rink each winter, the *Canadian Grand Prix* racetrack, *Gilles Villeneuve Circuit,* and the *Palais de la Civilisation* exhibition center. Exhibition center open May to October. Admission charge for exhibition center only.

Ile Ste.-Hélène – *La Ronde,* a rollicking amusement park, covers 135 acres of this island. In addition to rides, *La Ronde* has spirited restaurants and pubs that Montrealers frequent on warm summer evenings (especially from the end of May to mid-June when it's the launching pad for a 10-day *Fireworks Festival*), and an Aquapark with waterslides and swimming and wading pools. Open mid-June to *Labor Day.* Admission charge (phone: 272-6222).

The *David M. Stewart Museum* (formerly the *Military and Marine Museum*) in Ile Ste.-Hélène's Old Fort (built in the early 1820s by order of the Duke of Wellington) houses historic uniforms, military equipment, and model ships. It features special historical displays June to November (weather permitting); admission charge. In the summer, two colorfully uniformed resident companies of colonial troops — La Compagnie Franche de la Marine (French) and Fraser's Highlanders (Scottish) — perform authentic 18th-century drills and marches. Open daily, except Tuesdays year-round. Admission charge (phone: 861-6701).

The *Montreal Aquarium* is home to a wide variety of native and exotic fish and other aquatic animals, but the most popular residents are the penguins. They delight visitors with their antics in a simulated South Pole on the second floor. Open daily year-round. Admission charge. (phone: 872-4656).

The *Festin du Gouverneur* restaurant in the Old Fort invites diners to enjoy an 18th-century banquet served by costumed performers who sing, dance, and draw patrons into the act. Reservations required (phone: 879-1141). The island is also the site of *Hélène de Champlain* restaurant in an attractive mock Normandy–style building overlooking the river and the rose gardens that remain from *EXPO '67* (phone: 395-2424).

Every winter, in late January, Iles Ste.-Hélène and Notre Dame play host to *La Fête des Neiges,* a 10-day pre-*Lenten* snow carnival that includes costume balls on ice, skating races, sledding, and other outdoor sports, all aided and abetted by plentiful refreshments. Imaginative snow sculptures add so much to the fun that they seem to become contagious, often found across the St. Lawrence decorating Vieux Montréal as well. For information call 872-6093.

■ **Note:** The Laurentian Mountains — called Les Laurentides by French Canadians — extend from 20 to 80 miles (32 to 128 km) north of Montreal and contain some of the best ski slopes in eastern North America. Laurentides National Park is described in full detail in the Laurentian tour route of Quebec Province in DIRECTIONS.

SOURCES AND RESOURCES

TOURIST INFORMATION: The Greater Montreal Convention and Tourism Bureau and Tourism Quebec are both under the same roof in the Infotouriste building (Dorchester Square; phone: 873-2015; from eastern US, 800-443-7000). Visitors' information, maps, brochures, and a city guidebook for the handicapped are also available at the tourist bureau kiosks at the international tourist reception center in the Dorchester Square Building off Peel Street and in Place Jacques Cartier (phone: 871-1595).

Local Coverage – There is one daily English-language newspaper, the *Montreal Gazette* available at newsstands every morning, except Sundays. The free weekly English newspaper *Mirror,* available in restaurants, cafés, and bars, gives a complete listing of entertainment and cultural activities. The monthly *Montreal* magazine, available at newsstands, also has entertainment and restaurant listings.

Food – The *Shopping, Restaurants and Nightlife Guide,* available free at the tourist office, lists details on many of the city's restaurants.

Telephone – The area code for Montreal is 514.

Sales Tax – The 9% sales tax does not apply to hotel rooms, books, and clothing purchases below about CN$500; meals above CN$3.25 have a 10% tax.

TIPPING: At restaurants leave a 15% to 20% tip. Taxi drivers usually receive 15% of the fare. Airport porters and bellboys are given CN$1 per bag, and hotel maids should receive about CN$2, per person, per day.

CLIMATE: While there's no getting around Montreal's cold and snowy winters, its summers seem to make up for it, delivering pleasantly mild temperatures that usually range in the 70s F (20 to 25C). June and September evenings can be cooler, however, so a light jacket may come in handy. Spring temperatures average between the 50s and the mid-60s F (10 to 18C) and in fall drop to the 40s to mid-50s F (5 to 12C). December through March brings frigid temperatures — the low averaging about 10F, the high about 25F (−12 to −4C) — and plenty of snow (a monthly average of 23 inches). Montrealers cope by bundling up in fur couts, boots, hats, and gloves, and by going underground, as we described earlier.

GETTING AROUND: Métro and Bus – *STCUM,* the city transit system, is an efficient network linking various areas of the city with four different underground lines and 150 bus lines. (The same tickets are used on the *Métro* and the buses.) *Métro* trains are clean and quiet, whizzing underground on rubber-tired wheels. The price of the *Métro* ride (about $1.05 per ride; about $5 for six tickets) also includes admission to a veritable underground art gallery of murals, sculptures, stained glass windows, enameled steel frescoes, and ceramics built into exhibits in the 65 stations of the system. *STCUM* issues a helpful, complimentary map of the routes, available at hotel desks and all *Métro* station ticket booths. For 24-hour information about service, call 288-6287.

Car Rental – Montreal is served by *Avis* (1225 Metcalfe St.; phone: 866-7906); *Budget* (1460 Guy St.; phone: 937-9121); *Hertz* (1475 Aylmer St.; phone: 842-8537); *Thrifty* (1600 Berri St.; phone: 845-5954); *Tilden* (1200 Stanley St.; phone: 878-2771), and *Via Route* (1255 Mackay St.; phone: 871-1166).

Taxi – You can hail cabs on the street or at stands at the corner of main intersections near the railway stations and hotels. The drop fee is about $1.70.

Harbor Cruises – A scenic and restful way to see the entire island from the St. Lawrence; *Montreal Harbor Cruises* has six different tours departing from Victoria Pier at the foot of Berri St. from May 2nd through October 15th. Ticket prices vary with the cruise (phone: 842-3871). In addition, *Amphibustour* (phone: 386-1298) travels on both the streets and waters of the port; a ferryboat runs from Jacques Cartier Pier to Cité du Havre island park daily, from noon to 10 PM.

Horse-Drawn Carriage – A romantic way to see the town is by *calèche;* these are stationed at Dorchester Square, Place Jacques Cartier, and atop Mount Royal.

Tours – Some taxicab drivers are licensed tour guides (make sure you get a licensed guide); they can be found at stands around Dorchester Square. Sightseeing tours leaving from Dorchester Square are provided by *Autocar Connaisseur Gray Line* (1140 Wellington St.; phone: 934-1222) and *Murray Hill Sightseeing Services* (1001 Rue du Square Dorchester; phone: 937-5311). During the summer, guides from *Les Montréalistes* conduct daily walking tours of Old Montreal. The same group offers tours of Chinatown, downtown Montreal, and De la Commune Street along the Vieux Port. For rendezvous points and information, call 744-3009. Other private companies offering a variety of tours include *Guidatour* (phone: 844-4021), *Step-on-Guides* (phone: 935-5131), *Hertz Tourist Guides* (phone: 937-6690), *Visites de Montréal* (phone: 843-3308), and *Voyages Astral* (phone: 866-1001). For more information on private guided tours call the Greater Montreal Convention and Tourism Bureau (phone: 871-1595), or pick up a free copy of *A Walking Tour of Vieux Montréal* from the tourism bureau and go on your own.

SPECIAL EVENTS: Montreal hosts several big annual affairs. During the period prior to *Lent,* the island stages a 10-day snow carnival, *Fête des Neiges* (see *Montreal At-a-Glance, Extra Special*).

The 10-day *International Jazz Festival* draws jazz greats — and more than

400,000 of their fans — every year in early July. The major concerts are held at *Place des Arts,* with many more intimate events happening along St. Denis Street and St. Catherine Street around Place-des-Arts and in the *Théâtre St.-Denis* and the *Spectrum* (call 871-1881 for information).

The *Just for Laughs Festival* is a 10-day comedy event attracting stand-up comics from all over the world to test their wits against each other in French and English. It is held in early July at the *Comedy Nest* (1234 Bishop St.), the *Theatre St.-Denis* (St. Denis St.), and *Place des Arts.* For tickets and information, call 845-3155.

The *Palais de la Civilization* on Ile Notre Dame presents an outstanding exhibit every summer. Past exhibits include "China: Treasures and Splendors" and "Gold of the Thracian Horsemen," "*Cités Ciné,*" in 1989, and "*Cités Ciné Prise 2*" in 1990, which were both about film. Open daily, except Mondays, from mid-June until mid-October, 10 AM to 6 PM. (Hours may vary according to particular events.) For more information, call 872-4560.

During the last week in August, *The World Film Festival* brings the latest movies and their stars to Montreal's *Cinéma Parisien* and *Place des Arts* (phone: 848-3883). Another film event, nearly 20 years old, the *Montreal Festival of New Cinema and Video* presents avant-garde filmworks in late September (call 843-4725 for dates and places).

The *Grand Prix du Canada* is a Formula One racing car event held in mid-June at the 4.41-km *Gilles Villeneuve* track on Ile Notre-Dame. For information, call 392-0000.

Now in its fifth year, the *Tour de l'Ile de Montréal,* with over 35,000 cyclists competing, is fast becoming one of the most popular bicycle races in North America. Held in early June, the route encircles the island of Montreal via Sherbrooke St. (phone: 251-6955).

Place Bonaventure's exhibition hall is the site of numerous shows throughout the year, ranging from Canada's largest antiques show to boat and camping exhibits. For information, call 397-2222.

 MUSEUMS: For complete descriptions of the *Montreal Museum of Fine Arts, Château Ramezay,* the *David M. Stewart (Military and Marine) Museum,* and the *McCord Museum,* see *Special Places.* Other notable Montreal museums include the following:

Bank of Montreal Museum – Early currency and bank memorabilia. Open from 10 AM to 4 PM, Mondays through Fridays; closed weekends and holidays. No admission charge. 129 St. Jacques St. at Place d'Armes (phone: 877-6892).

Canadian Center for Architecture – This new museum, an architectural masterpiece in itself, is a study center devoted to architecture. It contains 20,000 prints and drawings, plus 45,000 photographs and important architectural archives, including works by Leonardo da Vinci and Michelangelo. Open Wednesdays and Fridays, 11 AM to 6 PM; Thursdays, 10 AM to 8 PM; Saturdays and Sundays, 11 AM to 5 PM; closed Mondays and Tuesdays. Admission charge. 1920 Baile St. (phone: 939-7000).

Fur Trade Museum – A historic home displays memorabilia from the area's rich fur-trading past. No admission charge. 1255 Saint Joseph Blvd. at 12th Ave., Lachine (phone: 637-7433).

Marc-Aurèle Fortin Museum – Works and memorabilia of the Canadian artist. Open daily except Mondays, 11 AM to 5 PM. Admission charge. 118 St. Pierre St. (phone: 845-6108).

Marguerite d'Youville Centre – Motherhouse of the Grey Nuns; guided tours are given of the chapel and crypt where the founder is buried. Open Wednesdays through Sundays from 1:30 to 4:30 PM. No admission charge. 1185 St. Matthew St. (phone: 932-7724).

Montreal History Center – Audio-visual tour through 11 display rooms describing Montreal's history. From mid-June to mid-September, open daily from 10 AM to 6 PM; from mid-September to mid-May, open Tuesdays through Sundays, 11 AM to 4:30 PM.

Closed Mondays and holidays. Admission charge. Place d'Youville at St. Pierre St. (phone: 872-3207).

Montreal Museum of Decorative Arts – International design from 1940 to the present, including glass and textile exhibits. Open Wednesdays through Sundays only, 11 AM to 5 PM. Admission charge. Corner of Piè IX and Sherbrooke St. (phone: 259-2575).

Museum of Contemporary Art – Canadian and international works. Open daily, 10 AM to 6 PM, except Mondays. No admission charge. Cité du Havre (phone: 873-2878).

Redpath Museum – An impressive anthropological collection, including Egyptian mummies and rare fossils. From September through May, open Mondays through Fridays, 9 AM to 5 PM; June through August, Mondays through Thursdays, 9 AM to 5 PM. No admission charge. 859 Sherbrooke St. W. (phone: 398-4087).

Saidye Bronfman Centre – Contemporary works by national and international artists. Closed Saturdays. No admission charge. 5170 Côte Ste.-Catherine (phone: 739-2301).

Saint Laurent Museum of Art – This arts and crafts center is housed in the old chapel that once served the Collège St.-Laurent school. Open daily, except Saturdays and Mondays, noon to 5 PM. No admission charge. 615 Sainte-Croix Blvd., St.-Laurent (phone: 747-7367).

Sir George-Étienne Cartier House – This national historic park was the Montreal home of one of Canada's founding fathers. Some of the rooms have been restored to their former Victorian glory and others are reserved for various exhibitions. Mid-May through mid-October, open daily, 9 AM to 5 PM; mid-October through mid-May, open Wednesdays through Sundays, 10 AM to 5 PM. No admission charge. 458 Notre-Dame St. E. (phone: 283-2282).

 SHOPPING: Since the duty-free allowance for US citizens returning from Canada has been raised to $338 (CN$400) and the US dollar is at a premium north of the border, there are some excellent values obtainable on a shopping spree in Montreal. Canadian import tariffs are different from those in the US, so in some cases this may mean even better buys. It also usually means a wider selection of imported products.

The underground shopping areas (see *Special Places*) provide a great variety of shops that could probably satisfy most shopping needs. But Montreal's department stores have fine selections of clothing, china, crystal, and furniture. Three of the best known in Canada are on St. Catherine Street West, between Mountain and Union Streets in the heart of downtown: *Eaton's, Ogilvy's,* and *The Bay.* In general, shopping hours are from 9 or 9:30 AM to 6 PM on weekdays, except on Thursdays and Fridays, when many stores stay open until 9 PM, and on Saturdays, until 5 PM.

Eaton's – This Montreal branch of the Canadian chain was founded by Timothy Eaton and dates back to 1925. Its merchandise runs the gamut from appliances to works of art, and a personalized-shopping service will do all the work for reluctant shoppers. The *Art Deco* restaurant on the ninth floor is modeled after the dining room of the *Ile de France,* the favorite vessel of Lady Eaton. 677 St. Catherine St. W. (phone: 284-8484).

Holt Renfrew – For true chic in furs. The firm traces its heritage to the 1837 furriers Henderson, Holt, and Renfrew. It is still known for its exceptional fur fashions as well as haute couture lines, its *Gucci* boutique, and stylish men's clothing. 1300 Sherbrooke St. W. (phone: 842-5111).

Ogilvy's – This once tartan-trimmed testament to days gone by has been transformed into a glossy new complex of chic boutiques and elegant counters. However, the columns and grand main-floor chandeliers have been retained, and traditional goods can still be found in many departments. The store's Scottish heritage continues to manifest itself every day at noon when shoppers hear the skirl of the bagpipes played by a kilted piper. Every *Christmas* since 1947 Montrealers have looked forward to *Ogilvy's* main window display of animated Steiff toys, a spectacle that ushers in the holiday season. 1307 St. Catherine St. W. (phone: 842-7711).

The Bay – Founded in 1845 as Henry Morgan and Company, it was purchased by the Hudson's Bay Company in 1960. It is strong on new trends, French boutique styles, and campus fashions. The variety of dining spots includes a buffet cafeteria, a licensed dining room, and *Le Soupière,* which serves soup, sandwiches, dessert, and coffee. 585 St. Catherine St. W., at Phillips Sq. (phone: 281-4631).

Devotees of fine antiques and delicate craftsmanship head for the fine (and expensive) shops on the aforementioned Sherbrooke Street and its attendant sidestreets, but the bargain hunters frequent the rather unimposing stalls along Notre Dame Street West between Atwater and Guy Streets.

A variety of shops around town carry typical Canadian crafts such as wood carvings, woven products, pottery, jewelry, and Inuit (Eskimo) art. One fine showcase for Canadian crafts is the *Canadian Guild of Crafts* (2025 Peel St.; phone: 849-6091); it carries crafts from all over Canada, including a notable selection of Eskimo art, and features Indian and Eskimo art galleries open during business hours.

 SPORTS: Baseball – The National League *Expos* baseball team plays at the spectacular *Olympic Stadium* (see *Special Places*) with a capacity of 53,858. For information, call 253-3434. Olympic Park is situated in the east end of the city, in the block bounded by Piè IX, Sherbrooke, Viau, and Pierre de Coubertin; take the *Métro* to Viau or Piè IX.

Biking – The Vieux Port rents bicycles to visitors who want to explore its waterfront trails. In addition, the island of Montreal has 20 bike paths, 12 of them city-run (phone: 872-6211). For information on commercial rentals, call *Vélo-Québec* (phone: 252-VELO). Rentals are also available from *Cycle Peel,* 6665 Saint-Jacques St. (phone: 486-1148) and *La Cordée,* 2159 St. Catherine E. St. (phone: 524-1515).

Golf – The 9-hole *Golf Municipal de Montréal* is located at Sherbrooke and Viau Sts. (phone: 872-1143, for information). Golfers can find more than 30 courses on the island of Montreal and in the surrounding area.

Hockey – From October through April, the ice is hotly contested at the *Forum* by *Les Canadiens* and their NHL challengers. 2313 St. Catherine St. W. (phone: 932-6131).

Horse Racing – Harness racing takes place nightly, except Tuesdays and Thursdays, at *Blue Bonnets Race Track.* Races begin at 7:30 PM, except on Sundays, when post time is 1:30 PM. 7440 Decarie Blvd. (phone: 739-2741).

Jet-boat Tours – Organized expeditions over the Lachine Rapids, in small hydrofoil-like crafts, leave from Victoria Pier at the foot of Berri St. in Vieux Montréal daily every other hour from 10 AM to 6 PM. May to late September (phone: 284-9607).

Jogging – Mount Royal Park and Angrignon Park both have paved trails for taking a pleasant run.

Swimming – The stunning Olympic-size pool at Olympic Park is open to the public year-round (phone: 252-4737); the city of Montreal also runs over 50 indoor and outdoor pools and the large public pools at Ile Ste. Hélène (phone: 872-6211). Two of the best indoor pools are the *Cegep du Vieux-Montréal* (255 Ontario St. E.; phone: 872-2644) and the *Centre Claude-Robillard* (1000 Emile-Journault; phone: 872-6900).

Tennis – The *Player's International Championships* alternate between men's and women's events; it's the men's turn this year. From early to mid-August at the *Jarry Tennis Stadium,* Jarry Park (phone: 273-1515). The City of Montreal operates more than 200 municipal courts that are open to the public, either at no charge or for a nominal fee. For information and court reservations, call 872-6763.

Winter Sports – Ice skating, snowshoeing, cross-country skiing, and tobogganing are practiced in parks all over town once winter sets in. All told, the city has 164 skating rinks; 11 cross-country ski areas, each with several trails; 11 large snowshoeing areas; 7 alpine slopes; and 9 toboggan runs among its facilities. From January to March, snowshoeing and cross-country skiing are popular on Notre Dame Island as well as skating along its 1.2-mile-long basin. Close to 1,000 Parks Department employees keep it all in condition. For information, call the municipal recreation department at 872-6211.

THEATER: Both English and French productions are presented at a dozen theaters around town. Local newspapers and in-hotel magazine guides list current attractions. English-language productions are most likely to be found at the *Centaur Theatre,* 453 St. François Xavier (phone: 288-3161).

MUSIC: Since music transcends all language barriers, you can enjoy all that Montreal has to offer, from grand symphony at the *Place des Arts* to French folk music at *boîtes à chanson,* Quebec-style cafés. Again, the guides mentioned above should have up-to-date schedules. The *Montreal Symphony Orchestra* performs at *Salle Wilfrid Pelletier, Place des Arts* (175 St. Catherine St. W.; phone: 842-2112), as do *Les Grand Ballets Canadiens, L'Opéra de Montreal,* and other guest soloists. Programs of chamber music are given at the *Place des Arts' Théâtre Maisonneuve* and *Théâtre Port-Royale* (same phone number). *Pollack Concert Hall* also regularly schedules varied musical programs (555 Sherbrooke St. W.; phone: 398-4547). Throughout the year rock stars perform at the *Forum* (phone: 932-6131) and *Olympic Stadium* (phone: 253-3434). Special productions, such as Handel's *Messiah* at *Christmastime,* are presented at Notre Dame Basilica (Place d'Armes; call the *Montreal Symphony* office, 842-3402), and at other Montreal churches.

NIGHTCLUBS AND NIGHTLIFE: Nightlife for the younger set centers around Crescent, Mountain, and St. Denis Streets. The supper club crowd can choose from among the many hotel and restaurant dining-entertainment spots. Among the more elegant nightspots are *Arthur's* in the *Queen Elizabeth* hotel (900 René-Lévesque Blvd. W.; phone: 861-3511), a dinner-theater that presents comic skits, shows, and music. The *Château Champlain*'s *Le Caf'Conc'* supper club is reminiscent of Paris's Moulin Rouge; you can go for dinner and the show or for drinks only at showtime. The hotel's *L'Escapade* restaurant on the 36th floor gives a good view along with music (1050 Lagauchetière; phone: 878-9000). *Le Stage Dinner Theatre,* at *La Diligence* restaurant, serves up a menu of supper and drama (7385 Décarie Blvd.; phone: 731-7771). *Solmar* (111 St. Paul St. E.; phone: 861-4562) has fado music and Portuguese cuisine. *Vieux Munich* (1170 St. Denis St.; phone: 288-8011) features a Bavarian orchestra and dancing every night after 6 PM, while the *Sabayon* (666 Sherbrooke St. W.; phone: 288-0373) features a dance band as well as Greek music and food.

Dance bands play at the the *Méridien*'s *Le Café Fleurie* restaurant (4 Complexe Desjardins; phone: 285-1450); and *Le Grand* hotel's revolving *Tour de Ville* restaurant (777 University St.; phone: 879-1370). The *Ritz Carlton's Café de Paris* (1228 Sherbrooke St. W; phone: 842-4212), features piano music.

Disco and bar-hopping abound around Crescent, Mountain, Bishop, and Mackay Streets and a number of side streets between René-Levesque Blvd. and Sherbrooke. Currently popular are *Au papillon gourmet,* a piano bar (2310 Guy St.; phone: 935-4255); *Biddles* for great jazz and ribs (2060 Aylmer St.; phone: 842-8656); *Le Business* disco (3510 St. Lawrence Blvd., above Sherbrooke; phone: 844-3988); *Cheers* (1260 Mackay St.; phone: 932-3138); for rock, *Déjà Vu* (1224 Bishop; phone: 866-0512) as well as the *American Rock Café* (2080 Aylmer; phone: 288-9272); *L'Esprit* (1234 Mountain St.; phone: 397-1711); *Kick's Bar* (2051 Mountain St.; phone: 288-2660); *Metropolis,* a turn-of-the-century theater with six bars and dancing on 3 floors (59 St. Catherine St. E.; phone: 288-5559); *Salsathèque,* for Latin music and dancing, (1220 Peel St.; phone: 875-0016); *Septembre* (2015-A Mountain St.; phone: 849-4544); *Sir Winston Churchill Pub* (1459 Crescent St.; phone: 288-0616); *Winnie's* (1455 Crescent St.; phone: 288-0623); and *Yesterday's* (1285 de Maisonneuve Blvd. W.; phone: 282-0220).

Vieux Montréal is fast becoming a hot nightspot area. Favorites include *Le Bijou* (300 Le Moyne St.; phone: 288-5508); *La Cage aux Sports,* a popular hangout with sports personalities (395 Le Moyne; phone: 288-1115); *Chez Brandy* (25 St. Paul St. E.; phone: 871-9178); *L'Air du temps* (191 St. Paul St. W.; phone: 842-2003); and *Zhivago* for caviar, vodka, and dancing (419 St. Pierre St.; phone: 284-0333).

BEST IN TOWN

CHECKING IN: With more than 16,000 hotel rooms in the Montreal area, there is no difficulty finding suitable accommodations. Hotels in all categories dot Montreal's downtown center, close to shopping, restaurants, and the city's other attractions. Even some of the luxury hotels offer weekend packages that are real bargains, including the small extras to make a stay more pleasant. Double room rates will run about $120 or more in the expensive category and about $60 to about $85 in the moderate category. A number of firms handle bed and breakfast lodgings; they include *Accommodations as at Home* (101 Northview Ave.; phone: 486-6910); *Bed & Breakfast de Chez Nous* (5386 Brodeur; phone: 485-1252); *Bed & Breakfast Downtown Network* (3458 Laval Ave.; phone: 289-9749); *Bed & Breakfast Montreal* (4912 Victoria Ave.; phone: 738-9410); *Bed & Breakfast Mount Royal* (4515 Royal Ave., phone: 484-7802); *Relais Montréal Hospitalité* (3977 Laval Ave.; phone: 287-9635); and *Welcome Bed & Breakfast* (3950 Laval Ave.; phone: 844-5897).

The downtown *YMCA* (1451 Stanley St.; phone: 849-8393) and *YWCA* (1355 René-Lévesque Blvd. W.; phone: 866-9941) as well as the youth hostel (3541 Aylmer; phone: 843-3317), McGill University (phone: 398-6367; see *Montreal At-a-Glance*), Université de Montreal (phone: 343-6531), MacDonald College in Ste.-Anne de Bellevue (phone: 398-7716), and the Collège Français on Fairmont St. W. (phone: 495-2581) all offer inexpensive accommodations. In addition, there are campgrounds in the immediate area: *L'Anse à l'Orme* (Gouin Blvd.; phone: 626-3268) is in the nearby suburb of Pierrefonds. *KOA* runs a campground on South Shore at St.-Philippe (phone: 659-8626). All telephone numbers are in the 514 area code unless otherwise indicated.

Bonaventure International – In a unique 3-story penthouse location — 17 stories above the *Place Bonaventure* — is Hilton International's 394-room establishment. Standing in the rooftop lobby, looking at the open-air gardens and heated outdoor pool, it is hard to believe that you are right above one of Montreal's busiest office and commercial complexes. The outside rooms have a lovely view of a good portion of the central city (often including the St. Lawrence Seaway). The inside rooms (preferred by many) look out on a contemplative, Japanese-style central garden that contains a brook, a multitude of trees and bushes, and a couple of waterfalls, all on the roof. *Le Castillion* restaurant is an elegant luncheon or dinner setting. 1 *Place Bonaventure* (phone: 878-2332). Expensive.

Le Centre Sheraton – This 824-room hostelry has posh suites on the top 5 floors, dubbed appropriately *Le Sommet de la Tour* (the Top of the Tower). Its *Point de Vue* restaurant is quickly gaining a reputation for fine nouvelle cuisine. 1201 René-Lévesque Blvd. W. (phone: 878-2000). Expensive.

Château Champlain – The huge, arched picture windows covering the 36-story façade of this Canadian Pacific property make it a distinctive landmark on Montreal's skyline (known to locals as the cheese grater). Its 617 rooms and suites are spacious and elegantly furnished, and there also is a health club and a swimming pool. 1050 Lagauchetière W. (phone: 878-9000). Expensive.

La Citadelle – An old Quality Inn high-rise has been completely refurbished to create this European-style hotel with 182 comfortable rooms, a health spa, and pool. *C'est La Vie,* the lobby bar, attracts a lively crowd for its happy hour. 410 Sherbrooke St. W. (phone: 844-8851; 800-263-8967 in US). Expensive.

Delta – Here is a luxury high-rise with 453 rooms (most with balconies), a health club, pools, and an innovative "Creativity Center"designed to keep young travelers occupied while their parents are sightseeing. Convenient downtown location. On the corner of Sherbrooke and City Councillors Sts. (phone: 286-1986). Expensive.

Four Seasons (Quatre Saisons) – This superb member of the Four Seasons group has 300 rooms, including deluxe suites and 2 extraordinary split-level penthouses. European touches include the efficient services of a 24-hour concierge and a free nightly shoeshine. Among the facilities are a heated outdoor pool, sauna, whirlpool bath, and exercise room. *Pierre de Coubertin* restaurant is now a private dining and meeting room, though the downstairs café, *Le Restaurant,* is open to the public. 1050 Sherbrooke St. W. (phone: 284-1110). Expensive.

Holiday Inn Crown Plaza – The largest and most convenient of the several *Holiday Inns* in the area, this 489-room link in the chain also has an indoor pool. 420 Sherbrooke St. W. (phone: 842-6111). Expensive.

Maritime – Centrally located, this place has 214 rooms, an indoor pool, and sauna. 1155 Guy St. (phone: 932-1411). Expensive.

Le Méridien Montréal – This 601-room property is the focal point of the enclosed commercial-business complex at Complexe Desjardins, adjacent to *Place des Arts,* Montreal's performing arts center. The atmosphere is French at this local link in the Air France hotel chain. There also are indoor and outdoor pools. 4 Complexe Desjardins, enter at 4 Jeanne Mance St. (phone: 285-1450). Expensive.

De la Montagne – This 132-room hostelry is within a stone's throw of the chic boutiques and restaurants in the Crescent Street–de la Montagne Street area. Its rooftop pool and terrace are popular for summer rendezvous, and its dining room, *Le Lutetia,* is highly regarded. 1430 Rue de la Montagne (phone: 288-5656). Expensive.

Queen Elizabeth (Reine Elizabeth) – A king-size, 1,046-room property, it is the city's largest. With direct access to underground *Place Ville Marie*'s shops and services and Canadian National's Central Station, it is one of the most conveniently located, too. In addition to the restaurants in the hotel itself, including the well-known *Beaver Club* (see *Eating Out*), the building features an elegant shopping arcade in the lower lobby, separate from the shops of *Place Ville Marie.* 900 René-Lévesque Blvd. W. (phone: 861-3511). Expensive.

Ramada Inn Centreville – Of the three in the Montreal area, this 205-room member of the chain is the most convenient to downtown. An outdoor pool and complimentary parking are among its attractions. 1005 Guy St. (phone: 866-4611). Expensive.

Ritz-Carlton – In the manner of the grand hotels of Europe, this 240-room property on a tree-lined street caters to a loyal international clientele by providing personalized service (two staff members to each guest) and impeccable decor. This is one of the rare instances where a Ritz hostelry was actually inaugurated by M. Cesar Ritz himself. During the summer, lunch, tea, and dinner are served alfresco at the garden restaurant, which overlooks the manicured lawn and flower-fringed duck pond in the hotel's center court. 1228 Sherbrooke St. W. (phone: 842-4212). Expensive.

Shangrila – This high-rise has a pleasant sidewalk café, *Café Park Express,* 167 well-appointed rooms, and an agreeable ambience. 3407 Peel Street (phone: 288-4141). Expensive.

Le Grand – An ambitious establishment with 737 rooms, it has a 40-foot-high atrium lobby with glass-enclosed elevators, an indoor pool, sauna, and massage room. *Chez Antoine,* an Art Deco oasis in the corridor linking the hotel to *Place Victoria,* serves an innovative menu featuring seafood and meat grilled over charcoal flavored with mesquite, applewood, sassafras, and hickory. *Le Tour de Ville* is the city's only revolving rooftop restaurant. 777 University St. (phone: 879-1370). Expensive to moderate.

Manoir LeMoyne – Just a few blocks from the *Montreal Forum,* it has 286 rooms, most of which are actually apartments with fully equipped kitchens, dining alcoves, and spacious balconies. *Le Frederic* is its fairly good restaurant and piano bar. There's an indoor pool and sauna, too. 2100 de Maisonneuve Blvd. (phone: 931-8861). Expensive to moderate.

Ramada Renaissance Du Parc – The hub of another major office-apartment-shopping complex at the base of Mount Royal, this 463-room hostelry, now a member of the Ramada Renaissance chain, has an attractive lobby lounge and piano bar, indoor and outdoor pools, sauna, and indoor tennis. The restaurant called *Puzzles* is a popular spot. 3625 Av. du Parc (phone: 288-6666). Expensive to moderate.

Château Versailles – A small, European-style hotel with 70 deluxe rooms, fast becoming a favorite with repeat visitors. It only serves breakfast, but its advantage is being in an area abounding in good, moderately priced restaurants. 1659 Sherbrooke St. W. (phone: 933-3611). Moderate.

De l'Institut – Located near the University of Quebec à Montréal, this 42-room establishment is part of the province's School of Tourism and is managed by teachers and students. Meals served here are said to be quite good. 3535 St. Denis (phone: 282-5120). Moderate.

Lord Berri – This 154-room hostelry is close to the Berri *Métro* station and Voyageur bus terminal in the city's east end. The *Café-Bistro* restaurant offers a reasonably priced menu. 1199 Berri St., near René-Levesque Blvd. E. (phone: 845-9236). Moderate.

 EATING OUT: For the Gallic gourmandizer, that unique gastronomic malcontent for whom foreign means nothing but French, Montreal provides a cornucopia of delights comparable to anything available on the far side of the Atlantic. Here is truly the opportunity to have your crêpe and eat it too. The predominant cuisines are French and French Canadian, but many of Montreal's ethnic restaurants, as well as seafood and steakhouses, are excellent. Montrealers seem to live to eat and they have high dining standards; the ambience of a restaurant is as important a consideration as its food. Our choices reflect this native concern. Expect to pay $55 or more for a dinner for two in the expensive range; $25 to $50 in the moderate category; and under $25 in the inexpensive category. Prices do not include drinks, wine, or tips. The 10% provincial tax is applied to all meals of $2.75 ($3.25 CN) and up, and the average tip is 15% to 20%. By law, all menus must be posted outside the establishment. All telephone numbers are in the 514 area code unless otherwise indicated.

Beaver Club – As the name implies, this was once a private club, exclusively for those hearty souls who had journeyed to the Northwest Territories in search of furs. Now the public is welcome (at very high prices), though trophies and pelts from the early fur trading days still decorate the dining room. Nouvelle cuisine selections have been added to the already extensive menu. The bouillabaisse — made with a whole Canadian lobster, halibut, scallops, and fish stock thickened with butter — served with fresh greens is delicious. For dessert, don't pass up the delightful fresh fruit sherbets. Open daily. Reservations advised. Major credit cards accepted. In the *Queen Elizabeth Hotel,* 900 René-Lévesque Blvd. (phone: 861-3511). Expensive.

Les Chênets – A small, intimate French place, decorated with copper pots. Try the oysters from France (called Portuguese), mussels marinière, fresh Pacific salmon, pheasant with mushrooms — but anything is fine. The wine list is also good and includes 60 kinds of cognac. Pricey, but one of the finest meals in town. Open daily. Reservations advised. Major credit cards accepted. 2075 Bishop St. (phone: 844-1842). Expensive.

Chez Delmo – Well-prepared seafood draws Montrealers to this restaurant in the financial district of Old Montreal. There is dining room service, and at lunchtime seafood is also served up at the Victorian-style mahogany bar. Closed Sundays and some holidays. Reservations advised. Major credit cards accepted. 211 Notre Dame St. W. (phone: 849-4061). Expensive.

Chez Desjardins – A Montreal favorite since 1892, it features a menu inspired by the sea. Open daily. Reservations advised. Major credit cards accepted. 1175 Mackay St. (phone: 866-9741). Expensive.

Chez la Mère Michel – In this fine old stone house converted to an attractive, dark-beamed, candlelit dining spot, French cuisine achieves authentic excellence. The lobster soufflé is a special treat, and don't miss a chance for a drink in the snug downstairs bar. Closed Sundays. Reservations necessary. Major credit cards accepted. 1209 Guy St. (phone: 934-0473). Expensive.

Claude Postel – One of Montreal's newest and finest French restaurants (formerly *Le Petit Havre)* is located in Old Montreal in the old *Richelieu* hotel. Specialties include venison with raspberry sauce; salmon in a sherry, shallot, and cream sauce; smoked seafood; and homemade pastries. Open daily. Reservations advised. Major credit cards accepted. 443 St. Vincent (phone: 875-5067). Expensive.

Daberto – Probably Montreal's most sophisticated Italian restaurant, it overlooks the *Museum of Fine Arts* and offers up true culinary artistry of its own. Be sure to try shrimps à la Berci; also fine are any of a multitude of pasta dishes. Closed Sundays except for groups with prior arrangements. Reservations advised. Major credit cards accepted. 1172 Rue de la Montogne (phone: 866-2191). Expensive.

Gibby's – If you are after good steak and atmosphere, try this spot in Old Montreal's restored, early-18th-century Youville Stables. While filling yourself on the large portions, you can take your time and enjoy the attractive stone-walled, beamed interior. Though most diners order a beef dish, there are other entrées as well, all accompanied by fresh, hot bread and a generous salad. Open daily. Reservations necessary. Major credit cards accepted. 298 Place d'Youville (phone: 282-1837). Expensive.

Les Halles – A special dining place in a converted, 2-story townhouse that has been divided into several intimate dining areas. You may be greeted at the door by an oversized cherub who will insist on planting the traditional French kiss of greeting on both your cheeks before letting you out of the foyer. That goes for both ladies and gentlemen. He will then lead you into one of several small dining alcoves and present a menu that is both classic and creative. Try the specialties such as *pamplemousse Marie Louise* (grapefruit stuffed with seafood) or the fine *tournedos.* Closed Sundays and holidays. Reservations necessary. Major credit cards accepted. 1450 Crescent St. (phone: 844-2328). Expensive.

La Marée – Housed in a carefully restored Old Montreal house and owned by the same gentleman who operates *Le Saint Amable,* this establishment specializes in *fruits de mer* (seafood). *Turbot au champagne,* imported French whitefish prepared in champagne, is one of the fine dishes. Open daily, but generally closed Sundays during the winter. Reservations necessary. Major credit cards accepted. 404 Place Jacques-Cartier (phone: 861-8126). Expensive.

Le Saint Amable – Located in a lovely old stone house overlooking Place Jacques Cartier in the heart of Old Montreal, this French dining place owned by Pierre Garcin has long held a high rank for its cuisine, service, and atmosphere. *Tournedos Opera* — filet mignon in a pastry crust — is a specialty. Open daily except *Christmas.* Reservations necessary. Major credit cards accepted. 188 Saint Amable St. (phone: 866-3471). Expensive.

Les Trois Arches – A highly rated restaurant in suburban Pierrefonds, about 15 minutes from downtown Montreal. Located in a century-old graystone mansion, formerly the home of Canadian Army Brigadier General Meighen, its specialty is fine French dishes. Of particular note are the *canard aux olives,* sorrel salmon, and sweetbreads with truffles. Closed Sundays. Lunch served weekdays only. Reservations advised. Major credit cards accepted. 11,131 Meighen St. (yes, that's the right street address) in Pierrefonds (phone: 683-8200). Expensive.

Vent Vert – An award-winning menu boasts such specialties as quail pâté layered in *mille feuilles* (puff pastry), freshly poached scallops, and watercress mousse in wine sauce. Dine on the glassed-in terrace at the front, the small, romantic main dining room or the back room, designed to accommodate larger groups. Open daily. Reservations advised. Major credit cards accepted. 2105 rue de la Montagne (phone: 842-2482). Expensive.

Auberge le Vieux Saint-Gabriel – Long favored for its good French Canadian food and old-time ambience, this restaurant rambles through an Old Montreal building that dates from fur-trading days, complete with a tunnel leading to a room (now a cozy bar) once used to hide furs from raiding Indians. For a taste of Old Quebec, this is the place. Open daily. Reservations advised. Major credit cards accepted. 426 Saint Gabriel St. (phone: 878-3562). Expensive to moderate.

Bonaparte – An attractive little dining room in the heart of Vieux Montreal, this place specializes in French cuisine and seafood. Ask for one of the balcony tables, overlooking the street. Open nightly for dinner, weekdays for lunch. Reservations advised for lunch. Major credit cards accepted. 433 St. François Xavier St. (phone: 844-4368). Expensive to moderate.

Le Fadeau – Seventeenth-century ambience and excellent food and service are offered at this classic French restaurant in an Old Montreal house. Selections from an excellent wine cellar complement the cuisine. Closed Sundays. Reservations necessary. Major credit cards accepted. 423 St. Claude St. (phone: 878-3959). Expensive to moderate.

LUX – This futuristic-style bistro in the up-and-coming neighborhood around Boulevard St.-Laurent is open 24 hours a day and serves French-influenced American food. Built in a converted textile mill, it has a spacious circular main room with a steel floor and a glass-enclosed second level, reached by two spiral staircases. Open daily. Reservations necessary for parties of 6 or more. Major credit cards accepted. 5220 Blvd. St.-Laurent (phone: 271-9272). Expensive to moderate.

Le Mas des Oliviers – If you're gearing up for a night in Montreal's best disco area (Stanley, Mountain, and Bishop Streets) start off the way Montrealers do —

by having dinner here. Try the lamb dishes — they're Chef Jacques Muller's specialty. Open daily. Reservations necessary. Major credit cards accepted. 1216 Bishop St. (phone: 861-6733). Expensive to moderate.

Le Pavilion de l'Atlantique – This seafood establishment, with its classic nautical decor, dominates the atrium of the Alcan building. Service, even on busy Sunday evenings, is friendly and efficient. Among the best dishes are the grilled scampi, lobster thermidor, and Arctic char. Open daily. Reservations advised. Major credit cards accepted. 1188 Sherbrooke St. W. (phone: 285-1636). Expensive to moderate.

Les Serres de Marguerite – A greenhouse dining room that is always humming, particularly in the summer when cooling ceiling fans spin lazily overhead. Full-course dinners, generous salads, and quiche are the fare. Closed Sundays. Major credit cards accepted. 417 Saint Pierre St. (phone: 288-9788). Expensive to moderate.

Arigato – The sushi and sashimi combinations at this Japanese restaurant draw a loyal lunchtime crowd. Open daily. Reservations advised. Major credit cards accepted. 75 de la Gauchetière St. W., on the Chinatown Mall (phone: 395-2470). Moderate.

Le Caveau – French food is served in this cozy little house in the heart of midtown. Checkered tablecloths and candlelight add an atmosphere of intimacy. The less expensive of the two menus offers good value and has almost the same selection as the regular menu. The *tournedos,* house wine, and crème caramel are all of high quality. Open daily. Reservations advised. Major credit cards accepted. 2063 Victoria St. (phone: 844-1624). Moderate.

Les Copines de Chine – This Chinese restaurant has an attractive setting in the tropical, plant-filled atrium of *Place Dupuis.* Its appetizing Szechuan dishes are served by an attentive staff. Open daily. Major credit cards accepted. 870 Maisonneuve Blvd. E.(phone: 842-8325). Moderate.

Le Latini – A different pasta dish is featured every day, and the veal specialties are tasty and tender. In summer, guests may dine alfresco on the new terrace. Closed Sundays. Reservations necessary. Major credit cards accepted. 1130 Jeanne Mance St., near *Complexe Desjardins* (phone: 861-3166). Moderate.

La Mer à Boire – Nestled in a historic house, this eatery serves hearty French Canadian dishes beside a cozy hearth. The decor is rough-hewn, early Montreal, but the walls display an impressive collection of contemporary Quebec art. Open daily. Major credit cards accepted. 429 Saint Vincent St. (phone: 397-9610). Moderate.

Le Paris – Yet another fine French eatery with an atmosphere that is truly Parisian. Closed Sundays and holidays. Reservations necessary. Major credit cards accepted. 1812 St. Catherine W. St. (phone: 937-4898). Moderate.

Les Filles du Roy – Another popular tourist haunt for French Canadian food in a 17th-century Quebec setting. The waitresses wear costumes fashioned after the period's "daughters of the king" who came to New France to marry eligible settlers. Open daily. Sunday brunch is a special treat. Reservations advised. Major credit cards accepted. 415 Bonsecours St. (phone: 849-3535). Moderate to inexpensive.

Bonsai – A Vietnamese restaurant named for the artistic miniature Japanese trees, it serves light meals accented with tasty soup and spring rolls. Ask for a table in the back dining room, which overlooks the Old Port. Closed Sundays. Reservations advised. Major credit cards accepted. 138 St. Paul St. E. (phone: 861-6640). Inexpensive.

Chez Vito – In the Côte-des-Neiges area, near the University of Montreal, this popular place has fine Italian fare and a good disco upstairs. Open daily. No reservations. Major credit cards accepted. 5408-12 Côte-des-Neiges (phone: 735-3623). Inexpensive.

Jardin Lung Fung – Located in Chinatown, this place has an extensive Cantonese and Szechuan menu and is fully licensed. House specialties include shrimp on toast as an appetizer; "Great Vegetable Mix," a combination of Chinese stir-fried vegetables; and chicken stuffed with chopped meat in oyster sauce. It also serves the best eggrolls in town. Open daily. Reservations unnecessary. Major credit cards accepted. 1071 St.-Urbain (phone: 879-0622). Inexpensive.

La Maison Greque – Very reasonable no-frills place featuring *moussaka* and *brochette au poisson*. Diners must bring their own wine, but it's worth a stop at the liquor store when a meal for two costs about $13. Open daily. Reservations advised. Major credit cards accepted. 450 Duluth St. E. (phone: 842-0969). Inexpensive.

Montreal Hebrew Delicatessen and Steak House – Known locally as *Schwartz's*, this deli is famous for its smoked meats (a sort of illegitimate product of the mating of corned beef and pastrami) and grilled steaks, and draws a cross section of Montrealers. You'll share a crowded table with other diners, and the French fries may be the best on this continent. No liquor license, but plenty of Dr. Brown's cream soda. Open daily. Closed *Yom Kippur.* No reservations. No credit cards accepted. 3895 St. Lawrence Blvd. (phone: 842-4813). Inexpensive.

Rotisserie Laurier – Chicken, Quebec-style. Open daily. No reservations. Major credit cards accepted. 381 Laurier W. (phone: 273-3671). Inexpensive.

Stash's Café Bazaar – Just beside Notre-Dame Church in Old Montreal, this establishment specializes in Polish food. The decor is simple and the atmosphere friendly. Open daily. No reservations. Major credit cards accepted. 461 Saint Sulpice St. (phone: 861-2915). Inexpensive.

Sucrerie de la Montagne – Anyone with a sweet tooth should make the trip to this sugaring-off spot 20 miles (32 km) southwest of the city. The maple sugar feast includes *tourtiere* (meat pie) and baked beans, finished off with the traditional maple syrup pie, more commonly served in Quebec City. A full meal runs about $6.50 per person. Open 11 AM to 8 PM all year. Groups need reservations. 300 Rang St-Georges, off Route 40 (phone: 451-5204 or 451-0831). Inexpensive.

Swensen's – An outlet of the San Francisco–based chain of old-fashioned ice cream parlors is serving some of the richest, creamiest ice cream found from the American West to the Canadian East. There are 27 flavors to choose from, including sticky chewy chocolate, black raspberry cheesecake, butterscotch marble, swiss orange chocolate chip — one better than the next. Open daily. At the corner of St. Catherine St. W. and Mansfield Ave. (phone: 874-0695). Inexpensive.

OTTAWA

Ottawa is Canada's national capital. Everything else about the city is merely supporting evidence for that simple but essential fact of Ottawa life.

Ottawa's role as the home base for the national government is so crucial to the city's existence, in fact, that if Queen Victoria had taken the expected course in 1858 and named one of the then more important cities — the front-runners were Toronto and Montreal — as the new capital of the merged colonies of Upper and Lower Canada (present-day Ontario and Quebec), Ottawa today would probably be just another dowdy, over-the-hill lumbering town. Instead, the capricious ruler chose Ottawa, encouraged by some wildly romantic watercolors of the community and fed up with all the petty bickering over which backwoods colonial outpost was more deserving of the honor. Her choice transformed the place overnight from a brawling, sprawling mill town into a reluctantly austere and dignified city. Nine years later, the colonies joined with a couple of Britain's other North American possessions to form Canada. Ottawa remained the capital of the new country because the government buildings, erected at great expense, were already in place and because few in the fledgling nation could stomach the thought of another interminable battle over which city should be the seat of the government.

The city is situated on the southern bank of the Ottawa River at its junction with the Rideau River. The impressive Parliament buildings rise from a hill above the Ottawa River to dominate the surrounding area and announce Ottawa's federal prominence in Gothic grandeur. Yet, despite its aura of power, Ottawa is very much a city of human proportions, with a population of just over 850,000 (the National Capital Region encompasses Hull, across the river in the province of Quebec). Because of its national significance, it has amenities other cities of its size might not be able to support. The city's role as the host for foreign embassies means almost unlimited access to the world's cuisines, and for a city of its size, it has a disproportionate number of good restaurants. French and French Canadian cuisine are the specialties, but visitors can sample ethnic food at an eclectic selection of restaurants, from Russian and Irish to Mexican and Lebanese. Culturally, the city is well set up. The *National Arts Centre* is a first-rate facility with an acoustically superb opera house, a theater, and a studio which draw Canadian and international stars. Cerebral stimulation is available at the *National Gallery of Canada* or at any of Ottawa's several national museums, and there's enough hiking, biking, skiing, and swimming to exhaust even the most physically fit.

Ottawa's current eminence, however, stands in stark contrast to its beginnings. If its selection as Canada's capital is not the stuff of heroic legend, its early history is even less awe-inspiring. The Outaouac Indians (from whom the city takes its name) used the area as a regular stopover on their nomadic jaunts, but the unwelcoming climate — Ottawa can be as hot and muggy in summer as Lagos, Nigeria, and colder in winter than Moscow — discouraged permanent settlement. Samuel de Champlain, the French explorer, paused briefly near the site of the present Parliament buildings in 1613 to admire the Chaudière Falls, pronounced himself much impressed, then hurried on in search of more interesting and rewarding discoveries.

Finally, in 1796, a hardy, puritanical New Englander, Philemon Wright, dragged along family and friends to a spot on the north side of the Ottawa River (now Hull), where he established a small settlement. Thirteen years later, another group began to hack out sprawling farms from the forests, swamp, and beaver meadow on the site that is now the city of Ottawa.

These settlers were joined in 1826 by Lieutenant-Colonel John By and the Royal Engineers, a rag-tag band of Irish laborers, army engineers, and British veterans of the Napoleonic and American wars who had been assigned the task of constructing a canal from Ottawa to Kingston, Ontario. Although the nearly 125-mile-long system of locks, dams, rivers, and lakes was originally intended to serve as a secure military route from Montreal to Kingston in the event of American attack, the threat never materialized, and the canal became a commercial venture almost as soon as it was completed in 1832. Today it is called the Rideau Canal.

Its good location at the midpoint of the then main water route between Montreal and the growing cities on the Great Lakes briefly gave Ottawa a sense of commercial purpose. That, in turn, attracted a group of American lumber barons, who set up mills, hired workers, and jammed up the Ottawa River with gigantic log booms.

It was this rambunctious wilderness town that Queen Victoria, with the flourish of a royal prerogative, made into a capital city. The choice was not a popular one, and, after the new legislature's first session in 1866, one disgruntled politician wrote to a friend that there was "an almost unanimous desire . . . to get away from Ottawa as soon as practicable."

Despite such carping, the city remained the capital and flourished. Under the watchful eye of a national government anxious to make it a vibrant hybrid of Canada's two founding cultures (35% of Ottawa's residents are of French descent, although most are bilingual), Ottawa has become — as officials like to boast — "a city of urban grace in which all Canadians can take pride."

Partly because it couldn't hope to compete with the elegant European sophistication of Montreal or the bustling cultural diversity of Toronto, Ottawa has staked out its own claim as a living, breathing model of what human-oriented urban planning is all about.

Modern Ottawa is a family place. The city is festooned with parks and open spaces, dotted with six national museums and many historic sites, and crowned with the *National Arts Centre,* a sparkling $36 million cultural showplace. Sprawling right in the middle of the city is a 1,200-acre experimental farm, with real cows and squealing pigs to delight city-bred kids and botanical and ornamental gardens to satisfy quieter tastes. For those who would rather act than observe, 65 miles of bicycle paths meander from the downtown core to the city's residential suburbs; in the winter, a 5-mile stretch of the Rideau Canal, extending from the Parliament buildings to the thoroughly modern campus of Carleton University, is transformed into the world's longest skating rink. To complete Ottawa's year-round picture, the city is neatly wrapped by a unique 2½-mile-wide greenbelt of dairy and beef farms, open spaces, and hobby gardens for the capital's apartment dwellers. Within easy reach of the city, nestled in the Gatineau Hills, a visitor will find the tranquility of Meech Lake. It is here, at the prime minister's residence, that the controversial Meech Lake Accord was drawn up in 1987.

Ottawa is, ultimately, as much a pleasant state of mind as it is a city in the conventional sense, and the result is an environment that is as rewarding to visit as it is to live in.

From the real-life theater of the daily House of Commons Question Period, which allows opposition politicians to grill the government of the day, to the serene beauty of Gatineau Park just 15 minutes away by car, Canada's capital — once snidely referred to as "Westminister in the wilderness" — measures up to true capital status.

OTTAWA AT-A-GLANCE

SEEING THE CITY: The best place to get an overview of the capital is from the lookout of the Peace Tower, a Parliament building, on Wellington Street, in the center of the city. Just a touch over 300 feet high, the tower opens up a panoramic view extending 40 miles in all directions. To the north stand the concrete and glass government buildings rising up from the Quebec side of the Ottawa River; beyond lies Gatineau Park, an 88,000-acre wilderness and recreation area popular with locals and visitors alike. To the east, you can catch a glimpse of the Rideau Canal. In the summer, pleasure boats wend their way along the calm channel; in the winter, skaters glide along its frozen length. To the south and west is the city itself, graced here, there, and everywhere by lush green parkland. Free English and French tours of the Parliamentary Centre Block, which include a trip to the top of the Peace Tower, start at the Info-Tent on the east side of the Centre Block. Tours are conducted daily (except *Christmas* and *New Year's Day*) from 9 AM to 4:30 PM (in the summer until 9 PM).

SPECIAL PLACES: Many of Ottawa's most interesting sights, including the must-see *National Gallery,* lie within a casual stroll of no more than a couple of blocks from the Parliament Buildings. Any downtown habitué will gladly point you toward the place of your choosing.

DOWNTOWN

Parliament Buildings – These impressive Gothic structures are Canada's single most famous landmark. Erected on a promontory above the Ottawa River, the Parliament Hill complex once housed the entire federal administration but now serves primarily as the meeting place of federal politicians. The East and West Blocks of the Parliament buildings (the only original, century-old structures remaining are on the Centre Block and were rebuilt after a disastrous fire in 1916) as well as the nearby Confederation Building contain offices for members of Parliament and are not open to the public. Visitors are welcome, however, to tour the Centre Block, which houses not only the chambers for the House of Commons and the Senate but also the opulent, domed Parliamentary Library and the magnificent Peace Tower. (Tour details are given above.) You also can visit the renovated East Block, which contains the old cabinet-meeting rooms. When Parliament is in session, you can watch the action from the public galleries overlooking the House of Commons and Senate chambers. At 10 AM daily from the end of June through *Labor Day,* the lawns in front of the Centre Block are the scene of a Changing the Guard ceremony, involving 125 soldiers dressed in bright scarlet uniforms topped with giant bearskin busbies. In spring, the tulip gardens are spectacular, particularly along the Colonel By Drive. The tulips were given to Canada by former Queen Juliana of the Netherlands to commemorate the sacrifices made by the Canadian First Army in the liberation of Holland and to thank Canada for protecting the Dutch royal family during World War II. Open daily. No admission charge. Wellington St. between Bank and Elgin (phone: 995-7771).

Rideau Canal – This 123-mile-long canal, linking Kingston on Lake Ontario with Ottawa, was constructed between 1826 and 1832 on the recommendation of the Duke of Wellington to provide safe lines of communication between Montreal and the new settlements on the lake in the event of war with the US. Despite its military origins, this inland waterway is now used as a recreational facility year-round. Much of the old stonework on the original locks and dams remains. Flower gardens, tall trees, and bike paths used by hikers and cross-country skiers in the winter line the 5-mile stretch in central Ottawa. During the summer, many Ottawans sail and canoe on the canal. From spring to fall, a 1½-hour boat tour cruises the central stretch, departing daily between 11:30 AM and 8:30 PM from a landing near the Government Conference Centre. In the winter, the canal is transformed into an excellently maintained 5-mile-long skating rink. South from the Ottawa River between Colonel By Dr. and Queen Elizabeth Driveway.

Rideau Centre – It cost $250 million, covers 14 acres, contains a *Convention Center* that can seat 4,000, boasts a 475-room luxury hotel, and has a multilevel shopping complex with over 200 stores, 18 restaurants, and 3 movie houses. On top of it, literally, there's a 5-acre park with winding paths, park benches, and real trees. The center has had an impressive impact on the heart of Ottawa, reversing the trend begun in the 60s when the city bled into the suburbs every night at 5 o'clock. 50 Rideau St. (phone: 236-6565).

Sparks Street Mall – An outdoor mall — 5 city blocks filled with boutiques, department stores, historic buildings, rock gardens, sculptures, live entertainment, and the best people-watching real estate in the capital — is Canada's first permanent pedestrian-only street, spruced up by a major facelift. The *Four Corners* (93 Sparks St.) and the *Davis Agency Canadiana Shop* (203 Sparks St.) are musts for Canadian crafts — everything from handwoven British Columbia blankets to Inuit carvings. During the summer, the mall comes alive with flower peddlers, fruit vendors, musicians, street corner orators, and armies of lunch hour civil servants trying to catch a little sun. At 240 Sparks is a giant glass enclosure housing federal government offices, a variety of lunch-on-a-bun spots, and stores selling elegant apparel. Open daily. Sparks St., between Elgin and Lyon.

Byward Market – This market has been an Ottawa institution since the mid-1800s, when local farmers first set up their stalls and began peddling fresh produce to city slickers. In recent years, the farmers have been joined by local artists and craftspeople who display their wares in the renovated market building. The market also houses an impressive array of specialty foreign grocery stores, fish markets, cheese shops, and cozy restaurants. On summer nights, its cobblestone courtyards and side streets become impromptu stages for sidewalk entertainers. The market itself operates daily May through October. Between Clarence and George Sts.

Nicholas Street Jail – Ottawa's last public hanging took place here in 1869, when the country's only political assassin, Patrick Whelan, was strung up for the murder of D'Arcy McGee, a member of Parliament. The forbidding structure served as the local lock-up for more than a century. In 1972 it was converted into a hostel for young travelers (see *Best in Town*). A 40-minute public tour every Sunday at 2 PM lets visitors view the tiny 3½-by-9-foot cells. Open daily. No admission charge. 75 Nicholas St. (phone: 235-2595).

National Museum of Natural Sciences – With 2 million zoological specimens, from the daspletosaurus (a 4-ton, 28-foot long tyrannosaur) on up the evolutionary ladder, this museum is particularly fascinating for children. The building that houses the exhibits is the castle-like structure where the House of Commons met after the Parliament buildings burned down in 1916. Open 10 AM to 8 PM Thursdays, 10 AM to 5 PM other days. No admission charge on Thursdays. Metcalfe at McLeod (phone: 996-3102).

National Museum of Civilization – The main hall of this $225 million museum (across the river in Hull) is the length of a football field and 5 stories high. Inside are a West Coast Indian village and rain forest, and a domed theater shows *IMAX* and *OMNIMAX* movies — the former projects crystal-clear images on a huge screen, while the latter has a 19,000-pound wrap-around screen. The museum also offers changing exhibitions, festivals, a resource center, and a children's museum. Open 10 AM to 8 PM Thursdays, 10 AM to 5 PM other days. (Closed Mondays in winter.) No admission charge on Thursdays. 100 Laurier St., Hull (phone: 995-8287).

National Gallery of Canada – A veritable glass mountain illuminated by natural light, the gallery is a breathtaking work of architecture — a major attraction in itself. It houses more than 25,000 paintings, sculptures, and drawings, including many by the world's great masters; the international photograph collection numbers around 15,000 pieces. The Canadian collection has works by the famous Group of Seven, including Paul Kane's paintings of native people and Cornelius Kreigoff's portrayals of pioneer life. Open 10 AM to 8 PM Wednesdays through Fridays, 10 AM to 5 PM other days. Closed Mondays from November to May. No admission charge on Thursdays. Sussex Drive (phone: 990-1985).

SUBURBS

Government House – Diagonally across the street from the prime minister's home is the 88-acre estate of the governor-general, the queen's official Canadian representative. In addition to a rambling mansion for the governor-general and a guesthouse for the queen and other foreign dignitaries, the tree-lined grounds also have gardens, a skating rink, and even a cricket pitch to add a little touch of Britain. Guided tours of the house and grounds are available by appointment only (phone: 992-5473).

Laurier House – Purchased by Canada's seventh prime minister, Sir Wilfrid Laurier, after his election in 1896, this 18-room brick house was also home to the tenth of the country's fifteen prime ministers — Laurier's fellow Liberal, William Lyon Mackenzie King. King was a popular leader and held power longer than any other prime minister, serving from 1921 to 1930 and again from 1935 to 1948. King bequeathed the house to the people of Canada; he died in 1950. Now the house is a showcase of the furniture and personal effects (right down to King's shaving mug in the bathroom) of the two men. Closed Mondays. No admission charge. 335 Laurier Ave. E (phone: 992-8142).

Canadian War Museum – Exhibits here are related to Canada's military history. Displays include skulls taken by the Indians as the spoils of war, a mock-up of a German bunker overlooking Normandy's beaches on *D-day,* and Goering's staff car. Open daily. No admission charge on Thursdays. 330 Sussex Dr. (phone: 992-2774).

Central Experimental Farm – Established in 1886 as the headquarters of the research branch of the federal Department of Agriculture, the farm sprawls over 1,200 acres within the city limits. The spectacular ornamental gardens are a favorite spot for local wedding photographs, and the arboretum is a showplace of rare trees. There are displays of more than 10 million insect samples in the farm's Neatby Building or visit the dairy barn and piggery. From spring through fall, you can jump aboard a horse-drawn wagon for a free tour of the grounds weekdays at 10 AM and 2 PM, weather permitting. Open daily. No admission charge. Prince of Wales Dr. between the Driveway and Base Line Rd. (phone: 995-5222).

Rockcliffe Park Village – A community of 22,000, set among stately mansions and narrow, tree-lined streets, it is the city's most elegant residential area. The village's first home was Rideau Hall, built in 1838. It has been the residence of all Canada's governor-generals since Confederation. Many of the other residents are also government officials (close to 600 diplomats live here). Most of the ambassadors' residences are identifiable by their country's emblems decorating the entranceways.

National Museum of Science and Technology – This popular museum encourages involvement; visitors can clamber aboard a train or ring the bell of a ship's wheelhouse. Exhibits range from a display of early motor cars to a non-radioactive, charred chunk of the Soviet satellite that crashed in northern Canada in 1978. Open 10 AM to 8 PM daily in summer. No admission charge on Thursdays. 1867 St. Laurent Blvd. (phone: 991-3044).

National Aviation Museum – Housed in dilapidated World War II hangars until 1988, this fine collection of aircraft dating back to the turn of the century is now displayed in an $18 million showplace at Rockcliffe Airport. More than 50 aircraft are exhibited in this new building, including the *Silver Dart,* the first plane ever flown in the British Empire, at Baddeck, Nova Scotia, in 1909. Closed Mondays during the winter; open daily the rest of the year. No admission charge on Thursdays. Rockcliffe Airport off St. Laurent Blvd. (phone: 993-2010).

Vincent Massey Park – This spot was named after the first native-born Governor-General of Canada. Offering a pleasant break from sightseeing, these 52 acres of country right in the city provide cycling paths, barbecue pits, picnic tables, ample parking, and plenty of grass and trees in which to frolic. You can also enjoy cross-country skiing and tobogganing in winter. Open daily. No admission charge. Base Line Rd. west of Riverside Dr.

Gatineau Park – An 88,000-acre wilderness and recreation area that has more than 60 miles of hiking and cross-country trails, 40 lakes for fishing, swimming, and boating, plenty of camping and picnic facilities, and a lion's share of the area's beautiful scenery. On the drive that wanders through the rolling hills of the park is Moorside, the summer home of former Canadian Prime Minister William Lyon Mackenzie King. The grounds are decorated with the ruins of old British and Ottawa buildings. Delightful lunches, afternoon tea, and dinners are served here. Open noon to 6:30 PM daily, from mid-May to mid-October. The park is just 15 minutes from the Parliament Buildings on the Quebec side of the Ottawa River (phone: 239-5000).

■**EXTRA SPECIAL:** Every evening at dusk from late May to early September a sound-and-light show, using 600 powerful spotlights and a synchronized soundtrack, brings Canada's history to life on the grounds of Parliament Hill. The National Capital Commission spent 3 years and $2.5 million developing the show. No admission charge. From 10 AM to 4:30 PM all summer, actors in period costume mingle with tourists on Parliament Hill and present historical vignettes. Some are controversial, and spectators are encouraged to heckle. Call 239-5000 for more information.

SOURCES AND RESOURCES

TOURIST INFORMATION: Ottawa and Hull Tourism Inc. (65 Elgin St., phone: 237-5158) in the *National Arts Centre* is where you'll find all manner of maps, brochures, and helpful hints. The National Capital Commission maintains two visitors' centers where you can pick up maps of the various NCC-operated cycling, hiking, and nature trails in the region. They are located opposite the Parliament buildings (14 Metcalfe St.); phone: 239-5000) and in Hull (25 Laurier; phone: 819-778-2229). Both centers are open weekdays from 9 AM to 5 PM and in the summer until 9 PM. From May to September, the NCC staffs an Info-Tent on Parliament Hill.

Local Coverage – The *Ottawa Citizen* and the *Ottawa Sun,* both dailies; *Ottawa Magazine,* monthly; *What's On in Ottawa,* monthly magazine. Ottawa also has eight local radio stations, as well as four TV stations and two cable TV centers.

Food – Two area dining guides are *Dining Out in Ottawa-Hull and Environs* by Marilyn Mannes (Borealis Press, about $3.80, and *The Consumer Guide of Restaurants of the National Capital Region* (SERPA Publications; about $4, which lists nearly 1,200 restaurants. The *Ottawa Citizen* has restaurant reviews and publishes an excellent restaurant ratings list twice a year (available free through hotels).

Telephone – The area code for Ottawa is 613; the area code for Hull is 819.

Sales Tax – The sales tax in the region is 8%. (Note: US citizens are eligible, under certain conditions, for a sales tax refund on accumulated purchases of CN$100 or more and a rebate of what they may have paid in hotel and motel tax. Stores and tourist centers can provide details.)

Currency – All prices are quoted in US dollars unless otherwise indicated.

TIPPING: Taxi drivers are generally given CN$2 to CN$4, depending on the length of the trip. Leave a 10% to 15% percent tip in restaurants. Hotel maids usually should be given CN$1 per day, per person, and bellboys and airport porters get about CN$2.

CLIMATE: Ottawa's weather is extremely variable. The temperature has been known to top 98F (37C) at the height of summer and to plummet to −25F (−31C) in the depths of winter. The warmest month is July and the coldest is January; there is rainfall about 100 days a year and snow during another 45.

GETTING AROUND: Daytime downtown parking is notoriously expensive, so look for the less expensive parking lots just outside the core area.

Bus – Although many places of interest are within walking distance, especially in summer, try the bus system anyway. The $450 million high-speed, modern, buses-only *Transitway* is a novelty as well as a way of beating traffic jams. Regular runs from 6 AM to midnight. *OC Transpo,* the city bus agency, offers tourists special rates. For information, call 741-4390.

Car Rental – There's a wide variety of companies, most of which offer airport pick-up and drop-off. All major North American firms are represented: *Avis* (phone: 230-2847 or 800-387-7600); *Budget* (phone: 521-4844 or 800-268-8900); *Hertz* (phone: 521-3332 or 800-263-0600); and *Thrifty* (phone: 737-4510 or 800-367-2277).

Sightseeing Tours – It's possible to view this lovely city by land, water, or air. *OC Transpo/Gray Line* (phone: 748-4426) offers excellent sightseeing bus tours of the city, starting near the *Château Laurier* daily on the hour from 10 AM to 7 PM, early May through late October. *Picadilly Bus Tours* (phone: 235-7674) offers tours of the city on London double-decker buses from Confederation Square (near Parliament Hill) from May 1 to October 23. Another wheeled conveyance to consider is a rickshaw from *Velvet Wheels,* pulled skillfully by fit young students who literally provide a running commentary. *Paul's Boat Lines* (phone: 733-5186) cruises the Ottawa River and Rideau Canal all summer; *Ottawa Riverboat Company* (phone: 232-4888) has party and brunch cruises aboard the *Sea Prince II.* Head toward Confederation Square, and ticket sellers for both companies will find you. Riding in hot air balloons has become a popular way of seeing the city from the sky, and four companies offer such excursions: *Alpha* (phone:

234-1221); *Great Canadian* (phone: 833-3101); *Skyview* (phone: 828-9605); and *Windborne* (phone: 233-1232). For those who prefer to keep their feet on the ground, daily walking tours are organized during the summer by the NCC (phone: 239-5000). For a nominal charge these expeditions explore areas of the Lower Town that are off-limits to traffic.

Taxi – All cabs in Ottawa are metered. Cab stands are located at major hotels. Otherwise, call *Blue Line* (phone: 238-1111), *Capital* (phone: 746-2233), *Diamond* (phone: 235-1821), *Blondeau* (phone: 749-5838), or *A-1* (phone: 746-1616). Hailing a cab is an uncommon practice in Ottawa.

SPECIAL EVENTS: The 10-day *Winterlude* celebration, held every February on the Rideau Canal, includes a parade, ice sculptures, sleigh rides, harness races on ice, and other events. Begun in 1977, it is one of Canada's biggest winter attractions, capped off on the final day by an international 55-km (88-mile) cross-country ski race in Gatineau Park. During the weeklong *Festival of Spring,* held every May, the city dazzles with millions of colorful tulips as well as crafts exhibits, fairs, concerts, boat shows, and community events. Other summer highlights include *Canada Day* (July 1), the *Jazz Festival,* during the first 2 weeks of July, and the *International Cycling Festival* in Hull, during the first 2 weeks of August. The *Ottawa Exhibition,* featuring an agricultural display, games of chance, rides, entertainment, and craft exhibitions, takes place at the end of August. Autumn brings the *Festival of Arts* for 2 weeks in October.

MUSEUMS: For complete descriptions of the *National Museum of Science and Technology,* the *National Aeronautical Collection,* the *National Museum of Civilization,* the *National Museum of Natural Sciences,* the *Canadian War Museum,* and the *National Gallery of Canada,* see *Special Places.* If you're not thoroughly exhausted by these, another notable museum is *Bytown Museum* (this is the city's oldest building and has displays of early Ottawa), on the Rideau Canal, under the bridge next to the *Château Laurier* (phone: 234-4570). Open Mondays through Saturdays from mid-May through September. Also worth a visit is the *Currency Museum* (a few blocks west at 245 Sparks Street; phone: 782-8914) and (also nearby) the *National Postal Museum* (365 Laurier). Both are open year-round. There is no admission charge at any of these museums.

SHOPPING: In addition to the *Sparks Street Mall* described in *Special Places,* there are a number of other prime shopping areas. Most notable is the downtown area's *Rideau Centre* with 220 stores. *Place de Ville* (320 Queen), an underground concourse linking the *Skyline* and *Holiday Inn* (Ottawa Centre hotels), houses 60 shops. *L'Esplanade Laurier* (181 Bank St.) has 12 clothing boutiques, 6 restaurants and delis, and 12 craft and hobby shops as well as a pharmacy and a liquor store. The main suburban malls are *Bayshore* (at the western end of the Queensway), with 90 stores, including *The Bay* and *Eaton*'s department stores; and the *St. Laurent Shopping Centre* (just off the St. Laurent Blvd. exit of the Queensway), which has 160 shops, including another branch of *The Bay* department store.

SPORTS: Though Ottawa has its share of spectator sports, it is much more a city of doers than watchers.

Biking – The National Capital Commission maintains more than 65 miles of trails. Bikes can be rented from *Rent-A-Bike* (phone: 233-0268). The best places to ride are on the Colonel By and the Ottawa River Parkways, which wind around the city. On Sunday mornings they are closed to auto traffic.

Football – The Ottawa *Rough Riders,* a professional team in the Canadian Football League, play home games in Lansdowne Park (phone: 563-4551). The city provides additional bus service on game days.

Golf – The NCC maintains two public 18-hole courses, the *Champlain* (Aylmer Rd.; phone: 777-0449) and the *Capital Golf Course* (Rte. 31; phone: 521-2612), while more than 30 private clubs within an hour's drive of downtown Ottawa are open to non-members for a greens fee.

Hiking – Information on trails, including Sarsaparilla Trail, especially designed for the aged and handicapped, is available from the NCC or the Ontario Ministry of Natural Resources (phone: 992-4231). There are bird watching trails starting at the *Ottawa-Carleton Conservation Centre* (phone: 828-3620). One trail stretches 125 miles (200 km) from the outskirts of Ottawa to Kingston, Ontario (phone: 828-1679, for information).

Hockey – The Ottawa area has two Junior A teams. The Ottawa *67s* (phone: 232-6767) play at the *Civic Centre* in Lansdowne Park and the *Hull Olympiques* (phone: 777-2791) play at *Guertin Arena* in Hull.

Horse Racing – Two racetracks offer harness racing: *Rideau-Carleton Raceway* (from July through November only), on the southern edge of Ottawa (phone: 822-2211); and the *Connaught Park Raceway* (year-round), in Hull (phone: 771-6111).

Jogging – Ottawa has many wonderful jogging paths. Among them are two that run along either side of the Rideau Canal, each about 5 miles long. There is also a path that runs parallel to the Ottawa River Parkway.

Skating – During the winter, the Rideau Canal freezes and is transformed into a 5-mile-long outdoor skating rink, stretching south from the Ottawa River between Colonel By Drive and Queen Elizabeth Driveway. During the day and at night, when the rink is lighted, thousands of people skate on what is the world's longest outdoor skating rink; in the morning, some people even skate to work.

Skiing – *Camp Fortune* in the Gatineau Hills is only minutes from downtown Ottawa (on Highway 5; phone: 819-827-1717). In addition, the region has numerous downhill courses, including *Edelweiss* (phone: 819-459-2859) and *Vorlage* (phone: 819-459-2301), both in Wakefield; *Mont Cascades* (on Highway 307; phone: 819-827-0301); and *Mt. Pakenham* (on Routes 17 and 29; phone: 819-624-5290). All of these places rent skis and offer instruction. There are also more than 60 miles of cross-country ski trails in the Gatineau Hills.

Soccer – Now the leading sport in the region, with 14,000 registered players, soccer games are played throughout the city from May to October. The *Ottawa Intrepid* plays in the professional Canadian Soccer League at the *Lansdowne Park Stadium* (Bank St.). See local papers for game times, or call 722-7774.

Tennis – Free courts are located throughout the city, many of them with floodlights for night play. Call the city recreation department for information (phone: 563-3222).

Water Sports – Canoes and paddleboats can be rented at many locations, including the Rideau Canal on Fifth Avenue and Dows Lake at the southern end of the main stretch of the canal (phone: 232-1001). Sailboat rentals and lessons are available on the Rideau and Ottawa rivers (phone: 733-5100). There's good swimming at Lac Phillippe, Lac Lapeche, and Meech Lake in the Gatineau Hills, though all three tend to get crowded and the NCC has begun charging daily fees for cars and motorcycles. Ontario and Quebec require fishing licenses, which are available for a modest fee at most fishing tackle stores.

 THEATER: For a complete list of current offerings and performance schedules, check the local publications. The *National Arts Centre* (965 Elgin St.; phone: 237-4440) maintains one repertory company that performs in French. Touring companies often appear at one of the *NAC*'s three theaters.

The *Ottawa Little Theatre* presents amateur productions with a professional flair in a 510-seat modern hall (400 King Edward Ave.; phone: 233-8948). The *Great Canadian Theatre Company* (910 Gladstone; phone: 236-5192) has a reputation for doing strong theme plays. *Théâtre de L'Ile* (1 Rue Wellington in Hull; phone: 819-771-6669) stages popular works in French.

MUSIC: Canada's *National Symphony Orchestra,* the local *Ottawa Symphony Orchestra,* and many guest artists perform at the *National Arts Centre* (65 Elgin St.; phone: 237-4440). The *Orpheus Operatic Society* stages musicals at the High School of Commerce Auditorium (Rochester St. at the Queensway; phone: 729-4318).

NIGHTCLUBS AND NIGHTLIFE: No more jokes about Ottawa rolling up the sidewalks at 6 PM. The city after dark has changed beyond recognition in recent years, with nightclubs offering everything from the big band sound to hot jazz, from male strippers to Second City–style comedy. The once dreary Elgin and Somerset Streets downtown are now stretches of chic sidewalk restaurants and boutiques. *Byward Market* is even livelier, with street entertainers on warm summer nights adding to the appeal of dozens of good restaurants and clubs. *Barrymore's* (323 Bank St.; phone: 238-5842) is the center for hard rock and big-name bands. Another hot rock spot is *Grand Central* (141 George St.; phone: 233-1216), which offers live dance music 6 nights a week. Local rock and blues bands are featured 6 nights a week at *On Tap* (160 Rideau St.; phone: 236-6827), a popular hangout for the university crowds. *Molly McGuire's* (130 George St.; phone: 235-1972) is an Irish pub that features rock bands on Sundays. In Hull, *Roxanne's* (721 St. Joseph Blvd.; 819-770-1525) is open until 3 AM nightly.

If your ears demand something a little more soothing, there also are lots of piano bars. Try *Perrier's* (*Delta Hotel,* Queen St.; phone: 238-6000), *Lautrec's* (*Radisson Hotel,* 100 Kent St.; phone: 238-1122), *Le Bar* (*Roxborough Hotel,* Metcalfe St.; phone: 237-5171), *Friday's Roast Beef House* (Elgin St.; phone: 237-5353), *Zoe's* (*Château Laurier,* Wellington St.; 232-6411), and *Full House Parlour* (Somerset St. West; phone: 238-6734).

Jazz is popular in Ottawa. For the latest jazz info, call the *Jazzline* (phone: 232-7755). Mainstream jazz groups play at the *Glue Pot Pub* (340 Queen St.; phone: 594-8222) on Monday evenings from 9 PM to 1 AM. Other jazz joints include *Vine's Wine Bar* (54 York St.; phone: 563-4270), *Applause* restaurant (246 Slater St.; phone: 594-4524), and the *Five-fifteen* restaurant and pub (779 Bank St.; phone: 235-6785). The *Downstairs Club* (207 Rideau; 234-9942) and the *Rainbow Bistro* (75 Murray; phone: 594-5123) are lively blues spots.

Folk and country can be heard live at the *Bank Café* (294 Bank St.; phone: 238-1757), *Cracker's* (3071 Carling; phone: 820-5464), *Cracker's Two* (175 Richmond; 722-3201), *Ozzie's* (85 Holland; phone: 722-8500), *Patty's Place* (1070 Bank; phone: 235-1020), *Rasputin's* (696 Bronson; phone: 230-5102), *T.J.'s Speakeasy* (91 Holland; phone: 729-4765), and *Whispers* (249 Richmond; phone: 722-9603).

Good dinner-dance spots include the *Canadian Grill* in the elegant *Château Laurier* hotel (Confederation Sq. at Rideau and Elgin; phone: 232-6411), *Talk of the Town* (50 Gloucester; phone: 238-6353), and the *Villa Lucia Supper Place* (3430 Carling; phone: 596-1346).

For stand-up comedy there's *Yuk Yuk's* (*Beacon Arms Hotel,* 88 Albert; phone: 236-5233). Reservations are needed for Friday and Saturday nights. *Komedy Knights* at the *Grand Central* (141 George; phone: 233-1435) features North American headliners Tuesday nights. There's improvisational comedy at the *Improv* (292-B Elgin; phone: 726-6339) Wednesdays through Sundays at 9 PM. Around midnight it's common for

Ottawans to head over to "the strip" — an area of Hull jammed with clubs and pubs that stay open until 3 AM and later.

BEST IN TOWN

CHECKING IN: Because Ottawa is almost always playing host to conventions and conferences, there are plenty of hotels and motels. But be warned — if there are a number of conventions in town at once, you may have trouble finding a room downtown. Expect to pay $72 or more for a double room (sometimes less on weekends) in the establishments listed as expensive; between $47 and $72 for a moderately priced room; and under $47 (as low as about $8 at the hostel) in those places classed as inexpensive. All telephone numbers are in the 613 area code unless otherwise indicated.

Château Laurier – This is the flagship property of the venerable Canadian National hotel chain. Named for former Prime Minister Sir Wilfrid Laurier, its doors opened in 1912. Its 500 rooms, including a number of ornate suites, have the comfortable feel of aged whiskey and fine cigars. Naturally, this is the favorite Ottawa hostelry of Canada's Establishment, and you'll probably spot Canada's movers and shakers being very sedate and dignified over lunch in the ritzy *Canadian Grill* or cocktails in the elegant *Zoe's* lounge. There is an indoor pool. On Confederation Sq. at Rideau and Elgin (phone: 232-6411). Expensive.

Four Seasons – Built by an innovative local millionaire-developer in the late 1960s, this is the epitome of modern comfort, and its 236 rooms are the city's most expensive. A fashionable dining room and an indoor-outdoor wine bar compete for attention. It also has a small indoor pool, a whirlpool bath, and a sauna. 150 Albert St. (phone: 238-1500). Expensive.

Minto Place – Six blocks from Parliament Hill, this impressive new apartment hotel offers daily, weekly, or monthly rates, with longer-stay discounts. The 418 attractive suites with 1, 2, or 3 rooms have everything from fully equipped kitchens to computer-compatible phones. Most also have 2 bathrooms. There are 2 restaurants — the *Dancing Mermaid* pasta bar and *Noah's* — an indoor pool, and a fitness center. 433 Laurier Ave. W. (phone: 232-2200 or 800-267-3377). Expensive.

Radisson – Formerly the *Holiday Inn Ottawa Centre,* this revised edition is more upscale than its predecessor. A modern high-rise, it has 504 spacious rooms that come equipped with such high-tech novelties as TV sets that will display your bill at the touch of a button and mini-bars that can be locked by a computer at the front desk (for times when the kids are by themselves). Other pluses include a pool and a fitness club; *La Ronde,* the revolving rooftop restaurant; and an underground shopping concourse. *Café Toulouse* is a popular lunch spot, with outdoor tables in summer, and *Lautrec's* piano bar is a pleasant place for cocktails. 100 Kent (phone: 238-1122). Expensive.

Westin – Part of a vast shopping and convention complex, this 24-story establishment has 475 rooms (10 specially equipped for the handicapped), plus a pool, gym, hot tub, and squash courts. Its restaurants serve good, moderately priced food as well as expensive haute cuisine (see *Eating Out*). At lobby level, the hotel connects with *Rideau Centre.* 11 Colonel By Dr. (phone: 560-7000). Expensive.

Lord Elgin – The "dean" of Ottawa accommodations, this imposing granite landmark just below Parliament Hill reopened in 1990 after being totally gutted and rebuilt. It has 312 rooms (48 fewer than before), so they're bigger, brighter, and better equipped. There also are a restaurant, a bar, and boardrooms. 100 Elgin St. (phone: 235-3333 or 800-267-4298). Expensive to moderate.

Beacon Arms – Thanks to a top-to-bottom renovation, this 158-room Ottawa landmark has staged a successful comeback. Considering its location, only a few blocks from Parliament Hill, the rates are a bargain. 88 Albert St. (phone: 235-1413). Moderate.

Cartier Place – One of an increasing number of apartment hotels springing up in Ottawa, offering good facilities at rates below those of the major hotels. There are 132 apartments (studios and 1- and 2-bedrooms) available for any length of stay; maid service is included. 180 Cooper St. (phone: 236-5000). Moderate.

Chimo Inn – A 10-minute drive from downtown Ottawa, this recently renovated spot is popular with families. It has an indoor pool, a sauna, a whirlpool bath, spacious lounges, and 2 reasonably priced restaurants. St. Laurent exit from Queensway, 1199 Joseph Cyr St. (phone: 744-1060 or 800-387-9779). Moderate.

Journey's End – Located on the main freeway at the east and west ends of the city and in downtown Ottawa, these three no-frills motels offer clean, pleasant, air conditioned accommodations. The west-end motel also has housekeeping units. East-end (St. Laurent Blvd. exit; phone: 744-2900); west-end (Eagleson Rd. exit; phone: 592-2200); downtown (290 Rideau St., next to the *Ottawa Little Theatre;* phone: 563-7511; or call 800-668-4200 for all three). Moderate.

Nicholas Gaol International Hostel – Sleep in a 19th-century jail cell, complete with bars (not locked) and bunk-style beds. Twentieth-century guests enjoy creature comforts, like carpeting, lockers, a laundry room, kitchen access, and enlarged cells. There are 160 beds in separate male-female dormitories, with a few family rooms available by reservation. Bike, canoe, and skate rentals. Open to everyone, though hostel members get reduced rates and discounts at about 20 stores and entertainment centers in the city. 75 Nicholas St. (phone: 235-2595). Inexpensive.

 EATING OUT: Ottawa is a great place for almost any kind of food you fancy because of the city's role as a host for foreign government missions. French and French Canadian fare are specialties in this bilingual, bicultural city, but there's also a strong showing of other ethnic foods, ranging from Russian to Chinese. Expect to pay $35 or more for a meal for two in restaurants classed as expensive; between $20 and $30 at those places listed as moderate; and under $20 in establishments categorized as inexpensive. Prices do not include drinks, wine, or tips. All telephone numbers are in the 613 area code unless otherwise indicated.

Chez Jean Pierre – Former US Embassy chef Jean Pierre Muller works culinary wonders in his own French dining spot. The prices are steep, but patrons usually don't mind the hefty check after such a pleasurable meal. Closed Sundays and Mondays. Reservations necessary. Major credit cards accepted. 210 Somerset St. (phone: 235-9711). Expensive.

Le Jardin – Widely acknowledged for its excellent food and consistent quality, it specializes in French cuisine and pledges never to use canned or frozen products. The decor is pleasing: an 1875 stone house that has won a Heritage Canada award for its renovation. Open nightly for dinner. Reservations recommended. Major credit cards accepted. 127 York St. (phone: 238-1828). Expensive.

L'Orée du Bois – A 15-minute drive across the river from Ottawa and up into the Gatineau Hills, near the Camp Fortune ski slopes, this restaurant enjoys a beautiful wooded setting and a reputation for excellent French cuisine. Specialties include *pavé au poivre vert, pot-au-feu de la mer, saumon a l'oseille,* and *canard au cidre.* Lunch for groups by reservation. Closed Sundays and Mondays. Major credit cards accepted. Reservations necessary on Saturday nights. Kingsmere Rd., Old Chelsea (phone: 819-827-0332). Expensive to moderate.

Bay Street Bistro – Though the waiters here can be a bit brusque at times, the "Italian-Californian" food is usually excellent. A sidewalk patio is open during the summer. Open daily; on Sundays for dinner only. Reservations necessary for weekday lunches. Major credit cards accepted. 160 Bay, near the Public Archives (phone: 234-1111). Moderate.

Daly's – Long and narrow so everyone can share the gorgeous view of the canal and the *National Arts Centre,* this pleasant eatery in the *Westin* hotel is classy without being pretentious or over-priced. Families will find their youngsters immediately occupied with crayons and drawing paper the moment they sit down. The staff is crisp, efficient, and friendly. Open daily. No reservations at lunch. Major credit cards accepted. Colonel By Dr. (phone: 560-7000). Moderate.

GuadalaHarry's – A Mexican village lurking behind a 19th-century stone façade. Incongruous, yes, but the noisy, harmonious atmosphere makes this a great place to go with the gang. Reservations advised. Open daily. Major credit cards accepted. 18 York St. (phone: 234-8229). Moderate.

Haveli – This East Indian restaurant has grown in size and popularity, with its much-talked-about specialties, including marinated leg of lamb and Ghandi's favorite — a complete vegetarian dinner. The decor is opulent dark wood and burnished brass. Lunch menu changes daily. Closed Sundays. Reservations advised. Major credit cards accepted. 87 George St., *Market Mall* upstairs (phone: 230-3566). Moderate.

Mamma Teresa – This firmly ensconced Italian restaurant has fine food and a comfortable atmosphere. Veal is the specialty, and dishes are served with home-made pasta, plenty of fresh bread, and deep-fried zucchini. There's a good selection of Italian wines. Open daily. Reservations advised. Major credit cards accepted. 300 Somerset St. W. (phone: 236-3023). Moderate.

Marble Works – Diners will enjoy the warm heritage atmosphere in this restored stone building. The interior is dominated by heavy oak beams and soft lighting. The menu offers the usual chicken, steak, and seafood, and a daily chef's dinner selection. Sunday brunch is very popular. Open daily. Major credit cards accepted. Reservations advised. 14 Waller St. (phone: 235-6764). Moderate.

Moroccan Village – Once a tiny, popular eatery on the outskirts of the city, it's now moved to larger premises in the busy *Byward Market* area. The atmosphere is as appealing as the traditional Moroccan food. Open daily. Reservations advised. Major credit cards accepted. 77 Clarence (phone: 230-2421). Moderate.

Opus Bistro – It doesn't look like much from the outside, but the attractive interior more than makes up for it. The food is well above average and the prices are reasonable. Cajun cooking is the specialty. Open Tuesdays through Saturdays for dinner only. Reservations necessary. Visa and MasterCard accepted. 1331 Wellington St. (phone: 722-9549). Moderate.

The Place Next Door – Tom Jones and Shirley MacLaine are among the celebrities who have eaten here, but the restaurant is also loved by locals who line up on weekends to get in. It's all because of some very good steaks and seafood and the presence of personable owner Dave Smith and his brother Scottie. Ample free parking in an area where parking is expensive. Open daily. Reservations advised. Major credit cards accepted. 320 Rideau St. (phone: 232-1741). Moderate.

Ritz 3 – There are five of them, actually, and each one is different and first rate. For example, the one on Clarence Street has pizza with unusual toppings — everything from scallops and mustard on watercress to figs and shrimp. Demand is so great, however, that they won't take reservations at some locations; call first: 15 Clarence St. (phone: 234-3499); 274 Elgin (phone: 235-7027); 1665 Bank (phone: 238-3270);

226 Nepean — known as *Tidbitz* (phone: 238-8752); and on the Driveway at the canal (phone: 238-8998). Major credit cards accepted. Moderate.

Khyber Pass – Noted for its authentic Afghan dishes (including vegetarian specials) and ample servings, this *Byward Market* restaurant has grown in both size and reputation. Open daily. Reservations advised. Major credit cards accepted. 271 Dalhousie St. (phone: 235-0881). Inexpensive.

Zak's – The 1950s are back. Highlighted by vinyl-swathed banquettes, metal paper napkin dispensers, and "Wake Up Little Susie" playing on the jukebox, the food at this real diner is exactly what you'd expect, with such "specialties" as burgers (great) and deep-fried clams. Open daily until midnight, at least. Major credit cards accepted. Reservations for groups of 15 or more. 14 *Byward Market* (phone: 233-0433). Inexpensive.

QUEBEC CITY

The key battle that determined the fate of French Canada lasted only about 20 minutes. It occurred on the morning of September 13, 1759, on the Plains of Abraham in Quebec City, the capital of New France. The city had been under siege by the British general James Wolfe since July, but had stood firm against the attacks. On the evening of September 12, however, Wolfe led a group of soldiers up the steep hill from Anse au Foulon (formerly called Wolfe's Cove) and assembled the force on the Plains of Abraham. That is where the astonished and horrified French found them the following morning when the Marquis de Montcalm, commander of the city's defenses, rushed his troops into battle. In the ensuing struggle, both Wolfe and Montcalm were killed (Wolfe died on the battlefield, Montcalm shortly after in the city) and the French were decisively defeated. Canada was to be British. But according to legend, as smoke obscured the battlefield and the dream of New France died with its last defenders, a voice was heard across the Plains, crying: *"Je me souviens"* — "I remember."

Those words have become the motto of Quebec Province, and nowhere do they resound with more conviction than in Quebec City, itself the most vivid and tangible remnant of New France in Canada. Rising on the massive cliff of Cape Diamond some 350 feet above the St. Lawrence River, Quebec City is the foundation of French culture and the rock upon which Canadian federalism often has come close to foundering. Though the English won control of Canada, Quebec City retained its French language, culture, and heritage. And through subsequent invasions by the British and Americans in the course of its history and the contemporary French-English controversy concerning the independence of Quebec, the city survives as a stronghold of French culture on an English-speaking continent.

Quebec City was the first French settlement in North America, and despite 2 centuries of English rule, it is still fiercely French today. Of the metropolitan population of 576,000, 95% is of French stock, primarily from Normandy and Brittany on the northwest coast of France. These Quebecois have a deeply rooted heritage. They are a family-oriented, provincial people, and their city reflects this attitude toward life.

Most everyone here speaks French; newspapers, plays, and conversations generally are in French, though many people can and do speak English, particularly those who work in businesses catering to tourists.

Many of the buildings in the old section of the city are restored 17th- and 18th-century stone houses, similar to those in the villages of provincial France. The cuisine is French or hearty Quebecois — thick pea soups, meat pies, and rich maple syrup pies for dessert. Street signs, store names, and customs attest to the city's French character. Even the walls that surround the Old City of Quebec (Quebec City is the only walled city on the continent) seem to protect its insular culture, and they demarcate historic Quebec from the newer parts of the city, where modern hotels, shopping malls, and office buildings acknowledge the 20th century.

The French-inspired architecture and the dramatic natural setting of Quebec City combine to make it one of the most beautiful cities in North America. Sometimes called the Gibraltar of America, Quebec City is carved into the 350-foot cliff of Cape Diamond.

At the foot of Cape Diamond is the St. Lawrence River, caught midway on its long journey from Lake Ontario to the Atlantic Ocean at the Gulf of St. Lawrence. As huge as the St. Lawrence is — and it is miles wide at points both above and below Quebec City — Cape Diamond almost seems to tame it, lunging eastward toward its confluence with a small tributary, the St. Charles, at the point where it narrows to a mere three-quarters of a mile.

To the southeast stands another promontory that forms the foundation of the town of Lévis. Some 25 miles (40 km) to the northeast, the hills culminate in the high peak of Mont Ste.-Anne, one of the finest ski areas in Canada. Quebec City is a city on a hill, with a spectacular panoramic view. Turn to the right and you're on your way to the Gaspé Peninsula, with its poor but picturesque villages; turn left and you are soon at Montreal, a mere 153 miles (246 km) away; go straight north and you bump into the fabulous Laurentian slopes, which the Quebecois call the Laurentides.

The history of Quebec City seems to be stratified, starting at the foot of Cape Diamond and progressing up the hill as the young settlement developed. Its history flows from the river, where the Amerindians inhabited the land for thousands of years, using the river as their main source of transportation. Jacques Cartier sailed by Cape Diamond in 1535 and gave the great rock its name. When Samuel de Champlain sailed down the St. Lawrence in the early 17th century, he was attracted by the strategically located site and founded the city in 1608. Champlain established his first "habitation" here, a trading post comprised of a store, a few houses, and surrounding fortifications. The site of this development, now known as Place Royale, is located at the foot of Cape Diamond near the river. Place Royale became the center of a fur trading colony — a meeting place for the merchants who governed the community as well as a commercial center and residential area where wealthy Quebec merchants built their homes. As more colonists and missionaries arrived, the settlement began to expand up the hillside. In 1647, the Château St. Louis was built as a governor's residence at the top of the cliff (today the spectacular *Château Frontenac* hotel occupies this site.)

The Canadian headquarters of the Roman Catholic Church also was established in Old Upper Town soon after Bishop Laval settled in Quebec City in 1659. The Church played a major part in the development and character of the province. For more than 3 centuries, the Church acted as a cultural force in the city, initially conservative, but becoming more liberal in recent years.

Quarrels between the Church and the trading company motivated the King of France to send over a royal *intendant* — a royal overseer of sorts — to administer the province in 1663. Jean Talon, the first intendant, and Comte Louis de Buade de Frontenac, the governor, dealt with this conflict and also settled problems with various Indian tribes that had been attacking the young settlement. Together they fostered an atmosphere of peace and security during which the town developed as the center of New France.

This period was cut short by a much more significant struggle for power — between the two major colonizing forces, France and England. In 1690, Frontenac subdued an attack on the city led by Sir William Phipps, the British Governor of Massachusetts. Three years later, walls were constructed to fortify the city's defenses. In 1759, during the Seven Years' War, Quebec City fell to the British as a result of the Battle of the Plains of Abraham. The settlement, known as the Act of Quebec (1774) guaranteed French Canadians, "as much as British laws would allow," in terms of cultural and religious rights. But the battle had a profound effect on the Quebecois psyche. Many members of the aristocratic class returned to France. Those who stayed taught their children what had been lost on the Plains of Abraham: "Je me souviens." It was the beginning of British rule.

But the British weren't the only ones with an interest in Quebec. The 18th century ended with the Quebecois resisting an invasion by American troops led by General Montgomery and Colonel Benedict Arnold. This siege lasted a little more than a month, ending with the arrival of the British fleet and the retreat of the exhausted American troops. Concerned over further attacks, the English completed the wall surrounding the city.

Throughout the 19th century, Quebec City remained an important political center and was named the provinces' capital in 1867. Peace also brought economic change. Timber and shipbuilding became the two major industries, and the city maintained its position as a significant commercial center until the mid-19th century when Montreal and Toronto surpassed it.

But Quebec City remains the most important historical center of Canada. In order for a community to flourish, it must have a sense of its past; to visit Quebec City is to know that all was not lost on the Plains of Abraham. The Old City walls, which the United Nations declared a historic site in 1985, have been restored, and they surround the most historic section of the city, Old Quebec. The Quebec government declared the area around Place Royale a special zone in the 1960s, and more than 90% of the 17th- and 18th-century houses and buildings have been restored. Museums, cultural centers, and restaurants now occupy these restored houses. The Old Upper Town is a well-preserved area of narrow cobblestone streets lined with historic buildings. You haven't really tasted Old Quebec until you go to one of its oldest buildings, now *Aux Anciens Canadiens* restaurant, for a hearty Quebecois meal topped off with maple syrup pie served with heavy cream.

Beyond the city walls, farther up the hill, lies 20th-century Quebec. Here is a concentration of all the amenities found in any other modern provincial capital — a convention center, an underground shopping gallery, Place Quebec, adjoined by the *Québec Hilton International;* several other luxurious high-rise hotels; and the stately National Assembly, as the legislature is called. Beyond spreads the suburb of Ste.-Foy, rapidly developed in the past 3 decades to accommodate a growing population. Many Quebecois work in Ste.-Foy at the suburb's two major shopping malls or at Laval University, a major employer and, with 35,000 students, also a big draw to the city. The largest employer of all is the provincial government, with more than 53,000 civil servants.

Around Parliament Hill you find that Quebec City's present is inextricably bound with its past. Sculptures of historically prominent Canadians are carved into niches on the National Assembly. These figures and the nearby Plains of Abraham and Citadelle — the star-shaped fortress that won the city the sobriquet "Gibraltar of America" — record Quebec City's struggle to become what it is today.

In many ways the struggle still continues, though its form has changed. The weapons are words rather than cannons, but the French-English controversy in Canada still simmers. During the late 1950s and early 1960s, what historians refer to as the Quiet Revolution swept Quebec. A liberal government headed by Premier Jean Lesage introduced major education and social reforms which are often associated with the growth of Quebec nationalism.

At the same time a growing feeling of exclusion from the mainstream of Canadian political-economic life gave rise to a new political party: the Parti Québecois. Headed by Réné Lévesque, it was determined to lead the province to political independence from English-speaking Canada, while still maintaining an economic link. The PQ was elected to power in 1976 and re-elected in 1981, though a provincial referendum on independence in 1980 was rejected. In the 1985 and 1989 provincial elections, the PQ was defeated by the less separatist-oriented Liberal Party, which strongly favors Quebec staying within the existing Canadian political system.

But Quebec's nationalism hasn't disappeared as an issue. There have been moments in its recent past when the province's secession seemed imminent. It is often said that "if you scratch the surface" you will find some level of nationalism in every Quebecois. Above all, the last decade has seen the emergence of a new era, one that finds the people economically confident and turning to the world at large for fresh opportunities. It is fair to say that this generation, well represented by a pragmatic government, aspires to economic stability rather than political turmoil.

At press time, the future of Quebec remained uncertain, as its drive toward separatism persisted. In response to Quebec's refusal to sign the Constitution in 1987, Prime Minister Mulroney proposed the Meech Lake Accord, designed to give all the provinces more power. Under the Accord, Quebec would have been recognized as a "distinct society" and been given the power to nullify the Constitution's Charter of Rights. When Manitoba and Newfoundland refused to ratify the agreement, the Accord, which requires unanimous approval, failed — giving rise to a new movement toward Quebec's secession from Canada. In a July 1990 poll, 60% of Quebecois said they favored sovereignty. Nearly 50% wanted full independence. Through almost 4 centuries and six invasions, Quebec City has remained authentically French. The strength of its collective memory ("*Je me souviens*") seems to be holding fast.

QUEBEC CITY AT-A-GLANCE

SEEING THE CITY: *L'Astral,* the *Loews Le Concorde* hotel's revolving rooftop restaurant-bar, situated on the highest point of Cape Diamond, has the best panorama of Quebec City and surrounding areas, day or night. On a clear day, you can see as far as Ile d'Orléans, the most picturesque island of the St. Lawrence River, and, some 25 miles away, a chain of mountains dominated by Mont St.-Anne, the region's best ski resort. *L'Astral* is open from 11:45 AM to 3 PM and 6 to 11 PM daily except Sundays, when it opens at 10 AM for brunch. 1225 Place Montcalm (phone: 647-2222).

There are many fine views of the river, but two of the best are from Dufferin Terrace, a boardwalk flanking the *Château Frontenac* hotel, and Earl Grey Terrace, an observatory adjoining the Plains of Abraham, between Wolfe and Montcalm Streets, in Parc des Champs de Bataille.

SPECIAL PLACES: The best way to see Quebec City is by strolling down its streets and alleys. Visitors definitely should ride the *funiculaire,* the outdoor elevator that links the Lower and Upper Towns. But Quebec City is more a feast for feet, a people-size place where the scale of sites is that of an easy day's perambulation. The rewards for lazy, languid strolls are quaint cobbled streets, historic houses, and the sort of secure claustrophobia conferred by a city that you can almost drape around your shoulders. But first arm yourself with a map. The streets are laid out in a haphazard fashion, particularly in the older sections. Old Lower Town centers around Place Royale at river level. If you walk north and west, you'll find a new cluster of cafés, pubs, art galleries, boutiques, and antiques stores in what used to be the city's financial district. The stock exchange and the old banks closed after Quebec's importance as a trading center waned. But just a few more blocks north, you'll find the spruced up port area, with old warehouses reincarnated as fashionable boutiques. Old Upper Town revolves around Place d'Armes, at the top of the funicular next to the *Château Frontenac.* Parliament Hill, farther up the hill, is the site of government buildings abutting sleek high-rise hotels. Beyond them all are the suburbs. The Plains of Abraham have been made into a lovely park, with miles of walking and jogging paths, picnic tables, bird-feeding stations, gardens, and great river views.

OLD LOWER TOWN

Place Royale – This small, cobblestone square is known as the Canadian "cradle of French civilization." It was here that Champlain built his first "habitation" in 1608, which included buildings for lodging, a store, a stockade, and gardens. During the French regime, the square was used as a marketplace, and successful merchants built their homes here. In the center of the square is a bronze bust of Louis XIV. The area has been declared a special historic zone by the Quebec government, and its restoration is almost complete. Despite the destruction of some of the houses, the place and the streets leading off it are lined with the greatest concentration of 17th- and 18th-century buildings in North America. Most of the buildings clustered around the Church of Notre-Dame-des-Victoires are architectural gems that began life as the houses of wealthy merchants. As the centuries slipped by, the area went downhill and the townsfolk simply forgot its history. Then, in 1960, a fire bared some strange brick walls. "They don't build walls like that anymore," noted assorted passersby until some of them realized that these were genuine historic treasures. The main floors of some of these homes are open to the public as museums, cultural centers, art galleries, and restaurants, while some of the upper floors are residential. Off Notre-Dame at the foot of Cape Diamond near the river.

Place-de-Paris – In 1984, France paid tribute to this city and province by inaugurating the Place au Quebec in Paris. To reciprocate, a monument was erected on the exact spot where the French first set foot on Quebec soil — at the corner of today's Rue de la Place and Rue de l'Union — and dubbed it Place-de-Paris.

Maisons Bruneau, Drapeau, and Rageot – The multimedia production, "Place Royale: Business Centre of New France," which describes the business activities of the area during colonial times, is presented here daily. No admission charge. 3A Place Royale, beside La Maisons des Vins.

La Batterie Royale – Built in 1691, this royal artillery, one of the oldest in Quebec City, has been entirely restored. On the corner of Rue sous le Fort and St.-Pierre.

Entrepôt Thibodeau – This house is now the Place Royale tourist reception center. Stop here first to pick up the "Place Royale" brochure, which describes points of interest in the area. Guided tours (in English) are available. Open daily from 10 AM to 6 PM June 24 to *Labor Day;* in winter, with reservations only (phone: 643-2158). No admission charge. Place Marché Finlay (phone: 643-6631, from June 1 to Sept. 3).

Maison Fornel – With foundations dating back to 1658 and vaulted cellars constructed in 1735, this restored house is now an atmospheric exhibition center. Its reconstruction in 1964 initiated the Place Royale restoration project. The exhibition "Place Royale: 400 Years of History," provides a good perspective on the area's past and ongoing restoration; a brochure in English is available. No admission charge. Rue St.-Pierre just south of Ruelle de la Place.

Notre-Dame-des-Victoires – Our Lady of Victories was built in 1688 and renamed to commemorate the triumph of the French over the English during the attacks of 1690 and 1711. The small stone structure was rebuilt in 1759, after the bombardment, in accordance with the original design. The exterior is quite modest, yet inside there is exquisite woodwork, including a main altar minutely carved in the shape of an old fort, paintings from the School of Rubens, and old battle flags. Mass is still said every Saturday at 7 PM, Sunday (call for hours). Open daily May 15 to October 15. Off season, closed Mondays. No admission charge. Place Royale (phone: 692-1650).

Maison des Vins – This restored home now houses an excellent wine store with an extensive selection of imported wines. The establishment is worth a visit for a look at its exposed brick walls, vaulted candlelit wine cellars, and its array of bottles ranging from a Mouton Rothschild 1879 (valued between about $13,000 and $21,000), to the local specialty, caribou, a mixture of wine and alcohol that is stronger than wine and, according to some Quebecois, more effective for getting through the long, cold winters. Open Tuesdays through Saturdays. Reservations are essential for guided tours. 1 Place Royale (phone: 643-1214).

Maison Chevalier – Three buildings, constructed in the 17th and 18th centuries for several merchants, including Jean Baptiste Chevalier, that have been linked to form an interesting ethnographic museum. Exhibits vary, but include old toys, costumes, furniture, and folk art, open daily from June 22 to September 3. No admission charge. Corner of Cul de Sac and Notre Dame (phone: 643-2158).

Maison Jolliet – This restored house was the home of explorer Louis Jolliet, who, accompanied by Jacques Marquette, discovered the Mississippi River in 1672. His house now contains the entrance to the *funiculaire,* which for 60¢ saves you the trouble of having to climb back up to Upper Town. In operation daily from 7:30 AM to 11 PM. Opposite Sous le Fort at the foot of Escalier du Petit Champlain (phone: 692-1132).

Musée de la Civilisation – Located between Place Royale and the Old Port near the St. Lawrence River, this building, designed by architect Moshe Safdie, won an award for the way in which its modern architecture is integrated into the historic neighborhood of the Old Port. Along with galleries, a stone house built in 1732 is enclosed in this large museum. Open Tuesdays through Sundays, except during the summer (June 24 to *Labor Day*), open daily. Admission charge for adults over 16. 85 Rue Dalhousie, near Place Royale (phone: 643-2158).

OLD UPPER TOWN

Place d'Armes – A small square that served as a meeting place and parade ground during the French regime. In the center of the square stands a Gothic fountain surmounted by the granite and bronze Monument of Faith, constructed in 1916 in memory of the Récolets (Franciscan) missionaries who arrived in 1615. Today the square is a good orientation point in Old Upper Town, the section of Old Quebec built above the cliff, where military, religious, and residential buildings from the 17th, 18th, and 19th centuries have been restored. One of the loveliest, La Maison Vallée (which dates from 1732), has become the home of the Tussaud-like wax museum *(Musée de Cire)*. For traditional French Canadian fare and decor, check out *Aux Anciens Canadiens* (see *Eating Out*) in a house built in 1677 and named after the classic Canadian volume whose author, Philippe Aubert de Gaspé, once lived on the premises.

Château Frontenac – This grand hotel owned by C.P. Hotels, Ltd., in all its classic French glory, is Quebec City's most recognizable landmark. Everything about this structure, built in 1893, announces its grandeur, from its broad, slanting copper roof, its turrets and towers, and its imposing red brick walls to its magnificent setting high above the St. Lawrence River. The site on which it is built has undergone numerous transitions. First a fort built by Champlain in 1620, it became a fortress in 1636, and eventually became known as Château St.-Louis, a regal residence of the Governors of New France. Two centuries later, in 1834, it was completely razed by a fire. History buffs will find an interesting display tracing the château's past in the main lobby. Spend some time strolling around the lobby, the inner courtyard, or taking in the excellent river view from the circular cocktail lounge. The Dufferin Terrace, built in 1834, with its spectacular view of the historic Old Lower Town and the Ile d'Orléans, is a favorite spot for relaxing on summer nights. At the north end of the terrace there's a statue of Samuel de Champlain, watching over the city he founded in 1608. 1 Av. des Carrières (phone: 692-3861).

Jardin des Gouverneurs – Originally the private garden of Château St.-Louis, it was opened to the public in 1838. Here stands the Wolfe-Montcalm monument, erected in 1828. It is one of the few monuments in the world commemorating both the triumphant and the defeated: "Their courage gave them the same lot; history, the same fame; posterity, the same monument." Open daily. No admission charge. Next to *Château Frontenac* at Av. des Carrières and Rue Mont Carmel.

Musée du Fort – This museum is a good place to get your bearings historically. A 30-minute sound-and-light show presented on a 450-foot-square model of the 18th-century city recreates the most important battles and sieges of Quebec, including the Battle of the Plains of Abraham and the attack by Arnold and Montgomery during the American Revolution. There's also a wide variety of guides and history books in English. Open daily (call for hours), except December 1 through *Christmas.* Shows alternate in English and French. Admission charge. 10 Rue Ste.-Anne (phone: 692-2175).

Notre-Dame-de Quebec Basilica – First built in 1647, this Roman Catholic church of the Cardinal Archbishop of Quebec once served the diocese of all French North America, and still serves the oldest parish north of Mexico. The façade is unusual for its two unequal towers; the vaulted interior contains an impressive number of religious works of art. Open daily. No admission charge. Rue Buade and Côte de la Fabrique.

Quebec Seminary – Beyond the iron gates lies a group of 17th-century buildings that were part of a training school for Catholic priests founded in 1663 by François de Montmorency Laval, the first Bishop of Quebec. The main chapel is worth a visit for a look at its marble altars, valuable relics, and the sarcophagus of Bishop Laval; the sundial over the door dates back to 1773. The museum here has a collection of religious and secular art from both Quebec and Europe as well as some early scientific instruments. The museum is closed Mondays. Admission charge. 9 Rue de l'Université (phone: 692-2843). Visits to other parts of the seminary are possible from June 1 to August 31 but must be arranged in advance; call 692-3981 for information.

Holy Trinity Anglican Cathedral – This stately structure was the first Church of England cathedral ever built (1804) outside of the British Isles. The pews, including the Royal Pew — which may be occupied only by the British sovereign or her representative — are composed of solid English oak; the large stained glass windows are awe-inspiring. Open daily except Mondays, 1 to 3 PM. 31 Desjardins (phone: 692-2193).

Ursuline Convent – Founded in 1639, it is the oldest school for women in North America. The convent itself was twice destroyed by fire, but some original walls still stand. A few of the present buildings date from the 17th century. The chapel contains a number of interesting relics and valuable paintings; its votive lamp, first lit in 1717, has never been extinguished. The defeated General Montcalm is buried in a tomb in the chapel. (His skull is preserved under glass at *Musée Marie des Ursulines,* 12 Donnaconna.) Open daily except Mondays; call for hours. Closed in December. Admission charge. Desjardins and Donnaconna (phone: 694-0694).

Montmorency Park – Named in honor of Bishop Laval — François de Montmorency Laval — this park, straddling the hill between the Old Upper Town and Old Lower Town, affords good views of the Lower Town, the harbor, and the surrounding area. A monument to Sir Georges Etienne Cartier, a French-Canadian political leader, and another to Louis Hébert (the first farmer to settle in Quebec City), stand in the center of the park. On the hill, off Côte de la Montagne.

Laval Monument – An impressive statue honoring Bishop Laval, Canada's first bishop, who arrived in 1659 and was one of the most prominent citizens of New France. He founded the Quebec Seminary, the predecessor of Laval University. The work, sculpted by Philippe Hébert, was unveiled in 1908. At Côte de la Montagne across from Montmorency Park.

PARLIAMENT HILL AND THE PLAINS OF ABRAHAM

La Promenade des Gouverneurs – This 2,200-foot-long walkway leads from Dufferin Terrace up Cape Diamond, beside the Citadelle, all the way to the Plains of Abraham. As you stroll, you have excellent views of the river upstream to the Quebec Bridge and downstream to the Ile d'Orléans. Open daily from late May to October (closed the rest of the year). No admission charge. Begins at the end of Dufferin Terrace.

Citadelle – A massive star-shape fortress that commands a strategic position at the highest point on Quebec's promontory, 350 feet above the St. Lawrence. The French built previous fortifications on this site, but the present citadel was constructed between 1820 and 1832 by the British government as a defense against American attack following the War of 1812. The fortress was never subjected to enemy fire. It was first occupied by British troops, then by the Royal Canadian Artillery, and since 1920 by the Royal 22nd Regiment. From mid-June to the first Monday in September, the Changing of the Guard is performed daily at 10 AM, and the Ceremonial Retreat is enacted at 7 PM on Tuesdays, Thursdays, Saturdays, and Sundays. Closed December through February except to groups with previous reservations (write *Musée de la Citadelle,* CP 6020, Haute-Ville, Quebec G1R 4V7), and weekday mornings in November and during *Carnaval.* Admission charge. Reached by Côte de la Citadelle (phone: 648-3563).

Plains of Abraham – Named for Abraham Martin, the first St. Lawrence River pilot, this is where Canada's French-English struggle was decided in 1759. Now part of the 250-acre Parc des Champs de Bataille, this was the scene of the battle between the British forces led by General James Wolfe and the French under General Montcalm that sealed the fate of New France. Both generals lost their lives in the struggle and the British gained control of Canada. Many Quebec residents returned to France; those who remained kept alive the idea of a French identity in North America, from which sprang the motto of the province: "Je me souviens." There is an observation post affording excellent river views and various monuments and statues. The *Quebec Museum* (see below) is also on the grounds. Open daily from June 15 to September 14, closed on Mondays for the rest of the year. Beyond the Citadelle to the west, off Grande Allée.

Quebec Museum – Dedicated to Quebec's history and its accomplishments in the fine arts, the museum contains the most significant collection of Quebecois paintings, sculptures, and decorative arts from the late-17th century to the 1980s. Restoration work in the late 1980s has doubled the size of the museum, which now also hosts major exhibits from around the world. Open daily. Admission charge. In Parc des Champs de Bataille, off Grande Allée (phone: 643-2150).

Regimental Museum – This 1750 structure holds an interesting display of ancient weapons, uniforms, and rare documents — some dating back to the time of the French regime. Closed January and February, except to groups reserving ahead, and during *Carnaval.* Admission included in the entrance charge to the Citadelle. Côte de la Citadelle off Rue St.-Louis (phone: 648-3563).

National Assembly – Also known as the Parliament Buildings, these imposing French Renaissance buildings were constructed between 1877 and 1886. The 12 bronze statues in niches on the façade, commemorating people prominent in Quebec and Canada's history, were executed by the Quebec sculptor Hébert. Guided tours, in French and English, are conducted daily in July and August and on weekdays from September to November and from January to May. The Assembly is not in session from June 24 to October or from December 22 to mid-March. Bounded by Rue Dufferin, Blvd. St.-Cyrille E., St.-Augustin, and Grande Allée (phone: 643-7239).

Complex G – This is an example of new Quebec, right down to its straightforward, no-nonsense name. At 31 stories, it is the city's highest building. It houses various ministries and provincial government services. An observation gallery on top is open weekdays from 10 AM to 4 PM and weekends from 1 to 5 PM. No admission charge. Bounded by Blvd. St.-Cyrille E., de la Chevrotière, St.-Amable, and Conroy. (phone: 644-9841).

Grand Théâtre de Québec – Another work of modern architecture, this sleek structure built in 1970 comprises a music conservatory and two entertainment halls. 269 Blvd. St.-Cyrille at the corner of Rue Claire Fontaine (phone: 643-8131).

SUBURBS

Ste.-Foy – This town has grown up quickly in the last 3 decades to become Quebec's major bedroom community. In addition to rows of neat wood and brick houses, the town supports two large shopping malls, *Place Laurier* and *Place Ste.-Foy* (see *Shopping,* below). Follow Grande Allée about 2 miles (3 km) west of the National Assembly.

Laval University – An outgrowth of the Quebec Seminary founded by Bishop Laval, it is the oldest French-language university on the continent. The construction of a sprawling 465-acre campus was begun in 1948 to accommodate the growing numbers of students. One of the school's 25 modern buildings is the physical education and sports complex. Its excellent facilities, including an Olympic-size pool, are open to the public at certain hours, mainly weekends. Off Blvd. Laurier (Rte. 175) and bounded by du Vallon, Myrand, and Chemin Ste.-Foy (phone: 656-2131).

Ile d'Orléans – This island in the St. Lawrence River below Quebec was relatively isolated until a suspension bridge connecting it with the mainland was built in 1935. Because of this, the island retains a great deal of its 18th-century French Canadian influence. Most of the islanders are of Norman or Breton stock, and like their ancestors, most are farmers. (Island apples and strawberries are especially good.) The island is only 21 miles long and about 5 miles wide. You can easily make a complete driving tour in a grand circle, stopping in village after village of 17th- and 18th-century houses and churches. (Route 368 is a 42-mile — 68-km — tour that circles the island.) Ste.-Famille has the most interesting church on the island — a triple-spired structure built in 1742. On the east side of the island are some summer cottages and Ste.-Pétronille, a summer resort village. 10 miles (16 km) northeast of Quebec. Take Autoroute Dufferin down the hill near the National Assembly, then

Route 138. *Beautemps Mauvaistemps* organizes personalized tours of the island, year-round (phone: 828-2275).

■**EXTRA SPECIAL:** Ste.-Anne-de-Beaupré is a small village near Mont Ste.-Anne dominated by a massive cathedral, which is an internationally renowned Catholic shrine. Millions of people have made pilgrimages here, and the piles of crutches, canes, and folding wheelchairs in the cathedral attest to healings that the faithful believe take place. The present basilica (1923) can accommodate 3,000 people. The fountain of Ste.-Anne in front is said to have the healing powers. The sanctuary has a marble statue of Ste. Anne, as well as other venerable religious items. An information bureau has been set up, and guides are available to lead tours.

Mont Ste.-Anne is the most popular winter sports center. Its downhill runs, night skiing, cross-country ski tracks, and lift facilities attract a different breed of pilgrim — in search of miraculous skiing (see below). To reach the ski area, head 5 miles (8 km) beyond the village on Rte. 138 and turn north onto Rte. 360.

Just east of Mont Ste.-Anne is the Réserve nationale de la faune du Cap Tourmente, developed by naturalists to protect the greater snow goose, along with 250 other bird species, which stop here during their seasonal migrations. The noisy October gatherings can easily attract 100,000 screeching birds. In May, ducks, herons, swallows, and red-winged blackbirds build their nests in the many pounds of the region. The reserve also offers a nature-interpretation center. To visit, head east on Route 138 after leaving Ste.-Anne-de-Beaupré and watch for signs for Cap Tourmente (phone: 827-4591, April to October; phone: 653-8186, other times).

En route to Ste.-Anne-de-Beaupré or on the return to Quebec City, stop off at the 274-foot-high Montmorency Falls. In 1759, the English general Wolfe established his headquarters near the top. These old buildings have been made into a beautiful, old hotel, the *Manoir Montmorency,* with a dining room offering a fantastic view over Ile d'Orléans in Quebec City (phone: 663-2877).

SOURCES AND RESOURCES

TOURIST INFORMATION: For tourist information, maps, and brochures, contact the Quebec City Region Tourism and Convention Bureau (60 Rue d'Auteuil; phone: 692-2471), or the reception office of the Quebec Department of Tourism (12 Ste.-Anne; phone: 643-2280 or 800-443-7000 in the Eastern US). The Place Royale restoration has its own information center in Entrepôt Thibodeau, open during summer only (Place Marché Finlay; phone: 643-6631). Another government tourist information center is in Ste.-Foy, off the Pierre-Laporte Bridge. Open daily, year-round (3005 Blvd. Laurier; phone: 651-2882).

English-language city guidebooks are hard to find; most are written in French. *Librairie Garneau* (a bookstore at 47 Buade) and *Musée du Fort* (10 Rue Ste.-Anne) have a fair selection. One useful (and free) publication is the *Quebec City Region* tourist guide published by the Quebec government. For information on its availability, call the Quebec City Region Tourism and Convention Bureau (phone: 692-2471 or 651-2882).

Local Coverage – *Le Soleil,* French morning daily; *Le Journal de Québec,* French morning daily; *Québec Chronicle-Telegraph,* English weekly that hits the newsstands on Wednesdays. *Voilà Québec* is a bilingual quarterly entertainment, sightseeing, and dining guide distributed free in hotels, at the various tourist information centers, or by calling 418-692-2471. For English television programs, tune to CKMI, Channel 5; the English radio station is CBVE at 104.7 FM.

Food – *Les Restaurants,* published by the Quebec Urban Community, lists restaurants in both the city and suburbs (free). Also check *Voilà Québec.*

Telephone – The area code for Quebec City is 418.

Sales Tax – In Quebec City there is a 9% sales tax only on clothing purchases above about CN$500. There is also a 10% sales tax on meals above CN$3.25.

Currency – All prices are quoted in US dollars unless otherwise indicated.

TIPPING: Waiters and waitresses should get 10% to 15% of the total bill, including tax. Hotel maids should be given CN$1 to CN$2 per person, per day, and bellboys, CN$1 per bag (although some hotels do not allow tipping). Taxi drivers usually receive 10% of the total fare. It is unneccessary to tip airport porters.

CLIMATE: Quebec City is generally clear and sunny and has relatively low humidity because of its altitude — about 350 feet above sea level. Summertime temperatures average in the low to mid-70s F (mid-20s C) and edge up to 90F (32C) highs; during the winter, temperatures average around 20F (−6C), though they can plummet to −10F (−23C) in January and February. In addition to cold weather, winter brings snow, and lots of it — 150 to 200 inches for the season. July has the most rainfall, with an average of 4.5 inches. For a 24-hour weather reporting service, call 872-2859; for winter road conditions, 643-6830.

GETTING AROUND: Bus – The *Quebec Urban Community Transit Commission (CTCUQ)* operates buses that serve the metropolitan area from approximately 5:30 AM to 1 AM. Exact change, CN$1.40, (about US$1.20) is required. For route information, call 627-2511. During the winter, *CTCUQ* also runs *Skibus,* which serves several ski areas around Quebec, from 7 AM to 9:30 PM. Look for the red and white snowflake symbol at bus stops throughout the city.

Calèche – Horse-drawn carriages tour Old Quebec, the Parliament area, and the Plains of Abraham year-round. The fare for the 45-minute tour is about $26 for up to five people. A tip is customary for the driver. The *calèches* line up at Rue d'Auteuil near Rue St.-Louis (phone: 687-9797).

Car Rentals – Major firms that serve the city are *Avis* (at the *Québec Hilton International;* 3 Place Quebec; phone: 523-1075; 2785 Blvd. Laurier, phone: 651-5087, and at the *Quebec Inn* hotel near the airport; 7174 Blvd. Hamel; phone: 872-2861); *Budget* (at the *Château Frontenac;* 1 Av. des Carrières; no phone; 29 Côte du Palais, phone: 692-3660; and Place Quebec, 5 Place Quebec, phone: 529-0966); *Hertz* (1200 Germains-des-Prés; phone: 658-6785; 44 Côte du Palais; phone: 694-1224; and the airport; phone: 871-1571); and *Tilden* (295 Rue St.-Paul; phone: 694-1727 and the airport; phone: 871-1224).

Cruises – You can take a cruise on the Saint Lawrence aboard the M/V *Louis Jolliet.* The boat leaves from Chouinard Pier (10 Dalhousie), in the Place Royale section of the city from June through September and by request only from May to mid-June and early September to October (phone: 692-1159). Also available for sailboat lovers are a variety of cruises and tours organized by *Vieux Port Yachting,* with cruises of up to 14 days to as far as the Saguenay River, one of the greatest fjords in the world. Information: *Vieux Port Yachting Inc.,* Quai Renaud, 80 St.-André. C.P. 1543, Terminus Quebec G1K 7H6 (phone: 692-0017).

Ferry – Year-round service links Quebec and Lévis, operating every half hour from 6 AM to midnight, then less frequently. The ferry ride affords panoramic views of both cities (phone: 644-3704).

Taxi – Generally they cannot be hailed in the streets. There are cab stands at the major hotels and in Old Quebec at Place d'Armes and at d'Youville Square. The principal cab companies are *Taxi Co-op* (phone: 525-5191); *Taxi Quebec* (phone: 522-2001); and *Taxi Co-op* in Ste.-Foy (phone: 653-7777). The 20-minute trip from downtown to the airport should run about $12. There's limited shuttle bus service to the airport from major hotels for about $5; check ahead, since service may not begin early enough for some morning flights.

Walking Tours – Quebec City is best seen on foot. To enrich your stroll, rent a tape-recorded tour tracing the city's history from *Sonore Tours* (Place d'Armes; phone: 694-0665); summers only. Or pick up a free copy of *Quebec City Region* — which includes walking tours — at the tourist office, and do it yourself. The Quebec Ministry of Cultural Affairs publishes this folder about Place Royale, which can be obtained at the Place Royale information center in Entrepôt Thibodeau, Place Marché Finlay. *Baillairgé Cultural Tours Inc.* (phone: 658-4799) offers 2¼-hour walking tours of the Old Town, with emphasis on history and architecture, departing from *Musée du Fort,* across the street from the *Château Frontenac,* at 9:30 AM and 2 PM daily. The tour guides are especially interesting and knowledgeable. Tours are available from late June to mid-October. Cost is about $9.35.

Note: You can walk down several flights of wooden steps from Dufferin Terrace, the 80-foot-wide boardwalk flanking the *Château Frontenac* in the Old Upper Town, to Place Royale in Old Lower Town. On the way back, rest your feet by returning on the *funiculaire,* an enclosed elevator–cable car that whisks you back and commands a splendid river view — for about 65¢.

SPECIAL EVENTS: Next to New Orleans's *Mardi Gras,* the *Carnaval de Québec,* a 10-day affair starting on the first Saturday in February, is the biggest blowout in North America. Over half a million people from all over Canada and the US flood the city to celebrate winter. A 7-foot snowman — Le Bonhomme Carnaval — presides over the festivities, which include two parades (one in Upper Town, one in Lower Town), international snow sculpture contests, fireworks, a queen's coronation and ball, a variety of theme parties, and lots of winter sports and events — hockey, skiing, and a canoe race on the frozen St. Lawrence River. The biggest events are scheduled over two weekends. Hotels are generally booked solid during *Carnaval,* so if you want to go, make arrangements several months in advance. Your best bet for last-minute reservations is through the *Carnaval's* lodging committee, which can sometimes book rooms in motels or guesthouses, from December 15 to *Carnaval* time. Note: the phone number changes every year). For general information, contact the *Québec Carnaval,* 290 Joly, Quebec City G1L 1N8 (phone: 626-3716).

For 2 weeks in July, between 600 and 800 artists from all parts of the world and all musical backgrounds gather in the city for the *International Quebec Summer Festival,* one of the largest cultural events in the French-speaking world. Rock, classical repertory, or jazz all can be heard in over 15 public squares and on stages around the city. Most presentations are free of charge. For information, contact the festival office: PO Box 24, Station B, Quebec City G1K 7A1 (phone: 692-4540 or 800-361-5405).

Although a more sedate event, the critically acclaimed *Quinzaine Internationale du Théâtre de Québec* (Quebec International Fortnight of Theater) is held every other year during the last 2 weeks in May. The next one is in 1992. Plays are presented in different theaters around the city in their original language. Admission charge (phone: 694-0206).

MUSEUMS: For complete descriptions of the *Musée du Fort, Musée du Quebec, Musée de la Civilisation,* and Maison Chevalier, see *Special Places.* Other interesting museums include the following:

Musée de Cire – Wax museum. 22 Rue Ste.-Anne (phone: 692-2289).

Musée du Québec – Showcase for Quebec arts and crafts. Parc des Champs de Bataille (phone: 643-2150).

Musée des Ursulines – An interesting permanent exhibition of very rare embroideries, some 500 years old. 12 Donnaconna (phone: 694-0694).

Parc Cartier-Breboeuf – A replica of Jacques Cartier's ship is moored on the St. Charles River. At 175 de l'Espinay near Parc de l'Exposition (phone: 648-4038).

 SHOPPING: Shops are generally open from 9:30 AM to 5:30 PM Mondays through Wednesdays; until 9 PM on Thursdays and Fridays; and until 5 PM on Saturdays. Shops are shuttered on Sundays except for some in Old Quebec. With its 63 shopping centers, numerous commercial streets and flea markets, the region offers a wide variety of shopping opportunities. The main concentration of commercial establishments in Canada is in the suburb of Ste.-Foy, about 2 miles (3 km) west of the *Château Frontenac* on Boulevard Laurier. You can't miss it: four shopping centers built next to one another and housing some 600 shops, boutiques, and department stores. *Place Laurier* is the largest with over 400 stores. *Place Ste.-Foy* (120 stores), *Place de la Cité* (60 stores), and *Place Belle-Cour* (34 stores) are smaller, but offer more sophisticated clothing stores and a pleasant ambience. Also in the suburbs (northwest of Quebec City on Blvd. de la Capitale) is *Les Galeries de la Capitales* (5401 Blvd. des Galeries; phone: 627-5800) with 230 boutiques and department stores, plus a vast indoor amusement park with rides, including a giant merry-go-round, an inside skating rink (open year-round), and a mini-golf course. Open daily. Admission charge for rides. Near the National Assembly is *Place Québec,* a multilevel shopping promenade connected to the *Québec Hilton International* that contains many chic boutiques, two cinemas, and restaurants.

For street shopping, favorite spots include St. Jean Street, Côte-de-la-Fabrique, and Cartier Street in the Old Upper Town, and le Quartier Petit Champlain and the Old Port sector in the Lower Town. Most of the boutiques in the shopping centers can be found on St. Jean Street, which also offers several pubs, cafés, and dining terraces. A continuation of St. Jean Street, Côte-de-la-Fabrique has some of Quebec's more venerable stores, including *Holt Renfrew* and *Simons* (established in 1840). The latter offers a variety of designer collections such as *Anne Klein, Ralph Lauren, Marithé,* and *François Girbaud,* plus an affordable private label collection. For Quebec handicrafts, try the stores along Rue Champlain and Rue du Petit-Champlain, which usually are open on Sundays.

Art lovers and antiques collectors should visit the Old Port section of the city, especially the shops and galleries on Rue St.-Paul where some of the country's best artists display their work. As for antiques, best bets are *L'Heritage* (109 and 111 St.-Paul) and *La Galerie 141* (145 St.-Paul).

The best places to find Eskimo or Indian art are the boutiques on St.-Louis, Desjardins, quartier Petit-Champlain, and Rue St.-Paul. Authentic Huron Indian craftwork, including prints, snowshoes, and moccasins can be found at Huron Village near Loretteville, a suburb of Quebec (about 20 minutes from downtown). Try *OKI* (152 Blvd. Bastien; phone: 847-0574), *Artisanats Gros-Louis* (125 Blvd. Bastien; phone: 843-2503), or *Artisanats Indiens du Québec* (540 Rue Max Gros-Louis; phone: 845-2150).

Finally, for the adventurous shopper, there's the Ste.-Foy flea market and marketplace (West of Quebec City on Blvd. des Quatre-Bourgeois). It is the biggest and most interesting. Open May to October (930 Place-de-Ville, Ste.-Foy; phone: 654-4070).

 SPORTS: Quebec City has an active sports scene for both spectators and participants.

Golf – Ten 18-hole and an equal number of 9-hole courses are within a 19-mile (30-km) radius of the city. Among the best are *Club de Golf Royal*

Québec (Bedard St. in Boischatel, near Montmorency Falls; phone: 822-0331); *Lorette Golf Club* (Cook St. in Loretteville; phone: 842-8441); *Club de Golf Mont Tourbillon* (in Lac Beauport, 12 miles/19 km north of the city; phone: 849-4418); and the two courses at Mont Ste.-Anne (25 miles/40 km northeast of the city; phone: 827-3778).

Harness Racing – They're off and running at the *Quebec Hippodrome* on the Exhibition Grounds. Follow Dorchester Blvd. until you see signs for Parc de l'Exposition (phone: 524-5283). Check ahead for days open during the winter.

Hockey – The National Hockey League *Nordiques* face challengers at the *Coliseum* on the Exposition Grounds (tickets, phone: 523-3333 or 800-463-3333; schedule information, phone: 529-8441).

Skating – Join the locals in Parc d'Esplanade, off Rue d'Auteuil. Other popular spots are the 3-kilometer circuit on the St. Charles River, between the Samson and Marie de l'Incarnation bridges and Place d'Youville, just outside the St. Jean Gate in Old Quebec. Village des Sports in Valcartier (Autoroute de la Capitale, then Rte. 371) offers skating paths through the woods, and *L'Anneau de Glace de Ste.-Foy* (see *Suburbs)* is an outdoor Olympic-size skating track made of artificial ice. Skating begins mid-October and usually lasts to the end of March (phone: 654-4462).

Skiing – Downhill skiing is best at Mont Ste.-Anne, a *World Cup* complex 25 miles (40 km) northeast of the city. The most direct route follows Route 138. You can also get there via Route 440. A more scenic route leaves 138 at Beaupré and continues along Route 360. Lac Beauport and Stoneham also have good slopes only a short drive from the city. All of them offer good night skiing. For information on buses to the ski areas, see *Getting Around.* For cross-country skiing and snowshoeing, try the Plains of Abraham or the nearby provincial parks with marked trails, and Réserve Faunique des Laurentides, northwest via Route 175. Mont Ste.-Anne, Lac Delage, and Duchesnay also have miles of groomed cross-country trails.

Swimming – Some of the hotels have pools; the *Physical Education and Sports Pavilion* (Laval University in Ste.-Foy, off Route 175; phone: 656-2807) has an Olympic-size pool that is open to the public; the *YMCA* (835 Blvd. St.-Cyrille W; phone: 527-2518) and the *YWCA* (855 Rue Holland; phone: 683-2155) also have pools the public can use for a fee at certain hours; call ahead.

Tennis – Indoor and outdoor tennis courts as well as squash courts are available from 7 AM to 11 PM daily at the *Montcalm Tennis Club* (901 Blvd. Champlain; phone: 687-1250). Courts are also available for rent at *Club de Tennis Avantage, Inc.* (1080 Bouvier, Charlesbourg W.; phone: 627-3343) and at *Tennisport* (4230 Blvd. Hamel; phone: 872-0111).

Tobogganing – There are slides at the *Village des Sports,* a vast outdoor amusement park near Valcartier, north of the city (phone: 844-3725).

 THEATER: A variety of plays is offered in French, rarely in English. Major theaters include the *Grand Théâtre du Québec* (269 Blvd. St.-Cyrille E; phone: 643-6976); *Palais Montcalm* (995 Place d'Youville; phone: 670-9011); and the French-language *Théâtre du Trident* plays in the *Grand Théâtre* (phone: 643-5873); *Bibliothèque Gabrielle Roy* (350 Rue St.-Joseph E.; phone: 529-0924); and *Salle Albert-Rousseau* (CEGEP Ste. Foy, 2410 Chemin Ste.-Foy; phone: 659-6629). Student productions are presented at the *Conservatoire d'Art Dramatique* (11 St.-Stanislas; phone: 643-9833), and at the *Théâtre de la Cité Universitaire* (on the Laval Campus in Ste.-Foy; phone: 656-2765). Summer theaters are *Théâtre de l'Ile* (Ile d'Orléans; phone: 828-9530); *Théâtre Beaumont-St. Michel* (on Rte. 2 between Beaumont and St.-Michel; phone: 884-2839); and *Théâtre du Bois de Coulonge* (Blvd. Laurier; phone: 681-4679). Among the small theaters are *Théâtre Petit Champlain* (68 Petit Champlain; phone: 692-4398) which often hosts folk-singing *chansonniers; Théâtre de la Bordée* (1143 Rue St.-Jean; phone: 694-9631); *Théatre de la Feniére* (1500 de la Feniére, Ancienne Lorette; phone: 872-1424); and *Théatre Paul Hébert* (1451 Av. Royale, St.-Jean, Ile d'Orléans; phone: 829-2202).

 MUSIC: The *Quebec Symphony Orchestra* performs at Louis-Frechette Hall in the *Grand Théâtre de Québec* (269 Blvd. St.-Cyrille E.; phone: 643-6976). Touring groups usually play at *Palais Montcalm* (995 Place d'Youville; phone: 670-9011) or at *Albert-Rousseau Hall* (2410 Chemin Ste.-Foy; phone: 659-6629). The small pubs along Rue St.-Jean between Rue d'Auteuil and Côte de la Fabrique, on Grande Allée, and in the Old Port area (see *Nightclubs and Nightlife*), have live music, ranging from Quebecois folk music to rock and blues. The bar in the *Clarendon* hotel (57 Rue Ste.-Anne; phone: 692-2480) has jazz.

 NIGHTCLUBS AND NIGHTLIFE: The pubs along and around St.-Jean attract a young crowd. One popular place is *Bar Elite* (54 Rue Couillard; phone: 692-1204). The bars and discos along Grande Allée near the National Assembly and in the Old Port area tend to be more sophisticated. Finally, check out some of the new pubs, some of which offer up to 135 brands of beer.

BEST IN TOWN

CHECKING IN: Quebec City has a wide range of hostelries, from the magnificent *Château Frontenac* — a landmark since it was built in the 1890s — to small family-run guesthouses. Four modern high-rise hotels dramatically altered the city's skyline during the 1973-1974 period, when the *Municipal Convention Centre* was being completed. The city and its immediate surrounding area have close to 10,000 rooms in major convention hotels, motels, inns, and guesthouses. The best bet for motoring visitors is to check into one of the motels in Ste.-Foy. If you are planning to visit Quebec City during *Carnaval* in early February or during the summer, make reservations as far in advance as possible. During the winter, rooms generally are available, and most places even offer discount rates. Expect to pay $100 to $170 and up per night for a double room in the expensive range; $70 to $100 in the moderate range; and about $65 in the inexpensive range. All telephone numbers are in the 418 area code unless otherwise indicated.

Auberge des Gouverneurs – Adjacent to the *Québec Hilton International,* this modern high-rise has 377 nicely appointed rooms, an elaborate dining room, a health club, and a heated outdoor swimming pool that is open year-round. 690 St.-Cyrille E. (phone: 647-1717). Expensive.

Le Château Frontenac – The grand dame of Quebec City hotels, this stunning 1892 French Renaissance structure is beautifully situated above the St. Lawrence River. It is no longer the best hostelry in town, but what the Champs-Élysées is to Paris and Red Square is to Moscow, this venerable property is to Quebec City — the point to which tourist tracks are inevitably drawn. The 500-room Canadian Pacific property continues to be refurbished, so modern comforts have been added without compromising its Old World appeal. Rooms are air conditioned and many have river views. *Le Champlain* is an excellent dining room (see *Eating Out*); there's also an attractive circular cocktail lounge overlooking the St. Lawrence; café-style restaurants; and a small gallery of shops. (For more information on its history, see *Special Places.*) 1 Av. des Carrières (phone: 692-3861). Expensive.

Hotel des Gouverneurs Ste.-Foy – A suburban hostelry, it has 318 attractive rooms, a sophisticated restaurant, a piano bar, and a heated outdoor pool that's open only in summer. 3030 Blvd. Laurier (phone: 651-3030). Expensive.

Loews Le Concorde – A dramatic pyramidal structure distinguishes this 424-room hotel. *L'Astral,* this city's only revolving restaurant, sits atop the 29-story pyramid. Other restaurants are available, too, and there is an outdoor pool. During the winter, guests may use the indoor pool at an adjacent club. 1225 Place Montcalm (phone: 647-2222). Expensive.

Québec Hilton International – With one of the best addresses in the city, this striking, modern high-rise has 565 rooms, including 38 suites and 2 executive floors that cater to businesspeople. Service is attentive and friendly. Facilities include a wide variety of restaurants (see *Eating Out*); a heated outdoor pool (closed in winter); a health club; and small liquor-vending machines. In addition, the hotel is connected by underground passages with an extensive shopping arcade and the *Convention Centre.* 3 Place Quebec (phone: 647-2411). Expensive.

Auberge Ramada Inn – This 99-room establishment, formerly known as *la Nouvelle-Orléans,* is a rustic-looking lodge done up in Canadiana. Rooms have all amenities and there are 28 split-level suites. It offers a choice of restaurants: *Le Leonardo* for continental and Italian specialties, *Le Vivier* for seafood. It has an outdoor pool. Near the Quebec bridge in Ste.-Foy. 1200 Av. Lavigerie (phone: 651-2440). Expensive to moderate.

Clarendon – Within the Old City walls, just opposite City Hall — very convenient for sightseeing — this hotel, built in 1870 is constantly undergoing renovations. The rooms have private baths, color TV sets, and phones but no air conditioning. The *Charles Baillargé* restaurant serves dinner accompanied by performances of classical music; *L'Emprise* bar, also on the premises, has the best jazz in town. 57 Rue Ste.-Anne, near Desjardins (phone: 692-2480). Expensive to moderate.

Holiday Inn Ste.-Foy – Formerly the *Châteaubriand,* this property reopened last June after extensive renovations. It now has 235 spacious rooms including VIP suites with Jacuzzis, an indoor swimming pool, a sauna, a health club, an elaborate dining room, and a cocktail lounge. Free limousine service to and from the airport is available. 3225 Hochelaga Blvd. Ste.-Foy (phone: 653-4901). Expensive to moderate.

Manoir Victoria – The most striking aspect of this new establishment in a lovely historical setting is its vast and richly decorated entry hall. It has 150 rooms, boutiques, an indoor pool, fitness center, and valet parking. Its 2 restaurants offer continental and French cuisine. Ski packages also are offered. 44 Côte-du-Palais (phone: 692-1030 or 800-463-4093). Expensive to moderate.

Le Château de Pierre – This 15-room English-style mansion (1853) was converted from a private residence to a guesthouse in 1960 and has much repeat business. The guestrooms are decorated with contemporary furniture; all have color TV sets, and air conditioning; most are large enough for two double beds. 17 Av. Ste.-Geneviève, a few steps from Rue Laporte (phone: 694-0429). Moderate.

Fleur de Lys – In the heart of Old Upper Town, 11 of the 33 units are equipped with kitchenettes. All have color TV sets, air conditioning, and direct-dial phone. Continental breakfast is served in the rooms; other facilities include a laundromat and parking garage. 115 Rue Ste.-Anne, near Desjardins (phone: 694-0106). Moderate.

Le Germain-des-Prés – Decorated in European Art Deco, this 127-room hostelry offers personalized service. Rooms include TV sets, AM-FM cassette radios, bathrobes, and fresh fruit. The hotel has a continental breakfast room and is near shopping centers. Transportation to and from the airport is complimentary. 1200 Germain-des-Prés, Ste.-Foy (phone: 658-1224). Moderate.

Manoir Ste.-Geneviève – One of the best things about this 9-room guesthouse is Marguerite Corriveau, the friendly proprietress. The house was built in the early 1800s and was one of the first in the Jardin des Gouverneurs. All the rooms are furnished with old English furniture but have modern baths, and three have kitchenettes. 13 Av. Ste.-Geneviève at Rue Laporte (phone: 647-9377). Moderate.

Auberge du Tresor – Formerly the *Hôtel Le Homestead,* this 300-year-old building has been renovated and now most of its 21 guestrooms — many overlooking Place d'Armes — are equipped with a private bath, a TV set, and air conditioning. Conveniently situated for those whose main objective is sightseeing, the hotel also has a cocktail lounge, a fine dining room with multi-ethnic menu, and a café in summer. 20 Rue Ste.-Anne at Rue du Tresor (phone: 694-1876). Moderate to inexpensive.

Château Laurier – Near the National Assembly, this 55-room hostelry is quiet and convenient, with a dining room and a coffee shop that's open until 5 AM — a rarity in Quebec City. 695 Grande Allée (phone: 522-8108). Moderate to inexpensive.

Belley – Situated in the Old Port area facing the harbor and marketplace, this small place has 8 rooms and 2 small apartments decorated with stylish, black-lacquered Oriental furniture and Quebecois artwork. Telephones, TV sets, and showers (but no baths) in every room. No restaurant on the premises, but continental breakfast is available at the *Tavern Belley* next door. 249 Rue St.-Paul (phone: 692-1694). Inexpensive.

 EATING OUT: Even if you don't know the difference between flambé and soufflé, Quebec City awaits you. At the myriad French restaurants here you can try both, as well as a broad selection of other Gallic dishes. Few restaurants still serve typical Quebecois meals of pea soup, meat pie, and maple sugar-based desserts. Although French nouvelle cuisine is on most menus, Quebecs' gastronomic landscape recently has grown to include a variety of ethnic establishments, including Chinese and Indian. Also new are tearooms (salons de thé) where one can enjoy the traditional ritual of tea or wonderful chocolate desserts. An added bonus is the relatively modest prices of the restaurants. Expect to pay $85 and up for a very expensive dinner for two; between $70 and $85 in the expensive range; $40 to $60 in the moderate range; and under $40 in the inexpensive range. Note that a provincial sales tax of 10% is added to your tab for meals costing more than $2.75 (CN$3.25). Prices given do not include drinks, wine, or tip. All telephone numbers are in the 418 area code unless otherwise indicated.

L'Âtre – The pride of Ile d'Orléans is this 1680 farmhouse-turned-fashionable-restaurant. The menu is Quebecois. Open daily from mid-June to early September only. Reservations necessary. Major credit cards accepted. 4403 Royal (Route 368) near Ste.-Famille, east of the island bridge (phone: 829-2474). Very expensive.

Le Croquembroche – This elegant, provincial-style restaurant has emerged as one of the top two or three dining rooms in town. It features beautifully prepared French nouvelle cuisine and Quebec City specialties. For starters, try the snails baked in grape leaves and puff pastry or the creamed Arctic char soup with orange zest. Grilled meats and fish, roasted on a spit in the dining area and served with suave sauces, are commendable entrées. Open weekdays for lunch; daily for dinner. Reservations advised. Major credit cards accepted. Lobby level of the *Québec Hilton,* 3 Place Quebec (phone: 674-2411). Very expensive.

Le Paris-Brest – Art Deco combined with stained glass windows and brass fittings creates an engaging decor in which to dine on the specialty here, French food. Open daily. Reservations necessary on weekends. Major credit cards accepted. 590 Grande Allée E. (phone: 529-2243). Very expensive.

A la table de Serge Bruyère – Possibly the best in town. Monsieur Bruyère constantly experiments with nouvelle cuisine and has come up with such dishes as *feuilletée de langoustine à la tomate fraîche* (prawns in puff pastry with tomato) and scallops with leek purée. Only one seating each evening, so reservations are essential. Serge Bruyère Entreprises also includes, in the same mid-19th-century house, a small tearoom (inexpensive), *La Petite Table de Serge Bruyère* for light lunches (inexpensive), and the more relaxed but excellent *Le Central* (moderate). Reservations advised for all three. Closed Sundays and Mondays. Major credit cards accepted. 1200 Rue St.-Jean (phone: 694-0618). Very expensive.

L'Elysée Mandarin – The best place in town for authentic Szechuan and other regional Chinese food. The dining room is spacious in a minimalist environment. The service is very courteous and discreet. Reservations advised. Open daily. Major credit cards accepted. 65 d'Auteuil (phone: 692-0909). Very expensive to expensive.

Le Marie Clarisse – A very good seafood spot near the bottom of the *funiculaire*. Closed Sundays and Mondays. Reservations necessary on weekends. Most major credit cards accepted. 12 Petit Champlain (phone: 692-0857). Very expensive to expensive.

Aux Anciens Canadiens – This house was built in 1675, and was at one time the home of Philippe Aubert de Gaspé. It's a wonderful place for a large lunch or brunch (dinner is served, too). Specialties include thick Canadian pea soup, *tourtière* (meat pie), meatball ragout, and, for dessert, sinfully delicious maple syrup pie served with heavy cream. Open daily. Reservations advised. Major credit cards accepted. 34 Rue St.-Louis (phone: 692-1627). Expensive.

Le Champlain – The *Château Frontenac's* dining room has changed over to nouvelle cuisine. Try the Brome Lake duckling with cassis vinegar, or the Dover sole soufflé with lobster sauce. Quiet harp and flute music adds to the serenity. Open daily. Reservations advised. Major credit cards accepted. 1 Av. des Carrières (phone: 692-3861). Expensive.

Le Continental – The cuisine could hardly be a surprise — an extensive menu of European specialties ranging from sweetbreads Madère to steaks *flambé au poivre*. The oak-paneled dining room is attractive and spacious and the service usually very good. For starters, try the *Gaspé en crêpe* (seafood crêpe). Open daily. Reservations advised. Major credit cards accepted. 26 Rue St.-Louis (phone: 694-9995). Expensive.

Apsara – A good place for adventurous dining in Quebec, it serves Thai, Cambodian, and Vietnamese foods. The plate of assorted appetizers is a wise and flavorful selection for the uninitiated. Open daily. Reservations advised. Major credit cards accepted. 71 d'Auteuil (phone: 694-0232). Expensive to moderate.

Auberge Louis Hébert – Offers friendly service and an attractive setting, with calico lampshades dangling above the tables. Specialties include fresh Quebec lamb and *confit d'oie,* a goose pâté. The outdoor terrace is open for summer dining. Open daily. Major credit cards accepted. 668 Grande Allée E. (phone: 525-7812). Expensive to moderate.

Café d'Europe – French and Italian dishes are served in cheery and cozy surroundings in Old Quebec. The café also has great little one-person pizza and a good dessert cart. Open daily. Reservations advised. Major credit cards accepted. 27 Rue Ste.-Angèle (phone: 692-3835). Expensive to moderate.

Café de la Paix – This is a small, friendly place with French food. The seafood plate, rack of lamb, and, in the fall, various kinds of game like bison and wild boar, are all good bets. Open daily. Reservations advised. Major credit cards accepted. 44 Desjardins (phone: 692-1430). Expensive to moderate.

L'Echaudé – In the Old Lower Town, its Art Deco interior is cool and relaxing, its nouvelle cuisine menu intriguing, and its desserts sumptuous. Try the *bavaroise aux framboises,* a raspberry custard with a tangy sauce. Open daily. Reservations advised. Major credit cards accepted. 73 Sault-au-Matelot (phone: 692-1299). Expensive to moderate.

Gambrinus – Just half a block from the *Château Frontenac,* this place serves fine Italian fare. The pasta dishes with seafood sauces are especially noteworthy, as is the cheesecake for dessert. Open daily. Reservations advised. Major credit cards accepted. 15 Rue du Fort (phone: 692-5144). Expensive to moderate.

Kyoto – The place to go if you've got a yen for Japanese food. It's decorated in bamboo, with Japanese prints on the wall, and has long tables that seat eight. On a gas burner right on your table, the chef — who loves to show off and make people laugh — prepares authentic Japanese chicken, steak, shrimp, or lobster dishes, with all the traditional accompaniments. Open daily; no lunch on weekends. Reservations advised. Major credit cards accepted. 560 Grande Allée E. (phone: 529-6141). Expensive to moderate.

La Ripaille – This long-established, well-run, small eatery specializes in French and Italian food. The things to try here are the crab dishes and veal escalopes. It's a good place for lunch. Open daily. Reservations advised. Major credit cards accepted. 9 Rue Buade (phone: 692-2450). Expensive to moderate.

Le Saint-Amour – An easy 5-minute walk from all the major hotels, this fine French dining spot specializes in nouvelle cuisine. Try the *lotte,* a white fish, in vinegar and honey sauce. There's also a better-than-average wine list. Open daily. Reservations advised. Major credit cards accepted. 48 Ste.-Ursule (phone: 694-0667). Expensive to moderate.

Balico – Off the usual tourist trail, this intimate little restaurant specializes in the food of the Provence region of France. The fish soups are quite delicious, and the *aïoli* (garlic mayonnaise) unforgettable. Closed Mondays. Reservations advised. Major credit cards accepted. 935 Rue Bourlamaque (phone: 648-1880). Moderate.

Le Chalet Suisse – For a change of pace, try the fondues at this festive, multi-storied place. Some suggestions: the Chinese fondue — thinly sliced beef served in a heated beef bouillon — grilled cheese *raclette,* or a traditional Swiss cheese fondue. One of the few restaurants in town open past 11 PM, hence its regulars include provincial politicians when the National Assembly is in session. Open daily. Reservations advised. Major credit cards accepted. 26 Rue Ste.-Anne (phone: 694-1320). Moderate.

Le Fiacre – For a congenial atmosphere, good service, and down-to-earth food — charcoal-broiled steaks or seafood — this large eatery in Ste.-Foy fits the bill and the budget. Open daily. Reservations advised Wednesdays through Saturdays. Major credit cards accepted. 1200 Germains-des-Prés, Ste.-Foy (phone: 651-4055). Moderate.

Fleur de Lotus – Near City Hall, this Cambodian restaurant also serves Vietnamese and Thai food. Bring your own wine. Open daily. Reservations advised. Visa and MasterCard accepted. 50 Rue de la Fabrique (phone: 692-4286). Moderate.

Mykonos – The total Greek population of Quebec City numbers 150, so it's surprising that there's a Greek restaurant here at all, let alone such a fine one. The menu features a wide variety of Greek dishes, but *agneau* (lamb) is the specialty — you can have a generous portion of roast lamb or shish kebab with lamb or beef. Accompanying the lamb is *briam,* fresh string beans, onions, potatoes, zucchini, and eggplant, baked in layers. *Galactobouriko,* custard served in *phyllo,* a thin pastry crust, tops off the meal. Open daily. Reservations advised. Major credit cards accepted. 1066 Rue St.-Jean (phone: 692-2048). Moderate.

Nupur – Outside the usual tourist trail, but well worth the 15-minute drive. Although the decor is modest, the atmosphere is warm and the service exceptional. Try any of the Tandoori or curried dishes. Open daily. Major credit cards accepted. Reservations advised. 850 Rue Myrand, Ste.-Foy (phone: 683-4770). Moderate.

Optimum – A recently renovated, luxurious, 2-story Victorian house with a Mediterranean deli on the first floor and a café on the second floor, where nouvelle cuisine is served and the desserts are sinful. Open daily. Reservations advised. Major credit cards accepted. 64 St.-Cyrille W (phone: 648-0768). Moderate.

Le d'Orsay – A restaurant-pub with a good location and an excellent selection of European beers. Open daily. Reservations advised. Major credit cards accepted. 65 Rue Buade, just across from City Hall (phone: 694-1582). Moderate.

Le Biarritz – It's an intimate place that can accommodate groups or twosomes for cozy dining. The escargots are a good choice for starters, and any of the many veal dishes will make a satisfying entrée. Open daily. Reservations advised. Major credit cards accepted. 136 Ste.-Anne (phone: 692-2433). Moderate to inexpensive.

Café Latin – A lovely place to dawdle over an espresso, sandwich, quiche, or salad to the accompaniment of taped classical music. It also has the best maple sugar pie in town. Outdoor dining on the terrace in summer. Open daily. Reservations unnecessary. No credit cards accepted. 8½ Ste.-Ursule (phone: 692-2022). Inexpensive.

Les Delices du Maghreb – Good and inexpensive Mediterranean and Provençal food in unpretentious surroundings. It's in a less than fashionable, but still interesting, part of downtown, surrounded by shops and cafés that seem left over from the 1960s. Bring your own wine. Open daily. Reservations unneccessary. Major credit cards accepted. 798 Rue St.-Jean (phone: 529-9578). Inexpensive.

La Garonelle – A tearoom and confectionary where only a strong will can keep you away from the chocolate desserts. Pâtés, salads, and fine cheeses also are offered. Two locations: 207 Rue St.-Jean (phone: 524-8154), closed Mondays; and 35 Rue Buade at the *Holt Renfrew* store — the only place that serves afternoon tea (phone: 692-3680). Closed Sundays. Reservations advised. Major credit cards accepted. Inexpensive.

Marie Antoinette – For fast food, Quebec-style. Breakfast is especially recommended. Open 24 hours daily. Reservations unnecessary. Major credit cards accepted. There are ten of these restaurants in the area, including ones at 2813 Laurier Blvd. (phone: 653-5993) and 44 Kennedy St., Lévis (phone: 837-5809). Inexpensive.

Le St.-Alexandre – One of a dozen English-style pubs to have opened in different fashionable parts of town. The object of the limited but excellent menu (sausages, sauerkraut, sandwiches, steaks) is to complement the 135 brands of beer that are served here. Reservations unnecessary. Open daily. Major credit cards accepted. 1087 Rue St.-Jean (phone: 694-0015). Inexpensive.

TORONTO

There was a time when Toronto was content with its position as Canada's second city, and willingly deferred to Montreal as the spicier, more intriguing Canadian travel destination. But anyone who visits the city today knows that the so-called Queen City's former lethargic attitude has changed dramatically. A vibrant rhythm has replaced the old puritanical chord, and a new spirit flows through the city's bustling streets. After-dark entertainment has a vital, exciting beat; restaurants have grown in number and variety; and modern structures are being built as rapidly as old neighborhoods are being restored. Toronto has truly developed a strong cosmopolitan personality.

The dreams of farm kids and immigrants and a surprising combination of economic and sociological factors have transformed Toronto from a minor North American city to the financial, commercial, and communications center of Canada. This change is reflected in the ethnic composition of the population, the character of the city, and even in its physical profile. Dominating the skyline are two structures, the CN Tower — an 1,815-foot communications tower that is the tallest free-standing structure in the world — and Royal Bank Plaza, two triangular towers that appear to be solid gold (actually, there's 2,500 ounces of gold in the windows). The construction and eminence of both structures symbolize the city's ascendancy, a rise that occurred during the past 2 decades.

One of the fastest growing cities in North America, Toronto has surpassed Montreal as the Canadian city with the largest metropolitan population (Toronto's is about 3.5 million, with over 2.1 million in the city itself). Toronto claims to have the greatest ethnic diversity of any major city in the world, with 70 percent of its residents non-white. Some 80 nationalities speaking 16 different languages are represented here. The city has the largest Italian population outside of Italy, and large numbers of Portuguese, Ukrainians, Germans, Asians, Caribbeans, and substantial other minority communities, all with their own newspapers and traditions.

Growth was spurred initially by a large influx of immigrants from the war-ravaged countries of Western and Central Europe who came in a great wave during the early 1950s in search of jobs. These immigrants, as well as the natives, have transformed Toronto from a minor city into the metropolis it is today. And the jobs are still here; some 6,200 industrial plants in and around the city account for one-fifth of all manufacturing in Canada. A third of the country's purchasing power is located within a 100-mile radius of Toronto; most national companies are headquartered here, and most international companies maintain offices here. Jobs brought people and people brought more jobs. Thus mass-scale immigration was responsible for Toronto's evolution as an international city.

Rising on the north bank of Lake Ontario, Toronto covers 244 square miles, six municipalities that stretch from the flat, central downtown section to numerous hills in the sprawling suburbs. The city is laid out on a rectangular grid, but the neat order of the plan is interrupted by a greenbelt of wooded ravines created by two small rivers — the Humber and the Don — that cut through the city with miles of wooded parkland. These stretches of green are regarded by residents as one of Toronto's prime recreational areas; summer and winter, they use the space to hike, jog, and cross-country ski.

The lake has a wide, deep harbor that can accommodate oceangoing vessels, making Toronto a major port on the St. Lawrence Seaway. The waterfront area close to downtown has been renovated and is now the site of Harbourfront, a government-funded complex that includes recreational, cultural, and crafts centers, restaurants, and residential and commercial complexes. Also bordering the lake are Harbour Square, exclusive, modern high-rise apartments, and the *Harbour Castle Westin,* a spectacular double-towered luxury hotel. Beaches, walkways, and marinas stretch along the lakefront.

Downtown rises to the north. Innovative architecture characterizes the city — the banking towers; a City Hall, with two curved towers surrounding a lower rotunda; *Eaton Centre,* the spacious shopping gallery that looks more like a huge greenhouse (inside are some of the best shops in Canada); the public library, designed by Raymond Moriyama; and numerous other avant-garde buildings.

All this has contributed to the transformation of a city that only 30 years ago was an almost provincial town. The Huron Indians set up camp at the end of their portage connecting Lake Huron to Lake Ontario. They called the site Toronto, the Indian word for "meeting place." French fur traders discovered it in the early 18th century and built a fort here in 1720. The fort was burned to the ground in 1759, and from that time Toronto's history and character were predominantly British.

In 1796 the site was proclaimed the capital of Upper Canada and welcomed Loyalist refugees from the US. They named the settlement York, after the Duke of York, the son of George III — the major opponent of the American Revolution.

During the War of 1812 between Britain and the US, the town was occupied by American troops who destroyed the Parliament buildings and archives and stole the mace, the symbol of British sovereignty and authority. The British retaliated by marching on Washington and burning all of its public buildings. (Before setting fire to the presidential mansion, a regiment of Scottish soldiers finished off a fine dinner prepared for the president, then proceeded to burn as much of the house as possible, leaving only a scorched outer shell. It was rebuilt quickly and painted white in such a hurry that it became known as the White House.) In 1934, President Franklin D. Roosevelt returned the mace to the government of Ontario as a gesture of international goodwill.

When the city was incorporated in 1834 and its name reverted from York to the original Toronto, the most remarkable aspect of it was its growth. By 1901 its population reached 200,000, and its business extended throughout Canada. It very much was an anglicized town — English-speaking — with its character heavily influenced by and indebted to classic English traits. People are civil, reserved, helpful when asked for help, but hardly gregarious, and there is a disproportionately low violent crime rate here in relation to cities of comparable size. Its business world was run like a very select British club, with the reins of financial and corporate power held tightly in a few hands. The view of what made a good and satisfying life was vividly perceived and rigidly maintained. Life in Toronto was a long series of Blue Laws. Until World War II, Toronto was a WASP town — white, Anglo-Saxon, and Protestant — and so immersed in the work ethic that anything that even looked like fun was assumed to be harmful, sinful, prideful, or all three. In the words of the late Gordon Sinclair, Toronto's outspoken radio and TV broadcaster, "Everyday life was dreary enough, but Sundays were murder. Everything but the churches shut down tight. *Eaton's* (the major department store) even drew its curtains to prevent the small enjoyment of window-shopping on the Sabbath."

What turned Toronto the Good into Toronto the Human was the infusion of cultures from several continents over the last 45 years. These groups have brought their customs, cultures, and cuisines with them, and they have utterly changed the city's character. Toronto has become a city of neighborhoods. Thousands of Greeks live in the East End around Danforth Avenue at the end of Bloor Street, and elsewhere there are large communities of Italians, Ukrainians, and Hungarians. Bordering Chinatown is a Portuguese neighborhood distinguished by its lovely pastel-painted houses. Toronto is home to a sizable German population as well, although its members tend not to live in any easily defined ethnic enclave. In nearby *Kensington Market,* most of these cultures meet to buy from and sell to one another. Strongly Portuguese and Caribbean, with some Italians and Jews, this market is where everyone can get everything. And as inexpensive as the goods always are, they get even less expensive if the buyer speaks the native tongue of the seller.

Toronto celebrates its ethnicity every year at the end of June in a 10-day blowout known as *Caravan.* Various groups set up pavilions in churches and community centers, offering the public food, drink, handicrafts, art, songs and dances, all from the old country. Visitors buy a "passport" and go from pavilion to pavilion on an around-the-world tour, stopping here for some Greek baklava, there for a demonstration of Ukrainian folk dancing, around the corner for an earful of Caribbean steel band music. In the course of a day's ramble, you can have Italian pasta washed down by Irish coffee or a potent Polish liqueur.

Caravan is a short-lived phenomenon, though a lot happens in its brief appearance each year. A more lasting gift from Toronto's newer residents has been the proliferation of theaters, clubs, and ethnic restaurants and, even more important, the effect such variety has had on living habits in the city. With so much to choose from, Toronto has opened up at night. Residents are determined that the city center should not be a daytime-only experience, and a good deal of the most recent construction — the last wave of which added so many of the buildings that now make the city's skyline unique — fosters and encourages this feeling. Mixed development downtown — commercial and residential complexes — keeps people in the heart of the city. So instead of becoming a ghost town after working hours, downtown Toronto remains vibrant, drawing people to its nightlife.

A concomitant movement has awakened in the city's neighborhoods. Until 35 years ago, Toronto appeared to be following the American model: a city center for business in the day, with rings of ever more affluent suburbs around it. When the great numbers of immigrants arrived, they moved into the older neighborhoods, where they established communities with strong bonds and natural cohesion. This movement has been extended to downtown commercial neighborhoods in recent years by the young middle class who years ago might have moved to the suburbs.

The phenomenon that sparked the revival of the decaying neighborhoods was the election in 1972 of a reform city council, which reversed developers' plans for massive demolition to make way for inner-city high-rises and instead promoted city-run nonprofit housing, rent control, and tenants' rights. (Today it seems inconceivable that old City Hall was almost torn down to make way for an earlier version of ultra-posh *Eaton Centre,* but it's true.) The mood of the residents changed, and with the support of the city, the restoration of the old neighborhoods began in earnest. One small group of 200 people managed to save their historic church — Church of the Holy Trinity — from destruction during the construction of *Eaton Centre.* Not only did developers revise their plans to protect the sanctity of the lovely little church, one of the oldest houses of worship in the city, but they changed the plans to ensure that sun would shine on the building.

Toronto residents created and maintain a lively and livable city. It boasts showplaces, like the spectacular *Ontario Science Centre,* the Toronto Zoo, where you can ZooSki — cross-country ski — around the building that houses the zoo's major indoor complexes, and the *SkyDome* stadium. But the city is worth a visit for even more fundamental reasons. Its number one tourist attraction is its healthy urban environment. As Canada's leading metropolis, it has achieved a balance between progress and preservation. Wherever Toronto's heading, much of the rest of urban Canada is likely soon to follow. And much of the rest of urban North America might do well to take note.

TORONTO AT-A-GLANCE

SEEING THE CITY: The best way to grasp the lay of the land is from the CN Tower, Toronto's most visible and famous landmark. The property of Canadian National, the publicly owned railway, this communication tower is the world's tallest free-standing structure. From the base of the reflecting pool, the tower stretches 1,815 feet and 5 inches. (There are taller TV antennas, but they're supported by guy wires and thus are not free-standing.) Four exterior glass elevators whisk visitors 1,122 feet up to the Sky Pod, which has an outdoor observation deck, an indoor deck with zoom lens peritelescopes, the world's highest revolving restaurant, *Top of Toronto,* and a nightclub called *Sparkles.* On a clear day, Buffalo, Niagara Falls, and everything in between is visible. The Sky Pod level also contains a broadcasting studio and communications equipment. Another elevator leads to the

1,500-foot level, where you can look up at the transmission mast and down on everything else, except the jets approaching Toronto International Airport. Open daily. Admission charge. 301 Front St. W. (phone: 360-8500).

Toronto is designed on a grid, which makes it easy to walk around downtown; however, nearly all streets have names not numbers, so finding a specific address can be difficult for a newcomer. At the north end of the city, you'll find Highway 401, and Lake Ontario borders the south. Yonge Street is the main north-south arterial, and other north-south streets are designated by blue street signs. Bloor Street is the main east-west thoroughfare, and other east-west streets have yellow signs. Downtown extends from Bloor south to Lake Ontario, between Spadina (Spa-*deena*) Avenue and Jarvis Street. Midtown covers the area north of Bloor to Eglinton Avenue.

 SPECIAL PLACES: Unless you have a special need to take your car into the central city, don't. Toronto streets can get very congested, and on-street parking is severely restricted during peak hours. Parking lots exist, but they are expensive. Overtime parking at meters can end in a CN$48 ticket, and parking in a restricted zone can result in towing and payment of CN$150 to retrieve your car. Your best bet is to use Toronto's modern, efficient, clean, and safe public transit system (see *Getting Around*). The *Toronto Transit Commission* has extensive routes and will get you anywhere you want to go in metropolitan Toronto for a single fare.

DOWNTOWN

SkyDome – Set on 8 acres, this 31-story amphitheater is one of the world's largest, with a capacity for 60,000 spectators and many other facilities. Home of the *Blue Jays* baseball team and football's Toronto *Argonauts,* it also hosts other major league sporting events, plus concerts, exhibitions, and more. The amphitheater has a retractable dome roof that covers the stadium during inclement weather and opens up when the weather is good. It also boasts the world's largest scoreboard/replay machine, SkyVision (35 by 115 feet), along with an 800-seat restaurant overlooking the football endzone, several bars, a health club, a 364-suite hotel with 70 rooms overlooking the stadium, a *Hard Rock Café,* and a *McDonald's* with seating for 500 people. Parking is limited, and most fans will have to reach the stadium via public transportation. 277 Front St. W. (phone: 341-3663).

Royal Ontario Museum – Affectionately referred to as the *ROM,* it's Canada's largest public museum — made even larger after an $83-million renovation and expansion project — which features collections drawn from 20 science, art, and archaeology departments. The *ROM* is well known for its Chinese collections, and the Bat Cave and Dinosaur Gallery are popular with kids of all ages. Several new galleries include the European Gallery, Gallery of Birds, and the Ethnology Gallery of Native Peoples of North America. Mummies are on exhibit in the Egypt-Nubia Gallery. The adjacent *McLaughlin Planetarium* presents Laserium shows Wednesdays through Sundays (call 586-5750 for show times and admission prices; children under 6 not admitted). Original star shows also are presented every few months; for more information, call 586-5736. The museum's Sigmund Samuel Building houses furniture, ceramics, and silver (14 Queen's Park Crescent; open daily; no admission charge; the main museum building is open daily and there is an admission charge). The *ROM* Shop is a cornucopia of gifts from around the world. 100 Queen's Park (phone: 586-5549).

Provincial Parliament Buildings – As you leave the museum, turn right. Located in Queen's Park, now synonymous with the provincial legislature, that pile of pink Romanesque rock is the back of the provincial parliament buildings; from the front they are striking brownstones. Enthroned beside the buildings is a statue of regally resplendent Queen Victoria. Her equally regal son, Edward VII, astride his sturdy steed, has become a shrine for local pigeons. Sir John A. Macdonald, Canada's first prime minister and the chief architect of Canadian Confederation, and George Brown, his political as well as personal adversary, also are represented here. Here's a bit of Canadiana to put these two characters in proper perspective: Once, during a legislative debate, Brown accused Macdonald of being drunk — a fairly safe accusation. Macdonald's reply was immortalized in the annals of Canadian history: "Better Sir John A. drunk," he said, "than George Brown sober." Queen's Park, with its sweeping lawns and old trees, is a favorite picnic ground with outdoor musical evenings held regularly during the summer and guided tours on weekdays during the winter (no admission charge; call for times); in summer, tours are conducted daily, every hour. The legislature convenes on Mondays through Wednesdays from 1:30 to 6 PM and on Thursdays from 10 AM to 12 PM. Queen's Park Crescent at University Ave. (phone ahead to book a tour: 965-4028).

Ontario Hydro – Up to the right of Queen's Park is the mirrored, concave building, headquarters of Canada's largest power-producing and distributing organization. It employs a radical heating system, eliminating the traditional boiler: Heat provided by interior lighting and old-fashioned body warmth is recirculated throughout the building. Technical tours only (not for the general public) are by appointment only. 700 University Ave. (phone: 592-3345).

University of Toronto – Before continuing south on University Avenue, detour 1 block west to one of North America's better universities, dating from 1827. The campus sprawls over several city blocks; the best route for a short tour is around King's College Circle. Take a look inside Hart House, the Gothic student center built with Massey money (the family of the late Hollywood actor Raymond and his brother, Vincent, former Governor-General of Canada). Among the other buildings are the Old Observatory, University College, Knox College, and the Medical Sciences Building. Many scientific firsts have happened in this last building: Dr. Frederick Banting and Dr. Charles Best isolated insulin in 1922; the first electric heart pacemaker was developed; and Pablum, the first precooked vitamin-enriched cereal, was formulated. Student guides lead free walking tours Mondays through Fridays during June, July, and August. Hart House (phone: 978-2452).

Tour of the Universe – For those who've always wondered what it's like to be an astronaut, this futuristic attraction is a must-see. The year is 2019. "Astronauts" are checked in by security, insert their 3-D pass into a computer terminal, and pass through customs. Then it's blast-off time, so fasten your seat belts for a bumpy ride through outer space. Upon returning from the solar system, reenter the earth with a visit to the gift shop. Open daily year-round. Admission charge. At the base of the CN Tower (phone: 364-3134).

Mary Pickford's Birthplace – Along stately University Avenue, with its wide, flowered median, you will find the city's most famous hospitals — Toronto General, Mt. Sinai, and Hospital for Sick Children. In the gardens of the "Sick Kids" on the east side of University Avenue is a plaque and bronze bust commemorating the birthplace of Gladys Marie Smith, better known as Mary Pickford, America's Sweetheart. Incidentally, Miss Pickford requested her Canadian citizenship back, which was granted in October 1978. 55 University Ave.

Chinatown – Several blocks downtown are the focal point of Toronto's Chinese, Korean, and Japanese communities: here you'll find many interesting grocery stores and restaurants. The best places to eat are *Macay Court* (405 Dundas St. W. — basement) and *Young Lok* (122 St. Patrick St. University Ave. and Dundas St. W.). See *Eating Out* for more information. The original Chinatown at Gerrard St. and Broadview Ave. has become "Vietnam Town." Another Chinatown is in the suburb of Scarborough.

City Hall and Nathan Phillips Square – This distinctive modern complex was designed by Finnish architect Viljo Revell. Two curved towers of unequal height focus on the low-domed Council Chamber, which, from an aerial view, resembles a giant eye. Surrounding the buildings is a square named for Toronto's longtime mayor Nathan Phillips, who initiated plans for a new City Hall back in 1957. The square is a popular gathering place and the site of special events during the summer. The reflecting pool and fountains circulate 12,000 gallons of water a minute. In summer, office workers dip their toes in the pool; in winter they skate on its frozen surface. *The Archer,* a bronze Henry Moore sculpture, was purchased by public donation to adorn the square after the city council refused to buy it. Free tours are conducted daily (call for times). Bay and Queen Sts. (phone: 392-7341).

Eaton Centre – A modern 4-level shopping gallery, it has a high glass roof, lots of space and light, marble floors, trees, plants, flowers, and benches. *Eaton's,* an institution in Canadian merchandising (whose founder, Timothy Eaton, first set up shop in Toronto in 1869), has its plush flagship store here. In addition, the center houses another 300 shops, boutiques, and restaurants. One entire level is underground. For a bite or a beer, drop into *Elephant and Castle.* You'll find the best ice cream in the city at *Swensen's.* The gallery was constructed in accordance with Toronto's policy for architectural preservation and was built around two of the city's oldest buildings, Trinity Church and Scadding House, the former home of an early Toronto historian. Shops are closed Sundays; some restaurants open daily. 220 Yonge St. (phone: 598-2322).

Bank Towers – Canada's five major banks have offices in these high-rise office-commercial complexes that dominate the Toronto skyline. All four complexes are linked underground by concourses that house shops, cinemas, and restaurants. The tallest of the buildings is the white marble, 72-story Bank of Montreal building, known as First Canadian Place because it was Canada's first chartered bank. Most striking is the Royal Bank Plaza, two triangular towers of 41 and 26 stories respectively with serrated walls and windows covered with 2,500 ounces of gold. Inside there's a cascading fountain and an international art collection featuring Venezuelan Jesús Soto's sculpture composed of 8,600 20-inch-long aluminum tubes. You can't miss it — the work is 100 feet high and 60 feet wide and occupies more than half the space in the hall. Commerce Court is a stainless steel skyscraper with 7,400 windows of double-glazed reflective glass. The three jet black buildings are the Toronto Dominion Centre; the lobby often has art exhibits. The fifth major bank tower is the Bank of Novia Scotia or "Scotia Bank" tower. King and Bay Sts.

Art Gallery of Ontario – The highlight here is the *Henry Moore Sculpture Centre,* the largest public collection of his work, displayed with related drawings, prints, studio material, and photography donated by Moore. Of the gallery's permanent collection, over half is the work of Canadian artists, including a wide variety of paintings and sculpture from the early 19th century through the present. Old Masters, Impressionists, and early-20th-century artists are also represented. (The gallery is currently undergoing an expansion.) Connected to the gallery by an underground walkway is the *Grange,* a charming museum that is Toronto's oldest remaining brick house (ca. 1817). Some say it's haunted, but the atmosphere is cheery and the furnishings delightful. Vera, the upstairs maid, often greets guests and goods baked fresh from the hearth are sold to visitors on Tuesdays, Thursdays, and Saturdays; facing the front lawn of Grange Park. Closed Mondays. Admission charge covers entrance to the gallery and the *Grange.* Gallery at 317 Dundas St. W., between McCaul and Beverley Sts. (phone: 977-0414).

Yorkville – Once a hangout for Toronto hippies before they headed west, this area is now the most chic in the city. Renovated townhouses, boutiques with designer fashions and expensive jewelry, quiet courtyards, wrought-iron lampposts, and art galleries flank the narrow streets. There are several cafés where you can sit by a window box sipping an aperitif and watching the world go by. Yorkville Village was incorporated in 1853, and eagle-eyed explorers will find the original coat of arms — brewer, smith, brickmaker, carpenter, and farmer — outside many of the specialty stores. Hazelton Lanes (55 Avenue Rd.) is a classy commercial-residential complex with some 70 boutiques and an outdoor courtyard that is transformed into an ice skating rink in winter. Some of the most expensive chocolate around is sold at *Teuscher of Switzerland* (55 Avenue Rd.), which imports its chocolates from Zurich; try the champagne truffles — you'll go broke happily. Bounded by Bloor St., Avenue Rd., Bay St., and Scollard St.

Queen Street West – The up-and-coming cousin to Yorkville, this once-moribund stretch just west of City Hall now hums with colorful street life, sidewalk jewelry vendors, and an assortment of shops selling everything from new and used furniture and books to state-of-the-art computers. Nearby is the Ontario College of Art, the proximity of which played a big role in the development of this area: When graduates from the acclaimed art school needed places to show their wares, they began opening shops along this street. High-fashion highlights include *Twinkle Toes* (No. 320) for men's and women's footwear; *Next* (No. 348) for boots; *Club Monaco* (No. 403) for sportswear, plus an inexpensive lunch counter offering sandwiches, salads, and cappuccino; and *Marilyn Brooks Boutique* (No. 383) for fine clothing from a top Canadian designer. From John St. to Spadina Ave.

Kensington Market – A colorful, artsy area jammed with cafés, street musicians, and shops where you can buy everything from salted fish and fresh produce to clothing and stereos. This outdoor market has character — lots of it — and a heavy ethnic flavor. Jewish, Portuguese, Caribbean, and Italian influences are apparent. The market is at its best on Saturday mornings. Closed Sundays. No admission charge. College and Dundas Sts., west of Spadina.

St. Lawrence Market – If you're into markets, this is another good one. Erected in 1844 to serve as Toronto's first City Hall, it's now a clearinghouse for farmers, butchers, and fishmongers. Saturday's the big day here, when the area farmers truck their produce to the *Farmer's Market* across the street. Open Tuesdays through Saturdays. 95 Front St. E.

Casa Loma – This magnificent, rambling, eccentric, turreted mansion — a 98-room mock medieval castle — was built between 1911 and 1914 by Sir Henry Pellatt — pioneer of the use of hydroelectric power in Canada — to house the collection of antique furniture and grandiose art he had collected from the greatest galleries of Europe during his career as one of Toronto's most successful financiers. He imported European craftsmen to build the secret staircase; the conservatory, with elegant bronze doors; Peacock Alley, running the length of the house, copied and named after the Peacock Alley in the royal residence of Windsor Castle; the Great Hall, with a 60-foot ceiling; the Oak Room, where three artisans worked for 3 years to chisel the French oak paneling; as well as the 15 bathrooms, 23 fireplaces, and a wine cellar with space for 1,700 bottles. In the 1920s, Toronto's electric utilities went public and the city took over his company. Sir Henry found the cost of upkeep beyond even his ample means; Casa Loma was taken by the city for back taxes, and Sir Henry had to auction most of his Chippendales and Reynoldses to keep body and soul together. For a while the place fell to the mice and disrepair. In 1937, the Kiwanis Club of West Toronto restored the castle and still runs it today as a tourist attraction with proceeds going to community projects. The Garden Club of Toronto renovated Casa Loma's 10 acres of gardens. Be sure to climb the two towers; the Norman Tower is open and the Scottish Tower is enclosed. Open daily. Handicap access. Admission charge includes self-guided audio tours. 1 Austin Terrace (phone: 923-1171).

Spadina – This house, whose Indian name means hill, is located just east of Casa Loma. Built in 1866 as a home for James Austin, major shareholder in Consumer Gas and founder of the Dominion Bank (now the Toronto Dominion), it has 50 rooms and halls which were completely restored by the Toronto Historic Board. Most of the Victorian and Edwardian furnishings belonged to the family, and many pieces were made by the Jakes & Haye Company in Toronto. The Garden Club of Toronto oversees the gardens and has replanted many of its original plant species. Open daily. Admission charge. Wheelchair access. 285 Spadina Rd. (phone: 392-6910).

Fort York – This restored fort from the War of 1812 re-creates the atmosphere of an early-19th-century garrison. Open daily. Admission charge. On Garrison Rd. off Fleet St. between Bathurst St. and Strachan Ave., near Exhibition Pl. (phone: 392-6907).

Mackenzie House – The mid-Victorian home and print shop of William Lyon Mackenzie, first Mayor of Toronto, has authentic 1850s furnishings. Open daily. Admission charge. Near *Eaton Centre* at 82 Bond St. (phone: 392-6915).

Colborne Lodge – An 1837 Regency country cottage, it was the home of John G. Howard, a city surveyor and architect. He donated his estate to the city, and now it's part of High Park. The lodge is furnished in period pieces, and there are some fine examples of early Canadian art. Open daily. Admission charge. Colborne Lodge Dr. in High Park (phone: 392-6916).

OUTDOORS

Ontario Place – This 96-acre theme park on the edge of Lake Ontario is part playground, part exposition and cultural center, and mostly lush green park. The cinesphere, a giant structure shaped like a dimpled basketball and spiked with luminous eyeballs, houses a curved movie screen, 6 stories high. At the *Forum* (capacity 10,000), you can listen to the *Toronto Symphony,* to jazz, or to popular performers. Children's Village is an imaginative area for kids up to 12 (there's even a height restriction of 58 inches). The Pavilion, a series of interconnected pods built right in Lake Ontario, houses good restaurants and exhibits. The west island features a wilderness flume ride and water stage facility showcasing Ontario talent. Open daily from mid-May to *Labor Day.* Films shown in winter. Admission charge. 955 Lakeshore Blvd. W. (phone: 965-7711).

Harbourfront – The federal government restored this 92-acre waterfront area and built a recreation/culture complex. The Metropolitan Toronto Convention and Visitors Association has its offices (with a designer foyer and contemporary art exhibit) in the Queen's Quay Terminal. At the refurbished terminal and surrounding park, you can shop, dine, listen to jazz, make crafts, participate in sports, examine old steam engines, feed the ducks, or just watch the ships go by. The area is divided into several sections: York Quay, with an art gallery, theater, and café for jazz and poetry readings; Spadina Quay, with a marina and picnic facilities; and Bathurst Quay, with a park and cooperative housing projects. There's also a year-round antiques and flea market, and in the summer there's a sailing school. Open daily. No admission charge, although sometimes there's a charge for specific events. 235 Queen's Quay W. (phone: 973-3000).

Toronto Islands – This group of islands off the Toronto shore of Lake Ontario encompasses Hanlan's Point, Ward's Island, Centre Island, Algonquin Island, and four small islands. The 15-minute ferry ride to the islands is the least expensive and quickest escape from the intensity of city life. You can't take your car; bicycles (bring your own on weekdays only) and legs are the standard modes of transportation. Centre Island, the most popular, has 612 acres of park, picnic grounds, restaurants, boating, a barnyard zoo, and Centreville, a child-size replica of a 19th-century Ontario village with lots of rides (open May 24 to *Labor Day*). Ward's Island and Hanlan's Point have fewer facilities and attract fewer people, but swimming is good at Ward's Island, and public tennis courts are available at Hanlan's Point. There also are boat rentals.

SUBURBS

Ontario Science Centre – A spectacular facility that was built in 1967 at a cost of $30 million as Ontario's contribution to Canada's centennial. Since then, it has attracted millions of visitors from all over the world for its scientific and technological exhibits, which stress interaction and participation and show that science can be fun. Designed by Raymond Moriyama, the structure itself is extremely well integrated with its environment. It is built into a ravine; visitors enter at the top of a cliff and work their way down on glass-enclosed escalators that open up a view of the natural surroundings in the lush, wooded valley. Inside, there are many different exhibits — Food/Earth Hall, Exploring Space, Hall of Communication, Hall of Life, Hall of Transportation, Science Arcade, Hall of the Atom — as well as demonstrations, films, and theaters with multimedia shows. There are far too many things to see and do to cover everything, even in several visits. There are no guided tours, so plot your own course from the *Science Centre*'s map and set your own pace. Wherever you head, you'll find numerous opportunities to participate: Pit your wits against a computer in a game of Hangman; make a machine talk; make your hair stand on end with a charge of static electricity; test your fitness, your reflexes, or your perception. Hosts knowledgeable about science are around to help you experiment if you want guidance. Open daily. Admission charge. 770 Don Mills Rd. (phone: 429-4100).

Metro Toronto Zoo – This impressive zoo is one of the largest in the world. Stretched between two arms of the Rouge River, these 710 acres of river valley and 8 pavilions have been shaped to simulate the natural habitats of the zoo's nearly 4,000 animal residents. The geographic regions represented include Africa, Australia, Eurasia, Indo-Malaysia, North America, and South America. The largest, the African Pavilion, is equipped with ponds and a jungle atmosphere to keep the gorillas, hippos, bongos, and monkeys feeling right at home. Orangutans and gibbons swing through trees in the rain forest environment of Indo-Malaysia. Other settings accommodate polar bears, alligators, zebras, Japanese macaques, and South African fur seals. A slow, rubber-wheeled train negotiates the 3½-mile path though the Canadian Domain, where deer, Arctic wolves, caribou, moose, and antelope play. The zoo easily can take up a full day. There are several ways to approach it: You can ride the train, take a variety of walking tours including the Round the World Tour, or in the winter try it by ZooSki — go cross-country skiing on trails through Africa and Eurasia (ski rentals are available at the zoo). Open daily. Admission charge. Just north of Hwy. 401 on Meadowvale Rd., 10 miles (16 km) east of the Don Valley Pkwy. (phone: 392-5900, or 392-5901 for recording).

Black Creek Pioneer Village – This restored 19th-century town depicts life in a rural Ontario village over a hundred years ago. The buildings include a homestead and farm, a general store, a blacksmith's shop, a town hall, and a flour mill. Costumed folk in last century's fashions perform tasks such as shoeing horses, making butter, and weaving rugs. Open daily in summer; buildings closed in January and February, but there's a sports program with skating, and horse-drawn sleigh rides. Admission charge. Jane St. at Steeles Ave. W. (phone: 736-1733 or 661-6610 for recorded message).

McMichael Canadian Art Collection – These attractive galleries built of hand-hewn logs and fieldstone, set amidst 100 acres of breathtaking conserved land overlooking the Humber River Valley, shelter many works of the Group of Seven, an informal school of artists who broke away from traditional British painting early in the 20th century and immortalized the Canadian landscape. There are also exhibits of Northwest Coast, Inuit, and contemporary Indian art. Closed Mondays, November through

April. Lively weekend programs include tours, talks, films, and Sunday afternoon jazz concerts. There's a full service restaurant and book and gift shop with exclusive, Canadian handcrafted goods. Admission charge. In Kleinburg, north of Toronto (phone: 893-1121).

Canada's Wonderland – Canada's major theme park is just 20 miles (32 km) northwest of downtown Toronto. The park features five live stage shows and some 30 thrilling rides, including the only stand-up looping roller coaster in Canada. Shops and restaurants line International Street, which leads to six theme areas. Top entertainers perform in the *Kingswood Music Theatre* (capacity 15,000). The children's and adult's pay-one-price passports allow unlimited use of the park for the day (*Kingswood* not included). Open daily June to September, weekends in May and September to mid-October. On Highway 400 between Rutherford Rd. and Major Mackenzie Dr. (phone: 832-7000 or 832-2205).

■ **EXTRA SPECIAL:** Just 82 miles (131 km) southwest of Toronto is Niagara Falls, one of the most powerful waterfalls in the world, as well as one of the Western Hemisphere's major tourist attractions. The falls are formed as the waters of Lake Erie race downhill to join Lake Ontario, becoming the Niagara River en route. The river gathers strength and power in the narrows and then plunges almost 200 feet to form the famous falls. A small island in the river splits this whitewater juggernaut at the point of its mighty dive, dividing it into two falls instead of one — the Horseshoe (Canadian) Falls, 176 feet high and 2,100 feet wide; and the American Falls, 182 feet high and 1,076 feet wide. There are several ways to see the falls — from a tower or helicopter ride; on the *Maid of the Mist* sightseeing boat that carries visitors to the base of the Horseshoe Falls; or from one of the restaurants that overlook them.

SOURCES AND RESOURCES

TOURIST INFORMATION: For general information, brochures, and maps, contact the Metropolitan Toronto Convention and Visitors Association (207 Queen's Quay W., Suite 509; phone: 368-9821 or 800-387-2999 from Michigan, New York, Ohio, and Pennsylvania). The association maintains several outdoor kiosks that provide quick information, and a permanent Visitor Information Centre outside the *Eaton Centre* (Yonge and Dundas Sts.; phone: 979-3133). Its city map has plenty of helpful information and an insert on the subway routes.

The *Toronto Guidebook,* edited by Alexander Ross (Grey de Pencier Publications; $4.95), is the best local guide. The *Toronto Book,* edited by William Kilbourn (Gage Publishing Co.; $35), is a good anthology of Toronto literature past and present.

Local Coverage – The *Globe* and *Mail,* morning daily except Sundays; the *Sun,* morning daily; the *Toronto Star,* morning and afternoon daily except weekends, when it comes out in the morning; *Toronto Life,* monthly magazine; *T.O. Magazine,* published ten times a year; *Metropolitan Toronto Events Guide,* a quarterly booklet with lists of what's going on in town. *Key to Toronto* is a monthly magazine distributed free to hotel guests by the Hotel Association of Metropolitan Toronto. CBC Radio (740) is the national network; CFRB (1010) is a major news, talk, and sports station; CHUM (104.5 FM) is the most popular rock music station.

Food – *Toronto Life* and *Metropolitan Toronto Events Guide,* list most of the established restaurants and many newcomers.

Telephone – The area code for Toronto is 416.

Sales Tax – There is an 8% tax on the sale of most goods.

Currency – All prices are quoted in US dollars unless otherwise indicated.

 TIPPING: Taxi drivers are generally given 10% of the fare. At restaurants tip 15% to 20% of the bill. Bellboys and airport porters usually receive CN$1 per bag, and hotel maids should be given about CN$1 per person, per day.

 CLIMATE: Toronto gets a lot of sunshine all year. Summers are warm, with average temperatures around 71F (21C); winters are cold, with average temperatures around 23F (−5C) and a fair amount of snowfall. For the latest weather information, call 676-3066, 24 hours a day.

 GETTING AROUND: Public Transit – The *Toronto Transit Commission* (*TTC*) operates an efficient, modern system covering over 700 miles of routes. The *TTC* publishes a handy pocketsize *Ride Guide* available free from station collectors, the *TTC* Center at Bloor-Yonge subway station, by phoning 393-INFO, or by writing to them (1900 Yonge St., Toronto, M4S 1Z2). The guide will help you easily find your way around. Subways are clean and safe. Some 2,300 vehicles — buses, trolleys, streetcars, and subways — make up this interconnecting system. The exact change or a token is required for the first fare, but additional transfers along the same route are free (including subway-bus transfers). Special family fares are available on Sundays and holidays. For information on routes and fares, contact the *TTC* information line between 7 AM and 11:30 PM at 393-4636.

Car Rental – All major North American firms are represented: *Avis* (Hudson Bay Centre, 80 Bloor St. E.; phone: 964-2051); *Budget* (141 Bay St.; phone: 364-7104); *Hertz* (39 Richmond St. W.; phone: 363-9022); and *Tilden* (at Union Station, 65 Front St. W; phone: 364-4191).

Taxi – Cabs are easy to hail on the street. Major cab companies are *Co-op Taxi* (phone: 364-8161) and *Diamond* (phone: 366-6868).

Sightseeing Tours – *Gray Coach* (610 Bay St.; phone: 979-3511), has excellent bus tours of the city during summer months with passenger pickups at all major hotels and the bus terminal.

 SPECIAL EVENTS: In May, the *International Children's Festival* features over 100 performances by international companies. Free activities include jugglers, mimes, and more. Harbourfront (235 Queen's Quay W.; phone: 973-3000). At the end of June, the *Caravan* festival is held, and 50 of Toronto's ethnic communities set up national pavilions in church basements, school gyms, and public halls for a 10-day orgy of international cuisines. For information, contact the *Metro Caravan* (263 Adelaide St. W.; phone: 977-0466).

The *International Picnic,* an annual free bash sponsored by the multilingual radio station CHIN, features free eating contests and games. For the exact date, check the publications noted above or contact CHIN, 637 College St. (phone: 531-9991).

Caribana is a 10-day West Indies carnival in mid-summer; for information, refer to *Metropolitan Toronto Happenings* or *Key to Toronto.*

The *Canadian National Exhibition* is the city's big fair, running for 3 weeks, mid-August to *Labor Day;* there's fine bandstand entertainment nightly. For information, contact *Canadian National Exhibition,* Lakeshore Blvd. (phone: 393-6000).

The *Royal Agricultural Winter Fair* at Exhibition Park on Lakeshore Boulevard is the showcase for what is billed as the largest agricultural fair under one roof (27½ acres). The fair runs for a week in mid-November, and its *Royal Horse Show* attracts international competition.

MUSEUMS: The *Royal Ontario Museum,* the *Ontario Science Centre,* the *McMichael Canadian Art Collection,* Fort York, Casa Loma, Spadina, and the *Art Gallery of Ontario* are described in detail in *Special Places.* At the *Art Gallery of Ontario* you can pick up an excellent guidebook to the art scene at more than 30 galleries around the city. For other interesting museums to visit include the following:

Gibson House – A restored 19th-century home. 5172 Yonge St. (phone: 225-0146).

Marine Museum of Upper Canada – History of shipping and waterways. Lakeshore Blvd., Exhibition Pl. (phone: 392-6827).

Museum of History of Medicine – Known for its Egyptian mummy, on which an autopsy has been performed, and for the Drake Collection of pediatric artifacts, this museum's exhibits span 5,000 years of health care, from the ancient world to the 20th century. No admission charge but donations requested. Academy of Medicine, 288 Bloor St. W. (phone: 922-0564).

Museum of Textiles – Tucked away in a condominium building, just a few blocks east of the *Ontario Gallery of Art,* is the only museum in Canada devoted to handmade textiles and carpets. Exhibits range from complex loom-woven tapestries to pounded and painted barkcloth. A special gallery is devoted to contemporary artists. Closed Mondays. Wheelchair accessible. Admission charge. 55 Centre Ave. (phone: 599-5515).

SHOPPING: Toronto is a good shopping city with stores carrying imported goods and native crafts — everything from Swiss chocolate to Eskimo soapstone sculpture. There's a broad selection of shopping areas as well, ranging from the exclusive *Hazelton Lanes,* which houses the biggest names in fashion and design, to *Kensington Market* (see *Special Places*). There's more to shopping here than initially meets the eye — some 1,400 shops are underground, many of them in *Eaton Centre* (see *Special Places*).

Antiques – The ideal spot for browsing in myriad antiques-cum-kitsch shops is on Queen St. West, between University Ave. and Bathurst St. *Pao & Moltke Ltd.* (118 Yorkville Ave.; phone: 925-6197) has an unusual assortment of Chinese antiques.

China – *Ashley China* (50 Bloor St. W.; phone: 964-2900) carries the finest and most distinctive English bone china dinnerware.

Chocolate – Swiss chocolates are air-expressed weekly from Zurich to *Teuscher Switzerland* in Hazelton Lanes at 55 Avenue Rd. (phone: 961-1303).

Cigars – *Winston & Holmes* (at several locations, including 138 Cumberland St.; phone: 968-1290) is Toronto's foremost tobacconist. Cuban cigars are on hand.

Crafts – The *Guild Shop* (140 Cumberland St.; phone: 921-1721) is a nonprofit retail outlet for Canadian craftspeople. Returning US residents do not have to pay duty on original works of Inuit art and are also reimbursed the Ontario sales tax of 8% (ask for the special form you must fill in and mail from home). *The Pottery Shop* (140 Yorkville Ave.; phone: 923-1803) specializes in handcrafted clay and glass pieces. *Yonge at Art* offers reasonably priced goods, including jewelry and toys, handcrafted by Canadians; the shop is run by the Inner City Angels, and proceeds support their charity programs. Scadding House, 6 Trinity Square, next to *Eaton Centre* (phone: 598-0245).

Eskimo Art – *The Inuit Gallery of Eskimo Art* features primitive Eskimo carvings, sculptures, prints, and wall hangings. 9 Prince Arthur Ave. (phone: 921-9985).

Fashion – Bloor Street is the Toronto equivalent of New York's Fifth Avenue, and you'll find several shops here with sophisticated fashions, including *Holt Renfrew & Co.* (50 Bloor St. W.; phone: 922-2333). Hazelton Lanes also features many shops with distinctive apparel. Also try *Chez Catherine* (20A Hazelton Lanes; phone: 967-5666).

Jewelry – Both casual shoppers and connoisseurs call at the *Gold Shoppe* (25 Bloor St. W.; phone: 923-5565) for antique jewelry and silver. At *European Jewellery* (390 Bay St.; phone: 369-0009 and 111 Bloor St. W.; phone: 967-7201), you can purchase elegant and distinctive pieces. *Fraleigh Jewelery & Gemologists* (21 Avenue Rd.; phone: 924-2296) in the *Four Seasons* hotel and other locations has estate and antique jewelry.

Leather Goods – *Lanzi of Italy* (123 Yorkville Ave.; phone: 964-2582) and *Hermès* (in Hazelton Lanes at 55 Avenue Rd.; phone: 968-8626) carry leather accessories.

Tweeds and Linens – *Irish Import House* (444 Yonge St. W.; phone: 595-0500) has Irish goods at lower-than-usual prices; 15% off Waterford and Belleek.

Women's clothing – *Canadian Signatures* features clothing and accessories, made exclusively by Canadian designers. 138 Cumberland (Old York Lane; phone: 975-0400).

Wool – *Norma* (116 Cumberland St.; phone: 923-5514) carries pure wool sweaters, jackets, and suits by Canadian designer Norma Lepofsky.

 SPORTS: Toronto is the home of baseball's American League *Blue Jays,* the National Hockey League *Maple Leafs,* and the Canadian Football League *Argonauts.* The Metro Parks Department maintains good facilities around the city for participatory sports.

Baseball – The *SkyDome* is home base for the Toronto *Blue Jays,* 277 Front St. W. (phone: 595-0077 or 341-1111).

Bicycling – There are some excellent bike paths around the Toronto parks. For folks who are really keen on biking, check *The Great Toronto Bicycling Guide,* by Elliot Kats (Great North Books, $3.95), which describes many of them. *Boardwalk Cycle* (748 Markham Rd.; phone: 431-1961) provides the wheels.

Football – The *Argonauts* play from June until early November at the *SkyDome* (phone: 595-1131 or 341-3663).

Golf – There are many pay-as-you-play courses in and around Toronto. *Lakeview Golf Course* (1190 Dixie Rd., ¾ mile/1 km south of the Queen Elizabeth Way; phone: 278-4411) is a good, narrow 18-hole course with pro shop, lockers, showers, and a snack bar. *Don Valley Golf Course* (4200 Yonge St., south of Highway 401; phone: 392-2465) is one of the most challenging public courses around.

Hockey – Hockey in Toronto means large crowds every time the *Maple Leafs* defend their home ice at *Maple Leaf Gardens.* Since 1927, when the team was established, the *Leafs* have won the *Stanley Cup,* the symbol of hockey supremacy, 11 times — a record second only to that of the Montreal *Canadiens.* Tickets for *Leaf* games are not as hard to come by as they used to be. For tickets, head to the *Gardens,* 60 Carlton St. (phone: 977-1641).

Horse Racing – At *Greenwood Race Track* (1669 Queen St. E.; phone: 698-3131), thoroughbreds and standardbreds take turns on the turf. There's an enclosed grandstand and dining room. *Woodbine Race Track* (Rexdale Blvd. at Hwy. 27; phone: 675-6110) is exclusively for thoroughbred racing. Every summer it is the scene of the *Queen's Plate* — the oldest continuously run stake event in North America at 132 years and the highlight of the Canadian racing season for Canadian-bred 3-year-olds.

Jogging – In downtown Ontario, City Hall has a jogging track. In central Ontario, jog at the University of Toronto or Queens Park. The Martin Goodman Trail along the harborfront is also pleasant, as are the stretches of wooded green cutting through the city along the Humber and Don rivers.

Skiing – Cross-country skiing is a way of life in Toronto, and you can do it around the Toronto Zoo, the Toronto Islands, or along the greenbelted ravines that run through the city from downtown to the *Ontario Science Centre.* Rental equipment is available at *Rudy's Sport Centre Ltd.* (1055 Eglinton Ave. W.; phone: 781-9196 and at the zoo; phone: 392-5900). The downhill picture right around the city is rather bleak — just some overcrowded mini-hills. Collingwood, 90 miles (144 km) north of Toronto, is the area's main ski resort. *Gray Coach* buses make weekend departures from the terminal (610 Bay and Dundas Sts.; phone: 393-7911).

Tennis – The Metro Parks Department (phone: 392-8184) maintains public courts in at least two parks, but the best courts are in private clubs, like the *Toronto Lawn Tennis Club,* to which you must be invited by a member. Hanlan's Point, one of the Toronto Islands, has good public courts, as does Ramsden Park on Yonge St.

 THEATER: For complete listings of current performances, check the publications listed above. Toronto has a large variety of theatrical offerings ranging from its own repertory groups to stagings of London shows by English performers. An organization called *5 Star Tickets* (phone: 596-8211) sells half-price tickets to events given by selected professional performing arts companies on the day of performance (tickets to out-of-town events are available the day before the performance). Outside *Eaton Centre* at Yonge and Dundas Sts. (open daily; cash only), or at the *Royal Ontario Museum.*

Two major theater festivals, focusing on the works of Shaw and Shakespeare, are held at theater centers within 2 hours of the city. Among the most prominent of the city's more than 30 theaters are the *O'Keefe Centre* (Front and Yonge Sts.; phone: 872-2262), home of the *Canadian Opera Company* and the *National Ballet of Canada;* the *Royal Alexandra Theatre* (260 King St. W.; phone: 593-4211), for Broadway, London, and local productions; the *Pantages Theater* (263 Yonge St.; phone: 362-3216); *Elgin-Winter Gardens* (189 Yonge St.; phone: 968-0455) is a fully restored historic theater; the *St. Lawrence Centre for the Performing Arts* (27 Front St. E.; phone: 366-7723), for Toronto repertory groups. *Second City,* Canada's version of "Saturday Night Live," presents a satirical revue in a nightclub-supperclub setting at the *Old Fire Hall* (110 Lombard St.; phone: 863-1111). *Toronto Workshop Productions* (12 Alexander St.; phone: 925-8640) and *Tarragon Theatre* (30 Bridgman Ave.; phone: 531-1827) stage new Canadian plays.

The *Stratford Shakespeare Festival,* in Stratford, Ontario, 98 miles (157 km) southwest of Toronto, is one of the foremost theater centers in Canada. The main *Festival* theater performs Shakespeare's masterpieces, as well as other productions; two smaller stages — the *Avon* and the *Third* stage — present a variety of plays. The festival runs from May through October. The *Visitors' Guide to Stratford* lists attractions, accommodations, and facilities and is available from the *Stratford Shakespeare Festival,* PO Box 520, Stratford, Ontario (or for more information call the Toronto box office at 364-8355).

The *Shaw Festival* is presented by one of the few professional theater companies concentrating mainly on the works of George Bernard Shaw and his contemporaries. The plays are supplemented with concerts, seminars, lectures, and exhibits, all in a country setting, at Niagara-on-the-Lake, 82 miles (131 km) from Toronto. The festival runs from April through October. For information, contact the *Shaw Festival Theatre,* 200 Picton St., Box 774, Niagara-on-the-Lake, Ontario (phone: 468-2172 or 361-1544 for the Toronto box office).

 MUSIC: The *Toronto Symphony* performs in the *Roy Thomson Hall* (60 Simcoe St.; phone: 593-4828). Musical performances are also given in the Edward Johnson Building by the University of Toronto music faculty (phone: 978-3744), and at Convocation Hall, also on campus (phone: 978-2100); Ontario Place (phone: 965-7711); and Nathan Phillips Square, downtown (phone: 392-7341). Classical concerts are also performed in the city's churches and schools.

NIGHTCLUBS AND NIGHTLIFE: The city has a growing number of night spots catering to every taste. *Bamboo* (312 Queen St. W.; phone: 593-5771) serves Thai food from noon to closing and features live reggae, salsa, and Latin music for dancing. Three of the largest and liveliest discos are *The Copa* (21 Scollard St.; phone: 922-6500); *RPM* (132 Queen's Quay E.; phone: 869-1462); and *The Diamond Club* (410 Sherbourne St.; phone: 927-9010). *Celebrities* (in the *Harbour Castle Westin;* 1 Harbour Sq.; phone: 869-1600) is a disco. *Beaton's* (in the *Westbury Hotel;* 475 Yonge St.; phone: 924-0611) is a chic lounge and bar. The city's most impressive big-name supper club is the *Imperial Room* (in the *Royal York Hotel,* 100 Front St. W.; phone: 368-6175), where top-name entertainers perform. Reservations necessary. *Barrister's Bar* (in the *Hilton International,* 145 Richmond St. W.; phone: 869-3456) is a quiet, elegant library lounge. For jazz aficionados, there's *Chick 'N' Deli* (744 Mt. Pleasant Ave.; phone: 489-3363); and *Café des Copains* (48 Wellington St. E.; phone: 869-0148). Try the piano bar, *George's,* at *Bigliardi's* restaurant and mingle with hockey players after a game (463 Church St.; phone: 922-9594). *Sparkles* is a nightclub located two-thirds of the way up the CN Tower (301 Front St. W.; phone: 362-5411). Since 1977, when the *Rolling Stones* recorded at *El Mocambo* (464 Spadina Ave.; phone: 961-2558), it has become *the* place for rock in Canada. The *Lounge* at the *King Edward* hotel is a popular meeting spot (37 King St. E.; phone: 863-9700).

BEST IN TOWN

CHECKING IN: As the up-and-coming major metropolis of Canada, Toronto has a proliferation of hotels to accommodate its large numbers of visitors. Even so, reservations are recommended. Choices can be made from a very wide selection. The *Hotel Association of Metropolitan Toronto* offers information about room availability and makes free reservations (call 596-7676). Expect to pay $130 and up for a double room in the places listed as expensive; from $95 to $125 in the moderate range; and under $90 in the inexpensive category. All telephone numbers are in the 416 area code unless otherwise indicated.

Four Seasons Inn on the Park – Within 30 minutes of downtown, this "resort" on 600 acres of parkland has 568 luxurious rooms (half of them for non-smokers), 24-hour concierge and room service, 5 restaurants, 2 lounges, and meeting facilities for over 2,000. For those bent on fitness, there is a health club, tennis, indoor and outdoor pools, toboggans, cross-country skis, and bicycles. There also are supervised children's programs. 1100 Eglinton Ave. E. (phone: 444-2541). Expensive.

Four Seasons Toronto – Nicely positioned right in the heart of Yorkville, a colorful area of boutiques, galleries, sidewalk cafés, and clubs, it has 381 beautifully appointed guestrooms and suites. Special touches include 24-hour concierge and room service, a health club, an indoor-outdoor pool, and a multilingual staff. There's good French dining in *Truffles* and continental dishes in *Le Café,* while *La Serre,* the hotel's cocktail lounge, is a nice choice for lunch. 21 Avenue Rd. (phone: 964-0411). Expensive.

Harbour Castle Westin – This sleek twin-towered structure dominates the Toronto waterfront. Its architecture is well integrated with its surroundings, creating a luxurious yet comfortable atmosphere. Its revolving *Lighthouse* restaurant has panoramic views of the area, and all 978 rooms have views of either Lake Ontario and the islands or the city skyline. The health club has an indoor swimming pool, whirlpool bath, sauna, steam room, gym, squash courts, and an outdoor track specially equipped to melt snow. In addition to the *Lighthouse,* the *Châteauneuf* restaurant serves French food (see *Eating Out*), the *Poseidon* has seafood, and there are 3 lobby lounges. Free shuttle bus service between the hotel and *Eaton Centre,* City Hall, and other downtown locations. 1 Harbour Sq. (phone: 869-1600). Expensive.

L'Hotel – A first class business property next to the CN Tower, it has 600 rooms and suites in a variety of styles — some specially designed for handicapped guests. Entrée Gold, the super service-oriented "hotel within the hotel," on the eighth and ninth floors, provides separate check-in and check-out facilities, complete concierge services, continental breakfast, limousine service, cocktails, hors d'oeuvres, and complimentary local calls and newspapers. *Chanterelles* offers nouvelle cuisine (see *Eating Out*), and the *Orchard Café* serves continental food; for lighter fare try one of the lounges, the *Skylight,* or *Le Bar.* Other facilities include a heated pool, whirlpool bath, saunas, squash courts, and an exercise room. (phone: 597-1400). Expensive.

Intercontinental – One of, if not *the* most luxurious of Toronto's lodging establishments, with 213 elegantly appointed rooms and a courtyard restaurant serving continental and French food. Its fitness center has a pool and sauna. Within walking distance of downtown. 220 Bloor St. W. (phone: 960-5200). Expensive.

King Edward – Warmly referred to by locals as "The King Eddy," this place is everything a first class establishment should be — from the elegant marble-columned lobby to the spacious and tastefully furnished rooms. Its *Lounge Bar* has greeted the Rockefellers and royalty; Prime Minister Margaret Thatcher even made her own tea in the Royal Suite. The *Café Victoria* is fine for breakfast or pre-theater dining; lunch and dinner are served at *Chiaro's.* 37 King St. E. (phone: 863-9700). Expensive.

Park Plaza – Situated at the crossroads of Toronto chic — Avenue Road and Bloor Street — this landmark property, built in the 1930s, has been renovated. The *Prince Arthur Lounge* has soft piano music and an intimate atmosphere as well as good food. The *Prince Arthur Dining Room* serves continental food. 4 Avenue Rd. (phone: 924-5471). Expensive.

Sutton Place – A member of the Leading Hotels of the World group, it has attracted such celebrities as Al Pacino, Faye Dunaway, Paul Newman, and Kim Bassinger. Guests who seek extra special service stay in Regency Floor suites, where 24-hour butler service is provided. All guests have access to the exercise, business, and banquet facilities. Visit *Alexandra's Piano Bar,* the hotel's chic lunch spot, filled with photos of stars who have eaten there. 955 Bay St. (phone: 924-9221 or 800-268-3790). Expensive.

Toronto Airport Marriott – This 423-room property is just 5 minutes from the airport and 20 minutes from downtown Toronto. For dining and entertainment, try the *Mikado* steak house, a Japanese steak and seafood restaurant with Teppanyaki-style display cooking. The *Terrace* is a large café, and *Toucans* is an entertainment lounge. For recreation, an indoor swimming pool, a hydrotherapy pool, weight room, and saunas are provided. 901 Dixon Rd. (phone: 674-9400). Expensive.

Hilton International – A striking Canadian showpiece, it has 601 large and lovely rooms and is conveniently located downtown near theaters, shopping, and most of the major office buildings. There's a good selection of restaurants on the premises: *The Garden Court* has complete meals or light dining; *La Cour* has fine dining; *Trader Vic's* has Polynesian drinks and food; and the *Barrister's Bar* has hearty snacks and nightly entertainment. There is a sauna and indoor and outdoor pools. 145 Richmond St. W. (phone: 869-3456). Expensive to moderate.

Royal York – With 1,408 fully renovated guestrooms, this grande dame has been a landmark since it was built in 1929. While its rooms may be a trifle cramped, its service facilities still remain among the best in Canada. Host to royalty, prime ministers, and visiting celebrities, it also has two floors for conventions. The *Imperial Room* offers dinner and dancing. There is an underground gallery of stores, airline offices (airport buses are at the west door of the hotel), and restaurants such as the *Acadian Room, Dick Turpin's,* and *Benihana of Tokyo.* 100 Front St. W. (phone: 416-368-2511). Expensive to moderate on weeknights; moderate to inexpensive on weekends.

Sheraton Centre – A city within a city, this establishment has 1,399 rooms, a waterfall cascading three stories into the lobby, gardens and paths on the grounds, over 60 stores and boutiques, 2 theaters, 18 restaurants and lounges, including the *Winter Palace* (see *Eating Out*). This is also home to *Good Queen Bess,* an intimate English pub literally shipped from Great Britain. The square shape of the hotel contrasts nicely with the curved structure of City Hall, to which it is linked by a footbridge. There is a sauna and an indoor-outdoor pool. 123 Queen St. W. (phone: 361-1000). Expensive to moderate.

Windsor Arms – Opened in 1928 as an apartment hotel, today it is owned by Canadian entrepreneur George Minden and, near Yorkville, it is a popular choice with the film, theatrical, and literary crowd. Each of the 81 rooms and suites still reflects the residential concept and is individually decorated. The *Three Small Rooms* restaurant (see *Eating Out*) has an elegant dining room serving haute cuisine, an informal grill, and a wine cellar. The *Courtyard Café* is a favorite venue for spotting famous actors, artists, and musicians. No recreational facilities. 22 St. Thomas St. (phone: 979-2341). Expensive to moderate.

Westbury – The twin towers house 545 spacious rooms, each of which has a color TV set, phone, and first-run movies. *Creighton's* serves French food in an elegant setting; *Beaton's Lounge* is for nightly entertainment, Mondays through Saturdays; and the coffee shop is for light fare. 475 Yonge St. (phone: 924-0611). Moderate.

Delta Chelsea Inn – An ideal place for families, because some of the rooms have kitchen facilities. Renovations and expansions last year made this Canada's largest hotel with 1,500 rooms. The property is conveniently located just 2 blocks north of *Eaton Centre.* There are 2 good restaurants (with special children's menus; children under 6 eat free), a lounge, a health club, sauna, a children's creative center, and an indoor pool. 33 Gerrard St. W. (phone: 595-1975). Moderate to inexpensive.

Bond Place – Very close to *Eaton Centre,* its 285 rooms are small, clean, and affordable. There is a coffee shop and lounge but no recreational facilities. 65 Dundas St. E. (phone: 362-6061). Inexpensive.

Carlton Inn – This establishment is right next door to *Maple Leaf Gardens.* Most of the 536 modern rooms have a small refrigerator, and there's also a dining room, 2 pubs, a pool, and a sauna. 30 Carlton St. (phone: 977-6655). Inexpensive.

 EATING OUT: The postwar immigration boom coupled with Toronto's flourishing economy has stimulated a proliferation of ethnic eating places, and today the city has over 4,000 restaurants. The choices of food, which formerly ran the gamut from roast beef to Yorkshire pudding, now include a host of cuisines — Chinese, French, Moroccan, Indonesian, Greek, Japanese, and Italian. The quality is generally high. Expect to pay $60 and up for a dinner for two in the expensive category, $35 to $60 in the moderate category, and under $35 in the inexpensive range. Prices do not include drinks, wine, or tips. All telephone numbers are in the 416 area code unless otherwise indicated.

Châteauneuf – Rich burgundy tones and lovely tapestries decorate this intimate dining place in the *Harbour Castle Westin* hotel. The menu is French, and favorites such as fresh lobster medallions and crêpes filled with golden caviar and sour cream are prepared and presented with care. For dessert, try cassis or raspberry sorbet. Closed Sundays. Major credit cards accepted. Reservations advised. 1 Harbour Sq. (phone: 869-1600). Expensive.

Glossops – The three dining areas in this renovated house are nicely decorated in soft pastels brightened by fresh flowers. Specialties are veal, lamb, and seafood, all served by a very attentive staff. Closed Sundays. Reservations advised. Major credit cards accepted. 39 Prince Arthur Ave. (phone: 964-2440). Expensive.

Scaramouche – Imaginative continental dishes featuring salmon, veal, and lamb are served in this elegant dining room with a lovely view of the city. There's also a pasta bar. A must for dessert is the bittersweet chocolate and praline truffle. Dinner only; closed Sundays. Reservations necessary. Major credit cards accepted. 1 Benvenuto Pl. (phone: 961-8011). Expensive.

Stelle – Located in the trendy Queen Street West area, the atmosphere — distinctly "artistic" — aims to capture the feel of a 1950s kitchen. Toward that end, diners sit on white vinyl chairs (which match one of the walls in color and material), and the waitresses are shod in white sneakers. The menu is an eclectic mix of southern Asian, northern Italian, and Latin American fare. Try the chicken Bangkok cloaked in ginger, shallots, chilies, and an orange-peanut sauce. Open daily for dinner. Reservations necessary. Major credit cards accepted. 807 Queen St. W. (phone: 868-0054). Expensive.

Three Small Rooms – The three dining rooms in the *Windsor Arms* hotel offer a variety of eating experiences. The *Restaurant* serves cuisine naturelle and privately imported wines in elegant surroundings. The *Grill* has a warm, cozy atmosphere and specializes in grilled meats and seafood. It's a great place for lunch. The *Wine Cellar* offers cheese fondue, supreme of grouper amandine, and a variety of wines poured into massive goblets. The *Restaurant* is closed Sundays; the others, open daily. Reservations advised. Major credit cards accepted. 22 St. Thomas St. (phone: 979-2212). Expensive.

Winston's – A tip of the hat to Paul Bocuse; this establishment serves rich haute cuisine in a flamboyantly grand setting. The city's patricians come here to see and be seen, and tourists may have to compete with the important regulars here for good tables and service. Specialties include duckling with fresh papaya, mango, rum, and wine, and Dover sole with shrimp, pine nuts, and green peppercorns. For dessert, don't pass up the grand marnier soufflé. Jackets and ties are mandatory for gentlemen. Closed Sundays. Reservations necessary. Major credit cards accepted. 104 Adelaide St. W. (phone: 363-1627). Expensive.

Winter Palace – Atop the 43-story *Sheraton Centre* complex, this place commands an excellent view of City Hall and Nathan Phillips Square. The interior is elegant, and the menu features French dishes with a Russian flair. Sample the *zakuska,* a dish of seven different hors d'oeuvres, including caviar, partridge pâté, and smoked salmon, followed by the veal tenderloin or scampi Fabergé. Dining is enhanced in the summer by the multicolored lights that shimmer from the reflecting pool 43 stories below, and in winter, by the soft glow that bathes the skaters on the frozen pool in front of City Hall. There's also an extensive wine list. Closed Sundays. Reservations necessary. Major credit cards accepted. 123 Queen St. W. in *Sheraton Centre* (phone: 361-1000). Expensive.

Chanterelles – Superb food, thoughtful service, and a handsome setting off the lobby of *L'Hotel* make this a fine dining choice. The menu includes everything from oysters and caviar to rack of lamb. There's a pre-theater dinner, but you may want to go after the performance just to try the *Chanterelles* cake — sinful but heavenly. Reservations advised. Major credit cards accepted. 225 Front St. W. (phone: 597-8142). Expensive to moderate.

Courtyard Café – Much more than a café, this is a good place for a late night nibble, where diners go to see and be seen. An award-winning chef prepares patés, fresh seafood, and continental fare served in a comfortable atmosphere of wood and brass, and a bounty of greenery. The service is impeccable. Open daily. Reservations advised. Major credit cards accepted. 22 St. Thomas St. (phone: 979-2212). Expensive to moderate.

Gatsby's – For elegant and intimate dining amidst late Victorian decor, this classy dining spot boasts a huge selection of continental cuisine. Closed Sundays. Reservations advised. Major credit cards accepted. 504 Church St. (phone: 925-4545). Expensive to moderate.

George Bigliardi's – Popular with the hockey crowd and high-powered business types, this elegant dining lounge serves steaks, seafood, pasta, and sausages — all with that special Italian touch. Enjoy the house cocktail, the "Midnight George," at the brass-railed bar or the new piano bar. Open for dinner only. Reservations advised. Major credit cards accepted. 463 Church St., 2 blocks north of *Maple Leaf Gardens* (phone: 922-9594). Expensive to Moderate.

Old Fish Market – A casual and comfortable place where the specialties are all kinds of fresh fish and seafood. There's also an oyster bar. Open daily. Reservations advised. Major credit cards accepted. 12 Market St. (phone: 363-0334). Expensive to moderate.

Bellair Café – Serving pasta, salads, seafood, and frozen yogurt and sorbet in a contemporary dining room, this is a popular spot for business lunches and shopping breaks. Celebrities are sometimes seen during dinner hours. Open daily. Reservations advised. Major credit cards accepted. 100 Cumberland St. at Bellair (phone: 964-2222). Moderate.

Doctor's House & Livery – Located 40 minutes north of dowtown Toronto, this 19th-century home has gone through several transmutations — from a doctor's house and barn to a tearoom to the restaurant and the gift shop it is today. The atmosphere is very homey. The menu includes Canadian specialties like salmon and duckling with sweet plums and maple syrup. The Sunday brunch features a wide range of light and heavy fare, from omelettes to prime ribs. Children's portions available. Closed Mondays in winter. Reservations advised. Most major credit cards accepted. Nashville Rd., Kleinburg (phone: 893-1615). Moderate.

Jacques' Omelettes – This Yorkville eatery, with a French à la carte menu, is frequented by devotees of the classic French omelette. Chef Jacques Sorin prepares fresh garnishes every morning and cooks omelettes to order perfectly. The omelette Niçoise is highly recommended. Closed Sundays. Reservations advised. Major credit cards accepted. 126 Cumberland Ave. (phone: 961-1893). Moderate.

Old House on Church Street – In a historic Toronto home, super atmosphere and delicious huge portions are offered. Guests may dine upstairs, or downstairs in the garden during summer months. Lamb, pasta, and seafood are all expertly prepared by the Greek chef–owner. Try the famous cheesecake for dessert. Open for lunch, dinner, and Sunday brunch. 582 Church St. (phone: 925-5316). Moderate.

Pink Pearl – Specializing in Hong Kong-style Cantonese food, the surroundings and service are distinguished, and dining is a leisurely affair. Highlights of the extensive menu include Rainbow Chopped in Crystal Fold — chopped meats and vegetables sautéed together and served with crispy noodles; Peking Supreme Beef Filet — sliced beef tenderloin sautéed with oyster sauce and served sizzling hot; and braised lobster prepared in black bean and garlic sauce. Open daily. Reservations advised for dinner. Major credit cards accepted. 120 Avenue Rd. and at Queen's Quay Terminal (phone: 966-3631). Moderate.

Select Bistro – With a French bistro atmosphere on trendy Queen Street, this spot has a real zinc bar, small tables set closely together, a super wine list, and baskets filled with homemade bread which are suspended on pulleys above diners' heads. The service is inconsistent, and the food varies from being super to mundane, but the music (jazz and classical tapes) and Canadian art posters on the walls still make it one of this town's favorites. Be prepared to wait in line. Open daily. Reservations advised for groups of 5 or more. Major credit cards. 328 Queen St. W. (phone: 596-6405). Moderate.

Top of Toronto – This revolving restaurant at the top of the CN Tower has incredible views and is best for Sunday brunch. Open daily; Sunday brunch from 10 AM to 2 PM. Reservations advised. Major credit cards accepted. 301 Front St. W. (phone: 362-5411). Moderate.

Ed's Warehouse – When entrepreneur Ed Mirvish bought and restored the *Royal Alexandra Theatre,* he also started a restaurant empire, seating 1,500 guests, next door. Garish, with Tiffany lamps and plush old-time autos, this restaurant is great for beef. Jackets are a must; no blue jeans allowed. Open daily. Reservations unnecessary. Major credit cards accepted. 270 King St. W. (phone: 593-6676). Moderate to inexpensive.

Filet of Sole – Fishing scenes of Peggy's Cove in Nova Scotia line the walls of this informal, top-rated seafood dining spot. Remarkably varied menu is printed twice daily. Try the shellfish platters. It caters to a theater crowd that likes to linger at their tables. Open weekdays for lunch and dinner; dinner only on weekends. Reservations necessary. Major credit cards accepted. 11 Duncan St. (phone: 598-3256). Moderate to inexpensive.

Masa – The focus here is on authentic Japanese food. Diners can sit in a standard booth or dine in traditional Japanese style on tatami mats in partitioned lounges. Open daily; weekends, dinner only. Reservations advised on weekends. Major credit cards accepted. 195 Richmond St. W. (phone: 977-9519). Moderate to inexpensive.

Sultan's Tent – For an intriguing change, try some authentic Moroccan food in the Yorkville shopping district. The decor looks genuine — rich tapestries, low round tables, and comfortable divans and brass vases. Specialties include lamb with honey and almonds, chicken with lemon and olives, and couscous — cracked wheat steamed and served with various meats and vegetables. For dessert try the pastries — dense combinations of honey, nuts, and layers of filo pastry — and some strong Moroccan coffee or mint tea. Arabic music and belly dancers. Closed Sundays. Reservations advised. Major credit cards accepted. 1280 Bay St. (phone: 961-0601). Moderate to inexpensive.

Church Street Café – Paintings by local artists hang on the walls, adding a bohemian touch to this informal, diner-style establishment. Continental fare includes rack of lamb, beef tenderloin medallions, and poached salmon. Open daily. Reservations necessary for groups of six or more. Major credit cards accepted. 485 Church St. (phone: 925-1155). Inexpensive.

Groaning Board – The gimmick here is the showing of award-winning commercials from the *Cannes International Advertising Film Festival.* While you're watching, pick something from a menu of hearty meat and vegetarian dishes, soup, salad, and sandwiches and homemade desserts. Open daily. Reservations advised for four or more. Major credit cards accepted. 131 Jarvis St. (phone: 363-0265). Inexpensive.

Ilie's – All dinners are *table d'hôte* in this Romanian eatery. Don't miss the *bors* — navy bean, bacon, and vegetable soup. For an entrée, try the crispy duckling or breaded veal cutlet in tomato and garlic sauce. Fully licensed. Closed Mondays. Reservations advised. Major credit cards accepted. 300 Eglinton St. W. (phone: 483-2654). Inexpensive.

Just Desserts – Virtually all manner of baked goods from oversize butter tarts to hefty pieces of an entire realm of cheesecakes as well as salads and quiche. The desserts are the cream of the crop of the best bakeries across town. The colorful assortment contrasts nicely with the tiled black and white decor. Sample one of the many coffees, teas, or juices. Open daily until 3 AM, 24 hours on Fridays and Saturdays. No reservations or credit cards accepted. 306 Davenport Rd. (phone: 922-6824). Inexpensive.

Korea House – The specialty here is succulent barbecued beef with pickled sesame leaves and cabbage. Fully licensed. Open daily. Reservations unnecessary. Most major credit cards accepted. 666 Bloor St. W. (phone: 536-8666). Inexpensive.

Silver Rail – It's Toronto's original tavern, the first bar to serve liquor legally in 1947. Here you'll see native Torontonians — including judges and shoppers — sipping beer at the "mile-long" bar, and eating plain, simple, mashed-potatoes-and-gravy style grub in booths. Across from *Eaton Centre* at 225 Yonge St. (phone: 368-8697). Inexpensive.

Vines – Across the street from the *St. Lawrence Centre* and the *O'Keefe Centre,* this wine bar is an ideal place to spend an hour or two dissecting the latest play or opera. Bistro-style hot dishes and light fare — cold roast beef, pâtés, and cheese plates — complement a wide variety of international wines. Wine is sold by the glass or by the bottle and a special vintage is featured daily. Closed Sundays. No reservations. Major credit cards accepted. 38 Wellington St. E. (phone: 869-0744). Inexpensive.

Young Lok – Peking and Szechuan regional food along with a tasty Mongolian grill, are the specialties served here, in what looks like an Oriental garden. Open daily. Reservations necessary for six or more. Major credit cards accepted. 122 St. Patrick St. (phone: 593-9819). Inexpensive.

VANCOUVER

In Vancouver, life is dominated by the elements — the sea, the mountains, and the weather that the two brew up between them. Pale buildings gleam in the marine air like opals set against varied hues of green — the green of the sea and the darker, truer green of the fir-covered slopes east of the city. The skyline is high-rise steel and glass, with snowcapped mountains for a backdrop. Around almost any corner is a glimpse of water, usually streaked by the white wake of an oceangoing freighter or dotted by white triangles of sailboats trailing colorful spinnakers.

Tucked into the southwestern corner of British Columbia, Canada's Pacific province, Vancouver is just about as close to the sea as it can be without leaving continental Canada. Downtown Vancouver sits on a peninsula bounded by English Bay to the west, the Fraser River to the south, and Burrard Inlet on the north. Across Burrard Inlet is the more securely land-locked residential suburb of North Vancouver. Flanking its lovely neighborhoods are the tall peaks of the Coastal Range — Grouse Mountain, Mt. Seymour, and Hollyburn. These 3,000-to-4,000-foot peaks do more than provide a magnificent background to the city; by capturing the storms that sweep in from the sea and down from the Alaskan panhandle, they create Vancouver's foggy, rainy climate, the gardener's delight and sun-worshiper's despair.

So the city spends its days between the towering certainties of mountain and the omnipresent sea. It would be tempting to say after a glimpse at the map that the mountains almost seem to be pushing the city into the waiting fingers of the sea, except that most residents embrace the surrounding elements and there is no hint of hostility in the relationship. They've *come* to Vancouver for the sea and the mountains, and those fingers of Pacific Ocean tickle their fancy and fill their leisure time with a diversity of activities unavailable anywhere else in Canada.

The sea, mountains, and moderate climate are prime forces in the city's development as part of Canada. Several thousand miles lie between Vancouver and Canada's other major cities, Toronto and Montreal (Vancouver, with just over a million residents in its metropolitan area, is Canada's third largest city and home to half of British Columbia's population.) This distance is further augmented by the Rocky Mountains, 400 miles (644 km) east of Vancouver, a psychological as well as physical barrier that isolates the city from eastern, urban Canada. Toronto and Montreal are 5 and 6 hours away by air. As a result, the city more resembles the US West Coast than the rest of Canada (the US border is only 30 miles (48 km) south; San Francisco is 2 hours away by air). It is as if the bonds of sea and mountain, which the city shares with the entire American Pacific coast, are stronger than the weight of culture and politics it shares with the rest of Canada.

The impact of the sea on life in Vancouver is enormous. The city has an excellent natural harbor that is active year-round. Wheat, timber, lumber, oil, and manufactured goods flow through the port in a steady stream, providing a crucial economic and transportation link with the rest of the world and maintaining an especially active trade relationship with Japan. Ships transport grain and lumber from Vancouver, returning with cars, appliances, and other Japanese consumer goods. The many rivers that flow from the Coastal Range into the sea along the Vancouver coast make the area prime salmon country. You'll be offered salmon everywhere — smoked or fresh, or frozen and packed to travel. It's part of the menu in many of the city's restaurants, from salmon sushi at the Japanese places to salmon Wellington in others. And if you fish, you may very well see it face-to-face.

When residents aren't on the sea or in it, they spend a good deal of their time over it. Because the city stretches over peninsulas and islands, most people have to cross water at least twice a day on one of the city's 20 bridges. And everywhere are seagulls — vying with pigeons for a place in the sun (or rain) on apartment ledges; scrambling after scraps at hamburger drive-ins; and battling with ducks and swans in the ponds of Stanley Park.

Still, with just over a million people, Vancouver is not any larger than a medium-size city by most standards. In the shadows of the aggressively new high-rise office buildings, there is a pulse of money and youth and drive. At the same time, the people — in full view of all these high-rises — stroll along the waterfront development at the foot of Granville Street and eat lunch on the grass at Stanley Park, all while speaking of that balance between work and leisure that gives life a certain grace.

Vancouver offers almost an embarrassment of riches for recreational activity, from boating and sailing out of Burrard Inlet or English Bay to skiing on Grouse Mountain. The thousand acres of Stanley Park offer miles of walking and biking trails through silent woodlands and over rolling lawns; cricket, tennis, lawn bowling, and putting; and less active sports, such as bird, water, and people watching.

The city itself is very much the product of the 20th century. The residents' interest and concern with the environment are reflected in the cleanliness of downtown streets. The newness of the city is reflected in its slick-as-glass skyline, a forest of high-rise buildings pricking the sky. The city's historic buildings are predominantly in the older sections of town — Gastown, where the city started, and Chinatown. Residential areas consist of nicely laid out streets with apartment buildings in the west end on the southern shore of English Bay; large, spectacular homes in Shaughnessy and Kerrisdale, south of downtown; sprawling contemporary homes in the southwestern suburbs of Richmond and Burnaby as well as in West Vancouver, on the north shore, where residents enjoy the highest per capita wealth in Canada.

Growth came quickly to Vancouver. Just over 100 years ago it was little more than tall trees stretching from the mountains to the sea. The Indians who lived here fished salmon and whale and traded furs with the white men, who first entered the area in June 1792, when explorer George Vancouver charted Burrard Inlet. Simon Fraser reached the Pacific from an inland route in 1808. But there was no permanent white settlement here until 1866, when a pioneer named "Gassy" Jack Deighton built a saloon and set up business near a very small sawmill where liquor was forbidden. A community grew up around the establishment, and two more saloons opened to serve the thirsty lumberjacks. The town lacked refinement, but it was certainly lively. Occasional sprees turned into community bashes that closed down the mill for days at a time. The area was so rich in potential resources, however, that the town kept growing. In 1886, with a population of 2,500 and 350 wooden buildings, it was incorporated as a city and named Vancouver. To celebrate, it ordered a brand-new fire wagon, but the city burned down 3 months later, 6 weeks before the new wagon arrived.

The city was soon rebuilt and began to thrive with the construction of the transcontinental railroad. A large influx of Chinese workers also came with the railroad, and thus began a number of ugly incidents between whites and the Chinese. When the city forcibly deported the Chinese from work camps to Victoria on Vancouver Island, the provincial government stepped in with constables to restore order. The deportation so outraged provincial officials that the city's charter was revoked for a period of time. As a result of such rabid racism, Vancouver's Chinese community segregated itself in Chinatown and established something of a parallel community.

The *Canadian Pacific Railroad* finally arrived in 1887, and Vancouver was on its way. Within the next few years several hotels and department stores were established. The first, the *Vancouver,* opened its doors in 1887, and *Hudson's Bay Company* opened the city's first department store. Now known as *The Bay,* it still is open for business.

In the 20th century, Vancouver has grown by leaps and bounds. The opening of the Panama Canal in 1914 strengthened the city by providing easy access to Europe for grain shipments from the western prairies. During US Prohibition, shipping took a new twist and rum-runners plied the coast for intrepid entrepreneurs who smuggled spirits southward. Today the situation is somewhat reversed. Because of lower liquor prices in the US, Vancouver residents often stock up before crossing the border from Washington State at Blaine.

Metropolitan Vancouver includes Burnaby, Richmond, New Westminster, Delta, and Surrey as well as North and West Vancouver. About 28% of the population are of British extraction; the others come from diverse backgrounds: some 100,340 Chinese, 60,435 Germans, 45,300 Indo-Pakistanis, 29,395 Italians, as well as smaller numbers of French, Japanese, Greeks, Scandinavians, Ukrainians, and Russians. In the last few years, there's been a large influx of Hong Kong Chinese as well. Many of these groups have their own newspapers, magazines, and clubs. Radio station CJVB caters exclusively to the ethnic community, with programming in many languages.

In spite of all the variety, though, you're always aware of Vancouver's basic Scottish-English heritage, on which the city was built. Labor and honor here are spelled with a "u"; the final two letters of words like theater and center are transposed. People queue up and are almost universally polite.

The ethnic community has made an impact on the restaurant scene, with representative cuisines of almost all the various national groups. Vancouver also has all the accoutrements of a major city — a symphony orchestra, an opera company, and several dance companies. The shopping is good here. West Vancouver's *Park Royal Shopping Centre* was the first big shopping mall in Canada. Malls have since become a Canadian rage, opening under, over, and alongside city streets and in suburban spaces from downtown Vancouver all the way to Underground Montreal. Old office buildings and warehouses have been converted into boutiques and studios. And there are antiques stores and galleries on South Granville Street, Asian crafts stores and vegetable markets in Chinatown, and delis, boutiques, and specialty stores in Gastown. But when you've had your fill of all these, there's plenty left of where Vancouverites spend their free time — the outdoors.

Leisure activity focuses on the sea year-round. From virtually any point in the city, it's a matter of minutes to the sandy beaches or rocky bays. Many people own boats and go sailing and fishing. During the summer, people swim in English Bay (every *New Year's Day* hundreds of hardy souls brave a dip in the cold depths, called the *Polar Bear Swim*).

Those more attuned to seasonal changes head for the mountains in wintertime. Grouse, Cypress, and Seymour mountains, approximately 20 minutes away, provide challenging slopes and equipment rentals. Other world-famous ski areas, such as Whistler and Blackcomb, are only 90 minutes from downtown.

Vancouver has a typical West Coast atmosphere in its high priority on outdoor activities. Perhaps this has something to do with the slower-paced, low-key feel of the whole city. Though business does get done in Vancouver, the pace is less hectic than that of eastern urban centers. Standing shoulder to shoulder with the wilderness and mixing races and nationalities, skyscrapers and ski runs, Vancouver is a delight to the imagination and the eye of the discerning visitor.

VANCOUVER AT-A-GLANCE

SEEING THE CITY: Grouse Mountain, rising 4,100 feet in North Vancouver, commands a spectacular view of the city and the surrounding coastal area. You can reach the top of the mountain and enjoy panoramic views along the way on the *Grouse Mountain Skyride,* an aerial tramway that runs from the parking lot to the summit. Open daily. Admission charge. At the top of Capilano Rd. in North Vancouver (phone: 984-0661).

Some 500 feet above the harbor, the Harbour Centre Observation Deck opens up a vista of waterfront activities. You can spend an hour or two watching the ships go by — oceangoing cruise ships, freighters, sailboats, yachts, seaplanes, and even rowing teams in training. Powerful telescopes are on hand for a closer look; staff members answer questions and point out special sights. After you've seen the city, take a half hour to view *Children of the Rainbow,* a marvelous panoramic film shown on a huge screen by a number of computer-directed projectors that produce stunning effects. Hours vary seasonally. Admission charge. 555 W. Hastings St. (phone: 689-0421).

And as if to emphasize what a beautiful town this really is, the drive from the airport along tree-lined Granville Street, with the North Shore mountains in the background, is a wonderful introduction.

SPECIAL PLACES: Walking is the best way to get a feel for certain sections, including Gastown, Chinatown, the Granville Island complex, Canada Place, and Stanley Park. But many of the area's attractions lie in the suburbs and outlying areas, to which it is most convenient to drive.

DOWNTOWN

Chinatown – The second-largest Chinese quarter in North America (only San Francisco's is larger or more energetic) encompasses a fair-size piece of downtown. This area has been the nucleus of the Chinese community for almost a century, first as a self-imposed ghetto in which the Chinese protected themselves from discrimination and physical abuse, today as a vibrant commercial community. Restaurants offer authentic Cantonese, Mandarin, and Shanghai cooking as well as Chinese-Canadian, which is virtually indistinguishable from Chinese-American. The stores range from large import emporiums to holes in the wall, with Mah-Jongg sets, jade and ivory carvings, dried lychee nuts, and dozens of items you never thought you wanted until you see them. The groceries feature smoked duck, bok choy, ginger root, and squid. At the Chinese newspaper office, the latest edition is posted in the window. Herbalists promise cures with roots and leaves and powdered bones. On Pender Street you can buy a cricket cage for $1 or a cloisonné vase for $100. There are also jade figurines of Kuan Yin, the goddess of mercy, or soapstone Foo dogs to guard your temple. Some highlights are the world's thinnest office building (Pender and Carrall); the Dr. Sun Yat-sen Classical Chinese Garden (578 Carral St.); the Kuomintang Building (529 Gore); the Chinese Cultural Centre (50 E. Pender St.); and Wong's Benevolent Society (121-125 E. Pender St.), exemplary of the balcony style. Two good places to eat are *Yen Lock* (67 E. Pender St.) and *Sun Tung Lock,* a seafood restaurant (127 E. Pender St.), both with appetizing dim sum and other Cantonese specialties. On Pender St. between Gore and Carrall Sts.

Stanley Park – Surrounded by the sea on three sides, this city park is one of the most beautiful in the world. The 1,000 acres are bespeckled with tall evergreens, gardens, lakes, lagoons, 50 miles of trails, tennis courts, a miniature golf course, bowling greens, restaurants, coffee shops, snack bars, a zoo, and the *Vancouver Aquarium* (see below). Residents use the park for hiking, jogging, biking, concerts, picnicking, and simple relaxing. The Seawall flanks the water for 5 miles and makes a lovely walk. Open daily. Some admission charges. At the foot of W. Georgia St.

Vancouver Aquarium – With over 9,000 aquatic inhabitants, this is Canada's largest and most famous aquarium. Attractions include the H. R. MacMillan Gallery of Whales, the Marine Mammal Center, and IMAQ, the Arctic Sea display. Popular exhibitions are the Amazon Gallery and the British Columbia Hall of Fish, displaying local sealife. There are killer whale shows throughout the day and public feedings of sharks, sea otters, and harbor seals. The gift shop features local craftwork. Open daily. Admission charge. In Stanley Park (phone: 682-1118).

Gastown – Named for "Gassy" Jack Deighton, first citizen and saloonkeeper, this is where Vancouver began as a rowdy milltown. Later it was the city's Skid Row and, still later, home of the drug culture. Today it is a living example of successful urban renewal. Extensive renovation has transformed the warehouses into antiques stores, boutiques, galleries, and restaurants with lovely brick façades and gaslight fixtures. *The Landing* (at the Cordova St. entrance to Gastown) is the latest trendy shopping center. The only steam clock in the world is at Cambie and Water Streets. *Umberto Al Porto* (321 Water St.) has homemade pasta and a harbor view from the upstairs lounge. Bounded by Water, Alexander, Columbia, and Cordova Sts.

Granville Island Market – Just under the south end of the Granville Bridge, this large indoor market has become the prime gathering spot for those in search of the freshest seafood and produce. You can get salmon packed to go, and a number of the stalls sell snacking food that can be consumed while watching the tugboats glide to and fro. Take any Granville Street bus and change at Broadway for the No. 51. Two independent ferry services, *Granville Island Ferries* and the *Aquabus,* run daily between Vancouver's West End and the Island. Granville Island itself is growing in importance each day — the complex is now home to two theaters, galleries, assorted shops, and a number of restaurants.

Robson Street – Once a charming, old European neighborhood with numerous small shops, Robsonstrasse has become Robson Street, a name change echoed by its metamorphosis into a fashion magnet for upscale boutiques. A few of the old-time businesses remain, however, and you can still buy knockwurst in bulk. The *Heidelberg* restaurant (1636 Robson; phone: 684-0817) continues to harken back to a bygone era and still serves up hearty cooking. But the street where shopkeepers once knew their customers by name is now primarily a haven for shops with names well known to the world at large: *Ralph Lauren, Rodier Paris, Ferragamo,* and the list goes on. A few bargains are still available but, in general, shopping here will require a well-stocked wallet.

Robson Square – The innovative complex designed by Arthur Erickson houses the provincial government offices, the courthouse, and shopping facilities in a multilevel galleria. The key attractions are a skating rink and a theater. Robson at Hornby.

Vancouver Art Gallery – The old courthouse is now an art gallery, the dramatic centerpiece of the Robson Square complex. There are four well-designed floors of exhibit space and numerous traveling shows; one entire room is devoted to the late Emily Carr, British Columbia's best-known artist. Closed Tuesdays. Admission charge, except Thursday evenings. 750 Hornby St. (phone: 682-4668).

Canada Place – Built for *Expo '86,* this building is known for its ship-like appearance and five sails on the roof. It houses the *Trade and Convention Centre,* the *Pan Pacific* hotel, and *CN IMAX* (Canadian National Image Maximum) *Theatre;* The special IMAX screen makes viewers feel as if they are in the picture (phone: 682-6422).

Science World – Vancouver's newest museum has an interesting and educational collection of participatory exhibits displaying a fascinating blend of art, science, and technology. There are special exhibits about space and the evolution of the Earth, plus a special dinosaur display. Films also are shown — on the largest Omnimax screen in the world. Open daily. Admission charge. 1455 Quebec St. (phone: 687-7832).

BEYOND DOWNTOWN AND THE SUBURBS

Van Dusen Botanical Gardens – Gardening is such a passion in Vancouver that it has been called the city's religion. If that's the case, Van Dusen must be the answer to a communal prayer. Its 55 acres of formal gardens and lakes are given over to displays of native and exotic plants. The fountain at the entrance is a gift from the Swedish Society and depicts the contribution of Swedish Canadians to the economic and cultural life of British Columbia. Open daily. Admission charge. 37th Ave. and Oak St. (phone: 266-7194).

Simon Fraser University – Sitting atop Burnaby Mountain, this campus commands beautiful views of the city and the surrounding coastal areas. Most of its striking modern buildings were designed by Arthur Erickson. Hourly tours of the campus are conducted during July and August and on weekends the rest of the year (no charge). The campus theater has frequent programs that may interest visitors. Open daily. No admission charge. In Burnaby on Burnaby Mountain (phone: 291-3210).

Museum of Anthropology – The University of British Columbia campus museum has fine collections of art and artifacts from British Columbian coastal Indians, and from elsewhere in the Americas, the Pacific Islands, Asia, and Africa. The entire collection is displayed in public galleries, with striking visible storage galleries designed around computerized data books for browsing or serious research. There's also a unique group of totem poles in the Great Hall. Closed Mondays. Admission charge, except Tuesdays. On NW Marine Dr. (phone: 228-5087).

Bloedel Conservatory – Under this ultramodern dome, you'll find some 350 exotic plants and flowers thriving in simulated desert, rain forest, and tropical environments. There are also 50 varieties of birds from throughout the world. Open daily. Admission charge. In Queen Elizabeth Park at 33rd and Cambie (phone: 872-5513).

H. R. MacMillan Planetarium – An unusual building that has sophisticated projection and sound equipment essential to its imaginative visual presentations of astronomical themes. The shows change frequently, and you should make reservations in advance. Here, too, is the *Centennial Museum,* depicting Vancouver's early history as well as native British Columbian cultures, and the *Maritime Museum,* permanent berth of the *St. Roch,* the first vessel ever to navigate the treacherous Northwest Passage in 1928. The Royal Canadian Mounted Police schooner has been restored and is now a national historic site. There's also a restaurant and gift shop. Closed Mondays. Admission charge. 1100 Chestnut St. in Vanier Park (phone: 736-7736).

Nitobe Memorial Gardens – This traditional Japanese garden on the University of BC campus is a serene, tranquil setting for contemplation. Though the gardens are small, you'll probably want to linger. There's a tea house for ceremonial occasions. Open daily from April to early October; otherwise, closed on weekends. Admission charge. On the campus at NW Marine Dr. (phone: 228-6038).

Lighthouse Park – Eight miles of trails lead through virgin forest, one of the most beautiful in the southwestern corner of British Columbia. The park is named for the 60-foot Point Atkinson Lighthouse, to which a short, half-mile hiking trail leads. It ends at a rocky bluff overlooking the beautiful Georgia Strait. Open daily. No admission charge. 5 miles (8 km) west of Lions Gate Bridge on Marine Dr., West Vancouver.

Old Hasting Mill Store – This small museum, with its collection of Indian artifacts, is one of the few buildings that survived the great fire of 1886. Originally built on Burrard Inlet, the store was relocated to its present site in 1930. Open daily June to September 15 and weekends only September 16 through May. Admission by donation. 1575 Alma Rd. at Point Grey Rd. (phone: 228-1213).

Grouse Mountain – In addition to the *Skyride* and stunning views of the city from the summit (see *Seeing the City,* above), this 4,100-foot mountain is only 20 minutes from downtown and has good ski runs with chair lifts, a chalet, a lounge, rentals, and a variety of slopes. In summertime its many paths are great for hiking. The *Grouse Nest* dining room serves lunch and dinner and has excellent views. Open daily. Admission charge. At the top of Capilano Rd. in North Vancouver (phone: 984-0661).

Capilano Suspension Bridge – One of the world's longest suspension foot bridges, hanging 230 feet above the Capilano River and stretching 450 feet across the canyon. The original bridge was erected in 1889; the bridge that stands now was built in 1956. If you walk the bridge you will feel its movement underneath. There's a gift shop and totem pole park. Open daily until dark, with illumination in July and August until 10:30 PM. Admission charge. 3735 Capilano Rd., North Vancouver (phone: 985-7474).

Capilano Salmon Hatchery – A working fish farm built to increase the declining salmon run in the Capilano River, and so far it has been extremely effective. You can see salmon in glass tanks and study the life cycle of this amazing fish as it is described in illustrated diagrams. Open daily. No admission charge. 4500 Capilano Park Rd., North Vancouver (phone: 987-1411).

Cypress Provincial Park – This mountain park overlooking the city has meadows, lakes, and forests spanning 7,037 acres of the North Shore mountains. Hiking, snowshoeing, and cross-country and downhill skiing are favorite activities here. Open daily (phone: 926-5612).

FARTHER OUT

Reifel Bird Sanctuary – Home and nesting ground of about 230 species of swans, geese, and ducks, this wild bird sanctuary has footpaths and observation towers for viewing. The 850-acre site is open daily. Admission charge. Take Hwy. 99 south to the

Ladner exit, then River Rd. west; cross the Westham Island Bridge and continue to the end of the road (phone: 946-6980).

Vancouver Game Farm – Lions and tigers and bears, monkeys, zebras, and giraffes, are among the 80 species from all over the world that inhabit these 120 acres of farmland. You can amble around the grounds or tour by car. The amiable elephants are available for rides during the summer. There also are picnic facilities and a gift shop. Open daily. Admission charge. 5048 264th St., Aldergrove (phone: 261-0225).

Fort Langley National Historic Park – Built in 1827 as the Hudson's Bay Company's fort, this park includes the original company store and restored gates, palisades, officers' quarters, and shops. The fort is historically quite interesting if for no other reason than it predates Vancouver by a number of years. Open daily. Admission charge. 30 miles (48 km) east in Fort Langley (phone: 888-4424).

Seabus – View the city from a different angle on twin-hulled catamarans operated as part of the city's public transit system. The *Burrard Otter* and the *Burrard Beaver* each shuttle up to 400 passengers between the North Shore's *Lonsdale Quay Market* and *Skytrain*'s Waterfront Station at the foot of Granville Street downtown. For schedule and fares, call 261-5100.

Royal Hudson Steam Train – A must for train buffs, this is a journey into the past aboard a genuine steam engine. Day trips aboard the *Royal Hudson Steam Engine 2860* leave from North Vancouver, follow Howe Sound, with its magnificent ocean and mountain views, and proceed up the coast to the logging community of Squamish, which is probably the least interesting part of the journey. The train is replete with a bar car and several refurbished passenger cars. The round trip takes a good 6 hours, including a lunch stop in Squamish. Another option provides what is perhaps the best way to see Howe Sound and to have a trip on this train. The boat-train day trip transports travelers one way on the train and they return by means of the M.V. *Britannia,* Canada's largest sightseeing vessel. Trips are made from May 21 to September 24, Wednesdays through Sundays. Reservations are mandatory. Tickets and details from *Harbour Ferries,* 1782 W. Georgia St. (phone: 687-9558).

■**EXTRA SPECIAL:** Just a 90-minute ferry ride through the spectacular Gulf Islands, and you're on Vancouver Island, 24 miles across the Strait of Georgia from the mainland. Some 285 miles in length, it is Canada's largest Pacific island and quite spectacular. Actually the top of a partially submerged mountain system, much of the island is heavily forested and mountainous. This is most dramatically apparent in the Pacific Rim National Park on the western coast. Here seals, sea lions, and shore birds inhabit 250 square miles of craggy headlands, white sandy beaches, interior lakes, and estuaries. There are campgrounds in the park and accommodations nearby.

From the terminal at Swartz Bay, it's a 45-minute drive to Victoria, the provincial capital. Victoria is beautifully situated on the shores of the Juan de Fuca Strait, surrounded by sea, with snowcapped mountains forming an impressive backdrop. This is the most English community on the continent, a haven of Sunday afternoon games of lawn bowling, well-loved gardens, and proper English high tea. The wealth of its 276,300 residents is reflected in the lovely residential districts of fine homes and carefully tended gardens. The main attractions are the dignified Parliament Buildings and the magnificent and justifiably renowned Butchart Gardens (phone: 652-5256) — 50 acres developed from an old quarry with six gardens, including the Sunken Lake with its fountains, an English rose garden, the lush Italian gardens, and a delicate Japanese garden. At night they're illuminated. There's a restaurant, coffee shop, and gift shop, and live entertainment during July and August.

Shops in Victoria offer good values in woolens, china, crystal, jade, antiques, and handicrafts. If you are staying over, reserve a room at the *Empress* (phone: 384-8111), the castle by the sea that is the grande dame of Canadian Pacific hotels. This elegant establishment recently underwent a $45-million restoration, fully recapturing her original charm and elegance. If you prefer something smaller and a bit out of town, try the charming *Oak Bay Beach* hotel (1175 Beach Dr.; phone: 598-4556). For more details on Victoria, see the Vancouver route in DIRECTIONS.

SOURCES AND RESOURCES

 TOURIST INFORMATION: For general information, brochures, and maps, contact the Greater Vancouver Visitors and Convention Bureau (562 Burrard St.; phone: 683-2000). The office is conveniently located just down the street from the *Hyatt Regency* hotel. City street maps are available at most newsstands and department stores.

For maps and general information on Victoria, contact the Tourism Victoria (812 Wharf St.; phone: 382-2127) in front of the *Empress* hotel.

Local Coverage – The *Province,* morning daily and the only Sunday paper; the *Sun,* afternoon daily except Sundays. *Vancouver; Western Living,* and *West* are monthly magazines concerned with the West Coast lifestyle; another monthly, *Key to Vancouver,* includes maps and information on shopping and entertainment.

Food – *Vancouver* contains short items on some of the city's restaurants, and the *Sun* and *Province* both have restaurant reviews. Vancouver *Gastronomique* ($9.95) describes a full range of options.

Telephone – The area code for Vancouver is 604.

Sales Tax – The basic sales tax is 7%.

Currency – All prices are quoted in US dollars unless otherwise indicated.

 TIPPING: At a restaurant generally leave 15% of the bill. Taxi drivers are usually given 10% to 15% of the fare. Airport porters and bellboys are given about CN$1 per bag. Hotel maids' service fee is usually included in the bill, but if you want to tip, leave CN$1 per person, per day.

 CLIMATE: Rain is a fact of life in Vancouver, so an umbrella and a raincoat are good ideas no matter what time of year you visit. Some snow usually falls during the winter months, although it rarely stays on the ground very long. Winter mornings can be nippy, but on a few days the mercury dips below 32F (zero C); the average winter temperature is around 39F (4C). Summers are warm and pleasant, with temperatures averaging in the 60s and 70s F (15-23C).

 GETTING AROUND: Airport Transportation – Both the *Airport Express* and *Perimeter Transportation* run a mini-bus service every 15 minutes from 5:45 AM with stops at major downtown hotels. For information, call 273-0071 or 266-0376.

Bus – The *BC Hydro* bus system covers most of Greater Vancouver with extensive downtown service; exact fare is required. Service is greatly reduced after midnight. For route information, call 261-5100.

Car Rental – All major North American firms are represented: *Avis,* near the *Vancouver* hotel (757 Hornby St.; phone: 682-1621); *Hertz* (*Pan Pacific Hotel,* 900 Canada Pl.; phone: 681-4333); and *Budget* (450 W. Georgia St.; phone: 685-0536).

Ferry – *Sea-Bus* is a ferry system that links the North Shore with downtown

Vancouver. Ferries depart every 15 minutes from the downtown terminal at the CP Rail station and from the North Vancouver terminal at the foot of Lonsdale. Transfers are available to connect with *Sea-Bus.* For information, call 261-5100.

For information on service to Vancouver Island, contact *BC Ferries* (phone: 669-1211) which sail to Victoria and Nanaimo, farther north on the Island.

Taxi – Major companies are *Yellow Cab* (phone: 681-3311); *Black Top Cabs* (phone: 681-2181); *Maclure's* (phone: 731-9211); and *Advance* (phone: 876-5555). Taxi stands are located throughout the city and at most hotels. Hailing cabs in the street is difficult. Almost any fare within the city will be under $10; a trip to the airport from downtown runs about $13.50.

Sightseeing Tours – *Gray Line* (phone: 681-8687) operates tours from most of the downtown hotels, and in summer, colorful British doubledeckers join the fleet.

SPECIAL EVENTS: For exact dates, check with the Visitors and Convention Bureau. At the *Polar Bear Swim,* held every *New Year's Day* since 1919, hardy souls of all ages dip into the Pacific at English Bay.

Considered one of the best of its kind in North America, the annual *Children's Festival* in May has a lively program of puppet shows, mime, dancers, singers, and plays — all performed under colorful tents in Vanier Park.

The *Vancouver Sea Festival* in mid-July is a series of parades, concerts, salmon barbecues, and sports events, topped off by a gigantic fireworks display over English Bay. Another highlight is the Nanaimo to Vancouver *Bathtub Race,* which draws contestants from around the world.

The *Vancouver Folk Music Festival* is a long weekend in mid-July filled with performances by musicians from all over North America; there are workshops and jam sessions as well.

The *Abbotsford International Air Show* features aerobatics and aircraft displays by everything from Piper Cubs to 747s. (You can fly your own plane in and take part.) It's held on a weekend in early August at the Abbotsford Airport, 45 miles (72 km) east of Vancouver. For information, call 859-9211.

Every year in late August, a grand parade through downtown Vancouver kicks off the *Pacific National Exhibition,* featuring concerts by renowned artists, logging sports exhibitions, livestock and agricultural displays, horse races, food fairs, and a good midway. For information, call 253-2311.

In December the *Christmas Carol Ship,* with a troupe of carolers on board, leads a flotilla of ships, all lit up for *Christmas,* around Vancouver Harbor from December 8th through the 17th. For information, call 683-2000.

MUSEUMS: The *Museum of Anthropology,* the *Vancouver Art Gallery,* the *MacMillan Planetarium,* the *Maritime Museum,* the *Centennial Museum,* and the *Vancouver Aquarium* are described fully in *Special Places.* Other interesting museums include the following:

Cap's Cycle Museum – Antique bicycles. 420 E. Columbia St., New Westminster (phone: 524-3611).

BC Sports Hall of Fame – Medals and memorabilia from *Olympic Games,* focusing on BC athletes. In the BC Pavilion of Exhibition Park (phone: 253-5655).

SHOPPING: Vancouver is a good city to shop in, with almost everything you need and some things you never even thought of buying. The three major downtown department stores — *Eaton's, The Bay,* and *Woodward's* — carry a full line of standard merchandise, and numerous shops have regional goods and unusual specialties — everything from salmon packed to travel to Indian and Eskimo art to railway paraphernalia. The following is a highly eclectic guide.

Antiques – *Deeler's Antiques* (832 N. Park Royal, West Vancouver; phone: 922-0213) is one of the largest importers and a good place to browse. *Uno Langmann Ltd.* (2117 S. Granville St.; phone: 736-8825), specializes in pre-1830 quality items. *Vancouver Antique Centre* (422 Richards St.; phone: 669-0089) features 20 shops.

Art – *Inuit Gallery,* (345 Water St., phone: 688-7323) carries a world-class collection on Inuit and Northwest Native Art. The *Equinox Gallery* (2321 Granville St., phone: 736-2405) has a notable collection of contemporary Canadian and international art.

Books – *Duthie's* is Vancouver's foremost bookstore, with several locations. *The Paperback Cellar* (919 Robson St.; phone: 684-4496) is the main store and has a broad range of titles.

Coffee – *Murchie's* (970 Robson St.; call 662-3776 for additional locations) is an old-fashioned coffee and tea shop that sells fresh-roasted coffee and a variety of teas. *Starbucks Coffee Company* has six locations in Vancouver offering the best cappuccino and fresh roasted coffees. The contemporary settings are a hit with the locals (phone: 685-9233).

Fashion – The *Pacific Centre* and *Vancouver Centre* shopping malls run underground for more than 2 square blocks and connect places such as the *Four Seasons* hotel and *Eaton's* department store. You'll find many shops in both complexes including *Holt Renfrew,* which features high quality men's and women's clothing and accessories. Robson Street has become a major fashion center, with elegant designer — as well as fun — fashion boutiques. Fine shops such as *Leone* can be found at the *Sinclair Centre,* a restored building (757 W. Hastings).

Furs – *Pappas Designers Ltd.* (449 Hamilton St.; phone: 681-6391) has a terrific array of high-fashion furs and a clientele from rock stars to jet setters. A classic selection is offered at *Amante Furs* (480 Granville St.; phone: 689-5929).

Games – If there's a game going, the *Games People* — at five locations around town, including one at *Pacific Centre* — has got it, from backgammon to computer chess and everything in between (phone: 986-5110).

Jewelry – *Brinkhaus* (705 Hornby; phone: 689-7055) features fine gems and Swiss watches. *Le Must de Cartier Boutique* is in *Pacific Centre* (phone: 689-9411). *Birks* (710 Granville St.; phone: 669-3333), Canada's major jewelry and silver supplier, has nine locations in town. Luxurious jewelry, sterling silver, and Royal Copenhagen china are available at *Georg Jensen* (648 Hornby; phone: 688-4744). For gold and silver jewelry handcrafted by a European master, try *Toni Cavelti* (692 Seymour St.; phone: 681-3481).

Leather – *Neto Leathers* (in Gastown at 347 Water St.; phone: 682-6424) features well-crafted garments in leather, suede, and fur.

Pipes – *Pipe Den* (714 West Hastings St.; phone: 688-5023) has a wide selection of pipes, a pipe reconditioning service, and more than 40 blends of tobacco. They also do custom tobacco blending.

Quilts – *Down 'n Under* (Park Royal in West Vancouver; phone: 926-2821) has an excellent selection of European-style eiderdown quilts.

Railway Paraphernalia – *Railway World* (150 Water St.; phone: 681-4811) is heaven for the train buff, with items ranging from models to books and calendars.

Sailing Supplies – The *Quarterdeck* (375 Water St.; phone: 683-7475) has everything for sailors and their vessels.

Salmon – Some of the world's best salmon comes from BC waters, and fresh or smoked salmon can be bought packed to go at *Longliner Seafoods* (on Granville Island; phone: 681-9016), or at *Jet Set Sam* (at the airport; phone: 273-9917).

Tuxedos – If you get an unexpected invitation to a formal occasion, *Black & Lee* (1110 Seymour St.; phone: 688-2481) can supply everything you need, including shirts, shoes, and accessories.

Woolens – *Edward Chapman Ltd.,* for men (833 W. Pender St.; phone: 685-6207); *Edward Chapman Ladies Shop,* for women (2596 Granville St.; phone: 732-3394).

SPORTS: Vancouver has become a major sports city in recent years, with plenty to participate in and watch.

Baseball – The *Canadians* have brought pro baseball back to the city with their home games at *Nat Bailey Stadium,* 4601 Ontario St. (phone: 872-5232).

Bicycling – Riding around Stanley Park is a good way to see this attraction or work off a big lunch. Rent 1- to 5-speeds, mountain bikes, and tandems (two-seaters) from *Stanley Park Bike Rentals,* 676 Chilco St. (phone: 681-5581).

Fishing – Vancouver is special in having easy access to both freshwater and deep-sea fishing. Take your pick — from the Capilano River, where you can catch trout, steel-head, and Dolly Varden, to any of the bays surrounding the city. The main catch is salmon. Fishing charter companies include *Westin Bayshore Yacht Charter* (1601 W. Georgia St.; phone: 682-3377) and *Malibu Yacht Charters* (at the foot of Bute St.; phone: 685-8468).

Football – The *BC Lions,* Vancouver's contenders in the Canadian Football League, take on all comers at the city's domed *BC Place Stadium,* 777 Pacific Blvd. S. (phone: 669-2300).

Golf – Eight excellent private golf courses, plus a dozen or more public links, dot the area. *Gleaneagles* (in West Vancouver; phone: 921-7353) is the best, with *Langara* (290 W. 49th Ave.; phone: 321-8013), a close second. Upgraded to one of the best public facilites in the entire country is the *University Golf Club* (5185 University Blvd.; phone: 224-7799).

Hockey – The National Hockey League Vancouver *Canucks* defend the ice at *Pacific Coliseum* in Exhibition Park (phone: 254-5141).

Horse Racing – The horses run at Exhibition Park, on the Pacific National Exhibi-tion grounds, from April through October. For information and reservations, call 254-1631.

Jogging – Stanley Park has a 7-km (4.3-mile) path that circles around the beautiful park. Jogging along the 1-mile West Vancouver Seawall is also popular.

Motor Racing – You can catch national and international race car action at *West-wood,* 12 miles (19 km) from downtown, from March to September.

Sailing – There are several yacht clubs, including the venerable *Royal Vancouver Yacht Club* (phone: 224-1344). Among the boat charter outfits are *Admiralty Yachts* (1666 Duranleau St.; phone: 685-7371) and *Pacific Quest Charters* (1521 Foreshore Walk; phone: 682-2205).

Skiing – At Grouse, Seymour, and Cypress mountains, you can ski down splendid slopes overlooking the city. For information and weather reports, call 926-5612. Some of the finest skiing in North America is at Whistler and Blackcomb mountains, about 1½ hours drive from Vancouver. For information, call 687-6761. Dozens of ski pack-ages are available, ranging from 1-day jaunts to week-long ski-ins. The Vancouver Visitors Bureau has full details.

Tennis – The city maintains an extensive number of municipal courts. Most popular are those in Stanley Park.

THEATER: The dailies and some city magazines give complete listings of what's on where and when. Among the most prominent theaters, repertory groups, and box offices are *Arts Club Theatre* (Granville Island; phone: 687-1644); *Theatre Sports/Back Alley Theatre* (751 Thurlow St.; phone: 688-7013); *Concert Box Office* (1304 W. Georgia St.; phone: 280-4444); *Metro Theatre* (1370 S.W. Marine Dr.; phone: 266-7191); *Orpheum Theatre* (Granville Mall; phone: 665-3050); *Punchlines* (15 Water St.; phone: 684-3015) for stand-up comedy; *Queen Elizabeth Theatre* (649 Cambie St.; phone: 665-3050); *Studio 58* (100 W. 49th Ave.; phone: 324-5227); *Vancouver East Cultural Centre* (1895 Venables St.; phone: 254-9578); *Vancouver Opera Association* (1132 Hamilton St.; phone: 682-2871); *Vancouver*

Playhouse (543 W. 7th Ave.; phone: 872-6622); the *Waterfront Theatre* (Granville Island; phone: 685-6217). An active program of dance performances appears at the *Queen Elizabeth Theatre* (Hamilton and Georgia Sts.) and offers some world class troupes, including the *Joffrey Ballet, Royal Winnipeg Ballet,* and BC's own troupe, *Ballet British Columbia.* For more information on the latter, call 669-5954.

 MUSIC: Almost any evening, there's some musical entertainment in Vancouver, from resident ensembles and orchestras to soloists and singers to visiting superstars. Rock concerts frequently take place in the *BC Place Stadium,* the *Pacific Coliseum,* the *Orpheum, 86th Street Music Hall,* and sometimes at the *Queen Elizabeth Theatre.* The *Vancouver Symphony Orchestra* offers a full season of music. The *Vancouver Opera Association* presents classic operas each year. A good reference for musical events is the *Canadian Music Centre* (phone: 734-4622).

 NIGHTCLUBS AND NIGHTLIFE: Vancouver has an eclectic after-hours scene offering something for everyone. The *Pelican Bay Bar* (in the *Granville Island* hotel; phone: 683-7373) is very lively and attracts a crowd ranging in age from early 20s to late 40s. Another big attraction is *Richard's on Richards* (1036 Richards St.; phone: 687-6794), which has 4 bars, videos, and dancing to both live and recorded music. In the same vein, *Systems* (350 Richards St.; phone: 687-5007) has an 1,800-foot dance floor. Other spots include the *Luv-A-Fair* (1275 Seymour St.; phone: 685-3288), where everyone meets to see rock videos and dance to live and recorded sounds.

Among the hotel meeting places are: *Le Meridien's Gerard Bar,* (845 Burrard St.; phone: 682-5511), the *Garden Lounge* at the *Four Seasons* (791 W. Georgia St.; phone: 689-9333), and the *Bacchus Lounge* in the *Wedgewood* hotel (845 Hornby St.; phone: 689-7777).

The *Commodore Ballroom* (870 Granville St.; phone: 681-7838) is another place to keep in mind for a wide variety of entertainment, ranging from the *New Glenn Miller Orchestra* and Cajun rocker Clifton Chenier to bluesman John Mayall.

Down in Gastown, the *Town Pump* (66 Water St.; phone: 683-6695) has brick walls and lots of brass trimmings, and features live bands that run from rhythm and blues to folk. *Hot Jazz Society* (2120 Main St.; phone: 873-4131) is where live Dixieland, swing, and big band sounds are produced by local and visiting musicians.

BEST IN TOWN

 CHECKING IN: Vancouver has a good choice of accommodations, from comfortable, old-fashioned smaller hotels to modern, luxury high-rises. During the past decade, especially in preparation for the wildly successful *1986 World's Fair,* numerous major hotels were constructed downtown. All hotels listed have room phones and color TV sets. Expect to pay $130 and up per night for a double room in the expensive range; $75 to $120 in the moderate range; and from $55 to $72 in the inexpensive category. All telephone numbers are in the 604 area code unless otherwise indicated.

> ***Delta Place*** – This lovely downtown hostelry has 197 well-appointed rooms. Amenities include a main dining room, a health club, a swimming pool, squash and racquetball courts, and a library. 645 Howe St. (phone: 687-1122). Expensive.

> ***Four Seasons*** – This leading establishment in the center of the city soars above

Pacific Centre. Everything is located right here or just an enclosed walk away. Among the features are 3 restaurants, including the elegant *Chartwell.* The 385 rooms and suites have spectacular city and mountain views. The *Garden Lounge,* with its piano bar, is a favorite meeting spot. There also is an indoor and an outdoor pool, and an exercise room. 791 W. Georgia St. (phone: 689-9333). Expensive.

Hyatt Regency – Quite lively, it sits atop the *Royal Centre* shopping mall. There are lots of luxurious touches in the rooms, 3 restaurants, an outdoor heated pool, lounges, plus a sauna and exercise rooms. 655 Burrard St. (phone: 687-6543). Expensive.

Méridien – One of the newest luxury hotels in town; gracious, appealing, and entirely satisfying. Although the rooms tend to be on the smallish side, they are exceptionally well done. Marble bathrooms are very luxurious, and corner rooms that end with the number 26 have especially good views. There's a substantial health and beauty center, plus a swimming pool and sundeck located in *La Grande Residence,* the adjacent luxury residential tower. Super service and extremely personal attention for a property with almost 400 rooms. 845 Burrard St. (phone: 682-5511 or 800-543-4300). Expensive.

New World Harbourside – Close to the downtown core, this sleek 19-story hotel has a revolving restaurant on top and good views of seaplanes and tugs from some rooms that overlook the water. 1133 W. Hastings St. (phone: 689-9211). Expensive.

Pan Pacific – Right on the harbor at Canada Place — the city's downtown waterfront development, which is the legacy of *Expo '86* — this place provides a view of harbor activity nearly as spectacular as the view in Hong Kong. A member of the Leading Hotels of the World group, it blends artfully with its location, since the design includes a pierlike wing jutting into the water. There are 507 luxurious rooms and suites, including some classed as ultra-deluxe (with special amenities such as a private concierge). The three restaurants here include one with casual dining and a harbor view, another with Japanese food, and the more formal *Five Sails,* with continental fare and panoramas of both the water and the North Shore mountains. Another highlight is the fitness club, with squash and racquetball courts, sauna, and aerobics classes. 999 Canada Place (phone: 662-8111; in the US, 800-663-1515). Expensive.

Vancouver – Now operated by Canadian Pacific, this property has long been a landmark on the downtown skyline. Stately, comfortable, and elegant throughout, it is not without its own informal touches. *The Roof* is a favorite weekend restaurant stop, with good food, entertainment, dancing, and a nice view. 900 W. Georgia St. (phone: 684-3131). Expensive.

Westin Bayshore Inn – It's in the heart of the city, but the ocean is at your doorstep; in fact, you can moor your yacht at the hotel dock. The late Howard Hughes once rented the top floors for a brief stay. There's a selection of elegant shops in the lobby, Beefeater-costumed doormen, a pool, a *Trader Vic's* restaurant and the *Garden* restaurant on the lobby level. 1601 W. Georgia St. (phone: 682-3377). Expensive.

Coast Plaza at Stanley Park – The primary attractions at this West End complex are a close proximity to the beach activity at English Bay and a 2-block stroll from the delights of Stanley Park. Some rooms come with a complete kitchen for an additional $10 per day. *Humphrey's* restaurant graces the 35th floor, and there is a shopping complex on the lower level. 1733 Comox St. (phone: 688-7711). Expensive to moderate.

Georgian Court – Many of the 180 rooms afford magnificent panoramic views, and if you intend to go to any of the sporting events or trade shows at the *BC Place*

Stadium, this is your best bet. The lounge is at once dignified and homey, and there is also a dining room. Of the 12 floors, 4 are designated for nonsmokers. 773 Beatty St. (phone: 682-5555). Expensive to moderate.

Granville Island – Situated near the city's popular covered market, this waterfront hostelry has a total of 54 rooms and suites. Also within are a popular nightspot and a restaurant (see *Eating Out*); outside are many seawall pathways on which to stroll. 1253 Johnston St. (phone: 683-7373). Expensive to moderate.

Wedgewood – Right across from the Robson Square complex, this intimate place has 94 attractively decorated rooms. There also is a lovely dining room which is popular for Sunday brunch. 845 Hornby St. (phone: 689-7777). Expensive to moderate.

Delta's Airport Resort – Convenient to the airport, this inn is just 20 minutes from downtown. Facilities include covered tennis and squash courts, pools, patios, and saunas. Rooms are modern, spacious, and comfortable. A courtesy bus will meet guests at the airport. 10251 St. Edward's Dr., Richmond (phone: 278-9611). Moderate.

Holiday Inn Downtown – Accommodations here offer good value. The 210 rooms are quiet, comfortable, and attractive; there's an indoor pool, a dining room, a coffee shop, and a cocktail lounge. 1110 Howe St. (phone: 684-2151). Moderate.

Georgia – The *Beatles* once stayed here, and if that's not enough, there's also plenty of Old World charm. Though the rooms are air conditioned, you can open the windows if you're a fresh-air fan. A streetside restaurant, *Night Court,* is busy at lunchtime and open to the wee hours. 801 W. Georgia St. (phone: 682-5566). Moderate.

Westbrook – Once host to many of the international participants at *Expo '86,* it boasts 200 studio suites, each with a queen-size bed, separate sitting area, and a kitchenette. Other amenities include *Page's Café,* a sports complex, and a good location. 1234 Hornby St. (phone: 688-1234). Moderate.

Park Royal – This small, quiet hostelry is nestled below the mountains on the banks of the Capilano River, across the Lion's Gate Bridge, 15 minutes from downtown. Beaches, golf, and ski lifts are nearby, as is the *Park Royal Shopping Centre.* There's a lovely terrace, surrounded by flowers and trees, where lunch, cocktails, and light evening meals are served. The *Tudor Dining Room*'s Sunday brunch is quite popular among the locals, as is the cozy pub. 440 Clyde St. at Sixth Ave., West Vancouver (phone: 926-5511). Moderate.

Barclay – Situated in the heart of the West End within strolling distance of most of the attractions of the city core, this small European-style property has 85 comfortable suites. *Barclay's,* the house restaurant, has notably reasonable prices. 1348 Robson St. (phone: 688-8850). Inexpensive.

Sylvia – Just a stone's throw from the Pacific Ocean, this 9-story West End hostelry offers great value. The ivy-covered building has been updated and its facilities include a well presented restaurant and bistro. Make reservations in advance, particularly in the summer. 1154 Gilford St. (phone: 681-9321). Inexpensive.

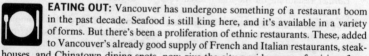

EATING OUT: Vancouver has undergone something of a restaurant boom in the past decade. Seafood is still king here, and it's available in a variety of forms. But there's been a proliferation of ethnic restaurants. These, added to Vancouver's already good supply of French and Italian restaurants, steakhouses, and Chinatown dining spots, now give the city a wide range of cuisines from which to choose. Expect to pay $40 and up for two for a dinner in the expensive range; $30 to $45 in the moderate range; and under $30 (in some cases, way under) in the inexpensive category. Prices do not include drinks, wine, or tip. All telephone numbers are in the 604 area code unless otherwise indicated.

Beijing – This place boasts northern and southern Chinese food at its best, with Szechuan, Shanghai, and Cantonese specialties. Seafood selections are plentiful and popular, and lunches offer Shanghai and Cantonese dim sum, noodles, and daily specials. Good service and regal atmosphere. Open daily. Reservations advised. Major credit cards accepted. 865 Hornby St. (phone: 688-7788). Expensive.

Cannery – This dockside place looks as if it has been around for a very long time, with its weathered woods, old brass, and nautical artifacts, but actually it's just about 15 years old. It's the seafood and the views of the harbor and mountains that make this a favorite spot in town. Open Mondays through Fridays for lunch; dinner daily. Reservations necessary. Major credit cards accepted. 2205 Commissioner St., about a 10-minute drive from city center (phone: 254-9606). Expensive.

Le Crocodile – Chef-owner Michel Jacob continues to win the hearts and palates of Vancouverites and critics alike with his world class French culinary talents. The freshest of seafood, lamb, and fowl are complemented by delectable sauces and graceful presentation. Impressive service, with consistent attention to detail. Lunch served Mondays through Fridays; dinner Mondays through Saturdays. Reservations necessary. Major credit cards accepted. 818 Thurlow (phone: 669-4298). Expensive.

Le Gavroche – Located in a charming West End house, it offers an interesting — and changing — menu. The game dishes are particularly notable, and the seasonal specialties all are good bets. Desserts are geared to send a weight watcher back to the drawing board. Closed Sundays. Reservations necessary. Major credit cards accepted. 1616 Alberni St. (phone: 685-3924). Expensive.

Imperial – This spacious, 320-seat place commands a harbor view; its opulent decor features crystal chandeliers and jade carvings. Hong Kong–trained chef Wei Sing Chow prepares creative Cantonese seafood specialties. Dim sum are served at lunch. Open daily. Reservations advised. Major credit cards accepted. 355 Burrard St. (phone: 688-8191). Expensive.

Umberto's – What began as an Italian eatery in an old yellow house has grown into three adjacent restaurants — the original *Umberto's,* (1380 Hornby St., phone: 687-6316) serves traditional northern Italian food nightly; *Umberto's Fish House* (1376 Hornby St., phone: 687-6621) specializes in fresh fish and seafood Tuesdays through Saturdays; and *Il Giardino di Umberto* (1382 Hornby St., phone: 669-2422) serves up equally delicious wild fowl and game. Umberto Menghi, the affable and energetic proprietor, divides his evenings between the restaurants. The food is decidedly Italian and eminently elegant, with close attention to detail. Reservations necessary, even for lunch. Major credit cards accepted. Expensive.

William Tell – Known as "the special occasion place," this dining spot serves haute cuisine in a luxurious atmosphere of traditional elegance. The delicious fare draws heavily on local delicacies, complemented by the chef's contemporary touch. Open daily. Reservations advised. Major credit cards accepted. 765 Beatty St. (phone: 688-3504). Expensive.

Bishop's – John Bishop is a true perfectionist and the output of his kitchen wins wide applause for its superior presentation and taste. While the place is small and located in residential Kitsilano, it is well worth the 10-minute taxi ride from downtown. Open for lunch Mondays through Fridays; dinner daily. Reservations advised. Major credit cards accepted. 2183 W. 4th Ave. (phone: 738-2025). Expensive to moderate.

Bridges – In a bright yellow building on a highly visible corner of Granville Island, this place offers a prize view of marine activities, the city skyline, and the bustle that makes the island such a lively spot. Seating is on numerous levels to take advantage of the view, and the menu of mostly seafood changes every day. A wine bar and pub fill the lower floor, and a wide deck is popular for fair-weather dining.

Open daily. Reservations necessary. Major credit cards accepted. 1696 Duranleau St. (phone: 687-4400). Expensive to moderate.

Caffè de' Medici – Classic fixtures, paintings, and attractive furnishings make this Italian eatery look as if it has been part of the scene for years. In reality, it's part of the modern Galleria complex near the central corner of Burrard and Robson Streets. The pasta is outstanding, and the chef is known for handling seafood with care. Open for lunch Mondays through Fridays; dinner daily. Major credit cards accepted. 1025 Robson St. (phone: 669-9322). Expensive to moderate.

Delilah's – Famous with the locals for serving the best martinis in town, this place blends modern comfort with 1930s Art Deco. Prix fixe menu with two- or five-course dinners. Open for dinner daily; Sunday brunch. Since reservations are not accepted (and it's a very popular place), try to get here early and, if necessary, remember that it's worth the wait. Visa, MasterCard, and Diners Club accepted. 1906 Haro St. (phone: 687-3424). Expensive to moderate.

English Bay Café – Once a beachfront fish and chip shop, this is now an elegant eatery with a fabulous ocean view. The lower level bistro offers casual dining, and on warm evenings dinner is also served on the outdoor deck. Specialties in the dining room include rack of lamb, fresh seafood, pasta, and chicken. Sunday brunch also is served. Open daily. Reservations necessary. Credit cards accepted. 1795 Beach Ave. (phone: 669-2225). Expensive to moderate.

Joe Fortes' Seafood & Chop House – In Vancouver's early days, Mr. Fortes was a well-loved character who lived on the beach and taught many youngsters to swim. Named in his honor, this attractive place, decorated with mahogany, brass, and greenery, is a favorite with young executives. Open daily. Reservations advised. Major credit cards accepted. 777 Thurlow St. (phone: 669-1940). Expensive to moderate.

Jonathan's Seafood House – Since it's next to a row of Granville Island houseboats, the seafood menu seems appropriate; thankfully, the kitchen staff is capable of not overcooking the fare. Guests have a lovely view from almost all the tables. Open daily. Reservations advised. Major credit cards accepted. 1333 Johnston St. (phone: 688-8081). Expensive to moderate.

A Kettle of Fish – The type of seafood place that people are always searching for — committed to serving *really* fresh seafood, not the ubiquitous "fresh frozen" kind. It has a convivial greenhouse feeling with skylights, lots of plants, and objects that would be at home in an English garden. The menu changes daily, as the owner never knows just what's going to be fresh. Open daily. Reservations advised. Major credit cards accepted. 900 Pacific St. (phone: 682-6661). Expensive to moderate.

Pelican Bay – Nesting on the east side of burgeoning Granville Island is a waterside eatery that's part of the *Granville Island* hotel. The menu is continental, with a slant toward seafood, and the view of houseboats, barges, and birds forms a very pretty picture. Open daily. Reservations advised. Major credit cards accepted. 1253 Johnston St. (phone: 683-7373). Expensive to moderate.

Prow – An aptly named place, it sits on the northeastern corner of Canada Place, surrounded on three sides by the waters of Vancouver harbor. The entire range of maritime activity can be observed from most tables: seaplanes, tugs, freighters, and the occasional seal all contribute to the scene. The food is creatively prepared, and the handling of vegetables an added plus. Open daily; no lunch served on Saturdays. Major credit cards accepted. 999 Canada Place (phone: 684-1339). Expensive to moderate.

Raintree – Specializing in the freshest of northwest coast cooking, a style that focuses on the hearty and healthy, everything at this place is good. To top it off, there is an award-winning wine list and a million-dollar view of Coal Harbour and the North Shore mountains. Live jazz and blues in the lounge, Thursday, Friday, and Saturday evenings. Lunch Mondays through Fridays; dinner nightly; Sunday brunch. Reservations advised. Major credit cards accepted. Complimentary underground parking. 1630 Alberni St. (phone: 688-5570). Expensive to moderate.

Salmon House on the Hill – Salmon is the specialty, but rack of lamb and Dungeness crab also are served. The magnificent view of the city, park, mountains, and sea lures tourists and locals alike. Open daily. Reservations advised. Major credit cards accepted. 2229 Folkestone Way, West Vancouver (phone: 926-3212). Expensive to moderate.

Teahouse – In Stanley Park at Ferguson Point, this airy and attractive spot has blossomed on a site that formerly housed a very British teahouse. Now the interior is all white and leafy green, and there's a separate conservatory, where the nicest tables are set. The menu changes often, and the seafood specials usually are the best choices. The sunsets here are breathtaking. Open daily. Reservations necessary. Major credit cards accepted. In Stanley Park overlooking the bay at Ferguson Pt. (phone: 669-3281). Expensive to moderate.

Quilicum – The only place in town featuring authentic dishes of Indians native to Canada's northwest coast. Try the salmon cooked over alderwood and garnished with cedar. Patrons sit at tatami-like tables, and Indian artwork (for sale) lines the dining room walls. Open daily. Reservations advised. Major credit cards accepted. 1724 Davie St. (phone: 681-7044). Expensive to moderate.

Bandi's – Located in a nice little clapboard house, it has an atmosphere that one might expect to find in a country inn — Hungarian-style. The food is hearty and very tasty, the soup delicious, and the homemade peasant bread addictive. Open for lunch Mondays through Fridays; dinner daily. Reservations necessary. Major credit cards accepted. 1427 Howe St. (phone: 685-3391). Moderate.

Café de Paris – The music, the decor — marble-topped tables and brass fixtures — and the French waiters all lend this convivial place an authentic Gallic bistro mood. The café has a menu that caters to various appetites, and it is a popular stop after a stroll in nearby Stanley Park. Closed Sundays. Reservations necessary. Major credit cards accepted. 751 Denman St. (phone: 687-1418). Moderate.

Café Splash – Tucked into a corner of a waterside apartment complex, the two main features here are a good view of Granville Island water activities and the superior efforts of a talented chef. The menu offers a variety of fresh, grilled seafood, steaks, veal, chicken, duck, and pheasant. There is alfresco dining during the summer. Open Mondays through Fridays for lunch, daily for dinner, and Sunday brunch. Reservations advised. Major credit cards accepted. 1600 Howe St. (phone: 682-5600). Moderate.

La Cote d'Azur – Vancouver's oldest French dining spot is situated in a vintage house with a huge fireplace, candles, and fresh flowers that set a romantic tone for leisurely dining. The menu offers classic French food prepared with the freshest ingredients, and includes traditional favorites plus changing daily specialties. A comprehensive wine cellar and friendly service add the final touches to a memorable meal. Closed Sundays, and for lunch on Mondays and Saturdays. Reservations advised. Major credit cards accepted. 1216 Robson St. (phone: 685-2629). Moderate.

Kamei Sushi – Many city sushi fans feel that this is the leading spot for the Japanese delicacy. You may sit at the counter to watch the chefs artfully construct the various dishes or in the dining room. The non-sushi items on the menu also are very good. Open daily. Reservations advised. Major credit cards accepted. 811 Thurlow St. (phone: 684-5767). Branches at 1414 W. Broadway (phone: 732-0112) and 601 W. Broadway (phone: 876-3388) provide both more room and a higher level of energy. Moderate.

The Kegs – The original of what is now an international chain. The fare is hearty, with an emphasis on steaks, plus a few seafood dishes. There's also a salad bar. It's good family value, although some people find the joviality a little taxing. Open daily. Reservations advised. Major credit cards accepted. Three locations: *The Keg*, on Granville Island (phone: 685-4735), and *Keg Coal Harbour* (phone: 682-5608) and the *Keg Downtown* (phone: 685-4388). Moderate.

Koji – Although the chef for whom this place was named no longer works here, other sushi experts have stepped up to his counter and continue to turn out superior dishes. The decor is attractive and there's a nice view of the downtown cityscape. Lunch Mondays through Fridays, dinner daily. Reservations advised. Major credit cards accepted. 601 W. Broadway (phone: 876-9267). Moderate.

Milestones – Boasting a fantastic view of English Bay, this is a casual spot where you can bring a big appetite to handle the huge portions. A six-page menu offers everything from breakfast entrées to gourmet burgers, hotdogs, pasta, and the best curly fries in town. Almost always packed full with locals. Open daily from 11 AM weekdays, 10 AM weekends. No reservations. Major credit cards accepted. 1210 Denman (phone: 662-3431). Moderate.

Prospect Point Café – Nearby Prospect Point has one of the best views in Stanley Park, and it is shared by this café. An inventive menu offering West Coast food — salmon, scallops, and salads, and an imaginative decor increase its appeal. Outdoor dining is available in good weather. Open daily. Reservations advised. Major credit cards accepted. Stanley Park (phone: 669-2737). Moderate.

Santa Fé Cafe – Fresh, innovative Southwest-California dishes are prepared in this open-air kitchen. Open for lunch Mondays through Fridays; dinner daily. Reservations advised. Major credit cards accepted. 1688 W. 4th Ave. (phone: 738-8777). Moderate.

Sawasdee Thai – Vancouver's original Thai dining spot, its two locations offer wonderful, spicy cooking at a very reasonable prices. There are four different levels of hot dishes. Lunch served Mondays through Fridays; dinner Mondays through Saturdays. Reservations advised. Visa and MasterCard accepted. 2145 Granville St. (phone: 737-8222) and 4250 Main St. (phone: 876-4030). Moderate.

Umberto al Porto – Homemade pasta and an array of Italian specialties are served at this Gastown establishment, and if seated on the upper level, you can get a terrific glimpse of the harbor and the distant mountains. Located in one of Gastown's most attractive buildings, it's close to most of the area's best shops. Open Mondays through Fridays for lunch; Mondays through Saturdays for dinner. Reservations advised. Major credit cards accepted. 321 Water St. (phone: 683-8376). Moderate.

Vassilis Taverna – At this family-run spot, a favorite with Grecophiles, all the usual favorites are offered, along with a few interesting adaptations. The Greek salad and roast chicken are special treats. Open daily. Reservations advised. Major credit cards accepted. 2884 W. Broadway (phone: 733-3231). Moderate.

Sun Tung Lock Seafood – Right in the heart of Chinatown, this place serves a delightful dim sum lunch that consists of about 40 items; the dinner menu also is quite extensive. Tiny local shrimp, kept in massive tanks, are delicious, as are seasonal specials like fried quail and stuffed oysters. Closed Thursdays. Major credit cards accepted. 127 E. Pender St., 2nd floor (phone: 682-3804). Moderate to inexpensive.

Afghan Horseman – Off the beaten track, diners may sit at tables or on the floor, Afghani style, while enjoying their meals. The Horseman's Platter provides a way for a couple to sample the best of Afghani food. Open for lunch Mondays through Fridays; dinner, closed Sundays. Reservations advised on weekends. Major credit cards accepted. 445 W. Broadway (phone: 873-5923). Inexpensive.

The Only (Seafood Café) – Firmly ensconced in the steambath and pawnshop district, this longtime institution serves some of the freshest seafood around. Inside are a few booths, a serpentine counter, dozens of gas burners, and huge frying pans. The menu includes clams, oysters, salmon, and sole. Every few minutes someone will truck a cartload of salmon through the place. (Mind your jacket!). No frills, no sauces, no appetizers, no liquor, no restrooms, no parking, no reservations, no credit cards accepted. Just incredibly fresh seafood. Closed Sundays. 20 E. Hastings St. (phone: 681-6546). Inexpensive.

Pink Pearl – Just about the most authentic Chinese food this side of Taiwan. The Sunday morning dim sum brunch is crowded, chaotic, noisy, and absolutely irresistible. The fresh local crab in black bean sauce is reason in itself to visit Vancouver. If you have time for only one Asian meal, make this your stop. Open daily. Reservations advised. Major credit cards accepted. 1132 E. Hastings St. (phone: 253-4316). Inexpensive.

WINNIPEG

No matter how you approach Winnipeg, it is hard to shake the impression that the city is no more than a small ship on a vast prairie ocean and, given a good, hard wind, could simply float away in all that space. The impression is certainly unfair to a city of Winnipeg's substance — 636,000 people, the provincial capital of Manitoba, and a city of no mean cultural and economic attainments — but it has the ring of psychological truth to it.

The nearest urban centers of any size are Toronto, 1,200 miles (1,920 km) to the east, Minneapolis, 430 miles (688 km) to the southeast, and Calgary, 800 miles (1,280) west; north of Winnipeg stretch the immense reaches of Manitoba, and to the west the equally huge prairie provinces of Saskatchewan and Alberta. Manitoba is a vast province of a quarter of a million square miles — 20% larger than France, stretching from Hudson Bay to the US border, from the eastern pine forests of Minnesota to an upland rise that leads eventually to the foothills of the Rockies. The capital of all this land is just 60 miles (96 km) north of the US border, at the junction of the Red and Assiniboine rivers.

In 1612 Captain Thomas Button, an English seafarer, spent the winter with his ships at what is now the site of Port Nelson on Hudson Bay. Button and other explorers had been looking for a northern passage to the Orient through the Arctic Ocean. They found their way blocked by the landmass of mid-Canada and discovered an area so rich in forest, streams, fish, and fur-bearing animals that the news they brought back of potential riches more than made up for the loss of easier access to the spice trade.

In 1670, King Charles II granted a franchise for all the lands draining into Hudson Bay to the *Hudson's Bay Company,* then a fur trading syndicate. (Today the *North West Company,* recently spun off from the original firm, operates a chain of fur and trading posts in northern Canada. The parent company, popularly called *The Bay,* lives on as a chain of department stores across Canada.) In the 19th century, to sustain its operation, the *Hudson's Bay Company* decided to develop an agricultural settlement at the junction of the Red and Assiniboine rivers, a floodplain north of what would become the US border. The deeply silted, rich soil of the Red River basin soon became an asset more important than the fur trade, and the agricultural industry of western Canada was born. By 1870, when Manitoba became part of the confederation of provinces comprising Canada, there were 12,000 settlers in the Red River Colony.

The union of Manitoba with Canada was, however, not without strife. The entire province had been the domain of several Indian tribes. In the course of the long years of trade between the Indians and the French voyageurs, a culture of French and Indian people called Métis developed. By the late 19th century, the Métis were relatively isolated from both the Indians and the white settlers who were coming to the area in increasing numbers. Louis Riel, a French-speaking Métis, opposed Manitoba's entry into the Confederation of Canada, but his opposition was brutally crushed by the Conservative (Tory) government of Prime Minister Sir John A. Macdonald. Riel's movement, in armed resistance to the government, was eventually put down and Riel himself was hanged. Today, the Riel Rebellion is one of the reasons that Quebec and French-speaking peoples in Canada usually vote for the Liberal party in preference to the Conservative.

The bitterness of the struggle was overlooked but never really resolved in the next decade, when the *Canadian Pacific Railroad* was under construction. The railroad changed life in every way on the prairies; nothing was the same afterward. It brought gangloads of immigrant Eastern European and Chinese laborers into western Canada, changing forever the demographics and ethnic politics of the provinces, and it turned small agricultural centers into boom towns, awash with prosperity and under siege by the gaudy ladies who decorated the bars and bedrooms of shanty hotels. The West opened up with a splash. And while the laborers laid track, the *CPR* laid its plans, becoming a colossus of land, mining, and transportation interests. In 1990, *CPR* discontinued its cross-continental routes.

Winnipeg was affected as deeply as any other city in the West and, because of its location as a gateway to the prairies, more than many. Laborers came with the railroad and stayed on; settlers from the East took the first trains out and did the same. The city that exists today in all its sophistication still carries the mark of that early development. And the center of Winnipeg's business and cultural life remains the settlers' crossroads, Portage Avenue and Main Street, only a few blocks from the junction of the Red and Assiniboine rivers.

For a city its size, it has an extraordinary spectrum of community-supported cultural activities. Opera, a highly acclaimed ballet, a symphony orchestra, several chamber music groups, two universities, professional sports, several legitimate theaters, and hundreds of restaurants feed the vitality of this city.

Not far from the Portage and Main crossroads are the *Manitoba Theatre Centre* and the *Warehouse Theatre,* venues for stage plays; the *Centennial Concert Hall,* home of both the *Winnipeg Symphony Orchestra* and the *Royal Winnipeg Ballet;* the Civic Centre, headquarters for the city's council and administration; the financial district; and the Commmodity Exchange, where Canada's grain crops are sold to the world. On the downtown mile of Portage Avenue, *Portage Place,* a trendy shopping center and office/residential complex, is linked by heated skybridges to virtually every major building on or near the thoroughfare, making it possible to visit almost every major downtown building in winter without getting cold.

Winnipeg remains, from its railroad boom town days, a city of great ethnic diversity. The leading population groups are English-Scottish, German, Ukrainian, French, native North American, Jewish, Polish, Dutch, and Italian. People of Icelandic descent make up a small but vital force in the city's business and government life. The newest wave of immigrants comes from the Far East. The Filipino community is close to 25,000, and more than 2,500

Vietnamese boat people have been resettled here, adding spice to Winnipeg's ethnic salad.

Some clustering of the ethnic groups has taken place through the circumstances of historical development and economic change. Winnipeg's North End was the traditional stopping place for newly arrived immigrants; today it is slowly turning into a corridor of high-rise developments and senior citizens' housing projects stretching several miles north on both sides of North Main Street. To the southeast, the suburb of St. Boniface is the home of Winnipeg's French-speaking citizens; to the northeast, the town of Transcona is a bedroom community for employees of the *Canadian National Railroad* and other working people.

Winnipeg's most prosperous suburbs lie south of the Assiniboine River. Winding along and leading from Wellington Crescent, home of some of the city's wealthiest and best-known families, River Heights, with old, stately homes, and Tuxedo, with sprawling mansions and enclosed grounds, remain the most prestigious addresses. Farther west, the suburb of Charleswood has recently attracted young families. North of the Assiniboine lies the pleasant suburb of St. James, with its picturesque homes and quaintly named streets.

The long, snowy months of winter take their toll, but residents take an almost perverse pride in their ability to handle whatever the Manitoba winter cares to dish out. When temperatures drop to the point that frostbite is an imminent danger on even the shortest outing, residents walk. When blizzards that in other places would shut down cities for weeks batter Winnipeg, residents take it in stride: they claim to have the best snow-removal system in western Canada, spending $12 million a year to plow the snow and repair the streets. Perhaps this stoic bravery harkens back to those early settlers standing at the crossroads of Portage Avenue and Main Street. Though today it is lined with banks, in those days it was quite desolate, and then as now it is the coldest intersection in Canada (winter temperatures can drop to −40F/−6C). If that didn't discourage their predecessors, it isn't going to discourage contemporary residents, though the underground shopping mall — *Lombard Place* — now makes it easier to traverse that infamous intersection. And so there is a common tradition of muddling through that reflects the city's survival of frontier hardships. Isolated on the vast Canadian prairies, Winnipeg has a sense of self-reliance that has given it financial and cultural vigor. That's the most remarkable thing about this very cosmopolitan urban island.

WINNIPEG AT-A-GLANCE

SEEING THE CITY: For a panoramic view of Winnipeg, visit the two *Royal Crown* revolving restaurants in the Gothic high-rise, Fort Garry Place. In Canada's only bi-level, revolving dining rooms, European food is served. Lunch daily from 11:30 AM to 2:30 PM, and dinner from 5 to 9:30 PM. 83 Garry St (phone: 947-1990).

SPECIAL PLACES: Winnipeg's downtown commercial center is a crazy quilt of odd-shaped blocks defined by streets, originally laid out more or less parallel to the meandering rivers that meet near the city's center. If you want to walk through this area of Victorian office blocks and soaring modern towers, it's best to park in a commercial lot. (City parking meters cost 50¢ an hour and at most of them there's a 1-hour limit; parking violators sometimes are towed and heavily fined.)

Downtown public transportation is frequent and excellent. A free weekdays-only bus called *DASH* rings the downtown area and connects the Legislative Building and its grounds with the many shopping areas near Portage Avenue. *DASH* runs every few minutes from 11:00 AM to 3:15 PM.

DOWNTOWN

Legislative Building – The legislative chambers and executive offices of the Manitoba government are open to the public year-round and serve as an excellent starting point for a tour of the city. The neo-classical architecture is set off by well-groomed, statue-filled lawns that surround the building. Atop the capitol's 255-foot dome stands *Golden Boy,* a 5-ton, 13½-foot gilded bronze statue holding a sheaf of wheat under his arm, a hardly demure symbol of the importance of this grain to Winnipeg's economy. Adjacent to the Legislative Building is the Woodsworth Building (405 Broadway). Off the lobby is an excellent cafeteria open to the public with just about the least expensive lunch in town — about $2.50 for several courses. Open from about 9 AM to about 4 PM, it's best to get there before or after the noon to 1 PM rush. Closed weekends and all government holidays. Broadway and Osborne Sts. (phone: 945-3777 or 800-665-0040 for guided tours).

Forks Market – Between South Main Street and the Red River, this 58-acre site, with elegantly restored old railway buildings, has been converted into a fashionable market with greengrocers, ethnic foods, antiques stores, and many restaurants. Archaeological digs often are in progress. Closed Tuesdays. Riverbank walkway to Legislative Building (phone: 943-7752).

Winnipeg Commodity Exchange – This is one of the largest grain exchanges in the world and the only commodity futures market in Canada. Visitors can view the trading from a gallery overlooking the floor. Open weekdays 9:30 AM to 1:15 PM; guided tours are available by calling 949-0495. Trizec Building at Portage Ave. and Main St.

Winnipeg Art Gallery – From small beginnings at the turn of the century, this museum has emerged as one of Canada's finest art showplaces. This triangular building, constructed in the early 1960s, houses the work of Canadian and European artists, as well as the largest collection of contemporary Eskimo sculpture and prints in Canada. The comprehensive collection of Eskimo work makes the gallery a must on any Winnipeg visit. The gallery also hosts frequent traveling shows. Closed Mondays. No admission charge. Portage Ave. and Memorial Blvd. (phone: 786-6641).

Portage Place – A swanky, friendly center joined by skywalk to major downtown shops, such as *The Bay* store. On the third level, the spectacular *IMAX Theatre,* with a 5½-story-high, 71-foot-wide screen, shows stunning wildlife and other films custom-made for its huge 70mm format. For program times, call 956-4629.

Exchange District – During the day on summer weekends, Old Market Square teems with produce vendors and antiques peddlers. At night, the action shifts to the discos, nightclubs, and restaurants bordering the square; this is also one of the city's red-light districts, so you'll see ladies of the evening here as well. King St. and Bannatyne Ave.

Western Canada Aviation Museum – A fascinating collection of aircraft from World War I to the jet age. Open daily. Admission charge. Hangar T2, 958 Ferry Rd. (phone: 786-5503).

SUBURBS

Osborne Village – This is Winnipeg's best shopping district. On each side of Osborne Street are small shops selling wicker furniture, books, Tiffany lamps, imported Pakistani carvings, handmade gold jewelry, records, fine clothing for women and children, and a variety of other exotica. Several excellent tea shops and restaurants are in the area, including the *Tea Cozy, Victor's,* and *Basil's* (see *Eating Out* for more information). Osborne St., just across the Osborne St. Bridge from the Legislative Building.

Assiniboine Park and Zoo – A 376-acre complex of recreational grounds, botanical gardens, a zoo, a miniature ride-along train, and ornate pavilions, this excellent park is just minutes from downtown. In the summer you can rent bicycles, including tandems, for a few dollars a day. But beware: Eating facilities within the park are limited to snack bars at the botanical gardens, the zoo, and a midpark pavilion; the food served is in the category of "only as a last resort." Located 4 miles (6 km) west of the city center off Wellington Crescent or Corydon Ave. No admission charge (phone: 888-3634).

Kildonan Park – One of Winnipeg's most interesting entertainment complexes, Kildonan has summertime swimming pools, Canada's only outdoor theater (the *Rainbow Stage,* open July and August), a dining pavilion with adequate luncheons, and a Hansel and Gretel Witches' Hut. In the summer, you can walk or cycle along the Red River through the dense trees of the park; in the winter, you can toboggan or skate. Approximately 5 miles (8 km) north of the city center on Main St.

St. Boniface Basilica – The original basilica was gutted by fire in 1968. The ruins of the building were left standing, and within them was built another cathedral of handsome contemporary design. Also of interest here is the gravesite of Louis Riel, the Métis resistance leader. Rue Taché, on the eastern side of the Red River.

Manitoba Museum of Man and Nature – This, the largest of Winnipeg's museums, recreates life on the prairies and in the north. Adjacent to the museum is a planetarium with science shows, dioramas, and animal and plant specimens. It also includes a replica of a 17th-century fur trading ship. Open daily. Admission charge. 190 Rupert Ave. (phone: 956-2830).

Lower Fort Garry – Built in the early 1830s by the Hudson's Bay Company, this is the only stone fur trade fort still intact in North America. In 1951 it was presented to the Canadian government and is now a national historic site. Costumed characters reenact the days of Lower Fort Garry's glory. Open daily from late May to late August and weekends in September. Admission charge. 20 miles (32 km) north of Winnipeg on Rte. 9 (phone: 983-3600).

Manitoba Children's Museum – The hands-on exhibits here include a model grain elevator, railroad switching yard, and a television studio. Open Tuesdays through Saturdays, 9:30 AM to 5 PM; Sundays and holidays, 11 AM to 5 PM. 109 Pacific Ave. (phone: 957-0005).

Royal Canadian Mint – Purported to be one of the most modern facilities in the world, the mint produces coins for a number of countries as well as Canada. It is laid out so visitors can see just how the money is made. Open weekdays from 9 AM to 3 PM for guided tours. Lagimodière Blvd. and the Trans-Canada Highway (phone: 257-3359).

Dugald Costume Museum – Canada's only historical display of clothing from 1765 to modern times. Open April to November, 10 AM to 5 PM Wednesdays through Sundays. On Highway 15, 30 minutes east of downtown (phone: 853-2166).

■**EXTRA SPECIAL:** Oak Hammock Marsh is a 8,705-acre wildlife management area in which you can view over 50,000 Canada and snow geese resting on their migratory flights. Spring and fall are the best viewing times. Guided tours are available except in winter (phone: 945-6784 for schedules). The area is also home to a plethora of mammals, including minks, weasels, deer, and coyotes. On Highway 67 between Stonewall and Selkirk.

SOURCES AND RESOURCES

 TOURIST INFORMATION: For general information, brochures, and maps, contact Travel Manitoba (155 Carlton St., 7th Floor, Winnipeg, Manitoba R3C 3H8; phone: 945-3777; in the US, 800-665-0040). The best Winnipeg city map is the *City of Winnipeg Tourist and Street Guide,* available free from Travel Manitoba. *The Manitoba Vacation Planner* is the best guide to the city. It is distributed at no charge by Travel Manitoba.

Local Coverage – The *Free Press,* daily; the *Sun,* daily (except Saturdays).

Food – The *Free Press* publishes restaurant reviews on Fridays.

Telephone – The area code for Winnipeg is 204.

Sales Tax – The basic sales tax is 7%.

Currency – All prices are quoted in US dollars unless otherwise indicated.

 TIPPING: Leave 15% to 20% of the bill at most restaurants. Taxi drivers aren't necesarily always tipped, but when you do, give 10% of the fare. Airport porters and bellboys generally receive CN$1.50 per bag, and hotel maids, CN$1.50 per person, per day.

 CLIMATE: Winter, from November through March, is a challenge. With average temperatures hovering around −11F (−24C) during December, January, and February, with readings of −20F (−29C) not uncommon, precautions against the cold are absolutely necessary. However, summers are warm, with temperatures averaging 68F (20C) and peaking in July at 79F (26C).

Winnipeg averages a substantial 50 inches of snow each winter. Drivers should carry a shovel, battery booster cables, and a tow rope at all times, and anyone driving in outlying areas or on the rural roads, including the Trans-Canada Highway, should carry some emergency rations, extra gasoline, and flares (if snowplows approach with their roar and blinding lights). Nevertheless, from about 10 AM to 2 PM during the remarkably sunny days of midwinter, it is possible to walk outside with only light winter wear. It's very sunny and very cold — that's the paradox of Manitoba's winters.

 GETTING AROUND: Bus – *Winnipeg Transit* operates bus lines throughout the city and suburbs. Maps of the system are available at gas stations, and additional information can be obtained directly from *Winnipeg Transit* at 284-7190.

Car Rental – All major national companies are represented.

Riverboats – Three companies conduct river cruises on the Red and Assiniboine rivers during spring, summer, and early fall. The MS *Paddlewheel Queen,* a replica of an old sternwheeler, brings an air of the Old South to Winnipeg. Evening cruises feature dining and dancing. The MS *Lady Winnipeg* and *Paddlewheel Princess* make sightseeing cruises down the Red River to Lower Fort Garry, a scenic 20-mile trip. Contact *Paddlewheel–Gray Line Tours* (PO Box 3930, Station B, or Water Ave. at Gilroy St.; phone: 942-4500); *River Rouge Ltd.* (312 Nairn Ave.; phone: 669-2824); or *Lord Selkirk II* (69 Birchbark Bay; phone: 582-2331).

Taxi – Cabs can be hailed in the street; taxi stands are located at the larger hotels throughout the city.

SPECIAL EVENTS: Every August, Winnipeg hosts the 2-week *Folkorama* international festival. More than 40 ethnic groups celebrate their diverse heritages in colorful pavilions throughout the city with native dances, songs, displays, and food. China, Greece, the Philippines, and the Ukraine are only a few of the many countries represented in addition to the pavilions dedicated to Canada's Indians. A *Folkorama* passport costs CN$8.50 (CN$4 for those over 65 or under 13) and provides access to all the pavilions, which are connected by frequent shuttle bus service provided by the city.

Another annual July event is the *Winnipeg Folk Festival,* a 4-day affair held at Birds Hill Park, about 20 miles (32 km) northwest of the city. The festival attracts top names in folk music and has an international reputation.

For children and the young at heart, Winnipeg offers an annual carnival, the *Red River Exhibition.* Held during late June and early July, the "Ex" site sprawls around the *Winnipeg Arena.* There are many roller coasters and other rides, numerous games of chance, and casino games.

Special seasonal festivals with an ethnic accent are the *Oktoberfest,* a German party for beer and sausage fans, and the *Festival du Voyageur,* a late winter event held in the French suburb of St. Boniface, featuring dogsled races, ice sculpture competitions, and hearty food.

 MUSEUMS: The *Manitoba Museum of Man and Nature* and the *Winnipeg Art Gallery* are described in *Special Places.* Also of interest is Manitoba's Provincial Archives Building, the lobby of which houses frequently changing exhibits of historical information, art, maps, and other memorabilia. The archives are open weekdays only. 200 Vaughan St. (phone: 945-3971). A moveable museum called the *Prairie Dog Central,* a restored 1900 locomotive with passenger cars, takes sightseers on a 2-hour ride on Sundays from June through September. Departures are at 11:30 AM and 3 PM from St. James St. at Portage Ave. station. Admission is CN$11 for adults, CN$9 for senior citizens and children ages 12 to 17, CN$6 for children ages 2 to 11. Reservations unnecessary.

 SHOPPING: Winnipeg's two largest department stores, *Eaton's* and *The Bay,* are located on Portage Avenue; both offer comprehensive services, dining facilities, and can provide tickets to sporting and theatrical events. Both are connected to most major downtown buildings and to each other by an enclosed skybridge.

Crafts Guild of Manitoba carries the work of Manitoban carvers, weavers, and jewelers and specializes in the leatherwork and carving of local Indians and Eskimos. Open Mondays through Saturdays. 183 Kennedy St. (phone: 943-1190).

St. Vital Shopping Center is a 10-minute drive southwest of Portage Ave. and Main St. Osborne Village and the Exchange District are interesting centers mentioned in *Special Places.* Note that most stores are closed Sundays in Winnipeg. *Polo Park,* an upscale shopping mall, is 10 minutes west of the city center on Portage Ave.

 SPORTS: Bicycling – A popular summer diversion in Winnipeg. City parks have marked bicycle paths, and bicycles may be rented in Assiniboine Park.
Boxing – Matches are held in the *Winnipeg Arena,* 1430 Maroons Rd. (phone: 780-7328).

Cross-Country Skiing – Most city parks support some cross-country skiing and snowshoeing, but the best for both activities are Assiniboine and Kildonan parks.

Curling – This Canadian game has Scottish origins and is somewhat related to shuffleboard. Played on an ice rink by teams of four, the players, or "curlers," slide squat, circular stones, each weighing 40 pounds, at goals 46 yards apart. Two "assistants" run ahead of the curlers, vigorously sweeping the ice with brooms along the path of the stone — one of the eyecatching features of the game. A team scores by getting the stones within the 6-foot circle surrounding the "button" (goal), and as close to it as possible. Curling is played at all city ice rink facilities from September to June.

Fishing – Good fishing is available at Lockport, 20 miles (32 km) north of Winnipeg.

Football – The Canadian Football League's *Blue Bombers* make their home in Winnipeg at the *Winnipeg Stadium,* adjacent to the *Polo Park* shopping center, just south of Portage Ave. at 1465 Maroons Rd. (phone: 786-2583).

Golf – Municipal courses dot the city; perhaps the best of the six public courses is *John Blumberg,* 4540 Portage Ave. (phone: 888-8860).

Hockey – The Winnipeg *Jets,* part of the NHL, confront their opposition at the *Winnipeg Arena,* 1430 Maroons Rd. (phone: 783-5387).

Horse Racing – Thoroughbred and harness racing are held year-round at *Assiniboia Downs,* 3975 Portage Ave. (phone: 885-3330).

Ice Skating – At any of the public ice rinks.

Jogging – Residents do it anytime, anywhere, even in midwinter. In the summer, many jogging paths are open in city parks.

Lacrosse – A sport more common to eastern Canada, lacrosse is nevertheless played in Assiniboine Park on summer Sundays.

Snowmobiling – Restricted to the frozen rivers in Winnipeg proper, it can be enjoyed at Birds Hill Park, 20 miles (32 km) northeast of Winnipeg.

Squash – City athletic clubs have courts as does the *YMHA,* 370 Hargrave St. (phone: 947-0601).

Swimming – Public municipal pools, mostly indoor, are located at: Sinclair and Dufferin Sts. (phone: 589-2005); Dalhousie and Baylor Drs. (phone: 269-7416); 25 Poseidon Bay (phone: 284-4030); 999 Sargent Ave. (phone: 986-3929); 381 Sherbrook St. (phone: 786-8475); and 644 Parkdale St. (phone: 832-1348).

Tennis – There are both public and private courts around the city. In summer, championship matches are held at the *Winnipeg Canoe Club,* 47 Dunkirk Pl. (phone: 233-4928).

Wrestling – Matches are held once a month during fall and winter at the *Winnipeg Arena* (phone: 783-7328).

THEATER: Most of Winnipeg's live performances — legitimate and musical — take place during the fall and winter months. The *Manitoba Theatre Centre* (174 Market St.; phone: 942-6537) has a season of serious and comic drama. A companion theater, *The Warehouse* (140 Rupert St.; phone: 943-4849) offers experimental drama with modest ticket prices. The *Prairie Theatre Exchange* (Portage Pl. at Portage Ave. and Memorial Blvd.; phone: 942-7291) features dramas for both children and adults. The *Actor's Showcase* (89 Princess St.; phone: 947-0394) offers children's drama. *Le Cercle Molière* (340 Provencher, in the French-speaking suburb of St. Boniface; phone: 233-8053) presents plays and revues in French. Avant-garde theater and plays for children are presented at the *Gas Station Theatre* (445 River Ave.; phone: 284-2757). The *Royal Winnipeg Ballet* has four major series, each consisting of six performances, at the *Centennial Concert Hall* (555 Main St.; phone: 956-1360), and offers a free summer performance at Assiniboine Park. The *Contemporary Dancers* perform at the *Playhouse Theatre* (180 Market St.; phone: 986-3003).

MUSIC: Major performances by the *Winnipeg Symphony Orchestra* and the *Manitoba Opera Association* take place in the *Centennial Concert Hall* (555 Main St.; phone: 956-1360). During the summer, musicals are performed at the *Rainbow Stage* (Kildonan Park; phone: 943-2929 or 338-4702).

NIGHTCLUBS AND NIGHTLIFE: Winnipeg's night scene has gone through a renaissance, and has emerged sophisticated and exciting. The poshest nightclub is *Norma Jean's* (115 Bannatyne; phone: 944-1600), a moderately expensive establishment with several bars, dance floors, and often, decorative buffets. There is a jazz guitar trio at *Hy's Steak Loft* (216 Kennedy St.; phone: 942-1000). Along Osborne St., between River Ave. and Stradbrook St., several bars and nightclubs offer entertainment. The latest meeting place is the cavernous *Rorie Street Marble Club* (65 Rorie St.; phone: 943-4222), in the financial district. Be prepared to wait in line to get in. Comedians perform at *Yuk-Yuk's* (108 Osborne; phone: 475-9857) and at *Rumor's* (2025 Corydon Ave.; phone: 488-4520). A European-style casino operates Mondays through Saturdays at the *Fort Garry* hotel (222 Broadway Ave; phone: 942-8251 or 800-665-8088). Formal dress required (see *Checking In*).

BEST IN TOWN

CHECKING IN: Winnipeg's accommodations range from turn-of-the-century establishments to ultramodern complexes. Many are located in the city center, within easy walking distance of Winnipeg's finer shopping, dining, and entertainment facilities. All the hotels listed are well managed, have phones in every room, and accept major credit cards. Expect to pay $75 to $155 for a double in those hotels classed as expensive; between $50 and $70 at places in the moderate category; between $30 and $50 at the inexpensive places. There also are various bed and breakfast accommodations — from modest homes to mansions — available in the Winnipeg area. For more information contact *B&B of Manitoba,* (3 Healy Crescent, Winnipeg, Manitoba R2N 2S2; phone: 256-6151). All telephone numbers are in the 204 area code unless otherwise indicated.

Delta Winnipeg – With 272 rooms atop a high-rise garage, this place has excellent parking and an indoor pool with a view of much of the city. 288 Portage Ave. (phone: 956-0410 or 800-268-1133). Expensive.

Fort Garry – Winnipeg's grande dame, built to resemble a French château, it has 264 guestrooms, suites, a stunning dining room, and French Canadian management. A sleek, European-style casino operates Mondays through Saturdays on the seventh floor, courtesy of the Manitoba Lotteries Commission. Formal dress (jacket and tie) required for men. Games offered include roulette, blackjack, la boule, and slot machines. 222 Broadway Ave. (phone: 942-8251 or 800-665-8088). Expensive.

Holiday Inn Downtown – This structure is part of a complex of office buildings and apartments, with an indoor swimming pool ringed by pinball machines. Several restaurants are available within the hotel, but savvy diners may visit either *Ichi Ban Japanese Steak House* or the *Market Grill* (see *Eating Out*), both located elsewhere in the complex. St. Mary's Ave. and Carlton St. (phone: 942-0551 or 800-465-4329). Expensive.

Relax Plaza – Centrally located, this medium-size property (with 157 rooms) has a pool and special facilities for handicapped guests. 360 Colony St. at Portage Ave. (phone: 786-7011 or 800-661-9563). Expensive.

Sheraton Winnipeg – Near *Eaton Place Shopping Centre* and the *Winnipeg Convention Centre,* this renovation of an apartment building features 273 expansive rooms with balconies, a pool, sauna, whirlpool bath, and outdoor sundeck. *Options* restaurant has an extensive continental menu, leaning on the Italian side. There is live entertainment nightly in *Windows* lounge. 161 Donald St. (phone: 942-5300 or 800-325-3535). Expensive.

Westin – In the middle of Winnipeg's financial district, near major department stores, the inn — with a good restaurant (see *Eating Out*) — is attached to an elaborate shopping and office complex, with ample parking nearby. 2 Lombard Pl. (phone: 957-1350 or 800-228-3000). Expensive.

Birchwood Inn – One of Winnipeg's major hostelries, it is in the rapidly expanding western suburb of St. James. Ample shopping opportunities exist at the nearby *Unicity Shopping Centre.* The 230-room hotel has several restaurants and bars. 2520 Portage Ave. (phone: 885-4478). Expensive to moderate.

Viscount Gort Flag Inn – Conveniently located near most places in Winnipeg. The *Polo Park* shopping center is a 5-minute walk, and the *Winnipeg Stadium and Arena* — home of many competitive sporting events — is only a 2-minute drive. 1670 Portage Ave. (phone: 775-0451 or 800-661-1460). Expensive to moderate.

Grant Motor Inn – Modern and well-managed, it has 65 rooms and a passable dining room. 635 Pembina Hwy. (phone: 453-8247 or 800-665-0087). Moderate.

Journey's End – Located just inside the city limits, this no-frills motel is close to the University of Manitoba. Pembina Hwy. at Perimeter Hwy. (phone: 269-7390 or 800-668-4200). Moderate.

Norlander – Near the University of Manitoba with an attractive Scandinavian-style decor. 1792 Pembina Hwy. (phone: 269-6955). Moderate.

Norwood – This turn-of-the-century institution in St. Boniface recently has been gentrified. It has 52 rooms, satellite TV, suites with oversize color TV sets, plus extensive bar and restaurant facilities. 112 Marion St. (phone: 233-4475). Moderate.

TraveLodge – Near the point at which the Trans-Canada Highway enters Winnipeg from the east, the motel is adjacent to a small shopping center. 20 Alpine, in St. Vital (phone: 255-6000 or 800-255-3050). Moderate.

 EATING OUT: For a seemingly isolated prairie town, Winnipeg boasts a large variety of restaurants that reflect its multi-culturism. Among the offerings are French, Italian, Danish, and Vietnamese cuisine, in addition to native Canadian fare. The restaurant cited as very expensive can run $85 or more for a meal for two, not including drinks; those in the expensive category will charge $40 and over; in the moderate range, $25 to $40; and in the inexpensive range, $15 to $20 without wine or drinks. (Inexpensive dining places in Winnipeg often have no liquor license.) All telephone numbers are in the 204 area code unless otherwise indicated.

Dubrovnik – Yugoslavian and continental dishes are the specialties of this place, which is housed in an old mansion along the Assiniboine River. Closed Sundays. Reservations necessary. Major credit cards accepted. 390 Assiniboine Ave. (phone: 944-0594). Very expensive.

Le Beaujolais – Located in the French-speaking suburb of St. Boniface, this graceful eatery offers nouvelle cuisine, elegant pastries, and deft service. Open daily. Reservations necessary. Major credit cards accepted. 131 Provencher (phone: 237-6276). Expensive.

Beefeater – This spot is popular with fans of charcoal-broiled steaks. Decor, to the chagrin of any self-respecting Beefeater, is Napoleonic. Open daily. Reservations advised for lunch and dinner. Major credit cards accepted. 437 Stradbrook at Osborne St. (phone: 475-8744). Expensive.

Churchill's – An elegant dining room in the *Marlborough Inn* that has been magnificently restored in the grand European castle tradition, but the menu remains basic steakhouse, with some elaborate soups and desserts added. Smooth service and a good wine list. Closed Sundays. Reservations advised. Major credit cards accepted. 331 Smith St. (phone: 947-1526). Expensive.

Le Couscous – North African food served by waiters in Tunisian dress. Closed

Sundays. Reservations advised. Major credit cards accepted. 135 Marion St. (phone: 237-3775). Expensive.

Ichi Ban Japanese Steak House – Beautifully decorated, this place has, among other things, a small artificial meandering river. It offers just what the name implies — steaks in the Japanese fashion — as well as sukiyaki, tempura, and a small selection of more exotic dishes. Open daily. Reservations necessary. Major credit cards accepted. 189 Carlton St. (phone: 942-7493). Expensive.

Market Grill – Surf 'n' turf and ambitious nouvelle cuisine are served in this elegant marble and glass dining spot. Open daily. Reservations advised. Major credit cards accepted. In the *Holiday Inn Downtown* complex, St. Mary's Ave. and Carlton St. (phone: 942-0551). Expensive.

Rae and Jerry's – Located west of the downtown core, it has good steaks, chicken, fish, and roast beef. Open daily. Reservations necessary. Major credit cards accepted. 1405 Portage Ave. (phone: 775-8154). Expensive.

Royal Crown – Located on top of Fort Garry Place, which has ancient Greek, Romanesque, and Renaissance-style architecture, this remarkable restaurant has 2 levels revolving in opposite directions. Dine on continental specialties while enjoying the superb view. Open daily. Reservations necessary. Major credit cards accepted. 83 Garry St. (phone: 947-1990). Expensive.

Sandpiper – An elegant grill with simple decor, avant-garde Euro-Californian food, interesting wines, and exquisite desserts. Closed Sundays. Reservations necessary. Major credit cards accepted. 2nd Fl., *Forks Market* (phone: 942-0918). Expensive.

Velvet Glove – A formal dining room with elaborate fare and harp music in the evenings. Open daily. Reservations advised. Major credit cards accepted. In the *Westin Hotel,* 2 Lombard Pl. (phone: 985-6255 or 957-1350). Expensive.

Victor's – In an elegantly restored block in Osborne Village, this spot offers good European food and excellent service. Interesting stained glass windows in the main dining room. Closed Sundays. Reservations necessary. Major credit cards accepted. River and Osborne Sts. (phone: 284-2339). Expensive.

Amici – A northern Italian *ristorante* with a luxuriously formal upstairs, and a café downstairs. Superb service. Closed Sundays. Reservations advised. Major credit cards accepted. 326 Broadway (phone: 943-4997). Expensive upstairs; moderate downstairs.

Old Swiss Inn – Rich, authentic alpine fare, fine service, and reasonable prices at lunch (more expensive at dinner). Closed Sundays. Reservations advised. Major credit cards accepted. 207 Edmonton St. (phone: 942-7725). Expensive to moderate.

Basil's – A charming, European-style coffeehouse in Osborne Village. Open daily for late afternoon coffee and dinner; lunch Mondays to Saturdays only. Reservations unnecessary. Major credit cards accepted. 117 Osborne St. (phone: 453-8440). Moderate.

Civita – Designer pizza, fashionable patrons, avant-garde decor. Closed Sundays. Reservations advised for evenings. Major credit cards accepted. 691-B Corydon Ave. (phone: 453-4616). Moderate.

Edohei Sushi – Recline on tatami mats to read the menu choices, which include sushi and excellent tempura. Lunch from 12 to 2 PM on Mondays, Wednesdays, Thursdays, and Fridays; dinner from 5 to 10:30 PM daily. Closed Tuesdays. Reservations advised. Major credit cards accepted. 355 Ellice Ave. (phone: 943-0427). Moderate.

Fork & Cork – Swiss fondue and Dutch fare are the staples of this intimate place. Open daily. Major credit cards accepted. Reservations unnecessary. 218 Sherbrook St. (phone: 783-5754). Moderate.

Mamma Mia – Southern Italian food served in a traditional setting. In summer, it's a popular sidewalk café. Open daily. Reservations essential in summer. Major credit cards accepted. 631 Corydon Ave. (phone: 453-9210). Moderate.

Tea Cozy – In Osborne Village, this shop serves tea and coffee, late breakfast, and lunch in a very English manner. The gingerbread cake with whipped cream is a favorite. Open daily. Reservations unnecessary. Major credit cards accepted. 99 Osborne St. (phone: 475-1027). Moderate.

Yamato – Japanese food — everything from sushi and sashimi to teriyaki and tempura. Open daily. Reservations advised. Major credit cards accepted. 667B Stafford St. (phone: 452-1166). Moderate.

Bistro Bohemia – Bright by day, intimate by night, this small establishment serves superb Czech food, as well as a more varied, authentic European menu. Desserts are magnificent. Closed Sundays. Reservations advised. Visa and MasterCard accepted. 159 Osborne St. (phone: 453-1944). Moderate to inexpensive.

Bistro Dansk – A frequently changing Danish menu and knowing service keeps this one of Winnipeg's favorite eateries. Closed Sundays. Reservations advised. Visa only accepted. 63 Sherbrook St. (phone: 775-5662). Moderate to inexpensive.

Carlos and Murphy's – Built to resemble a Wild West saloon, this Mexican restaurant and bar has good food, a devoted clientele, and an atmosphere conducive to mingling. Open daily for dinner. Reservations unnecessary. Major credit cards accepted. 129 Osborne St. (phone: 284-3510). Inexpensive.

Le Croissant – A French bakery, butcher shop, and cheese shop in one, this Gallic spot is a great place to stop for picnic food as it serves take-out food only. Closed Sundays. No credit cards accepted. 268 Blvd. Taché in the French suburb of St. Boniface (phone: 237-3550). Inexpensive.

D'8 Schtove – The name is a Low German pun and the food is Mennonite peasant fare. Sausages are homemade and desserts are undeceivingly rich. Open daily. Reservations unnecessary. MasterCard and Visa accepted. 1842 Pembina Hwy. (phone: 275-2294). Inexpensive.

Kelsey's – This large bar and eatery serves an extensive selection of foods, from Tex-Mex to Italian. Open daily. Reservations unnecessary. Visa and MasterCard accepted. 580 Penbina Hwy. (phone: 452-4944). Inexpensive.

King's Head Tavern – This authentic British pub serves endless kegs of ale, along with superb fish and chips, sausages prepared in several ways, and excellent desserts. Open daily. Reservations advised on weekends. Visa and MasterCard accepted. 120 King St. (phone: 957-1880). Inexpensive.

Nibbler's Nosh – A Jewish delicatessen with delicious, authentic fare and very tasty pastries. Open daily. No reservations. Major credit cards accepted. 973 Corydon at Stafford (phone: 284-0310). Inexpensive.

Old Spaghetti Factory – In an old warehouse restored with many turn-of-the-century antiques, including a genuine cable car, it serves inexpensive lunches. Open daily. No reservations. Major credit cards accepted. 291 Bannatyne (phone: 957-1391). Inexpensive.

Thanh Huong – Fine Vietnamese food, including soup, noodle dishes, native beverages, and desserts, served in an informal setting. Open daily for lunch and dinner. Reservations unnecessary. Major credit cards accepted. 534 Sargent Ave. (phone: 774-8888). Inexpensive.

DIVERSIONS

DIVERSIONS

For the Experience

Festivals, Fairs, and Fancy Acts

 No matter where or when you travel in Canada, you're apt to find the citizenry celebrating — always with spirit and panache. Some festivities honor a town's European heritage. Others — like the rodeos, the lobster festivals, and even the mining festivals — fete the local industry. Some are meant to build up the community's public image, to put it on the map, or to indulge the citizenry's fondness for music, dance, and the other arts. As you would expect, there are plenty of winter festivals, many of them in February.

Provincial tourist authorities can provide you with lists of the various fairs, exhibitions, and festivals taking place at any given time. Even the smallest is worth a detour. Here are a few suggestions.

EAST

FESTIVAL BY THE SEA, St. John, New Brunswick: Some 500 entertainers, many representing other Canadian provinces, perform over 1,200 shows during 2 weeks in August in this festival honoring New Brunswick's marine heritage. Information: *Festival by the Sea,* PO Box 6848, Station A, St. John, NB A2L 4S3 (phone: 506-632-0086).

ACADIAN FESTIVAL, Caraquet, New Brunswick: Centers around the *Acadian National Holiday* on August 15, the day of the "tintamarre" — the rushing noise that ducks and geese make as they swoop over the marshes. Custom has it that at 6 PM, everybody stops work and makes noise with drums, horns, bells. The festival includes dance performances, the blessing of the fleet, and folk singing — all in French. Information: *Acadian Festival,* Town of Caraquet, Box 420, Caraquet, NB E0B 1K0 (phone: 506-727-3423).

MIRAMICHI FOLK SONG FESTIVAL, Newcastle, New Brunswick: The oldest festival of its kind in North America, this 5-day event is a gathering of old-timers who indulge in enthusiastic accompanied and unaccompanied singing of lumber camps and days at sea, in French and in English and occasionally in other languages as well. Sometimes there's some clickety-clackety spoon playing and tap dancing, but each night a noted entertainer from the province appears. The festival offers a good opportunity to gather some knowledge of New Brunswick folkways and soak up the atmosphere of this unusual province at the same time. Held annually the first week in August. Information: *Susan Butler,* PO Box 13, Newcastle, NB E1V 3M2 (phone: 506-773-4469).

SHEDIAC LOBSTER FESTIVAL, Shediac, New Brunswick: One of the hot spots of coastal sailing, this community, long famous for the lobsters brought ashore by its fishermen, is called the "Lobster Capital of the World." So the annual 6-day, mid-July bash celebrating the delectable crustaceans seems entirely appropriate. You'll find all the goings-on that are usual at such small-town festivities — as well as lobster-trapping and boiling exhibitions, lobster-eating contests, and, well worth the trip, plenty of lobsters for all. Information: *Shediac Lobster Festival,* PO Box 969, Shediac, NB E0A 3G0 (phone: 506-532-2421).

ANTIGONISH HIGHLAND GAMES, Antigonish, Nova Scotia: The Scottish yearning to link arms with kith and kin, near and far, under the shield of the family clan is expressed at this colorful gathering that takes place for a few days annually in mid-July. The oldest Scottish games in North America are held here, but you don't have to be a Scot to enjoy the fun: There are competitions in caber tossing and weight throwing and Highland dancing and piping, and plenty of refreshments, including tea and oatcakes. Information: *Nova Scotia Department of Tourism* (phone: 902-424-5000).

MUSKOKA WINTER CARNIVAL, Bracebridge, Gravenhurst, and Huntsville, Ontario: This 4-day festival held each February in the Muskoka Lakes district 100 miles (160 km) north of Toronto, is known for the assortment of wild and wacky contests that are on the agenda — motorcycle races, bed races, a *Wreck-um Derby,* snow sculptures, and a talent contest — just to name a few. Information: *Muskoka Tourism Office* (phone: 705-645-3088).

KITCHENER-WATERLOO OKTOBERFEST, Kitchener, Ontario: The German and Pennsylvania Dutch settlers who founded this town around 1800 and named it Berlin never would have imagined that the settlement would give rise to anything like this event, which attracts some 600,000 and ranks among the biggest celebrations of its kind in North America. German clubs and area service groups sponsor nearly 25 festhalls groaning with sausage, sauerkraut, and beer, and, while diners and guzzlers partake, oompah bands merrily entertain. There are concerts, folk-dance shows, performances by brass bands and drum corps, sports tourneys, Canada's largest *Thanksgiving Day* parade, and more — even *Thanksgiving* church services. The event starts during the weekend in October that is Canadian *Thanksgiving.* King Ludwig's Castle at Speakers' Corner is the information center. Information: *Kitchener-Waterloo Oktoberfest, Inc.,* 17 Benton St., PO Box 1053, Kitchener, Ontario N2G 4G1 (phone: 519-576-0571).

SHAW FESTIVAL, Niagara-on-the-Lake, Ontario: With some help from an energetic citizenry instrumental in restoring the many old buildings and homes of this historic Upper Canada capital, George Bernard Shaw has done for Niagara-on-the-Lake what Shakespeare did for Stratford. Every year, from May to October, three separate theaters are given over to productions of ten plays by the celebrated playwright and his contemporaries. What began as a small community of devoted actors has become one of the most successful professional theaters in North America. Information: *Shaw Festival,* PO Box 774, Niagara-on-the-Lake, Ontario L0S 1J0 (phone: 416-468-2172). Also see *The Heritage Highways,* DIRECTIONS.

WINTERLUDE, Ottawa, Ontario: No matter how scenic, around about February snow and cold can wear on the nerves of even the most stoic. So Ottawa has created *Winterlude* to help lift the spirits of citizens and winter visitors alike. The second week of February finds this lovely capital alive with harness races on ice, skating shows, music races, and contests of many descriptions. Elaborate ice sculptures delight the eye and fireworks quicken the blood. Hot air balloons provide one mode of transportation, but then so do the ubiquitous skates — everyone in Ottawa, it seems, skates on the Rideau Canal. Information: *Canada's Capital Visitors and Convention Bureau,* 222 Queen St., 7th Floor, Ottawa, Ontario K1P 5V9 (phone: 613-237-5158), or visit the information center at 65 Elgin St., in the *National Arts Centre.* Also see *Ice Skating.*

FESTIVAL OF SPRING, Ottawa, Ontario: To commemorate the exile of the Dutch royal family in Ottawa during World War II, the people of the Netherlands presented the capital city with 100,000 tulip bulbs in 1945. An additional 20,000 tulip bulbs have been sent every year since, making the Ottawa display the largest of its kind in North America. The blossoming of these Dutch flowers, themselves spectacular enough to lure folks from afar, also serves as the impetus for a 10-day, mid-May program of outdoor entertainment for all ages, including the 10-kilometer *National Capital Marathon,* a procession of decorated boats on the Rideau Canal, a huge crafts market, aerial events, firework displays, and more. Information: *Festival of Spring,* 1743 St. Laurent Blvd., Suite 226, Ottawa, Ontario K1G 3V4 (phone: 613-238-2345).

NIAGARA GRAPE AND WINE FESTIVAL, St. Catharines, Ontario: Here in the heart of Ontario wine country, the last 10 days of September are dedicated to celebrating the grape harvest. Over 200 events include a charity pancake breakfast, the crowning of the Grape King, a *Pied Piper Parade,* arts and crafts shows, concerts, a royal ball, an amateur wine making contest, and a family Teddy Bear's picnic (where members of the Victorian Order of Nurses "patch up" damaged teddy bears). Topping it all off is one of the largest parades in North America. Information: *Niagara Grape and Wine Festival,* 145 King St. (Carlisle St. entrance), St. Catharines, Ontario L2R 3J2 (phone: 416-688-0212).

STRATFORD FESTIVAL, Stratford, Ontario: This event, held from May to October, produces some of the best theater in the world. Originally known for its fine star-studded productions of Shakespeare, the festival now presents a fine program including plays by other classical writers, world premieres, musicals, and modern contemporary classics; the fame of the *Festival* has attracted actors like Maggie Smith and Peter Ustinov, and the conception brought Alec Guinness and Irene Worth here in the early years. Guest celebrity lectures and other related events also are part of the program. A trio of performing halls houses productions running in repertory throughout the season — so much theater that you could stay for days and still not see everything. The *Festival Theatre,* with a thrust stage, which seats 2,262 within 66 feet of it, presents four or five plays per season; the *Avon Theatre,* with a traditional proscenium arch stage, features contemporary works and classics; the *Third Stage* (another thrust), spotlights the work of the *Young Company.* Information: *Stratford Festival,* PO Box 520, Stratford, Ontario N5A 6V2 (phone: 519-271-4040).

CANADIAN NATIONAL EXHIBITION, Toronto, Ontario: The world's largest annual exposition, this enormous Canadian version of a state fair keeps over 2 million visitors entertained with everything from a mile-and-a-half midway to agricultural displays and competitions. Artisans compete for prizes with their quilts and other handiwork. There are grandstand shows with name performers, daily water shows, many major league sports events, and the *Canadian International Air Show* during the last 4 days of the fair. The *CNE,* founded in 1879, runs from mid-August to *Labor Day.* Information: *Canadian National Exhibition,* Exhibition Pl., Toronto, Ontario M6K 3C3 (phone: 416-393-6019).

CHARLOTTETOWN FESTIVAL, Charlottetown, Prince Edward Island: Devoted primarily to showcasing large-scale musical productions, this festival also presents the long-running *Anne of Green Gables,* as well as children's entertainment, arts and crafts exhibits, and art classes (some of which can be joined on a single-lesson basis). The June-through-September program was begun by the *Confederation Centre of the Arts* in 1964. Information: *Public Relations, Confederation Centre of the Arts,* PO Box 848, Charlottetown, PEI C1A 7L9 (phone: 902-566-2464; box office, 902-566-1267).

LOBSTER CARNIVAL AND LIVESTOCK EXHIBITION, Summerside, Prince Edward Island: Every year the population of this small town of 10,000 swells eightfold as former residents come home and tourists throng here to watch the Miss PEI Beauty Pageant and enjoy daily harness races (the highlight is the Governor's Plate), a mammoth parade, talent contest, daily stage entertainment, and delicious lobster suppers. Held in July. Information: *PEI Tourism,* Visitors Services Division, PO Box 940, Charlottetown, PEI C1A 7M5 (phone: 902-368-4444).

TYNE VALLEY OYSTER FESTIVAL, Tyne Valley, Prince Edward Island: If you like oysters, this 4-day event, held in early August in an old, picture-pretty community, is for you. In addition to all the fiddling, step dancing, songfests, and parades found in similar fairs in the area, you get oysters — fried, raw, in chowder, and prepared just about any other way you can imagine. Oysters are served at down-home oyster dinners, Friday and Saturday, and Sunday is the day for harness racing. Information: *PEI Tourism,* Visitors Services Division, PO Box 940, Charlottetown, PEI C1A 7M5 (phone: 902-368-4444).

QUEBEC WINTER CARNIVAL, Quebec City, Quebec: Quebec fairly explodes for 10 days early each February. Tens of thousands of visitors jam the hotels and crowd the twisted streets of the Old Town. Parades, ice-carving exhibitions, and snowshoe races fill the calendar, not to mention the crazy canoe race across the ice-choked St. Lawrence River. Information: *Quebec Winter Carnival,* 290 Rue Joly, Quebec City, Quebec G1N 1L8 (phone: 418-626-3716); or *Quebec City Region Tourism & Convention Bureau,* 60 Rue d'Auteuil, Quebec City, Quebec G1R 4C4 (phone: 418-692-2471).

WEST

CALGARY EXHIBITION & STAMPEDE, Calgary, Alberta: Canada's self-styled "Greatest Outdoor Show on Earth" draws people from all over the world for 10 days annually, around the first or second week of July. The *Half Million Dollar Rodeo,* which takes place daily, ranks among the top events on the circuit, and cowboys compete hard for prize money in bareback-bronc riding, saddle-bronc riding, bull riding, steer wrestling, calf roping, barrel racing, wild-horse racing, wild-cow milking, and Indian-buffalo riding. But there also are *World Championship Chuckwagon Races,* live entertainment, a casino, Indian dance competitions, rock concerts, agricultural exhibits, a midway, a big parade, a vast array of free entertainment, and much more. This is the Wild West at its 20th-century best. Information: *Calgary Stampede,* PO Box 1860, Calgary, Alberta T2P 2M7 (phone: 403-261-0101 or 800-661-1260) for tickets; *Calgary Tourist and Convention Bureau,* 237 8th Ave. SE, Calgary, Alberta T2G 0K8 (phone: 403-263-8510) for details on accommodations.

KLONDIKE DAYS, Edmonton, Alberta: The fact that Edmonton is on the map today is almost exclusively the result of the turn-of-the-century gold rush to the Yukon, when the community became a supply depot and departure point for north-bound fortune seekers. So when the town fathers were casting around for a theme for a community celebration, this colorful bit of local heritage was a natural choice. Everyone dresses in Gay Nineties garb, and buildings all over town disappear behind 19th-century storefronts. All very colorful. What makes the festival so much fun — for the residents as well as the tourists — is the lively program of activities that features everything from marching bands and flapjack breakfasts to river raft and bathtub races, street entertainment, community dances, and sporting events, as well as a midway — Canada's biggest. *Klondike Days* takes place during the last half of each July just after the *Calgary Stampede.* Information: *Edmonton Klondike Days Association,* 1660-10020-101A Avenue, Edmonton, Alberta T5J 3G2 (phone: 403-426-4055).

FRINGE THEATRE FESTIVAL, Edmonton, Alberta: What started as a daring experiment a few summers ago is now regarded as the largest, most exciting festival of alternative theater in North America. *Fringe*-goers can choose from among an eclectic selection of 150 new plays in 14 theaters, plus dance, music, mime, and street entertainment by performers from around the world. Theater buffs have been known to spend the last 9 days of August racing feverishly from one play to the next. Information: *Fringe Theatre Festival, Chinook Theatre,* 10329 83rd Ave., Edmonton, Alberta T6E 2C6 (phone: 403-448-9000).

WORLD CHAMPIONSHIP OUTHOUSE RACE AND LAC LA HACHE WINTER CARNIVAL, Lac La Hache, British Columbia: This one-of-a-kind affair, featuring one- and two-holers mounted on runners, skis, or skate blades and fitted out with doors (for the sake of modesty), keeps Lac La Hachians thinking outhouses all year-round. Losers can compete in grudge matches; and, lest outsiders feel left out, race planners have included a borrow-an-outhouse match. All sorts of other winter activities also are on the agenda for the 4 days of this February event. Information: *Visitor Information,* PO Box 252, Lac La Hache, BC V0K 1T0 (phone: 604-395-5353).

WORLD CHAMPION BATHTUB RACE, Nanaimo to Vancouver, British Columbia: The madcap race across the 34 miles of the Strait of Georgia, under the aegis of the Loyal Order of the Bathtub Society, is one of those things you have to see to believe. Why would anyone want to watch a bathtub race, you ask? Suffice it to say that this contest, held every July in conjunction with the *Vancouver Sea Festival,* in "The Bathtub Capital of the World," has spawned dozens more, and, to this day, every bathtub race follows Nanaimo rules. Information: *Tourism Vancouver,* Pavilion Plaza, 4 Bentall Centre, 1055 Dunsmuir St., PO Box 49296, Vancouver, BC V7X 1L3 (phone: 604-683-2000).

VERNON WINTER CARNIVAL, Vernon, British Columbia: This Okanagan Valley community, 110 miles (176) from the international border near Penticton, hosts one of Canada's wildest and wackiest events annually in February — 10 days of old-fashioned skating parties for kids, competitions in broomball, snowgolf, jogging, bed-racing, ice sculpture, and racquetball. In the evening, there are parties given over to *Mardi Gras*–type merriment, Hawaiiana, Ukrainiana, Klondikiana, MASH-mania, and the like. Some 100-odd events are staged, but despite the scope, there's a friendliness and a homespun feeling here that you won't find at similar events in the big cities in the East. While you're here, you can stay to ski the lovely Silver Star Mountain with fine dining and on-hill accommodations for 600 (phone: 604-545-2236). Information: *Vernon Winter Carnival,* 3303 35th Ave., Vernon, BC V1T 2T5, or phone the *Tourist Information Centre,* 604-545-0771. Also see *Downhill Skiing.*

NATIONAL UKRAINIAN FESTIVAL, Dauphin, Manitoba: Cabbage rolls and pirogi, painted *Easter* eggs and intricate hand-carvings: The culinary and artistic traditions brought by this group of immigrants is extraordinarily rich, as you'll see at this 4-day event which takes place annually during the last weekend in July and the first weekend in August. The events include music, dance, workshops, authentic Ukrainian foods, displays, four grandstand shows, and a colorful parade. It ought to give you a new appreciation for Canada-as-melting-pot. Information: *National Ukrainian Festival,* 119 Main St. S., Dauphin, Manitoba R7N 1K4 (phone: 204-638-5645); or *Dauphin Chamber of Commerce,* 107 Main St., N., Dauphin, Manitoba R7N 1C1 (phone: 204-638-4838).

FESTIVAL DU VOYAGEUR, St. Boniface, Manitoba: Every year during the third week in February, this district of Winnipeg stages 10 days of parades, concerts of French Canadian music, and all manner of contests (in snow sculpture, jigging, fiddling, hockey, and dog-sled racing) in an effort to beat the midwinter blahs. And it seems to work. Information: *Festival du Voyageur,* 768 Taché Ave., St. Boniface, Manitoba R2H 2C4 (phone: 204-237-7692).

NORTHERN MANITOBA TRAPPERS' FESTIVAL, The Pas, Manitoba: The oldest festival in western Canada — originated in 1916 — the *Trappers' Festival* is a celebration of the heritage and traditions of the northern pioneer. This 5-day event takes place in the third week of February and includes the *World Championship Dog Race,* a 105-mile, 3-day-long dog sled race that carries over $24,000 in prize money. Events in the King Trapper category include contests in bannock baking, flour packing, log climbing, animal calling, and a marathon snowshoe race. Other goings-on include craft shows, beerfests, ice fishing, and more. Information: *Trappers' Festival Inc.,* PO Box 475, The Pas, Manitoba R9A 0N2 (phone: 204-623-2912); or *Travel Manitoba,* 155 Carlton St., 7th Floor, Winnipeg, Manitoba R3C 3H8 (phone: 800-665-0040).

National Parks

 A visit to one of Canada's national parks gives you a glimpse into a world of natural beauty that exists scarcely anywhere else on earth: From the rainy coast of the Pacific Rim, with its dense vegetation, to the imposing Canadian Rockies, from rolling prairies to storm-pounded Atlantic shores, the Canadian park system preserves the precious and sometimes fragile ecology of some of the nation's most distinctive regions. Its 70,000 square miles are a vast playground for nature lovers and a rich example of Canada's diverse natural and cultural heritage.

But the system also is designed to please anglers, boaters, golfers, hikers, skiers, campers, swimmers, and photographers. All but the most remote have campgrounds, hiking trails, scenic driving routes, and lively interpretive programs that everyone can enjoy. Details are available from *Environment Canada* (Parks, Ottawa, Ontario K1A 0H3; phone: 819-997-3736), or from the individual park offices. A checklist of all the parks follows. For more detailed information about your visit, consult the appropriate section in DIRECTIONS.

EAST

FUNDY NATIONAL PARK, near Alma, New Brunswick: Some of the world's highest tides rise and fall here and, retreating, leave behind vast tidal flats full of periwinkles, limpets, and other sea creatures that make a stroll in the area a delight. The cave-pocked, 200-foot cliffs that the surf pounds elsewhere and the rolling terrain inland, cut by deep valleys whose steep rocky walls are ribboned with waterfalls, are among the park's other features. You can see it all on some 80 miles of hiking trails, which range from a 30-minute loop trail to a 4-day backpacking adventure. Be sure to write ahead for tide schedules to help plan your visit. Information: *Fundy National Park,* PO Box 40, Alma, NB E0A 1B0 (phone: 506-887-2000).

KOUCHIBOUGUAC NATIONAL PARK, Kent County, New Brunswick: The name means "River of the Long Tides," and the water — among the warmest north of the Carolinas — is shallow and gentle. There also are a multitude of environments: rivers, beaches, bogs, salt marshes, lagoons, fields, forests, and sand dunes. The area hosts a profusion of migrating waterfowl in spring and fall, and also features trout, flounder, and striped bass (anglers need a park fishing license). Fees are modest and attention has been given to providing considerable access for the physically challenged. At the visitors' reception center, you can view an award-winning slide presentation about the park. Information: *Kouchibouguac National Park,* Kouchibouguac, Kent Co., NB E0A 2A0 (phone: 506-876-2443).

GROS MORNE NATIONAL PARK, near Rocky Harbour, Newfoundland: Situated on the province's west coast at the base of the Great Northern Peninsula, this 703-square-mile preserve dominated by the 2,644-foot Gros Morne Mountain is home to some of the nation's most spectacular scenery — fjord-like ponds, barren expanses of volcanic rock, heavily wooded forests and alpine meadows, bogs and beaches, tide pools and surf-washed headlands, and waterfalls that cascade for such long distances that the stream turns to spray before it hits bottom. The plant and animal life is equally diverse, and the fishing is good. There are several miles of hiking trails to show it all off. Be aware that there are no electrical hook-ups within this park. Information: *Gros Morne National Park,* PO Box 130, Rocky Harbour, Newfoundland A0K 4N0 (phone: 709-458-2066 or 709-458-2417).

TERRA NOVA NATIONAL PARK, near Glovertown, Newfoundland: Canada's easternmost national park, this 153-square-mile expanse of ponds, peatlands, spruce, and fir rolls westward from the rugged, rocky coastline adjoining Bonavista Bay and the Labrador Sea, punctuated by natural arches, notched by inlets, and fronted by steep cliffs, from which you can often spot bluish-white icebergs, carried south by the Labrador Current in spring and early summer, or you may spy some of Terra Nova's inhabitants, such as moose, lynx, and bald eagle. In addition to virtually all the outdoor pursuits — bird watching, hiking, camping, swimming, sailing, snorkeling, scuba diving, cross-country skiing, snowshoeing, golfing, fishing, and canoeing — Terra Nova offers free winter camping at Newman Sound, with heated washrooms and showers, and an enclosed kitchen. Information: *Terra Nova National Park,* Glovertown, Newfoundland A0G 2L0 (phone: 709-533-2801).

AUYUITTUQ NATIONAL PARK, Baffin Island, Northwest Territories: The 8,290 square miles of this national park ("the land that does not melt") are dominated by the spiky, 7,000-foot-high Penny Ice Cap, which covers a 2,200-square-mile area. Plants have a tenuous hold on existence in such terrain, but the bright blossoms that polka-dot the meadows in June and July, when the May-through-July midnight sun has worked its magic, are among the park's real beauties. And though there are 40 species of birds, and other wildlife abounds, rocks and mountains are what people come here to enjoy. The celebrated Pangnirtung Pass trek is a must for experienced hikers. April, May, and early June are perfect for winter activities such as snowmobiling and cross-country skiing; in July and August, there's excellent fishing for the prized Arctic char in the tidewater of Cumberland Sound. Information: *Superintendent, Auyuittuq National Park,* Pangnirtung, Northwest Territories X0A 0R0 (phone: 819-473-8962). Also see *Mountain Climbing.*

CAPE BRETON HIGHLANDS NATIONAL PARK, near Ingonish Beach, Nova Scotia: One of the most scenic of the Canadian national parks, this one occupies a stretch of tundra-, bog-, and forest-covered highlands between the Gulf of St. Lawrence and the Atlantic Ocean. The 180-mile-long Cabot Trail winds along a famous stretch of coastline, where the mountains meet the sea in awe-inspiring cliffs dotted by bizarrely twisted spruce trees. Equally lovely sights greet those who wander down the park's hiking trails. Stay at the charming *Keltic Lodge* (phone: 902-285-2880), near the *Cape Breton Highland Links,* one of Canada's best 18-hole courses. Information: *Cape Breton Highlands National Park,* Ingonish Beach, NS B0C 1L0 (phone: 902-285-2270). Also see *Special Havens* and *Golf.*

KEJIMKUJIK NATIONAL PARK, near Maitland Bridge, Nova Scotia: These rolling, forested 147 square miles are a paradise for backcountry campers and canoeists, thanks to a good system of canoe routes and hiking trails. There's a variety of activities available year-round. The hospitable climate and abundance of wetlands make survival possible here for many species not found elsewhere in Atlantic Canada. Information: *Kejimkujik National Park,* PO Box 36, Maitland Bridge, Annapolis County, NS B0T 1N0 (phone: 902-682-2772).

GEORGIAN BAY ISLANDS NATIONAL PARK, near Honey Harbour, Ontario: Lake Huron's immense Georgian Bay is only about 2 hours north of Toronto, but its waters are sparklingly clear and island-dotted. Fifty-nine islands in the southeastern part of the Bay belong to this preserve, a favorite of swimmers, fishermen, boaters, hikers, and campers. If you don't have your own boat, you can hire a water taxi or join a tour boat in nearby mainland towns. Information: *Georgian Bay Islands National Park,* Box 28, Honey Harbour, Ontario P0E 1E0 (phone: 705-756-2415).

POINT PELEE NATIONAL PARK, near Leamington, Ontario: The most southern point on Canada's mainland is a huge sandspit jutting into Lake Erie. Internationally known for its spring and autumn concentrations of migrating birds and stunning monarch butterfly migration each fall. There are miles of sandy beaches, marshes to explore by canoe, and a theater program at the visitor center. Information: *Point Pelee National Park,* RR1, Leamington, Ontario N8H 3V4 (phone: 519-322-2365).

ST. LAWRENCE ISLANDS NATIONAL PARK, between Brockville and Kingston Ontario: Canada's smallest national park is scattered over 21 of the famous Thousand Islands in the region between Brockville and Kingston, Ontario. Major activities include boating, hiking, camping, fishing, and plain old relaxing. Wide-ranging facilities include individual and group campsites, beaches, and interpretive trails. The mainland base at Mallorytown Landing has parking, campsites, playground, and general day-use facilities. Access to the islands is by private boat, boat rental, or water taxi, and faciliities are available at most of the many local marinas along the river. Information: *St. Lawrence Islands National Park,* Box 469, RR3, Mallorytown, Ontario K0E 1R0 (phone: 613-923-5261).

PUKASKWA NATIONAL PARK, near Marathon, Ontario: Located 15 miles east of Marathon, Ontario, and accessible by Highway 627, Pukaskwa encompasses a boreal wilderness of 725 square miles on the rocky landscape of the Canadian Shield. The major reception area at Hattie Cove offers 67 semi-serviced campgrounds (with showers), a visitors' center, and walking trails on the nearby headlands and beaches of Lake Superior. The coastal hiking trail (40 miles long) provides opportunities for day and overnight hikes. The bays, harbors, and coves of the park coastline afford limited protection to sea kayakers, canoeists, and boaters. Information: *Pukaskwa National Park,* Hwy. 627, Hattie Cove, Heron Bay, Ontario P0T 1R0 (phone: 807-229-0801).

PRINCE EDWARD ISLAND NATIONAL PARK, near Charlottetown, Prince Edward Island: A prime example of the kind of sandy Atlantic shoreline that Americans prize on Cape Cod, this stretch of northern PEI is all scalloped bays and inlets, sand dunes, sandy beaches, and salt marshes. More than 200 species of birds have been recorded along the park's 25 miles of coast. There also are eight supervised beaches, three campgrounds, lots of recreational activities, and the farmhouse immortalized in Lucy Maud Montgomery's *Anne of Green Gables.* Information: *Prince Edward Island National Park,* PO Box 487, Charlottetown, PEI C1A 7L1 (phone: 902-672-2211).

FORILLON NATIONAL PARK, Gaspé Peninsula, Quebec: The foghorns moan and the gulls wheel and cry as Quebec meets the sea at this splendid preserve set on a needle-headed, 92-square-mile triangle of land that pokes roughly southeastward into the Atlantic. In the easternmost section, 600-foot-high limestone cliffs slice into the sea. The wildlife here is abundant and varied: some 200 species of birds live in the park, and thousands of sea birds visit annually in summer; whales can usually be spotted off the coast from mid-May to around October; and gray and harbor seals are year-round residents. Inland, there are forests, peat bogs, dunes, lakes, and dozens of streams. Besides the camping, hiking, biking, scuba diving, and sightseeing cruises that keep summer visitors busy, there's snowshoeing, winter camping, and cross-country skiing in winter months. A park interpretation center and an interpretive program help visitors to discover the treasures and beauties of the park. Information: *Forillon National Park,* PO Box 1220, Gaspé, Quebec G0C 1R0 (phone: 418-368-5505).

LA MAURICIE NATIONAL PARK, near Shawinigan, Quebec: The scenic St. Maurice River flows along the eastern border of this 210-square-mile expanse of glacier-scoured, forest-covered wilderness, and the interconnected lakes and streams forming the river's watershed make for some very good canoeing. Thirteen-mile-long Lake Wapizagonke, contained between two high rocky escarpments, is a principal beauty spot. Hiking, camping, canoeing, canoe-camping and fishing, and cross-country skiing are popular. Two winter shelters provide 44 beds for cross-country skiers. Information: *La Mauricie National Park,* PO Box 758, Shawinigan, Quebec G9N 6V9 (phone: 819-536-2638).

WEST

BANFF NATIONAL PARK, Banff, Alberta: Established in 1885 on the site of hot sulfur springs discovered by three railway construction workers, this park takes in 2,500 square miles of Canada's most spectacular mountains, alpine meadows, glaciers, forested slopes, rivers, and lakes. And, though the springs are still there — delightful for soaks — getting out into the mountains is the real attraction. The park's network of hiking trails is well developed, and you can go canoeing, riding, skiing, fishing, boating, sailing, scuba diving, and climbing as well. Information: *Banff National Park,* Box 900, Banff, Alberta T0L 0C0 (phone: 403-762-3324). Also see *Golf, Tennis, Downhill* and *Cross-Country Skiing, Mountain Climbing, Ice Skating,* and *Special Havens.*

WATERTON LAKES NATIONAL PARK, near Cardston, Alberta: It's been said that this Canadian section of the Waterton-Glacier International Peace Park crams a maximum of scenery into a minimum of space. For while the park is only 204 square miles, its scenery varies greatly as a result of its location in a transitional zone between the prairie and the peaks. There's good hiking on 108 miles of prairie and mountain trails, plus riding, biking, fishing, tennis, golf, swimming, and boating (rentals are available at Cameron Lake). Waterton has three campgrounds. In addition, nightly interpretation programs are offered at *Townsite* and *Crandall* campgrounds. Information: *Waterton Lakes National Park,* Waterton Park, Alberta T0K 2M0 (phone: 403-859-2224).

ELK ISLAND NATIONAL PARK, near Edmonton, Alberta: In the early 1900s, when the elk in the Beaver Hills were in danger of extinction, a few conservationists banded together and successfully lobbied for the government to establish a fenced-in preserve to save the animals from hunters. Now, some 1,200 elk, as well as 500 plains bison and 250 rare wood bison, make the park their home. Summer activities include camping, canoeing, sailing, hiking, picnicking, and golf (9 holes); in winter, hiking trails are trekked by snowshoers and cross-country skiers. Information: *Elk Island National Park,* Attention: Visitor Services, Site 4, RR1, Fort Saskatchewan, Alberta T8L 2N7 (phone: 403-998-3781).

JASPER NATIONAL PARK, Jasper, Alberta: Named for Jasper Hawes, a fur trader of the early 1800s, these 4,200 square miles of lofty peaks and alpine valleys, clear lakes and thundering falls are a backpacker's paradise, thanks to the extensive trail system. On horseback treks, riders often spot all manner of big game. All-weather parkways provide access to such scenic highlights as Maligne Lake, Athabasca Falls, and the renowned Columbia Icefield area. Information: *Jasper National Park,* Jasper, Alberta T0E 1E0 (phone: 403-852-6161).

WOOD BUFFALO NATIONAL PARK, near Fort Smith, Northwest Territories: One of the world's largest national parks, with some 17,300 square miles, this wilderness preserve is home to the largest extant herds of free-roaming bison in the world and is the only natural nesting ground of the whooping crane. Named a UNESCO World Heritage Site in 1983, it also contains most of the spectacular Peace-Athabasca Delta, one of the planet's biggest freshwater deltas, a staging area for millions of waterfowl. Salt flats with beautiful and unusual vegetation extend throughout the northeastern part of the park. Access is by car or boat, and regularly scheduled flights land at Fort Smith, NWT, and Fort Chipewyan, Alberta. Information: *Wood Buffalo National Park,* PO Box 750, Fort Smith, Northwest Territories X0E 0P0 (phone: 403-872-2349).

YOHO NATIONAL PARK, Field, British Columbia: Named by the Cree Indians ("Yoho" is an expression meaning *awe*), this 507-square-mile preserve near the top of the Rockies takes in about 25 peaks over 10,000 feet, countless cascading streams and spectacular falls, plus lush forests. The 250-odd miles of hiking trails take you through areas inhabited by the park's abundant wildlife. Or you can take in the park's glories from your car as you drive along the Trans-Canada Highway. Information: *Superintendent, Yoho National Park,* PO Box 99, Field, BC V0A 1G0 (phone: 604-343-6324).

KOOTENAY NATIONAL PARK, Radium Hot Springs, British Columbia: The Banff-Windermere Highway, the focal point of this long, skinny preserve, makes its beauties remarkably accessible. There in front of you are towering peaks by the score, the 128-foot depths of Marble Canyon; the rusty-colored paint pots whose iron-rich mud the Indians used as body paint; and all manner of wildlife. In May and October, as many as 300 elk may congregate alongside the road at any given time. A complex of swimming and soaking pools also is available. Information: *Kootenay National Park,* Box 220, Radium Hot Springs, BC V0A 1M0 (phone: 604-347-9615).

GLACIER NATIONAL PARK, near Rogers Pass, British Columbia: A trip to this 521-square-mile preserve in the rugged Selkirk and Purcell ranges is a fascinating geography lesson where you learn that glaciers are dynamic, ever-moving forces, able to slice off whole sections of mountains and carve out their peaks, dig valleys, and polish rock faces as smooth as glass. Evidence of eons of this slicing, carving, and polishing is what makes Glacier so special. But there are wonderful wildflowers as well. Be sure to visit the information center at Rogers Pass. Information: *Glacier National Park,* PO Box 350, Revelstoke, BC V0E 2S0 (phone: 604-837-5155 or 6274).

MT. REVELSTOKE NATIONAL PARK, near Revelstoke, British Columbia: The views in this 99-square-mile park — particularly from the lookout atop Mt. Revelstoke itself — are what will astound you, because the mountains, which surround the area, are exceptionally rugged and the forests unusually dense. Alpine meadows bloom bright in late summer — as you'll see when you head out on the park's hiking trails that cover over 39 miles. Information: *Mt. Revelstoke National Park,* PO Box 350, Revelstoke, BC V0E 2S0 (phone: 604-837-5155).

PACIFIC RIM NATIONAL PARK, near Ucluelet, Vancouver Island, British Columbia: This is a wet world. Heavy rains and salt spray produce dense vegetation on the mountains that rise abruptly from the sea on the western edge of this 150-square-mile park. Tidal pools trap clusters of hermit crabs, starfish, limpets, and mussels. But inland the peaks are often snow-capped. The West Coast Trail, chopped out of the storm-pounded sea cliffs, is one of the nation's great hiking adventures, and 14-mile-long Long Beach among its finest strands. Offshore, you can fish, canoe, and camp — in utter solitude — at the Broken Group Islands. Information: *Pacific Rim National Park,* PO Box 280, Ucluelet, BC V0R 3A0 (phone: 604-726-7721 or 4212).

RIDING MOUNTAIN NATIONAL PARK, near Dauphin, Manitoba: Riding Mountain isn't a mountain at all, but a huge, 2,000-foot-high plateau. Covered with the kind of thick forest more commonly found in the east, as well as the grasslands that are typical of the surrounding prairies, the park's 1,150 square miles are laced with hiking and cross-country ski trails, and a spectrum of wildlife can be spotted. Many visitors come to battle the feisty, voracious northern pike, which is the main game fish, but pickerel, trout, perch, and whitefish also can be caught. Information: *Riding Mountain National Park,* Wasagaming, Manitoba R0J 2H0 (phone: 204-848-2811).

NAHANNI NATIONAL PARK, near Fort Simpson, Northwest Territories: The first area to be named to UNESCO's World Heritage List of natural sites that form part of our collective heritage, this 1,840-square-mile wilderness surrounding the South Nahanni River is spectacularly beautiful. Unusual plants, high mountains, and incredible canyons manage to dazzle you as much as Virginia Falls — an immense cataract that plunges about 400 feet to the river and shows a 4-acre face of whiteness in the process. Access is by chartered aircraft from Fort Simpson, Fort Liard, Fort Nelson, or Watson Lake; you can run the river and its tributaries in canoes or rafts, on your own, if you are very experienced, or with groups, and explore the mountains and valleys on foot. Since this area is very remote, you must book ahead if you plan to use the services of an outfitter. Information: *Nahanni National Park,* PO Box 300, Fort Simpson, Northwest Territories X0E 0N0 (phone: 403-695-3151).

PRINCE ALBERT NATIONAL PARK, near Prince Albert, Saskatchewan: Wildlife — moose, deer, elk, caribou, black bear, bison, and beaver — is abundant, and over 200 species of birds have been recorded (one of Canada's largest white pelican colonies being located at Lavallee Lake in the park's secluded northwest corner). Located 30 miles (48 km) north of Prince Albert — the Waskesiu Lake Visitor Services Center is an additional 30 miles (48 km) north — this million-acre wilderness park is near the geographical center of the province. Here, a rolling glacial terrain dotted with spruce bogs, large, cold lakes, and aspen uplands is preserved. Interpretive programs explain the fascinating ecosystems you'll see if you go hiking or canoeing. Information: *Prince Albert National Park,* PO Box 100, Waskesiu Lake, Saskatchewan S0J 2Y0 (phone: 306-663-5322).

KLUANE NATIONAL PARK, near Haines Junction, Yukon Territory: A good deal of this park's 8,500 square miles is given over to glaciers and mountains, including 19,520-foot Mt. Logan, Canada's highest peak. The world's largest ice fields outside the polar regions are here. Consequently, Kluane is a mountaineer's dream — even though climbing in the Icefield Ranges always means an expedition. But the park's eastern section is unglaciated, and using the old mining roads and some newly constructed trails, you can get a good feeling for a less forbidding Kluane, a preserve that boasts an amazing variety of flora, fauna, and terrain. Kluane's interpretive program, based at a fine visitors' center, includes a number of special events and campfire talks at the Kathleen Lake, Pine Lake, and Congdon Creek campgrounds. Guided hikes are available throughout the summer. Information: *Kluane National Park,* Haines Junction, Yukon Territory Y0B 1L0 (phone: 403-634-2251).

Special Havens

 Since standardization has begun to overtake the Canadian hotel industry, finding acceptable accommodations is usually not a problem. But a question arises: Where are all the hostelries with unique atmosphere, distinctive personality, style, and histories all their own? Not to worry. They're still around, though scattered, from the Maritimes to the Pacific Coast; and sometimes hard to find. A few resorts in this class are better advertised, but putting your finger on one with the facilities and activities that suit you can be a taxing chore.

The Canadian havens described here — our favorites — are places you'll want to visit when the locale is as important as what you do there. Among them are both resorts and inns. Most of the resorts feature stables, championship golf courses, biking and hiking paths, swimming pools, beaches, and often nightclubs and similar after-dark diversions. The inns, usually tucked away in some beautiful part of the country for which the innkeeper has a special affinity, are quieter and smaller. In either case, accommodations will cost more than at a less interesting establishment. If money is an important consideration, ask about off-season rates, normally offered in spring or fall; summers are always busy, and many properties fill to the rafters with skiers just after the first snowfall. Some hostelries also offer lower rates during the week. It's also wise to inquire whether activities will cost extra at resorts, and don't forget to budget for tips.

EAST

MARATHON INN, Grand Manan Island, New Brunswick: The bird life that Audubon admired when he visited here in the early part of the 19th century is as rich as ever, and some 300 species feed on the wild strawberries, blueberries, and blackberries that fairly blanket the island — the largest of the trio of Bay of Fundy isles — in summer. You'll certainly want to watch the birds, but you'll also want to gather the berries to eat with cream at the inn, admire the lupine and other wildflowers that polka-dot the meadows, and join one of the whale-watching tours conducted from August 1 to mid-September. Other activities include: tennis, swimming, beachcombing, hiking, and bicycling. The hotel itself was built (in 1871) atop a hill, so that there's almost always a breeze. It's a delight — well kept, from the wide hallways that lead to the 32 gleaming, lofty-ceilinged guestrooms to the widow's walk that tops the 3-story structure. All but 6 of the rooms have views over the harbor, and most rooms share a bath. The experience is well worth the little extra effort it takes to get to the island, which is accessible only by ferry from Black's Harbor, east of Calais, Maine, on the Canadian side of the border. Open May to October. Information: *Marathon Inn,* North Head, Grand Manan Island, NB E0G 2M0 (phone: 506-662-8144).

MARSHLANDS INN, Sackville, New Brunswick: Built around 1850 and owned by the same family from 1895 until a few years ago, the house has been a hostelry for nearly

6 decades. A staircase and hallways leading to the guestrooms are carpeted with richly colored Oriental rugs, and accented with dark woodwork. Before you're packed off to bed at night, innkeepers John and Mary Blakely will ply you with hot chocolate and gingersnaps. Later, if you get chilly, you've only to reach for the fluffy down comforter lying at the foot of your bed. In the morning, you're stuffed like a Périgord goose with goodies like baked apples and porridge, country sausage patties and buckwheat pancakes, and homemade bread and gooseberry jam. For lunch and dinner, choices include all manner of specialties — steak-and-kidney pie, grilled Atlantic salmon (often with an egg sauce), boiled salt cod and pork scraps, and fiddleheads, the top portion of the ostrich fern, a New Brunswick specialty. The Blakelys grow many of the foods that are served in the dining room, which is set in the large gardens behind the inn. The rooms vary; one of the nicer ones has a high four-poster and Oriental rugs. The Tantramar marshes, the summering site for thousands of Canada geese whose honks fill the air during spring and fall migrations, are on the nearby isthmus connecting New Brunswick and Nova Scotia. No wonder Queen Elizabeth took tea here when she toured New Brunswick. Open February through November. Information: *Marshlands Inn,* 73 Bridge St., PO Box 1440, Sackville, NB E0A 3C0 (phone: 506-536-0170).

ALGONQUIN, St. Andrews-by-the-Sea, New Brunswick: One of the loveliest of the Canadian Pacific hotels, this rambling English country manor of a hostelry, ringed by immaculately manicured lawns and well-tended flower gardens, sits on the edge of Passamaquoddy Bay on a hill overlooking the town, a short walk from the main street. Golfers make pilgrimages to the *Algonquin*'s 9- and 18-hole courses. Guests can swim in Katy's Cove or in the hotel's heated outdoor pool, play tennis or croquet, or go cycling. After such physical exertion, there are several restaurants and evening entertainments from which to choose for unwinding. Another way to relax is to visit the town for some of Canada's most interesting shopping or for a walking tour of the many late-18th- and early-19th-century houses built by the Loyalists who first settled the area. Information: *Algonquin Hotel,* St. Andrews, NB E0G 2X0 (phone: 506-529-8823). Also see *Golf* and *The Fundy Trail,* DIRECTIONS.

ROSSMOUNT INN, St. Andrews-by-the-Sea, New Brunswick: Victorian England must have been a lovely place, or so you would judge from the antiques and portraits of British royalty at this century-old inn, nestled in the woods at the foot of Chamcook Mountain. There's even a dartboard in the taproom. The 16 bedrooms, all with private bath, are comfortable, but plainer than the public rooms. Owners Robert and Lynda Estes left California for a richer, simpler life, and found it here. Robert runs the inn and Lynda is the chef. Dining tables are graced with linen, crystal, and antique china. The menu features fresh fish, fruits and berries from the inn's gardens, and bread and desserts baked with whole grains, raw sugar, and honey. (Vegetarian meals are offered, too.) Walking, hiking, and jogging on trails on the private 87-acre wildlife sanctuary, shopping in town, and playing golf on the nearby course are the favored pastimes. There's also a swimming pool. (Smoking is confined to certain areas, with none permitted in the dining room.) Information: *Rossmount Inn,* RR2, St. Andrews, NB E0G 2X0 (phone: 506-529-3351).

KELTIC LODGE, Cape Breton Island, Nova Scotia: The lonely site of this provincial government resort in magnificent Cape Breton Highlands National Park, on a rocky peninsula, assures each room a marvelous view over a landscape of rugged, heavily wooded highlands reminiscent of the Scottish Hebrides. That alone, or the hotel's proximity to the Cabot Trail, the scenic highway that rings the island, would make *Keltic Lodge* worth a visit. But it also is a relaxing place for far longer stays. You can swim in the large pool or in a fresh water lake, or soak up the salt air on a mile-long beach not far away. The surrounding woods are full of hiking trails, ideal for peaceful rambles. And there's the epic Stanley Thompson–designed golf links and a tennis court. And when you've worked your appetite up to monstrous proportions, you can satisfy it in a big way: The fresh seafood caught by local fishermen and prepared by French chefs can't be beat. Accommodations are offered in the sedate *Main Lodge* with its 32 rooms, the modern 40-room *White Birch Inn,* or in one of the well-appointed cottages (2 or 4 bedrooms, plus a sitting room with fireplace, in each). Information: *Keltic Lodge,* PO Box 70, Ingonish Beach, NS B0C 1L0 (phone: 902-285-2880). Also see *Golf* and *National Parks.*

KILMUIR PLACE, Cape Breton Island, Nova Scotia: This lovely little country house just off the Cabot Trail on Nova Scotia's Cape Breton Island is the kind of place to which we would all retire if life were fair. Since it is not, we can only hope to visit, and with only 5 guestrooms, you'd better book a place early if you hope to do even that. Once you get there, innkeepers Nancy and Guy Parry will make you abundantly welcome, whether you are having a salmon dinner in the dining room or sampling freshly baked goods in the friendly kitchen. The real reason for a visit — besides the utter peace of the place and the beauty of the island — is salmon fishing. The house is filled with family heirlooms, and the atmosphere is warm and loving. Open from the end of June to mid-October. Information: *Kilmuir Place,* Northeast Margaree, Cape Breton Island, NS B0E 2H0 (phone: 902-248-2877).

MILFORD HOUSE, South Milford, Nova Scotia: Located in the province's lake district just 15 miles (24 km) from Kejimkujik National Park, this 600-acre country resort was founded in the 1860s as a stopping-off place for travelers. The main lodge, site of the dining room and the parlors, is a comfortable sort of place with polished wood floors and old-fashioned fireplaces. Guests stay in 27 scattered waterside 2- to 5-bedroom, fireplace-equipped cottages; each comes with its own dock. Hearty country fare — home-baked bread and pastries, fresh vegetables and native berries, homemade soup and fresh fish and roasts — is the specialty of the house. Though you'll find clean linens and fresh flowers on your table every day, this is a very informal establishment. Families can bring their squalling babies and find themselves welcomed with open arms, so many return year after year until the children are grown. In fact, when the original owners sold it in 1969, it was to some longtime guests who have continued the traditions they'd grown to love. Canoeing, swimming, and fishing have always been the popular activities, but the tennis courts are starting to catch on, too. Golf is nearby. To get the space you want, you must count on having your reservations confirmed by season's opening in mid-June. The dining room closes in mid-September, but two off-season cabins are equipped for housekeeping and are open year-round. Information: *Milford House,* South Milford, RR4, Annapolis Royal, NS B0S 1A0 (phone: 902-532-2617). Also see *National Parks.*

MILLCROFT INN, Alton, Ontario: This has to be one of the continent's best examples of adaptive use of an old building. The structure is an 1881 knitting mill, a stone version of the kind that glowers resentfully at municipalities like New Bedford, Massachusetts, and Providence, Rhode Island, which have all but forgotten them. The Toronto movers and shakers behind the Millcroft project restored the mill, installed a bayed, glass-walled "dining pod" to provide guests with a profoundly stomach-churning view of the falls below, and then furnished the whole from stem to stern with a delightful blend of the contemporary and the antique. Lodgings are in rooms in the mill or in "crofts" (contemporary condominium-type loft units that can accommodate four). And the dinners include specialties like Atlantic salmon with either clover honey and saffron glaze or tandoori spices and Jasmine tea sauce, salad ragout, and tropical champagne sorbet. The 100-acre property also boasts a heated outdoor pool, sauna, whirlpool bath, Jacuzzi, tennis courts, and ice skating on the mill pond. And the cross-country skiing is great here in winter. Information: *Millcroft Inn,* Alton, Ontario L0N 1A0 (phone: 519-941-8111).

AROWHON PINES, Algonquin Park, Ontario: Smack in the center of a 3,000-square-mile wildlife preserve, this resort's draw is its natural beauty and tranquillity.

Seclusion is prized, as guests must travel a 5-mile private road to reach Arowhon, which is situated on the shore of its own lake. Each of the 2- to 12-bedroom cabins, furnished in Canadiana, has a communal lounge with a fireplace; or you can opt for 1 of 3 suites in a private cabin with a stone fireplace. Moose, deer, red fox, wolf, bear, and over 100 species of birds call the preserve home, and many hours can be spent seeking out these creatures while hiking the marked trails, picnicking in the woods, or boating. At night there are movies in the main lounge, or you can listen to the call of the loon in front of a blazing bonfire. A member of the Relais & Châteaux group, and known for its fine food fresh from the Canadian North Woods, it is open from May 16 to October 10. Full American Plan and use of all recreational facilities — tennis courts, canoes, and windsurfers — are included. Information: *Arowhon Pines,* Algonquin Park, Ontario P0A 1B0 (phone: 705-633-5661/2), in summer; 297 Balliol St., Toronto, Ontario M4S 1C7 (phone: 416-483-4393), in winter.

BENMILLER INN, Goderich, Ontario: Like so many inns, this one was the result of the owners' love affair with the locality — in this case, a London, Ontario, man and his sister fell in love with an area near Lake Huron, on the banks of the Maitland River, where they used to come as children. They acquired the area's woolen mill, then followed that with the purchase of a flour mill. When both mills had been restored and furnished with antiques, the mill owners' homes were bought, refurbished, and expanded to include 48 rooms. The complex now occupies some 70 acres of rolling woodlands by the river. Each of the four buildings has its own character, and each room is different; but the whole is furnished with antiques and items ingeniously crafted from the old mill machinery. Spindles, for instance, are used for room dividers, and wheels for the bases of coffee tables. The old beams and barnboard add to the rustic charm. There's great fishing in the surrounding stream and on the river during spring and fall, when the salmon run, and you can go trout fishing in the pond on the premises, swim in an indoor pool, play tennis (there are 2 outdoor courts), or relax in the whirlpool bath or sauna. Stratford is only 45 miles (72 km) away. Information: *Benmiller Inn,* RR4, Goderich, Ontario N7A 3Y1 (phone: 519-524-2191; 800-265-1711).

INN AT MANITOU, McKellar, Ontario: This small, ultra-luxurious Relais & Châteaux resort located on a semi-wilderness shore of a north central Ontario lake, not far from the beautiful Georgian Bay area (and some 160 miles/256 km north of Toronto) offers a perfect spot for the active tennis enthusiast and nature lover alike. Sixty-five guests can be accommodated in 32 doubles and one single. There is a staff of 16 pros to instruct guests on the 13 outdoor courts and one indoor court. Facilities include ball machines and video equipment, a heated pool, sauna and spa, and boats for sailing on the lake. The suites each have a wood-burning fireplace (and many have whirlpool baths and sauna). The food is delicious, featuring nouvelle cuisine and special "spa cuisine" for the health conscious. A health and beauty spa with aerobics classes and hydrotherapy baths also are available. The inn offers special rates from late May to late June and from *Labor Day* to mid-October. Closed from November to April. Information: *Inn at Manitou,* McKellar Centre Rd., McKellar, Ontario P0G 1C0 (phone: 705-389-2171); off-season: 251 Davenport Rd., Toronto, Ontario M5R 1J9 (phone: 416-967-3466).

PINESTONE INN AND COUNTRY CLUB, Haliburton, Ontario: The fact that you never have to travel very far in Canada to get away from the urban rat race is proved once more at this year-round resort, with a total of 124 rooms in the hotel, villas, chalets, and 5-bedroom executive house. Although it is modern and almost citified — with tennis courts, indoor and outdoor swimming pools, 18-hole golf course, sauna, whirlpool bath, 2 lounges with live entertainment, and 2 fancy restaurants with a long wine list — the atmosphere is decidedly low key. Flanking either side of the hotel are a pond and a lake (great for swimming, fishing, boating); and surrounding it all are more woods than you could possibly explore on foot even in a whole summer. In winter, there's cross-country skiing on a 150-mile trail network on the golf course and in the forests along with snowmobiling, sleigh rides, and ice skating. Downhill skiing is within a half-hour drive. Information: *Pinestone Inn and Country Club,* Box 809, Haliburton, Ontario K0M 1S0 (phone: 705-457-1800 or 800-461-0357).

DEERHURST INN AND COUNTRY CLUB, Huntsville, Ontario: A favorite with summer guests since the turn of the century, this friendly resort on the shores of Peninsula Lake in the heart of the Muskoka tourist area (or Muskoka lakes district) will give you good reasons to join the applause: 2 fine 18-hole PGA-level golf courses, heated indoor and outdoor pools, 8 outdoor and 4 indoor tennis courts, just about any kind of boat rental for which you could wish, wooded hiking trails, horseback riding, saunas and whirlpool baths, and a big living room fireplace for quiet nights at the end of busy days. Sixty miles of interconnecting waterways in the area make for great fishing. Then, once the snow falls, the place is transformed into "The Complete Cross-Country Skier's Resort," with over 17 miles of double-track set trails traversing the rolling pine forests. Also available are snowmobiling, skating on the new rink, dog-sledding, and snowshoeing, with alpine skiing just a half-mile away. Accommodations — many with fireplace and whirlpool bath — are in the main lodge, two modern buildings, separate cottages, or timeshare villas and condominiums. Meals are served in any of a number of dining areas, and there's also nightly live entertainment in three different sections of the inn year-round. Information: *Deerhurst Inn and Country Club,* RR4, Huntsville, Ontario P0A 1K0 (phone: 705-789-5543).

WINDERMERE HOUSE, Muskoka, Ontario: This stately, 78-room resort, with all the charm of a country inn, has been a fixture on Lake Rosseau since it was built in the 1870s. Overlooking the lake, the "Grand Lady of the Muskoka Lakes" was renovated and refurbished 5 years ago. There are fine views of the beach and the water from the verandah of the main house, many of its rooms, and from the Settlers Bay units. (Other rooms overlook charming gardens.) A wealth of diversions include fine dining, dancing, and theater and lounge entertainment. The social director stays busy organizing games, movies, and special children's programs. Sports enthusiasts can enjoy tennis, canoeing, windsurfing, sailing, and the 18-hole championship golf course. Open mid-May to mid-October. Information: *Windermere House,* Windermere, Ontario P0B 1P0 (phone: 705-769-3611).

SHAW'S, Brackley Beach, Prince Edward Island: The proximity of Brackley Beach, Canada's best strand, to this onetime farm run as a hotel since the mid-19th century by the Shaw family, is among its prime attractions — and for good reason: The beach is 5 miles long, pinkish-tawny, hard-packed, dune-backed — and, more to the point, lapped by waters warm enough for swimming. When you've had enough of the sand and sea, you can golf, play tennis, take in horse races or a play, or go fishing, swimming, or sailing nearby. From June through September, the *Charlottetown Festival* is in full swing not far away. Accommodations are in 28 rooms, some with private bath, and 18 cottages, and there's a main dining room (the food here is a draw in itself). Reservations well in advance are a must. Information: *Shaw's Hotel,* Brackley Beach, PEI C0A 2H0 (phone: 902-672-2022). Also see *Festivals, Fairs, and Fancy Acts, National Parks,* and *Blue Heron Drive, Prince Edward Island,* DIRECTIONS.

DALVAY-BY-THE-SEA, Dalvay Beach, Prince Edward Island: This small resort hotel, with its pine-paneled, fireplace-warmed, 2-story foyer, has a lot to offer in the way of Victorian charm — which will probably come as a surprise. Since it was designed around a lovely mansion constructed in 1895 by a partner in the Standard Oil Company, most visitors expect a more formal and elegant interior decor. But it's not a bit stuffy. There are no planned activities, since guests always manage to make their own good times — a fact that gives immense pleasure to the management, the Canadian-born grandsons of the Swiss couple who ran the place beginning in 1959. There are 2 cottages, but 2 dozen of the resort's 26 rooms, most paneled in island pine, are in the mansion proper. Those on the second floor are the loveliest, and some have views over both Dalvay Beach, situated 200 yards away on the least-crowded part of Prince Edward Island National Park, and Dalvay Lake, which is at the hotel's doorstep. You can swim or splash in either one, go canoeing or rowing on the lake, play tennis on the hotel's 2 courts, or try your hand at lawn bowling on its green. The attractions at Cavendish, setting for native author Lucy Maud Montgomery's *Anne of Green Gables,* and its golf course are nearby. Closed mid-September until June. Information: *Dalvay-by-the-Sea Hotel,* PO Box 8, Little York, PEI C0A 1P0 (phone: 902-672-2546 in winter; 902-672-2048 in summer). Also see *Golf, National Parks,* and *Blue Heron Drive, Prince Edward Island,* DIRECTIONS.

LA PINSONNIÈRE, Cap à l'Aigle, Quebec: A lovely setting for a lovely inn: in the heart of Charlevoix, a mere fathom from Pointe-au-Pic, between the St. Lawrence River and the mountains. A crisp, white mansion that was once a private home, it has 28 rooms and suites, some with fireplace and canopied bed, most with a river view. Whale safaris, cruises on the Saguenay Fjord, swimming in the new indoor pool, riding, sailing, tennis, sleigh rides, downhill and cross-country skiing fill your days; theater, concerts, and dining, fill your nights. Like other Relais & Châteaux group properties, the owners rely on fresh produce and foodstuffs to produce their fine cuisine. Closed in November. Information: *La Pinsonnière,* Cap à l'Aigle, Charlevoix, Quebec, G0T 1B0 (phone: 418-665-4431).

LE TREMBLANT CLUB, Mont Tremblant, Quebec: Facing Mont Tremblant, the highest peak in the Laurentians, this resort on the shores of Lac Tremblant has immediate access to some of Canada's best cross-country ski terrain, snowshoeing trails, and downhill skiing. It even has its own live-in ski instructors to accompany students to the slopes every morning. The various incarnations of the main inn as private home, boarding house, and drinking establishment have given a patina to an already lovely structure — a typically Canadian mix of big stones and massive beams centered upon a gigantic fireplace — one that is carried through to its 15 rooms and 16 suites. Having added 70 condominiums, the present owners have fixed its place firmly up at the top among Laurentians resorts — the year round. For though the decor seems as if it was arranged to warm the soul when the winds of winter hurled themselves at the windowpanes, *Cuttle's* sparkles in summer as well. It's small enough to be cozy but large enough to give you plenty of things to do: There's swimming, sailing, boating, windsurfing, and fishing on the lake; 4 tennis courts and a beautifully situated swimming pool also are available. Golf and riding are nearby, and the forest around the lake is great for walks and hikes. For the kids, the club has a playground and hosts a social program. The award-winning dining room speaks with a definite French accent — impeccably. Information: *Le Tremblant Club,* Mont Tremblant, Quebec J0T 1Z0 (phone: 819-425-2731). Also see *Tennis, Downhill* and *Cross-Country Skiing,* and *The Laurentians, Quebec,* DIRECTIONS.

STATION MONT TREMBLANT LODGE, Mont Tremblant, Quebec: This old, well-established resort, with 50 rooms in small chalets and condominiums, the only one actually on Mont Tremblant, is still the favorite it used to be, and now and then you'll spot a famous face — no surprise since a complement of the kind of facilities that are required by the rich and famous await them. There's plenty of privacy (most lodgings are in a scattering of cottages), and the hotel sets a good table. And you can ski to the slopes. Information: *Station Mont Tremblant Lodge,* Mont Tremblant, Quebec J0T 1Z0 (phone: 819-425-8711; 800-567-6761). Also see *Downhill* and *Cross-Country Skiing* and *The Laurentians, Quebec,* DIRECTIONS.

LE CHÂTEAU MONTEBELLO, Montebello, Quebec: The brochures describing this Canadian Pacific-owned hotel 40 miles (64 km) east of Ottawa in the Ottawa River Valley as a magnificent playground aren't stretching the point. The baronial 210-room log palace was once a private club, and when you step across the threshold, you feel just a little bit grander, a little bit more important, for being there. The scenes are impressive indeed: Fires that burn in the massive six-sided, 3-story stone fireplace cast their flickering light over rafters that look as if they've come from the 15th century. You've never seen anything like it before, and won't for a while to come. Outside, there are 65,000 acres of dense woodlands dotted by over 70 lakes. There's golf, tennis, hiking, fishing, horseback riding, croquet, indoor and outdoor swimming, cross-country skiing, skating, snowshoeing, sleigh riding, and curling — and on and on. The fitness area, complete with squash courts, exercise room, saunas and whirlpool baths, rounds things out. New this year are the executive suites. This is a *seigneurie,* as the French Canadians say, on a very grand scale. Information: *Le Château Montebello,* Montebello, Quebec J0V 1L0 (phone: 819-423-6341). Also see *Downhill* and *Cross-Country Skiing.*

HOVEY MANOR, North Hatley, Quebec: The story is told often enough that it's probably true, sad though it may be: After the US Civil War, the small groups of Southerners who had summered up north in antebellum days continued to head for Yankeeland — but when the trains arrived there, the travelers pulled the blinds, kept going, and didn't stop until they had crossed the international border. Summer homes were eventually built by a couple of these Southerners, including one Henry Atkinson of Atlanta, who always showed up in North Hatley with two private railway cars, ten horses and several carriages, and 18 servants. The turn-of-the-century home he had built for himself — broad of verandah and white of pillar, inspired by George Washington's Mount Vernon — now lends its very considerable charm to Hovey Manor. All of its 35 rooms — installed not only in the main house but also ingeniously fitted into the former servants' quarters, Ice House, Pump House, and Electrical House — are furnished with Canadian antiques. All rooms have private bath, most face the lake, and many have fireplaces. Each has its own special decor. The Tap Room, where you'll find a vast, 10,000-brick fireplace which is one of 16 of varying sizes scattered throughout the inn, used to be the stables. Sitting atop an 18th-century diamond-pointed Quebec pine armoire in the reception lobby is the inn's celebrated haunted clock, a Gothic-style 80-day chimer that rings only when someone mentions Plumley LeBaron, an early North Hatleyite known for having worn a raccoon coat in the summertime. The site itself is lovely — along a sloping garden down to a private beach facing 10-mile-long Lake Massawippi, surrounded by maples, birches, beeches, and evergreens. In summer, you can canoe, sail, windsurf, water-ski, fish, swim, play tennis on the inn's single court, or golf on any of five courses within a 20-minute drive. In winter, skiers schuss the substantial Eastern Townships slopes or take on the manor's 22 miles of cross-country trails. All year-round, you'll enjoy the creations of the inn's Belgian chef. Information: *Hovey Manor,* PO Box 60, North Hatley, Quebec J0B 2C0 (phone: 819-842-2421). Also see *Downhill Skiing.*

AUBERGE HATLEY, North Hatley, Quebec: A romantic country inn overlooking Lake Massawippi, this 1903 hostelry is a charming reminder of the colonial grandeur created by 19th-century Confederates who, following their defeat by the Yankees (see *Hovey Manor,* above), summered here with their entourages. Each of its 24 rooms is individually appointed in period antiques, floral wallpaper, quilted bedspreads, and, in some rooms, fireplaces. Original artwork, leather sofas, beamed ceilings, and an old brick fireplace furnish the spacious living room. Guests work up an appetite playing tennis or golf, boating, sailing, boardsailing, or fishing on beautiful Lake Massawippi. Guy Bohec, a 1985 gold medal winner for nouvelle cuisine at the Grand Salon Quebecois d'Art Culinaire, creates magic with his Duck Aiguillettes with Morriolo cherries. The inn, a member of the prestigious Relais & Châteaux group, is closed November 15–30. Information: *Auberge Hatley,* PO Box 330, North Hatley, Quebec J0B 2C0 (phone: 819-842-2451).

AUBERGE GRAY ROCKS, St. Jovite, Quebec: This massive 252-room inn, opened in 1906 when the surrounding Laurentians were still virgin forestlands, occupies 2,600 acres on the shores of Lac Ouimet, with a commanding view of Mont Tremblant, and it is almost as lively as it is large: There are facilities for swimming and diving on the lake, a complete marina that rents sailboats, windsurfing, and canoes, a 5,000-foot airstrip, 22 Har-Tru tennis courts, a fine 18-hole championship golf course, a complete health club, all manner of other sporting facilities, and exceptionally varied nightlife. Tennis clinics by Dennis van der Meer are a big drawing card in summer, and the program is among Canada's best. In winter, the Snow Eagle Ski School, based on the hotel's own Sugar Peak, 100 yards from the main inn, attracts guests from all over the states, and graduates will tell you without equivocating that the school (begun in 1938) is one of North America's best. Big-mountain skiing at Mont Tremblant is only a short drive away. In the capacious dining room, international cuisine is the order of the day. Information: *Auberge Gray Rocks,* PO Box 1000, St. Jovite, Quebec J0T 2H0 (phone: 819-425-2771). Also see *Downhill* and *Cross-Country Skiing, Tennis, Golf,* and *The Laurentians, Quebec,* DIRECTIONS.

AUBERGE HANDFIELD, St. Marc-sur-Richelieu, Quebec: Accommodations at this charming hostelry in the heart of the peaceful Richelieu River Valley not far from Montreal are in nine old Canadian farmhouses rescued from destruction at the hands of local farmers who were modernizing, then transported to the Auberge Handfield's woods-rimmed property and fitted out with Canadian antiques. There is a total of 55 rooms in the establishment. The main lodge — where you'll find the dining room — is charming as well, with a big stone fireplace in the lobby. The inn is just the right size — small enough so you don't get lost, large enough to give you some privacy and to support a goodly number of facilities, including a kidney-shape swimming pool, a marina, and an activities program that includes corn-on-the-cob parties in fall and sugaring-off parties (at the inn's own sugar shack) from the beginning of March to the end of April. The restaurant is noted for both its nouvelle cuisine and its French Canadian dishes. In winter, there's cross-country skiing, and in summer, summer theater (mainly comedies, performed in French, on a steamboat moored nearby). Information: *Auberge Handfield,* 555 Chemin du Prince, St. Marc-sur-Richelieu, Quebec J0L 2E0 (phone: 514-584-2226). Also see *Canoeing and Rafting.*

LES TROIS TILLEULS, St. Marc-sur-Richelieu, Quebec: Overlooking the Richelieu River, a 20-minute drive from Montreal, this property was originally a 19th-century mansion. A 21-room rustic inn has been added, and the whole is a member of Relais & Châteaux, the exclusive association of hostelries who abide by the following criteria: courtesy, calm, comfort, cuisine, and character. To that list can be added warmth and relaxation. In each air conditioned room, guests find a color TV set, radio, and balcony from which they can plot the day's activities in the marina or the pool, on the links or the courts. The inn's highlight is its French cuisine; the outstanding menu becomes self-explanatory once you know that both owners are French. Information: *Hostellerie les Trois Tilleuls,* 290 Chemin du Prince St. Marc-sur-Richelieu, Quebec J0L 2E0 (phone: 514-584-2231).

LA SAPINIÈRE, Val David, Quebec: In this Laurentians hotel and restaurant, the first Canadian member of France's prestigious Relais & Châteaux group, the primary distinction is the kitchen. Between meals, there's canoeing and rowing on a private lake, swimming in an outdoor heated pool, tennis, badminton, shuffleboard, miniature golf, and, in winter, cross-country skiing in the maple, pine, and fir woods that surround the hotel and downhill skiing at myriad nearby areas. The 70 rooms and suites are large, clean, and comfortably appointed — and must be reserved several months in advance. There also are several private "salons" with fireplaces, 5 meeting rooms with air conditioning, and audio-visual and sound equipment. Information: *Hôtel la Sapinière,* PO Box 190, Val David, Quebec J0T 2N0 (phone: 819-322-2020 or 514-866-8262). Also see *Downhill* and *Cross-Country Skiing* and *The Laurentians, Quebec,* DIRECTIONS.

WEST

BANFF SPRINGS, Banff, Alberta: Imagine a snow queen's castle rising at the base of an evergreen-covered mountain slope with ice-capped peaks all around in the distance. This establishment, with 841 rooms and suites and situated in Banff National Park, is like that. As the focus of tour groups and conventions, the interior accommodations and amenities haven't always been the equal of the exterior architecture, but a major renovation of its guestrooms and eating facilities, along with its new health club, have made the inside more appealing — albeit more modern. And the site remains remarkable: It's surrounded by hundreds of square miles of lofty mountains, deep valleys, stunning glaciers, and crystal lakes. In addition to the hotel's 4 dining rooms, it has a café and deli, sushi and wine bars, an outdoor heated pool, an indoor Olympic-size pool, a health club with 3 Jacuzzis and a sauna, a spectacularly scenic championship golf course, and 5 tennis courts. In winter it's a skier's delight, and there's also ice skating, ski touring, and snowshoeing on the property. Information: *Banff Springs Hotel,* PO Box 960, Banff, Alberta T0L 0C0 (phone: 403-762-2211). Also see *Downhill Skiing, Ice Skating, Golf, Tennis,* and *Calgary to Banff and Jasper National Parks, Alberta,* DIRECTIONS.

NUM-TI-JAH LODGE, Bow Lake, Alberta: Situated between Jasper and Banff national parks, amidst the mountains and overlooking a lake, this rustic log lodge has a crusty, western flavor, with its chairs crafted of antlers, huge stone fireplaces, and good simple food. Horseback riding and hiking are favored pastimes. Closed November through March. For reservations and information: *Num-Ti-Jah Lodge,* Bow Lake, Box 39, Lake Louise, Alberta T0L 1E0 (phone: 403-761-7020). Also see *Calgary to Banff and Jasper National Parks, Alberta,* DIRECTIONS.

JASPER PARK LODGE, Jasper, Alberta: Towering snowcapped peaks surround this alpine lodge on the shores of Lac Beauvert deep inside Jasper National Park. Guests stay in what amounts to a small village of modern cedar chalets and original log cabins — there are 400 rooms in all, many with patios and fireplaces. For recreation the choices are golf, tennis, horseback riding, cycling, white-water rafting, boating, fishing, or going for a guided tour of sections of the park. Excellent food is served in several dining rooms or in the comfort of your own cabin, and a variety of evening entertainment, including dancing, is offered. During the summer months, a daily social and cultural program is made available, as is one for children. Open year-round. Ski packages available. Information: *Jasper Park Lodge,* Box 40, Jasper, Alberta T0E 1E0 (phone: 403-852-3301).

CHÂTEAU LAKE LOUISE, Lake Louise, Alberta: This large, French-style château, one of the Canadian Pacific hotels, has a breathtaking setting on the shores of world-famous Lake Louise — blue-green, beautifully clear, rimmed by mountains, and backed by the blue-white Victoria Glacier. The setting alone would recommend the hotel. But like its fellows, this Gallic beauty is no garden-variety establishment. The resplendence of the interiors almost matches the beauty of the scene outside. Witness the regal pillars in the palatial lobby and the soaring arches of the Victoria Room. The front desk is of carved oak, the lobby furniture is carved and heavy, and though the lobby itself is cavernous, it manages to be warm and welcoming. The recently opened Glacier Wing added 140 bedrooms and suites, for a total of 525, and renovation of many of the older rooms has made them fresher as well. Though there is no golf course, the excellent layout at the *Banff Springs* hotel is only 39 miles (63 km) away. On-site diversions include an indoor pool, tanning salon, Jacuzzi, and a steam room, as well as a pub, pizza parlor, and a rooftop restaurant. Also available are ice skating, sleigh rides across frozen Lake Louise, pony trekking in the mountains, canoeing and hiking in pollen-free woods, and downhill and cross-country skiing. Open year-round. Information: *Château Lake Louise,* Lake Louise, Alberta T0L

1E0 (phone: 403-522-3511). Also see *Calgary to Banff and Jasper National Parks, Alberta,* DIRECTIONS.

FAIRMONT HOT SPRINGS, Fairmont Hot Springs, British Columbia: This hostelry — a long-established resort now housed in a handful of newish buildings — is a delight for families. Kids, especially, love the 10,000 square feet of steaming natural mineral pools. And then there's the setting — on the side of a mountain in the lovely Kootenay district of the Rockies, surrounded by woods, lawns, and gardens, with nice views over the valley below. There's skiing in winter on its own slopes, which have a 1,000-foot vertical, or nearby at big Kimberley and Panorama. In summer, you can play tennis (there are 4 courts), golf on two 18-hole courses, or go riding. The resort also has a recreation center with a pool, Jacuzzis, racquetball and squash courts, work-out room, and sauna. Additional accommodations are provided at the property's 265-site campground (30 spaces are open in winter). Information: *Fairmont Hot Springs Resort,* Box 10, Fairmont Hot Springs, BC V0B 1L0 (phone: 604-345-6311 or 800-663-4979).

HARRISON HOT SPRINGS, Harrison Hot Springs, British Columbia: Nestled in the Coast Range, in the upper Fraser River Valley some 90 miles (144 km) east of Vancouver, this impressive old 361-unit resort sits on the shores of Harrison Lake, in a rural area dotted by farmhouses and speckled with lakes. Though the economics of modern hotelkeeping have affected the place, many of the traditions begun in the hotel's early days are intact. Tea and homemade cakes are still served every afternoon in the upper lobby. Dancing to live music in the well-loved Copper Room is as spirited as ever; the band leader, a fixture here for years, has retired — but the band plays on. And a prime attraction is still the hot springs. A circular sulfur indoor pool heated naturally to 100F, a curved indoor swimming pool kept at 90F, and an outdoor pool, with a combination of fresh and mineral water, surrounded by a large sundeck are available. There are Roman and whirlpool baths, a Universal gym and an outdoor fitness course, and registered masseurs and masseuses are on duty at the plush health pavilion. (And the sauna and 2 of the pools are open around the clock.) Sports facilities abound: tennis, shuffleboard, golf on a 9-hole course; plus bicycling, water skiing, fishing, boating, and boardsailing. Off the property are scenic boat cruises, helicopter trips, and tours of the area's many attractions. Information: *Harrison Hot Springs Hotel,* Harrison Hot Springs, BC V0M 1K0 (phone: 604-796-2244).

Farm and Ranch Vacations

 Holidays at a Canadian farm or ranch can take you back quickly to a childhood you wish you had had — if not to your own youth. They can help introduce your youngsters to a way of life that city and suburban kids simply don't encounter elsewhere. They'll milk a cow, talk to the small animals that many farmers keep, prowl through the woods with a dog at their heels, learn to ride, swim in a creek, and explore to their hearts' content without getting into trouble. For them, as for you, the long summer days fill up quickly with berry picking, horseback riding, haying and combining, visits to auctions in tiny towns you'd otherwise have no reason to visit, or just hanging out in the kitchen while the bread is being baked or the red raspberries, harvested by the gallon from the garden, are being turned into jam. (A farm visit can be a regular cooking school.) The food that shows up on the table — usually simple fare — is meant to satisfy the hearty appetite so easily worked up wherever the air is fresh. Your hosts are friendly folk who learn from you as much as you do from them. They like the stream of strangers that passes through their homes, and they have almost infinite tolerance for the ignorance of people from the city.

Among them, you'll find more than a few who speak English with an accent —
not just the French Canadians, but also the new Canadians from Germany, the
Ukraine, and other parts of the world: Canada is still a melting pot.

The nature of the farms changes with the landscape. In the east, you'll find smaller,
old-fashioned places of around 200 acres that specialize in dairy or mixed farming, some
owned by French Canadian families who can teach you a little of their language. In
the Maritimes, you'll find farms of 200 to 2,000 acres specializing in apples, potatoes,
or beef and dairy cattle. On Prince Edward Island, as an added bonus, you can wake
up to a view of the ocean. The larger spreads out west fall into two basic categories:
guest (or dude) ranches, where the guest business contributes substantially to the
property's income; and working ranches, where guests are a sideline. Guest ranches
may offer more luxurious surroundings, a more extensive roster of planned activities,
and a wider variety of facilities. Working ranches are make-your-own-fun places,
although since they're generally smaller as well, your hosts will always give you plenty
of personal attention and many suggestions to keep you busy. Prices can run anywhere
from $30 to $85 per night, depending on whether meals are included and on the size
and facilities of the farm or ranch; there is usually a discount for children.

Provincial tourism departments can give you information about dude ranches in their
province. Farms also are represented by associations. All the members of these associations are inspected regularly and thoroughly and then listed in provincewide directories
that are updated annually. When you're picking a farm or ranch, first determine the
province you want to visit, then write for the listings, and phone the farms that interest
you to get a more specific idea of what they're like and to see how you like your potential
hosts. Farms and ranches without children tend to be a little quieter than those with
children at home, and you may prefer them if you and your spouse are coming alone.
Otherwise, you'll probably want to stay with a family whose children are about the
same ages as your own. For a complete listing of approved farms in Canada, contact
these provincial offices:

ALBERTA: *Travel Alberta,* Dept. E, PO Box 2500, 15th Floor, 10025 Jasper Ave.,
Edmonton, Alberta T5J 3Z3 (phone: 800-661-8888).

BRITISH COLUMBIA: *Tourism British Columbia,* Recreation and Culture, Parliament Bldg., Victoria, BC V8V 1X4 (phone: 800-663-6000) or *Williams Lake Travel
Infocentre,* PO Box 4900, Williams Lake, BC VoJ 2NO (phone: 604-392-2226).

MANITOBA: *Manitoba Farm Vacations Association,* 525 Kylemore Ave., Winnipeg,
Manitoba R3L 1B5 (phone: 204-475-6624).

NEW BRUNSWICK: *Tourism New Brunswick,* PO Box 12345, Fredericton, NB E3B
5C3 (phone: 800-561-0123 or 506-453-2377); *New Brunswick Farm Vacations,* RR3,
Port Elgin, New Brunswick E0A 2K0 (phone: 506-538-2597).

NOVA SCOTIA: *Jane Reid Stevens, Nova Scotia Farm & Country Vacations Association,* Newport Station, Hants Co., NS B0N 2B0 (phone: 902-798-5864).

ONTARIO: *Sharon Grose, Ontario Vacation Farm Association,* RR2, Alma, Ontario
N0B 1A0 (phone: 519-846-9788).

PRINCE EDWARD ISLAND: *Prince Edward Island Department of Tourism and
Parks,* Visitor Services, PO Box 940E, Charlottetown, PEI C1A 7M5 (phone: 902-368-
4444).

QUEBEC: *Fédération des Agricotours du Québec,* 4545 Ave. Pierre-de-Coubertin, CP
1000, Succ. M, Montreal, Quebec H1V 3R2 (phone: 514-252-3138 or 800-361-3585).
This organization will help you find the kind of farm you have in mind in the area you
want to visit; it also runs a rural bed and breakfast program.

SASKATCHEWAN: *Beatrice Magee, Saskatchewan Country Vacations Association,*
Box 54, Gull Lake, Saskatchewan (phone: 306-672-3970).

FAMILY FARMS

LIIVAM FARMS, Eckville, Alberta: A lot of Mrs. Liivam's visitors just stop for the bed and breakfast accommodations on their way to the mountains, which are not far away. But when they see what there is to do, they exclaim that if they'd only known, they would have planned to stay longer. Many return on their way home, even though that usually means backtracking. The attraction of the place is not hard to understand. Mrs. Liivam's home is a very peaceful place, with its berry patch, its fruit trees, and its beautiful lawns planted with big trees 40 or 50 years old — not so common in this part of the province; in mid-July, the blooming of the rapeseed, an oil-producing grain that is common in these parts, turns the fields beyond the house bright yellow for months. There's haymaking in July, harvesting in mid-August or so, and, any time, riding on the farm horses, swimming in a fine pool, fishing in three lakes nearby, plus biking and motor biking, with cross-country skiing in winter. Information: *Mrs. A. Liivam, Liivam Farms,* RR1, Eckville, Alberta T0M 0X0 (phone: 403-746-5438).

GWYNALTA FARM, Gwynne, Alberta: With 400 acres, this central Alberta dairy farm about 40 miles (64 km) from the provincial capital at Edmonton is not tiny, but it's not particularly big and wealthy either. Yet, when you visit, you never seem to be able to get around to reading the books you brought along, thinking there'd be nothing to distract you. When you sit on the banks of the farm's own lake, you won't see a single car or house — but the fishing is fine and the water, hills, and forests are too lovely to ignore; cutting into the trees, you spot the bare trace of an old buffalo trail. The place is secluded, but every morning there are deer in the yard. Nights are quiet, too — you often spend them sitting out on the big deck of the Glasers' comfortable old house; it might be nice to turn in early and read — but then the northern lights begin to dance across the sky. Hiking and bird-watching are popular in summer, and in winter you can go cross-country skiing, snowmobiling, or ice fishing. And whenever you have a mind to, you can taste the milk collected from the herd of very contented black-and-white cows. The farmhouse can accommodate up to four adults, or two youngsters and two adults. Information: *Mrs. M. Glaser, Gwynalta Farm,* Gwynne, Alberta T0C 1L0 (phone: 403-352-3587).

ASPEN RIDGE, Clear Lake, Manitoba: Robert Sopuck has not been taking in guests for very long, partly because he spent just over 3 years building the house where he lives with his guests — a log structure that one visitor dubbed a log palace, complete with beamed ceilings and a big stone fireplace. That each of the dozen beds has its own down comforter begins to explain the "palace's" appeal to cross-country skiers, though you can't ignore the attraction of heavy snow accumulations and the vastness of the available terrain — Sopuck's 320 rolling acres adjoin government and private land that also is available to skiers, and Riding Mountain National Park is just 2 miles (3 km) away. From mid-May through late June and from late August to early October, the area is equally fine for bird-watching, since the farm lies right on the Central and Mississippi flyways. And there's always horseback riding at nearby stables. Meals are prepared using indigenous ingredients — geese, ducks, garden vegetables — and include specialties like kielbasa and cabbage rolls, typical fare of the area's large Ukrainian population. Sopuck also is knowledgeable about wild foods and is willing to teach any guests who are interested. Information: *Robert Sopuck, Aspen Ridge,* Lake Audy, Manitoba R0J 0Z0 (phone: 204-848-2964).

DEERBANK FARM, Morris, Manitoba: If you arrive at this 320-acre spread in early July, you can ride atop sweet-smelling bales of hay, fresh from the baler, as the wagon creaks its way through the fields. If you come in August, you can watch the farm's wheat, barley, and oats being combined to separate grain from straw, which is then baled and stacked; and you don't have to be a strong man to help stack those straw bales, as many a past guest has done, or to drive the farm truck from field to bins, where the grain is stored. Whatever chore you choose, you'll work up an appetite for the noon feast — usually a roast with lots of vegetables and a filling dessert — and again for supper, a more modest repast, usually of hash browns, cold sliced beef, salad, more vegetables from the garden, fruit, and cake. The beef is butchered on the property. Accommodations are in the 3 clean, simply furnished spare rooms in the modern farmhouse or in a camper outside; campsites with some hook-ups also are available. Information: *Kathleen and Ed Jorgenson, Deerbank Farm,* Box 23, RR2, Morris, Manitoba R0J 1K0 (phone: 204-746-8395).

LA FERME DES ERABLES, Aroostook, New Brunswick: This 1,200-acre grain-and-potato farm and cattle ranch not far from the Maine border, a couple of miles off the Trans-Canada Highway in the province's northwest corner, belongs to a family that numbers around 41, when you figure all the sons, daughters, wives, husbands, and grandchildren — and though they don't all live in the farmhouse, there are always quite a few of them around, making the place very lively. The entire family is bilingual, and the kids will babysit or take you around to see the various neighborhood sights — among them the photogenic 225-foot-high Grand Falls and, in Hartland to the south, a 1,282-foot-long covered bridge, the world's longest. There is a heated indoor swimming pool. Catered bus tours, which place guests in different well-organized homes in the neighborhood, also can be arranged. There are plans for a campground to accommodate both tents and trailers. Information: *Aurèle and Fernande St. Amand, La Ferme des Erables,* Aroostook, NB E0J 1B0 (phone: 506-273-3112). Also see *The St. John River, New Brunswick,* DIRECTIONS.

ALLEN'S HOLIDAY FARM, Port Elgin, New Brunswick: The three television sets in the big, early-19th-century white frame farmhouse aren't turned on much in summer, simply because there are so many other things to do: helping out in the garden, day-tripping to a nearby beach or to PEI via ferry (20 minutes away), chowing down on big meals of roast meats or fish fresh from the not-too-distant sea, or helping with farm chores. One Montreal woman managed to find time to put up some raspberry jam, using the fruit from the garden. Information: *Christopher and Dorothy Kean, Allen's Holiday Farm,* RR3, Port Elgin, NB E0A 2K0 (phone: 506-538-2597).

BROADLEAF FARM, Hopewell Hill, New Brunswick: This 1,400-acre beef cattle farm — a big one by New Brunswick standards, operated by the horse-happy Hudsons, their married daughter, her husband, the Hudson's married sons, and their wives — is a lively, spic-and-span place. The main attractions are the 80 horses. Western riding lessons, hayrides, and trail rides that take you out by the water and through the woods are all available. But because the farm's marshy sections attract migrating geese and ducks, the place also is good for bird watching. It also makes a good base for trips to nearby Fundy National Park and Moncton, for tours of the coastline, and for antiques-hunting trips. The old-fashioned country house is comfortable, and the food is good and simple, though occasionally you'll be treated to harvests from the marshes — cranberries and mushrooms as well as exotica like samphire and goosetongue greens. Relax at *Broadleaf Too,* the home of Vernon and Joyce Hudson, which is right next door and also has guestrooms. A small area for tents and 8 trailer hook-ups is available; reservations for these sites are necessary. And there's a week-long summer camp for the kids. Open year-round. Information: *Phyllis and Danny Hudson, Hopewell Hill,* Albert Co., NB E0A 1Z0 (phone: 506-882-2349); *Joyce and Vernon Hudson, Broadleaf Too,* Hopewell Hill, Albert Co., NB E0A 1Z0 (phone: 506-882-2803). Also see *The Fundy Trail, New Brunswick,* DIRECTIONS.

ANDERSON'S HOLIDAY FARM, Sussex, New Brunswick: There are sheep, beef cattle, and a variety of fowl on this 200-acre farm in the heart of dairy country about an hour's drive from Fundy National Park. But kids love the farm's menagerie of ducks, Canada geese, rabbits, ornamental pheasants, and even peacocks. Nearby golf and curling, as well as swimming, tennis, and sightseeing, can keep you so busy you'll need a rest when you get home. They also offer bed and breakfast arrangements. Information: *Tom and Laura Anderson, Anderson's Holiday Farm,* RR2, Sussex, NB E0E 1P0 (phone: 506-433-3786). Also see *The Fundy Trail, New Brunswick,* DIRECTIONS.

WASHA FARM, Alma, Ontario: The grandma's country kitchen of your dreams becomes reality at the farm of Walter and Sharon Salm-Grose, located in the rich, gently rolling hills of southern Ontario, an hour's drive west of Toronto. Not only is the food all home-cooked, but it's also all home-grown — if not at Washa Farm, then at a relative's spread. Feast on fresh sweet corn, beets, spinach, Swiss chard, and peas and potatoes, steamed and garnished with butter. The grilled veal steaks come from pigs raised by Walter's brother. The pure maple syrup that drenches the French toast and blueberry pancakes is supplied by an aunt and uncle in Quebec. Strawberries, blueberries, raspberries, and currants grow wild, and many find their way into Sharon's locally renowned pies. Her coffee cake, muffin, and cookie recipes are the legacy of her mother and grandmother. On weekends, Walter takes over the cooking on the outdoor barbecue grill. It all adds up to a rural gastronomic delight. Open year round. Information: *Sharon Salm-Grose, Washa Farm,* RR 2, Alma, Ontario NOB 1AO (phone: 519-846-9788).

AMBLEWOOD FARM, Orton, Ontario: There's a distinct pioneer touch to this farm vacation spot, where guests lodge in an 1820 log home built by Irish settlers — and painstakingly restored by Erin Township craftsmen, neighbors, friends, and members of Barry and Carol Tyler's family. Visitors are welcome to help churn the butter and dip the beeswax candles. For another kind of dipping, there's also a pond. Visit the barnyard animals, stroll through gardens and woods, collect honey and eggs, make soap and cider, and spin and weave. At day's end, as the hearth cools, you trundle off to bed and experience the delight of sliding off to sleep under a huge patchwork quilt. Open year-round. Information: *Barry and Carol Tyler, Amblewood Farm,* RR 1, Orton, Ontario LON 1NO (phone: 519-855-4705).

MOLDENHAUERS, Allan, Saskatchewan: You can ride one of the farm's horses when visiting here, but not on trail rides: Guests are on their own to strike out across the pastures or wend down one of the nearby country roads on the farm's horses. There's no worry about traffic, since Allan, the nearest settlement — 4½ miles (7 km) away — is too small to generate very many vehicles. After a ride, there are rabbits and goats and sheep to be fed and petted, eggs to be gathered, beautiful fields to be photographed, vegetables to be picked and weeds to be pulled in the garden, and more. As soon as guests find out about the old wooden churn, most can hardly wait to make butter. Some courageous souls try milking the cows by hand. Then there are those big meals — traditional country food like fried chicken, home-baked bread and homemade jam, fresh apple pies juicy with the fruit of the farm's own apple tree, topped with whipped cream courtesy of the farm's own cows. Information: *Moldenhauers,* Box 214, Allan, Saskatchewan S0K 0C0 (phone: 306-257-3578).

WORKING RANCHES

POPLAR BLUFF STOCK FARM, Chauvin, Alberta: At this working farm in east central Alberta, near the Saskatchewan border, the land rolls into the distance in great swells, as far as the eye can see; the skies above are bigger than you ever remember them when you're confined in the city. Oats and barley are the primary business here, but there are some 50 head of beef cattle as well. It makes a fine setting for a relaxing, country vacation. The trails through the small hills near the place are good for hiking, as is nearby Dillberry Provincial Park. Trail rides also are on the activities roster in summer, and there's help if you need it; in winter, cross-country skiing and snowmobiling keep you busy. Year-round, you can visit the communal Hutterite colony 25 miles (40 km) distant, and the hosts often take guests to see the oil field with its little pumps and the big grain elevator not far away. Open all year. Information: *Poplar Bluff Stock*

Farm, Harold and Georgina Taylor, RR1, Chauvin, Alberta T0B 0V0 (phone: 403-858-2234).

TL BAR RANCH, Trochu, Alberta: This central Alberta horse and cattle ranch, located between the towns of Red Deer (pop. 55,000) and Drumheller (pop. 6,300) along the Red Deer River in the "Valley of the Dinosaurs," offers accommodations in a log ranch home and a private cottage. Fishing and swimming are as popular as helping out with the ranch chores, but the surrounding Drumheller Valley, carved over the ages by the Red Deer River, is such a fascinating place that exploring — in canoes, on foot, or on horseback — can be the most interesting activity of all. Sometimes, for instance, you'll find dinosaur bones, fossils, and petrified wood that the river has uncovered. The *Tyrrell Museum of Palaeontology,* named for the geologist who found the first dinosaur bones in the area in 1884, explores the prehistory of the area with films and please-touch computer terminals; it's just a 45-minute drive away. June is the month for cattle branding on the ranch, July for the *Calgary Stampede* not far away. Open May through October. Off-season rates November to April on weekends. Information: *Tom and Willie Lynch, TL Bar Ranch,* PO Box 217, Trochu, Alberta T0M 2C0 (phone: 403-442-2207). Also see *Festivals, Fairs, and Fancy Acts* and *Cypress Hills Provincial Park to Edmonton via the Dinosaur Country, Alberta,* DIRECTIONS.

K J 5 RANCH, Rapid City, Manitoba: At this 320-acre spread, you'll find some 150 head of Appaloosas and quarter horses, and there are plenty of trail rides, picnics, and, for those who need them, riding lessons. Boating, water skiing, swimming and golf are nearby, and this is another place where the produce in the garden in the afternoon is on the table at dinner. When the farm begins its 4-month season in June, newborn colts are still wobbly legged. The family's Dalmation is very fond of guests, and you'll be able to tell right away that she enjoys having company. Information: *Ken and Janie Bridgeman, K J 5 Ranch,* PO Box 209, Rapid City, Manitoba R0K 1W0 (phone: 204-826-2078).

GUEST RANCHES

BLACK CAT, Hinton, Alberta: This is a wonderful place, just big enough to give you some privacy — but not too big. It's also beautifully situated so that each of the 16 guestrooms faces the first range of the Rockies. A large, central living room also has a view, plus a fireplace, library, many comfortable chairs, and a pine floor for dancing; the coffee pot is always on. In summer, you can go out for riding, hiking, and fishing at places like Solomon Creek and the Wild Hay River or canoeing on the Athabasca River; or you can go sightseeing to nearby areas like the Columbia Icefield. Upon return, unwind in the outdoor hot tub with a view of the mountains. Winter's main attraction is cross-country skiing on some 40 miles of poplar- and spruce-lined trails that surround the lodge, sometimes along old logging roads. The ranch is better suited for singles and couples than for families. Information: *Jerry Bond, Black Cat Guest Ranch,* Box 6267, Hinton, Alberta (phone: 403-865-3084).

RAFTER SIX, Seebe, Alberta: A good-size operation in the mountainous Kananaskis country, about 25 miles (40 km) from Banff, it can accommodate about 60 guests in its solid-log lodge and cabins. Ordinarily, an establishment of this size doesn't nurture spontaneity. But here, the staff numbers around 25 in the summer, so when a few guests decide they want to go out on a trail ride or take a nature walk or play volleyball, there's always someone from the ranch available to make sure they do it — and have the best time ever. Breakfast rides, hayrides, and barbecues are regular activities, and occasionally a group of the local Stoney Indians (the owner is a blood brother) drops by just to visit or, by request, to dance, in full-dress regalia, for guests. There's also a licensed dining room, cocktail lounge, swimming pool, whirlpool bath, and a game room, and the surrounding mountains are appealing enough to have been chosen — not once, but several times — as movie locations. Open May 1 through

October. Information: *Rafter Six Ranch Resort,* Seebe, Alberta T0L 1X0 (phone: 403-673-3622 or 403-264-1251).

SUNDANCE, Ashcroft, British Columbia: This 31-room ranch in the Thompson River Valley is living proof that the wild west is not so wild anymore. Though there's sagebrush for miles around, things at the ranch are eminently civilized. Everything is air conditioned, and swimming in the well-kept heated pool, enjoying hot showers, and sampling mealtime creations of the accomplished chef are as much a part of your experience here as the trail dust and sounds of coyotes howling at night. But horseback riding is still the raison d'être here, and there are daily trail rides (the ranch usually runs about 100 horses), gymkhanas (athletic equestrian events), cookouts, barbecues, and hayrides. Open year-round. Information: *Cynthia Rowe, Sundance Guest Ranch,* PO Box 489, Ashcroft, BC V0K 1A0 (phone: 604-453-2554/2422).

CHILKO LAKE WILDERNESS RANCH, Williams Lake, British Columbia: It takes a four-wheel-drive vehicle about 4 unforgettable hours to drive the 180 miles (288 km) from Williams Lake to this spread bordering glacier- and stream-fed, 52-mile-long Chilko Lake. But it's easier and even *more* scenic to arrive by plane, across the ice-covered Coast Mountains wilderness. Once at the rustic timber lodge, there's more of the same, either on day-long horseback, hiking, fishing, or canoeing trips or on longer overnight trips in the area. But unless you're a glutton for real wilderness, you may opt for the former. The area immediately surrounding the ranch, covered with dense bush, is wild enough, but the lodge and outlying cabins are most comfortable. Inside the lodge you'll find an indoor pool, sauna, outdoor Jacuzzi, table tennis, pool tables, convention facilities, and a lounge. The food is Canadian-style, with terrific picnic lunches, and there's usually fish or meats from the ranch's own smoker. The fishing and hunting are exceptionally good here. Heli-skiing, cross-country skiing, and snowmobiling are available in winter. Maximum 60 guests. Information: *Chilko Lake Wilderness Ranch,* PO Box 4750, Williams Lake, BC V2G 2V7 (phone: 604-398-8828 or, if you can't get through, radio phone H678596 on the Chilanko 55 channel).

For the Body

Downhill Skiing

 Canadians can probably be classified in two major groups: Those who ski and those who intend to learn. That's not surprising, considering the usually abundant quantities of snow north of the international border, the mountainous terrain up there, and the number of mountains developed for skiing.

Natural snowfall can be expected from late November to late March, but sometimes — particularly in eastern Canada — the "Great White North" is not quite white enough, so many of the major ski areas have installed supplementary snowmaking machinery to ensure good ski conditions even during periods of light snowfall.

In any case, a skier in Canada is seldom very far from a good run. There's skiing in Newfoundland or in the Maritimes, for instance — though the atmosphere may be better than the ski slopes. In Ontario, the picture is brighter, with large ski areas close to both Ottawa and Toronto. Even the prairie provinces of Manitoba and Saskatchewan have some lift-serviced verticals. All of these places are of principal delight to skiers from the cities nearby. But Canada has many more ski areas that are worth traveling a long distance to savor — some because of their unique ambience, some because of the world class slopes. Quebec is undoubtedly the queen of eastern Canada skiing with Parc du Mont Ste.-Anne, a giant area outside Quebec City; the Eastern Townships, a quartet of mountains with first class runs for all levels of ability and with a less hectic pace than at some of the older, more popular resorts; and the grand Laurentians, mountains that offer a vacation experience as notable for the excitement quotient of the nearly 1,000 slopes and runs of its 125-odd ski areas as for the elegant cuisine and the regional specialties (meat pies, vinegar-splashed French fries) served in the restaurants of the quaint villages at the lift base. That the Laurentians must be one of the few ski areas in the Western Hemisphere where the chef is held in as much regard as the head ski instructor is more important for many skiers than the fact that the runs are shorter and conditions frequently icier and rockier than those in Canada's other great ski region, the ineffably beautiful Rocky Mountains.

In the Rockies, powder-drenched bowls and trail-cut forests provide skiing so dazzling, runs so unique, that Europeans forsake the cozy slopeside villages of their own Alps to enjoy it. The scenery inspires awe; the snow quality and the variety of slopes are equaled in few other places in the world. Yet in Alberta and British Columbia, more than a few Canadian ski areas — particularly the ones in British Columbia's interior — have long been considered just local operations. Opening up the mountains with lifts, and attracting skiers from outside the area with extensive lodging facilities and nightlife, has been a relatively new endeavor, and only in the last few years has money gone into development programs that have brought the mountains the fame they deserve. The ultimate dollop of recognition was acquired in February 1988, when the *Winter Olympics* were held on the slopes surrounding Calgary. Meanwhile, helicopter skiing, in ranges of the Rockies known as the Cariboos, Bugaboos, and others has soared in popularity, and the seemingly endless runs and the fluffy, untrammeled powder snow of a number of nearby mountain ranges (which have never known the hum of a ski lift) have been discovered by thousands of brave and hardy skiers. Skiing of the sort found here is quite simply unavailable anywhere else in the world.

For more information about helicopter skiing and for rundowns of the facilities of all the major Canadian resorts, consult the regional ski directories published by the Canadian Government Office of Tourism and available from its offices in major US cities. The various consulates can provide further information. Or browse through issues of the magazine *Ski Canada* (277 Front St. E., Suite 100, Toronto, Ontario M5A 1E8; phone: 416-368-0185). The *White Book of Ski Areas, US & Canada* (Inter-Ski Services, Inc., PO Box 3635, Georgetown Station, Washington, DC 20007; phone: 202-342-0886) lists all the ski areas in both countries, with brief descriptions. It's revised annually and can be found in ski shops and bookstores ($13.95) or by mail through the publisher ($16).

EAST

WEST QUEBEC, near Ottawa, Ontario, and Hull, Quebec: There are four ski centers within a 30 minutes drive of downtown Ottawa-Hull: Camp Fortune, Mont Cascade, Vorloge, and Edelweiss. Although they're not world class in vertical drop, among them they offer something for everyone, including some advanced level slopes not for the timid or inexperienced. Younger, more aggressive skiers tend to favor Edelweiss; Vorloge is ideal for beginners and families with toddlers. Fortune and Cascade offer a good range of hills from beginner to advanced. All have night skiing (except Sundays), and good facilities including ski schools, equipment rentals, and cafeterias. Mont Ste.-Marie is another 30 minutes' drive, but worth it. At 1,250 feet, it has twice the vertical drop of the others, and its longest run is just over 2 miles. Two new high-speed detachable quad chairs and the installation of snow-making equipment to cover 100 percent of the 17 runs are part of a $10 million investment that has made the resort, Auberge L'Abri, number one in the region. The ski chalet has been expanded, and there's an attractive resort lodge known for its excellent food and good ski packages. All these centers have two-for-one ticket days during the week. Information: *Camp Fortune* (phone: 819-827-1717); *Mont Cascade* (phone: 819-827-0301); *Vorloge* (phone: 819-459-2301); *Edelweiss* (phone: 819-459-2328); *Mont Ste.-Marie* (phone: 819-467-5200 or 800-567-1255 in Canada).

LAURENTIANS (LES LAURENTIDES), near Montreal, Quebec: Beginning about 35 miles (56 km) from the city, along the high-speed Laurentian autoroute leading into the hills to the northwest, there is a succession of ski communities one after another — more than 20 major ones in all, each the center of a cluster of ski areas situated just minutes apart. If only for the sheer number of runs in the area — some 300 in the space of 40 square miles, a concentration greater than that of any other area of comparable size in the world — the Laurentians would be unique. But the frills of a skiing vacation here also stand out. The region's charming French villages are full of lovely inns, pleasant resorts, and small hotels so close to the skiing that it's easy to schuss right to your doorstep — or, more to the point, to your dining room, where good food is the order of the day. (Especially endearing are local specialties like *tourtière,* a meat pie, and the sweet, maple-sugar-flavored pie known as *tarte au sucre.*)

Every one of the ski areas has its special charm. At the northern end of this string of resorts is Mont Tremblant, the dowager queen of Canada's winter resorts, which, with a vertical drop of 2,100 feet and runs that extend up to 2 miles in length, offers plenty of good skiing for experts and intermediates. A detachable quad chairlift and jet T-bar have been erected; restaurants on top and at the base of the mountain have been renovated; the beginner's area has been relocated; a nursery has been installed; and snowmaking facilities have been extended to the very top of Mont Tremblant's south side. It has a number of first-rate hotels, including the big *Station Mont Trem-*

blant Lodge and the smaller *Cuttle's Tremblant Club.* Some 3 miles (5 km) away in St. Jovite is the *Gray Rocks Inn,* a friendly sprawl of a 252-room Victorian hostelry on 2,600 acres with its own ski hill, Sugar Peak, 100 yards from the inn. The vertical here is a mere 620 feet, but the proprietors never wasted time deluding themselves that they had the Matterhorn on their hands. Instead, they touted the mountain as ideal for learning and, in 1938, developed the *Snow Eagle Ski School,* with a teaching program so thorough that there are even a couple of instructors whose sole job is keeping the others on their toes. Consequently, there are hundreds of graduates who will testify that the school is North America's best. Among the many aspects that make the lodge outstanding are its new sports complex, indoor swimming, whirlpool bath, saunas, its nightlife (which is vigorous enough to make the place a good bet for the solo vacationer), and its lunches (served on white-linen-covered tables in a dining room practically at the lift base). Other ski areas offer similar delights. Belle Neige in Val-Morin, a small hill with a vertical of only about 520 feet and 2 T-bars and 2 chair lifts, is distinguished by the proximity of the *Hôtel la Sapinière,* a member of the Relais & Châteaux group and the proud possessor of one of Canada's finest kitchens (see *Special Havens*).

And so it goes. The Laurentians are far from being Canada's biggest mountains, but the plenitude of amenities goes a long way toward taking the sting out of foregoing, for the moment, the steeper-and-wilder-and-more-dazzlingly beautiful slopes Canada offers in such abundance.

For general information and lists of small hostelries: *Association Touristique des Laurentides,* 14142 Rue de Lachapelle, RR1, St. Jérôme, Quebec J7Z 5T4 (phone: 514-436-8532). The following resorts can be contacted in Mont Tremblant: *Station Mont Tremblant* (phone: 819-425-8711 or 800-567-6761); and *Cuttle's Tremblant Club* (phone: 819-425-2731). Write the *Gray Rocks Inn;* PO Box 1000, St. Jovite, Quebec J0T 2H0; phone: 819-425-2771). Also see *Special Havens* and *Ice Skating.*

EASTERN TOWNSHIPS (ESTRIE), Montreal, Quebec: Unlike the Laurentians, which were initially built up to serve as summer resorts and were then strung with lifts to help the communities make it through the winter, the mountains in this northern extension of the Appalachians, 44 miles (71 km) southeast of Montreal and just north of the Vermont border, were developed primarily for skiing, because of the suitability of the terrain. Each one is the peer of Mont Tremblant or any comparable Vermont resort. Mont Sutton, near Sutton, has 54 trails, 9 chair lifts, a 1,509-foot vertical, and unique glade skiing. Owl's Head, near Mansonville, has a 1,770-foot vertical. Mont Orford, near Magog, has a 1,772-foot vertical and 32 trails. Bromont, with a 1,328-foot vertical and 26 trails, is the fourth member of the quartet of major mountains in the area. Headquarter at any one of the four mountains, ski there, and then use your interchangeable lift ticket to sample the other three. Wherever you go, you're going to find runs to suit everyone in the family, varied terrain, and good lift service; each area has its own unique character.

Where should you lodge? That will depend on the kind of town you like best. Owl's Head has a small lodge right at the base, plus apartment-hotels and condominiums with ski-in/ski-out access to lifts and trails. It will be interesting to see what effect Owl's Head's multimillion-dollar expansion project will have on the tenor of the place (with not much of anything around it, Owl's Head has been valued by people who enjoy making their own après-ski entertainment). The expansion includes more snowmaking, 2 new trails, and a detachable quad chairlift. Those who go for Owl's Head usually go for it in a big way and return year after year after year. The *Auberge Bromont* at Bromont is a cozy place with views of the night-lighted runs. The areas around Mont Sutton and Mont Orford are livelier; they're both close to a couple of other small towns that boast restaurants and other nighttime activities. (Among the more interesting hostelries in this area are *Village Archimède* at Sutton, *Hovey Manor* at North Hatley, and Magog's *Cheribourg Resort.*) Although the Eastern Townships don't bustle with as much activity as the Laurentians, and although this is still very much the farming area that it was before the lifts went in just over 20 years ago, these mountains offer an abundance of amenities for those who've come first and foremost to ski. What's more, the quality of the skiing is among the best in the East.

Information: *Quebec Ski East,* 2883 W. King St., Sherbrooke, Quebec J1L 1C6 (phone: 819-564-8989). For reservations and local information: *Mont Orford Resort Centre,* Box 248, Magog, Quebec J1X 3W8 (phone: 819-843-6548); *Owl's Head,* Mansonville, Quebec J0E 1X0 (phone: 514-292-5592); *Sutton Tourist Association,* for lodging, CP 418, Sutton, Quebec J0E 2K0 (phone: 514-538-2646 or 514-538-2537); for skiing, CP 280, Sutton, Quebec J0E 2K0 (phone: 514-538-2339); and *Bromont Ski Area,* CP29, Bromont, Quebec J0E 1L0; phone: 514-534-2200 or 800-363-8920).

QUEBEC CITY: The Old Capital is so close to good skiing that many of the city's major hotels offer ski packages. Mont Ste.-Anne, mountain enough to have hosted the first *Canadian Winter Games* in 1967 and now a regular stop on the *World Cup* circuit, is the biggest of the local areas. Located at Beaupré, a rather nondescript one-street town about half an hour's drive east of the city, it boasted terrain that was already considerable before development of its north and west sides a few years ago doubled the skiable area; today 50 slopes and 12 lifts of varying types allow for an uphill capacity of over 17,761 an hour. Consequently, there's now the option of enjoying the sunny conditions on the southern slopes (the top three-quarters of them as challenging as any of Vermont's steepest and hairiest), or the intermediate and novice north-facing runs, or even the intermediate and expert trails of the mountain's western exposure. Every year more runs are being backed up by an elaborate new snowmaking system; well over 85 percent of the skiable terrain is currently covered. With the addition of 12 lighted trails, Mont Ste.-Anne now claims to have the highest vertical night skiing in Canada. It also offers the cross-country skier over 110 miles of double-track, groomed and patrolled trails equal to the very best in North America. The base village provides 140 condo units in two 5-story buildings, plus an assortment of boutiques and restaurants. A children's center was added last year as was a 3-story day lodge adjacent to the existing base chalet with a 550-seat cafeteria and a bar with multi-level sundecks. Over the last 5 years the park has developed into a year-round resort, with two 18-hole golf courses, camping facilities, and 157 miles of cycling and mountain bike trails. On clear days, year-round, a gondola climbs 2,640 feet to the summit providing a breathtaking view of the St. Lawrence River, Quebec City, and Ile d'Orléans. There also is Le Massif, the most unusual ski center east of the Rockies. A 2,614-foot-high escarpment that plunges toward the St. Lawrence River, it has ten 2½-mile intermediate and expert trails that boast some of the best powder snow in eastern Canada. Instead of the usual ski-lift, it has 8 or 9 buses that transport skiers from the base of the mountain to the top of the slopes. Because the center can accommodate only 300 skiers a day, reservations are a must.

The region's next most extensive skiing is to be found at Stoneham, with a 1,380-foot vertical. In addition, it's possible to ski the two areas at longtime favorite vacation center Lac Beauport — Le Relais and Mont St.-Castin, whose verticals measure 750 and 550 feet respectively. As is inevitable due to these areas' proximity to the city, every one of them is busier still on weekends; only Mont Ste.-Anne would, in its own right, warrant traveling a long distance to ski. But the city's food, lodging, and lively après-ski activity is as exceptional as Aspen's; and for beginners, intermediates, and even experts for whom what goes après is as important as what happens right on the slopes, Quebec City is hard to equal, providing an all-around vacation that includes some skiing. The attractions are such, in fact, that it's probably best to headquarter in the city and schlep to the ski area every day, rather than the other way round.

Most ski resorts provide good accommodations right at the base of (or close to) the mountain, but for those who want to combine the best of all worlds, the place to lodge is in Quebec City. The historic old *Château Frontenac* (phone: 418-692-3861) in the center of town has the most atmosphere, while the *Québec Hilton International* (phone: 418-647-2411) is more modern and rather elegant. The *Quebec Winter Carnival* turns the city upside down in February. Enjoy it — or avoid it if you hate hubbub and crowds.

Information: *Quebec City Region Tourism and Convention Bureau,* 60 Rue d'Auteuil, Quebec City, Quebec G1R 4C4 (phone: 418-692-2471) and *Parc du Mont Ste.-Anne,* PO Box 400, Beaupré, Quebec G0A 1E0 (phone: 418-827-4561); *Le Relais,* 1084 Blvd. du Lac Beauport, Quebec, GOA 2CO (phone: 418-849-1851); *Mont St.-Castin,* 82 Chemin le Tour-du-Lac, Lac Beauport, Quebec, GOA 2CO (phone: 418-849-4277); *Stoneham,* 1420 du Hibou, Stoneham, Quebec, GOA 4P8 (phone: 418-848-2411); *Le Massif,* Route 138, CP 68, St. François, Quebec G0A 2L0 (phone: 418-435-3593); a Central Reservation Service for Quebec City and the Charlevoix region, RESERVO-TEL, can be reached at 800-463-1568). Also see *Quebec City,* THE CITIES, and *Festivals, Fairs, and Fancy Acts.*

WEST

So special and inclusive are the opportunities for winter recreation in the Canadian Rockies that the province of Alberta was chosen to host the *1988 Winter Olympics.* But much fine skiing also can be found in other parts of western Canada.

The heart of the Canadian Rockies offers just about everything a skier could want — great slopes, deep powder, some of the continent's most glorious scenery, and a ski season that consistently extends into June. Mount Norquay is known as Banff's challenge to advanced skiers, but it does offer some easy skiing for beginners as well. At Sunshine Village, an alpine resort in a bowl above the treeline, you'll find tons of powder, the longest season in the area, and on-hill accommodations. Canada's largest ski location is Lake Louise, with a variety of terrain — bowls, moguls, open runs, and forested slopes.

With shuttle buses linking the three big ski complexes, and the availability of interchangeable lift tickets, mountain-hopping is a common practice here. It's probably more convenient to set up a base in the town of Banff and travel to each of the three ski areas. Mt. Norquay, site of the celebrated mile-long chute known as the North American, as well as a couple of other hair-raisers that are nearly as steep, also boasts some of the finest novice terrain anywhere — acres of broad fields covered with ultralight, carefully groomed powder. Accommodations are available in a variety of more than 30 hotels in 4-mile-distant (6-km) Banff, including the modern and very comfortable *Banff Park Lodge* (phone: 403-762-4433), or the spired-and-turreted *Banff Springs* hotel (phone: 403-762-2211), one of the dramatic hotels that the *Canadian Pacific Railway* built in the late 19th century in its efforts to develop traffic on the line. "The Springs," as it's called, boasts a good breakfast buffet, an Olympic-size indoor swimming pool, a heated outdoor pool, skating rink, innumerable places to eat, and a health club with three Jacuzzis and a sauna. For slopeside resort life, look to Sunshine Village, a complex of forest runs and above-timberline snowfields with a 3,420-foot vertical that is served by just under a dozen lifts. All resort facilities are in a complex of buildings at the lift base (at 7,200 feet), which is accessible by gondola from the parking lot at the end of an access road branching off the Trans-Canada. There's also plenty of programmed après-ski activity. The most extensive terrain in the area, however — indeed, the nation's largest lift-serviced downhill ski area, our northern neighbor's answer to Aspen and Squaw Valley — is to be found at Skiing Louise, 35 miles (56 km) and 45 minutes down the Trans-Canada from Banff. There, skiers find 17 square *miles* of mogul fields, steep chutes, vast glacial bowls, gentle trails through the glades —

and just about any other kind of ski terrain imaginable — on four mountain faces. Some 43 designated runs, ranging up to 5 miles in length, are draped down 3,250 vertical feet of hillside and served by a panoply of lifts. Here all lodgings are about 2 miles (3 km) from lift base; for charm, the best bets are the expanded *Post* hotel (Box 69, Lake Louise, Alberta T0L 1E0; phone: 403-522-3989), known for its kitchen, and the winterized *Château Lake Louise* (phone: 403-522-3511), the grandest of all the Canadian Pacific hotels. Banff is also the jumping-off place for some of the finest helicopter skiing in the world.

Information: *Banff/Lake Louise Chamber of Commerce,* Box 1298, Banff, Alberta T0L 0C0 (phone: 403-762-3777), and *Banff Club Ski,* Box 1085, Banff, Alberta T0L 0C0 (phone: 403-762-4561). Also see *Wilderness Skiing, Special Havens,* and *Ice Skating.*

NAKISKA AT MOUNT ALLAN, Kananaskis Village, Alberta: The Kananaskis-Nakiska area, site of the *1988 Olympic* alpine competition, is one of the newest ski destinations in Canada. It boasts tremendous fall-line skiing, first class facilities, state-of-the-art snowmaking, Western Canada's first two detachable quad chair lifts. Kids have their own ski area, with a handle tow and a day-care center. Kananaskis Village includes a general store, ski rental shop, post office, and a new complex of restaurants, shops, and three hotels. The *Kananaskis* hotel offers 69 luxury suites. The *Lodge at Kananaskis* has 255 rooms with a health club; guests can swim from the pool area to the hot tub located outside under the stars. There's also a sauna outside and plenty of snow to roll in. For more moderately priced accommodations, try the *Kananaskis Inn,* which has 96 units. Other winter activities there include horsedrawn sleigh rides, tobogganing, ice skating, and cross-country skiing. For more information, write or call *Kananaskis Village Resort Association,* Box 100, Kananaskis Village, Alberta TOL 2HO (phone: 403-591-7555).

MARMOT BASIN, Jasper, Alberta: The Canadian Rockies' third-largest downhill center provides some of the West's finest open slope and bowl skiing off its 7,930-foot summit and delights skiers of all levels. Thirty-five of the trails are gentle enough that even the most fearful novice can snatch a look at the scenery, and there are sunny bowls that make intermediates feel like hotshots. A memorable 30% are rated expert, including an extraordinary deep-powder run accessible via the Knob Chair. With the recent addition of a high-speed T-bar, the area now offers 7 varied lifts, which means less waiting and more skiing. Marmot Basin also offers a nursery for children from 19 months to 5 years of age, a ski improvement center with ski week vacation packages, and a rental and retail ski shop. But for all that, Marmot Basin would be just another wonderful ski resort were it not for its location inside the boundaries of spectacular Jasper National Park. When you've had enough of the vast downhills, join a cross-country ski tour, snowshoe tour, "canyon crawl," or walking tour guided by park naturalists — or take a day off from skiing altogether for the 60-mile (96-km) drive down the Columbia Icefields Parkway, right through the middle of one of the most gorgeous parts of the awe-inspiring Rockies, to the Columbia Icefield. Marmot Basin's lodging is all of 12 miles (19 km) from lift base in Jasper, a family-oriented community of 3,270, offering a satisfying lineup of après-ski activities. But for those who want to sample the skiing and activities at Banff, a weekly bus service provides transportation, offering the chance to take in the scenery on the 172-mile (275-km) round trip.

Information: *Marmot Basin Ski-Lifts Ltd.,* PO Box 1300, Jasper, Alberta T0E 1E0 (phone: 403-852-3816); *Jasper Park Chamber of Commerce,* Box 98, Jasper, Alberta T0E 1E0 (phone: 403-852-3858); or for ski packages, *Marmot Experience,* Box 1570, Jasper, Alberta T0E 1E0 (phone: 403-852-4242, or 800-661-1931, in Western Canada).

TOD MOUNTAIN, Kamloops, British Columbia: One of a number of Canadian Rockies ski areas in the interior, with 3,100-foot-plus verticals and slopes, Tod Mountain, 33 miles (53 km) from British Columbia's third-largest city, a lumber-and-mining center that some 65,000 souls call home, has stepped over the threshold into the big time with the initiation of a major development that will soon put it in a league with only a few other ski areas in North America. The deep, dry powder snow, a specialty of the BC interior, the extra-long beginner and intermediate runs (5 and 7 miles, respectively), the steep mogul fields that shoot toward the base, and the "Challenger," which ranks among North America's steepest slopes, are as satisfying as ever. Tod has as close to an ideal distribution of terrain for skiers of all ability levels as any other mountain anywhere, and it can comfortably handle 12,600 skiers a day. But with just 5 lifts, it hasn't even come close to maximizing its potential. However, its current construction program promises much, much more in the future. On-mountain accommodations feature bed and breakfast options and RV hookups. Buses are available to carry skiers between the mountain and Kamloops, which is accessible by rail, air, bus, or car. The season runs from mid-November until May. Information: *Tod Mountain Development, Ltd.,* PO Box 869, Kamloops, BC V2C 5M8 (phone: 604-578-7222).

OKANAGAN VALLEY (BIG WHITE SKI RESORT, APEX-ALPINE, SILVER STAR), Kelowna, British Columbia: The region of pine-clad, lake-dotted mountains whose valleys yield the prodigious harvests of fruit for which the province is so famous is blessed in winter with what some people call Canada's best snow — the famed, fast-and-fluffy Okanagan Powder. A good deal of it falls at night, especially during the month of February, so days seem to be almost predictably sunny and the valleys stay green almost all winter long. Kelowna, a town of some 64,000, is at the midpoint of a trio of good-size ski resorts that stretch up and down the valley: Big White Ski Resort, Apex-Alpine, and Silver Star. Silver Star, an area 11 miles (18 km) from Vernon, has a total of 35 runs — some narrow and tree-lined, some wide-open alpine slopes — with a vertical drop of 1,600 feet; each lift gives access to skiing of all degrees of difficulty. On-mountain accommodations are relatively new and include three hotels (with Swiss, railway, and saloon themes) and three apartment-style condominiums. Big White, a resort not unlike Colorado's fine Keystone, is also a favorite with families, but the variety of runs wrapping around the mountain down its 2,050 feet of vertical is somewhat greater; it's 35 miles (56 km) from Kelowna. Meanwhile, Apex-Alpine, located about 20 miles (32 km) west of Penticton, offers 36 runs (something for every level of skier, with more advanced terrain than many areas) ranging down 2,000 vertical feet; there are on-mountain accommodations for up to 500.

Information: *Okanagan Similkameen Tourist Association,* 104-515 Highway 97 S., Kelowna, BC V1Z 3J2 (phone: 604-769-5959); *Silver Star,* Box 7000, Vernon, BC V1T 8X5 (phone: 604-545-2236); *Big White Central Resort Ltd.,* PO Box 2039, Station R, Kelowna, BC V1X 4K5; 604-765-3101); *Apex-Alpine,* PO Box 488, Penticton, BC V2A 6K9 (phone: 604-292-8221).

KIMBERLEY, Kimberley, British Columbia: Before 1972, the community 2 miles (3 km) from this British Columbia ski resort in the East Kootenays — 50 miles (81 km) north of the international border — was just another mining town. Then the citizens got together and put Bavarian façades on their shop fronts and converted the downtown area into a pedestrian mall, now known as the Platzl. Condominiums at the base of the lifts were designed to carry out the theme. But the mountain that rises 2,300 vertical feet above needed no such cutesification. Kimberley management instead threw its energy into extensive summer grooming of the 40 major runs (which are served by a pair of chairlifts, a trio of drag lifts, 2 pony tows, and a T-bar); combined with extensive snowmaking early in the season, this manicure assures good conditions around the heavily trafficked lift base area, where all runs converge, through season's end in mid-April. The careful year-round slope preparation also makes Kimberley such a joy for novices and intermediates that many of them can't get enough, and after dark, they go out to ski some more on one of North America's longest illuminated downhill ski runs (vertical, 1,800 feet). Other facilities include lodges at the top of the hill and, at the base, winterized campsites, two racquetball courts, and 5 tennis courts (2 indoor, 3 outdoor). Information: *Kimberley Ski & Summer Resort,* Box 40, Kimberley, BC V1A 2Y5 (phone: 604-427-4881).

PANORAMA, Invermere, British Columbia: Nestled in a high mountain valley near Invermere, this self-contained village provides condominium and hotel accommodations right on the mountain. There are 33 runs and the highest vertical rise (3,800 feet) in the Canadian Rockies. *Hal Bavin Heliplex* offers Heli-Ski day packages. Information: *Panorama,* PO Box 7000, Invermere, BC V0A 1KO (phone: 604-342-6941).

RED MOUNTAIN, Rossland, British Columbia: Named for the color of the tailings of the old Rossland gold mines, this relatively uncrowded mountain a few miles beyond the Washington State border in the southern Monashees is where *1968 Olympic* gold medalist Nancy Greene went from snowplow to slalom. As a result, it was pegged for many years as a hotshot's mountain; ski weekers who had grappled with the terrain, a good many of them from 120-mile-distant (192-km) Spokane, went back home to confirm the truth of the locally popular saying that if you could master Red, you could handle any other slope in the world. In 1965, 18 years after the first trails were cut on Red itself, lifts were strung up on nearby Granite, which now provides 30 runs for beginners and intermediates ranged down 2,800 vertical feet. The mountain's Main Run is one of Canada's *World Cup* downhill race courses. All trails from both Granite and Red converge at the lift base, where you'll find a day lodge and, nearby, overnight accommodations in chalets, cabins, and one of the most charming ski hotels anywhere, the 9-room *Ram's Head Inn* (Box 636, Rossland, BC V0G 1Y0; phone: 604-362-9577). Still other lodging places as well as the area's nightlife are in Rossland proper; the fanciest spot is the 67-room *Uplander* hotel (Box 1510, Rossland, BC V0G 1Y0; phone: 604-362-7375). Night skiing is available, and ski races are scheduled throughout the season, which runs from late November through mid-April. Every year in late January there's a lively winter carnival. Information: *Red Mountain,* Box 939, Rossland, BC V0G 1Y0 (phone: 604-362-7384; 604-362-7700 for central reservations).

VANCOUVER, British Columbia: The three Coast Range ski areas situated just a half hour's bus ride from this lovely city offer urban skiing at its most fantastic: thousand-foot verticals, unbelievable accessibility, spectacular views. Grouse Mountain, the best-developed of the trio, has a 1,200-foot vertical and some satisfyingly steep expert skiing. There are also fine runs for beginners and intermediates, along with snowmaking to ensure top conditions throughout the mid-December-to-March season, and long hours — that is, from early every morning until 11 PM. More recently developed Cypress, 5 miles (8 km) from the Upper Levels Highway in West Vancouver, has 18 runs (the longest is 1,700 feet) and night skiing on its expert and intermediate runs. Some people like it best — but Seymour Ski Country specializes in family skiing. It features one of the largest ski schools in the Pacific Northwest, the highest base elevation of the three areas, night skiing, and four double chair lifts. Seymour is about 10 miles (16 km) from the Upper Levels Highway in North Vancouver in an area known for its sunshine and winter warm spells. For those who like skiing hard-packed, Vancouver can provide some pleasant slope time.

Information: *Grouse Mountain Resorts, Ltd.,* 6400 Nancy Greene Way, North Vancouver, BC V7R 4N4 (phone: 604-984-0661 for ski conditions); *Cypress Bowl Recreations,* Box 91252, West Vancouver, BC V7V 3N9,(phone: 604-926-5612 or 926-6007 for ski conditions); *Mt. Seymour Resorts,* 1700 Indian River Rd., North Vancouver, BC V7G 1L3; phone: 604-986-2261); and *Tourism Vancouver,* Pavilion Plaza, 4 Bentall Centre, 1055 Dunsmuir St., PO Box 49296, Vancouver, BC V7X 1L3 (phone: 604-683-2000 for lodging and après-ski details).

WHISTLER RESORT, Whistler, British Columbia: Nestled in the mountains 75 miles (120 km) north of Vancouver, along the spectacular Sea-to-Sky Highway, this resort has long been one of the giants of North American skiing. Yet, surprisingly enough, it was long known mainly to locals and day-trippers and Whistler Village was the sort of unspoiled Western place frequented by youths investigating alternative lifestyles. This situation has changed — dramatically. Thanks to a multimillion-dollar development program, Whistler Village is full of shops, restaurants, nightspots, hotels, galleries, and more. The skiing remains unparalleled. The resort's two ski mountains boast North America's longest lift-served vertical drops — 5,280 feet at Blackcomb and 5,006 feet at Whistler Mountain. Side by side, this pair offers close to 2,000 acres of world class ski terrain with over 180 trails up to 5 miles long served by more than 2 dozen lifts, and every type of skiing from forest-edged trails and paths through the glades to broad groomed slopes and breathtaking high alpine powder bowls. Whistler's snowfall often tops 450 inches a year. Open year-round, with a special ski camp in summer. Information: *Whistler Resort Association,* Box 1400, Whistler, BC V0N 1B0 (phone: 604-932-4222).

WILDERNESS SKIING

Austrian-born skier and mountain guide Hans Gmoser fell in love with the wild, untamed mountains of Western Canada when he came here in 1951 and almost immediately began to explore on skis some of the peaks and slopes that no one before him had ever seen in winter. Before long he was leading tours on a commercial basis.

But getting uphill involved such arduous climbs that, for a dozen years, one run a day was the norm — two at the most. Gmoser was continually frustrated by being unable to take full advantage of the immense concentrations of skiable terrain in the area, until he began using helicopters to get his skiers uphill. Heli-skiing was born, and it boomed. In some ways, heli-skiing's popularity is surprising. Prices are high — from a little more than $2,000 to around $3,400 for a week-long, all-inclusive package, around $225 for a day trip. Then, too, not every skier is strong enough, advanced enough, or gutsy enough to handle the wide-ranging conditions — everything from rain to neck-deep powder to corn snow. Three-quarters of the time the snow is very good — of a quality about which most mortal skiers can only dream — but sometimes it is even worse than anyone might imagine. There is also the ever-present danger of skiing in terrain where avalanches are apt to occur.

But for all that, heli-skiing outfits do their best to keep their guests happy and safe. Guides not only seek out the best snow but also lead skiers around crevasses on the glaciers, keep them out of areas of probable avalanche danger, and lend their experienced help to first-time deep-snow skiers to turn what could be a frightening and frustrating day into an unforgettable experience. (*Canadian Mountain Holidays* — see below — even offers a week-long program for first-time heli-skiers who would like to build up their confidence in skiing this type of terrain.) Guests always ski with others of similar ability and can rent special powder skis that will make the going easier. As for safety, avalanche rescue transceivers are carried by every member of the heli-skiing parties, and radios linking the skiing groups to the helicopters, the base, and the outside world are standard equipment for the guides.

All of which makes a good case for the contention made by Mike Wiegele, operator of *Mike Wiegele Helicopter Skiing* (see below), that his brand of operation is as safe as any well-established, efficiently operated, lift-serviced ski resort.

And besides, the lure of the mountains themselves is powerful. They offer absolutely extraordinary ski terrain. For instance, along the skiable part of the Columbia Mountains' Purcell Range known as the Bugaboos, in the southeasternmost segment of the Canadian Rockies, the skiable area encompasses some 600 square miles. And if you have your fill of skiing there, there are always the Cariboos, the Monashees, Valemount, Revelstoke, and the Bobbie Burns to tackle. *Each one* of Hans Gmoser's six operations is bigger than 40 conventional resorts combined, and optimum snow conditions prevail from December until May. There is none of the heavy, wet snow found at times on the

West Coast. Nor are there the dry, cold, and fierce winds of the Rockies' eastern slopes. The flakes come in generous quantities — some 1,200 centimeters, or about 39 feet, every year — but there's rarely too much at any one time, and for the most part it is the lightest, driest powder imaginable.

Moreover, it's not necessary to be Billy Kidd to tackle it. Advanced intermediates experienced with a variety of terrains should find heli-skiing slopes within their abilities — even if they've never before skied powder. Consequently, for anyone with an adventurous spirit and a little loose cash, heli-skiing is certainly an option. Some good operations include the following:

CANADIAN MOUNTAIN HOLIDAYS, Banff, Alberta: Hans Gmoser's operation, staffed by experienced guides, runs 7-day helicopter ski tours to six areas in British Columbia. Sometimes skiers headquarter at an isolated mountain lodge; sometimes in a facility in a nearby town. Information: *Canadian Mountain Holidays,* PO Box 1660, Banff, Alberta T0L 0C0 (phone: 403-762-4531).

MIKE WIEGELE HELICOPTER SKIING, Banff, Alberta: Mike Wiegele's operation offers 3-, 5-, and 7-day packages in the Cariboos and the Monashees, covering an area of 3,000 square miles of wilderness. Accommodations are in Blue River, 130 miles (208 km) from Kamloops, where a new lodge and chalets recently have been built. Ski weeks can also be arranged for private parties. Information: *Mike Wiegele Helicopter Skiing, Ltd.,* PO Box 249, Banff, Alberta T0L 0C0 (phone: 403-762-5548 or from the continental US, 800-661-9170).

MOUNTAIN CANADA (*Purcell Helicopter Skiing Ltd.***), Golden, British Columbia:** This company has 3-, 5- and 7-day heli-skiing packages, as well as day trips into the Purcell Mountains. Skiers lodge at the *Golden Rim Motor Inn,* which has a great view of the Purcells and the Columbia River Valley. Information: *Rudi Gertsch, Mountain Canada (Purcell Helicopter Skiing Ltd.),* Box 1530, Golden, British Columbia V0A 1H0 (phone: 604-344-5410).

SELKIRK WILDERNESS SKIING, Meadow Creek, British Columbia: Those with a helicopter phobia can still experience this unique brand of deep-powder skiing. Selkirk Wilderness Skiing transports skiers to the top of the mountain via deluxe heated snowcat. A limited number of guests per week are accepted, and they share 20 square miles of varied terrain. Information: *Selkirk Wilderness Skiing Ltd.,* Meadow Creek, British Columbia V0G 1N0 (phone: 604-366-4424).

Cross-Country Skiing

It's not necessary to be an Olympic-caliber athlete to enjoy ski touring — cross-country skiing. Nor is it necessary to go anywhere special in Canada to enjoy the sport. You can ski in city ravines, suburban vest-pocket parks, farmers' fields, and on frozen lakes. But with a long weekend or a week to spare, you'll want to head for the more attractive trails on Canada's hundreds of square miles of public lands. There, given some wisdom in the ways of the winter wilderness, it's a great adventure to break your own trails through the powder. Or tackle one of the many areas where special cross-country ski trails are marked, groomed, and patrolled. The latter can be found at a variety of hostelries: downhill ski resorts; luxury resorts (where après-ski means swimming in a big pool and relaxing in a sauna); dude ranches and guest farms; simple housekeeping cottages in the woods; cozy country inns; and rustic mountain lodges heated by wood stoves and lit by kerosene lanterns. Or you might want to try a lodge-to-lodge or hut-to-hut (tents, actually) tour with accommodations that are a day of skiing apart, on an interconnecting trail (luggage is transported separately by road). For the truly adventurous, there's even helicopter cross-country skiing. Interesting articles dealing with various areas where cross-country skiing is big are published in *Ski Canada* (CN$16.45, about US$14, annually), 227 Front St. E., Suite 100, Toronto, Ontario M5A 1E8 (phone: 416-496-8413).

EAST

Because of Canada's current cross-country skiing boom, most provincial and municipal parks have developed at least one trail and try to keep campgrounds open for die-hard winter lovers. Even the Atlantic provinces have gone in for the sport. Mactaquac Provincial Park, 15 miles (24 km) from Fredericton, New Brunswick, keeps locals happy on its small network of trails. There are 40 miles more at Poley Mountain, north of Saint John, not far from Sussex. In Nova Scotia, the *Old Orchard Inn Ski Touring Centre* (Box 1090, Wolfville, NS B0P 1X0; phone: 902-542-5751) at Annapolis Valley caters exclusively to cross-country skiers. Wentworth Valley, the wooded area surrounding the *Canadian Hostelling Association*'s handsome, century-old *Wentworth* hostel (RR1, Wentworth, Cumberland Co., NS B0M 1Z0; phone: 902-548-2379) is a delight. The hostel accommodates 45 people (bring your own sleeping bag) and has a cross-country ski rental shop. Reservations are necessary.

In Quebec, the Gaspé Provincial Park and the Forillon National Park attract a trickle of experienced skiers looking for a superior wilderness experience. There's an extensive trail network at Parc du Mont Ste.-Anne — known for its downhill runs — and at a few other areas just outside Quebec City. Quebec's Eastern Townships, also usually thought of for fine alpine skiing, are sprinkled with lodges catering to kick-and-gliders. The massive and elegant *Château Montebello,* at Montebello, 40 miles (64 km) east of Ottawa, has gained an international reputation as the annual operational headquarters for the 160-km *Canadian Ski Marathon* — a giant, anyone-can-enter Nordic competition. (For hotel information, contact *Le Château Montebello,* Montebello, Quebec J0V 1L0; phone: 819-423-6341. Also see *Special Havens.*)

Meanwhile, in Ontario, there are myriad resorts in the Huronia district, around Barrie. There's wilderness skiing in the glorious Algonquin Provincial Park, while the nearby *Deerhurst Inn and Country Club* (described in *Special Havens*) and the *Bear Trail Inn* (Box 158, Whitney, Ontario K0J 2M0; phone: 613-637-2662) both have good touring trail systems.

In addition to these areas, most of the inns and resorts described in *Special Havens,* and many of the guest farms sketched in *Farm and Ranch Vacations* either maintain their own cross-country ski trail networks or have access to terrain in nearby provincial and national parks. For more ideas, in every case, contact the various province tourist offices. A number of areas in eastern Canada merit special attention for the unique experiences they offer.

ALGOMA COUNTRY, north of Sault Ste.-Marie, Ontario: Northward from this city at the junction of Lake Superior and Lake Huron, there is a vast wilderness full of cross-country skiing opportunities, many of them in four provincial parks and one national park. The forests are deep and silent and bring to mind the days when Indians roamed the land. Establish a base at a hotel in Sault Ste. Marie and then head out for day trips into these preserves or to the big *Hiawatha Lodge II* (RR5, Landslide Rd., Sault Ste.-Marie, Ontario P6A 6J8; phone: 705-949-9757). There are no overnight accommodations at the lodge, which is home base for the famous *Sault Finnish Ski Club,* but cross-country skiers can stop here to enjoy the cocktail lounge and other day facilities. In addition to about 21 miles of immaculately groomed trails, there is a 3 mile loop lighted for night skiing. Alternatively, it's possible to headquarter at any one of a number of small, secluded cabins and lodges north and east of Sault Ste. Marie and north of Thessalon in the Mississagi River valley. The trail networks are not extensive, but the lodges themselves are long on charm. (For details, contact the *Algoma-Kin-niwabi Travel Association,* 616 Queen St. E., Suite 203, Sault Ste.-Marie, Ontario P6A 2A4; phone: 705-254-4293).

LAURENTIANS, Quebec: Twenty-five years ago, cross-country skiing here had the reputation of being for kamikaze-types only. Trails were severe, with frequent cliff-like descents. Today, most of the trails have been redesigned, upgraded, and mechanically tracked. This vast sweep of mountains may well be the ultimate cross-country ski resort area, the Aspen of cross-country skiing. The main attraction, besides the skiing, is the abundance of wonderful restaurants and lodging places. But when you consider their diversity and the variety of the skiing terrain, putting together a Laurentians ski vacation can become terribly confusing. A few basic facts about the area may be helpful. To wit: The northern Laurentians' trails are not quite so well marked as those in the south; and the farther east or west you travel from the Laurentians autoroute, which bisects the region from north to south, the wilder and less well marked are the ski routes. The trails at the better-known hostelries of the more northerly St. Jovite–Mont Tremblant area — the *Tremblant Club,* the *Station Mont Tremblant Lodge,* and the *Gray Rocks Inn* (all described in *Special Havens*) — are enjoyable. Most people make their headquarters at one establishment, then spend their vacations exploring its trails and those of its neighbors, accessible via interregional trails. But the very concentration of inns and the proliferation of long-distance trails also suggest the possibility of inn-to-inn touring, and in the south, where the hostelries are situated practically on top of each other, innkeepers are generally quite obliging about transporting your luggage via hotel bus or taxi to your next overnight stop.

Regional trail maps are available from local hotels and ski shops, as is the interregional trail map published by the Laurentian Ski Zone. The Laurentians are also well known for hosting the *Canadian Ski Marathon,* a mammoth, anyone-can-enter 2-day cross-country ski event, usually held in mid-February, that ranks among the biggest of its kind in the world. Entrance fees range from about $38 to $55, depending on your age group. (For details, contact the *Canadian Ski Marathon,* P.O. Box 98, Montebello, Quebec J0V 1L0 (phone: 819-423-5157). Information: *Association Touristique des Laurentides,* 14142 Rue de Lachapelle, RR1, St.-Jérôme, Quebec J7Z 5T4 (phone: 514-436-8532). Also see *Downhill Skiing* and the *Laurentians,* DIRECTIONS.

QUEBEC CITY, Quebec: One of the great charms of this endlessly fascinating city is its proximity to the great out-of-doors. You can spend days pursuing your favorite sports — and your nights in the comfort of the city's splendid hotels, sleeping off the effects of a bountiful French Canadian repast eaten in one of its cozy restaurants. Cross-country skiers will find some of the province's best skiing within an hour's drive of the city. Quebecois themselves take to the Plains of Abraham — like New Yorkers to Central Park — to keep in shape; and though the skiing isn't the best, the views are fine. However, Quebec's best ski terrain — more than what's possible to explore in a 2-week vacation (let alone a 2-week vacation that leaves time to enjoy the delights of the metropolis) — is at Mont Ste.-Anne, 25 miles (40 km) to the east; at Duchesnay Forestry Station, 25 miles (40 km) northwest; and at Camp Mercier, just inside Laurentides Park, 36 miles (58 km) from downtown. Located in the picturesque village of St.-Férreol-les-Neiges, 5 miles east of the alpine ski center, Mont St.-Anne's cross-country ski center has 134 miles of trails in the heart of the Laurentian Forest. The trails have been specifically designed to meet the needs of beginner and intermediate skiers. Expert trails are found at the competition center of Parc Mont St.-Anne. Duchesnay's more varied woods trails, through mixed hardwood and fir, are better suited to beginners, while the trails at Camp Mercier, far less windy than at either of the other areas, are flatter still; the snow is also better there. Inexpensive group overnight trips are also available. Information: *Quebec City Region*

Tourism and Convention Bureau, 60 Rue d'Auteuil, Quebec City, Quebec G1R 4C4 (phone: 418-692-2471).

WEST

The cross-country skiing mania means, in Manitoba, Saskatchewan, and Alberta, that scarcely a snowy weekend passes without swarms of skiers descending on municipal and provincial parks near the cities and every ski lodge in sight. Guest farms in the area get some of the traffic, and not a few have reported repeat business all the way from Europe. The woodland trails in Prince Albert National Park, smack in the center of Saskatchewan, are also popular. In Manitoba, the major magnets are Duck Mountain Provincial Park, a major wintering ground for elk; Riding Mountain National Park, near Wasagaming; and Whiteshell Provincial Park, where ski trails lead through black spruce woods, aspen groves, and such. In Alberta some 24 miles of double track have been added at Nakiska. Canadians casting about for a really special cross-country skiing vacation often look to several quite distinctive mountain ranges in the west, where they can base themselves in luxury resorts and backcountry lodges and go out for tours in the valleys or the mountains, with or without guides, depending on the extent of their wilderness savvy. For high-country trips, some skiers rent alpine skis with special touring bindings; others tackle the long downhills with their own skinny skis — and they keep up just fine.

ROCKIES, western Alberta: These high and rocky glaciated mountains are well known for the wealth of downhill skiing opportunities they offer — but some of the continent's most dazzling cross-country skiing can be done here as well, in Banff and Jasper National Parks and in outlying regions. Relatively inexperienced skiers can stick to the marked and mapped trails in the more accessible areas of the parks and consult local ski shops and park personnel for help in planning other day trips — and never run out of new trails to explore. The dramatic *Banff Springs* hotel and the equally imposing *Château Lake Louise* offer good access to the best of all levels of skiing. For information on ground packages, including lift tickets and accommodations, contact *Banff Club Ski* (Box 1085, Banff, Alberta T0L 0C0; phone: 403-762-4561). Long-celebrated *Skoki Lodge* — a group of half-century-old log structures situated in a mountain-rimmed valley 8 miles (13 km) from the nearest road, lit by lanterns and candles and heated by fireplaces — makes a wonderful retreat. Guests ski all day in the serene woods and meadows in the immediate area and in valleys above timberline and then come back to delicious meals prepared on real wood stoves and friendly conversations with other guests around the fireplace. (For information on this lodge as well as all the others in the Lake Louise area, contact *Skiing Louise,* PO Box 5, Lake Louise, Alberta, T0L 1E0; phone: 403-522-3555) There are a half dozen such cozy places in the Rockies — though the setup varies a little from one to the next. You will have to ski into the *Lake O'Hara Lodge,* so pack light. The timbered lodge, about 7 miles (11 km) west of Lake Louise, was built by the *Canadian-Pacific Railroad* company in 1925 (Box 1677, Banff, Alberta T0L 0C0; phone: 403-762-2118 or 604-343-6418); and beautifully situated *Mt. Assiniboine Lodge,* built of logs in about 1928 (Box 1527, Canmore, Alberta T0L 0M0; phone: 403-678-2883). In Jasper National Park, the spectacular Tonquin Valley — edged and overlooked by the renowned "Ramparts," rock cliffs that soar up to 10,000 feet in height — is home to *Tonquin Valley Ski Tours,* a 14-mile back-country trip from Jasper to the lodge (Box 550, Jasper, Alberta T0E 1E0; phone: 403-852-3909). The *Alpine Club of Canada* (Box 1026, Banff, Alberta T0L 0C0; phone: 403-762-4481) operates 15 back-country huts within easy reach of Banff or Jasper, including the *Wates-Gibson Hut* in the Jasper park's Eremite Valley. They also offer accommodations for 67 people in their clubhouse at Canmore. The *Sunshine Village*

Inn, perched at the top of the gondola, is the single source for on-slope accommodations at one of Banff's big-time ski resorts (PO Box 1510, Banff, Alberta T0L 0C0; phone: 403-762-6500). There are a number of marked loop trails in the area and some longer overnight tours. Organized tours are available from *Banff Alpine Guides* (Box 1025, Banff, Alberta T0L 0C0; phone: 403-762-2791); For details about skiing in the parks, contact *Banff National Park* (PO Box 900, Banff, Alberta T0L 0C0; phone: 403-762-3324) and *Jasper National Park* (Box 10, Jasper, Alberta T0E 1E0; phone: 403-852-6161).

CARIBOOS, British Columbia: This province's Interior Ranges — the Cariboos, Purcells, Selkirks, and Monashees — are well known for the heli-skiing operations found there. But the area is also liberally sprinkled with operations that specialize in cross-country skiing and mountain touring; in fact, the 100–108 Mile area (yes, that's its name) alone hosts a ski trail network of approximately 124 miles. The Cariboos, the most westerly of these four groups of peaks, are most like the Rockies in their relatively smooth contours, but snowfall — though it varies considerably from valley to valley — is generally higher. Of the resorts and lodges in the area that offer cross-country skiing, the fanciest are the *Hills Health and Guest Ranch,* with indoor swimming pool, whirlpool bath, saunas, and chalets that sleep six (*C-26, 108 Ranch,* 100 Mile House, BC V0K 2E0; phone: 604-791-5225); and, across the road, the *108 Golf and Country Inn Resort,* a modern 62-room motor lodge with all the trimmings (*C-26, 108 Ranch,* 100 Mile House, BC V0K 2E0; phone: 604-791-5211; also see *Farm and Ranch Vacations*). Eight miles (13 km) south, in 100 Mile House — the cross-country capital of BC — the *Red Coach Flag Inn* (PO Box 760, 100 Mile House, BC V0K 2E0; phone: 604-395-2266) and many other motels offer fine facilities (including lighted night skiing) and are particularly packed the first weekend in February, when the town hosts the annual 50-km *Cariboo Ski Marathon.* There are also a number of smaller, more rustic places here. The *Circle H Mountain Lodge* (Box 7, Jesmond Rd., Clinton, BC V0K 1K0; phone: 604-459-2565), situated at the base of Mt. Bowman, 25 miles (40 km) outside of a blink-and-you-miss-it town called Clinton, is among them. Installed in an old log-and-frame hunting lodge and a number of outlying log cabins, it has about 46 miles of trails with a good mix of terrain for every level of skier. For a list of other lodges in the area, contact the *Cariboo Tourist Association,* PO Box 4900, Williams Lake, BC V2G 2V8 (phone: 604-392-2226).

WILDERNESS MOUNTAIN SKIING IN THE PURCELLS AND THE SELKIRKS, British Columbia: The Purcells, just west of the Rockies, and the Selkirks, just west of the Purcells, are some of British Columbia's most rugged mountains. Compared to the Rockies, the slopes are steeper, the tops more pointed, the rocks more jagged, the snow much deeper. This is not the sort of terrain easterners envision when they think of cross-country skiing. Yet once you've mastered the turns, your skis can take you all sorts of places, and the high mountains are as beautiful as any. Most of the activity in this particular area centers on a handful of tiny mountain lodges of varying degrees of rusticity and remoteness, from which guests go out on guided day trips with the host, who is invariably a confirmed mountain lover. A rustic and rugged experience is offered by *Valhalla Mountain Touring* (PO Box 284, New Denver, BC V0G 1S0; phone: 604-358-7714). Skiers are transported by heated snowcat to a cozy subalpine cabin, the base for the daily ski tours. *Mountain Canada* (Box 1530, Golden, BC V0A 1H0; phone: 604-344-5410) offers both guided ski tours and heli-cross-country ski tours of the 1-day variety, as well as a seven-day package that also includes 1 day of heli-cross-country skiing. Accommodations and meals are included with the 3-, 5-, and 7-day packages.

The Best Tennis Vacations

For many years, Canadians simply weren't interested in tennis. The climate didn't help. Building courts was an expensive proposition. Long, hard winters that precluded play for much of the year wrought havoc even on all-weather surfaces; expensive indoor courts were the only alternative, and there was little demand. Promoters, sensing an uncertain return on their investment, steered clear of tennis, at least as far as vacation facilities went.

But gradually tennis has been taking hold north of the US border. Rare indeed is the area without tennis facilities. Courts are now found in all resort hotels and many big-city hotels, as well as in just about all the country's townships and municipalities. (Write to the chamber of commerce or local tourist authority of the area you intend to visit for a list.) And bit by bit, the number of resorts devoted exclusively to tennis has been increasing. Most are located in marvelously scenic country, and most offer private lessons or clinics and other facilities — which you can enjoy even if you've never held a racket in your life. Clinics and intensive instruction programs will teach you the correct way to play right from the beginning, and even experienced players can benefit from a little additional coaching once in a while.

Far more common in Canada than the tennis-only resort, however, is the resort with a few courts and a pro — and these are, in any case, far more relaxing places to spend a vacation. Just check in, sign up for a couple of lessons here and there, play tennis when you want, and spend the rest of your time taking advantage of the resort's saunas, shops, whirlpool baths, swimming pools, golf courses, and waterfront activities.

BANFF SPRINGS HOTEL, Banff, Alberta: The tennis season runs from May, when the weather clears, until October, when temperatures begin to drop, here in the heart of the Canadian Rockies where this turreted 841-room château of a hostelry is situated. The 5 plexi-pave hard-surface courts are used by guests from all over North America as well as by members of a Banff Springs club (whose members pay an annual fee for the privilege), so the setup is exceptionally convivial — somewhat less transient in feeling than at most hotels, but not so stuffy as a good many country clubs. A ball machine and pro are available to help perfect your strokes, and, though the courts aren't lighted, you can play until 10 almost every night — because that's when the sun sets in these parts. Consequently, this establishment is one of your best bets for a tennis vacation that involves pursuing other activities as well. There are plenty to enjoy: fishing in mountain streams, canoeing and rafting, climbing, golf on one of North America's most scenic courses (bar none; see *Golf*), as well as swimming in either of 2 pools. You can relax after all this activity in one of the health club's 3 Jacuzzis or its sauna. Information: *Banff Springs Hotel,* PO Box 960, Banff, Alberta T0L 0C0 (phone: 403-762-2211).

JASPER PARK LODGE, Jasper, Alberta: Here, the same situation prevails: a great hotel (really a lodge surrounded by old-fashioned log cabins and modern cedar chalets), a fine golf course (see *Golf*), lots of climbing (see *Mountain Climbing*), good fishing, hiking, canoeing and rafting, and all the other Rocky Mountain highs as off-the-court entertainment — plus wonderful tennis. There are 4 hard-surface courts at your disposal. No clinics are offered, but you can take lessons from the pro. Information: *Jasper Park Lodge,* Box 40, Jasper, Alberta T0E 1E0 (phone: 403-852-3301).

LAKE OKANAGAN RESORT, Kelowna, British Columbia: This is a 300-acre condominium resort hotel on the shores of 90-mile-long Lake Okanagan. There are 7 courts here (3 lighted), and two teaching pros to help you improve your game. You get about 3 hours on the court every day (including work with ball machines and video equipment). Accommodation (for up to 350) is in guestrooms, suites, studios, and 2- and 3-bedroom apartments in Bavarian-style chalets scattered widely around the wooded grounds and at the edge of the 9-hole, par-3 golf course. Access to local championship courses is available through the pro shop. There's also a stadium court with seating for 300 on the property. All sorts of other activities are available in the area, which is Canada's fruit-growing center. Open April to October. (See *Okanagan Orchard Country,* DIRECTIONS.) Information: *Lake Okanagan Resort,* PO Box 1321, Station A, Kelowna, BC V1Y 7V8 (phone: 604-769-3511).

ELGIN HOUSE, Port Carling, Ontario: There are 4 tennis courts at this 640-acre turn-of-the-century resort in the Muskoka Lakes district, and there's a pro who holds clinics. But clinics here are not like those you find anywhere else. Most guests come to stay a week, with the express purpose of playing and studying tennis. Just after they've all checked in, the pro gathers them together to find out their strengths and weaknesses, then groups them accordingly. Private lessons are available at any time you and the pro deem mutually desirable. Flexibility, in other words, governs the program, and the high percentage of return business would indicate that the guests are happy with the arrangement — and with the resort's other features. Spread out as it is on a lawns-and-woods-blanketed peninsula poking into one Lake Joseph, this is a relaxed sort of place, and even when the house is full — that is, with all 350 guests who can be divided between the various balconied hotel rooms, suites, and 4-bedroom cottages — you don't feel hemmed in by people. In fact, sometimes the management looks around and wonders where everybody has gone. The answer: They're swimming in the pool, wielding their irons on the 9-hole golf course, sailing, canoeing, water skiing, windsurfing on the lake, playing shuffleboard or field games — or, after dinner, enjoying movies, bingo games, pool parties, a popular dinner theater with professional actors, or other social programs cooked up by the full-time recreation director. The resort also offers a nursery with a complete children's program. Information: *Elgin House,* RR2, Port Carling, Ontario P0B 1J0 (phone: 705-765-3101).

DEERHURST INN AND COUNTRY CLUB, Huntsville, Ontario: Almost a century old, this Muskoka Lakes resort keeps growing to meet demand. It now has 8 hard courts outdoors and 4 indoor courts in a new entertainment complex that also features a swimming pool, 3 squash courts, a raquetball court, fitness room, men's and ladies' spas, beauty salon, 350-seat dinner-theater, and pro shops to go with the club's two PGA-level golf courses. Tennis lessons are available from a pro. Information: *Deerhurst Resorts Ltd.,* RR4, Huntsville, Ontario P0A 1K0 (phone: 705-789-5543).

HIDDEN VALLEY RESORT, Huntsville, Ontario: Set all by itself on the shores of what is affectionately known as Pen — for Peninsula — Lake, this establishment boasts 4 tennis courts (2 lighted), indoor and outdoor pools, racquetball, squash, a universal gym, a whirlpool bath, sauna, and tanning room. There is a tennis pro and an instructor for popular aquatic exercise classes. Sailboats, windsurfers, water skis, and jet boats also are available. In winter, the ski slopes of Hidden Valley Highlands land you almost at the hotel door. Information: *Hidden Valley Resort,* RR4, Huntsville, Ontario P0A 1K0 (phone: 705-789-2301).

CLEVELANDS HOUSE, Minett, Ontario: Tennis is the major attraction at this handsome older lodge — a 175-room families' delight on 100 lakeside acres in the Muskoka Lakes district, about 140 miles (225 km) north of Toronto. You'll find 16 courts here and a structured program — available for rank beginners, novices, intermediates, advanced and team players, and children under 14 — which give you court time and time for viewing indoor films, learning the rules of the game, and discussing tactics and strategies. You use ball machines and video equipment when appropriate. Other activities include golf on the challenging 9-hole course, plus boating, fishing, swimming. Rooms are located in 5 lodge buildings and a scattering of bungalows. Information: *Clevelands House,* Minett, Muskoka, Ontario P0B 1G0 (phone: 705-765-3171).

INN AT MANITOU, McKellar, Ontario: This small, ultra-luxurious Relais & Châteaux resort located on a semi-wilderness shore of a north central Ontario lake, not far from the beautiful Georgian Bay area and some 160 miles (256 km) north of Toronto, offers a solid program of 3-, 4-, and 7-day clinics that stand out particularly because of their high teacher-pupil ratio: A staff of 16 pros is always on hand to provide instruction for the 65 guests who can be accommodated at any given time. Facilities include 13 outdoor courts and an indoor court, a complement of ball machines and video equipment, a heated pool, sauna and spa, and boats for sailing on the lake. The suites each have a wood-burning fireplace (and many have whirlpool baths and saunas). The food is delicious, featuring nouvelle cuisine. This is one of North America's best-established tennis resorts, well worth traveling a long distance to experience — and a lot of first-rate tennis players do just that. New fitness facilities include a health and beauty spa with aerobics classes and hydrotherapy baths plus special "spa cuisine" for the calorie conscious. A "value season" prevails from late May to late June and from *Labor Day* to mid-October; if your budget is average, you will probably want to time your visit accordingly. Information: *Inn at Manitou,* McKellar Centre Rd., McKellar, Ontario P0G 1C0; phone: 705-389-2171; off-season: 251 Davenport Rd., Toronto, Ontario M5R 1J9 (phone: 416-967-3466).

LAURENTIANS, Quebec: St. Jovite's *Gray Rocks Inn,* a complete tennis resort destination, is the grand old lady of the Laurentians. Well known to skiers for many years for its outstanding teaching program, it offers tennis clinics on a par with those of the *Inn at Manitou,* described above. However, management here goes for volume as well as quality; the resort, situated on some 2,600 acres on the shores of Lac Ouimet, can accommodate close to 500 guests. Tennis clinics follow the methods developed by Billie Jean King's former coach Dennis Van der Meer — that is, plenty of stroke work. Usually, this means 20 hours of instruction (4 hours per day, for 5 days) with a pair of instructors for each student on the court at any given time. If you don't want to throw yourself entirely into the game, you don't have to: A fee of approximately $30 entitles you to a week's unlimited use of the resort's 22 Har-Tru courts. And when you're not lobbing balls, you can golf on the 18-hole course, enjoy water sports and a fitness center, play badminton and other lawn games, go riding, or, more to the point in this gourmand's paradise, indulge in good French Canadian food in a lovely dining room practically paved with white linen. There's live entertainment nightly. The main lodge includes rooms and small suites, some with fireplaces or balconies and patios. More than fifty 1-, 2-, and 3-bedroom condominums are also available. *Le Chantecler* in Ste.-Adéle, and *Villa Bellevue,* on Lake Ouimet, both offer tennis weeks and weekends, private lessons, and clinics. *Villa Bellevue* also has a pro available for lessons and guests have access to four new clay courts and can take full advantage of the resort's lakeshore setting and watersports. The resort has recently added an indoor pool, spa, exercise room, and 14 deluxe rooms. *Station Mont Tremblant Lodge* at Mont Tremblant has a half dozen Har-Tru courts, and both private and group lessons and seminars for children are available. You lodge in a variety of deluxe rooms or in chalets of varying sizes, some with fireplaces. *Cuttle's Tremblant Club,* on the edge of Lac Tremblant, has 4 courts and a tennis pro located at its beach club. Information: *Gray Rocks Inn,* PO Box 1000, St. Jovite, Quebec J0T 2H0 (phone: 819-425-2771); *Station Mont Tremblant Lodge,* Mont Tremblant, Quebec J0T 1Z0 (phone: 819-425-8711 or 800-567-6761 in the US and Canada); *Cuttle's Tremblant Club,* Mont Tremblant, Quebec J0T 1Z0 (phone: 819-425-2731); *Villa Bellevue,* Mont Tremblant, Quebec J0T 1Z0 (phone: 819-425-2734 or 800-567-6763).

MONT STE.-MARIE RESORT AND CONFERENCE CENTRE, Lac Ste.-Marie,

Quebec: This ski-and-summer resort in the Gatineau Hills some 55 miles (88 km) north of Ottawa offers tennis on 4 courts that are available daily from 8 AM to 10 PM. When you've had enough on the courts, you'll find plenty of other sports to enjoy on the resort's 4,500 acres, such as a round of golf on the 18-hole course. Lac à la Truite here is reserved for fishing. You can windsurf, swim, canoe, and kayak on Lake Fournier (canoe and windsurfing equipment can be rented.) There's a health club with sauna, gym equipment, and a full complement of after-dark activities — a must for any complete destination resort that is as relatively remote from the bright lights as this one. Information: *Mont Ste.-Marie,* Quebec J0X 1Z0 (phone: 819-467-5200).

Golf in Canada: A Land of Links

 Canada's British heritage is nowhere more obvious than in its abundance of first class golf courses. That they have not exactly reached international renown is much more a by-product of a relatively short grass-growing season than any inadequacy in design, and though the overall playing season may be similarly short, there are more good golfing challenges within Canada's borders than the average golfer could conquer in a lifetime.

As in the US, there are many private golf clubs that bar transient players. But even these enclaves are more pleasant to tourists than their stateside counterparts, especially if you show up on slack days — that is, during the week. A letter from your own golf club president or home course professional requesting playing privileges at a Canadian club, together with your own membership card, often provides more ready access to private clubs than you might suppose.

You needn't go to such trouble, however, for the courses listed below. Most are located at resorts or in public parklands — and they're some of Canada's finest.

EAST

EDMUNDSTON GOLF CLUB, Edmundston, New Brunswick: The main 18-hole championship layout stretches 6,666 yards and plays to par 73, with one long par 3 over a railway spur. There's also a 5-hole par-3 junior course for youngsters or adult practice. This semi-private course also features a clubhouse and pool overlooking the river and the city. Information: *Edmundston Golf Club,* PO Box 263, Edmundston, NB E3V 3K9 (phone: 506-735-7266 or -3086).

ALGONQUIN GOLF COURSE, St. Andrews, New Brunswick: Part of one of Canada's traditional summer resort hotels, the course borders on Passamaquoddy Bay, due east of Calais on the Maine border. There are a total of 27 holes here, set in rolling seaside terrain. The name of the town in which the course is situated is hardly gratuitous since it's quite reminiscent of its famous namesake on the east coast of Scotland. The 9-hole course has narrow fairways and the 18-hole stretch is very scenic with 13 holes along the bay. Information: *Algonquin Golf Club,* St. Andrews, NB E0G 2X0 (phone: 506-529-3062).

BALLY HALY GOLF AND CURLING CLUB, St. John's, Newfoundland: Its narrow fairways, side-hill lies, and well-contoured greens would make this 5,800-yard, par-71 course difficult enough, but because of its coastline location, rigorous winds add to its toughness. The course has 18 scenic holes, many with views of the North Atlantic from the tees and fairways. Information: *Bally Haly Golf and Curling Club,* PO Box 9185, St. John's, Newfoundland A1A 2X9 (phone: 709-753-6090).

BRIGHTWOOD GOLF AND COUNTRY CLUB, Dartmouth, Nova Scotia: Located smack in the center of the city, looking much like Central Park in the center of New York City, this 18-hole course is perched high on a hill on what must surely be the choicest site in the area, and the views are as beautiful as the golf holes are difficult. Information: *Brightwood Golf and Country Club,* 227 School St., Dartmouth, NS B3A 2Y5 (phone: 902-466-7688).

PINES GOLF CLUB, Digby, Nova Scotia: This club is owned by the provincial government and operated by the Nova Scotia Department of Tourism, which also runs the fine adjacent hotel. At least as appealing as the course's rolling acreage are the famous scallops caught hereabouts, and this is one of the best places in Canada to combine good golf and gastronomy. Information: *Pines Golf Club,* c/o *The Pines Resort Hotel,* PO Box 70, Digby, NS B0V 1A0 (phone: 902-245-2511).

OAKFIELD GOLF AND COUNTRY CLUB, Grand Lake, Nova Scotia: With Ashburn, this is one of the prime sites for golfers who live in and around Nova Scotia's capital of Halifax. It's as wide open as Ashburn is wooded but no less difficult. The constant breeze that blows over the lakeside setting makes each hole a bit trickier than it initially appears. The fourth hole here is unique, since the scene off the tee seems to indicate no green immediately at hand. But one *is* tucked in just beyond the far left corner of the seemingly empty square in front of you, and a caddy's advice as to the direction of your drive is indispensable. Information: *Oakfield Golf and Country Club,* Enfield Post Office, Enfield, Hants County, NS B0N 1N0 (phone: 902-861-2777).

HIGHLAND LINKS, Cape Breton Highlands National Park, Ingonish Beach, Nova Scotia: One of the great adventures in golf, the course is one you play many times to savor its true challenge. The setting is superb, combining seaside, valley, and mountainous terrain in perfect proportion. Tees and greens are placed only in the most perfect positions, and architect Stanley Thompson included walks as long as a half mile between holes to assure maximum enjoyment of this unique layout. Anyone considering a round on this course should enjoy walking; motorized golf carts are prohibited in order to maintain the physical challenge and spirit of the old Scottish links. Information: *Cape Breton Highlands National Park,* Ingonish Beach, Victoria County, NS B0C 1L0 (phone: 902-285-2600 May through October, or 902-285-2270).

LINGAN COUNTRY CLUB, Sydney, Nova Scotia: Golf pros who really know Nova Scotia consider this one of the hardest tracks in all of the Maritimes on which to score. The course measures 6,657 yards and you play every foot of it, for the distances on the scorecard are deadly accurate — your short iron game had better be also. Definitely not for the timid. Information: *Lingan Country Club,* PO Box 1252, Grand Lake Rd., Sydney, NS B1P 6S9 (phone: 902-562-5100).

UPPER CANADA GOLF COURSE, near Morrisburg, Ontario: Operated by The St. Lawrence Park Commission, the course boasts unusually large greens and rather rolling fairways. The setting is especially picturesque. A driving range, dining facilities, and a pro shop are also on the premises. Information: *Upper Canada Golf Course,* The St. Lawrence Parks Commission, PO Box 740, Morrisburg, Ontario K0C 1X0 (phone: 613-543-2003).

GLEN LAWRENCE GOLF AND COUNTRY CLUB, Kingston, Ontario: Don't let the rather flat front 9 here lull you into a false sense of security. The back 9 are considerably more rolling, and the course represents a fine test. (There's water to conquer on 7 holes.) Information: *Glen Lawrence Golf and Country Club,* RR1, Kingston, Ontario K7L 4V1 (phone: 613-545-1021).

WHIRLPOOL GOLF COURSE, Niagara Falls, Ontario: The course gets its name from the famous Niagara Whirlpool, and the scenery includes a view of the Niagara Gorge. There are many trees, many traps, and very challenging green positions. Information: *Whirlpool Golf Course,* Niagara Parks Commission, PO Box 150, Niagara Falls, Ontario L2E 6T2 (phone: 416-356-1140).

DON VALLEY GOLF COURSE, Toronto, Ontario: Actually 6½ miles (10 km) from the center of downtown Toronto, this difficult municipal course has the Don River as its main hazard. This winding brook traverses the course and comes into play on at least 11 holes. Information: *Metropolitan Toronto Parks and Property Dept.,* 365 Bay St., 8th Floor, Toronto, Ontario M5H 2V1 (phone: 416-392-2465).

BRUDENELL RIVER PROVINCIAL GOLF COURSE, Roseneath, Prince Edward Island: Part of Brudenell River Provincial Park, this course, built in 1969 and the site of five *Canadian National Championships,* was designed to open this area to tourism. The seaside setting is well used, with fully half of the 18 holes requiring some passage over a portion of the watery landscape. It is just one of the features of a major recreation complex that also includes a marina, tennis, swimming, canoeing and boardsailing, horseback riding, camping, and 50 chalets. Information: *Brudenell River Provincial Golf Course,* c/o Harry Simmonds, Department of Tourism and Parks, PO Box 2000, Charlottetown, PEI C1A 7N8 (phone: 902-652-2342 for the pro shop; or, between October and June, 902-652-2356).

GREEN GABLES GOLF COURSE, Cavendish, Prince Edward Island: One of the oldest courses on the island (opened in 1939), it owes its name to PEI's leading literary light, Lucy Maud Montgomery. Early in this century, Miss Montgomery's story of a young orphan girl, *Anne of Green Gables* entranced the world, and the house in which her fictional heroine lived is adjacent to the golf course. Literary lives notwithstanding, the course itself is a rare blend of rolling terrain with seaside dunes and ponds. The course opens each year in mid-May and closes at the end of October. Information: *Green Gables Golf Course, Island Coastal Services Ltd.,* PO Box 151, Charlottetown, PEI C1A 7K4 (phone: 902-892-1062); or *Environment Canada,* Parks-PEI, PO Box 487, Charlottetown, PEI C1A 7L1 (phone: 902-672-2211).

MILL RIVER PROVINCIAL PARK GOLF COURSE, Woodstock, Prince Edward Island: Here's another course that's part of a larger provincial park-and-recreation complex. The course is absolutely superb, and if you have only one round of golf to play on PEI, this is the place to tee off. It's worth the trip just to play the eighth hole, where a bubbling brook boils down the middle of the fairway all the way from tee to green. Information: *Mill River Provincial Golf Course,* Department of Tourism and Parks, Woodstock RR3, O'Leary, PEI C0B 1V0 (phone: 902-859-2448).

CARLING LAKE GOLF CLUB, Lachute, Quebec: Designed by Harold Watson, this challenging course occupies a rolling site in the foothills of the Laurentian Mountains. Though it's not the longest course in Canada (at 6,650 yards), it boasts many difficult holes that will challenge the talents of even the lowest-handicap player. Information: *Carling Lake Golf Club,* PO Box 670, Brownsburg, Quebec J0V 1A0 (phone: 514-437-4653).

LE CHÂTEAU MONTEBELLO, Montebello, Quebec: The resort courses of the Outaouais area have one thing in common — their challenging, rolling terrain. Naturally sculpted ravines and valleys make the most forbidding hazards here, and the entire course is surrounded by dense pine and spruce woods. Information: *Le Château Montebello,* 109 Rue Notre-Dame, Montebello, Quebec J0V 1L0 (phone: 819-423-6341).

MANOIR RICHELIEU GOLF CLUB, Pointe-au-Pic, Quebec: The precipitous high and low points of this site overlooking the Laurentians make the course both scenic and challenging. Information: *Manoir Richelieu Golf Club,* 19 Rang Terrebonne, Pointe-au-Pic, Charlevoix, Quebec G0T 1M0. Out of season, write to 181 Rue Richelieu, Pointe-au-Pic, Charlevoix, Quebec, G0T 1M0 (phone: 418-665-3703, year-round).

LE CHANTECLER GOLF CLUB, Ste.-Adèle, Quebec: Again, part of a sizable Laurentian resort with abundant mountain scenery to provide a spectacular golfing backdrop. The 18-hole, par-72 course is next door to the *Chantecler* hotel. Information: *Le Chantecler Golf Club,* 2520 Chemin du Golf, PO Box 165, Ste.-Adèle, Quebec J0R 1L0 (phone: 514-229-3742 or, in Montreal only, 800-363-2587).

GRAY ROCKS GOLF CLUB, St.-Jovite, Quebec: Part of the large *Gray Rocks Inn* complex, the 18-hole course covers gently rolling, wooded terrain not far from Mont

Tremblant. Information: *Gray Rocks Golf Club,* PO Box 1000, St.-Jovite, Quebec J0T 2H0 (phone: 819-425-2771).

WEST

BANFF SPRINGS GOLF CLUB, Banff, Alberta: Set in a valley more than a mile high, this course is surrounded by snowcapped mountains, and you often aim shots at one of the cloud-shrouded peaks. The baronial *Banff Springs* hotel provides a striking background, and every fairway is framed in tall, deep green pine and spruce. The Bow River winds its way down the length of the valley, occasionally throwing up freshets of white water. This is perhaps one of the most beautiful (to say nothing of one of the most difficult) golfing sites in all Canada. Information: *Banff Springs Golf Club,* c/o *Banff Springs Hotel,* PO Box 960, Banff, Alberta T0L 0C0 (phone: 403-762-2211).

JASPER PARK LODGE GOLF COURSE, Alberta: This course is as beautiful in its own way as Banff Springs. Both were designed back in the 1920s by Stanley Thompson and are of indisputable quality. The fairways are carved into and out of the slopes of the Canadian Rockies, and despite the course's northerly location, the greens are as manicured and lush as any in this hemisphere. Many fairways have been designed specifically to align themselves with one of the surrounding mountain peaks. Information: *Jasper Park Lodge Golf Course,* c/o *Jasper Park Lodge,* Box 40, Jasper, Alberta T0E 1E0 (phone: 403-852-3301).

KANANASKIS COUNTRY GOLF COURSE, Kananaskis, Alberta: Alberta's only double set of 18-hole golf courses feature some of the most spectacular scenery in the Canadian Rockies. These finely sculptured greens, bunkers, and fairways are a real challenge. Information: *Kananaskis Country Club Golf Course,* Box 100, Kananaskis Village, ALberta TOL 280 (phone: 403-591-7282; 800-372-9215 in Alberta).

WATERTON PARK GOLF CLUB, Waterton Park, Alberta: The rolling fairways are a by-product of the Rocky Mountain location, with the surrounding peaks serving as a spectacular background. Information: *Waterton Park Golf Club,* Waterton Lakes National Park, Box 128, Waterton Park, Alberta T0K 2M0 (phone: 403-859-2383).

FAIRMONT HOT SPRINGS GOLF CLUB, Fairmont Hot Springs, British Columbia: Beyond the condominiums surrounding the course, the mountains compete with the Columbia Lake and Valley to provide the most compelling vista and views. Information: *Fairmont Hot Springs Resort Ltd.,* PO Box 10, Fairmont Hot Springs, BC V0B 1L0 (phone: 604-345-6514).

108 GOLF COURSE, 100 Mile House, British Columbia: This spread in central British Columbia's Cariboo country, transformed in the 1970s into a 1,500-home development with one of the most luxurious of all Canadian guest ranches, offers magnificent golfing among its many other activities. There is an 18-hole, 6,800-yard, par 71, CPGA-approved golf course that has been the site of one of western Canada's largest tournaments in the past few years as well as a pro, a putting green, chipping green, and outdoor driving range. You can take some time away from your golf game to play tennis, volleyball, or horseshoes; go horseback riding; swim in a heated pool; or relax in a sauna or whirlpool bath. Information: *108 Golf & Country Inn Resort,* Compartment 2, RR1, 100 Mile House, BC V0K 2E0 (phone: 604-791-5211).

RADIUM BEST WESTERN GOLF COURSE, Radium Hot Springs, British Columbia: The Canadian Rockies provide an impressive backdrop for this 18-hole, 5,271-yard, par 69 course, at the southern edge of Kootenay National Park, just minutes from the mineral waters of Radium Hot Springs. (The 126-room *Radium Best Western* is between the 16th and 18th fairways.) After a challenging round, guests can enjoy the resort's well-equipped sports complex, which offers tennis, racquet ball, squash, an indoor swimming pool, hot tub, exercise gym, sauna, and a massage therapist for those who overdo it. Information: *Best Western Radium Resort,* Box 310, Radium Hot

Springs, BC V0A 1M0 (phone: 604-347-9311) or *Rocky Mountain Visitors Association of British Columbia,* PO Box 10, 495 Wallinger Ave., Kimberley, BC V1A 2Y5 (phone: 604-427-4838).

VANCOUVER UNIVERSITY GOLF CLUB, Vancouver, British Columbia: Situated on the university's Endowment Lands, this 18-hole, par 72, 6,584-yard course is open year-round. It has been upgraded to one of the best public facilities in the entire country. Information: *Vancouver University Golf Club,* 5185 University Blvd., Vancouver, BC (phone: 604-224-7799).

UPLANDS GOLF CLUB, Victoria, British Columbia: The wind always blows off the surrounding Pacific around here and probably provides the most difficult resident hazard. The 18-hole, 6,246-yard course was the site of the *Canadian Senior Championships* in 1972 and 1985. Information: *Uplands Golf Club,* 3300 Cadboro Bay Rd., Victoria, BC V8R 5K5 (phone: 604-592-7313; Pro Shop, phone: 604-592-7313).

VICTORIA GOLF CLUB, Victoria, British Columbia: This 18-hole course is the oldest in the province, founded in 1893, and has about 75 bunkers set beside the Pacific Ocean. Information: *Victoria Golf Club,* 1110 Beach Dr., Victoria, BC V8S 2M9 (phone: 604-598-4321).

GLENEAGLES, West Vancouver, British Columbia: This 9-hole, par 35, 2,785-yard course is rated the best public course in Vancouver. Open year-round. Information: *Gleneagles,* 6190 Marine Dr., West Vancouver, BC VCW 2S3 (phone: 604-921-7353).

WHISTLER GOLF CLUB, Whistler, British Columbia: Adjacent to Whistler Village, this beautiful course was designed by Arnold Palmer. The 18-hole, par 72, 6,400-yard championship course is surrounded by breathtaking views of snow-capped mountains, and is open from early May to mid-October. Reservations necessary well in advance. Information: *Whistler Golf Club,* Box 1700, Whistler, BC V0N 1B0 (phone: 604-932-4544).

WASAGAMING GOLF COURSE, Riding Mountain National Park, Wasagaming, Manitoba: This province is best known for its rather flat terrain, but this 6,072-yard, par-72 course overlooking the 9.5 square miles of central Canada's beautiful Clear Lake is unusually testing, because of the rolling terrain. Then, too, there are the difficult lies, the blind approaches to the greens, and the fairway-crossing ravines and creeks you have to contend with. It's about 175 miles (280 km) northwest of Winnipeg. Information: *Wasagaming Golf Course,* c/o Jim Dudman, Box 52, Wasagaming, Manitoba R0J 2H0 (phone: 204-848-2925).

FALCON BEACH GOLF COURSE, Whiteshell Provincial Park, Manitoba: A creek running through this fine 7,000-yard championship course provides a severe hazard on four of the holes. Fairways are tree-lined and bunkered, greens are large, undulating, and well-trapped, and the eighth hole was voted the best par 3 in the province. Information: *Falcon Beach Golf Course,* c/o Department of Natural Resources, Falcon Lake, Manitoba R0E 0N0 (phone: 204-349-2201).

WASKESIU LAKE GOLF CLUB, Waskesiu Lake, Saskatchewan: Well-trapped and famed for its rolling, wooded terrain, an irrigation system makes this course, designed by Stanley Thompson in the 1930s, a jewel of the north. It's located in 1,496-square-mile Prince Albert National Park, some 143 miles (229 km) north of Saskatoon. Information: *Lobstick Golf & Tennis Club, Inc.,* PO Box 1134, Prince Albert, Saskatchewan S6U S57 (phone: 306-663-5488 or 306-663-5301).

MURRAY MUNICIPAL GOLF CLUB, Regina, Saskatchewan: This hilly public course is kept in top shape through an extensive watering system. You'll find it 7 miles (11 km) northeast of downtown Regina. Information: *Murray Municipal Golf Club,* c/o City of Regina Community Services and Parks Department, PO Box 1790, Regina, Saskatchewan S4P 3C8 (phone: 306-777-7739).

Where They Bite: Fishing in Canada

 This immense land of bays, lakes, streams, and rivers has the most plentiful and prolific fishing grounds in the world. There are lakes in the northern wilderness that no one has fished, streams flush with brook trout where no line has fallen. With a little patience, more than a little cash, and some generous help from the outfitters listed below (or any of the hundreds of others whose names are on file with provincial tourist authorities), you can arrange a fly-in wilderness fishing expedition to virtually virgin fishing grounds.

But that isn't the only lure of fishing in Canada. The true splendor of Canada's waters is that you can have superior fishing without flying anywhere. Within driving access of any major Canadian city are splendid fishing grounds; a 2-day drive will take you into country that feels as untouched as wilderness, where you will nonetheless find guides, fishing lodges of every degree of comfort and luxury, all the back-up facilities you need, and, best of all, hundreds of thousands of fish. Every area of the country has its own specialties: Atlantic salmon in the rivers of the Maritimes (and bluefin tuna in the ocean), muskie and pike in Ontario, Arctic char in the Northern Territories, steelhead trout and salmon on the Pacific coast, and lake trout everywhere. The fishing is unlimited.

Each province has its own licensing requirements, bag limits, and fishing seasons. Regional tourist offices provide this information (for addresses, see *Tourist Information,* GETTING READY TO GO), as do the fishing bureaus of the provinces (addresses in this section). *Fishing Canada's Mountain Parks* by James R. Butler and Roland R. Maw (Falcon Press; $8.95, paperback) tells you everything from what waterways are worth hiking to the best national parks for fishing. It also gives advice on what kind of bait to use, the kind (and size) of fish to expect to bring home, and how to be sure the big one doesn't get away. The book can be ordered from the publisher, Falcon Press (PO Box 1718, Helena, MT 59624; phone: 800-582-2665) for $8.95, plus $1.75 postage and handling.

EAST

Atlantic salmon, the classic game fish of the East, is called the king of fish in this part of the country, and they are most abundant in the rivers of New Brunswick, and in many areas along the St.-Lawrence River, especially around the Gaspé Peninsula. Salmon also can be caught in Nova Scotia, Newfoundland, and Labrador. Prince Edward Island has them as well, although in smaller numbers. Catches are strictly controlled almost everywhere.

The fishing in eastern Canada is hardly limited to the king; there are plenty of less regal but equally exciting inland river and lake fish running. New Brunswick's rivers and lakes are one of North America's best resources for small-mouthed bass. Brook trout and lake trout are common on the seaboard and inland; speckled trout also is found in the eastern part of Quebec; oauananiche (pronounced *wah-nah-nish,* a breed of landlocked salmon) in Labrador; and walleye and the hard-fighting pike in Ontario and Quebec. Because of the chill of its fresh water, Prince Edward Island has great brook trout fishing. Brook trout is also popular in Nova Scotia, but the waters most accessible by car are fished pretty heavily, so you'll do better scouting out the wilds. Early in the season (in spring), try bait and lures or streamers; later on, wet and dry flies are more effective.

The Maritimes used to be known for huge bluefin tuna; however, their numbers have diminished in the last 5 years. Throughout the Maritimes, charter boats aren't readily available until the end of the lobster season, usually around mid-July, and the fishing gets richer as the summer progresses. Other saltwater fish caught in numbers are halibut, hake (off Prince Edward Island), cod, and haddock.

The regulations on licenses and bag limits change yearly from province to province; for current regulations check with the provincial tourism department.

MIRAMICHI RIVER, near Fredericton, New Brunswick: The Miramichi is a classic salmon stream, one of the very best salmon rivers on the continent, and its name alone conjures up images of quiet mornings on serene pools and that fabled fish, the Atlantic salmon. The season for spring salmon — black salmon — lasts from mid-April until mid-May, while the Miramichi is still high, and fishing is done from a boat. Bright salmon, freshly run from the sea, can be taken from mid-June until the end of September. The waters have receded by then and the river can be waded in most places. Almost needless to say, the only way a salmon can be taken on any New Brunswick river is with a fly rod; and that's as it should be since only a fly rod is appropriate for such an elegant fish. (Anglers should be sure to check the latest regulations on catching large salmon. Immediate release is required for any salmon of at least 2 feet (63 cm) from the tip of the snout to the fork in the tail, measured along the side of the fish.) There are a number of excellent fishing lodges on the Miramichi, each with its own "beat" on the river. To mention a few: *Wilson's Sporting Camp Ltd.* (McNamee, NB E0C 1P0; phone: 506-365-7962); *Pond's Chalet Resort* (PO Box 8, Ludlow, NB E0C 1N0; phone: 506-369-2612); and *Wade's Fishing Lodge* (Blackville, NB E0C 1C0; phone: 506-843-2288 from April through mid-October, or 143 Main St., Fredericton, NB E3A 1C6; phone: 506-472-6454) the rest of the year). Information: *Tourism New Brunswick,* PO Box 12345, Fredericton, NB E3B 5C3 (phone: 506-453-2377 or 800-561-0123); and the *Department of Natural Resources and Energy,* Fish and Wildlife Branch, PO Box 6000, Fredericton, NB E3B 5H1 (phone: 506-453-2440).

HUMBER RIVER, near Corner Brook, Newfoundland: The most productive salmon river on the island, this stream full of vast pools annually gives up, between early July and late August, some 4,000 salmon averaging around 5 or 6 pounds, with 20-pounders not uncommon. The river empties into the Bay of Islands and can be fished upstream by boat or from the shore for about 20 miles from its mouth. Information: *Department of Development and Tourism,* PO Box 2016, St. John's, Newfoundland A1C 5R8 (phone: 800-563-6353).

GANDER RIVER, near Gander, Newfoundland: This is one of Newfoundland's top salmon rivers, and more than 3,000 salmon, averaging about 6 pounds, are landed annually; fish up to 18 pounds have been netted. The fishing, best from early July to September, is mostly done out of riverboats with outboard motors, but some of the pools on the Gander can be fished from shore. Information: *Department of Development and Tourism,* PO Box 2016, St. John's, Newfoundland A1C 5R8 (phone: 800-563-6353).

EXPLOITS RIVER, near Grand Falls, Newfoundland: Here is another of Newfoundland's biggest salmon rivers, emptying into Exploits Bay of Notre Dame Bay. There are about 30 miles of fishable water on the Exploits, and about 1,800 salmon are taken annually, their size running up to 18 pounds. Enhancement projects may eventually produce annual returns of 100,000 salmon. The best fishing period runs from early July to late August. Information: *Department of Development and Tourism,* PO Box 2016, St. John's, Newfoundland A1C 5R8 (phone: 800-563-6353).

RIVER OF PONDS, near River of Ponds, Newfoundland: Here is yet one more lure for salmon fishermen, and about 2,500 salmon are landed annually between early July, when the first run of fish enters the river, and the end of August; best fishing is usually from about July 10 to August 10. A good run of sea trout enters the river in early August. Of the many excellent pools in the River of Ponds, wide and island-dotted Hayward's Pool and Highway Pool are notable, but good fishing can also be had in the Steady, between River of Ponds Lake and Barrister's Pool, and in Island Pool, Rock Pool, Flat Pool, Dashwood Pool, Cran's Pool, and Mid-Dam Pool. Information: *Department of Development and Tourism,* PO Box 2016, St. John's, Newfoundland A1C 5R8 (phone: 800-563-6353).

EAGLE RIVER, near Goose Bay, Labrador, Newfoundland: This river — 100 miles of foaming rapids, spectacular waterfalls, placid riffles, and beautiful still pools — sees its peak salmon run beginning about mid-July. It's accessible only by float plane. The nearby White Bear River, which also empties into Sandwich Bay, gets a good run of salmon as well, though somewhat later in the summer. The tidal waters at the mouths of both these rivers are noted for their abundance of big sea-run brook trout. Information: *Department of Development and Tourism,* PO Box 2016, St. John's, Newfoundland A1C 5R8 (phone: 800-563-6353).

ALBANY WATERSHED, north of Geraldton, Ontario: The wilderness streams and lakes that are part of the Albany River watershed offer a combination of brook trout, walleye, and northern pike fishing. Walleye and brook trout average 2 to 4 pounds — and the hard-fighting northern pike from these cold, clean waters occasionally weigh in at 25 pounds. The guides here are Ojibway Indians from the Indian villages of Fort Hope, Webequie, and Lansdowne House. They still live largely off the land by trapping and hunting and are master woodsmen. Limits on the size and number of fish continue to change, so check first with the Ministry of Natural Resources. Information: *Ministry of Natural Resources,* Geraldton District, PO Box 640, Geraldton, Ontario P0T 1M0 (phone: 807-854-1030).

NORTH CHANNEL, near Little Current, Ontario: When Franklin Delano Roosevelt wanted to go on a Canadian fishing trip after the historic Quebec Conference in 1943, Canadian government officials took him to the North Channel, a rock-studded passage of water between Lake Huron's Manitoulin Island and Ontario's mainland, where FDR reportedly caught as many as 36 bass a day. Though the creel limit is now a mere half dozen daily, splake (a lake trout–brook trout hybrid) are rapidly growing in population, and the limit is 3 per day. North Channel also has good pike, muskie, and excellent jumbo perch fishing in spring and summer, plus magnificent scenery. A family vacation here will keep even non-anglers happy. Information: *Espanola District Office, Ministry of Natural Resources,* Box 1340, Espanola, Ontario P0P 1C0 (phone: 705-869-1330); and for a list of fishing lodges, the *Northern Ontario Tourist Outfitters Association,* PO Box 1140, North Bay, Ontario P1B 8K4 (phone: 705-472-5552).

GEORGIAN BAY, north of Midland, Ontario: This large bay, part of Lake Huron, which stretches some 200 miles (320 km) from Wasaga to Great Cloche Island off Little Current, offers some of the province's best fishing — not so much because of its size as its irregular shoreline and the profusion of rocky reefs, bars, and deep channels creating an excellent habitat for smallmouth bass, northern pike, walleyes, muskies, and trout. The eastern shoreline, where the water is especially shallow, offers the most productive smallmouth and pike fishing on the Bay. Parry Sound, on the eastern shore, provides good fishing for lake trout and lake trout backcross (a hybrid that is 80% lake trout and 20% brook trout); daily limit was reduced for Parry Sound from 3 to 2 in January 1988. Honey Harbour, Moon River–Woods Bay, Twelve Mile Bay, Sturgeon Bay, and Magnetawan River areas provide good to excellent muskie action. Largemouth bass are plentiful in select areas along the eastern shore. Severn Sound, to the south, is important for smallmouth, northern pike, and black crappie throughout the summer, and, in the spring and late fall, for walleye. Still farther west, the southwestern section from Wasaga Beach to Wiarton offers good rainbow and lake trout backcross angling during the spring, late summer, and fall; in winter, you can fish for them through the ice from Lion's Head to Collingwood. The northeastern area, where the

French River enters the bay — accessible only by boat — provides the best walleye action. In winter, there's good ice fishing for black crappie in the Honey Harbour and Twelve Mile Bay areas, and for walleye (in February and March) in the Port Severn, Waubaushene, area.

For information, contact the Ministry of Natural Resources: *Huronia District Office,* Midhurst, Ontario L0L 1X0 (phone: 705-728-2900); *Owen Sound District Office,* 611 Ninth Ave. E, Owen Sound, Ontario N4K 3E4 (phone: 519-376-3860); *Sudbury District Office,* Box 3500, Station A, Sudbury, Ontario P3A 4S2 (phone: 705-522-7823); and *Parry Sound District Office,* Lloyd Thurston, District Biologist, 7 Bay St., Parry Sound, Ontario P2A 1S4 (phone: 705-746-4201).

EAGLE LAKE, near Vermilion Bay, Ontario: Until recently, the angler who wanted to fish for big muskellunge considered Eagle Lake an absolute must. Although its rocky reefs and bars with sudden drop-offs are a perfect habitat for these fish, the lake has been so heavily fished for the muskies, lake trout, and walleyes, that the fish are no longer as plentiful as they once were. Outfitters, anglers, and the Ontario Ministry of Natural Resources are working together to implement regulatory changes and undertake habitat improvements that should help return Eagle to its former status as an ideal fish habitat. Information: *Dryden District Office, Ministry of Natural Resources,* PO Box 730, Dryden, Ontario P8N 2Z4 (phone: 807-223-3341); for a list of lodges on the lake, the *Patricia Regional Tourist Council,* Box 66, Dryden, Ontario P8N 2Y7 (phone: 807-223-6792).

NORTH LAKE, Prince Edward Island: Hoping to land one of the behemoths of the sea, big-game fishermen from all over the world have fished out of this small seacoast community, and it has won a reputation as the bluefin tuna capital. Until recently, 200 to 300 fish were boated off the coast of PEI, and some years it was as many as 1,200, a catch consistently higher than that from anywhere else in Atlantic Canada, often weighing in at 900 to 1,000 pounds per fish. (The largest tuna caught here to date weighed about 1,400 pounds.) But the number of bluefin tuna is declining, and lately the catch has fallen off. Some epic battles between anglers and bluefin have lasted over 10 hours. Once boated, the tuna by custom becomes the property of the boat captain. But there's always time for photographs at the weigh-in ceremony before the fish is taken to the processing plant. About ten tuna charter boats cater to big-game fishermen out of North Lake, as well as several other ports. Information: *North Lake Tuna Charters,* South Lake, PEI (phone: 902-357-2055).

QURLUTUK RIVER, near Kuujjuaq, formerly Fort Chimo, Quebec: The battling Arctic char is king of this stream running through the sub-Arctic tundra country of the northern part of the province, and fishing can sometimes be so good that anglers get tired of reeling them in. The average catch runs up to 10 to 15 pounds, and in August, when the spawning season is on, the males are bright red — spectacular. Qurlutuk also has lake trout and brook trout. The guides are Inuit, and they know the river like a Montrealer knows restaurants. Information: *Tourism Quebec,* 1010 Ste.-Catherine W., Office 430, Quebec H3B 1G2 (phone: 514-873-2015 or 800-363-7777 outside the Montreal area).

CEDAR LAKES, near Messines, Quebec: For a mixed creel, it's hard to beat the easily accessible Cedar Lakes — 4-mile-long, 2-mile-wide Big Cedar and 3-mile-long, mile-wide Little Cedar. Smallmouth bass, which pound for pound fight harder than just about any other species, are abundant here; in fact, they are the mainstay of summer fishing. Most catches weigh in at around 3 pounds, but bigger ones, ranging up to 5¾ pounds, are not unknown. The Cedars also offer good lake trout fishing (best in May and June) and fairly lively northern pike action (especially in May and June and again from July through September). Lake trout fishing in Cedar Lakes can be combined with a spring black bear hunt in the surrounding wilderness. *Moosehead Lodge* is the only establishment on the lakes. Information: *Moosehead Lodge,* PO Box 61, Messines,

Quebec J0X 2J0 (phone: 819-465-2050) or *Tourism Quebec,* 1010 Ste.-Catherine W., Office 430, Quebec H3B 1G2 (phone: 514-873-2015 or 800-363-7777 outside Montreal).

GEORGE RIVER, northeast of Schefferville, Quebec: One of the world's great, barely fished salmon rivers, this spectacular stream flows from Michikamau Lake north through the sub-Arctic wilderness and finally drains into Ungava Bay. The season's first angling, right after ice-out when the streams are swollen with melt water, is for "black" salmon; silvers appear, fresh from the sea, in late July and run through August and September. Resident brook trout and lake trout can be taken all summer. In September, the salmon fisherman can combine a fishing trip with a hunt for caribou, which migrate through the George River valley by the thousands at that time of year. During July and August, only fly fishing is allowed on Quebec's designated salmon rivers (the George among them). Information: *Ministry of Tourism,* Michael Leblanc, 800 Square Victoria, Room 260, Montreal, Quebec H4Z 1C3 (phone: 514-873-7977).

WEST

Western Canada can fulfill an angler's greatest expectations. Great Bear and Great Slave lakes in the Northwest Territories have become legendary for trout fishing. British Columbia's superabundance of trout and salmon have made bass seem run-of-the-mill to local anglers. Lake trout thrive in the Yukon, while the prairie provinces are rich with walleye and northern pike as well as big lake trout and, in Manitoba, even trophy brook trout.

KNIGHT INLET, Minstral Island, near Campbell River, British Columbia: From April to September, spring salmon are the rule here rather than the exception, but there's a limit to the number of large spring you can catch. Big tyees are regularly caught from May through August, while coho are taken from July through September. April and May are the best months to go after trout and steelhead. And given the plentiful population of Dungeness crab, anglers and their families can go crabbing in the bays. Accommodations, and fishing guides who know the best spots intimately, are available at the *Hoeya Hilton* (accessible only by float planes from Vancouver or Campbell River), and at *Spring Island.* Information (for both Hoeya Hilton and Spring Island): *Hoeya Hilton,* Blair McLean, Box 818, Campbell River, BC V9W 6Y4 (604-286-6016).

DISCOVERY PASSAGE, Quadra Island, near Campbell River, British Columbia: The Inside Passage, from the Queen Charlotte Islands to Vancouver, is salmon country, and there are concentrations around Rivers Inlet to the north and the Vancouver-Victoria area to the south. But if big chinook salmon is your game, the Discovery Passage — the 15-mile-long, mile-wide stretch of water that runs from the bottom of Quadra Island to Seymour Narrows — is where you should fish. Chinooks over 30 pounds — which the area Indians call tyee, or big salmon — have been taken. Bucktailing — trolling a bucktail fly with fly-fishing tackle — is generally the method to use from April through June, and fly casting is the sport in September and October. Some locals say that the best time for tyee is during August and the first week in September. Most fishermen, however, go for the ferocious coho, which hit hard and then run, leaping like acrobats as the end approaches; it's not uncommon to see schools of them slashing through herring and shrimp from April to October. The best time for casting to them, both from the shore and from boats, is September and October.

Almost as outstanding as the fishing is the scenery — miles and miles of fir-clad mountains that rise majestically from the ocean, hundreds of islands tucked away in inlets and bays, tiny beaches where you can dig for clams and oysters and cook your catch. And there are miles of rivers and streams full of steelhead and cutthroat. The area is well known for its killer whales, seals, and sea lions, and the population of bald eagles is one of the world's largest. The celebrated *April Point Fly Fishing Club* makes its headquarters at *April Point Lodge and Fishing Resort,* a first class operation owned and operated by the Peterson family for 40 years. The fresh seafood in the dining room is one of the great après-fishing bonuses of a fishing excursion here. Information: *April Point Lodge and Fishing Resort,* PO Box 1, Campbell River, BC V9W 4Z9 (phone: 604-285-2222).

UPPER SUSTUT AND FINLAY WATERSHEDS, northwest of Fort St. John, British Columbia: For wilderness fishing, with both fly tackle and spinning gear, nothing can beat the mountain streams, rivers, and lakes of the rugged Cassiar Mountains. The Dolly Varden and rainbow trout run big here. The best time for trout is from May to mid-September; Dolly Varden are plentiful from spring through summer. There is a feeling of remoteness here that is seldom found farther south. The striking scenery and abundant wildlife — including moose, caribou, mountain goats, stone sheep, and grizzly bear — are an added bonus. Information: *Ministry of Environment,* Information Services Branch, 780 Blanshard St., Victoria, BC V8V 1X5 (phone: 604-387-9420).

NUELTIN LAKE, north of Thompson, Manitoba: On this 120-mile-long lake astride the Manitoba–Northwest Territories border, you'll find superb angling for Arctic grayling averaging a good 3 pounds, and, in the many secluded, underfished bays, fine northern pike action. But the lake trout you pull in are what really put this place on the map. There are strains of lakers here that have learned to use river currents so that they fight like fish twice their size — and when you have a fish on the line as big as the ones in Nueltin, commonly up to 40 pounds, you have a real battle on your hands. Nueltin has outclassed every other Manitoba lake in the lake trout *Master Angler Award.* The place to stay is *Nueltin Fly-In Lodge,* Manitoba's most northerly lodge. Located on the fringe of the province's most northerly stand of black spruce, only 20 miles (32 km) from the Northwest Territories border, it can be reached only by air. Information: in winter, *Nueltin Fly-In Lodge,* P.O. Box 1561, Morden, Manitoba R0G 1J0 (phone: 204-822-4143); in summer, Box 1229, Thompson, Manitoba R8N 1P1 (phone: 204-284-3247); or *Travel Manitoba,* Dept. 9043, 155 Carlton St., 7th Floor, Winnipeg, Manitoba R3C 3H8 (phone: 800-665-0040).

BRABANT ISLAND, Mackenzie River, near Hay River, Northwest Territories: This section of the Mackenzie River, not far from Great Slave Lake, is outstanding for northern pike and walleye fishing, with superb Arctic grayling angling in both the river and local feeder streams. For pike fishing, you should bring a good selection of big Red Devil and Pixie spoons; for walleyes, an assortment of jigs and spinners. Arctic grayling, a fly fisherman's delight, are best attracted with black ant or black gnat fly patterns and small Mepps lures. The area's *Brabant Lodge* has modern, fully equipped cabins. Information: *Brabant Lodge,* PO Box 1095, Hay River, Northwest Territories X0E 0R0 (phone: 403-874-2600); and *TravelArctic, Government of the Northwest Territories,* Yellowknife, Northwest Territories X1A 2L9 (phone: 403-873-7200), or its *Tourism Industry Association* (phone: 800-661-0788).

GREAT BEAR LAKE, north of Yellowknife, Northwest Territories: For many North American anglers, any mention of this small ocean, 150 miles long and 250 miles wide, is going to conjure up visions of giant lake trout — as well it should. Great Bear Lake has produced more trophy lakers on rod and reel than any other lake on the continent, and the world records for lake trout (65 pounds), as well as those for grayling and lake whitefish, were set in the area. Most lake trout that are taken — and you can expect to catch hundreds in a week — weigh in at 8 to 12 pounds, while grayling run in the 1- to-2-pound class, with 3½- and 4-pounders not all that uncommon. Arctic char is found a short hop away in the Tree River, accessible through *Plummers Great Bear Lodge* (phone: 204-774-5775), an outpost camp. Reaching any of these fishing grounds is not that difficult, and most lodge owners offer transportation from Alberta as part of their package price. Information: *TravelArctic, Government of the Northwest*

Territories, Yellowknife, Northwest Territories X1A 2L9 (phone: 403-873-7200), or its *Tourism Industry Association* (phone: 800-661-0788).

GREAT SLAVE LAKE, near Yellowknife, Northwest Territories: Great Slave was the first of the great far northern lakes to be discovered by fishermen and is now famous for excellent lake trout and northern pike. Arctic grayling abound in many feeder streams. Fly fishermen can test their skill trying to land whitefish, which can be as challenging as trout. Information: *TravelArctic, Government of the Northwest Territories,* Yellowknife, Northwest Territories X1A 2L9 (phone: 403-873-7200), or its *Tourism Industry Association* (phone: 800-661-0788).

LAC LA RONGE AREA, north central Saskatchewan: This massive lake and surrounding waters, including the Churchill River system, provide northern pike, walleye, lake trout, whitefish, and grayling. Lac la Ronge Provincial Park, Saskatchewan's largest (931,000 acres), encompasses 100 lakes. Drive in to this center of northern aviation on an excellent paved highway. Fly-ins are available to 200-plus outfitting camps in the province. Information: *Tourism Saskatchewan,* 1919 Saskatchewan Dr., Regina, Saskatchewan S4P 3V7 (phone: 800-667-7191).

HANSON LAKE ROAD AREA, northeastern Saskatchewan: Winding some 240 miles through magnificent Canadian Shield country, this route takes anglers to some of the best fishing in the north. Lakes like Little Bear, Deschambault, Jan, and Big Sandy offer some of the most diverse fishing in the province. The route also provides access to the Churchill River system. Many parks, campsites, resorts, and outfitters provide excellent services and access to remote fly-in camps. Information: *Tourism Saskatchewan,* 1919 Saskatchewan Dr., Regina, Saskatchewan S4P 3V7 (phone: 800-667-7191).

Sailing Canada's Many Waters

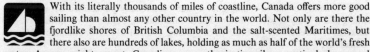 With its literally thousands of miles of coastline, Canada offers more good sailing than almost any other country in the world. Not only are there the fjordlike shores of British Columbia and the salt-scented Maritimes, but there also are hundreds of lakes, holding as much as half of the world's fresh water. As you might expect, Canadians are enthusiastic sailors, particularly around Halifax, Vancouver, and Toronto, where there are delightful sails to be had through the channels and lagoons of the idyllic Toronto Islands at the harbor's mouth, and in the area around Vancouver Island and the nearby Gulf Islands. Either area offers immense variety, so if you like to sail, these could well keep you happy. But depending on your inclinations, you might look farther afield, at areas more remote from population centers such as those described below. For a list of the provincial yachting associations, contact the *Canadian Yachting Association,* 1600 James Naismith Dr., Suite 504, Gloucester, Ontario K1B 5N4 (phone: 613-748-5687).

And when you do begin planning in earnest, be sure to contact the following: the provincial tourist authority for lists of marinas; and *Transport Canada* (Public Affairs, Tower C, Place de Ville, Ottawa, Ontario K1A 0N5; phone: 613-990-2309) for a copy of the *Canadian Coast Guard Safe Boating Guide,* the *Directory of Nautical Information,* and other useful brochures. Canadian Hydrographic Service offices have chart catalogues showing chart coverage, related nautical publications, and an international dealership list. You can contact them at either the Chart Distribution Office (Department of Fisheries and Oceans, PO Box 8080, 1675 Russell Rd., Ottawa, Ontario K1G 3H6; phone: 613-998-4931), or the Department of Fisheries and Oceans (Institute of Ocean Sciences, Patricia Bay, 9860 W Saanich Rd., PO Box 6000, Sidney, BC V8L 4B2;

phone: 604-356-6358). Also, *Canadian Yachting* magazine (227 Front St. E., Suite 100, Toronto, Ontario M5A 1E8; phone: 416-368-0185) and *Pacific Yachting* (202-1132 Hamilton St., Vancouver, BC V6B 2S2; phone: 604-687-1581) both publish cruising and charter guides in every issue.

GREAT CRUISING, EAST TO WEST

NOVA SCOTIA'S COAST: The shipbuilders of this ocean-washed province were famous for making square-riggers; today, they build smaller boats — both fishing and pleasure craft — and rent many of them by the day or the week, with or without crew, for cruises along the province's over 4,500 miles of coastline. There's good cruising all along the rocky bay- and inlet-notched headlands and among the scattered off-lying islands from Halifax to Shelburne, particularly around St. Margaret's and Mahone Bay just west of Halifax. But during the summer, fog rolls in with regularity, and because of the numerous rocks and shoals, you have to know what you're doing. The Northumberland Strait between Pugwash and Canso Strait is another good bet. There's no fog to speak of and very little tide; the water is warm — warmer, in fact, than anywhere else on the Atlantic coast north of the Carolinas — so you can take a dip after you drop anchor. The Bras d'Or Lakes offer the area's most sheltered saltwater cruising and lovely scenic shoreline without the problems of fog or tide. Throughout Nova Scotia's cruising area, anchorages are generally just a few hours' sail apart, and a dozen or more yacht clubs welcome visitors. Information: *Nova Scotia Department of Tourism,* PO Box 130, Halifax, NS B3J 2M7 (phone: 902-424-5000).

COASTAL NEW BRUNSWICK: The coasts of Prince Edward Island, Nova Scotia, and New Brunswick — so compactly arranged to shelter each other from the blustery Atlantic — together offer some of Canada's finest cruising waters, and sailors head with equal readiness for destinations such as Summerside on Prince Edward Island; Mahone Bay, Nova Scotia; and Pointe-du-Chêne, New Brunswick. Here, the prime cruising area is up and down the Northumberland Strait between New Brunswick and PEI, where you can tie up in tiny fishing villages or little coves, or just cruise along and enjoy the view — mainly of flat-to-rolling countryside occasionally punctuated by a pier or a wharf and a spiky cluster of fishing boats. Information: *Tourism New Brunswick,* PO Box 12345, Fredericton, NB E3B 5C3 (phone: 800-561-0123 from mainland US and Canada).

ST. JOHN RIVER SYSTEM, New Brunswick: This is unusual cruising for the Maritimes — ideal for families, for dinghy sailors who want to cruise, and for just about anybody else who wants to see what it's like to charter before getting into really big craft. Twenty- and thirty-foot craft are fine on these inland streams. They're tree-lined for the most part — pastoral on the upper reaches, fjordlike lower down. Charters can be arranged. Information: *Maritime Bareboat Charters, Ltd.,* PO Box 99, Grand Bay, NB E0G 1W0 (phone: 506-454-3525).

SHORES OF PRINCE EDWARD ISLAND: The most fantastic thing about the view of this 150-mile-long, 25-mile-wide island, as seen from the water, is the patchwork quilt effect of the fields — bright red when they're freshly plowed — and the forests and the grasslands, whose greens, especially in early June, will dazzle you with their brightness. The land is relatively flat to low and rolling; here and there you'll pass a cluster of farm buildings or a little fishing village, a conglomeration of white houses, piers, wharves, masts, and hulls. The north shore, sparsely settled and relatively barren, is characterized by longer stretches of beaches and more heavily breaking seas than the south shore; there are fishing harbors in the north, but navigation there is tricky because shifting sands often fill them up. Because of the protection afforded by New Brunswick and Nova Scotia to the south, such difficulties plague the south shore less frequently; this is where you'll probably do most of your sailing. The Magdalen Islands, some 80 miles (129 km) to the north, are another favored destination. Information: *PEI Sailing*

Excursions, Victoria By-The-Sea, PEI C0A 2G0 (phone: 902-658-2227); the *Charlotte-town Yacht Club,* PO Box 1024, Charlottetown, PEI C1A 7M4 (phone: 902-892-9065); and the *Silver Fox Curling and Yacht Club,* 110 Water St., Summerside, PEI C1N 1A9 (phone: 902-436-2153).

THOUSAND ISLANDS AND THE BAY OF QUINTE, Ontario: This province has its fair share of lakes and waterways, from the Great Lakes north to Hudson Bay. Toronto citizens are such wildly enthusiastic sailors, in fact, and the harbor is so full on weekends that some locals assert they'd rather contend with a highway. But for vacation cruising, one of the prime destinations is this area at the eastern end of Lake Ontario, where the lake flows into the St. Lawrence River. The Thousand Islands — over 1,700 pink granite or limestone outcroppings ranged between Kingston and Brockville — offer good fishing, fine swimming, delightful scenery. St. Lawrence Islands National Park provides mooring, camping, picnic facilities, and interpretive programs throughout the Islands (see listing later in this section). The Bay of Quinte — long, narrow, and irregular — ranks among the province's prettiest backwaters, and some people prefer it to the Thousand Islands nearby because of the near absence of commercial and power-cruising traffic. The bay, in the heart of historic Prince Edward County, is flanked by prosperous farmlands, wooded slopes, limestone escarpments, sandy beaches, and several of Ontario's oldest towns; occasionally, you'll sense yourself in the heart of the Canadian North. To get to the Bay of Quinte from the west, you can travel around the Isthmus of Murray or, like most boaters, traverse the straight-as-an arrow, 7-mile Murray Canal, near Trenton — a lovely trip. The bay is also the southern terminus of the Trent-Severn Waterway, a 240-mile inland waterway connecting Lake Ontario to Georgian Bay through the heart of central Ontario. Most services are to be found in Kingston. Information: *Eastern Ontario Travel Association,* 209 Ontario St., Kingston, Ontario K7L 2Z1 (613-549-3682); *Ontario Tourism* (phone: 800-ONTARIO, from the continental US and Canada, except Yukon); *St. Lawrence Islands National Park,* Box 469, RR3, Mallorytown, Ontario K0E 1R0 (phone: 613-923-5261); *Venture Yacht Charters,* Portsmouth Olympic Harbour, 53 Yonge St., Kingston, Ontario K7M 1E4 (phone: 613-549-1007); the *Portsmouth Olympic Harbour,* 53 Yonge St., Kingston, Ontario K7M 1E4 (phone: 613-544-9842); and the *Murray Canal,* c/o the Trent-Severn Waterway, PO Box 567, Peterborough, Ontario K9J 6Z6 (phone: 705-742-9267).

ONTARIO'S GEORGIAN BAY AND NORTH CHANNEL: For fine vacation cruising, a Toronto sailor is apt to travel to Lake Huron's spectacular Georgian Bay, which lies about 60 miles (96 km) northwest of Toronto across the neck of land that separates the city from the lake. The vast, bay- and cove-notched, island-dotted expanse of water known as the North Channel — contained to the south by hundred-mile-long Manitoulin Island and to the north by the Ontario mainland — ranks among the prime cruising areas of the world. You can sun yourself on a lonely rock, pick blueberries the size of grapes, fish, swim, explore long fjordlike bays, and spend your nights anchored in the lee of an island or tied up in a tiny cove where it's just you, the water, and the stars. Or you can dock at one of the many resorts and marinas concentrated around Killarney, on the mainland, and Little Current, on Manitoulin Island, for a good meal and some friendly conversation. Powerboating has always been popular, but sailing is taking over, as it is costly to gas up engines; a few 25-to-35-foot sailboats are available for charters. Information: *Ontario Travel,* Queen's Park, Toronto, Ontario M7A 2E5 (phone: 800-ONTARIO or 416-965-4008); and *Ontario Sailing Association,* 1220 Sheppard Ave. E., Willowdale, Ontario M2K 2X1 (phone: 416-495-4240).

LAKE OF THE WOODS, Ontario-Manitoba: Discovered by Jacques de Noyon in 1688, this longtime section of the fur traders' canoe route between Montreal and the prairies, the largest link in an intricately interconnected chain of lakes, is a mere 70 miles in length and 50 miles in width. But when you figure the multitudinous zigs and zags in the ragged shoreline of the mainland and the over 14,000 scattered islands, the coastline measures 65,000 miles. So complex is the layout that you could sail for an entire season and still be a stranger to the many winding bays, cinched channels, and unexplored landfalls and still not have had your fill of the marvelous scenery — spruce forests scattered with handsome boulders, clear waters: classic Canadian Shield country. Sailing is extremely popular, and there are wide-ranging facilities for boaters in Minnesota at Warroad, along the north shore of Lake of the Woods and in Kenora, Ontario. The latter, a handsomely sited town of about 10,000, which was once known as Rat Portage because of the muskrats that lived in the area, is the home of a museum devoted to local history and the like; during the summer, there's a lively schedule of fairs, festivals, and regattas, including *Lake of the Woods International Sailing Association* (*LOWISA*), one of North America's biggest regattas (probably the very biggest staged on an inland lake). There are also cruises on the M.S. *Kenora* four times a day, covering about 18 miles in and around the islands of the north end of the lake. Fishing — for muskies, lake trout, pickerel, and bass — is almost as productive as it was back in fur trading days. In addition, if Lake of the Woods isn't enough for you, travel farther down the Winnipeg River to the west. The *Keewatin Boatlift* will put you into the Winnipeg River system in a matter of minutes. Information: *Kenora Sailing Club,* c/o R. H. Aitken, 1511 Beach Rd., Keewatin, Ontario P0X 1C0 (phone: 807-547-2533); the *Publicity Board of Kenora Information Centre,* 1500 Highway 17 E., Kenora, Ontario P9N 1M3 (phone: 807-468-8233 or 807-468-9441); and the *Ontario Ministry of Natural Resources,* PO Box 5080, Kenora, Ontario P9N 3X9 (phone: 807-468-9841).

LAKE WINNIPEG, Manitoba: This 9,421-square-mile lake, 260 miles long and cinched at the center like a Gibson girl's corseted waist, is the largest body of water lying entirely inside Canada south of the sub-Arctic. And though you won't spot all that many sails in the northern basin even on a sunny day, that's mostly owing to the relatively small size of the province's population — just over a million. The lake's potential for cruising is practically unlimited. The waistline is the site of a cluster of islands, a number of beautiful natural harbors, the handsome Hecla Provincial Park, and the modern *Gull Harbour Resort and Conference Centre.* South of these, the lake's western shore is flat and prairie-like enough that you think immediately of Big Sky country; east of there, and north of Hecla Island, you're in Canadian Shield country again. But here, unlike at Lake of the Woods, the shoreline is smooth rather than jagged, and there are long sails between anchorages. The fact that there are few settlements in the north only heightens the sense of isolation you can feel as a result, and brings home most strongly how it must have been for the earliest trappers who settled here in the days of the founding of the Hudson's Bay Company. The few communities that you encounter nowadays are, for the most part, connected with the several reservations that border the lake, except in the south. There are marinas and yacht clubs at Winnipeg Beach, Selkirk, Victoria Beach, Silver Harbour, and Gimli, site of North America's largest Icelandic settlement, and, in early August, of a boisterous celebration of this heritage. A good deal of the history of Canada — and, indeed, of all of North America — was played out around Lake Winnipeg, and you can't fail to get interested when you come for a visit. Information: *Manitoba Sailing Association,* 1495 St. St. Matthews, Winnipeg, Manitoba R3G 3L3 (phone: 204-985-4106), and *Travel Manitoba,* Dept. 9043, 155 Carlton St., 7th Floor, Winnipeg, Manitoba R3C 3H8 (phone: 800-665-0040).

KOOTENAY LAKE, British Columbia: Snow-capped mountains plunge right to the water's edge, and sandy beaches edge the shoreline. The scenery is indescribably dramatic. This area is growing, albeit slowly, and many people have just begun to take a look at sailing as a boating option. Kootenay Lake is a place whose time has come, and one of the local marinas has opened a branch at Woodbury, which is one of the largest facilities of its kind on any inland lake in the country. You can sail the lake year-round here, because Kootenay never freezes; and the kind of winter day when the mercury hits 50F (10C) and the wind blows from the south is more than a sometime thing. In summer, a number of the owners of the 120 sailboats moored here head for Crawford Bay and its popular beach; anyone can join the informal good times. But if you want to keep to yourself, there's no dearth of tiny coves within a quarter hour's sail — or, for that matter, of productive fishing holes: The cold, clear waters are full of lingcod, Rocky Mountain whitefish, kokanee (landlocked sockeye salmon), Dolly Varden, and world-famous trophy rainbow trout. Because of the cross valleys that cut through the mountains at frequent intervals, the prevailing northwest-southeast breezes are occasionally interrupted by squallish winds, sometimes doing a complete reversal in a matter of minutes. Most facilities are in Kaslo, Balfour, and Nelson. For information on chartering a sailboat: *Kokanee Yacht Charters,* RR3, Nelson, BC V1L 5P6 (phone: 604-825-9235 or 825-9364). For general information: *Kootenay Country Tourist Association,* Site 2-11, Castlegar Airport, RR1, Castlegar, BC V1N 3H7 (phone: 604-365-8486); *Kaslo Marina,* Box 700, Kaslo, BC V0G 1M0 (phone: 604-353-2341).

COASTAL BRITISH COLUMBIA: Here, along some of the province's 4,390 miles of coastline, there's scenery on a grand scale, like practically nowhere else on earth, in spades, all the way from Victoria on Vancouver Island, and Tsawwassen, in the south, to the Queen Charlottes and Prince Rupert, which face them across Hecate Strait just south of the Alaska border: some 2,000 square miles of water in all. The mountains plunge practically to the water's edge; the shores of the little bays and inlets and the literally thousands of islands are upholstered with forests of primeval evergreens. Then there's the sky: Blue. Bluer. Bluest. You can stop to sun yourself on pebbled beaches, go for a swim, fish for salmon or other finny creatures in the channels, dig for clams, play the rockhound in the coves. You can travel for hundreds of miles and never see a soul. But you've only to detour a little to hit a settlement — a yacht club, a government marina, a fishing village, or any one of a couple of dozen provincial marine parks. And because of the moderating influence of the Pacific Ocean, you can enjoy all of this year-round; sometimes your views take in white-blanketed ski slopes with little skiers moving around like microbes above and water skiers down below. Though the number of pleasure craft owners in British Columbia, some hundred thousand in all, pretty much ensures that there will be activity all up and down the coast, there are some areas that seem to be favorites: the Gulf Islands in the Strait of Georgia around Vancouver; the hundred miles or so beyond that; the Juan de Fuca Strait around Victoria; and the very isolated Queen Charlotte Islands, 400 miles (640 km) to the north, a superb cruising ground in their own right. Information: *Ministry of Parks,* Mt. Seymour Rd., North Vancouver, BC V7G 1L3 (phone: 604-929-1291) for a list of marine parks, and the *British Columbia Sailing Association,* 304-1367 West Broadway, Vancouver, BC V6H 4A9 (phone: 604-737-3113).

CRUISING SCHOOLS

There are nearly 600 establishments that teach sailing of a small boat or dinghy — but learning to cruise is a lot more complicated, and there are proportionately fewer organizations willing to train the novice. A complete list can be obtained from the *Canadian Yachting Association* (1600 James Naismith Dr., Suite 504, Gloucester, Ottawa, Ontario K1B 5N4; phone: 613-748-5687). Here is one of the best:

ATLANTIC YACHTING ACADEMY, headquartered in Dartmouth, Nova Scotia:
At the school's various locations, good sailors (with experience on the Great Lakes and other fresh waters) can learn to deal with ocean currents and tides; beginners can get acquainted with the difference between port and starboard; and Pacific coast dwellers and Midwesterners alike can experience the waters of Atlantic Canada. These include small, secluded coves, where people can anchor and never see another boat, and the

pretty fishing villages — not to mention the wonderful Bras d'Or lakes — where it's possible to tie up in a cove, within arm's reach of a stand of spruce trees whose scent fills the air with an aroma you won't soon forget. Ken Isles, the school's founder and representative of the Cruise Training of the *Nova Scotia Sailing Association,* has been active in the movement to standardize sailing instruction in the US and Canada, and he uses these national guidelines in his day- and week-long courses as well as in his navigation and seamanship programs. Registered and certified by the *Canadian Yachting Association,* the academy's instructors are certified by the *CYA* and the Department of Transport. The academy is affiliated with the *International Sailing Schools Association* and awards national and international certification. Information: *Atlantic Yachting Academy,* PO Box 972, Dartmouth, Nova Scotia B2Y 3Z6; or at the academy's location, Dartmouth Marina, 1 North St., Dartmouth, Nova Scotia B2Y 1H1 (phone: 902-424-1661 or 902-465-7245).

Canoeing and Rafting

 Eons ago, when the glaciers crawled across Canada, they scraped the bedrock bare of soil, gouged out great gaping holes and filled them with water, polished giant boulders and scattered them willy-nilly across the land. The so-called Canadian Shield, the 1.6-million-square-mile horseshoe-shaped expanse of rock that was created in this way is Canada's single most characteristic geological feature. Its vast network of river- and stream-linked lakes has been shaping history here since the days of the Indians.

The rivers, streams, and lakes were the highways along which the French and the English explored the land. Later, to facilitate shipping in strategic areas where rapids or waterfalls made navigation difficult, canals and lock systems were added. When thus combined, Canada's network of waterways ranks among the most extensive in the world. In the Northwest Territories alone, there are enough streams that 100,000 people could canoe through 100,000 lifetimes and still not cover them all. The Mackenzie River — Canada's Mississippi, the trunk of the nation's longest river system — flows some 10,071 miles from its source into the Arctic Ocean. The Quetico area of southern Ontario seems immense when you're paddling through, but it's hardly more than a freckle on a map compared to even such relatively small areas as the Algonquin Provincial Park in southeastern Ontario, or Quebec's La Vérendrye Provincial Park. Of Ontario's 250,000 lakes and 20,000 miles of streams, the Ministry of Natural Resources has documented some 14,000 miles of the most practical water routes.

No two areas are quite alike. In the southernmost parts of Ontario and Quebec, the Canadian Shield is upholstered with the northernmost reaches of the deciduous forests, which present a striking contrast to the so-called boreal forests of conifers that you find farther north, which differ yet again from the tundra of northern Quebec, Labrador, and the Northwest Territories. The farther you go from the cities, the fewer people you'll see.

The canoeing waters described below are only representative of those detailed voluminously elsewhere. *Canoe Canada,* by Nick Nickels, covers some 600 canoe routes, their water conditions and history, and the outfitters that serve them. (Although the book is now out of print and no longer available from its publisher, Van Nostrand Reinhold, you may be able to find it in your local library.) Just where you decide to go will depend ultimately on the kind of fishing you enjoy, the time of year you're going, your own canoeing and camping experience, the time you have to spend, and your desire or reluctance for rapids and portages. Once you've fixed on a route or an area, the provincial tourism offices can furnish you with lists of canoe outfitters and rental agencies whose brochures usually provide excellent descriptions of what you'll find when you get there. A note to a few of them will yield stacks of material.

Most outfitters can provide maps, but in some areas you may find it necessary to order the special Canadian National Topographic Survey Maps — cartographic reproductions of aerial photographs that pinpoint lakes, rivers, roads, buildings, bridges, and some 90 other manmade and natural features. Those scaled at 1:250,000 will give you the general location, while the 1:50,000 series, each map covering approximately one day's paddle, is good for details. To order them and the map indexes that tell you which maps you need, contact the *Canada Map Office* (615 Booth St., Ottawa, Ontario K1A 0E9; phone: 613-952-7000). Also, ask for their two useful brochures, *How to Use a Map* and *Maps and Wilderness Canoeing,* free of charge.

ONTARIO'S VAST PROVINCIAL PARKS: The hardwoods in the forests that cover the ridges and hills of this part of the Canadian Shield just across the US border give the area a look and smell all its own, and for many people canoeing here and canoeing in Canada are one and the same. The Algonquin, Killarney, and Quetico provincial parks are immensely popular, yet there is plenty of room to roam even in the busy summer months. Algonquin Provincial Park, which occupies some 2,925 square miles of highlands between the Ottawa River and Lake Huron's Georgian Bay, boasts over a thousand miles of canoe routes and good fishing for lake and brook trout. Some of the notable destinations here include ultra-deep, cliff-ringed Lake Eustache; the breathtaking Natch Rapids on the Petawawa River (towered over by 300-foot-high cliffs); and Hailstorm Creek, where you may see moose browsing. But that's not the end of it. To the northwest, there's Quetico Provincial Park, with 900 miles of its own water routes that are essentially as the Ojibwa Indians and the voyageurs found them; the portages you use (generally speaking, shorter than those in Algonquin) are often the same ones trod by the famous fur trade governor Sir George Simpson, the explorer La Vérendrye, and the itinerant artist Paul Kane. Additional routes are found in 118,600-acre Killarney Provincial Park, near Georgian Bay. Day trips are possible here, but the area is more appropriate for outings of about 3 days or longer, and the scenery is stunning: white quartzite ridges and crystal-clear waters. Outfitting services are in Atikokan and Thunder Bay for trips into Quetico and the lakes to the west and north outside the park; in Dwight, South River, and Whitney for Algonquin Park trips; in Killarney Village for trips into the Killarney park (due to Killarney Park's popularity, visitors are encouraged to make reservations); and, for paddles in the park proper, at the Portage and Opeongo stores (*Algonquin Park,* Ontario P0A 1B0; phone: 705-633-5622 in summer only), which have been equipping canoeists for decades.

Information: For overviews of canoe routes in the three parks, write to *Ministry of Natural Resources, Algonquin Park District Office,* Box 219, Whitney, Ontario K0J 2M0 (phone: 705-633-5572); the *Atikokan District Office,* 108 Saturn Ave., Atikokan, Ontario P0T 1C0 (phone: 807-597-2735) for Quetico details; and, for Killarney information, the *Sudbury District Office,* Box 3500, Station A, Sudbury, Ontario P3A 4S2 (phone: 705-522-7823). For listings of outfitters, contact *Ontario Travel,* Queen's Park, Toronto, Ontario M7A 2E5 (phone: 800-668-2746 or 416-965-4008). Guided trips are offered by *Black Feather Wilderness Adventures,* 1341 Wellington St. W., Ottawa, Ontario K1Y 3B8 (phone: 613-722-9717) or 40 Wellington St. E., Toronto, M5E 1C7 (phone: 416-861-1555).

NORTHERN ONTARIO: The northern reaches of this 412,582-square-mile province, south of James and Hudson bays, lie in Canadian Shield country. There are literally hundreds of thousands of lakes and as many more streams here, and the huge expanses of cool silent forests, patched here and there with outcroppings of polished rock and scattered with huge glacial boulders, are often impenetrable except by canoe. Many of the waterways are virtually unexplored, and there are areas where you can paddle through clear streams that are seen by only a handful of people in a year. Some 53,000 square miles are drained by the swift-flowing Albany River and its tributaries. Among the province's great wilderness waterways, the Albany was once a major fur trade route between York Factory on Hudson Bay, Lake of the Woods, and Winnipeg. On the upper reaches of the river, which flows through the middle of northern Ontario from its headwaters at Lake St. Joseph, you can still portage the many rapids and falls on wide pathways used by the oversize canoes known as York boats. The pools at the base of the rapids and falls make for some of the river's best fishing. Tributaries include the Kabinakagami, Kenogami, Little Current, Nagagami, and Ogoki rivers. But there are hundreds of routes you can follow. Most canoe trips here are fly-in propositions. Outfitters are located in the areas around Geraldton, Hearst, Longlac, Nakina, Armstrong, and Sioux Lookout.

Information: For a list, contact *Ontario Travel,* Queen's Park, Toronto, Ontario M7A 2E5 (phone: 800-268-3735 or 416-965-4008). *The Ministry of Natural Resources Public Information Centre* (Room 1640, Whitney Block, 99 Wellesley St. W, Queen's Park, Toronto, Ontario M7A 1W3; phone: 416-965-3081) publishes the helpful *Canoe Routes of Ontario* ($9.95), which gives an overview of the principal watersheds and canoeing possibilities. For information about both guided and unguided trips, contact *Wildwaters Nature Tours & Expeditions,* 119 N. Cumberland St., PO Box 2777, Thunder Bay, Ontario P7A 4M3 (phone: 807-345-0111).

RIDEAU CANAL, Kingston to Ottawa, Ontario: This 123-mile-long waterway between Lake Ontario and the Ottawa River was built in the early 19th century as a part of Canada's defense against the US. It now is in use as a recreational waterway, as gradually increasing numbers of boats cruise its waters every summer. Above all, the trip is a pleasant one. You'll go through 45 locks, masterpieces made of hand-hewn stone blocks, all but three of which are still operated by hand. Everyone stops at Jones Falls for the awe-inspiring view of the massive horseshoe dam built more than 150 years ago by the British army under the supervision of Lt. Colonel John By. The lockmasters can tell you about the odd-shaped buildings at some of the lock stations, originally designed as fortified structures, and fill you in on other points of interest in the area. Newboro Lock brings you to the full height of the canal where you begin a gradual descent through the Rideau Lakes. One of Ontario's fine cruising and fishing grounds, with a wealth of tree-tufted islands, it is surrounded by forests, fields, weedy shallows, sleepy little villages and towns, cottages, and marinas. At the canal's northern extremity, the Ottawa Locks, you begin a fascinating 79-foot descent through 8 flight locks to the Ottawa River. Information: *Superintendent* (Rideau Canal, 12 Maple Ave. N., Smiths Falls, Ontario K7A 1Z5; phone: 613-283-5170), and, for rental information, *Ontario Travel* (Queen's Park, Toronto, Ontario M7A 2E5; phone: 800-268-3735 or 416-965-4008).

OTTAWA RIVER, near Pembroke, Ontario: Canada has bigger rivers than this tributary of the St. Lawrence, which was once used by the voyageurs on their journeys between Montreal and Lake Huron, and many of the paddle-snapping rapids that challenged the early Canadians have been tamed by hydro dams. But the island-sprinkled Rocher-Fendu area, 1½ hours west of the nation's capital and just east of Algonquin Park, is a stretch of water so rough you'd want to run it only in a large rubber raft — even when it's at summer levels. When the river is at flood stage during May and June, the towering explosion waves are the equal of wild water anywhere in the world. If you can't sample Canada's whitewater in the West, don't miss the 1- and -2-day trips on the Ottawa. There's also lots of off-water activity. Information: *Wilderness Tours,* Box 89, Beachburg, Ontario K0J 1C0 (phone: 613-646-2241 or 800-267-9166); and *Ottawa Whitewater Rafting,* Box 179, Beachburg, Ontario K0J 1C0 (phone: 613-646-2501 or 800-267-8505).

BRITISH COLUMBIA'S THOMPSON, FRASER, AND CHILCOTIN RIVERS BY

RAFT: Raft tour operators on these three dynamic streams have been turning city slickers into river rats for years. The big, swift-flowing Fraser, the granddaddy of Canadian streams and one of the largest and deepest in all of North America, flows at an average of 150,000 cubic feet per second, as compared to the mighty Colorado, whose maximum flow is regulated at 25,000 cubic feet per second. In some areas, the Fraser dips and dives past the ruins of Gold Rush towns, and sometimes it roars through deep canyons over roller-coaster rapids. Those at Hell's Gate, below Boston Bar, are the most famous, and sometimes have the rafts practically airborne, but the Moran and Bridge River rapids are even wilder. Alone, the Fraser would make an exciting trip.

But most operators in the area offer floats that combine a number of miles on the big streams with sections on one or more of its tributaries and interconnected lakes. One such trip, on the upper reaches of the Fraser system, takes you from turquoise, 54-mile-long Chilko Lake, ringed on all sides with hanging glaciers and mountains, to its outlet and the crystal-clear Chilko River, then down the Chilko and into the Chilcotin, which flows into the Fraser; scenery ranges from arid benchlands to cool forests of evergreens, and in canyons you'll see rare California bighorn sheep, moose, bear, deer, and more. Shorter versions of this trip, which begin on the Chilcotin, about 20 miles upstream from its confluence with the Fraser, just above the lower of the Chilcotin's two best stretches of whitewater, are also available. Or you can sign up for still shorter trips on the powerful Thompson, a more southerly Fraser tributary that flows roughly southward from Savona via Ashcroft to Lytton through an arid sage-brush-and-bunchgrass land dotted by abandoned mines and cabins. The climate here was aptly described by one tripper as "hotter than a devil's esophagus" — but the whitewater spray will keep you cool enough. Information: *Kumsheen Raft Adventures,* PO Box 30, Main St., Lytton, BC V0K 1Z0 (phone: 604-455-2296) and *Canadian River Expeditions,* 1-35 4 W. 16th Ave., Vancouver, BC V6R 3C1 (phone: 604-738-4449).

BOWRON LAKES PROVINCIAL PARK, near Barkerville, British Columbia: Located in the northernmost Cariboos near the Fraser River some 70 miles (112 km) east of Quesnel, this rectangularly shaped, 304,000-acre preserve offers one of Canada's classic wilderness canoe trips — a 73-miler that takes in a chain of mountain lakes and portions of the Bowron and Cariboo rivers, past meadows and through thick forests of spruce, lodgepole pine, western hemlock, western red cedar, and occasional decidu-ous trees, which make the area especially beautiful in the fall. Moose feed in the marshes, beavers build dams in the flats, bears feed on abundant salmon in the streams, and your chances of seeing them all as you paddle silently along are quite good. The clear waters, which flow roughly in a clockwise direction, offer good fishing for Dolly Varden, Kokanee, rainbow trout, whitefish, and lake trout. One of the chief beauties of this trip, however, is that there are only about 5 miles of portaging on the whole circuit, with no single portage longer than 1.5 miles. Early June through October is the season; insects are least prevalent beginning in September. Information: Canoe rentals are available from *Becker's Canoe Outfitters,* Box 129, Wells, BC V0K 2R0 (604-492-2390 or Prince George radio operator N698552, Wells channel); and *Bowron Lake Lodge and Resorts Ltd.,* 672 Walkem St., Quesnel, BC V2J 2J7 (phone: 604-992-2733). Other information: *Ministry of Parks,* 540 Borland St., Williams Lake, BC V2G 1R8 (phone: 604-398-4414).

SOUTH NAHANNI RIVER, southwestern Northwest Territories: One of the continent's finest wild streams takes in incredible vertical-walled canyons 4,000 feet high, karst landforms and caves, high mountains sprinkled with hot springs, and larger-than-life Virginia Falls, which shows a 4-acre face of white spray and foam where it plunges about 300 feet — over twice the distance of Niagara. Unusual plants, luxuri-ant growths of grasses, balsams, poplar, and spruce, and all manner of wildlife — including grizzlies and Dall's sheep, golden eagles and trumpeter swans — can be seen here. The ridge walking that some canoe-trippers undertake for a break from their paddling is some of Canada's finest. And the local history, which concerns aboriginal peoples, mysterious murders, and Gold Rush characters, is as fascinating as the landscape. The 1,840-square-mile Nahanni National Park, through which the river flows, publishes a booklet detailing a 183-mile-long section of the South Nahanni, which takes in waters ranging in difficulty from Grade I to Grade IV, and a 78-mile-long section of the Flat River — mostly Grades I and II, except for the Cascade of the Thirteen Steps, which must be portaged. Outside the park, the South Nahanni flows into the Liard, which joins the Mackenzie at Fort Simpson; both of these former fur-trade arteries can be canoed, and the tributaries of the Liard, particularly the Beaver, Grayling, Rabbit, Red, and Toad rivers, offer fine Dolly Varden and Arctic grayling fishing. If you feel that waters of this level in such a true wilderness are beyond your abilities, sign up for a group raft or canoe trip run by outfitters on shorter sections of the stream.

Information: *Nahanni River Adventures,* PO Box 8368, Station F, Edmonton, Alberta T6H 4W6 (phone: 403-439-1316); *Black Feather Wilderness Adventures,* 1341 Wellington St. SW, Ottawa, Ontario K1Y 3B8 (phone: 613-722-4229); *Nahanni Wilderness Adventures,* Box 879, Nanton, Alberta T0L 1R0 (phone: 403-646-5768); *TravelArctic, Government of the Northwest Territories,* Yellowknife, NWT X1A 2L9 (phone: 403-873-7200); and the *Nahanni National Park,* Postal Bag 300, Fort Simpson, Northwest Territories X0E 0N0 (phone: 403-695-3151).

GREAT BARREN GROUND RIVERS, Northwest Territories: Canada's northernmost region — the more than 1 million square miles of tundra between the forest-clad Mackenzie Valley and Hudson Bay to the east, plus the Northern Yukon and the Ungava Plateau of northern Quebec and Labrador — are so finely veined with hundreds of thousands of miles of rivers and so liberally dotted with lakes that the area is as much water as land. During the brief summer, you have a canoeing ground that is unequaled anywhere else on earth. Much of the land is rolling tundra, upholstered with dwarf shrubs, mosses that are sometimes emerald in hue, plus lichens, grasses, and sedges; here and there, this palette of greens is spattered with the brilliant blues, reds, and yellows of tiny Arctic flowers. Stunted spruce trees huddle together along the shores of some of the rivers. This is all as you would expect. But occasionally, too, you'll spot trees standing tall along the eskers (ridges of gravel deposited by rivers that flowed underneath the glaciers so many ages ago). In the hundred or so miles south of tree line, you'll find forests of widely spaced spruce, pine, and birch. The wildlife is every bit as abundant as you'd expect. Herds of caribou file across the tundra every spring and fall on their way to and from the tree line in a mysterious migration that, even now, no one understands thoroughly. The tens, or even hundreds, of thousands of caribou often seen traveling together constitute the largest herds of wild animals left on earth. Ducks, geese, and wading birds breed in the kettle ponds and lakes. Canada geese, grizzlies, white tundra wolves, loons, musk oxen, falcons, and tundra swans are commonly seen. Because man is unknown to many of the wild creatures here, they are more readily approached than elsewhere. The fishing can be spectacular. In midsummer, you can paddle through the wee hours of the morning, if you're so inclined, by the eerie half-light of the midnight sun. In late summer the northern lights play magically across the sky. All in all, a trip in the Barren Grounds will be one you won't ever forget — whether you take it on the well-known Coppermine; the Thelon, which flows through a wooded game sanctuary; the Thelon's tributary, the short, swift Hanbury; the furious 615-mile-long Back River, which flows into the Arctic; or the Anderson, Burnside, Dubawnt, Horton, or Kazan. All these rivers are described in some detail in materials available from *TravelArctic,* Box 1320, Yellowknife, Northwest Territories X1A 2L9 (phone: 403-873-7200). For information on guided trips — and, because of the remoteness of the Barren Grounds, this is the only way to go if you're not an expert canoeist and outdoorsperson — contact *Canoe Arctic Inc.,* Alex Hall, PO Box 130, Fort Smith, Northwest Territories X0E 0P0 (phone: 403-872-2308).

Mountain Climbing

 Stunning as they are from the ground, Canada's mountains are still more bewitching when seen up close. Vast expanses of glaciers, whitish-blue ice-falls, and breath-stopping peak-behind-peak views are things that some people can't get enough of. And, while well-trained climbers with good judgment and a sound understanding of their own limitations usually encounter little real danger, there is still an element of daring in every meeting with the mountains. That's also part of the attraction.

MOUNTAIN CLIMBING SCHOOLS

Good training at the hands of a competent guide can make the difference between life and death in the mountains when you go on a climb. Good training gives you the solid knowledge of skills and instills a mountain sense and the judgment that will keep you from getting into scrapes to begin with — and help you get out of them safely when they do occur unexpectedly.

But you don't really have to plan to make real climbs to sign up for a course at one of Canada's several mountaineering schools. They can be a lot of fun in their own right, and, believe it or not, even for acrophobics. A good way to see for yourself is to join one of the several day-long beginning rock-climbing courses that are widely available. These will teach you the basics.

If the experience pleases you, you might consider a climbing week where you'll cover more of the same in lecture-practice sessions and on several peak ascents in the area of the base camp. The cost can be $475 or more, including accommodations and meals. Rental equipment is usually extra. Or you could go for 1-day intermediate programs, or 1-day or 2-day snow-and-ice courses aimed at intermediates and beginners with some experience.

The organizations listed below offer a good variety of programs.

ALPINE CLUB OF CANADA, Banff, Alberta: Canada's only national mountaineering club, established in 1906, annually sponsors a variety of week-long mountain-lovers' get-togethers. Training weeks are organized to teach snow-, rock-, and ice-climbing skills to beginners and leadership skills to those with experience. General mountaineering camps, set up in areas that offer a variety of exceptional mountaineering opportunities, give you the chance to go out on daily climbs or form your own climbing parties with kindred spirits. At family camps, parents take turns organizing their own excursions out of the base and squiring each other's youngsters on hikes or scrambles. Venues for all *Alpine Club of Canada* programs change from year to year. Information: *Alpine Club of Canada,* Box 1026, Banff, Alberta T0L 0C0 (phone: 403-762-4481).

BANFF ALPINE GUIDES SCHOOL OF MOUNTAINEERING, Banff, Alberta: Between May and September, a group of certified professional mountain guides offer a huge variety of rock and ice climbing schools and private guided climbs. Information: *Banff Alpine Guides School of Mountaineering,* Box 1025, Banff, Alberta T0L 0C0 (phone: 403-762-2791).

FEDERATION OF MOUNTAIN CLUBS, Vancouver, British Columbia: This year-round school offers weekend to 6-day courses for beginners, intermediates, and advanced climbers in hiking, climbing, and back-country travel. Information: *Federation* *of Mountain Clubs,* Nos. 336-1367 W. Broadway, Vancouver, BC V6H 4A9 (phone: 604-737-3053).

CANADIAN SCHOOL OF MOUNTAINEERING, Canmore, Alberta: The *CSM* recently celebrated its 18th year in operation. Chief Guide Ottmar Setzer, is also part-time proprietor of the *Haus Alpenrose Lodge* (phone: 403-678-4134), which bills itself as "the first no-smoking lodge in the Rockies," and is where most students are housed. Summer courses include: rock climbing weeks or weekends, snow and ice climbing, mountain discovery weeks, Rockies challenge weeks, and special mountaineering weeks. Winter courses include a winter challenge week and waterfall ice-climbing weekend, among others. Information: *Canadian School of Mountaineering,* 629 9th St., PO Box 723, Canmore, Alberta T0L 0M0 (phone: 403-678-4134).

SOUTHERN ALBERTA HOSTELLING ASSOCIATION, Calgary, Alberta: Among the varied outdoor programs presented in collaboration with area operators, the *SAHA* offers mountaineering, hiking, and trekking with the University of Calgary's Campus Recreation Department. Information: *Southern Alberta Hostelling Association,* Suite 203, 1414 Kensington Rd. NW, Calgary, Alberta T2N 3P9 (phone: 403-283-5551).

JASPER CLIMBING SCHOOL AND GUIDE SERVICE, Jasper, Alberta: Hans Schwarz, the local authority on Mt. Robson, shares his knowledge and experience at his climbing school for summer and winter courses. Information: *Jasper Climbing School,* Box 452, Jasper, Alberta T0E 1E0 (phone: 403-852-3964).

CANADA'S CLASSIC CLIMBING

You'll begin to grasp the incredible scope and variety of the climbing available here when you flip through the pages of the climbing guides published by the *Alpine Club of Canada.* The books are thick, the details multitudinous, the descriptions concise, and the type small. The possibilities are mind-boggling.

Canada's loftiest peak, 19,850-foot Mt. Logan, and the surrounding St. Elias Mountains — within Kluane National Park — generally fall into the category of expedition climbs.

But the sheer number of mountains in Canada also guarantees the general mountaineer an abundance of peaks to assail — substantial peaks with many routes to the top; peaks which have had a special allure from Canada's earliest days. While the kind of extremely difficult north face routes that challenge very experienced climbers can be found, the summits of these giants are also accessible by easier routes that vary in difficulty from perhaps a scenic route that is ultimately little more than a walk involving some scrambling to the standard routes that pose satisfying mountaineering challenges.

Novice climbers always should go out with a more experienced person or a registered guide. Otherwise, you can discuss routes with climbers from a local club. There are no age limits at hostels; everyone is welcome. The *Canadian Hostelling Association* (Northern Alberta District, 10926 88th Ave., Edmonton, Alberta T6G 0Z1; phone: 403-439-3089), and the *Southern Alberta Hostelling Association* (Suite 203, 1414 Kensington Rd. NW, Calgary, Alberta T2N 3P9; phone: 403-283-5551), can be very helpful. They maintain a number of hostels just off the Icefields Parkway within walking distance of the starting points for several of the great climbs. (For information on informally organized outdoor trips and mountaineering resources in the southern Alberta area, contact the *Calgary Area Outdoor Council* (1111 Memorial Drive NW, Calgary, Alberta T2N 3E4; phone: 403-270-2262). The council will forward queries to an organization that can offer assistance.

MT. TEMPLE, MT. VICTORIA, AND MT. LEFROY, next to Lake Louise, Alberta: Ascents of these three 11,000-foot-plus peaks — the ones you see in standard postcards of Lake Louise — mean a long climb that most mountaineers prefer to make in 2 days. First climbed in 1897, Lefroy's summit is accessible via several routes. The Mouse Trap Route to Abbot's Pass (where you camp overnight in a stone structure that accommodates 30 and was built by Swiss guides in 1922; you'll cross Abbot's Pass on both the Victoria and Lefroy climbs), a snow route known for its changing glaciers, is moderately difficult but fairly straightforward. Behind the hut, there is a 2½-mile (4-km) traverse to the north peak of Mt. Victoria. The three peaks (southern, center, and northern) of Mt. Victoria make a spectacular ridge, popular for climbing and photographing. Temple, one of the bigger of the Rockies' 11,000-foot peaks, is most frequently climbed by the moderately demanding route up its southwest face from Sentinal Pass. Its particular challenges arise from the regularity with which you encounter deceptively dangerous snow patches. When you make it to the top, and if the weather holds, you see an unforgettable view of Paradise Valley below and the scattering of tiny lakes surrounded by wave after wave of mountains. Consult *Alpine Club of Canada,* (PO Box 1026, Banff, Alberta T0L 0C0) publications for detailed information. Information: *Banff National Park,* Box 900, Banff, Alberta T0L 0C0 (phone: 403-762-3324).

MT. ROBSON, near Jasper, Alberta: Located in eastern British Columbia alongside the Alberta border in Mt. Robson Provincial Park, this 12,972-foot giant, the highest in the Canadian Rockies, is so big that it creates its own weather. Clouds so often hang over Robson when the skies are clear for miles around that some locals quip they've never yet seen the summit. The climb would be difficult for that reason alone, but there are other problems. There's the huge difference in altitude between the 2,800-foot base and the summit, so most climbs last from 3 to 10 days. The standard route, up the south face, is heavily glaciated and leads over a series of ledges; here the climber will encounter many séracs and crevasses in unstable icefalls, unique frosted cornice formations called the Gargoyles, and ice and snow that can be very dangerous. Most of the mountain is raked by avalanches. To climb Robson by any route is a major mountaineering challenge — even experienced climbers frequently turn back. There is no easy way to the top, nor local certified guides for this mountain — Banff is the nearest place to hire one — however, Hans Schwarz of Jasper is a recognized authority on the mountain's idiosyncrasies. Information: *Jasper Climbing School and Guide Service,* Hans Schwarz, Box 452, 806 Connaught Dr., Jasper, Alberta T0E 1E0 (phone: 403-852-3964); *Mt. Robson Provincial Park,* PO Box 579, Valemount, BC V0E 2Z0 (phone: 604-566-4325).

MT. EDITH CAVELL, near Jasper, Alberta: The summit of this namesake of a British nurse, which has been famous since the early days of exploration, gives you views over the Tonquin Valley that are especially fine because, at 11,033 feet, the peak is by far the highest in the Jasper townsite vicinity. Getting there is within the skills of most competent mountaineers in good shape, weather permitting. The western slopes, for instance, are technically easy, requiring little more than scrambling with an ice axe, and perhaps crampons. The East Ridge, known for the exposed position it often puts you in, with sheer drop-offs on either side, is a mixed snow-and-ice route, not technically difficult but requiring rock, snow, and ice work in quickly changing sequences, so that you can count on spending 16 to 18 hours round-trip. Expert mountaineers tackle several routes on the North Face. Information: *Jasper National Park,* PO Box 10, Jasper, Alberta T0E 1E0 (phone: 403-852-6161).

COLUMBIA ICEFIELD, near Jasper, Alberta: Shaped somewhat like a saucer and rimmed with some of the highest peaks in the Rockies, this tremendous, 120-square-mile accumulation of ice lying astride the Continental Divide in Jasper and Banff National Parks sends its melt water to three oceans — the Arctic, 765 miles (1,224 km) away via the Athabasca, the Slave, and the Mackenzie rivers; the Atlantic, by way of the Saskatchewan River, Lake Winnipeg, and Hudson Bay; and the Pacific, via the Columbia River through British Columbia and Washington State. The 11,340-foot Snow Dome, a bland-looking peak where all these river systems originate, is, in specialists' terms, the hydrographical apex of the continent. But the Snow Dome takes a back seat, in the popular mountaineering imagination, to a number of other peaks in the area, among them 12,294-foot Mt. Columbia, the highest in Alberta, and Mt. Athabasca. The latter gets special attention because, though only 11,452 feet high, it is so accessible from the Icefields Parkway, and probably, too, because the North Glacier route, the standard route to the summit, is fairly straightforward for someone experienced in glacier travel and snow climbing. The Silverhorn Route is also particularly pleasant and only moderately difficult. A score of other popular peaks also offer fine challenges. Information: *Jasper National Park,* PO Box 10, Jasper, Alberta T0E 1E0 (phone: 403-852-6161).

AUYUITTUQ NATIONAL PARK, Baffin Island, Northwest Territories: Baffin Island, above Hudson Bay, is home to some of the most unusual and demanding of Canada's climbs, and big-wall climbers from Yosemite, Europe, and Japan, come here to test themselves on the extremely difficult rock walls and just to get away from it all. In most cases, it's not that the peaks are so technically tough (although a recent American expedition rated the direct west face of Mt. Thor Peak 5.10 A4 Grade 7). Rather, climbing here poses problems simply because of the isolation. The park's outstanding features are Mt. Ascard, with its beautiful peak and the spiky 7,000-foot Penny Icecap that covers a 2,200-square-mile area. Information: *Superintendent, Auyuittuq National Park,* Pangnirtung, Northwest Territories X0A 0R0 (phone: 819-473-8962).

Hiking and Backpacking

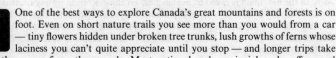

One of the best ways to explore Canada's great mountains and forests is on foot. Even on short nature trails you see more than you would from a car — tiny flowers hidden under broken tree trunks, lush growths of ferns whose laciness you can't quite appreciate until you stop — and longer trips take you farther away from the crowds. Most national and provincial parks offer good opportunities for hiking; some have really extensive trail systems. In addition, Canada offers a number of scenic long-distance trails. Consult Elliot Katz's *Complete Guide to Backpacking in Canada* for a comprehensive look at what's available (about $11 from Doubleday Canada, 105 Bond St., Toronto, Ontario M5B 1Y3; phone: 416-340-0779). Here's a sampling of some of the nation's hiking hot spots, from west to east:

BANFF NATIONAL PARK, Banff, Alberta: Some 950 miles of trails cut through this 2,500-square-mile preserve and take you through forests of spruce and pine, over high alpine meadows filled with delicate colored flowers, and under high peaks ribboned with waterfalls. Some lead to areas of scenic beauty known around the world — Lake Louise, Skoki Valley, Sunshine Meadows, Egypt Lake, and Moraine Lake and the Valley of the Ten Peaks. Information: *Banff National Park,* Box 900, Banff, Alberta T0L 0C0 (phone: 403-762-3324). Also see *The Canadian Rockies Trail Guide* (about $13 plus $5 postage and handling, from the *Book and Art Den,* PO Box 1420, Banff, Alberta T0L 0C0 (phone: 403-762-3919).

WATERTON LAKES NATIONAL PARK, near Cardston, Alberta: The 108 miles of trails in this 204-square-mile preserve explore the prairies-to-mountains transitional country that gives the area its distinctive character. Most of the trails can be hiked in a day, but backcountry camps are available. There are three main trail systems, one radiating from the town of Waterton Park, one from the Akamina Highway and Cameron Lake, and one from the Red Rock Canyon area. Information: *Waterton Lakes National Park,* Waterton Park, Alberta T0K 2M0 (phone: 403-859-2224). Also see *National Parks.*

JASPER NATIONAL PARK, Jasper, Alberta: With some 4,200 square miles, and a network of over 600 miles of trails, the hiking possibilities here make your head spin. Some of the more famous take in Brazeau Lake, Jonas Pass, and Amethyst Lake in the Tonquin Valley, with its towering ramparts. The three national parks — Banff, Kootenay, and Yoho — double the available terrain. Information: *Jasper National Park,* Box 10, Jasper, Alberta T0E 1E0 (phone: 403-852-6161); and *Information Services,* Parks Canada, Western Region, Room 522, 220 4th Ave. SE, P.O. Box 2989, Station M, Calgary, Alberta T2P 3H8 (phone: 403-292-4440).

TWEEDSMUIR PROVINCIAL PARK, near Bella Coola, British Columbia: This 2.4-million-acre wilderness is British Columbia's largest provincial park. The South Park lies some 229 miles (369 km) by gravel road from the nearest town of any size. Consequently, much of the south area of the park has changed little since the area's first explorations, over a century and a half ago, affected the landscape. For the hiker, this means that self-sufficiency is paramount. You will not find a dense network of trails like those of the Alberta national parks, but there is plenty of space for wilderness travel. Nearly every North American landform is to be found somewhere within the park boundaries — glaciers and snowfields, lakes and rivers, plains and forest-clad hills. With its large lake system, the northern area is a marine park, accessible only by boat, helicopter, or floating plane. The brightly tinted peaks of the Rainbow Mountains, in the east central part of the park, are especially striking. Licensed guides are available — hiring one is advisable unless you're a very experienced outdoorsperson. Information: *Park Supervisors, South Tweedsmuir Provincial Park,* Box 126, Bella Coola, BC V0T 1C0 (radio phone: Williams Lake Radio Operator Tweedsmuir Park N692224) or *Visitor Services Coordinator Skeena District,* Bag 5000, Smithers, BC V0J 2N0 (phone: 604-847-7565).

CHILKOOT TRAIL, from Dyea, Alaska, to Bennett, British Columbia: From the winter of 1897 until the fall of 1898, some 30,000 men and women trekked the 33 often-steep and usually rocky miles between these two towns: The promise of gold lured them on. Today's motivations seldom grip hikers with the same force, but the trip remains more magical than most. In addition to the sweeping views of rocky peaks and mirror-still lakes, the trail also turns up traces of the Gold Rush days. The hike is a demanding one, so hikers should come well prepared. The *White Pass & Yukon Railway,* with service between Skagway and Fraser, BC, where bus transportation is available to the trail's end at Bennett, allows hikers to use it to return to their starting point. From May to September, bus service is also available between Whitehorse and Skagway. Information: *Klondike Gold Rush National Historical Park,* PO Box 517, Skagway, AK 99840 (907-983-2921), or *Superintendent, Yukon National Historic Sites,* Canadian Parks Service, Box 5540, Whitehorse, Yukon Y1A 5H4 (phone: 403-668-2116).

YOHO NATIONAL PARK, Field, British Columbia: In the heart of the Rockies, this park is famous for its towering peaks, alpine valleys, thundering waterfalls, and turbulent streams. A network of trails, some 250 miles of them, takes you into the high country, where the views go on forever, and through the valleys, threaded with glacial streams. Backcountry lodges within the park boundaries can be incorporated into your walks. Information: *Superintendent, Yoho National Park,* PO Box 99, Field, BC V0A 1G0 (phone: 604-343-6324).

MT. ASSINIBOINE PROVINCIAL PARK, near Invermere, British Columbia: Matterhornlike 11,870-foot Mt. Assiniboine dominates the scenery in this fine 96,350-acre expanse of jagged peaks and shining lakes, blue-white glaciers, and wildflower-dotted meadows. Although the preserve is one of the Rockies' loveliest, it's also among the wildest. You can get there only on foot or, by permission, on horseback, or by helicopter from Banff. Although supplies and equipment are not available, there is a concessionaire-operated resort, *Mount Assiniboine Lodge,* and four alpine shelters known as the *Naiset Cabins.* Reservations are required at the lodge (Box 1527, Canmore, Alberta T0L 0M0; phone: 403-678-2883). The wilderness experience you can have here ranks among Canada's finest. Banff and Kootenay national parks adjoin Assiniboine. Information: *Ministry of Parks, Southern Interior Region,* 101-1050 W. Columbia St., Kamloops, BC V2C 1L4 (phone: 604-828-4501).

MANNING PROVINCIAL PARK, Manning Park, British Columbia: This 176,000-acre (71,400-hectare) preserve, situated some 140 miles (225 km) east of Vancouver just north of the international border, is somewhat more developed than many BC parks. Several self-guiding nature trails, many guided walks, and a variety of day hikes are available in the area. The park itself is the southern terminus of the Canadian leg of the Pacific Crest Trail, which ends in Mexico. Information: *Ministry of Parks,* 1610 Indian River Dr., North Vancouver, BC V7G 1L3 (phone: 604-929-1291).

KOKANEE GLACIER PROVINCIAL PARK, near Nelson, British Columbia: Preserving some 158,000 acres of rugged Selkirk Mountains country, and accessible only by gravel road and by trail, this park's craggy peaks, canyons, glaciers, and jewellike tarns are well worth the effort it takes to reach them. The main trail, from Gibson Lake to Joker Mill, winds through some of the most spectacular countryside past five crystal-clear lakes. Another trail, beginning at the Slocan Chief hut, takes you up to 9,000 feet and the Kokanee Glacier. This is not the wildest of BC's parks, but some degree of expertise is required to handle the terrain, even in summer. Information: *Parks and Outdoor Recreation Division,* 101-1050 W. Columbia St., Kamloops, BC V2C 1L4 (phone: 604-828-4501).

GLACIER NATIONAL PARK, near Rogers Pass, British Columbia: Most trails here begin at or near the Trans-Canada Highway, which bisects the park, and then climb steeply into jagged mountains covered with lovely forests of conifers below and spectacular glaciers and snowfields above. Its immensity overwhelms you. Trails lead you near the 10-square-mile Illecillewaet Icefield, one of the park's most awe-inspiring, and to Mt. Abbott, Mt. Sir Donald, and the Asulkan Glacier. Most are short enough for a day's hike, but overnight trips are also possible. A visit to the Rogers Pass Information Centre is well worth a break in the day's hiking. Here, exhibits and movies are offered about the world's largest active avalanche control program, or about the park and people. Park staff members are on hand to help plan hikes and answer questions. Information: *Glacier National Park,* PO Box 350, Revelstoke, BC V0E 2S0 (phone: 604-837-5155).

WEST COAST TRAIL, PACIFIC RIM NATIONAL PARK, Vancouver Island, British Columbia: The western shore of this island is rocky and cliff-bound, and it often happened in days gone by that storms drove ships onto the rocks and that the sailors who survived later died because they couldn't get up the cliffs. Indeed, the area was once known as the Graveyard of the Pacific. The 48-mile-long West Coast Trail, carved out as an escape hatch, has become one of the nation's most popular hiking trails. Now a part of Pacific Rim National Park, it is also one of the most spectacular for the fine views it gives of foamy surf and sky. The northern terminus is at Bamfield, on Pachena Bay; the southern trailhead is in Port Renfrew. Information: *West Coast Trail Information Centres,* open mid-May through September (phone: at Pachena Bay 604-728-3234, or at Port Renfrew 604-647-5434); or *Pacific Rim National Park,* PO Box 280, Ucluelet, BC V0R 3A0 (phone: 604-726-7721).

RIDING MOUNTAIN NATIONAL PARK, Wasagaming, Manitoba: Part of the Manitoba Escarpment, Riding Mountain is actually a plateau rising up from the surrounding prairie, with undulating hills, meadows, lakes, and streams accessible via over 30 hiking trails in summer and over 20 cross-country ski trails in winter. Information: *Superintendent, Riding Mountain National Park,* Wasagaming, Manitoba R0J 2H0 (phone: 204-848-2811).

DOBSON TRAIL, near Moncton, New Brunswick: Meandering for 37 miles from Riverview into Fundy National Park, this is one of the more beautiful of Canada's long trails because of the primitive Albert County woods-and-valleys landscape it covers. In the park, the trail becomes the Cross Fundy Hiking Trail and gives you access to other trails that lead to the bold, irregular coastline and along quick-flowing streams. The Dobson Trail, marked with blue blazes, is recommended only for experienced hikers. Information: *Outdoor Enthusiasts,* PO Box 254, Moncton, NB E1C AK9 (phone: 506-855-5089).

BRUCE TRAIL, near Hamilton, Ontario: This 430-mile hiking trail winds over the scenic Niagara Escarpment from Queenston on the Niagara River to the village of Tobermory on the tip of the Bruce Peninsula between Lake Huron and Georgian Bay. A complete guide and maps are available. Information: *Bruce Trail Association,* Box 857, Hamilton, Ontario L8N 3N9 (phone: 416-529-6821 or 416-529-6823).

ALGONQUIN PROVINCIAL PARK, near Huntsville, Ontario: This immense preserve has long been known for its extensive canoeing. But the Ministry of Natural Resources, which is responsible for the area's administration, has begun cutting trails into the dense forests of hardwoods and conifers that cover the Canadian Shield in the area. Two of these are the Western Uplands Backpacking Trail, made up of three loops of 19, 33, and 42 miles; and the Highland Backpacking Trail, whose two loops are 11 and 22 miles long. Some trails skirt the edges of the lakes, some meander around boggy areas, and some climb ridges. The scenery is always lovely, and a permit system preserves the isolated feeling. Information: *Algonquin Park District Office,* Ministry of Natural Resources, Box 219, Whitney, Ontario K0J 2M0 (phone: 705-633-5572).

RIDEAU TRAIL, at Kingston, Ontario: A 235-mile-long system that follows trails and secondary roads on its meandering way from the shores of Lake Ontario, through marshes, forests, and fields, to Chaudière Falls in Ottawa, to the north. The scenery varies from serene to spectacular, and historic sites and wildlife are widely in evidence. Come prepared for mosquitoes, which you may find in the swampy areas in late spring and early summer. For about $10 plus $2 postage, you can buy a copy of the new *Rideau Trail Guidebook.* Information: *Rideau Trail Association,* Box 15, Kingston, Ontario K7L 4V6 (phone: 613-545-0823).

GATINEAU PARK, near Hull, Quebec: This preserve's 88,000 acres are crowded between the Gatineau and Ottawa rivers, not far from Ottawa, a region well known for its hills. They rise as high as 1,367 feet from the valleys, which are at about 600 feet, and most are crisscrossed with hiking trails — more than 120 miles of them. Meandering to waterfalls and beaver ponds, to historic ruined buildings and overlooks of the valleys to the south, some trails loop back to Lac Philippe, where you'll find beaches, picnic grounds, a campground, and semi-wilderness campsites. Zero-impact canoe-camping is possible at Lac La Pêche. Information: *Gatineau Park Division, National Capital Commission,* 161 Laurier Ave. W., Ottawa, Ontario K1P 6J6 (phone: 613-827-2020).

Guided trips provide good opportunities for acquiring camping skills if you don't already have them. For information on organizations offering camping trips in Canada, see *Camping and RVs, Hiking and Biking,* GETTING READY TO GO.

Hunting

Canada's untracked wilderness is just about any hunter's dream. Modern man can return to a more primitive age to stalk big game, such as elk, moose, caribou, and bear, or smaller prey, like grouse, partridge, geese, and ducks. Canadians view their wildlife as a precious natural resource. Game species are professionally managed to ensure their future well-being, and government regula-

tions strictly control hunting seasons. Each province has its own licensing requirements, and the federal government restricts the hunting of migratory birds (a permit
can be obtained from any post office for about $8.50, $42.50 for non-residents; a
mandatory habitat stamp for about $5.50). It is absolutely essential that the hunter
contact the province and/or the Ministry of Natural Resources to obtain hunting
regulations for specific areas. Hunting regulations and license requirements vary from
province to province, and they can be quite complicated.

In general, hunting is an autumn activity, when game populations are at their peak.
(Sunday hunting is prohibited in many areas.) Bag limits for small game and birds are
generous across the country, but the numbers of larger game are strictly limited.
Non-resident hunters have no problem bringing rifles, shotguns, and hunting dogs into
Canada, provided they observe the regulations outlined in *Travel Information,* available from the provinces, Ministry of Natural Resources, or Canadian Customs (for
addresses, see *Tourist Information,* GETTING READY TO GO).

EAST

Hunting in eastern Canada centers around upland game birds, such as partridge,
grouse, and woodcock, but some areas are also outstanding for moose, caribou, whitetail deer, and black bear. Hunters from all over the world are drawn to the picturesque province of New Brunswick in pursuit of woodcock. These long-billed game birds are
especially common in Kent, Charlotte, Albert, Westmorland, Kings, Queens, York,
Victoria, and Northumberland counties; guides with good dogs are available.

NEW BRUNSWICK: Charlotte County (which includes Grand Manan Island) as
well as Victoria, Kings, and Queens counties are some of the best spots in eastern
Canada to hunt whitetail deer. While the length of the deer season varies from area
to area (either 3 or 4 weeks), it generally opens in late October or early November.
Non-resident hunters must be accompanied by a guide. Information: *Fish and Wildlife
Branch,* PO Box 6000, Fredericton, NB E3B 5H1 (phone: 506-453-2440).

CHAPLEAU AREA, in Chapleau, Ontario: This expanse of rugged, lake-dotted,
boreal forest, is one of the top hunting spots in eastern Canada. Black bear hunting is
excellent in both the spring and fall, and hunting for moose and small game is best in
the fall. Several lodges and outfitters in the area handle fly-in trips, accommodations,
and equipment rentals. There are also six Ontario provincial parks, four with developed
campsites and two waterway parks. The Town of Chapleau is the gateway to the
Chapleau Crown Game Preserve, the largest wildlife preserve in the world. Information: *Ministry of Natural Resources,* 190 Cherry St., Chapleau, Ontario P0M 1K0
(phone: 705-864-1710).

PELEE ISLAND, in Lake Erie, Ontario: Among sportsmen who prize pheasants
above all other game birds, this island is justly famous. The pheasant season is split into
two periods of two days each during the fall. An additional season is scheduled during
winter. Pelee Island takes on an almost holiday-like atmosphere as all the islanders
welcome visiting hunters. There are some guides with hunting dogs on the island, but
hunters are advised to bring their own if possible. Information: *Township Clerk-Trea-
surer,* Township of Pelee, Pelee Island, Ontario N0R 1M0 (phone: 519-724-2931); and
the *Chatham District Office,* Ministry of Natural Resources, Box 1168, Chatham,
Ontario N7M 5L8 (phone: 519-354-7340).

JAMES AND HUDSON BAY, Moosonee, Ontario: Snow geese, blue geese, and
Canada geese breed and rest in huge numbers along the rugged, unspoiled western
shores of James and Hudson Bay. In September and early October during migration,
when geese and ducks mass along the coastal flats to feed, the hunting is superb. Cree
goose hunting camps operate during this peak season and have cabins and canoes.
Based in these comfortable spots, hunters go out with Cree Indian guides. For details

about hunting here, contact the *Moosonee District Office,* Ministry of Natural Resources, PO Box 190, Moosonee, Ontario P0L 1Y0 (phone: 705-336-2987).

ILE AUX GRUES (Crane Island), near Quebec City, Quebec: This split of grass and mud in the St. Lawrence River is one of the best hunting grounds for water fowl in eastern Canada. When greater snow geese by the thousands stop over on the tide flats during their southward migration in October, hunting conditions are ideal. The area is also rich in black ducks, teal, and snipe. *Quebec Fishing and Hunting Packages,* a government publication, provides all the information needed on services offered in the region. See phone numbers listed below. Information: *Tourism Quebec,* PO Box 22,000, Quebec City, Quebec G1K 7X2 (phone: 514-873-2015 in Montreal or 800-873-2015 elsewhere). Questions of a more technical nature can be directed to the *Recreation, Hunting and Fishing Department,* Ministère du Loisir de la Chasse et de la Pêche, 150 Boul. St.-Cyrille E., Quebec City, Quebec G1R 4Y3 (phone: 418-643-3127).

UNGAVA, near Kuujjuaq (formerly Fort Chimo), Quebec: The rolling, tundra-covered hill country south of Ungava Bay is the best caribou area in Canada, thanks to careful management that has allowed the herds to grow to some 700,000 strong. As a result, the number of available hunting licenses has been increased (but there's a two-caribou-per-license limit), and several Inuit from Kuujjuaq have started outfitting hunters. An adult bull caribou makes a magnificent trophy, and a hunt with the Inuit is a supreme outdoor adventure. Hunting season is August 1 through October 31, but most lodges close by the end of September. Information: *Tourism Quebec,* PO Box 20,000, Quebec City, Quebec G1K 7X2 (phone: 514-873-2015 in Montreal or 800-363-7777 elsewhere); *Quebec Inuit and Indian Outfitters,* Louis Brousseau, Marketing Director, 2525 Watt St., Local 12, Ste.-Foy, Quebec G1P 3T2; phone: 418-659-6009).

WEST

Western Canada is stocked with an unparalleled variety of game. The mountains of Alberta, British Columbia, the Yukon, and the Northwest Territories are internationally famous for their big-game hunting, while the prairies of Manitoba and Saskatchewan have abundant waterfowl and upland game, such as grouse, pheasant, Hungarian partridge, and snipe.

WILLMORE WILDERNESS, north of Jasper National Park, Alberta: This vast Rocky Mountain wilderness is one of the largest strongholds of trophy bighorn sheep on the continent. What makes a mountain hunt here such an unforgettable experience is that, because no motorized transport is allowed in the area, you either hike in or trek in on horseback, with a string of pack horses in tow, much like the country's earliest explorers. The park is home to an abundance of elk, mountain goats, deer, and moose. Information: *Alberta Forest Service* (phone: 403-427-3582). For information on hunting and wildlife, contact *Alberta Fish and Wildlife Division* (phone: 403-427-6757). Both departments can be contacted by mail at Main Floor, North Tower, Petroleum Plaza, 9945-108 St., Edmonton, Alberta T5K 2G6.

SPATSIZI PLATEAU, near Kinaskan, British Columbia: Together with the Level Mountain Range, located west of Dease Lake, this area just east of the Stewart Cassiar Highway, a provincial park that allows hunting within its boundaries (though by special permit only) offers some of the province's best hunting for mountain goat and caribou. The season starts early to mid-August and runs through mid-October, but the best time to hunt is from mid-September on, after the animals have acquired their thick winter coats. *Spatsizi,* an Indian term meaning red goats, refers to the color the normally white goats' fur takes on when they roll around in the area's red volcanic dust to protect themselves from insects. Information: *Ministry of Environment and Parks,* Fish and Wildlife Branch, Information Services, 780 Blanshard St., Victoria, BC V8V 1X5 (phone: 604-387-9731).

QUEEN CHARLOTTE ISLANDS, off the coast of British Columbia: The black-tail deer are abundant on these islands because they have no natural predators here, except for the occasional black bear. In an effort to control the population, the British Columbia Fish and Wildlife Branch allows hunters to bag ten deer per year with a possession limit of three. Information: *Ministry of Environment,* Fish and Wildlife Branch, Information Services, 780 Blanshard St., Victoria, BC V8V 1X5 (phone: 604-387-9731).

INTERLAKE REGION, between Lake Manitoba and Lake Winnipeg, Manitoba: Sharp-tailed and ruffed grouse have always been a primary hunting attraction in this area, and they are still. In good years, the sharp-tailed grouse are unbelievably abundant, especially during peak season in late September and through October. (The town of Ashern, so enamored of the sharp-tailed grouse that it has erected a 17-foot, 3,800-pound statue of the creature alongside Provincial Highway 6, annually stages its celebrated International One-Box Sharp-tail Hunt, in which teams of selected VIP guests race to bag the largest number of birds with one box of shells.) In 1989, the population of ruffed grouse peaked. Lately, however, because of a resoundingly successful habitat management program, the Interlake Region has become one of the nation's best spots for goose hunting. An estimated 1 million snow geese and 1.4 million Canada geese migrate through Manitoba, and the two lakes act as a funnel, so that most of the birds stop to feed and rest in the area; around Grant's Lake and Oak Hammock Marsh, within sight of the Winnipeg skyline, several hundred thousand birds can be seen at any given time. As a result of the healthy population, bag limits are liberal — much to the delight of hunters from more restrictive, more southerly areas. Information: *Department of Natural Resources,* 1495 St. James St., Box 22, Winnipeg, Manitoba R3H 0W9 (phone: 204-945-6784).

POTHOLE COUNTRY, from Minnedosa to the Assiniboine River, Manitoba: Thanks to an abundance of sloughs, potholes, and other wetlands, this area has been a prime place for duck hunting; however, the number of mallard and pintails has declined annually, and hunting is good only in islolated spots. A habitat management program is being introduced, so with hope the birds' population will multiply in the near future. Goose hunting is excellent throughout much of southern Manitoba. The province's snow goose and Canada goose populations are healthy and expanding. Roughly 1 million snow geese and 1 million Canada geese wing their way through southern Manitoba each fall. Information: *Department of Natural Resources,* 1495 St. James St., Box 22, Winnipeg, Manitoba R3H 0W9 (phone: 204-945-6784).

MACKENZIE MOUNTAINS, near Norman Wells, Northwest Territories: Sheep still die of old age without ever having seen a human being in the rugged Mackenzies — probably among the best Dall's sheep ranges on the continent — and rams with full-curl horns measuring 35 to 38 inches are common, while trophies with 40- to 42-inch horns are bagged in season, between July 15 and October 31. The snow white Dall's ram has to be the most regal trophy a hunter can take. Information: *TravelArctic,* Government of the Northwest Territories, Yellowknife, NWT X1A 2L9; or call the *Arctic Hotline* at 1-800-661-0788.

Ice Skating and Hockey

 Canadian winters and ice go together. From December until May, ponds, lakes, rivers, and streams turn into natural rinks. The tradition of bundled-up businessmen skating to their offices originated with the French traders who skated over the frozen waterways from one trading post to another with their goods. Then, inspired by the ingenuity of the French, the Iroquois strapped bones to their feet and joined the sport, and English soldiers in turn began holding competitions for the most creative and intricate patterns cut into ice. Indoor rinks first appeared in Quebec City and Montreal in the 1880s.

Today, skating is enormously popular all over the country. Hockey tends to dominate the scene, and aspiring professionals begin early: There are leagues for tykes aged 7 and 8, atoms aged 9 and 10, peewees aged 11 and 12, bantams aged 13 and 14, midgets aged 15 and 16, juveniles aged 17 to 19, juniors aged 15 to 20, intermediates over 20, and seniors over 21. (Players are delegated to the last four categories on the basis of their ability.) In the last 15 years, the sport of ringette — a fast team sport played by girls with bladeless sticks and a rubber ring — has taken off; there are some 40,000 players in Ontario, the sport's home province, and in a pair of recent exhibition games played against boys' hockey teams, the girls came out ahead. Figure skating is also booming. The Canadian Figure Skating Association has 157,000 members, and some 1,400 clubs based in municipalities nationwide stage seminars for skaters and interclub competitions, sending the winners on to sectional, divisional, national, and international contests. A top Canadian skater in training usually winters in Toronto and summers in the Rockies or England, buying private ice time (usually to the tune of $15,000 annually).

You'll find fine recreational skating in just about every province, in literally hundreds of rinks. But one of the joys of skating in Canada is the preponderance of lakes and rivers that freeze over and the fact that, because of the sport's popularity, warming huts and hot sandwich stands pop up here and there along the shores.

CANADA'S UNIQUE OPEN-AIR SKATING

BANFF SPRINGS HOTEL, Banff, Alberta: Like many big mountain resort hotels, this one provides its guests with an ice-skating facility. But this is a special hotel with a very special setting, and though the rink isn't of Olympic caliber, it's worth taking a few spins just to enjoy the grand scenery: Jagged, snow-capped peaks rising steeply at the edge of the mile-wide Bow River Valley, where the hotel sits. And after a respectable few minutes of invigorating exercise, reward yourself by heading over to the hotel's winterized golf clubhouse, a Tudoresque mini-château, and sit by one of those enormous fieldstone fireplaces and warm up over a hot buttered rum or a bowl of soup. Information: *Banff Springs Hotel,* PO Box 960, Banff, Alberta T0L 0C0 (phone: 403-762-2211). Also see *Downhill Skiing, Special Havens,* and *Calgary to Banff and Jasper National Parks,* DIRECTIONS.

VANCOUVER, British Columbia: The climate here is so delightful that pleasure boaters can explore the islands offshore all winter long; when snow falls, it never stays around very long. So you might not expect to find much of an outdoor ice-skating scene here. But every November, the city fathers install a rink in the big bubble-covered sunken plaza at the Provincial Courthouse Complex downtown. From then until March, everybody ice skates. Office workers twirl and whirl on their lunch hours and after 5 PM; the rink is open every day until 11 PM. And there are more than usually interesting places to snack or have a meal — a pub-restaurant called the *Old Bailiff* (phone: 604-684-7448) and the European-style *Mozart Konditori* (phone: 604-688-6869) on one side and, on the other, the informal *Food Fair* (closed evenings) where you can prowl for Mexican, Ukrainian, Chinese, and other fast food (or, if you must, hot dogs), then take it to a pleasant area nearby to eat. Information: *Tourism Vancouver,* Pavilion Plaza, 4 Bentall Centre, 1055 Dunsmire St., PO Box 49296, Vancouver, BC V7X 1L3 (phone: 604-683-2000).

OTTAWA, Ontario: The 5 miles of the 125-mile-long Kingston-to-Ottawa Rideau Canal between Colonel By Drive and Queen Elizabeth Driveway, south of the Ottawa River, becomes the world's longest skating rink every winter, and you'll find hot chocolate stands, skate-sharpening operations, benches, safety patrols, even changing rooms — not to mention thousands of skaters. Students, their packs full of books, skate to school. Office workers skate to work. Friends head for the canal instead of the movies, and kids haul their parents out on the ice on weekends. Information: *Ottawa-Hull Tourism Inc.,* 111 Lisgar St., Ottawa, Ontario K2P 2L7 (phone: 613-237-5158), or visit the information center at 65 Elgin St., in the *National Arts Centre.* Also see *Festivals, Fairs, and Fancy Acts.*

LAURENTIANS, Quebec: You're in luck if you arrive after a spell of weather long enough and cold enough to ice over the myriad ponds, lakes, and streams of this lovely area — but before the snow. Then you can skate for miles, play hockey to your heart's content, or trace figures large enough that giants might have made them. The great outdoors is one vast skating rink. But even after the snowfall, there's no dearth of places to skate in this skate-happy region. Almost every village has its rink — if not a man-made oval set up in the schoolyard, then a section of a nearby lake kept plowed for the season. Sections of the lakes at several of the area's best resorts (among them *Gray Rocks* at St. Jovite and the *Hôtel la Sapinière* at Val David) are usually kept clear, for instance, as are the lakes at Ste. Adèle and Ste. Agathe. The former has a half-mile oval to speed around as well as the regular rink-sized area. And there are indoor rinks as well. The delight of skating here also derives from what goes après: the unique "European flavor" of the après ski in the Laurentians; long sessions at the hearthsides of cozy inns; satiation of galloping appetites in one of the many fine restaurants in the quaint villages, not to mention the gayer-than-Paris-in-springtime nightlife — some of the happiest to be found at any winter resort on earth. For more information contact: *Association Touristique des Laurentides,* 14142 Rue de Lachapelle, RR1, St.-Jérôme, Quebec J7Z 5T4 (phone: 514-436-8532).

MONTREAL, Quebec: Canadians are as enthusiastic about their skating as they are about their sailing, and they don't reserve their ice time exclusively for weekends out of town. Throughout the week, by day and by night, they throng to open-air rinks that the city government maintains for their pleasure — in Montreal at La Fontaine Park and Parc Mont-Royal (both lighted at night and near downtown), and on Ile Notre Dame, where you can skate along its 1.2-mile-long canal. Parc Mont-Royal, whose 530 acres wrap around the sides of a still active volcano, is as terrific in winter as it is for summer strolls and calèche rides. The skating all takes place on Beaver Lake (Lac des Castors), and there are fine views of the city. After you've unlaced your skates, you can go cross-country skiing, slide down one of a couple of slopes in a toboggan, ride a horse-drawn sleigh, or warm up over an interesting meal. Information: *Greater Montreal Convention and Tourism Bureau,* 1010 St. Catherine St. W., Room 410, Montreal, Quebec H3B 1G2 (phone: 514-871-1595).

QUEBEC CITY, Quebec: Beautiful as it can be under a hot summer sun, Quebec occasionally appears to have been built to look its best swathed in a cloak of snow. Quebecois put on skates almost as soon as they learn to walk, and there are hundreds of free skating rinks throughout the region on which to practice. To see for yourself, you've only to step into your skates and head for the St. Charles River between Samson and Marie de l'Incarnation bridges, where you'll sail along beside one of the city's many parks, serene under its mantle of white. Within walking distance of all major hotels, the new *Carré d'Youville* (Pl. d'Youville; phone: 418-691-6284) outdoor skating rink has become a favorite of local residents. Those who stay at one of the many hotels and motels in the suburb of Ste.-Foy can enjoy skating at the *Gaétan Boucher Speed-Skating Rink* (Pl. de Ville; phone: 418-654-4462). About 20 miles (32 km) north of the city, in Valcartier, you can have another sort of skating experience entirely. An unusual family business, known as the *Village des Sports* (Valcartier Village; phone: 418-844-3725), has cut a circle-trail through the woods, then iced it over. It's 1½ miles long, about as wide as a country road, and lighted at night; speakers concealed in bird houses provide MUZAK to skate by (or rock music, depending on the crowd). The complex is open every day in winter, and rentals are available. There are still other trails for tobogganing, cross-country skiing, and snowshoeing. In summer, the ice rink is given over to roller skating. Located at the center of a vast indoor amusement park, the younger crowd will enjoy this year-round skating facility. At *Les Galeries de la Capitale* (phone: 418-627-5800). Information: *Quebec City Region Tourism & Convention Bureau,* 60 Rue d'Auteuil, Quebec City, Quebec G1R 4C4 (phone: 418-692-2471).

HOCKEY MUSEUMS

INTERNATIONAL HOCKEY HALL OF FAME AND MUSEUM, Kingston, Ontario: People have been playing hockey in Kingston ever since it was called shinney, back in the 1880s, and the collections here record the history of the game through the present. There's the stick used in the big game between Queen's and Royal Military College on Kingston harbor ice around 1886, the first colored hockey cards (1906–1909), an early NHA player contract signed by Alf Smith of Ottawa for $500 a year, the famous No. 9 sweaters of Rocket Richard and Gordie Howe, and Dit Clapper's No. 5, retired by the Boston *Bruins* in 1947 — not to mention the battered skates of Scotty Davidson and referee Mike Rodden, Gordie Howe's gloves, and much more. Open weekends in winter, daily from June through September; admission charge. Information: *Doug Nichols, Executive Director, International Hockey Hall of Fame and Museum,* York and Alfred Sts., PO Box 82, Kingston, Ontario K7L 4VS (phone: 613-544-2355).

HOCKEY HALL OF FAME AND MUSEUM, Toronto, Ontario: For the serious hockey fan, a visit to this historical museum is a must. The *Stanley Cup,* the oldest of North America's professional sports trophies, is housed here. So are most of the sport's other famous trophies — *Challenge Cup, Canada Cup,* and all of the National Hockey League's major trophies. Officially endorsed by the NHL, the CAHA, and the International Ice Hockey Federation, the *Hockey Hall of Fame* has sections devoted to famous goalies, famous hockey skates and sticks, and other celebrated impedimenta of the sport; a number of audiovisual presentations and regular programs are also part of the show. Information: *Hockey Hall of Fame and Museum,* Exhibition Pl., Toronto, Ontario M6K 3C3 (phone: 416-595-1345).

DIRECTIONS

DIRECTIONS

Alberta

Perhaps the most beautiful drive in western Canada starts at Calgary, Alberta's second-largest city (pop. 670,000; Edmonton, the provincial capital, has 576,000 people) and follows the spine of the Rocky Mountains north through Banff to Lake Louise and Jasper National Park. These mountains, shared with the Pacific province of British Columbia, are part of the diversified geography that distinguishes Alberta from its sister prairie provinces, Saskatchewan and Manitoba. Covering 255,285 square miles, Alberta is the largest and most westerly of the prairie and plains provinces, but it is the least prairie-like. In the west, on the Alberta-British Columbia border, are the Rocky Mountains; in the southeast corner of the province are badlands and desert; and along the border with the Northwest Territories (of which the province was a part until 1905) are wildernesses of forests, lakes, and rivers.

Nor is the economy devoted exclusively to the traditional prairie concerns of farming and ranching. Oil discoveries in central and southern Alberta, especially the Leduc Fields find in 1947 propelled the province into a period of soaring growth. Although the prosperity Albertans enjoyed during the 1970s has dimmed somewhat with the slide in oil prices, residents are confident of the prospect of steady — if slower — growth in the future. Not the richest of Canada's provinces, Alberta's oil business grew to such proportions that the provincial government set up a trust fund to assure future development as oil reserves wane. Edmonton and Calgary are the centers of the province's oil industry. Some 75% of Alberta's 2.4 million people live in its cities, and the two major oil centers account for the greatest proportion of them. Alberta is the only province with no sales tax, affording its residents one of the lowest tax rates in the country.

Where there is oil there are fossil remains, and, true to form, archaeological excavations in Alberta's badlands earlier in this century turned up more than 100 dinosaur skeletons, four of which have been completely reassembled and put on display in Dinosaur Provincial Park, near the southeastern town of Brooks. In the same part of the country is the Blackfoot Indian Reserve, one of the largest communities of native North Americans in Canada.

Visitors with a yen to enjoy Alberta's natural beauty up close can take advantage of the province's numerous opportunities for trail riding, river rafting, cycling, mountain climbing, and even dog sledding. Farm and ranch vacations offer families a chance to milk cows, ride horses, gather farm-fresh eggs, and smell the country air. Consult *Travel Alberta's* (address below) excellent accommodations guide, winter vacationers' guide, touring guide, and adventure guide; also available from this agency is a comprehensive guide to campgrounds and parks in the province. While national parks don't offer reservations, many provincial parks do. Phone numbers for each location are in the campground guide. For complete reports on Calgary and Edmonton, their hotels, restaurants, sights, and activities, see the appropriate chapters of THE CITIES.

The following pages outline four distinct driving routes, each lasting 3 or 4 days, that take you to the most compelling sights and dramatic scenery of this varied, vast western province. Southern Alberta is thoroughly explored in the Lethbridge-Calgary drive, which includes beautiful Waterton Lakes National Park. The high point of any Alberta trip is Banff and Jasper national parks, and the drive through them from Calgary is described in the second Alberta route. Edmonton is the ultimate destination of the third route, from Cypress Hills Provincial Park through the dinosaur-ridden badlands and the Blackfoot Reserve. Finally, for a taste of northern Alberta, we have included the circular Edmonton-Slave Lake journey, a long and exciting trek into Alberta's more northerly wilderness.

Information: *Travel Alberta,* 10025 Jasper Ave., 15th Floor, Edmonton, Alberta T5J 3Z3 (phone: 403-427-4321 in Edmonton; 800-222-6501 elsewhere in Alberta; 800-661-8888 elsewhere in Canada or the US); mailing address: Dept. E, PO Box 2500, Edmonton, Alberta T5J 2Z4.

Lethbridge to Calgary via Waterton Lakes National Park

This 250-mile (400-km) route begins at the prairie city of Lethbridge, swings through southwestern Alberta, then heads north to Calgary. It crosses Waterton Lakes National Park in the Rocky Mountains at Alberta's southwestern corner and passes several places of interest elsewhere along the route. Cardston, on the way to Waterton Lakes, has Canada's only Mormon temple, the Alberta Temple. North from Waterton Lakes, fishing is good around Pincher Creek, and at Fort Macleod stands an original prairie fort. The route is easily traveled, and you can take it at your own pace. The whole area enjoys bright blue sky and clean air. The best time for traveling this route are from spring to fall; many attractions close down for the winter. A map of Alberta may be obtained from Travel Alberta (address above). For maps specifically of Waterton Park, Lethbridge, and other parts of this area, write *Chinook Country Tourist Association,* 2805 Scenic Dr., Lethbridge T1K 5B7.

LETHBRIDGE: This city of 60,600, the commercial center for the surrounding farm and ranch country, sits on the banks of the Oldman River. A pleasant, orderly place, it has blossomed over the last 20 years and is now a far cry from its first days in the 1860s, when Fort Whoop-Up was set up by whiskey traders from the US to sell liquor to whites and Indians, often with tragic results. A reconstruction of the fort stands in Indian Battle Park, in town on the riverbank. All that is missing is the rotgut. The park, which is not on the original site of Fort Whoop-Up, was the site of a battle between the Cree and Blackfoot Nations in 1870 that lasted for days. Details of the epic battle are explained in exhibits inside the fort. The park also has a coal train that will carry you through a simulated entrance to a mine tunnel.

Cross the Oldman River just south of Indian Battle Park and continue south on the bypass road to gain an excellent view of the University of Lethbridge campus. The university's unusual buildings were designed to complement the coulees (deep, sharp, trench erosions in rock) in the surrounding terrain. From the western end of the bypass road, the university looks like a large ship nestled in the folds of the surrounding hills.

On the east side of town, on Mayor Magrath Drive, Exhibition Park offers a variety of diversions, including a golf course and Henderson Lake, with swimming, boating, and fishing. On the shore of the lake is Lethbridge's premier attraction — Nikka Yuko Garden, a beautiful Japanese garden, designed and constructed in Japan under expert supervision and shipped in pieces and assembled without nails in Lethbridge. Nikka Yuko guides are Japanese women in traditional dress who explain the philosophy of the intricate pebble designs, the manicured trees and shrubs, and the miniature pools and waterfalls. The centerpiece is a replica of a Japanese teahouse, but, alas, it does not serve refreshments.

If you're hungry, head south on Mayor Magrath Drive for one-half mile to *Sven Ericksen's* restaurant (phone: 403-328-7756) on the east side of the road. The large, family-style dining room serves home-style cooking at moderate prices.

> **En Route from Lethbridge** – Mayor Magrath Drive becomes Route 5, the direct road to Waterton Lakes park 81 miles (130 km) southwest of Lethbridge. You will cross rolling prairie and coulees beneath an incredibly blue, seemingly infinite sky on the way to the next major town, Cardston, 48 miles (77 km) south of Lethbridge.

WRITING-ON-STONE PROVINCIAL PARK: For a fascinating day trip or overnight camping expedition, travel southeast of Lethbridge to the Writing-On-Stone Provincial Park. Drive about 50 miles (80 km) south on Route 4 to Milk River, then 20 miles (32 km) east on Route 501 to the park turnoff, and 6 miles (10 km) south to the park. This archaeological preserve is rich in ancient Indian rock paintings and carvings, and features a reconstructed Northwest Mounted Police outpost once used to control whiskey smuggling. These parched sandstone hills have been a sacred spot for Indian tribes for at least 700 years. Surrounded by rare cottonwood trees and the wind-carved rock pillars known as hoodoos, the campground offers opportunities for swimming, canoeing, and fishing. This is rattlesnake country, but don't be alarmed. The rangers keep the campground clear, and assure visitors that the local rattlers are timid creatures, unlike their aggressive relatives farther south. Be on the safe side, though, wear boots when hiking in wilderness terrain. Information: *Administrative Office,* 297 Milk River, Alberta T0K 1M0 (phone: 403-647-2364).

CARDSTON: This small town is the home of the Alberta Temple, the country's first Mormon temple, dedicated in 1923. The temple and visitors' center have just undergone a 2-year restoration. Information on the Mormon church and its history is available at the center, but the temple itself is open only to pre-approved church members. On Main Street, the *C. O. Card Home and Museum* preserves the house of the leader who first brought the Mormons from Utah to Alberta in the 1880s. The interior accurately reflects the decor and furnishings of early Alberta pioneer homes, providing a fine sense of the atmosphere of a Mormon household. If the temple and the museum don't make the point that the town is Mormon, note that Cardston also is "dry." Look elsewhere for a cold beer.

Cardston also marks the southern border of the Blood Indian Reserve, with 7,000 residents, the largest reserve in Canada. Every June, the Blood perform the *Sun Dance* religious ritual; it is one of the few plains tribes maintaining this tradition. However, this dance is not a tourist attraction, nor a public event.

If you need gas, fill up in Cardston. Gas stations are few and far between on the next stretch of highway.

> **En Route from Cardston** – Except for a couple of small towns, Leavitt and Mountain View, this is mostly open country, the approach to the foothills of the

Rockies. Thirty-one miles (50 km) after leaving Cardston, you arrive at the gate of Waterton Lakes National Park.

WATERTON LAKES NATIONAL PARK: This little sister of Banff and Jasper shows little family resemblance to the two larger, more popular parks. A more ancient part of the Rockies, Waterton has jagged mountains and ridges; layered rock of contrasting purple, red, and green; chains of connected valleys; and innumerable mountain streams, waterfalls, and lakes. The four largest lakes, connected by small streams, run across the middle of the park. The center of many of its recreational activities, they are the Maskinonge, the Lower Waterton, the Mid-Waterton, and the Upper Waterton. A few miles farther west is Cameron Lake, apart from the other four. The Waterton Lakes townsite is on the northern shore of the Upper Waterton, several miles in from the park gate at Route 5. Waterton Lakes National Park joins the US's Glacier National Park at the US border in Montana. The two parks have been named the International Peace Park, commemorating and celebrating the long open border shared by the two countries.

The town of Waterton is an active park center of motels, restaurants, stores, and campgrounds. *Shoreline Cruise* (phone: 403-859-2362) boats offer leisurely 2-hour cruises of Upper Waterton Lake, crossing the international border and stopping briefly at Goat Haunt, Montana. *Shoreline Cruise* also rents boats. The town has docking facilities and a boat launch. (Motorboats are restricted to the main lakes.) Just north of town is the starting point of the Red Rock Canyon hiking trail, which leads through successive stages of canyon rock, a living exhibition of the geology and ecology of this part of the park. Before heading into the wilds, however, visit the *Bayshore Inn* in town (see *Best en Route*); its beautiful view of the area is surpassed only by its old-fashioned dining room and the mountain trout served there. Alberta beef is on all local menus. The *Prince of Wales* hotel, a château-like hostelry up the hill from town, is worth a visit (see *Best en Route*). It has a magnificent view of the lake, huge fireplaces, and an open foyer that rises six floors. A great, formal dining room overlooks the lake. Meals are expensive, but if you want to splurge, this is the place to do it. Waterton has a golf course, tennis courts, riding stables, fishing, an outdoor swimming pool, a lakefront campground, and lake swimming. If you do swim in the lake, be prepared: It is fed by mountain glaciers and is extremely cold.

A short drive from the townsite brings you to Cameron Lake. Apart from the parking lot and picnic spots, the lake is almost in its original pristine state. There are driving and hiking trails that give access to park wilderness and its wildlife — buffalo, elk, deer, moose, bear, Rocky Mountain sheep, cougar, coyote, badger, and skunk. The usual rules about letting the animals go about their own business apply.

During the winter, snowdrifts often block the roads to Waterton Lakes National Park. But if the roads are open and you don't mind that many facilities are closed, the snow-covered mountains are a wonderful sight. If you do visit in the winter, bring food with you, and be sure that you arrive with enough gas in your car to get you to the nearest service station outside the park. You can enjoy a stay at the *Kilmorey Lodge* (see *Best en Route*), open year-round and offering cross-country skiing in winter. It is located near the *Bay Shore Inn.*

En Route from Waterton Lakes – To continue the journey to Calgary, take Route 6 north from the northern exit of the park. After 30 miles (50 km) you will reach the town of Pincher Creek, reputed to be the windiest spot in Alberta. The chinook (the prevailing strong westerly wind from the Rockies) hits Pincher Creek full force as it whistles off the mountains. In town, the *Pincher Creek Museum* and Kootenai Brown Historical Park (James Ave. and Grove St.; phone: 403-627-3684), have several restored pioneer log cabins, one of which was built in 1889 by Kootenai Brown, the area's most illustrious pioneer. The trout fishing is good in the rivers around Pincher Creek and in Beauvais Lake Provincial Park, just west of town. Open summers only.

A detour west at Pincher Creek on Route 3 will provide a peek into an interesting chapter of Alberta's past. About 20 miles (32 km) west of the Pincher Creek junction lies Crowsnest Pass, birthplace of the province's earliest coal mining and the scene of one of its greatest tragedies, the Frank Slide. The *Frank Slide Interpretive Centre* (also on Route 3; phone: 562-7388) tells the story of the night in 1903 when 90 million tons of rock broke off Turtle Mountain and buried part of the mining town of Frank and an estimated 75 people. The nearby *Leitch Collieries* stone ruins are now an interpretive center depicting the history of the coal mining industry. Open year-round.

Returning eastward on Route 3, the road heads northeast of Pincher Creek toward Fort Macleod, 29 miles (46 km) away. On the way, the road passes through part of the Peigan Indian Reserve and its main town, Brocket. From here, Fort Macleod is a half-hour drive.

FORT MACLEOD: The authentic reconstruction of the original Fort Macleod stands on 25th Street and gives a glimpse into early frontier life that is thought-provoking. The first fort was built in 1874 by the Northwest Mounted Police. The Mounties were the umpires of the territories, standing between the settlers, Indians, whiskey traders, ranchers, and immigrants. They were hardly impartial, being essentially forces of eastern expansionism, but they represented what law existed. Exhibits in the fort museum detail the history of the NWMP and local Indian cultures, and Mounties in the uniform of the period perform original horseback drills.

Be sure to take a stroll through downtown Fort Macleod, where the streets are lined with historic buildings dating back to the turn of the century. The downtown core has been declared a provincial historic site — the first such designation in Canada — and protected buildings include an old sandstone hotel, a Roman Catholic church, a Town Hall, and a post office.

The *Fort Macleod Rodeo* is one of the better small-town rodeos. It usually takes place during the first 10 days of July.

En Route from Fort Macleod – About 9 miles (14 km) northwest of Fort Macleod on Route 516, nestled in the Porcupine Hills, is Head-Smashed-In Buffalo Jump. Named a World Heritage Site by UNESCO, the 5,700-year-old jump was used by Blackfoot Indians, who would stampede buffalo herds over the cliffs and then slaughter them for food. Open year-round. An interpretive center (also open year-round) has five display galleries, an audio-visual presentation, and guided tours (phone: 403-553-2731).

Route 2 heads north from Fort Macleod on a direct line to Calgary, 103 miles (165 km) away, and passes through several interesting small towns. About 23 miles (37 km) north of Fort Macleod, Claresholm, a town of just over 3,400, is mainly a service community for area farmers and ranchers. Its small museum in the old *Canadian Pacific Railroad* station on the main highway is worth a stop.

At this point, you can continue north on Route 2 or take Route 520 west for a winding, 80-mile (128-km) tour of the foothills that will eventually return you to Route 2 at Nanton, 24 miles (38 km) north. Most of the roadway is unpaved and passes through remote territory, but you will see real ranching country and fantastic scenery. Take Route 520 until it meets Route 517. Go north on Route 517, and it will join the Forestry Trunk Road (Route 940) in the Rocky Mountains Forest Reserve. Traveling north on the Trunk Road, you will pass the spectacular Livingstone Falls. Shortly beyond Livingstone Falls, turn east on Route 532, which takes you out of the forest reserve. At the junction with Route 922, head south for a few miles to Chain Lakes Provincial Park, which has 140 picnic sites, cooking shelters, fishing, and a boat launching in an isolated, relaxing environment (phone: 403-646-5887). From Chain Lakes, Route 533 goes directly to Nanton in about 45 minutes. Nanton is famous for its sparkling, ice-cold water, available from taps beside the highway. Fifteen miles (24 km) north on Route 2 is High River.

HIGH RIVER: Many Albertans believe this little town typifies western life. Always a center for ranchers, it also has become home for many people who work in Calgary but want to live in a small town. Many of its shops carry arts and crafts made in the area, so if you're looking for a special souvenir, High River might be able to supply it. The unique Western articles produced by stores such as *Eamor's Saddlery* and *Olson's Silver and Leather Co.* are prized around the world. Each August, the town hosts the *North American Chuckwagon Championships.* These races attract the same drivers and rigs that appear in the famous *Calgary Stampede,* but here you get a much closer view of the action. During the championships, there also are horse races, a midway, and a country dance and beer hall. The *Little Britches Rodeo,* the last 2 weeks of May, features junior cowboys and cowgirls, as young as 7 years, bronco busting, steer wrestling, and calf roping. The *Museum of the Highwood* (First St.) is open year-round and has a good geological collection and exhibits on local history. A quaint house at 153 Macleod Trail is home to the *Briar Rose Tea Room and Gift Shop.* Enjoy lunch or afternoon tea in pleasant, pastel surroundings (phone: 403-652-3226).

En Route from High River – It is a simple, 24-mile (38-km) drive on Route 2 to Calgary. For a bit of homey sustenance, head west on Highway 7 (off Route 2) about 5 miles (8 km) until you reach the small town of Okotoks. On South Railway Street, you'll find the new *Ginger Tea Room* serving Saskatoon berry pie, cream cheese and cucumber sandwiches in season, and their own blend of Okotokian tea. Open for lunch and afternoon tea (403-938-2907). Back on Route 2, just before Calgary, turn west on Route 22 to see Spruce Meadows, one of the finest equestrian facilities in the world. For a complete report on Calgary, its hotels, and restaurants, see THE CITIES.

BEST EN ROUTE

There are plenty of motels and campgrounds along this route, but except for those in Waterton and Lethbridge, quality is limited. Most motels are simple, functional, and little else. Similarly, the overnight campsites meet only basic needs. There's also little difference in room rates. Expect to pay $50 or more per night for a double in a hotel listed as expensive; $30 to $50 in the moderate range; and $20 to $30 in the inexpensive category. All prices are quoted in US dollars.

LETHBRIDGE

Lethbridge Lodge – This modern, 190-room lodge has a a plant-filled atrium, a spectacular view of the Oldman River Valley and features a dining room, a country-western tavern, a pool and Jacuzzi. 320 Scenic Dr. (phone: 403-328-1123). Expensive.

Sandman Inn – With 138 rooms with color TV sets and telephones, facilities here include an indoor swimming pool, dining room, cocktail lounge, gift shop, and a tavern. Holiday Village, 421 Mayor Magrath Dr. (phone: 403-328-1111). Expensive.

Lodge – This 94-room motel features a dining room, outdoor pool, hot tub, sauna, and satellite TV. Mayor Magrath Dr. and 7th Ave. (phone: 403-329-0100). Moderate.

Park Plaza – Just a few blocks from the Japanese gardens and Henderson Lake Park, this 64-room hotel has a dining room, cocktail lounge, coffee shop, telephones, and color TV sets. 1009 Mayor Magrath Dr. (phone: 403-328-2366). Moderate.

Sundance Inn – Telephones, color TV sets, an indoor swimming pool, kitchenettes, and complimentary coffee are found in this 54-unit motel. 1030 Mayor Magrath Dr. (phone: 403-328-6636). Moderate.

Henderson Lake Campground – Just across the road from the park and the lake, at the east end of the lake, there are 100 camping sites, many with sewer, electric, and water hook-ups. There also are stoves, fireplaces, tables, showers, flush toilets, and laundry facilities. Privately owned (phone: 403-328-5452). Inexpensive.

CARDSTON

Flamingo – At the south end of town, this 38-unit motel has color TV sets, telephones, kitchenettes, and an outdoor pool. All units feature queen-size beds. Major credit cards accepted. 848 Main St. S., or PO Box 92 (phone: 403-653-3952). Moderate.

Lee Creek Campground – Twenty-six camping sites, no hook-ups are available, but there are cooking facilities, tap water, and flush toilets (no phone). In the town of Cardston. Inexpensive.

Police Outpost Campground – Operated by the provincial department of recreation and parks, there are 46 camping sites, cooking facilities, a boat launch, pump water, and pit toilets. There are no hook-ups. 10 miles (16 km) west and 11 (18 km) miles south of Cardston (phone: 403-653-2522). Inexpensive.

WATERTON

Bayshore Inn – This 70-unit motel overlooks the lake and has a dining room, cocktail lounge, and color TV sets. Open May 1 to October 1. 111 Waterton Ave. or PO Box 38, Waterton Park (phone: 403-859-2211). Expensive.

Prince of Wales – The best in the area. A château on a hill with a splendid view of the mountains and the lake, this is a perfect headquarters for a park visit. There are 82 rooms, a dining room, cocktail lounge, and telephones. Open June 1 to September 14. Waterton (phone: 403-859-2231). Expensive.

Crandell Mountain Lodge – With 11 units, some kitchenettes, and family units, this motel is open from April to November. 102 Mount View Rd. or PO Box 114, Waterton Park (phone: 403-859-2288). Moderate.

Kilmorey – Right on the lake at the entrance to Waterton townsite, this motor lodge has 25 rooms, a dining room, and a cocktail lounge with fireplaces. Open year-round. Major credit cards accepted. 117 Evergreen Ave. or PO Box 100, Waterton Park (phone: 403-859-2334). Moderate.

Waterton Homestead Campground – Here are 250 camping sites, including 70 trailer spots with electric, sewer, and water hook-ups, showers, flush toilets, and laundry facilities. Two miles (3 km) north of the Waterton National Park on Route 6 (phone: 403-859-2247). Inexpensive.

Crooked Creek Campground – Seven miles (11 km) east of Waterton Park, it's a small campground, but it's free and open year-round. Operated by Alberta Transportation (no phone). No charge.

PINCHER CREEK

Foothills – A 30-unit motel, it has color TV sets, a whirlpool bath, a sauna, and telephones. On the east side of Route 6. 1049 Waterton Ave. or PO Box 2347 (phone: 403-627-3341). Moderate.

FORT MACLEOD

Sunset – At the west entrance to town, this motel has 22 units, color TV sets, kitchenettes, and air conditioning. PO Box 398 (phone: 403-553-4448). Moderate.

CLARESHOLM

Sportsman – This inn has 42 units with a dining room, direct-dial phones, cable TV sets, and plug-ins for cars; some units have queen-size water beds. PO Box 1328 (phone: 403-625-3347). Moderate.

Calgary to Banff and Jasper National Parks

Immense as they are, stretching from the Yukon Territory to New Mexico, the Rocky Mountains are only part of a much larger chain that reaches deep into Mexico, sending two arms of peaks along Mexico's eastern and western coasts, gathering the country into a stony embrace that comes to fingerpoints of peaks cupped protectively around Mexico City. This huge mountain chain — from the Arctic to the jungles of Chiapas — tells the story of creation; and one of the most revealing and beautiful chapters of that story is open for the reading on the drive between Banff and Jasper national parks, the showpieces of the Canadian West.

These two vast, adjoining parks cover 200 square miles of the Rocky Mountains on the Alberta-British Columbia border, some of the finest mountain scenery in the world. Like fingers caressing a backbone, the 259-mile (414-km) road from Calgary to Banff, past the beautiful Lake Louise, the Columbia Ice Fields, and to Jasper follows the spine of the Continent. Whether for summer or winter sport or because it is simply one of the most wonderful drives in North America, this is the most popular destination in the West.

Banff is a nature sanctuary as well as a major resort. Around the town itself are luxurious hotels, elegant restaurants, galleries, craft shops, ski resorts, and entertainment centers. Since it is one of Canada's most popular vacation areas, be prepared for crowds at the major attractions and considerable traffic on the park's winding roads.

Jasper is somewhat less commercially developed, although the town of Jasper has creature comforts aplenty. And for those who want to commune with nature in peace and quiet, both parks have miles of uncrowded hiking trails, secluded riverside picnic sites, and wilderness paths into the raw, undeveloped Rockies.

Information: A map of Alberta may be obtained from *Travel Alberta,* 10025 Jasper Ave., 15th Floor, Edmonton T5J 3Z3. Write Dept. E, Box 2500, Edmonton, Alberta T5J 2Z4. For maps of Banff and Jasper, write *Banff-Lake Louise Chamber of Commerce,* PO Box 1298, 93 Banff Ave., Banff T0L 0C0 (403-762-3777), and *Jasper Park Chamber of Commerce;* PO Box 98, 632 Connaught Dr., Jasper T0E 1E0 (403-852-3858).

En Route from Calgary – The entrance to Banff National Park lies about 70 miles (112 km) west of Calgary. Both the four-lane, divided Route 1 (the Trans-Canada Highway) and the parallel Route 1A lead directly to the park entrance.

If you take the Trans-Canada Highway, stop at Canada Olympic Park, on the west edge of the city, site of the *1988 Winter Olympic* games and the world's only *Olympic Hall of Fame.* Route 1A passes through several small towns and the Stoney Indian Reserve. If you have time, it's a relaxing way to go. Our route follows Route 1A.

The Crowchild Trail in Calgary becomes Route 1A as you head west. Just outside Calgary, the small town of Cochrane is worth a stop if you want to ramble over the grassy site of the first large ranch in Alberta, established in 1881, and climb to the rocky perch of the Cochrane Ranch's famous horse and rider statue. Cochrane has several new housing developments, built mainly for people who work in Calgary but who prefer to live in Cochrane's small-town atmosphere. The town also boasts a growing community of artists and craftspeople. Look for unique antiques and gifts at *Old and Crafty* (404 First St. W.) and reproductions of Victorian dolls at the *Doll Gallery* (in the *Cochrane Centre Mall*). You can watch the owners of *Studio West* (205 2nd Ave. SE; phone: 403-932-2611) create sculptures of horses and riders from molten bronze, and view the paintings of talented Alberta artists.

THE STONEY INDIAN RESERVE: About 10 miles (16 km) from Cochrane, on Route 1A, is the Stoney Indian Reserve. You may recognize some of the surrounding landscape from films. *Little Big Man,* with Dustin Hoffman, and *Buffalo Bill and the Indians,* starring Paul Newman, were filmed here. Located on the highway, the main village on the reserve is Morley, settled in the 1800s by Methodist missionary George McDougall. It is the site of the tribe's schools, administrative office, and recreation center. The tiny McDougall Memorial United Church, built in 1875, is the second-oldest building on its original site in Alberta. While there are no restaurants, or major retail stores here, it is possible to purchase leather goods, feather and bead work, and jewelry made by the men and women of the reserve at the *Nakoda Lodge,* a large cedar-log facility built by the Stoney on the shore of Hector Lake, 10 miles (16 km) west of Morley. An addition to the lodge includes 50 motel units. The building is the site of workshops and educational retreats for anyone interested in native culture. Sunday brunches are offered in summer and fall (phone: 403-881-3949). The Stoney value their privacy. While you are welcome to visit the town and other places open to visitors, don't wander off the main highway. The residents have the right to ask you to leave; the reserve is their property.

A few miles west of Morley, near the banks of the Bow River, the Stoney have set aside land for a public campground. The facilities are rudimentary (fire pits, picnic tables, and outhouses), but they include some beautifully wooded camping spots. And the scenery is spectacular. Some of the sites overlook a fenced buffalo paddock, and, to the west, the mountains seem close enough to touch. During the summer, more than a dozen teepees set up in the park make the area feel even more removed from the present day.

Each August the Stoney host a conference of Native Americans interested in the preservation of their religious tradition (by invitation only).

Stoney Indian Park and Morley also can be reached from the Trans-Canada Highway.

En Route from the Stoney Indian Reserve – Route 1 and Route 1A draw closer together as they approach Banff National Park. Just past the town of Exshaw — its large Canada Cement factory visible from both highways — the two roads join and continue a few miles to Canmore. Within a mile or two of this intersection are two guest ranches, *Kananaskis* (see *Best en Route*), and the *Rafter 6* (phone: 403-673-3622). The latter's Sunday brunches and dinners are legendary feasts of western fare — anyone is welcome to sample the prime rib roasts and turkey with stuffing, cooked just the way Mother used to do. Originally a coal mining town, Canmore has become a thriving center, with many grocery stores, shops, motels, and fast-food outlets serving Banff's overflow tourist industry. For a leisurely meal, try *Gallagher House* (phone: 403-678-5370), downtown. It offers fireside tables, afternoon tea, lunch, and dinner in an Old World atmosphere.

KANANASKIS COUNTRY: From Canmore, it's easy to explore Kananaskis Country, a year-round recreational area developed by the provincial government. This 2,400-square-mile mountain wilderness has facilities for hiking, biking, horseback riding, cross-country skiing, fishing, and snowmobiling. The *Canmore Nordic Centre,* on the town's outskirts, hosted the *1988 Winter Olympic* cross-country and biathlon events. The center's 34 miles of skiing and hiking trails are open to the public (phone: 403-678-2400).

If you follow Route 1 east of Canmore to Route 40 and travel 13 miles (22 km) south, you come to Mount Allan, site of the *1988 Olympic* alpine events. Call Ski Nakiska (phone: 403-591-7777) for public skiing information. Only 2 miles (3 km) farther south on Route 40 is the challenging and beautiful 36-hole *Kananaskis Country Golf Course* (phone: 403-591-7070).

BANFF NATIONAL PARK: The gates to Banff National Park are just beyond Canmore. The entrance fee depends on which park facilities you plan to use. Although you may drive nonstop through the park or a portion of it, you will have a more enjoyable trip if you view the sights at leisure and participate in some of the activities. Plan at least an overnight stay; 2 days is even more desirable. Campers will find sites throughout the park. (And remember, all national park campsites are first-come, first-served.) For those who prefer motels or hotels, there are adequate accommodations in the town of Banff; at Lake Louise, 35 miles (56 km) beyond; and along the longer stretch of road between Lake Louise and the boundary of Jasper National Park (see *Best en Route*). Reserve rooms well in advance; this is a popular area.

The town of Banff, about 10 miles (16 km) beyond the park entrance, is the center of the park's attractions and the home base for exploring the southern portion of the park.

Banff is the fount of the area's tourist industry. In 1841, Sir George Simpson, governor of the Hudson's Bay Company, was the first white man to explore the area. It remained untouched until the 1880s, when the Canadian Pacific Railway prepared to lay track nearby and businessmen decided to exploit the hot springs at Sulphur Mountain by building a hotel and spa. As the resort gained popularity, the town grew.

Today, Banff is a major tourist center in the summer and the winter ski center, and its stores, bookshops, art galleries, and restaurants are often crowded, but endlessly intriguing. The *Banff National Park Natural History Museum* (93 Banff Ave.) has exhibits explaining the area's geological structure and wildlife.

The *Whyte Museum of the Canadian Rockies* (housed in the Public Library on Bear Street) shows the work of both local and national Canadian artists. The library also houses the Archives of the Canadian Rockies, a collection of rare books and photographs.

The Canadian Pacific's *Banff Springs* hotel (see *Best en Route*) on Spray Avenue is the descendant of the original resort that first established Banff as a vacation spot. It was built between 1910 and 1928, but 18 years was apparently not enough time to complete the job, because when the new hotel was opened to the public, one room still had no door. Three architects worked on the hotel's design, creating a style that can only be described as 16th-century French château with touches of Scottish manse. Part of the 850-room property was recently renovated. The hotel can arrange rafting trips and sleigh rides, in season. Amenities also include indoor and outdoor swimming pools. Fossilized stone used throughout the structure emphasizes its castle-like appearance. Nearby, on Mountain Avenue, you can still take a dip in the Upper Hot Springs Pool.

The pool is not intended for swimming but for soaking in the soothing natural sulfur waters. The water — not just warm, but hot — is especially relaxing after a day of hiking or skiing. The outdoor pool is open year-round. The Cave and Basin Hot Springs, discovered 100 years ago by three railway workers, are open from June to September. Special displays reveal the springs' effect on local flora and fauna.

A number of quality stores sell clothing, ceramics, weavings, paintings, and sculptures. But a word of warning: Some of the items are overpriced and can often be found for less money in Calgary. Check the labels if you buy Indian handicrafts; some of them may be made in Japan. Authentic Canadian Indian handicrafts are identified with a label. The *Quest* (Banff Ave.) has a good collection of Inuit prints and soapstone carvings, jewelry, and wood, clay, and leather crafts.

Banff also is the home of the Banff Centre, one of the best fine arts schools in North America. The original theater school is now only one division of an education complex serving more than 1,600 students annually. The center offers instruction in dance, music, writing, and management. All year, in two modern theaters, films, concerts, theater, dance, and recitals are offered. Its annual *Banff Festival of the Arts* is held June through August and features a variety of concerts, exhibitions, and other productions. For information on current events, call 403-762-6300.

Despite Banff's many attractions, the real interest lies in the mountains, lakes, and forests that surround it. A good way to begin exploring the countryside is to take either of the gondola lifts on the two mountains near town. To the northwest, the *Mount Norquay Scenic Lift* goes to the top of Mt. Norquay, providing an opportunity to enjoy its commanding view of several mountains; picnic tables and a restaurant at the summit station are open from mid-June to September 1. Even if you don't take the cable car to the top, it's worth driving to the base station. This road goes high on the mountain, with great views and stopping points along the way. To the southeast, the *Sulphur Mountain Gondola* runs much the same operation, with a teahouse and hiking trails at the top. It operates year-round.

Several short hiking trails lead out from Banff. A fascinating 1½-mile loop in Sundance Canyon crosses streams and climbs rocks. Behind the parking lot at Upper Hot Springs is a 2½-mile climb that takes about an hour and brings you back to the hot springs. Two miles (3 km) down Spray Avenue, you can walk around the sulfur springs at Cave and Basin Pool. Guided horseback trail rides are available from *Warner and MacKenzie Guiding and Outfitting* on Banff Avenue.

Rocky Mountain Raft Tours (phone: 403-762-3632) offers — on a large rubber raft — a 3-hour tour of the Bow River. Tickets may be obtained at the bus station or at the *Banff Springs* hotel. A few miles west of town, at Lake Minnewanka, are 2-hour motorboat tours of the lake, and canoe rentals. For skiers, Mt. Norquay has excellent downhill slopes. *Sunshine Village,* 14 miles (22 km) west of town, has full ski facilities and overnight accommodations. In summer, a 25-minute gondola ride takes nature lovers to a beautiful and rare sub-alpine meadow. The lofty site can be cold and wet, even though the sun is shining down in the parking lot, so dress warmly.

One of the easiest ways to enjoy the park's splendid scenery is simply to drive through it. A number of major peaks, like Cascade Mountain, Castle Mountain, and Mt. Brett, are short distances away, and there are plenty of seldom-traveled trails throughout the area for easy hikes. Park personnel will help you to find them. A word of caution that can't be repeated too often: The constant presence of human beings has made the animals unafraid of people. Nevertheless, they are still wild; they can be dangerous and unpredictable. Also, in feeding or attempting to play with wild animals, you risk harming them. It is cruel and stupid to feed park animals, here or in any park. Don't do it.

Lake Louise, 35 miles (56 km) northwest of Banff, must not be missed. You can make it a separate overnight stop, a day's round-trip journey from Banff, or the first stop in a full day of driving northward. Lake Louise early in the morning is a special treat. It is a beautifully clear, blue-green lake, surrounded by mountains and backed by the Victoria Glacier. As the sun rises, the mountains and the glacier are mirrored on the lake's surface. Since sunrise can be as early as 4 AM, it helps to stay overnight. The only hotel right on the lake is the *Château Lake Louise* (see *Best en Route*), the Canadian Pacific's landmark hotel, which has added a new wing and undergone major renovation. Guests can leave a wake-up call to see the sunrise spectacle. (The hotel serves coffee to those who get up to watch.) Rooms with a view of the lake (as opposed to the mountains) are slightly more expensive.

For years, the lake was an undisturbed preserve of the rich and the powerful, but over the years democracy (and economics) caught up with it. Lake Louise is now accessible to all, and remains beautiful at any time, sunrise or midday. And if you want to get away from other people, rent a canoe or a horse. There is ample privacy and serenity around here for everyone.

The *Lake Louise Inn* and the *Post* hotel (see *Best en Route*), a few miles from the lake, are both charming. Although neither is inexpensive, both are more reasonable than *Château Lake Louise.*

En Route from Lake Louise – From Lake Louise, Route 93 heads north toward Jasper through the large remaining section of Banff park and some of the most striking scenery you will ever see. This section of Route 93 is called the Ice Field Parkway. From the road you will be able to see 12 of the 25 highest peaks in the Rockies and glaciers up to 1,000 feet thick. Be prepared to take your time, because the highway winds and climbs. It's also a good idea to switch drivers once in a while so everyone can get a good look at the scenery. About 22 miles (35 km) past Lake Louise, you can stop for coffee and a meal at *Num-Ti-Jah Lodge* (phone: 403-761-7020) on Bow Lake. Open May to October. You also should stop to absorb the views at Hector Lake, Peyto Lake (which has a mysterious blue tint), and Bow Summit. Forty-six miles (74 km) north of Lake Louise, you reach the boundary with Jasper National Park.

JASPER NATIONAL PARK: Less crowded than Banff, Jasper emphasizes its natural wonders, which complement rather than repeat those of Banff. It's a long 92 miles (147 km) from the park entrance to the town of Jasper, but the sights along the way are amazing.

Immediately after crossing into Jasper you are still in glacier country. Directly inside Jasper's boundary is the Columbia Icefield, from which the Saskatchewan, Columbia, and Athabasca rivers rise. The ice field, covering 160 square miles, lies across the Continental Divide. One toe of the Athabasca Glacier, which is 600 to 1,000 feet thick, spills down the mountain; visitors can ride across the ice in specially-equipped vehicles at the mountain, or park their car and follow the foot trail leading to an excellent view of the mountain's cliffs and the abutting Angel Glacier. Back on Route 93A, it is a short drive to Jasper.

Although the town of Jasper has been growing rapidly in recent years, it still has a more relaxed, less formal atmosphere than that of Banff. One of the first objects to attract your attention will be the large totem pole in the center of the open square near the railway station. From the Queen Charlotte Islands of British Columbia, it is one of the finest examples of a nearly extinct art. Elsewhere in Jasper are many activities similar to those in Banff. The *Jasper Tramway Ltd.* (phone: 403-852-3093) ascends Whistlers Mountain, 7,500 feet. There is a café at the top station and hiking trails leading even higher. Since this is the treeline, there are lovely specimens of rock flowers and moss. Numerous marmots — a type of groundhog — scurry from burrow to burrow. *Jasper Raft Tours* (phone: 403-852-3613), *Maligne River Adventures* (phone: 403-852-3370), and *Whitewater Rafting* (phone: 403-852-7238) offer whitewater excursions on the Athabasca in large rubber rafts. *Pyramid Riding Stables* (Pyramid Lake

Rd.; phone: 403-852-3562) and the *Jasper Park Riding Academy* (phone: 403-852-5794) at the *Jasper Park Lodge* (phone: 403-852-3301) provide guided trail rides (see *Best en Route*). The town has a luxurious golf course. And if you want a quiet picnic and an opportunity to appreciate the scenery, there's a tiny island in Pyramid Lake that can be reached by footbridge. For a plain but satisfying meal, try *Becker's Bungalow* at *Becker's Roaring River Chalets* (phone: 403-852-3779) on the Jasper-Banff Highway. Its reputation has spread far beyond Jasper.

The Miette Hot Springs, 25 miles (40 km) away, near the park's eastern boundary, has three naturally hot pools, including the hottest one in the mountains. Marmot Basin, 13 miles (21 km) from town, is one of the finest ski areas in the Rockies. A worthwhile trip is to take the side road from Jasper south to Maligne Lake for the popular 1½-hour motor cruise. Fishing is good and boats are for rent. Nearby, Maligne Canyon is one of the best examples of canyon landscape. Trails lead part of the way into the gorge. Like Banff, Jasper has many hiking trails and lots of pristine nature.

BEST EN ROUTE

Although motels, hotels, and campgrounds are plentiful along this route, during the summer you should make reservations. The chambers of commerce in Banff (403-762-3777) and Jasper (403-852-3858) can recommend a reservations service. Campsites operate on a first-come, first-served basis. Room rates here are higher than elsewhere in Alberta, but this is the only area in Alberta there is have a real choice of accommodations. Expect to pay $90 to $170 per night for a double room in the expensive range (and even more than this in the high season); $55 to $90 in the moderate category; and up to $55 in the inexpensive range. Following are just a few of the accommodations available; in Banff alone, there are over 30 hotels, motels, and apartment-style accommodations to choose from. All prices are quoted in US dollars.

CANMORE

Rocky Mountain Chalets – Fireplaces, bedroom lofts, and kitchenettes are found in these alpine lodgings. On Highway 1A, Box 725 (phone: 403-678-5564). Moderate.

Rundle Ridge Chalets – There are 20 cedar chalets with fireplaces here, just a half mile east of the Banff park gates at Harvie Heights. PO Box 1847, Banff (phone: 403-678-5387). Moderate.

Cee-Der Chalets – The 8 individual cozy cabins have kitchenettes and sleep two, four at the most. Some have fireplaces, TV sets, and mountain views. At Harvie Heights, 1 mile (1.6 km) east of the Banff park gates. PO Box 525 (phone: 403-678-5251). Inexpensive.

Spray Lakes Campground – Twenty miles (32 km) south of Canmore, this property has 50 tent sites with stoves, tables, and outdoor toilets. It's run by the provincial recreation and parks department (phone: 403-678-5533). Inexpensive.

KANANASKIS COUNTRY

Lodge at Kananaskis – This luxurious facility in a pristine wilderness setting has 255 rooms, some suites with fireplaces, an indoor pool, whirlpool bath, and sauna. Reports about the restaurant, however, have been less than favorable, so you may want to dine elsewhere. Located near Mount Allan's Nakiska ski resort, 13 miles (21 km) south of Route 1 on Route 40 (phone: 403-591-7711 or 800-268-9411). Expensive.

Mount Engadine Lodge – An alpine lodge that sits alone in primal forest and mountain country. Amenities include a dining room, living room, lounge, and fireplace. You get your choice of dormitory or private accommodations, plus wholesome meals and opportunities for alpine hiking, cross-country skiing, mountain climbing, and wind-surfing. Take Smith-Dorrien Rd. south of Canmore to Mount Shark turnoff (phone: 403-678-4080). Moderate.

BANFF

Banff Park Lodge – The downtown area is only 2 blocks from this modern, quiet, 210-room hostelry, with dining rooms, a cocktail lounge with live entertainment, heated indoor pool, saunas, and a whirlpool bath. All rooms have queen- or king-size beds. 222 Lynx St. (phone: 403-762-4433). Expensive.

Banff Springs – This castle of a hotel has 841 rooms, indoor and outdoor swimming pools, an exercise room, sauna, 3 Jacuzzis, ice skating, sleigh rides, a golf course, tennis courts, riding stables, several dining rooms and cocktail lounges, and a posh Presidential Suite. Spray Ave. (phone: 403-762-2211). Expensive.

Homestead Inn – A small basic motel off the main drag where you can get a good night's sleep. With 27 units, color TV sets, and telephones. 218 Lynx St. (phone: 403-762-4471). Moderate.

Mount Royal – A pleasant hostelry in the center of town, it has 92 rooms, color TV sets, a dining room, and a cocktail lounge. 138 Banff Ave. (phone: 403-762-3331). Moderate.

Swiss Village – On the eastern outskirts of Banff, this lodge has 47 motel units with color TV sets and telephones, some with kitchenettes and fireplaces; also 22 bungalows. 600 Banff Ave. (phone: 403-762-2256). Moderate.

LAKE LOUISE

Château Lake Louise – In addition to its spectacular Lake Louise setting, there is a newer wing — bringing the total number of rooms to 525 — outdoor and indoor swimming pools, a tanning salon, Jacuzzi, exercise room, dinner and dancing, cocktail lounges, and a tavern. Reservations necessary. Off Highway 1, on Lake Louise (phone: 403-522-3511). Expensive.

Lake Louise Inn – This 186-unit motel has 38 kitchen apartments, 56 standard rooms, laundry facilities, a tennis court, pool, Jacuzzi, sauna, and an exercise room. Open all year. PO Box 209 (phone: 403-522-3791). Expensive.

Post – A charming, Bavarian-style jewel, this log-constructed building was remodeled in 1987, and now houses an excellent dining room. There also is a pool, Jacuzzi, and sauna. The 93 rooms include suites with lofts, kitchens, and fireplaces. 200 Pipestone, Box 69 (403-522-3989). Expensive.

JASPER

Jasper Park Lodge – This sprawling lodge on Lac Beauvert has 400 rooms with adjoining sitting rooms, color TV sets, a golf course, tennis courts, boating, fishing, stables, saunas, whirlpool baths, and car rentals. Open year-round. Ski packages are available. Rates soar during peak season — mid-April to mid-October. Lodge Rd., Box 40, Jasper (phone: 403-852-3301). Expensive.

Lobstick Lodge – Five blocks from the center of town, this 138-unit motel has kitchenettes, sauna, executive suites, game rooms, telephones, and TV sets. Geikie St. or PO Box 1200 (phone: 403-852-4431). Moderate.

Pyramid Lake Bungalows – A terraced lakeside property, 3½ miles (5 km) northwest of Jasper, with 10 units, each with a kitchenette, as well as fishing and boating facilities. Ski packages available. Open mid-April to mid-October. PO Box 388 (phone: 403-852-3536). Moderate.

Whistlers – This 41-room motel with a dining room, cocktail lounge, telephones, and TV sets, is across the street from the Jasper train station. Open year-round. PO Box 250 (phone: 403-852-3361). Moderate.

Cypress Hills Provincial Park to Edmonton via the Dinosaur Country

Modern technology has taken the bad out of badlands. These marginal desert areas were places where, years ago, a man on foot or horseback could well die without due precaution, native intelligence, and desert savvy. Today there is nothing bad about them. In the distances a car can cover, they need hardly be dangerous, and chances are, unless you've done desert driving, the image you carry in your mind of an area named "badlands" doesn't begin to account for its color, the striking rock formations, or its severe beauty.

All the better reason to make this drive from Cypress Hills Provincial Park in southeastern Alberta across the province's badlands and plains to Edmonton, in the center of the province. It is a drive of about 400 miles (640 km) and in its course you will encounter all the surprises, all the grave beauty, all the harsh splendor referred to so cavalierly as "the badlands."

Alberta's badlands contain many surprises. Cypress Hills Provincial Park, in the middle of a desert, is a teeming, green forest with a crazy-quilt ecology. Northwest of Cypress Hills, the city of Medicine Hat provides a variety of urban attractions. West through the badlands, at the towns of Brooks and Drumheller, are the skeletons and fossils of dinosaurs and other extinct creatures discovered in this area. There are excellent opportunities to see these remains and to explore the fossil beds yourself.

At the Blackfoot Indian Reserve, between Brooks and Drumheller, you can look back into Indian history and also see something of present Indian culture. In Alberta's midlands, the desert gives way to rich farm country. Near Red Deer, several lake resorts well equipped for recreation provide a welcome contrast to the arid terrain. North from Red Deer, an easy trip through Alberta's farm communities brings you to the major city of Edmonton. While there is much driving on this route — and in the summer the weather is apt to be hot — there are excellent facilities all along the way, including many farms offering bed and breakfast services, and the sights make the driving worth it. If necessary, you could travel the whole route in two crowded days, just glimpsing at the scenery. But since the best attractions lie slightly off the main roads, a more leisurely pace makes sense. A three- or four-day drive allows you to see each sight thoroughly and to stay overnight at spots you find particularly attractive.

Information: A map of Alberta may be obtained from *Travel Alberta,* 10025 Jasper Ave., 15th Floor, Edmonton T5J 3Z3. Write Dept. E, Box 2500, Edmonton, Alberta T5J 2Z4. For more detailed maps of the Cypress Hills-Medicine Hat-Brooks area, write *Southeast Alberta Travel and Convention Bureau,* PO Box 605, Medicine Hat T1A 7G5; for the Drumheller area, write *Big Country Tourist Association,* PO Box 2308, Drumheller T0J 0Y0; for the Red Deer area, write *David Thompson Country Tourist Council,* 4836 Ross St., Red Deer T4N 5E8.

CYPRESS HILLS PROVINCIAL PARK: Cypress Hills Park lies just west of Saskatchewan and north of Montana. From the US, take Montana's Route 232; this will become Canada's Route 41. Cypress Hills is 50 miles (80 km) beyond the border. West from Saskatchewan on the Trans-Canada Highway (Route 1) is a turnoff south onto Route 41, shortly after you enter Alberta. Another 21 miles (34 km) brings you to Cypress Hills.

This is one of nature's startling oddities. Surrounded by the prairie's rolling hills, Cypress Hills is a wide plateau, 2,000 feet higher than the surrounding countryside and nearly 5,000 feet above sea level. It is covered by a heavy pine forest, supports a wide variety of wildlife, and contains three lakes, the largest of which is Elkwater. This landscape should, by all reason, exist only hundreds of miles farther south. Here in abundance are mountain and woodland orchids, hawthorne, violets, and crocus. Coyotes, moose, deer, and all manner of birds are found in the forest. (As in all Alberta's provincial parks, hunting is forbidden.)

Near the park's northern boundary are Elkwater Lake and the town of Elkwater. The lake has swimming, boating, windsurfing, and bicycling and canoe rentals. The town has a service station and one motel, the *Green Tree* (phone: 403-893-3811), with 19 units. The campgrounds have 540 sites for both trailers and tents (for campground reservations, call 403-893-3811). During the winter, there are facilities for cross-country skiing and Hidden Valley, a downhill course, with a lodge and quad-chair lift.

En Route from Cypress Hills Provincial Park – Take Route 48 north to Route 1 (Trans-Canada Highway). Head west on Route 1, and within 45 minutes you will arrive at Medicine Hat.

MEDICINE HAT: Medicine Hat is a tree-filled city (population 43,000), its prosperity based on being built on 780 billion cubic feet of natural gas. The city is said to have "all hell for a basement." This gas reserve, the largest in Canada, is 99% pure and pumped directly into the turn-of-the-century gas lamps that light the revitalized downtown area. Legends concerning the origin of the city's name abound. According to one story, a Cree medicine man lost his headdress during a battle with the Blackfoot, and the Cree consequently lost the battle. Medicine Hat contains more than 70 parks connected by 67½ miles of trails for hiking, biking, and cross-country skiing. The Cultural Centre is on the Trans-Canada Highway at College Drive. The Clay Products Interpretive Center (Medalta Avenue) depicts the history of clay products native to Medicine Hat. The *Medicine Hat Museum and Art Gallery* (1302 Bomford Crescent SW) provides a history of the Canadian West through exhibits, reconstructions, and photographic displays. The Tourist Information Centre (on the Trans-Canada Highway at Southridge Drive) includes an interpretive center and dump station. Medicine Hat boasts three excellent golf courses, including one that is a par 3.

En Route from Medicine Hat – Continue west on Route 1. For the most part, it is open country until you reach the town of Brooks, 70 miles (112 km) west of Medicine Hat. This stretch of highway gives you a chance to appreciate the scenery of Alberta's badlands. Prominent here and throughout much of southern Alberta are coulees, sharp trenches worn by wind and water into masses of rock. You will see a few of the formations of curiously columned rock called hoodoos. There are plenty more of them farther along. In Brooks, the Alberta Horticultural Research Centre conducts tours of its gardens. The *Brooks and District Museum* (568 Sartherland Dr.; phone: 403-362-5073) takes you back in time, as you walk through an old church and schoolhouse with maps, schoolbooks, and inkwells intact. *Ecos Fine Food,* next to the town fire department, is a trendy eatery and art gallery displaying the works of Alberta artists. The main attraction, however, is Dinosaur Provincial Park, containing the largest dinosaur fossil bed in the world, northeast of Brooks.

DINOSAUR PROVINCIAL PARK: The park lies about 15 miles (24 km) outside Brooks. Take Route 873 north at Brooks and follow the signs. Located on the banks of the Red Deer River, the park, named a world heritage site in 1979, was once lush seaside swampland, the home of 11 species of duck-billed dinosaurs. Although its valleys and hills are now covered with juniper, sagebrush, and prickly pear cactus, it is Canada's — and one of the world's — richest fossil grounds. The action of the river has gradually eroded the rock bed, creating spectacular hoodoos and revealing layer upon layer of colored minerals. In the process, the river uncovered the remains of the dinosaurs.

Be sure to stop at the Field Station of the *Tyrrell Museum of Palaeontology* in the park. There is an interpretive center where visitors can watch paleontologists at work and visit a nearby winter campground.

Scientists began excavations here late in the last century, ultimately finding the skeletons of 120 dinosaurs, which were duly distributed to museums around the world; only four skeletons remain in the park — three duck-billed dinosaurs and one horned dinosaur, all of which were recovered and restored by Dr. H. C. Sternberg, the world-famous paleontologist. The park has been kept as natural as possible, with the skeletons on display in the badlands, housed in protective buildings. Visitors are welcome to roam around the parkland, and although access to certain areas is restricted, tours are available. Note that all fossils and bones are protected by law; you are not allowed to keep any you may find.

The park also is the site of John Ware's cabin, a museum depicting life on an early Alberta ranch. A former slave from South Carolina, Ware settled here in the late 1800s, when little was known of this valley. He eventually ran a thousand head of cattle on the Red Deer River.

En Route from Dinosaur Provincial Park – The next major destination is Drumheller, to the northwest, where there are more dinosaurs. Pick up Route 1 again at Brooks and continue west. You will be traveling gradually out of the badlands. After about 48 miles (77 km), the highway passes the Blackfoot Indian Reserve. The towns of Cluny and Gleichen on the reserve are well worth your attention. Off the Trans-Canada Highway, a few miles south of Cluny, is Blackfoot Crossing. Here, in 1877, Crowfoot, chief of the Blackfoot Nation, signed Treaty No. 7, which provided peace between the Indians and white settlers. On the way back to the Trans-Canada you will pass a marker indicating Crowfoot's grave. Up the ridge from the marker is an Indian burial ground containing the graves of many Indians who died of starvation and poverty after the treaty was signed. At the edge of the graveyard, surrounded by a black fence, is the grave of Crowfoot. Eight miles (13 km) past Cluny on Route 1 will be a turnoff for Gleichen. For locally made Indian crafts, visit the *Buffalo Jump Arts and Crafts Centre* (at the junction of Route 1 and the Gleichen turnoff; phone: 403-734-3882) and *Early Thunder Creations,* (phone: 403-734-2535) located about 10 miles (16 km) east of town. On the south side of town are the buildings of Old Sun College. Here the Blackfoot operate a museum of Indian history and culture intended to be a major center for the study of Indian civilization. Many exhibits are completed, and work is continuing to bring back artifacts dispersed throughout Canada over the past century. To view the museum's collections, write or call the Blackfoot Cultural Studies Department (Old Sun College, Gleichen T0J 1N0; phone: 403-734-3862) in advance. To continue on to Drumheller, return to the Trans-Canada Highway. A turnoff to Route 21 appears 18 miles (29 km) later. Head north on Route 21 for 23 miles (37 km) and turn east on Route 9. Another 29 miles (46 km) will bring you to Drumheller. Over the course of this route, you will have reentered the badlands.

DRUMHELLER: This city of 6,300 boasts an excellent museum — the *Royal Tyrrell Museum of Palaeontology* (Dinosaur Trail; phone: 403-823-7707) and spectacular landscape. Here, over the ages, the Red Deer River has carved the Drumheller Valley deep into the plains. The region is filled with hoodoos and exposed layers of stone, gullies, and canyons. And, as at Brooks, the river has uncovered the remains of prehistoric animals.

Drumheller's other major attraction is the Dinosaur Trail, a 29-mile (46-km) tourist road that begins at the outskirts of town, travels through the badlands north and west of the city, and brings you back to town. Despite its name, the Dinosaur Trail contains a mixture of attractions relating to local life and history and is more commercial than Dinosaur Provincial Park. Entering through the north gate, you come first to the *Homestead Antique Museum* (phone: 403-823-2600), a collection assembled by local farmers of just about anything that relates to life in the Drumheller area. The road travels through badlands to the *Royal Tyrrell Museum of Palaeontology* (phone: 403-823-7707), a $30-million provincial museum and research center where you can wander among some 45,000 dinosaur specimens and watch scientists preserving and mounting fossil skeletons. One of the museum's prize pieces is the Albertosaurus skull that geologist Joseph Tyrrell (for whom the center is named) discovered in the area in 1884. The museum also boasts a garden of tropical plants similar to those that thrived in Alberta between 70 and 300 million years ago. The facility is open year-round, and admission is free. Next, you come to the Little Church, a universal house of worship that accommodates six worshipers at a time. Somewhat beyond the Little Church is Horsethief Canyon. From the road there is an excellent view of the canyon's fine desert landscape. After Horsethief Canyon, a ferry takes you across the Red Deer River, and on the opposite bank you pass by thousands of fossilized oysters.

The road has now turned south and continues through more badlands terrain. Drumheller Prehistoric Park contains life-size replicas of dinosaurs and a rock and fossil shop.

Six miles (10 km) southwest of town, off Route 9, Horse Shoe Canyon is an excellent example of desert landscape. From the canyon floor the rock piles rise in strange shapes, and the canyon's walls are layers of contrasting green, red, and gold. There are fine vantage points along the canyon's rim, and trails lead down into the canyon itself. You also can take an hour's drive east from Drumheller, along Route 10, to East Coulee. This route goes deeper into the river valley, passes some abandoned coal mine shafts, and reveals more hoodoos and some mushroom-shaped rock formations. There is an interpretive center and a walking trail around the mine site. Near East Coulee, a swinging bridge spans a deep portion of the valley. At East Coulee you will find the Atlas Mines. Although closed now, they were once the region's major working coal mine. Some East Coulee citizens are now working to revive the old 1940s mine as a museum, and surface tours are available. *The East Coulee School* (ca. 1930) has been restored and is now a museum. There also is a crafts store, tearoom, and art gallery. Motel rooms and campsites are readily available in Drumheller.

En Route from Drumheller – To reach the city of Red Deer and, from there, the highway to Edmonton, head north and west. The quickest way is Route 9 west from Drumheller, which becomes Route 72, and 72 miles (115 km) west of Drumheller, intersects Route 2. Go north on Route 2, a four-lane highway, another 57 miles (91 km) to Red Deer. One worthwhile detour along the way is Stephansson House, the historic residence of Iceland's national poet. It's just north of Markerville (turn west off Route 2 onto Route 592). It also is possible to make the trip to Red Deer by way of secondary roads through countryside that lacks any major tourist attractions but does have interesting scenery. Follow Route 56 north from Drumheller for about 25 miles (40 km) and then cut west on Route

585. After 22 miles (35 km), Route 585 intersects Route 21 at Trochu. Head north on Route 21 for 19 miles (31 km) until it intersects Route 42. Take Route 42 west for 24 miles (38 km), and it crosses Route 2 just south of Red Deer.

RED DEER: This city of nearly 55,000 and its vicinity are worth a visit, perhaps an overnight stay. It is the convention capitol of the province and a fast-growing industrial center. Although Red Deer is not a major touist attraction, there is a museum worth seeing: the *Red Deer and District Museum* (47th Ave. and 45th St.) is devoted to pioneer history. If hunger strikes, there's *Phil's Steaks and Pancakes* (*Port O'Call Shopping Centre*) as well as *Smitty's* — an attractive alternative to the standard gas station restaurants (on Route 2 south of the city). The *Red Deer Lodge* (49th Ave.) and the *Black Knight Inn* (50th Ave.) both have dining rooms (see *Best en Route*).

Of greater interest to a vacationer is the area just west of the city on Highway 11. Here in wooded countryside is the town of Sylvan Lake, a resort popular with Albertans, with six commercial campgrounds and a public beach, on the south shore of the lake. This area is popular and may be crowded, so those in need of some serious solitude should drive around to the north shore of Sylvan Lake, where Jarvis Bay Provincial Park has been established. Less crowded and more peaceful, the park has trailer sites, picnic facilities, swimming, fishing, and boat rentals.

En Route from Red Deer – From Red Deer it's an easy 93 miles (149 km) north to Edmonton on either Route 2, the major highway, or Route 2A, which passes through towns along the way. The countryside is pleasant, at times spectacular. Sights include two more lake resorts west of the highways. Red Deer also can be the starting point for a trip west on Route 11, the David Thompson Highway. Rocky Mountain House on Route 11, the only national historic park in western Canada, is built on the site of several former trading posts. This 154-mile (246-km) road crosses unspoiled country through the Rocky Mountain Forest Reserve and terminates at the boundary of Banff and Jasper national parks.

Fifteen miles (24 km) north of Red Deer is the town of Lacombe, home of the Canadian Agriculture Department's research station, where scientists develop new varieties of wheat and grain. The station is open to visitors. Seven miles (11 km) west of Lacombe, at Gull Lake, is Aspen Beach Provincial Park, the best of the area's lake resorts, with more than 400 campsites in two campgrounds, swimming, fishing, and boat rentals. Continuing north for another 19 miles (30 km), Routes 2 and 2A both cross Route 13. Follow Route 13 west from Route 2, and you will shortly arrive at Pigeon Lake Provincial Park, with campsites, swimming, fishing, and boat rentals. Route 13 east from Route 2 leads to the town of Wetaskiwin, at the junction of Route 2A. Here, the *Reynolds Museum* (403-352-6201), an agricultural and transportation museum, has assembled one of North America's largest collections of antique and classic cars, fire engines, and airplanes. The final 42 miles (67 km) north take you through farmland, past the town of Leduc, to Edmonton. For a complete account of Edmonton, its hotels and restaurants, see *Edmonton,* THE CITIES. From Edmonton, you can take Route 16 west to Jasper or you can head north and explore the Slave Lake-Peace River region.

BEST EN ROUTE

Medicine Hat, Brooks, Drumheller, and Red Deer have good motels and there are several good campgrounds. There are no truly luxurious or major resort motels, but most are pleasant and comfortable, with the fanciest at Red Deer. Expect to pay $55 to $75 per night for a double room in the expensive range; $40 to $50 in the hotels we list as moderate; $35 and under in the inexpensive range. All prices are quoted in US dollars.

MEDICINE HAT

Imperial – This motel has 104 units, telephones, exercise room, an indoor pool, sauna, and whirlpool bath. At the east entrance to the city on Highway 1. 3282 13th Ave. SE (phone: 403-527-8811). Moderate.

TraveLodge – At the junction of Routes 1 and 3, this 92-unit motel has both outdoor and indoor swimming pools, telephones, and color TV sets, as well as a dining room and cocktail lounge. 1100 Redcliff Dr. SW (phone: 403-527-2275). Moderate.

Gas City Campground – Considered one of the best in the province, this 97-site property is open May through September (403-526-0644). Inexpensive.

BROOKS

Heritage Inn – Color TV sets, telephones, and air conditioning in all of its 64 rooms. There is a restaurant and cocktail lounge. On Main St., just off the Trans-Canada Highway, or write PO Box 907 (phone: 403-362-6666). Moderate.

Tillebrook Provincial Park – On 344 acres, its 120 tent and trailer sites have electrical hook-ups, showers, flush toilets, and piped water. Open year-round. Five miles (8 km) southeast of Brooks on Route 1 (phone: 403-362-2962). Inexpensive.

DRUMHELLER

Drumheller Inn – Features include an indoor pool, whirlpool bath, color TV sets, 100 rooms, executive suites, dining room, and lounge. 100 Railway Ave. SE (phone: 403-823-8400). Expensive.

RED DEER

Red Deer Lodge – Considered the best in Red Deer. Built around an indoor courtyard featuring many plants and a swimming pool, this 233-room motel has color TV sets, telephones, a hot tub, a surprisingly good dining room, tavern, poolside coffee shop, and cocktail lounge. There also are a number of lovely duplex suites. 4311 49th Ave. (phone: 403-346-8841). Expensive.

Black Knight Inn – This 98-room hostelry has an indoor swimming pool, sauna, dining room, cocktail lounge, color TV sets, and telephones. 2929 Gaetz Ave. (phone: 403-343-6666). Moderate.

Edmonton to Slave Lake and Peace River

This long route, 717 miles (1154 km), may not suit everyone's taste. Forming a great circle, it begins at Edmonton, heads north to Athabasca, then turns northwest along the edge of Alberta's northern wilderness past the shores of Lesser Slave Lake until it reaches the town of Peace River. At Peace River the route turns southwest until it reaches the town of Grande Prairie, where it heads south and east back to Edmonton. Although this northern area has few major tourist attractions, it has plenty of farmland and open country, with good hunting and fishing. The area also is rich in history; the first European explorers came here in the 1700s. It is a good place to escape to the serenity of unspoiled nature. The population is small, but the residents are friendly. There are numerous points from which the adventurous traveler can venture farther north, deeper into the forest wilderness. However, the route outlined here remains well within the bounds of civilization and can be comfortably traveled by anyone. The roads usually remain passable during the winter, and the area is good for ice fishing, skating, and cross-country skiing.

Information: A map of Alberta may be obtained from *Travel Alberta,* Dept. E, Box 2500, Edmonton, Alberta T5J 2Z4. Consult their *Adventure Guide* for the names of companies offering rafting trips, nature treks, dog-sledding, canoeing, and fishing experiences in Alberta's northern wilderness. For specific maps on the St. Albert–Slave Lake region, write *Midnight Twilight Tourist Association,* 1 Sturgeon Rd., St. Albert, Alberta T8N 0E8; for the Peace River region, write *Land of the Mighty Peace Tourist Association,* PO Box 3210, Peace River, Alberta T0H 2X0; for the Grande Prairie region, write *Game Country Travel Association,* c/o George Keen, 9932-111 Ave., Grande Praire, Alberta T8V 4C3. For a list of outfitters and guides serving the area, write *Alberta Fish and Wildlife,* North Tower, Petroleum Plaza, 9945-108 St., Edmonton, Main Floor, Alberta T5K 2G6 (phone: 403-427-3574).

ST. ALBERT: Just beyond Edmonton on Route 2 north is St. Albert. Here in 1861 Father Albert Lacombe, one of the great figures in Alberta's history, founded a mission in a log cabin. Lacombe's ministry was, for his time, both progressive and visionary. He aided the Métis (Canadians of European-Indian ancestry) in their efforts to develop the first farms in this area. He worked for peace between the Blackfoot and the Cree nations, and he gave of himself tirelessly during smallpox epidemics. Lacombe's cabin mission still exists, in the Father Lacombe Mission, on St. Vital Avenue off St. Albert Trail. The museum's exhibits include many tools and relics from frontier days as well as material on the history of the Oblate missionary order, to which Father Lacombe belonged.

En Route from St. Albert – North from St. Albert, Route 2 follows the route of an old forest trail, the St. Albert Trail, which dates back to the early 1800s. Unfortunately, no signs of this early trail exist. The road passes by several French Canadian towns — Villeneuve, Rivière Qui Barre, and Vimy — until it arrives at Clyde, 40 miles (64 km) north of Edmonton. From Clyde, Route 2 follows the path of the old Landing Trail north to the town of Athabasca. Along this stretch, efforts are being made to recreate the historical trail: A parallel trail exists for certain stretches, and there are historical markers, historical collections, playgrounds, and modern recreational facilities along the way. Soon you notice fewer and fewer towns and houses and more and more pine trees. At Athabasca, you are beyond the edge of the great northern forests.

ATHABASCA: Located at the southernmost point of the winding Athabasca River, this town has traditionally been both a crossroads and jumping-off point for travelers. In days gone by, Athabasca saw hundreds of fur traders, gold seekers, and missionaries board the sternwheelers heading north or west. The coming of the railway put an end to all that, and today Athabasca is of interest because of several beautiful lakes nearby. For fishermen, two large lakes containing perch and pike can be reached from Athabasca. Lac la Biche lies 54 miles (86 km) east on Route 55. It has several commercial campsites and Sir Winston Churchill Provincial Park, with campsites. Swimming is allowed. *Diesel's Owl Hoot Cabins and Campground* (phone: 403-623-7073) rents boats to guest. Call ahead to reserve a camping spot, or 1 of the 11 cabins. About 40 miles (64 km) north of Athabasca on Route 813 is Calling Lake Provincial Park, a far less developed, quieter locale, with about 25 tent and trailer sites. If the extra driving does not appeal to you, consider three smaller but excellent lakes just off our main route leaving Athabasca, discussed below.

En Route from Athabasca – Leaving Athabasca, Route 2 swings west for 10 miles (16 km) to Baptiste Lake. You can fish and swim in the lake, and boating is allowed, although there are no boat rentals. As the road turns north from Baptiste Lake, it changes from pavement to a packed surface for about 30 miles (48 km), but it remains easily travelable. Ten miles (16 km) north of Baptiste Lake is Island Lake, another fishing spot. And another 10 miles (16 km) north is Lawrence Lake, with fishing, a beach, swimming, and a boat launch but no boat rentals. Island Lake and Lawrence Lake both have small campgrounds.

The next point of major interest is the town of Slave Lake, on the shore of Lesser Slave Lake. When Route 2 becomes paved once again, several miles past Lawrence Lake, you are about 35 miles (56 km) away from Slave Lake. On the way you may want to stop and see the village of Smith, a bustling river town until the railroad passed it by. Some forlorn examples of the original cabins are still standing.

SLAVE LAKE: Slave Lake and its vicinity are essentially places to relax and to enjoy the lake and the woods. The town, with a population of 5,600, sits at the southeastern corner of Lesser Slave Lake. The lake itself is a vast expanse of water over 40 miles long. Unlike many of the lakes of southern Alberta, which are fed by the icy waters of mountain glaciers, Lesser Slave warms up during the summer and is quite comfortable for swimming. It also has fine sandy beaches and, during the summer, daylight lasts late into the evening hours, making for great late-night picnics. The shoreline is thick with berry bushes — raspberries, wild strawberries, Saskatoon berries — as well as delicate wild flowers and ferns. There are several motels in town and at least two commercial campgrounds in the area. On the eastern shore of the lake, north of town, Lesser Slave Lake Provincial Park covers 18,000 acres. There are picnic facilities, a beach, and a hiking trail, and swimming and fishing are permitted. From the top of Mt. Marten to the east of the park, you have a commanding view of the length of the lake and of the Swan Hills, a nearly untouched wilderness area out to the south.

If you are a serious hunter or angler, or just a wilderness buff, you may enjoy a side trip from Slave Lake to Desmarais and Wabasca, deeper in the wilderness. To get there, drive north through the provincial park and head northeast on Route 754, for some 40 miles (64 km). There is virtually nothing but unsettled land until you arrive at the two small townsites, located between North and South Wabasca lakes. This is primarily a fishing area — for perch and pike in the lakes and trout in the streams. Write in advance to *Eric Alook* (General Delivery, Wabasca, Alberta TOG 2K0; phone: 403-891-2262) or consult the list of guides and outfitters provided by Alberta Fish and Wildlife in Edmonton to inquire about fishing, hunting, and tour guiding services in the area. Again, this is not a trip for everyone. And once at Desmarais you will be literally in the middle of nowhere; there are no connecting routes or other towns. Therefore, it is advisable to write to or call the guide service well in advance of your trip.

En Route from Slave Lake – Route 2 travels westward along the southern shore of Lesser Slave Lake. After 25 miles (40 km) a turnoff onto Route 33, an unpaved road, leads down into the Swan Hills. Humans have left the Swan Hills pretty much alone, and the area is full of deer, moose, duck, elk, bear, trout, and pike. It can make an interesting side trip, but keep in mind that much of the area is inaccessible by car.

Returning to Route 2, the road continues west for another 70 miles (112 km). It passes the western end of Lesser Slave Lake at mile 40 (64 km) of this distance. Throughout this area it passes by towns rooted in the early history of the white man in the province. The town of Joussard near the southwestern end of the lake was named after Bishop Joussard, a respected, 19th-century missionary in the

Northwest Territories and Alberta. Grouard, near the lake's northwestern corner, bears the name of another missionary. The town's history goes back to 1801, when it was a fur trading outpost. It became a bustling city in the late 1800s, when it gained a large Métis population and the Hudson's Bay Company made it its district headquarters. But after the railroad went well south of the town, Grouard's glory faded. While you may want to visit these towns out of curiosity, you will find little that calls to mind their lively pasts.

At High Prairie, directly on Route 2 about 15 miles (24 km) past the western shore of Lesser Slave, displays showing the area's history can be seen at the *High Prairie and District Centennial Museum.* However, the best museum lies farther along the route at Girouxville (see below). Also at High Prairie is a turnoff onto Route 749, which takes you to Winagami Lake Provincial Park, a few miles to the north. The park has swimming, fishing, and tent and trailer sites. About 15 miles (24 km) west of High Prairie, Route 2 turns north and intersects Route 49 after 18 miles (29 km). A side trip west for 8 miles (13 km) and a turn north on Route 744 will bring you to Girouxville.

The *Girouxville Museum* has exhibits on virtually all aspects of the area's history. In addition to remarkably good and complete collections of tools, household items, Indian artifacts, old books, and documents, the museum has a reconstruction of a trapper's cabin, a chair used in the first meeting of the Alberta legislature, and a 1914 version of a snowmobile. From Girouxville, continue north on Route 744 for a scenic drive to Peace River, or backtrack to Route 2. If you wish, you can stop at Falher, considered to be the honey capital of North America, and tour a honey plant. Once back on Route 2, it's another 38 miles (61 km) north to the town of Peace River.

PEACE RIVER: The Peace River itself and local history are the attractions in this town of about 6,355, located at the point where both the Smoky and the Heart rivers flow into the Peace. Its history reaches back to the days when the Cree called it Sagitawa — the place where one views the meeting of the waters. The fur traders knew it as the Forks, and many a fort was built here. In 1792 Alexander Mackenzie fashioned a shelter and spent the winter here while making his pioneering journey across North America.

An excellent view of the confluence of the waters can be seen from Sagitawa Lookout on Judah Hill on the southeast bank. The confluence is an impressive sight, a vista of calm beauty. You can watch the Peace River, nicknamed "the Mighty Peace," emerge from far back in the countryside. At the points of confluence the river is interspersed by sandbars and green islands. The waters then draw together into a narrower channel and flow north. The sight is all the more impressive if you keep in mind that the Peace rises in British Columbia and flows far to the northwest to join the Slave River. Another excellent spot from which to view the confluence is the top of an 800-foot hill on the east side of town. That hilltop also is the gravesite of the local folk hero, Twelve-Foot Davis. Davis came here during a gold rush in the 1840s. Finding that the best claims had been staked, he took advantage of a surveying error and staked a claim on a 12-foot strip that had been missed between two lots. Thus he won both his fortune and his name.

The *Peace River Centennial Museum* (10302 99th St.; phone: 403-624-4261), open year-round, is in many ways similar to Alberta's other small historical museums, although its collection emphasizes the fur trade. In addition to displays of a fur press and animal traps, there are several Hudson Bay journals kept by early traders and a replica of a paddlewheel boat.

We urge you to think twice before renting a boat. WARNING: The waters at the confluence of the rivers are treacherous; don't take out a boat unless you are expert in boating on rivers. A safer way to travel the Peace is to take the *Tar Island River Cruise.*

The *Tar Island* boat crew will take you on a scenic overnight cruise downriver, fix you a barbecue dinner, let you fish, take you ashore for trail hikes, and bring you back to town. The cruises only operate during the summer. Write ahead for reservations to: *Tar Island River Cruises,* Box 2070, Peace River T0H 2X0 (phone: 403-624-4295).

En Route from Peace River – Head west on Route 2. In about 16 miles (26 km) you will reach Grimshaw. Just west of town is Queen Elizabeth Provincial Park. There are 200 acres with 56 sites for overnight camping and swimming and boating (no boat rentals) at Cardinal Lake. The junction of Routes 2 and 35 just north of Grimshaw offers another side trip for hunters. The town of Manning, 47 miles (75 km) north on Route 35, is a center for wilderness hunting. There also is good trout fishing in the rivers.

From Grimshaw, Route 2 heads southwest for 42 miles (67 km) and reaches Fairview, another good spot from which to launch hunting trips. South of Fairview on Route 2, the town of Dunvegan has restored the St. Charles Mission, a log church and rectory built by missionaries in 1884. The interior has been turned into a museum and interpretive center depicting the town's history as one of the earliest fur trading posts. A small campground is next to the mission. About 22 miles (35 km) farther south on Route 2 is the town of Rycroft. From Rycroft, Route 2 travels through mostly open country to Grande Prairie, 42 miles (67 km) to the south.

GRANDE PRAIRIE: With a population of about 26,800, Grande Prairie is the chief city of an area of farms, ranches, and forests. It has most of the urban amenities that may be welcome after a succession of small towns; these include a golf course, an Olympic-size swimming pool, and a large shopping plaza. The *Pioneer Museum* (in Muskoseepi Park in town) has, along with the usual artifacts and fossils, a good display of the wildlife that abounds in the region. Twelve miles (19 km) west of town on Route 2, Saskatoon Island Provincial Park has campsites and allows swimming in its lake. Part of the park has been set aside as a nesting area for trumpeter swans.

The area all around Grande Prairie and that stretching from Valleyview to White-court to the southeast is good hunting country, and there are many hunting and fishing guides in this region. Contact the Fish and Wildlife Division in Edmonton for a list of names.

En Route from Grande Prairie – To return to Edmonton, backtrack on Route 2 and turn east on Route 34 just north of Grande Prairie. You will again be driving through sparsely populated farmland and forests. About 48 miles (77 km) along Route 34, you will reach Williamson Provincial Park, on Sturgeon Lake. The park has swimming and fishing and contains 62 campsites. Another 11 miles (18 km) will bring you to Valleyview, a good spot from which to begin a hunting trip into the countryside. From Valleyview, head south on Route 43. The 97 miles (155 km) to Whitecourt are virtually open wilderness. Along the way you will see the Swan Hills reappearing in the east. There is a road, Route 32, into the hills just before you reach Whitecourt. At Whitecourt, pause to see the McLeod River join the Athabasca River in a roar of waters. Beyond Whitecourt, Route 43 travels for 72 miles (115 km) past the small towns of central Alberta until it joins Route 16 outside Edmonton. At the junction, you can either turn east for the 19-mile (30-km) drive to Edmonton or head west on Route 16 toward Jasper.

BEST EN ROUTE

This route has few motels and campgrounds, although most of the moderate-size towns on the major roads have motels. And there is overnight camping near most of the major scenic attractions. There's little elegance about the motels, but they are comfortable and have the usual amenities. One or two do have more elaborate facilities. The campgrounds tend to be a little more primitive than many in the US. Expect to pay $40 and up per night for a double room in the expensive range; $20 to $40 in the moderate range; $15 to $20 in the inexpensive range. All prices are quoted in US dollars.

ATHABASCA

Athabasca Inn – A 64-room establishment with TV sets, telephones, a dining room and cocktail lounge, and a tavern. No charge for children under 12 occupying the same room as their parents. 5211 42nd Ave. or PO Box 1526 Athabasca, Alberta TOG 0B0 (phone: 403-675-2294). Expensive.

Athabasca Lodge – This motel has 22 units, some with kitchenettes and all with telephones, plug-ins, and color TV sets, and a refrigerator in every room. On Highway 25, PO Box 1560 (phone: 403-675-2266). Moderate.

Athabasca Municipal Campground – A city-run spot that has 15 tent and trailer sites, showers, flush toilets, a boat launch, and fishing. Open May 1 through October 15. Along Athabasca River, 1 block east of Main St.; PO Box 450 (phone: 403-675-2967). Inexpensive.

SLAVE LAKE

Nash's Cabins – Three log cabins near a private beach, 3 miles (5 km) north of Slave Lake. Open May to October. PO Box 86 (phone: 403-849-3977). Expensive.

Sawridge – This property has 183 rooms featuring color TV sets, telephones, a dining room, and coffee shop. There also is a gift shop. PO Box 879 (phone: 403-849-4101). Expensive.

PEACE RIVER

Traveller's – Another motel, this one has 149 rooms with telephones and color TV sets. There's a tavern, dining rooms, a cocktail lounge, coffee shop, sauna, and the use of an exercise room a block away. Major credit cards accepted. 9510 100th St. or Box 459 (phone: 403-624-3621). Expensive.

Crescent – This motel has 95 units, some with kitchenettes and all with color TV sets, telephones, and plug-ins. Close to the center of town. Major credit cards accepted. 9810 98th St. or PO Box 670 (phone: 403-624-2586). Moderate.

GRANDE PRAIRIE

Alpine – There are 62 units, some kitchenettes, telephones, color TV sets, and an outdoor swimming pool. Major credit cards accepted. 10901 100th Ave. (phone: 403-532-1680). Moderate.

Grande Prairie Inn – This hostelry has 212 rooms, an indoor swimming pool, tropical garden, winter plug-ins for warming up car engines when the weather is cold, telephones, a dining room, and a cocktail lounge. Major credit cards accepted. 11633 100 St. (phone: 403-532-5221). Moderate.

British Columbia

The third-largest province in Canada, British Columbia also is the wettest and most westerly. (Neighboring Yukon juts a few miles farther west, but it is a territory.) BC is bordered on the south by the state of Washington and bits of Montana and Idaho, to the east by Alberta, to the north by the Northwest and Yukon territories and Alaska, and to the west by the Pacific Ocean and the Alaskan Panhandle. The province covers 366,255 square miles, enough land to make 73 Connecticuts or 300 Rhode Islands. Despite the highly visible — to tourists — fruitlands of the Okanagan Valley, the trim pastures of Vancouver Island's east coast, and the truck farms of the Fraser River delta east of Vancouver, less than 10% of the land is now or ever will be arable or grazeable. The rest is covered by virgin forests, towering mountains, and vast expanses of semi-arid sagebrush land.

That immense wilderness is most sparsely inhabited, for three-quarters of the province's population lives at the southwest tip in two cities, the provincial capital of Victoria (population over 270,000) and the Pacific port city of Vancouver, the third-largest Canadian city with more than 1 million inhabitants. (For a detailed report on Vancouver see THE CITIES.) Overall population density averages about 13 to every 2 square miles, scarcely more than thinly populated Alaska.

Motoring routes that provide the most sightseeing with the greatest comfort include a drive up Vancouver Island, a trip up the Fraser River road, a tour of the Okanagan fruit country between Kamloops and the US border, another from Kamloops eastward through the stunningly beautiful mountain parks on the Alberta border, and two wilderness routes starting in midprovince at Prince George, one going to the Pacific Ocean at Prince Rupert, the other to the Alaska Highway and the Yukon.

Running between Vancouver Island and the mainland is a protected channel the length of the mainland's coast, protected from the Pacific's rollers by a chain of barrier islands. The channel is called the Inside Passage and is crisscrossed by routes of comfortable automobile ferries that make possible linking the Vancouver Island drive to several of the mainland routes. The ferry rides — around the forested Gulf Islands and through the densely wooded fjords of the northern reaches — are themselves among the province's most picturesque and pleasant voyages. Eagles and sea birds abound. Porpoises, killer whales, seals, and sea lions swarm in those waters. With luck, occasional ferry passengers see the rare humpback whale, and, on the shore, bear and deer. (For routes and fares, write: *British Columbia Ferry Corporation,* 1112 Fort St., Victoria, BC V8V 4V2.)

The island drive begins at Victoria. (To clear confusion: Victoria is on Vancouver Island, but the city of Vancouver is across the Strait of Georgia on the mainland.) That pretty little capital city at the island's southernmost tip has a climate strikingly like that of southern England, and the locals exploit their supposed English way of life as a prime tourist draw. The road runs northwest on Route 19 through some of the province's rare farmland. Impeccably kept pastures and barns, manicured row crops, and blooded stock make as pretty a bucolic scene as Kentucky's bluegrass or Pennsylvania's Amish country. On the Inside Passage side of the drive, tugs tow immense log rafts through whitecaps whipped up by a spanking breeze, and fishing boats putter about the sparkling waters on mysterious errands. The drive from Victoria to Port Hardy encompasses more than 300 miles (480 km) of this rugged picturesque island that has captured the hearts of countless travelers ever since Captain Cook first met the native people off Nootka Sound in 1778. At Port Hardy, the *Queen of the North* loads cars and passengers for a 15-hour trip to Prince Rupert, terminus of one of the wilderness drives through northern British Columbia. Equipped with a dining room, lounge, and staterooms, the ferry makes a comfortable crossing. Reservations are required. Contact *BC Ferries* (1112 Fort St., Victoria, BC; phone: 604-386-3431), well in advance.

The Fraser River route runs east from Vancouver on the Trans-Canada Highway, Route 1. In its lower reaches, the Fraser River runs serenely through a flat delta of its own building, an alluvial bottomland that supports rich truck and dairy farms. About 75 miles (120 km) east, the delta runs out and mountains close in on the road. The Trans-Canada turns sharply northward here to Yale, the head of navigation on the Fraser. From here on, the river loses its peaceful nature and becomes one of the most turbulent, brawling streams in North America, trying to ram a full-size river through gorges barely wide enough to accommodate a babbling brook. The route runs through former gold-mining country and ends in Bowron Lake Provincial Park, where the forests teem with moose, bear, and trout.

The Okanagan Valley drive is through fruit orchard country transformed from a sagebrush desert to lush farmland by irrigation. With the grape industry utilizing much of the land, this area now boasts 11 wineries and is sometimes known as Canada's "Napa Valley."

The national park route eastward on Trans-Canada from Kamloops runs through the Rockies in a cluster of national parks of majestic beauty. The highest peaks in Canada, great ice fields and glaciers, cobalt blue lakes, and virgin forests make the mountain section of the route a strong competitor for the most beautiful drive in North America.

Starting at Prince George, Route 16 (the Yellowhead route) runs through a sparsely settled wilderness to the terminal at Prince Rupert. From there, the BC ferry will carry travelers to Vancouver Island so they can make the island drive to Victoria. Alaskan ferries also call at Prince Rupert, making possible a side trip further up the Inside Passage to Alaskan ports like Sitka, Juneau, and Skagway.

From Prince George north on Route 97 and the Alaska Highway to the Yukon border, the road runs through a magnificent game-filled wilderness.

Information: *Tourism British Columbia,* 1117 Wharf St., Victoria, BC V8W 2Z2 (phone: 604-382-2127 or 800-663-6000 from both US and Canada).

Vancouver Island

Some Americans still grumble about the Oregon Treaty, ratified by Britain and the US in 1846, which established the 49th Parallel as the line of demarcation for most of the US-Canada border. The complaint is the little blink in the Far West where Vancouver Island drops just below the 49th, putting the beautiful town of Victoria firmly into what should be — but is not — American territory. It makes some Americans nostalgic for Manifest Destiny.

This island of sunken mountains and soaring, snowcapped peaks gives way to sandy beaches carved out by coves, inlets, and fjords. The waters of the Pacific and the Juan de Fuca Strait splashing against the beaches and rocky edges of this island are so gentle and clear that what a US navy lieutenant said more than 100 years ago is still valid: "Nothing can exceed the beauty of these waters . . . I venture nothing in saying there is no country in the world that possesses waters equal to these."

For some, long white beaches, waters teeming with salmon, fine deep harbors, and a year-round mild climate (in the southeast, summer temperatures rarely rise above 90F, or 32C, and winter temperatures seldom fall below freezing) are reason enough to travel the eastern edge of the island. But this 310-mile (496-km) trip from Victoria to Port Hardy reveals more than the soothing sands of the coastal resort towns of Qualicum Beach and Parksville, the salmon runs in the renowned Campbell River, and the stately harbor in Victoria. This island also has a history stretching back to the Haida, Kwakiutl, Sooke, and Cowichan Indians who lived in fishing villages along its coasts. Although their populations have been nearly wiped out by disease, war, and treaties, the Cowichan Indians still fish for salmon in the Cowichan River in much the same way as did their ancestors for thousands of years. But, for the most part, you will feel the spirit of the Indians in the giant totem poles (Thunderbird Park, Victoria), in the petroglyphs on the edges of evaporating pools, and in the legends surrounding geographical landmarks like Forbidden Plateau in Courtenay.

In contrast to the Indian spirit is the very real presence of the Canadians — many of English descent — living in the provincial capital. Although you won't see a bobby on every corner, afternoon tea at the *Empress* hotel is a tradition, not just a show the natives put on for tourists. You could easily spend days visiting Victoria's museums and ornate castles or sampling its very English pubs. Victoria is known as the most British city in Canada, and if it is a little bit stuffy and formal, it sets a tone to the journey along the island's Route 19 that is distinct. The road shoots the full length of the island along its eastern shore, with various side trips across the island. It's a favorite drive of residents.

VICTORIA: This provincial capital jutting into the Juan de Fuca Strait is named after Queen Victoria, and true to her memory, it is perfectly, immaculately British. Victorian architecture, spacious parks, manicured gardens with flowers blooming year-round, and its people (many of British descent) make this harbor city the most British in all Canada.

Established as a Hudson's Bay Company post in 1843, the city went through a rowdy boom-town period almost 2 decades later when fortune seekers stopped on their way to pan for gold in the Fraser River. Bastion Square downtown — with its renovated criminal courthouses, a supply center for miners, a maritime museum, restaurants, and shops with modern items but mid-19th-century architecture — recaptures the years from 1843 to 1889.

But thousands of years before any white person set foot on the North American continent, Indians on the island used deer antlers to chop down the cedars growing nearby to build homes and canoes. Visitors to Thunderbird Park (across from the provincial buildings) will not only see a Kwakiutl Dance House but will feel the awesome power of the mythical thunderbird, thought to be a representation of the huge California condor. Carvings of this creature crest totem poles (some are originals, some copies) throughout the park. Indians believed the bird created thunder by fluttering its wings and lightning by flashing its eyes.

Visitors to the nearby *Royal British Columbia Museum* (675 Belleville St.) can see one of the best collections of Northwest Coast Indian art and view re-created street scenes and turn-of-the-century storefronts.

Considered one of Canada's finest art museums, the *Art Gallery of Greater Victoria* (1040 Moss St.) is home to the only Shinto shrine in North America. There also is a large Japanese and Chinese art collection, and European art from the 15th to the 20th centuries.

The *Royal London Wax Museum* (470 Belleville St.) contains many suprisingly realistic likenesses of some of the prominent people in history and fantasy, a cast of characters ranging from Queen Victoria to Pinocchio.

As the museums and art gallery symbolize the city's past, the Parliament Buildings (corner of Government and Belleville Sts.) exemplify the future of the province. These ornate Victorian structures are built of andesite and native granite. You can visit during working hours.

More of the English influence is evident in the city's Victorian residences; some are far more luxurious than others. Craigdarroch Castle (1050 Joan Crescent) was once the home of a wealthy matron lured to Victoria by her husband's promise of a palatial abode. Robert Dunsmuir, a coal baron, built the castle for his Scottish wife but died before its completion.

Protocol is the name of the game at another posh residence, Government House (1401 Rockland Ave.), the residence of the Lieutenant Governor of British Columbia, the Queen's official representative. The lawns and hall of the mock-Tudor building are open to visitors. And any visitor who signs the guest book in the hall receives an invitation to join the lieutenant governor and his wife for a tea party each July. One recent guest said women are not required to wear a hat and gloves, but they may feel out of place if they don't.

In an old English setting complete with a Chaucer Lane and a 17th-century Plymouth tavern stands a replica of William Shakespeare's birthplace and his wife Anne Hathaway's thatch cottage (429 Lampson St.). Bring a copy of the master's sonnets, spread a blanket on the lawn, and you've got the perfect setting to wonder about Shakespeare's "Dark Lady."

Although the city's English influence is well preserved, it is not completely frozen in architecture or buried in museums. A visitor to the *Empress* hotel (721 Government St.) can partake of one of the most British and genteel customs, afternoon tea (see *Best en Route*). A recent $45-million restoration has fully recaptured the hotel's original charm and elegance.

If you want something more substantial after a spot of tea, head for *Barb's Place* (Fisherman's Wharf) or *Old Victoria Fish & Chips* (1316 Broad), where you can get heaping helpings of this moderately priced meal. Other restaurants cater to every whim — *Taj Mahal* (679 Herald St.) for Indian food; *Japanese Village* (734 Broughton St.) for genuine Japanese cuisine; and *La Petite Colombe* (604 Broughton St.) for French fare. Or, instead of eating indoors, order a box lunch from *Sam's Deli* (805 Government St.) and picnic under the oaks in Beacon Hill Park. Although any place in the city is good for bird watching (sparrows and purple finches perch on apartment windowsills downtown), in the park you can watch native wild ducks and black (English) swans sail serenely across the ponds. From this 154-acre city park, you may hear the distant clanging of the Carillon, a 62-bell gift from the people of the Netherlands for the *1967 Canadian Centennial.*

From the leisurely pace of the people you may get the impression that little work goes on here, but a trip to the inner harbor will put such thoughts to rest. This is a fishing and lumbering center, and ships from all over the world use the harbor as a port of call. For a view of what goes on under the harbor without getting your toes wet, descend to the bottom of the sea at the *Underseas Gardens* (490 Belleville St.) and watch Pacific salmon, wolf eels, and octopi through windows.

SEALAND: From Victoria, head east on the Marine Drive through a district of modern and mid-Victorian homes on the cliffs overlooking the Haro Strait. About 10 miles (16 km) along this road, you will reach *Sealand* (Oak Bay Marina, 1327 Beach Dr.), where killer whales perform with seals, sea lions, and porpoises.

Nearby, anglers can rent a boat at Oak Bay and have a fine day of fishing for rockfish, lingcod, sole, and flounder. It also is possible to cast a lure off the rocks for the salmon and black sea bass that thread their way through the kelp beds in search of small herring or needlefish.

BUTCHART GARDENS: Take Route 17 or 17A north from Victoria, then pick up Benevenuto Ave. to Butchart Gardens, where on 50 acres of manicured lawns, ponds, and lakes bloom exotic and native flowers. More than 88 years ago the estate of Jennie Butchart was a limestone quarry. Through the years, Jennie transformed this dismal scene into a horticulturist's dream: an English garden with thousands of rose beds, arches, and arbors; a Japanese garden with maple trees, hydrangeas, bamboo, and the rare Tibetan blue poppy; and a formal Italian garden with a cross-shaped lily pond and sculptured trees and hedges. A restaurant on the estate offers breakfast, lunch, and afternoon tea, and the *Seed and Gift Store* offers seeds of many of the flowers on the site. Often, on summer evenings, concerts are held at the Gardens. Follow Route 1 to Duncan.

DUNCAN: On the banks of the Cowichan River, this small, bucolic town survives on lumbering — its traditional industry — and farming and fishing. The river is known for European brown trout and Pacific and Atlantic salmon. Surrounding Cowichan Valley is lumbering country, and the economics and ecology of lumbering are the underpinnings of Duncan's prosperity. All of this, and a great deal more, is explained in the *British Columbia Forest Museum* (just a mile/1.6 km outside town), open May to late September. The museum is organized around the theme "Man in the Forest: Yesterday, Today, and Tomorrow," and exhibits explore all aspects of the industry, from the raw beauty and power of forests of 250- and 350-year-old Douglas firs to reseeding and replanting operations in contemporary forests. In addition, the museum has a wonderful collection of early lumbering equipment, including donkey engines, hand carts, and various kinds of saws used when the industry got under way here in 1860.

En Route from Duncan – About 4 miles (6 km) west on Route 18 is Cowichan Bay. Once a prime (and still reasonably good) area for sport fishing, the bay is now covered with log booms to feed nearby mills. You can rent a boat and fish for salmon in late summer and early fall. But the best fishing is off limits to visitors. Local Indians, within whose reserve most of the Cowichan River runs, expelled white anglers from the stretch of the river where steelhead, cutthroat, and brown trout swim.

From Cowichan Bay, you can head back to Route 1, north to the town of Chemainus. Once sustained by its lumber mill, Chemainus seemed doomed when the mill closed. But in a project involving many of the residents, artists took over the sides of stores and buildings to turn the main street into a festival of murals. Each mural depicts an aspect of the area's history from steam locomotives and general stores to loggers and seamen.

Beyond Chemainus, the mountains and sea close together again, funneling travelers through Ladysmith. This town lies on the 49th Parallel, the Canada-US border for mainland British Columbia. Continue on Route 1 to Nanaimo.

NANAIMO: More than a century ago, seven tribes of Indians lived in harmony along the shores of the Georgia Strait. The discovery of coal in 1852 and the arrival of countless British miners destroyed that peace. Less than a decade after an Indian showed the coal and its whereabouts to a Hudson's Bay Company employee trading in a fort here, the company added a turreted bastion with cannons to protect the workers from Indian attacks. Visitors can follow a narrow cowpath-like road uphill to view the bastion, now a museum. Forest products have since replaced coal mining as Nanaimo's main industry.

Recently, tourism has become important to Nanaimo, and the city's waterfront facilities have been redeveloped. The latest addition is Swy-a-Iana Lagoon, the world's only mammal tidal lagoon, which draws observers four times daily. Nanaimo also boasts its own professional theater company with a summer program featuring BC playwrights.

In mid-July, the harbor is the site of one of the wackiest races in Canada. Contestants race, or in some cases float, 35 miles over the often stormy Strait of Georgia to the mainland in motorized bathtub-like contraptions. This popular event, the *World Champion Bathtub Race,* attracts entrants from around the world (see DIRECTIONS).

Those who forgo the tub trip can use the strait for the more traditional sport of fishing. (Salmon, trout, and steelhead proliferate here all year.)

En Route from Nanaimo – Just north along the waterfront on Route 19 is Departure Bay, with marina facilities for boats and yachts. At Parksville, follow Route 4 over a small mountain pass descending into the Alberni Valley and running west to Port Alberni. Along the way the mountain pass cuts through MacMillan Park, one of the best examples anywhere of virgin forest. It's also the home of Cathedral Grove, a cluster of tall west coast cedars and Douglas fir rising high above the forest floor.

PORT ALBERNI: Visitors to this mill city are usually more interested in the sport fishing than the city life. Near here, an angler can find sockeye salmon and cohos in the harbor or follow a narrow paved road 6 miles (10 km) northwest to Sproat Lake, noted for its trout. From Sproat Lake, take Highway 4 to the Pacific Rim National Park. Miles of curving, sandy beaches greet you in this national park with some of the best beachcombing in North America.

En Route from Port Alberni – At the end of Route 4 is Tofino, a pretty little fishing village, which is the site of the annual whale watching festival (late March to April). Retrace Route 4 to Parksville, a resort town with long sandy shores splashed by shallow warm water. Rathtrevor Beach Park, just south of town, has camping and picnic facilities. North of Parksville on Route 19 is Qualicum, with more beaches. South of Qualicum on Route 4A, the Little Qualicum Falls Provincial Park offers a day's hiking or overnight camping.

From Qualicum, head north on Route 19 to Courtenay, the southeastern portion of the Comox Valley. Bounded by high mountains and carved out by clear lakes and the river, this area is home to grouse, duck, geese, and pheasant.

COURTENAY: The British established this town as a major farming community in the late 1880s. (It's now a popular recreational area, with golf courses, lodges, and restaurants.) Before this, Indians lived here atop a mountain known as the Forbidden Plateau, haunted by the legend of a mysterious monster, still feared today. While the tribe's braves were away, the legend says, an enormous monster slew every squaw and child on the plateau. It is believed no Indian has ever returned.

Those not frightened by the legend may make the trip up the plateau by foot for world class wilderness climbing. Both Forbidden Plateau and Mt. Washington offer challenging ski runs during the winter months.

En Route from Courtenay – Head 14 miles (22 km) north along the coast to Miracle Beach Park, a public campsite for 193 tents and a great beach to comb for driftwood. Take Route 19 north to Campbell River.

CAMPBELL RIVER: Although this town is a mining and lumbering port, its fame comes from its excellent salmon fishing. In fact, the most sought-after honor among the fishing fraternity here is membership in the *Tyee Club*. Only those who have caught a tyee salmon weighing more than 30 pounds from a rowboat, on light tackle, in one of two local ponds can become members.

The town enjoys the advantage of the largest river on the island. If you want to rent a boat, tackle, or any other fishing equipment, just walk to the shores of the river, which flows through Strathcona Provincial Park (head west on Rte. 28). Mountain climbers will be challenged by Mt. Albert Edward and Mt. McBride, both over 6,000 feet tall.

About 81 miles (130 km) north on Route 19 is Port McNeill, known for its Vanishing River, a river that disappears into the earth, indicating the existence of a vast subterranean maze of caves and tunnels. Continuing on this portion of Route 19, you'll reach Port Hardy, where visitors can board the *Queen of the North* ferry for a 274-mile (438-km) voyage through the Inside Passage to Prince Rupert on the mainland (contact *British Columbia Ferries,* 1112 Fort St., Victoria, for information). Completion of this highway has opened up North Island all the way to Cape Scott and San Josef provincial parks.

BEST EN ROUTE

This island is one of the most popular vacation spots in Canada, with a wide variety of accommodations from basic modern motels and numerous clean campsites to elaborate hotels. This also means that during the peak season (May to October) it is wise to book ahead. Prices range from around $8 for a place to pitch your tent in a campsite to the expensive hotels (from $110 to $265 for a double) in Victoria. Between these are the moderately priced hotels, bungalows, and cottages ($60 to $110 for a double). Bed and breakfast establishments and inexpensive inns are another lodging alternative ($30 to $40 for a double). For a complete listing of accommodations, write *Tourism BC* (1117 Wharf St., Victoria, BC V8W 2Z2; phone: 604-387-1642). All prices are quoted in US dollars.

VICTORIA

Empress – Built in 1906 on the harbor, this Gothic giant reigns as the largest and best-known hotel on the island. This 480-room bulwark of British custom has completed extensive renovations, but it still retains its old charm. Facilities include 3 bars, a dining room, a pool, and an exercise room. 721 Government St. (phone: 604-384-8111). Expensive.

Laurel Point Inn – An addition to the inner harbor that offers plush, modern facilities, including an indoor/outdoor pool, tennis, a dining room and bar, and balconies with views. Expansion has added banquet facilities and 70 additional rooms. 680 Montreal St. (phone: 604-386-8721). Expensive.

Captain's Palace – This converted mansion has a Tudor exterior, hand-painted fresco ceilings, and antique furniture. The dining room, overlooking the inner harbor, specializes in seafood and steaks. 309 Belleville St. (phone: 604-388-9191). Expensive to moderate.

Oak Bay Beach – A short drive from downtown, this Victorian seaside resort hotel showcases its priceless antiques throughout. Afternoon tea with scones and Devonshire cream is served in the lobby. Gardens, golfing, and a marina are nearby. 1175 Beach Dr. (phone: 604-598-4556). Expensive to moderate.

Olde England Inn – In a renovated 17th-century English village, this gabled Tudor hotel offers rooms with furnishings similar to those in an old carriage house. Set on acres of lawns, it is a tourist attraction but not a typical one. It's a rare hostelry that offers a guest sleeping accommodations in the same bed that King Edward VII supposedly used in Warwick Castle, England. Breakfast, lunch, dinner, and tea are served. In the suburb of Esquimalt at 429 Lampson St. (phone: 604-388-4353). Expensive to moderate.

LADYSMITH

Yellowpoint Lodge – After a fire destroyed this popular resort a few years ago, the owners didn't take long to rebuild, preserving the original form. It remains one of the island's top getaway spots, on 180 acres overlooking the sea. Book one of the rustic log-and-sandstone cottages or a room in the main lodge. Walking trails, tennis, a swimming pool, dining area, and rumpus rooms with fireplaces are all here. RR #3 (phone: 604-245-7422). Expensive to moderate.

NANAIMO

Coast Bastion Inn – Part of the town's revitalized waterfront, this 15-story hotel features a well-equipped health club with Universal gym, a whirlpool bath, sauna, and an outdoor deck. There also are full dining facilities as well as a popular nightclub. 11 Bastion St. (phone: 604-753-6601).

PARKSVILLE

Bayside Inn – Just minutes off the highway on sandy Parksville Bay, this full-service place offers ocean and mountain views. Also, a dining room, lounge, indoor pool and whirlpool bath, aerobics room, tennis, racquetball, and squash are available. 240 Dogwood St. (phone: 604-248-8333). Expensive to moderate.

QUALICUM BEACH

Qualicum College Inn – A modern resort with a pool, whirlpool baths, sauna, and lounge entertainment. The dining room was once an English-style boys' school. Despite the resort atmosphere, this sprawling 4-acre vacation site is reminiscent of its original incarnation. 427 College Rd., PO Box 99 (phone: 604-752-9262). Moderate.

CAMPBELL RIVER

Painter's Lodge – The oldest and the best-known fishing property in town, its guest list includes celebrities and plain folk drawn to the great salmon fishing. It's composed of a main lodge, cottages with fireplaces, a heated pool, boats, guides, access for float planes, a dining room, and a lounge. PO Box 460 (phone: 604-286-1102). Expensive to moderate.

Strathcona Park Lodge – This family-oriented resort, on the edge of Strathcona Provincial Park, offers 4 chalets made up of 50 rooms, plus 12 cabins. The main dining hall serves buffet-style meals daily. Visitors can enjoy boats, kayaks, canoes, and swimming on the 50-mile lake system. Rock-climbing and hiking nearby. Special packages available. PO Box 2160 (phone: 604-286-3122). Moderate.

QUADRA ISLAND

April Point – This fishing resort with a view of the fjords and snow-fringed mountains on the island has a tackle shop, boats, guides, licensed diningroom, heli-fishing, and heli-hiking (helicopter trips to fishing and hiking destinations), swimming, water skiing, and sailing. (From Campbell River, take a 10-minute ride on the *Quadra* car ferry, which operates from May to October.) PO Box 1, Campbell River (phone: 604-285-2222). Expensive.

Fraser River

From the time Indians were the sole inhabitants of this continent to the last century, when prospectors were struck with gold fever, the Fraser River, with its deadly whirlpools, jagged shoals, and white rapids, blocked the road to the promised land — the deer and elk hunting grounds, fur trading routes, and gold mines of the Cariboo Mountains. Though still as wild and fierce as in earlier days, the Fraser is no longer an obstacle to the modern explorer's promised land of calm rivers and lakes stocked with trout and salmon and of rolling sagebrush hills where ruggedly independent folk tend dude and cattle ranches. In fact, the Fraser, boiling rapids and all, may be the choicest oasis in the promised land. This 850-mile (1,360-km) journey is dominated by the narrow, twisting flow of the Fraser: from the Fraser Valley delta around Hope, rich in fur trading history and alive with farm fairs and festivals, through the scenic but perilous Fraser Canyon slashed out by the raging river, to the cattle ranching country north of Cache Creek, where the spirit of the Wild West is as alive today as it was when gold fever hit more than 100 years ago.

In the farmlands to the south, the Fraser is calm, a source of water that makes the countryside lush with vegetation; but farther north at Hell's Gate and Devil's Cauldron (names worthy of the river's wrath), the river puts on its splashiest performance as it winds its way through narrow cliff walls. Although most people watch this show from an aerial tramway at Yale, others, in defiance of Simon Fraser's caution — "It's so wild I cannot find words to describe it" — don life jackets, cling tightly to a rubberized raft, and hurtle over and through the boiling cauldron.

Each July, the river is the site of another spectacular show. Millions of salmon streak the water red as they force their way upstream through rapids and over rocks to spawn and die. For anyone who prefers salmon smoked and filleted at reasonable prices, a trip farther north may be in order.

Here is cowboy country, where the locals act as if it were only yesterday that the West was unsettled and law and order meant each man dealt with transgressors on his own terms. Here the beer flows freely on a Saturday night, when a clean white shirt and red bandanna dress up the usual pair of jeans. But for all its wild spirit, this region's pace is slow, its tensions few. As expressed by one wrangler, a descendant of a man who outfitted prospectors in the mid-1850s: "Our biggest fear is that a moose will break our fences — we've got miles and miles of the barbed wire — and eat our hay. So big deal. No one's ever been mugged by a moose."

A trip through prairie country is a trip through the living West — cattle rustlers and wrestlers are not just movie stereotypes here — you can live on a ranch, pitch hay in the stables, round up the cattle, or just ride through the bush. And it's also a trip through gold rush country, where a reconstructed village (Barkersville) puts you in the heart of the west when the mountains of the Cariboo and the banks of the Fraser promised, with one lucky gold find, a lifetime of easy living.

En Route from Vancouver – Travel east on Route 1 to Langley, a dairy and truck farming community overlooking the Fraser River. Nearby is Fort Langley, now a national historic park, a restored Hudson's Bay Company fort located on the last point on the Fraser River that seagoing vessels can navigate. A visit here brings back days of this site's boom period in 1859, when gold seekers spent as much as $1,500 daily outfitting themselves. At that time the camp was dominated by the Hudson's Bay Company, which even organized dances for the prospectors. But this was more than a company town; it was the site of the founding of British Columbia. Each November 19, Langley sponsors a banquet and historical program in tribute to the day in 1858 when Governor James Douglas signed the decree making British Columbia a British colony.

Heading southeast on Route 1, the road passes Abbotsford, noted for its international air show (one of the biggest on the continent), held here each August.

Traveling east on Route 1, the road skirts the Vedder River, where anglers fish for spring salmon in May and June, coho in the fall, and steelhead trout from December to July. A few miles east, the road cuts through Chilliwack, a small farming town on the Fraser delta abutting the cliffs at the foot of the Coastal Range. From the snowcapped peaks of Mt. Slesse and Mt. Clemme, melting snow cascades over the dark green pines of the range, veiling the rocks and trees underneath and inspiring the name Bridal Falls. Near the town runs the 35-mile Chilliwack River, swimming with Dolly Varden trout. Although the town is in the heart of dairy farming, cattle ranching, and deep river country, it's most noted for its horses. Visitors and residents often parade through the streets and surrounding countryside on the backs of every type of horse, from Arabian stallions to old nags. And each May the town hosts an elaborate *Chilliwack Horse Show.*

South of Chilliwack is Sardis, where Salish Indians sell handwoven mats, aprons, and other garments in old Indian designs. Farther south is Cultus Lake, within a provincial park with camping sites and picnic areas. Each June, crews race war canoes across the 3-mile-wide lake as part of the *Indian Festival.*

Continue east on Route 1 to Hope.

HOPE: This small town, surrounded by mountains and alongside the Fraser River (at this point still calm), is known as the entrance to the Fraser River Valley. Here in 1848 the Hudson's Bay Company established Fort Hope — a fitting name, considering the dangers of the Fraser River just upstream. The name stuck until the town was incorporated in 1965, becoming just Hope. Although the site enjoyed a burst of growth in 1858, when miners stopped before paddlewheeling up the river to the gold fields, it has since shrunk (it has 4,000 residents today). Visitors often stop to stock up on supplies and get a good night's rest before venturing into the interior.

The town has the *Hope Museum* (Water St. off Route 1; phone: 604-869-7322), which has relics of pioneer days, two of the oldest churches in the province, and a major festival celebrating settlement days. On the second weekend in September, tourists are invited to join the populace in 3 days of logging sports, parades, and motorcycle races commemorating *Brigade Days*.

The area around Hope offers first-rate hiking and climbing, and, due to the updrafts caused by the mountainous terrain, soaring and hang gliding also are popular.

From this town, 5,400-foot Mt. Ogilvie is visible. Goats scamper on its ledges, and black bear, deer, and raccoon live within its forests.

En Route from Hope – The opening of a new highway gives travelers a choice of two routes to Kamloops. The faint of heart can head northeast on the Coquihalla Highway for a shorter and less adventurous trip to the interior city of Kamloops. While wildlife and scenery abound, gas stations do not. Fill up in Hope. Or head north on Route 1 to Yale, the gateway to Fraser Canyon, where the Fraser rages in all its power. It is such a twisting, treacherous run of water because the mountains in the center of the continent (the Rockies, Selkirks, Cariboos) receive extraordinary amounts of snow. And when the warm Pacific breezes waft eastward, the vast snow fields melt, unleashing a fierce torrent flowing in one direction, carving sheer canyon walls and craggy mountain bluffs. At Yale, the water, squeezed between the reddish bluffs of the Cascade Mountains and the Coastal Range, forms swirling, churning rapids.

These bluffs and rapids mocked the dreams of gold-struck prospectors in the last century. Genteel storekeepers and farmers from eastern Canada and the US forsook families and friends; sailors jumped ships; soldiers deserted regiments. They joined priests, prostitutes, and even shiploads of refined English ladies lured here by the promise of marriage to prospectors, making their way up the Fraser on rough-hewn log rafts. These adventurous, courageous, avaricious (take your pick) people arrived at Yale and found the natural barrier of cliff and water almost insurmountable — almost, but not quite, for their ingenuity was fired by lust. Prospectors used rope ladders to hoist themselves and their horses, mules, and camels over sheer cliff walls that at some points rise 7,000 feet. (An enterprising outfitter introduced camels to lug heavy loads of mining gear. But the beasts' stench so repelled the mules, horses, and prospectors that they were let out to pasture in fields and valleys along the way.) They also built a makeshift road (Cariboo Road) along the bedrock of the canyon. Although still precipitous in parts, today's route is made infinitely easier by paved highways overlooking the Fraser and by the tunnels drilled through the canyon walls. When the river is quiet, a traveler can still see an occasional contemporary gold seeker, with manual sluices and gold pans, searching for pay dirt below.

A few miles north of Yale, the canyon constricts to form Hell's Gate, where visitors can board an aerial tramway (open April to November) and peer down at the federal fisheries (constructed by the US and Canada after blockages in the river threatened the lives of the sockeye salmon). Each July, battered and exhausted salmon make their tortuous 24-day journey over rocky riverbeds, through fierce rapids, and over the federal fishway steps to spawn and then die at the mouth of the Adams River.

North on Route 1 is Boston Bar, noted for its gold mining in the last century and for its jade today. Nineteen miles (30 km) north is Jack Ass Mountain, a precipitous ridge on the canyon cliffs where (so the story goes) a donkey laden with heavy gold-mining gear jumped 1,500 feet to the river below rather than carry his burden to Cariboo. A few miles farther north is Lytton, where the Fraser Canyon ends and the Thompson River valley begins.

The Thompson and Fraser rivers converge here, and at their banks fortune seekers still pan for gold and search for jade. But a more reliable quest is for the steelhead trout swimming in these fast-flowing waters from late October to spring.

The Thompson River knifes through mountains, revealing 10,000-year-old rocks and nurturing semi-arid terrain of sagebrush, bunch grass, and prickly pear cactus. An exciting way to experience both the tranquillity and the turbulence of the river is to board a motorized rubber raft in Lytton.

Either rafting the Thompson or traveling Route 1 will lead you to "Gold Pan Campsite" on the banks of the Thompson. From here you can see mountain sheep scampering along the stratified edges of the cliffs.

From Lytton, travel north to Spences Bridge. During the summer, vendors sell honey, fruit, and apple juice along the highway. The town is an Indian reserve, where remains of the "wikiups" (houses used by nomadic Indians) still stand. In a ravine stand apricot trees, part of the orchards an early settler planted. Although chukar, partridge, deer, and grouse still inhabit this region, avid hunting has greatly reduced their numbers. From Spences Bridge, Route 1 rises to what was once a sagebrush plain but is now irrigated ranching country. Some 27 miles (43 km) north is Ashcroft, the entrance to the Bethlehem Copper Pits. A mile (1.6 km) out of town is Ashcroft Manor, a pioneer ranch settled by the first Lieutenant Governor of British Columbia, Clement Cornwall. Although Cornwall was the very personification of the pioneer spirit — his courage and energy were indomitable — his Englishness was equally indelible. When he led guests on "modified" foxhunts, everyone wore traditional garb. (Hunts were modified because the quest was coyote, not fox, of which few exist in BC.) The riding habits and hunt gear are on display in the manor, now restored and open to the public.

A few miles north is Cache Creek, at the junction of Routes 1 and 97.

CACHE CREEK: A stopover for prospectors seeking gold in the Cariboos in the last century, today this city acts as a halfway point between the lower Fraser and Cariboo region. Surrounded by the semi-arid ranching country of the Thompson Flats, Cache Creek is a center for cattle ranching and copper mining. It also often is a base for freshwater sport fishermen.

Although no gold is found here today, the legends of the boomtown era live in the town's name. An ignominious (and perhaps fictional) bandit stole 80 pounds of gold from a successful miner and cached it here before disappearing. It's never been found. Some tell of disbanded camel caravans grazing on the Thompson Flats after an unfortunate run on the Cariboo Trail, where they frightened both man and beast.

En Route from Cache Creek – Follow Route 97 north through the dry hills surrounding Cache Creek. Take a side trip east to Loon Lake for small rainbow trout or follow a dirt road farther northeast to Lake Bonaparte for the bigger trout.

Route 97 runs through Clinton, an up-to-date version of the Old West.

CLINTON: Although its name comes from a British duke, the character of this spunky settlement comes from its history as a roadside stop on the trail to the Cariboo gold fields — 47 Mile House on the Gold Rush Trail.

Travel 5 miles (8 km) north and 22 miles (35 km) east to 808 acres of wooded and rolling terrain interspersed with lakes for fishing and swimming.

En Route from Clinton – North on Route 97 about 10 miles (16 km) you pass through Painted Chasm. Amid heavily forested areas and grassy meadows with cattle grazing is the chasm, a multicolored gorge rising out of the lowlands with rocks thought to be 10,000 years old.

North of the chasm, a road leads east to Bridge Lake, surrounded by lakes for fishing and waterfowl hunting. In season, grouse and small game thrive here.

Driving farther north on 97 brings you to 100 Mile House.

100 MILE HOUSE: The men who blazed the Cariboo wagon road from Lillooet to the gold fields of Cariboo were paid by the mile. This may explain why 100 Mile House is a good deal short of 100 miles from the start of the trail. Although 100 Mile House (an official designation) is preserved as a testimony to man's chicanery, greed, and ingenuity, it is a sprawling ranch that sets the tone of the town. In 1912, the Marquis of Exeter purchased a ranch here. His son, Lord Martin Cecil, ran it and the Emissaries of the Divine Light, a religious group, until his recent death. The town is known for its annual 50-kilometer *Cariboo Marathon,* which draws upward of 2,000 hale and hearty cross-country skiers every February.

En Route from 100 Mile House – Back on Route 97, the road runs through rolling, wooded country dotted with lakes, where waterfowl live on the marshy borders. One of these lakes, Lac La Hache, beside the highway, has some of the best kokanee (landlocked salmon) fishing in the province.

Drive north on 97 (watch out for chipmunks and squirrels crossing the highway) to Williams Lake.

WILLIAMS LAKE: During the Chilcotin Indian War of 1864, Willy'um, chief of the Shuswap Indians (now the Sugar Cane tribe) saved the white settlers here from being massacred. To show their thanks, the settlers named the town after him. Although a stone marks the spot where the Indians held their tribal meetings (Colunetze, "gathering place of lordly ones"), the Indian spirit has been violated here (as in most other towns) by the rowdier and more aggressive culture of the western gold panners. Typical of the Wild West atmosphere is the *Williams Lake Stampede* each July, in which top riders, many of them Indian ranch hands, compete in such traditional rodeo events as bronco riding and cattle wrestling.

Running parallel to this hillside town is 6-mile-long Williams Lake.

En Route from Williams Lake – Head east on a series of dirt roads to the forested rolling terrain around Horsefly and Quesnel lakes, surrounded by the mountains of Big Timoth and Mt. Stevenson, both over 7,000 feet. You'll find lake trout and kokanee, and a hiker may sight a moose, deer, or black bear roaming through the cottonwoods.

Head north on Route 97, which leads through about 75 miles (120 km) of ranching, logging, and mining country along the edges of the Fraser River to Quesnel, a former Cariboo gold rush town, now a booming lumbering center. During the summer months the main streets are lined with colorful petunia blossoms. Salmon fishing is good where the Quesnel River enters the Fraser.

Head east from here on Route 26 to Barkerville, a restored gold mining boom town near 1,300-acre Bowron Lake Provincial Park.

BARKERVILLE: In 1862, a Cornish fortune seeker named Billy Barker jumped ship, came here, and staked a claim on a small parcel of land. After digging 40 feet down and finding nothing but dirt, Barker was almost ready to give up and head north. But he and his mates persisted and 2 feet deeper they found a pocket of gold nuggets worth $600,000 ($9 million by today's standards). Attracted by Barker's find, thousands of prospectors swarmed here, making this town the biggest city north of San Francisco and west of Chicago. Like the city named for him (now a ghost town restored for tourists), the fate of Billy Barker was sad. He married a more successful gold digger than himself and died penniless in a Victoria nursing home.

Visitors can pan for gold nearby, ride a stagecoach, or watch a period melodrama at the *Theatre Royal.*

A few miles east is Bowron Lake Provincial Park Wilderness Area, where moose, beaver, caribou, mountain goat, grizzly bear, and wolf live in a wildlife sanctuary. In the lakes and streams swim Kamloops, Dolly Varden, and lake trout. If not the most satisfying activity in the park, certainly the most strenuous is canoeing on such lakes as Bowron, Indianpoint, and Isaac, and portaging equipment among them.

BEST EN ROUTE

Sagebrush ranges and wooded plateaus are the backdrop for some of the best vacation bets in the region: ranch holidays. Here are working cattle ranches, where hundreds of head of branded cattle graze on the short grasses of the arid ranges. When cattle hands round them up, you're usually more than welcome to help. One ranch owner describes it as riding like the wind, circling and circling the cattle. Or you can stay on a ranch where expensive, sleek Arabian horses are the main attraction. Here you ride on blazed trails and live in up-to-date accommodations. Wherever you stay, the food is fresh and plentiful. For example, there's roast beef off the range (a freshly slaughtered specialty you're not about to find at your supermarket). The nightly entertainment is usually a gathering of cowpokes — both urban and authentic — sitting around the fireplace listening to cowboy music. The range of prices is wide, from luxury accommodations for $1,300 a week (expensive!) to less fancy ones for about $400 a week (moderate). Although most ranches are open all year, the horseback riding is sometimes replaced by cross-country skiing during the bitterly cold winters.

ASHCROFT

Sundance Guest Ranch – A luxury dude and working cattle ranch for people who like to go out on the trail and rough it up, then have a nice hot bath or a swim in the heated pool when they return. Early every morning, wranglers wake up the guests and take them out to the trails, riding everything from Arabian to quarter horses. Guests are divided according to their riding abilities, some galloping over small rivers, others trotting or walking on the sagebrush prairies on half-day or day-long supervised trail rides. The nightlife is centered around the giant stone fireplace and bar. (Bring your own liquor; mixers, glasses, and ice are supplied.) Each room, with wall-to-wall carpeting, bath, and TV set, is located in the main lodge on the Thompson Flats within view of the river snaking below. Open year-round. Five miles (8 km) south off Highland Valley Rd.; write PO Box 489 (phone: 604-453-2554/2422). Expensive.

100 MILE HOUSE

108 Golf and Country Inn Resort – Fans of cross-country skiing, horseback riding, swimming, golfing, or tennis should know about this 62-room motor lodge. For riding the open range, late August, September, and October are best. Let them know you're coming and they'll take you along on a real cattle roundup. After a hard day's ride, relax in the whirlpool bath and sauna. Walks and drives will take you to some incredible bird-watching, and there's fishing right on the property. The resort's 62 rooms all have private balconies or patios, color TV sets, and private baths. As for wintertime, the Canadian Olympic team called the ranch's rolling Cariboo rangelands some of the greatest cross-country ski terrain in the entire world. And there are, sleigh rides, tobogganing, and ice fishing as well. For those guests whose taste in food also is more basic, European cuisine often takes a back seat to west coast favorites like smoked salmon. Open year-round with a 4,800-foot paved airstrip. Box 2, RR 1 (phone: 604-791-5211). Moderate.

Okanagan Orchard Country

If you rode a horse through British Columbia's Okanagan orchard country in the mid-1850s, you would have galloped through tall green grass and patches of sagebrush, forded rivers and streams, and passed azure lakes. From low mountain plateaus you would have viewed a variety of grouse feeding beside the lakes. Although much of the terrain has changed little in centuries, this valley sandwiched between the Cascade Range and the Monashee Mountains now supports countless apple, pear, and apricot orchards.

The best time to travel this route (a 184-mile/294-km trip from Kamloops south to Osoyoos) is spring, when the direct rays of the sun have not yet singed the grass. Spring also is the best time of year to head from Osoyoos north 117 miles (187 km) to Vernon, through a fairyland of pink peach blossoms misting the borders of lakes and mountains.

You will drive through Kelowna, where in 1869 the Oblate Father Pandosy landscaped his Indian mission with a tiny orchard fed from nearby lakes by a crude irrigation system. Farther south is Penticton, now known as the fruit capital of the region, but little more than a one-horse town before Thomas Ellis, a former Oregonian, buried some peach pits here in 1874. Here, farmers and the cattle ranchers are further exploiting their natural resources of sun (it shines almost daily in the spring and summer), water, and land by setting up boating and fishing facilities and resorts around the lakes, renting horses for prairie rides, and holding fairs to celebrate the fruit harvests.

The route starts in Kamloops, then goes southward into Okanagan country, which is dotted with roadside stands where vendors sell cool fruit drinks that taste as if they have come straight from the tree. They have. The valley also is one of Canada's few wine producing regions.

KAMLOOPS: This city, sprawled across the sagebrush hills and dry brown mountains is a major junction for motorists driving on Highways 1 and 5. But more significant to the visitor is the name the Indians gave this site — Cumcloups, "the meeting of the waters" — where the north and south branches of the Thompson River converge, creating Kamloops Lake. (A strain of trout that jumps a few feet into the air after being hooked, Kamloops trout, is found in the lake.)

The pioneering spirit of the Overlanders who, struck by gold fever, crossed the Rockies, journeyed through forests, and rafted the rapids of the North Thompson to reach Kamloops is commemorated in many of the city's festivals and celebrations. Kamloops has an indoor rodeo, a bluegrass country music festival, a sunfest, and an international air show in spring and summer.

Nearby mountains are rife with deer, moose, grizzly bear, caribou, and elk, and the lakes teem with trout. For hunting, fishing, and other tourist information, contact the *Kamloops Travel Info Centre* (phone: 604-374-3377).

En Route from Kamloops – Follow Route 5 south and turn east on a gravel road to Douglas Lake. Here, in the center of miles of prairie grass broken by cactus and an occasional cottonwood, is Douglas Lake Cattle Ranch, one of the largest in Canada. A few miles south, the road skirts Nicola Lake, one of the roughest and deepest in the province and noted for good trout and kokanee fishing. Nearby is an entrance to the *Quilchena* hotel (see *Best en Route*), built in 1908 and a fine example of the architecture of the era. South on Route 5 is Merritt, home of the *Nicola Valley Rodeo* (September) and an indoor rodeo (February). Although copper and molybdenum mining is a multimillion-dollar industry here, amateur rockhounds can explore the nearby Coldwater River and Mill Creek for everything from intrusive batholiths and stream gravels to jade, agate, gold, and platinum.

Head south to Princeton and northwest along a dirt road to Coalmount, a mining ghost town. Before the mountains were gouged out in 1860, the town was known as Vermillion Forks because of the red ocher outcroppings, used by the Indians for paint.

Return to Princeton and take Route 3 southeast to Hedley, once the site of an enormously rich base metal and gold mine. Hummocks of stone and bricks lie where buildings were once a hive of activity; now the only signs of life are the grouse and mountain sheep on the surrounding mountains.

Farther southeast, separated from the Okanagan Valley by a small mountain range, is Keremeos. The road through town is edged with blossoming fruit trees in spring and roadside stands selling fruit, apple cider, and honey during the summer. Head south on Route 3 to Osoyoos, a combination ranching-fruit growing town. From Anarchist Mountain Lookout along the road, you can see orchards and deep Osoyoos Lake contrasting with "Desert Gardens," 1 mile (1.6 km) south of town, an arid area of semidesert. This is a resort town where you can fish for trout and bass along the lakeshore or swim among the painted turtles. The town holds a variety of festivals, including the *Golden Age Jamboree* (April/ May); *Warm Water Open Ski Tournament* (May 24); the *Cherry Fiesta* (July); and the *International Powerboat Races* (September).

As you head north on Route 97 toward Penticton, plains dotted with lupine and some fruit trees give way to the orchards of the Okanagan Valley.

PENTICTON: Since the first orchard was planted here in 1874, this settlement has grown from a few fruit picking, cattle grazing families to a city of some 24,000 people. Located on the southern shores of Okanagan Lake and surrounded by orchards of peach trees, the site of a large fruit packing plant and winery, Penticton is known as the city of beaches and peaches. In fact, each July and August the city celebrates a *Peach Festival,* during which peach brandy is consumed in quantity and visitors and natives alike are coaxed into dancing in the streets.

Besides, with almost 150 miles of shoreline, Lake Okanagan is home to rainbow trout and an old sternwheeler, the SS *Sicamous,* once the only means of transportation on the lake. And, like so many large lakes, the Okanagan has its yet-to-be-seen monster, Ogopogo.

Follow route 97 north across a bridge floating on Lake Okanagan to Kelowna, where Father Pandosy planted the first peach pit in front of his mission house. This city of parks, beaches, gardens, and broad streets is partly encircled by terraced orchards. It's a well-water greenness thanks to lakes hidden in the mountains ringing the valley. A combination of virtually unlimited water resources and nearly 2,000 hours of sunshine a year makes Kelowna not only a major fruit and wine producing region, but also a playground for both tourists and residents.

Heading north to Vernon, the road ascends over Kalamalka Lake (Indian for "lake of many colors"), whose waters change color with every passing cloud. A few miles farther is Vernon, a town with more orchards, sunshine, and lakes, the end of the Okanagan journey.

BEST EN ROUTE

Accommodations range from modern hotels and motels in a fair-size city to dude ranches and beach bungalows. Prices for a double in the expensive category range from $100 to $195; moderate, from $50 to $95; and for an inexpensive room, from $30 to $45. All prices are quoted in US dollars.

KAMLOOPS

Coast Canadian Inn – This place offers the most modern facilities available in this interior city. There's a heated outdoor swimming pool (seasonal), a pub, and a dining room. 339 St. Paul St. (phone: 604-372-5201). Expensive to moderate.

QUILCHENA

Quilchena – A hotel on the shores of Nicola Lake that was built in 1908 and has retained its turn-of-the-century decor. Facilities include a licensed dining room, golfing, horses, and boating on Nicola Lake. Open May to October. Located on the lake in Quilchena (phone: 604-378-2611). Inexpensive.

PRINCETON

Riverside – On the Tulameen River, the motel offers a cluster of rustic log cabins. Open year-round. PO Box 368 (phone: 604-295-6232). Inexpensive.

NARAMATA

Sandy Beach Lodge – Nestled among peach trees, the cottages here overlook Okanagan Lake. The resort has a swimming pool and tennis courts. Open mid-May to October. PO Box 8 (phone: 604-496-5765). Moderate.

PENTICTON

Lakeside Resort – On the shores of Okanagan Lake, this first class establishment has become a favorite get-away for discriminating Vancouverites. Each of the 204 rooms has a private balcony, and there's outdoor dining, an indoor pool, a whirlpool bath, sauna, tennis courts, and exercise room. Boardsailing, parasailing, and water skiing facilities are on the lake. 21 Lakeshore Dr. (phone: 604-493-8221). Expensive.

KELOWNA

Lake Okanagan Resort – A half-hour drive from Kelowna proper, this lakeside resort has both suites and housekeeping units. Recreation facilities abound: a par-3 golf course, horseback riding, water skiing, boardsailing, sailing, 3 heated pools, and the warm waters of Lake Okanagan. Open April to October. 2751 Westside Rd. (phone: 604-769-3511). Expensive to moderate.

VERNON

Tiki Village Motor Inn – This motor hotel has a Polynesian decor, a 1-acre garden courtyard, heated outdoor pool, sauna, and restaurant. 2408 34th St. (604-545-2268). Moderate to inexpensive.

The Pacific National Parks

One hardly thinks of national parks coming in groups, like an exaltation of larks or a clowder of cats, but on British Columbia's eastern border that is exactly what happens. Several mountain chains tumble together — the Purcell, Selkirk, and Rockies — and the result is a jagged tangle of glaciers, chasms, peaks, and snow fields unparalleled in the Western Hemisphere. The Trans-Canada Highway cuts like a blade through this wondrous knot, connecting Kamloops in the west with Banff across the Alberta border. To protect the sanctity of these mountains, huge areas have been made national parks, with access through Revelstoke on the Trans-Canada.

The mountains themselves — Mt. Revelstoke, Glacier, Yoho, Kootenay, and Bugaboo — make up parts of the long chain that separates British Columbia from the rest of Canada, creating its unique weather systems and that touch of isolation responsible for its Pacific coast culture. The 280-mile (448-km) trip from Kamloops on Route 1 (the Trans-Canada) skirts Mt. Revelstoke, bisects Glacier National Park and Yoho National Park, and passes near the entrance to Kootenay Park.

For thousands of years the mountains of the Continental Divide stood in splendid isolation. Few Indians ventured into them, awed by the size of the glacier-torn peaks and chasms. Certain lakes were fished, and ocher beds in the Kootenay Mountains were used for their natural paint. Oddly, early fur traders approached the mountains with the same circumspection, and it wasn't until the railroad came through that the mountains were even partially explored by white men. An expedition of explorers, construction workers, and engineers threaded the railroad over precarious mountain passes, through the densely wooded forests at lower altitudes, and beside lakes and rivers.

This conglomeration of mountains was considered quite special, and the federal government was persuaded to preserve these lands as national parks. Preservation, however, does not preclude the human presence. There are luxurious baths near the hot springs of Kootenay and numerous well-maintained hiking trails linking the most interesting spots in the parks.

En Route from Kamloops – (For more on Kamloops, see the *Okanagan Orchard Country* route.) Head east along Route 1 to the world's richest 300 acres (or so the roadside sign says). Here are the Adams River spawning beds, where in late October millions of salmon spawn and die after fighting their way up the Fraser and Thompson rivers. When the early settlers arrived, the salmon were pitchforked out of the water and used for fertilizer.

Traveling east, the road follows the Columbia River through the mountains of the Monashee Range to Revelstoke. The town, a stop on the Canadian Pacific Railroad, is near the eastern entrance to Mt. Revelstoke park.

MT. REVELSTOKE NATIONAL PARK: So enchanted were the citizens of Revelstoke with the variety of natural rock formations, trees, and animals in the nearby Clachacudainn Mountains that they persuaded the government to designate 100 square miles of it a national park. Thanks to their efforts, a visitor can walk 40 miles of trails, including one 16-mile trail meandering through valleys cloaked in trembling aspen, black cottonwood, and Rocky Mountain maple and over hillsides covered with rain forests of western white pine, western red cedar, western hemlock, Douglas fir, and spruce below the timberline. Other trails lead to mountain meadows of blazing Indian paintbrush, arnica, and valerian to Eva Lake, teeming with trout, and to masses of colorful rock, thought to be 500 million years old.

Although the extensive snowfalls (between 30 and 40 ft.) scare off most of the big animals, a variety of birds, including the wren, finch, Canada jay — and even the golden eagle — fly above.

Before you climb the peaks, including Mt. La Forme (8,400 ft.) and Mt. Cyr (8,520 ft.), or camp in the wild, contact the Superintendent of Parks in Revelstoke.

GLACIER NATIONAL PARK: Between Revelstoke and Golden on Route 1, high up in the Selkirk and Purcell ranges, is this 521-square-mile park, where huge snowfalls occur each year. While some of this snow melts and cascades down waterfalls and rivers or evaporates, much of it never melts. Earlier snows compact, harden, and through their sheer weight create glaciers that crawl down the mountainside. Ragged summits, including the 10,818-foot Mt. Sir Donald, and steep canyon walls have been carved out and polished by the slow-motion flow of countless rivers of ice, forming and descending to the plains over thousands of years.

If you've always wanted to see a glacier nose-to-ice this is the place. There are more than 400 glaciers here, with trails leading to two of them, Illecillewaet and Asulkan. Another trail leads to the Nakimu Caves of Cougar Valley, a seemingly endless maze of limestone passages underground. While trekking through the dense forests of western red cedar and hemlock on any of the hundreds of miles of trail, be careful:

Avalanches sometimes close the highway, and the underbrush is too thick to pass in places. Although the snowfall limits the growth period below the timberline to 2 months, the glacial lily, alpine anemone, and heather grow well during summer.

For a map of trails, lakes, glaciers, and campgrounds, contact *Parks Canada Administration Offices,* Yoho National Park, Box 99, Field, BC V0A 1G0 (phone: 604-343-6324).

En Route from Glacier National Park – Head east on Route 1 to Golden, the gateway to Yoho National Park and the beginning of the Rocky Mountain Range, looming high above the east. This city changed its name from the Cache to Golden after a silver rush in nearby Cathedral Park panned out.

YOHO NATIONAL PARK: Even after other mountain ranges in the province had been smoothed by wind, snow, and rain, the Rockies still had not erupted from the earth. This may explain why the younger range (when the Selkirks were 105 million years old, the Rockies had not yet been born) has 28 peaks soaring more than 10,000 feet into the air. The astounding heights of these peaks have given the park its name, Yoho — "awe" in Cree. Long before the Palliser expedition penetrated Kicking Horse Pass, the Crees had plied the pass from east to west, camped around Emerald Lake, and fished for cutthroat, brook, and lake trout.

More than 250 miles of hiking trails crisscross this 507-square-mile region in the heart of the Rockies. A trip on the Yoho Valley Trail extends from the evergreen forests surrounding the Laughing Falls to the Yoho Glacier.

From the twin-spired Mt. Goodsir, more than 11,000 feet high, to the craggy ridges where mountain goat, hoary marmot, and pika graze, and below, to the wet regions inhabited by ducks and Canada geese, the park is an untamed wilderness.

KOOTENAY NATIONAL PARK: On the southern end of Yoho is this 543-square-mile park, running parallel to the Continental Divide on the western slopes of the Rockies. Marked and wilderness trails lead to Marble Canyon, created by the power of the waterfall at Tokumm Creek; to glaciers on the sides of the mountains; and to grassy alpine meadows dotted with wild flowers, marshes, and lakes.

Other trails lead to the ocher beds southwest of Marble Canyon. Kootenay, Stoney, and Blackfoot Indians dipped into these natural paint pots to stain their bodies, decorate their teepees, and draw pictures on rocks. Near Sinclair Canyon at the southwest end of the park paintings of elk, bighorn sheep, bear, and horses adorn the limestone ledges.

At the base of Redstreak Mountain in the valley carved out by Sinclair Creek is the source of the Radium Best Western, one of the more developed, popular places in the park. Water seeps through faults deep in the earth where the rock masses are hot. When it meets this hot mass, it turns to steam and quickly rises through fissures to meet the cool air. The steam condenses to water at a temperature of 113F (45C) and is channeled to the Aquacourt, which is a modern bathing pool.

BEST EN ROUTE

All of these establishments are near the national parks and range in price from about $45 for an inexpensive room or cottage for two people to $70 for a moderately priced establishment, and $160 for an expensive one. Glacier, Yoho, and Kootenay national parks offer developed campsites on a first-come, first-served basis. For wilderness camping in Revelstoke, check with the park supervisor. All prices are quoted in US dollars.

REVELSTOKE

Three Valley Gap Motor Inn – This sprawling lakefront resort is a ghost town — and a place to sleep. From the gold mining towns of Canada, owner Gordon

Bell transported bits and pieces of gambling halls, gin mills, and cabins and reassembled them here to preserve a slice of the Wild West. The structures are filled with authentic furnishings of the period — a long bar, roulette wheels, and spittoons. Open April to October. PO Box 860 (phone: 604-837-2109). Moderate.

YOHO NATIONAL PARK

Emerald Lake Lodge – A rustic lodge overlooking the lake, it is 5 miles (8 km) north of Highway 1. Open year-round. There's a licensed dining room, game rooms, outdoor hot tubs, and a sauna. Box 10, Field (phone: 604-343-6321). Expensive to moderate.

KOOTENAY NATIONAL PARK

Radium Hot Springs Lodge – Overlooking the hot springs, this motor hotel is built on solid rock in the midst of dense pine forests. The lodge has dining facilities, whirlpool baths, sauna, and in-room movies. Golf packages are available. PO Box 70, Radium Hot Springs (phone: 604-347-9622). Moderate.

Blakley's Bungalows – Each secluded cottage has its own fireplace and bath or shower. PO Box 190, Radium Hot Springs (phone: 604-347-9918). Inexpensive.

Prince George to Prince Rupert

This region was one of the last in the province to be penetrated by the white man, and it has yet to fall prey to modern "civilization" and development. The Rocky Mountains (which separate this area from the rest of British Columbia) have always posed a natural, almost insurmountable barrier to explorers, traders, and loggers.

Although there are some large, modern cattle ranches and mining and lumbering operations, this 456-mile (730-km) trip from Prince George — the crossroads of the province — west to Prince Rupert — dubbed the Halibut Capital of the World — takes in a string of small fishing and hunting villages that seem frozen in time. These settlements and the surrounding area are almost as unspoiled as when the Indians hunted moose on the densely wooded foothills and speared salmon in the deep rivers years ago.

Heading west from Prince George, you will drive through river canyons with semiprecious stones at the base to parks where driftwood lines the bottom of deep canyons. You will enter the village of Hazelton, where the Indians have erected a Kwakiutl longhouse to commemorate their past. South of this town is Fort St. James, settled as a Hudson's Bay fort by Simon Fraser when he explored the region. Around the fort are dense evergreen forests and some of the best big-game hunting in the province. The area's large lakes (Burns and Babine are just two) offer boating and fishing.

As the tour proceeds west to the Pacific Ocean, the climate changes drastically. In the interior, 15 to 25 inches of rain fall in a year, but the coastal city of Prince Rupert gets more than 100. As one native remarked, "It's a great place when it's sunny."

PRINCE GEORGE: Before railway and road workers extended the *Canadian Pacific Railroad* and paved Routes 97 and 16 through the heart of the city, this site was a slumbering Hudson's Bay Company trading post. Today, however, it is the crossroad of the north, south, east, and west. Truckloads of timber, farm produce, and minerals cross the heart of this city daily. To the visitor, all this activity means modern hotels, restaurants, museums (*Prince George Art Gallery;* 2820 15th Ave., 604-563-6447), historic sites (*Fort George Regional Museum;* 20th Ave. entrance of Fort George Park; phone: 604-563-6447), and a taste of city life with emphasis on recreational facilities.

One of the main attractions is the par-71 golf course at the *Prince George Golf Club* (phone: 604-563-0357). During the summer and spring, golfers ply the course in the usual manner, but come February, ingenious enthusiasts dress up in costumes and whack purple golf balls across the snow-covered course in the *World Championship of Snow Golf.*

But it is the city's location near the confluence of the Nechako and Fraser rivers that gives this town its special appeal. From here, anglers can travel to nearby lakes swimming with rainbow and steelhead trout or hike to the backwoods to bag the big game — grizzly bear, black bear, caribou, deer, and moose.

For all tourist information, including a list of hunting guides, visit *Prince George Tourism Office,* 1198 Victoria St. (phone: 604-562-3700).

En Route from Prince George – Drive west along Route 16 to Vanderhoof, noted for its Nechako Bird Sanctuary, a stopover for Canada geese in the spring and fall. Then head north on Route 27 to Fort St. James, founded in 1806 by Simon Fraser and the original capital of New Caledonia, which was the name of the territory before it became British Columbia. Several of the old Hudson's Bay Company buildings are still standing on the banks of nearby Stuart Lake. There's excellent moose and grouse hunting.

Head back south to Vanderhoof and west on Route 16 through forests of poplar to Fraser Lake, the site of Endako Mines and Fraser Lake Sawmills. At nearby Stellako River, the rainbow trout fishing is excellent.

Head west to Burns Lake, noted for the Pinkut artificial salmon-spawning grounds. The back roads radiating from this town lead to good hunting territory and fishing lakes.

Tschesinkut Lake, 10 miles (16 km) south of town with some of the cleanest water in the province, supports lots of lake and rainbow trout. Another nearby lake is Francois Lake, 80 miles long and teeming with freshwater fish. The area around Burns Lake also is fine moose hunting country.

TWEEDSMUIR PROVINCIAL PARK: Follow Route 35 south to Tweedsmuir Provincial Park, a mixture of semi-arid prairie lands, icecapped mountain peaks, and lush meadows sprouting purple lupine and yellow black-eyed Susans. Running through the park are such rivers as the Bella Coola and Dean, where Dolly Varden and cutthroat swim all year. In the undeveloped thick forests of spruce, moose, mountain caribou, and grizzlies roam.

Return to Route 16; head west toward Hazelton and its Indian village of Ksan.

HAZELTON: Before a Hudson's Bay Company employee renamed the village after the abundant hazelnut trees covering this fertile farmland, Indians called the site Kiran-maksh, "where people fish by torchlight." Beside this modern Indian town is a replica of the Gitksan Indian village (Ksan) that stood there before the white man arrived. It has six Indian longhouses, birchbark canoes, and numerous totem poles, including one carved in 1850.

Continue southwest on Route 16 to its terminus at Prince Rupert.

PRINCE RUPERT: Because of its position on the western coast of the province, this site was chosen as the terminus of the *Grand Trunk Pacific Railway.* It also was chosen by urban planners to become a city as large and developed as Vancouver. Although, like many artificially created cities, it failed to fulfill the ambitions of its founders, it is still worth a visit.

Situated on lightly hilly terrain in the midst of thick pine forests, Prince Rupert overlooks an ice-free harbor, and its economy is centered around its halibut and salmon canning industry. You may visit these canneries (if you can stand the smell). The city also has a museum (*Museum of Northern British Columbia,* with Tsimpsian and Haida Indian artifacts). In June it celebrates an annual *Sea Fest.*

There is car and passenger service to Port Hardy on Vancouver Island.

BEST EN ROUTE

Although this part of British Columbia is one of Canada's more remote areas, you don't need to suffer the pains of primitive accommodations. In fact, most hotels seem to go out of their way to make sure their facilities match those of the busier tourist areas — and each hotel is really a self-contained visitors' center. The price range in the area is pretty established, with most of the hotels falling into the moderate category — charging around $60 per night, double occupancy. Very few places are inexpensive — under $40 per night for two people — and almost none of the hotel facilities are expensive, charging more than $70 per night for two. All prices are quoted in US dollars.

PRINCE GEORGE

Coast Inn of the North – Offers everything a traveler could possibly want, from restaurant and lounge to pool and health club. 770 Brunswick St. (phone: 604-563-0121). Expensive to moderate.

Holiday Inn – Located right downtown, this full-service hostelry has a licensed lounge, a pub, a casino, and free covered parking. Other facilities include an indoor pool, sauna, and a whirlpool bath. 444 George St., Prince George, BC V2L 1R6 (phone: 800-405-4329). Moderate.

Sandman Inn – This spot provides a wide range of facilities in a modern building, including a restaurant, pool, and sauna. 1650 Central St. (phone: 604-563-8131). Moderate.

TERRACE

Inn of the West – A fairly small establishment with very nice rooms; the management provides a full range of creature comforts and really cares about its guests. 4620 Lakelse Ave. (phone: 604-638-8141). Moderate.

Sandman Inn – Located in the downtown area of western Terrace, across from the *Skeena Mall,* with spacious rooms, a restaurant, pool, and other niceties. 4828 Hwy. 16 W. (phone: 604-635-9151). Moderate.

PRINCE RUPERT

Prince Rupert – Overlooking the harbor, room service and nightly entertainment in the cabaret are offered. Second Ave. and Sixth St. (phone: 604-624-6711). Moderate.

Raffles Inn – Also overlooking the harbor, this soundproofed motel guarantees a quiet night's slumber and a hearty breakfast in the morning in its restaurant. 1080 W. Third Ave. (phone: 604-624-9161). Inexpensive.

Prince George to the Yukon

For thousands of years, the northern part of British Columbia has been wilderness — snowcapped mountains; forests of spruce and pine alive with caribou, moose, and grizzlies; deep lakes choked with Arctic grayling and Dolly Varden trout; and churning rivers carving out mountain passes. It's a great place for hunters, fishermen, and hikers who believe the farther away from cities and towns the nearer to heaven.

However, civilization is following the gravel and the blacktop of the Alaska Highway, creeping north and south, east and west, into the wilderness. Within this rough, awesomely beautiful mixture of mountain, prairie, and wood lies the raw stuff of commercial interests — oil, minerals, and lumber. Explorers have already dug for oil and found it. Mining companies have begun to extract minerals. Lumber companies have cut forests. This means instant towns, more modern accommodations, more restaurants, and more people — mostly in boom towns hugging the highway. What this will do to the wilderness is anybody's guess. It is doubtful that in this age of ecological sensitivity the wilderness will be mortally threatened, but there is a pristine purity to BC's northern expanses right now that is as delicate as it is virginal. This is a good time to make the 860-mile (1,376-km) trip from Prince George up Route 97 to Dawson Creek and north along the Alaska Highway.

This is a region of extremes: from the valleys of the Peace River region with rich farmlands to the 7,536-foot peak of Mt. St. George in Stone Mountain Park; from the cold waters of Muncho Lake swimming with Arctic grayling to the 120F (49C) Liard Hot Springs, soothing stiff tendons; from dense forests of spruce and pine to oceans of wheat near Dawson Creek; from 20 hours of darkness in cruel, frigid winters to 20 hours of sunlight in pleasant, mild summers.

But before you journey to the northern part of the province, some words of caution. The Alaska Highway is not the New Jersey Turnpike, though 90% of it is now paved. And whether you go in the winter, when the highway is a frozen, snow-covered surface, in the summer, when it's muddy, or during autumn, when the roadbed is fairly good, never wander far from the road unless you've got a guide or have extensive wilderness training. The area beyond has few trails and few facilities for the trekker.

This trip may not be for everybody, but it is for those who prefer the hush accompanying the kaleidoscope of colors as the Northern Lights streak across the unpolluted black sky to the blare of the jukebox and the flashing strobes of a discotheque.

For complete hunting, fishing, and touring information, and for road condition reports to the Yukon border, contact the *Peace River Alaska Highway Tourist Association* (P.O. Box 6850, Fort St. John V1J 4J3; phone: 604-785-2544). To fly into the wilderness, contact *Air B.C.* (Dawson Creek Airport; phone: 604-782-1661). Guides, licenses, and tourist information are available year-round from the chambers of commerce in towns along the Alaska Highway.

En Route from Prince George – (For information about Prince George, see the Prince George to Prince Rupert route.) Follow Route 97 (John Hart Highway) from Prince George north 32 miles (51 km) to Summit Lake, on the Continental Divide. From this Rocky Mountain ridge, water flows either north to the Arctic Ocean or south to the Pacific or Atlantic. Follow Route 97 north and take Route

39 to MacKenzie, established in 1966 to process the dense forests nearby. Those interested in the lumber industry may tour the town's two pulp mills. But its prime attraction is the 5,960-foot lookout on Morfee Mountain. From here, Williston Lake (the largest manmade lake in the province) and its miles and miles of wilderness can be seen. The lake is rich in lake trout, while within the jackpine forest roam black bear and moose. Return to Route 97.

After cutting through the lowest crossover point in the Rockies, the road passes Chetwynd, on the slopes of the Rockies. Following the wave of prospectors who searched for gold here in 1861, the site slumbered for more than 100 years until a new wave of explorers found coal and natural gas. Beyond the coal mines are good moose and deer territory and fine grayling and jackfish lakes. For hunting and fishing information, contact the *Chetwynd Chamber of Commerce*, PO Box 1000 (phone: 604-788-3345).

From Chetwynd, Route 97 stretches from the foothills of the mountains to the vastness of the prairies. Dawson Creek is the center of the province's most vital grain-producing region and also is on the edge of fine moose grazing terrain dotted with lakes stocked with northern pike, Arctic grayling, whitefish, and Dolly Varden and rainbow trout. All wilderness information is available from the *Dawson Creek Tourist Centre*, 900 Alaska Ave., V1G 4T6 (phone: 604-782-9595).

Dawson Creek also is the start (Mile 0/Km 0) of the Alaska Highway, a paved road built during World War II by the US Army Corps of Engineers as a defense measure.

Follow the highway to Fort St. John (Mile 49/Km 79).

FORT ST. JOHN: Although the town is a busy lumbering, oil exploration, and cattle ranching center, tourists are drawn to the fine hunting, fishing, hiking, and canoeing in the environs, rugged mountainous terrain topped by forests of spruce. But before venturing far from the Alaska Highway to seek mountain caribou, mountain goat, and black bear, to blaze your own wilderness route, or to canoe the boiling rapids of the Peace River, stop at the chamber of commerce to hire a guide or get a map. Hunting, fishing, and all tourist information is available from the *Tourist Information Centre*, 9323 100th St. (phone: 604-785-6037).

For many years after this site was settled as a fur trading center (Rocky Mountain House, now an Indian reserve, was the fort), these Northerners depended upon fishing and hunting for their livelihood. A few years back, oil was discovered nearby and this northern community went through a building boom, with new restaurants and hotels going up almost daily.

Although the oil discovery brought a new degree of sophistication to the wilderness, the town still stages some traditional events. In March, the *Spring Ice Carnival;* in June, a rodeo; and in August, the *World Goldpanning Championship.*

En Route from Fort St. John – About 8 miles (13 km) north of town is Charlie Lake, filled with Arctic grayling and gray trout. As the road winds through forested hills and valleys to Pink Mountain (during autumn the multicolored leaves take on a pinkish hue from a distance), do not be surprised to see a moose, black bear, or grizzly parade across the gravel road. Also, stargazers rave about the view of the Northern Lights in the late fall and early winter.

Head northwest to the last fairly large city on the highway, Fort Nelson (Mi 300/Km 483). Beyond this gas-processing and shipbuilding center on the river of the same name is the wilderness, inhabited by grizzlies and olverines. For information, contact the *Fort Nelson Bag Service 399*, V0C 1R0 (phone: 604-774-2541).

Continue west over Summit Pass, the highest elevation on the highway, through Stone Mountain Provincial Park. From the highway, hikers can follow a 4-mile trail (one of the few improved ones) alongside the North Testa River to Flower

Spring Lake, where caribou graze in meadows around the banks. Although the towering peaks of Mt. St. George and Mt. St. Paul may be too taxing for any but the most experienced climber, smaller neighboring mountains may appeal to others. Summit Lake, by the side of the road, is the park's biggest lake and has boating facilities and lake trout and Arctic grayling.

MUNCHO LAKE PROVINCIAL PARK: At Mile 456 (Km 734) this provincial park, 218,476 acres of white spruce and lodgepole pine forests, thins to scrub alpine spruce, lichen, and moss above the timberline. Dominating the park is Muncho Lake (Indian for "big water") ringed by forests inhabited by moose. A hike along an 8-mile trail following Nonda Creek (near the northeastern boundary of the road) will reveal goat, beaver, black bear, and Stone sheep.

A few miles north of the park is the Liard River, Mile 496 (Km 798). From here you can rent equipment and hire a guide to canoe the river, once a prime trade artery for the fur traders and named Liard (French for "poplar") for the trees lining its banks. Here, too, are the Liard Hot Springs, soothingly hot no matter how cold the air. During the winter, visitors don bathing suits and slip into the thermal waters. In the summer, bathers soak in the waters within view of the miniature orchids growing wild on the nearby hills. Near the springs is an 80-unit free campsite; lodging and guide service is available from *Muncho Lake Lodge,* Mile 463/KM 745 (phone: 604-776-3456).

BEST EN ROUTE

As one government tourist official put it: "You're not beating a path through one of the last wilderness regions in the world to find a luxury hotel." But what most of the establishments along the route lack in luxury (and for that matter, character, too, since most are concrete, boxy structures) they make up for in cleanliness and efficiency. New hotels and motels were added to this northern stretch of BC at an astonishing rate a few years ago, after black gold was found in the wilderness. While the oil boom no longer has BC in its grip, the wise traveler will make reservations.

The establishments listed below are moderate: $40 to $55 for a double. All prices are quoted in US dollars.

For those purists who scoff at hotel and motel accommodations, there are plenty of campsites in and around the towns on the tour. Check with the chambers of commerce in the towns for locations. The sites are rented on a first-come, first-served basis.

MACKENZIE

Alexander MacKenzie – This hotel has just about everything — a shopping center, laundromat, beer parlor, dining facilities, and nightly entertainment. PO Box 40 (phone: 604-997-3266). Moderate.

Powder King Ski Village – Within walking distance of the slopes, the resort features a 55-room hotel, with 2 dining rooms, a bar, day-care facilities, and triple-chair and T-bar lifts. PO Box 2405 (phone: 604-561-1776). Moderate.

DAWSON CREEK

Peace Villa – At Mile Point Zero, this motel has carpeted rooms, a sauna, color TV sets, complimentary coffee, and water beds. 1641 Alaska Ave. (phone: 604-782-8175). Moderate.

FORT ST. JOHN

Alexander MacKenzie Inn – A 7-story, modern motel that has an indoor pool, a sauna, and nightly entertainment. 9223 100th St. (phone: 604-785-8364). Moderate.

FORT NELSON

Fort Nelson Motor Hotel – This hotel-motel complex has dining facilities, color TV sets, an indoor pool, and a shopper's arcade. But what places this establishment a notch above the others is its main dining room, where 70 stuffed beasts, from moose to grizzlies, keep an eye on the diners. PO Box 240 (phone: 604-774-6971). Moderate.

Manitoba

Rugged, sparsely settled, and vast, the province of Manitoba covers 251,000 square miles of diverse terrain. Bordered by the US states of North Dakota and Minnesota to the south, the Canadian province of Saskatchewan to the west, Ontario to the east, and the Northwest Territories to the north, Manitoba is home to 1 million inhabitants, many of whom make their living by farming or mining. Most, however, live in the capital, Winnipeg.

Manitoba got its name from its original inhabitants, the Cree Indians, who believed in the spirit Manitou, whose drum was the voice of rushing water. White people came through in the early 17th century in search of the Northwest Passage. The first settlers were French, but in the 19th century communities of Mennonites, Icelanders, and Ukrainians built settlements through the plains.

Although there is plenty of wilderness that will appeal to outdoor sportspeople, the climate in Manitoba certainly is a factor to consider before planning a visit. Bone-chilling winters drop the mercury well below −40F/−40C. In the southern part of the province, summers can get as hot as the 90s F (30s C).

The four driving routes in this chapter are Whiteshell, which travels from Winnipeg east on the Trans-Canada Highway and south to the Mennonite town of Steinbach, Whiteshell Provincial Park, Falcon Lake, Winnipeg River, and Pinawa; the Wheat Belt, which runs west on the Trans-Canada Highway across Whitehorse Plain to Brandon, south through Turtle Mountain Provincial Park to the International Peace Garden; Interlake, which takes you north from Winnipeg along the western shores of Lake Winnipeg past Netley Marsh, Gimli, and Hecla Provincial Park; and the North, which goes west from Winnipeg on the Trans-Canada Highway to Portage La Prairie, northwest to Neepawa, a fur trading post of old, then north through picturesque river valleys to Riding Mountain National Park, The Pas, and Flin Flon, home of the *Flin Flon Trout Festival.*

Information: *Travel Manitoba,* 155 Carlton St., 7th Floor, Winnipeg, Manitoba R3C 3H8 (phone: 800-665-0040, or in Winnipeg, 945-3777).

Whiteshell

Millions of years ago, glaciers covered the high mountains and plains in the eastern part of Manitoba. The movements of the huge ice sheets eroded deep craters and gullies that were eventually filled with crystal-clear water. The ice, sliding through the mountains, exposed quartz and granite layers and ground them down to form gentle hills. Later, the exposed rocks were covered with a thin layer of soil supporting thick forests of barely rooted evergreens. This is the topography of the Canadian Shield.

The Whiteshell tour begins in Winnipeg and runs 209 miles (334 km) east on the Trans-Canada Highway to Falcon Lake. In this region — the Canadian Shield — the hills, valleys, forests, lakes, and streams provide some of the best fishing, hunting, hiking, and recreation in the province. You will see a replica of a Mennonite village near the town of Steinbach, where villagers still grind grain in a wind-powered grist mill. The resort communities of Falcon Lake and West Hawk Lake have fine beaches, sailing, and water skiing. In Whiteshell Provincial Park, the wilderness is traversed by the fast-flowing Winnipeg River. In fact, most of this tour winds through the park, where you'll find hiking trails alongside moose, deer, and black bear territories and deep lakes where trophy-sized northern pike, walleye, and smallmouth bass can be caught. To the north are granite bluffs topped with precariously balanced evergreen and spruce trees. Within the park are the remains of those glacier days — shallow marshy lakes, now speckled with nesting geese and ducks. In the winter, tobogganists and downhill skiers careen down the park's snow-covered hills; cross-country skiers slide along the forest trails; and anglers drill holes in the lakes' frozen surfaces to ice fish.

En Route from Winnipeg – As you head east on Route 1 from Winnipeg, the rich, expansive farmlands of the southwest gradually give way to the jagged granite outcroppings of the Precambrian Shield. At the junction of Routes 1 and 12, take a short side trip south for a glimpse of two towns — Ste. Anne and Steinbach — as different from each other in lifestyle as this century is from the last.

Ste.-Anne, one of the few predominantly French-speaking communities outside of Quebec, is the first town south of Route 1. The *Musée Pointe des Chênes* exhibits the cultural artifacts of the ancestors of these people.

Ten miles (16 km) south brings you to Steinbach, the center of thriving grain farms where Mennonites, escaping religious persecution in Russia, have lived and farmed since 1873.

STEINBACH: Strictures based on religious teachings are the rule of the town. But religion does not ban an annual festival — *Steinbach Pioneer Days* — in which these people demonstrate for visitors such old-time farming methods as reaping, flailing, and plowing and such homemaking chores as spinning, weaving, and churning butter. It's held during *August Long Weekend,* the weekend preceding the first Monday in August, in the *Mennonite Heritage Village* (a museum complex), 1½ miles (2 km) north of Steinbach on Route 12.

Regardless of when you visit this village, you can watch and talk to the Mennonites — who are mostly bilingual (English and a Low German dialect) — as they grind whole-wheat grains in one of Canada's few wind-powered grist mills. You also can buy the flour here to bake your own bread. Or forgo the baking and eat bread and other Mennonite food (try the *varenyky,* a cheese- or potato-filled dumpling) at the livery barn, which along with the blacksmith shop and houses, make up the village complex.

En Route from Steinbach – Return to Route 1. Traveling east, you soon reach Sandilands Provincial Forest, filled with acres and acres of pine, spruce, and other evergreens. Its nursery raises trees to landscape parks throughout the province.

Beyond the forest, a bit north of Route 1 on Route 11 and 51 miles (82 km) from Winnipeg, is Hadashville, an excellent spot to reel in northern pike while canoeing on the Whitemouth River. Then continue east on Route 1 to Falcon Lake, the southern entrance to Whiteshell Provincial Park.

WHITESHELL PROVINCIAL PARK: Here are 1,065 square miles of one of Canada's best wilderness, canoeing, fishing, hunting, and vacation lands. The park stretches from Falcon Lake to the south to the swiftly flowing Winnipeg River on the north, and east to the streams and granite hills of the Canadian Shield. Dramatic waterfalls — such as Rainbow Falls on the northeastern tip of White Lake — splash and crash over granite and snowy quartz before tumbling into rivers, lakes, and streams edged by forests of jackpine, spruce, and elm. Ruffed grouse feed in the vast wild rice beds encircling small lakes, and Canada geese and ducks make the marshes around Hart, Betula, White, and Jessica lakes their home. Atop a layer of caribou moss and spots of muskeg (decayed vegetation), hunters search in spring and fall for the black bear, in recent years the only big game allowed to be taken in the park. For those who prefer driving a golf ball, smashing a tennis ball, or catching the rays on a beach, the resorts of Falcon Lake and West Hawk Lake are the places to stay. For a rundown on everything the park offers, read *The Manitoba Vacation Planner,* free from *Travel Manitoba,* 155 Carlton St., 7th Floor, Winnipeg, Manitoba R3C 3H8.

FALCON LAKE: In Falcon Lake's less wild sections are sophisticated sailing and water-skiing facilities and a guarded swimming beach; a major shopping center; an 18-hole golf course on rolling hills; and tennis courts. But the Beaver Creek circular hiking trail (at the entrance to Falcon Beach) penetrates the more pristine wilderness of the Canadian Shield, where beavers construct dams and an occasional deer whizzes through the spruce. Despite the popularity of this resort, an angler can still find an isolated inlet on the lakes in which to reel in a smallmouth bass, northern pike, and walleye.

During the winter, travel east on Route 301 to *Falcon Lake Ski Resort* (see *Best en Route*), where you can ski down 14 slopes of beginner and intermediate trails.

WEST HAWK LAKE: Thousands of years ago, a meteor fell to earth and formed this lake (also known as Crater Lake), the deepest in Manitoba, at 365 feet. No matter how hot the summer day, this lake is spine-tingling cold. The swimmers may mind, but it certainly doesn't bother the smallmouth bass that inhabit this rockbottomed lake. If you don't care to try to land one of these fighting fish (and then fry it up at one of the area's 150 campsites), you can still savor it at one of the resort's restaurants.

En route from West Hawk Lake – Leave the Trans-Canada Highway and head northwest on Route 44. Just west of Caddy Lake, where you can rent canoes and boats to fish for its smallmouth bass, is the Lily Pond. A small, shallow lake lined with hard rock visible on all shores, it gets its name from the yellow and white water lilies floating on the surface. Across the road is a cliff consisting of light-colored "lenses" of granite formed about 2½ million years ago, when molten rock forced its way in between layers of the harder, older stuff.

At the junction of Route 307 near the town of Rennie (the site of hunting and drive-in fishing lodges) is the Alf Hole Goose Sanctuary. In 1937 a trapper named Alf Hole nursed four sick, abandoned Canada goslings back to health in his home. These four returned the next year, bringing more of their flock. Now, 200 geese return here each spring. At the sanctuary's center are exhibits on the life cycle of the Canada goose.

Return to the junction with Route 307 and head north, driving in between Jessica Lake and White Lake, with its Rainbow Falls cascading over the granite ledge.

Continuing along the route, you come to the Bannock Point petroforms about 2 miles (3 km) north of Betula Lake. Archaeologists believe the petroforms of people, turtles, snakes, fish, and birds were arranged by the Ojibwa in configurations to track the movement of the sun and the moon. Cree, Saulteaux, and Ojibwa Indians once rode over and through these hills and valleys, but all that remains of them in the area are their weapons and stuffed replicas of the bison and elk they once pursued.

From here, the highway cuts through Precambrian country at its best — sparkling lakes, verdant evergreen forests and towering granite cliffs. At the end of Natalie Lake is Seven Sisters Falls on the Winnipeg River. This is not the same river on which trappers, adventurers, and Indians canoed. That river was treacherous — filled with rapids, sudden swirling pools of water, and dangerous obstacles like decaying evergreen trees felled by lightning storms. Today the river is calmer, its rapids tamed by several power dams, of which the largest is in Seven Sisters Falls . . . and there are fewer mosquitoes. Even though canoeing on these waters is not like paddling the uncharted wilderness waters in the northern bush, it does have its moments: You glide on cool fresh water teeming with sturgeon and smallmouth bass, through sheltering forests of birch, bur oaks, and evergreens. Along the rugged cliffs are granite and rock formations that geologists believe to be among the oldest in the world — 2½ billion years. When you've had enough canoeing for the day, you can camp at one of the many sites dotting the Winnipeg River from here to Lake of the Woods in Kenora, Ontario, and dine on some fried smallmouth bass filets.

PINAWA: Ten miles (16 km) west on the Winnipeg River is the Whiteshell Nuclear Research site. During the summer months, general tours of the plant (including a portion of the reactor building and laboratories) are conducted at 10 AM and 1:30 PM. For reservations, call 204-953-2311. Off limits to pregnant women and children under 11 years old. Open Mondays through Fridays year-round, and Saturdays in July and August.

En Route from Pinawa – Returning to Route 44, the road meanders through tall cliffs of dolomite limestone. (Chunks of it were used to build the Legislative Building in Winnipeg.) If you're making this trip in late February, stop at Beausejour for the *Canadian Power Toboggan Championship*. The race is a commercial event in which major snowmobile manufacturers from the US and Canada demonstrate their sophisticated equipment in heart-stopping races.

At the junction with Route 59 at Lockport (see the *Interlake* route), turn south toward Winnipeg. On the last leg of this journey you drive past Birds Hill Provincial Park — 8,300 acres of aspen, poplar, and cedar groves and thickets of strawberries and blueberries. The park offers opportunities for camping only half an hour from the big-city bustle of Winnipeg.

BEST EN ROUTE

Most of the hotels, inns, and camping sites along this route take advantage of the beautiful natural settings of pine and spruce forests and clear lakes. In some of the expensive resorts, expect to pay between $50 and $75 for a room for two. The moderate-priced will range from $25 to $45 for a room. Camping will cost from $6 to $10 per person, per night. On summer weekends, some of the more popular camping sites fill up fast. You can't make reservations, so get there early on Friday. All prices are quoted in US dollars.

STEINBACH

Dutch Connection – A 16-unit motor inn with European touches, color television sets, and full baths. Its restaurant serves authentic Low Countries food in a dining room that's right out of a Rembrandt painting. 88 Brandt Rd. at Highway 12 (phone: 204-326-2018). Moderate.

Frantz – A 20-unit modern motel with color TV sets and full baths was built outside the town limits to avoid a ban on alcoholic beverages. Facilities include a cocktail lounge and bar. South of Route 52 (phone: 204-326-9831). Moderate.

WHITESHELL PROVINCIAL PARK

Falcon Lake – Close to Falcon Lake, the resort is open year-round, but most units are condos. However, 35 units are available and each has a full bath and a color TV set. There's also a cocktail lounge, restaurant, and swimming pool. Open year-round. Falcon Lake (phone: 204-349-8400). Expensive to moderate.

Tallpine Lodge – Near the 15 rustic housekeeping units — some with baths and fireplaces — is a quaint souvenir shop selling Indian crafts and jewelry. Open year-round. West Hawk (phone: 204-349-2209). Moderate.

Caddy Lake Campground – If you crave peace and quiet, camp here in one of 26 sites near Caddy Lake, with a playground, store, and boat ramp. Six miles (10 km) west of West Hawk on Route 44 (no phone). Inexpensive.

Falcon Beach Campground – On summer weekends this is one of the most popular spots in the park. There are 175 tent sites and 117 trailer sites. From here you can rent equipment and boats for fishing on the lake. Falcon Lake (phone: 204-349-2201). Inexpensive.

West Hawk Campground – The 89 campsites and 71 trailer sites are close together, but the tall pines give each a degree of privacy. Often noisy on summer weekends, this provincial government camping facility has picnic shelters and boat rentals. West Hawk (phone: 204-349-2245). Inexpensive.

RENNIE

Inverness Fall Resort – This resort offers 4 deluxe cottages and 6 spartan cabins in a spacious, wooded setting. The complex has a coffee shop and store, tackle and bait shop with fishing and hunting licenses for sale, fly-out fishing service, and canoe and boat rentals. Closed December. Brereton Lake (phone: 204-369-5352). Moderate.

The Wheat Belt

Just as the fertile black soil of these prairies attracted the first settlers to Manitoba, so the beautiful farm and ranch lands beckon vacationers today. The following 500-mile (800-km) route — stretching from Winnipeg west to the Brandon Hills and south to the International Peace Garden on the Canada–North Dakota border — cuts through the heart of the wheat belt, thousands and thousands of acres devoted to wheat, barley, oilseeds, and oats. This "breadbasket of the world" also is fast becoming an important center of dairy farming and cattle ranching.

The breadbasket appeals to city dwellers seeking a change of pace — vast fields of wheat waving in the breeze, cows grazing in green pastures and, in fall, combines sweeping across the plains. Many farmers and ranchers invite visitors to share their homes, their work (pitching hay, milking cows), and their natural resources: lakes, rivers, streams, and countryside.

Spring, the busy season for farmers, is the best time to see how a farm works. In high summer — June, July, and August — the temperature often rises to 100F (38C), and you're likely to be more comfortable visiting an agricultural fair or putting in hard time under an elm tree fishing for perch or walleye. Yet even in winter, when the mercury drops to 20F/−6C (and below) at night, many of the province's farms welcome travelers, offering a place by the family fire and tales of the early prairie days.

En Route from Winnipeg – Leaving Winnipeg on the Trans-Canada Highway (Route 1), the road cuts through the Whitehorse Plain, which Indians believed was haunted by the spirit of a murdered Assiniboine Indian maiden. Just off the highway, near the town of St. François Xavier, a statue of a horse immortalizes the white stallion that the maiden and her equally hapless Cree bridegroom rode to escape the arrows of her jealous suitor, a Sioux. Although the lovers were killed, the ghostly white horse escaped with the soul of the maiden and is believed to roam the plains today.

The route continues along Route 26 to Portage la Prairie, 44 miles (70 km) from Winnipeg, passing several small prairie towns. Along this route is the town of Poplar Point, site of St. Anne's Church. Built about 1864, it is one of the oldest log churches in continuous use in western Canada.

PORTAGE LA PRAIRIE: Many of the early French explorers carried canoes through this area on their way to Lake Manitoba in unsuccessful searches for northwest trade routes to the Far East and its riches. More than a century later, a different type of explorer settled here after discovering that the rich black soil of the prairies nourished wheat. The transient life of explorers — such as Pierre Gaultier de La Vérendrye, who built Fort La Reine here in 1738 — and the more settled ways of farmers — such as John Sutherland Sanderson, who established the first homestead in western Canada here — are dramatically and effectively revealed at *Fort La Reine Museum* (Highway 1A E.; phone: 204-857-3259) and Pioneer Village. A trading post, blacksmith shop, and stable make up the museum, and the village includes an early log homestead, a trapper's cabin, and a "farm of the century" home. Open mid-May to mid-September; admission charge.

There is much more to Portage la Prairie than its past. In July, the town puts on a strawberry festival and, in the same month, the lively *Portage Fair*. A permanent attraction is Island Park and Crescent Lake, a preserve with a horseshoe-shaped lake, sanctuaries for deer, one of the largest captive flocks of Canada geese, hiking trails, tennis courts, and a golf course. The park is on Saskatchewan Avenue at Royal Road, and is open only during summer months.

En Route from Portage la Prairie – Travel west on Route 1 to Austin and its Fort Ellice–Edmonton Trail. Just south of town on Route 34 is the *Manitoba Agricultural Museum* and Homesteaders Village, with its large collection of steam engines, three log buildings, and a grist mill. At the end of July, the *Threshermen's Reunion and Stampede* is marked on the museum grounds with a rodeo and agricultural fair. From Austin, follow the Trans-Canada west to Carberry, where artist, naturalist, and writer Ernest Thompson Seton once lived. This is the center of a unique, desert-like region (see Spruce Woods Provincial Heritage Park, below). The town of Glenboro, south of here, erected a fiberglass camel to give visitors a larger-than-life hint of the terrain (but not the creatures) that awaits them. For excellent and abundant German food, drive 15 miles (24 km) west of Glenboro on Highway No. 2 to Wawanesa, where you'll find *Kurt's Schnitzel House,* 4th St. (phone: 204-824-2472).

SPRUCE WOODS PROVINCIAL HERITAGE PARK: Assiniboine Indians once rode bareback through forests of elm, oak, and trembling aspen (west of the park) to the sloping plains of the Assiniboine River basin. They rode over huge beds of moss, through clumps of fern, and among hazelnut bushes and grapevines to hunt bison, antelope, and mule deer. Like scientists today, they were mystified by the Spirit Sands, a region so similar to a desert that the Canadian Armed Forces simulate desert fighting on it, much to the dismay of environmentalists. (The site of the artillery and tank maneuvers, Camp Shilo, is off limits to tourists.) This region, also known as the Carberry Sandhills, was formed 12,000 years ago when the Assiniboine River flowed into glacial Lake Agassiz, leaving sandy sediment in its wake. Winds whipped the sands into constantly shifting dunes where today rare and endangered desert creatures — the prairie skink and hognose snake — live among the barrel cactus. Although it may appear to be a desert, topographically speaking, it's not. When rain falls in the surrounding countryside, it rains here as well. Spongy sands trap the water and humidity beneath a drier top layer, creating a fascinating phenomenon of sudden springs and thick pots of quicksand. Because of the unique, fragile topography in the park, be careful along the 1-mile Isputinaw and Oxbow Lake trails. Don't expect to see the mainstay of Assiniboine life (bison, antelope, and mule deer). They were slaughtered years ago, mostly by the pioneers.

The park is open year-round, with an extensive winter program. Return via Highway 5 north to Route 1 west to Brandon.

BRANDON: "The Wheat City" lies in the Pembina Valley surrounded by the blue hills of Brandon and divided by the Assiniboine River. On the borders of some of the main streets, golden wheat grows on experimental farms. In the summer the eastern bluebird is an annual visitor. Just outside the city limits, farmers wake at 5 AM to milk cows, beekeepers care for their hives, and children ride their horses before school. But for all this, Brandon — the central terminal for shipping grain — is the second largest city in the province, with a population of 39,000. There are creameries, packing plants, and even oil refineries here. And recently Brandon has become a recreational and cultural center, with good, if not grand, hotels, restaurants, and nightspots (see *Best en Route*). Athletes (even the armchair variety) should visit the 84-acre *Keystone Sports Complex*, built for $5 million as a site for the *1979 Canada Winter Games*. The *Sportsplex* has an indoor swimming pool, racquetball courts, a speed-skating oval, and a hockey arena. It also is the site of three agricultural fairs — the *Royal Manitoba Winter Fair* the last week in March, the *Provincial Exhibition* in mid-June, and the *Ag-Ex* in late October.

For good classical music and ballet, make reservations for programs playing at Brandon University's *West Man Auditorium* (270 18th St.). The *Royal Winnipeg Ballet* and the *Winnipeg Symphony* perform here occasionally.

Also at Brandon University is the *B. J. Hales Museum of Natural History*, featuring Sioux and Plains Indian artifacts — pipes, pottery, arrowheads, and tools made of bone — and 250 indigenous species of birds set in displays of prairie grass and simulated snow and ice. Long-time curator of the museum, the late Dr. Jack Lane was the legendary Bluebird Man who saved the eastern bluebird from extinction. By the 1930s their numbers had dwindled to a couple of dozen. Dr. Lane organized children in birdhouse-building brigades and set the houses up around the city. Thanks to him, more than 15,000 of the creatures now nest in birdhouses dotting the city and countryside.

In most grain markets of the world, Manitoba No. 1 Hard means fine wheat. A tour of the Agriculture Canada Research Station may show you there's more to good wheat than hard work and rich soil. The station conducts research in plant nutrition, herbicides, barley genetics, and the controlled breeding and feeding of beef, cattle, swine, and poultry. Tours available weekdays upon request.

En Route from Brandon – Heading west from Brandon on Route 1, you come to Griswold, a Sioux Indian reserve, the home of the ancestors of the Indians who fought General George Armstrong Custer in the Battle of Little Bighorn in 1876. In the reserve is a crafts store.

A worthwhile side trip is Virden, less than 25 miles (40 km) west on Route 1. In 1951, California Sun Oil struck black gold here and the place has never been the same. Pump-jacks in surrounding fields and in the town itself draw crude oil from the natural subterranean reservoirs.

From either Virden or Griswold swing back toward Winnipeg. Head south on 21 from Griswold and pick up Route 2 east to Souris, at the junction of Provincial Highways 2 and 22.

SOURIS: In this small, hilly town is perhaps the most famous wedding gift in Canada. More than 75 years ago, a homesteader built a 582-foot suspension bridge across the Souris River for his bride. A huge flood tore it apart in 1976, but the town repaired it. The brave can still cross the Souris River by walking the swaying footbridge, but the acrophobes in the crowd had better stick to photographing the longest suspension bridge in Canada. Nearby is the *Hillcrest Museum,* an early settler's spacious home filled with pioneer heirlooms.

A mile (1.6 km) from town are the Souris Agate Pits, where rockhounds will have no trouble collecting agates (from clear to red), petrified wood (beige, brown, or black), and jaspers (mostly red and green). Although scarce, an emerald green epidote veined in pink may be found, too. Before you go to the pits, which are open year-round, stop at the *Souris River Gem Shop* (8 First St. S.) for directions, digging equipment, and a license (about $4), allowing each family to take home 10 pounds of rock. The shop sells natural stone jewelry and guides to identifying your finds.

En Route from Souris – Head south on Route 22 to Route 23. Head east to Route 10 and then south to Boissevain, home of the zany *Turtle Derby,* an annual event held one weekend in mid-July. A few years back, a North Dakota turtle named Watergate crept his way to glory, winning the $100 prize for his owner. He did even better for those who wagered on him — a $1,000 sweepstake prize.

TURTLE MOUNTAIN PROVINCIAL PARK: The park gets its name from the western painted turtle that lives in the many shallow lakes — ranging from pothole size to massive — on these 47,000 acres. Here, too, are a variety of waterfowl, such as ducks, grebes, coots, herons, and cormorants, which feed on the grassy shores. In the spring and fall, migratory waterfowl swell their numbers. Hikers can pace the park's rolling hills through trembling aspen, black poplar, ash, and birch, and at the edge pick chokecherries, cranberries, and pinchberries in clearings perfumed by wild plum trees. Max Lake has excellent perch and walleye. And nearby William Lake has produced trophy-size catches of rainbow trout. There are campgrounds at Max Lake, Adam Lake, and William Lake Recreation Park. Open year-round.

INTERNATIONAL PEACE GARDEN: Just south of the park on the North Dakota–Manitoba border is this park dedicated to peace and goodwill between the US and Canada. Formal gardens, conceived half a century ago by a Canadian horticulturist, include beautiful flower beds and sunken pools surrounded by rosebushes. Visitors in winter snowshoe and ski on the trails that lead to a series of lakes connected by ornamental spillways and surrounded by terraced panels. Also in the garden are the All Faith Peace Chapel, available to any religious group for services, and the *International Music Camp,* held each summer. Students from the camp perform concerts and plays each summer Sunday in an open-air amphitheater.

En Route from the Peace Garden – Heading north from the border on Route 10, you'll reach Route 3. Traveling east, you can see Killarney Lake, a pleasant spot for a quick dip, an afternoon of boating, or a picnic. On the shore is Killarney, where the Irish Canadian community stages a spirited *St. Patrick's Day* parade. But if you miss it, don't despair — you can still kiss a Blarney stone and photograph the leprechaun perched on top of the shamrock-shaped fountain in Erin Park — or maybe even catch a glimpse of the town's green fire engine. Just north of town on Route 18 is the Pelican Lake Recreation Area, pleasant for camping. Continuing east on Route 3, the road leads to Pilot Mound, whose Assiniboine burial mound dates back 11,000 years. Exhibits at the *Pilot Mound Museum* explain the 1908 excavation that uncovered the site; the museum is open Tuesday, Thursday, and Saturday afternoons.

Back on Route 3, you reach La Rivière and the *Holiday Mountain Ski Resort*

(204-242-2172). Expert skiers will find the gentle hills no challenge, but beginners and intermediates will get a workout. Continue east to Morden, where the Agriculture Canada Research Station has a 627-acre farm dedicated to developing new strains of early-maturing crops, fruit trees, and grains. In the spring the town hosts *Blossom Week* (the date changes each year, as fruit trees flower), and in late August the *Corn and Apple Festival,* with free corn on the cob and apple cider. Southwest of town lies Lake Minnewasta, one of the few spots in the province where you can catch largemouth bass. Camping and picnicking facilities can be found at Colert Beach.

From Morden, head east on Route 3, then north at the junction of Route 75; 12 miles (19 km) away is the town of Morris, home of the *Manitoba Stampede and Agricultural Exhibition,* the second-largest rodeo in Canada, held in mid-July. Besides bronco riding, bareback riding, and steer wrestling, the rodeo features toga-clad racers (even before the film *Animal House* made toga parties popular) who compete in the unique *Ben Hur Suicide Chariot Race.* From Morris continue north to Winnipeg.

BEST EN ROUTE

If pitching in with farmwork or just savoring the rural life attracts you, spend a night, week, or summer on a farm. Some of the farms along the route are listed below, but for a complete roster write the *Manitoba Farm Vacations Association* (525 Kylemore Ave., Winnipeg; phone: 204-475-6624). Be sure to make reservations because most farms accommodate only a few guests. If you live in the family's house and share their meals, the most this will cost adults is about $50 per person, per day, and children, $25 per person, per day.

If you decide to use public lodging, a night's stay in a double room in an expensive hotel will cost from $35 to $40 (a few dollars more in Brandon), and a moderately priced establishment will cost between $17 and $35. In the moderate range, many bed and breakfast accommodations can be found throughout Manitoba. Contact *B & B of Manitoba,* 93 Healy Cr., Winnipeg (204-256-6151). All prices are quoted in US dollars.

GLENBORO

Hiwin Glen Farm – Ron and Mazo Black run this working dairy farm that accommodates 20 guests in a separate farmhouse. Not far from Spruce Woods Provincial Heritage Park, it features an outdoor pool, and meals can be taken with the family on advance notice. Associate member of *Canadian Hostelling Association.* Open year-round. On Provincial Trunk Highway 2, 2½ miles (4 km), west of the junction with Provincial Trunk Highway 5, Glenboro (phone: 204-827-2891). Moderate, with meals; inexpensive, for lodging only.

SPRUCE WOODS PROVINCIAL HERITAGE PARK

Kiche Manitou Campground – This is a provincial government camping facility with 76 tent sites and 45 trailer sites at the foot of a hill in the park. Open May to October (phone: 204-827-2458). Inexpensive.

BRANDON

Victoria Inn – The plushest in the city, this place has an indoor swimming pool surrounded by tropical plants and trees. There are lounges, small shops, a sun deck, sauna, and the *Tropical Garden Café.* The hotel offers babysitting services and accommodates wheelchairs. 3550 Victoria Ave. (phone: 204-725-1532, or 800-852-2710, from anywhere in Manitoba). Expensive.

Royal Oak Inn – This 100-room luxury hotel boasts a liquor-serving restaurant,

Winsor's. The indoor swimming area, decorated with tropical plants, has a sauna and whirlpool bath. 3130 Victoria Ave. (phone: 204-728-5775, or 800-852-2709, from anywhere in Manitoba). Expensive.

Redwood Motor Inn – With a fairly central location, this hotel has 60 rooms and a coffee shop. 345 18th St. N. (phone: 204-728-2200, or 800-255-3050, from anywhere in Manitoba). Moderate.

Little Chalet – Here you'll find 28 air conditioned A-frame cabins with color TV sets, an outdoor swimming pool, and a coffee shop. At the junction of Route 1 and 18th St. (phone: 204-725-1574). Moderate.

TURTLE MOUNTAIN PROVINCIAL PARK

Adam Lake Campground – This government camping facility has 64 tent and 25 trailer sites. Open May to September. Route 10 (phone: 204-534-2578). Inexpensive.

MORDEN

Valley View Farm – Help a family of six with milking cows and feeding chickens on this farm in the Pembina Hills. The farm also has horses for riding and a yard in which to park campers. Contact Virginia McKerlie, PO Box 140, RR 1 (phone: 204-822-3731). Moderate to inexpensive.

Interlake

In 1875, Iceland suffered severe and destructive volcanic eruptions, and many Icelanders fled their beautiful but harsh and unpredictable home to seek a land similar but more hospitable where they could continue their lives as fishermen and farmers. When they arrived, these pioneers thought Manitoba promising, with its vast fertile plains and many lakes. So they traded the cold rough waters of the Atlantic Ocean — teeming with saltwater catches — for the gentle, shallow waters of Lake Winnipeg and Lake Manitoba — both brimming with goldeye, whitefish, and walleye. And instead of fjords lashed by harsh waves, the settlers found grassy marshes alive with ducks and geese. Most important, instead of active volcanoes, the immigrants found deep, silent pine forests and fertile land.

The first leg of this 190-mile (304-km) trip from Winnipeg, along the western coast of Lake Winnipeg to an archipelago of wilderness islands, encompasses a region that was once New Iceland — an independent country in the heart of Canada, governed and inhabited by the descendants of the Icelandic settlers. The Icelandic people and their traditions still live here. In Gimli, the area's unofficial capital, the fishermen and farmers may talk to each other in their native tongue, but they will welcome you to festivals of Icelandic poetry and plays, with native food and costumes. And, on Hecla Island, you can stay at an Icelandic-style resort, built smack in the middle of spruce, aspen, and jack pine forests alive with deer and beaver. (On smaller islands, where no cars may penetrate, moose and black bear also thrive.)

The roads are open in the Interlake region all year unless a winter storm closes them. (In winter, when temperatures plunge below –18F/–28C, it's wise to pack extra blankets, food, and a flashlight into your car.) In spring, geese and ducks flock to this well-watered region from the south to feed and mate. In summer, numerous festivals and fairs are held, and the lakes are splendid for sailing and swimming. But autumn is the time of most special scenic beauty. The trees change to a myriad of colors — gold, orange, brown, and rust; the farmer's crops are ripe; and the villagers sponsor fowl suppers, where you'll find tables heaped high with turkey, chicken, fish, vegetables, and such calorie-filled Icelandic desserts as *vinarterta* (prune cake) and *ponnukukur* (sweet pancake).

En Route from Winnipeg – Leave Winnipeg by way of Main Street north to the Perimeter (a route skirting the city) and continue on it as it becomes Route 9. Follow this road 9 miles (14 km) north to Lockport, noted for its locks, historic Anglican church, and, some say, the best hot dogs in Canada.

LOCKPORT: Near the St. Andrews Locks, which are used for the passage of freight and pleasure vessels along the Red River, try your luck at catching some of the many species of fish. (One angler caught a 34½-pound trophy-rating catfish here.)

If you prefer something other than the white, tender, and flaky meat of the catfish for supper, pick up a *Skinner's* hot dog, voted the best in the country by national magazines. Underneath the usual sauerkraut and mustard lurks a unique blend of meats, creating a wiener that people praise from Quebec to British Columbia. (*Skinner's* is on River Road, north of St. Andrews Locks.)

Just south of town on the River Road is the oldest stone church in western Canada that is still in use — St. Andrews-on-the-Red, built in the 1800s. Worshipers still use the original prayer kneelers, covered with buffalo hide.

Down the road from the church and overlooking the Red River is the *Kennedy House Museum* (1866), once the home of Captain William Kennedy, the first Canadian-born person and the only Métis (son of a Cree mother and Scot father) to command an Arctic exploration.

Return to Route 9 and proceed northeast toward Selkirk. Just outside town, at Lower Fort Garry National Historic Park, is the only stone fort of the fur trade era still intact in North America. Selkirk, north of the fort, is known for its beautiful homes and excellent marina on Lake Winnipeg (see *Winnipeg,* THE CITIES). Head north on Route 9 to Petersfield and the base of Netley Marsh, one of the continent's great waterfowl nesting areas.

NETLEY MARSH: This 100 square miles of briny green marsh grass, bullrush, cattail, and tall cane grass is home to duck, tern, western grebe, and goose. The best way to tour the narrow channels is by canoe, but with a strong gust from Lake Winnipeg, you'll be wading instead of paddling. If an occasional dunking alarms you, take your gear and board the MS *Lady Chesley,* a sightseeing boat. Or if you've left your sea legs in Winnipeg, hike along the dike road skirting the edge of the marsh. Early (4 to 6 AM) risers who venture into the marsh will spot many of the 100 species of aquatic birds eating breakfast. Common terns dive for minnow, great blue herons swoop down and carry off silver fish, and pelicans skim the marsh for surface fish. Throughout the feeding, each bird adds its individual sound to the ear-splitting cacophony. The season for jump, pass, or decoy shooting opens in mid-September. From early spring, when transients swell the bird population, to early fall, when marsh foliage bursts with gold, red, and orange, the marsh is the turf of hunters and birders. Conventional hunting weapons must be declared to Canada Customs. Hunting licenses can be obtained from the *Manitoba Department of Natural Resources* (191 Broadway, Rm. 500, Winnipeg R3C 4B2; phone: 204-945-6762). Dogs may be brought into Canada only if they have rabies innoculation certificates that are no more than 36 months old. See "Border Crossing" in GETTING READY TO GO.

En Route from Netley Marsh – Return to Petersfield and follow Route 9 for 43 miles (69 km) to Winnipeg Beach, a revived family summer vacation spot with a large marina, beaches, and boardwalk. Nine miles (14 km) north, you enter Gimli, the gateway to Icelandic country.

GIMLI: This harbor town by the sandy southwestern shores of Lake Winnipeg so enchanted its Icelandic settlers a century ago that they named it after the home of the mythological Norse gods. If fishing for whitefish, walleye, and goldeye; sailing on a windswept lake near an excellent marina; or soaking up some Icelandic culture appeals to you, summertime in Gimli may be your corner of heaven. (More than half the population of 1,600 is of Icelandic descent. A huge statue of a Viking with his back to the lake never lets you forget it.)

Gimli Historical Museum on the waterfront of Gimli Harbor displays Icelandic and Ukrainian pioneer material and relates the history of fishing on Lake Winnipeg. Open late May to end of June, Wednesdays through Sundays 10 AM to 5 PM; July through August, daily 11 AM to 6 PM. Admission charge.

Many people still fish and farm here, the largest town of Icelanders outside of Iceland. On the weekend before the first Monday of August, the *August Long Weekend,* they doff their fishing and farming apparel and don colorful Icelandic costumes to host the *Islendingadagurinn,* or *Icelandic Festival,* as a tribute to their ancestors. At the festival, you can feast on smoked *rula pylsa* (lamb) and *vinarterta* (torte with prune filling); watch or join a 10-mile walking race called *glima;* enjoy the water sports from the harbor; choose an ethnic artifact from the arts and crafts display; and look for the Maid of the Mountains, called *Fjalkona.* She's not your average teenage festival queen, but a respected woman of outstanding merit whose physical appearance is immaterial.

En Route from Gimli – North on Route 9, the road passes (never far from Lake Winnipeg) through the Camp Morton Provincial Recreation Park, with its beaches, picnic tables, and 12 rustic log cabins. Farther north you pass through more lakefront communities settled by Icelanders. The first is Arnes, birthplace of Vilhjalmur Stefansson, the first explorer to report on Arctic climatic conditions (a commemorative statue in town honors him). Beyond this point, Route 9 degenerates to a gravel roadway, and although construction is expected to improve the roadway (and maybe pave the area), switch over to Route 8 to continue north to Hecla Provincial Park.

HECLA PROVINCIAL PARK: This is a vast archipelago of wild and wooded islands thoroughly rimmed by reedy marshes, of which only Hecla Island, the largest, can be reached by car. Canoes will take you to see wildlife preserves where deer, elk, and moose thrive in island habitats isolated from one another and their predators. The rare western grebe, the bald eagle, the blue heron, and the black tern give even the most seasoned bird-watcher an eyeful. Hecla Island is a year-round resort community, named by the Icelandic immigrants for Mt. Hecla, the volcano whose eruption drove them from their homeland. Breathtakingly beautiful granite and limestone cliffs buttress the shores of this largely uninhabited island, offering some of the finest hiking and camping in the province. Badger, fisher, deer, and moose live in the dense forest of spruce, aspen and jack pine surrounded by miles of prairies. In winter, snow buffs don showshoes or cross-country skis to hike through well-mapped and maintained trails. At the north end of the island is the *Gull Harbour Resort* (see *Best en Route*), an Icelandic-style luxury hotel with large picture windows overlooking the great outdoors. During the summer, 50,000 ducks, Canada geese, and snow and blue geese make the surrounding marshes home. *Gull Harbour* has facilities for hunters searching out the upland game and waterfowl. But the big attraction on the island is the *Gull Harbour Golf Course* (204-475-2354), an 18-hole course. Duffers beware the notorious par-4, No. 17, known as *Langa Tjorn* (Long Pond) and par-5 *Grjotagja* (rocky ravine) holes that make even the pros sweat.

En Route from Hecla – Return to the junction of Routes 8 and 68 and proceed west on Route 68 through sparsely settled "cowboy country." The terrain is slightly rolling, with short, scrubby grasses and wild strawberries and blueberries near enough the road to pick. (Before you eat any, check carefully the free booklet *Edible and Poisonous Berries,* available from Manitoba Department of Natural Resources, Room 201, 1495 St. James St., Winnipeg R3H 0W9.) Where Routes 68 and 6 join, 121 miles (194 km) along, is Eriksdale, an outfitting center for anglers who fish in the Manitoba Narrows and for hunters seeking upland waterfowl and game. The many shops specialize in fishing, hunting, and camping equipment and also will provide licenses.

From Eriksdale, follow Route 417 west to Route 418, then north to Route 68. Then proceed west along the southern portion of Dog Lake, following the road to Oakview, within walking distance of the Narrows.

MANITOBA NARROWS – Waves crashing against the limestone shores of the narrowest part of the lake gave the province its name. The Ojibwa Indians believed that Manitou, the spirit of good and evil, banged his drum during stormy weather to create the resounding sound.

In these narrow, often rough straits, a skilled angler can haul in a 14-pound walleye and a 35-pound fierce, northern pike. And hunters bag many Canada geese feeding by the marshy shores of the numerous inlets.

Return to Eriksdale.

En Route from Eriksdale – Travel south on Route 6 to Lundar, another Icelandic community. As you drive, you can't miss an 8-foot Canada goose pointing the way the wind blows. With several towns vying for the title "goose capital of Canada," the Lundar folk erected this giant Fiberglas statue to stake their claim — and with good reason. Every spring and fall, flocks of Canada geese pause during their migrations at a wild goose sanctuary in Lundar. There you can feed them; north of town, you can shoot them and eat them. Many shops in town provide equipment and licenses.

Follow Route 6 along the southeast shore of Lake Manitoba to Twin Lake Beaches, a popular swimming, picnicking, and camping spot. From here, follow Route 6 to Winnipeg, the last leg of your Interlake odyssey.

BEST EN ROUTE

Lodgings on this route range from the plush *Gull Harbour Resort and Conference Centre,* with just about every recreational facility you can think of, to the spartan lodges where hunters snatch a few hours of shut-eye before rising at 5 AM to fish and stalk game. For a double room, expect to pay $50 to $70 for hotels we list as expensive, $25 to $45 for moderate, and $15 to $20, inexpensive. All prices are quoted in US dollars.

PETERSFIELD

Chesley's – On the fringes of Netley Marsh, these 7 units and cottages provide comfortable all-service accommodations for avid duck and upland game hunters. The lodge supplies guides and a trip up the Netley River in the MS *Lady Chesley.* After a duck dinner, sportsmen gather in the cedar lodge to discuss the day's hunting. Weekly rates are available. For reservations, write PO Box 220, Petersfield, Manitoba ROC 2LO (phone: 204-738-2250). Inexpensive.

GIMLI

Shoreliner – The 11 spartan units provide a spectacular view of the harbor and the Viking statue. 39 First Ave. (phone: 204-642-5992). Moderate.

HECLA ISLAND

Gull Harbour Resort and Conference Centre – This modern complex epitomizes Icelandic architecture, with its large picture windows, welcoming *setustofa* (lobby), and wooden furniture. Facilities include 93 comfortable rooms, a gymnasium, indoor swimming pool, and sauna. During the winter, the hotel is a perfect base from which to cross-country ski, skate, and snowmobile. Open all year. Reservations essential. (phone: 204-475-2354 or 800-442-0497). Expensive.

Gull Harbour Campground – After a day of fishing, swimming, or hiking, camp out in this 213-site provincial government facility. Open May to September. (phone: 204-475-2354). Inexpensive.

LUNDAR

Lundar – The main attraction at this 23-unit motor inn is its bar, where local hunters may enlighten a transient about the best hunting spots. Rte. 6 (phone: 204-762-5855). Moderate.

The North

Where the dark, dense forest meets the clear blue lake, rabbit, deer, and fox peep from the bush; a fish leaps in the lake; a bird calls; the scent of pine is in the air; a campfire crackles as bacon and eggs sizzle on the grill; and a cushion of lichen feels soft underfoot. From the sight of the blue sky on the horizon to the taste of the fried, just-caught walleye on your tongue, this is the northern wilderness.

And then there's that other world of the north — the shouts and whoops at the *Flin Flon Trout Festival;* the crack of the mushers' whips over the heads of the lead dogs during the *World Championship Dogsled Derby* at The Pas; the clatter of chain saws and the crunch of trees felled in the pulp and paper operations; the delicate embroidery and brightly colored *Easter* eggs in the Ukrainian town of Dauphin; and the camaraderie of a people more than willing to share their good times with visitors.

The tour route outlined below takes you from the wheat farming communities of the interior to the flatlands of Hudson Bay. En route you will visit Riding Mountain National Park, its extensive wilderness preserves, and the lumber and mining towns of Flin Flon and The Pas. From The Pas you may want to hop a plane and visit *real* pioneer country, the subarctic seaport of Churchill.

After The Pas, the trip is no luxury excursion. As you go north, you'll find cedar bogs with a few spindly dwarfed spruce clinging to gray rocks and tundra. This region's frigid winter extends from mid-October to June 15. But the cold climate and pitifully short summer are no reason to skip this leg of the journey.

En Route from Winnipeg – Leaving Winnipeg, head west on the Trans-Canada Highway (Route 1) to Portage la Prairie, where a fair is held each July in remembrance of Thomas Spence, a settler who was a strong advocate of confederation (see Portage la Prairie in the *Wheat Belt* route). From Portage, follow the Yellow-head Route 16 northwest to Neepawa, where a plaque commemorates the 900-mile (1,440-km) road that fur traders trod from the Red River settlement to Fort Edmonton, Alberta.

Neepawa is noted for its salt mines; the Canadian Salt Company once pumped brine out of an underground salt lake near the center of town; the lake still exists. During July, Neepawa culture buffs (14 years and older) paint, sing, or play instruments under the tutelage of top-notch teachers in the week-long *Holiday Festival of Arts.* Students and teachers (some from the *Winnipeg Symphony and Ensemble*) perform concerts and plays.

Continuing west, in the Minnedosa River Valley — an area of rolling hills decked with oak trees — lies the small town of Minnedosa (population 2,500). Hunters flock here each autumn for the fine goose and duck hunting. For those not interested in the sporting life, there's Minnedosa Lake, northeast of town, offering delightful swimming, picnicking, and camping. Each July Minnedosa puts on the *Country Fun Festival,* a family fair at which local musicians stage every-thing from square dances (fiddlers and all) to rock concerts.

North on Route 10, the road climbs from the valley into sandy, hilly country, then through grassy plains onto the plateau of Riding Mountain National Park.

RIDING MOUNTAIN NATIONAL PARK: Surrounded by the prairies of the Cana-dian plains, this is a recreational park and nature preserve of prairies and rolling hills, hardwood and evergreen forests, and crystal-clear lakes and streams.

Northern pike and rainbow trout swim in the park's deep cold lakes — Clear Lake, Lake Katherine, and Deep Lake, to name a few — while beaver build dams in marshy, shallow creeks. On the meadow to the west bloom the bright yellow blossoms of shrubby cinquefoil and the purplish Gaillardia. On the prairies around Audy Lake, herds of buffalo roam through the scrubby grasses. An exhibit nearby relates the history of the bison — almost extinct except for one species. Throughout the park are wolves, elk, whitetail deer, and moose. A walk along one of the numerous hiking paths will bring you to the log cabin of Archibald Belaney — more commonly known by his Indian name of Grey Owl — a British naturalist who, in the early 20th century, drew and wrote about the creatures living in the forest around him.

During the winter, you can don cross-country skis and follow several trails through the park. If the prospect of schussing down the steepest downhill ski slope in the province attracts you, take a trip to Mt. Agassiz, on the east side of the park near McCreary.

Adjoining the park in the town of Wasagaming is the *Elkhorn Resort* (see *Best en Route*), where horses may be rented for trail rides through the park.

The southeastern entrance to the park is at the resort community of Wasagaming (Indian for "clear water") on the shores of Clear Lake. The lake, regularly stocked with trout, has facilities for fishing, boating, and sailing. Wasagaming also boasts an 18-hole, par-72 golf course (so near Clear Lake that a misguided long drive may cost you a ball), tennis and badminton courts, a roller skating rink, dance pavilion, and cinema.

For information about overnight and day hikes and trails (including one for the blind), visit the interpretive center at Wasagaming. Most of the park's facilities are accessible to people in wheelchairs. The information center is open from mid-May to mid-September and on weekdays during the ski season.

From the park, follow Route 10 to Dauphin.

DAUPHIN: After the transcontinental railroad was finished in 1896, Ukrainian immigrants moved north with visions of fertile farming land and homesteading grants. They were not disappointed. Over the years the rich soil of the Dauphin Valley nurtured their crops of wheat, barley, and potatoes. Today, the town is noted for its flour and lumber mills as well as its farming.

Each *August Long Weekend,* the town holds the annual *Ukrainian Festival* as a tribute to its ancestry. The festival offers much to see and do. Ukrainian Cossack riders in traditional garb ride through the valley; artisans demonstrate *pysanka* (*Easter* egg decorating); and people gather for Ukrainian dancing, singing, and eating delicious home-cooked foods. These last include *pirogi* (boiled or fried pastry stuffed with potatoes and/or cheese), borscht (beet soup), and kielbasa (sausage). If you miss the festival, you may treat yourself to these dishes at the *Dauphin Allied Arts Centre* (in the old Town Hall).

Another Dauphin attraction includes the five professional horseshoe pits in *Dauphin Memorial Community Club,* where anyone can have a fling with a horseshoe.

En Route from Dauphin – Follow Route 10 as it veers west and then north. At the junction with Route 367 in Garland, head west to Duck Mountain Provincial Park for wilderness camping and excellent fishing. In 1961, a forest fire ravaged much of the park's jack pine and spruce. But as you hike the several well-mapped trails, you will see numerous shrubs, part of the continuing process of forest renewal. The highest point in Manitoba is Baldy Mountain (2,727 ft.), where in late fall you can hear the bugling of elk. The Nicholas Copernicus Observance Committee has mounted a sundial on this mountain to help those hiking the Copernicus Hill Trail keep track of the hour.

Back on Route 10, head north and west to the town of Swan River, where between 1787 and 1821 the Hudson's Bay Company tried to compete with the Northwest Company's franchise to trade with the Plains Indians. The *Swan River Museum* (a mile/1.6 km north of town on the banks of the Swan River) depicts the history of that era through its collection of old photographs and Plains Indian artifacts.

At the end of July, the town sponsors the *Northwest Roundup,* when farmers exhibit beef cattle, cowboys rope steer, and everybody eats pancake breakfasts at sidewalk buffets.

From Swan River, the road runs through miles of evergreen forests and skirts clear lakes, including the second largest in the province, Lake Winnipegosis. If you stop to fish, you may catch great northern pike; you also may hear black bear, moose, or deer rustling the leaves of the trees behind you.

On Route 10 north of Lake Winnipegosis you'll pass a stretch of floating muskeg (partially decayed vegetable matter) known as "the bog." It's 144 miles (230 km) from Swan River to The Pas.

THE PAS (pronounced *Pah*): The Pas not only has the finest fishing and hunting but also some of the liveliest festivals in the country.

In mid-February the town puts on the 5-day *Trappers Festival,* when mushers from all over Canada and the US race teams of Canadian huskies and other breeds through a 105-mile course. (The fastest dogs win $3,500 for the musher.)

Townspeople compete in log-wrestling and log-felling events as well as in the less-rugged contests of moose and goose calling. There's even a muskrat-skinning contest.

For both spectators and participants, there are buffet dinners with continuous entertainment, beerfests, and pancake breakfasts. Lumberjacks, miners, fishermen, trappers, and all other Pas citizens get in the festival spirit by wearing beads and buckskin while hunting the mythical "ice worm" (visitors can buy the album *When the Iceworms Nest Again*) and by crowning one woman Miss Fur Queen of the North.

For a fur of your own, stop at *The Bay Co.* (333 Edwards St.; phone: 204-623-5428). Also sold here are handmade mukluks (warm furry boots), Eskimo parkas, and coonskin hats.

In mid-August, the Opasquiak Indians host the *Opasquiak Indian Days* festival. One of the most popular events is a race in which contestants carry heavy bags of flour and canoes on their backs. Visitors are welcome to compete or, if less energetic, to browse in the reservation shopping mall and buy beaded moccasins and jackets.

En Route from The Pas – Continue north on Route 10. The road skirts Clearwater Lake Provincial Park, known for its crystalline, blue, unpolluted water (bush pilots flying 1,500 feet above have reported spotting rocks lying 35 feet below the surface). The trout living in these waters are so healthy that experts use the lake water as an index by which to measure pollution in other waters. The shores of the lake are home to ducks and geese; moose and other big game roam in the nearby woods.

FLIN FLON: In 1915, gold miners here found an old, tattered novel about Josiah Flintabbatey Flonatin, the discoverer of a city of gold. They named this town after him, soon shortening it to Flin Flon. A statue of Flonatin, designed by cartoonist Al Capp, welcomes visitors. Although little gold is found here now, the industry of the town is dominated by the Flin Flon mine, where visitors can visit the surface operations of the nonferrous metal mines.

Flin Flon is now much more than a mining community. Lumbering has become the other major industry; in the vicinity, the sounds of lumberjacks sawing large evergreens can be heard. And Flin Flon also is a great place for fishing (the town claims to be the "fishing capital of Manitoba"). The first weekend of July, the town hosts the *Flin Flon Trout Festival,* with cash prizes for the biggest lake trout and northern pike. A festival queen presides over the event, which includes pancake breakfasts and a canoe race.

En Route from Flin Flon – Return south on Highway 10 to the junction with Route 391 and follow the road as it enters Grass River Provincial Park. Here you will be awed by the truly untouched wilderness: The terrain is composed of layers of limestone bedrock, Precambrian granite, and permafrost, and is covered with somewhat stunted, dense evergreen forests. You may even see caribou darting about with their young. The park is open from mid-May to the end of September.

CHURCHILL: This subarctic seaport lies on the southwestern shore of Hudson Bay, a vast arm of the Atlantic Ocean extending deep into Canada's north. A town of 1,200 winter-hardened people, Churchill has no road connection to the south and can be reached only by rail, air, or, in summer, ocean-going ship. Along the bleak shore of the bay, trees grow to be little more than wind-worn stumps, yet a thriving world of wildlife, some that cannot be seen anywhere else in the world, dwells near — and even in — the town. In the long subarctic night, the Aurora Borealis, or northern lights, are vivid, illuminating the town with the brightness of street lamps. In spring, which comes in mid-June, arctic flowers create a riot of color.

Though Inuit or native peoples lived in the Churchill region as early as 1700 BC, European settlement began in the winter of 1619–1620 when the Danish seafarer Jens Munck wintered near the present townsite during his fruitless search for the Northwest Passage. Of the original crew of 65, only Munck and two sailors survived to return to Denmark. In 1717, the Hudson's Bay Company established a trading post at Churchill. Later in the 18th century, Fort Prince of Wales (now a national historical site that can be reached by tour boat) was built to defend British colonial fur trading interests.

Today, vast numbers of snow geese, Canada geese, sandhill cranes, and 200 other species of birds migrate through Churchill on their way to and from summer breeding grounds in the high arctic and along the shores of Hudson Bay. Four species of fur seals visit Churchill harbor, fishing for abundant char, grayling pike, and cisco. Beluga whales, now protected against commercial hunting, frolic in the Bay's waters near Churchill from June to early September. And polar bears, which migrate to the frozen ice of the Bay from surrounding land in the fall, often roam Churchill's streets from September to November, making it the only town in the world with an itinerant population of *Ursus maritimus.* At the peak of the bear migration, which occurs around Halloween, the beasts, drawn by smells of food and garbage, are kept under control by Royal Canadian Mounted Police patrols and environment officials armed with tranquilizer dart guns. Tundra buggies, huge vehicles with immense tires and tracks, provide tours to the polar bears' haunts. Souvenirs, including 8-foot-long narwahl tusks, eskimo-carved tombstones, and moosehair earrings, can be bought at the *Arctic Trading Company*, Kelsey Blvd. and Bernier St. (phone: 800-665-0431).

To get to Churchill by air, take *Canadian Airlines International* from Winnipeg (phone: 204-632-1250), The Pas (phone: 204-624-5218), or Thompson (phone: 800-592-7303). Three days a week, a 2-night, 1-day train journey begins in Winnipeg. Accommodations range from coach to bedrooms and a dining car offers spirits and sustenance. Contact *VIA Rail* (123 Main St., Winnipeg R3C 2P8; phone: 800-561-8630). Organized tours are operated by the *Great Canadian Travel Company* (54 Donald St., Winnipeg R3C 1L6; phone: 204-284-1580).

BEST EN ROUTE

Lodging for doubles ranges from expensive ($35 and up) hotels and inns with restaurants and cocktail lounges to the more moderately priced ($15 to $25) bungalows and hunting/fishing lodges. Camping in provincial or federal campsites averages about $5 per person, per night and is on a first-come, first-served basis. If you want a truly rustic experience, grab your sleeping bag and camp out under the stars near Audy Lake, home of the bison. It's free, and it might be the most memorable night of your trip. All prices are quoted in US dollars.

RIDING MOUNTAIN NATIONAL PARK

Elkhorn Resort – An ideal spot for those who want to combine ranch living with all the accoutrements of a resort. Besides horseback riding, hayrides, and horseshoe pits, this ranch, with 58 rooms in the lodge and 16 chalets, has a dining room, cocktail lounge, indoor pool, and sauna. Open year-round. Near Clear Lake and *Clear Lake Golf Course* (phone: 204-848-2802). Expensive.

Thunderbird Bungalows – These 22 log cabins surround a spacious lawn and are separated from one another by thick clumps of pine trees. Although within walking distance of Clear Lake, the complex has a heated outdoor swimming pool. Open May to October (phone: 204-848-2521). Expensive.

Aspen Ridge – Close to Riding Mountain National Park, this farm is very popular with cross-country skiers. The attraction is not only in the farm's 320 rolling acres but also because accommodations are in a lovely log home complete with beamed ceilings, a huge stone fireplace, and puffy down comforters on every bed. Lake Audy (phone: 204-848-2965). Moderate.

Wasagaming Campground – Not far from the bustling resort community of Wasagaming is this federal government campground with space for 379 tents and 158 trailers. The facilities include barbecue pits, wood stoves, a playground, store, laundromat, and boat rentals. Open May to mid-September. Near Clear Lake (phone: 204-848-2811). Inexpensive.

DUCK MOUNTAIN PROVINCIAL PARK

Blue Lakes Campground – Thick forests of pine and spruce shelter and create privacy for the 89 tent sites. At night, the dark, dense forests, unlit by electricity or trailer lights, make the provincial campgrounds pitch black. The grounds have a boat ramp and store. Open May to October. Near Blue Lake (no phone). Inexpensive.

THE PAS

Wescana Inn – One of the newest hotel in town has 80 deluxe units and a sauna, but no pool. 425 Fischer Ave. (phone: 204-623-5446). Expensive.

CLEARWATER LAKE PROVINCIAL PARK

New Vickery Lodge – With modest accommodations for serious fishers, the lodge has a guide service, canoes, boats, and a fly-out fishing service. Open May to October. Write to PO Box 2670, The Pas, Manitoba R9A 1M5 (phone: 204-624-5429). Expensive.

Carpenter's Clearwater Lodge – This simple property caters to hunters and fishermen who get their licenses here. Weekly rates are available. Open year-round. Write to PO Box 695, The Pas, Manitoba R9A 1K7 (phone: 204-624-5467). Moderate.

FLIN FLON

Victoria Inn – This modern, 76-unit motel is near a park in which stands the statue of Josiah Flintabbatey Flonatin. It has an indoor swimming pool, sauna, dining room, cocktail lounge, and airport limousine service. Off Route 10 (phone: 204-687-7555). Expensive.

CHURCHILL

Churchill Motel – A well-equipped facility in the heart of town with a licensed restaurant and cable television. On Kelsey Blvd. near Munck St. (phone: 204-675-8853). Expensive.

Tundra Inn – Comfortable accommodations with full bath, satellite TV, radio, and a dining room. 34 Franklin St. (phone: 204-675-8831 or 800-661-1460). Expensive.

Seaport – A full-service facility with 21 rooms, a licensed dining room, and satellite TV. It can be noisy. Munck St. and Kelsey Blvd. (phone: 204-675-8807). Expensive to moderate.

New Brunswick

Many New Brunswick residents have an inferiority complex about their province. They assume that visitors travel through New Brunswick only to get to Prince Edward Island or Nova Scotia. But others recognize the vast, natural bounty of their land — a rugged coastline, healthy forests, rich agriculture, and a friendly, unpretentious population with roots in rugged Loyalist and Acadian stock. New Brunswick is tucked under the Gaspé Peninsula and shares a long western border with Maine. Its maritime status is firmly established by its extensive seacoast on the Gulf of St. Lawrence and reiterated in the Bay of Fundy, where 50-foot tides crash against the southeastern shore. This land of forested hills is crossed by rivers, which enrich the earth and encourage agriculture. Potato farming is the major industry after lumbering and mineral production.

Conservation is vital to a province so dependent for survival on its natural resources, and a strict program has been enacted to protect the forests from depletion. The province's real natural wonder, the Fundy tide, is in no danger of depletion. Tides in the Bay of Fundy are the highest in the world and are the primal force behind the province's main water-linked phenomena — the reversing falls at Saint John and Hopewell Rocks, a striking formation carved by water out of indigenous limestone.

This land of woods and water was settled by French-speaking Acadians in the early 18th century. The French built forts to protect these settlers, but when the British captured the forts in 1755, the Acadians were expelled. Some returned 30 years later and were given land. In fact, over 35% of the current population of 710,600 is French-speaking. The other early settlers were New Englanders, British immigrants, and Loyalists who came from the US during and after the American Revolution.

Much of New Brunswick is rural, but its major urban areas are Moncton (pop. 102,084 in the metropolitan area), a distribution center; Saint John (pop. 121,265), a manufacturing center; and Fredericton (pop. 65,768), the provincial capital and gathering place of artists and craftspeople who produce and sell wares.

New Brunswick is a paradise for hikers and bird watchers. The *New Brunswick Travel Guide* details hundreds of miles of hiking trails, trail lengths, and things to see along the way. (The guide is available from *Tourism New Brunswick,* PO Box 12345, Fredericton NB E3B 5C3; phone: 800-561-0213). Some 250 species of birds are to be found in the province.

The Acadian Trail follows the eastern coast through fishing, farming, and lumbering villages. In the summer you can start this trip out with a bang at the mid-July *Shediac Lobster Festival,* which celebrates the homely crustacean. The Fundy Coast links the cities along the southern coast of New Brunswick, where the Loyalist heritage is still devoutly maintained. At Saint

John, Canada's oldest incorporated city, you can watch the river run upstream, forced by the strength of the Fundy tide. The St. John River route includes Fredericton, Grand Lake (the province's largest freshwater lake), and the beautiful rolling hills of the region's low-tide farming area.

Information: *Tourism New Brunswick,* PO Box 12345, Fredericton, NB E3B 5C3 (phone: 506-453-2377 in the US or Canada; 800-561-0123 outside of New Brunswick). Any New Brunswick Tourist Information Center can make reservations for your stay in the province during the high season, from June 1 to mid-September. Most tourist attractions close from early September through May, and the phones may be disconnected during that time.

The Fundy Coast

When open warfare broke out between Great Britain and the American colonies in April 1775, not all of George III's American subjects grabbed a musket to fight for independence. Some salvaged what they could of their estates and dashed across the border into New Brunswick. The Fundy Coast follows the path of those who fled the rebellious colonies. These were the Loyalists — or British Loyalists — who remained loyal to the Crown. Along the southern coast of New Brunswick, you will explore cities where this proud heritage is maintained.

This route runs beside the Bay of Fundy, whose 50-foot tides dash the coast with awesome power. At Hopewell Cape and at St. Martins, it has sculpted giant "flowerpots" out of sandstone. The tide plays such an important role in this area that it definitely is recommended to write to the provincial tourism office and request a timetable to help plan the best time to arrive so that you see the magnificent tidal action. A word of caution about swimming in the Bay of Fundy: High tides mix the water so that the temperature never gets much above 65F (16C). Swimming in New Brunswick is much better on the eastern coast, along the Northumberland Strait, where the water is shallow and warm (see *The Acadian Trail*).

The small communities along the coast developed a strong shipbuilding industry in the early 1800s. The famous *Marco Polo,* the fastest sailing ship of the mid-19th century, was built in Saint John. When wooden sailing ships became obsolete, deep-sea fishing became the main industry of smaller coastal centers.

Even though commercial fishing is the fourth largest industry in the province (behind forestry, mining, and agriculture), the Bay of Fundy still yields cod, halibut, flounder, herring, crab, scallops, lobster, and sardines in abundance. Deep-sea fishing enthusiasts can hire boats in St. Andrews. For a real taste of the sea, try the Fundy Isles, all of which are accessible by sea. Grand Manan and Deer Island from the mainland by ferry; and Campobello by ferry from Deer Island and by bridge from Lubec, Maine. Whale watching is an opportunity not to be missed. Check with *Osprey Travel and Promotion* (in St. Andrews; phone: 506-529-8844) for an environmentally conscientious charter.

The Fundy Coast is also a farming and dairy region; a land of covered bridges; a place to catch speckled trout or landlocked Atlantic salmon; and it goes by Fundy National Park, for canoeing, backpacking, and 50 miles of hiking trails. The route begins at St. Stephen, on the US-Canada border, and winds for 210 miles (336 km) to Moncton near the Nova Scotia border. The route does not have four-lane highways, although the roads are excellent. Nor does it have a boisterous nightlife, though Saint John is fairly sophisticated. When you explore the Fundy Coast, you enter a region where life is not only touched by the dignity of the sea, but by a long and proud history.

ST. STEPHEN: Your introduction to colonial history begins immediately across the border. Residents of the two border communities — St. Stephen and Calais, Maine — ignored the War of 1812, which Canadian historians regard as an attempt by the US to annex Canada. The atmosphere was so doggedly nonviolent that gunpowder sent by the British to defend St. Stephen was loaned to Calais for their *July Fourth* festivities. You can visit a landmark named after the war's local peacekeeper, the Duncan McColl United Church. The friendship is renewed each August at the *International Festival.*

A popular British Loyalist settlement in the 1780s, it is now known for its chocolate, lumber, and canning industries. Arthur Ganong invented the chocolate bar here in 1910, and Ganong Brothers Ltd. is still turning out candy. Stop in at *Ganong's Chocolatier* (Water St.) for some delicious bites. A chocolate festival is held here in early August. The *Crocker Hill Herb Garden* (on the St. Croix River) is a pleasant stop for a cup of herbal tea.

British Loyalist memorabilia are on display at the *Charlotte County Historical Society Museum* (in the James Muerchie Building, 443 Milltown Blvd.; phone: 506-466-3295), open daily from June to September.

Those who can't wait to sink their hooks into some of the famous landlocked salmon in the Chiputneticook Lakes region to the north of St. Stephen should plan ahead with outfitters in that area (for the booklet *Accommodations,* see *Best en Route*).

En Route from St. Stephen – Oak Bay Provincial Park is only 8 miles (13 km) from the US-Canada border. Oak Bay has 112 campsites, with services for trailers. It also has an excellent saltwater beach on the bay.

Take Route 127 south for 10 miles (16 km) to St. Andrews. Along the way, stop for the exceptional view of Dochet's Island, where in the winter of 1604, Champlain lost half his temporary settlement to scurvy.

ST. ANDREWS: At the close of the Revolutionary War in 1783, British Loyalists in Castine, Maine, were horrified to learn that the US-Canada border had been moved to the other side of the St. Croix River. Almost the entire community moved across the Bay of Fundy to the havens of British protection. Those who could afford it moved their homes — lock, stock, and barrel — along with their possessions, and some are still standing in the center of town. Fourteen of the 280 buildings in St. Andrews erected before 1880 date back to the 1700s.

The local Canadian Club organizes walking tours of the historic homes in odd-numbered years, 1 afternoon in late July. The Historical Society arranges limited tours for conventions at the famous *Algonquin* hotel. Information on walking tours is available from the *St. Andrews Civic Trust* (PO Box 484, St. Andrews). Local boat cruises, whale watching, bird watching, and diving can be arranged through *Osprey Travel and Promotion* (222 Water St., St. Andrews; phone: 506-529-8844).

Other historic sites within easy walking distance include: the Blockhouse, which is the last of 12 built to defend St. Andrews during the War of 1812, and the Greenock Church (1822) on Montague Street, with a pulpit built without using a single nail, copied from one in Greenock, Scotland. St. Andrews is a great place to tour by bicycle; several places offer rentals, including the *Algonquin* hotel (phone: 506-529-8823).

Since St. Andrews is an extremely popular resort area, reservations are advisable in summer at most hotels and restaurants. Four excellent seafood restaurants are the *Evening Star Dining Room* (in the *Tara Manor,* Route 127), *Conley's Shore House* (Conley's Wharf), *Whale of a Café* (173 Water St.), and *The Gables* (143 Water St.). Just outside town is *The Rossmount Inn* (see *Best en Route*), noted for its Victorian decor and pleasant dining. It offers elegant rooms for bed and breakfast in historical surroundings. The town boasts some of the best shopping in New Brunswick. *Sea Captain's Loft* (211 Water St.) features handblown glass and woolens; *Cottage Craft* (in the town square, phone: 506-529-3190) offers locally made and imported woolens; *St. Andrews Woolens Handweaving Ltd.* (22 Douglas St.) weaves 100% virgin wool blankets and sweaters in its own shop; *Tom Smith's Studio* (136 Water St.) has fine quality pottery; *The Canadian Trading Co.* (224 Water St.) offers a good selection of crafts; and the *Pansy Patch* (59 Carlton St.; phone: 506-529-3834) sells unusual antiques and rare books.

The *Sunbury Shores Arts and Nature Centre* (139 Water St.) sponsors shore walks and gives presentations on marine ecology (phone: 506-529-3386).

If you enjoy antiques, don't miss the *Ross Memorial Museum,* a restored home (188 Montague St., phone: 506-529-4270) with one of the finest collections in eastern Canada.

The *Huntsman Marine Science Centre* (Brandy Cove Rd.; phone: 506-529-8895) is a 15-minute walk from town. The laboratory itself is a large oceanographic institute that is, unfortunately, closed to the public. Its aquarium, however, is open from May to September, and has tanks with sturgeon, salmon, sea cucumbers, and other local marine life. There is also an excellent film on the area's sealife and a playful group of seals in residence. The nonprofit research and educational institute charges an admission fee to cover expenses.

The *Algonquin* hotel (see *Best en Route*) has two golf courses open to the public: a 9-hole woodland course and an 18-hole, par-71 course, with 13 fairways near Passamaquoddy Bay.

Five of New Brunswick's 76 covered bridges are near St. Andrews. Ask for directions before rejoining Route 1 toward St. George.

Letete, reached through St. George, is the jumping-off (or floating-off) point for the first major side trip from the Fundy Coast: a chain of beautiful islands nestled between the US and Canadian shores.

FUNDY ISLES: A trip to these little-known islands in the Bay of Fundy takes time and planning (which explains why they remain little known and unspoiled). Each is reached from a different point of embarkation: all from the Canadian coast, including Campobello, which is also accessible by the International Bridge in Lubec, Maine. During late summer, it's very common to see whales in this area. Most of the 350 Right Whales (also called Greenland Whales) are thought to migrate to the Bay of Fundy in August and September. Other varieties of whales here include the humpback and finback. This is also a popular bird-watching area.

Grand Manan – The largest of the Fundy Isles can be reached by ferry from Black's Harbour, 6 miles (10 km) south of St. George on Route 778. The reasonably priced MV *Grand Manan* ferry leaves Black's Harbour five times daily (three times on Sundays) from July through September; less frequently the rest of the year. Often dolphins will ride the bow waves in a watery escort.

Grand Manan is just the place if you want to see whales cavorting offshore and can appreciate the beauty of a delicate wildflower. Or pick up a copy of the *Hiking Guide to Grand Manan,* available in gift shops, and enjoy some of the island's 19 trails, many of which wind near spectacular seascapes.

The island's 2,000 residents live off the sea. Its fishermen take tons of herring, scallops, clams, and lobsters daily. A paved road runs the 15-mile length of the island. The village of North Head boasts the *Shorecrest Lodge,* run by two naturalists, and the

Compass Rose, a smaller inn with highly regarded food (see *Best en Route*). Additional accommodations can be found at Grand Harbour and Seal Cove. Stop at the island's only beer and liquor store in Castalia, 5 miles (8 km) south of Grand Harbour, if you plan to provide your own entertainment.

Dark Harbour on the west coast is the "dulse capital of the world." Dulse is edible seaweed sold for its high iodine content in health food stores all over the continent. You can pick your own dulse and dry it on the beach — just ask a local resident how to do it. Dulse production is now the second most lucrative industry on the island. The dried product is an acquired taste, and while most New Brunswick residents swear by it, expect mixed reviews on your first bite. But certainly give it a try. The *Manan Island Inn and Spa* (in North Head; phone: 506-662-8624), uses dulse in its pricey health treatments.

People come from all over to photograph the tall, spiky wildflowers called lupens. Other wildflowers, strawberries, blueberries, and blackberries can be found in the meadows and near the picturesque lighthouses at either end of the island.

A free government ferry takes visitors from Ingall's Head Village to White Head Island. Residents claim that a 33-foot great white shark, the largest catch ever recorded, was landed just off White Head. Boats can also be chartered at Ingall's Head for trips to the Three Islands, home of the Bowdoin Scientific Station, a sanctuary for many of the 250 species of birds on Grand Manan. Boats can also be chartered for a 2-hour trip to Machias Seal Island, where you can see seals, puffins, and an occasional whale. Inquire at the *Shorecrest Lodge* (phone: 506-662-3216) about whale watching expeditions; sightings are practically guaranteed in the mating season.

Deer Island – From St. George, take Route 772 south to Letete, and hop on the free government-run ferry to Deer Island. There is a quiet campground on the island and the world's three largest lobster pounds. From July to *Labor Day,* a private ferry makes the journey to Campobello Island. From the ferry you can see the Old Sow, the second largest whirlpool in the world. *West Isles World Bed and Breakfast* offers rooms, cottages, and whale watching cruises (phone: 506-747-2946).

Campobello Island – You can get to Campobello either by the ferry just mentioned or from US Route 1 at Lubec, Maine. The island features good hiking and walking trails, a lighthouse, and a great 9-hole golf course.

Like most other Fundy Coast history, the island was originally settled by the French and later by British Loyalists from New England. Campobello was given to Captain William Owen in 1767 in exchange for an arm he lost in battle. Benedict Arnold and his wife lived at Snug Cove for a while, but the island draws its fame from an American president who spent many summers here, Franklin Delano Roosevelt. The Roosevelt-Campobello International Park on the southern end of the island encompasses the former 11-acre Roosevelt estate. Many of Roosevelt's artifacts are on display, including the leather chair he used for Washington cabinet meetings, and a childhood letter to Santa Claus. Open year-round; guided tours are available from May to October.

When you return to the continent from Grand Manan or Deer Island, rejoin Route 1 toward Saint John.

NEW RIVER BEACH: If you cross the border too early in the day to stop at Oak Bay, perhaps this 835-acre provincial park will sound attractive. From New River Beach, facing the Bay of Fundy, there are spectacular ocean views, and the park has 115 campsites, as well as services for trailers.

Lepreau Falls is 3 miles (5 km) beyond New River Beach on Route 1. The falls are 80 feet high, but can be significantly shorter at high tide. They are not one of the seven wonders of New Brunswick, but it is a good place to stop and relax for a few minutes. Another peaceful spot is Dipper Harbour, just off Route 1 toward Saint John, where you'll find *Fundy Haven,* an excellent little restaurant.

As you approach Saint John from the west, note that Route 1 merges with Route 7 and becomes the Saint John Throughway. By the way, Saint in the name of the *city* is always spelled out; Saint in the name of the *river* is not. The most serious offense, however, is adding "'s" to "John." St. John's is the capital of Newfoundland.

SAINT JOHN: This is New Brunswick's largest city (pop. 121,265), one of its most historic, and the heart of Loyalist country. Thousands of Loyalists arrived in this port in 1783 after the US was officially recognized by the Treaty of Paris. The city celebrates *Loyalist Day* each July. Saint John harbor is open year-round, so a bulk of the activity in its commercial port comes after the St. Lawrence Seaway freezes in winter. It has been a shipping center since British Loyalists built a shipbuilding center here in the early 19th century. Although similar maritime cities failed with the obsolescence of wooden sailing ships, Saint John thrived. At the Saint John Drydock you will see tankers under construction. A special observation booth overlooks the work area. The drydock is the largest facility of its kind in North America. The Irving Oil refineries are also located here. A good way to see New Brunswick's oldest city is to obtain a brochure at the tourist information center detailing walking tours of the area's many historic buildings. When you arrive in Saint John, find out the times for both high and low tides at the "reversing falls" (phone: 506-635-1238). For optimum viewing, it is best to observe the tidal action twice — at or near both high and low tides. During low tide in the Bay of Fundy, the water drops 15 feet below river levels, forcing the river to crash through a narrow gorge in the harbor. At high tides, the rush reverses and bay waters flow upriver. A 13-minute interpretive film explaining the phenomenon is shown regularly at the Reversing Falls Tourist Centre on Route 100 at the Reversing Falls Bridge.

Market Slip, the site of the first Loyalist landing on May 18, 1783, is a good point of orientation to downtown Saint John and the city's historical beginnings. The *Ocean Hawk II,* a tugboat that served the city from 1940 to 1976, is a tourist information center (phone: 506-658-2410), open from mid-May through mid-October. Available here are brochures that give excellent directions and historical information for three walking tours of Victorian homes, merchant heritage, and Saint John's Loyalist history.

Most of the Loyalist sites are within easy walking distance of the harbor. *Barbour's General Store,* with staff in period costumes, is just a few feet from the "tourist tug." Tours of Loyalist House — ca. 1810 — (120 Union St.; phone: 652-3590) provide an excellent introduction into family life, culture, and skills of early Saint John craftsmen. Other Loyalist sites include the Old Loyalist Burying Ground (1783) and the Old County Courthouse (1825) on Sydney Street facing King Square. Inside, a 3-story spiral staircase made of more than 100 tons of freestone from Scotland is fitted without a central support pillar. Historians believe that the fitting was done by Robert Barbour, a local stonecutter of that time.

Adjacent to Market Slip with its sidewalk cafés is Market Square, a colorful restoration, featuring the public library and 70 shops, boutiques, and restuarants, including *Grannan's* (phone: 506-634-1555), as well as a series of fast food bars serving international fare. *Café Creole* (King St.; phone: 506-633-8091) serves New Orleans–style food, and *Incredible Edibles* (Princess St.; phone: 506-633-7554), a short walk from Market Square, features pasta, salad, and seafood.

Enter the block-long *Old City Market* from either Charlotte or Germain Streets. The market has been open since 1876. Vegetables, meat, fresh lobster, and fish, as well as hand-knitted items and various crafts for both infants and adults are sold here.

Relics of the shipbuilding era can be seen at the *New Brunswick Museum* (277 Douglas Ave.). In the 1880s, detailed models were built before the actual construction of the ship. These replicas are displayed in a special exhibition at the museum. Don't miss the miniature of the 1,625-ton *Marco Polo,* the fastest sailing ship of its time. In August, the city's *Festival by the Sea* draws more than 1,000 song-and-dance performers from all over Canada.

Direct ferry service to Nova Scotia from Saint John begins at the foot of Lancaster Street. The trip takes almost 3 hours. The *Princess of Acadia* plies the bay three times daily in summer, twice on Sundays. About 40 miles (64 km) east along Route 111 (detour on to Route 825 to see more of the Bay of Fundy) is St. Martin's, a very quiet, undeveloped village, home of the *Quaco Inn* (see *Best en Route*).

En Route from Saint John – The most direct road to complete the Fundy Coast is Route 1 toward Sussex. However, a short drive through the farming district of the Kingston Peninsula and the Kennebecasis River Valley is recommended. You will see many of New Brunswick's remaining covered bridges as well as some of the best countryside the province has to offer. A complete list of covered bridges can be obtained from *Tourism New Brunswick,* PO Box 12344, Fredericton NB E3B 5C3.

Take Route 100 through Rothesay to Gondola Point and cross the Kennebecasis River by ferry (free, year-round, 24 hours) to Reeds Point. Follow Route 850 north to Route 124 east and rejoin Route 1 at Norton. Continue along Route 1 for 12 miles (19 km) to Sussex, through the heart of the dairy district. Try a stay at *Anderson's Holiday Farm Bed and Breakfast,* (phone: 506-433-3786) to experience dairy life. The *Broadway Café* is directly across from the train station in the middle of town. From Sussex, pick up the Trans-Canada Highway (Route 2) toward Moncton. Drive 10 miles (16 km) to Route 114, also known as the Fundy Tidal Trail, and take the road south to Fundy National Park.

FUNDY NATIONAL PARK: Most of this 80-square-mile park sits on a plateau 1,000 feet above sea level. Its thick forests are laced with 50 miles of hiking trails used by the resident moose, black bear, fox, deer, bobcat, and beaver as well as by two-footed visitors. Its interior streams are excellent for trout and salmon fishing. Guides are available for the nature trails, but you can explore for yourself with relative ease.

The entrance from the northwest on Route 114 is through dense forests, but 2½ miles (4 km) before Alma, a small city at the southeastern corner and home of park headquarters, stop at Hastings Hill for the view, for the road opens suddenly for a vista of the Chignecto Bay. Campers can stock up on supplies at Alma (lobster is plentiful), and you can eat at the *Fundy Park Chalets and Coffee Shop.* For a snack, try the sticky buns at the aptly named *Sticky Bun Shop* (470 E. Main St., Alma; phone: 506-532-3137).

A heated, saltwater swimming pool is close to the chalet for those who have tried the icy waters of the Bay of Fundy. Visit the beach, however, even if you don't plan to swim. The coastline is dotted with caves cut into the side of the 200-foot cliffs by the pounding surf. This exploration can be dangerous: Park officials warn that should you lose track of the time, the tide will rise faster than you can climb to safety. Check at park headquarters for a timetable.

A 9-hole golf course, tennis courts, and a lawn-bowling green are available for use through the provincial government. For more information write to the Superintendent, Fundy National Park, Alma, NB, or call 506-887-2000.

En Route from Fundy National Park – Follow Route 114 east from Alma to Hopewell Cape, where the mighty tides have created sculptures from sandstone known locally as the "flower pots." You can take Route 915, which follows the coast and offers great bird watching. From Hopewell Cape, proceed north on Route 114 for 50 miles (81 km) to Moncton, "the hub of the Maritimes." At Hillsborough, you can board a train on the *Salem and Hillsborough* line for an hour-long dinner excursion through picturesque marshlands (phone: 506-734-3195).

MONCTON: The second-largest city in New Brunswick, Moncton is an important distribution center for the other Maritime Provinces. Rail connections to Montreal, Nova Scotia, Prince Edward Island ferry, and the Northumberland coast pass through the city. It has been an important rail center since its designation as maritime headquarters of the *Intercolonial Railway* in 1872.

The Free Meeting House (Steadman St. and Mountain Rd.) was built in 1821 as an interdenominational place of worship until churches could be built. *Moncton Civic Museum,* just across the street, has displays on the city's history as a rail center. From the museum, walk down King Street toward the Petitcodiac River to Boreview Park. The action of the Fundy tide creates a phenomenon similar to the reversing falls in Saint John: Twice daily a wave — known as the Tidal Bore — rushes upstream as the tide rises in the Bay of Fundy 25 miles (40 km) away. But for all this activity, the wave is usually only one foot high. At Magnetic Hill, cars seem to be pulled uphill. For the most part, though, Moncton's manmade attractions prevail — its plenitude of large shopping malls, and a huge water theme park, *Magic Mountain,* which has boats, wave pools, and slides.

For a taste of the sea, try *Cy's Seafood* restaurant (170 Main St.; phone: 506-382-0032; closed Sundays). For sophisticated, but expensive, dining *à la française,* splurge at *Chez Jean Pierre* (21 Toombes St.; phone: 506-382-0332).

BEST EN ROUTE

Most of the accommodations listed here are older establishments, with a friendly staff and homey atmosphere. In heavily traveled areas, we also note some standard accommodations where you have a better chance of getting a room without reservations. In the popular resort areas, you must have a reservation for July and August — with the exception of the *Algonquin* in St. Andrews, where reservations are advisable during the entire summer season. Unless otherwise noted, hotels are open year-round.

The price range is based on double occupancy: expensive, $50 and up; moderate, $27 to $50; inexpensive, below $27. All prices are quoted in US dollars.

The government publication *New Brunswick Accommodations and Campground Guide* lists hundreds of smaller hotels, cabins, guesthouses, and bed and breakfast establishments. These generally have between 5 and 15 rooms with fewer but less expensive facilities. For a copy of the *Accommodations* guide, write to *Tourism New Brunswick,* PO Box 12345, Fredericton NB E3B 5C3.

ST. STEPHEN

Wandlyn Motor Inn – This hostelry has 50 modern rooms and a dining room specializing in seafood and steaks. 90 King St. (phone: 506-466-1814). Moderate.

ST. ANDREWS

Algonquin – One of the best hotels in the Canadian Pacific chain, it has 200 rooms, a restaurant, coffee shop, 2 lounges, and a clubhouse adjoining the 2 golf courses — a 9-hole and an 18-hole (guests pay no greens fees). There is tennis and bicycles for touring the city. Open from late May to early October. Reservations are a must during the entire summer season. 184 Adophus St. (phone: 506-529-8823). Expensive.

Pansy Patch – This bed and breakfast establishment looks like a fairy-tale cottage and also houses an antiques store with silver, china, linens, and books. 56 Carleton St. (phone: 506-529-3834). Moderate.

Rossmount Inn – The decor is eclectic in exactly the fashion of a well-traveled Victorian gentleman's home: Persian rugs, French art, colorful English wallpaper in the parlor and 16 guestrooms. Dining from 6:30 to 9:30 PM. For information, simply write to the *Rossmount* in St. Andrews (phone: 506-529-3351). Moderate.

GRAND MANAN

Shorecrest Lodge – This old-fashioned country inn with 15 guestrooms, a lounge, and dining room, is run by two naturalists who give plenty of direction and information on exploring Grand Manan. North Head (phone: 506-662-3216). Expensive.

Compass Rose – Nine guestrooms in two charming old houses look out to the sea. The dining room faces a deck overlooking the harbor. North Head (phone: 506-662-8570). Moderate.

SAINT JOHN

Delta Brunswick – This modern motel with 255 rooms is centrally located and has a pool, sauna, whirlpool bath, game room, lounge with live entertainment, bars, and a good, moderately priced dining room. 39 King St. (phone: 506-648-1981). Expensive.

Saint John Hilton – Here is a luxury hotel nicely situated in the renovated historic harborfront area — the best of the 197 rooms overlook the bay. The *Turn-of-Tide* dining room is first class. Market Sq. (phone: 506-693-8484). Expensive.

ST. MARTINS

Quaco Inn – An old sea captain's home, lovingly restored. There are 9 guestrooms with great beds. The dining room serves excellent local foods for breakfast and dinner (phone: 506-833-4772). Moderate.

ROTHESAY

Shadow Lawn Inn – Built in 1871, this old inn has 8 guestrooms furnished with a mixture of antiques and cast-offs. The dining room, which serves breakfast, and dinner by reservation, is elegant, but the owner makes the gratuity a mandatory part of the bill instead of an offering. Route 100 (phone: 506-847-7539). Moderate.

SUSSEX

Rory's Mountain Inn – This motel has been expanded to include a lounge, restaurant, a log-constructed convention center, and 22 rooms and housekeeping units. 1019 Main St. (phone: 506-433-1558). Moderate.

FUNDY NATIONAL PARK

Caledonia Highlands Inn and Chalets – These 44 units are modern with spectacular views. Fundy National Park, PO Box 99, Alma, NB (phone: 506-887-2930). Moderate.

MONCTON

Beausejour – Reservations are a must at one of New Brunswick's finest establishments. The 316 rooms are decorated in early Acadian style; also featured are a lounge, 2 restaurants, and an outdoor pool. The *Windjammer Room* specializes in steaks and seafood, and *L'Auberge* serves Acadian dishes. Special rates are available with vouchers from the tourist information centers. 750 Main St. (phone: 506-854-4344). Expensive.

Canadiana – This century-old house contains 20 rooms, a dining room, and cable television. 46 Archibald St. (phone: 506-382-1054). Moderate.

SACKVILLE

Marshlands Inn – Some 25 miles (40 km) southeast of Moncton, in the neck of land that connects New Brunswick and Nova Scotia, are the Tantramar marshes, the launching pad for thousands of Canada geese each year. On the edge of the marshes, this inn, built around 1850 is the launching pad for people traveling between the two provinces or bird watchers and naturalists haunting the marshes. There are 20 rooms in this lovely old home, and even if you can't stay overnight, come for a meal (breakfast: 7-10 AM; lunch: noon-2 PM; dinner: 6-9 PM). Treat your tastebuds to a fiddlehead (the top portion of the ostrich fern), a local delicacy cooked until it's fork-tender, then served with lemon juice and butter. Other taste treats are local mushrooms, and rhubarb punch. Write to PO Box 1440, 73 Bridge St., NB E0A 3C0 (phone: 506-536-0170). Expensive to moderate.

Different Drummer – This bed and breakfast establishment has 8 rooms and loads of charm. 146 Main St. (phone: 506-536-1291). Moderate.

The St. John River

The St. John River once served as a major Indian waterway between the St. Lawrence River and the Bay of Fundy. This was the territory of the powerful Maliseet, the nomadic tribe that wandered throughout the northernmost Allegheny Mountains. Their swift canoes carried them all the way to Nova Scotia in the warm months. In fact, most of the canoes in use today are based upon the Maliseet design. There are six Indian reserves along the route.

This drive along the St. John River Valley, from the busy commercial port of Saint John to the pulp and paper center at Edmundston, is 264 miles (422 km) long. It starts in the rolling hills and agricultural region of the Kingston Peninsula, passes New Brunswick's largest freshwater lake and the provincial capital of Fredericton.

The river turns north at Meductic toward Hartland — with the world's longest covered bridge — and continues through New Brunswick's potato growing district (where you can enjoy a farm vacation at Aroostook — see *Best en Route*) to Perth-Andover. A pleasant sidetrip to the undeveloped 43,000-acre Mt. Carleton Provincial Park returns to Route 2 at Grand Falls.

One of the two best Atlantic salmon and canoeing rivers in North America is the Restigouche — accessible from St. Leonard — which leads to Chaleur Bay on New Brunswick's northern border. Other spots for canoeing and fishing are pointed out along the way. Tourism New Brunswick can send you a free fishing guide (phone: 800-561-0123). Topographical maps of any section of the province are available at modest prices. The *Outfitters* brochure will help plan a fishing or canoeing expedition. It's available from *Tourism New Brunswick,* PO Box 12345, Fredericton E3B 5C3.

The drive starts in Saint John (described in detail in *The Fundy Coast*).

En Route from Saint John – There are two options at the beginning of this route, depending on how you entered Saint John. If you came from the east through the dairy district surrounding Sussex, take Route 7 directly to Fredericton to avoid repetition. From there, you can do some of the things listed in the area as side trips, such as camping and boating on Grand Lake. If you came from the west along the Fundy Coast, a trip through the Lower St. John River valley on the Kingston Peninsula is recommended. Many of the province's 133 covered bridges can be found on the peninsula. The rolling countryside has not yet been touched by industrialization.

KINGSTON PENINSULA: From Saint John, take Route 100 north for 12 miles (20 km) to Quispamsis. The road is well marked to Gondola Point, where you take the ferry (free, year-round, 24 hours) to Reeds Point. Take Route 850 north for 18 miles (29 km) to a second ferry across the Belleisle Bay (free, year-round, 24 hours). Route 124 west will take you to the ferry at Evandale.

Don't be afraid to ask residents for directions to the covered bridges or to the best place to stop for a leisurely picnic. This drive through the pastoral countryside of New Brunswick seems to make the hours fly by.

THE LOWER ST. JOHN RIVER: From Evandale take Route 102 north for 17½ miles (28 km) to Gagetown, home of the *Queens County Museum* (Front St.; phone: 506-488-2966) and a handful of crafts shops, as well as the Loomcrofters, weavers of tartans and other fabrics whose workshop is in a blockhouse dating from the late 18th century. The old *Steamers Stop Inn,* (Front St.; phone: 448-2903), run by friendly owners, Vic and Pat Stewart, features 7 antiques-furnished rooms and a good restaurant. Also in Gagetown: *Colpitt's* marina and old-fashioned general store; and the *Loaves and Calico Tearoom,* which features tasty homemade treats.

Look for cattle grazing on the interval islands in the middle of the St. John River. If you pass at the right time of day, you can see the cattle being transported back and forth on wooden flatboats, as they have been for over 100 years. Apple orchards dot the meadowlands.

Route 102 skirts the southern bank of the river as it bends to the west toward Fredericton. At Oromocto, 24 miles (39 km) from Gagetown, the Canadian Forces Base Gagetown (open to the public) has an army museum. There are some craft, gift, and antiques shops in the area.

Route 102 joins Route 7 into Fredericton.

GRAND LAKE: Lakeside Provincial Park at Jemseg has 132 campsites, services for trailers, and a beach. Grand Lake seems to have fallen into disfavor since the completion of Mactaquac Park on the west side of Fredericton. But so much the better: The facilities around Grand Lake — several bed and breakfast inns and farm vacation accommodations — are relatively uncrowded.

FREDERICTON: The French were the original settlers here until driven out by British troops in 1759. British Loyalists sailed up the St. John River in 1783 and promptly established a British city. Fredericton was the first major settlement in the "interior" and is still a prosperous city, with many small industries in addition to the major employers, the University of New Brunswick and Provincial Government offices. Officer's Square, part of the original British military compound, has been restored, complete with soldiers in red coats and an hourly changing of the guard, accompanied by a piper, in summer.

This "city of the stately elms" was designated the provincial capital in 1785 by Governor Thomas Carleton to the chagrin of Saint John. The Old Government House (1828) on Woodstock Road, until 1893 the official residence of provincial governors, was the headquarters of the district's Royal Canadian Mounted Police.

Other sites of note are centrally located on Queen Street. The Anglican Christ Church Cathedral (1853) is considered one of the best examples of Gothic architecture in North America. The cathedral's east stained glass window was donated by Trinity Church in New York City.

The Legislative Building's silver dome dominates the skyline. Its Assembly chamber has two giant Reynolds portraits of King George III and Queen Charlotte (the provincial capital was named after their second son, Frederick). A 1783 edition of the *Domesday Book* and a complete set of king-size Audubon bird books are displayed in the Legislative Library annexed to the rear of the main building.

You can't visit Fredericton without being aware of the city's admiration for Lord Beaverbrook (1879–1964). Born William Maxwell Aitken in Maple, Ontario, and raised in Newcastle, New Brunswick, Lord Beaverbrook became a self-made millionaire before the age of 30, making his fortune in the merger of Canada Cement from 13 smaller companies. Beaverbrook owned London's *Daily Express,* was a member of British Parliament from 1910 to 1916, and served in Winston Churchill's cabinet during World War II.

Lord Beaverbrook's legacy in Fredericton is in the buildings he left the town, including several on the University of New Brunswick campus such as the University Library; the *Playhouse,* home of *Theatre New Brunswick* (on Queen St.); and the *Beaverbrook Art Gallery* (also on Queen St.).

The *Beaverbrook Art Gallery* has works by Botticelli, Sir Joshua Reynolds, Thomas Gainsborough, Constable, Turner, and Hogarth. Its pride and joy is the 10-by-13½-foot *Santiago El Grande,* by Spanish surrealist Salvador Dali.

The Fredericton area has become a center for craftspeople working in materials of various kinds. You'll find batik, pewterware, stained glass, hooked rugs, handwoven clothing, sterling silver jewelry, enamelware (such as miniature paintings on copper buttons), wooden toys, candles, and fine pottery. A list of handicraft studios throughout the province is available from *Tourism New Brunswick* (address above). In Fredericton, visit *Aitken's Pewter* (81 Regent St.) for tableware, jewelry, and collectibles; *Shades of Light* (228 Regent St.) presents a smorgasbord of New Brunswick crafts; and *Regent Craft Gallery* (72 Regent Promenade) feautures a large selection of maritime crafts.

Just behind the art gallery is the "Green," a massive landscaped park between Queen Street and the St. John River. *The Pioneer Princess,* a riverboat replica, docks here and offers daily cruises and dinner cruises.

A few of the best places to eat are nearby: *Eighty Eight Ferry* (88 Ferry St.; phone: 506-472-1988) is set on the sunny porch of an old-fashioned farmhouse. It has lots of greenery, chintz, and genuine hospitality. In summer, cocktails are served on the lawn beside the garden and the brook. *The Barn,* a trendy spot (540 Queen St.; phone: 506-455-2742) features chicken, ribs, escargots, and crêpes; and *Mei's* (Regent St.) is a good, small Chinese restaurant. Fredericton's farmers' market on Saturday mornings (on George St. between Regent and St. John Sts., 6 AM to noon) is a must for crafts, produce, and local color — especially for breakfast afterward. For this, visitors should make a beeline to *Goofy Roofy's.* This restaurant, which is part of the market complex, has become something of an institution for its informality and affordability, and is popular with the artistic and political crowds for breakfast and brunch.

En route from Fredericton – Highway 8 runs north out of Fredericton along the Miramichi River, world famous for its abundance of Atlantic salmon. Doaktown is about 2 hours north of Fredericton. Like many New Brunswick towns, it is small, but it is a headquarters for hunting, fishing, and canoeing outfitters. For the *Outfitters* brochure, write *Tourism New Brunswick* (PO Box 12345, Fredericton, NB E3B 5C3). Even if you don't fish, Doaktown's *Atlantic Salmon Museum* attractively protrays the history of Atlantic salmon, and displays of myriad colorful flies used to lure the fish and conservation policies necessary to protect them. Costumed guides provide interpretive tours of the house, farm, and Doak Historic Park. The Doak family came from Ayershire, Scotland, and had planned to sail south and settle in Kentucky, but storms forced their ship off course to a port on the Miramichi and the area they settled later was named Doaktown. The bed and breakfast *Inn by the Pond* (see *Best en Route*), is comfortable and attractive. Dinners can be served if reservations are made well in advance. West from Fredericton, the Trans-Canada Highway (Route 2) runs beside the St. John River almost to the Quebec border. Follow Route 2 west 15 miles (24 km) to Mactaquac Provincial Park.

MACTAQUAC PROVINCIAL PARK: This "super park" is one of the newest and largest of the provincial parks. Because of its wide range of facilities and close proximity to Fredericton, it also is crowded most of the summer. In the late 1960s, the New Brunswick Electric Power Commission built the hydroelectric dam from which the park takes its name. The dam's headwaters flooded the St. John River Valley for 60 miles (96 km), all the way to Woodstock.

Boating, water skiing, swimming, and fishing are among the popular pastimes at this mammoth, 1,400-acre park. Pickerel, smallmouth bass, and trout are among the fish in the 34-square-mile headpond of the dam. Sailboat and powerboat marinas serve the lake, which has two long beaches.

There are guided nature trails, programs for children, playgrounds supervised by qualified counselors skilled in arts and crafts instruction, and 296 campsites with kitchen shelters, heated washrooms, and showers. The *Park Lodge* has both a bar and restaurant. The lodge also rents clubs for its championship 18-hole golf course, one of the best in the province. *Chickadee Lodge* (phone: 506-363-2759), nearby, offers a bed and a hearty country breakfast, a great view of Mactaquac Headpond, and a proprietor who acts as a hunting guide during hunting season.

　　En Route from Mactaquac – Continuing on the Trans-Canada Highway, the route intersects with Route 3 to the US border at St. Stephen. Route 3 also leads to Harvey Station. A farmer's market is nearby, and, in addition to fruits and vegetables in season, the market offers patchwork quilts, canned goods, and freshly baked bread. Kings Landing is only 10 miles (16 km) away.

KINGS LANDING: This is the last example of Loyalist tradition along the St. John River route (3 miles/5 km west of the Route 3 intersection on the Trans-Canada Highway). Kings Landing Historical Settlement was constructed when the rising waters of Mactaquac Dam threatened to wash away several sites of historic value along the river. Over 50 buildings, including a school, church, carpenter's shop, and forge, were moved to higher ground. In historic shops, costumed staff of the settlement are busy making horseshoes, planing lumber, and practicing other early crafts. Children will enjoy an hour-long, behind-the-scenes tour, where they can don period costumes, see how buildings were constructed, and eat cookies made on the premises (phone: 506-363-3081).

The *Kings Head Inn* (phone: 506-363-5613) offers wholesome meals from 1800-vintage recipes. The settlement is open from June 1 to mid-October.

　　En Route from Kings Landing – Route 2 runs east along the south bank of the river for 29 miles (46 km) and turns north at Meductic. Just before Meductic, Route 122 leads to the Chiputneticook Lakes region, with landlocked salmon and trout. When you get to Canterbury on Route 122, ask outfitter Albert Conklin of *Skiff Lake Inn Sporting Camps* (phone: 506-279-2119) about canoeing on Eel River. Depending on the time of year, Eel River is the penultimate whitewater in New Brunswick.

MEDUCTIC: This is the site of a Maliseet Indian fort built for protection against the raiding Mohawks. Until recently, excavations were made of the ancient Maliseet burial grounds. Living Maliseets petitioned the Department of Indian Affairs to cease this digging and the excavations were brought to a halt. Indian crafts are available at some reserves along the way.

WOODSTOCK: The streets of this quiet town on the St. John are lined with elms. Its primary activities are agricultural. Visit the restored Old Courthouse (1833) in Upper Woodstock, which doubles as the *Carleton County Historical Society Museum.* If you return to the US at the Woodstock-Houlton, Maine border, note that there are comprehensive duty-free shops here with English woolens, china, and crafts from Canada and all over. Open daily in summer, 24 hours a day.

　　En Route from Woodstock – Route 2 leads to Hartland, site of the world's longest covered bridge (1,282 ft.). Hartland is where many of the New Brunswick potatoes come from and is a popular resort for salmon and trout fishing. Route 2 crosses to the east bank of the St. John River above Hartland for 12 miles (19 km), returning to the west bank at Florenceville. The Tobique Indian Reserve, near Perth-Andover, is another good place to buy Indian handicrafts, and is home to *York's* restaurant (phone: 506-273-2847). Take Route 109 north to Plaster Rock, home of several outfitters for canoeing, hunting, and fishing on the Tobique River, and the gateway to New Brunswick's largest park.

Strange as it may seem, one of Canada's more famous restaurants is located in Perth-Andover on old Highway 2. *York's* draws people back again and again for its simple, hearty — indeed immense — fixed-price (moderate-price) meals. The waitress offers a choice of lobster, duck, crab, turkey, steaks, clams, scallops, chicken, or pork chops, and with it you get five kinds of bread, soup, salad, and either strawberry shortcake or pie for dessert. Second helpings are free and are literally pushed at you — even the steaks. Open May to October, there's no menu, no credit cards accepted, no liquor, and no reservations, but it's a great treat. Just be sure to arrive with an empty stomach.

MT. CARLETON PROVINCIAL PARK: This new 43,000-acre park is reserved for wilderness campers. Be forewarned: There are no accommodations in this park, aside from its 88 campsites (phone: 551-1377). There are, on the other hand, moose, deer, otter, muskrat, brook trout, and Atlantic salmon. Mt. Carleton is the highest peak (2,690 ft.) in New Brunswick. A canoe set down on one of the Nepisiguit Lakes will take you all the way to the Bathurst Power Dam by way of the Nepisiguit ("Angry River").

The drive into the park from Plaster Rock takes about an hour. There is a 30-mile (48-km) stretch of gravel road, but even here speeds of 50 to 60 miles (80 to 90 km) per hour are safe except in the early spring. Interior roads are plentiful — although not marked on most maps — thanks to extensive logging in the area. The logging trucks also travel 50 miles (80 km) per hour on the narrow road, so be careful.

To plan your trip through this wilderness, write Park Superintendent (Box 180, St. Jacques, NB E0L 1K0) or contact a local outfitter in Plaster Rock.

When you return to Plaster Rock, take Route 108 north to Grand Falls. En route, drive through scenic New Denmark, the largest settlement of Danish people in Canada. Spectacular scenery surrounds New Denmark. The *Valhalla* restaurant serves good Danish food (phone: 506-553-6614).

GRAND FALLS: The 75-foot Grand Falls are among Canada's highest cataracts. The best view is from the newly constructed walkway along the gorge, higher than Niagara's. Tours are available of the hydro-electric powerhouse.

En route from Grand Falls – Route 2 runs north from Grand Falls. Just in case you haven't had your fill of canoeing and fishing on this route, the best is last. The Restigouche River winds for almost 100 miles (160 km) to Chaleur Bay on the Quebec border. After the Miramichi River on the east coast, this is the best salmon river in the province.

Route 17 leads to Campbellton on Chaleur Bay. Edmundston is 25 miles (40 km) north on Route 2.

ST. LEONARD: This hamlet between Grand Falls and Edmundston is home to *Madawaska Weavers,* producers of fine hand-woven products, who boast that Princess Anne is a customer (phone: 506-423-6341). Hours: 9 AM to 5 PM.

EDMUNDSTON: The inhabitants of the northern part of the province are predominantly of French origin, since British soldiers drove them out of southern New Brunswick in 1784. Although logs are no longer floated to the pulp and paper mills, the St. John River is polluted for many miles below Edmundston (from mills on the US side, locals will tell you). If you visit in August, don't miss the *Foire Brayon Festival* — the largest Canadian French festival outside of Quebec.

The spires of the Roman Catholic Cathedral of the Immaculate Conception (145 Pine St.) can be seen from all over the city. Lac Baker and Les Jardins provincial parks are nearby. The *Laporte Art Museum* at St. Louis Maillet College is excellent.

Whitewater canoeing on the St. John River above Edmundston is the best in the province. There is excellent skiing at Mont Farlagne, along with some good restaurants and motels. Worth special mention in the eating department is *La Tulipe Blanche* (9 Hill St.; phone: 506-739-9008), a modern little café with an unusual black and white decor. It has excellent food with regional specialties such as *ployes* (a buckwheat pancake) and *créton* (a chopped-pork pâté). *Le Baron* (174 Victoria St.; phone: 506-735-3329), is a fine restaurant with a touch of haute cuisine.

BEST EN ROUTE

Except for Fredericton and Edmundston, there are no large cities on this route. Many small lodges and tourist homes can be found along the way. This route follows the Trans-Canada Highway, which means reservations are necessary during July and August. If you find the motels full, consult the *New Brunswick Travel Guide,* available from *Tourism New Brunswick* (PO Box 12345, Fredericton NB E3B 5C3; phone: 800-561-0123). For hotels we list as expensive, expect to pay $50 and up; for moderate, $26 to $50; and for inexpensive, less than $26. All prices are quoted in US dollars.

Accommodations in Saint John are listed in the *Best en Route* section at the end of *The Fundy Coast.* There are no accommodations in Mt. Carleton Provincial Park.

PRINCE WILLIAM

Chickadee Lodge – Fine bed and breakfast accommodations are found in this 5-room facility. There are 2 lounge areas with fireplaces and a dining area. It also boasts a spectacular view of Mactaquac Headpond. The proprietor acts as a guide during hunting season. Closed late November through April. Route 2 (phone: 506-363-2759). Moderate.

FREDERICTON

Lord Beaverbrook – With 165 rooms, this is part of the Keddy's Motor Inn chain and has an indoor pool with a bar, hot tub, and sauna. The hotel's *Maverick Room* (open 5 PM to midnight) is a popular restaurant. 659 Queen St. (phone: 506-455-3371). Expensive.

Carriage House Bed and Breakfast – Built in 1875 for the then-Mayor of Fredericton, this 2-story, 32-room mansion includes 2 balconies, a ballroom, coffee bar, and 7 guestrooms. 230 University Ave. (phone: 506-452-9924). Moderate.

Wandlyn Motor Inn – This 116-room family motel features a dining room, lounge, pool, sauna, and conference rooms. 58 Prospect St. (phone: 506-452-8937). Moderate.

GAGETOWN

Steamers Stop Inn – This hostelry with a spacious verandah overlooks the St. John River. All 7 guestrooms are furnished with antiques. There is a licensed dining room. PO Box 155 (phone: 506-488-2903). Moderate.

WOODSTOCK

Wandlyn Motor Inn – Located on Route 95 near the US-Canada border, this motel has 50 rooms, a dining room, and is usually crowded during July and August. PO Box 1191 (phone: 506-328-8876). Moderate.

AROOSTOOK

La Ferme des Erables I and II – Watch a real potato farm in action, fish for trout, hike, swim in an indoor pool, or golf nearby. Just 2 rooms at each farm. On Route 1 (phone: 506-273-3112). Inexpensive.

GRAND FALLS

Lakeside Lodge and Resort – Eight rooms are featured in the lodge and 7 chalets on 65-acre Pirie Lake, where many outdoor activities are available. The dining room serves three meals daily and Sunday brunch. PO Box 2753 (phone: 506-473-6252). Expensive.

Près du Lac – Noted for its hospitality (it received a special award for service), this motel has 100 attractive rooms, indoor pool, whirlpool baths, sauna, gym, and miniature golf. It also features some nonsmoking rooms and a nonsmoking section in its restaurant. Trans-Canada Highway (phone: 506-473-1300). Expensive to moderate.

EDMUNDSTON

Howard Johnson's – Located in the heart of town, this motel features 103 rooms, a pool, sauna, whirlpool baths, a family restaurant, and a dining room. 100 Rice St. (phone: 506-739-7321). Expensive to moderate.

Le Brayon – A hospitable and attractive motel, it has 32 rooms, 7 chalets, and a dining room serving breakfast and dinner. Ste. Basile, Route 2 E (phone: 506-263-5514). Moderate.

Lynn – This motel is centrally located and has 21 rooms. It is within walking distance of shopping and restaurants, and just a mile (1.6 km) from the ski slopes. Ski packages are available. 30 Church St. (phone: 506-735-8851). Moderate.

The Acadian Trail

Acadia, the name France gave its holdings on the Atlantic seaboard in the 17th century, suffered bitterly 100 years later at the hands of the British.

Acadian residents of Nova Scotia and southern New Brunswick who refused to pledge allegiance to the British Crown fled to northeast New Brunswick in 1755, when British soldiers burned settlements under orders from colonial Governor William Shirley in Massachusetts. The Expulsion routed thousands of French settlers, making Nova Scotia and New Brunswick "safe" for the British Loyalists. This saga is immortalized in Henry Wadsworth Longfellow's *Evangeline, A Tale of Acadia.* The tenacious French slowly drifted back to their northeast corner, establishing settlements in the forest, out of sight of marauding British soldiers. Without help from the Micmac Indians, many Acadians could not have survived the harsh winters. The people on the eastern coast of New Brunswick still rely largely on fishing, farming, lumbering, and mining, despite the growth of new industry nearby.

The climate of eastern New Brunswick is tempered by the Gulf Stream, a stark contrast to the Bay of Fundy. Long sandbars at several points along the coast create some of the best and warmest beaches north of Virginia.

The 270-mile (432-km) drive starts at Shediac, host of an annual lobster festival, and follows Route 11 to Bathurst on the northern coast. Cocagne, a tiny village on the other side of the Caissie Cape, comes alive in summer, when hydroplanes speed down the Cocagne River estuary at 200 miles per hour in an annual regatta.

Two small communities, Rexton and Richibucto, were once the home of a flourishing shipbuilding company. At Big Cove Indian Reserve, 5 miles (8 km) inland, some of the remaining Micmac Indians still make canoes. Nearby Kouchibouguac National Park, one of the richest ecosystems in the world, has been set aside to preserve a coastal timberland that harbors moose, black bear, and a variety of waterfowl. The park features a 16-mile-long beach.

The people of Chatham and Newcastle are proud of their British past, especially of Lord Beaverbrook, the British newspaper magnate who grew up in the area. Chatham and Newcastle sit on opposite sides of the Miramichi River, famous for its Atlantic salmon and trout.

Along the northeastern coast of New Brunswick is some of the best deep-sea fishing in the province. A world-record bluefin tuna, 1,200 pounds, was caught off Miscou Island in Chaleur Bay in 1976.

The Acadian Trail ends at Bathurst, a wood pulp and paper industry center on Chaleur Bay. Route 11 continues to the Quebec border at Matapedia.

SHEDIAC: One of the province's most hospitable communities, this town of 4,370 claims to be the "lobster capital of the world," hosting a 6-day *Lobster Festival* annually in mid-July. A lobster-eating contest, bicycle and 10-km foot races, entertainment, and a big parade, with the requisite fireworks, are all part of the festivities. (For details, see *Festivals, Fairs, and Fancy Acts,* DIVERSIONS.)

Nearby is Parlee Beach Provincial Park, with a 142-site tent and trailer campground, close to the province's largest beach. If you've tested the icy waters of the Bay of Fundy on the south shore, these waters will seem ideal. The long sandbars and shallow water make it perfect for children.

Shediac also has some of the best seafood spots in the province. *Fisherman's Paradise* (Main St.; phone: 506-532-6811) is exceptional both in food and service. The unforgettable lobster rolls make a complete dinner; eat in one of the three lavish dining rooms, or take your food out. The chowder is considered the best in the region, portions are gigantic, and prices moderate. *Chez Françoise,* (93 Main St.; phone: 506-532-4233) is another excellent seafood restaurant, located in an old mansion, now an inn.

COCAGNE: This picturesque fishing village is 13 miles (21 km) north of Shediac on Route 11. Cocagne (pronounced Ko-*kann*) was settled in 1767 by Acadians expelled from Nova Scotia by the British. Even today most residents speak French as well as English.

The *International Hydroplane Regatta* is held here in early August in the wide Cocagne River estuary. The regatta annually draws entries from all over the US and Canada and over 40,000 spectators.

From Cocagne, drive north on Route 530 to Caissie Cape, where there are several lighthouses and a good beach, less crowded than Parlee in Shediac.

About 11 miles (18 km) north of Cocagne on Route 11 is Bouctouche.

BUCTOUCHE: (Pronounced Book-*tush*). If you haven't sampled oysters yet, try some in "the oyster bed of New Brunswick," as this small fishing village and busy port is known. Some of the best are at the *Bouctouche Bay Inn.* (See *Best en Route*).

There are several good beaches on the coastline north of Bouctouche. Also nearby is the Bouctouche Indian Reserve, with a small handicrafts shop, open by appointment. Route 11 goes directly to Rexton; Route 134, however, is the prettier drive, winding close to the coast and through small communities along the way.

REXTON: This pretty coastal village was settled by a group of Scots early in the 19th century. Among the earliest residents were the Jardine brothers — Robert and John — from Dumfriesshire, Scotland, who established one of the first shipbuilding companies in the town and built Kent County's first squarerigger in 1820. Rexton's relationship to the sea has never faltered. John Jardine, incidentally, returned to Great Britain in 1844 to settle in Liverpool, where his son David became chairman of the *Cunard Line* some years later. A small museum, open daily in summer in the Town Hall of nearby Richibucto, traces the history of wooden shipbuilding in the area. Rexton is also the birthplace of Andrew Bonar-Law, who became Prime Minister of Britain in 1922.

His home is now a museum. *L'Habitant* (phone: 506-523-4421), in Richibucto, is one of the best places to eat between Shediac and Bathurst. The cooking is plain but reliable, and fish is the best bet.

KOUCHIBOUGUAC NATIONAL PARK: New Brunswick's "other national park" offers a mixture of forest, open fields, and beach. An offshore sand bar, the primary swimming area, runs the entire length of the shoreline. With sand dunes dotted with tufts of sea grass, the area resembles Cape Cod, but without the crowds and commercialization.

Three rivers flow through the park into the Kouchibouguac Bay, forming tidal estuaries and quiet lagoons on the coast.

The park is a flat coastal plain with no stunning vistas, except along the shore at low tide, but the spruce, pine, and birch forests have a varied wildlife population. On the hiking and nature trails, watch for black bear, moose, and deer. Some of the smaller streams have beaver dams. And if you run short of provisions during your stay, try your hand at clam digging. The Northumberland Strait is free of the poisonous red tides that occasionally plague the Bay of Fundy. If you prefer to have your dinner caught for you, try the lobster suppers at *Bon Accueil* (phone: 506-876-4310), a restaurant in the park. Open June through September, noon to 10 PM daily. Kouchibouguac National Park features an outdoor theater, self-guided trails through fragile habitats, and awareness programs on acid rain and other subjects. An award-winning audio-visual presentation is shown at the information center.

Kouchibouguac has 218 sites for tents and trailers, and 4 wilderness campgrounds for backpackers and canoeists (free). Canoes, boats, sailboards, and bicycles can be rented; sailboarding lessons are also available. At 93 square miles, this park is slightly larger than Fundy National Park, and because it is off the heavily traveled route to Nova Scotia, it's not as crowded. Open May to October. For more information, write to the Superintendent, Kouchibouguac National Park, Kouchibouguac, NB E0A 2A0, or phone 506-876-2443.

En Route from Kouchibouguac – The trip to Chatham via Route 117 through the seaside Acadian villages — Point Sapin; Escuminac, where there is a monument to lost fishermen; and Baie Ste.-Anne — home of former world champion boxer Yvon Durelle — is twice as long as the more direct Route 11, but more enjoyable. The coastal road has lighthouses, several good beaches, and, occasionally, home-cooked Acadian food; the 22-mile (35-km) drive on Route 11 passes through wilderness forest.

CHATHAM: This area provided timber for Joseph Cunard's shipbuilding industry in the early 19th century, before the invention of the steamship led to the demise of wooden ships in the late 1800s.

The Miramichi River, runs into the Miramichi Bay at Chatham. Jacques Cartier landed here in 1534, when Micmac Indians ruled the area. Micmac means "river of the long tideway."

According to legend, Chatham's Middle Island was lifted from the forest (forming a lake there) and dropped into the river. Sure enough, just a mile away is a lake the exact size and shape of Middle Island. In 1847, Irish immigrants fleeing the potato famine were quarantined on Middle Island after an outbreak of cholera on their ship. The island became first a hospital and then a burial ground for most of the ship's passengers and crew. It is now a park with a beach for swimming.

NEWCASTLE: Just up the river from Chatham on Route 8 is Newcastle, a wood pulp- and lumber-exporting center, with some lovely old homes that reflect its booming shipbuilding days under the Cunards. Max Aitken, who became Lord Beaverbrook, was a British newspaper magnate and New Brunswick's great benefactor. He was raised here in the Old Manse (225 Mary St.), the parsonage of his Presbyterian minister father. When Aitken was made a peer in 1917, he took his new name from the Beaver Brook stream north of Newcastle. He restored the Old Manse in 1950 as a library and donated it to the town, along with a copious collection of books. He also donated the Town Hall, theater, and town square, where his ashes rest.

En Route from Newcastle – Route 8 south goes to Doaktown, site of fabulous fishing (see En Route from Fredericton). Route 8 north intersects Route 11 at Ferry Road. Continue north on Route 11 on the shore of Miramichi Bay. Eight miles (13 km) east of Chatham at Bartibog Bridge, you can visit the MacDonald Farm Historical Park, a restoration of an early-19th-century farm. Costumed guides provide interpretive tours of the farm site and the sandstone farmhouse, built around 1820 by Alexander MacDonald. There also are self-guided nature trails on the property.

Burnt Church, 22 miles (35 km) north on a tiny side road off the main highway, is now an Indian reserve. It was the site of a French church burned in 1759 by British troops on their way to Quebec. Excellent sandy beaches are found all along the shore.

Continue north to Tracadie.

TRACADIE: Although the name sounds French, Tracadie is a Micmac Indian name meaning "a good place to camp." Many French settlers, divested of everything during the infamous Expulsion, moved back to this area in the 1780s. This corner of New Brunswick is almost entirely French-speaking, but communication is rarely a problem. Fish are plentiful. There are salmon in the Tracadie River and deep-sea fishing charters are available. Or if a charter is too ambitious, just go down to the beach and dig up some clams. If you come up empty-handed, try one of the local takeouts, which are often very good. A leper colony once existed here, and an odd museum recalls those days.

The small Val Comeau Provincial Park, 5 miles (8 km) south of Tracadie, has 55 campsites, a beach, and a picnic area.

From Tracadie, Route 11 wanders away from the coast to Pokemouche. Take Route 113 east to Shippegan.

SHIPPEGAN: The fishing industry in the northeast corner of New Brunswick employs many people, but there is another industry as well: Peat moss is harvested out of the earth and piled to dry in the sun to reduce its weight. The government is experimenting with a peat-burning electrical plant in the area. The Marine Centre, a tribute to the fishing industry, illustrates sea life in the Gulf of St. Lawrence and the Northumberland Straits. It features a replica of a lighthouse, a "touch tank" and displays of live fish and seals (506-336-4771). On Lamèque Island, accessible by bridge from Shippegan, the village of Lamèque hosts the *International Baroque Music Festival* in early July and the *Peat Moss Festival* in late July.

MISCOU ISLAND: From Little Shippegan, on the northern tip of Lamèque Island, take the toll-free ferry to Miscou Island, where you'll find endless white sand beaches and a fish restaurant. Deep-sea fishing boats can be chartered in the quest for giant bluefin tuna, averaging 800 pounds. *Miscou Island Camping* has 56 campsites and a few cabins (phone: 506-344-8638).

Returning to Route 11 at Pokemouche, drive north 10 miles (16 km) to Caraquet.

CARAQUET: On Chaleur Bay, this small fishing community is rich with Acadian tradition. Caraquet, which was settled in 1757, is home to one of the largest commercial fleets in New Brunswick. You can buy reasonably priced fresh seafood at the wharf. Small wooden fishing boats bob in the water as their owners sit on the wharf preparing lobster traps. Just east of Caraquet is a wooden shipbuilding company, one of the last of its kind.

In mid-August Caraquet hosts the *Acadian Festival,* with a traditional *Blessing of the Fleet* (to protect the fishermen) conducted by Catholic priests. Residents will tell you of a fiery ghost ship often seen in Chaleur Bay on stormy nights. Sightings of the ship with sails ablaze have also been reported across the bay in Quebec. The town's small *Acadian Museum* will introduce you to the Acadian way of life.

The dining rooms of the unpretentious *Paulin* hotel (143 Blvd. St. Pierre; phone: 506-727-9981) have some of the best scallops on the north coast (see *Best en Route*). By calling ahead, you can arrange to have an authentic Acadian meal, such as chicken *fricôt*, a thick, savory stew, or in season, a fresh-from-the-sea lobster feast.

ACADIAN VILLAGE: This 500-acre village was built in 1977 to commemorate the hardships endured by French settlers expelled by the British. Early Acadian homes, a working tavern, a school, and a blacksmith's ship were dismantled piece by piece from other parts of the province and reassembled here. Craftsmen demonstrate how to make cedar shingles, soap, and candles. All clothing worn by staff is produced on site.

Since there was little arable land in the Caraquet area, the tenacious French exiles created an ingenious alternative. They built a system of dikes to recover swampy marshland from the sea, a skill they brought from their homeland on the coast of Brittany. The site for the re-creation was chosen, in part, because it has a number of these 18th-century engineering marvels. Other features include a restaurant serving Acadian fare — such as *poutine rape,* grated potatoes wrapped around pork and then steamed or fried. The Acadian Village is open daily from 10 AM to 6 PM, early June to early September. Admission charge. In nearby Grand Anse, the unique *Pope's Museum* features portraits of all the popes, a replica of St. Peter, and nuns' and priests' habits. Open daily, 10 AM to 6 PM; admission charge.

BATHURST: Until the mid-1950s, Bathurst's economy was shackled to pulp and paper production. When zinc and copper deposits were discovered in 1953, Bathurst's faltering economy boomed. Because of this heavy industry, much of Bathurst is not particularly attractive, but there are several good beaches nearby on Nepisiguit Bay at Youghall, Caron Point, and Chaleur, and the city has lively discos and taverns. A free tour of the world's largest zinc mine can be arranged by calling 506-456-6671.

Five rivers tumble off the plateau into the Nepisiguit Bay.

Another of New Brunswick's top eating places is in Nigadoo, 9 miles (14 km) north on Route 134. *La Fine Grobe* is 1,000 feet off Route 134, by the Nigadao River Bridge, with a pretty view of the Nepisiguit Bay. The fine menu is mainly French with some Acadian dishes. The restaurant usually closes in September, and then the owners of *La Fine Grobe* begin their "real" work: Georges and Hilda Frachon are artists specializing in pottery, painting, and silk screening; fine examples of their work are on display in the restaurant. *La Fine Grobe* is relatively expensive because the table is yours for the evening. During the summer a more affordably priced luncheon menu is served on the terrace. Dining room hours: 6 PM to whenever. It is advisable to make reservations at least a day in advance (phone: 506-783-3138).

Route 11 goes to the Quebec border at Matapédia, 81 miles (130 km) to the west. Again, Route 134, following the coast, is more scenic. At Petit-Roc, northwest of Bathurst, the new *Mining and Mineral Museum* gives visitors "hands on" experience with geologic resources of the area (506-783-8714).

Continuing on Route 11 or 134, the Eel River bar is one of the longest natural sandbars in the world, with salt water on one side and fresh water on the other. A few miles away on Route 134 is Dalhousie, an attractive town known for processing wood products; its shoreline boasts interesting rock formations that attract rock hounds. The *Restigouche Regional Museum* (437 George St.; phone: 506-684-4685) depicts the area's pioneering days, as well as the development of fishing and farming. The *Chaleur Phantom* departs daily for tours of the beautiful Bay of Chaleur and there is a ferry from Dalhousie to Misquasha, Quebec. Chaleur Provincial Park and Inch Arran Municipal Park and are popular for swimming and camping.

Campbelltown, at the western end of the Bay of Chaleur, is an important outfitting and service center for sport fishermen. In the city's waterfront park, you can see a lighthouse and a 28-foot long model of an Atlantic salmon. The *Restigouche Gallery* (39 Andrew St.; phone: 506-753-5750) is a national exhibition center for regional artists. The last naval engagement of the Seven Years' War was fought offshore at Campbelltown in 1760. The city was founded 13 years later and named after Sir Archibald Campbell, the lieutenanat governor of the province.

Sugarloaf Provincial Park features camping, tennis, hiking, downhill skiing and Canada's only alpine slide. Visitors can ride up a chairlift and make the downhill run on sleds.

BEST EN ROUTE

Moncton has the best accommodations at the beginning of this route (see *The Fundy Coast* for a complete report on Moncton). You should note festivals and other special events before deciding whether reservations are necessary. For example, the *International Hydroplane Regatta* draws 40,000 spectators, but Cocagne is so tiny that residents take in guests during the festival. It's a good way to meet the Acadians. Contact the *Festival Committee,* Hôtel de Ville, Cocagne, NB E0A 1K0.

In French-speaking northeastern New Brunswick, most hotel and motel staff members are bilingual. They are good sources of information on restaurants, shops, and events. For two, expect to pay $53 for accommodations listed as expensive, $26 to $53 in the moderate category, and under $26 in the inexpensive range. All prices are quoted in US dollars.

BOUCTOUCHE

Bouctouche Bay Inn – The main building here is over 100 years old, and some of the 14 rooms are furnished with antiques. The dining room serves lobster and shrimp in season. Route 11 (phone: 506-743-2726). Inexpensive to moderate.

DOAKTOWN

Inn by the Pond – Five beautifully restored rooms with antiques in a gracious old home built in 1917. Bathrooms are shared. 2 Central St. (phone: 506-365-7942). Moderate.

CHATHAM

Morada – A pleasant motel that features 28 rooms, and serves breakfast in its dining room daily. 64 King St. (phone: 506-773-4491). Moderate to inexpensive.

NEWCASTLE

Wharf Inn – This modern inn has 70 units including 16 executive units, an indoor pool and saunas, and a dining room with live entertainment. 1 Jane St. (phone: 506-622-0302). Expensive to moderate.

Miramiche Manor – Hosted by a charming young couple, the Douchets, this bed and breakfast establishment is an experience in Victorian elegance. The 3 guestrooms are furnished with antiques and feature heavenly scented potpourri. Breakfast is served on antique china and glassware in a dining room with classical music playing in the background. PO Box 23, Main St. (phone: 506-622-8837). Moderate to inexpensive.

CARAQUET

Auberge de Baie – Highlighted with oak and brass trim, this 53-room motel is *the* most convenient to the beach in Caraquet. Additions include a new lobby, restaurant, lounge, and conference room. The moderately priced restaurant specializes in seafood. 139 Blvd. St. Pierre W. (phone: 506-727-3485). Expensive.

Paulin – Built in 1890, this hotel has been in the Paulin family for years. Most noteworthy are the dining rooms; one is quiet and cozy with fresh seafood, daily specials, and the other is a bright, cheerful breakfast room. The owner/chef will prepare special Acadian or lobster dishes for groups, with advance notice. Guestrooms are sparsely furnished, the doors and latches creak, and the bath is down the hall. But if you are hunting for a bargain, this is it. 143 St. Pierre Blvd. W. (phone: 506-727-9981). Inexpensive.

BATHURST

Atlantic Host – Here are 106 attractive, modern rooms, an indoor pool, sauna, Jacuzzi, racquetball courts, game room, restaurant, lounge, and crafts shop. Route 11 (phone: 506-548-3335). Expensive to moderate.

Fundy Line – Formerly a seminary, this hostelry features sandstone construction with beautiful woodwork and heavy beams. It offers 52 units and a splendid dining room with genuine down-home seafood dishes. 855 Ste.-Anne St. (phone: 506-548-8803). Moderate.

Newfoundland

When Newfoundland finally joined the Canadian Confederation in 1949, it ended a long, on-again, off-again flirtation with that larger political entity. Like many an island, Newfoundland prides itself on self-sufficiency and independence, and for decades that pride kept it at arm's length from the confederation of provinces. Many consider the fact that Newfoundland is in a separate time zone (half an hour ahead of mainland Canada) a symbol of her independent spirit. It was the tenth — and so far the last — region to become a province of Canada.

The province includes the island of Newfoundland, numerous smaller islands around it, and the huge mainland territory of Labrador. It is the most easterly of the Canadian provinces, with an area of 156,648 square miles, almost three-quarters of which is Labrador. The island is the political and population center of the province, and when people refer to Newfoundland (unless they add "province") they usually mean the island; Labrador is generally referred to simply as Labrador. Some 600,000 people live in the province, all but 30,000 or so on Newfoundland. What is most unique about this population is its homogeneity; 99% of Newfoundland's residents speak English, and something over 95% were born on the island. This says much about the singular cohesiveness of its culture and society, still British to the core.

Newfoundland is in the Atlantic just off the northeastern coast of Canada, separated from the northern tip of Nova Scotia by the Cabot Strait and from Labrador by the narrower Strait of Belle Isle. Legend has it that the Irish explorer St. Brendan sailed to Newfoundland in the 6th century. Maritime Artic settlements date back more than 3,000 years and the island's mysterious Beothuck tribe are thought to have been the first Red Indians of North America. From the beginning it has been a fishing island, living off the Grand Banks' rich schools of cod. The island, the tenth-largest in the world, was discovered in 1497 by the Venice-born explorer John Cabot, sailing under the British flag, who found an opening into a protected harbor that he promptly named St. John's. In 1583, the island was claimed by Sir Humphrey Gilbert for Britain, and then from 1933 to 1949, Newfoundland was governed by a British-appointed commission. The *Book of Lists* says that Newfoundland is one of two countries to volunteerily give up its independence in this century.

Today, the port city of St. John is the provincial capital, with 160,000 people. The Grand Banks have been one of the richest fishing grounds in the world and have supported the island for centuries as it was settled and colonized by Irish, Basques, and West Men — settlers from the west of England. Recent disoveries in the Grand Banks, however, have shown massive oil deposits, which some expect eventually will displace the fisheries as the main source of provincial income. This constellation of oil deposits has been much heralded as the economic salvation of the province, but Newfoundland has yet to see any tangible benefits from them. In 1855, the island was made a self-governing dominion of the British Commonwealth, but it reverted to colony status when it went bankrupt in the Great Depression. (The provincial government seriously considered selling Labrador during the Great Depression in an attempt to resolve its debts.) It remained aloof from Canada until the debate over joining the Confederation was finally settled in 1949, on *April Fool's Day*. (This was the official date, but Premier Joseph Smallwood moved it back to March 31 to avoid derision.)

The island is a series of mountains and forests dropping precipitously to the sea — a rugged, rocky landscape of hard splendor and icy power. Labrador is even more isolated. It is part of the oldest section of the Canadian Shield, that underpinning of ancient rock that surrounds immense Hudson Bay; it has huge spruce and fir forests, intercut with many lakes and streams, and incredibly good fishing and hunting, although much of it is accessible only by bush plane. The northern coast is home to several Indian and Inuit communities. Western Labrador, the deep interior, handles the bulk of Canada's iron ore mining. The climate here is what's called "temperate Maritime," meaning winters are usually mild, with the average temperature at 32F (0 degrees C); the average summer temperature is 68F (20C). However, extreme variations are possible. Labrador is much colder.

Our routes follow the natural configuration of the island, which is essentially a large central section with a prominent, nearly separate area on the east called the Avalon Peninsula. Though small in comparison to the rest of the island, Avalon nonetheless claims a disproportionate share of attractions for the traveler, including St. John's, headquarters for any excursions in eastern Newfoundland. The routes that follow are divided into a tour of Avalon's southern shore; a drive across the central part of the island and its west coast on the Trans-Canada Highway, the only road to cut clean across the island's width (this route includes a tour of the more navigable parts of Labrador); and a tour of northern Avalon. To reach Newfoundland by car, you have to go to North Sydney, Nova Scotia, where *Marine Atlantic* operates car ferries to the island. The 6-hour trip to Port aux Basques, on the southwest tip of Newfoundland runs year-round. The 18-hour trip to Argentia, near St. John's, is available only in summer. The speed limit on the highway is 55 mph (90 kph); in cities and towns it's 30 mph (55 kph). For information and reservations, call *Marine Atlantic,* in Maine, 800-432-7344; in the continental US, 800-341-7981; hearing impaired, call 800-794-8109 in the US and Canada. For further information, contact the *Newfoundland Department of Development and Tourism,* PO Box 2016, St. John's, Newfoundland A1C 5R8 (phone: 709-576-2830 or 800-563-6353).

Avalon's Southern Shore

This tour of the Avalon Peninsula follows the eastern and southern shore from St. John's to the ferry landing at Argentia. Two sanctuaries, at Bay Bulls and Cape St. Mary's, are among the most important seabird sanctuaries in the world. The tour starts on Route 10 south of St. John's and circles a large wilderness area. The trout fishing is excellent, and caribou thrive on the southern shore.

CAPE SPEAR NATIONAL HISTORIC PARK: This is the easternmost point of land in North America. Seven miles (11 km) south of St. John's on Route 11, it is bare, windswept, surf-washed, and wildly picturesque.

Cape Spear derives an unearthly atmosphere from its immense World War II gun emplacements in a state of semiruin. The barrels of two 10-inch guns, weighing 30 tons each, remain on-site. They were originally mounted on "disappearing" carriages and had a firing range of 8 miles. The park service has restored a 19th-century lighthouse, the oldest in Newfoundland, where two lightkeepers and their families lived year-round in dramatic isolation. The park also displays a reassembled skeleton of a humpback whale. The sea is spectacular here, but if high seas are running, heed the posted warnings and stay within the prescribed area; visitors who have ventured too close to the breakers have been washed off and drowned.

    En Route from Cape Spear – Petty Harbour, 10 miles (16 km) south of Cape Spear on Route 10 (access from Route 11), is a compact, busy fishing village and a favorite of photographers (and filmmakers such as Dino de Laurentiis who shot *Orca* here) for its quaint houses, which cling to steep hills.

    Continuing south on Route 10 (the Southern Shore Road, as Newfoundlanders call it), you first reach Bay Bulls. Cannons used for fighting off French raiders in the 18th century are now gateposts for a local church.

BAY BULLS: From here you can visit the great seabird sanctuary offshore. The three islands just offshore are world-famous among birders and ornithologists for their immense colonies of petrels, dovekies, guillemots, puffins, razor-billed auks, murres, terns, kittiwakes, and gulls.

A permit is required if you intend to land on the islands, but none is needed to visit them in a boat. *Bird Island Charters* offers a 2½-hour tour of the islands (phone: 709-334-2355). *Gatherall's Sanctuary Boat Charters* also operates out of Bay Bulls. The sanctuary offers a 5-room hospitality center with home-cooked meals (even homemade jam). Proprietor Rosemary Gatherall (phone: 709-334-2887) can arrange whale watching excursions, cod and squid jigging, and tours of the bird colony. There are thousands of nesting seabirds almost within arm's reach, and the air is filled with birds in flight. A visit to this great nesting colony is unforgettable and especially rewarding for the amateur photographer. The islands are at their best before mid-August, with colonies of puffins, murres, northern gannets, black guillemots, kittiwakes, and Leach's storm petrels. Later in the summer the bird population decreases rapidly, and by autumn the islands are almost deserted.

    En Route from Bay Bulls – Every cove along this section of Route 10 south to Cape Race figures in at least one story of high adventure, complete with pirates, wrecks, and buried treasure. Interestingly, the people of the area are of almost pure Irish descent. The eastern shore, once inhabited by outlaws known as "the masterless men," later became a favorite haunt of rum runners bringing tax-free booze from the French islands of St.-Pierre and Miquelon. Many ships, carried off course during transatlantic runs, have been wrecked along this shore, and many of their remains are visible still.

    En route to Ferryland, just past the community of La Manche, you'll pass *Great Island Tours* of Cape Broyle. They offer bird and whale watching, cod jigging, and moonlighting tours. They also provide shuttle service from St. John's (on the southern shore of Cape Broyle, Box 20; phone: 709-432-2355 or 800-563-2355, in Canada only).

FERRYLAND: This was once the English capital of Newfoundland, attacked repeatedly by both the French and the Dutch. Isle au Bois, which plugs the mouth of its harbor, still has the remains of forts and movable guns that rolled from the cliffs into a rocky gulch now washed by the sea. Relics of battles going back to the 17th century litter the area. The old courthouse overlooking Ferryland harbor houses a charming community museum with exhibits on shipwrecks and fishing.

The Ferryland Downs is perfect for leisurely hiking (bring a sweater), and there's always a chance you'll spot a minke whale as you picnic. The Downs provided artistic inspiration for nationally known Newfoundland painter Gerry Squires, who lived for a while in the lighthouse poised over the dramatic harbor entrance.

En Route from Ferryland – The southern shore, especially from Ferryland south, is one of the best trout fishing areas in Newfoundland. The most plentiful species is the eastern brook trout, but landlocked salmon and sea-run salmon also are found here, especially in the rivers running into Trepassey Bay, just west of Cape Race.

THE TREPASSEY BARRENS: The great sweep of barren land at the southern tip of the Avalon Peninsula is remarkably like the inhospitable lands of the Canadian Arctic. Until 1987, this wild area was thought to be the most southerly caribou habitat in the world, but since then, a herd of about 20 Avalon caribou have made their home in the high and remote ranges of the state of Maine, transplanted from these barrens in a dramatic cooperative effort by US and Canadian wildlife officials. From the high road crossing the Trepassey Barrens, you might see as many as 100 of these magnificent animals at once; the whole herd in this region numbers about 3,000. (Use caution when driving wherever caribou are plentiful.)

Trepassey itself was once a major cosmopolitan center, being one of the "golden triangle" ports for ships engaged in British/American Trade (Liverpool-Trepassey-Boston). Later it played a big role in the fledgling aviation industry. Amelia Earhart set her first record from Trepassey as the first female to cross the Atlantic in an airplane.

Another attraction is the great flocks of curlews that pause here briefly during migration. These storklike Arctic birds with sickle-shape beaks are often found by the hundreds beside the road.

En Route from Trepassey Barrens – You come to the sea at Holyrood Pond, an inlet of the ocean crossed by Route 10 on a causeway. Route 10 becomes Route 90 at St. Vincent's, leading back to the Trans-Canada Highway 30 miles (48 km) west of St. John's.

On St. Mary's Bay shore, Route 90 passes through a number of lovely fishing villages. The landscape along this drive heading north into the bay is lush and gentle — an unexpected respite from the raw power of the scenery that precedes it. Midway to the Trans-Canada is the Salmonier Nature Park, with its 1.2-mile woods walk, unique in Canada, along which you can see moose, caribou, beaver, otter, and other wildlife of Newfoundland and Labrador in spacious, natural enclosures. Butter Pot Provincial Park is just off the highway between the junction of Route 90 and St. John's. Besides excellent camping and swimming, this park offers fine hiking trails to the crest of Butter Pot Mountain, another barrens with a splendid view of Conception Bay.

This loop drive on southern Avalon has a counterpart to the west by way of Routes 91, 92, and 100. About half of this 120-mile (192-km) route is gravel road. Pavement extends from the Trans-Canada Highway to St. Bride's, approximately 9½ miles (15 km) from Cape St. Mary's. The access road to the seabird sanctuary from Route 100 is rough and requires careful driving.

The sanctuary is one of two outstanding attractions on the loop: Cataracts Park, on Route 91 west of Colinet, a series of waterfalls in a small rocky gorge with platforms and bridges for viewing; and the lovely sand beaches along the Placentia Bay Shore on Route 100.

BIRD ISLAND: The province's only major seabird sanctuary that is accessible by land. Because of a natural cleft that protects the birds from visitors, you can walk right to the edge of the colony from the parking lot and see such splendid birds as the goose-size gannets incubating eggs and raising chicks almost under your nose.

Few experiences can be more impressive than a visit to the colony during the nesting season in July. There also are kittiwakes, remarkable for their courage to live among the much larger gannets, and murres, duck-size black and white birds.

PLACENTIA: In the late 17th century, this was the base for the French fishery in Newfoundland. For 50 years the French built numerous fortifications around the harbor as they extended their hostilities with Britain (based in St. John's) to the new world. Fort Royal, the centerpiece of Castle Hill National Historic Park, was built in 1693 but ceded to the British 20 years later. Its ruins have been preserved, and an interpretation center provides some of the history of the area. At nearby Argentia, a plaque commemorates the Atlantic Charter, signed by Roosevelt and Churchill in 1941 aboard a British warship anchored in the bay. Now an important American naval base, Argentia recently was the focus of an international spy scandal. From Argentia, you can return to St. John's via Routes 100 and 1.

BEST EN ROUTE

Accommodations are not plentiful on the Avalon Peninsula's south shore, so you may have to settle for whatever you are near at the end of the day. Plan ahead by consulting the brochures *Newfoundland and Labrador Accommodations Guide* or *Newfoundland and Labrador Hospitality Homes,* both available from the *Department of Development and Tourism* (PO Box 2016, St. John's, Newfoundland A1C 5R8). For motels and guesthouses along this route listed as moderate, expect to pay $45 to $55; for inexpensive, $20 to $30. All prices are quoted in US dollars.

CALVERT

Sullivan's – Mrs. Sullivan runs this comfortable guesthouse and provides home-cooked meals. Near Ferryland, 1¼ mile (2 km) from Route 10 (phone: 709-432-2474/2372). Inexpensive.

TREPASSEY

Gorden's Tourist Home – Handy to superb salmon fishing rivers, the evening meal here often centers on fish or local wild game. An expanded "hospitality home," it now offers wheelchair access. Pets are allowed. Route 10 (phone: 709-438-2934). Inexpensive.

PLACENTIA

Harold – Located near 17th-century French fortifications, it has 23 quiet, clean rooms. Route 91 (phone: 709-227-2107 or 2108). Moderate.

Central Newfoundland

This 420-mile (672-km) drive cuts across the island almost to the isthmus of Avalon, then swings south to the Burin Peninsula. The Trans-Canada Highway, the only east-west road across Newfoundland, skirts Notre Dame Bay at Springdale, with access to scenic fishing villages.

Gander is a prime salmon fishing area just south of Notre Dame Bay. Outfitters take visitors to the interior by float plane, but reservations should be made in advance. The town, an important air base during World War II, has an aviation exhibit at the airport.

Terra Nova National Park, on Bonavista Bay, can be reached easily from St. John's if you ferry to Newfoundland's eastern port at Argentia. The 153-square-mile park has a variety of facilities including boat rentals for exploration of the shoreline. The Burin Peninsula, dotted with beautiful fishing villages, is the jumping-off point for St. Pierre and Miquelon, French territorial islands where a taste of France can be had at modest expense.

En Route from Deer Lake – Route 1 skirts the north shore of Grand Lake and Sandy Lake between two arms of the Long Range Mountains. Lobster House (1,916 ft.) and Mt. Sheffield (1,640 ft.) loom in the distance on the other side of the lakes. Route 410 leads to the Baie Verte Peninsula, 60 miles (96 km) east of Deer Lake.

NOTRE DAME BAY (WEST): This vast network of waterways and islands was created 7,000 years ago, when the last great ice sheet tilted Newfoundland to the northeast, causing deep depressions at the same time. Route 1 makes a wide bend past the bay, touching it at only two points — Halls Bay and Norris Arm. The rest of the bay is served by 800 miles of secondary roads.

On the western side of the bay, the Baie Verte Peninsula has been a major center for mining copper, silver, gold, lead, zinc, cadmium, and asbestos. Because of its unique geological formation, the whole peninsula is a rockhound's delight, with thousands of noncommercial outcroppings of collectible rocks. However, major mining companies have recently staked claims throughout the peninsula following the promising discovery of gold deposits.

A more scenic trip for the motorist is a beautiful drive around landlocked waters on Route 390 (13 miles/21 km farther east on Route 1) and Route 391, to such lovely villages as King's Point and Rattling Brook. If you head east on 390, past the area's commercial center, Springdale, you can pick up Route 392, which is mostly unpaved but will take you, in only a few miles, to the ferry to Little Bay Islands. Just 8 miles (13 km) further east on Route 1, Route 380 leads to Roberts Arm, Pilley's Island, Brighton, Cards Harbour, and the ferry to Lushes Bight. Lovely, wooded islands are linked by causeways which span calm channels of clear water filled with shellfish and other marine life.

En Route from Notre Dame Bay (West) – From the Route 380 intersection at South Brook, Route 1 swings inland 49 miles (78 km) to Grand Falls. Less than 2 miles (3 km) west of this paper-mill town, there is an entertaining logging museum at Beothuck Provincial Park; ask the park interpreter about "G'arge's Bullet Proof." At the *Mary March Museum and National Exhibition Centre* in Grand Falls, visitors learn the sad story of the museum's namesake and her now extinct race, the Beothuck Indians. From Grand Falls, Route 1 continues east 32 miles (51 km) to Notre Dame Junction, where you'll find Notre Dame Provincial Park. With 100 campsites and swimming, fishing, and boating facilities, it is an ideal stopover before heading north to Notre Dame Bay (east). Only 7 miles (11 km) from the junction along Route 340 is Lewisporte, home of the By the *Bay Museum* and its craft shop, run by the local Women's Institute. You can go "down" (north) to Labrador by taking the Lewisporte–Goose Bay ferry, the new

Northern Ranger, which makes a stop at Cartwright on the Labrador coast. The sojourn takes the better part of 2 days and is probably the closest one can get to the long coastal steamer trips that were once the only transportation to numerous isolated outports. Coastal trips can be booked only from within Newfoundland. For information contact *Marine Atlantic* at the numbers listed above.

NOTRE DAME BAY (EAST): The eastern end of Notre Dame Bay is a beautiful place to spend a few days. Several chains of islands large and small are easily accessible from Boyds Cove on Route 340.

Route 340 crosses Dildo Run, known to be confusing for boatmen who try to negotiate the maze of islands, to Chapel and New World islands. The most attractive settlements on New World Island are Herring Neck and Cobb's Arm. Dildo Run Provincial Park, on Route 340 just across the road from Virgin's Arm, has more than 30 picnic sites overlooking the bay.

TWILLINGATE: New World Island is connected by causeway to Twillingate, the fishing and well-known sealing capital of bygone days. A bell cast in 1862 commemorates the Great Haul of Swiles ("swiles" are seals in local parlance), when an iceberg carrying a large herd of harp seals came so close to shore that the townspeople walked across the ice pans and killed 30,000 of the animals. During summer, icebergs can often be seen floating in the bays and coves surrounding Twillingate. In fact, Newfoundland's northeast coast is one of the very few places in the world where the awesome natural phenomena of icebergs can be viewed from accessible and populated areas.

A burial ground of the Maritime Archaic People, nearly as old as the site at Port au Choix, was found in nearby Back Harbour. The community museum is in the Old Anglican Rectory (PO Box 124; phone: 709-884-2825). Its shop sells quality local crafts and souvenirs. Jasper, one of the gems mentioned in the Bible, is plentiful in gravel pits near Twillingate. Return to the Trans-Canada Highway at Gander via Routes 331 and 330.

GANDER: The first thing that strikes most visitors to Gander is that there seem to be too many shopping centers, parking lots, and hotels for a town of its size. Such surprise disappears, however, when they discover that it is a center of commerce for the whole northeast coast, an important international airport location serving numerous transatlantic flights, and that it is a popular outfitting station for anglers and hunters heading inland by floatplane. Gander's history is closely tied to the pioneer days of aviation. Because of its proximity to Europe, many early transatlantic flights originated here, and the Allied forces maintained an important airstrip in Gander during World War II. An aviation exhibit has mementos of early flights.

The Gander River, one of the island's most important salmon rivers, flows under Route 1 at Glenwood, 14 miles (23 km) west of the airport town. A beautiful river, passing through idyllic boreal wilderness, it is known for its deceptive shoals and rapids. Many canoeists owe their lives to the guides who work these waters. *Gander River Tours* (no phone) is one of many guide services that are equipped to provide safe and pleasurable excursions for anglers, sightseers, canoeists, or photographers. River tours of any duration are available, with package deals that include all the wilderness comforts you desire.

Campers can replenish supplies at stores in town, but, as in the rest of Newfoundland, the dining facilities are very limited. Two good restaurants are the *Albatross* motel (on Route 1), and *Sinbad's* (in town on Bennett Dr.). Avoid the airport cafeteria; the food is institutional in character and overpriced.

TERRA NOVA NATIONAL PARK: The older of Newfoundland's two national parks is 48 miles (77 km) east of Gander on Route 1. Terra Nova's specialty is its beach, tidal flats, and abundant wildlife. The provincial flower, the carnivorous pitcher plant, grows in inland peat bogs. Black bear and moose can frequently be seen from the road (be very alert for moose crossing the highway); and beaver, muskrat, red fox, lynx, and

Canada geese can be seen along the 50 miles (80 km) of nature trails. Maps of the walking trails are available at park headquarters. *Ocean Watch Tours* (phone: 709-533-2801 or 709-677-2327) offers wildlife and moonlight cruises.

Terra Nova hosts a variety of activities, including a 9-hole seaside golf course (slated for expansion) in a beautiful wilderness setting. Cabin, canoe, and bicycle rentals are available at park headquarters. Besides many primitive campsites, there are serviced campgrounds at Newman Sound and Malady Head with over 550 camping sites total, and there is free winter camping at Newman Sound with heated washrooms and an enclosed kitchen. There also are two outdoor theaters. From a boat launch at Salton's Brook on Newman Sound, visitors can explore miles of coastal inlets. Whales and seals cavort among the icebergs in Bonavista Bay in early summer. For more information, write to the *Superintendent, Terra Nova National Park,* Glovertown, Newfoundland A0G 2L0 (phone: 709-533-2801).

Before leaving this beautiful park, take a short drive on Route 310 to Salvage and Eastport. Salvage, a small fishing village, is situated on a harbor ringed by white houses among bare headlands and surf-washed islands. The *Lane House* has been converted into a fishermen's museum, where you can purchase locally made, traditional handicrafts. *Happy Adventure,* just south of Eastport, has a lobster pool from which you can buy live lobsters in July.

BONAVISTA PENINSULA: From Clarenville, 55 miles (88 km) south of the Terra Nova exit on Route 1, Route 230 leads to Bonavista, the site of a crucial 18th-century battle between the French and English. Michael Gill, a fishing master from Charlestown, Massachusetts, held off French raiders with only two armed ships and assistance from local fishermen. The lighthouse at nearby Cape Bonavista dates back to 1843 and is a provincial historic site. Port Union, one of the neighboring communities, is named for Newfoundland's first Fishermen's Union. There is an imposing monument to William Coaker, organizer of the union and founder of the town. Trinity, 20 miles (32 km) south of Port Union, is an old fishing and mercantile town, first visited by the Portuguese João Vas Corte Real in 1500. It is considered a showcase in Newfoundland for its success in preserving its historic character. The Ryan Premises (a provincial historic site), a blacksmith shop (privately owned but open to visitors upon request), and other buildings now look much as they did in the 19th century, when Trinity was the commercial center of Bonavista Bay. At Hiscock House, guides in costumes from 1910 interpret the life and times of a local merchant household of the area.

BURIN PENINSULA: Route 210 to the Burin Peninsula leaves the Trans-Canada Highway (Route 1) at Goobies, 100 miles (160 km) west of St. John's. Most of the road runs inland with short access roads to beautiful coastal villages.

Swift Current, 15 miles (24 km) from the turnoff, has beautiful sea beaches and a very fine river, Piper's Hole.

Pass up Route 211 to Terrenceville and English Harbour East; it has little to offer. Route 212, paved for most of its length, runs out to Bay l'Argent and Little Bay East, settlements of enduring beauty. Bay l'Argent has no silver, despite its name, but has long stretches of silvery rocks and water. Along this shore you may see inshore fishermen splitting and cleaning their catch as it comes out of the water.

Baine Harbour and Rushoon, on the opposite side of the peninsula, are beautiful villages with strong ties to the sea. Still farther south you come to the best of them all — Jean de Baie, Little Bay, and Beau Bois. Beau Bois is one of those places almost too good to be true: Photographs of it have appeared around the world.

MARYSTOWN: Most of Newfoundland's large fishing vessels are constructed in the Marystown Shipyard. Picturesque and placid Mortier Bay, together with neighboring Burin Bay and Burin Bay Arm, turn the area surrounding Marystown into an intimate mixture of land and sea. Burin is a collection of villages scattered among coves and inlets. No single piece of land anywhere in the area is big enough for a town. It is so rugged and hilly that villages only a few hundred yards apart are hidden from one another.

A shipbuilding center, the region also is home to great fleets of trawlers and some of the largest fish processing plants on the island. Millions of pounds of fish are produced annually by the towns that ring the bottom of the peninsula.

The country's quest over the past decade to secure oil and gas reserves has brought imposing symbols of a new industry to the area. Lovely Spanish Room Peninsula, across the bay from Marystown, is now the site of a maintenance and repair facility for the huge semi-submersible oil rigs that probe deep into the earth's mantle on Newfoundland's Grand Banks.

En Route from Marystown – Using Marystown as an anchor point, take Routes 210 and 220 to circle the "boot" of the peninsula, stopping at the other outports — St. Lawrence, Lamaline, and Fortune.

Much of the 99-mile (158-km) drive around the boot goes through barren, windswept countryside. The surf on the south shore at Allan's Island, High Beach, and Point au Gaul can be spectacular. The *Golden Sands* resort at Lewin's Cove (see *Best en Route*), near Salt Pond, has 18 cabins and 86 campsites with a fine swimming beach.

ST. PIERRE ISLAND: From Fortune, 34 miles (54 km) west of Marystown on Route 220, you can visit the French islands of St.-Pierre and Miquelon. Information on daily ferry service is available from the *Department of Development and Tourism* in St. John's or by calling the *Newfoundland/St, Pierre Ferry Service* (phone: 709-738-1357 or 709-832-0429). There are flights between St. John's and St.-Pierre three times weekly. Eight passengers can fly on the small plane (phone: 709-576-4100).

Since the islands are French territories, you must clear customs during your visit. But passports are unnecessary: All you will need is the identification used to cross the US-Canadian border.

St.-Pierre is one of the most European towns in North America: From its wrought-iron balconies to the tips of its Parisian sandals, it radiates the quiet charm of a slightly seedy French provincial town. Until recently, the islands were famous for their terrific duty-free eating and drinking bargains that made bootleg liquor St.-Pierre's major export. Since losing that special tax status, prices have gone up considerably, although most liquor is still less expensive than in Canada and French wines remain an attractive buy.

If you have more than a day to spend in St.-Pierre, stay in a pension and plan a short visit to the nearby islands of Miquelon and L'Anglade. You can charter a boat or take one of the tours arranged by the St.-Pierre Tourist Office (PO Box 4274, St.-Pierre; phone: 011-508-412222 or 011-508-412384). *SPM Tours* (phone: 709-722-3892) also offers packages that include daily boat services in the summer. At the northern tip of Miquelon is a small fishing settlement inhabited by pure Basques. Miquelon is joined by 10 miles of sand dunes to wild and picturesque L'Anglade Island. The toll in lives and ships the dunes have taken over the centuries is one of the saddest chapters in North Atlantic sailing history. By contrast, the lagoon at the northern end of the dunes is a haven for a large colony of seals.

Going through customs at St.-Pierre takes but a moment; upon your return, the delay may be as long as half an hour, especially if you arrive at Fortune with a full shipload. Visitors have to stand in line to declare their purchases and perhaps open their bags for inspection.

BEST EN ROUTE

On Notre Dame Bay, there are accommodations in many of the coastal fishing villages, and since the Trans-Canada Highway was constructed, these are becoming even more tourist-oriented. Public and private campgrounds are listed in the *Newfoundland and Labrador Accommodations Guide* or *Newfoundland and Labrador Hospitality Homes,* both obtainable from the *Department of Development and Tourism,* PO Box 2016, St. John's, Newfoundland A1C 5R8.

Grand Falls and Gander are outfitting centers for excursions to the interior. Outfitters in Newfoundland are listed in the *Hunting and Fishing Guide,* available from the address listed above. This brochure includes up-to-date hunting and fishing regulations.

Expect to pay $70 to $80 and up per night for a double room in the expensive range; $45 to $65 in the moderate; under $45 is inexpensive. All prices are quoted in US dollars.

SPRINGDALE

Pelley Inn – This modern, 23-room motel is 4 miles (6 km) off Route 390. It's a good access point for the ferries to Little Bay Islands and Lushes Bight. Cyril Pelley will arrange boat or land tours of the area. Little Bay Rd. (phone: 709-673-3831). Moderate.

GRAND FALLS

Mount Peyton – A contemporary motel with 150 immaculate rooms, it has a pretty good steakhouse. Route 1 (phone: 709-489-2251 or 800-563-4894). Expensive.

TWILLINGATE

Anchor Inn – Directly overlooking the harbor; the owner has added 8 housekeeping units to the original 14 rooms. Route 340 (phone: 709-884-2776). Moderate.

GANDER

Albatross – One of the best in central Newfoundland, this spot has 111 wheelchair-accessible rooms and is 187 miles (299 km) from Deer Lake, making it a good place to stop the first night of the tour. Facilities include a lounge, convention room, and babysitting services. There also is a restaurant with excellent service, which specializes in delicious local seafood. Pets are allowed. On Route 1 (phone: 709-256-3956 or 800-563-4894). Expensive.

TERRA NOVA NATIONAL PARK

Weston's Terra Nova National Park Chalets – If roughing it in the park's campgrounds is not for you, here are 24 self-contained cabins at a reasonable rate. Extra charges for more than two people. Grocery store and babysitting service are available. Route 1 (phone: 709-533-2296; off-season, 709-651-3434). Moderate.

TRINITY

Village Inn – The proprietors describe themselves as "publicans," the British term for innkeepers. It has only 8 rooms and serves very good meals. Whale watching excursions can be arranged. Route 239 (phone: 709-464-3269). Inexpensive.

LEWIN'S COVE

Golden Sands – This fine resort has 18 cabins and 86 semi-serviced and unserviced trailer sites, with excellent swimming nearby. Just off Route 222 (phone: 709-891-2400). Inexpensive.

ST.-PIERRE

Robert – Breakfast comes with a night's stay in this modern 56-room hostelry which offers Old World hospitality. Call ahead and someone will meet you at the boat. (Phone: Ask operator for St. Pierre 2419.) Expensive to moderate.

The West Coast

Contrary to popular belief, Newfoundland is not a wasteland enshrouded in fog (although approaching Port aux Basques on the gulf ferries will seem to confirm such preconceptions); this North Atlantic island has splendid wilderness areas, as this 444-mile (710-km) route along the western shore proves. It is an awesome combination of wild surf, rugged mountains, and quiet rivers teeming with salmon.

The tour starts at Port aux Basques, the ferry landing from North Sydney, Nova Scotia. Just up the road at Cape Ray, the surf pounds the shore in a relentless effort to reclaim the entire island. As you drive north along the Trans-Canada Highway, St. George's Bay and then the Gulf of St. Lawrence are on the left and, in striking contrast, the barren Long Range Mountains are on the right.

Roughly halfway between Port aux Basques and Corner Brook is the Port au Port Peninsula. Corner Brook is a popular outfitting center for excursions to the interior and connections to Labrador. The Humber River, which flows into the gulf at Corner Brook, is famous for salmon.

Also between Port aux Basques and Corner Brook is the Barachois Provincial Park, on Route 1, 30 miles (48 km) south of Corner Brook. It's one of the largest and most lovely of the provincial parks, with 158 sites, swimming, and hiking. It's also one of the few places in Newfoundland where chipmunks live.

The next stop is 697-square-mile Gros Morne National Park, with the most spectacular fjords in North America. The park's interior has peat bogs, pristine lakes and streams, and a variety of wildlife, including bald eagles and Arctic hare.

From Gros Morne, Route 430 hugs the shore of the Great Northern Peninsula. At Port au Choix, a 5,000-year-old burial ground of the Maritime Archaic People is on display, and at the northern tip of the peninsula is a Viking settlement thought to have been established around AD 1000.

All waterfront in Newfoundland is open to the public. You will appreciate this, especially on the northern coasts, where you may stop suddenly and head for the beach to better photograph a drifting iceberg. Although there are no private beaches, be sure to ask anyway should you appear to be encroaching on someone's privacy.

Dining facilities on this tour are mediocre, but seafood is the best bet. Be sure that "fresh" fish on the menu does not merely mean not salted, but also not frozen.

CAPE RAY: The ferry from Nova Scotia lands at Port aux Basques, named for the Basque fishermen who began making annual voyages to Newfoundland as early as 1500. The Basques were gradually supplanted by Norman and Breton French, who also fished the waters of Cabot Strait. Until the 19th century, this area was exclusively French-speaking. Today, Port aux Basques and neighboring Channel are important fishing centers.

When you disembark, drive west from Channel along the Cape Ray shore on Route 1. Exit at Cheeseman Provincial Park for a look at the spectacular surf. Waves move swiftly along the smooth, shallow ocean shelf in Cabot Strait and crash against the rocky shoreline.

A word of caution: The surf can be extremely dangerous. On several occasions, people have been swept into the sea by the impact of an unexpectedly high wave. The thrilling spectacle is best watched from a safe distance.

TABLE MOUNTAIN: From Route 1, the hale and hearty can climb 1,700 feet above the ocean to the plateau of Table Mountain, just a few miles north of Cheeseman Provincial Park. Even in midsummer you may find snow fields in its crevasses. Caribou graze on the plateau. On rare occasions the gyrfalcon can be spotted — the only place south of Labrador the great Arctic bird of prey is known to hunt. Hiking boots are recommended for the arduous climb, as are a sweater and lightly packed rain gear, for weather on the plateau is very changeable.

Table Mountain is the first of the Long Range Mountains, once part of the Appalachian chain on the eastern seaboard of North America. Successive ice ages have worn down the Long Range Mountains to less than 3,000 feet.

GRAND CODROY RIVER: The region between Cape Ray and Corner Brook — a 136-mile (218-km) stretch of wooded hill and valley — is the best area in Newfoundland to find moose, caribou, and Atlantic salmon.

The Grand Codroy River, with its two tributaries — the North Branch and South Branch — is 25 miles (40 km) from Port aux Basques on Route 1. Approximately 1,000 salmon are taken annually from the river and its 30 miles of accessible pools.

Seasons vary from river to river, but the best salmon fishing on most rivers is from late June through July. There is no limit on the number of licenses issued, and arrangements with outfitters should be made well in advance. Fishing lodges and cabins have surprisingly modest rates — often lower than those of motels — but few outfitters accept credit cards. There are extra charges for guides. All rivers in the province are subject to closure to anglers on short notice, depending on water depths and temperatures that can affect salmon migration. In recent years, there have been limits on the maximum as well as minimum size of salmon that fishermen are allowed to keep (12 in. to 24.8 in.). It is hoped that when they spawn, the larger salmon's greater egg volume will help maintain one of the healthiest stocks in the world. The rivers of Labrador, being more remote, have no upward limit on the size of fish that may be kept. For current conservation regulations, write Department of Fisheries and Oceans, Newfoundland Region (PO Box 5667, St. John's, Newfoundland A1C 5X1, or call 709-772-4421 and ask for that season's *Angler's Guide*). For more information, see *Where They Bite: Fishing in Canada,* DIVERSIONS.

The western coast also is one of Canada's prime moose, black bear, and caribou hunting areas. Hunters with local guides are virtually guaranteed success because big-game populations in Newfoundland have been well managed by the government.

The Newfoundland caribou is the largest of its species in the world. Hunters from the island claim all the world record heads (measured in spread and number of points to the antlers). The season opens in mid-September for both moose and caribou. Licenses must be obtained well in advance from outfitters listed in the brochure *Newfoundland and Labrador Hunting and Fishing Guide,* issued by the Newfoundland Department of Development and Tourism.

PORT AU PORT PENINSULA: With its sea-battered cliffs along its southern shore (Route 460 via Route 490 from Route 1), and sandy beaches in the north (Route 463), Port au Port Peninsula is one of the island's best kept secrets. It is home to descendents of Channel Island French fishermen who jumped ship during the 18th and 19th centuries to take up a free life, away from the hardships of conscripted seamen. They inherited a place of beautiful seaward vistas, particularly that from Piccadilly Head, the site of a provincial park which is known for its lack of flies (a point worth noting) and sandy saltwater beach. To the west, an ancient raised reef projects 14 miles northward. At its tip, Long Point is a resting spot for numerous bird species during their spring migration. To the east, the Lewis Hills rise near vertically to 2,674 feet, the highest point on the island of Newfoundland and home to bald eagles and osprey.

CORNER BROOK: This city of 30,000 is set on an arm of the sea among mountains. It was transformed from a small coastal village to a busy industrial center in the 1920s, when a pulp and paper mill was built. A Fine Arts College also is here.

Near Corner Brook are scenic drives on both shores of the Bay of Islands. Route 450 follows the south shore 40 miles (64 km) to the public beach at Bottle Cove and Blow Me Down Provincial Park, with 27 campsites and a hiking trail into the Blomidon Mountains. A lookout tower offers a magnificent view of the bay. Route 440 tours the north shore of the bay to Cox's Cove. Each summer, Corner Brook also hosts the *Hangashore,* the island's most popular folk festival.

On both shore routes you may visit fishing villages and see fishermen at work. For a small fee, you usually can rent a boat to go angling for codfish. Cod in the Bay of Islands average between 5 and 20 pounds.

The Humber River, which empties into the Bay of Islands at Corner Brook, is another famous salmon river. Catches as large as 20 and 30 pounds have been landed in the pools of the Lower Humber. Besides salmon rivers and hunting areas accessible by car, Corner Brook is an outfitting center for excursions to the interior lodges that can only be reached by small plane.

The *Glynmill Inn* (Cobb's La., off Route 1, see *Best en Route*) is a beautiful old hotel in the European style. Its dining room features seafood in season.

MARBLE MOUNTAIN SKI RESORT: Newfoundland's only major ski area with modern tows and lifts is 5 miles (8 km) east of Corner Brook. Marble Mountain has consistently good snow surfaces from January to early April on a range of slopes from easy to difficult. Cabins are available at Steady Brook but are not a good buy, considering the superior accommodations available at lower rates in nearby Corner Brook. A new, but fast-growing resort, the *White Hill* (off the Trans-Canada Highway, PO Box 1118; phone: 709-466-7773) has opened in Clarenville.

En Route from Marble Mountain – At Deer Lake, 30 miles (48 km) east of Corner Brook, you leave Route 1 for the 275-mile (440-km) drive to St. Anthony and L'Anse-aux-Meadows. This coastal road — now entirely paved — offers some of the most scenic driving in the province. Except for the first 20 miles (32 km), Route 430 hugs the shore all the way to the northern tip of Newfoundland. As you drive north, the Gulf of St. Lawrence is on your left and the Long Range Mountains, on your right. Every so often awesome fjords cut into the mountains.

GROS MORNE NATIONAL PARK: The results of 400 million years of continental drifting and of the successive ice ages that ended 12,000 years ago are dramatically evident in this 697-square-mile park on Route 430. The most spectacular park in eastern Canada, its hiking trails pass through the habitats of Arctic animal and plant species rarely found this far south.

The 2,644-foot slopes of Gros Morne end in a 2,000-foot plateau whose cliffs drop to deep fjords on the Gulf of St. Lawrence. (Gros Morne is French for "big knoll," with connotations of dismal and bleak.) A rugged 2½-mile climb to the top of Gros Morne on the James Callaghan hiking trail is rewarded by a magnificent view of the sea and windswept tundra. Be prepared for climatic changes during the ascent, even in summer.

At the Wiltondale entrance to the park, an alternate road, Route 431, skirts the south shore of beautiful Bonne Bay. The road then skirts a massive flat-topped and desolate mountain of orange rock, named the Tablelands, which resembles a Martian landscape on its descent through ancient uplifted beaches to the existing Trout River shoreline.

Returning from Trout River, proceed to Woody Point, perhaps the most picturesque village on the west coast. Do not return to Wiltondale without first checking the status of the Woody Point–Norris Point ferry. The exquisite 15-minute ride used to be an alternate link to Route 430 on the far side of Bonne Bay. It was curtailed in 1985 when its provincial government subsidy was withdrawn. If it is running, the trip is an unequalled opportunity for photographers and whale watchers. If it is not in service, never mind; the stretch on Route 430 from Wiltondale north to Rocky Harbour, through the fjord of East Arm, is no less spectacular. Continue north along the shore to St. Paul's Inlet, a rock-girt fjord with cliffs rising more than 2,000 feet from the water. En route, you will see a parking lot marking the hiking trail into Western Brook Pond. By all means take it. Round-trip, it's a 5-mile hike on a boardwalk through beautiful woods and open marshy fields. When winds from the upland plateau are not too severe, a tour boat plies the 9 miles to the end of the land-locked fjord. On the way, waterfalls pour over the lip of the plateau 2,000 feet above and turn into a fine mist before reaching the pond. Boat trips should be arranged in advance; inquire at the park information center. The dining room of the *Ocean View* motel (phone: 709-458-2730) in Rocky Harbour has good food. Be sure to ask if fresh salmon and lobster are available.

Swimming in the Gulf of St. Lawrence is for the hardy only: water temperatures at the Shallow Bay and Western Brook beaches rarely exceed 59F (15C). However, the beaches are their own attraction. Their dunes engulf the coastal forests to the treetops and threaten the delicate marshland ecology inland. Berry Hill has 150 semi-serviced campsites, and there are other unserviced campgrounds in the park. On the hiking trails, you should look for black bear, moose, otter, beaver, caribou, bald eagle, osprey, rock ptarmigan, and Arctic hare.

En Route from Gros Morne – On the remainder of Route 430, you are rarely more than a stone's throw from the sea. Remember: All beaches are public and have public access. There is no such thing as a private seafront in Newfoundland; feel free to stop wherever to swim, picnic, or beachcomb.

The beaches on the western shore of the Great Northern Peninsula hold a special fascination for beachcombers, because prevailing winds and currents wash ashore natural flotsam (starfish, shells, and false corals) and manmade artifacts (nets, net floats, and deck gear from ships).

Genuine traditional handicrafts can be purchased on this section of Route 430: individually designed Newfoundland hooked mats as well as "workshop" handicrafts produced under the supervision of the International Grenfell Association. The *Straits Development Association* sells local knitting, sealskin goods, and embroidered duffel parkas at Flowers Cove, 90 miles (144 km) north of Daniels Harbour.

RIVER OF PONDS: This salmon fishing region is 50 miles (80 km) north of Gros Morne. The salmon run a bit later here than those farther south: The best fishing is between July 10 and August 10. Sea trout up to 30 pounds enter the river in early August. Sadie House rents inexpensive river cabins (*House's Cabins,* River of Ponds, Newfoundland A0K 4M0; phone: 709-225-3301); reserve in advance.

The 150-acre River of Ponds Provincial Park has 40 campsites on a long sand beach with facilities for boating.

PORT AU CHOIX: The Maritime Archaic Indians flourished here from 4,300 to 3,200 BC, contemporary with the Pyramid Age in Egypt. The Dorset Eskimos, whose stone tools are among the most delicate and beautiful ever made, lived here for 2,000 years until they were supplanted by the Beothuck Indians in about AD 1100.

Three Maritime Archaic cemeteries were excavated in 1962. Along with the remains of 100 individuals, weapons and other artifacts were found. Relics are on display in the visitors' center, open from June to *Labor Day.*

As you drive north past St. John Bay, the Long Range Mountains melt into the coastal flatlands of the northern peninsula.

LABRADOR COAST: St.-Barbe Bay, 60 miles (96 km) north of Port au Choix, has ferry service to Labrador. The 22-mile run is made twice daily during the summer; reservations are not necessary. If you take the first ferry in the morning, it's possible to explore the 50 miles (80 km) of Labrador coastline with some wide, white-sand beaches, which can be reached by road, and return the same evening.

There are accommodations at L'Anse-au-Clair and L'Anse-au-Loup and a provincial park at Pinware River, if you choose to stay overnight in Labrador. Fishing and hunting excursions to the interior of Labrador are arranged by outfitters on the coast.

From St.-Barbe Bay, Route 430 continues along the shore for another 21 miles (34 km) and then crosses the tip of the Great Northern Peninsula. Take Route 436 north after you pass Pistolet Bay for 10 miles (16 km) to L'Anse-aux-Meadows National Historic Park.

L'ANSE AUX MEADOWS: In 1978, this park was declared the first UNESCO World Heritage Site. The distinction derives from the 1960 discovery of a tiny Norse settlement established on this site around AD 1000, the only confirmed Norse settlement in North America and possibly the one founded by the Icelandic trader Thorfinn Karlsefni. If so, then this is the birthplace of North America's first European child, Snorri Thorfinnson, mentioned in the Viking sagas.

Three sod-roof buildings, of the original six, have been reconstructed, and other artifacts are on display in the visitor center. Open June 1st through September.

En Route from L'Anse aux Meadows – The northern tip of Newfoundland is known for its icebergs. Every summer, numerous icebergs, towering up to 300 feet above the water, float south along Labrador from their birthplace on the west coast of Greenland. Many ground in shallow water for weeks until dislodged by a storm.

This area is close to the ice floes where harp seals deliver their young each spring and an annual seal hunt follows. Beginning in the mid-1950s, several groups have tried to halt the yearly kill of seal pups and have won wide support. Since then, stiff rules have been imposed to ensure that the seals are killed humanely, and quotas have successfully reversed the decline of the herd, which now stands at 1.4 million. In some recent years, the hunt has been suspended because of poor markets in Europe, where the protest is centered. Newfoundlanders regard the hunt as economically essential and resent the protest. Seals also consume huge quantities of fish, the main industry of Newfoundland. To the people here, life is a matter of wresting a precarious living from the resources of the sea and land around them.

ST. ANTHONY: Only a short drive south of L'Anse-aux-Meadows, St. Anthony is the headquarters of the famous Grenfell Mission, established in the late 1800s. Dr. Wilfred Grenfell tried, with partial success, to improve the poor living conditions of Newfoundland and Labrador fishermen. Although he built hospitals and missions, his vision and fanaticism, compassion and dictatorial ways, made him both loved and hated on the Labrador coast.

Upon his retirement, Dr. Grenfell founded the International Grenfell Association, which today is involved in community work.

The Grenfell workshop and store at St. Anthony sell a wide range of handcrafted products from postcards to parkas. The parkas, made of strong "Grenfell cloth" and embroidered by hand, are an exceptional buy. Grenfell also promoted Labradorite jewelry, which can be purchased at many Newfoundland craft outlets. Labradorite (also called firestone) is a beautiful opalescent stone with green, bronze, and blue highlights (a similar stone is mined in Madagascar). Some inferior stone is polished; you should examine many pieces to find a really good one.

Dr. Grenfell and his successor Dr. Curtis are buried on a hill above St. Anthony. The shrine, overlooking Hare Bay, can be reached by a trail through the woods.

BEST EN ROUTE

For many years the scarcity of paved roads in western Newfoundland depressed tourism. The construction of the Trans-Canada Highway spurred the development of some accommodations, but there is still a dearth of high-quality hotels and motels. Expect to pay $60 to $75 and up per night for a double room in the expensive range; $45 to $55 in the moderate category; $25 to $40 in the inexpensive range. All prices are quoted in US dollars.

PORT AUX BASQUES

Port aux Basques – A fairly modern place with 50 rooms, all with TV sets and radios, a lounge, and a restaurant specializing in regional seafood. Pets are allowed. Grand Bay Rd. and Trans-Canada Highway (phone: 709-695-2171). Expensive.

CORNER BROOK

Glynmill Inn – Overlooking a pond and its resident swans in a quiet section of town, this inn provides 92 rooms in a Tudor-style building dating back to 1924. Among the facilities are a lounge, a restaurant specializing in seafood, and a romantic wine cellar serving steaks with an extensive wine list. 1 Cobb La. (phone: 709-634-5181 or 800-563-4894). Expensive.

GROS MORNE NATIONAL PARK

Parsons Hospitality Home and Harbour View Cabins – Florence Parsons rents 2 rooms in her home, 3 housekeeping cabins, and 3 motel units. Her cooking and friendliness are renowned. Pets on leashes are allowed. Just off Route 430 in Rocky Harbour (phone: 709-458-2544). Inexpensive.

ST. ANTHONY

Viking – On Pistolet Bay, 5½ miles (9 km) from the airport and 14 miles (22 km) from town, this motel provides 11 standard rooms, a restaurant, bar, and dancing on Saturday nights. At the intersection of Routes 430 and 437 (phone: 709-454-3541). Moderate.

Northern Avalon

This short tour of the Avalon Peninsula can be covered in a day or two. Beginning at St. John's, the provincial capital and one of the oldest cities in North America, the drive follows Avalon's northern shore through picturesque fishing settlements.

St. John's was the reception point for the first transatlantic wireless signal in 1901. Its annual regatta in August is the most popular event of the year. St. John's also is the cultural center of Newfoundland, with several art galleries, museums, and outdoor concerts.

Routes 20 and 30 follow the shore to Flat Rock and Pouch Cove, whose surf is equal in violence to that of Cape Ray, in Newfoundland's southwestern corner. Farther west, via the Trans-Canada Highway and Route 70, Harbour Grace is the only place in the world with a monument to a pirate.

ST. JOHN'S: This city is a gem. Its small harbor, surrounded by high, protective hills, is one of the best in the world. A slim channel, called the Narrows, gives access to the sea and it's a rare moment that there isn't a ship or a fishing boat gliding in or out of the harbor's mouth. Fishermen have been coming to St. John's since the late 15th century, but today their vessels are joined by an incredibly diverse fleet that seeks refuge or engages in commerce in the harbor. On any given day, visitors may walk along the waterfront (more like an esplanade than a harbor service area) and examine a variety of fishing boats from half a dozen countries. These are docked among oceanographic research ships, sleek and imposing navy vessels, giant US and Soviet satellite tracking craft, cruise ships, oil drilling ships, offshore supply ships, and the boats of transatlantic adventurers (which seem to get tinier and tinier with each record-breaking crossing). Through much of its history the town was ruled by ruthless fishing admirals. Savage fires in the 19th century wiped out the town several times, so the oldest buildings in the city date back only to the Victorian period. Square, flat-topped, wooden houses, painted in a variety of colors, cling to each other as they staircase up the hills leading away from the harbor. The fine, old architecture that remains generally is Gothic Revival, Second Empire, and Queen Anne–style. Of special note is Rothwell House on Circular Road. Two eccentric sisters occupied this house and neither wanted her side of the building to remotely resemble the other; each is designed in a totally different period (phone: 709-576-8109).

Signal Hill National Historic Park is a good place to begin a tour of St. John's because it offers a splendid panorama of the city to the west and has many walking trails. Best known as the site of the first transatlantic reception of a wireless signal, sent by Marchese Guglielmo Marconi on December 12, 1901, Signal Hill actually got its name centuries earlier when company flags were raised to alert merchants, dockworkers, and customs officials of ships approaching the harbor. Time is still marked by a cannon fired at midday on the hill. From mid-July to the end of August, visitors can see — and hear — a military tattoo on Signal Hill which commemorates the last battle between the French and the English in Canada. The event takes place 4 days a week at 3 and 7 PM, weather permitting. Call the *Newfoundland Tourism Office* (phone: 800-563-6353), for specifics.

Horticulturists must visit the *Memorial University Botanical Gardens* (just off Mount Scio Road, which circles the city; phone: 709-737-8590) where rock gardens, heritage plants, and cottage gardens are among the displays. There also are a variety of walking trails.

Nearby Quidi Vidi Village, reached by car 2 miles (3 km) north of Signal Hill, has a restored fort and a small cottage built around 1740. The cottage, possibly the oldest in English Canada, was used as a dressing station for the English forces at the Battle of Quidi Vidi. The town has a pocket-size harbor enclosed by hills and is a good place to buy fresh fish and lobster in season.

A regatta is held every year during the first week of August at Quidi Vidi Lake. *Regatta Day* has been held every year since 1828, making it the longest running annual sports event in North America. It is a gala event with sideshows, gambling, games, food, drink, and other entertainment that attracts as many as 50,000 people. The course record on Quidi Vidi Lake, set in 1901 by a crew of fishermen from Outer Cove, stood for 80 years.

Prince Phillip Drive, the eastern extension of Route 1 through St. John's, leads to Confederation Hill and the Confederation Building, the seat of the provincial government. Half a mile west of the Confederation Building are the *Arts and Culture Centre,* which contains the province's largest public art gallery, and the campus of Memorial University. While the foyers, halls, and grounds of the Confederation Building display the finest examples of works by Newfoundland's traditional and experimental artists as part of its permanent collection, the art gallery of the neighboring facility hosts new works as well as visiting exhibitions.

The *Newfoundland Museum* (directly across Duckworth Street from the Anglican cathedral) has both prehistoric and colonial exhibits. In its annex at the *Murray Premises* (a building on the waterfront which includes gift shops and a liquor store), the museum covers the marine, military, and natural history of the province.

Duckworth Street hosts two commercial art galleries — *The Gallery* and *Pollyanna Gallery* — and, like the *Murray Premises* (Water St.) is known for its luxury shops and cafés. In the shops and boutiques on Duckworth and Water Streets, you can buy everything from specially designed stained glass bird cages, to warm mittens, hologram watches, and books of poetry by Newfoundland authors. (Keep in mind there is no provincial sales tax on locally made crafts; also, tourists who purchase Newfoundland artwork are exempt from the tax.) Across from the *Pollyanna Gallery* is the War Memorial, on the site where Sir Humphrey Gilbert took possession of the colony in the name of Queen Elizabeth I on August 5, 1583. This is the central area for craft shops: *Cod Jigger* (252 Duckworth); *The Salt Box* (194 Duckworth) and *Livyers* (also at 194 Duckworth), just downstairs from *The Salt Box,* is filled with beautiful and unusual antiques. *Duckworth Lunch* (191 Duckworth) serves fresh bagels, healthy soup, and the best chocolate chip cookies in town. For more information on local crafts, call the *Newfoundland and Labrador Crafts Development Association* (phone: 709-753-2749).

The dining room at the *Battery Inn,* which looks over the harbor, has the best view in the city. The *Stone House* restaurant is a restored early-19th-century cottage (8 Kenna's Hill near Quidi Vidi Lake). Fresh fish and produce are turned into such wonders as iced crab and ginger soup and cod tongues with chive and cream sauce. It probably has the best wine list in St. John's. For quality dining on a restricted budget, the *Continental Café* (George St.) offers an international menu, with something for vegetarians, in a casual but intimate atmosphere. The pan-fried cod is choice; for breakfast, the freshly baked muffins are the best in town. A favorite local spot is the *Woodstock Colonial Inn* (7 miles/11 km out of town on Route 60). The cooking is superb, the atmosphere pleasing, and you can get such rarities as game dishes and seal flipper pie. The prices are reasonable, the portions generous. The *Kenmount* (75 Kenmount Rd.; phone: 709-753-8385) is a good Chinese restaurant, and for Mexican fare, try *Casa Grande* (on the east end of Duckworth Street), a small, charming restaurant near the *Newfoundland* hotel, or *Zapata's* (10 Bates Hill). The *Cavendish Café* (across from the *Newfoundland* hotel) is a cafeteria-style restaurant with a wonderful view of the harbor. *Alan's Donair* (27 Cookstown Rd.) is known for its generous, inexpensive servings. Next door is *Bridgett's Pub,* which regularly features the best in local music, including jazz, folk, rhythm and blues, and rock.

Until recently, George Street, in the heart of downtown, was a service lane for businesses fronting on major commercial streets on either side. However, the City Fathers decided it should be developed as a major downtown attraction. Now, it is the social hub of the city, with a diverse selection of pubs, nightclubs, restaurants, and the *Emma Butler Gallery,* at 111 George St.

Several major construction projects are reshaping the downtown skyline. Chief among recent new buildings is the *Radisson Plaza* hotel and convention center, a 276-room hotel operated by Commonwealth Holiday Inns of Canada, with a convention facility that can accommodate 2,000 people. See *Best en Route.*

The grand old Longshoreman's Protective Union Hall, at the foot of Victoria St., is now home to Newfoundland's flourishing indigenous theater. This lively downtown cultural center is known simply as "The Hall," and is the theatrical home of the comedy troup *CODCO.* During the summer it stages free, outdoor concerts.

The *Arts and Culture Centre,* a modern structure (that some call beautiful and others call hideous) has a truly exceptional theater and hosts a summer festival of the arts that includes both professional and amateur theater, concerts, and crafts shows. There are free outdoor concerts by musical groups playing traditional Newfoundland music. The center also has an art gallery and three libraries. In even-numbered years, St. John's features The *Sound Symposium*, an international exhibit of sound, art, and concerts. Some events are free, including a daily harbor symphony.

Hilly downtown St. John's is a crowded city in the style of Queen Victoria, full of fanciful buildings clustered around the harbor guarded by Signal Hill. You need no directions to reach Duckworth and Water Streets, the heart of downtown: Head downhill till you get there.

A new site is *Apothecary Hall*, a restored drugstore on the west end of Water Street. Even if you're not a pharmacist, you'll appreciate the Art Deco and Art Nouveau styles.

Apart from Signal Hill and the *Arts and Culture Centre*, downtown St. John's is where everything is located — good restaurants, craft shops, the principal museum, the magnificent old churches, and the best specialty food store in the Atlantic provinces.

Mary Jane's (377 Duckworth St.) is a 2-story establishment purveying anything from dried Chinese lily flowers to vine leaves pickled in Lebanon, brown rice, soy beans, fresh-baked cookies, and every herb and spice known sold in bulk.

St. John's has two major churches, both with splendid interiors — the Roman Catholic basilica (no one can miss its twin towers, built deliberately on the most conspicuous spot in the city) and the Anglican cathedral (straight downhill from the basilica). The cathedral is one of the finest examples of pure Gothic architecture in North America.

En Route from St. John's – The Marine Drive, one of Newfoundland's oldest roads, following the cliffs of the Atlantic shore past Logy Bay, starts from St. John's on Route 30 and joins Route 20 at Torbay. Middle Cove, 8 miles (13 km) from St. John's, has a public beach.

FLAT ROCK: The surf at Flat Rock is so violent at times that it damages houses on the far side of the highway. A huge flat stone, acres in area, forms a natural rock pier and beach. Mass is celebrated in summer at an outdoor shrine built into the rocks of a cliff beside the village church. Pope John Paul II said Mass here during his visit to Canada.

POUCH COVE: The surf at Pouch Cove also displays impressive violence. In this important fishing community, boats have to be winched out of the water on skids because there is no safe place to anchor them.

The lighthouse at Cape St. Francis can be reached only by a narrow, one-lane dirt road from Pouch Cove. It is a wild and picturesque spot.

The road between Pouch Cove and Portugal Cove on the west shore of the peninsula is very poor. You might return to St. John's and drive to Portugal Cove on Route 40.

PORTUGAL COVE: One of the oldest fishing settlements in Newfoundland, Portugal Cove is 16 miles (26 km) south of Pouch Cove. Trap boats and oceangoing fishing boats unload their catches on the wharf, where you may buy fresh salmon and cod.

A ferry connects Portugal Cove to Bell Island, an immense, cliff-ringed rock rising out of the bay, once the site of Canada's most productive iron mine. Though the supply of iron ore has been exhausted, thousands of people still live on the barren island.

En Route from Portugal Cove – Route 41 continues south through scenic Beachy Cove to St. Phillips, a small boat harbor, and Topsail, a town with a stony beach that is a popular Sunday drive destination for area families. At this point, you can return to St. John's within 20 minutes via Route 60, or continue south on Route 61 to the western shore of Conception Bay. The first stop on the west shore is Brigus, almost directly across the bay and 37 miles (59 km) from Topsail.

BRIGUS: If you look, you may find a plaque commemorating Captain Bob Bartlett (1875–1946), Newfoundland's greatest explorer, who made 30 Arctic expeditions, including three attempts to reach the North Pole with Robert Peary. Mementos of the expeditions are preserved in Bartlett's house, Hawthorne Cottage, which Parks Canada has declared a National Historic Site.

PORT-DE-GRAVE PENINSULA: A short drive beyond Brigus via Routes 70 and 72, the Port-de-Grave Peninsula has several small fishing villages worth visiting. At Hibbs Cove, on the eastern tip of the peninsula, the *Fisherman's Museum* is filled with artifacts of the colonial fishing industry.

HARBOUR GRACE: This crusty fishing and mercantile town is 10 miles (16 km) north of the Port de Grave Peninsula on Route 70. Harbour Grace is probably the only town in Canada with a monument to a pirate, Captain Peter Easton, who established his headquarters here in 1610 and built a private navy by enlisting hundreds of Newfoundlanders. In 1611, his navy of pirate ships defeated a French squadron in the harbor. After amassing vast wealth by preying on international shipping, Easton retired as a marquis in Savoy, France, with a fortune estimated at more than $50 million. Four miles north of Harbour Grace is Carbonear, said to be the home and burial palce of Sheila Na Geira. This Irish princess was en route to the New World when her ship was captured by the adventurer Gilbert Pike. Happily, they fell in love and settled in Carbonear.

> **En Route from Harbour Grace** – Route 74 leads across the peninsula to Trinity Bay and joins Route 80 at Hearts Content. The first transatlantic cable was landed at Hearts Content in 1866; by the turn of the century, it carried 3,000 messages a day to Europe. Route 80 south from Hearts Content passes through Hearts Desire and Hearts Delight, rejoining Route 1 at the head of Trinity Bay for the 50-mile (80-km) drive back to St. John's.

BEST EN ROUTE

Using St. John's as an anchor point, with the best hotels and motels on the Avalon Peninsula, you can cover most of this route in a day's drive. If you go farther along the north shore, there are inexpensive motels on the way. This is the most heavily traveled tourist route in Newfoundland, so reservations are advisable. Expensive lodging runs from $70 to $140; moderate from $35 to $65; inexpensive rooms, under $35. All prices are quoted in US dollars.

ST. JOHN'S

Radisson Plaza – An 11-story property overlooking the harbor, it is swathed in pastels and marble and has 267 rooms, 9 suites, 3 concierge floors, nonsmoking floors, 24-hour room service, a casual restaurant, specialty dining room, and an entertainment lounge. Fitness facilities include a health club, squash courts, indoor pool, sauna, and a whirlpool bath. New Gower and Casey Sts. (phone: 709-739-6404 or 800-228-9822). Expensive.

Newfoundland – The grandest property in Newfoundland, it has 288 rooms and 14 suites on Cavendish Square, within easy walking distance of most downtown attractions. The elegant building has a wide range of modern services including a family restaurant, formal dining room, lounge, indoor pool, sauna, and gym. Duckworth St. (phone: 709-726-4980 or 800-268-9411). Expensive.

Battery – This is a lovely establishment with 152 rooms and a splendid view of the harbor. Signal Hill (phone: 709-726-0040 or 800-267-STEL). Expensive to moderate.

Prescott Inn – Only steps away from the posh residence of the province's lieutenant governor, this is an award-winning heritage property. The proprietors have produced a wonderful blend of turn-of-the-century architecture, the best of contemporary Newfoundland art, and various modern amenities, including a whirlpool bath. The 5 large bedrooms, with period furniture, are available year-round. Smoking is allowed on balconies only. Military Rd. (phone: 709-753-6036). Moderate.

Victorian Station – An inn with 10 suites, most with kitchen and fireplaces and some with offices, they are comfortable and well-appointed. The first-floor restaurant offers fine meals. 290 Duckworth St. (phone: 709-722-1290). Moderate.

Parkview Inn – Ensconced in a pleasant downtown residential area, this 16-room property has a fair dining room and reasonable prices. Military Rd. (phone: 709-753-2671). Inexpensive.

The Northwest Territories

To grasp the elemental fact of the Northwest Territories, consider a couple of simple but eloquent statistics: The Territories account for one-third of the total area of the world's second-largest country; that means they cover a little over 1.3 million square miles from east to west, north to south, stretching from Ellesmere Island, just off Greenland's northern coast, to the Mackenzie Mountain range at the Yukon border. The human population of this immense area is 52,000, nearly 25% of which lives in the capital, Yellowknife, with another 18% living on the other shores of Great Slave Lake.

If those figures speak to you of huge expanses of untouched wilderness, of life-and-death encounters with nature, of hunting and fishing for survival, of caribou and bear, moose and walrus, whale and trout, you are quite right. But it is not unexploited, and it is not an unpeopled paradise where modern life has had no impact. The most marginal areas of the Territories are hunted and fished by tribes of Métis, Dene, and Inuit. The life and livelihood of these native North Americans are under greater and greater pressure as new areas open up for development and wildernesses are explored for mineral deposits — especially for oil — by mining companies. So far, much of this human traffic of business and enterprise spins around the Yellowknife area near the Alberta border (which is by far the best route for entering the province and visiting its most accessible areas). But when new roads cut into the wilderness, they carry with them modern life.

Of this huge area, we have chosen to concentrate on Great Slave Lake, circled by smaller and larger towns, providing a wonderful introduction to both the human and natural environment of the Territories; a side trip to Nahanni National Park in the southwestern corner of the province, north of British Columbia (now more accessible since the building of the Liard Highway); and the Dempster Highway, the 460-mile (736-km) route between Dawson City in the Yukon and Inuvik in the Northwest Territories, a road cutting through what had been virgin territory previously unmarked by roadway, crossing the traditional wandering grounds of one of the largest herds of wild caribou in the world.

Information: *TravelArctic*, Box 1320, Yellowknife, NWT X1A 2L9 (phone: 403-873-7200, or 800-661-0788 to reach the Arctic hotline).

The Hay River to Yellowknife

To journey in the Northwest Territories is to travel between two cultures — one driven by the needs and technologies of contemporary society, the other a traditional, native way of life fast disappearing. The northern frontier is a land of bustling towns and cities not so very different from those towns farther south, with most of the amenities and some of the worries of any even slightly urban environment. The northern Homelands, however, are the small settlements scattered in the North and elsewhere where native people still rely on the traditional pursuits of hunting, fishing, and trapping to live, even while incongruous aspects of modern life appear and impinge on their society. Here traditional arts and crafts exist in the face of increasing pressure to urbanize a way of life that has changed little in thousands of years. And yet, in the last 25 years, the deep currents of change have undercut traditional lifestyles in a way unimaginable to the grandparents of the Inuit alive today. (Inuit — pronounced *In*-oo-it — means "the people" and is the proper term for native Americans of the Far North. The term Eskimo is a derogatory appellation picked up by early settlers, and which today is discouraged by the Inuit.)

Nowhere are all these forces more evident than around the Northwest Territories' mighty Great Slave Lake. The Chipeweya people live here, a tribe of the Dene (pronounced De-*nay*, also meaning "the people") of the large Mackenzie district. Here too is thriving Yellowknife, the capital of the Territories since 1967. And the drive around the lake from Hay River to the capital crosses the Mackenzie River and gives the visitor a glimpse of the majesty of the area. And through it all run the winds of change, as gas and oil discoveries, in the wake of the Alaska pipeline project, have brought to the relations between government and people — especially native people — a new edge and urgency.

En Route from Hay River – Drive 27 miles (43 km) south on Highway 2 to Enterprise. There is one gas station and one restaurant in case you need a break. Turn west on Highway 1 to start the 307-mile (491-km) drive skirting Great Slave Lake, the third-largest lake in North America, to the NWT capital of Yellowknife. Gas up either in Hay River or Enterprise — it's a 125-mile (200-km) drive to the next gas station in Fort Providence. You should also check to see if the ferry is running across the Mackenzie River to Fort Providence.

The highway is gravel, but the driving is good. Here the road follows a ridge overlooking a wide, wooded plain covered with the familiar jack pine. In the distance, you can see the wide expanse of Great Slave Lake. For a spectacular view — and a look at one of the North's many paradoxes — turn off into the Hart Lake fire tower access road, 29 miles (46 km) from Enterprise. The well-marked road leads to a picnic site, 500 yards beyond which, along the marked path, is a 250-foot escarpment, the remains of a coral reef.

Another 23 miles (37 km) brings you to the well-marked turnoff to Kakisa and the Lady Evelyn Falls campsite, with 10 tent sites and 5 RV pads. Drinking water and firewood are available. Fishing is good below the 48-foot falls and grayling are common. A 10-minute drive past the campsite is the small (pop. 30) village of Kakisa, where the Slavey still live off the land, hunting moose, fishing for pike and whitefish, and trapping muskrat and beaver. The small but well-kept log cabins are nestled in groves of pine and birch. There are no services here. Inquire first if you want to launch a boat because fishing nets are strung out around the lake. Keep your eyes open for the net floats when boating to avoid tangling your outboard in the nets and damaging both.

Eleven miles (18 km) from the Kakisa turnoff on Highway 1 is the junction of Highways 1 and 3. Turn north on Highway 3 for the Mackenzie River ferry crossing, Fort Providence, and Yellowknife. Highway 1 takes you to Fort Simpson and access to Nahanni National Park (see *The Nahanni*).

At the ferry crossing, 15 miles (24 km) from the junction, the *Merv Hardie* takes vehicles across the mile-wide river. The free service is available after break-up and before the freeze-up. Winter travelers drive right across the river on the 4-foot-thick ice, which supports up to 55 tons. When highway communications are interrupted during break-up and freeze-up, perishable goods must be flown into Yellowknife. Before the road to Yellowknife was built, goods were freighted across the ice of Great Slave Lake from Hay River to Yellowknife.

Free ferry service is provided during the summer; in winter, ice bridges make safe crossings possible. There are delays each spring and fall during break-up and freeze-up when these rivers cannot be crossed at all. For information on ferry operations, call 800-661-0751. For information on the Mackenzie or Yellowknife Highway call 800-661-0750 or ZENITH-2010.

FORT PROVIDENCE: Across the river, a 5-mile (8-km) drive takes you to the Fort Providence access road. A motel, restaurant, bar, gas station, and store are located between the junction and the settlement of 663, 3 miles (5 km) up the road. Two excellent craft shops in the village produce some of the best Dene handiwork in the valley. You can buy made-to-measure parkas, moosetufting, porcupine quill, and bead-work designs. Each settlement in the valley has its own style of artwork. One craft shop is in the *Snowshoe Inn,* across the street from the motel. The other is in the Dene Band office. If it's closed, inquire around, and someone will open it for you.

At the west end of the village is a monument to Sir Alexander Mackenzie, who passed through here in 1789 in his search for the Pacific Ocean. He didn't find the Pacific, but he was the first white man to get his baggage wet in the Arctic Ocean: He had camped on a beach in the Mackenzie Delta, just out of sight of the ocean. Everyone was sleeping when the tide came in, flooding out the camp. But this had no bearing on Mackenzie calling this, the river that now bears his name, the River of Disappointment. The Dene along the river call it the Mother River or the River of Life.

Father Henri Grollier, a Catholic priest, built a mission on Big Island in 1858, but after he moved it here 3 years later, the settlement gradually grew around it.

You can rent boats at either of the service stations for some excellent grayling and pike fishing, but watch out for the blackflies. These pesky bugs love to bite anywhere; bring a good insect repellent or head net. A mile from the junction of the access road, a beautiful campsite on the top of the river bluffs has secluded tenting and RV pads and a dumping station for RVs. You can watch tugs pushing laden barges downriver, heading for the High Arctic.

En Route from Providence – Head north on Highway 3 for the 144-mile (230-km) drive to Rae and Edzo, where you can gas up for the additional 62-mile (99-km) drive into Yellowknife. On the east side of the highway is the Mackenzie Bison Sanctuary. The government transplanted 19 wood buffalo here from the Fort Smith area in 1963. Now the herd numbers well over 500, the only pure herd of wood buffalo left in North America. You probably won't see any near the highway since the animals tend to range closer to the shores of the lake. But you will see an occasional moose browsing in the numerous lakes and sloughs along the highway. And if you're lucky, you'll see a sandhill crane.

There is a picturesque view of Great Slave Lake's North Arm, dotted with numerous islands, at North Arm picnic site, 112 miles (179 km) north of Fort Providence.

There is a popular fishing spot on Mosquito Creek, 7 miles (11 km) south of Edzo on the highway. Pickerel (walleye) and grayling run in springtime. Black bear are also common in the area at that time. Extra care should be taken then, because bears just out of hibernation, still not quite awake, are particularly hungry.

RAE and EDZO: These towns make up the largest Dene community in the NWT (pop. 1,378). The Dogrib tribe was mostly a nomadic people following the migratory caribou in winter and fishing the plentiful lakes in summer. At the turn of the century, this area produced tons of dried meat for Hudson Bay traders. Dr. John Rae established a post on the North Arm, several miles from the present settlement in 1852. It was moved in 1906 to its present site, where it's possible to see some log cabins, the only remains of old Fort Rae.

Edzo was intended as a replacement community when it was built in 1965 on the south side of Frank's Channel. The government established this model community with a modern school, a nursing station, and housing at the same time the Mackenzie Highway was being built to Yellowknife. However, the residents refused to move to the new community, even though it was built at a higher, drier, and more sanitary location. They refused to abandon their homes built on the rocks and muskeg, where they could launch canoes into Marian Lake from their own backyards. Some finally did move, but the old community survives, strong as ever. There are no services in Edzo, but there are two gas stations in Rae. Walking around the village you see snowmobiles, dogs tied up waiting for winter snows, and fish hung up on drying racks.

Edzo was named after a famous Dogrib chief who brought peace to the area in the mid-1800s. His antagonist was Chief Akaitcho of the Yellowknife Indians, who ranged from Yellowknife Bay north almost to Coppermine. The Yellowknife preyed on the Dogrib, chasing them out of hunting and fishing grounds. In a confrontation between the two, according to legend, Edzo spoke so long and eloquently that Akaitcho was afraid to wage war again. Akaitcho helped Captain John Back in his trek to the Arctic Ocean up the Back River in 1832. The Yellowknife Indians disappeared as a distinct tribal unit after their ranks were decimated by a great flu epidemic in 1928. The survivors gradually moved into other settlements and were assimilated into other tribal groups.

Frank's Channel, between Rae and Edzo, also marks the geological dividing point between the sedimentary basin, an extension of the Canadian prairies, and the Precambrian Shield. The highway takes on a few more curves as it skirts lakes and sloughs nestled among hard rock outcrops. The familiar spruce and pine grow shorter here as they struggle for footholds in any dip and crevice that can hold a few inches of soil. This is also the area of permafrost, where only a few top feet of ground thaw in summertime.

Proceed north on Highway 3 and drive 62 miles (99 km) to Yellowknife.

YELLOWKNIFE: This city of 1,200, the capital of the Northwest Territories, owes its existence to two gold mines, and owes its growth to government offices administering a territory comprising one-third the landmass of Canada. Nearly 25% of all NWT residents live in this city (the population of the entire territory is 52,000).

This city of high-rises and office buildings sprouting out of the surrounding taiga is the most cosmopolitan of all NWT communities. It's come a long way since Laurent Leroux, a Northwest Company trader, first built his trading post on Yellowknife Bay in 1789. Alexander Mackenzie passed through here in his roundabout search for the river that now bears his name. And John Franklin, famous for discovering the Northwest Passage, traveled up the Yellowknife River to the Arctic coast via the Coppermine River in 1819. Franklin later triggered one of the biggest manhunts in British naval history when he disappeared during his exploration in 1848.

The Hudson's Bay Company closed down the Yellowknife trading post in 1823, after the Bay amalgamated with its longtime fur trading rival, the Northwest Company. Little attention was given to the area for the next 75 years. Prospectors on their way to the Klondike via the Mackenzie River found traces of gold in the hard rock in 1896. In 1930, a major discovery precipitated a boom in the area. Con Mines, on the southern edge of Yellowknife, became the first mine to produce in the area in 1938. The second, Giant Yellowknife Mines, began production in 1945. Surface tours can be arranged by calling the mine office (phone: 403-873-6301). Those who come at the right time may even see molten gold being poured into 70-pound bricks.

Take a walk around Old Town Yellowknife on the peninsula where, in the 1930s and 1940s, shacks fought for space on the bare rocks. Today, the Bush Pilot's Monument is perched on one of these rocks, overlooking the waters of Great Slave Lake. The shacks are long gone, but a cairn commemorates the legendary bush pilots who opened the North with their daring exploits in rickety planes. From the vantage point offered by the Bush Pilot's Monument, visitors can watch the floatplanes take off, flying tourists to remote fishing lakes and prospectors to another potential bonanza. Below the monument on the Back Bay side is the restored *Wild Cat Café*, one of the few surviving landmarks in Old Town. *Raven Tours* (phone: 403-873-4776) offers walking tours.

On your drive into Yellowknife, you will probably notice the Bristol Monument, a *Bristol* freighter set atop a prominent rock outcrop. This plane made aviation history in May 1967, when *Wardair* pilot Don Braun touched down on the North Pole, the first wheeled aircraft to do so. The *Bristol*, a relic of World War II, helped open many an isolated camp and mine in the NWT by freighting in construction materials, even bulldozers.

The Prince of Wales Northern Heritage Centre on the shore of Frame Lake is just a 3-block walk from downtown. It houses extensive displays of northern artifacts, ranging from Inuit carvings to dioramas of northern wildlife. Also in this well-rounded collection is a piece of *Cosmos 954,* the Soviet satellite that crashed into the Barrenlands 300 miles (480 km) east of Yellowknife on January 24, 1978.

And for something really different: Golf buffs arriving in Yellowknife around the longest day of the year, June 21, can participate in the Midnight *Golf Tourney* at the *Yellowknife Golf Club* (phone: 403-873-4326). This annual event draws participants and celebrities for a teeoff under the light midnight sky. The course is unique — the turf, sand; the greens, oiled sand; and the biggest hazards, ravens. The large plucky birds have been known to steal a golf ball from under the nose of a golfer. Contestants get a special repellant, liquid refreshment, and extra golf balls, among other things. This event is held in conjunction with *Raven Mad Days,* when stores remain open past midnight and the *Daughters of the Midnight Sun* carry on their tradition of zany entertainment wherever they can find a crowd, be it in a bar or on the street. The *Folks on the Rocks* music festival is held in mid-July.

Yellowknife has numerous hotels and motels that cater to a wide service and price range. Its stores can fill just about every need, but it's well to remember that prices in far-off Yellowknife are about 30% higher than in southern Canada because of the transportation costs. Many stores sell soapstone carvings and handicrafts. The largest collections can be found in *Northern Images* in the *YK Mall* (corner of Franklin and 48th Sts.) and the *Toa Chen's Art Gallery* in the *Scotia Centre* (corner of Franklin and 51st Sts.). Both stock the internationally famous Holman Island and Cape Dorset prints and etchings.

There's a large number of campsites within easy reach of Yellowknife. The Fred Henne Park across from the airport, the closest to town, has drinking water, tenting sites, and pads for RVs, with dumping facilities. Also, while at Long Lake consider taking the interesting "Trail of the Early Prospector," a self-guided, 2-hour interpretive hike that explains the area's unique geology as well as some of its flora and fauna. Fred Henne Park can get crowded on weekends because it has the only sandy swimming beach close to town, attracting residents enjoying the short but sunny summers.

Those wishing to get away from the crowds can drive the 50-mile (80-km) Ingraham Trail, named for the Yellowknife hotelier Vic Ingraham. The trail was to be the start of the ambitious Roads to Resources, skirting Great Slave Lake and linking many potential mine sites. However, the project was abandoned in the late 1960s.

Along the Ingraham Trail you'll now find hiking paths, boat launches, picnic sites, and camping (with drinking water and firewood) at Prelude Lake and Reid Lake territorial parks. Fishing is a popular area pastime, with lake trout, northern pike, walleye, whitefish, and Arctic grayling the primary catches in the waterways off the trail. It's also a very good place for canoeing. If you venture out here in winter, you might see the Bathurst Caribou herd, which migrates as far south as this road. You can also engage in activities like ice fishing, cross-country skiing, and snowshoeing. (Fishing licenses are necessary; they are available at the Northwest Territories border information booths, most sport fishing lodges, sporting goods and hardware stores, and the RCMP district offices of the Northwest Territories Wildlife Service and the Department of Fisheries and Oceans offices.)

En Route from Yellowknife – Drive 2 miles (3 km) past the Giant Mines property on Highway 4. The first site is the Yellowknife River Park across the bridge. A boat launch provides access to the northern pike-rich river. Or you can fish for grayling and whitefish at Tartan Rapids, 7 miles (11 km) upstream, where Prosperous Lake empties into the river. There are plenty of pike in the shallows and weed beds that will rise to a homemade lure, but red devils are a favorite.

There are three other picnic sites over the next 12 miles (19 km), each providing hiking trails and fishing. Prelude Lake Territorial Park at the end of a 1-mile (1.6-km), well-marked turnoff has a boat launch, a beach, and good trout fishing. The *Prelude Lake Lodge* (phone: 403-873-8511) provides commercial accommodations, boat and motor rentals, and a café. Fishermen should watch for sudden shifting winds when boating on the larger lakes. If you get into difficulty, make for the nearest land and wait out the weather; even the smaller lakes kick up sizable waves, and the water here is extremely cold.

At Kilometer 48 you'll find a parking area at the beginning of the well-marked scenic trail leading to the Cameron River Falls. The ¾-mile trail leads to a 45-foot waterfall, and side trails lead to another, smaller waterfall downstream.

Another 8-mile (13-km) drive takes you to Reid Lake Territorial Park, the best along the Ingraham Trail. Water, wood, and a boat launch are available, plus plenty of good fishing. This 27-site camping area is only 7 miles (11 km) from the end of the road at Tibbet Lake.

BEST EN ROUTE

Due to the scarcity of accommodations in the Northwest Territories, make reservations as far in advance as possible. In addition, you should expect to pay $50 and up per night for a double in the hotels we've listed here. All prices are quoted in US dollars.

■ **NOTE::** There are more than 25 dining establishments in Yellowknife; some are licensed premises.

YELLOWKNIFE

Discovery Inn – This downtown establishment has 41 rooms, a family-style restaurant, a lounge, and conference facilities. Box 784, Yellowknife, NWT X1A 2N6 (phone: 403-873-4151).

Explorer – Modern, with 110 guestrooms, all with color TV sets and air conditioning, the facilities include the *Treeline Café*, fine dining in the *Factors Club*, a cocktail lounge, and a game room. Postal Service 7000, Yellowknife, NWT X1A 2R3 (phone: 403-873-3531).

Northern Lites – Located 1 block from downtown, Yellowknife's newest motel has 20 guestrooms, all with cable-equipped color TV sets. PO Box 2532, Yellowknife, NWT X1A 2P8 (phone: 403-873-6023).

Twin Pine – This motel halfway between Old and New Towns accommodates 100. There is no café, but breakfast is available. Some rooms also have kitchen facilities. Franklin Ave. Mailing address: PO Box 596, Yellowknife, NWT X1A 2N4 (phone: 403-873-8511).

Yellowknife Inn – Conveniently located downtown, with 150 rooms, it has a café, bar, lounge, newsstand, and one of the best dining places in town, the *Mackenzie Dining Room*. The menu includes a selection of northern Canadian dishes such as arctic char, caribou steaks, and musk ox. The café is a crossroads of the north, frequented by businessmen, travelers, and by the mining and aviation fraternity. The inn is the site of the *Annex Conference Centre* and home of the NWT Legislative Assembly. Franklin Ave. Mailing address: PO Box 490, Yellowknife, NWT X1A 2N4 (phone: 403-873-2601).

YWCA – Here are 32 rooms (for men and women), many with kitchenettes. Weekly and monthly rates are available. 5004 54th St, Yellowknife, NWT X1A 2R6 (phone: 403-920-2777).

The Nahanni

The 450-mile (720-km) journey from Great Slave Lake's western shore to Nahanni National Park in the southwestern corner of the Northwest Territories is a trip that will appeal primarily to hard-core wilderness trekkers, for the main purpose of a visit to Nahanni, besides the lure of burying oneself in its 1,840 square miles of mountains, lakes, and wilderness, is South Nahanni River, one of the purest, wildest, roughest stretches of white water left in the world. All motorized craft are forbidden on the river. Because it is a wilderness destination, the park and river are most accessible by charter aircraft (see below). The two jumping off places for flight access are Fort Liard and Fort Simpson. Visitors need to make travel arrangements in advance (outfitters are listed at the end of this section). Usually, visitors fly into the north end of the park and paddle canoes or rafts downstream. To reach either Fort Liard or Fort Simpson, take the Liard Highway, which starts at Fort Nelson, BC, and runs through the fabled Liard Valley to Fort Simpson.

The following air services depart from Fort Liard or Fort Simpson: *Liard Air Ltd.* (PO Box 3190, Fort Nelson, BC V0C 1R0; phone: 604-774-2909 in summer and 604-986-8941 in winter); *Deh Cho Air Ltd.* (Liard Valley Band Development Corp., Fort Liard, NWT X0G 0A0; phone: 403-770-4103); and *Simpson Air* (Box 260, Fort Simpson, NWT X0E 0N0; phone: 403-695-2505) will transport both you and your canoe into Nahanni National Park. *Simpson Air* also has a canoe rental service.

Because there is no way to drive to the park, the Nahanni can be a difficult destination for the non-rugged traveler. Motorists can drive the Liard Highway to Fort Liard and on to *Blackstone Territorial Campground* where there is an information center, campsites for tents and RVs, and a boat launch and float plane station. From here, *Liard Air* can arrange flight-seeing trips over the park and the river.

> **En Route to Fort Simpson** – From the junction of Routes 1 and 3 near Fort Providence, it's a 180-mile (288-km) drive to Fort Simpson on the well-graveled, all-weather highway. If you're going straight through, figure on 4 to 5 hours' driving. The park at Whittaker Falls, 93 miles (149 km) from Fort Simpson, has a nice view of Coral Falls, a short hike away. The well-laid-out campsite has wood supplies but no drinking water. Trees are much taller in this area, a favorite moose hunting region. The road is relatively level and straight. A free ferry takes you across the Liard River into Fort Simpson, 10 miles (16 km) away.

FORT SIMPSON: The Northwest Company established the Fort of the Forks here in 1804 to trade for the rich beaver and marten furs that fashion-hungry Europe demanded. This town of 987 at the confluence of the Liard and Mackenzie rivers is named for Sir George Simpson, governor of the Hudson's Bay Company when it amalgamated with its rival Northwest Company in 1812. If you walk around town, you'll see an occasional small, steam river tug lying on the shores, a remnant of the day when Simpson was an important stopping point for river barges that loaded up here with food, fuel, and furs for their voyages up and down the Mackenzie. Simpson has great potential for agriculture, and for many years the church missions grew their own potatoes and grains and raised cattle. The federal government established an experimental farm here but closed it in 1969. When the highway was built, it cost less to import all the food needed from outside.

NAHANNI NATIONAL PARK: The Nahanni National Park is a long, skinny area of land designed to ecologically protect the Nahanni River. The river flows past natural hotsprings, hills of soft calcium, canyons twice as deep as the Grand Canyon and other features so unusual that the United Nations has designated the park a World Heritage Site. At 312 feet, the river's Virginia Falls is twice the height of Niagara Falls.

Legends tell of a lost tribe of Indians (Nahanni means "the people over there"), tropical valleys, and sightings of Sasquatch, the legendary Bigfoot. The legends arose from prospectors traveling up the Liard on their way to the Klondike gold rush in the Yukon. In 1904, three McLeod brothers entered the Nahanni Valley looking for gold. Rumor had it that they found gold nuggets the size of grapes. The following year, two of the brothers returned to the valley and disappeared. Three years later their headless bodies were found, giving the name to Headless Valley, where they had their cabin. Their fate remains a mystery, with legends mushrooming — of cabins mysteriously burning, of murders, and many tall tales. Others have followed, looking for the McLeod brothers' mother lode, but no one has found it. Albert Faille spent his life looking, making more than 30 trips into the valley; as you portage around Virginia Falls, you use the route he cut on his travels.

You can find orchids growing around the falls, take a dip in sulfur hot springs, hike the trails into the mountains, or stalk wildlife with your camera. Dall's sheep can be seen on the mountainsides, moose and bear in the valley, and woodland caribou in the upper valleys.

Those planning to canoe the river must be experienced in white water. Register your travel plans with the national parks warden at the Fort Simpson headquarters or the

Nahanni Butte warden station at the entrance to the park. The Royal Canadian Mounted Police also offer a wilderness travel registration service throughout the North. If you're heading into the bush, tell them where you're going and when you expect to return. If something happens, help will be on the way once you're reported overdue.

Good outfitters that offer canoeing and rafting trips on the Nahanni River in summer months are *Nahanni River Adventures* (PO Box 8368, Station F, Edmonton, AL T6H 4W6; phone: 403-439-1316) and *Black Feather Wilderness Adventures* (1341 Wellington St., Ottawa, Ontario K1Y 3B8; phone: 613-722-9717).

If you decide to canoe yourself, first study the literature on canoeing this valley.

BEST EN ROUTE

Due to the scarcity of accommodations in the Northwest Territories, you should make reservations as far in advance as possible. Expect to pay $40 and up per night for a double in the hotels listed here. All prices are quoted in US dollars.

FORT SIMPSON

Maroda – A 15-room motel with TV sets and kitchenettes, it also has a gift shop. Open year-round. PO Box 67, Fort Simpson, NWT X0E 0N0 (phone: 403-695-2602).

Nahanni Inn – This sturdy hotel that sleeps 70 is open year-round. All rooms have private bath, cable TV, and a telephone; 4 suites are equipped with kitchens. A restaurant and cocktail lounge are on the premises. The property overlooks the Mackenzie and Liard rivers. PO Box 248, Fort Simpson, NWT X0E 0N0 (phone: 403-695-2201, 403-695-2202, 403-695-2203, 403-695-2204).

Nahanni National Park – For information on accommodations, campsites, and outfitters, contact the Superintendent, Nahanni National Park, Postal Bag 300, Fort Simpson, NWT X0E 0N0 (phone: 403-695-3151).

Dawson City to Inuvik

The Dempster, one of the newest of NWT highways, snakes 475 miles (760 km) from the rolling hills around historic Dawson City, Yukon, to above the Arctic Circle. The road ends at Inuvik, NWT, on the eastern edge of the majestic Mackenzie River delta, so it is necessary to drive out on the same route you came in on. The highway, named after a Royal Canadian Mounted Police corporal who found the ill-fated Dawson patrol, is the only public access highway reaching this far north in North America.

Since the highway is in such a remote area, facilities are scarce, and drivers should carry enough fuel to reach the next gas pump. Although only two places between Dawson and Inuvik provide accommodations, there are plenty of campsites to pitch a tent.

The drive takes you to the top of the world, from the forested slopes of the Yukon across the Eagle Plain wintering grounds of the Porcupine caribou herd to the alpine tundra of the Richardson Mountains. There will be plenty of opportunity to photograph and observe wildlife along the route, so have your camera ready.

Before making this trip, inquire about the state of the highway, whether the ferry is operating across the Peel and Mackenzie rivers, and whether the gas and lodge facilities at Eagle Plains are open. For information on ferry operations, call (toll-free, within the Northwest Territories) Zenith 2022; in Inuvik, 403-979-3828. For information on the Dempster Highway, call 800-661-0752 (in NWT and Alberta).

The migration of the 150,000 head of Porcupine caribou across the highway may also temporarily close the road. But since this massive movement coincides with freeze-up and break-up periods, when the ferry is not in operation, the highway will probably be closed anyway. Check with either the Yukon or NWT Department of Highways before proceeding.

The Dempster Highway is also open from December to late April; however, travelers should be well prepared for adverse driving conditions on this road in winter months.

Make sure your tires are good, and carry extra gas in the trunk. In case of breakdowns, there are garages in Dawson and Inuvik; one has recently opened in Fort McPherson. It's wise to have a down-filled jacket as well. The nighttime temperatures can get chilly in high altitudes and near lakes and rivers. A wide variety of food and supplies is available in both Dawson and Inuvik, and you can get the basics in Fort McPherson and Arctic Red River.

En Route to Dawson Creek – From Whitehorse in the Yukon, take Routes 1 and 2 to Steward Junction, 214 miles (342 km) away. Instead of following Route 2 here, turn off to Highway 3 and follow it 114 miles (182 km) to the gold rush town of Dawson Creek. The turnoff to the Dempster is 26 miles (42 km) back, but since you've driven all the way up here, Dawson is worth seeing too (see "The Dawson Circle Route," *The Yukon*).

En Route from Dawson – Drive east on Route 3 to its intersection of Route 11 and turn north. There is a gas station at this junction where you can fuel up and you can stay at the *Eagle Plains* hotel (123 miles/371 km farther on). The next gas available beyond Ogilvie River is at Fort McPherson, 337 miles (539 km) past the lodge. Also check to see if the ferries at Arctic Red River and Fort McPherson are operating (phone: 403-873-0158 or 800-661-0752).

The *Tombstone Campgrounds,* on a ridge above the Klondike River 45 miles (72 km) north of the junction, offer minimal conveniences. Another 78 miles (125 km) through rolling, forested hills takes you to the Ogilvie River (named for the Yukon commissioner at the time of the Yukon gold rush) campsite. The lodge is across the river.

Caribou stragglers are sometimes visible on the Eagle Plains. The Porcupine herd migrates from the North Slope of Alaska into the Yukon interior. This herd was the subject of much debate during Judge Thomas Berger's public inquiry into the building of the Mackenzie Valley gas pipeline and will also affect the building of a gas pipeline down the Dempster, linking gas reserves in the Mackenzie Delta with the Alaska Highway gas pipeline. As you near the NWT border and the Richardson Mountains, you might see Dall's sheep. In June, snowbanks will still line the side of the road. Once you hit the NWT-Yukon border, the cable-operated ferry across the Peel River is only 47 miles (75 km) away.

FORT McPHERSON: This is a Dene settlement of 760 people on the Peel River. The Loucheux rely on hunting, trapping, and government work for survival. The area is rich in mink, muskrat, lynx, and beaver. The present site, originally called Fort Bell, was established in 1840 by Alex Isbister and John Bell, Northwest Company fur traders. Later its name was changed to honor Murdoch McPherson, chief trader for the Hudson's Bay Company. The RCMP established this as one of their main patrol posts in the early 1900s to bring justice to whalers wintering on Herschel Island off the Yukon's north coast.

In the winter of 1910–1911, Inspector F. J. Fitzgerald of the RCMP attempted a patrol from McPherson to Dawson with three companions. Usually the patrols came from Dawson over the Richardson Mountains; reversing the route would have been a historic first. The patrol, without competent guides, lost its way. With heavy snows and bad weather obscuring landmarks, they missed the turn that would have taken them through a pass. Hopelessly lost, they turned back after running low on food. Starvation and cold took their toll, although two made it to within 20 miles of home. The bodies were found by Corporal W. D. Dempster, en route from Dawson to McPherson in search of the lost patrol. Fort Fitzgerald, formerly Smith's Landing (south of Fort Smith), was renamed to honor the inspector.

For provisions, stop at the *Co-op* (phone: 403-952-2417).

En Route from Fort McPherson – The Arctic Red River lies just east of Fort McPherson, and between the two communities are two picnic areas that offer excellent views of the river rapids; both are real hot spots for whitefish and grayling. As you approach the ferry crossing at Arctic Red River, you'll come to a ridge with a splendid view of the Arctic Red River pouring into the MacKenzie River. Unbelievably, swans nest in this area.

ARCTIC RED RIVER: This is a traditional fishing camp for the Loucheux, who catch their winter supply of northern pike and whitefish for themselves and their dogs here. You can see fish drying on racks around the town. The settlement gained some permanence when Father Jean Seguin, OMI, established a Roman Catholic mission here in 1868. Eventually, the Hudson's Bay set up a trading post here. Only three families lived here 40 years ago. Now the population is 108.

En Route from Arctic Red River – A government-run ferry takes passengers across the mile-wide river. Across the mighty Mackenzie are four sites along the next 84 miles (134 km) for picnics, fishing, shutterbugging, and relaxing before you arrive at the next territorial campground, Chuk Park, with the basic conveniences of territorial parks. To view the scenery along the highway, most travelers just pull off on the shoulder of the road.

INUVIK: This Inuvialuit word means "place of man." The Inuvialuit are the Delta and Western Arctic Eskimo, or Inuit. Located in the Mackenzie Delta, this is a modern town as towns in the North go. Construction began in 1955, and it officially opened on July 18, 1958, as a replacement community for Aklavik, on the western side of the delta. Government engineers thought Aklavik would be swept into the Mackenzie because of the constant erosion of the riverbanks. Aklavik's motto is "The Town that Wouldn't Die," so few moved to the new center despite promises of better services and housing. Aklavik is still alive and well, but all government offices moved to the new site, 35 miles (56 km) west. Inuvik, mainly a government town of 3,400, enjoyed a boom period when oil companies were drilling into the delta to find oil and gas reserves. Most of the petroleum exploration now is in the Beaufort Sea, centered out of Tuktoyaktuk (more commonly known as Tuk), 70 miles (112 km) to the north, a modern town with most conveniences. Inuvik is a good example of how people adapt to a frigid northern environment. Until the main street was paved in 1978, wooden boardwalks protected one's boots from the thick, springtime mud. (Vestiges of these wooden sidewalks can still be found in some areas of town.) Buildings are built on piles driven into the permafrost — ground permanently frozen to depths of 300 feet. (If they were built on top of the ground, heat from the building would melt the permafrost; soon the ground would settle and the building sink.) It's impossible to bury sewer and water lines for the same reason. Digging through permafrost is like digging through rock, and if you did bury the lines, they would have to be heated to prevent them from freezing. Instead, service lines are laid on top of the ground in utilidors, insulated corridors connecting buildings.

Permafrost has some advantages. The hunters and trappers association tunneled into a ridge to make a community freezer. Thirty feet underground, meat stays frozen no matter how hot the summer. Summer temperatures may reach the high 80s F (30s C); the summer mean is in the 50s F ('teens C).

The Inuvik branch of *Northern Images,* the retail arm of the northern cooperatives, is housed in an octagonal building. Here you'll find soapstone carvings by internationally recognized Inuit carvers; silkscreens and soapstone lithographs from Holman Island and Sachs Harbour, 400 air miles (640 km) to the northeast; wolf, muskrat, and coyote parkas and coats made in the shops of Tuk and Aklavik. Or you can purchase the finely made Inuvik duffle parkas. Inquire at *Northern Images* about seeing the native craftswomen at work.

Boats and guides are available for fishing the twisting channels of the resource-rich Mackenzie Delta. The fishing is splendid in nearby lakes, accessible by chartering a small plane. Inuvik's *Happy Valley Campground* is a good choice if you'd like to pitch your tent where there are views of the lakes and channels of the Mackenzie Delta.

Inuvik is the transportation center for the delta and western Arctic region, providing regularly scheduled flights to such Inuit centers as Sachs Harbour, Holman Island, Tuk, Aklavik, and Coppermine. Each of these has accommodations if you want to spend a day or two watching how the Inuit live off the land, sealing, whaling, and hunting.

BEST EN ROUTE

Due to the scarcity of accommodations in the Northwest Territories, it is necessary to make reservations as far in advance as possible. Expect to pay at least $60 per night for a double room in the hotels we've listed here. All prices are quoted in US dollars.

INUVIK

Eskimo Inn – A downtown establishment with 78 rooms and a wide range of services, including a café, lounge, and dining room. Mailing address: PO Box 1740, Inuvik, NWT X0E 0T0 (phone: 403-979-2801).

Finto – This 51-room motel is between the airport and downtown. Mailing address: PO Box 1925, Inuvik, NWT X0E 0T0 (phone: 403-979-2647).

Inuvik Inn – There are only 3 rooms here so it's best to call ahead. The inn features a café, catering service, and a gift shop. On the airport road. Mailing address: Box 1557, Inuvik, NWT XOE 0T0 (phone: 403-979-2631).

Mackenzie – This hostelry has 33 rooms, 2 licensed lounges, a coffee shop, a large dining room with a fireplace, and a 150-seat nightclub. Mailing address: PO Box 1618, Inuvik, NWT XOE 0T0 (phone: 403-979-2861).

Hay River to Fort Smith

The 174-mile (278-km) drive along Highway 5 from Hay River to Fort Smith and Wood Buffalo National Park delights photographers, naturalists, and active adventurers. You won't find polar bears this far south, but in the thickets of birch and poplar alongside the road you can photograph the last free herd of bison roaming in their natural habitat. The park is the nesting home for more than 200 species of migratory birds after their winter vacations in warmer climates. Bird watchers can view many varieties, including the whooping crane whose wild population now numbers nearly 200. Once thought to be extinct, "whoopers" are making a slow comeback. You can contact licensed flight-seeing operators in Fort Smith. Try *Canoe Arctic Limited* (phone: 403-872-2308), *Subarctic Wilderness Adventures* (phone: 403-872-2467), *Jewell's River Tours* (phone: 403-872-2089), and *River Trails North* (phone: 403-872-2060). In late August and September the numerous lakes, sloughs, and lush deltas are alive with birds gathering in flocks for their flight south, but it is unlikely that motorists will see them.

Travelers driving here can do so in relative comfort. The all-weather gravel highways from the NWT border are well maintained, wide, relatively straight — and sometimes dusty. For more information on road conditions, call 403-874-3780 (Hay River) or, toll-free, ZENITH-2018 or 800-661-0751 for communities in the NWT on the southern Mackenzie road system (Fort Smith, Pint Point, Fort Resolution, Enterprise, Fort Liard, Fort Simpson, Fort Providence, Yellowknife, Rae and Edzo). There is a tourist information center and exhibit at the Alberta-Northwest Territory border.

The Southern Mackenzie may not be far enough north for you to enjoy the pleasure of the sun overhead 24 hours a day. But during the summer there is more daylight than dark for you to pack more sightseeing into your day. For instance, in June in Fort Smith the sun rises at 3 AM and sets at 11 PM to midnight — and it hardly gets dark during the 4-hour nights.

Dress as you would for camping in the mountains. Mean summer temperatures range from the upper 30s F ('teens C) to the low 60s F ('teens C). Highs in the 90s have been recorded in many areas — and most also have records of summer freezes, so bring along a warm jacket. It will also help keep away the mosquitoes. Since the bugs can be a nuisance, take steps to avoid discomfort: Camp in dry, open areas where breezes can sweep them away. A long-lasting mosquito coil is effective if you burn a couple upwind.

All of the camp and picnic sites along this route have drinking water and are well stocked with firewood. The towns of Hay River and Fort Smith can meet most of your needs. If you're not camping, there are hotels, motels with restaurants, and bed and breakfast accommodations. Inquire at the tourist information center at the Alberta-Northwest Territory border.

On the banks of the Slave River, Fort Smith developed from a portage around a series of four rapids. This was the favorite and easiest route for early explorers and traders penetrating the Far North. Both overland and water-based trips are available with licensed companies, which cater to active adventurers as well as those who prefer more passive touring. For air tours try *Northwestern Air Lease* (phone: 403-872-2216). Boat tours are offered by *Jewell's River Tours* (phone: 403-872-2089) and *River Trails North* (phone: 403-872-2060).

The gently rolling countryside is an extension of the prairies. Near Fort Smith, approaching the Precambrian Shield, the terrain becomes more rocky.

En Route from Edmonton, Alberta – There are two routes through Alberta to the NWT.

The quicker one is via the Yellowhead Highway 16. Drive 25 miles (40 km) west out of Edmonton and turn north on Highway 43. At Valleyview turn north on Highway 34 to Donnelly. As you go north the road becomes Highway 2. Follow this through the rolling countryside to Peace River, then 16 miles (26 km) farther to Grimshaw. This is Kilometer Zero of the Mackenzie Highway. A monument and plaque just north of the village commemorate the explorer Alexander Mackenzie and the construction of the highway. It's 300 miles (480 km) from Edmonton to Grimshaw and 340 miles (544 km) farther to Hay River, hub of the NWT. Poplar and birch gradually crowd out the farmland as you drive north, with balsam, pine, and spruce taking over near the NWT border.

The second route, via Lesser Slave Lake, is only 25 miles (40 km) longer, and more picturesque. (You'll also find excellent northern pike fishing in the lake.) Follow Highway 2 north out of Edmonton through the towns of Slave Lake, High Prairie Peace River, and on to Grimshaw.

The well-kept Mackenzie Highway, paved all the way north to Hay River, is wide and straight, unlike the twisting Alaska Highway. Maps, information, and a detailed *Explorers' Guide* are available at the border tourist information center.

Driving and passing other cars on gravel highways require extra caution. Dust, which can impair your view of oncoming traffic, is a special problem. There are 2-mile stretches of straight highway that are oiled and spread with a dust suppressant to make passing safer. Watch for these areas; they are well posted. If you get caught in dust from an oncoming or passing vehicle and you can't see the road, slow down, but don't stop.

NWT drivers are courteous and willing to help those stranded by the roadside. It's more than goodwill; in winter, when temperatures hit 40F below (-40C), it's a matter of survival.

HAY RIVER: This junction community of 3,000 on Great Slave Lake provides access to all the settlements on the Mackenzie Highway system. The Hudson's Bay Company built the first trading post here in 1868, but the population didn't grow until the Mackenzie Highway system was completed and oil and gas exploration begun. A railway finished in 1964 to carry lead-zinc ore from Pine Point to smelters established the town as a transportation center. Freight bound for High Arctic settlements is transhipped here onto barges for the 1,200-mile voyage down the Mackenzie River to the Arctic Ocean, a precarious lifeline depending heavily on the weather: Mackenzie River and High Arctic communities depend for survival on these once-a-year supply drops of food, fuel, and construction material.

Drive past the airport into Hay River's Old Town, where wharves of the barging companies are piled high with supplies for exotic places like Holman Island, Fort Good Hope, and Tuktoyaktuk. Old Town is also the home of the commercial fishermen who ply the waters of Great Slave Lake, winter and summer, bringing in trout, whitefish, northern pike, and inconnu. Some of the pike is shipped to France, where it's made into pâté.

Old Town is an area of small, old frame houses built on the flood plain of the Hay River delta. After two disastrous floods, the townsite was moved to high ground upriver. New Town is dominated by a 14-story high-rise, built in anticipation of a gas pipeline down the Mackenzie Valley. Hay River would then have become a staging area for the project. The Diamond Jenness School, across the street from the high-rise, is a striking example of northern-flavored architecture. Students were given their choice of color for the building, thus, a shocking purple building has become a landmark. Disconcerted at first, everyone is now quite proud of it. (The school was named after the anthropologist who first studied northern native culture around 1910.)

Although relatively small, the town provides most amenities. Several motels and hotels offer good, clean service, and some have restaurants and bars. The *Back Eddy* restaurant (phone: 403-874-6680), just a block from downtown, has the best steak in town. Unleaded gas is available in the gas stations and garages, and tourists can find just about any camping supplies.

En Route from Hay River – Travel south on Highway 2 for 5 miles (8 km) and turn east onto Highway 5 for the start of the 174-mile (278-km) drive to Fort Smith and Wood Buffalo National Park. Two miles (3 km) from the junction, a road turning north leads to the Hay River Indian Reserve. At the end of the 6-mile (10-km) road, at the original site of Hay River, old churches and the remains of the Hudson's Bay post offer quiet testimony to the two major influences on early northern life.

Highway 5 forks 34 miles (54 km) past the reserve turnoff. Turn south on Highway 5 for 130 miles (208 km) to Fort Smith.

Take Highway 6 to Fort Resolution, 41 miles (66 km) east, where you will find a fur trapping center of 550, most of the inhabitants of Chipeweya descent. This is the last band of North American Indians to hunt wild, free-roaming bison on land adjacent to Wood Buffalo National Park as a food source. A sawmill provides employment, but many still support themselves by hunting, trapping, and fishing in the fur-rich Slave delta. Fort Resolution was an important center at one time, when barges plied the Slave River, bringing goods from Fort McMurray. The large mission hostel and school are no longer used.

WOOD BUFFALO NATIONAL PARK: With more than 17,300 square miles, this is Canada's largest national park. Straddling the Alberta-NWT border, it's the home of the world's last free-roaming bison herd, the last refuge for the endangered whooping crane, and the world's only river rookery of white pelican. These birds normally nest in lakes, but in a deviation of the evolutionary process some birds adapted to the white waters of the Slave River rapids.

The park was created in 1922 to protect the estimated 1,500 surviving wood buffalo, a longer-legged, darker, and hardier cousin of the plains buffalo. Six years later the government herded 6,000 plains bison from Wainright, Alberta, into the park when their grazing grounds became a military range. The park is also home to the Sweetgrass Station Naturalist camp, an area where Canadian Wildlife Service staff and park staff rounded up buffalo to inoculate them against anthrax, tuberculosis, and other diseases. Although it was to protect the animals, the effort caused them stress and was discontinued during the mid-1970s. At one time, the area had a human population approaching 4,000, supported in part by a large logging operation nearby. Today, it's possible to walk about 9 miles of trail that was once built as an access road from the Sweetgrass Landing to the Sweetgrass Station. An alternative is to paddle in on canoes on Sweetgrass Creek. In addition, some of the buildings on the edge of the corral are still standing, and can be booked at no charge by contacting the park service: *Superintendent, Wood Buffalo National Park* (Box 750, Fort Smith, NWT X0E 0P0; phone: 403-872-2349). The buildings provide a site from which it's still possible to view the black bear, wolves, and bison in their native habitat.

The wood and plains bison interbred to produce a hybrid that adapts well to the cold. They are frequently visible lounging beside the road or wallowing in the dust to get rid of flies and mosquitoes. Photographers should be prepared: Bison and black bear normally will dash out of view when they see a car (buffalo may merely ignore you); nevertheless, don't get out of your vehicle.

When camping, keep your food in the vehicle or tied up high, never in your tent, unless you want unwelcome visitors. There are special regulations for camping and hiking in national parks. If you're hiking one of the many trails in the park for a couple of days, you'll need a special campfire permit (free), available from a park officer or park headquarters in Fort Smith. Schedules for hikes, lectures, films, and arrangements for licensed, private naturalist guides for day or overnight trips are available at the park office. For further information contact: *Superintendent, Wood Buffalo National Park,* Box 750, Fort Smith, Northwest Territories X0E 0P0 (phone: 403-872-2349).

A variety of features are rare to the area — northern areas of the park are dotted with sinkholes typical of Karst topography, and in the eastern central area, near Fort Smith, here are expansive salt plains encompassing some 250 square miles. Early traders and natives used the salt in their diets and as a medium of trade.

On the highway near the Angus fire tower, 6 miles (10 km) inside the park, there's a sinkhole 80 feet deep and 120 feet across. Sinkholes are created by the collapse of underground caves. Pine Lake, south of Fort Smith, is composed of three adjoining sinkholes 70 feet deep filled with water. If spelunking is what you're after, the park office can direct you to little-explored caves.

Highway 5 takes you into Fort Smith, 1 mile (1.6 km) north of the Alberta-NWT border. Five miles (8 km) south of town the highway splits into the 185-mile (296-km) loop road through the southeastern portion of the park. Forty miles (64 km) south of the junction on the west fork of the loop road is the Pine Lake campground, with graveled tenting pads and services for RVs. (A special permit required for fishing in national parks is available for a nominal fee at the warden's station, 1 mile (1.6 km) from the campground and at Fort Smith headquarters.)

The west fork of the loop road continues south 50 miles (81 km) to Peace Point on the Peace River. If you want to travel the entire loop, check first at the warden station — the section past Peace Point can become impassable after heavy rains, but in dry conditions, you may well continue toward Carlson's Fire Tower on a back country road busy with bison.

Starting back at the junction of the loop road, the east fork takes you on a 15-mile (24-km) drive along Slave River past Mountain, Pelican, and Cassette rapids to Fort Fitzgerald, the southern terminus of the portage around this navigation bottleneck. The road is in good shape for another 40 miles (64 km), to the Hay Camp forest fire control base. Inquire before proceeding farther.

Goods shipped on barges from Fort McMurry once portaged 23 miles from Fort Fitzgerald, more commonly known as Fitz, to Bell Rock, just north of Fort Smith. The four rapids have taken the lives of several unwary travelers who thought they could shoot the white water. The name Rapids of the Drowned speaks for itself. Goods stopped coming through Fort Smith after terminal facilities were built in Hay River in the mid-1960s. Although some people live here, Fitz is almost a ghost town. Originally called Smith's Landing, the town was renamed in honor of RCMP Inspector F. J. Fitzgerald, who died in 1911 along with three companions attempting a patrol by dog team from Fort McPherson to Dawson City. (See Fort McPherson in the *Dawson City to Inuvik* route for more about Fitzgerald.)

The Mountain Rapids also are the nesting site for the world's northernmost rookery of white pelicans. You can see these graceful birds in the rapids, although they feed mostly in the surrounding lakes. Many trails lead from the road to the bluff overlooking the rapids and the pelican's nesting site, which may be endangered if plans go ahead for a mammoth hydroelectric project on the Mountain Rapids south of Fort Smith.

For information on naturalist-oriented hiking, paddling, rowing, dog sledding, and year-round outdoor gear rentals for Wood Buffalo National Park and vicinity, contact *SubArctic Wilderness Adventures,* PO Box 685, Fort Smith, NWT X0E 0P0 (phone: 403-872-2467).

FORT SMITH: This town, like many other northern settlements, started out as a Hudson's Bay post in 1874. Its strategic position on a portage contributed to its growth. Everyone traveling north on the main water route of Peace River passed through here. The federal government established Smith as the main administrative center for all the NWT in 1911. In 1967, when the government decided to administer out of the Territories instead of Ottawa, Yellowknife was chosen as the NWT capital. Many residents were upset by this at the time but now feel it was the best thing to happen to the town. It is now a regional administrative center for the NWT government as well as the territory's academic and vocational training center.

Fort Smith was named after Donald Alexander Smith, the first Baron of Strathcona, who drove the last spike in Canada's transcontinental railroad in 1885. Ironically, the railroad was built to Hay River, which stunted the growth of Fort Smith. The major barge company, Northern Transportation Ltd., moved its transshipment point to Hay River so barges no longer had to make the trip from Fort McMurray, Alberta, to Great Slave Lake via the Slave River.

The town of 2,500 is large enough to meet most travelers' needs. There's a motel, a hotel, 12 bed and breakfast guesthouses, and 2 restaurants for those who are not camping. Food supplies are available at either the *Hudson's Bay* or *Kaeser's* general store. Several gas stations sell fuel and can service your vehicle. All stores are clustered in a 2-block section of downtown.

Visit *North of 60 Books* (71 Portage Ave.; phone: 403-872-2606), where Ib and Lillian Kristensen sell northern handicrafts and gifts. The workshop-bookstore features the largest and best collection of books about the north. A big attraction is the mounted head of a "muffaloose," a cross between moose and buffalo that has become the town's symbol. This rare animal was discovered under curious circumstances after a year of bad forest fires — but you can hear the story at the workshop. Open year-round.

Another must for visitors is the *Northern Life Museum* (110 King St., 403-872-2859) which houses one of the best collections in the north of traditional native crafts, photographs, and artifacts of a disappearing way of life. Open year-round.

There's a public campground beside the Slave River on the northern side of town. Drinking water and showers are available, and there is a dump station for RVs.

BEST EN ROUTE

Due to the scarcity of accommodations in the Northwest Territories, make reservations as far in advance as possible. Expect to pay $40 and up per night for a double room in the hotels listed. All prices are quoted in US dollars.

HAY RIVER

Caribou – In the new section of Hay River (built up since a big flood in 1967), this motel features 29 rooms, kitchenettes, phones, TV sets, steam baths, whirlpool baths, and car plug-ins. Licensed dining, lounge. Open year-round. Mailing address: PO Box 1114, Hay River, NWT X0E 0R0 (phone: 403-874-6706).

Cedar Rest – Right on the highway, this motel has 28 suites and 12 rooms with kitchenettes; all have waterbeds and satellite TV. Mailing address: PO Box 540, Hay River NWT X0E 0R0 (phone: 403-874-3732).

Harbour House – A bed and breakfast establishment with 6 rooms, it also has a crafts center. Boats, canoes, and surfboards are also available, as is take-out food. Mailing address: PO Box 54, Hay River, NWT XOE 0R0 (phone: 403-874-2233).

Hay River – On Hay River in Old Town, this cedar-log place has 16 renovated rooms available in winter, 38 in summer. TV sets, phone, licensed dining, a café, a lounge, entertainment, and a convenience store. Mailing address: PO Box 487, Hay River, NWT X0E 0R0 (phone: 403-874-2951).

Migrator – This motel has 24 rooms, and if you prefer to do your own cooking, 6 have kitchenettes. On the main highway between the Old and New Towns. Mailing address: PO Box 1847, Hay River, NWT X0E 0R0 (phone: 403-874-6792).

Ptarmigan Inn – A 41-room hotel downtown that is in a complex housing a restaurant, dining lounge, downstairs bar, barbershop, and a bank. Mailing address: PO Box 1000, Hay River, NWT X0E 0R0 (phone: 403-874-6781).

FORT SMITH

Pelican Rapids Inn – Some of the 50 rooms are equipped with kitchens; all have private bath, radio, a TV set, and carpets. In the center of town. Mailing address: PO Box 52, Fort Smith, NWT X0E 0P0 (phone: 403-872-2789).

Pinecrest – Most of the 28 rooms have TV sets and private baths. There also is a cocktail lounge, a restaurant, and showers on the premises. Near Wood Buffalo National Park. Mailing address: PO Box 127, Fort Smith, NWT X0E 0P0 (phone: 403-872-2320).

■ **Note:** For half the price of hotels in the Fort Smith area, you can enjoy bed and breakfast in the home of a NWT family. A dozen families lease out their rooms and, by arrangement, will prepare extra meals and do laundry. Contact *SubArctic Wilderness Adventures,* PO Box 685, Fort Smith, NWT (phone: 403-872-2467).

Nova Scotia

Nova Scotia is a province of two parts: the peninsula of Nova Scotia, which is connected to the mainland by a narrow isthmus over the Bay of Fundy, and Cape Breton Island, the northern extreme of the province, linked to the rest of the peninsula by a mile-long causeway. The Atlantic Ocean beats against the long eastern shore of this Maritime Province while the Bay of Fundy and Gulf of St. Lawrence lie to the west. With the sea all around, this long, narrow strip of land naturally has an economy based largely on the fishing trade. From its southern tip in the Bay of Fundy to the northern St. Lawrence Gulf coast, Nova Scotia encompasses 21,425 square miles of fishing villages, ferry towns, and cities with excellent harbors. The Bay of Fundy slope in the southwestern section, the isthmus, and southern Cape Breton are the most lush and fertile parts of the island, while the rural and rocky northeastern reaches of Cape Breton support coal mining and steel production.

Nova Scotia is a mosaic of half a dozen cultural influences. The French and the English struggled for decades to control the land that some 18th-century cynics called "Nova Scarcity." During the 1600s, settlement by both countries was sporadic. In 1720, when the French built their strategic Fortress of Louisbourg on Cape Breton Island, the tussle over Nova Scotia began in earnest. Twenty-five years later, a band of New Englanders captured the fort. Rather than rejoice, Britain handed it back to France in return for French opposition to Bonnie Prince Charlie's claim to the British throne. Enraged, the New Englanders demanded an English base in Nova Scotia — the result was Halifax. As Britain's control over the peninsula tightened, they expelled the French-speaking Acadians and destroyed Louisbourg. These moves helped to steer the rest of Canada into the arms of the British empire.

Other groups began arriving in Nova Scotia: Germans settled on the Atlantic shore, southwest of Halifax, turning Lunenburg into a thriving port; waves of Loyalists rushed in after the American Revolution; shiploads of Irish came, seeking relief from the potato famines of the 1840s; Scots, displaced by the Highland Clearances, landed at Pictou County on the northwestern shore and at Cape Breton with its highlandlike glens; and blacks settled near Halifax after the War of 1812.

Halifax is the capital of Nova Scotia and the commercial, administrative, and military center of the four Maritime Provinces. Its metropolitan population of about 290,000 (including Dartmouth and surrounding communities) encompasses almost one-third of Nova Scotia's 874,000 people. Even so, it retains its small-town flavor — shady, tree-lined streets, stately Georgian buildings, and active pubs. For a complete report on *Halifax,* see THE CITIES.

Although Halifax and Dartmouth (facing one another across Halifax Harbour), midway on Nova Scotia's long Atlantic coast, are the province's largest urban centers, many people start their tours of the area from Yarmouth, on the southwestern coast where the Atlantic and the Bay of Fundy meet. This is the docking point of ferries from both Portland and Bar Harbor, Maine. We have divided the province into three routes: from Yarmouth along the Bay of Fundy to Amherst, through Nova Scotia's Acadian country; from Yarmouth south and east along the Atlantic shore to the Strait of Canso, through the Atlantic coast uplands scenery and a series of ever more fascinating fishing villages; and from Amherst across the Strait of Canso through Cape Breton Island, including a stop at the restoration of Fort Louisbourg and a drive along the beautiful Cabot Trail. This last route goes through Scottish Nova Scotia, an area settled by Scots and so filled with lochs and glens that it is almost a miniature of Scotland.

Information: *Nova Scotia Tourism,* 136 Commercial St., Portland, ME 04101 (outside Maine within the Continental US, 800-341-6096; from Maine, 800-492-0643); or *Nova Scotia Department of Tourism and Culture,* 4th Fl., Cornwallis Pl., 1601 Water St., Halifax, NS B3J 3C6 (phone: 902-424-5000).

Yarmouth to Amherst

The 324-mile (518-km) drive from Yarmouth to Amherst along the Bay of Fundy shore is a ramble through French Nova Scotia along the stunning coastline forged by the powerful tide of the Bay of Fundy. It passes through Acadian villages where the daily language is still the odd French dialect brought by the region's first French settlers. Crossing Annapolis Valley, it skirts the province's most prosperous farmlands. Near the end of the route stands tragic Springhill, where a 1958 mining disaster claimed 76 lives; the town's survival is a testament to the determination and character of the townspeople. The Bay of Fundy always is within easy access.

The route virtually traces the province's history. Here you can walk through the first settlements established in the early 1600s; view the battlegrounds where the French and the English vied for new lands; and remember Longfellow's star-crossed lovers, Evangeline and Gabriel, whose story represents the fate of the Acadians.

Along the route, there's a gradual change of atmosphere that coincides with the changing landscape. As French turns into English, rocky, wind-blown fishing villages are replaced by thriving agricultural communities. The 170-mile (272-km) Bay of Fundy, always nearby on the left, gradually narrows as its bottom imperceptibly rises. This results in the highest tides in the world at the bay's eastern end, the Minas Basin. Generations of Nova Scotians have watched these tides with fascination, some dreaming of the day when that enormous power might be harnessed to provide inexpensive energy for industry.

Although the roads along the Bay of Fundy are sometimes narrow and winding, they are generally good. The road most often follows Routes 1 and 2 and the Evangeline Trail and the Glooscap Trail, signposted routes set up by the Nova Scotia Department of Tourism. The gastronomic attractions of the route are enormous, featuring fish and Acadian dishes in French Nova

Scotia and, a bit farther on, fresh fruit and vegetables in abundance from roadside stands in the Annapolis Valley. And there are countless opportunities to pull over and watch the fishing boats in the weirs, see the gulls diving, or simply to enjoy the cool bay breeze.

To get to Yarmouth, you can take a ferry from either Portland, Maine, or from Bar Harbor. Some ferries have rooms for cars and overnight berth accommodations. Reservations on the Bar Harbor–Yarmouth run aboard the MV *Bluenose* can be obtained by calling 800-423-7344 (from Maine) or 800-341-7981 (in the continental US). The Portland-Yarmouth ferry, the *Scotia Prince,* also includes cruise features such as duty-free shopping, a casino, formal dining room, and nightclub with live entertainment; for bookings, call 800-482-0955 (from Maine) or 800-341-7540 (from the rest of the US). Advance reservations on both the Bar Harbor–Yarmouth ferry and the *Scotia Prince* are subject to cancellation if tickets are not picked up 1 hour before sailing. *Air Canada* also has direct flights to Yarmouth from Boston.

At Yarmouth, a major gateway, arrange for membership in the Order of the Good Cheer, the oldest social club in North America. Samuel de Champlain, the great explorer and historian, formed the club more than 375 years ago in an attempt to cheer up his men in the face of the loneliness, disease, and harsh weather of the New World. Today, the order is open to all those who visit Nova Scotia for at least 3 days. There are no initiation fees or dues, and members of the order never meet formally. Members are, however, required to have a good time, remember Nova Scotia pleasantly, speak of the province kindly, and come back again. You can join the club at the Nova Scotia Government Tourist Bureau located at the ferry dock. You might as well; you're bound to fulfill club requirements in any case.

YARMOUTH: This attractive town's narrow, lighthouse-guarded harbor serves as a haven for ferries and herring seiners. (The latter are boats named for seines, the large, weighted nets used by fishermen to trap their catch.) These craft can be seen as they come and go in the harbor or docked below Main Street. With a population of 7,600, Yarmouth is the largest community in the province west of Halifax. It is a transportation, commercial, and shopping center for much of western Nova Scotia. A former global shipping capital — with the world's highest per capita ship tonnage — Yarmouth today relies on fishery and fish processing plants, two textile mills, machine shops, and a woodworking plant. The downtown has maintained much of its 19th-century architecture. A walking-tour guide is available from the municipal tourist information center (phone: 902-742-6639) and leaves from the *Yarmouth Historical Museum* on Collins St. Bus tours also are available, leaving from the *Rodds Grand* hotel (Main St.). The town also features the *Fire Fighters Museum of Nova Scotia* (451 Main St.), with some equipment over 100 years old. At the *Yarmouth County Historical Society Museum* (22 Collins St.), a runic stone linked to the Norse explorations of AD 1000 is on display. This relic is cited as evidence that visitors came to North America long before Columbus.

Yarmouth offers some fine seafood restaurants. A noteworthy example is *Harris' Seafood,* (Highway 1 in Yarmouth). Its delicious fish, lobster, and fresh vegetables are popular with Nova Scotians and visitors alike.

En Route from Yarmouth – Travel along Route 1 through the Hebron area's "lupine trail," named for the wild herbs growing on both sides of the road. In June, a blanket of white, pink, and blue spreads back from the road into the fields.

Passing by Port Maitland, you might see oxen. On the rocky but highly successful commercial dairy farms, they were more suitable than horses in the days when draft animals were used. Located just over 4 miles (7 km) east of Route 1, the Lake George fish hatchery annually provides millions of trout and salmon for release in the lakes and streams of western Nova Scotia. Thousands of black-backed gulls nest on the islands in Lake George. As you cross into the municipality of Clare, you enter the district settled by Acadians, the early French settlers who named Nova Scotia "Acadie." They were expelled from the province in 1755 by the British; later they returned. In fact, 335 Acadian families are said to have walked from Boston to Digby in the summer of 1768. In Clare, you'll feel as if you've entered a different country. The residents still speak a French quite different from that spoken in Paris or Quebec. And just as the language has been preserved, so have the culture and traditions. Even the smallest communities along the "French shore" are dominated by a large Catholic church; wooden homes and farmhouses all look out to sea. As you follow Route 1, consider a side trip to North Bear Cove and South Bear Cove, where cliffs meet the ocean. After returning to Route 1, you soon reach Clare Park at Smuggler's Cove. During prohibition, when liquor was shipped illegally to the US, the maze of coves here provided rum-runners with hideaways. You'll find their lair at the bottom of the footpath leading down to the picnic area.

METEGHAN: This small town of about 900 people is typical of communities along the coast. It was settled in 1785 by the Acadians; La Vieille Maison, one of the oldest homes, has been preserved. (Privately owned, the home is occasionally open to visitors.) This is a shipbuilding town, and Meteghan's skilled craftsmen gained international recognition in 1966, when they built a 165-foot, three-quarter-size replica of Donald McKay's famous American clipper ship *Flying Cloud* for Arthur Johnston of Philadelphia. The original was built in East Boston in 1851 and destroyed after going aground in 1874.

En Route from Meteghan – Upon entering the community of Saulnierville, look for the Acadian bakery, *Le Pain de Chez Nous,* and turn right to St. Benoni. Along the road you will see waterwheels and, perhaps, a logjam in the river. The jams still serve as bridges for the local lumbering industry.

CHURCH POINT: This tiny village has the tallest wooden church in North America. On the campus of Université Ste. Anne, the church and its small museum are open to visitors. From May to mid-October, tours are available with bilingual guides. The province's only French degree-granting institution, the college was founded in 1891 by Eudist (the Congregation of Jesus and Mary) priests from France and has traditionally attracted local students or those of Acadian descent from neighboring Canadian provinces and American states. Lately, however, the college has begun to interest larger numbers of English-speaking students eager to learn Canada's other official language. The *Acadian Festival of Clare,* held annually at Church Point, usually in the second week of July, features local crafts, music, and French Canadian specialties such as *rappie pie* (grated potatoes and chicken or rabbit baked in a crust). The celebration is the oldest Acadian festival in the Atlantic province.

En Route from Church Point – Less than a mile from Church Point is Grosses Coques, meaning "large clams." It's said that the clams in this district are the largest on the North American coast. Reportedly, they were so plentiful that the first settlers lived on them throughout their first winter. Just a 1½-mile drive to the left of Grosses Coques bridge takes you to Major's Point and its long, blue slate beach. The site of the first Acadian cemetery, this driftwood-studded beach is thick with clams. And it's a great spot for bird watching. In the village (pop. 357), a stone memorial marks the place of the first chapel. There's also a tablet on the site of the first frame house built in the town of Clare.

ST. BERNARD: Even though its population is only 322, St. Bernard supports a large stone cathedral with a seating capacity of 1,000. Construction of the church was started in 1910 and finished in 1942, and all material and work was supplied by local laborers. It is an interesting example of local conviction, if nothing else. Visitors are welcome.

En Route from St. Bernard – As you leave St. Bernard, look for a road off to the left that takes you to New Edinburgh, a bit over 2 miles (3 km) away. A loop will return you to Route 1, but along the way are beautiful views of the rustic seashore and countryside. Traces of the first townsite, settled by three Scottish Loyalists in 1783, still remain.

WEYMOUTH: Continuing along Route 1 (which becomes Route 101 in several miles) you come to Weymouth, settled by Loyalists in 1783 and named after Weymouth, Massachusetts. Colonel Moodie of North Carolina, a famous Loyalist, settled in this district and wrote an interesting diary of his experiences in the American Revolution. Weymouth is situated on St. Mary's Bay at the mouth of the Sissiboo River (an Indian name meaning "big river"); trading schooners formerly loaded there. Stores in the town are built on logs to allow the river's tides to pass underneath. Periodically, the first floors of the stores flood.

Just past Weymouth, at Weymouth North is a wharf off Fort Point Road; it's frequented by lobster and herring fishermen. Foreign ships load logs here for ports around the world. From the wharf you can see New Edinburgh across the Sissiboo River and Sandy Cove across St. Mary's Bay.

En Route from Weymouth – Five miles (8 km) from Weymouth North is Plympton, with an interesting variety of antiques and crafts shops. Just past Plympton is Savary Park, a provincial picnic site with a fine tidal pool beach and large groves of white birch and evergreen.

Five miles (8 km) farther is Marshalltown, former home of the late Maud Lewis, a primitive painter who won international acclaim. The Lewis residence, decorated with her work, has been removed for restoration by the *Nova Scotia Museum,* in Halifax. To the right off Route 101 is Acaciaville (pop. 141). From the Acaciaville hills there are fine views of Digby on the east and the Bay of Fundy on the west.

DIGBY: Like Yarmouth, Digby is a ferry town, served by Canadian National's MV *Princess of Acadia,* which carries cars and passengers to and from Saint John, New Brunswick, three times a day. Digby was named after Robert Digby, a British admiral who commanded the HMS *Atlanta,* the ship that conveyed 1,500 Loyalists from New England in 1783. Digby is one of Nova Scotia's more popular summer resorts, offering horseback riding, canoeing, and swimming. It also is the center of the highly profitable scallop fishery in the Bay of Fundy. Take a few minutes to walk to the end of the government wharf downtown to get a close look at the scallop draggers; perhaps you'll also see pulpwood and lumber being loaded onto ocean vessels for export. If you climb to the top of the hill by the high school, you'll get a beautiful view of Annapolis Basin. The *Pines Resort* hotel (see *Best en Route*) serves breakfast, lunch, and dinner. This government-owned establishment is open only in summer. *Digby Scallop Days* are held in August, and deep-sea fishing and whale watching excursions are available; check with municipal or provincial tourist bureaus.

En Route from Digby – It's a good idea to take a scenic side trip along the spit of land known as Digby Neck to its end at Brier Island. The trip, on Route 217, includes two short ferry rides, a distance of about 86 miles (129 km). Depending how often your ferry stops (it varies), it could take as long as 7 hours. Heading out on Digby Neck, you'll pass a number of sheep farms. Make a right turn downhill toward the Bay of Fundy into Centreville, one of the prettiest fishing villages in the province. There are several beautiful old churches along the road. In Centreville, *Les Raymond* sells smoked fish and other sea treats from his roadside smoke shop. Back on Route 217, just past Centreville, there is a well-kept picnic park at Lake Medway — a good spot for a swim. The lake water is usually 15 to 20 degrees warmer than that of the numbingly cold Bay of Fundy. (The lake is also stocked with trout.) Sandy Cove, 4 miles (6 km) farther down the road, is at the bottom of a big hill.

SANDY COVE: Leaving Route 217, take the road to the right and follow its meandering path to the long sandy beach on the Bay of Fundy side. At this beach you can have the best view of weir fishing, a style of fishing common only in the Bay of Fundy area. The weirs are long, thin trees driven into the seabed and lined with fishnet. Stretching out from the shore in a straight line, the weirs form a semicircle at the end. Fish are trapped in the large, rounded area after meeting and following the straight section of the weir to its end. If you are lucky, you might see the fishermen enter the weir with their boats to scoop up the fish. For good seafood and homemade bread in a dignified setting, try the *Olde Village Inn* (phone: 902-834-2202), a restored 1890 inn.

Sandy Cove also is the setting of the mysterious story of Jerome. This man was found on the beach one summer morning in 1854 with both legs freshly amputated above the knees. Two fishermen carried the man to a home, where he was made warm and given hot drinks. But he remained unresponsive and only muttered something that sounded like "Jerome." Since people believed he did not understand English, Jerome was later taken to Meteghan to converse with John Nicholas, a man who spoke to him in French, Italian, and German. Still he did not answer. Living with Nicholas and his family, Jerome eventually learned to walk on his stumps. And occasionally he had brief conversations with children. But most of the time Jerome crouched behind the kitchen stove with his head in his hands. Jerome's case was eventually brought to the attention of the provincial government, and an allowance of $2 per week was established for his keep and given to the Nicholas family. In 1912, 58 years after he was found on Sandy Cove beach, Jerome died, taking his mysterious past with him forever.

En Route from Sandy Cove – Continuing on Route 217, you pass Mink Cove and Little River, two prosperous fishing villages. Mink Cove is well known for its amethyst and quartz, often sought by rockhounds. The next village is East Ferry, where you can board the Joshua Slocum ferry for the 10-minute trip to Tiverton on Long Island. The round-trip fare is about 85¢ (CN$1) per car; pedestrians travel free. A 10-mile (16-km) trip brings you to Freeport and the second ferry ride to Brier Island.

BRIER ISLAND: Brier Island was the home of Joshua Slocum, who in July 1895 bade good-bye to his mother and set off to become the first man to single-handedly circumnavigate the earth. He accomplished this feat in his 36-foot, 9-inch sloop, *Spray,* which he had built himself. Slocum sailed for 3 years to complete his journey, arriving finally at Gloucester, Massachusetts. A plaque on the southern end of the island memorializes the solitary navigator. From here, follow the short walking trail along the cliffs with the waves crashing below. The island is a popular spot for bird and whale watchers.

You'll also want to wander about Westport, the small community where the ferry docks. Stained glass windows grace many of Westport's more well-to-do homes; these were brought from faraway lands long ago by seamen of the community. The waterfront is lined with fishing shacks and wharves on which lobster traps and orange floats are piled high, and to which bright Cape Island boats are moored. In the late afternoon, fishermen clean their catch along the wharf. If you want an easy opening gambit for conversation, ask any Brier Islander about the *Groundhog Day* storm. On February 2, 1976, a violent and largely unexpected storm devastated buildings along the waterfront and caused millions of dollars' damage. The memory has not easily faded. Birdwatchers will be impressed with the many species of both land and sea birds that concentrate in the area during migration periods. For advice on the province's best birding spots, check with the *Nova Scotia Bird Society,* through the *Nova Scotia Museum,* Halifax.

Before heading back on the ferry (which runs 24 hours a day), you may want a snack from the takeout counter by the ferry wharf, which features fish and chips — naturally, the fish are right out of the water.

En Route from Digby – When you return to Route 1, consider stopping at Smith's Cove. Here you can see the St. Anne's Birchbark Chapel on the grounds of Harbourview Inn. The chapel, over 60 years old, was built by a local craftsman in honor of a longtime summer visitor, an Anglican bishop. Nearby on Route 1 is the old *Methodist Church Museum* (1885).

The better restaurants on this leg of the journey are all located in the vicinity of Route 1 at Smith's Cove. *Hedley House* (phone: 902-245-2585), on the grounds of the *Hedley House* motor hotel, offers fresh fish and vegetables; the atmosphere is on the formal side. *Harbourview Country Inn* (phone: 902-245-5686) is well known for its Saturday night lobster boil around the swimming pool and its Sunday buffets. *Mountain Gap Inn* (phone: 902-245-5841 or 800 565-5020, in summer) also offers good meals.

BEAR RIVER: Route 1 crosses Route 101, the road to the river town of Bear River, known as the Switzerland of Nova Scotia (by the time you have crossed Acadian Nova Scotia, Scottish Nova Scotia, English Nova Scotia, and Swiss Nova Scotia, you may well feel it is the most international spot in the Maritimes). The river itself fronts the charming street of 100-year-old shops, each built on stilts as a precaution against untimely floods. The town's fondest folly is a full-scale, wood Dutch windmill, built a few miles out of town. It has a pleasant view of the river and a tearoom from which to enjoy it. Bear River is especially beautiful during the annual *Cherry Carnival* in July.

En Route from Bear River – Head back to Route 1 and Deep Brook. You'll pass Canadian Forces Base Cornwallis on the way to Clementsport. This community was settled by United Empire Loyalists in 1784. Many of its homes were formerly occupied by sea captains. The old Loyalist church of St. Edward, consecrated in 1788, houses many relics and is worth a visit. In a few miles you arrive at Fort Anne National Historic Park at Annapolis Royal.

FORT ANNE NATIONAL HISTORIC PARK: This 28-acre park was the first national historic park in the country. A section of the first fortress, built here in 1635 by d'Aulnay de Charnisay, is still maintained. Since its construction, the fort (then known as Port Royal) has been the scene of attacks by the English, the French, New Englanders, Indians, and even pirates.

In 1690, brigands burned the church and destroyed 28 homes, cremating a mother and her children in one fire. During the winter of 1709, after three attacks by New Englanders had been repulsed in the previous 5 years, three privateers sheltered at Port Royal. They had with them 55 Boston ships that they had seized during the summer. Stung by this latest outrage, the New Englanders launched another expedition in 1710, and in 8 days the fort was captured. It was renamed Annapolis Royal after Queen Anne. The key to the fort was carried to Boston (it was returned in 1922 and placed in the *Fort Anne Museum*). After its capture in 1710, it was attacked many more times, and England maintained a garrison of soldiers here until 1854.

Things have been preserved pretty much as they were then. The British officers' quarters, erected by the Duke of Kent, father of Queen Victoria, originally consisted of 30 rooms, each with a fireplace and a view of the fort and Annapolis Basin. Now the officers' quarters are a museum open to the public. An Acadian room with its original wall beams and ceiling and a complete collection of Acadian kitchen utensils and clothing is part of the museum's displays. There is also a historic library. Fort Anne is open year-round. The museum is open mid-May to mid-October, 9 AM to 6 PM; remainder of the year, weekdays 9 AM to 5 PM. No admission charge.

Two miles (3 km) from Annapolis Royal, turn left for the 7-mile (11-km) drive to Port Royal National Historic Park.

PORT ROYAL NATIONAL HISTORIC PARK: The tiny village of Port Royal is the oldest permanent white settlement north of Florida in North America. A replica of the original Port Royal Habitation that Samuel de Champlain and Pierre du Gua de Monts built in 1605 is on the original site. The replica is exact in size and detail. The building's timber framing was mortised, tenoned, and pinned together in the old manner; no spikes or nails were used. It was here that Champlain founded the Order of the Good Cheer. The park is open year round, but the buildings are open only from June to mid-October, 9 AM to 6 PM.

   En Route from Port Royal – Drive back to Route 1 and continue to Bridgetown, traveling into the Annapolis Valley, framed by the North and South Mountains. As you proceed farther into the valley, you'll probably note an increase in the temperature; the mountains protect the area from the winds and the fog off the Bay of Fundy. The warmer weather has helped make the valley an area that's famed for its produce, particularly apples. The region is probably most beautiful at apple blossom time in late May or early June. Bridgetown (pop. 1,037), a pleasant dairying and fruit farming community, is situated at the head of the Annapolis River. Paradise, at the junction of the Paradise and Annapolis rivers, marked the eastern limit of French settlements in the Port Royal region. Near Paradise is the 9-hole *Eden Golf and Country Club*. Greens-fee players are welcome. As you explore the area, keep an eye open for signs of fairs and church suppers. They have terrific home-cooked food.

LAWRENCETOWN: This is the regional headquarters for sport fishing and hunting. Signs in the town direct you to where you can hire guides with canoes. The town also has a land surveying and photogrammetry school, the only such school in the country. The 5-day *Annapolis County Agricultural Exhibition* is held here in August.

   En Route from Lawrencetown – The next main community along the way is Middleton, so named because it stands about halfway between Annapolis Royal and Kentville. Just 5 miles (8 km) off the road from Middleton, at Mt. Hanly, there is a scenic view of the Annapolis Valley. Passing into Kings County, you enter the best farmland in the province. In addition to apples, plums, pears, and cherries, the area supports a substantial dairy industry. Along the rivers flowing into the Minas Basin great stretches of diked marshes yield roots, grain, and hay. Kingston, a key agricultural service area, hosts the province's largest steer barbecue on the second Saturday in July. The *Paragon Golf Course* also is in Kingston. Canada's largest antisubmarine air base is located at Greenwood, just off Route 1. The military community totals about 9,000 and has what amounts to its own village, including schools, churches, and recreational facilities. Alfred C. Fuller, who founded the Fuller Brush Company, was born in this region; his home, near Berwick, is a private residence. Berwick, just off Route 1, has two fruit- and vegetable-processing plants, a bakery serving all of mainland Nova Scotia, large fruit packing warehouses, and a meat-processing plant.

KENTVILLE: This shire of Kings County is the home of the *Apple Blossom Festival,* held in late May or early June. The *Old Kings Courthouse Heritage Museum* (37 Cornwallis St.) houses a collection of social and natural history of Kings County, the community history, and the genealogy of the Kings Historical Society (at the courthouse, 37 Cornwallis St.; phone: 902-678-6237). Open year round. No admission charge. The *George Warden Railway Museum* has hundreds of rail-related items. Memorial Park has tennis courts, baseball diamonds, a public swimming pool, and a football field. Between Kentville and Wolfville, there is a lovely side trip for rockhounds, photographers, and hikers. Route 358 winds through several attractive communities before coming to The Lookoff, a spot which offers a spectacular view of Minas Basin, the valleys of six rivers, and parts of five counties. Farther down the road is Scots Bay, with a broad rocky beach and low cliffs, where agates and other stones continually wash up on shore, particularly in spring and early summer. From the end of the road, a hiking trail leads to Cape Split, one of the best walks in the province. Much of the trail is inland, but it emerges at the tip of the cape and ends with a breathtaking panorama from 150-foot cliffs.

WOLFVILLE: This town, the center of Henry Wadsworth Longfellow's Land of Evangeline, also is the home of Acadia University, which was founded by the Nova Scotia Baptist Education Society in 1838. Wolfville is the closest town to Grand Pré and is a convenient base for explorations in this historical area. Nearby Evangeline Beach offers saltwater bathing that is almost warm.

GRAND PRÉ: The name Grand Pré ("great meadow") refers to the large number of dikes in the area, but the community is better known as the site of one of the oldest French settlements in the province and the setting for Longfellow's famous poem *Evangeline.* Between 1755 and 1763, nearly 14,000 Acadians were expelled by the British, who feared that the peaceful Acadians would challenge their military authority. On September 5, 1755, standing on the steps of Grand Pré's Acadian church, Lieutenant-Colonel John Winslow announced the Expulsion. In the next 4 months, 6,000 Acadians were torn from their homes and deported. Longfellow imagined that among those sent away was a girl named Evangeline, and her lover, Gabriel. Separated by the Expulsion, Evangeline spent the rest of her life searching unsuccessfully for Gabriel.

Grand Pré National Historic Park, a memorial to the deported Acadians, features a statue of Evangeline. Viewed from the right side, the bronze statue depicts Evangeline as a young girl, but as the viewer moves left, the face seems to change to that of an old woman, still searching. The story of the Acadians is recounted by the park staff in a reconstructed Acadian church serving as a museum and interpretative center. Although the park is open year-round, its buildings are open to the public only from June to mid-October. No admission charge.

Following the subsequent peace, many of the exiled Acadians came back to Nova Scotia. But most residents of Grand Pré are descendants of New Englanders.

Be sure to visit the *Grand Pré Pottery* shop, then treat yourself to *Evangeline Snack Bar*'s luscious strawberry shortcake, pies, and other good food.

Also see the Church of the Covenanters, constructed by New England planters in 1790, with its quaint box pews and pulpit halfway to the ceiling. Worth a visit, too, are the estate vineyards of Grand Pré Wines, which are open to visitors, preferably by appointment.

HANTSPORT: You soon pass into Hants County, where agricultural land changes into a lumbering and light industry area. In the middle of the last century, Hantsport, along the Avon River, served a large number of oceangoing clipper ships. Today it is a major shipping port for the gypsum quarried near Windsor. Observation Lookoff provides an excellent view of the river tides and the loading of the gypsum boats. William Hall, the first black to win the Victoria Cross for heroism, died in Hantsport. The son of an escaped Virginia slave, Hall was rewarded for heroism during the relief of Lucknow during the Indian Mutiny.

WINDSOR: The remnants of Fort Edward, built by the British in 1750, are here. Off King Street and Fort Edward Street stands the oldest blockhouse in Canada. The *Haliburton Memorial Museum* (Clifton Ave.) is the former residence of Judge Thomas Charles Haliburton, known as the founder of North American humor, who created the fictional character Sam Slick. The *Hants County Exhibition* is held here annually in September. Started in 1765, it's believed to be the oldest fair in Canada. King's College School, the oldest educational institution outside the United Kingdom in the British Commonwealth, also is located here.

En Route from Windsor – Take Route 1 to Three Mile Plains before turning left onto Route 14 toward Brooklyn. At Brooklyn, take Route 215 toward Summerville along the Glooscap Trail. This route parallels the drive from Grand Pré to Hantsport and Windsor on the other side of the Avon River. The area, like Hantsport, has active gypsum and barite mines and an anhydrite quarry. As you pass Tennycape, look to your left to Economy Point, on the other side of Minas Basin. Plans for a dam between Economy Point and Burntcoat Head to harness the power of the Bay of Fundy high tides are under discussion. The tides here have been measured at 54 feet — the highest in the world. The small town of Noel, settled by families from Northern Ireland in 1762, is farther along the shore. Local lore has it that the legendary Captain Kidd brought his pirate ship to Noel to be remasted. It's said that although he threw bars of silver to those who supplied timbers, the locals would not touch the pirate's ill-gotten gains. The road then follows the path of the Shubenacadie River to South Maitland, where a pronounced tidal bore appears twice each day. This wall of white water advances over the muddy bottom, signaling the advent of another high tide. From Shubenacadie, pick up Route 2 north. Head for Stewiacke's provincial wildlife park, which contains a large variety of native Nova Scotian animals and birds. The area around Shubenacadie and Stewiacke — located halfway between the Equator and the North Pole — is headquarters for the Micmac Indians of Nova Scotia.

TRURO: This town (pop. 12,500) is a major service community for the surrounding area. Victoria Park, a 1,000-acre natural playground, has two picturesque waterfalls. At the Nova Scotia Agricultural College (on Bible Hill), there's a demonstration farm open to visitors. In August, Truro hosts the *Nova Scotia Provincial Exhibition,* the largest attraction of its kind in the province. From June through October, visitors also can take in harness racing at Truro. *Glengarry House* in the *Glengarry* motel (138 Willow St.) serves good food, especially fish, in a colonial atmosphere. Equally good is the food at the *Palliser* restaurant in the *Tideview* motel (Tidal Bore Rd.); it also offers a view of the tidal bore. To check on the arrival of this natural phenomenon, which rolls into the Salmon River at the rate of a foot a minute, call *Dial-A-Tide* at 902-426-5494.

    En Route from Truro – Take Route 2 west following the Glooscap Trail through Masstown, where a number of dikes built by the Acadians still function. There's also good striped bass fishing near the mouth of the Bass River. Continuing on Route 2, you climb Economy Mountain. From the peak, there is a spectacular view of Minas Basin. At Five Islands (pop. 199), you can see the five pieces of land the town is named for. According to Indian tradition, the god Glooscap hurled these great chunks of earth at a beaver in anger. Moose Island, one of the five, is supposed to be the hiding place of pirate treasure; the others are called Egg, Diamond, Pinnacle, and Long. Still on Route 2, you now pass through a narrow gorge between two wood-covered hills to Parrsboro.

PARRSBORO: A port town, Parrsboro is across the Minas Basin from Cape Blomidon. The basin features the world's highest tides. Weir fishing, like that done in the Bay of Fundy near Digby, is carried on here. In August, amateur geologists from across the continent gather for the annual Rockhound Roundup. Amethysts, agates, and other attractive minerals may be found along the shores. Follow the main street through Parrsboro and, about 1 mile (1.6 km) from town, on the left, you'll see Ottawa House, once the summer home of Sir Charles Tupper. Born in Amherst, Tupper became Prime Minister of Canada in 1896.

    There's a museum and tourist bureau at the three-way intersection near the center of Parrsboro. Check here for tide times and get a complimentary guide for a beach tour and rockhounding. Outside the museum, a cairn commemorates the plane that left Parrsboro in 1919 to fly the first airmail service between Nova Scotia and the US. A giant statue of Glooscap stands nearby. By pushing a button, you can hear the legend of the Indian god.

The *White House* (Upper Main St.) is open all year and serves home-cooked dinners from 5:30 to 7 PM.

En Route from Parrsboro – Take a short side trip to Advocate Harbor along Route 209. This winding road, rising from sea level to 750 feet, unveils a series of extraordinary vistas. At Fox River you can see the picturesque rock formation of Cape Split across Minas Channel. The high hills on the right are known as Woods Mountain. Port Greville was at one time a great shipbuilding center, and yachts and motorboats are still built here. Pollock, haddock, and halibut are caught along this shore, and charter boats are readily available.

SPENCER'S ISLAND: This tiny community is misnamed — it's not, in fact, an island. One of the world's great mystery ships, the *Mary Celeste,* was built here in 1861. Eleven years later, on October 27, Captain Ben Briggs and ten others, including his wife and their 10-year-old daughter, left New York for Genoa in the 100-foot-long brigantine. Twenty-seven days later the Nova Scotian brigantine *Del Gratia,* sailed by Captain Morehouse of Bear River, Digby County, came upon the *Mary Celeste,* sailing erratically. It was soon found that there was nobody aboard and its one lifeboat was gone. Although there were no signs of violence, the compass was knocked out and ruined, and the navigation instruments had been removed. There had not been any storms, and the last entry in the log was marked for 8 AM, 2 days earlier. No trace of any of the 11 people or of the lifeboat was ever found.

En Route from Spencer's Island – At nearby Advocate, there's a rock formation known as the Three Sisters; legend claims it is the spot that Glooscap's three sisters were all turned into stone. Turn back to Parrsboro to rejoin Route 2 toward Springhill. Mapleton is the center of the local maple sugar industry. It's said that Indians of the area discovered that maple sap becomes sweet and thick through boiling while cooking potatoes in the sticky substance. Maple sugar and superior maple cream are sold in most candy stores.

SPRINGHILL: This town of 4,900 holds a special place in the hearts of all Nova Scotians. Coal mining began here in 1872, and the 4,000-foot No. 2 mine was the deepest in Canada. In 1891, 125 miners lost their lives in a mining accident. In October 1956, an explosion occurred in No. 4, trapping 118 miners; 39 eventually died in the pits. Just after *Christmas* the following year, fire destroyed half of the downtown business district. Then, on October 23, 1958, a "bump" (a great disturbance of the earth in a mine) in No. 2 trapped 174 men. A desperate attempt to reach the men began, and 81 were found alive in the first few days. After 6 days of searching, the rescuers had almost abandoned hope, when 12 more miners were found alive; 2 days later, 7 more were rescued. In all, 76 miners died. And in the 2 years following the disaster, 2,400 people left the town to seek employment elsewhere. The tragic events of 1958 are told in "Springhill Mine Disaster," a song made popular by the *Brothers Four.* Springhill's suffering did not end there: On July 20, 1975, another fire destroyed 75% of the downtown business district. The mines are now closed.

En Route from Springhill – The next town is Amherst, 22 miles (35 km) northwest, the inland gateway to Nova Scotia and the geographical center of the Maritime Provinces. It is built on rising ground above the famous Tantramar marshes. Set in a 187-year-old house with period decor, the *Drury Lane Steak House* is 3 miles (5 km) from Amherst just across the border in New Brunswick, at the junction of Routes 2 and 16. Some claim it's one of the best restaurants in Canada.

BEST EN ROUTE

The road from Yarmouth to Amherst includes a variety of interesting accommodations: a grand old hotel that used to be run by a railroad, an inn tucked away in an apple orchard, and a motel built by Nova Scotia Indians. And equally as various are the prices of these establishments. We've rated places charging over $35 for a double room as expensive; from $17 to $35 as moderate; and below $17 as inexpensive. All prices are quoted in US dollars.

YARMOUTH

Rodd Colony Harbour Inn – This has a lovely view of Yarmouth Harbour and facilities that include a licensed lounge and dining room with entertainment, a sauna, and mini-bars in the rooms. Open year-round. At the ferry terminal (phone: 902-742-9194). Expensive.

Rodd's Grand – One of the most modern hostelries in Yarmouth, it has 138 rooms, each with bath and color TV set. Some rooms have lovely views of the harbor. Open year-round. 417 Main St. (phone: 902-742-2446). Expensive.

Gateway Farms Bed & Breakfast – Accommodations are available in 3 rooms and 2 shared baths, open May 1 to November 1. Breakfast is served from 7 to 8:30 AM. Chegoggin Rd., off Route 1 (phone: 902-742-9786). Moderate.

DIGBY

Pines – By far the best-equipped in the area, this is a grand old place. Originally operated by the *Canadian Pacific Railway,* it's now run by the provincial government. There are 83 rooms, 60 cottages, an excellent golf course, tennis courts, and shuffleboard. Open only in summer. PO Box 70 (phone: 902-245-2511). Expensive.

Westway House Bed & Breakfast – This spot offers 5 rooms (1 with private bath and 2 shared baths). View of Fundy tides and whale watching can be arranged. 6 Carleton St., Digby (phone: 902-245-5071). Moderate.

SOUTH MILFORD

Milford House – Very close to Kejimkujik National Park, due south of Port Royal in the center of the province, is this country lodge devoted primarily to the joys of canoeing, fishing, swimming, and the like. There is a main lodge and lakeside cabins, each of which has a dock. Open mid-June to mid-September. RR 4, South Milford, Annapolis Royal B0S 1AO (phone: 902-532-2617). Expensive.

WOLFVILLE

Old Orchard Inn – Nestled in an apple orchard, overlooking the university town of Wolfville, this inn has 110 rooms and 30 rustic chalets. There also is nightly entertainment, cross-country skiing, an indoor swimming pool, saunas, tennis courts, bicycle rentals, and a children's playground. Open year-round. Take Exit 11 off Highway 101 or Route 358 off Route 2. Mailing address: PO Box 1090 (phone: 902-542-5751). Expensive.

TRURO

Best Western Glengarry – This 90-unit motel has spacious grounds, a heated outdoor swimming pool, and complimentary use of cribs. 150 Willow St. (phone: 902-893-4311 or 800-528-1234). Expensive.

Palliser – This resort's flood-lit view of the tidal bore is a main draw. Facilities include a licensed restaurant, 41 units, and 1 cottage. Route 102 (phone: 902-893-8951). Expensive.

Walker House – A small bed and breakfast establishment with 3 rooms, 1 full bath. No pets allowed. Open year-round. 74 Walker St. (phone: 902-895-1076). Moderate.

PARRSBORO

Glooscap – An 11-unit motel with a children's playground, fishing, boating, swimming, and hunting nearby. Open May 1 through November 30. Crossroads. Mailing address: PO Box 640 (phone: 902-254-3135). Moderate.

BRIDGETOWN

Bridgetown – Part of the Friendship Inns organization, the 33-unit motel is well situated for excursions around the Annapolis Valley. Facilities include a dining room, lounge, heated outdoor pool, sauna, and games room. 83 Granville St. (phone: 902-665-4491). Expensive.

Yarmouth to the Strait of Canso

Traveling along the southern and eastern shores of the province, you'll pass through dozens of quaint, hospitable fishing villages. These communities have held great significance for Nova Scotia's economy since the province was first settled, and they could become even more important as Canada asserts greater control over its offshore waters. In addition, the route offers some most impressive scenery. But don't be too put off if, just as soon as you start, you run into fog. All of Nova Scotia's Atlantic coast can be foggy. Yet it rarely lasts long, often burning off before noon. And if you do run into fog, it will help you appreciate the dangers faced daily by the fishermen of the villages you pass on your journey. Certainly mist creates the right mood for this drive; as you explore Oak Island, for instance, where the infamous Captain Kidd is thought to have hidden treasure, wraiths of mist and fog only increase the drama and plausibility of the story. (Look for the treasure if you want, but be warned, you won't be the first. Lives have been lost and fortunes spent in fruitless search.)

Starting at Yarmouth, the 477-mile (763-km) route weaves along Atlantic coastal highways, then proceeds via the well-forested eastern shore to Cape Auld on the Strait of Canso. The area's economy is profoundly affected by its proximity to the Grand Banks fishing grounds off Canso in the Atlantic Ocean. The first part of the journey, appropriately named the "lighthouse route," includes several stretches of good white sand beach. The second part — or "marine drive" — begins on the other side of the Halifax-Dartmouth metropolitan area, an area of brooks, streams, sheltered coves, and forests. Throughout the trip, you'll sense a New England influence in the architecture, a reminder of the thousands of New Englanders who came here after the American Revolution because of their loyalty to England. You'll pass through areas where descendants of Scottish, French, and German settlers maintain their cultural heritage.

YARMOUTH: To get to this gateway port, you can take a ferry from either Bar Harbor or Portland, Maine, or one of *Air Canada*'s daily direct flights from Boston.

Yarmouth itself is a resort attraction, and you can swim, go salmon or trout fishing, or take a boat trip here. Formerly the town was one of the world's shipping leaders;

it's still a commercial center for western Nova Scotia. Marked by a lighthouse, Yarmouth's harbor is a good place to watch the ferries and fishing boats cruise by. Other attractions are the *Fire Fighters Museum* (451 Main St.) and the *Historical Society Museum* (Collins St.). For information on the town's restaurants, see the Yarmouth entry in the *Yarmouth to Amherst* route.

En Route from Yarmouth – Take Route 3 to Tusket, a community settled in 1785 by Dutch United Empire Loyalists from New York and New Jersey. Passing through Argyle and Central Argyle, you'll see rugged coast and largely uninhabited countryside. Located at the head and on both sides of Pubnico Harbour are the Pubnico communities. Middle East Pubnico and Lower East Pubnico both have herring plants capable of processing 1,000 tons a day. Crossing into Shelburn County, you soon come to Shag Harbour. Here, at the top of Chapel Hill near the United Baptist Church, there's a splendid view of the water and Cape Sable Island. At night five lighthouses are visible from this point.

Past Shag Harbour, at Barrington Passage, you'll find the only tourist bureau in the province with a Cape Island fishing boat tied alongside. From here take Route 300 toward Clark's Harbour, crossing over the 4,000-foot Cape Sable Island Causeway built in 1949. Continue along Route 220 through Newellton to West Head, turning right to the government wharf. On the right, just before the wharf, the Cape Sable Island Fisherman's Cooperative has a lobster pound capable of storing 50,000 crustaceans and a salt fish processing operation. Visitors are invited to tour the plant. Continue on Route 330 to Clark's Harbour.

CLARK'S HARBOUR: As you drive into this town, look for a road on the right to K. D. Smith and Sons Boatbuilders. It was in Clark's Harbour that the Cape Island boat, a particularly seaworthy craft, was designed in 1907. The broad-beamed wooden vessel is quite popular with fishermen because it doesn't tip over. Keith or George Smith will be happy to explain the intricacies of the boat's construction.

En Route from Clark's Harbour – Continue on Route 330 past Lower Clark's Harbour and South Side. You'll see countless lobster traps stacked on the shore (it's open season here from November to May) before coming to Barrington Passage and Route 3.

BARRINGTON: Buildings here are preserved as museums. The Old Meeting House, built in 1765 and used by settlers for public meetings and later as a place of worship, is now the oldest nonconformist church in the country. It is located on Route 3 just to the west of the bridge in Barrington. The Old Woolen Mill is just to the east of the bridge. Built in the early 1880s, the mill dyed and spun its own yarns from the wool of sheep raised on the neighboring headlands and islands. After yarn was prepared and dyed, the clattering looms produced yards and bolts of twills and flannels to be used for blankets and suits. It was the last water-powered woolen mill to operate in eastern Canada and was in private use until 1962.

En Route from Barrington – As you head north, you will see the Clyde River. It passes through the villages of Upper and Middle Clyde, hamlets that once consisted of homesteads for lumbermen. Today, the homesteads are used as summer residences or hunting and fishing lodges. Just before Shelburne is Birchtown, first settled by 1,000 black servants who came to Shelburne with their Loyalist masters in 1783.

SHELBURNE: This town was founded in 1783 by a contingent of United Empire Loyalists, many of whom were members of the New York aristocracy. To a great extent it retains the feel and atmosphere of its origin, especially in the *Ross-Thompson House* (Charlotte La.), both a house and a shop — the only extant shop from the 18th century in the province. At one time the store sold necessities — yard goods, rum, china; today it sells items especially associated with the Loyalist period. The rest of the house also is open, filled with period furniture and the delicious odor of pungent spices from around the world, exactly what an enterprising and wide-ranging sea captain might bring home to amuse his patient and long-suffering wife. The town always has been associated with the sea. It was here that many of the world's great yachts have been built, and here that Donald McKay, one of the greatest yacht builders, learned his trade. Appropriately, one of the oldest lighthouses in Nova Scotia, Cape Roseway Light, is here, on McNutt's Island in the entrance to Shelburne's harbor. The island is a lovely place for summer picnics, but only sailors need apply — you must get there by boat. The route so far may have put you in the mood for a fishing expedition of your own.

En Route from Shelburne – Continue on Route 3, also called Route 103 in this area. You'll pass through Jordan Falls, a tiny community where the novelist Zane Grey once caught a record tuna.

From Jordan Falls take Route 3 to Lockeport.

LOCKEPORT: Founded in 1755 by settlers from Plymouth, Massachusetts, Lockeport is known for its crescent beach, more than a mile of hard sand. Near the beach is the *Little School Museum* (1845), the town's first schoolhouse. The school has been refurbished by the Lockeport Garden Club and contains many artifacts of the time.

En Route from Lockeport – Proceeding on Route 103, you soon enter Queens County and travel past Port Joli. In the winter and spring this area, with its plentiful supply of eel grass, lures large numbers of beautiful Canada geese. Shooting — in season — is allowed only when the birds fly over the hills that separate the Port Joli and Port Hebert harbors. A few miles farther is White Point Beach, a popular resort area. There's an attractive beach near *White Point Beach Lodge* (phone: 902-354-2711), but the water is usually cold. Nearby is the 9-hole seaside course of the *Liverpool Golf and Country Club* (phone: 902-683-2485). Greens-fee players are welcome.

LIVERPOOL: Situated on the banks of the Mersey River, Liverpool, once the site of an Indian village, was founded in 1760 by New Englanders of Pilgrim stock. The town has an exciting history. It was visited by Samuel de Champlain and Pierre du Gua de Monts in 1604, and was the home of the privateer Joseph Barss, Jr. In the War of 1812, Barss captured more than 100 American vessels. The Barss home is still standing. On the grounds of Old Fort Point there are monuments to the exploits of Barss and others. The Simeon Perkins House (Main St.) was built in 1766 by Colonel Perkins, a famous Nova Scotia merchant and diarist. Today the Cape Cod-style home contains rare artifacts, books, and furniture of that fascinating period of trading, Yankee privateering, and the American Revolution. Perkins's dairy, on display at the Royal Bank of Canada, gives an account of the town between 1766 and the War of 1812.

BROOKLYN: This town near Liverpool is the site of the 125,000-ton Mersey paper plant, owned partly by the *Washington Post*. The Nova Scotia Power Corporation on the Mersey River supplies power for the plant, which employs 1,000 people.

En Route from Brooklyn – Take Route 331 just past Mill Village and pass through the delightful fishing villages of Vogler's Cove and West Dublin. Farther along the road, in a major provincial park, you'll find Risser's Beach, one of the many excellent beaches in this area. The water's warm enough for a summer swim. There are many summer homes in the region. You'll see some of them as you begin to follow the LaHave River toward Bridgewater. This river is called the Rhine of Nova Scotia, both for its beauty and because the surrounding area was settled by people of German descent. The area is of particular historic interest as the scene of numerous attempts by the French to build settlements in the 1600s.

BRIDGEWATER: The *DesBrisay Museum* (Jubilee Rd.) was completed in 1967 as a project honoring Canada's centennial. It contains a collection of old coins, possessions of the early settlers, Indian artifacts, and curios from the sea. Also worth seeing is the Dean Wile Carding Mill (1860), a water-powered wool operation that cleans and untangles fibers before spinning. Bridgewater is situated on the LaHave, a river noted for its good salmon fishing. The town's name refers to the bridge over the river. The *South Shore Exhibition and International Ox Pull,* featuring oxen from the US competing against local champions, is held here annually in early July.

Just past Bridgewater take Route 332, following the LaHave toward the ocean.

RIVERPORT: The Ovens, Feltzen South Road, is a series of caverns worn into the rocky cliffs by the pounding surf, twisted by the incessant work of the water into fascinating geological formations. A park at the Ovens marks the site of a brief but furious gold rush. For 6 months in 1861, the Ovens yielded $120,000 worth of gold without the aid of machinery (most of the gold was washed from the beach). A town developed, but was soon abandoned; almost as quickly as the gold appeared it disappeared. The park contains old pits and workings, and there is a good lookout point.

LUNENBURG: Probably the most important fishing port in North America, Lunenburg is the home of the Highliner Division of National Sea Products, a Nova Scotia company with fish plants from Florida to Newfoundland. Here you're certain to get an indication of the enormous part fishing plays in the economic and cultural life of the province. According to estimates, national sea-related companies employ 10,000 people, with twice that number indirectly dependent on the firms. In Lunenburg, you'll be able to trace the industry's progress. The town is the home of the original fishing schooner *Bluenose,* which went undefeated in international schooner races between 1921 and 1946 and is remembered with pride by all Nova Scotians and depicted on the back of the Canadian dime. It's honored in Lunenburg with a monument that reads: "1921–1946 Champion of International Schooner Races and symbol of the transformation of an inland people into leading deep-sea fishermen of the North Atlantic. Planted here as farmers in 1753, the German, French, and Swiss immigrants, after clearing the wilderness and practicing the coastal fisheries, gradually went onto the Banks where they vied with the fishermen of Gloucester, their competitors in the International Schooner Races."

A replica of *Bluenose, Bluenose II,* was constructed at the Smith and Rhuland yard in Lunenburg and launched in 1963. Built by a brewery for promotional purposes, the replica is an exact duplicate of the original except for the addition of some modern conveniences. It is now owned by the provincial government. Although it tours around the province and goes to coastal cities of the US, *Bluenose II* spends most of the summer in Halifax, from where it makes daily cruises. The Smith and Rhuland yard also built the *Bounty* for use in the film *Mutiny on the Bounty,* starring Marlon Brando. In addition, the Lunenburg *Fisheries Museum* is at the water end of Duke Street. The museum is housed in two ships, the *Theresa E. Connor,* the last Lunenburg schooner to fish the Grand Banks with dories, and the *Cape Sable,* a steel-hulled trawler. The museum also has an aquarium. The *Nova Scotia Fisheries Exhibition and Fishermen's Reunion* is held in Lunenburg in early September. Among the annual exhibition events is the international two-person dory race in which the US *Gloucester* fishing fleet challenges that of the Lunenburgers. Have dinner at the *Boscawen Inn* (150 Cumberland St.), a restored Victorian mansion. It specializes in fresh local seafood and home-cooked meals.

MAHONE BAY: Founded in 1754, Mahone Bay is a scenic town at the head of a bay sprinkled with no less than 365 islands. During the War of 1812 an American ship, the *Young Teazer,* was chased into Mahone Bay by a British man-of-war. On board the American vessel was a British deserter. Realizing that the *Young Teazer* couldn't escape and that he would be hanged if captured, the Briton threw a torch into the powder magazine and blew the ship apart. Legend has it that on the anniversary of the explosion, June 27, a ghost ship, engulfed in flames, can be seen in the bay. Three pretty churches standing side by side at the head of the bay make an attractive photograph. Stop for lunch at *Zwicker's Inn,* a refurbished 1805 posthouse, or take tea at *Tingle*

Bridge Tea House. Both serve a fine array of made-on-the-premises specialties that certainly won't disappoint.

OAK ISLAND: According to another legend, an enormous treasure is buried here. Some say it's the plunder of Captain Kidd. But the treasure also has been linked to British military engineers attempting to hide valuables during the American Revolution as well as to pirates who used the island as a communal bank. In any event, millions of dollars have been spent, and six men killed, trying to unearth the cache. But nothing of consequence has been found. The search for the treasure began in 1796, when three hunters from Chester noticed a depression in the land and thought someone had been digging there. The next day they began their own excavation. At 10 feet they discovered a layer of planks; at 20 feet they found a second layer. And more layers were found at a depth of 90 feet. Using more sophisticated methods, the diggers went to 96 feet. Then water rushed in and flooded the pit. Subsequent drillings met the same fate, although oak casks and loose metal were encountered. It was later discovered that an ingeniously constructed shaft stretches from the pit to the ocean. This apparently permitted water to enter the main shaft. The original pit has long since collapsed. But the hunt goes on. In the most recent attempt, in late 1978, a private treasure hunter tried to hit paydirt by drilling a new shaft, 8 feet in diameter, 180 feet away from the pit. The island, now pockmarked by drilling, is accessible by car, and tours are offered at a small charge.

CHESTER: A scenic town popular with the many American families who have summered here for generations, Chester was settled in 1759 by New Englanders. Graced with both back and front harbors, Chester also has tennis courts and a golf course open to visitors. A yacht club hosts some of the province's most spirited regattas. *Race Week* in late August features dozens of yachts, many flying beautiful spinnakers — a delightful sight, even for the landlubber. From Chester a ferry travels to Big and Little Tancook islands, famed for cabbages and sauerkraut; the ferry can be picked up at Water Street. Check locally for schedules. The *Captain's House* restaurant (phone: 902-275-3501) has good meals, and the view of the Back Harbour is splendid. Others of note are *The Rope Loft* (Water St.) in an old fish shack and *Windjammer* (attached to the motel on Route 3 at the southern turnoff to the town). Both have quite good seafood at reasonable prices. For fresh take-out seafood try *Hilchie's,* (Water St.).

HUBBARDS: The pleasant community of Hubbards has a small fish plant and is the home of many summer residents. There is a nice private beach to which you can have access for a small charge. It has a snack bar and picnic facilities.

> **En Route from Hubbards –** As you head toward Halifax on Route 3 you will see many attractive sea views and clean, supervised beaches. Queensland Beach is particularly popular because the water usually reaches 70F (21C) by late summer. At Upper Tantallon look for the turn to your right on Route 333 toward Glen Haven and Peggy's Cove. At one time, many of the houses here were occupied by a species now disappearing — the lone fisherman. Now, commuters travel from their homes here to jobs in Halifax, and summer homes dot the roadside. Even so, old fishing villages, like Indian Harbour and Paddy's Head, are still thriving.

PEGGY'S COVE: This rustic fishing village is probably the most photographed spot in the province. A barren landscape of granite projections and piled boulders stands in stark contrast to the brightly painted homes of Peggy's Cove. Although few of the townspeople are actually engaged in fishing, the provincial government has sought legislation to preserve the maritime character of the village. In St. John's Anglican Church at the entrance to Peggy's Cove are two murals painted by the late William deGarthe, a town resident and one of the province's best-known artists. To enter the church, get the key from the house next door. If you walk on the rocks near the water, don't go too close to the edge. Particularly after storms and during an advancing tide, the waves can crash unexpectedly high up the rocks. In recent years a couple of

wave-watchers have been drowned. Visit the post office in the lighthouse. The *Sou'*
Wester nearby features hearty chowder and delicious gingerbread.

En Route from Peggy's Cove – It seems as if giants have dropped the huge
boulders you'll see as you head toward Halifax through the bare countryside on
Route 333. They are the result of glacial movements; the boulders lie where they
were when the ice melted. Weeping Widow's Island in Shad Bay has been the scene
of several unsuccessful treasure hunts. At White's Lake, take the short drive out
to Prospect, a hardy fishing village facing out to sea from a spit of land. Each July
the village has a chowder-ama, with lots of hearty fish chowder and baked goods.
When you reach the end of Route 333, look for signs to Route 102. This will take
you, via the Bayer's Road Exit, into Halifax. This city, the largest on the east coast
of Canada, merits a tour of its own. (For complete details, see *Halifax,* THE
CITIES.) While in Halifax, amble down to the waterfront to Historic Properties.
The selection of quality specialty shops is good, but more enticing is the atmosphere on a warm, sunny day. It's definitely a stroller's paradise. Lots of people
congregate to watch the scenery, have an ice cream, or just pass the time. If time
allows, take a trip into the harbor aboard one of the tour boats. For the budget-
minded, even a trip on the ferry that runs between the twin cities of Halifax and
Dartmouth can be a welcome experience; it's less than the cost of a city bus ride.

Just after you pass *Halifax Shopping Centre* on the right-hand side of Bayer's
Road, look for Connaught Avenue, and make a left turn at this corner. Continue
on Connaught until you see signs to the A. Murray MacKay Bridge. Cross the
bridge (toll 25¢) and follow Route 111 to the Micmac Rotary, with its lakes on
both sides. From the rotary continue on Route 111. Now you've begun the marine
drive, which is marked with distinctive signs. At Woodlawn, near the *Penhorn*
Mall Shopping Centre, look for Route 207 to Cole Harbour and Lawrencetown.
There's good shooting for Canada geese and other sea birds in the Cole Harbour
Dike area. Lawrencetown has a fine sandy beach; although the beach is supervised
in season, bathers are warned of a sometimes strong and dangerous undertow.
Waves are sometimes adequate for surfing, though hardly challenging to an expert.
Three Fathoms Harbour, Seaforth, and West Chezzetcook are all picturesque
villages. Early in the morning, the villagers go to sea in small boats; in the
afternoon you can see them cleaning their catch on the wharves. At Musquodoboit
Harbour you enter a lumbering area, the center of which is Head of Jeddore. Lake
Charlotte is one of the province's best hunting and fishing districts.

TANGIER: This was one of the province's first gold mining areas. Nearby, at the
Moose River Gold Mines, one of the most famous dramas in Nova Scotia history was
acted out on April 12, 1936, the day before *Easter,* when three Toronto men were
trapped in the 141-foot shaft of the gold mine they were inspecting. Six days later,
signals indicating that the three were alive came through a hole drilled by rescue crews.
Five days later, the men were finally reached. One of them had died. The story received
worldwide attention.

At Tangier, look for signs to *Willy Krauch's Smoke Shop.* Krauch is internationally
known for the quality of his smoked fish. (He has supplied smoked salmon to Queen
Elizabeth II.)

En Route from Tangier – On the way to Sherbrooke, you'll pass through Sheet
Harbour, a thickly wooded area known for deer. Inland from Sheet Harbour is
the 200-square-mile Liscomb Park Game Sanctuary where moose, mink, muskrat,
and other animals roam the forests; it's an ideal spot for camera buffs. Trout fishing
also is excellent, but fishermen must be accompanied by registered guides. Port
Dufferin, named after the Marquis of Dufferin, is another area where gold has been
found. Farther along the route is Necum Teuch, Indian for "a beach of fine sand."
Before reaching Ecum Secum, "red bank," you'll cross into Guysborough, main-

land Nova Scotia's easternmost county. At Liscomb Mills, look for *Liscombe Lodge* (see *Best en Route*). The restaurant at this government-owned riverside lodge is attractive yet informal. The lodge owners also are complete outfitters for trout and salmon fishing (phone: 902-779-2307).

SHERBROOKE: While you're here, be sure to visit the Sherbrooke Village restoration. Seventeen buildings, including a post office, drugstore, jail, school, church, blacksmith's shop, and sawmill have been restored to their appearance between 1860 and 1880, when Sherbrooke boomed with gold mining, shipbuilding, and lumbering activity. Costumed guides provide tours.

En Route from Sherbrooke – At the junction of Routes 7 and 276, take Route 276 right to Goshen. Then proceed on Route 316 south toward 15-mile (24-km) Country Harbour, with Harbour Island at its mouth. Although its magnificent waters are virtually unspoiled by commerce, the harbor has been mentioned as a possible site for marine industrial development. From Country Harbour you pass through numerous other small fishing towns of rugged beauty. At the junction of Routes 316 and 16, take a swing east to Canso, the closest mainland point to the rich Atlantic fishing grounds. First inhabited by the French in the 1500s, Canso always has been heavily dependent on fishing for its prosperity. Return on Route 16 to Guysborough, an important lumber and pulpwood center. Then take 344 to Mulgrave on the Strait of Canso. Mulgrave faces Port Hawkesbury across the strait; the two towns have benefited from the ice-free, deepwater harbor resulting from the construction of the Canso Causeway, the world's largest, which was built from 1952 to 1955. Auld Cove, the mainland end of the causeway, also is the last stop on this route.

BEST EN ROUTE

The hotels and motels on this route provide generous facilities for the region's favorite forest and sea sports: canoeing, camping, fishing, and swimming. You'll pay $17 to $25 for accommodations we've listed as moderate and over $25 for those we've rated expensive. Prices are subject to fluctuation and are based on the cost for two persons for 1 night. All prices are quoted in US dollars.

SHELBURNE

Ox Bow Motel – On the shores of Lake George, this place has 47 spacious rooms, a heated swimming pool, game room, and an enclosed children's playground. RR No. 2 (phone: 902-875-3000). Expensive.

LIVERPOOL

Lanes Privateer – At the east end of the Liverpool Bridge spanning the Mersey River, this 28-room motel comes with all the usual conveniences. Lounge and licensed dining room. PO Box 509 (phone: 902-354-3456). Expensive.

White Point Beach Lodge – Open year-round with 47 rooms and 40 cottages, this resort offers daily beach parties and barbecues on a white sandy beach. A freshwater lake, boats, tennis courts, golf course, nature trails, and horseback riding also are available. Off Highway 103, Exit 20A or 21 on Route 3 (phone: 800-565-5068). Expensive.

Pat's Overnight Guests – Three rooms, 1 shared bath. Breakfast is served from 7:30 to 9:30 AM. Open May 1 to October 15. 388 Main St., Milton (phone: 902-354-4071). Moderate.

BRIDGEWATER

Auberge Wandlyn Inn – Part of an eastern Canadian motel chain, it has an indoor swimming pool and a sauna. 50 North St. (phone: 800-561-0006). Expensive.

Best Western Bridgewater – This 50-unit motel has a heated indoor swimming pool. 35 High St. (phone: 902-543-8173 or 800-523-1234 in Nova Scotia). Expensive.

WESTERN SHORE

Oak Island Inn – Overlooking Oak Island and Mahone Bay, this 74-unit inn has a full-service marina, boat and sailboat rentals, and deep-sea fishing charters. Western Shore, Lunenburg County (phone: 902-627-2600 or 800-565-5075). Expensive.

CHESTER

Windjammer – An 18-unit motel located west of town on Route 3 near Chester; the landscaped grounds are set back from the highway. PO Box 240 (phone: 902-275-3567). Expensive.

Big Oaks Inn B & B – Four rooms, 1 shared full bath/shower, and a private powder room. Full breakfast is served from 7 to 8:30 AM. No pets allowed. No smoking. Open May 15 to October 15. Located in Chester Basin, 3 miles (5 km) west of Chester (phone: 902-275-4542). Moderate.

HUBBARDS

Anchorage House and Cabins – Gordon and Judy Morrison are the friendly proprietors of this lovely, old house with 4 snug guestrooms decorated with homemade quilts and antique furnishings. There also are 3 cabins and 5 housekeeping cottages. Trout ponds, fishing charters, and small boat and bicycle rentals are all available. 6612 Shore Club Rd. (phone: 902-857-9402). Expensive.

LISCOMB MILLS

Liscombe Lodge – The best accommodations on the eastern shore are provided at this government-owned facility on the Liscomb River. The attractive property has 35 units, including cottages and cabins. Boating and freshwater and saltwater fishing are nearby. Tennis, marina boat and canoe rentals, playground, lawn games, freshwater fishing, guides and equipment, yacht mooring, hiking trails — are all on the premises. Open May to late October. Liscomb Mills, Guysborough County (phone: 902-779-2307). Expensive.

Amherst around Cape Breton Island

Beginning in Amherst, this 530-mile (848-km) route passes through farmlands bordering the warmest salt water north of the Carolinas, crosses the Strait of Canso, then swings around Cape Breton Island to its terminus in Port Hawkesbury. Alexander Graham Bell, who spent his summers on the island, thought this was the most beautiful scenery in North America: rolling hills plunging into verdant valleys, stony cliffs overlooking the ocean, and inland lochs and glens that are purely Scottish. The trip culminates in Louisbourg, where Canada's largest historical restoration project is in progress, offering an authentic picture of a major French military stronghold in the New World.

The first part of the route leads through lands mostly settled by Scots. It was at Pictou that the *Hector* landed in 1773 with 33 families and 25 unmarried men, all refugees from the Highlands of Scotland. On the 11-week journey across the Atlantic, 18 passengers died. But *Hector*'s voyage was just the start of the migration; thousands more followed, giving the area its decisively Scottish character. One of the first communities outside Amherst is Pugwash, birthplace of the great American industrialist Cyrus Eaton. Although Cape Breton has Nova Scotia's highest unemployment rate, you'll see people here who seem to thrive, with a way of life that is fulfilling and comfortable.

Along the way, keep an eye out for good meals in out-of-the-way places. Along Route 6, bordering the Northumberland Strait, look for signs advertising lobster suppers, often sponsored by church groups. The waters around the island contain some of the world's richest lobster grounds, and during the summer months local groups sponsor community suppers of absolutely fresh lobsters. Of particular note is the *Pictou Lobster Carnival* (usually in early July).

AMHERST: This town is named after Lord Jeffrey Amherst (1717–1797), the English baron and Governor-General of British North America from 1760 to 1763 who also gave his name to the Massachusetts town and college as well as to Amherstburg and Amherst Island in Ontario. Amherst is the first community on the Nova Scotia side of the Nova Scotia–New Brunswick border. The major provincial tourist bureau is on Route 104 on the New Brunswick side of Amherst.

> **En Route from Amherst** – Take Route 6 on the Sunrise Trail, a stretch of highway following the Northumberland shore to the Canso Causeway. Head for Heather Beach on Northumberland Strait, where you'll find a saltwater beach typical of many along Route 6.

PUGWASH: In Pugwash — with street signs in English and Gaelic — you'll feel the first tangible evidence of the Scottish influence in the area. Pugwash is the site of a major salt mine, which produces 1,000 tons of salt a day. The salt is moved out by ship from Pugwash Harbour, one of many in Nova Scotia capable of handling large ocean vessels. The town of 640 is known internationally as the site of the annual *Thinkers Conference* sponsored by the late American industrialist Cyrus Eaton, who was born in Pugwash in 1883.

> **En Route from Pugwash** – Continue on Route 6 to Wallace, known for over 100 years for sandstone quarries that have provided material for such famous buildings as the Houses of Parliament in Ottawa and Province House in Halifax. Wallace is the birthplace of Simon Newcomb, the great American scientist and astronomer, who immigrated to the US at the age of 18.
>
> From Wallace, you'll pass Malagash Peninsula, known for its lobsters and oysters and for a salt mine discovered in 1916. The discovery was a key one for Nova Scotia, since the fishing industry required thousands of tons of salt yearly. Most of the province's salt mining is now done in Pugwash.

TATAMAGOUCHE: Anna Swan, an 8-foot-tall giantess, was born near this village (pop. 553) in 1846. She went on to star in P. T. Barnum's show and marry Captain Martin Van Buren Bates, who also was 8 feet tall. In Tatamagouche, you can see Anna Swan's skirt and other mementos at the *Sunrise Trail Museum.*

From Tatamagouche, take a side trip on Route 311 to Balmoral Mills.

BALMORAL MILLS: The *Nova Scotia Museum* (Main St.; phone: 902-429-4610) operates a grist mill (phone: 902-657-3016) here dating from 1830. Privately owned until 1966 and now completely restored, the mill still grinds grain into flour with old-fashioned water wheels providing the power. You can buy the products of the mill. The *Balmoral* hotel (Main St.; phone: 902-657-2000) has pastries and pies made from the mill's stone-ground flour, as well as huge helpings of hearty country food. The 23-foot Drysdale Falls, with a marvelous swimming area below, is nearby.

En Route from Balmoral Mills – Travel back to Route 6 and head for Brule, known for its warm water, sandy beaches, golf course, and campgrounds. As you cross into Pictou County, you enter an increasingly industrialized area; people rely more on factories than on the sea or farmlands for their livelihood. At Toney River you might see Irish moss being bailed and dried.

PICTOU: This small city, along with four surrounding towns, forms the third largest industrial area in the province, ranking behind Halifax-Dartmouth and Sydney. It has a shipbuilding yard, a lobster cannery, and a knife manufacturer. In 1773, the *Hector* brought the first settlers from Scotland. In 1973, major ceremonies were held in Pictou to mark the bicentennial of the arrival. One of the key participants was former US Supreme Court Justice William O. Douglas, a descendant of people who traveled on the *Hector.* Pictou is the site of the annual 3-day *Lobster Carnival* early in July. It also hosts the *Pictou County–North Colchester Exhibition* early in September. Thomas McCulloch's house, overlooking the junction of West River and Pictou Harbour, was built in the early 19th century and today is a museum devoted to tracing the lives of prominent Pictonians of Scottish ancestry. On Shore Road, 2 miles (3 km) east of Pictou, is the *Micmac Indian Museum.* Open during daylight hours in summer, the museum has Indian relics from a nearby 17th-century burial ground.

Continue on to Route 104 (the Trans-Canada Highway) and turn west briefly.

STELLARTON: Coal was discovered in Stellarton in 1798; the Foord Seam here, at 48 feet, is believed to be the thickest seam of coal in the world. A small miners' museum and an 1854 steam locomotive, *Albion,* located near the center of town in Albion Park, commemorate the history of the area.

Continue back east on Route 104 to New Glasgow.

NEW GLASGOW: Named after Glasgow, Scotland, this town was originally the center of Pictou County coal mining. Today it's known for its steel foundries, clay works, and machine shops. The first settlers along the banks of the East River were mostly bachelors. It's reported that once, when a ship bearing new settlers docked in Halifax, three of the single men trekked all the way there on foot to find brides. After the Halifax weddings, the new couples hiked the entire distance back. Along nearby Abercrombie Road, you'll find the *Abercrombie Country Club,* featuring an 18-hole golf course and a curling rink.

En Route from New Glasgow – At Sutherland's River, take Route 245 north toward Merigomish. At Malignant Cove (named for a British man-of-war wrecked here), follow Route 337 to Cape George. Beautiful sea views grace the road here, and there's a lighthouse at the tip of the cape.

ANTIGONISH: Each year, around the middle of July, this pretty town hosts the *Highland Games.* This traditional celebration — a kind of *Olympics* of the clans — features tests of the Scots' brawn like the caber toss (in which hefty competitors heave a large pole as far as they can). In addition to track and field events, there's even a kilted golf tournament. Marching bagpipe bands, a Gaelic choir, a Highland dance competition, and a whiskey-tasting event are part of the week-long festivities.

Antigonish also is the home of St. Francis-Xavier University and its sister institution, the Coady Institute. The university won recognition in 1920 for the Antigonish Movement, a self-help program for community development that stressed the use of cooperatives and credit unions. Today, students from more than 80 countries study community development at the Coady Institute on the Antigonish campus. Antigonish, halfway between Halifax and Sydney, was founded by Loyalist soldiers and their families after the American Revolution. *The Lobster Treat* (241 Post Road), a converted schoolhouse, has fresh, well-prepared food, and the kitchen serves only what's in season.

En Route from Antigonish – Continue east on Route 104 to the Strait of Canso and the Canso Causeway. Completed in 1955, the causeway replaced the ferry service that used to operate from Auld Cove. The causeway, almost a mile long, took 3 years to build and required over 10 million tons of fill, mostly from Cape Porcupine on the mainland side of the Strait of Canso.

STRAIT OF CANSO: Canso Causeway is an ice-free "superport" that permits the world's largest ships to enter the 13 mile long Strait of Canso and dock with ease. The strait area was once considered as a possible site for huge petrochemical developments to handle liquefied natural gas being shipped out of the high Arctic.

En Route from the Strait of Canso – Take Route 19 north along the western shore of Cape Breton Island through Inverness County. At the start, at Creignish, the road rises to 850 feet, a good point from which to see the whole Strait of Canso and St. George's Bay; then it's down again past the farms that support most residents, who farm and fish for a living. The Judique communities were once known in this region for the size and violence of their male residents. These huge Highlanders challenged each other at dances and other social events with the call: "Judique on the floor. Who'll put him off?"

Port Hood (pop. 500) used to be much larger during its coal mining days. The pits have been closed for some time since the mines flooded. From Port Hood, you pass through the farming and sheep raising area of Mabou and Strathlorne. Then the road proceeds through Inverness, a coal mining center since 1865. Farther along, at Margaree Forks, you join the Cabot Trail, a highway named after explorer John Cabot, who's said to have landed here just after Columbus discovered America.

Before heading off to Cape Breton Highlands National Park, you can visit the *Salmon Museum* at North East Margaree. *Margaree Lodge* (phone: 902-248-2506) offers dignified country dining — good fresh fish and vegetables in an attractive setting (see *Best en Route*). The *Margaree Salmon Museum*, only a stone's throw from the river, has marvelous displays of old fishing equipment, legal and illegal. Operated by the Margaree Anglers' Association, the museum also has a display depicting the life cycle of that king of fish, the salmon. The Margaree River, by the way, yielded the largest salmon ever caught in the province: a 45-pounder nabbed in 1933.

As you leave Margaree Forks, you enter an area of the province where French is the first language. Belle Côte might be called the Acadia of Inverness County, for the inhabitants retain the language and tradition of their Norman ancestors. At St.-Joseph du Moine there are large, undeveloped deposits of limestone and extensive, untrammeled cranberry bogs. At Grand Etang there is a cooperative lobster canning plant controlled by local fishermen.

CHÉTICAMP: Opposite St. Peter's Church at the south end of the village is the *Acadian Museum*, with frequent demonstrations of spinning and weaving. Crafts, including hooked rugs, are on sale. Acadian meals also are served. *Laurie's* motel (Main St.; phone: 902-224-2400) has homemade mincemeat and fresh fish. Three miles (5 km) past Chéticamp you enter Cape Breton Highlands National Park.

CAPE BRETON HIGHLANDS NATIONAL PARK: Forming part of a vast tableland, this 370-square-mile area contains the island's most spectacular scenery. It's a landscape reminiscent of the coast of Scotland: steep cliffs, often hundreds of feet high, loom over a stony shore. Barrens give way to deep, green valleys crisscrossed with rivers and streams. Fox, lynx, and bear roam the park's forests, and over a hundred bird species nest here. Facilities include many hiking trails and a number of campgrounds and picnic parks. And golfers can test their skills on an 18-hole course that is quite challenging.

Although it often climbs mountains only to drop suddenly back to sea level, the road is good and an alert driver will have no difficulty. The curves are sharp and the grades steep, though. French Mountain, at an elevation of 1,492 feet, is the highest point on any highway in the province. The road also climbs MacKenzie Mountain (1,222 ft.), descending, by a series of switchbacks, to Pleasant Bay. Three rivers — the MacKenzie, the Pond, and the Red — converge here. From the bay, the road swings to the east up the side of North Mountain, climbing 1,460 feet. You'll have good views of the park's spectacular gorges as you descend into Sunrise Valley. Heading south for the first time on the Cabot Trail, turn left to Neil Harbour.

Named after an early settler, Neil Harbour is an English-speaking fishing village; it's one of the best spots on the island to plunge into a way of life as dependent on the sea as it was a century ago. Steep grades and more dramatic sights are on the Cabot Trail before Ingonish.

Local legend says that the name "Ingonish" is Portuguese, and that the Portuguese had a fishing base here as early as 1521. Early in the 17th century, the French established an active settlement here, and by 1740, 54 fishing vessels were sailing out of Ingonish. From here continue to Ingonish Beach, the site of the administrative quarters for the park. The community also is a major provincial resort area, with the impressive, provincially owned *Keltic Lodge* (phone: 902-285-2880; see *Best en Route*) as its centerpiece. The lodge, with a swimming pool, tennis courts, championship golf course, superb cuisine, and spectacular setting, is well worth a visit. Stroll along the nearby beach, with its large breakers and cold water. The lodge lays one of the best tables in the province.

En Route from Ingonish Beach – The road passes Cape Smokey, a winter ski area, from which a chair lift is available in the summer if you want to take in the view from the mountaintop. From this peak, you can clearly see the results of a disastrous forest fire that occurred in June 1968.

The villages of Wreck Cove, Skir Dhu, Briton Cove, and North Shore are next along the trail. In Wreck Cove is the last major hydroelectric power source that can be developed in the province; the lack of this power forces reliance on imported crude oil and coal-fired thermal generating plants, the main reason for Nova Scotia's high electrical costs.

Just south of Indian Brook, take Route 312 toward Jersey Cove. From here, a short ferry trip (it operates 24 hours a day) takes you to Englishtown. Just to your right as you disembark is the grave of Angus MacAskill, the fabled Cape Breton giant who died in 1863 at the age of 38. MacAskill grew to a well-proportioned height of 7 feet, 9 inches and weighed 425 pounds. His boot, on display at the *Nova Scotia Museum* in Halifax, is 14½ inches long. From Englishtown you can soon pick up Route 105 to Sydney, Nova Scotia's steel center. But instead of going directly to Sydney, make a side trip to Baddeck.

BADDECK: This is the community where Alexander Graham Bell summered the last 35 years of his life. During that time, he worked on a host of experiments. Bell's descendants still live in the area, occupying the home at Beinn Bhreagh (Gaelic for "beautiful mountain") where Bell and his wife lived. (Although visible from the government wharf in Baddeck, his home is not open to visitors.) Nearby are the Bells' graves. The fascinating *Alexander Graham Bell Museum* (at the east end of town on Route 205) is open, however. The building itself is tetrahedral in design, a form of four triangular faces used by Bell in his huge man-carrying kites. Inside the museum are photos and artifacts donated by the Bell family. These give an indication of the extraordinary range of Bell's interests, including sheep breeding, medicine, aeronautics, and — the telephone. Aided by Bell, J. A. D. McCurdy flew the *Silver Dart* across icy Bras d'Or Lake near here on February 23, 1909. It was the first flight made in the British empire. This fishing and sailing center is extraordinarily picturesque, especially when the harbor is filled with summer yachts.

En Route from Baddeck – Take Route 105 back to Sydney. Passing over Kelly's Mountain (again), you'll have excellent views of St. Ann's Bay and Bras d'Or Lake. Cross the Bras d'Or Bridge, completed in 1961, and proceed to North Sydney, where ferries travel to Newfoundland. Route 125 leads to Sydney.

SYDNEY: On its deep natural harbor facing Newfoundland across the Cabot Strait, Sydney is a center of shipping and industry. Its first settlers were Loyalists from New York led by Abraham Cuyler, a former Mayor of Albany, New York. Scottish Highlanders were the next group to put down roots. The third-largest city of Nova Scotia, Sydney has a population of 29,400; the University College of Cape Breton here has over 1,000 students. Steel production, the main industry, is dominated by the Sydney Steel Corporation (SYSCO), owned by the provincial government since the previous owners abandoned the mill in 1967 — and no blessing. The plant has created difficult economic and social problems for three provincial administrations, losing hundreds of millions of dollars but crucial to the whole economy of Cape Breton, where generations of men have worked at steel-related jobs.

FORTRESS OF LOUISBOURG: Just a few miles outside the town of Louisbourg on the Atlantic coast is the largest restoration project ever undertaken in Canada. Originally built by the French between 1720 and 1745, the Fortress of Louisbourg was the headquarters of the French fleet. It became an important trading community and was the most formidable French military establishment on the Atlantic. In 1745 Colonel William Pepperell, enraged over the constant, French-inspired Indian massacres of New England fishermen stopping in Nova Scotia, led a volunteer force of New Englanders in an attack on Louisbourg. The success of the New England force shocked the world. But shortly after it became meaningless, for the fortress was returned to France as part of a treaty with the English. In 1758, hostilities again broke out and the fort was captured by the British, who reduced it to rubble. From that mess, one-quarter of the huge fort has been restored. Comfortable shoes are advised, along with a sweater or jacket to cope with the cool temperatures. The modern site resembles the 18th-century French fort as much as possible. Guides dressed in period costume give the place particular authenticity: even the untidy dress of certain soldiers seems true to the times. The imposing château, a 365-foot-long building with walls 2 feet thick, is topped by a 250-pound wrought-iron fleur-de-lis. The object was made in the fortress's present forge from early French designs. Inside the walls, four periods of furniture — Louis XIII, Louis XIV, Regency, and Louis XV — are displayed in the governor's sumptuous apartments. After touring the fort, drive to Lighthouse Point, Careening Point, and Royal Battery — other areas of scenic beauty and historical importance in the 20-square-mile Fort Louisbourg park. A trip to Kennington Cove, constructed by American volunteers during the siege of 1745, also is a worthwhile stop.

En Route from Louisbourg – A loop diversion from Route 22 proceeds through Main à Dieu. This small, quaint fishing village was almost wiped out by a huge forest fire in the summer of 1976. As you approach the town, you'll see the charred trunks of trees in the surrounding forest. It's easy to imagine the terror the villagers felt as the fire advanced from the woods toward the town. Although flames destroyed a beautiful old church — long a landmark for mariners — and several homes, the fire was extinguished before it could destroy Main à Dieu.

On the road back to Sydney, look for the exit to Route 125 that quickly takes you to Route 4 heading south. Route 4 passes along the shore of saltwater Bras d'Or Lake, a favorite yachting site on the Atlantic coast. At Chapel Island, near Soldier's Cove, is an Indian shrine where Micmac Indians hold an annual 3-day religious festival in July. Next, you pass through St. Peter's across St. Peter's Canal, which was built in 1869 to connect the 400-square-mile Bras d'Or Lake and St. Peter's Bay on the Atlantic.

ST. PETER'S: The first Europeans to occupy this area were the Portuguese. They called the community San Pedro and used it as a fishing base between 1521 and 1527. In the next century, Nicholas Denys exploited the fishing grounds and exported lumber to France. Located on the west side of St. Peter's Canal, the *Nicholas Denys Museum* contains Micmac Indian artifacts and mementos of the early French and British settlers. Until 1745 the port, known first as St. Pierre and later renamed Port Toulouse, was a stronghold of French power. But in that year New Englanders attacked Louisbourg and sank four warships. Louisbourg fell for the second time in 1758, at which time British settlers ousted the French and changed the town's name to St. Peter's. Visit the 90-acre provincial picnic and camping park on the east side of St. Peter's Canal. Here you can hike to the top of Mt. Granville, the original site of Fort Granville, built in 1793. The remains of its ramparts are still visible.

En Route from St. Peter's – Before reaching Port Hawkesbury, take a short side trip to Isle Madame, linked to the mainland by a bridge. The paved loop passes through several scenic Acadian villages. One of these, Arichat, features a cathedral (1838), the century-old Bishop's Palace (now a hospital), and *Le Noir Forge Museum*. Returning to the mainland, take Route 4 through Cleveland, a tiny lumbering community named after US President Grover Cleveland, to Port Hawkesbury.

BEST EN ROUTE

An interesting alternative to hotels and motels is overnight accommodation at one of Cape Breton Island's bed and breakfast houses. To make a reservation at one of these homes, contact any Cape Breton Tourist Information Bureau.

Some of the accommodations listed below offer an American Plan (meals included) and/or a Modified American Plan (dinner and breakfast) in addition to the conventional European Plan (no meals). Expect to pay about $17 per night for two at the hotels listed as inexpensive, $18 to $25 as moderate, and $35 to $70 as expensive. All prices are quoted in US dollars.

ANTIGONISH

Best Western Claymore – Almost anywhere along the route will be within striking distance of Antigonish and its midsummer *Highland Games*. There are some very attractive inns and lodges on Cape Breton Island with more atmosphere, but to be in the center of the action, try this comfortable motel near the town's shopping center. Nearby St. George's Bay can be chilly, making the motel's heated pool all the more attractive. Church St. (phone: 902-863-1050 or 800-528-1234). Expensive.

PORT HASTINGS

Skye – On the Canso Causeway, connecting Cape Breton Island with the rest of Nova Scotia, this place is most interesting for its kitchen — specifically, the simple seafood prepared there. Catches from the Gulf of St. Lawrence and the Atlantic end up on its table. At the junction of Routes 105, 4, and 19 (phone: 902-625-1300). Expensive.

INVERNESS

Inverness Beach Village – There are 40 fully equipped cottages with kitchens and a total of 52 bedrooms. Open June 15 to September 15. A quarter-mile north of Inverness on Route 19 (phone: 902-258-2653). Expensive.

MARGAREE FORKS

Kilmuir Place – The real reason to visit this tiny farmhouse just off Cape Breton's Cabot Trail (besides its utter peace) is salmon fishing, and the innkeeper can tell you where the salmon are running in the nearby salmon river as well as make judicious suggestions on the most effective fly. There are only 5 guestrooms, so book early in season (June–October 15). Northeast Margaree (phone: 902-248-2877). Expensive.

Margaree Lodge – Overlooking the Margaree Valley, this 46-unit establishment can arrange deep-sea fishing trips, salmon and trout fishing excursions, and guides. Facilities include a dining room and a swimming pool. Open early June to mid-October. Junction of Route 19 and Cabot Trail, Margaree Forks (phone: 902-248-2193). Expensive.

MARGAREE VALLEY

Normaway Inn – Besides the charming 9-room country inn on this lovely estate there are 14 comfortable cabins. Good food and hospitality are to be found; the owner often shows films about the local area, and sometimes there's live entertainment — one or two local Cape Breton fiddlers. In the inn lobby are listings of local concerts and square dances. Facilities include badminton, tennis courts, bicycle rentals, and equipment for salmon fishing. Situated 2 miles (3 km) off the Cabot Trail on Egypt Rd. (phone: 902-248-2987 or 800-565-9463). Expensive.

CHÉTICAMP

Park View – With rooms looking over the Gulf of St. Lawrence and the Cape Breton Highlands, there are facilities here for both deep-sea and freshwater fishing. And if you prefer your water contained, the motel has a pool. Open May 24 to mid-October. At entrance to Cape Breton Highlands National Park. Mailing address: PO Box 117 (phone 902-224-3232). Expensive.

PLEASANT BAY

Beachside – A motel with 20 units that are available on a daily and weekly basis. Fishing, hiking trails, swimming, a playground, and a barbecue are available (phone: 902-224-2467). Expensive.

INGONISH AND INGONISH BEACH

Glenghorm – This resort has two parts: "Complex 1" comprises 15 acres of landscaped property, including beach frontage, with 36 motel units, 5 efficiencies, and 11 cottages; "Complex 2" spreads over 6 adjacent acres, also with some beachfront property, plus a swimming pool and 32 more motel units. Guests have access to all facilities. PO Box 39, Ingonish (phone: 902-285-2049). Expensive.

Keltic Lodge – The provincial government runs this resort set on a peninsula sticking out into the Atlantic. The surrounding country looks astoundingly like the Scottish Hebrides. A tough, long 18-hole golf course, superb dining, and a spectacular setting are featured, as are nature trails, tennis courts, and other activities. Open year-round, except from mid-October to late December; reopening depends on snow conditions since alpine and cross-country skiing are offered. Near the east gate of Cape Breton Highlands National Park. Herman Falls, Ingonish Beach (phone: 902-285-2880). Expensive.

BADDECK

Inverary Inn – A charming inn with 24 rooms, 14 cottages, 50 motel units, and lots of room for children to play. Good food is served in a dignified dining room. Shore Rd., Route 205 (phone: 902-295-2674). Expensive.

Silver Dart – Overlooking Bras d'Or Lake on a hill above the road, this motel has 82 modern units, waterfront area, walking trails, and bicycle rentals. It's just across the road from the *Inverary Inn.* PO Box 399 (phone: 902-295-2340). Expensive.

LOUISBOURG

Louisbourg Motel – Just 2 miles (3 km) from the fortress and the national historic site, this motor inn is hardly historic, but it is convenient, with 46 units. Main St. (phone: 902-783-2844). Moderate.

PORT HAWKESBURY

Auberge Wandlyn Inn – Five miles (8 km) west of Canso Causeway, near a small shopping center, it has 74 units, a heated swimming pool, sauna, whirlpool bath, suntan bed, badminton, volleyball courts, and exercise facilities. 717 Reeves St. (phone: in the US, 800-561-0006; in central and eastern Canada, 800-561-0000). Expensive.

Ontario

More than any other province, centrally located Ontario offers a cross section of Canada's past and present, its dual heritage, and its diverse appearances. Its coastal areas, lying on four of the five Great Lakes, were explored in the early days of the fur trade and provided access to the trapping lands of the north and west. The coastal settlements that began as trading posts have become the industrial heart of Canada — and have brought the province's population to over 9 million, the largest in Canada.

The industrial and commercial center of Ontario is that odd peninsula of land surrounded by three Great Lakes — Ontario, Erie, and Huron — that seems to be anchored with a kiss to New York State at Niagara in the east and to Detroit in the west. The peninsula dominates the economic life of the province and is itself dominated by Toronto, the provincial capital, on Lake Ontario. With 2.5 million people, Toronto is the country's most populous metropolitan area (for a detailed report, see *Toronto,* THE CITIES). Above Toronto, in a small nubbin of Ontario jutting into neighboring Quebec, sits Ottawa, the national capital (for a complete report, see *Ottawa,* THE CITIES). This corner of the province is exceedingly fertile, and most of Ontario's vegetables come from its gardens.

Ontario, with 412,000 square miles, is Canada's second-largest province. (Quebec is the largest; the Northwest Territories — which cover more than a million square miles, or one-third the total area of Canada — is not a province.) The Great Lakes Peninsula is just a small part of Ontario: The province reaches above the lakes all the way to Hudson Bay, from rich lake districts and mining and lumber country to wilderness accessible only by foot, canoe, or plane.

Culturally, geographically, and historically, Ontario divides rather neatly into four driving routes. First is certainly a tour of the peninsula's "little England": from Windsor, on the Canadian side of the Detroit River, to Stratford, through the heart of Canada's English culture, where architecture, historic sites, and even the green, green gardens conspire to be as much like an English shire as possible. French Ontario is not far away. The traditional "heritage highway" of the voyageurs starts at Niagara and follows the western shore of Lake Ontario north to Hamilton and Toronto and ultimately to the St. Lawrence and its Thousand Islands. The third route leads north and west, along Ontario's compelling Great Lakes' shores: across to Manitoulin Island to Sault Ste.-Marie and around the beautiful northern shore of Lake Superior. And following the shape of this shore in a broad inland arc is the fourth route, Toronto's Yonge Street — reputed to be the longest street in the world. Yonge (pronounced *Young*) Street starts in downtown Toronto and wanders over 1,000 miles (1,600 km) north and then west, the only link between civilization and Ontario's vast wilds.

Camping is offered in 220 provincial parks, 4 of the 6 national parks, and in some of the 304 conservation areas, as well as in hundreds of private sites. Hunting and fishing licenses for non-residents are available at provincial government offices and sporting goods stores. Visitors from the US are eligible under certain conditions for a sales tax refund on accumulated purchases of CN$100 or more and a rebate on their hotel and motel tax. Stores and tourist centers have details.

Remember that highway distances (and speed limits) are measured in kilometers, not miles, and gas is sold by the liter (roughly one US quart).

Information: *Ontario Travel,* Queen's Park, Toronto, Ontario M7A 2E1 (from the continental US and Canada, except Alaska, Yukon, and Northwest Territories, phone: 800-ONTARIO or 416-963-2992 for daily recorded reports on alpine ski conditions and summer campground vacancies).

Windsor to Stratford: Ontario's England

Just as Quebec is the guardian of Canada's French culture, the southern tip of Ontario — that odd foot of land that drops into the Great Lakes like an anchor — is the citadel of British culture and tradition in Canada. On the route from Windsor, across the river from Detroit, the place names tell the story: Chatham, London, Woodstock, Brantford, Stratford, Waterloo, Kitchener, and on and on. The route ends at Stratford on the River Avon, the site of the summer-long *Shakespearean Festival,* the best presentation of the playwright's work in North America.

Certainly Stratford and its festival make a fitting culmination to this ramble through British Canada, but there is much else to see in this populous and busy section of Ontario. In counterpoint to other areas of the province, the cities and sites are close to one another. The entire route is only 160 miles (256 km) long; it could be driven in a few hours.

Here, in the most southerly part of Canada, where the fertile land is threaded with grass-banked streams, quiet creeks, and flowing rivers for picnicking, swimming, or fishing, is Canada's vegetable garden. This is one of the most temperate areas of the country, and the miles of flat farmland form a vast prairie, washed on all sides by lakes and rivers. This unusual bit of Canadian geography lies between Lake Erie on the south, Lake Huron on the north, and Lake St. Clair and the Detroit River on the west. To the east is Hamilton and the shores of Lake Ontario. The sandy soil of Elgin and Norfolk counties (southeast) is Ontario's tobacco belt, and the clay soil of Essex and Kent counties (southwest) yields corn and sugar beets. In this area the Indians grew pumpkins, beans, and maize; contemporary gardeners have added a tremendous variety of fruits, vegetables, and flowers.

This is the southernmost portion of what were the lands of the Huron Nation before their agricultural development led them to leave the more violent Iroquois Confederacy and turn to farming as a way of life. Their withdrawal from that alliance turned this area into a no-man's-land, crossed frequently by warring Indian nations. Only a tribe called the Neutral Indians, who supplied tools and weapons of flint to all combatants, were able to dwell in this embattled area.

Settlers began occupying the area shortly after the British took control in 1763, but not until the 1820s, when the Canada Company was formed to promote development of the Huron Tract, did the "land between the lakes" really begin to thrive. Windsor itself began as the first agriculturally based European settlement in Ontario, and today some of the country's most beautiful gardens thrive in its rich soils.

The route we outline below is designed to take a couple of days and to include the most interesting sites and cities on the peninsula. From Windsor, you travel through Amherstburg and around the point of the peninsula to the north shore of Lake Erie, lined with small fishing villages and farming communities, like Leamington and Port Stanley, before turning north.

Farther inland are the rural metropolitan towns of London and Stratford. Each of these cities grew as a farming center and still has the aura of a giant farmers' market, as if a bustling marketplace had been imposed on a quiet village. The effect is of a rural English town: acres of farmland punctuated by inns, taverns, and hostelries, all marked by their English origins.

WINDSOR: On a small peninsula surrounded by Lake Erie and Lake St. Clair, the sheer beauty of Windsor's position belies its place as the hub of Canada's automotive industry, one of the country's busiest points of entry from the US, and the southernmost city in all of Canada, across the Detroit River from the automotive capital of America. This busy city, with its shops, parks, and recreational areas, is actually *south* of Detroit, connected via the only international underwater tunnel as well as by conventional bridges.

Windsor's little corner of land has been crucial to the area's development and economy ever since European explorers first sailed up the St. Lawrence River and it became a major passage for fur traders penetrating deeper into the new continent. They could portage across the Niagara Peninsula and continue by water past Windsor and Amherstburg on the Detroit River. From such beginnings, Windsor developed into an industrial city closely interlocked with American industries in Detroit.

The city is filled with spacious, colorful parks like Dieppe Gardens, overlooking the river at Ouillette Avenue and Riverside Drive. Here, in 1749, French settlers began the first agriculturally based European community in Ontario. Nearby plaques also establish Windsor's involvement in the Mackenzie Rebellion (1838) and in the growth of the Great Western Railway, which connected Windsor with Niagara Falls in 1854.

Whether or not you're an avid gardener, you will thoroughly enjoy a stroll in Jackson Park Sunken Garden (Tecumseh Rd. and Route 3B). With its formal garden and sunken rectangular pool, the park is lovely at all times, but it is especially bewitching in the evenings, when it is transformed into its own world of light and color. Some 400 custom-designed lights have been installed among the flower beds and shrubs, highlighting the most exquisite blooms and delicately sculptured floral designs. Underwater lights turn fountains into rainbow machines; the focal point of the display is the unique sculpture *Coordination*, donated by Windsor artist Hans Hennecke. Residents come mainly for the shady picnic areas, to play tennis, or to visit the Memorial Rose Test Gardens immediately adjacent, but the park is an absolute bonanza for ambitious photographers. The gardens are laid out in the shape of a compass and contain 12,000 rosebushes of 450 different varieties. This certainly explains why Windsor is called the City of Roses and attracts rose lovers from all over North America. A battle-scarred *Lancaster* bomber plane, in tribute to the 398 RCAF flyers who died during World War II, is in the center of the garden. No admission charge.

The *Art Gallery of Windsor* (445 Riverside Dr. W.; closed Mondays) is in a 3-story, $2.25-million structure converted from the old Carling Brewery and Warehouse. A permanent collection of Canadian paintings and sculpture tracing various styles and themes from the 18th century is on display as well as traveling exhibits and a children's gallery of pioneer toys and furniture. A notable collection of Inuit sculpture also is on exhibit. The gallery has a restaurant that offers good food in old heritage surroundings and a stunning view of parkland, ocean-going ships, and the Detroit skyline. There is no admission charge. During the second and third weekends in June, the *Carousel of Nations* (at locations throughout the city) features ethnic food, entertainment, and dress. It's a warm-up for the big *International Freedom Festival* which runs from late June to early July, celebrating *July Fourth* as well as Canada's national day (*Canada Day*) on July 1.

If you like "sight-sipping" tours, visit the Hiram Walker distillery, open May through September (phone: 519-254-5171, ext. 537); Colio Wines at nearby Harrow (phone: 519-738-2241) on Wednesdays at 1 PM and Saturdays, on the hour, noon to 4 PM; reservations necessary for 10 or more; and Pelee Island Winery at Kingsville (phone: 519-733-6551), open daily except Sundays, May through December; January through April, open Saturdays only.

Golfers have a choice of numerous public courses, including *Little River* (phone: 519-945-3912), *Roseland* (phone: 519-969-3810), *Fox Glen* (phone: 519-726-6076), *Dominion* (phone: 519-969-4350), *Belleview* (phone: 519-839-4372), and *Lakewood* (phone: 519-735-9171). The nearby countryside is fairly lined with places where horse-back riding can be arranged. Less strenuous, but much more exciting, are the harness races at the *Windsor Raceway* — with completely enclosed and heated seating areas since they're mostly winter events (6 miles/10 km south on Route 18; phone: 519-969-8311 late October to June, Tuesdays, Thursday through Sunday evenings, and Saturday afternoons.

A magnet for visitors is the *Oullette Avenue Mall,* which in summer is lined with leafy trees and musicians in addition to its array of interesting stores. Nearby is a 4-block area boasting a dozen fur stores (there is a sales tax rebate for US visitors). Look for Erie and Ottawa Streets if you like shopping in an Asian or European atmosphere. The largest shopping center in the city is *Devonshire Mall* (3100 Howard Ave.; phone: 519-966-3100), with 175 stores, including *Sears* and *The Bay. Windsor Market* (over several blocks in the downtown area) is a great place to go for fresh fruits, vegetables, meat, and bread. There is a wide variety of good restaurants, including outdoor cafés, and an abundance of ethnic foods — from schnitzel to curried goat.

En Route from Windsor – Amherstburg is only 15 miles (24 km) south of Windsor via Route 18, through a section of Essex County deeply involved in the short war between British Canada and the US. A plaque about 5 miles (8 km) north of the town marks the site of the first major battle.

AMHERSTBURG: Fort Malden, erected here in 1797 by the British after they lost Detroit to the Americans, rapidly became a strategic point in the defense of Canada and was involved in both the War of 1812 and Mackenzie's Rebellion. It was here that General Isaac Brock met with Shawnee Chief Tecumseh to plan the capture of Detroit, which was accomplished by a joint expedition. However, their loss of control over Lake Erie forced the British to abandon and burn the fortifications at both Detroit and Amherstburg. The fort was partially rebuilt following the war, then converted into a government asylum for mental patients in 1857. The property was used by a private company after the asylum was moved some 13 years later, and in 1939, Fort Malden (open year-round), some of its original earthworks intact, was declared a national historic park.

Dalhousie Street offers a string of charming stores. Try *Huntley's Emporium* (at No. 239), importers of the very best of British candies, cookies, and other upper-crust sins, and *Phoenix Interiors* (at No. 259) for its delightful antiques.

The *Waterfront Restaurant* (and ice cream parlor) at Navy Yard Park is worth a visit. The dining room at *Duffy's* motel (phone: 519-736-2101) is highly regarded, and the kids will go for *Rosa's Italian* restaurant across from *Duffy's*.

Also on Dalhousie is the *Park House Museum* (212 Dalhousie), a doubly interesting structure because of its pre-1800 construction and because it was moved here from Detroit in 1799. The house interior is done in 1850s style.

The *North American Black Historical Museum* (277 King St.) traces the black heritage from its origins in Africa through slavery to emancipation and settlement in Essex County. Open Wednesdays through Sundays.

Nearby *Bob-Lo Island Amusement Park* is a 240-acre island located in the Detroit River slightly south of Amherstburg and is served by three 250-passenger ferries. One of Canada's best amusement parks, it features an arts and crafts colony, a miniature golf course, a safari zoo trail, rides, a spacious dining room, and 6,000 picnic tables and benches. Open daily, late May to *Labor Day*. All rides and shows included in admission charge (phone: 519-252-4444).

    En Route from Amherstburg – Take Route 18A due south to Holiday Beach Provincial Park. Here you can camp overnight, enjoy the sandy beach, the picnic area, and stocked fish pond — or simply watch the boats go by. During the migration seasons, this is one of the best places in Ontario for viewing hawks and waterfowl.

    Returning to Route 18, you will pass through the small agricultural town of Harrow, where a research station has been established that specializes in crop studies of tobacco, hybrid corn, white beans, peaches, and apricots. You'll see dozens of fruit and vegetable stands along the way.

    Continue east until you reach Kingsville, 35 miles (56 km) southeast of Windsor and the home of the world-famous Jack Miner Bird Sanctuary.

KINGSVILLE: This is Canada's most southerly town, 35 miles (56 km) south of Detroit. Its dominant landmark, founded in 1904 by naturalist Jack Miner, OBE, is the Jack Miner Bird Sanctuary (phone: 519-733-4034), which continues under the guidance of his son, Jasper, and grandson, Kirk.

The sanctuary and its founder have become internationally recognized for one of the earliest and most successful efforts in conservation. When Jack Miner began banding birds with his name and address, hunters would return the bands to him, giving the location of their kill. Miner was then able to follow the birds' migratory flight patterns. Most of what is known about migration routes comes from the work of Jack Miner and his family.

The sanctuary is located on the great central flyway; this protected region of 300 acres is used by waterfowl, including an estimated 30,000 geese, during their seasonal migrations to and from breeding grounds in the Hudson Bay area. The most dramatic time to visit the sanctuary is late March and late October to early November, when you also can catch glimpses of a large variety of songbirds. Try to visit at feeding time, at 3 and 4 PM sharp every day. The sanctuary and its museum are open to the public all year from daylight to dusk, daily except Sundays. No admission charge.

For the best lunch served for miles around, try the *Rose and Thistle Tea Room* (64 Main St. E.; phone: 519-733-5228). Open 10 AM to 5 PM; closed Mondays.

Immediately south of Kingsville and west on Route 18A are two beautiful sandy beaches on Lake Erie. Linden Beach has about 2,640 feet of shoreline; Cedar Beach has about 413 feet. They are free and excellent for swimming and sunning; neither beach maintains a lifeguard.

En Route from Kingsville – Follow Route 18 east from the bird sanctuary for 3 miles (5 km) to the turnoff going north (about 5 minutes' driving time) to the tiny village of Ruthven on Route 3.

The Colasanti Cactus Garden and Farm at Ruthven is a major attraction for plant lovers. Acres of greenhouses feature one of the largest North American displays of tropical house plants. If you have a weakness for cacti, you'll be in your element here, and you may be compelled to make a purchase or two. The plants have been cleared for customs and may be taken to the US. Parrots and tropical birds also are on exhibit. The farm is famous for its oranges, lemons, bananas, and grapefruit. In the fall, they serve up apple cider and donuts. Open daily all year except *Christmas* and *New Year's* (phone: 519-326-3287).

From Ruthven, continue east on Route 3 to Leamington, at the junction of Routes 18 and 77.

LEAMINGTON: Billed locally as the "tomato capital of Canada," this canning center almost floats in a sea of surrounding vegetable fields.

The keystone of Leamington's economy is the H. J. Heinz Company of Canada, which has been processing food for worldwide markets from its Leamington plants since 1914. Tours of the plant are available through the tourist information center on Main Street. (You can't miss this booth maintained by the chamber of commerce: it's in the shape of a huge tomato, painted a vivid red.)

The *Thirteen Russell Street Steak House* (13 Russell St.; phone: 519-326-8401) is a charming restaurant, built at the turn of the century by Adolphus D. Broun. The *Dock* restaurant (at the end of Erie St. S.; phone: 519-326-2697), built on the edge of the wharf, offers a great view of the lake.

POINT PELEE NATIONAL PARK: Located on the southernmost tip of contiguous Canadian land, the park is a 4,000-acre sandspit, supporting trees, grass, and some small animal life — and 14 miles of beaches. Though the park has no camping facilities, it is thoroughly crisscrossed with trails and boardwalks for viewing all year (some services are closed in winter).

PELEE ISLAND: Floating between Ontario and Ohio, Pelee is the largest Lake Erie island, with 10,000 acres of farmland. The island is a popular summer resort, with sandy beaches, cottage rentals, and the famous *International Pheasant Hunt.* Only a limited number of hunters — US and Canadian — are allowed a crack at the 18,000 pheasants released each fall (late October to early November; contact the township clerk for information, 519-724-2931). The island is accessible by boat from Leamington (for schedule and information, call *Pelee Island Ferry Services* (phone: 519-724-2115).

It's only about 85 miles (136 km) on Route 3 to St. Thomas, following Lake Erie's north shore.

WHEATLEY: The village of Wheatley claims to have the largest freshwater fish processing plant in the world, operated by Omstead Foods. You can photograph the picturesque harbor and chat with fishermen. There's also a mile of sandy beach, picnic grounds, a 9-hole golf course, and nearby Wheatley Provincial Park, with 210 wooded campsites.

En Route from Wheatley – There are several picturesque commercial ports along Route 3, but dominating any traveler's attention are the area's splendid fruit orchards and crops — corn, tomatoes, soybeans, and wheat — which represent a gross annual return of several million for the area. Roadside stands are numerous, and you could do worse than stop to savor some of the sun-ripened pears, peaches, plums, and apples.

ERIEAU: Another stop is the village of Erieau, a renowned center of commercial and recreational fishing with a fabulous 1,900-foot beach. (From Route 3 take County Road

12 southeast to Erieau.) Check with *Rondeau Bay Marina* (phone: 519-674-5931) for information on boat rentals and fishing charters. Tiny Erieau, fronting on both Lake Erie and Rondeau Bay, has swimming, boating, and excellent fishing for muskie, pike, coho salmon, bass, perch, and smelt during the runs in April.

RONDEAU PROVINCIAL PARK: Accessible from the junction of Routes 3 and 51, this park is another of Lake Erie's famous sandy spits and is Ontario's second-oldest park (1894). It encloses sheltered, 9-mile Rondeau Bay. Located within an 80-mile radius of 5 million people, the park is a major preserve for birds, reptiles, whitetail deer, and Carolinean forest. There are sandy beaches, a swimming area, nature and hiking trails, picnic grounds, tennis courts, a riding stable, bicycling, miniature golf, a fishing dock, a store, and interpretive programs. During the fall, hunting of waterfowl is allowed, and winter activities include skating, icefishing, and iceboat racing.

En Route from Rondeau Park – From Rondeau, for a distance of about 30 miles (48 km), Route 3 continues to parallel the north shore of Lake Erie and leads to another park.

John E. Pearce Provincial Park has the appeal of secluded picnic sites, a wood-land hiking trail, and a superb view over Lake Erie. Situated at the top of steep clay cliffs, there is no shoreline for swimming. But if you happen to be there during migration season, you can see (and photograph) a variety of hawks. For day use only.

Before you have traveled much farther along Route 3, you will notice the frequency of the name Talbot in Elgin County.

In 1791, Colonel Thomas Talbot became a member of Lieutenant-Governor John G. Simcoe's staff. The two men traveled throughout western Ontario, and Talbot was deeply impressed by the fertile land that lay between Lake Erie's north shore and the Thames River. He left Canada in 1794 to serve in the Napoleonic Wars, but the memory of the land stayed with him, and he returned in 1800. At the Colonial Office he insisted that the departed Simcoe had promised him 5,000 acres of this rich farmland. Finally, the office yielded to his persistence, and he received the land on the condition that he would divide it into 50-acre farms for settlement. Talbot drove a hard bargain, demanding an additional 200 acres for himself for every settler he located. Ultimately, he controlled 60,000 acres of Ontario's finest agricultural land and became known as the "pasha of the wilderness," in part because of his quarrelsome and difficult disposition. In all, he managed to organize 27 townships from Long Point to the Detroit River. Talbot's settlement project began May 21, 1803, in the Port Talbot area. Conveniently, he chose Iona Station as the site of a grandiose log cabin, which he called Malahide, after his ancestral castle in Dublin. It was here that the settlers applied for their land grants, and Talbot was far from gracious in fulfilling their needs — especially with the Scots, whom he despised for their frugality.

At Talbotville Royal, you can take Route 4 either north to London or south to St. Thomas and Port Stanley for a delightful diversion.

ST. THOMAS: Set in the gently rolling landscape of Elgin County's tobacco belt, St. Thomas is one of the prettiest cities in southwestern Ontario. It was the capital of the Talbot settlement and seems to have been named in honor of the cantankerous colonel, though one might be justified in reading a touch of irony into the naming.

The city is well known for its examples of fine architecture, which date back some 120 years. One of the most interesting of these early buildings is the Elgin County Courthouse, which took over a year to build. For this lovely old building, the pioneer taxpayers absorbed a construction charge of double the $20,000 estimate! Forty-four years later, on *Dominion Day,* 1898, a fire destroyed all but the ediface of the building. Within 12 months, the citizens of St. Thomas began rebuilding. They managed to incorporate the front of the old structure, with its Grecian columns, into the new building, and it now stands as a testimony to the perseverance and Victorian sensibilities of Ontario's pioneers.

Another example of early architecture is the St. Thomas Anglican Church. This white clapboard building, with its quaint covered entrance gate, was built in 1824 on a plot deeded by Captain Daniel Rapelje, founder of the city and a descendant of Huguenots from New England. The bell in the old steeple still summons the faithful to evensong.

Also of interest is the *Elgin County Pioneer Museum* (32 Talbot St.). This beautiful old home, built in 1848 and 1849, was the residence of a pioneer physician, Dr. Elijah Duncombe. The displays here relate to the early development of the community, with exhibits of numerous pioneer tools and crafts. A special section is devoted to Colonel Thomas Talbot, and the *Native Room* has a fascinating display of regional birds. The museum is open daily, except Mondays, February to December.

St. Thomas's 100-acre Pinafore Park (Elgin and Elm Streets) features a wildlife sanctuary, picnic area, tennis courts, baseball diamond, and, on weekends, a genuine steam locomotive that rides on a narrow-gauge railway. If you are in St. Thomas the first Sunday of the month, stop at the *St. Thomas Memorial Arena* (80 Wilson Ave.; phone: 519-631-4015) to take in the antiques show.

PORT STANLEY: On the north shore of Lake Erie, no more than a 15-minute drive south on Route 4, is Port Stanley. This picturesque fishing village of 1,700 warrants at least a few photographs along the waterfront. The port is renowned as a boaters' haven, and you'll find pleasure craft of all sizes and types.

If you happen to be an enthusiastic angler and are out on the pier at an early hour, you could catch a tasty perch or two for breakfast as well as a prize-winning photograph of the fishing trawlers heading out onto Lake Erie for their daily commercial harvest.

Port Stanley holds a summer festival called *Calipso* (the name stands for Come and Live in Port Stanley, Ontario), in early August, featuring bonfires, an outdoor market, a boat parade, and dancing to a steel band. In late September, the apple harvest is celebrated during *Ciderfest,* with lots of hot apple cider and apple pies.

Port Stanley has a thriving summer theater which runs from June 28 to August 26, Tuesdays through Saturdays (302 Bridge St.; phone: 519-782-3211). The *Kettle Creek Queen* (phone: 519-782-3566), a paddle wheeler, offers 90-minute afternoon cruises May 1 through September 30 at 1:30 and 3:30 PM.

The town also boasts the only privately owned passenger train service in Canada. Run by volunteers, the 45-minute round trip links Port Stanley and Union. The service operates afternoons, Wednesdays through Sundays, from May to October.

Follow Route 24 along the north shore of Lake Erie to Port Bruce, where the road connects with Route 73. In another 15 minutes you'll reach the tobacco town of Aylmer.

AYLMER: Located in the heart of a thriving agricultural area, the heavily fertilized and irrigated fields of sandy soil are prime for the production of flue-cured tobacco. From early spring to mid-August, when the tobacco leaves are harvested, whole families work in the fields. At harvesttime, leaves must be picked, tied in bundles, and hung in the drying sheds. Regulated heat dries them at the proper temperature, which is the crucial step in the production of flue-cured tobacco. Aylmer also plays host to some 60,000 whistling swans who stop here on their yearly migration to the Artic during April and May.

Take Route 3 west back to its junction with Route 4 at St. Thomas, and follow Route 4 (joined by Route 2) until it becomes Wharncliffe Road, inside London.

LONDON: This city sits at the fork of the north and south branches of the Thames River. The river, originally called Aspenesippi by the Indians, reminded Governor Simcoe of the English Thames, and, with his usual disregard for the established, he promptly changed its name. The Thames, capable of sudden floods, meanders through the heart of London, passing commercial enterprises and gracious old homes on quiet, tree-lined streets.

London is known as the "Forest City," the product of a far-sighted and extensive tree-planting program undertaken almost a century ago and continued today. The city still plants 1,000 trees in its civic squares, 1,500 acres of parkland, and along busy thoroughfares every year. As you stroll along these shady streets, you'll discover museums, art galleries, antiques shops, specialty stores, some excellent restaurants and hotels, and, of course, like its namesake, a surprising variety of parks.

Springbank Park, with 350 acres on the banks of the Thames, is a source of justifiable pride to London. There are broad expanses of lawn, colorful flower beds, a careful selection of trees, picnicking facilities, and *Storybook Gardens,* a theme park designed especially for children, with the Old Woman in a Shoe, Old McDonald's Farm, the Three Bears, a Climb to the Top of the Tree House, a thrilling slide down the slippery throat of Willie the Whale, and bells ringing in the Children's Peace Chapel. From the dock, you can take a summer cruise along the Thames River on the paddlewheeler *Storybook Queen* or a 20-minute ride on the *Tinkerbell* (open daily, May to September; boat schedules vary).

Reservoir Park, on the highest point of land in London, offers a beautiful vista of the Thames Valley and the downtown area. As natural woodland, the park represents one of the finest stands of native trees within the urban limits. Historically, it was the site of the city's original water reservoir (1878). At that time, residents were drinking spring water that was piped up the hill from Springbank Park and pumped by a water-driven wheel.

Fanshawe Park, operated by the Upper Thames Conservation Authority, was established to combat the traditional problem of flooding in the Thames's watershed. The dam and reservoir, built in 1953, remain the largest flood control structure in Ontario. The lake, although normally used at its low level for recreational activities, is capable of holding 38,880 acre-feet of water in emergencies. While functioning as flood control protection for downstream communities, the 4-mile lake and park area provide beaches, swimming, sailing, fishing, hiking, picnicking, campgrounds (May 1–September 30), an 18-hole golf course, and Fanshawe Pioneer Village (off Clarke Road in London; phone: 519-451-2800). This museum complex authentically reproduces a typical crossroads Canadian community in the pre-railway era of the 19th century. Buildings include early log cabins, a barn, blacksmith's and weaver's shops, carriage makers, a general store, a Presbyterian church, and a replica of the original Free Press Building. Open daily late May to September; weekdays only September through December.

Sifton Bog (on Oxford St., east of Sanitorium Rd.) is a 15,000-year-old black spruce floating bog that contains rare specimens of orchids and certain medicinal plants; the round leaves of the sundew, for instance, can be dried and powdered for use as a cold medication. There are huge masses of bright green sphagnum moss, 60 feet deep in places, floating in the bog; the moss was used by Indian mothers as a disposable diaper, by medicine men as an antiseptic, by World War I medics as a field dressing. The center of the bog can be reached on a boardwalk, from which the bottom is visible through crystal-clear water. Carnivorous plants seem to do well around the edges of the area, and attentive bog-watchers may spot lemmings.

The *Royal Canadian Regiment Museum* (Wolseley Hall; phone: 519-679-5102) has a spectacular collection of weapons, uniforms, and personal memorabilia from Canada's oldest regular infantry regiment. Closed Mondays and holidays.

The *London Regional Children's Museum* (21 Wharncliffe Rd. S.; phone: 519-434-5726) is the ultimate kids' playground — a place where they can climb down a manhole and see underground telephone cables, or study the stars, or rummage through a huge box of props and come up dressed as a Roman soldier or North American Indian. Open 10 AM to 5 PM Mondays through Saturdays, 10 AM to 8 PM Fridays, 1 to 5 PM Sundays and holidays.

The *Museum of Indian Archaeology and Pioneer Life* (1600 Attarwandaron Rd.; phone: 519-473-1360), on a bluff overlooking Snake Creek and the Medway River, shows life as it was for the Indians before the explorers and settlers arrived. Open daily.

The *London Regional Art Galley* (421 Ridout St.; phone: 519-672-4580) is an architectural gem in a superb natural setting. It features the works of leading national and international artists, plus a permanent collection of more than 2,000 historical and current works. Open from noon daily, from 10 AM on Saturdays.

The *Guy Lombardo Museum* (205 Wonderland Rd. S.; phone: 519-473-9003) traces the story of Mr. New Year's Eve and his *Royal Canadians.* Born in London, Guy, along with his brothers and sisters, formed a band that played for presidents at the White House and became synonymous with "Auld Lang Syne" and ringing in the *New Year.* Open May through September, 10 AM to 8 PM.

London's pride and joy is its *Grand Theatre* (471 Richmond St.; phone: 519-672-8800). Restored to its turn-of-the-century glory in 1977 at a cost of $5 million, its professional productions range from serious drama to comedy and musical theater.

Those who enjoy a nice walk should avail themselves of the four walking tours prepared by the historians of London's public library. Check with the visitors' bureau at City Hall (on the corner of Wellington St. and Dufferin Ave.) or the library, (305 Queens Ave.). Less active folks can catch the double-decker English bus from City Hall, which runs 7 days a week (phone: 519-672-1970).

Shopping in London is bountiful; the city is reputed to have a larger shopping area per capita than any other Canadian metropolis. Stop into the *Antiquarian* (corner of Richmond and Horton), famous for its antiques and wide variety of figurines unavailable elsewhere. The *Wicked Wick Candle Shop* (478 Richmond St. near Queens Ave.) claims to stock the largest array of handcrafted candles in North America. For something special for the kids, try the *Toy Chest* (255 Dundas St., near Wellington St.); then go over to the *Covent Garden Market* (just off Market Lane in the center of London), for some fresh fruit, a block of cheese, perhaps some still-warm, crusty bread, and homemade cookies to round it off. If you plan to relax after dinner one evening, pick up something interesting at *The Country Mouse,* London's favorite bookstore (621 Richmond St.).

This same part of downtown London teems with good restaurants of all kinds. There are family- and country-style cooking at *Mr. Abernathy's* (299 King St.) and traditional Canadian meals in the *Friar's Cellar II,* formerly the *Friar's Cellar* (267 Bathurst St. at Wellington), noted for its good service and quiet atmosphere. The buffet at *The Garage* (73 King St.) can be a real lifesaver, soothing strained appetites after a long day of shopping.

In the Longwoods Road Conservation Area, is Ska-Nah-Doht Indian Village (Oneida for "a village stands again"). Here, reconstructed with longhouses of cedar and elm bark, a village is perched on a sandy bluff overlooking the forks of a stream. The Attawandaron tribe occupied this area 400 years ago. An agricultural band, they were as rooted to this place as their carefully tended fields and refused to become involved in the Iroquois-Huron conflict. They became known as the Neutrals, and, like neutrals in so many wars, they traded their skillfully made flint tools and weapons to combatants throughout the area. Ska-Nah-Doht strives to recreate faithfully the activities of the entire village. Crops of corn and squash are planted and harvested on plots cleared by felling trees and burning out the stumps. A stockade encircles the central village, complete with a sweat lodge (similar to a sauna), council chamber, fish-drying racks, and the special dwelling belonging to the shaman, the tribe's spiritual leader. Open daily, late May to *Labor Day;* other times by appointment. The park area is open year-round and located 12 miles (19 km) west of London, off Route 2.

Depending on where you're staying in London, take either Route 4 (from the west side of town) north to its junction with Route 7 at Elgenfield and follow Route 7 into Stratford, or Route 90 or Route 2 east from downtown London as far as Ingersoll, where Route 19 leads north into the Stratford area. Routes 7 and 19 intersect outside of Stratford and enter the festival city as one road.

STRATFORD: Scottish novelist John Galt, dispatched to Canada in 1820 to deal with claims arising after the War of 1812, cast his eye on the undeveloped lands held as "clergy reserves" in then Upper Canada and saw a wealth of possibilities. He recommended that the Canada Company be set up to buy these churchlands and resell them to British settlers. The Anglican clergy fought this plan in court and achieved only one small victory: The terms of Canada Company's charter provided that one-third of the profits be earmarked for the building of roads, bridges, and schools to further the area's growth. The company acquired 1 million acres of Huronia's prized farmland at the rate of 3 shillings an acre and sold the kingdom of the Huron Nation for double the price.

Galt hired a fellow Scot, Dr. William ("Tiger") Dunlop, to survey the land, by then called the Queen's Bush or the Huron Tract, and plan the roads. Dunlop, a fiery redhead with a distinct liking for a "wee drap," rapidly became as enchanted with the area as Galt had been, and he took a millsite on a small tributary of the Thames as payment for laying a trail from Guelph to Goderich — now parts of Routes 7 and 8. The area around Dunlop's mill site soon became known as Little Thames. Around 1830, William Sargint, proprietor of the local inn, hung a sign bearing the likeness of William Shakespeare over his doorway, and, in the English custom, it soon became the Shakespeare Inn. That sign caused the community, which included a post office by 1835, to change its name to Stratford. The small river, dammed to power Dunlop's grist mill, was named the Avon.

It wasn't until the early 1900s that a Stratford citizen, R. Thomas Orr, convinced the town's council to replace the old wooden dam and clean out the marsh created by the brackish water it retained, turning the area into a 175-acre park and the clear waters of Lake Victoria. The new dam is named for this civic-minded individual.

Shortly after World War II, journalist Tom Patterson of Stratford initiated his plan to establish a counterpart of Britain's Stratford-on-Avon in Ontario. With the help of Sir Tyrone Guthrie, the first Stratford *Shakespearean Festival* opened in July 1953. The temporary tent enclosing the permanent stage was 98% filled the first season, and the festival's popularity has increased steadily. In 1957, John Fairfield designed a permanent theater along the lines of the familiar tent; it won him the Massey Gold Medal for Architecture.

From the beginning, the festival has followed a policy of casting regional talent as well as international stars in its productions. The festival stages numerous plays each season (June to October), not exclusively Shakespeare's, taxing the actors' talents as they perform in two or three revolving programs while learning two more roles for later in the summer. The 1963 addition of the *Avon Theatre,* a converted movie house, allowed the festival to expand its schedule. It also sponsors Shakespeare seminars, discussions, lectures, and an experimental theater workshop; contact the *Stratford Festival* (Box 520, Stratford, Ontario N5A 6V2; phone: 519-273-1600 or 519-271-4040) for details on these activities and play schedules. Although the festival sells out regularly, "rush reserved seats" are sold at 9 AM the day of each performance.

Queens Park, within sight of the *Festival Theatre,* is a tranquil place to pass a few hours between picking up your tickets and showtime. Picnic with the ducks by the shore or take a canoe or paddleboat for a brief outing. West of the theater is a footbridge leading over some train tracks to Confederation Park, where an attractive brick building houses *The Gallery* (54 Romeo St. N.; open daily in summer, closed Mondays from September to May), a continually changing series of art and sculpture exhibits.

Staging and establishing a sense of time and place in Stratford are not limited to the theaters. *The Church* (70 Brunswick St.; phone: 519-273-3424) is a century-old church converted into a restaurant serving French food; allusions to the church's past are sensed in the staff's religious dedication to Old World serving traditions. Overlooking the dining area is a lounge-bar called, naturally enough, the *Belfry*. The *Old Prune* (151

Albert St.; phone: 519-271-5052) is a fairly small restaurant in a beautifully renovated home serving the best and freshest of this farmland's produce in a variety of light, tasty, and well-prepared dishes including fresh fish, quiche, and soup. Dinners are on a fixed-price basis. In addition to the fine service in its dining area, *Rundles* restaurant (9 Cobourg St.; phone: 519-271-6442) also will prepare box lunches during the festival, ranging from the most basic fare to dinners of fresh salmon with watercress *mousseline*, fresh bread, cheese, and pâté. Bring your own *Rubaiyat* and turn a picnic on the Thames into an occasion.

From here, it's a 95-mile (152-km) drive to Toronto.

BEST EN ROUTE

If you're traveling during the summer, make reservations as early as possible; good places are booked far in advance. Fortunately, there is no shortage of good motels and campgrounds in this area, and you can expect all creature comforts to be available — this isn't the North Woods. In the expensive range (over $65 per night for two) you can expect the best in the house. The moderate price range ($45 to $60 per night, double occupancy) covers the vast majority of establishments, even most of the better inns; many places that offer excellent accommodations are inexpensive (under $45 per night for two people). All prices are quoted in US dollars.

WINDSOR

Holiday Inn – A 238-room motel overlooking the Detroit River that offers standard accommodations and many facilities, including a heated outdoor pool, air conditioned rooms, color TV sets, radios, phones, wheelchair access, and golf nearby. There's a dining room and a coffee shop that serves a good Sunday morning buffet. 480 Riverside Dr. W., just east of the Ambassador Bridge (phone: 519-253-4411). Expensive.

Red Oak Inn – This downtown property has 150 pleasant air conditioned rooms, color TV sets, radios, and phones. There's also a dining room, a heated outdoor pool, and a sauna. 430 Ouellette Ave. (phone: 519-253-7281). Expensive.

Cadillac Motel – The 47 rooms (including bridal suites) here have water beds. There's also a heated pool and a whirlpool bath. 2498 Dougall Ave. (phone: 519-969-9340). Moderate.

National Traveller – Near the entrance to the Windsor-Detroit tunnel, you'll find 104 pleasant, well-equipped rooms, a dining room, and an entertainment lounge. Popular with businesspeople. 675 Goyeau (phone: 519-258-8411). Moderate.

Relax Plaza – A pancake house and indoor pool make this 150-room hostelry an appealing place for families. 33 Riverside Dr. E. (phone: 519-258-7774). Moderate.

Ivy Rose – Reasonable prices make this 69-room motel another good place for families. The setting is landscaped and quiet; the rooms, spacious and pleasant. Facilities include water beds, air conditioning, color TV sets, radios, phones, a heated outdoor pool, playground, and a dining room. 2885 Howard Ave., opposite the *Devonshire Shopping Mall* (phone: 519-966-1700). Moderate to inexpensive.

Windsor South KOA – This 25-acre site has 145 campsites (89 with electrical and water hook-ups), a dumping station, flush toilets, showers, fireplaces, a shelter, a store, ice, and a pool. Laundry, restaurant, and golf course are all within a mile of the campground. Reservations are accepted. Seven miles (11 km) south on Howard Ave., west off Route 401 (phone: 519-726-5200). Inexpensive.

AMHERSTBURG

Duffy's – This attractive and well-equipped motel overlooking the Detroit River has been renovated and expanded from 17 to 35 rooms, all with TV sets and air conditioning. There are 3 Jacuzzi suites. It has a dining room popular with the locals, a swimming pool, and a marina with 70 boats. 296 Dalhousie St. (phone: 519-736-2101). Expensive to moderate.

Holiday Beach Conservation Area – Formerly owned by the province, this campground on a beautiful 2,000-foot sandy beach on Lake Erie offers 32 sites for seasonal rent, 59 tent sites, and 10 overnight sites with water and power hookups. Central facilities include a dump tank, flush toilets, fireplaces, a store, and a shelter. Trail motorcycles and all-terrain vehicles are not permitted. In addition to a bird sanctuary and bird-observation platform, a pond is stocked with rainbow trout for fishing derbies. Nine miles (14 km) south of Amherstburg off Route 18 (phone: 519-736-3772). Inexpensive.

KINGSVILLE

Lakeshore Terrace – Set on the shores of Lake Erie, this place has 40 rooms with air conditioning and TV sets. There's a golf course nearby. 85 Park St. E. (phone: 519-733-4651). Moderate.

Adams Golden Acres – The 27 rooms and efficiency units are laid out on grounds set back from the road. All are air conditioned and have TV sets and radios. There's also a playground and a golf course nearby. One mile (1.6 km) west on Rte. 18 (phone: 519-733-4496). Inexpensive.

Pleasant Valley Trailer Park – This campground on Lake Erie has 125 sites with electrical and water hook-ups, fireplaces, a dump station, flush toilets, showers, a shelter, and a swimming pool. Nearby are a laundromat, restaurants, riding, hiking trails, and golf. One mile (1.6 km) west on Route 18 (phone: 519-733-5961). Inexpensive.

LEAMINGTON

Sun Parlor – A quiet motel that has 17 units, 6 with kitchens, and all with air conditioning, TV sets, and phones. Water beds are a newer feature. Close to tennis and a sports complex. 135 Talbot St. W. (phone: 519-326-2214). Moderate to inexpensive.

Pelee – Amenities at this 94-room motel include a sauna, whirlpool bath, indoor pool, coffee shop, dining room, beach, and a nearby golf course. Just a few minutes' drive south of town on Route 33 (phone: 519-326-8646). Moderate.

Wigle's – Set on spacious, landscaped grounds, this attractive motel has 24 air conditioned units, color TV sets, phones, and a playground. There's a coffee shop and dining room. 135 Talbot St. E. (phone: 519-326-3265). Inexpensive.

PELEE ISLAND

Pelee Island – Right on the lakefront, this 2-story establishment has its own beach for swimming and fishing, a pleasant dining room and lounge, and a dock a few steps down the beach. The dining room serves breakfast, lunch, and dinner. Rooms have TV sets and showers. Open year-round. At the West Dock (phone: 519-724-2912). Moderate to inexpensive.

Westview – Next door to the *Pelee Island* hotel, this small motel has 5 comfortable rooms with TV sets and 1 cottage with 3 bedrooms, a living room, dinette, kitchen, and bath. Closed during the winter. West Dock on the west side of the island (phone: 519-724-2072). Moderate to inexpensive.

Anchor and Wheel – This inn has 6 rooms, 5 motel units, and a campground with showers, plus boating, swimming, fishing, and golf. Closed during the winter. Special rates for large groups. On the northwest end of the island (phone: 519-724-2195). Inexpensive.

BLENHEIM

Rondeau Provincial Park – There are 226 campsites here, but only 12 have electrical hook-ups. Other facilities include flush toilets, fireplaces, a store, shelter, sanitary dump, launching ramp, and a natural beach. There are restaurants, boat rentals, a marina, hiking trails, and riding nearby. Reservations accepted. Four miles (6 km) south on Route 51 (phone: 519-674-5405). Inexpensive.

Queen's – Though small (17 rooms), this motel has been receiving high ratings. All units have air conditioning and TV sets; a restaurant, playground, and a golf course are nearby. On Highway 3, a mile (1.6 km) west of Blenheim (phone: 519-676-5477). Inexpensive.

ST. THOMAS

Dalewood Conservation Area – This 130-acre conservation area has 165 sites, most with electrical, water, and sewer connections. There are flush toilets, showers, fireplaces, shelter, laundry, launching ramp, swimming, fishing, picnicking, and walking trails. Three miles (5 km) north on Dalewood Rd. (phone: 519-631-1270). Inexpensive.

Sleepy Time – A good choice for budget-minded families. All 11 rooms have air conditioning, TV sets, and free in-room movies. Miniature golf is on the grounds. Babysitting service. Exit Highway 401 at 177A, then 5 miles (8 km) on Highway 4 (phone: 519-633-0471). Inexpensive.

PORT STANLEY

Kettle Creek Inn – Built in 1849, this delightful European-style inn won the London Free Press award for excellent dining in 1984 and 1989. In summer, it serves dinner in the gazebo on the lawn as well as in its dining rooms. Its 10 air-conditioned rooms have shared bathrooms for men and women, with private areas. An annex, opened in 1989, contains 8 rooms with private bathrooms and balconies, 3 with whirlpool baths and gas fireplaces. Maine St. (phone: 519-782-3441). Expensive.

Invary Heights Trailer Park – On a hilltop overlooking Lake Erie are 79 campsites, 42 with electricity and water hook-ups; a dumping station, flush toilets, showers, fireplaces, and a beach. Nearby there's a laundry, restaurants, boat rentals, a marina, and riding. Off Route 4 (phone: 519-782-3441). Inexpensive.

AYLMER

Aylmer – These 17 rooms have air conditioning and TV sets. There's also a coffee shop, an adjacent restaurant, and a municipal park and swimming pool 1 block away. 300 Talbot St. W. (phone: 519-773-3262). Inexpensive.

Red Oak Trailer Park – A 30-acre campground with 100 campsites, most with water hook-ups and electrical connections, and 23 with sewer hook-ups. Other facilities include flush toilets, showers, fireplaces, a store, ice, a shelter, and a pool. There's a laundromat, restaurant, and hiking trails within a mile. Nine miles (14 km) east on Route 3 (phone: 519-866-3504). Inexpensive.

LONDON

Golden Pheasant – All 41 rooms come with extra-long beds, air conditioning, TV sets, phones, and radios. Other pluses include facilities for the handicapped, a heated outdoor swimming pool, playground, restaurant, and coffee shop. Route 22, 1 mile (1.6 km) west of Route 4 (phone: 519-473-4551). Moderate.

Hyland – Set on spacious landscaped grounds, this motel has 33 air conditioned rooms, satellite TV, phones, and baths. There's also a heated pool and a playground; a restaurant is adjacent. 750 Wharncliffe Rd. S (phone: 519-681-5901). Moderate.

Motor Court Motel – Facilities here include water beds, air beds, and family and honeymoon suites. 1883 Dundas St. E., near the airport (phone: 519-451-2610). Moderate.

Fanshawe Park Conservation Area – This 1,500-acre park has lovely wooded areas and a large manmade lake. There are more than 660 campsites, 400 with electrical hook-ups and 475 with water. There also are flush toilets, showers, ice, fireplaces, a store, a shelter, launching ramps, and a beach. Nearby are boat rentals and hiking; pets are allowed. 691 Ontario St. (phone: 519-451-2800). Inexpensive.

Happy Hills – On 175 acres there are 325 sites, all with electrical and water hook-ups; a dumping station, flush toilets, showers, ice, fireplaces, a shelter, and a pool. Motorbikes are not allowed. Mini-golf, a horseshoe pitch, and hayrides are recent additions. From Route 7 take Embro Rd. 11 miles (18 km) southwest (phone: 519-475-4471). Inexpensive.

The Heritage Highways

The Heritage Highways are a network of roadways originating at the popular border-crossing of Niagara Falls, skirting Lake Ontario, and extending along the banks of the St. Lawrence River to the tip of the Gaspé Peninsula in Quebec. These highways follow the trails and byways developed from the Indian paths used by early explorers and settlers.

There are 377 miles (603 km) of these historical highways in Ontario, both high-speed express routes and meandering roadways. From Niagara Falls, the route takes you quickly back to Ontario's past, into the 1800s village of Niagara-on-the-Lake, home of the *George Bernard Shaw Festival*. It then traverses the extensive wine- and fruit-producing district spanning the Niagara peninsula.

The metropolitan areas of Hamilton, with its impressive Burlington Skyway Bridge, and Toronto are on the route as it rounds the western end of Lake Ontario and proceeds along the north shore toward Quebec. The outlying areas of Toronto are filled with beautiful old homes and estates that once belonged to early settlers and later to rich industrialists.

Whatever your interest — historic homes, battlefields of the War of 1812 and the French and Indian Wars, stone fortresses, sand castles — it is here on the shores of Lake Ontario.

The Isle of Quinte, in the eastern part of the Great Lake, has four beach-parks: Sandbanks Park is a gigantic 894-acre sandbar. From here it's only a short hop to Kingston, guarding the passage between Lake Ontario and the St. Lawrence River as it has since Count Frontenac first established his trading post here in 1673. Fort Henry, erected to protect the sanctity of Canada's borders against thieves during the War of 1812, has been restored; it overlooks one of the world's most impressive shipping routes. At the narrows of the river, just past its juncture with Lake Ontario, lie the beautiful Thousand Islands, where the Indians came to "the place of good health" for peaceful relaxation. And beyond is the oft-challenged war zone of Canada's southern border: Across this river the Americans attempted time and again to strike out at their British adversaries through colonial Canada.

All of this transpired in the footsteps of the pioneers who first opened this countryside to settlement in their search for furs and precious metals. By traveling in their paths, the development and history of this country will come alive.

Population growth and herd depletion have limited hunting in the coastal areas to deer and small game, but game is more prevalent in the North. The fishing, on the other hand, couldn't be better: northern pike, muskie, walleye, smallmouth and largemouth bass, brown bullhead (catfish), and rainbow, lake, and brown trout all fill the lakes and rivers throughout southeastern Ontario. Small wonder that this varied countryside is immensely popular with residents and visitors alike.

NIAGARA FALLS: Canada's most famous border city, Niagara Falls, generally makes things seem larger than life. Even though its commercialism is more crass than that of other areas in Canada, most residents of the American side will grudgingly, but honestly, admit that the Canadian side is more pleasant (meaning less commercial). The falls are formed as the waters of Lake Erie race downhill to join Lake Ontario, becoming the Niagara River en route. The river gathers strength and power in the narrows, then plunges almost 200 feet over the limestone cliffs at the rate of 34 million gallons a minute, creating the world-famous falls. A small island on the river splits the whitewater juggernaut at the point of its mighty dive, dividing it into two falls: the straight-crested American Falls — 182 feet high and 1,076 feet wide; and the Horseshoe (Canadian) Falls — 176 feet high and 2,100 feet wide. A smaller falls, Bridal Veil, lies on the American side.

The little island responsible for parting these rushing waters is New York's Goat Island, named for its former residents. Its 70 acres are a prime viewing location, making it a popular attraction. In addition to scenic walks almost to the brink of the falls, the island features a heliport for sightseeing "copter rides" and an elevator to the base of the falls. From here the fearless may don the heavy-weather gear provided by tour leaders and walk along a path just behind the wall of water — as drenching as it is deafening. The Indians originally christened the falls Onigara, "thunder of waters," and sacrificed at least one beautiful maiden over the falls. This gave rise to the legend of a "maid in the mist," whose image is sometimes visible in the spray.

It is ironic that the single most devastating threat to the future of the falls comes not from the abuses of man but from a weakness in nature. The shale and limestone foundations of the riverbed are slowly being washed away by the sheer force of the plunging water. As this erosion continues, the falls will be forced backward until they flatten out entirely, becoming just a series of rapids in the river.

If you can dream up an off-beat angle from which you'd like to view the falls, chances are someone has already thought of it and has turned it into a prosperous business. The *Horseshoe Falls Incline Railway* (phone: 519-356-0943) provides transportation up and down the escarpment in twin cable rail cars. Would you like an aerial view? Take your choice: *Niagara Spanish Aerocars* (cable cars that make a dizzying 1800-foot trip over the Whirlpool Rapids; phone: 519-354-7511), helicopter rides, or any of several observation towers. The two best viewing towers are on the Canadian side on a 250-foot bank across from the falls. The taller one is the 524-foot Skylon Tower (viewing height about 770 feet above the base of the falls), complete with a revolving dining room, a lounge, and an indoor/outdoor observation deck all housed on three levels atop its structural base. A variety of shops and an amusement area are located below. The shorter one, the 416-foot Minolta Tower (viewing height of about 665 feet), features the *Top of the Rainbow* restaurant.

At ground level there are any number of ways to approach the falls. People Movers are miniature trams that run a 30-minute course between Prospect Point and Goat Island, allowing passengers to get on and off at any of several stops. Of the various boat trips, the *Maid of the Mist* is the most famous. (Actually, there are four sightseeing boats named *Maid of the Mist,* so you won't have too long to wait.) Wearing hooded raincoats (supplied), you can enter the Table Rock Scenic Tunnels to view points behind the falls. There's also a viewing station halfway down the cliff; expect to feel the spray in your face. Open daily, year-round. Queen Victoria Park. Admission charge.

And don't forget night viewing. The Horseshoe Falls is lighted by 4 billion candle-power in rainbow colors every night.

Rainbow Bridge crosses the river just below the falls and makes an excellent vantage point. From the end of the bridge, parallel to the falls area, a stretch of parking lots and flower gardens extends past the American Falls to the viewing towers near Horseshoe Falls.

The commercial area in the immediate vicinity of the falls tends to get congested at times. In the first few blocks occupying the hillside opposite the falls, beginning near the end of the bridge and extending a block or two on either side of the main road, are the *Niagara Falls Museum* (5651 River Rd.), including the Daredevil Hall of Fame, honoring the greats who challenged the falls in barrels and on rafts (some made it, others perished). There's also a collection of Egyptian mummies; *Ripley's Believe It or Not Museum* (4960 Clifton Hill); *Louis Tussaud's Waxworks Museum* (4915 Clifton Hill), with life-size statues of kings, presidents, and other notables and nasties; and the *Houdini Museum* (4983 Clifton Hill). *Marineland* (7657 Portage Rd. Open daily, except Fridays mid-December to mid-March, year-round) offers popular daily shows featuring whales, dolphins, and sea lions. The admission charge also includes access to an adjacent game farm and midway (boasting the world's largest roller coaster).

Gift stores in the area get plenty of business, although prices are sometimes out of line. Either wait until you've had time to check prices at other shops or postpone your shopping for one of the smaller towns along the route: those little pillows, key rings, medallions, and other prized items with NIAGARA FALLS emblazoned on them are available for miles around. Use care in selecting choice import items like English china, Scottish plaids, Irish woolens, and Inuit soapstone carvings (native Canadian, but foreign to this area).

En Route from Niagara Falls – The Niagara Parkway parallels the river northward toward Lake Ontario, running through a delightful system of parks and historic sites on its 18-mile (29-km) route to Niagara-on-the-Lake.

Plan on spending at least a half an hour at the Niagara Parks Commission's School of Horticulture, among the acres of magnificent flowers and gardens. Beyond the school at Sir Adam Beck Generating Station is the Floral Clock, a working timepiece some 40 feet across comprised of thousands of brilliantly colored plants that bloom from early spring to the first frost.

Queenston Heights Park at Queenston, just a few miles north of Niagara Falls, marks the slopes where the British eventually defeated American troops attempting to overtake Queenston in October of 1812. British General Sir Isaac Brock, one of Upper Canada's most prominent war heroes, died here while leading the first counterattack against American soldiers.

Nearby, in Queenston Village, is the Laura Secord Homestead, a restored 1800s dwelling. Laura Secord became a heroine during the War of 1812 by walking 19 miles to reveal the plans of an American attack to a British officer. Although the officer knew of the attack already from other sources, her courage in defying the soldiers who had occupied her home was rewarded in later years by the Prince of Wales (later Edward VII). Open daily, mid-May to mid-October.

NIAGARA-ON-THE-LAKE: This historic village (1781), on the west bank of the Niagara River at its mouth on Lake Ontario, was one of the earlier settlements in southern Ontario. Originally called Butlersburg, its name was changed to Newark in 1792 when it became the first capital of Upper Canada (as Ontario was then called). During this period, Fort George, the principal British outpost on the Niagara frontier, was erected nearby. The town was occupied by American soldiers during the War of 1812, and both the town and Fort George were destroyed in 1813 when the troops abandoned the area.

The town was rebuilt and is an excellent example of 19th-century architecture. Stately homes with wide doorways adorned with decorative transoms and sidelights line avenues shaded by ancient trees. The revived community, the point of entry to Canada for many Mennonite and Amish settlers, was dubbed Niagara-on-the-Lake in 1906. Today the main street, Queen Street, houses several crafts shops selling quilts, handcrafted furniture, and other period items. *McClellands* store has been serving the community since 1835, and *Greaves Jam* (staffed by its fourth generation of cooks) still produces jam in the small kitchen behind the store. The *Niagara Apothecary Museum* no longer dispenses the medicaments on its shelves but merely displays them as a living museum.

Fort George, on the outskirts of town, was rebuilt in 1815, and it was reconstructed as a tourist attraction in the 1930s after a period of disuse. Now it is manned by colorfully dressed troops who regularly display their expertise. The fort is open all year, from 9 AM to 6 PM in summer, shorter hours in early spring and late fall, and tours only by appointment during the winter (phone: 416-468-3938).

The town's biggest attraction, which draws theater-lovers from all over and presents top-name talent in several productions, is the annual *George Bernard Shaw Festival* held at the *Festival Theatre* late April through October; group packages for 20 or more are available (phone: 416-468-2172). The acclaimed mime group *Theatre Beyond Words* performs at the *Royal George Theatre,* Queen Street (phone: 416-468-2151) during the winter when not on tour.

The *Prince of Wales* hotel is a restored 1864 structure with period furnishings in its dining area and guest rooms (6 Picton St.; phone: 416-468-3246), and the *Oban Inn* (160 Front St.; phone: 416-468-2165), considered by residents a guide by which other restaurants are measured, lives up to its reputation for style and taste in both appearance and food. For more information on both hotels, see *Best en Route.*

A special attraction are the *Niagara River Boat Company* cruises aboard the *Senator,* an elegant Edwardian-style cruise ship with brass railings, plush carpeting, and rich mahogany trim. The ship offers moonlit dances, champagne brunches, and pre-theater dinners, as well as daily sightseeing trips. Sails May through October from the Olde Boatworks (phone: 416-468-4219 or 416-468-4291).

En Route from Niagara-on-the-Lake – The Queen Elizabeth Way, a high-speed auto route, is easily accessible via the Stone Road (Route 55) about 7 miles (11 km) southwest of town. The QEW leads into St. Catharines and then follows the shore of Lake Ontario toward Hamilton.

The Scenic Blossom Route (Route 87) follows the lakeshore west from Niagara-on-the-Lake through a broad fruit-growing area where roadside stands sell the season's crop at favorable prices. Small towns, many of them founded by German settlers, appear almost as frequently as the fruit stands. The area is well known among antiques collectors searching for unusual pieces. Canal Road leads right into St. Catharines, about 16 miles (26 km) from Niagara-on-the-Lake.

ST. CATHARINES: Located among the vines and orchards of Ontario's prime fruit- and wine-producing district, St. Catharines has been nicknamed the Garden City. A visit to the *Farmer's Market* (outdoors near the City Hall and federal buildings; Tuesdays, Thursdays, and Saturdays) demonstrates how well the town and region have earned their name and claim to unusually abundant harvests. Settled by English Loyalists before the American Civil War, the city was an important terminal of the Underground Railroad. Today it is a major stop for travelers to the many festivals in the area.

The *Niagara Grape and Wine Festival,* in late September, celebrates the ripening of the grapes in true bacchanalian style, with 10 days of eating, drinking, parades, and contests of strength and skill. The Bright's–St. Michelle Winery gives tours of the plant and product tastings Mondays through Saturdays, 10 AM, 1 PM, and 3 PM; reservations required for groups of 15 or more. (120 Ridley Rd.; phone: 416-641-8770).

Second only in size to the famous regatta in England, the *Royal Canadian Henley Regatta* in August attracts champion rowers from all over the world. It celebrated its 100th anniversary in 1982. Local newspapers provide details on the best vantage points for spectators.

The Welland Canal facilitates passage to and from inland ports of ships unable to negotiate the Niagara River (and Falls). Originally built between 1824 and 1829, the canal cuts across the peninsula from Port Weller on Lake Ontario to Port Colburne on Lake Erie. A series of locks compensate for the 326-foot variation in water level between the two lakes. The present canal was opened in 1933. An observation platform, near Lock 3, provides a close look at the lock as seagoing freighters rise and fall with the water level (take the Glendale Ave. exit from the QEW eastbound or Niagara St. exit westbound and follow signs).

Peter D's (Louth St.) is a pleasant and reasonably priced family eatery near Bright's winery. There also is a wide variety of restaurants on Ontario Street: *The Parkway* and *Berto's* are good bets.

> **En Route from St. Catharines** – Use Canal Road to get back onto Route 87, the Scenic Blossom Route, and continue west along Lake Ontario, bypassing several boat launching areas and beaches. To go swimming, try one of the smaller lakes on the north shore; Lake Ontario has a well-earned reputation for being cold. Near Henley Island, Route 87 becomes Route 34 and turns south to intersect Route 818. Follow Route 818 for a side trip to Jordan, a few miles inland.

JORDAN: Before the construction of the canal, Jordan was an important shipping center, providing access to Lake Ontario through Twenty Mile Creek. The area's economy is now based on its prominence as a wine-producing center. A group of early structures is part of the *Jordan Historical Museum of the Twenty,* named after the creek responsible for the settlement's growth. The Vintage House (ca. 1840) and the Jacob Fry House (ca. 1815) display many items used by the early Mennonite settlers, including a wedding dress, and several of the patterns and equipment used by Samuel Fry, a weaver. There are other period pieces like Franktur paintings and a primitive wine press.

The Balls Falls Conservation Area, just off Route 8, features two medium-size waterfalls, the larger about 90 feet high, and an 1809 grist mill. The Bruce Trail, one of the original routes through the peninsula, cuts across the Balls Falls area on its 430-mile (688-km) stretch from Niagara Falls to Lake Huron.

> **En Route from Jordan** – Return to Route 818 and continue along the lakeshore toward Hamilton.
>
> The highlight of Vineland, a tiny vacation community, is Tivoli-on-the-Lake, a miniature village featuring replicas of world-famous landmarks (St. Peter's Basilica, the Eiffel Tower, the Tower of Pisa, and the Kremlin) in perfect 1:50 scale. Besides being an excellent way to visit these diverse places at once, think of the fun you can have with your photos.

The town of Grimsby is situated in farmland about 10 miles (16 km) farther, a total of 17 miles (27 km) from Jordan. There are several historical buildings, including an 1800s blacksmith shop, which houses the *Stone Shop Museum* (271 Main St. W.).

From here, take the high-speed Queen Elizabeth Way on to Hamilton, about 10 miles (16 km) west.

HAMILTON: History credits United Empire Loyalists with selecting this site in 1778, but not until businessman George Hamilton laid out a pattern of lots and roadways in 1813 did the city begin to sprout. Shortly after a canal was cut through the sandbar (which had landlocked the city's most usable port area), Hamilton rose to prominence as a Great Lakes shipping port and the largest steel-producing city in Canada. If you've never seen steel being made, you should arrange a tour of either the Dominion Foundries (phone: 416-544-3761) or the Steel Company of Canada (phone: 416-528-2511) plant. Both advise that you make reservations at least 2 or 3 weeks in advance; no one under 16 is admitted.

Dundurn Castle — built in 1832 by Sir Allan MacNab (later Prime Minister of pre-Confederation Canada) and named for his ancestral homeland in Scotland — is a 36-room Regency villa restored in 1967. The mansion and grounds, overlooking Hamilton Harbour, were then opened to the public for concerts and other outdoor events. The gatekeeper's cottage has been converted into a museum detailing local involvement in the War of 1812, the Fenian Raids of the 1860s, and other military activities. Open 10 AM to 5 PM daily from mid-June through September; 1 to 4 PM the rest of the year (phone: 416-522-5313). A short distance northwest are the Royal Botanical Gardens, with over 2,000 acres of gardens and special plantings and a 1,200-acre wildlife sanctuary among the marshes and woods just outside town. The Lilac Garden blooms in May and June; Hendrie Park, dedicated to roses, blooms later in the summer, and in the fall Coote's Paradise, the wildlife area, blazes brightly. The *Sugaring-off Festival,* held in March, is a 2-week celebration of maple syrup making and pancake eating. The park is open daily all year.

Whitehern, the home of the McQuesten family, was built in the 1840s and purchased by Dr. Calvin McQuesten in 1852. It remained in the family until it was given to the city in 1968, and it now serves as a fine example of Canadian-Georgian architecture. Open 11 AM to 4 PM daily from June through August; 1 to 4 PM daily from September through May. Admission charge (41 Jackson St. W. at McNab; phone: 416-522-5664).

En Route from Hamilton – Take the Queen Elizabeth Way east across Hamilton Harbour on the Burlington Skyway Bridge, heading toward Toronto, 44 miles (70 km) northeast. You are now entering the heart of Ontario's economy, the Golden Triangle, which stretches from Hamilton to Oshawa (on the far side of Toronto). Try to avoid driving through this congested area during afternoon rush hour. Take time out in Burlington, if possible, to visit the *Joseph Brant Museum,* a tribute to one of the most powerful Indian chiefs. It is housed in a replica of the cedar home built for him about 1800 (open daily; 1240 North Shore Blvd. E.). In mid-July, check out the *Highland Games,* a week-long festival including bagpipe contests, dancing, and the traditional throwing of the caber.

Halfway between Hamilton and Toronto is the community of Oakville, filled with beautiful parklands and the homes of the wealthy. The *Glen Abbey Golf Course* (1306 Lakeshore Rd. E.), designed by Jack Nicklaus for championship play, is the permanent site of the *Canadian Open,* held every June. Its clubhouse is a former monastery. Gairlock Gardens, a fashionable 1922 residence on the lake, houses an art gallery. On the grounds is a wild bird sanctuary (open weekends, year-round).

Nearby Bronte Provincial Park will please children after a day of looking at "old houses," since it contains a special children's farm full of animals waiting to be played with; a collection of farm implements adds to the fun (open all year, although hours are limited in winter).

In Toronto over a weekend? Look for Canada's largest year-round indoor flea market, held Sundays in Dixie Plaza in Mississauga (a suburb of Toronto). The plaza is right off the south side of the QEW.

If you stop over in Toronto, continue on the QEW to the Gardiner Expressway and take the Yonge Street turnoff into the downtown area. Otherwise, take Route 427 north from Mississauga to Route 401, which cuts across the northern part of Toronto much more efficiently, bringing you right to Oshawa.

TORONTO: See the *Toronto* chapter in THE CITIES.

En Route from Toronto – From downtown Toronto, take the Gardiner Expressway east from Yonge Street and pick up the Don Valley Parkway north to the MacDonald Cartier Freeway (Route 401) toward Oshawa. From the north end of town, you can pick up Route 401 directly. Either way, you will find yourself traveling through a broad district of suburban housing, a sign of Toronto's growth. At the Pickering Nuclear Power Station (Brock Rd. exit from Route 401; phone: 839-0465), 22 miles (35 km) from Toronto, visitors are welcome. Displays explain the conversion processes in words and pictures. Open daily. Oshawa is 13 miles (21 km) beyond the plant.

OSHAWA: Called Canada's Detroit, Oshawa is the center of the Canadian automobile industry. The McLaughlin Carriage Company (1867) was one of the largest in the British Empire. In 1907, the same family founded the motor car factory that produced the McLaughlin Buick; it was later sold to GM in 1918. A third of the city's workforce is employed by General Motors and thousands more work in associated industries. The McLaughlin mansion, Parkwood, is open to public viewing of the formal gardens and the household furnishings, most of which are rare antiques (270 Simcoe St. N.; phone: 416-579-1311). Open Tuesdays through Sundays, June through August; open afternoons on Wednesdays and Sundays, September through November and April and May; winter months by appointment only.

The *Canadian Automotive Museum* (99 Simcoe St. S.; phone: 416-576-1222) contains exhibits of the town's history and economy and an interesting collection of early Canadian automobiles, including an 1898 Redpath runabout. Open daily. Admission charge.

En Route from Oshawa – Continue driving east on Route 401, passing through the outer ring of Toronto suburbs and into the Great Pine Ridge Tourist Area, the 64-mile coastline between Oshawa and Trenton. This area, used heavily by residents, is filled with weekend vacation spots, camp grounds, picnic areas, and small, quiet communities. The Darlington Provincial Park, just off the roadway, is fine for camping or picnicking and has a beach for swimming and boat-launching ramps. About 9 miles (14 km) from Oshawa is the cutoff to *Mosport,* Canada's *Grand Prix* racing track. Exit 75 from Route 401; events are scheduled between April and October.

Port Hope, a small town on Lake Ontario, dates back to the 1700s, when French missionaries began frequenting the area. In the past, leather and woolen goods, iron, and whiskey were produced here; now it's just a quiet little community with several historic buildings, a good place to relax from driving.

Cobourg, just 7 miles (11 km) past Port Hope, has become a popular resort area over the years, aided by the town's typical Canadian flavor. Ancient maples along the avenues enhance the beauty of the 19th-century homes and traditional churches. An important transportation center during the 1800s — when lake steamers docked here and coaches on the Toronto-Montreal roadway stopped to change horses and allow passengers to refresh themselves — none of the town's beauty or appeal has faded.

From here toward Trenton you can either remain on Route 401 or take the older (and more pastoral) Route 2, running closer to the waterfront. The Presqu'ile Provincial Park at Brighton, just outside Trenton, has 500 sites for camping among its 2,000 acres of woodlands, plus a small natural history museum (in an old lighthouse) and a wildlife sanctuary for the migratory birds who make this an annual stop.

If you approach Trenton on Route 401, take Route 33 south into town; if you're on Route 2, it will bring you right into Trenton.

TRENTON: This town sits astride the Trent River at the southern terminus of the Trent-Severn Waterway, a 240-mile recreational inland waterway system cutting diagonally across the narrow neck of this huge peninsula (which separates Lakes Ontario, Erie, and Huron) to Port Severn, on an inlet of Lake Huron's Georgian Bay. The waterway follows the original Indian route — later used by fur traders — along the Trent River and across Lake Simcoe (and several other rivers and lakes). Today it is augmented by canals, locks, and even a rail line to make travel and portage easier for 20th-century voyagers. Samuel de Champlain used the route in 1615, when he traveled from Port Severn to attack the Iroquois at Oswego, New York.

Trenton also marks the southwestern end of the Bay of Quinte, separating the Isle of Quinte, a peninsular extention lying in Lake Ontario. Route 33, providing access to this beautiful area, runs along its coastline to bring us back to the mainland near Bath, just south of Napanee. The island deserves a full day's exploration, but if you must hurry east (toward Kingston and Quebec), stay on either Route 2 or 401 rather than taking Route 33 south to Trenton and Quinte's Isle.

QUINTE'S ISLE: Route 33 travels south onto Quinte's Isle and down to its southern coast before swinging east toward Glenora and the Adolphustown peninsula, which extends west from the mainland. An island tour is a peaceful and relaxing day's drive through several of the area's oldest settlements. The nomads of the Laurentian Group are thought to have roamed the island around 1000 BC, and the Point Peninsula culture occupied the area from about that same time until AD 1000. Europeans started to come during the early 1600s, and groups of United Empire Loyalists began to farm the island during the late 1700s (many of their descendants still farm the land). The general impression of the island is of a land unchanged by the years, of a more restful way of life than most of us know.

The island is one of the largest vegetable- and fruit-growing areas in Ontario, with roadside stands everywhere. Route 33 passes through Carrying Place (about 4 miles/6 km south of Trenton). A secondary roadway, Route 19, leads 6 miles (10 km) east toward Ameliasburgh.

The *Ameliasburgh Museum* is a collection of early settlement structures — an 1868 church, two more recent barns, and a reconstructed log cabin, all complete with crude furnishings. Indian and pioneer relics, such as blacksmithing tools, are on view in most of the buildings (open Tuesdays through Sundays during July and August; weekends only from *Victoria Day* — late May — through *Thanksgiving* — early October). Return to Route 33 and head south to the southwest corner of this little island and North Beach Recreation Area, a small beach for swimming and sunning (no camping).

Just below North Beach, about 22 miles (35 km) south of Trenton, Route 33 turns sharply east and traces the coast toward Bloomfield.

There are four provincial parks on the island. The two on the western coast boast the most beautiful sand dunes in Ontario. Take the marked secondary roads, Route 12 to Sandbanks and Route 18 to Outlet.

Sandbanks Provincial Park consists of an 894-acre sandbar extending 5 miles (8 km) across a wide bay to create West Lake under its sheltering wing. The dunes decorating the sandbar are spectacular. (There are boat rentals and designated swimming areas.) Camping is available at 411 campsites.

In the morning, return to Route 33 near Bloomfield to continue to the mainland.

PICTON: Located on Route 33 about 8 miles (13 km) east of Bloomfield is the island's major town, Picton. Sir John A. Macdonald, Canada's first prime minister, grew up and successfully defended his first case here, in the District Courthouse and Gaol. Built in 1832, it is still used as the county courthouse and is, therefore, open to the public weekdays, year-round. Although it's the commercial center of the island, Picton is by no means big or bustling; it's quite peaceful and has attracted many fine craftspeople in a variety of fields. A brief walk about town is sure to end in front of somebody's studio, where a fine bit of leatherwork or silverwork or a painting catches your eye. A 10-mile (16-km) side trip to the *Mariners' Museum Lighthouse Park* is worthwhile (south of Picton at the intersection of County Roads 9 and 13). The museum features a collection of marine artifacts salvaged from local waters, and heirlooms of the days of steam and sail power on nearby Bay of Quinte. Open daily mid-June through September, weekends for about a month before and after these dates.

En Route from Picton – Your direction of travel will depend on what you want to see. North on Route 49 toward the mainland takes you past the 1,700-acre Tyendinaga Indian Reserve, with several native craft centers. About mid-May, an annual reenactment of the Mohawk landing is staged, complete with full battle array and traditional costumes. From here it's possible to continue north on Route 49 to either Route 2 or 401, both of which pass through the historic town of Napanee en route to a reunion with Route 33 at Kingston.

Route 33 east brings you to the Lake on the Mountain, a little lake 200 feet above Lake Ontario that local legend holds is fed by an underground connection with Niagara Falls, about 120 miles (192 km) away. The view from this little mountain is worth the short drive.

Route 33 continues east for a short distance to Glenora, where a free ferry takes you across the Adolphus Reach to Adolphustown on the mainland. The stone mills seen around the docks in Glenora were built in the 1800s as flour and carding mills by Sir John A. Macdonald's father. They're now the Fisheries Research Station. On the mainland, Route 33 travels 32 miles (51 km) along the shore toward Kingston, passing through Adolphustown and Bath, bypassing Amherst Island.

The origins of Adolphustown are evident in the Loyalist Memorial Church (1822) and in the *United Empire Loyalist Museum,* which describes the influx of Loyalist settlers in great detail. The Hay Bay Church (1792) is the oldest Methodist church in Upper Canada; even older are the Quaker Burying Grounds at Hay Bay (both about 2½ miles/4 km north of Adolphustown proper), established by some of the town's original settlers.

NAPANEE: For those traveling east on Routes 2 and 401, Napanee — just 7½ miles (12 km) east of the Route 49 junction — is a natural stop. A grist mill (1786) became the basis of the settlement's economy, and Scotsman Allan McPherson (who made a nice profit on the milling) built a magnificent home with the proceeds. The house (on Elizabeth St.), overlooking the Napanee River, has been restored to the state McPherson himself demanded in the early 1800s. Open Tuesdays through Sundays, *Victoria Day* (late May) to *Thanksgiving* (early October), and the first week in December for a Victorian *Christmas.*

Whether you take Route 2 or 401, it's still only 20 miles (32 km) east to Kingston.

KINGSTON: French fur traders quickly realized the importance of this point of land at the mouth of the Cataraqui River, where Lake Ontario meets the St. Lawrence River. An outpost was established here in 1673 by Louis de Buade, the Count of Frontenac, to control the fur trade with the Indians of the North and West who came down the Ottawa River as well as those of the Lake Huron and Ontario areas. A marker in the archway of the Tête de Pont Barracks (at the west end of Cataraqui Bridge) commemorates the site of the original Fort Frontenac (as the fortified trading post was called) and its later rebuilding under explorer and fellow fur trader Robert Cavelier, Sieur de La Salle.

Long before the French came, the site had been used as an Indian trade center. A small Iroquois village stood nearby. Fighting between the Iroquois Confederacy and the Huron Nation kept French traders from dealing with area tribes, but this outpost, established during a peace that lasted from the late 1660s until 1680, gave the French a strong foothold from which to trade with the interior. The profitable trade alliances of the French and the Huron on the one hand, and of the English and Dutch in New England and New York with the Iroquois of Upstate New York on the other, aggravated hostilities between the Indian groups. Fort Frontenac stood in the midst of the fighting. Shortly before the Treaty of Paris put an end to both the century-long series of French and Indian wars and the larger British-French conflict over the possession of Canada, a force of 3,000 British-American colonials and their Iroquois allies destroyed the fort and took control of Lake Ontario. Quebec was taken the following year.

Count Frontenac, crusty, autocratic, and likable from all accounts, did not live to see his fortress's demise. He died in 1698 at 76, 2 years after successfully leading a force of Hurons and fur traders against the Oneida and Onondaga tribes of the Iroquois Confederacy to relieve hostile Indian pressure on French holdings in the area.

Many structures date back to the period following the 1763 treaty, when United Empire Loyalists began to resettle in British-occupied Canada, fearing the loss of British control over the American colonies they inhabited. Brock Street, the main thoroughfare of Kingston (as the British christened the settlement), still lives as a commercial center, with many of the original stores still transacting business in the old manner. A century of aging has enhanced the color and depth of the locally quarried limestone used to build these buildings. A stroll down this street is a step into the past. Turn left at the foot of the street, along the waterfront and Ontario Street, to get to the site of Frontenac's original structure.

One of the city's highlights is Old Fort Henry, a reconstructed fort erected during the War of 1812 as the key defense of the southern end of the St. Lawrence River. The original Fort Henry fell into disrepair in the late 1890s after it was abandoned in the interest of Canadian-American cooperation. Nowadays the fortress is staffed by a fife and drum corps, tour guides, and a small detachment of gunners who fire salutes to match the precision of the drill team on the parade field. The *Sunset Retreat Ceremony,* performed each Monday, Wednesday, and Saturday at 7:30 PM during July and August, weather permitting, is impressive. The fort is located east of town, on the far side of both the harbor and Navy Bay (open daily, mid-May to mid-October). On Point Fredrick, which separates Navy Bay from Kingston Harbour and the mouth of the Cataraqui River, stands the circular Martello tower of Fort Fredrick, one of the early fortifications protecting Kingston. Now the tower houses the *Royal Military College Museum* and the *Douglas Small Arms Collection* (open daily, June through *Labor Day*). Another stone Martello Tower, located at the corner of Barrie & King Streets facing Lake Ontario, is the Murney Redoubt, which also contains a museum of pioneer artifacts and military history (open 10 AM to 8 PM July and August, 10 AM till dusk from mid-May through mid-October).

The importance of Kingston, Fort Frontenac, and Fort Henry to Canadian history is documented by numerous plaques about town detailing the contributions of individuals and the histories of many of the older buildings. The 1840 *Firehall* (251 Ontario St.; phone: 613-548-8888) has been restored and is now a privately run restaurant offering lunch and dinner daily, and Sunday brunch. There are several dining areas within the structure, but everything is geared toward local history and culture. Even the menu is based on local produce and regional dishes, such as Wolfe Island pheasant.

From Kingston Harbour, cruises north into the Thousand Islands area can be arranged through *Thousand Islands Cruises* (phone: 613-549-1123) from their dock about 5 miles (8 km) east of the town off Route 2.

Take Route 2 eastbound about 18 miles (29 km) to Gananoque, the "gateway to the Thousand Islands."

GANANOQUE: Although a plaque by the Town Hall of Gananoque credits United Empire Loyalist Joel Stone as its founder, it's likely the Indians were responsible for establishing this beautiful resort overlooking the fabulous Thousand Islands area. Their names for this coast, "place of good health" and "land that slopes toward the water and disappears under it," are both embodied in its anglicized name, pronounced Gan-non-*ock*-way.

The *Gananoque Historic Museum* (10 King East St.; open 2 to 5 PM, Mondays through Saturdays from June to September, with evening hours from 7 to 9 PM during July and August) contains many Indian relics discovered nearby and a large number of military items from the War of 1812 to World War II. Several historic plaques, placed around town by Ontario's Heritage Foundation, tell of the area's past — of Pirate Johnston (who attacked British shipping in the 1830s), and of the September 21 attack on the city by American soldiers during the War of 1812, to name two.

■ **EXTRA SPECIAL:** It's not history that attracts hundreds of visitors to this bank of the St. Lawrence each year, it's the islands. Legend has it that a French explorer (unnamed) first called this area Thousand Islands, although there are actually about 1,700 separate bits and pieces of land in the chain. They vary in size from a few square feet to a few hundred square feet. Houses on these islands are prized for their beauty and privacy, and many of the stone dwellings date back to the early 1800s.

On Heart Island stands Boldt Castle, begun in the late 1890s by George Boldt (owner of the *Waldorf-Astoria* hotel in New York) as a gift for his wife. She died, the castle was never completed, and the magnificent stonework fell into disrepair. The castle has been renovated, and the charm and scale of Boldt's undertaking can be easily appreciated.

Cruises of the Thousand Islands can be arranged through *Gananoque Boat Line* (phone: 613-382-2144) and *Sea Fox* (phone: 613-384-7899), both in Gananoque; or try *Island Queen* (phone: 613-549-5544); and through several smaller lines on both sides of the St. Lawrence. (Not all cruise boats stop at Heart Island.)

Two fine restaurants in Gananoque offer a true 19th-century atmosphere: the *Golden Apple Inn* (45 King St. W.; phone: 613-382-3300), in an 1830s farmhouse, and the dining room of the *Athlone* motor inn (250 King St. W.; phone: 613-382-2440), in an 1874 home. *The Golden Apple* specializes in prime ribs and seafood and does all its own baking. Open April through December 31.

En Route from Gananoque – Take Route 2, the Heritage Highway, east toward the Quebec border. The village of Ivy Lea and the Thousand Island Bridge to New York State are about 10 miles (16 km) away. *Skytown,* a combination viewing tower and entertainment complex, stands 400 feet above Hill Island, the central support for the bridge. This mid-river platform, Hill Island, also houses duty-free shops for travelers and Never-Never Land, a children's park with a fairy tale and nursery rhyme theme. Cruises of the islands are available from the docks at Ivy Lea through *Snider Thousand Island Boat Tours* (no phone).

At Mallorytown Landing, just 9 miles (14 km) beyond Ivy Lea, the St. Lawrence Islands National Park, comprised of 18 scattered areas, maintains a 97-acre visitor center on the mainland with visual displays of the history of the Thousand Islands and a War of 1812 gunboat, the HMS *Radcliff,* part of which is open to visitors.

BROCKVILLE: The industrial center of Brockville, 32 miles (51 km) east of Gananoque, marks the eastern end of the Thousand Islands area. While the town is worth a quick stop, there are few sightseeing highlights: Even the historical markers are less than inspiring. One marks the site of Canada's oldest railroad tunnel (just south of Town Hall) and a second reminds all visitors of the night of February 6, 1813, when the town was raided by Americans under the command of Major Forsyth (on the waterfront of Blockhouse Island). One good reason to see Brockville is the *Towne Haus* tavern (32 Apple St.; phone: 613-345-1182), in a building dating back to "sometime before 1826." The catch-of-the-day is the high point on an excellent menu. Open for lunch Mondays through Fridays, and dinner, Mondays through Saturdays.

The small town of Prescott lies 32 miles (51 km) farther east along Route 2.

PRESCOTT: One of the few deepwater ports along this section of the river, Prescott has risen in importance as a port over the last 100 years. Its principal fortification, Fort Wellington, overlooking the St. Lawrence River, played a crucial part in the War of 1812 when both Canadians and Americans vied for control of the valuable waterway. It also was involved in the fighting during the 1837 Rebellion and the Fenian Raids of the late 1860s. The fort (right off Route 2; phone: 613-925-2896), restored to its original condition, hosts a military pageant each July, with Canadian, British, and American troops dressed in period uniforms. Open daily from mid-May through mid-October; by appointments at other times. No admission charge.

En Route from Prescott – The banks of the St. Lawrence between here and Montreal, in Quebec, are dotted with small communities that date back to the early days of French exploration of the lands beyond the fortress of Mont Royal. The land has lost none of its appeal and beauty. When the village of Iroquois, 6 miles (10 km) from Prescott, was partially relocated to allow the construction of the St. Lawrence Seaway, many of the old homes were reconstructed in fine detail. One of the dwellings on its original site is the Carman House (Carman Rd., off Route 2, en route to the seaway locks), thought to have been built in 1825. Open 1 to 8 PM daily, June 28 to September 2).

MORRISBURG: Located 8 miles (13 km) closer to Montreal, this town also was settled in the early 1800s. About 40 of the best-preserved pioneer dwellings were restored when the town was moved to accommodate the rising waters of the St. Lawrence Seaway. A choice cross section of the early-19th-century buildings have been grouped together, 7 miles (11 km) east of the newly positioned Morrisburg, to form a typical, almost self-sufficient, 1850s community. The houses, mills, taverns, and shops are joined with hand-forged nails and dowels; the shingles have been split by hand, and the corduroy road is comprised of trees cut and dragged into place manually. Upper Canada Village (in Crysler Battlefield Park; phone: 613-543-2911), as this working settlement is called, is inhabited by a group of talented craftspeople keeping the old trades alive: Flour is ground with stone; an 1840 water-powered mill is the closest thing here to "mechanized"; women hook rugs and weave blankets by hand; and bread is baked in wood-fired ovens. Open daily, mid-May through mid-October.

Crysler Battlefield Park also is the site of one of the most decisive battles of the War of 1812, a major turning point in Canadian history. Here about 800 British and Canadian civilians and soldiers and Indians battled over 4,000 American troops and forced their withdrawal on November 11, 1813. This defeat, coupled with another loss at Châteauguay, destroyed American hopes of capturing Canada.

En Route from Morrisburg – If you want to fish in an area where you have the advantage over the fish, then stop in the village of Ingleside or Long Sault, about 15 miles (24 km) from Morrisburg on Route 1: 11 islands, formed by the expanded St. Lawrence Seaway (and the dam at Cornwall), create an angler's heaven. The islands are linked by bridges and causeways, allowing easy access to almost any point in the group. A wildlife sanctuary and Canada goose compound are located on nearby Nairne Island. The whole area, with its beautiful river views and secluded inlets, is perfect for picnicking and camping.

CORNWALL: The St. Lawrence Seaway, with its extraordinary system of dams and power plants, was created to ease navigation through hazardous parts of the 800-mile St. Lawrence River and to harness the power of this tremendous river more efficiently. The headquarters of the Seaway Authority is located here in Cornwall, where Thomas A. Edison first installed a plant for lighting an entire factory by electricity. Today, the Robert H. Saunders–St. Lawrence Generating Station, a $6 billion section of the US-Canadian hydroelectric power system, is open for tours Sundays through Thursdays during the summer. A plaque at Lakeside Park, just outside of Cornwall proper, is a sad reminder of the numerous small communities and historic homes submerged by the altered watercourse.

Among the old structures that survived the flood are St. Andrew's Church, one of the oldest remaining stone buildings in Ontario (now used as the parish hall of the current church); the District Courthouse and Gaol, completed from the early 1830s; and the "Wood House," which serves as the *United Counties Museum,* with a collection of Canadian artifacts and some of the original electrical equipment Edison used in the Canada Mills plant (731 2nd St. W.). Open 10 AM to noon and 1 to 5 PM, Mondays through Saturdays; Sundays, 2 to 5 PM only; May through October.

The boundary of Ontario is just 20 miles (32 km) beyond Cornwall, and Routes 2 and 401 both continue eastward, toward Montreal, Quebec, and the Atlantic.

BEST EN ROUTE

Due to the high volume of tourist traffic flowing through the province, most hotel accommodations tend to fall into an average price category. While you're not going to find many rooms at bargain rates, very few hotels exceed the going rate except when premium services or especially desirable rooms are involved. Those with rates over $65 per night (double occupancy) are considered expensive. The majority of hotel space falls into the moderate ($45 to $65 per night) range, and any establishment charging under $45 per night for two occupants is listed as inexpensive. These rates apply to the summer high season. Reservations are advised at all times and should be made weeks in advance during the summer and fall. Recent developments in the Ontario park system allow (and encourage) advance registration for camping areas, and it is advisable to plan your trip accordingly. All prices are quoted in US dollars.

NIAGARA FALLS

Ameri-Cana – About 4 miles (6 km) outside the hustle and bustle of downtown, amid spacious grounds with a play area, this motor inn has 110 rooms, including honeymoon suites, as well as several efficiencies and kitchen units. A good base of operations if you've got a small mob with you. 8444 Lundy's La. (phone: 416-356-8444). Expensive.

Brock – Probably the best-known hostelry in town, with a good view of both sets of falls from many of its 238 rooms. The *Rainbow Room* is a popular dining spot. 5685 Falls Ave. (For reservations call 800-263-7135). Expensive.

Foxhead Inn – Slightly closer to the falls than its neighboring cousin, the inn has over 400 modern rooms, many of which overlook the falls, and a full range of features — pool, excellent dining room, sports complex, and facilities for the handicapped. 5875 Falls Ave. (For reservations call 800-263-7135). Expensive.

Michael's Inn – A comfortable motor inn overlooking the river and gorge, it has a pool and dining facilities. Many of the 130 rooms offer good falls views from their balconies. 5599 River Rd. (phone: 416-354-2727). Expensive.

Parkwood – All 32 rooms have air conditioning, TV sets, and refrigerators. There is an outdoor pool and a picnic area nearby. 8054 Lundy's La. (phone: 416-354-3162). Moderate.

Niagara Falls KOA – This appealing 340-site campground has many wooded areas and grassy tent sites as well as RV facilities; it also has miniature golf. If you like tent camping, this is the one. Most sites have power and water hookups. There also are fireplaces, flush toilets, and a pool. One mile (1.6 km) west of Queen Elizabeth Highway on Route 20 (phone: 416-354-6472). Inexpensive.

NIAGARA-ON-THE-LAKE

Angel Inn – Originally built as a 3-room log cabin in 1779, the inn always has been a center of local history and politics. Let one of the staff members fill you in on the events that took place here. It has been a hotel since 1823 and is full of authentic colonial pieces and collector's items. The beds in all 12 rooms are canopy-style, embellished with petit-point. Queen St. at Regent (phone: 416-468-3411). Expensive.

Oban Inn – Erected in 1824, it wasn't until a few years later that the 23-room building became a hotel and began a tradition of excellence which has made it one of the town's landmarks in terms of both grace and beauty. 160 Front St. (phone: 416-468-7811). Expensive.

Pillar and Post – There are fireplaces in half of the 90 rooms of this interesting place, and a sauna, whirlpool bath, and an outdoor pool for creature comforts, plus a dining room and a crafts and antiques shop. Complimentary morning coffee and a newspaper are provided. King and John Sts. (phone: 416-468-2123). Expensive.

Prince of Wales – A truly magnificent restored inn highlighted by a royal suite (and bed) occupied by the Prince of Wales in the 1920s. The other 103 rooms have yet to be blessed. Theater and winter packages are available. 6 Picton St. (phone: 416-468-3246). Expensive.

ST. CATHARINES

Parkway Inn – An attractive and convenient downtown spot, with 125 rooms and enough amenities to satisfy anyone: sauna, whirlpool bath, bowling, indoor pool, and good dining facilities. 327 Ontario St. at QEW (phone: 416-688-2324). Expensive to moderate.

Highwayman – Noted for its cozy atmosphere, this inn has 50 rooms with TV sets, and an outdoor pool. Winery tours can be arranged. 420 Ontario St. (phone: 416-688-1646). Moderate.

Lorenzi's Motor Inn – Minutes from Niagara Falls and the famous Seaway twin locks, this place has 27 pleasant, well-furnished rooms and a dining room. Exit 406 at Glandale Ave. W. to Merritt St. (phone: 416-227-1183). Moderate.

PICTON

Tip of the Bay – Overlooking Picton Bay, it has 28 rooms, a dining room, lounge/bar, and *Misty's* — the liveliest bar and dance spot in the area. Fishing packages are available and docking has just been doubled to accommodate 60 slips. 35 Bridge St. (phone: 613-476-2156). Moderate.

KINGSTON

Confederation Place – One of Kingston's newest hostelries and a member of the Howard Johnson family, this modern, 101-room establishment is in the heart of downtown, overlooking the harbor. In fact, the Thousand Islands boat tours dock right here. 237 Ontario St. (phone: 613-549-6300). Expensive.

Seven Oakes – Just outside Kingston, this motel offers about the best accommodations, dollar for dollar, in the area. The 40 units occupy about 2 acres of the motel's

11 acres, so there's plenty of space for kids to play in addition to the Olympic-size pool and a tennis court. Also, the owners will arrange charters for fishing or just cruising the lake. 2331 Princess St. (phone: 613-546-3655). Expensive to moderate.

Highland – Near historic Fort Henry, this 44-room establishment has spacious grounds, a heated pool, and tennis courts. Route 15 at Route 2, RR 1 (phone: 613-546-3121). Moderate.

Beaver – Sixteen of the 22 clean, quiet rooms are now efficiency units. There's an outdoor pool, a playground, and an antiques-and-other-collectibles store. Just off Highway 401 on Route 15 (phone: 613-546-6674). Moderate.

GANANOQUE

Country Squire Family Inn – An activity-oriented resort with everything from tennis to a trampoline to an 85-foot indoor pool. Fifteen cottages are available as well as 51 motel rooms. The honeymoon suites have fireplaces. Open April through November. 715 King St. E. (phone: 613-382-3511). Expensive.

Glen House – This resort lodge lies right on the St. Lawrence and has a beach, an indoor pool, 72 rooms, and 4 cottages. The view of the river from the dining room is excellent. Open year-round. On the Thousand Islands Parkway, (phone: 613-659-2204). Expensive.

1000 Island – A clean and cozy motel with honeymoon suites and suites with Jacuzzis, water beds, and an outdoor pool. Babysitting is available. Tickets for the Thousand Islands boat tour are available here. 550 King St. E. (phone: 613-382-3911). Expensive to moderate.

IVY LEA

Ivy Lea Inn – Set on 35 acres, with 1,700 feet of St. Lawrence River shoreline, the inn has 23 rooms, 8 cottages, a pool, tennis courts, a fishing pier, and a yacht harbor. One mile (1.6 km) west on Thousand Islands Parkway (phone: 613-659-2329). Expensive to moderate.

Caiger's – This quiet resort with 35 rooms is fully dedicated to the fine art of relaxing and casting a few fishing lines. They will arrange everything from boats and guides to licenses and bait. There's a pool and good dining facilities. Thousand Islands Parkway (phone: 613-659-2266). Moderate.

The Western Lakeshores

The 660-mile (1,056-km) route follows almost mile for mile — with a few inland departures — the spectacular shoreline of Lake Huron and Lake Superior, one of the most scenic drives in Canada. Less than 20 years ago, this wilderness area of thick forest, gorges, fjords, lakes, and rivers was passable only by rail, canoe, or air (bush pilots served various fishing and hunting lodges throughout the area). Today a road stretches from Owen Sound, on the peninsula of land that divides Georgian Bay and Lake Huron, to Nipigon on the southern shore of huge Lake Nipigon. At Nipigon the road joins Yonge Street, the long road from Toronto that is discussed in the following route.

This is a land of rushing rivers, untamed waterfalls, vast deposits of mineral wealth, thickly wooded bush, and deep forests. It is a tortuous landscape of canyons and gorges punctuated by tiny crystal lakes, with the mighty inland sea forever washing its shores. It is the country of the backpacker, canoeist, camper, camera enthusiast, rockhound, skier, angler, hunter, and anyone who enjoys unspoiled nature in its full beauty. For the adventurous, rough feeder roads along the route lead deeper into the wilderness, to remote fishing spots and wildlife habitats. It is, however, no place for a novice alone.

The many moods of Lake Superior dictate weather conditions deep into the surrounding interior. Fog is common, and the weather is changeable. The nature lover will find all its moods impressive, but there is a special purity to the vast expanse of azure blue on a sunny summer day. Winter comes early and stays late, and on occasions the overnight temperatures drop to the freezing mark as early as mid-August. On the other hand, daytime temperatures can reach the 90s F (30s C) in midsummer. And summertime visitors should include a good insect repellent in their luggage.

Hidden in the massive rock formations that line Lake Superior's shores are the Indian petroglyphs that influenced Longfellow when he wrote *Hiawatha,* and there are indications that the Indians who lived along the coastline were making copper tools long before Europeans visited this part of the country.

The original native American inhabitants were the Ojibwa Indians; they were joined by French fur traders in the early 1700s in a few locations around the lake, and soon after, British fur traders also discovered the area and established communications with the Ojibwa. The three cultures existed side by side (dominated by the Ojibwa, who far outnumbered the scattered French and British) for almost 100 years, until prospectors discovered the region's vast lode of mineral wealth — copper and silver, some gold, and heavy concentrations of iron ore — in the early 1800s.

That ended the halcyon days of the fur trade and brought the decline of the Indian culture. Between 1845 and 1870 mining was extremely heavy, focusing primarily on copper and silver. With the mines came the railroad, and the wild region began to open up. (Mining remains a significant part of the area's business, with uranium the most recent discovery.)

Visitors will be more interested in one particularly significant aspect of the region. Ontario's Great Lake shoreline is part of the transitional zone between northern and southern life forms. The Great Lakes–St. Lawrence Forest Region extends to just south of Wawa, where it begins to merge into the Boreal Forest Region of the north, thus representing a transition between northern and temperate climates. In the southern region the mixed hardwood forest is composed of sugar maple, yellow birch, and a mixed forest cover of conifers, white birch, and mountain ash. The northern sector of boreal mixed forest has birch, spruce, aspen, and balsam fir. On the floors of deep canyons of this region, where little sunlight falls, Arctic flowers, mosses, and lichens, normally found only in the extreme north, maintain a precarious existence.

The Owen Sound–Nipigon route is doubly delightful; conscientious observers of nature will be fascinated by the combinations of northern and southern life forms in the area. And you need no special knowledge to be awed by the massive rock formations along the lake; the cascades of waterfalls and necklace braids of lakes that lace the area's forests; the gorges and fjords chiseled out of the rocks; and the inpenetrable silence of the woods. From Owen Sound on the Bruce Peninsula, the route crosses the mouth of Georgian Bay to Manitoulin Island, where an annual Indian powwow is held. On the mainland, Route 17, part of the 5,000-mile Trans-Canada Highway, continues along the shoreline to the great locks at Sault Ste. Marie, which connect Lake Huron with Lake Superior.

Beyond "the Soo," as Sault Ste. Marie is known, most of the highway has only two lanes, and the stretch between Lake Superior Park (85 mi/137 km from the Soo) and Marathon (124 mi/198 km east of Nipigon) wasn't even built until the 1960s. In some places the road slices 60 feet into the crest of a mountain in an effort to climb over the top, and pits 80 feet deep had to be filled to provide footing for the road. This highway is one of the few in the world traveled not as a means of getting from one point to another but for the pure joy of the trip.

OWEN SOUND: This attractive community on its own inlet just within Georgian Bay is 74 miles (118 km) west of Barrie, Ontario, and 116 miles (186 km) northwest of Toronto. On the fringes of the historic Huron Indian district, its original population was nonetheless Ojibwa Indians, who were deeply influenced by the agricultural successes of the Hurons (one of the few Canadian Indian tribes to farm rather than hunt). Today, Owen Sound has a fine museum of local native history. The three buildings of the *County of Grey and Owen Sound Museum* (975 Sixth St. E.) date from a period of white settlement early in the 19th century. The museum not only has exhibits from that period and the era of the Ojibwa, but also presents even more interesting "living history" — demonstrations on spinning and weaving, the cooking styles of both Indians and early settlers, and blacksmithing. The museum staff has made a special study of the technology of Algonquin birchbark canoe construction, and you can see the 26-foot "express" canoe — built for speed, the kind used by Indians and voyageurs in the fur trade — that was built by the museum. Open Tuesdays through Fridays, 9 AM to 5 PM, and on weekends from 1 to 5 PM. During July and August, open daily from 9 AM to 5 PM, except on Sundays, 1 to 5 PM (phone: 519-376-3690). Admission charge.

Photographers will love the Inglis, Jones, and Indian Falls beauty spots close to the city (just about anyone will direct you), while *Story Book Park* (off Routes 10 and 6, on Story Book Rd.) is the place to burn off youthful energy.

For a calmer end to the day, the *Tom Thompson Memorial Art Gallery* (840 First Ave. W.; closed Mondays), dedicated to one of Canada's most innovative landscape painters, displays Thompson's work as well as that of his well-known contemporaries, the Group of Seven, and others. Thompson spent his boyhood here, and the colors of the area's farms and countryside and the views of Georgian Bay heavily influenced his work.

En Route from Owen Sound – From Route 7, pick up Route 6 north and west of Owen Sound, leading out of the Bruce Peninsula separating Georgian Bay (on your right) from Lake Huron (on your left). About 40 miles (64 km) from Owen Sound, just beyond Wiarton and its bustling shopping districts, is the Cape Croker Indian Reserve. Here, a reconstructed Indian fortress still guards the Ojibwa village on Georgian Bay; the village and fortress are open year-round, and campsites on the shore are available during the summer. Fishing in the bay once supported the community and is still too good for most anglers to resist. Many of the shoreline villages — on both shores — have developed into fishing-oriented resorts; two of the best are Lions Head and Tobermory.

TOBERMORY: At the very tip of the Bruce Peninsula, Tobermory is, first and always, a fishing village. Its wood-frame homes and harbors are quite peaceful, but it is a busy resort center. Whether you're fishing for rainbow trout, fighting northern pike, walleye, or bass in Lake Huron or Georgian Bay, or scuba diving for a glimpse of one of the 50 or so known wrecks that lie in nearby waters, charter boats are available in Tobermory's twin harbors. Water taxis will always take you out to fantastic Flower Pot Island, about 4 miles offshore, where wind- and water-carved rock formations look like giant flower pots in the distance. Also on the island are caves that can be explored for hours and a campground so you can spend some time here comfortably.

   En Route from Tobermory – The Manitoulin Island car ferry crosses the main channel of Georgian Bay's mouth onto Lake Huron, passing among the beautiful Georgian Bay Islands. The crossing takes about 2 hours and operates daily, May through October. Make reservations during the summer (*Owen Sound Transportation Company* (1101 1st Ave. W., Owen Sound; phone: 519-376-6601). There is a charge for the ferry.

MANITOULIN ISLAND: Stretching west from the mouth of Georgian Bay toward the mainland, the island forms part of the landmass that actually separates Georgian Bay from Lake Huron and makes it a distinct body of water. From its first habitation, the history of Manitoulin Island has been inextricably bound to its surrounding waters. Early Indian residents lived by fishing; current residents live primarily by fishing or the tourists that fishing attracts. At the South Baymouth Fish Research Station, north of South Baymouth off Route 68, and at the Sandfish Hatchery, 22 miles (35 km) northwest of South Baymouth, you can get a close view of the modern fishing industry. And just as fishing always has been a part of island life, Manitoulin is still very much an Indian area as well.

   Time your visit to coincide with the *Wikwemikong Indian Powwow* (the first weekend in August), when the Manitoulin Indians host a conclave of some 18 tribes of six distinct Indian Nations. It's a spectacular colorfest of dancing, crafts shows, and traditional tribal ceremonies. For information, contact the Wikwemikong Band Administration Office, Wikwemikong Unceded Indian Reserve, Wikwemikong (phone: 705-859-3122).

   Take time to tour the quiet communities that line the island shores. Little Current, in the northeast corner, began as a Hudson's Bay Company trading post; just outside town is McLean's Mountain (1,075 ft.), and the views of the bay from there are eye-popping. Gore Bay, also on the north shore, is a major shopping stop for residents and visitors alike, but the calm and quiet of its old-fashioned streets keep that aspect in the background. On the south shore, opposite Gore Bay, is the long sandy beach of Providence Bay. At Meldrum Bay, on the western tip of the island, the *Mississaugi Strait Lighthouse Museum* has been guarding the hazardous strait since 1874. La Salle's ship, the *Griffin,* shipwrecked here in 1670, and relics are displayed in the old lighthouse.

   En Route from Manitoulin Island – By a series of bridges and causeways, Route 68 leads across the Bay of Islands from Little Current to the industrial hub of Espanola on the mainland. If mining or geology are among your interests, drive east 1 hour on the Trans-Canada Highway to Sudbury, one of the country's biggest mining towns and home to the *Science North* exhibition center.

SUDBURY: Was it a meteorite or volcanic explosion that created the Sudbury Basin? Expert opinion is divided. Whatever the answer, this phenomenon — measuring 37 by 17 miles — is the largest source of nickel in the world, and Sudbury is the site of the world's largest integrated nickel mining, smelting, and refining complex. The region has other mineral wealth, too: platinum, copper, cobalt, silver, and gold. Its natural treasures include beautiful lakes — some within the city limits — and forests. But most visitors make the trip to Sudbury to check out *Science North,* a $28-million science center opened by the Queen in 1984. Perched on a rock outcropping on the shores of Lake Ramsey, 1 mile (1.6 km) south of the Trans-Canada, the snowflake-shaped structure is set over a cavern blasted out of the rock to represent the probable creation of the Sudbury Basin. In a vast rock cavern, a stunning wilderness film is projected in

3D, and in the weather station, visitors can see the earth from 23,000 miles up and count lightning strikes during a storm. *Science North* has a restaurant, lounge bar and cafeterias. Open year-round, with extended hours in the summer (phone: 705-522-3700).

En Route from Sudbury – Backtracking west on the Trans-Canada leads to Elliot Lake, a modern boom town, created in 1954 by industries attracted to the spectacular lake district by the discovery of uranium. Limited tours of the facilities are available by contacting the Corporation of the Town of Elliot Lake (phone: 519-848-2888), Mondays through Fridays, July and August only. The town of Blind River, west on Route 17, is nestled at the mouth of the Mississaugi River in a way that hid it from lake travelers during the violent early years of exploration. The westernmost island of the Manitoulin group is accessible over a toll-free bridge from Route 17. An early British fort of the same name as the island, St. Joseph, has been reconstructed (it was burned by Americans in 1814), and parts of the large trading center here are in operation (May through September, daily). Route 68 ends at Espanola, where it joins Route 17 for the 143-mile (229-km) drive west to Sault Ste. Marie.

SAULT STE. MARIE: At this narrow point of land separating Lakes Huron and Superior, the rapids of the St. Mary's River separate the twin cities of Sault Ste. Marie — one in the US, the other in Canada. A settlement was established by Jesuit missionaries at this crucial juncture in 1668, and the British and French clashed over possession of the site several times. The Soo (as the city is known, because *Sault* is pronounced *soo*) is currently Canada's second-biggest steel producer, its mills fed directly from the mines just north of here. The giant freighters that sail the Great Lakes to and from the port of Thunder Bay must pass through the locks here on either side of the St. Mary's River, making the Soo Locks among the busiest on the St. Lawrence Seaway. You can view these oceangoing ships from shore or take a cruise through the locks yourself. Contact *Chief Shingwauk Cruises* (phone: 705-253-9850), daily from mid-May to mid-October. The locks operate only from April to December due to the winter freeze.

The biggest attraction of the area is the day-long excursion train trip into wild Agawa Canyon, 114 miles (182 km) north of the city. The *Algoma Central Railway* takes you deep into the unspoiled Ontario wilderness, crossing gorges on trestle bridges and dipping into wide river valleys. The tracks wind around lakes and mountains where no roads exist. The 9-hour round trip to Agawa Canyon includes 2 hours to explore this beautiful area, which has ample opportunities for picnicking, fishing, and photography. Advance reservations are not accepted, but tickets may be purchased at the depot one day in advance. The train leaves the Algoma Central Railway Terminal (129 Bay St.; phone: 705-254-4331) daily at 8 AM from early June to mid-October. A special *Snow Train* — a cross-country ski special — runs between January and March, Saturdays and Sundays only, leaving the Soo at 8:30 AM and returning at 5:30 PM (call 705-254-4331 for reservations).

In Sault Ste. Marie, visit the Old Stone House, built in the early 1800s by Charles Ermatinger, a fur trader with the Northwest Company, for his Indian princess wife. The restored first story is furnished as it was when the house was originally built, and the second floor has been turned into a museum. Ermatinger's house is the oldest extant dwelling in northwest Ontario (open daily, May to mid-October, 831 Queen St. E.).

The Soo waterfront is the berth of the last overnight passenger cruise ship built on the Great Lakes, the MS *Norgoma,* and the headquarters of the Firebirds, the aerial firefighters who protect the vast timberlands around Sault Ste. Marie. At the headquarters, you can inspect the planes and see some of the gear vital to their work. The headquarters is open to the public Tuesdays and Fridays from 2:30 to 4 PM during July and August only.

The Great Lakes Forestry Centre (1219 Queen St. E.), one of six around the country, conducts research programs to solve forestry problems. Tours of the facilities are free and are offered weekdays between 10 AM and 2 PM from June to September.

For a meal in an informal setting, try *Guffin's Chaw-Chew and Steer Stop* (Bay St. at the Algoma Central Railway Station; phone: 705-942-1535); an interesting mix of railroad and western themes with delicatessen overtones. The nearby *Station Mall Shopping Centre* has good specialty shops, including the *The Bay Fur Store*.

En Route from Sault Ste. Marie – Take Route 17 for 133 miles (213 km) north toward Wawa. Population centers will dwindle as you draw away from the influence of the city, but tiny communities are scattered along the way as far as Montreal River Harbour (65 miles/104 km from the Soo), which is close to the boundary of Lake Superior Provincial Park. These small towns generally are able to provide basic services — gasoline, food, and lodging. Once you enter the park area, however, there are very few services, and accommodations are limited to government campgrounds.

Just north of Sault Ste. Marie, the *Algoma Central Railway* passes over the highway as it winds 236 miles (380 km) north to Hearst (on Route 11) to join the *Canadian National Railway*. The *Algoma Central* was a key tool in opening up the area.

If you are in the mood for some wilderness camping, leave Route 17 at Heyden, about 8 miles (13 km) north of the Soo, for Route 556, which leads to the Ranger Lake Game Preserve deep in the Ontario interior. Paved part way, most of Route 556 is gravel. Camping is primitive, and you will need to bring your own supplies.

Continuing 8 miles (13 km) beyond Heyden on Route 17 is the Goulais River turnoff. After a short drive along a gravel road on the left (toward Lake Superior), you could find a large swamp; if you are quiet and patient, you have a good chance of spotting moose here. There also are numerous waterfowl and some rare swamp orchids in the area. The spotted coral root (about 12 inches tall), which grows only in the Lake Superior region, also is found here.

By the time you reach Batchawana Bay on Route 16, you will really begin to experience Lake Superior. As the land starts to rise, large portions of the lake are visible. The rocks of the Canadian Shield become apparent, and the forest is thicker as you follow the lake shoreline for 50 miles (80 km). From here on, the coastline offers many deserted picnic and swimming spots. At Batchawana Bay itself there is a beautiful stretch of beach, once a government-run campground, now open for day use only.

BATCHAWANA BAY: The Batchawana Bay area is a huge bay encompassing both Havilland and Marmony bays. Its name comes from the Indian *Obajewunung,* which means "narrows and swift waters there," an appropriate description of the swift waters that pour through the narrow mouth of the bay when a strong wind whips across Lake Superior. The village of Batchawana was once an Ojibwa settlement, and Indians still live here, though they are now outnumbered by non-Indians working the local copper mines, logging operations, and a growing tourist industry.

On nearby Batchawana Island, off the mouth of the Batchawana River, a trading post was established in 1824, and it remained in operation for 70 years. The waters of the bay here are the warmest on Superior's east coast, and the rivers that empty here offer good access to the fishing and hunting areas inland.

En Route from Batchawana Bay – Just a few miles north, hidden by forests of black spruce, lies Pancake Bay. The bay was named by a party of fur traders who stayed only long enough to cook breakfast near the mouth of Pancake River. A small park (1,500 acres and 50 campsites) allows visitors to do the same. Before the railroads began laying track through here, all supplies came via the lake; from December freeze-up to April thaws, settlers were isolated by the winter ice. Pancake Bay is rough country and has rough waters: a lighthouse just north of the bay marks the loss of one lake freighter that went down here in 1902; it was not alone. From here the road stays close to Superior's irregular shore, passing the commercial fishing fleets at Hibbard Bay and the site of Indian copper mines at Point Mamainse, where the "Old Copper" Indians may have worked these mines as early as 6000 BC; commercial mining began here in 1889 and lasted only 5 years.

North of Hibbard Bay the terrain changes drastically — volcanic lava coated the surface a billion years ago, and when it hardened, trapped air bubbles became natural collection points for agates and copper. It is rockhound heaven, and you can collect interesting samples almost anywhere along the road simply by pulling over and looking.

The Montreal River powers four hydroelectric generating stations before draining into Lake Superior. Its 65-mile course winds through some of the most dramatic country in the region and has been painted from several different perspectives by artists of the Group of Seven.

Uranium was discovered in this area in 1847, but apparently the vein was lost soon after because it was "discovered" again in the 1950s, when a mining operation was set up. The Ranwick Uranium Mine, 3 miles (5 km) north of Montreal River Harbour on Route 17, permits public tours of its site from mid-May to mid-October.

LAKE SUPERIOR PROVINCIAL PARK: Established in 1944 to preserve this spectacular shoreline and the surrounding area, this park is 601 square miles of shore, forest, and rising hills. Its highest point, 1,950 feet, is about halfway through the park on Route 17 near Gamitagama Road. Except for the 50-mile (80-km) ribbon of Route 17 that cuts through the park, this is a natural environment, established for hiking, boating, and camping. One of the newer trails leads into spectacular Agawa Canyon, but it's a pretty rough hike. The Agawa Bay section of the park, part of the shoreline around which the park was formed, is protected by several rocky hills. The curved beach is dotted with multicolored pebbles worn smooth by sand and waves.

A little farther into the park, Route 17 crosses the Agawa River and climbs to the Agawa Bay Lookout high over Lake Superior. Just a mile beyond here are the Agawa Rock Pictographs, a place of eerie and awesome proportions, which has been recognized for ages as a site of religious and spiritual significance. The 35 paintings around the cliff base include fish, mythical serpents, canoes, caribou, bears, and a turtle.

There is no real evidence of the age of these paintings, but they appear to span a broad period of time. By a curious and unlikely series of events, the stories told by the pictographs became the basis of Henry Wadsworth Longfellow's epic *Hiawatha* without the poet knowing where they were. In 1851, a government Indian agent named Henry Schoolcraft wrote down various myths and legends told by local Indian tribes. The stories actually came from the pictographs, but Schoolcraft knew nothing of their existence. A copy of Schoolcraft's version of the tales came to Longfellow, who was inspired to write *Hiawatha*. Unfortunately, no one mentioned *where* the pictographs were, and not until 1958 (12 years after the park was established) did Selwyn Dewdney end a 14-month search when he directed his canoe toward the massive rock point on which they appear.

En Route from Lake Superior Provincial Park – There are additional park facilities north of the pictographs and picnic grounds near the mouth of the Michipicoten River. This intersection of a water route leading north with the principal east-west access of the Great Lakes was the site of a trading post — erected by the French in 1725 — fought over by the Hudson's Bay Company and its economic rival, the Northwest Company. Ownership of the post was disputed constantly until the firms merged in 1821. The trading post was closed in 1904 and has since been reconstructed.

Take Route 101 east into Wawa, just a few miles away. At the intersection of Routes 101 and 17 stands the Wawa Goose — a 28-foot-tall, 22-foot-long steel sculpture of a goose weighing in at over 2 tons. You can't miss it.

WAWA: On the western shore of its own lake, also called Wawa (Ojibwa for "wild goose"), is this annual stopping place for flocks of Canada geese during migration. Although hunters have followed the geese here for ages, the town wasn't established until the accidental discovery of gold in 1896. Since that time Wawa has experienced two more gold rushes, all three of which burned out quickly. Today, iron mining is the basis of local industry, but you're welcome to try starting a fourth gold rush: Just explore the Old Gold Mine Road that lies between Routes 17 and 101. The town is very popular with waterfowl and big-game hunters and sport fisher folk as a starting point for treks and fly-in trips to the Ontario interior wilds, and a variety of shops, provisioners, guides, and accommodations are nearby.

En Route from Wawa – Back on Route 17, turn right at the Wawa goose and head for Nipigon, in Lake Superior's northwest corner. It's a fairly long trip — 220 miles (352 km) — on a road that didn't even exist until the 1960s. The highway curves inland, and the lakeshore lies far to the west, beyond reach except by foot; it is still as wild and desolate as ever. Part of this coast is included in the Pukaskwa Park (Puk-o-saw), Ojibwa for "place for the cleaning of fish." Even the park area is only accessible either from Lake Superior or overland by foot, since the streams leading in are mostly impassable even by canoe except during the spring thaws. It's the patient backpacker who really benefits from this park. One of Ontario's tallest mountains, 2,120-foot Tip Top, is deep in the park, and there are a couple of small herds of woodland caribou in the area.

As the land begins to flatten out, muskeg, bog, and swamp break up the forests, creating a virtual playground for beaver, waterfowl, and moose. Except for isolated communities and a few Indian reservations, this area is uninhabited and is beautiful beyond belief. Fungus Lake, excellent for pike and walleye, and Obatanga Park, a 36-square-mile primitive park, are accessible from Route 17, as are Bogh, Hammer (another pike hot spot), and Marion lakes. The patches of bright lavender and pink flowers are you seen everywhere are fireweed; they spring out of the earth scorched by a forest fire in the late 1950s.

WHITE RIVER: Ever since that day in 1935 when the mercury hit 72F *below* freezing ($-22C$), White River has been known for its cold winters. But the locals get upset at claims that it's consistently the coldest spot in Canada. In any case, they argue (correctly), the dry cold is much more comfortable than the humid, higher temperatures near lakes and rivers. What the place should be known for, they say, are the pollen-free summers (it's a haven for those with hay fever), the magnificent scenery, and the abundance of game: black bear and moose, pike, walleye, lake trout, and whitefish. The *White River Trading Post* (106 Superior St.; phone: 807-822-2366) can equip hunters for expeditions, arrange for fishing licenses and guides, and keep fish on ice. The store now has a deli and laundrette. *White River Air Services* (phone: 807-822-2222 or 705-856-2753 in winter) flies hunters into camps. It operates several American-plan lodges of its own in the area.

En Route from White River – Alongside this still-recent roadway are the tracks of the *Canadian Pacific Railway,* the first lifeline into this wild area. The small communities that huddle around the tracks testify to the importance of this steel network to the development of the land.

Most of the lakes visible from the road are nameless, just secluded places where you can take a break or cast for the "big one" hiding on the bottom somewhere. Route 17 runs right past the Mobert Indian Reservation, and the White Lake Provincial Park lies about 6 miles (10 km) beyond Mobert. The lake itself is pretty big, and if rumors are to be believed, it supports enormous walleye. Settle for a couple of 8- or 10-pounders. If fishing bores you, try some of the hiking trails or just stretch out on the lake's sandy beach.

About 10 miles (16 km) west of the park on Route 17 is the intersection of Manitouwadge Corners. Here Route 614 extends 36 miles (58 km) north to Manitouwadge, or "cave of the Great Spirit," a small mining town hidden in the bush. An Ojibwa Indian guided prospectors here in 1931, and they found copper, gold, zinc, silver, lead, and cadmium. By the mid-1950s a town had grown around the hastily erected camps. So far there are four mines here, and engineers are still "sounding out" the area.

Over the next 20 miles (32 km) the landscape becomes hilly, and the Black River cuts a rocky path along the highway in its rush to Lake Superior. Route 17 also runs toward Lake Superior, through hills of pink granite as old as the river.

Here the Pic River crosses the highway to empty into the lake, and a small roadway, Route 627, leads south along the shore to the Pic River Indian Reservation. The reservation was the site of an 18th-century trading post, and it is the closest thing to "access" to Pukaskwa National Park, which lies south of here on the far side of the White River. Be sure to check with the tribal chief or administrator about arranging guide services or right-of-way passage through their lands if you go to the park overland.

MARATHON: When you see thousands upon thousands of logs piled on the waterfront, you'll be in Marathon, a fairly large town founded recently in connection with the lumber industry.

On a broad peninsula 20 miles (32 km) west of Marathon are the sandy beaches of Neys Provincial Park, some of the most beautiful on Superior's north shore, but too cold for swimming most of the time. Fishing in this area is excellent, though, and the park shelters a herd of woodland caribou who feed (partially) on the wild blueberries that grow here. During World War II, the park was used as a prisoner-of-war camp because of its almost escapeproof location.

En Route from Marathon – Continuing west on Route 17, with the offshore islands of Lake Superior on the left and a mountain ridge on the right, an unfortunate scene offends all who pass — the sight of a foaming, chemically polluted river making its way to the lake, a dumping ground for the paper processing industries in the area.

About 50 miles (80 km) west of Marathon is Terrace Bay, whose road winds among the coastal hills that surround Lake Superior.

TERRACE BAY: When the glaciers formed Lake Superior, the ice also cut a series of sand and gravel terraces into the shoreline. The exposed sides of these steps are full of amethyst, opalite, quartz, and other minerals, all of which are visible from Terrace Bay's Centennial Park, where a plaque describes the geological process that gave birth to these brilliant glacial scars. The town's main industry is a pulp mill, supported by the region's abundant forests. A few miles offshore are the twin Slate Islands, shelter for a herd of caribou.

En Route from Terrace Bay – Less than a mile west of town, off Route 17 on a marked access road, is the Aguasabon Falls and Gorge. The Aguasabon River cascades over the edge of a 100-foot drop, plunging into a deep gorge as it courses toward nearby Lake Superior. Schreiber is only 9 miles (14 km) farther.

SCHREIBER: If you start seeing double, pull over and check — you're probably in Schreiber. The town has gained a certain notoriety for the incredible number of twins born here. A few years back there were 28, which doesn't include broken sets — some twins have moved away because of the absurdity of it all. There's no way of explaining this phenomenon.

En Route from Schreiber – At the scenic Lookout Point about 6 miles (10 km) west of town is a plaque telling a small part of a very large story. During the 1800s, the lands of the Hudson's Bay Company, originally granted by the Crown, were given over to the Dominion of Canada. Fearing that this voided their agreements with the company, many Métis, trappers, and Indians who occupied the Northwest Territories and Saskatchewan rebelled against the government and white settlers. The open fighting that broke out on the frontier contributed to the unwillingness of the railroad companies to run lines into this area. It also fueled the French-English antagonism within the country because many eastern French Canadians supported the leader of the rebellion, Louis Riel, in his claims for the rights of the Métis. Riel was executed in November of 1885. The use of rapid transit rail systems, relatively new in this area at the time, was crucial to the government's defeat of Riel's forces. In this area the rail line was incomplete, and the troops had to make a forced march across it to reach the fighting farther west. Their march is commemorated in the Lookout Point plaque.

Rainbow Falls Provincial Park, just outside Rossport, has a lovely set of falls, white sand lakes, and fishing and swimming facilities. From Rossport to Nipigon, then down a few miles toward Thunder Bay, the sheltered waters of Nipigon Bay are separated from Lake Superior by St. Ignace Island, just across the mouth of the bay.

Skirting the bay, Route 17 passes through Cavers, Gravel, and Dublin to Kama Lookout, 17 miles (27 km) east of Nipigon, where the view of the bay is considered to be the best on the shoreline. Here a plaque tells travelers about the "Old Copper" Indians, who by all evidence were making metal tools long before Europeans began exploring the New World.

At Nipigon, Route 17 intersects Yonge Street (Rte. 11) as it curves southward from its path across the northern frontier toward Thunder Bay, farther south and west. Yonge Street crossed Route 17 at North Bay as it climbed to Cochrane before bearing west, paralleling Route 17 on its journey through Ontario. See the *Yonge Street: Toronto to Thunder Bay* route for a complete report on Nipigon and Routes 11 and 17 (which run concurrently through Thunder Bay).

BEST EN ROUTE

Since this route covers such a varied area, there are wide discrepancies in the prices listed for any given location. In many areas you're actually comparing rates that include guide services, fishing permits, and equipment in addition to the rooms themselves. Those charging more than $60 per night for two are listed as expensive. The bulk of the establishments fall into the moderate category, $40 to $60 per night, double occupancy, and places charging under $40 per night for two are considered inexpensive. All prices are quoted in US dollars.

The price ranges cannot reflect the level of service, so be sure of what you're buying when you call to make reservations. Make your plans as far in advance as possible, and don't expect to find many vacancies; hotel and even camping space can be scarce in the summer.

SUDBURY

Journey's End Motel – Canada's largest motel chain (122 in Ontario alone) has a very good reputation for cleanliness and comfort. Morning coffee and newspaper are complimentary, and the must-see *Science North* is 5 minutes away by car. 2171 Regent St. S., off Highway 69 (phone: 705-522-1101). Moderate.

SAULT STE. MARIE

Holiday Inn – Overlooking St. Mary's River and conveniently located near shopping and the *Algoma Central* depot, this large inn provides 194 rooms and 6 suites, an indoor pool, sauna, dining room, and a lounge. 208 St. Mary's River Dr. (phone: 705-949-0611). Expensive.

Ramada Inn – On the city's "golden mile" of shopping centers, this place has 218 rooms and just about every facility you can think of — including a bowling alley and an indoor *Wilderness* miniature golf course. 229 Great Northern Rd. (phone: 705-942-2500). Expensive.

Water Tower Inn – This modern 5-story member of the Best Western chain is part of Water Tower Place, a complex containing the inn and several good restaurants and lounges. The 180 rooms are large and impeccably clean; furnishings are contemporary, and each room has an original batik on the wall. Among the restaurants here is *Jimmie John's,* which specializes in seafood, steaks, and shish kebab. Facilities include indoor and outdoor pools and whirlpool baths, a wading pool, sauna, and exercise room. In the winter, the hotel offers special ski packages for Search Mountain (20 miles/32 km away) and the many cross-country trails in the area. Route 17B at junction of Route 50 (phone: 705-949-8111). Expensive.

Empire – The area is noted for its many reasonably priced motels, and this is one of them. With 120 rooms, an indoor pool, and a sauna, it's the largest and best-equipped. 320 Bay St. (phone: 705-759-8200). Expensive to moderate.

Blueberry Hill Motel – This two-in-one spot on the Goulais River offers a pleasant 10-room motel and a 100-site campground with hookups, shelter, flush toilets, showers, a pool, playground, store, and boat rentals. Fifteen miles (24 km) north of the city off Route 17 (phone: 705-649-5631). Moderate.

WAWA

Normandy – This wilderness resort has 4 rooms and 10 cottages, a dining room, fly-in services, and hunting and fishing guides. Rate includes meals. Open from May to November. Route 17, 30 miles (48 km) north of Wawa. (phone: 705-856-2644). Expensive.

Wawa – A motel with 70 rooms and 18 secluded rustic log cabins, all with fireplaces. There's also an indoor pool, sauna, dining room, and exercise room. Route 101, 1 mile (1.6 km) east off Route 17 (phone: 705-856-2278). Expensive (cottages) to moderate (rooms).

Kinniwabi Pines – Its 12 rooms and 3 two-bedroom chalets are set in an attractive wooded location; some have a river view. There's fishing, a restaurant across the road, and boat rentals nearby. Open from May to October. Route 17, 4 miles (6 km) south of town (phone: 705-856-7302). Moderate (chalets) to inexpensive (rooms).

Camp High Falls – Ten units, including 7 cottages with fireplaces and 3 air conditioned motel rooms, set back from the highway in a grove of trees. Open from May to October. Highway 17, 2 miles (3 km) south of town (phone: 705-856-4496). Inexpensive.

WHITE RIVER

Continental – Open year-round, this motel has 33 clean rooms with color TV sets, radios, and phones. There's a restaurant across the road. Route 17 (phone: 807-822-2500). Inexpensive.

MARATHON

Pic – Overlooking Lake Superior, this motel has 23 large, clean rooms with color TV sets. There's a 2-level dining room; the top area serves full meals, and the bottom is a more informal disco serving pizza and subs. A golf course is nearby. Marathon Rd. off Route 17 (phone: 807-229-0130). Moderate.

Peninsula – Set back from the highway, this 21-unit inn is open year-round. Route 17 (phone: 807-229-0651). Moderate.

TERRACE BAY

Imperial – Overlooking Lake Superior, this in-town motel has 21 units and a dining room. A golf course is nearby. Open year-round. Route 17 (phone: 807-825-3226). Moderate.

Red Dog – In the center of town, this inn has 40 large rooms with color TV sets, and a licensed dining room. It offers tennis on the spot and golf nearby. Open year-round. Route 17 (phone: 807-825-3286). Moderate.

SCHREIBER

Nor-West – This quiet motel is set well back from the highway. The 11 rooms (some kitchenettes included) have color TV sets, and there's an adjacent restaurant. Open year-round. Route 17 just west of town (phone: 807-824-2501). Moderate.

Circle Route – Some of the 31 rooms in this motel have kitchenettes. There also is a dining room, and a laundromat. Open year-round. Route 17 (phone: 807-824-2452). Moderate.

Yonge Street: Toronto to Thunder Bay

Toronto's Yonge Street, listed in the *Guinness Book of World Records* as the longest street in the world, runs 1,142 miles (1,827 km) from downtown Toronto on Lake Ontario to the province's far southwestern border with Minnesota and Manitoba. It is a trip from urban sophistication to an almost frontier-like austerity, through the rich farmland of southern Ontario's "English counties," across the harsh, mineral-rich mining districts of the Canadian Shield, and through the trapping and fur country north of the Great Lakes. Called Route 11 once it leaves Toronto, Yonge Street cuts like a surgeon's knife across the width of southern Ontario, touching all the features that have forged Ontario's special culture. It is one of the major factors that knitted this diverse province into a political entity.

Lieutenant-Governor John Simcoe began planning the route in 1793, and construction of the roadway began the following year. Its original purpose was to provide a rapid military and commercial route to northern Ontario and the Upper Great Lakes; it became a major force in the settlement of Ontario.

The road grew as Ontario grew. Built along traditional Indian paths used long before Europeans came to Canada, the first leg of the road crossed the fertile lands of the southern Ontario peninsula, reaching from Lake Ontario to what was called the lakelands, near Georgian Bay. It served the fur trading routes, for voyageurs could bring furs from the west to be transported overland. But as people poured into the area, the rich mineral deposits of the Canadian Shield, north and west of the lakelands, became known, and the road was pushed northward, past Lake Nipissing. It crossed the "height of the land," the central crest of the Canadian Shield, past lumber and mining towns like Cobalt and Kirkland Lake, where the main street is called the Golden Mile because the roadbed is filled with raw gold ore. Most of the towns in this area were side effects of discoveries of gold or silver or offshoots of the lumber trade, and the growth of these industries brought first railroads and later settlers. As Ontario's development pushed back the frontiers, Yonge Street grew segment by segment.

At its western end, Route 11 cuts south, skirting the shores of Lake Nipigon to reach the city of the same name, on the far northwest corner of Lake Superior. Nipigon and the twin cities of Fort William and Port Arthur (now united as Thunder Bay) had been major trading posts and gateways to the lands of western Canada. Here are the spectacular rock carvings of nature — Sleeping Giant Mountain and Ouimet Canyon. This section of Ontario is pure heaven for hunters, anglers, and rockhounds.

Everything past North Bay is outdoors territory, for here Yonge Street is nothing more or less than a thin line through which hunters, miners, trappers, loggers, and others maintain contact with the outside world.

TORONTO: This active international business and cultural center is a highlight of any vacation or business trip. For a detailed report on the city, its sites, hotels, and restaurants, see *Toronto,* THE CITIES.

   En Route from Toronto – The 60-mile (96-km) journey to Barrie, on the shore of Lake Simcoe, begins on Yonge Street (Rte. 11) going north. About 13 miles (21 km) from downtown Toronto is suburban Richmond Hill, known as Mt. Pleasant until the Duke of Richmond renamed it in 1819. Yonge Street runs right by Town Hall, where a marker recalls this period of Richmond Hill's history. On the grounds of the *Summit Golf and Country Club* (11901 Yonge St., about 2 miles/3 km north of town), a marker names Lieutenant-Governor John G. Simcoe as the planner of this extensive roadway. A nearby historical plaque tells of the efforts of French Royalists to establish the De Puisaye settlement here.

   Newmarket, just 11 miles (18 km) beyond Richmond Hill, is the site of a Quaker meetinghouse, the first church erected in the lands north of Toronto; it has stood on the west side of Yonge Street since 1810. Another early 1800s structure, also built by Quakers, has been incorporated into the Pine Orchard Union Church (RR 3, Newmarket). The history of Newmarket's settlement is detailed in the *Whitchurch-Stouffville Museum,* located slightly southeast of the town on Vivianside Road, near Woodbine Avenue (open May through September, Wednesdays through Sundays, holidays from 10:30 AM to 5 PM; or by appointment).

   Continuing on Yonge Street, the route leads toward the Holland River, with its thousands of acres of rich, black farmland that were reclaimed by patient Dutch farmers during the early 1930s. The broad swath of bottomland opening to view as the road approaches is Holland Marsh. Careful management of this once unproductive swamp and flood plain by residents of this still very Dutch district has resulted in one of Ontario's prize vegetable growing areas. The view is breathtaking, but don't get so engrossed that you miss the turnoff to Holland Landing at the foot of the hill.

HOLLAND LANDING: A little over 25 miles (40 km) from Toronto, here was the original terminus of Simcoe's Yonge Street. From the settlement of Holland Landing, soldiers and settlers would follow the route of the early trappers to Georgian Bay by taking the Holland River to Lake Simcoe and connecting with the Severn River to the north. This water route comprises the upper section of the Trent-Severn Waterway, which begins on Lake Ontario at Trenton. Before leaving Holland Landing, visit the hamlet of Sharon, about 1 mile (1.6 km) east. This settlement was established by a Quaker splinter group known as the Children of Peace, or Davidites, so named because they were led by one David Willson. Central to the community was the Temple of Peace, erected from the late 1820s to early 1830s and designed to reflect in its architecture aspects of the sect's beliefs. The structure fell into disrepair following Willson's death in 1866, when the sect began to wane. It has been partially restored and is now a museum of local history (18974 Leslie St.; phone: 416-478-2389). Open daily, except Tuesdays, 10 AM to 5 PM during the summer, weekends only during the fall.

En Route from Holland Landing – Bradford, the commercial hub of Holland Marsh, is only 6 miles (10 km) beyond the Holland Landing turnoff. Yonge Street goes through the town, passing acres of the fertile black muck that in its manicured form produces such beautifully precise rows of fruits and vegetables.

Beyond Bradford, the road crosses a series of river valleys that carry just a hint of the northern highlands to come; you will see occasional glimpses of distant Lake Simcoe as the road nears Barrie. This region, between the Toronto suburbs and the resort areas of Lake Simcoe–Huronia, contains clusters of hardwood forest, small dairy and cattle farms, and a few rural villages.

BARRIE: This gateway to Ontario's pleasant lakeland district, a year-round tourist center, is on Kempenfeldt Bay, an inlet of Lake Simcoe, Ontario's sixth largest lake. As you would expect, summers in Barrie are devoted to sailing, swimming, water skiing, and just about every other water sport, but the attraction doesn't end with the summer sun. Winters are given over to snowmobiling and alpine and crosscountry skiing as well as ice fishing on the lake. Smallmouth bass and lake trout live in Lake Simcoe, and they are just as likely to bite in winter as summer.

An afternoon stroll through downtown Barrie is bound to lead to one of the town's many crafts shops. *Artifact* (123 Dunlop St. E.) offers weaving, handblown glass, and cotton clothing made by artisans across Canada.

If you'd like a look at old Barrie (ca. 1840) the *Simcoe County Museum and Archives* has a replica of an 1840s street, with shops and buildings carefully reconstructed. Several restored pioneer buildings and other exhibits detail changes in the area from 2000 BC until today. The museum is 5 miles (8 km) north of town on Route 26 and is open daily; the Archives are open Tuesdays through Saturdays. (phone: 705-726-9300).

Springwater Provincial Park and the adjacent Midhurst Forest Station comprise an area aimed at preserving the natural environment that created this resort area a century ago. Some of the park's animals roam free, but for visitors' safety others are caged. The beaver dam, continually being expanded and improved by its residents and architects, is one of the most interesting sights (6 mi/10 km west of town on Route 26; the park is open daily; the forest station is open weekdays from April to October).

The *Canadian Forces Base Borden Military Museum,* incorporating six collections of military hardware ranging from small arms to heavy artillery and tanks, contains equipment dating back to the "Big War" (World War I). The base is 10 miles (16 km) west of Barrie on Route 90, near Angus. Look for signs with a simple military "M," for museum. Open Tuesdays through Fridays; afternoons only, Saturdays and Sundays. Proof of vehicle ownership and insurance is required to enter Base Borden.

The *Crazy Fox* restaurant on the waterfront makes wonderful pasta and seafood. For exotic desserts, try *Michael and Marion's* (on Bayfield). Barrie's favorite nightspot is the *Raceway* (Essa Rd.), rebuilt in 1985 after being flattened by a tornado. Track facilities, including a dining room, are all top-notch, and the grandstand is completely glass-enclosed for year-round viewing. The track usually runs ten harness races per program, Wednesdays and Saturdays.

MIDLAND: In the early years of Canada's development, Jesuit missionaries established one of the first inland European settlements in the heart of the Huron Nation. The town of Midland, 24 miles (38 km) northwest of Barrie on Route 27, was established in the 1630s, when French Jesuits made it their headquarters for spreading Christianity through Canada. During the Iroquois Wars against the Huron and their French allies in the 1640s, half a dozen Jesuits were killed by the Iroquois: Fathers Jean de Brebeuf and Gabriel Lalament, put to the torture fires at St. Ignace in March 1649, are buried here at the Martyrs' Shrine. The shrine commands a spectacular view of Georgian Bay and the Wye River and overlooks the mission of Ste.-Marie-among-the-Hurons. The mission, completely rebuilt with a museum, illustrates the lives of the Indians and their Jesuit guests. (Both are on Route 12, about 3 miles/5 km east of Midland, on opposite sides of the highway. Hours are from 10 AM to 6 PM, late May through *Labor Day,* until 8 PM during July and August; *Labor Day* to *Thanksgiving* (early October), 10 AM to 5 PM. The shrine holds Mass daily for pilgrims.)

Across from the shrine is the Wye Marsh Wildlife Centre, 2,500 acres of forests, fields, and marsh, with an interpretive program detailing the importance of this varied terrain to the development of the area, past and future. There are boardwalks, an observation tower, and even an underwater window, all of which are explained in a program of movies, slides, displays, and explanations by the guides. The center is open from late May to mid-October; by appointment at other times (phone: 705-526-7809).

To explain and describe something of the Huron life before and after the coming of the French, Midland has reconstructed a 1615 Huron village in Little Lake Park (King St. S) and an accompanying *Huronia Museum;* together they provide an excellent picture of both early Indian and fur trader life.

En Route from Midland – Back on Route 11, Yonge Street traces the shore of Lake Simcoe for 19 miles (30 km) to the narrows that separate it from Lake Couchiching to the north. In Samuel de Champlain's notes, he tells of this place, called Michekum by the Indians, meaning "fence." The fence consisted of a series of stakes driven into the lake bottom, almost closing the passage, much like a vertical dam. The Indians set fishnets in the breaks, capturing Lake Simcoe's fish bounty. This particular weir, recorded by Champlain, resulted in the lake being called Lac aux Claies (Lake of Sticks) or simply Le Clie until Governor Simcoe renamed it in honor of his father.

ORILLIA: Known as both an industrial city and a summer resort, Orillia has grown considerably since its days as an Indian homeland. A plaque at Couchiching Park relates the story of Chief William Yellowhead's Mississauga tribe of Ojibwa Indians (called Chippewa in the US), who fought with the British during the War of 1812 and settled in the Orillia area in 1830, at the traditional fishing grounds. White settlers came to Orillia less than a decade later, however, and forced the Indians to abandon their lands at the juncture of Lakes Simcoe and Couchiching (now called Atherley Narrows) and relocate at Rama Indian Reserve.

The city has made two important contributions to Canada's cultural heritage: Painter Frank Carmichael (the youngest artist of the original Group of Seven) was born and raised in Orillia, and Stephen Leacock (well-known humorist and Canada's favorite writer, who has more books in print than any other Canadian author) lived in the Lake Simcoe area from the age of 6, and built a 19-room mansion on Old Brewery Bay in 1908. Here he spent some of the most productive years of his life, writing his most famous works. On display at the Leacock home are the author's letters, notes, manuscripts, fishing rod, desk, and other memorabilia. In all likelihood, Leacock's *Sunshine*

Sketches of a Little Town is based on life in Orillia. Open daily, late June to *Labor Day;* tours by appointment from May to mid-June and *Labor Day* to *Thanksgiving* — early October (phone: 705-326-9357).

Orillia's *Ossawippi Express* (210 Mississauga St. E.; phone: 705-325-1559) is a special restaurant located in antique and turn-of-the-century railway cars (complete with brass fittings and Tiffany lamps); it has a marvelous view of Lake Couchiching and serves continental dishes. Closed Sundays. A good way to get an overview of the entire Lake Simcoe area is to take one of the sightseeing flights available from *Orillia Aviation* (phone: 705-325-6153); the company also runs two fishing camps on nearby lakes and will fly passengers in for 1-, 2-, or 5-day stays. For those who feel squeamish about flying around in small planes, the *Lady Belle* cruises through 25 miles of islands in and about Lake Couchiching. Both 1½- and 3-hour cruises leave from the dock at the foot of Mississauga St. (phone: 705-325-5252 or 705-326-2379). Golden Creek Game and Bird Farm features exotic and domestic birds, with flight demonstrations by falcons and hawks on summer weekends. South Sparrow Lake Rd. Exit Highway 12 at Concession Road 12. Open daily mid-May to early September.

En Route from Orillia – The scenery begins to change north of Orillia — farms grow smaller, fewer, and farther apart as rocky outcroppings become more frequent and wooded hills, rivers, and streams tumble after one another in surprising profusion. It's an easy 23 miles (37 km) along Route 11 to Gravenhurst, at the southern tip of Lake Muskoka.

GRAVENHURST: This town began as a hard-working and rambunctious lumber town, but it became a favorite summer home and resort area during the early 1900s. Rumors persist that its name originated in Washington Irving's *Bracebridge Hall* (which indulges in some mischievous and fictitious geography), but its appeal to those seeking a quiet corner of the world is very real. It is the doorway to the fall foliage route, the Cavalcade of Color, when the changing season paints the trees of Muskoka's lakeside district a blaze of reds and oranges. The northern tip of the great forests of southern Ontario, filled with deciduous trees like birch and maple, extends only a few miles farther north before being replaced by firs and pines, and so the autumnal change begins early here — accompanied by dances, country fairs, parades, and firework displays to match the bright colors of the leaves. RMS *Segwun,* 100 years old in 1986 and the oldest steamship still operating in Canada, has daily cruises, June through October from Segwun Park in Gravenhurst (phone: 705-687-6667).

Gravenhurst's favorite son is Norman Bethune, a doctor who became famous as a medical officer with the Chinese Communists. Mao dedicated an essay to Bethune after the Revolution, and his home is a destination for Chinese diplomats to this day. Bethune Memorial House, a former church manse (235 John St.; phone: 705-687-4261) where Bethune was born, has been restored to its original 1890 appearance and contains exhibits depicting Bethune's life and accomplishments. Open daily, except legal holidays in winter.

The 4-day *Muskoka Winter Carnival,* held the last weekend in February, is a lively, popular event, with everything from motorcycle races on ice to a jazz festival.

Sloanes restaurant (155 Muskoka St.; phone: 705-687-4611) is as much a historic landmark as it is a benchmark by which other area restaurants are judged, and none in town surpasses it. *Sloanes* serves delicious meals in the old-fashioned manner — even the breads, rolls, and cakes are homemade (and available for sale to take out).

En Route from Gravenhurst – Only 10 miles (16 km) north of Gravenhurst, on the east side of Lake Muskoka, lies Bracebridge, which also may (or may not) have derived its name from Washington Irving. Just north of Gravenhurst at the *Reay Road KOA* campsite, thousands take part in a cross-country ski race the first week in March. A highway sign claims Gravenhurst is "halfway to the North Pole," and a *Santa's Village* theme park capitalizes on the idea. Children can ride a paddlewheel boat or miniature train, see Santa and his helpers, and play with a farm full of animals (west of town, on Santa's Village Rd., open mid-June through August, daily from 10 AM to 6 PM; weekends only from late May to mid-June and September to mid-October; closed *Labor Day* and *Thanksgiving* (celebrated in Canada in early October). A new attraction in Bracebridge is the *Kite Festival,* held in Jubilee Park the first week in May.

Instead of heading straight to Huntsville, take Highway 169 to Parry Sound and enjoy a real treat — a sightseeing cruise aboard the *Island Queen.* The navigational skills of the crew in some tight and spectacular rocky channels are as breathtaking as the scenery. A snack bar and washrooms are available on board. The ship makes trips from from June 1st to mid-October. From Parry Sound, take Highway 141 to Rosseau and then Highway 3 to Huntsville (phone: 705-746-2311).

HUNTSVILLE: Twenty-two miles (35 km) beyond Bracebridge on Yonge Street, Huntsville is located between the Lake of Bays and Lake Vernon and serves as the western entrance to Algonquin Provincial Park and as a resort center for this watershed area. Anglers can try their skill on lake, rainbow, and brook trout, which are plentiful in these waters, and hunters will find some moose and deer in the woods but may have better luck going after waterfowl. An international triathlon (swim-cycle-run) takes place the second week in May.

ALGONQUIN PROVINCIAL PARK: Created in 1893 as a wildlife sanctuary to protect the headwaters of five major rivers, Algonquin is a natural environment park, and, as such, it is one of the most varied recreational areas in the province. Only one road, Route 60 (which intersects Route 11 at Huntsville) actually runs through the park, although other access roads lead to the park grounds. The southern third of the park, those parts closest to the highway, are fairly heavily developed, with a logging museum, visitors' center, tent and trailer sites, and basic sanitation facilities. The remaining sections of this 2,910-square-mile park are dedicated to hikers and canoeists and are crossed by two major hiking trails and 1,000 miles of canoe routes over calm lakes, rushing rivers, and an occasional portage over rough ground. No motor vehicles are allowed in the back country. Information on outfitters associated with the park, the lodges and campgrounds along Route 60, and seasonal activities is available from the *Park Superintendent, Algonquin Provincial Park,* Ministry of Natural Resources, Whitney, Ontario K0J 2M0.

En Route from Huntsville – Yonge Street, Route 11, continues for a little over 74 miles (118 km) north into the hills of the Canadian Shield toward North Bay on Lake Nipissing. Burk's Falls, on the Magnetawan River, is about 24 miles (38 km) from Huntsville; Sand Lake, a few miles east of town, is within canoeing distance of the backwaters of Algonquin Park. Sundridge, 12 miles (19 km) farther north, also provides a water route (from Bernard Lake) into the park area. The lakes that surround South River, 6 miles (10 km) past Sundridge, are filled with sheer joy for fishing enthusiasts and are excellent testing grounds for more rigorous expeditions into the Great North.

NORTH BAY: Popular with hunters, trappers, and anglers as a staging area for expeditions into the northern and western reaches of Ontario, North Bay began as a camp along the portage used by the Indians, explorers, and fur traders between the Ottawa River and Georgian Bay. Nearby Mattawa, 40 miles (64 km) east of North Bay at the junction of the Mattawa and Ottawa rivers, began as a Hudson's Bay Company trading post. This marked the turnoff point of the canoe-trade routes leading west rather than due north.

Today you can trace one of these routes aboard an excursion boat across Lake Nipissing to the French River, then down to the Dokis Indian Reserve. The *Chief Command II* cruise (phone: 705-495-2236) from the Government Dock off Main

Street, North Bay, lasts 6 hours and departs daily on Tuesdays, Wednesdays, Thursdays, Saturdays, and Sundays, and twice on Fridays, from late May until early September.

North Bay's popularity with travelers of long-ago is probably due to the mile-long sand beach, around which the community grew, as well as the excellent fishing. And, lest the overabundance of trout in these waters begins to wane, the North Bay Fish Hatchery raises hundreds of brookies, lakers, and rainbows to keep the population up — and give sport fishers an even chance.

MARTEN RIVER PROVINCIAL PARK: Once past North Bay, the Bunyanesque proportions of the Ontario that lies beyond the urban and even rural areas begins to reveal itself. The Yonge Street route literally defines the limits of organized society in the province. Along its path towns become infrequent, roadways leading north trail into nothing, and travel into the backcountry is either by rail or more often by air. Viewed in these terms, Marten River Park, only 36 miles (58 km) "up the road," could easily be considered close to North Bay. The park lies in a transitional zone where the yellow birch of the southern forests (used by the Indians for canoe building) merges with the northern black spruce, balsam fir, and pines. Displays of logging tools and tales of the lives of lumberjacks comprise an accurate history of the park area, a story told at the *Northern Ontario Trappers Museum,* a few miles north on Route 11. The museum, built around a trapper's cabin, contains among other things exhibits of pelts and trapping gear. It is open daily from May to mid-October.

En Route from Marten River – Route 11 enters the Temagami Forest Reserve, traveling through its 4.2 million acres of protected forests, lakes, and rivers. This is the entrance to northeastern Ontario's mining and timber resources, and many of the towns on the route were founded in connection with the development of these industries.

TEMAGAMI: The town of Temagami appears out of the wilderness about 60 miles (96 km) past North Bay on the outstretched arm of Lake Temagami (which means "deep lake"). This oddly shaped lake, which extends long fjords and bays in every direction, encompasses some 1,600 islands and 370 miles of shoreline and varies from treacherous shallows to depths of 1,500 feet, making it closely akin to heaven for boaters, canoeists, and fisherfolk.

Temagami began as a fur trading post and grew as trapping and fishing, and later lumbering and then mining operations, started harvesting the wealth of the Canadian Shield. At the Sherman Mine, the largest in this area, visitors see first hand how iron ore is extracted from the four open-pit mines that began production in 1968. Although the iron is of a fairly low grade, only 25%, the ore — in red and black bands — is unusually beautiful, and tourists are invited to take home samples. Tours run Mondays through Fridays from May through August, and reservations are a must; other times by appointment; children under 14 must bring parents with them. Visitors without reservations are limited to a lookout point from which they can see the pit and some mine buildings. Inquire at *Northland Traders* for details, Highway 11, in town, (phone: 705-569-331).

En Route from Temagami – From the prosaic industrial iron ore at Temagami to the glamorous richness of the silver ore at Cobalt is a brief drive of 18 miles (29 km) on Route 11 to the 11B Bypass, then a few miles farther on Route 11B. Slightly south of the 11B cutoff is the *Highway Bookshop* (phone: 705-679-8375). In addition to carrying a variety of area maps, excellent canoe-route guides, and works by Canadian and Indian authors, the shop stands squarely on the portage between the Montreal River, heading west, and Lake Timiskaming, on the route down the Ottawa River toward Montreal.

COBALT: Fate often dictates "strange happenings" that produce spectacular results, and one night in September 1903 a rather unusual chain of "happenings" led blacksmith Fred LaRose to throw his hammer at (he thought) the glittering eyes of a fox — striking the world's richest silver vein. At least two lumberjacks made similar discoveries before a provincial geologist examined the area; he found traces of cobalt (hence the name) mixed into the wealth of silver, and miners flocked to the site. The mining boom died out in the 1930s but revived in the late 40s, when newer methods made additional silver extraction feasible, and the cobalt ore, once discarded as waste, became important for medical, military, and manufacturing uses.

Cobalt's birth as a boom town and its existence as a modern frontier community is outlined in the town's cobalt- and silver-filled *Mining Museum* (24 Silver St.), where tours can be arranged of area mines from May to October, daily.

The frontier lifestyle that characterized Cobalt's origins are remembered in the *Miner's Festival* (first week each August) with rock-breaking, canoeing, and fiddling contests, flea markets, French Canadian step dancing, a parade, and a beauty contest.

En Route from Cobalt – If you continue north on the Route 11B Bypass to its reunion with Route 11 just past New Liskeard, you'll pass the beaches of Lake Timiskaming at Haileybury and go through the dairy farms of New Liskeard — a bit unusual in these chilly northern woods. It's about 70 miles (112 km) from Cobalt to Kirkland Lake, a short distance east of Route 11 on Route 66.

KIRKLAND LAKE: The legendary "streets paved with gold" sought by the Old World explorers are almost true here: The road construction crew accidentally used rock from the piles of gold ore rather than waste rock when filling in the roadbed of Kirkland Lake's main thoroughfare — Government Road, otherwise known as the Golden Mile. By the time they knew what had happened, it would have cost more than the value of the ore to recover the gold. Since the discovery of gold in 1912, the Kirkland Lake district has yielded over a billion dollars of the prized metal, and the three area mines are rated among Canada's largest. The chamber of commerce can arrange tours of the mines for you, but tours and schedules are limited, so plan this visit as far ahead as possible (contact the *Kirkland Lake Chamber of Commerce,* 20 Duncan St. N., Kirkland Lake, Ontario P2N 3L1; phone: 705-567-5444).

The old mining assay office has been converted into a museum and contains a variety of Eskimo and Indian carvings, weapons, and clothing, plus some interesting pieces of old mining gear.

En Route from Kirkland Lake – Double back (westbound) on Route 66 to Route 11, then travel about 9 miles (14 km) north to the signpost that marks the crest of the Arctic watershed. You'll recognize the spot easily: From here on, all the lakes and rivers flow *north* toward James and Hudson bays. A little fancy footwork on the nearby slopes puts you in position to photograph incredible expanses of countryside and streams flowing away to the north or the south in whichever direction you look. The area is rugged and rocky, another rich mineral stockpile of the Canadian Shield, producing silver, zinc, nickel, copper, lead, tin, cadmium, and more gold than any other source in North America. This region, known as the Porcupine-Timmins district, also is popular for big-game hunting, fishing, swimming, golf, and other outdoor activities. It is a little over 27 miles (43 km) on Yonge Street from the Route 66 intersection to the Route 101 access into Timmins.

TIMMINS: Europeans explored and traded in this area during the 1700s, but it was the discovery of gold in 1909 that created the Porcupine Gold Rush and drew settlers to the site. A forest fire, which took over 70 lives and destroyed more than 500,000 acres of timberland in 1916, dampened the miners' enthusiasm only slightly, and today over 40,000 people live and work in the area. The town is quite proud of its importance as a major mineral-producing center, and the chamber of commerce will be happy to arrange tours of various locations (*Timmins-Porcupine Chamber of Commerce,* PO Box 985, Route 101, Timmins, Ontario P4N 7H6; phone: 705-264-4321).

Kettle Lakes Provincial Park, on the Route 101 access east of town, is a beautiful area for camping, hiking, canoeing, and fishing — and blueberry picking. To maintain the park's environment, no motorboats are allowed.

En Route from Timmins – Take Route 610 east to Route 67 to return to Yonge Street; stop at the plaque marking the site of a 1700s Hudson's Bay trading post on Barber's Bay. The fur trade started its growth here and modern mining operations continually explore the area, but timber has remained the constant in the economy. Canada's forests cover about 1.25 million square miles (half the country's surface area), and Ontario's timber industries employ some 75,000 people. Many of the area mills welcome visitors, and the pulp- and paper-making process, converting the tall forests into broad sheets of high-grade paper, is really something to see.

IROQUOIS FALLS: It's a little startling, to say the least, to find a planned community, with parklands and broad avenues, in the midst of these forests and hills. Nonetheless, here it is. This mill town has been carefully planned as a model community and is quite interesting to visit, especially because of its contrast to the surrounding wilds.

One of Ontario's newsprint producers, Abitibi Paper Company, was founded here in 1912 and offers tours of its mill, displaying how logs are manufactured into paper. Contact Florian Prouly (phone: 705-258-3931).

En Route from Iroquois Falls – Yonge Street continues north toward Cochrane, some 30 miles (48 km) from the Iroquois Falls access road. Route 11 has begun to arch slightly west ever since New Liskeard, but here it takes a definite turn and begins its journey across the frontiers of western Ontario.

COCHRANE: A major industrial, mining, lumbering, and rail center, Cochrane was established at the turn of the 20th century in the opening days of the area's mineral discoveries. It was the railroad that made, and still makes, Cochrane an important jumping-off point for mineral exploration and for hunting and fishing expeditions into the Far North and the Hudson Bay region.

The *Polar Bear Express* still crosses the wide Arctic watershed from Cochrane to the remote community of Moosonee, near the mouth of the Moose River on James Bay. Here, on a river island called Moose Factory, a lone fortress was erected in the early 1670s, the second such "trading post" under the auspices of the Hudson's Bay Company. A plaque near the site of the original post, which was destroyed in the closing days of the century, commemorates English explorer Henry Hudson, who first sailed into Hudson Bay — and was set adrift here with his sons. Several early buildings, including a smithy and a gunpowder magazine, are grouped together with a museum describing the post area's growth over the centuries. St. Thomas Church, on the small island, has floor "plugs" that are released during periods of flooding to prevent the rising waters from floating the church away. Inside are prayer books in Cree. Another aspect of the area's history is explained on the riverbank in Moosonee at the *Révillon Frères Museum* (Hudson's Bay Company's French rivals). The British-French conflict for control of the New World focused on the choice territory around this extensive inlet more than once; the museum describes much of the conflict. Only the tracks of the *Ontario Northland Railway* share the immense territory around Moosonee with the prints of moose, bear, caribou, deer — and an occasional person.

This excursion into Ontario's — and Canada's — heritage can be packed into one day; overnight accommodations also can be arranged at the isolated camp. It's a long walk back (186 miles/298 km from Moosonee to Cochrane), so contact the *Ontario Northland Railway* (Passenger Service Department, North Bay, Ontario P1B 8L3; phone: 705-472-4500), well in advance of your trip. A "local" train, which stops anywhere upon request by trappers, hunters, or campers, takes a full day in each direction; the express runs 3 days a week in winter, and daily, except Fridays, in summer. Group fares for families available.

In keeping with Cochrane's background as a rail center, a locomotive and several cars dating back to the days of the railway construction have been set aside and filled with memorabilia of the era. In forthright frontier style, the *Railway Museum* is on a spur track at Union Station in Cochrane. Another aspect of Cochrane's development is a specialized facet of Ontario's timber industry — one of Canada's largest plywood plants. If you think that changing giant trees into newspaper took some incredible machinations, just wait until you see how these magicians turn tall trees into broad sheets of plywood (Cochrane Enterprises Plant, Railway St., PO Box 1059; phone: 705-272-4321; open July to early September, Mondays, Wednesdays, and Fridays).

En Route from Cochrane – Yonge Street wheels westward at Cochrane, tracing 285 miles of thinly settled frontier outlining the Hudson Bay lowlands to the north and the fringes of the population centers around the westernmost Great Lake, Superior, to the south. The small towns along Route 11, such as Smooth Rock Falls, Kapuskasing, Mattice, Hearst, Longlac, and Geraldton, all cater to the camper, sport fisher, hunter, and canoeist. For a truly memorable experience, thousands of miles of unspoiled rivers and untrampled forest await an adventurous vacationer. And those who prefer a little less strenuous adventure will find innumerable fly-in hunting and fishing camps operated by experienced outfitters. Some of the best of these are operated by the Cree Indians in the James and Hudson bays areas, where the fall goose and duck hunting is superb.

Take advantage of the half-dozen provincial parks along the way; they encompass a wide variety of terrain and geographical oddities. A quick survey includes the following:

Greenwater Park – Centered on a 200-foot esker ridge (glacial gravel deposit) formed over 15,000 years ago, 26 small lakes are all filled with trout (20 miles/32 km west of Cochrane).

Remi Lake Park – In the midst of a belt of clay earth, this oasis of fertile land in the rocky Canadian Shield has good beaches. It is 45 miles (72 km) from Greenwater Park.

Fushimi Lake Park – The clay belt extends here from Remi Lake, but the cooler climate keeps the growing season too short for farming. The fish, however, seem to thrive.

Nagagamisis Park – South of Route 11 at the lake of the same name, offering boating, fishing, swimming, and a bit of history, the lake area was the site of an Indian camp. It is 25 miles (40 km) beyond Fushimi Lake, off Yonge Street via Route 631.

Klotz Lake Park – A 30-mile canoe trip down the Flint River begins here at the river's headwaters and courses north through an area where the banks are lined with flint, used by the Indians for arrowheads. It is 60 miles (96 km) west of the Nagagamisis Park access road.

Macleod Park – On the shores of Kenogamisis Lake, an extremely popular park for swimming and boating; the numerous islands and inlets around the lake harbor pike and pickerel, whitefish and yellow perch. It is 45 miles (72 km) from Klotz Lake Park, on the eastern outskirts of Geraldton.

GERALDTON: This small timber and mining community was founded in the wake of gold discoveries in the 1930s; Geraldton today is the western starting point for expeditions into the James Bay area. Here, Yonge Street begins to curve toward the western extremity of Lake Superior and its coastal towns and cities.

En Route from Geraldton – Originally a divisional point for rail lines leading north from the Thunder Bay tributary into the James Bay–Hudson Bay region, Jellicoe, about 30 miles (48 km) west of Geraldton, later became a mining town for a short time. Semiprecious gemstones like agate and jasper can often be picked up beside the highway by sharp-eyed rockhounds between here and Beardmore, some 16 miles (26 km) west and south on Route 11. The timber and gold resources of Beardmore, on the southeast shore of Lake Nipigon (the largest inland lake in Ontario), preceded the town's current industries — hunting and fishing outfitting and tourism.

Yonge Street continues south from here, along the shore of Lake Nipigon through Macdiarmid, Orient Bay, Reflection Lake, and Gorge Creek. It's about 50 miles (80 km) to Route 11's juncture with Route 17 at Nipigon, on the northwest shore of Lake Superior. Between Beardmore and the fisheries at Macdiarmid, Lake Nipigon becomes visible to the west, and the tall palisades of the Pijitawabik region peer down upon the highway from the eastern side.

BLACKSAND PARK: Overlooking Pijitawabik Bay on Lake Nipigon, the beach of black sand that gives the park its name lies across from the legendary nesting place of the Thunderbird. Ojibwa stories tell of the wrath of the Thunderbird, who abandoned his home and destroyed his secluded mountaintop retreat as whites began invading the remote territory. Occasionally he still vents his rage through summer thunderstorms.

En Route from Blacksand Park – The area around the lakeshore of Nipigon and farther south to Lake Superior and the Minnesota border has yielded Indian artifacts (mostly pre-Ojibwa, or pre-Chippewa) and enough archaeological evidence to substantiate the presence of Norsemen — Vikings — in the Minnesota–Thunder Bay lands around Lake Superior.

NIPIGON: Spread across three terraces created by glacier-wrought changes in the water level, the city lies at the mouth of the Nipigon River on Nipigon Bay. The river always has been a major route inland, and this sheltered area near the river mouth was inhabited by the Ojibwa for ages before the European fur traders turned Nipigon into the first year-round white settlement on Superior's north shore. The fur trade no longer draws explorers, but the opportunity to hook a champion trout beckons many. The world's largest brook trout, a 14-pound, 8-ounce monster, was taken here.

The *Nipigon Museum,* incorporating the *L. M. Leim Gallery of Archaeology,* has displays of native cultures, logging and timber industries, and a history of the area. Nipigon's earliest history is told by the intriguing rock formations and the structure of the area itself. Open daily mid-June to September (Newton St. at Second). East of town, along Route 17, markers designate some of the formations, like the Kamahill Mesa, that fringe the Nipigon Bay–Lake Superior shore. The marker at the Kama Bay Lookout relates the history of the "Old Copper" Indians, who were making metal tools here long before the first European explorers arrived.

En Route from Nipigon – The 64 miles (102 km) explored by Routes 11 and 17 between Nipigon and Thunder Bay are filled with the fantastic rock formations that characterize the area. Red Rock Cuesta, a wall of red cliffs south of the roadway, is 2 miles long and about 700 feet high. The red hue is caused by horizontal layers of limestone tinted by hematite.

Ouimet Canyon is an amazing earth carving 500 feet wide, almost 2 miles long, and 300 to 500 feet deep into volcanic rock and red mudstone. Several tall columns have broken away from the sheer cliff walls and stand by themselves. One of these is called Indian Head because of its classic profile; other columns have tumbled, breaking into huge boulders hundreds of feet below. There are few guard rails, and if you happen to venture to the edge and peer straight down, you'll see large cracks in the canyon floor. No one knows which section will break free next.

The canyon floor is an environment all its own. Little sunlight warms these depths, and the cold holds back the flowering and greening of spring until late summer. In deeper areas, where even the summer sun brings no warmth, snow and ice cover the ground most of the year, and Arctic plants like firs, Arctic moss, and a type of liverwort thrive miles south of their southernmost growing areas.

This is not a place to allow children to run around unsupervised, and many adults may find some of the canyon trails a little hair-raising, especially when it comes to stepping over crevices that seem to extend to the canyon floor. From the trail along the canyon's south rim Lake Superior is visible in the distance, its surface dotted with tiny islands. At this point, Superior's Black Bay lies opposite, formed between Nipigon Bay's sheltering southern peninsula and Thunder Bay's northern Sibley Peninsula.

The Dorian Fish Hatchery, just off Route 17/11 near Ouimet, breeds speckled and lake trout to keep area population levels high. A few miles farther is the Thunder Bay Amethyst Mine (about 35 miles/56 km northeast of Thunder Bay or 30 miles/48 km south of Nipigon, 5 miles/8 km off Route 17/11 on E Loon Rd.; open daily May–October), uncovered by a crew cutting a logging road into the woods. You can climb into the pits and collect your own stones or purchase samples for about 65¢ a pound. Route 587 travels the length of Sibley Peninsula from the village of Pass Lake, on Route 17/11, to Sibley Provincial Park.

SIBLEY PROVINCIAL PARK: Although the park lies outside the town's boundaries, the port of Thunder Bay claims Sibley Park's most visible and memorable landmark as its own — the Sleeping Giant. The natural sculpture is as perfect as anything created by man, carved into exposed surfaces of the Canadian Shield over a span of centuries. Ojibwa legends, however, tell of the Son of the Great West Wind, Nanibijou (or Nanabozho), a giant demigod who had led the tribe north of Lake Superior in search of sanctuary from a violent tribe of the Sioux Nation. While exploring the peninsula, Nanibijou (who dwelled on the peak of nearby Mt. McKay, from which he could survey the entire region) discovered a rich vein of silver. He warned the tribe not to reveal the metal's presence to anyone, saying that if a white man were to learn of it, the tribe would perish and he would turn to stone. The silver was buried on a tiny island at the far end of the peninsula and the tribe sworn to secrecy; nevertheless, one warrior made himself silver weapons that fell into the hands of the Sioux. Nanibijou spotted the Sioux bringing white traders as they approached Sibley Peninsula across Lake Superior and caused a windstorm to sink their canoes, drowning both the Sioux and the whites. Fulfilling his own destiny, Nanibijou was turned to stone by the Great Spirit, and the next morning the Ojibwa tribe looked out upon him, transformed into the 1,000-foot-tall, 7-mile-long mountain peninsula called the Sleeping Giant.

It wasn't until 1868 that someone stumbled onto the Indian silver cache on Silver Islet, an island barely large enough to be worthy of notice. A haphazard pick stroke exposed $10,000 worth of silver, and a 14-year boom began. During that time, many lives were lost as miners were trapped in frequently flooded shafts, and even more were lost in Lake Superior's sudden storms. Today, a causeway built in the 1930s makes access to the isle a lot safer, and the island's century-old houses, general store, and rare photographs of the desperate miners and their families are an interesting adjunct to the park and its legend.

En Route from Sibley Park–Silver Islet – Back on Yonge Street, Route 17/11, it's about 24 miles (38 km) to Thunder Bay, traveling along the bay's shoreline under the watchful eyes of Sleeping Giant Mountain.

THUNDER BAY: Created when two separate communities sheltered by Sibley Peninsula merged in 1969, Thunder Bay is one of Canada's largest and busiest ports and one of the best harbors on the Great Lakes. Route 17/11 approaches from the northeast, through the gentle hills above the city; Lake Superior and the massive grain elevators that characterize the lakehead dominate the city's south; and Mt. McKay stands, taller than its fellow mountains, toward Thunder Bay's southwest corner. The Kaministikwa River, which runs past Mt. McKay, empties into the harbor through a broad delta divided into three navigable channels.

This sheltered river mouth was the meeting place, the Great Rendezvous, of Indians and fur trappers bringing their skins to barter with the fur buyers carting European goods up the St. Lawrence. Fort Kaministquia, a French outpost, was erected here in the 1670s; in 1801 the British (who had assumed control of the area) built Fort William, the main supply post for the Northwest Company after the settlement of the US-Canadian boundaries showed the company's earlier headquarters to be in US territory. For the next 20 years, all of the Northwest Company's goods moved through this point until it merged with the Hudson's Bay Company. Each summer, more than 2,000 voyagers gathered here.

The famous old fort has been extensively rebuilt on the bank of the Kaministikwa River, 9 miles (14 km) upstream from the original site, together with an entire village of about 50 buildings and an Ojibwa camp. The active trading center is staffed with a full complement of trappers, voyageurs, traders, and Indians, all going about as if it were still the early 1800s. There are demonstrations of Indian crafts, blacksmithing and tinsmithing, even a cooper (barrel and wheel maker), and boatbuilders making Indian birchbark canoes and European split-wood hulls. In late June and early July, the *Great Canadian Rendezvous* is celebrated with a week-long festival.

A 140-acre section of Thunder Bay North is devoted to Centennial Park, a wooded area with trails along the Current River and a working 1910 logging camp. The camp and some other facilities are open in summer only, but in winter there's day and night skiing and sleigh rides. The peak of Mt. McKay lies in the Fort William Indian Reservation, where the Ojibwa tribe operates a ski resort on the 1,800-foot mountain. There are six ski areas, including Mt. McKay, in the mountains of this compact alpine ski region, all just a short drive southwest from downtown Thunder Bay.

Cruises of the harbor, or of the whole area including Sleeping Giant and Old Fort William, can be arranged through *Welcomship Ltd.* (467 Parkwood Dr.; phone: 807-344-2512 or 807-577-7875) or *Mary Ethel Cruises* (467 Parkwood Dr.; phone: 807-577-7875).

Thunder Bay does have its own waterfall, Kakabeka Falls, and it is spectacular — but only on weekends! A hydroelectric dam on the Kaministikwa River controls the water flow, and during the week the fall is usually no more impressive than a drainpipe in a drought. Locally, the fall is called "Only on a Sunday Falls," because that's when it is let loose in full force (or almost), and the water tumbles over the 128-foot-high, 225-foot-wide ledge into the gorge below. In the days before the dam, according to legend, an Ojibwa princess captured by a band of Sioux was forced to lead her captors to her tribe. Instead, she guided the Sioux warriors over the falls, and all were killed. Her spirit is said to be visible in the spray, although the dam has probably cut down the frequency of her appearances (Kakabeka Falls Park is 18 miles/29 km northwest of Thunder Bay on Route 17/11).

There's no lack of variety in Lakehead restaurants. *Hoito's* (314 Bay St.; phone: 807-345-6323) has excellent Finnish food, while *Chan's* (130 May St. N.; phone: 807-622-2601) is the place to go for Chinese. Both are open daily and are easy on the budget. The *Circle Inn* (686 Memorial Ave.; phone: 807-344-5744) is moderately priced and offers good fare, including Sunday brunch, in pleasant surroundings. Open daily.

One of Thunder Bay's most popular camping-activity areas is Chippewa Park, 300 wooded acres with a beach, a small zoo, several rides for children, and a wide variety of facilities for travelers (south of town, off Route 61, on access road 61B; open mid-May to early September).

En Route from Thunder Bay – From the Lakehead to the US border at Rainy River, it is about 270 miles (432 km) through territory ideal for canoeing and fly-in hunting and fishing. Routes 17 and 11 travel together as far west as Shabaqua, about 25 miles (40 km) from Thunder Bay. Route 17 bears off to the northwest, past the tip of the Lake of the Woods and on into Manitoba. Yonge Street, Route 11, parallels the international border until it finally crosses into the US at Rainy River, Ontario–Baudette, Minnesota.

BEST EN ROUTE

Yonge Street covers a lot of territory, and along its route there's a wide range in hotel prices. In the northern areas you may well be comparing rates that include guide services, fishing permits, and equipment in addition to rooms. Accommodations farther north tend to be a little less fashionable and more rustic than in southern Ontario. After all, most visitors to this area are outdoor people, on their way to or from a moose hunt or fishing trip. In the stretch between Hearst and Geraldton, virtually the only places to stay are park campgrounds.

The price ranges cannot reflect the level of services, so be sure of what you're buying when you make reservations. Don't plan on finding any vacancies on the road in summer; hotel and camping space can be scarce then. Any establishment charging over $60 per night for two is considered expensive. The moderate category covers the $43 to $60 per night range, and those charging less than $43 per night, double occupancy, are listed as inexpensive. Prices for resorts listed as expensive usually include meals. All prices are quoted in US dollars.

Ontario offers advance registration for camping in provincial parks and makes only 40% of its campsites available for those with no reservation, so it's a good idea to plan your trip as far ahead as possible. Contact the *Provincial Parks Branch, Ministry of Natural Resources,* Whitney Block, Room 3321, Queen's Park, Toronto M7A 1W3, to obtain advance registration forms and a listing of those areas for which you must register.

BARRIE

Continental – This very comfortable inn has 124 rooms, an indoor pool and sauna, a whirlpool bath, tennis courts, and a fireplace in the lounge area. At the Dunlop St. interchange (phone: 705-726-1834). Expensive.

Journey's End – Sixty rooms offer air conditioning, TV sets, and all the comforts you'd expect from Canada's largest motel chain. Exit Highway 400 at Dunlop St. to Hart Drive (phone: 705-722-3600). Moderate.

Willow Creek Trailer Park – In addition to 175 campsites, most with water and electrical hookups, there are showers, flush toilets, fireplaces, a pool, and a store. In Spring Water Park (phone: 705-726-0817). Inexpensive.

ORILLIA

Fern – A family-oriented resort with 72 rooms and 31 cabins that has something for everybody — fishing, water skiing, a sauna, lake swimming, 3 pools (one indoors), programs for adults and for kids, a babysitting service, and conference facilities. In winter, there is snowmobiling and skiing. Complimentary coffee 24 hours a day. Rama Rd. (phone: 705-325-2256). Expensive.

Sundial – This is a popular motor inn with 94 rooms and a view of Lake Simcoe. It has an indoor pool, a sauna, and a whirlpool bath. 600 Sundial Dr. (phone: 705-325-2233). Expensive to moderate.

Friendship Knight's Inn – "Friendliness and cleanliness" is the motto here. All 40 rooms are air conditioned and have TV sets. 265 Memorial Ave. (phone: 705-326-3554). Moderate.

GRAVENHURST

Pine Dale – A pleasant resort made up of 21 efficiency units and 1 cabin, it's surrounded by pine groves on the shore of Gull Lake. It has a beach and a dock, and fishing or water skiing on the lake can be arranged. There is a recreation hall and boat rentals are available. Pinedale Rd. (phone: 705-687-2822). Moderate.

BRACEBRIDGE

Aston Villa – This is a comfortable 67-room resort with a dock and a beach on Lake Muskoka for fishing, free windsurfing and water skiing, or just sunning and swimming. It also has an outdoor pool, and golf and tennis (with instruction), for the dry-land set. No-tipping policy. Open June to October. Off Route 118 (phone: 705-764-1111). Expensive.

Bangor Lodge – Six tennis courts, a private 9-hole golf course, and an outdoor pool go with 98 fully equipped rooms and 5 cottages. Open June to September. Golden Beach Rd. (phone: 705-645-4791). Expensive.

HUNTSVILLE

Deerhurst Inn – This northern property has been catering to the whims of summer guests for almost a century, and it does an equally good job summer and winter. It has an indoor pool, an outdoor pool, and nearby Peninsula Lake for every conceivable water activity — sailing, boating, canoeing, fishing; two types of tennis courts (clay and asphalt); a sauna and whirlpool bath; an 18-hole golf course; a billiard table; and fireplaces galore to warm skiers' frozen limbs. There is a choice of 122 rooms or 14 cottages. Muskoka Rd., PO Box 1950 (phone: 705-789-5543). Expensive.

Hidden Valley – It's a lot more like a family inn than part of a hotel chain. In the center of the skiing area, surrounded by a lake and golf course, this 100-room establishment offers racquet sports, a sauna, an indoor pool, and a whirlpool bath. It also has an outdoor pool, beachfront, a dock, and boats for water skiing or fishing. Hidden Valley Rd. (phone: 705-789-2301). Expensive.

Highland Court Motel – Located at the west end of town, it offers spotless, well-furnished accommodations, including 15 rooms and 2 cottages, each room is equipped with a small refrigerator, a kettle, and coffee. 208 Main St. W. (phone: 705-789-4392). Moderate to inexpensive.

Lake of Two Rivers Campground – Set in Algonquin Park, the Route 60 corridor provides access to the park's 8 campgrounds and this one (with 243 sites) has the most facilities, including showers, a store, a laundry area, and fireplaces. (phone: 705-633-5572). Inexpensive.

NORTH BAY

Ramada Inn – One of many reliable hostelries located on this part of the lake shore, it has 130 rooms, an indoor pool, sauna, a good restaurant, and a coffee shop. Arrangements can be made for guests to play on a nearby golf course. 700 Lakeshore Dr. (phone: 705-474-5800). Expensive.

Ascot – Considered a high-quality inn, the 31 rooms have air conditioning and TV sets, and there's also a sauna. Central location to bus, rail, beaches, sports, shopping, and entertainment. 255 McIntyre St. W. (phone: 705-474-4770). Moderate.

Champlain Trailer Park – A full range of services is available, including electrical hook-ups at many of the 56 sites, showers, flush toilets, fireplaces, and a store, all set on Lake Nipissing. 1202 Premier Rd. N. (phone: 705-474-4669). Inexpensive.

MARTEN RIVER

Land O'Lakes – In addition to a cluster of campsites around a store, a swimming pool, showers, toilets, a beach, boats, and space for fishing, there are 13 cottages. The season runs from May to October. On Rte. 11 (phone: 705-892-2206). Moderate to inexpensive.

Rock Pine Motel – It has only 8 rooms, but it's in a picturesque setting and there's a restaurant, gift shop, and boat rentals. Located 31 miles (50 km) north of North Bay on Route 11 (phone: 705-892-2211).

COBALT

Marsh Bay – On beautiful Marsh Bay on the Montreal River, this establishment has 5 housekeeping cottages, campsites, boat rentals, and guide services. Marsh Bay Rd., off Route 11 (phone: 705-679-8810). Moderate.

KIRKLAND LAKE

Commodore – This is Kirkland Lake's smaller establishment, with 27 rooms, but it's quite up to the standards of most people. There's a coffee shop and a tennis court. 1 Duncan Ave. N. at Government Rd. (phone: 705-567-9386). Inexpensive.

Esker Lakes Park – About a half-hour from town, the park lies just within the Arctic watershed on Panagapke Lake. Thirty-two of the 137 campsites have electric hookups. There are showers, flush toilets, and a store, and boat rentals are available in the park. Access from Route 66 (phone: 705-567-4849). Inexpensive.

TIMMINS

Best Western Colonial Inn – Set on the Mattagami River, near cross-country and downhill skiing, here are 27 well-equipped rooms and a coffee shop. 1212 Riverside Dr. (phone: 705-268-5200). Moderate.

Ramada – Special attractions in this 116-room hostelry include an indoor pool, nearby golf, free local phone calls, and rooms with king-size beds and refrigerators. There's a good dining room and a bar with a 6-foot video screen. Within walking distance of *Timmins Square Shopping Centre*. 1800 Riverside Dr. (phone: 705-267-6241). Moderate.

COCHRANE

Westway – There are 42 units with color TV sets and air conditioning and a mini-putt course next door. 21 First St., on Route 11 (phone: 705-272-4285). Moderate.

Greenwater Provincial Park – You should have no trouble getting one of the park's 135 sites since this fairly remote area is not one of Ontario's busiest. All the basic facilities are here, including showers, a laundry, and a beach. Access from Route 636, off Route 11 (phone: 705-272-6335). Inexpensive.

KAPUSKASING

Apollo – A popular place, with 38 large rooms, 9 housekeeping cottages, an indoor pool, and a sauna. Route 11 (phone: 705-335-6084). Moderate.

Two Bridges – En route to the spectacular *Polar Bear Express* train ride, this motel has 23 rooms, some of which are housekeeping units. Refrigerators in rooms and complimentary morning coffee and newspaper, plus use of the mini-putt course. Route 11 (phone: 705-335-2281). Moderate.

GERALDTON

Park Bay View – Twenty rooms are equipped with all the necessities, and the dining room offers good home cooking. A beach picnic area and golf are nearby. There's also a centralized video system, from which you can order movies. Open May to October. Route 11 (phone: 807-854-1716). Moderate.

Wild Goose Lake Resort – Twelve cottages on 600 feet of private lakeshore, with boat rentals and hunting and fishing packages. Two fly-in cabins are available for some incredible fishing trips. Route 11 (phone: 807-854-0482). Moderate to inexpensive.

NIPIGON

Chalet Lodge – An original Canadian Pacific Railroad rustic lodge, it offers 32 chalets set among the trees. There is a dining room. Hunting and fishing packages are available. Open May to October. Highway 17 (phone: 807-887-3030). Moderate.

THUNDER BAY

Airlane – South of the town itself, close to the airport, this is one of Thunder Bay's top hostelries. It has 170 rooms and a full array of creature comforts, including a heated indoor pool, a sauna, a whirlpool bath, and a fine dining room. Complimentary limo service to the airport. 698 Arthur St. W. (phone: 807-577-1181). Expensive.

Landmark – Another of Thunder Bay's aces, this metropolitan establishment, with 106 rooms, matches any other in its range of amenities and excellence of service. Close to the shopping areas. Dawson Rd. and Thunder Bay Expressway (phone: 807-767-1681). Expensive to moderate.

Prince Edward Island

This crescent-shaped island in the gulf of the St. Lawrence River attracts over half a million visitors every summer. Unspoiled by modern freeways and heavy industry, Prince Edward Island is called the Garden of the Gulf. Visitors constantly remark on the island's charming appeal — its ubiquitous farmlands and cliffs, rich red soil, its evergreen forests, its views of the sea, its red sand beaches, its long-legged blue herons along the shores, its fishing villages, its community lobster suppers, and its lovely Cavendish area described in Lucy Maud Montgomery's *Anne of Green Gables.* In short, for visitors seeking an enchanting, uncrowded, unhurried land, Prince Edward Island is a small utopia.

Once described humorously as two long beaches with potato fields in between, Prince Edward Island is the tiniest of Canada's ten provinces. Some 128,000 people live in the province, which encompasses 2,184 square miles. In 1864 Charlottetown, its seat of government, was the site of the first discussions on the Canadian Confederation (Canada became a confederation in 1867; PEI entered the Confederation in 1873). Outside the capital, rural Prince Edward Island is noted for its peaceful landscape, across which the provincial government has mapped out many scenic drives.

Over half the island is tidily cultivated farms, the soil famous for its rich, red clay color. Northern evergreen and hardwood forests are cut by excellent clam-digging inlets and stretches of abandoned beaches. Wild blueberries ripen along roadsides during the month of August. The island has several picturesque inland and coastal villages, and exploring its period churches alone has occupied more than one photographer.

Accessible to motorists by two ferry routes across the Northumberland Strait (just 1½ hours from Caribou, Nova Scotia, to Wood Islands; 45 minutes from Cape Tormentine, New Brunswick, to Borden), the island stretches 140 miles long and from 4 to 40 miles wide. It is served almost entirely by one-lane roads (which make for wonderful car or bicycle expeditions).

It is hard to know exactly how to describe the shape of Prince Edward Island; looking at it on the map, it seems not so much one piece of land as three small islands that drifted together — barely — in a moment of forgetfulness. Most touring on the island starts at Charlottetown, the provincial capital, in the southern corner of the center "island." From there, travelers have two major choices: to go east, spanning the Hillsborough Bridge and the river that almost splits the island, along the Kings Byway Drive; or to go north and west along the Blue Heron Drive. The third alternative, from Kensington about three-quarters along the Blue Heron Drive, is to explore the westernmost section of the island, a route known as Lady Slipper Drive.

Information: *Prince Edward Island Department of Tourism,* Visitor Services, Box 940, Charlottetown, PEI C1A 7M5 (phone: 902-368-4444; or from the eastern US, 800-565-0267; from Nova Scotia and New Brunswick, 800-565-7421).

Blue Heron Drive

The Blue Heron Drive leads north and east out of Charlottetown to the island's northern shore, a stretch of 25 miles (40 km) of national park beaches and red sandstone capes, ending at the tourist town of Cavendish. Just beyond is New London Bay, the home of the beautiful blue herons for which the route is named. From here the drive begins turning south toward the southern shore of the island to return to Charlottetown. This route, which forms a loop that begins and ends at Charlottetown, circles the island's center and is 110 miles (176 km) long. At Kensington is the turnoff west that opens the third PEI route — Lady Slipper Drive — for exploration of the island's western third.

CHARLOTTETOWN: The provincial capital is just 38 miles (61 km) from the ferry landing at Wood Islands and 34 miles (54 km) from the ferry landing at Borden. Charlottetown's downtown area features beautiful tree-lined streets and rows of wood-frame houses. The city, concerned about preserving the character of its central core, has passed an ordinance restricting the demolition of its historic buildings. The only incorporated city in the province, Charlottetown still retains its original colonial seaport feeling despite a full array of 20th-century conveniences.

The French, under Comte St. Pierre, originally settled Port la Joie across the harbor from Charlottetown in 1720. In 1758, the British took control of the fort at Port la Joie and, as was the custom, renamed the island St. John's Island. Charlottetown became its capital in 1768 but grew slowly, even with an influx of British Loyalists at the close of the American Revolution. Today, Greater Charlottetown's population stands at 29,000, roughly one-fourth of the island's entire population.

The *Confederation Centre of the Arts* is the city's focal point. Built in the mid-1960s on the location of the original city market, this national museum, art gallery, and theater makes up for its stark architecture (tons of concrete) with its impressive exhibits and acclaimed theater.

In the foyer of *Confederation Centre,* you can pick up a free map of the city, which you can then study over a bowl of clam chowder at the indoor restaurant.

Theatergoers should plan to see the *Confederation Centre's* annual summer festival performance of *Anne of Green Gables.* The touching story of a freckled, pigtailed orphan growing up in the splendor of rural Prince Edward Island is one of the world's most popular children's tales. The play, adapted from the Lucy Maud Montgomery novel, has been translated into 17 languages. Bordering the *Confederation Centre* is the city's downtown shopping district. Some of Charlottetown's oldest retail stores now form part of the *Confederation Court Mall.* Nearby is the century-old, red-brick City Hall, with its mansard roof and 66-foot tower, which has retained most of its historic character in spite of renovations and modernization. A visitors' information center is located on the ground floor.

Just behind *Confederation Centre* is Province House (phone: 902-566-7627), built from Nova Scotia sandstone in the 1840s. In 1864, this Georgian building was the site of the discussions that led to Canadian Confederation and the establishment of the Dominion of Canada in 1867. Ironically, Prince Edward Island did not join the dominion until pressured into doing so in 1873. Visited by thousands of people every year,

Province House contains in its second-floor Confederation Chamber the original chairs and table around which the founders of Canada sat 127 years ago, along with other mementos of island history. Province House is now the home of the provincial legislative assembly and is a national historic site.

Guided walking tours of the city depart each daylight hour during summer from in front of Province House. People who wish to explore the city on their own can begin with a walk down Great George Street. Its old brick and wooden buildings have been restored, and the street is lined handsomely with old-fashioned lanterns. (To purchase a variety of crafts and artifacts made on the island, visit the *Island Crafts Shop,* 156 Richmond St., which is operated by the PEI Craftsmen's Council. Closed Sundays.)

Along Great George Street, is St. Dunstan's Basilica, the seat of the province's Roman Catholic diocese. Built in 1919, the present-day St. Dunstan's is the fourth Roman Catholic church on this site; its two Gothic spires rise to a height of 200 feet and still dominate the city's skyline. Charlottetown has several other churches worth exploring: St. Paul's Anglican Church (Richmond St., 1 block east of Province House), established in 1747 and the oldest Protestant church on the island; St. James Presbyterian Church (Pownal and Fitzroy Sts.), with impressive stained glass windows and relics of Iona, Scotland; and St. Peter's Anglican Church (Rochford and Fitzroy Sts.), with murals by Canadian painter Robert Harris.

At the very bottom of Great George Street, on Water Street, lies the section of the city known as Old Charlottetown. Historic wood and brick buildings have been renovated as part of a major waterfront restoration called Project Harbourside.

Along Water Street is the *Prince Edward Hotel and Convention Centre* and the Sir Louis Henry Davies Law Courts. Below the courthouse is the *Charlottetown Yacht Club.* The *Root Cellar* (34 Queen St.) is one of the best natural foods stores in eastern Canada. The island's alternate-lifestyle community likes to chat with owners Joe and Gail Kern, to browse through the books, and to enjoy the good food. Island products sold here include fresh eggs, goat's milk, cheese, organic grains, and honey.

No stay in Charlottetown would be complete without a stroll through beautiful 40-acre Victoria Park, overlooking the harbor. At suppertime, islanders play softball (virtually every thriving business in Charlottetown has a team in the league) or ramble through the white birch woods. (Watch for raspberry canes along the pathways during early August.) Along the southern shore, you'll pass the old cannons guarding the harbor; from here you can see the city's striking silhouette.

Bordering the grounds of Victoria Park is Government House (1835), the official residence of the province's governors. Directly ahead at the corner of West Street is Beaconsfield, an old wood-frame house with an expansive porch, the current home of the Prince Edward Island Heritage Foundation.

Every August, Charlottetown sponsors *Old Home Week,* 7 days of livestock and handcraft exhibitions, country music, a midway, and harness racing day and night at the *Charlottetown Driving Park.* The highlight is a huge, 2-hour parade through the streets of Charlottetown, and the *Gold Cup and Saucer Race* featuring some of the best trotters in eastern Canada. For information contact PEI Tourism, Visitors Services Division, PO Box 940, Charlottetown, PEI C1A 7M5 (phone: 902-368-4444).

Charlottetown has two movie theaters, an 18-hole golf course, and many good restaurants and lounges. The *Lord Selkirk Room* at the *Prince Edward* hotel (18 Queen St.) is the city's most formal and expensive dining room. The menu features salmon, lobster, chateaubriand, and seasonal dishes like quail, rabbit, and roast duckling. Less formal and more moderately priced, but also highly regarded, is the *Queen Street Café* (52 Queen St.), operated by one of the city's finest chefs, Larry Wilson. The *Griffon Room* at the *Dundee Arms Inn* (200 Pownal St.) is expensive, but the menu justifies the prices: lobster, scallops, and pepper steak are among the most popular entrées. *Pat's Rose & Grey Room* (132 Richmond St.) has a restaurant and bar, with mahogany-stained walls and leaded glass windows. This establishment, which specializes in Italian food, steaks, and salads, is operated by the Kenny family, who also own *M. P. Hogan's* (134 Richmond St.), the city's most attractive nightspot. Here, wide pillars and archways separate a long bar from a table and dance floor area. The *Claddagh Room* (129 Sydney St.) has the city's widest selection of seafood, and the *Olde Dublin Pub* upstairs has imported draft beer from Ireland and Scótland. The *Off Broadway Café* (125 Sydney St.) is inexpensive and features seven kinds of crêpes, Acadian meat pie, and rich desserts. In the wee hours, *Cedar's* (81 University Ave.) has low-priced, hefty sandwiches and Lebanese food; open until 2 AM daily, except Sundays.

En Route from Charlottetown – Take Route 2 north 5 miles (8 km) to Marshfield. Turn left on Route 25 to York. *Jewell's Gardens and Pioneer Village* is a restored early-19th-century village surrounded by floral gardens, a natural pond, and rolling lawns. Admission charge. From York, take Route 220 to Grand Tracadie and turn left to Prince Edward Island National Park.

PRINCE EDWARD ISLAND NATIONAL PARK: Here are miles and miles of dunes, fronted by the sea, backed by salt marshes and beach grass, cliffs and sea-torn rock formations, and more than 200 species of birds, the most compelling and commanding of which are the great blue herons, those exquisitely gangling beasts of the wetlands. Like the Cape Cod National Seashore, this 25-mile stretch of shoreline — one of the most popular tourist destinations in Canada, though never as crowded as the great national parks in the US West are at high season — is at once delicate and durable, a wonder of ecology and balance. The park begins at Tracadie Bay and Dalvay Beach and ends at Cavendish Bay. The herons are easiest to find at Rustico Island and New London Bay.

DALVAY BEACH: This is the least crowded area of the national park. It has only one bathhouse and a sheltered cooking facility. Nearby, on the shores of Dalvay Lake, is the stately *Dalvay by the Sea* hotel, built almost a century ago as the summer residence of a business associate of John D. Rockefeller (see *Best en Route*). Along the Gulf Shore Road, watch for the nature trail, with a bubbling spring, pioneer cemetery, and log bridge. (Don't try the nature trail in the summer without a liberal application of insect repellent.) From Dalvay Beach, walk 2 miles (3 km) east along the shoreline to the Tracadie Harbour area, where you may be able to talk a local boater into taking you water skiing.

STANHOPE BEACH: Over 3 dozen cottage operations, many of them along Gulf Shore Road, provide ample accommodations for the thousands of visitors who spend summers here. Weekly housekeeping rates range from $350 to $800. For those on more modest budgets, the 25-acre national park campground, cut out of a spruce forest, has 104 campsites and 14 sites for trailers. Roadside shopping, laundry facilities, and bicycle rentals are available in the area.

BRACKLEY BEACH: The area has a wide range of cabins, farm tourist homes, and campgrounds. *Shaw's Hotel & Cottages,* located next to the national park on Route 15, has been under the same family management since 1860 (see *Best en Route*). The national park campground at Rustico Island is just west of Brackley Beach on the Gulf Shore Road. Overlooking beautiful Rustico Bay are 148 campsites set in 113 acres of evergreen forest.

En Route from Brackley Beach – Follow Route 6 west to Oyster Bed Bridge. On your right at the Route 223 intersection is a drag strip, popular with young people on summer weekends. For a pleasant, short side-trip, take Route 251 to the picturesque community of Wheatley River. Just 100 yards before the crossroads at Wheatley River is *The Weathervane* antiques store. Lynn and Cynthia Foley are among the most knowledgeable antiques dealers on the island and are always willing to give helpful tips to visiting antiques hunters. The *PEI Preserve Company* (on Route 224 in New Glasgow) makes its own preserves and mustards, and has a pleasant tearoom serving imported teas and coffees and home-baked desserts.

On the drive between Oyster Bed Bridge and North Rustico, you will see blue herons along the inlets formed by the Wheatly and Hunter rivers. These long-legged birds have spearlike beaks and resemble cranes, though they aren't related; the herons can usually be seen wading near the shore in search of small fish. They are alert and wary of intruders; they are best viewed through binoculars and photographed using a telephoto lens.

NORTH RUSTICO: This fishing village has the reputation of being one of the most picturesque on the island; it isn't, but it is worth a look in passing. The Prince Edward Island Wildlife Park is a popular children's attraction (don't miss Santa in Santa's Woods). Deep-sea tuna fishing charters can be arranged from here.

CAVENDISH: Native author Lucy Maud Montgomery set her novel *Anne of Green Gables* in this area. Some of the rustic paths that the fictional Anne explored have been turned into a golf course, but visitors can still see the Lover's Lane, the Babbling Brook, the Haunted Woods, and the Lake of Shining Waters. "Green Gables," the country farmhouse immortalized in the children's classic, is open daily. No admission charge.

Cavendish Beach is the busiest of all Canada's national park beaches, and Route 6 between Cavendish and Stanley Bridge is almost a continuous strip of motels, lodges, and summer cottages, as well as a variety of roadside shopping and attractions for children.

En Route From Cavendish – Route 6 leads to Stanley Bridge, an area famous for its beautiful inlets and excellent inland fishing on the Stanley and Trout rivers. This part of Prince Edward Island has a tradition of community lobster suppers, held nightly during the summer, which has become a cherished part of island life. The tradition began in the community and parish halls of New Glasgow, St. Ann's, and New London, and is still going strong today. For about $20, lucky guests have a choice of hot or cold lobster, New York sirloin, or pork chops, accompanied by seafood chowder, several styles of potatoes, corn, coleslaw, and rolls, finished off with three varieties of pie and ice cream. Call St. Ann's at 902-964-2351, or look for the signs pointing the way.

From Stanley Bridge, you can take a short side trip south on Route 254 to Devil's Punch Bowl Provincial Park. According to tradition, in 1771 a liquor transporter encountered the devil here (perhaps he was sampling his wares) and was so startled that his liquor fell off the wagon, creating this crater in the earth.

Route 6 leads to New London, Lucy Maud Montgomery's birthplace. The house in which the author was born contains her wedding dress, veil, shoes, and personal scrapbook. Open daily. Admission charge (phone: 902-886-2596).

Along Route 20 is the *Anne of Green Gables Museum* at Park Corner. Located in a house where Lucy Maud Montgomery lived at various times during her life, the museum contains the island's largest collection of Montgomery memorabilia, including autographed copies of the first edition of her world-famous novel. The museum has a gift shop, and outside a playground for children. Open daily. Admission charge (phone: 902-886-2884).

SOUTH SHORE: The Dunk River, near Ross Corner on Route 1A, is the best salmon and trout river on the island. The ferry landing from New Brunswick is at Borden Point, on Route 10 on the south shore. Follow Route 10 and then Route 1 to Victoria, a quaint seaside village. The *Victoria Village Inn* (Main St.) is a restored, century-old sea captain's house with comfortable guestrooms and a licensed dining room specializing in home cooking. Next door is the *Victoria Playhouse,* which stages local productions. *Time Was* (River St.) is one of PEI's most interesting antiques shops. Proprietors Gary and Jo Friesen restore antique clocks and go on annual buying trips to Europe.

En Route from Victoria – Turn off Route 1 onto Route 19 at DeSable for a picturesque drive along the south shore. At Rocky Point, Fort Amherst is the site of the first French settlement on the island (1720). Only the earthworks built by the British after they captured the settlement in 1758 remain today, and the site now has been turned into a national historic park with a museum and picnic area. Open daily. No admission charge.

At Meadowbank, *McCrady's Green Acres* (see *Best en Route*) is a motel set among 34 acres of pastoral farmland. Its restaurant is known for home-cooked meals and English-style cream teas. From Meadowbank, Route 19 returns to Route 1, which leads back to Charlottetown.

BEST EN ROUTE

Prince Edward Island has an ample supply of accommodations of every sort: hotels, motels, bed and breakfast establishments, farms that take visitors, cottages, and lodges. Along the Blue Heron Drive, because of the national park, there is a preponderance of small cottages and tourist homes which are available for rental; and they should be booked early for July and August. They are listed in the comprehensive *Visitors Guide,* available free from the *Department of Tourism,* PO Box 940, Charlottetown, PEI C1A 7M5.

Listed below are our suggestions for accommodations. Expect to pay $80 and up for two in any place in the expensive category; $50 to $80 in the moderate range; and under $50 in the inexpensive range. All prices are quoted in US dollars.

CHARLOTTETOWN

Dundee Arms – Some of the rooms in this 80-year-old refurbished house have antiques and brass beds and are slightly less expensive than the modern rooms. Try to get one. The *Griffon Dining Room* serves excellent food. 200 Pownal St. (phone: 902-892-2496). Expensive.

Prince Edward – Overlooking the waterfront, this 10-story Canadian Pacific establishment is Charlottetown's finest, with 2 restaurants, a lounge, heated indoor pool, saunas, and fully equipped exercise room. It is joined to a convention center and a small indoor shopping plaza, where visitors can purchase everything from men's and women's clothing to imported chocolates, antiques, paintings, crafts, and gift items. 18 Queen St. (phone: 902-566-2222). Expensive.

Duchess of Kent Inn – An antique clapboard-and-shingled house, just a block and a half from the center of the city. The spacious rooms have period furnishings and hardwood floors, and kitchen facilities are available. Continental breakfast is provided on request. 218 Kent St. (phone: 902-566-5826). Inexpensive.

DALVAY BEACH

Dalvay-by-the-Sea – A lovely resort on Dalvay Lake with tennis courts, lawn bowling, and rowboats. Its dining room serves French and English dishes. Route 6, in Prince Edward National Park, near Dalvay Beach. Winter address: PO Box 8, Little York, PEI C0A 1P0 (phone: 902-672-2048, in summer). Expensive.

BRACKLEY BEACH

Shaw's – The Shaw family has been welcoming guests here for over 130 years. Adjacent to the national park, it has 23 rooms, 12 cottages, and 6 chalets, one with a sauna and two with whirlpool baths. Rates includes two meals a day. A licensed dining room and lounge are on the premises. Sailboats and windsurfing are available. Route 15 (phone: 902-672-2022). Expensive.

RUSTICO ISLAND

Rustico Island Campground – This 113-acre parkland with small fir trees overlooking Rustico Bay has more secluded campsites than any other campground in the area. There are 148 campsites only a short distance from Brackley Beach. It is administered by the park, write PO Box 487, Charlottetown, C1A 7L1 (phone: 902-672-2211). Inexpensive.

SOUTH SHORE

McCrady's Green Acres – A small motel overlooking the West River, the dining room serves home-cooked food, right down to rolls and dessert. Route 19, at Meadowbank (phone: 902-566-2814). Moderate.

Lady Slipper Drive

The westernmost third of Prince Edward Island is an odd piece of geography. Attached to the rest of the island by a small umbilical cord of land at Summerside and twisted into right angles like a bent paper clip, it appears to be doing its best to wriggle away from the rest of Prince Edward Island altogether, like an eel or a snake just disappearing. But for all its apparent reluctance, it shouldn't be missed. This is Acadian country, home of the island's French-speaking population, the descendants of the early French settlers who established villages here before the British took over in 1758. Two Acadian museums, the *Acadian Museum* (phone: 902-436-6237) and the *Acadian Pioneer Village* (phone: 902-854-2227), along the 171-mile (274-km) Lady Slipper Drive route recreate the way of life of the French settlers.

Although Lady Slipper Drive really begins at Summerside, most travelers will reach that point from Kensington if they have been on the Blue Heron Drive just described or from Borden, if they have taken the ferry from Cape Tormentine, New Brunswick. From Summerside, the route drops south to Cape Egmont and the *Acadian Pioneer Village,* then shoots north to the fabulous fishing centers of Tignish and Alberton on the northwestern cape. Tons of tuna, lobster, and cod are caught every year in the Gulf of St. Lawrence. It was near Alberton that Jacques Cartier landed in 1534, naming the whole island Isle St. Jean. Farther down the coast is Malpeque Bay, where oyster beds produce the famous Malpeques. Making a large loop, the route returns to Summerside.

SUMMERSIDE: This town of well-kept residential streets and wood-frame houses is sometimes referred to as Prince Edward Island's western capital. Residents (pop. 8,000) are mainly employed in fishing, farming, and at a nearby military installation. Town Hall (1886), with a fine old clock tower, makes the perfect starting point for a walking tour of the neighborhood, where every house looks like a stately château. *The Eptek Centre* in the *Waterfront Mall* features art and other exhibits open to the public. The building also houses the island's *Sports Hall of Fame.* Nearby, the yacht club offers a view of Bedeque Bay and Holman's Island, the site of a 125-room hotel destroyed by fire in 1904. *The Brothers Two* (618 Water St.) is the town's best steak and chop house. *Shakers Lounge* (250 Water St.) is a popular rock 'n' roll dance bar, and the *Regent Lounge* (12 Summer St.) is another popular night spot. The *Summerside Lobster Carnival* in mid-July is the town's popular annual festival.

En Route from Summerside – Follow Central Street to Route 2. A left turn will take you through suburban St. Eleanor's and past the Canadian Forces Base, which employs many residents. At Miscouche, the *Acadian Museum* displays antiques from the early 19th century, including a collection of farm implements, trade tools, and portraits.

For 6 miles (10 km) beyond Miscouche, Route 2 cuts through a barren stretch of swamp and scrub. A left turn on Route 124 brings you to Mont Carmel.

MONT CARMEL: Overlooking Egmont Bay and dominated by the two black spires of Notre Dame Church, this city might serve nicely as the gateway to Acadian Prince Edward Island. Certainly Mont Carmel and its surrounding villages are staunchly French Canadian (and French-speaking). A favorite way to tour the whole area is by bike, tooling along the little roads between villages like a French *curé* visiting parishioners. Photographers should note the cemetery adjacent to Notre Dame, with several ornate statues standing on stone pillars.

Cape Egmont, just 3 miles (5 km) west of Mont Carmel on Route 11, is the site of the Acadian Pioneer Village, a re-creation of an early-19th-century log cabin settlement, with a church, common house, blacksmith shop, school, and water well. *Etoile de Mer,* in a spacious log building, is the island's most authentic Acadian restaurant. Its dishes include meat pies and *rapure,* a dish of grated potatoes wrapped around pork, then steamed or fried.

En Route from Mont Carmel – Follow Route 11 north for 14 miles (23 km) to Route 2 at Mt. Pleasant. Take Route 2 to Route 14 at Carleton, and proceed south to West Point. This drive around Egmont Bay takes you to Prince Edward Island's westernmost shore. Cedar Dunes Provincial Park at West Point has 33 campsites, 10 sites for trailers, and a beach on the bay. The West Point Lighthouse, inside the park, was built in 1875, and has a museum, chowder house, crafts shop, and 10 guestrooms. Route 14 follows the shoreline north to Cape Wolfe, named after General James Wolfe, who stopped here in 1759 on his way to lay siege to Quebec.

From Cape Wolfe to Christophers Cross, the island's western shore is dotted with small fishing villages and provincial parks. If you want to "get away from it all," the campgrounds and beaches here are uncrowded even at the height of summer. Seacow Pond on North Cape is named after the seacow, or manatee, which at one time lived here in great numbers.

The Atlantic Wind Test Site, at North Cape, is Canada's national laboratory for testing wind energy systems. Testing is done on traditional turbines with propeller blades and vertical "eggbeater" models. Visiting hours are 10 AM to 6 PM, daily (phone: 902-882-2746).

TIGNISH: The western terminus of the *Canadian National Railway,* Tignish is a busy fishing village from which large quantities of cod and lobster are shipped every year. The massive red brick Tignish Parish Church is the focal point of town life.

ALBERTON: Years ago this quiet little town was the center of Prince Edward Island's silver fox trade; today the remnant of that prosperous era is a heritage of tree-lined streets fronting large, lovely homes.

From Alberton, Route 12 winds south through rolling farm country. At Route 172, turn right to Route 162, along the banks of the Mill River.

MILL RIVER RESORT: This 500-acre park and camping area has facilities similar to those at Brudenell (see below), including a heated indoor pool, tennis courts, and an 18-hole golf course. River Resorts, an Atlantic Canada chain, has completed an 80-room hotel, *Rodd Mill River Resort* (phone: 902-859-3555), adjacent to the park.

MILL RIVER FUN PARK: On Route 2 at Woodstock, this park is especially worth visiting if you're traveling with children. Highlights include an outdoor pool and water slides, miniature golf, paddle and bumper boats, a petting zoo, and a 650-seat amphitheater for daytime entertainment. Admission charge (phone: 902-859-2071).

En Route from Mill River – Route 12 winds around the north shore. Lennox Island, accessible from Route 163, is the site of the island's largest Indian reserve, where many of the island's 350 surviving Micmac Indians live. At Bideford, government biologists work with oysters at the Ellerslie Research Station. The oyster beds in Malpeque Bay have made Prince Edward Island famous for bivalves. Nearby Green Provincial Park is perhaps the island's most beautiful camping spot. On the way into the park, the road winds through spruce and white birch forests and open fields. From here the route returns to Summerside.

BEST EN ROUTE

The western section of Prince Edward Island is sparsely populated, except for Summerside. Many smaller accommodations are listed in the *Visitors Guide,* available free from the *Department of Tourism* (PO Box 940, Charlottetown, PEI C1A 7M5). For the places we list as expensive expect to pay $80 and up for two; for moderate, $50 to $80; and inexpensive, under $50. All prices are quoted in US dollars.

There are many places to camp, including provincial parks along the shore. Campsites usually cost $10 to $15 per night.

PORT HILL

Senator's House – Formerly the home of a Canadian senator, this turn-of-the-century mansion has 8 guestrooms, a dining room, and is just over a mile (1.6 km) from Green Provincial Park. Open year-round. Route 12 (phone: 902-831-2071). Moderate.

SUMMERSIDE

Best Western Linkletter Inn – Summerside's largest motel has 108 rooms, a convention center, a licensed dining room, and a comfortable lounge. 311 Market St. (phone: 902-436-2157). Expensive.

Silver Fox – On a residential street, this is another restored house that's decorated with antiques — it's one of PEI's nicest inns. There are 6 rooms with private baths; rates include a continental breakfast. Open year-round. 61 Granville St. (phone: 902-436-4033). Moderate.

TYNE VALLEY

Doctor's Inn – About 20 miles (32 km) west of Summerside is this fine example of a traditional PEI country home. Owners Paul and Jean Offer operate a 7-acre market garden and have just 2 rooms available on a bed and breakfast basis. The owners are excellent cooks and will serve guests and others with reservations a delicious dinner in the dining room. On Route 167 off Route 12 (phone: 902-831-2164). Inexpensive.

WEST POINT

West Point Lighthouse – Located in the Cedar Dunes Provincial Park, this restored, century-old lighthouse has 10 guestrooms furnished with antiques. A licensed chowder house and crafts shop are on the premises. Off Route 14 (phone: 902-859-3605). Moderate.

WOODSTOCK

Rodd's Mill River – This resort, about 35 miles (56 km) west of Summerside, is considered one of the most scenic in Atlantic Canada. Among the amenities are tennis and squash courts, an 18-hole championship golf course, a heated indoor pool, a dining room, and a lounge. Off Route 2 (phone: 902-859-3555). Expensive.

The Kings Byway

The eastern portion of Prince Edward Island is almost detached from the rest of the island by the Hillsborough River. Most of this 220-mile (352-km) drive transverses Kings County, from which it takes its name.

The Kings Byway starts in the strawberry fields across the river from the provincial capital of Charlottetown (pick an armload of berries for next to nothing). It turns south to the original Scottish settlement founded by Lord Selkirk at Eldon, then cuts across the island's hilly interior tobacco-growing region to the eastern shore. At Moore's Migratory Bird Sanctuary you can observe Canada geese, blue geese, and black ducks in their natural habitat or test your angling skills in the Sturgeon River for rainbow and speckled trout.

The many provincial parks along the route have facilities for camping and swimming; the largest is Brudenell Park, with 90 campsites. The adjacent 1,700-acre *Brudenell Resort* (see *Best en Route*) also is the home of the best golf courses on Prince Edward Island.

Route 16 follows the coastline of PEI to North Lake, the "tuna capital of the world," from which several companies offer chartered boats for deep-sea tuna fishing. Catches of 1,000-pound bluefin tuna are common. From North Lake, the Kings Byway returns to the Charlottetown area along the island's rugged northern coast through several tiny coastal fishing villages.

En Route from Charlottetown – For a detailed report on Charlottetown, see the *Blue Heron Drive* route, the first Prince Edward Island route. Follow Grafton Street east over the Hillsborough Bridge to the village of Southport. Take Route 1A approximately 2 miles (3 km) to the top of Tea Hill for a spectacular view of Hillsborough Bay. Tea Hill and Alexandra are noted for their neatly kept country houses and thriving berry farms. During July, self-pick farms in this area sell strawberries and raspberries for about 75¢ per pound. Free picking boxes are provided; you do the work and reap the benefits.

Continue along Route 1A for 8 miles (13 km) beside Pownal Bay and take the Trans-Canada Highway (Route 1) east at Mt. Mellick. Proceed 6 miles (10 km) east to Orwell.

ORWELL CORNER: This tiny restored farm village depicts the life of the early settlers on PEI. The pioneer mood and setting of the mid-19th-century village are recreated by the historic site's store, post office, keeper's house, church, and barn. Open daily. Admission charge.

Campers visiting Orwell Corner can pitch a tent up the road at Sir Andrew MacPhail Provincial Park. MacPhail, a well-known writer born on PEI, was associated for years with McGill University, and his home is at the end of a magnificent tree-lined drive. The 24-site campground is located just opposite in an open field circumscribed by woods. The park has no facilities for trailers.

From MacPhail's home, walk back to the red clay road past the park entrance. In the valley below, a stream runs beneath a grassy mall — a perfect place for a picnic.

ELDON-BELFAST: These two tiny villages lie 6 miles (10 km) south of Orwell on Route 1. Lord Selkirk of Scotland led 800 Highlanders to settle the area in 1803. The small settlement at Eldon has remained a farming village through the years. On the opposite side of Route 1, Lord Selkirk Provincial Park overlooks Orwell Bay. There is a pioneer cemetery in the park, but unfortunately only a few memorials remain, their inscriptions all but indecipherable.

From Eldon take Route 207 east for the half-mile drive to Belfast, originally a French settlement called La Belle Face ("the beautiful face"), whose name was deeply distorted by the influx of Highlanders. Here, Selkirk settlers who moved inland built St. John's Presbyterian Church with timbers dragged uphill and squared with a broadax. Inside the church are memorials to Mary Douglas, the only daughter of Lord Selkirk, and to the Reverend John MacLellan, the church's first pastor.

Belfast was the site of an election day riot on March 1, 1847. Anxious for their respective candidates to win at the polls, Scottish and Irish factions exchanged words and then blows. Several men died during the fight, and the polls had to be reopened later under military supervision. A stone in the village cemetery marks the grave of Malcolm MacRae, the only Scot killed in the melee.

En Route from Belfast – Route 2 continues southeast along the shoreline to the Nova Scotia ferry landing at Wood Islands. Route 206 inland from Belfast meanders through the island's profuse tobacco district. At the intersection of Route 24, you have the choice of proceeding east on Route 316 or turning right through a stretch of hardwood forest to Caledonia and Murray River. Farther east, at the intersection of Routes 4 and 317, is Milltown Cross. Nearby is Buffaloland, with real buffalos, and Moore's Migratory Bird Sanctuary, with good freshwater fishing.

Panmure Island, 7 miles (11 km) farther east on Route 347 off Route 17, has one of the island's finest white sand beaches. In all, the drive from Belfast to the east coast is only 20 miles (32 km).

MONTAGUE: On the scenic Montague River, this town has a notable seafood restaurant, the *Lobster Shanty North* (Main St. S.; phone: 902-838-2463), which features lobster, scallops, and many other fish dishes. Be sure to glance through the guest book, in which the names of Queen Elizabeth II and Prince Philip are written, dated July 1, 1973.

At Poole's Corner, 3 miles (5 km) north on Route 4, stop at the Kings Byway Interpretive Centre. The center is a multimedia encapsulation of Kings County history and culture and worth some time to enhance the drive. Turn right on Route 3 to the Brudenell Provincial Park.

BRUDENELL RESORT: This 1,700-acre resort (see *Best en Route*) is the perfect spot to spend a few days relaxing. The resort has 50 chalets, including 36 overnight and 14 housekeeping units. *Brudenell* has the island's best 18-hole golf course, 2 tennis courts, open playing fields, and a small-craft marina on the river. The resort is family-oriented, with scheduled activities for children.

Nearby is the Brudenell Provincial Park, with 90 campsites (some with services for trailers). Guests staying in the park are entitled to use the resort's facilities.

Although the red sand bank of the Brudenell River offers only mediocre swimming, its placid inlets are ideal for canoeing and rowing (rentals are available at the marina).

GEORGETOWN: Recovering from some hard times, PEI's once thriving seaport is experiencing a revival. Georgetown's shipyard and fish plant are still active, along with its theater on the main street. The Brudenell River Provincial Park and *Roseneath* resort are contributing to its recent popularity and comeback. The *King's Playhouse* features local amateur productions.

En Route from Brudenell – For a picturesque drive through rural Prince Edward Island, follow Route 311 through Cardigan along the shore of the Boughton Peninsula. At Launching, its eastern point, you can very easily walk, at low tide, across to Boughton Island. At the western end of the island, look for Boughton's Natural Armchair, a freak of nature where the tide has cut an area out of rock at the foot of a cliff.

At Dundas, scene of the province's annual plowing match in late August, turn right on Route 310 along the north shore of Boughton Bay to Annandale. Named after a pioneer shipbuilder who established a business here in 1855, Annandale has a beautiful harbor — one of the few on PEI that does not freeze during winter.

From Annandale, follow Route 310 north to Souris.

SOURIS: This town got its name from the French word for "mice" after an invasion of these rodents early in the province's history. (The mice were passengers on ships bringing provisions to Prince Edward Island and, because they had no natural enemies, they multiplied with frightening speed.) A small park with beach access has been built just off Route 2 as you enter Souris. Some of the island's finest white sand beaches are found on the 9-mile (14-km) stretch between Souris and Bothwell. The town's *Bluefin Restaurant* (10 Federal Ave.) has good homemade fish chowder.

Souris is the jumping-off point for a side trip to the French-speaking Magdalen Islands, located 84 miles (134 km) north of Prince Edward Island in the Gulf of St. Lawrence. The Magdalens, part of Quebec, can be reached by ferry from a pier just beyond the outskirts of Souris.

En Route from Souris – Nearby Red Point Provincial Park has 26 campsites nestled behind a small woods close to the shore. The park has a picnic area, a large children's playground, and an excellent beach.

The *Basin Head Fisheries Museum* is nearby, with exhibits on the history of fishing in the province — and in many respects the history of fishing is the history of the province. The museum is open daily from June to September. Admission charge. There are shacks along the shore, an old lobster canning factory on the wharf, and a fine white sand beach below the museum.

At East Point, so named because it is the most easterly tip of the island, a lighthouse is stationed on a cliff overlooking the gulf, and Nova Scotia can be seen on a clear day. From East Point, Route 16 follows the north shore for 6 miles (10 km) to North Lake, which is both a lake and a seaport on the Gulf of St. Lawrence and Prince Edward Island's deep-sea tuna fishing center.

NORTH LAKE: Bluefin tuna are attracted to the seas of the Gulf of St. Lawrence by huge schools of herring and mackerel; men are attracted to the same seas by the bluefin tuna. Good charter fishing boats are available at the piers of North Lake for one to six people at about $255 per day. Charters should be booked in advance by calling *North Lake Tuna Charters* (phone: 902-357-2055). The bluefin in these seas are big — spelled BIG — and the fishing can be physically demanding: Tuna weighing more than 1,200 pounds have been caught off North Lake. Bringing a tuna to gaff can take as long as 10 hours.

En Route from North Lake – The coastline along Route 16 turns rugged as it winds back toward Charlottetown. Fishermen in the tiny village of Naufrage, 15 miles (24 km) west of North Lake, harvest a unique product — Irish moss, a red algae used as a thickening and emulsifying agent, and a common ingredient in many food products under the better-known name of its extract, carrageenain.

Route 16 runs into Route 2 at St. Peters, from which you can return to Charlottetown or join the Blue Heron Drive on Route 6.

BEST EN ROUTE

While there are few large accommodations along this route, there are many lodges and cottages with no more than five rooms all along the drive. Many of these are listed in the *Visitors Guide,* available free from the *Department of Tourism* (PO Box 940,

Charlottetown, PEI C1A 7M5). For places listed as expensive, expect to pay $50 and up for two; for moderate, $30 to $50; and inexpensive, under $30. All prices are quoted in US dollars.

BAY FORTUNE

Inn at Bay Fortune – Once the summer home of playwrights, actors, and actresses, this place has 11 cozy rooms, some with fireplaces, and a dining room. Route 310 (phone: 902-687-3745). Expensive.

ROSENEATH

Brudenell Resort – This resort is just west of Georgetown. The 1,700-acre park and resort area has 50 one-room chalets, each equipped with phone, television set, and bath. The property has the island's best golf course, 2 tennis courts, a small-craft marina on the Brudenell River that meanders through the park and resort, and a swimming pool — really preferable to swimming in the river. Open mid-May to mid-October. For information, write the *Brudenell Resort, c/o Rodd Inns,* PO Box 22, Cardigan, PEI C0A 1G0 (phone: 902-652-2332); in winter, *Rodd Inns,* PO Box 432, Charlottetown, PEI C1A 7K7 (phone: 902-892-7448). Expensive.

KINGSBORO

Sea Breeze – Overlooking Basin Head Harbour, 7 miles (11 km) east of Souris, this motel is an ideal overnight spot for tuna fishermen. There are 13 rooms and 3 housekeeping units, and fine home-cooked meals. Open all year. Mailing address: Souris RR2, PEI C0A 2B0 (phone: 902-357-2371). Moderate.

Quebec

Known as "La Belle Province," Quebec is the bastion of French nationalism and culture in Canada. At one time Quebec was part of New France — an area extending from the Hudson Bay to the Gulf of Mexico, and from the St. Lawrence nearly to the Rockies — which Louis XIV made into a French colony in 1663. In spite of a long battle to protect the French colony and its fur trading companies, in 1759 the British defeated the French and officially gained the land through the Treaty of Paris of 1763. To appease the French Canadians, the Quebec Act of 1774 was passed, allowing the French to maintain their feudal system, along with their language, religion, legal system, and other customs. But after the American Revolution many British Loyalists settled in Quebec, and by 1791 the British government had divided the colony into two regions — Upper and Lower Canada. The first elective assembly also was formed, but it provided little actual power for French Canadians. What followed was a revolt headed by Louis Papineau in 1837. The British defeated the French, but the uprising ultimately led to the creation of a truly self-governing body for Canada. Upper and Lower Canada were reunited and Canada East was made the province of Quebec. Under the new Canadian constitution, English and French were made the official languages of both Quebec and the Canadian Parliament. In 1974, though, French became the only official language of Quebec. Today, still, Quebec proudly maintains its French heritage. And, last year with the rejection of the Meech Lake Accord by Manitoba and Newfoundland, Quebec revived its drive toward independence. As the largest Canadian province, Quebec covers 594,860 square miles. More than 80% of the province's 6,580,000 residents are French Canadians. Its capital, Quebec City (pop. 580,000), one of the most beautiful cities in North America, is its second-largest city; Montreal (pop. 2,862,000) is the first. (For individual reports on Quebec City and Montreal, see the appropriate chapters of THE CITIES.) Outside these urban centers, the terrain consists of hilly agricultural land in the south along the banks of the St. Lawrence River and rocky, barren mountains in the north. Quebec's summers are hot and on the humid side. Winters are often cold, relatively long, and renowned for the quality of snowfall.

We have divided Quebec into six driving routes: the Eastern Townships, Beaupré/Charlevoix and Saguenay, the North Shore, the Laurentian Mountains, the Gaspé Peninsula, and the islands called Iles de la Madeleine.

The Eastern Townships consists of a fertile region between Montreal and New England that is dotted with ski resorts, glacial lakes, and country inns. From Montreal, our route follows Autoroute 10 or the slower, more scenic, Route 112 to Granby, which has a worthwhile zoo and, every October, a 26-day-long food festival. Bromont, a few miles south of Granby, is one of Canada's top ski resorts. Not far from Bromont is Cowansville, with a popular nature center. A detour west from Cowansville leads to Farnham, which boasts an interesting church and art collection. Backtracking east through Cowansville, the route goes to Sutton, which offers great downhill skiing and plenty of cross-country ski trails. Cottage country spreads along the shore of Lac Brome, which has a museum, and a renown for raising ducklings that make good eating. Swimming, picnicking, and regular boat tours are among the summer diversions possible at nearby Lake Memphremagog. Mont Orford, farther along this route, is both a good winter and summer holiday destination. Mont Orford Ski Area has everything for snow-lovers, and the *Orford Arts Centre* hosts an ambitious music festival every summer. Summer theater and three well-known inns are found in North Hatley, on Lake Massawippi. The route ends in Sherbrooke, the industrial center of the Eastern Townships, with a university, numerous galleries, and museums.

The Beaupré/Charlevoix and Saguenay route goes from Quebec City, northeast along the banks of the St. Lawrence River and finally to the Laurentian Mountains. It passes the historic French villages of Giffard, Beauport, Courville, Montmorency Falls, Ile d'Orléans, and the shrine of Ste. Anne de Beaupré. From a detour to Parc du Mont Ste.-Anne — where you can ski during the winter and visit the Ste.-Anne Falls in spring, summer, and fall — the road continues to St.-Tite des Caps, a mountain village; past Baie St.-Paul; to St.-Joseph de la Rive, where you can ferry to Ile aux Coudres. Along the way, the drive goes through La Malbaie, a popular fishing area, and Cap à l'Aigle, where eagles nest. The wilderness begins at Havre St.-Pierre, on the North Shore, and for those who prefer festivals, the friendly town of Chicoutimi is the site of an annual winter carnival.

The North Shore exploration picks up the route at Tadoussac and runs past Saguenay Fjord along the St. Lawrence River toward Labrador. This is a sparsely settled area (five inhabitants per square mile along the coast and only one person per square mile inland) of mountains, trout-filled lakes, and forests full of bear, caribou, and moose. The route continues through the lakes and farms of Petites Bergeronnes to Ilets Jérémie, a former Hudson's Bay Company trading post; past the hydroelectric plant and wildlife reserve Baie Comeau; through the fishing village of Franquelin at the foothills of the Laurentians; and alongside the rivers and lakes of Port Cartier and Sept Iles.

The Laurentian Mountains lie along the southern boundary of the glacial formation known as the Canadian Shield between the Ottawa and Saguenay rivers. It is a region made up of parks, reserves, and resorts. The first route begins at Trois Rivières, halfway between Montreal and Quebec at the mouth of the St.-Maurice River, and takes you to La Mauricie National Park, St.-Maurice Wildlife Reserve, and Parc St. Louis in La Tuque. Another route runs north from Quebec to Laurentides Wildlife Reserve, a camping and canoeing area; or, from north of Montreal to the ski slopes and resorts of St.-Sauveur and Ste.-Agathe des Monts, and on to St.-Jovite and Mont Tremblant. A third route runs from the town of Hull through the Gatineau Valley to La Vérendrye reserve at the western end of the Laurentian range, where you can hunt moose and fish for trout.

One of the oldest landmasses on earth, the Gaspé Peninsula is an area of old-fashioned fishing settlements where people still cast with homemade nets.

The route leaves Quebec City along the south bank of the St. Lawrence and encircles the peninsula, ending at Ste.-Flavie and Mont Joli. You will pass St.-Jean Port Joli, a handicrafts center; Rimouski, a deep-sea and river fishing port; Matapédia Lake, a salmon fishing center; the Micmac Indian reservation cooperative in Maria (where handmade snowshoes are sold); Port Daniel Park (for tuna fishing); Percé, home of Percé Rock; the town of Gaspé, where wildlife enthusiasts gather to observe animals and birds; and the salmon hatchery at Ste.-Anne des Monts.

The section on Iles de la Madeleine in the Gulf of St. Lawrence, 180 miles (288 km) east-southeast of the Gaspé Peninsula, describes a remote archipelago of about 12 islands, only 7 of which are inhabited. The residents make their living from fishing: Herring, mackerel, scallops, cod, halibut, and lobster are the main catch. In spring and fall, naturalists observe migratory birds and animals. During the summer, many vacationers make their way to these islands via the Cap Tourmentine ferry and Borden, PEI.

Information: *Ministère du Tourisme du Québec,* CP 20,000, Quebec City, Quebec G1K 7X2 (phone: 514-873-2015 in Montreal, 800-363-7777 from elsewhere in Canada and the United States).

The Eastern Townships

Sometimes called Quebec's best-kept secret, this scenic area of woods and glacial lakes, in the upper reaches of the Appalachian range, is just an hour's drive from Montreal. Long a popular vacation cottage area among Montrealers, the Eastern Townships region has gained an enthusiastic new following during the last 15 years. Now a busy resort area, it features such popular diversions as horseback riding, swimming, sailing, and festivals galore in summer; brilliant foliage worth biking or hiking through and vineyards and cider mills fragrant with fresh-pressed apples in the fall; and alpine (downhill) and Nordic (cross-country) skiing, snowmobiling, and snowshoeing all winter. Winter facilities have grown to meet the increased demand: There are now some 14 alpine ski centers (such as Bromont, Orford, Owl's Head, and Sutton), more than 800 miles of cross-country ski trails, and close to 100 miles of snowshoeing tracks. (For more details, see *Downhill Skiing* in DIVERSIONS.) It also is prime snowmobile country. The vehicle was invented in this area, and every February in the village of Valcourt an international snowmobile festival celebrates this sport. The townships' proximity to the American border states of Maine, New Hampshire, and Vermont, just across the road in some cases, makes it a favorite stopping-off place for New Englanders on their way to Montreal, and for Montrealers traveling in the opposite direction.

The Eastern Townships gets its name by virtue of its location east of Montreal. It was largely settled and developed by former New Englanders — known in Canada as United Empire Loyalists — who poured over the nearby border between 1774 and 1840 to escape, first, the American Revolution and, later, the government of the independent United States of America.

Loyal to the King of England, settlers came to British North America and set up farms similar to their former homes south of the US-Canada border. Prior to this influx, the earliest townshippers were the Abnaki Indians and other, smaller tribes who gave the region its romantic place names: Coaticook, Massawippi, Megantic, and Memphremagog. When Quebec was New France, a portion of the region known as Haut Saint-François was a trapping area that remained undeveloped until the Loyalists arrived. Town names like Granby, Sherbrooke, and Waterloo attest to the region's British heritage. However, following the construction of a rail network in 1852, increasing numbers of French-speaking Quebecois were drawn to this fertile land. Today, the area's residents are practically 95% francophones, and they refer to their home as "Estrie," a combination of the word "est" meaning east and "patrie" for homeland.

The region extends north and west from the New England border states and is flanked by the Yamaska and Chaudière rivers on either side. It begins at the town of Granby in the west, embracing Richmond and Asbestos to the north and Lac-Mégantic and Thetford Mines to the east. Although small compared to other vast spaces in the province, the townships make up for their diminutive size with spectacular scenery and a surplus of activities. Sherbrooke, the eastern terminus of this route, is 100 miles (160 km) from Montreal, so exploring the area is an easy day or weekend excursion from there.

En Route from Montreal – Head east from Montreal on either the high-speed Eastern Townships Autoroute, Route 10, or the winding (and far more scenic), older Route 112. The latter passes through Rougemont, a small town often considered a suburb of Montreal, known for its apple orchards and cider mills. If you follow this route in the fall, it is a great place to pick, buy, and eat apples, and to watch them being pressed into cider; you can purchase apple products, breads, and crafts all year. The town's apple interpretation center (11 Chemin Marieville; phone: 514-469-3600 or 469-3967), in a former refrigerated warehouse, has an audiovisual presentation on the fruit's cultivation and arranges apple-picking excursions in the fall. Open August through October. Closed Mondays.

GRANBY: The townships truly begin in Granby, on Route 112, just off the autoroute. Formerly known for its zoo, Granby more recently has been dubbed the Gastronomic Capital of Quebec, thanks to a month-long food festival staged here every October; regional specialties and dishes are created by guest chefs for visitors to sample at a number of restaurants, hostelries, and community centers in town (phone: 514-378-7272). Granby's zoo — in addition to 1,000 animals, a children's petting section, plenty of rides, and a picnic area — claims to have the only reptile farm in Canada. Located at 347 Bourget St. (phone: 514-372-9113), the zoo is open from May through October. The Lac Boivin nature preserve, (700 Drummond St.; phone: 514-375-3861), features a collection of European fountains and nature trails that wend through the city's parks. Nearby Yamaska Provincial Park (Rural Route 2; phone: 514-373-3204), is worth a short detour for its swimming, windsurfing, hiking, and picnicking facilities. A few miles south of Granby, just off the autoroute, is Bromont, one of a quartet of major mountains developed for skiing in the Eastern Townships.

BROMONT: This resort area is most popular during the winter, thanks to the Station Touristique Bromont, which has the longest illuminated night ski runs in Canada.

There are 24 slopes in all, 12 of which operate at night, plus a ski school, rental shop, and restaurant. The entrance to the ski center is at 150 Champlain St. (phone: 514-534-2200). During the summer, Bromont's visitors take to its alpine water slides, also at the tourist station, or enjoy the lake's fine swimming and sailing. Bromont also is a great place for horseback riding at *Centre Equestre Bromont* (100 Laprairie St.; phone: 514-534-3255). The *Bromont Equestrian Festival* in mid-July is one of the top events of the summer.

En Route from Bromont – Highway 241 South goes to Cowansville and its nature center (corner Church and McKinnon Sts.), where water lovers can sail, windsurf, kayak, or swim on Lake Davignon from mid-June to *Labor Day* (phone: 514-263-4311). A detour west from Cowansville — via Jean-Jacques Bertrand Blvd. to the junction of Highway 104 West — leads to Farnham, worth a stop to visit Saint-Romuald Church (1904) and its collection of works by Quebec painter Ozias Leduc. From Cowansville, a short drive east on Route 104 to the junction of Routes 139 and 215 puts you in Sutton, virtually in sight of the Vermont border. Some of the best skiing in eastern Canada can be enjoyed at Mont Sutton, which has a 1,500-foot vertical drop and 54 downhill trails. The woods and meadows surrounding the ski area have extensive cross-country trails as well. During warmer seasons, the public market, held every Saturday morning, harkens back to the farm life of an earlier time. From Sutton, head north on Route 215 to the town of Lac-Brome, formerly Knowlton (and still called that by many locals).

LAC-BROME: A choice vacation spot, this cottage country sprawls along the shore of Lac-Brome, made famous by its delicious ducklings. Summer activities center around the lake, and during the winter there is skiing at nearby Mont Glen. The *Brome County Historical Museum* (130 Lakeside Rd.; phone: 514-243-6782) is housed in buildings dating back to the turn of the century, and its exhibits of furnishings and tools re-create the life of the Loyalist settlers. Open mid-May through September.

En Route from Lac-Brome – Stay on Route 215 north — past the autoroute — until you reach Waterloo, a little valley village set against the rolling Eastern Townships mountains. Founded by Loyalists during the 1790s, Waterloo claims to be the mushroom-growing capital of Canada. It also is the site of North America's only hunting museum, the *Musée Québécois de la Chasse* (45 Horizon Rd.; phone: 514-539-0501), which features a large taxidermic collection. Open from late-May to mid-September. From Waterloo, hop on the autoroute and head west about 15 miles (24 km) to the Magog-Orford area.

MAGOG: Pronounced *Ma*-gog, from a corruption of the Abnaki term Memrobagak, meaning "great expanse of water," this town lies at the northernmost tip of Lake Memphremagog. It is busy all summer long with tourists and seasonal residents, who often picnic and swim at the public beach on Merry Point. The motor launch *Adventure II* makes regular tours of the lake, while the *International Swim Marathon* attracts thousands of spectators in July. To celebrate the turning of the leaves at the end of September, the town hosts the *Magog Festival of Colors. Auberge de l'Étoile,* right in the heart of town (1133 Principale W.; phone: 819-843-6521), is an excellent spot to sample the area's Lac Brome duckling.

MONT ORFORD: Both exits 115 and 118 off the autoroute lead to Mont Orford, known for its ski center, scenic Stukely Lake, a provincial campground, and an ambitious summer music festival. The highlight here is the 2,600-foot peak of the Mont Orford Ski Area (phone: 819-843-6548), which has 35 trails traversing its 1,772-foot vertical drop. Mont Orford Provincial Park is much more than just a summer sports paradise: Since 1951, it also has been the site of a leading Canadian art center. A 500-seat concert hall, surrounded by scattered chalets hidden amid the trees, is the focal point of the *Orford Arts Centre,* which is the scene of *Festival Orford.* One of Canada's best-known annual music festivals, this event begins at the end of June and concludes at the end of August. The summer home of the country's national youth orchestra, *Les Jeunesses Musicales,* the Orford hills come alive daily with the sound of classical, jazz, and popular music at both indoor and outdoor locations, including Victoria, Blanchard, Jacques Cartier, and Camirand parks. (The festival's Sunday brunch and supper concerts are extremely popular.) Students from all over the world attend the center's summer music school, and the public is invited to listen in on some of the master classes. The *Orford Arts Centre* is just off the Eastern Townships Autoroute, exit 118 on Route 141 North (phone: 819-843-3981).

The area also includes the *Mont Orford* 18-hole public golf course, open May to mid-October (phone: 819-843-5688), summer chairlift rides (phone: 819-843-6548), and a number of resorts.

En Route from Mont Orford – The autoroute goes directly to Sherbrooke, the heart of the Eastern Townships, but a more scenic circular route involves a quick backtrack to Magog to pick up Route 141 to Ayer's Cliff, then to Hwy. 143, around the jagged shoreline to Lake Massawippi and its resort community, and lastly to North Hatley. Ayer's Cliff, on the lake's southern banks, offers a wide range of summer and winter facilities and equipment, including cottages, pedal boats, kayaks, rowboats, and fishing tackle. It is home to the *Ripplecove Inn,* an old-fashioned resort complex of cottages and a main house overlooking the water. Montrealers don't seem to mind driving an hour or so just to enjoy the hostelry's award-winning food; guests also make good use of the pool, tennis and shuffle-board courts, and the sailboats and paddleboats (phone: 819-838-4296). The town has a public beach and a number of antiques stores.

NORTH HATLEY: One of the area's most popular destinations, the village is spread out along the northern banks of the lake. This is the site of two of the Eastern Townships' better-known inns and a summer theater. The *Piggery Theatre,* Quebec's only English-language summer theater, has a wide-ranging repertoire, from Broadway hits to Canadian productions. The theater's restaurant serves tasty country suppers prior to curtain time at 8 PM. The *Piggery* is off Route 10 at exit 21 (phone: 819-842-2191). Both *Hovey Manor,* with its art gallery, and the *Auberge Hatley* (see *Best en Route* for both hotels), a member of the Relais & Châteaux group, are in North Hatley, as are a number of craft studios and galleries. The *Lake Massawippi Festival,* held from late April to late June, is highlighted by organ recitals at St. Barnabas Church and Sunday brunch "Sons et Brioches" concerts at the United Church.

SHERBROOKE: Often called the Queen of Estrie, Sherbrooke is the area's industrial and cultural center. With just over 100,000 inhabitants, this small city, dating back to 1791, is home to the University of Sherbrooke. It also is the site of a number of art galleries and museums, such as the *Sherbrooke Museum of Fine Arts* (Palais St.; phone: 819-821-2115), which features a collection of 19th-century art inspired by local scenery. The town also has an imposing cathedral and an old seminary. During the winter, Sherbrooke is served by its own alpine and cross-country skiing facilities in several scenic municipal parks and at Mont Bellevue, a mountain just blocks from the downtown core. The city also takes advantage of activities at nearby Mont Orford — roughly 20 miles (32 km) east — with its ski slopes, cross-country runs, and summer festival.

The neighboring small town of Lennoxville, south of Sherbrooke on Route 143, is the site of one of Canada's leading universities, Bishop's (1843). The buildings that spread over the peaceful little campus were inspired by the architecture at Oxford University in England; visitors to both institutions have remarked on their similarities. Lennoxville's main street harbors a number of well-stocked antiques shops, while the *Musée Uplands* (50 Park St.; phone: 819-569-1179; or 562-4949 in summer) houses displays relating to the area's history.

BEST EN ROUTE

The area is known for its excellent inns, but there also is a variety of accommodations in resort hotels, motels, and bed and breakfast establishments. The hostelries listed here all feature basic services and amenities. Prices vary with the fluctuation of exchange rates and the season. Expect to pay over $70 for a double room in the expensive range, $55 to $75 in the establishments listed as moderate, and under $55 in the inexpensive category. All prices are quoted in US dollars.

GRANBY

Bon Soir – Within walking distance of most Granby restaurants, this 44-unit motel has a pool but no dining room. 1587 Principale St. (phone: 514-378-7947). Moderate.

Le Castel de l'Estrie – This comfortable, 137-unit motel has kitchenettes and a satisfactory dining room. 901 Principale St. (phone: 514-378-9071). Moderate.

Motel du Lac – Here is a 36-unit motel with a full-service restaurant and a swimming pool. Bargain ski packages are available in the winter. 255 Denison St. E. (phone: 514-372-5930). Inexpensive.

BROMONT

Auberge Bromont – An inn with motel units (55 rooms, all told) close to ski slopes, cross-country ski trails, and a golf course. It has an outdoor pool and a fairly good restaurant. 95 Montmorency St. (phone: 514-534-2200). Moderate.

Loft Acres – A country inn in an old farmhouse is the centerpiece of this complex. Around it is a condominium community with studio and 1-bedroom units available for overnight lodging. Popular bar and restaurant. Near Bromont and Mont Sutton. Route 139, West Brome (phone: 514-263-3294). Expensive.

La Petite Auberge – A 6-room inn, near ski hills, with very good dining. 360 Pierre La Porte Blvd. (phone: 514-534-2707). Inexpensive.

SUTTON

Centre Paulette Hiriart – Close to downhill and cross-country skiing, this 9-room establishment has a dining room and a pool. McCullough Rd. (phone: 514-538-2903). Expensive.

La Paimpolaise – This 28-room property is close to ski slopes and has good guest services and a fair dining room. In the summer, tennis and swimming are available. Chemin de Ski (phone: 514-538-3213). Moderate.

Horizon – A modern place with 48 rooms, an indoor pool and sauna, and a dining room that features old-fashioned roast pig every Thursday night. Cross-country ski trails ribbon the property. Chemin Mont Sutton (phone: 514-538-3212). Inexpensive.

MONT ORFORD

Auberge Chéribourg and Villas – This 97-room hostelry has an outdoor pool and first-rate dining room. 2603 Chemin du Parc (phone: 819-843-3308). Expensive.

Auberge Estrimont – The best place to stay in the area, this 46-unit resort features rooms in the main house or accommodations in 50 completely equipped chalets with fireplaces and kitchens. The main house has a good dining room. Squash and racquetball courts, 2 golf courses, a sauna, and a swimming pool round out the facilities. Exit 118 off the Eastern Townships Autoroute. 44 l'Auberge Ave. (phone: 819-843-1616). Expensive.

Auberge du Parc Orford – Right in the park, with 42 units equipped with kitchenettes. There also is a restaurant, café, swimming pool, and grocery store on the premises. 1259 Rue Montagne (phone: 819-843-8887). Moderate.

NORTH HATLEY

Auberge Hatley – A member of the Relais & Châteaux group, this country inn was built in 1903 as a summer house on a beautiful piece of property overlooking Lake Massawippi. The 23 colonial-style rooms are comfortably furnished with antique pieces; some have fireplaces. Sports include swimming in the pool or lake, sailing, golf, and riding. Award-winning chef Guy Bohec oversees the excellent dining room. On Magog Hwy. (phone: 819-842-2451). Expensive.

Hovey Manor – Formerly a private estate, this manor house is furnished with antiques. Most of the 35 rooms have views of Lake Massawippi and special suites feature wood-burning fireplaces, whirlpool baths, and private balconies. Water sports and tennis are available all summer. The inn's dining room is highly regarded, rating "four forks" from the Quebec government's tourism department. Hovey Rd. (phone: 819-842-2421). Expensive.

For more details on either the *Hatley Inn* or the *Hovey Manor*, see *Special Havens* in DIVERSIONS.

AYER'S CLIFF

Ripplecove Inn – Situated at Lake Massawippi, this intimate 27-room country inn is just minutes away from five major alpine ski centers. It has one of the best restaurants in the entire region. 700 Ripplecove Rd. (phone: 819-838-4296). Expensive.

Beaupré/Charlevoix and Saguenay

The Beaupré/Charlevoix coast is the section of the St. Lawrence River shoreline that stretches from Quebec City north to Tadoussac, the former Indian trading post at the mouth of the Saguenay River where it pours into the St. Lawrence. This is the St. Lawrence at its most pristine, skirting the foothills of the Laurentian Mountains (called the Laurentides by French Canadians) to the west, growing ever wider as it gets nearer the Gulf of St. Lawrence, lined with fishing villages and farms, small houses and ancient estates, 18th-century churches and long vistas of unparalleled beauty. The 130-mile (208-km) road between Quebec City and Tadoussac faithfully follows the northern shore of the St. Lawrence. At Tadoussac the route turns inland to follow the Saguenay River for 70 miles (112 km) along Route 172 to Chicoutimi, near Lac St. Jean; it returns to Quebec on Route 175 through Laurentides Provincial Park. Along the way, several alternative routes can extend or shorten the journey, including a driving route around Lac St. Jean or a continuation of the drive along the northern bank of the St. Lawrence — see *The North Shore* — as far as Havre-St. Pierre, after which the roads degenerate to unpaved and irregular tracks that may not be passable. Along this stretch, coastal transport is usually via all-terrain vehicles, small boats, or light aircraft.

This route covers a wide variety of terrain. North of Quebec City, beyond the gentle meadows of the St. Lawrence River Valley, the land becomes hilly and turns mountainous inland along the Saguenay River. Lac St.-Jean is a huge mountain pond, a basin among the peaks. The return cuts across one of the world's oldest mountain ranges, the magnificent glacier-ravaged Laurentian Mountains. Within Laurentides Provincial Park alone, the earth's convulsions have created more than 1,500 lakes and 700 streams.

The Saguenay Fjord, carved into the mountains by glacial activity, is a rarity outside the frozen northlands of Alaska and Scandinavia. A giant crack in the earth's crust — the largest fjord in eastern North America — it cuts a narrow but deep tributary through the mountains from Lac St.-Jean to the St. Lawrence. Saltwater tides from the Gulf of the St. Lawrence, channeled through the St. Lawrence River, gush into the mouth of the Saguenay with tremendous force. Greenland sharks and other ocean-dwellers are found in its waters as far as 60 miles (96 km) upstream. This junction of the two rivers also is a playground for whales, often seen cavorting in late July and August.

The Beaupré/Charlevoix region, Lac St.-Jean, and the Saguenay River area are extremely popular with sportspeople and nature-lovers alike. The coastal marshes harbor many varieties of edible fowl in such abundance that bag limits are usually generous. Numerous sanctuaries help preserve the large flocks and provide natural viewing environments.

Sensible wildlife management programs limit the hunting of bear, moose, and caribou in the populated shoreline areas along the St. Lawrence, but farther north, in Nouveau Quebec, they are fair game. Guides/outfitters are mandatory — and dictated by common sense. But anglers need not travel the least bit out of their way. Not only are many of the rivers of this province known for their challenging Atlantic salmon fishing (considered one of the hardest-fighting gamefish), but the large speckled trout seem to be just waiting to be coaxed out of the water.

The French navigator and explorer Jacques Cartier, discoverer of Canada, first traveled this coast in 1534–1535. His exclamation "Quel beau pré!" ("What a lovely meadow!") was the source of the name of this pastoral coast between what is now the eastern edge of Quebec City and Cap Tourmenté (about 25 miles/40 km north). The borders of the Charlevoix region — named after the Jesuit historian the Reverend Pierre Francois Xavier de Charlevoix, who traveled the St. Lawrence and Mississippi rivers between 1719 and 1722 — extend from here to the Saguenay River area.

The first Europeans to inhabit the area were mostly French as well as English and Scottish; they settled during the late 1500s and early 1600s. These settlers lived in isolated communities, struggling to survive in much the same way as the Abnaki and the Algonquin Indians who preceded them — by trapping, hunting, fishing, and farming the fertile valley of the St. Lawrence River. The means of survival have changed little here. The Saguenay Fjord area wasn't settled until the late 18th century, and it was not until the mid-19th century that settlers made their way up the Saguenay River to Chicoutimi, now the capital of the region, and farther north to Lac St.-Jean. Only recently have tourists had easy access to these remote parts of the province and their distinctive French North American culture.

En Route from Quebec City – Traveling northeast from Quebec City, Route 138 passes through the historic villages of Giffard, Beauport, and Courville —

all of them being swallowed by Quebec's expanding suburbs. Giffard (once part of Beauport) has a group of 18th-century structures. Two of the best known are the Côté House (3200 Av. Royale) and the Parent House (2040 de Lisieux St.). Within Beauport itself are the Aimé Marcoux House (Rue de l'Academie) and the Bellanger-Girardin House (600 Av. Royale). The Marcoux house is a 4-story mill in which one room has been restored in 19th-century style; it also houses an artisans' boutique, art gallery, theater, and *boîte à chansons* (cabaret). Open daily except Mondays, May to September. Once in Courville (7 miles/11 km from Quebec City), stop by the *Manoir Montmorency* (2490 Av. Royale, Beau Port; phone: 418-663-2877). Originally built as the Kent House in 1781 and occupied by the Duke of Kent between 1791 and 1794, its lookout provides a spectacular view of Montmorency Falls and the river gorge and its restaurant provides a pleasant lunch. The site includes picnic grounds, a handicrafts boutique, and a tourist information center. Then drive back to Route 138.

MONTMORENCY FALLS: About 9 miles (14 km) outside of Quebec City on Route 138, Montmorency Falls appear to the left and Ile d'Orléans (Island of Orléans) to the right. The falls cascade 274 feet to their base, considerably farther than Niagara's 193 feet. A terraced lookout (and some rain gear) allows visitors to get within 100 feet of the falls. During the winter, the water spray freezes into a gigantic cone that grows to 100 feet in diameter before the spring thaw. The cone is called *pain de sucre* (sugar loaf). From here, hop across to Ile d'Orléans on Route 368.

ILE D'ORLÉANS: Until the bridge was built in 1935, the only access to this pictur-esque isle was by boat in the summer and across a precarious ice bridge in winter. Cartier called the island Bacchus because of the abundance of wild grapes in the rich soil. Later the island was renamed for the Duke of Orléans, but the apples, strawberries, raspberries, and other fruits and vegetables that grow here still seem to be blessed by a god of fertility. Roadside stands and village shops sell local produce as well as quilts, blankets, and other items made on the island. The long isolation of Ile d'Orléans added to the strength of local legends of Loup-Garou and Feux-Follets. The "Old Ones" of the island believed (and taught) that the howling of the winter winds was the cry of supernatural wolves and that the lights that danced on the river waters at night (caused by phosphorus) were spirits. A circular tour of the 5½-by-21-mile island covers about 42 miles (67 km) and takes about 2 hours.

Turn right onto the road at the foot of the bridge (traveling counterclockwise), and go along the cliff to the village of Ste. Pétronille. Its wharf affords one of the best views of Quebec City and Cap Diamond. There are island walking tours in English (phone: 418-828-2275) along Chemin Royale. Tours leave from the Ste. Pétronille wharf but are for groups only, with reservations, May 1 through October 31. Be sure to visit the orchards — especially in late summer, when the apples ripen in the warm sun — before going on to St.-Laurent, where the strawberries grow as large as small apples and taste heavenly. Just past St.-Laurent's village church, which hosts regular folk and classical music concerts from July through September, is *Le Moulin St.-Laurent* (phone: 418-829-3888), a fine French restaurant in a renovated mill, open from June to September. Reservations necessary for this special place; ask to be seated at a table near the cimballa, which is a horizontal harp, sort of a cross between a pedal-steel guitar and a vibraphone.

The village of St.-Jean and its boatyards lie at the halfway point of the island's southern shore. Not only has St.-Jean been involved in the construction of boats since the French first settled the island, but many of the villagers became captains and navigators on the St. Lawrence waterway. Walking tours (in English) of St.-Jean leave from the church; for groups only, with reservations (phone: 514-346-4945), from May 1 to October 31. The *Mauvide-Genest Manor,* one of Quebec's most beautiful rural estates, has been converted into a private museum and a fine restaurant (phone: 418-

829-2915). Also on the grounds is the *Théâtre Paul-Hébert,* which hosts French productions. (For summer reservations, call 418-829-2202.) The museum, restaurant, and theater are open May to October.

St. François, with its scenic church (1735), old schoolhouse, and picturesque little cemetery, occupies the eastern tip of the island, overlooking the smaller islands of the Orléans archipelago as well as the coast of Charlevoix County. Here salt water from the Gulf of St. Lawrence 600 miles (966 km) away taints the freshwater river and the tide achieves its greatest height of 25 feet.

Continue through the village of Ste.-Famille to St.-Pierre. The village church (1718) is a historical monument open to visitors, and the *Presbytère* is a museum filled with household artifacts from the 18th century. St.-Pierre was the home of the late poet and singer Felix LeClerc. The *Théâtre de l'Île* (phone: 418-828-9530) presents summer theater (in French) and entertainment. *Les Ancêtres de la Petite Canadienne* (391 Chemin Royal) is an excellent restaurant in an old farmhouse, but it is open to tour groups only, on special occasions. The cook specializes in Quebecois dishes. From here, it's back across the bridge and onto Route 138 through Château-Richer toward Ste.-Anne de Beaupré.

STE. ANNE DE BEAUPRÉ: Local legend holds that this world-renowned Roman Catholic shrine began as a chapel built by a grateful group of Breton sailors. Caught in a violent storm, the sailors vowed to build a chapel upon reaching land safely. Three survived to start the project, and the chapel became an object of devotion even before it was completed when a crippled parishioner working on it was miraculously cured. The original wood chapel was replaced in 1676 with a stone church. By 1700 thousands of pilgrims were journeying to the shrine, and numerous cures were documented. That first stone church no longer exists, although a replica, incorporating material from the old church, serves as a Memorial Chapel. Both the Memorial Chapel and the newer Basilica, inaugurated in 1934, contain 18th-century art and silverwork. The wax museum near the Basilica illustrates the sanctuary's history (phone: 418-827-3781).

En Route from Ste.-Anne de Beaupré – Parc du Mont-Ste.-Anne (phone: 418-827-4561), host to the *Du Maurier International-Skiing Competitions* in 1966, catapulted into the skiing public's eye only a year after its opening and has been the site of skiing competitions ever since. The park now boasts 43 ski trails and 14 lifts as well as the province's only gondola lift, and $8 million worth of snow-making equipment keeps the slopes operating from early November through May. In summer, visitors can ride along the park's scenic bicycle path or play golf on its 18-hole course. Just 4 miles km) from the ski resort, there is *Camping Parc du Mont-Ste.-Anne* (phone: 418-826-2323), a 166-site campground open from mid-June through *Labor Day.* The *Château Mont-Ste.-Anne,* a luxurious, 258-room property at the foot of Mont-Ste.-Anne, is considered by many to be the best winter resort hotel in the region (see *Best en Route*). It is accessible from Route 138 via Route 360, about 3 miles (5 km) northeast of Ste.-Anne de Beaupré.

A well-marked secondary road off Route 138 just beyond the park access leads to St.-Joachim and Cap Tourmente. This fertile area, the first portion of the Beaupré coast to be settled, lies within a triangle formed by two arms of the Laurentian range (known as Les Caps) and the St. Lawrence River. The first buildings erected here in 1626 were destroyed during the French-British conflicts; however the Petit Cap, built in 1777, remains, as do two other structures: the Château Bellevue and its chapel. Except for a later addition (1870), these buildings have not changed since they housed seminary students during their summer vacations 200 years ago.

The Cap Tourmente National Wildlife Reserve (phone: 418-827-4591) in the migratory path of greater snow geese (or white geese), is a haven for geese and other birds. Each spring and fall, the Cap Tourment offers a fine view of about

150,000 white geese looking like a bed of live snow floating on the river. The reserve's interpretative center offers guided tours from mid-April through October. The information center at the entrance of the reserve offers information on the the different trails, tours, and observation points.

The 213-foot St. Anne Falls are located on a small road leading north from Route 138.

Outside St.-Joachim, Route 138 climbs sharply, bypassing the village of St.-Tite des Caps as it traverses the 2,300-foot crest of one of Les Caps. This vantage point, with a fantastic view of the river, marks the official boundary between the Beaupré region and Charlevoix County. Baie St.-Paul, 26 miles (42 km) away, is barely visible from the peak through the spruce-forested hills.

BAIE ST.-PAUL: This shallow, sheltered bay, guarded by tall promontories to the southwest and northeast, and Ile aux Coudres offshore in the St. Lawrence, has been a favored port since it was first settled in 1678. Many of the homes here are more than 200 years old. Just inland, outlining its valley of farms, are the highest mountains of the Laurentian range (4,000 ft.). The mountain peaks and the rivers flowing into their valleys — notably the du Gouffre and du Bras — irrigate the soil and beautify the town's setting. The lookouts at Cap-aux-Corbeaux and Rang Ste.-Catherine, with their stunning views of the bay, are popular attractions. The cliffs and beach draw hang-gliding enthusiasts all summer. Many artists, drawn by the calm, colorful scenery, live here; others visit. Their numbers and talents account for the quality and quantity of art available at the town's many galleries. The *Clarence Gagnon Art Gallery* (61 St. Jean-Baptiste St.; phone: 418-435-2428), named for famous Quebec painter Clarence Gagnon (1881-1942), is one of the better ones. The *Centre d'Art Baie St. Paul* (4 Fafard St. (phone: 435-3681) shows off Quebecois works.

The 18th-century *César Mill* (730 Rang St.-Laurent; phone: 435-5340), houses a workshop and sculpture gallery used by Quebecois sculptor Lucien Bouchard and others. Turning right onto Route 362 upon entering Baie St.-Paul via Route 138, follow it through town to a secondary road, Rang St.-Laurent. The mill is a little over 1 mile (1.6 km) from Route 362. Both the de la Rémi Mill (1826) and the Michel Perron Mill (ca. 1770), on the Rémi River and Michel Brook, respectively, still operate, but visitors are not allowed inside.

En Route from Baie St.-Paul – Upon entering Baie St.-Paul, Route 138 turns inland. The driving time from here to La Malbaie (25 miles/40 km) is less than 1 hour. Route 362, the old coast road, winds through town and then on to the villages of Les Eboulements, Cap aux Oies, and St.-Joseph de la Rive. The route is hilly and some of the hairpin turns are tight. This area served as the backdrop for the popular French-language television show, "Le Temps d'une Paix." One of the spots where scenes were shot — the forge in Les Eboulements — is open to visitors.

The name Eboulement means "landslide," and one occurred here in 1663 after an earthquake. This is another Quebec village noted for its period architecture that contains an array of art galleries and handicraft shops. The village church, from its elevation of 1,204 feet, offers a good view of Ile aux Coudres. Past the village, a dirt road leads to Cap aux Oies. From here you can see schools of porpoises playing in the St. Lawrence.

Also in Les Eboulements is a small, unnamed paved road to St. Joseph de la Rive, steep and treacherous when wet. About 300 people live in St. Joseph all year. The altar in the Church of St.-Joseph de la Rive is mounted on four sea anchors and the baptismal fonts are made of seashells. The St.-Gilles paper mill, which uses few machines, produces a luxurious parchment comparable to the finest of China, Japan, and France. The Ile aux Coudres ferry docks at a wharf lined with people year-round, fishing for the many varieties of smelt in the St. Lawrence. There are three small motels and one inn in St. Joseph de la Rive.

ILE AUX COUDRES (HAZELTREE ISLAND): Christened by Cartier for its thick copses of hazel trees, it was here in 1535 that the first Mass was celebrated on Canadian soil. The early settlers on the island were whalers and shipbuilders. Now the mining of peat moss, 20 feet thick in some areas of its vast bogs, is the principal industry of this island's 1,600 inhabitants.

Until the recent establishment of a year-round ferry, ice floes in the river cut off the island from the mainland in winter. By necessity, island people, seafarers like most island dwellers along the St. Lawrence, mastered the art of ice canoeing, now a competitive team sport at Quebec City's *Winter Carnival.*

This romantic island — just 35 miles in circumference — attracts many visitors lured by its isolation and scenery. The *Centre Artisanal de l'Ile aux Coudres* (Artisans' Center; 605 Rue des Coudres; phone: 418-438-2231) sells a wide range of pottery, leatherwork, sculpture, painting, knitted clothing, quilts, blankets, and other items crafted by the islanders. The *Leclerc House* (114 Principale St., La Baleine; phone: 418-438-2240), one of the island's first, also sells such arts and crafts. In addition, it now displays a collection of regional antiques and objets d'art. Open daily from June 24 to *Labor Day.*

The Moulins de l'Ile aux Coudres (windmills, on Moulin Road) are open for guided tours from June to September. An interpretive center, the *Musée Les Voitures d'Eau,* or "ship museum" (203 des Coudriers Rd. phone: 418-438-2208), explains the history of the area and its fabled schooners through a slide show, exhibitions, and tour of the boats, or *goélettes* as they are called here. Tours of the schooner *Mont-St.-Louis* are given June through September.

En Route from Ile aux Coudres – After the ferry returns you to St. Joseph de la Rive, drive up the hill to Les Eboulements and turn left onto Route 362. A secondary road leads inland to St.-Hilarion and Route 138, but Route 362 continues along the coast to the resort area of Pointe-au-Pic, passing through the village of Ste.-Irénée, the birthplace of Adolphe Routhier, composer of the Canadian national anthem.

The *Manoir Richelieu* (see *Best en Route*) has dominated this international resort area for over 60 years. Set high on a cape overlooking the St. Lawrence, the 400-room gray stone hotel has hosted such dignitaries as former US President William Howard Taft (who had a summer home nearby) and Senator Robert Taft, and many Canadian and American luminaries own or rent summer villas here. The rooms of the hotel retain their traditional atmosphere. There is a golf course at the manor, another at the *Murray Bay Club* (phone: 418-665-2494). The manor also has tennis, horseback riding, swimming, and facilities for shooting clay pigeons. There also is summer theater. For first class dining, try the classic French cooking at the *Les Trois Canards* hotel-motel (phone: 418-665-3761) on Côte Bellevue, or the French and regional dishes at *Des Falaises* (18 Rue des Falaises, Pointe-au-Pic; phone: 418-665-3731), an inn with a stunning view of Malbaie.

LA MALBAIE: Ideally located at the mouth of the Malbaie River, with the summer resorts of Pointe-au-Pic (southwestern) and Cap à l'Aigle (northeastern) on either side, this town has attracted summer visitors and anglers since the 1760s. Champlain dropped anchor in this bay one evening in 1608. The morning low tide left him nearly beached on the clay flats, hence the name Malbaie ("bad bay"). The area's great forests of cedar and white pine gradually have been depleted since the establishment of a sawmill here in 1672. In 1759, two officers of General Wolfe's invasion force landed here, presumably to raze the town, but they decided to settle instead. Their attempt to rename the town and river in honor of their commanding officer General Murray

(Wolfe's successor) failed, but unofficially the area is called Murray Bay by both French- and English-speaking people. The town is home to the *Laure-Conan* regional museum (30 Patrick Morgan St.; phone: 418-665-4411) which contains the recreated Victorian parlor of Quebec's first author; periodic art and history exhibitions are presented year-round.

En Route from La Malbaie – Follow Route 138 northeast toward Tadoussac and the Saguenay River, about 75 miles (120 km) away. There are fewer villages along this section of the coast.

Five miles (8 km) beyond La Malbaie is the tiny resort of Cap à l'Aigle, named by Samuel de Champlain in 1608 for the many eagles nesting on the rocky cape. These magnificent birds are still here, their numbers sadly reduced. Though a tiny village, Cap à l'Aigle is home to *La Pinsonnière,* a member of the prestigious Relais & Châteaux group (see *Special Havens,* DIVERSIONS).

At the village of St.-Siméon, you may turn left onto Route 170 and go north (and west) to Chicoutimi, but this means skipping Tadoussac and the mouth of the Saguenay River, which are well worth seeing. One of the several ferries on the St. Lawrence crosses from here to Rivière du Loup on the south shore. Ste.-Catherine, at the edge of the mountains, marks the border of Charlevoix County. On the clay flats of this village, Champlain met with representatives of the Huron tribes and other inhabitants of the northern shore of the St. Lawrence to form an alliance. This put the French into direct conflict with the Iroquois Nation, the traditional enemies of the northern tribes. Eventually this treaty helped cause the downfall of New France because it was used by the British to funnel the hostilities of the violent Iroquois Nation against the French and their allies. The northern tribes, no match for the Iroquois, were decimated.

TADOUSSAC: This village, one of the oldest settlements north of Mexico, dates to when Cartier visited the site in 1535 and pronounced it the "gateway to the Kingdom of Saguenay," a land of precious metals and stones. In 1599 Pierre Chauvin became the first Frenchman to build a house in Canada by erecting a trading post here. Chauvin, a fur trader, arranged for 16 men to remain at the site during the winter of 1600-1601. As a colony, the attempt failed, but as a trading post, business boomed. By 1603, when Champlain stopped here on his way up the St. Lawrence, Tadoussac ("rounded hillock," or "knoll") was the supply port for ships traveling to and from Europe. The *Chauvin Museum* (157 Rue du bord de L'eau), an exact replica of that first house, was constructed from a description written by Champlain. Open daily, June 1 to September 30, 10 AM to 10 PM (phone: 235-4657). Next to it stands Canada's oldest wooden church, a chapel that dates from 1747 (open all summer). The brothers Kirke (David, Lewis, and Thomas), British merchant-explorers commanding a fleet under royal patent to expel the French from Canada and establish their own trade monopoly, captured the post in 1628.

Tadoussac owes part of its growth to its location at the mouth of the Saguenay, which flows 471 miles (754 km) from Lac St. Jean, which connects with several other rivers to the north, creating a network of waterways. From Tadoussac, it was possible to establish trade with trappers and Indians halfway to Hudson Bay. The traders and explorers may have been attracted to the site because the Saguenay Fjord is a deepwater channel (750 ft.), wide enough to sail, or because of the whales (belugas, blue, and finback) that congregate in the St. Lawrence during late July and early August. The blue are the largest, averaging 99 feet long and weighing 118 tons. The refurbished *Tadoussac* hotel (see *Best en Route*) arranges boat trips upriver to see the whales, as well as cruises on the *Marie Clarisse,* a tall ship plying the river during the summer. Film buffs will be interested to know that the hotel was one of the settings for the movie *Hotel New Hampshire.*

Tadoussac is prime hunting and fishing territory. The forests are filled with moose, and farther north, with caribou, grouse, ptarmigan, and small game. The waters are rich with pike, walleye, landlocked salmon, and speckled trout. For music lovers, the town bursts into song in mid-August when it presents the *Festival De La Chanson Québécoise* for North Shore and Quebec composers and singers. It is centered around the *Café du Fjord* (152 Bateau-Passeur; phone: 418-235-4372 or 235-4626), which also stages art exhibitions.

En Route from Tadoussac – At a strategic point on the river, Tadoussac can be the final goal, midpoint, or jumping-off spot for any vacationer. From here it is possible to follow Route 138 along the north bank of the St. Lawrence (see *The North Shore*) to Havre St.-Pierre, where the road ends. Beyond that is wilderness. North and west from Tadoussac is Lac St. Jean, source of the Saguenay. Beyond that, light aircraft and an outfitter-guide are necessary to hunt and fish the wilds that extend toward Hudson Bay. A ferry at Escoumins, 24 miles (38 km) past Tadoussac, goes to Trois Pistoles on the south shore. Our choice is to take Route 172 north and west to Chicoutimi (70 miles/112 km) and on to Lac St.-Jean; the turnoff is about 6 miles (10 km) outside Tadoussac.

The drive from Tadoussac takes in wild and splendid scenery, but the fjord is not visible from the highway. About 43 miles (69 km) north of Tadoussac, a road leads down a cliff to Ste. Rose du Nord, near Chicoutimi. The road is quite tricky, but the town has an awe-inspiring view of the high cliffsides of the fjord and the rushing waters beneath. Every year hordes of photographers and artists flock to this spot for a glimpse of these near-vertical walls torn from the mountainous earth by glaciers countless years ago. There is a rest area, a few services, a wharf and a camping area (*Campground La Descente des Femmes;* phone: 418-675-2348), and little else — no hotels or motels.

About 30 miles (48 km) past the Ste.-Rose du Nord turnoff is the village of St. Fulgence and the small park/rest area of Mont Valin, which offers a breathtaking view of the Saguenay Fjord.

CHICOUTIMI: Chicoutimi means "as far as it is deep" in the language of the Montagnais Indians who inhabited the area; beyond this point the fjord was unnavigable. Peter McLeod, a Scottish settler, founded this thriving community on August 24, 1842. Shipbuilding was a major industry of the time, wood its principal material. McLeod brought a small group to this forested land to open a sawmill. From this venture grew one of the province's largest cities (pop. 60,000). A major convention city, it abounds with good Quebecois dining, generous watering holes, and, as befits this still-young frontier town, an active nightlife. Two large shopping centers, *Place du Saguenay* and *Place du Royaume,* are both on Racine Street.

The *Lac St.-Jean Museum* provides a good introduction to the region's history and geography (534 Jacques Cartier E.; phone: 418-545-9400), and the Old Pulp Mill (300 Dubuc; phone: 418-543-2729) has displays on the city's industrial origins.

In mid-February the city hosts a week-long *Winter Carnival,* with skiing and snowshoe races, tobogganing, and singing, dancing, and riotous partying to rival the *Quebec Carnival* for excitement. In summer, there's the *International Swimming Marathon* and a series of regattas in July. And all summer the *Marjolaine II* (phone: 418-543-7630) leaves from the Chicoutimi dock for cruises along the Saguenay.

En Route from Chicoutimi (the Lac St.-Jean circle) – If your time is limited, take Route 175 back to Quebec City (120 miles/192 km; driving time less than 3 hours). If you have time, however, continue north and west on Route 172 toward Làc St.-Jean through a small agricultural district to the industrial town of Alma. Alma stands in the midst of several smaller lakes and rivers at the headwaters of the Saguenay River, its back to Lac St. Jean. Aluminum, pulp, and paper are the town's major industries.

The cruise ship *La Tournée* departs daily, except Mondays, during the summer from the town's marina for tours of the Saguenay. At Alma, Route 172 intersects Route 169, which circles Lac St.-Jean; bear to your right, traveling counterclockwise, and head north and west on Route 169.

Péribonka, 30 miles (48 km) from Alma, was the home of Louis Hémon (1880–1913), author of *Marie Chapdelaine*. A Marie Chapdelaine museum is located in the house Hémon occupied, 3 miles (5 km) east of the village. On the last Saturday in July there is a swimming race across the lake starting at the town's waterfront.

Twelve miles (19 km) farther around the lake, on the bank of the river of the same name, is Mistassini — "big rock" in Cree. The village holds a *Blueberry Festival* the first week of August, with contests for such local specialties as blueberry wine and blueberry pie. Across the river is a monastery of the Trappist fathers (phone: 418-276-0491); a slide presentation about the monastic lifestyle is available to visitors, but no guests are permitted in the monastery itself. Ask for Père Marcel Carrier.

At the far end of Lac St.-Jean is St.-Félicien. Here, on Chamouchouane Island, in the Saumon River, is the most beautiful zoo in the province, open from June to September. More than 2,600 animals representing 130 different species roam the open area. From St.-Félicien, Route 167 leads to the Chibougamau Reserve and beyond it the Mistassini Reserve. These areas attract many hunters and anglers. Route 169 bears south and east here, beginning its swing back toward Alma.

Roberval, the first parish settled on Lac St. Jean (1855), is about 25 miles (40 km) beyond St.-Félicien. It is now a small commercial center, providing access to the Pointe-Blue Indian Reserve and its *Amerindian Museum* 3 miles (5 km) away on the lakeshore at 407 Amishk St. (phone: 418-275-4842). In late July, the town hosts 8 days of entertainment and sporting events culminating in a marathon swim from Péribonka the last Sunday of the month.

Six miles (10 km) from Roberval is Val Jalbert, erected as a company town servicing the paper, pulp, and lumber industry in 1901. It failed when the company went bankrupt in 1927. The site remained vacant until 1960, when it was turned into a park and historic museum (open late May to October 1; phone: 418-275-3132). A terrace café and a handicraft center operate out of the old mill. About 35 miles (56 km) outside Val Jalbert, Route 169 abruptly turns south toward Quebec and intersects Route 175 (from Chicoutimi) in the middle of the Laurentides Park. This final leg of the route, about 120 miles (192 km), takes about 3 hours to drive.

BEST EN ROUTE

Outside Quebec City and Montreal, the province's accommodations take on a rural flavor. Although services may be limited, all the necessities and the niceties of life are available. The hostelries listed here have services and amenities enough for any traveler. Remember that prices fluctuate with exchange rates and the season. In the listings below, $55 (double occupancy) is expensive; $40 to $55, moderate; and under $40 for two is inexpensive. All prices are quoted in US dollars.

ILE D'ORLÉANS

Auberge Le Chaumonot – This plush 8-room inn is about 18 miles (29 km) from the Pont de Ville bridge, on an isolated stretch of waterfront. There is a heated pool, a bar, and the rooms are very comfortable. The French restaurant on the premises is quite good. Open April to October. 425 Chemin Royal, St. François (phone: 418-829-2735). Expensive.

STE. ANNE DE BEAUPRÉ

Château Mont-Ste.-Anne – Sitting right at the foot of Mont-Ste.-Anne and facing the hill, this place is the best winter resort in the region. Of its 258 air conditioned rooms, 18 have fireplaces and 50 are split-level suites. All have just been redecorated and offer cable and pay TV. The property also features 2 restaurants and a formal dining room. Ski week packages, as well as transportation from the airport, are available. 500 Blvd. Beaupré (phone: 418-827-5211 or 800-463-4467). Expensive to moderate.

BAIE ST. PAUL

Auberge La Pignoronde – A popular bayside hostelry with 27 rooms, a swimming pool, and a fine dining room. 750 Blvd. Mgr-de-Laval (phone: 418-435-5505). Expensive.

Belle Plage – As its name suggests, this small place with a restaurant is located at the water's edge. 192 St. Anne St. (phone: 418-435-3321). Expensive.

Maison Otis – A 28-room inn that has a highly rated restaurant and comfortable accommodations. 23 St. Jean-Baptiste St. (phone: 418-435-2255). Expensive.

ILE AUX COUDRES

Auberge de la Roche Pleureuse – At the eastern tip of the island, this 90-room motel has a good restaurant, tennis courts, and a pool. Closed in winter. La Baleine, 238 Route Principale E. (phone: 418-438-2232). Expensive.

Cap-aux-Pierres – This property has 60 motel units and 35 rooms in the main house, as well as a swimming pool, tennis courts, and special facilities for the handicapped. Canadian and international folk dancing shows are staged here on Saturdays, and there is a lively *boîte à chanson* (cabaret) from June to September. 220 Route Principale E. (phone: 418-438-2711 or 800-463-5250). Expensive.

POINTE-AU-PIC

Auberge Au Petit Berger – This comfortable inn with just 20 rooms dispenses especially good and reasonably priced food. 1 Côte Bellevue (phone: 418-665-4428). Expensive.

Auberge Les Trois Canards – Small and comfortable with 44 rooms, it's known for its fine French and Quebecois food. There is tennis and swimming. 49 Côte Bellevue (phone: 418-665-3761). Expensive.

Manoir Richelieu – One of the most popular resorts in the province, with very accommodating service, it has golf, tennis, a pool, a deluxe dining room, bars, and 390 traditional rooms. Make early reservations. 181 Manoir Richelieu Ave. (phone: 418-665-3703 or 800-463-2613). Expensive.

LA MALBAIE

Auberge Charlevoix – An attractive, 42-room inn with a restaurant, tennis courts, and a pool. 1030 St. Etienne St. (phone: 418-665-4413 or 800-463-5776). Expensive.

TADOUSSAC

Tadoussac – This popular hostelry — the largest in town with 149 rooms — has a dining room and full services; the management organizes various expeditions, including summer whale-watching trips on the Saguenay River. Totally renovated by the Famille Dufour Cap-aux-Pierres hotel group during the mid-

1980s, the property has retained the charm of an old-fashioned summer resort. Summer theater and other entertainment are offered every evening during the summer. 165 Bord de l'Eau St. (phone: 418-235-4421/4343 or 800-463-5250). Expensive.

Georges – A small hotel-motel that offers 23 comfortable units and complete restaurant services. 135 Bateau-Passeur St. (phone: 418-235-4393). Inexpensive.

CHICOUTIMI

Auberge des Gouverneurs – Just outside town, this plush establishment with 167 rooms has a pool, good restaurant, bar, and fine service. 1303 Talbot Blvd. (phone: 418-549-6244 or 800-463-2820). Expensive.

Universel – A 119-room complex, with a pool and good restaurant; it is a member of the Quebec chain of efficiently run lodgings. 250 Sagueneens St. (phone: 418-545-8326 or 800-463-4495). Expensive to moderate.

Chicoutimi – Centrally located, this older 99-room property features a dining room and full services. 460 Racine St. (phone: 418-549-7111 or 800-463-9656). Moderate.

Le Montagnais – This large, modern complex has 292 rooms plus exhibition and conference halls. There also are 2 swimming pools (indoor and outdoor) and a restaurant. 1080 Talbot Blvd. (phone: 418-543-1512 or 800-463-9160). Moderate.

ALMA

Universel – A pleasant place close to the lake, it has 60 rooms. 1000 Cascades Blvd. (phone: 418-668-5261 or 800-463-4495). Expensive to moderate.

Cascades – This comfortable hotel-motel has 58 rooms and a decent restaurant. 140 Pont Nord Ave. (phone: 418-662-6547). Moderate.

Dequen – A 56-unit motel with a dining room serving local dishes. 800 Pont Nord Ave. (phone: 418-662-6649). Inexpensive.

The North Shore

The North Shore route explores the edge of that immense, remote region extending east from Tadoussac and the Saguenay Fjord along the north bank of the St. Lawrence River toward Labrador.

The principal overland access, Route 138, extends to Havre St. Pierre, on the bank of the Gulf of St. Lawrence opposite Ile d'Anticosti. Previously, this blacktop highway went only as far as Moisie, augmented by an irregular series of unpaved (and periodically impassable) roads linking the tiny villages along the rugged coast. Route 138 runs for 385 miles (616 km), from Tadoussac to its end at Havre St.-Pierre, along a sandy seashore wedged between capes and mountains and through fewer and ever more remote villages.

Beyond Havre St.-Pierre, the coast is accessible only by small boats or light aircraft. North, into the immense wilderness of the province toward Hudson Strait, small aircraft are necessary for efficient, long-distance transportation, although all-terrain vehicles manage some of the logging roads and dirt trails through some areas.

The isolation, the abundance of fish and game, and the enormous volume of natural resources that have attracted hunters, anglers, and explorers for more than two centuries continue to dominate life in this vast land of mountains, lakes, and forests. The scarcity of settlements along the St. Lawrence is compounded by the lack of natural population centers beyond it. The population density ranges from five people per square mile near the coast to roughly one per square mile inland. There are only a handful of interior settlements in this area, and, for the most part, those that exist are either by-products of industrial exploration or modern equivalents of the 17th-century Hudson's Bay trading posts, outposts in the wilderness to which hunters and anglers journey in search of legendary prizes. Large portions of land just beyond the coastal strip are open to hunters, although outfitter services are necessary. Moose, caribou, and even bear can be taken in the forests of Nouveau Québec, as the northern area is called. Speckled and Quebec red trout dominate the river waters. Commercial exploration has led to the opening of this isolated frontier, with expansion of the coastal settlements encouraged by the growth of mining, fishing, lumber, and hydroelectric power companies tapping the resources of the Canadian Shield. For example, the power project at James Bay has created 1,000 miles of roads and three power stations.

Travel arrangements in this region must be made in advance. Because of the rapid industrial growth, service facilities (particularly lodging, guides and outfitters, and aircraft and boat transportation) may be strained by the flow of traffic in coastal villages used as jumping-off points for hunting and fishing as well as construction and exploration expeditions. The following service the North Shore: *Canadian International* serves Radisson (phone: 418-692-0912 or 800-361-7413); *Québecair* (phone: 418-692-1031 or 800-361-0200); *Air Inuit* (phone: 514-636-9445 or 800-361-5933 in Quebec province); and *Air Creebec* (phone: 819-825-8355). Other charter services can be picked up at Kuujjuak, Val d'Or, Schefferville, Fermont, La Sarre, and Sept Iles.

At Tadoussac, the massive Saguenay Fjord, its cliffside walls rising 1,500 feet, joins the St. Lawrence River, where ocean-dwelling giants like the blue whale play in the river waters every summer just as they did when the Basque whalers hunted them during the 15th and 16th centuries. The route crosses the mountains and forests stretching along the St. Lawrence's edge toward Labrador, a cold barren tract often called the Land of Cain. This trip has just a taste of the extraordinary beauty and overpowering size of the land beyond the northern horizon. It will alter your conception of size and distance.

En Route from Tadoussac – Take Route 138 northeast from Tadoussac through a lovely area filled with lakes into the farming valley of Petites Bergeronnes. The village of Grandes Bergeronnes is about 15 miles (24 km) from Tadoussac; a secondary road on the far side of the tiny village leads to Cap Bon Désir Bay. The bay (now a park) had been a meeting place for whalers and seal hunters. On nearby Anse à la Cave (Hollow Cove), remains of 16th-century furnaces used by Basque whalers to boil animal fat have been found. Les Escoumins, a town by comparison, is 9 miles (14 km) farther on Route 138. Champlain examined the site in 1603 and noted in his log, "This is the place where the Basques go whaling." Evidence of a Basque whale oil processing furnace has been found on (and since removed from) Pointe Escoumins. The first European to settle here, around 1825, was Joseph Moreau, a Hudson's Bay Company employee. Not until 1845 was a village established, in conjunction with the expansion of the timber industry into the area. Now the village is the point where inbound ocean ships pick up river pilots to navigate the hazardous waters of the St. Lawrence.

Exactly who named the river (and village) and when is unknown, but it appeared on maps as early as 1611. In 1860 the area was developed by John Edmund Barry, who established a lumber business.

FORESTVILLE: Forestville is a born-again industrial center. Originally settled in 1844 as Sault au Cochon, a lumber camp with a sawmill, the town died during a decline in the lumber trade at the turn of the century. It was revived by a timber boom in 1937 and renamed Forestville in honor of Grant Forest, who had managed private lumber interests here before the decline. The dam and 1837 forest house are open to the public.

Route 385, paved as far as Labrieville, leads north to the Forestville and Labrieville park/reserves.

En Route from Forestville – On Route 138 eastbound about 2 miles (3 km) outside of Forestville is a turnoff toward Colombier. The town, which has an excellent beach at Anse à Norbert, is about a mile (1.6 km) from the highway. Return to Route 138 and continue through the tiny hamlet of Ilets Jérémie. Like many of these villages, this began as a Hudson's Bay trading post (established by Joël-Jérémie de la Montagne). Peter McLeod, founder of Chicoutimi, was stationed here during the late 1820s and Napoleon-Alexandre Comeau, a well-known North Shore personality and naturalist, was born here in 1848. East of the Bersimis River, Route 138 skirts the Betsiamites Indian Reservation. The Montagnais Indians who inhabit the reservation are self-governing, manage their own logging and sawmill operation, and, with the consent of the tribal chief, organize and guide hunting and fishing trips on reservation land. During the summer, the Indians also operate a handicrafts boutique and a gallery with a permanent collection of Amerindian work in Les Escoumins (29 Rue de la Réserve; phone: 418-233-3096). Less than 20 miles (32 km) from the reservation is the town of Chutes aux Outards and the Manicouagan Peninsula. The peninsula has several fine sandy beaches.

The city of Baie Comeau-Hauterive, including the ruins of its predecessor, the industrial village of St. Eugène de Manicouagan, 8 miles (13 km) east of Chute aux Outardes on Route 138, is another born-again community.

BAIE COMEAU: Enthusiasts of great technological achievements will enjoy Baie Comeau. Established by *Chicago Tribune* publisher Colonel Robert R. McCormick during the 1930s, the city (ten times the size of most coastal communities) began on this isolated site with the construction of a pulp and newsprint plant. The highway (Route 138) was built later as was the Hydro-Quebec Highway (Route 389), which leads to a series of giant hydroelectric dams. A Hydro-Quebec reception center at the intersection of Routes 138 and 389 arranges visits to the installations during July and August. This service road (Route 389) of 135 miles (216 km) is partially paved; the remainder is well-maintained gravel. There is a campground near the Manic 2 dam — about 15 miles (24 km) from Baie Comeau. Manic 5, the Daniel Johnson Dam, is considered one of the world's largest multiple-arch structures (4,310-foot crest length). The *Baie Comeau Museum* (43 Mance St.; phone: 418-296-8199) has regular art and cultural exhibitions during the summer. The museum is part of the town's *Centre-Socio-Culturel,* which also houses the *Baie Comeau Summer Theater;* the season runs from July 1 to September 5.

The Hydro-Quebec Highway (Route 389) also provides access to Baie Comeau. The town, honoring the naturalist and favorite son of the North Shore, Napoléon-Alexandre Comeau, is 123 miles (197 km) from Tadoussac. The harbor serves more than 700 ships per year, and a ferry links this industrial town with Matane on the south shore.

En Route from Baie Comeau – Even with 20th-century transportation and communications, the isolation of this land becomes readily apparent after you leave Baie Comeau. The tiny fishing village of Franquelin, nested amid slopes of the Laurentian Mountains on three sides and the St. Lawrence River on the fourth, is 20 miles (32 km) beyond Baie Comeau on Route 138. During the early 1900s, the village grew with the logging industry. Following the construction of the highway from Baie Comeau to Sept Iles, both the industry and the population moved eastward. About 600 inhabitants remain in this village. Continue on Route 138 through the village cemetery to Godbout.

Route 138 crosses the Godbout River and swings north, but an access road leads east into one of the most beautiful sites on the North Shore. Embracing the east bank of the Godbout River on one side and extending to the promontory of Pointe des Monts on the other, with an enticing bay on the St. Lawrence, the village of Godbout began as a trading post in the mid-1600s. The river and village honor Nicholas Godbout, a sailor and river pilot, who lived on Ile d'Orléans in the 1670s. Godbout has an Indian and Inuit museum containing a number of artifacts; open daily, June through September, from 9 AM to 10 PM (phone: 418-568-7724). There's also a nearby beach and picnic area.

A secondary roadway 18 miles (29 km) past Godbout leads to the tiny village of Pointe des Monts, 7 miles (11 km) off Route 138 on a point jutting into the Gulf of St. Lawrence. This spot, where the bank of the St. Lawrence abruptly widens to the gulf, was the first harbor in the gulf. The lighthouse, reputedly the oldest in Canada (1830), has been declared a historical landmark and is now an interpretive center offering excursions, open daily, 10 AM to 8 PM, from late June to late September. There also is a bar and a restaurant. Before the lighthouse's construction (and occasionally since), the rocky coves and inlets on the eastern face of the shore saw numerous shipwrecks, inbound vessels blown by ocean storms onto the unseen rocks. Picnic grounds also are on the site, and an outfitter's service can provide fishing gear.

Return to Route 138 and proceed north to the village of Baie Trinité, which includes the hamlets of Pointe à Paulin, Petit Mai, and Ilets Caribou. Cartier supposedly christened the river when he visited here on Trinity Sunday, 1536, but this may be inaccurate. Regardless, the names Trinité River and Baie Trinité appear on maps dated 1682. These hamlets, settled in the late 1830s, were active in the lumber trade during the late 1920s. This entire area was once known for caribou hunting, but the wildlife has been greatly depleted, and the small islands that once sheltered game are now barren sand dunes. In response to the crisis, the government has converted some 200 square miles of territory bordering on the Grande- and Petite-Trinité rivers into a salmon fishing reserve. Baie Trinité has one campground right on the bay.

Pointe aux Anglais, 20 miles (32 km) from Baie Trinité, was founded by a group of French settlers in 1873, who were joined by about 15 Acadian families from Anticosti Island 20 years later. The settlement followed the construction of a lighthouse (which remains) in 1870 on nearby Ile aux Oeufs. This point marks the spot where, on August 22, 1711, part of Admiral Walker's fleet was wrecked en route to laying siege to Quebec.

PORT CARTIER: Incorporated in 1958, Port Cartier is a lumber community with a good deepwater harbor. The lumber industry gave the area its start in 1915, when Colonel McCormick ventured to the outpost known as Portage des Mousses (and later Rivière aux Rochers), renamed it Shelter Bay, and established a sawmill. The city, 228 miles (365 km) from Tadoussac, borders on the Port Cartier-Sept Iles Reserve. This entire region is known for its rivers and lakes. Moose, bear, wild duck, and partridge are plentiful, and speckled trout is the most popular attraction for anglers. Access to the reserve is via a 17-mile (27-km) secondary road. During the summer, the beaches on the east bank of the St.-Margaret River are excellent swimming areas.

En Route from Port Cartier – It is only 22 miles (35 km) along Route 138 to Clarke City, a suburb of Sept Iles. Established as a pulp mill by the Clarke brothers — William, James, John, and George — in 1908, the next generation of Clarkes expanded into gulf and North Shore shipping. The city of Sept Iles is 18 miles (29 km) farther.

SEPT ILES: In the northwest corner of the Gulf of St. Lawrence, the Baie des Sept Iles provided a perfect location for Basque fishing vessels and French explorers seeking refuge from the rough waters of the Atlantic and the Gulf of St. Lawrence. Pointe Noire, on the western side of the harbor, curves to form a breakwater on the west and south sides of the bay, while a protruding point forms the east side of the harbor mouth. The seven small islands that named the bay (and city) protect this passage. A trading post and mission were established here during the 1650s, but the first settlers were the Smith, Brochu, and Levesque families shortly after 1860.

Camping is allowed at rustic sites on one of the islands at the mouth of the bay (contact *Côte Nord;* phone: 418-583-2710), as is coastal (saltwater) fishing for cod, mackerel, and halibut. Inland, speckled trout and ouananiche (landlocked salmon) are the angler's game; and moose, bear, wolf, hare, partridge, wild duck, and goose attract hunters. Two airports and a seaplane base make this a good takeoff point for expeditions farther into the wilds. The original trading post, *Le Musée Vieux Poste,* reconstructed on a bank of the Vieux Fort River (with a restaurant added), is part of the *Musée Régional de la Côte-Nord.* Open daily, summer only, from 9 AM to 5 PM (phone: 418-968-2070).

En Route from Sept Iles – From Sept Iles to Havre St.-Pierre is about 140 miles (224 km) via Route 138, which is now paved for its entire length. Air or sea transport is more suitable than the coast road for any travel farther into this region.

Beyond Sept Iles lies the coastal area known as the Mingan Coast and the coastal Iles de Mingan. The San Sebastian Basque whalers who visited these islands during the 16th century named one long island Min Gain ("tongue of land"). Five dry-stone ovens and assorted utensils for the preparation of whale oil have been found on two of these islands. The coast was the site of bloody border wars between the Inuit people from the north and the Iroquois, and later Montagnais, Indians who occupied the area to the south. The region was bought by Parks-Canada and is now a federal national preserve. A welcome center at Havre St. Pierre has audiovisual presentations on the Mingans and arranges guided tours (phone: 418-538-2512).

BEST EN ROUTE

Even though Quebec is visited by more people than any other Canadian province, accommodations outside the larger towns are sometimes limited. Although there are enough places that provide all the amenities, deluxe accommodations are few and far between. Most of the hotels listed here fall into the moderate price range — $40 to $50 per night, double occupancy, with no meals. Those that cost more than $50 are listed as expensive, and those under $40 are considered inexpensive. Off-season rates are lower, and sometimes they're cut in half. All prices are quoted in US dollars.

ESCOUMINS

Complexe Hôtelier Pelchat – A comfortable 25-unit motel with a restaurant. Route 138 (phone: 418-233-2401). Moderate.

Gagnon – Family-run with 14 rooms, a comfortable atmosphere, and home cooking. 87 Marcellin St. (phone: 418-233-2010). Inexpensive.

FORESTVILLE

Danube Bleu – A modern hotel-motel with excellent services and a restaurant. Route 138 (phone: 418-587-2278). Expensive to moderate.

L'An 2000 – The basic 20-unit motel has air conditioning and a TV set in every room. No dining room, but a restaurant is across the street. 164 Principale St. (phone: 418-587-4431). Inexpensive.

BAIE COMEAU

Le Manoir – A plush stone manor house in a beautiful garden setting, overlooking the St. Lawrence. It offers one of the best tables on the North Shore, with French specialties and seafood. 8 Cabot St. (phone: 418-296-3391 or 800-361-6162). Expensive to moderate.

Caravelle – On a hill overlooking town, this modern hotel-motel has an indoor swimming pool and sauna, plus a restaurant and a bar with dancing. 202 La Salle Blvd. (phone: 418-296-4986). Moderate.

PORT CARTIER

Château – A nice hotel-motel that includes a restaurant and a sauna. 30 Elie Rochefort St. (phone: 418-766-3444). Moderate.

SEPT ILES

Auberge des Gouverneurs – This is a luxurious 122-room inn with all services, a good restaurant, and a pool. 666 Laure Blvd. (phone: 418-962-7071 or 800-463-2820). Expensive.

Sept Iles – A large establishment with a satisfactory restaurant. 451 Arnaud St. (phone: 418-962-2581 or 800-463-1753). Moderate.

The Laurentians

The Laurentian Mountains, with extensive parks and wildlife reserves, play a crucial role in maintaining the high quality of Canadian life. They are at once a magnificent playground, a bulwark against misuse of the land, and a vital part of the heritage of Canada.

The Laurentians are the wilderness backyard of the populated section of the St. Lawrence shoreline. Cutting a broad swath across southwestern Quebec, this group of modest but ancient mountains provides huge areas of lakes and rivers for outdoor activities; the slopes closer to Quebec and Montreal have become world-famous ski resorts. There are 26 alpine ski areas within a 40-mile radius capable of handling up to 100,000 skiers per hour. The mountains comprise a natural reserve, their rugged slopes having deterred inquisitive explorers and thwarted industrial developers. As the coastal settlements became cities and wildlife began to take refuge deeper and deeper in the mountains, great sections of the Laurentians were made game reserves. Many of the area's parks are based on the historical boundaries of the Crown lands established as early as the 1600s; others have been created in response to recent trends in land use.

Carefully controlled hunting is permitted in some reserves and in certain areas is often restricted either to native Indian tribes or to Quebec residents. Although large sections of the Laurentian Mountains have been set aside as parks and reserves, there also are commercial skiing centers and private (owned or leased) hunting and fishing grounds. All wildlife is carefully monitored, and hunting and fishing guidelines are established to ensure that no species is threatened. With equal care, development in and around the parks and wooded areas is controlled to preserve this pristine environment where harried victims of modern life can retreat to mend soul and body.

The Laurentians are one of the oldest mountain ranges in the world, skirting the southern boundary of the part of the Canadian Shield that lies between the Ottawa and Saguenay rivers in Quebec. The Shield, formed by the first permanent rise of the North American landmass during the Precambrian era, outlines the Hudson Bay watershed. The glaciers that followed it carved out thousands of lakes and rivers and helped shape Hudson Bay itself. Continuous upheaval and erosion gradually defined the fringe of this U-shaped plateau into the low-level mountains of today. Few Laurentian peaks exceed 2,500 feet; the famous ski resort of Mont Tremblant is a relative giant at 3,000 feet. The mountains rise within sight of the St. Lawrence River in many places, and nowhere are the Laurentians more than 100 miles from the river, making this immense recreation area easily accessible from any of the metropolitan sections along the shoreline.

If you're planning to do any hunting other than in parks, the help of an outfitter is recommended. Because of the unique service and the close interaction between hunter (or angler) and outfitter, much of your enjoyment of the trip depends upon personalities; it's wise to talk to one or two outfitters before making arrangements. The *Quebec Outfitters Association Directory* (phone: 514-687-0041) details names and numbers according to region, so make a few calls.

CENTRAL QUEBEC: THE ST. MAURICE VALLEY

One of Quebec's major industrial cities, Trois Rivières, halfway between Montreal and Quebec, straddles the mouth of the St. Maurice River. The city's French name is based upon the three channels formed by the islands in the river delta where it meets the St. Lawrence. The Indians had called the river Métabéroutine, "sheet of water exposed to all winds." It was renamed for Maurice Poulin, who was granted control of the valley in 1668. The rich timberlands, providing the logs, and the river, providing transportation and power, were a vital combination in the creation of this busy city. It is fitting that this hectic industrial and shipping center with a past as old as Canada itself — Cartier toured the St. Maurice River Valley in 1535 and Champlain erected a trading post here in 1615 — should guard the entrance to one of the most beautiful sections of Quebec.

TROIS RIVIÈRES: This prosperous industrial city warrants at least an afternoon's stop to tour its much-improved historic district, which is toward the river. The tourist information center is housed in the beautifully restored Manoir Boucher de Niverville (168 Bonaventure St.; phone: 819-375-9628), a 1730 house that was once home to the first *seigneurs* of the town. It also features two rooms of antique French Canadian pine furniture and artifacts. Guided tours of the city begin here, June to *Labor Day*. Maurice Duplessis, controversial premier of Quebec from 1936 to 1939 and again from 1944 to 1959, is Trois Rivière's most famous native son, and he is honored with a statue in the square adjacent to the Manoir Boucher de Niverville. Another attraction is the archaeology museum at the University of Quebec (5030 Forges Blvd.; phone: 819-376-5032). From the end of June to mid-July the city stages a cultural festival — *Festival des Trois Rivières* — with concerts, shows, historical tableaux, and art exhibitions. These events take place at Champlain Park, Place Niverville, and Place d'Armes; for information, call 819-372-4614.

En Route from Trois Rivières – Take Route 55 north about 25 miles (40 km) to Grand Mère, where the road becomes Route 155, or bypass Trois Rivières via Route 153 if you're approaching along the coast from Montreal or via Route 159 if you're coming from Quebec.

The growth and development of the St. Lawrence shoreline contrasts sharply with the rural atmosphere of this valley. Although many of the towns are industrial centers drawing upon neighboring resources, they maintain a deep and protective respect for their roots. They are dedicated to preserving the forests and rivers that surround them as part of a life of outdoor activity and a relaxed pace.

Most of the route runs past small farms or through forests, with the river rarely out of sight. It is not unusual to see logs, a staple of local industry, floating down toward the sawmills. You may see a logjam — thousands upon thousands of uniformly cut logs piled every which way until the river is covered with a floor of pine, not a glint of blue water to be seen. When an explosion clears the blockage, thousands of logs break loose and are swept downriver by the current. It's a sight you'll never forget.

The southeast entrance to La Mauricie National Park is a secondary road from St.-Jean des Piles, about 8 miles (13 km) from Grand Mère.

LA MAURICIE NATIONAL PARK: Encompassing some 200 square miles of glacier-torn mountains, including 60 lakes and an untold number of rivers, the park is currently being enlarged to accommodate increasing numbers of visitors. There are now 208 campsites near the park entrance at Lac la Pêche as well as 218 at Lac Wapizagonke and 91 at Mistagance; perhaps a dozen wilderness sites, accessible only by boat, surround the lake. Beyond this small area, a canoe is the only feasible means of transportation to the many wilderness campsites in the backcountry. It is necessary to portage both canoe and gear about 1¼ miles to reach the next lake, and frequent portages are required to explore the area. Canoe rentals are available in the park along with detailed maps indicating 3-, 4-, and 5-day canoe-camping trips through the area. A license is necessary if you plan to catch trout dinners while you camp — a 4-day food supply can be heavy. Hunting is not permitted. Even if you don't spend your vacation tramping through the woods, take a day trip (by canoe) on Lac la Pêche. At the north end of the lake is half a mountain, sheared away by a passing glacier, with its solid rock interior exposed. There are several sandy shores along the lake where you can beach your canoe and walk in distant forests. But paddle close to the exposed mountainside, look straight up its rocky wall, and try to imagine the force that cut through it. Then back away and try to take a picture of this cliff, from water level to forested peak and end to end; capturing a bear with your hands would be easier. Lac Wapizagonke lies between two such rocky walls 8 miles long. Exploration has revealed Indian pictographs on these cliffs, but their origins are unknown. The park is open year-round, and there is an admission charge of US$3.40 (CN$4) per car, per day (phone: 819-536-2638).

If this area is too tame or confining for your taste, bear in mind that it borders on the wilder reserves of St. Maurice (to the north) and Mastigouche (to the west).

ST. MAURICE RESERVE: If it's really untamed woodland you're looking for, this is a fine place to start. For 150 years, hunters and fishermen from Quebec, Ontario, and the US have come here to engage in their favorite outdoor pursuits. The reserve covers 617 square miles of wild mountains, rivers, and woods. There is no access road; you must take a ferry across the St. Maurice River at Matawin — about 42 miles (67 km) from Grand Mère — then proceed by jeep and boat to your campground. Some cottages (hunting lodges) are available, but tents may be necessary in some areas. A guide is recommended but not required. Small-game hunting is permitted (moose are controlled for residents), although it's really not feasible to hunt in this area without a guide, and the abundance of speckled trout almost takes the challenge out of fishing. Canoeing is encouraged, but only a few rentals are available in the park. The area has been leased to local hunting and fishing clubs, which have kept development (like roads) to a minimum. Line up an outfitter and let him direct you to non-park lands where moose and bear can be hunted.

LA TUQUE: Some 75 miles (120 km) from Grand Mère along Route 155, this town provides its own *Domaine Touristique de La Tuque* (public tours of La Tuque; phone: 819-523-4424 or 819-523-5533), with seven camps where hunting and fishing are *the* activity (depending on the season). The park is relatively small — 40 square miles — but with 18 outfitters controlling 138 additional camps and lodges, there are places for almost everyone. Area game includes moose, deer, and bear, plus rabbit and various fowl. From here, Lac St. Jean is 82 miles (131 km) north, past the huge St. Maurice Reserve; the Chibougamau Reserve's access roads are only a short distance away.

NORTH OF QUEBEC CITY: RÉSERVE FAUNIQUE DES LAURENTIDES

En Route from Quebec City – Take Route 175 north from downtown for the 30-mile (48-km) drive to the Laurentides' (Laurentians') southern entrance. The 5,637 square miles of Laurentides Réserve began as a Montagnais hunting ground until infringement by Huron tribes turned the peaceful mountains into a battleground. When the fighting died down in 1895, the Quebec government opted to use the land as a park to preserve the natural forests and wildlife of this area as much as possible, but the caribou that once dominated the region have been severely depleted. The park is currently used to reacclimate animals from other areas and to encourage breeding to rebuild the herds. Only moose hunting is permitted (under controlled guidelines), but fishing is easily arranged. Several cottages are available summer and winter. There are two camping areas totaling 258 sites at Belle Rivière and Lac Loutre, plus a wilderness camping-canoeing area in the Jacques Cartier Valley. Guides are mandatory in many areas.

The reserve covers a wide variety of terrain, with the eastern peaks averaging between 3,120 and 4,025 feet. The western area is considerably less mountainous. All sectors are reasonably accessible, thanks to the network of roads serving the park. Route 175 travels a north-south path through the park. The southern entrance is only 30 miles (48 km) north of Quebec, the northern entrance only 13 miles (21 km) south of Chicoutimi. Route 169 from Alma, east of Lac St. Jean, leads to the park entrance only 24 miles (38 km) south and intersects Route 175 in the middle of the park.

NORTH OF MONTREAL: SKI COUNTRY

En Route from Montreal – Two routes lead north toward the entrance to Mont Tremblant Park. One leads into the heart of the Laurentian ski country, the other into more of a hunting area, although the skiing is equally good there.

Take either Route 117 or the high-speed Route 15 north from Montreal into the Laurentian foothills. The small city of Rosemere is only 15 miles (24 km) from the metropolitan area, yet the timeless peace of the mountains is apparent in the 2,800-acre forest in the heart of the town. Several of the houses in the area were built in the 17th and 18th centuries. The city of St. Jérôme, the gateway to the Laurentians, is only 15 miles (24 km) away. Farther north and east, along Route 125, is Canadiana Village (phone: 514-834-4135), a reconstructed 19th-century farm community in the Lanaudière region, a scenic area about 45 minutes northeast from Montreal that also is the site of the *Wilfrid Laurier National Park and House,* the former home of Canada's seventh prime minister and now a museum (phone: 514-439-3702). In the town of Joliette, the heart of the region, the annual Lanaudière summer festival fills local parks, theaters, and churches with the strains of classical music and jazz from June until late August. The event has attracted such performers as Oscar Peterson and Marilyn Horne. Most venues charge admission (phone: 514-759-7636). *Tourisme Lanaudière* (phone: 514-834-2535 or 800-363-2788) can provide more details on the area's attractions and the summer-long music festival. For information on the Laurentians, stop at the tourist center at exit 39 off Route 15 or near the junction of Route 117 and 158 (phone: 514-436-8532).

ST.-JÉRÔME: St.-Jérôme was established in 1830, its development greatly aided by Curé Labelle, who attracted settlers to this community and others during the latter half of the 1800s. He also is credited with bringing the rail line to St.-Jérôme and as far north as Mont Laurier. His fervent efforts to open the wild lands of Canada's north and west and his explorations to establish new communities made him a well-loved folk hero throughout the country. Many ski areas and summer resorts are hidden in the mountains just north of here.

St.-Jérôme's de la Durantaye Park is the site of outdoor concerts from late June to mid-August. The art gallery in the Vieux Palais, or Old Courthouse (185 Palais St.; phone: 514-432-7171), is open year-round.

PREVOST: The Shawbridge resort area begins only 37 miles (59 km) northwest of Montreal. It was here, in 1928, that Jack Rabbit Johanssen, considered the father of Laurentian skiing, laid out the slalom run that started it all. The famed Maple Leaf Trail, covering 60 miles (96 km) of cross-country trails from Shawbridge to Mont Tremblant, was established by Johanssen during the early 1930s.

Together with Piedmont, just 5 miles (8 km) away, and nearby Ste. Adèle, this area comprises a convenient change of pace. There are 21 ski runs at Morin Heights (Bellevue, Chemin du Lac Echo) and 20 at Mont Gabriel (Mont Gabriel, *Auberge Mont Gabriel;* phone: 514-229-3547), plus 2 resorts in the area of Ste. Adèle, with a total of 27 slopes. *Le Chantecler* (phone: 514-229-3555 or 800-363-2420) is the largest (see *Best en Route*), and *Cotes* (phone: 514-229-2921) follows. Around Piedmont are Alpine-style slopes at Monts Avila (Avila) and Olympia (Mont Olympia), and more than 2 dozen cross-country trails. At St. Sauveur, 4 ski resorts provide some 42 slopes, with maximum vertical drops averaging 530 feet. The largest is Mont St.-Sauveur (Rue St. Denis; phone: 514-227-4671 or 514-971-0101), with 26 slopes, followed by Mont Christie (Christieville, St.-Sauveur; phone: 514-226-2412) with 12 and Mont Habitant (12 Blvd. des Skieurs; phone: 514-227-2637) with 8. St.-Sauveur also is a prime area for nighttime activites, thanks to its many fine restaurants and discos.

Although the village of Piedmont has existed since 1853, it is gradually becoming associated with a broad resort area called St. Sauveur-des-Monts, which also includes Mont Gabriel and several other communities. During the summer months, golf courses bloom near many of these resorts (18 holes at Piedmont, Ste.-Adèle, and Mont Gabriel respectively; 9 holes at Prévost), and there are dozens of private campgrounds. In Bellefeuille, just south of Prévost, are the *Lac Claude* (phone: 514-438-7532) and *Lac Lafontaine* (phone: 819-431-7373) campgrounds, with 75 and 250 sites respectively. The 150-site *Au Pin d'Erable* grounds (phone: 514-436-8319) and the 47-site *De l'Iris* grounds (phone: 514-563-2790) are located in St.-Hippolyte. This area's popularity has attracted (and has been helped by) several excellent dining establishments. The *Alpine Inn* hotel (phone: 514-229-3516 or 800-363-3623) in Ste. Marguerite Station and the *Estérel* (phone: 514-228-2571) rate among the best (see *Best en Route*).

Mont St.-Sauveur has a water-slide park, the Parc Aquatique (phone: 514-871-0101 or 800-363-2426), which includes a pool with 4-foot waves. The village's main street, dominated by the white church steeple, is lined with boutiques, crafts shops, and good restaurants — all favorites with Montrealers out for a weekend drive. On summer Saturday evenings, music lovers flock to the classical concerts held at the church (call 514-227-6664 for information).

STE. AGATHE DES MONTS: The Val Morin and Val David sport centers are less than 20 miles (32 km) away, and the city of Ste.-Agathe des Monts, on Lac des Sables, is the hub of this resort area (60 miles/97 km from Montreal), which dates back to the 1850s. There are 11 slopes at Alta (2114 Route 117), and another 12 at Vallée Bleue, all in Val David; Belle Neige (Route 117) also has 14 slopes, and Mont Sauvage (2nd Ave.) has 9, bringing the village of Val Morin's total to 23. Nearby, in St.-Adolphe d'Howard, L'Avalanche (not exactly a choice name) has 7 slopes. As popular for its tables as its slopes is Val David, which takes the culinary awards for this area. Leading the way is the restaurant of *La Sapinière* hotel (phone: 819-322-2020; see *Special Havens* in DIVERSIONS and *Best en Route*). St.-Adolphe d'Howard's *Auberge La Soupière* (1944 Chemin du Village; phone: 819-327-2525) and *La Légende* (1510 Rue de l'Avalanche; phone: 819-327-2055) also are highly regarded dining establishments.

For summer activities, there are campgrounds at Val David (*La Belle Etoile,* 100 sites, phone: 819-322-3207; *Laurentian,* 42 sites, phone: 819-322-2281; and *Le Montagnais,* 35 sites, 819-322-2921), as well as a massive municipal campground (556 sites) in Ste.-Agathe des Monts (phone: 819-326-5577). *Alouette Boat Tours* of Lac-des-Sables (phone: 819-326-3656) leave from the dock in the center of town daily during the summer.

En Route from Ste.-Agathe des Monts – The village of St. Faustin, 14 miles (22 km) north on Route 117, marks the location of one access road to the giant Mont Tremblant Park. This small resort area is popular with hunters; Mont Blanc, with 24 ski slopes, is equally attractive to skiers (in Mont Blanc). St.-Jovite, a major resort area, is 6 miles (10 km) farther on Route 117.

ST.-JOVITE: Three ski centers provide a total of over 50 slopes in the St.-Jovite/Mont Tremblant area: *Station Mont Tremblant Lodge* (phone: 819-425-8711 or, from anywhere in the US except Massachusetts, 800-567-6761) is the biggest, with 34 slopes and a maximum vertical drop of over 2,100 feet, and Gray Rocks (phone: 819-425-2771 or 800-567-6767) follows, with 18 slopes. The smallest is Mont Blanc (phone: 819-688-2444). For more complete information on skiing in this region, see *Downhill* and *Cross-Country Skiing,* DIVERSIONS.

Camping in the area is plentiful, with a 242-site provincial campground at Mont Tremblant, in the Lac Monroe district, and backed up with 158 sites in the private *Vert et Blanc* area (phone: 819-688-2828), and 93 sites in the *Domaine Desjardins* (phone: 819-688-2179) in St.-Faustin. For serious diners, there are excellent choices: the *Gray Rocks Inn* (Lac Ouimet; phone: 819-425-2771) and the *Tremblant Club* (Lac Tremblant; phone: 819-425-2731), both in Mont Tremblant (see *Best en Route*). From St.-Jovite, Route 117 runs northwest to La Vérendrye Reserve, 94 miles (150 km) away.

An alternate approach to Mont Tremblant Park is via Route 125, through the villages of Chertsey and St.-Donat, a total of 83 miles (133 km). This route also provides access to the Joliette Park, and although there are five ski centers — the two major hills of Mont La Reserve with 13 slopes and Mont Garceau with 12 — in St.-Donat, the area is definitely better outfitted for hunting and fishing. *La Corniche* (Route 329 in St.-Donat; phone: 819-424-7966), takes top table honors in the area, but there's a special satisfaction to a meal prepared over an open fire in the woods, especially if you caught (or shot) dinner yourself. Make arrangements with one of the many outfitters in the area to start hunting or fishing expeditions from here.

MONT TREMBLANT PARK: Created in 1984 as a recreation center for residents of Quebec Province, this park is used almost all year. Skiing, snowmobiling, and snowshoeing are the principal winter activities, with camping, canoeing, and moose hunting in season. (The park harbors some 30 animal species. Bear, deer, marten, mink, and porcupine are easily visible if you travel some of the more remote trails.) Only 22 cottages are available for rent, but provincial campgrounds at Lac Monroe, Lac Chat, and Lac Lajoie provide plenty of space for camping.

JOLIETTE: This small reserve is primarily devoted to fishing and small-game hunting, and the bear, deer, and moose you'll see wandering about appear to *know* this.

There are cottages available around most lakes to make your hunting or fishing comfortable, but there are no canoe rentals in the park.

NORTH OF HULL: THE GATINEAU VALLEY AND LA VÉRENDRYE

Fur trader Nicholas Gatineau from Trois Rivières explored this valley in 1650. Lumberjacks and hunters followed his lead, opening a broad pathway to the north for settlers. The city of Hull, its sawmills fed with timber floated down the Gatineau River, grew quickly in what had been Indian hunting grounds.

A large group of Americans, including Philemon Wright from Massachusetts, settled the town in 1800. Wright is credited with establishing the first commercial enterprise in town, and another American, Ezra Eddy, started the match factory that made Hull known throughout the world in the 19th century.

Route 105 leads from Hull through the valley to La Vérendrye Reserve, 110 miles (176 km) north.

En Route from Hull – The Gatineau Park, which preserves part of the hunting grounds of the Iroquois and Algonquin Indians, is just outside Hull. There are four principal lakes and ten times that number of smaller ones. Although hunting is prohibited, fishing is allowed in all lakes and rivers, and canoe rentals are available. Protected wildlife — easily spotted while walking the trails — include deer, mink, marten, porcupine, beaver, and an occasional bear. Lac Philippe has an attractive campground with 306 sites (phone: 819-456-3016) as well as a large public beach, picnic tables, and boat rentals.

Also in the park is Moorside, the 575-acre summer estate of former Canadian Prime Minister William Lyon Mackenzie King, which he willed to the public. On the grounds is an interesting and impressive collection of ruins brought here by King, such as parts of the Canadian and British houses of parliament. Open May through mid-October. In the park, just off the Gatineau Pkwy.

Gracefield, Bouchette, and Messine, grouped together about 60 miles (96 km) from Hull, constitute a staging area for hunting and fishing trips. Approximately 30 outfitters based around these towns can point out the best spots for hunting moose, bear, deer, rabbit, partridge, fox, and duck. Fishing will bring in rainbow, speckled, brown, and lake trout, pike, and walleye. A secondary roadway from Gracefield leads to the Pontiac Reserve.

MANIWAKI: Set up as a Hudson's Bay Company trading post, this town is now a major hunting and fishing center. There are many outfitters in the surrounding area, controlling 642 campsites, chalets, and lodges, ranging from primitive to luxurious. A seaplane base is a jumping-off point for expeditions far north. The rustic feel of this community belies its location only 85 miles (136 km) from Hull and the 20th century.

En Route from Maniwaki – Continue on Route 105 to its end at Grand Remous, 20 miles (32 km) north, where Route 117 from Mont Laurier intersects and leads west into the La Vérendrye Reserve. There are about 100 hunting and fishing camps in the immediate area, served by 13 outfitters. Consult the *Quebec Outfitters Directory* or call 819-771-4840.

LA VÉRENDRYE: Established in 1939 to protect wildlife from the onslaught of hunters invading this area, the park preserves the natural habitat of moose, bear, wolf, mink, beaver, marten, rabbit, loon, and many other species. Route 117 travels through the heart of the 5,174-square-mile expanse. Hunting is limited to moose (for residents only), but fishing is encouraged because even these extensive waterways can support only so many pike, walleye, smallmouth bass, lake, and speckled trout. Contact *Le Domaine* (Reserve La Vérendrye; phone: 819-435-2216 or 438-2017) for details and access rights. Limited numbers of canoe rentals and cottages are available, and there is one inn within the park: *Auberge de Domaine* (phone: 819-435-2541). The reserve is located in the western extremity of the Laurentian Mountain Range.

BEST EN ROUTE

The Laurentians have some of the most pleasant and some of the most rustic accommodations in Canada. In the ski resort areas north of Montreal — around Val David, for instance — are several of the best hostelries in the country; in the backcountry, facilities are little more than basic, and prices are quite reasonable.

The selection below singles out the best in any given area, though not necessarily the least expensive. If your budget is tight, avail yourself of one of the many inexpensive roadside motels, but be prepared for less than perfection. For the hotels that follow, inexpensive refers to places in which a double-occupancy room costs less than $35; moderate runs from $35 to $55 for two; and expensive, anything over $55 per day. In the prime ski resort areas, seasonal prices can be as high as $170 per day for two but may not include extras, like skis and lifts. Check to see what is included before making reservations. Note that Mont Tremblant has a central reservation service (phone: 819-425-8681 or 800-567-6760) for booking rental accommodations at any of its chalets or condomininiums, or lodgings at a select number of other area hotels. All prices are quoted in US dollars.

SHAWINIGAN

Auberge L'Escapade – An excellent place to stay — good facilities, comfortable, and conveniently located. There is a dining room. 3383 Rue Garnier (phone: 819-539-6911). Moderate.

LA TUQUE

Le Gîte – A good place to recover from the woods. Well-appointed rooms and good motel services, though the dining room tends to detract a little. 1100 Blvd. Ducharme (phone: 819-523-9501 or 800-361-6162). Moderate.

STE.-ADÈLE

Alpine Inn – A fairly large resort facility with a wide variety of extras — including tennis, swimming, and skating. Chalets also are available. 1455 Chemin Ste.-Marguerite (phone: 514-229-3516 or 800-363-2577). Expensive.

Altitude – This attractive 55-unit complex includes 22 rooms with fireplaces. A congenial ski resort, it also features indoor and outdoor pools and a hospitable dining room. Ste.-Adèle Blvd. (phone: 514-229-6616 or 800-363-3683). Expensive.

Le Chantecler – This resort has 287 well-appointed rooms, as well as squash and racquetball courts, saunas, and a whirlpool bath. It provides a full schedule of summer and winter sports. Lac Rond, Chemin du Chantecler (phone: 819-229-3555). Expensive.

VAL DAVID

La Sapinière – An hour's drive from Montreal, this is one of the exceptional inns of eastern Canada and the first Canadian member of the association of international country hotels, the Relais & Châteaux group. Its primary distinction is its kitchen, run by Chef Marcel Kretz, who with pastry chef Jean-Pierre Monjon rules the roost. Plan to reserve a few weeks in advance for weekend dining. For more details, see *Special Havens* in DIVERSIONS. Val David, 1344 Chemin de la Sapinière (phone: 819-322-2020 or 866-8262, in Montreal). Expensive.

VILLE D'ESTEREL

L'Esterel – Near Ste.-Marguerite Station, this place offers very good services, 135 rooms, an indoor sports complex, and convention facilities. Pool, sauna, golf, tennis, fishing, and boating are available. Fridolin Simard Blvd. (phone: 514-228-2571 or 800-363-3623, in Montreal). Expensive.

MONT TREMBLANT

Le Tremblant Club – This 32-room inn faces Mont Tremblant, the highest peak in the Laurentians, and has "one step from the door" access to some of the best ski slopes in eastern Canada. The inn, which also has condominium units, sits on Lac Tremblant and is a year-round center of activities — cross-country and downhill skiing in winter; swimming, sailing, fishing, golf, tennis, and riding in summer. It participates in a dining exchange program with the other excellent inns in the area should you tire of its award-winning kitchen, an unlikely event. Mont Tremblant (phone: 819-425-2731 or 800-567-8341). Expensive.

Auberge Villa Bellevue – The Dubois family has owned this 120-room lodge for three generations. Luc Dubois, head coach of the Canadian ski team from 1973 to 1976, is now director of the hotel ski school, while the rest of the family concentrates on keeping the accommodations cozy and comfortable and maintaining the restaurant's very high standards. On Lac Ouimet (phone: 819-425-2734 or 800-567-6763). Expensive.

Station Mont Tremblant – Skiing is serious business here, with bars, boutiques, and excellent food to enliven après-ski. On Lac Tremblant, the lodge is open summer and winter; closed about a month between seasons. Mont Tremblant (phone: 819-425-8711 or 800-567-6761). Expensive.

ST. JOVITE

Auberge Gray Rocks – Accommodations include rooms in the main inn or in intimate, romantic cottages. The resort has 18 ski runs and a well-known ski school. Also on a lake — Lac Ouimet — with canoeing and swimming and sailing and other summer delights. There is a complete fitness center in the main lodge featuring a heated indoor pool, gym, and jogging facilities. (phone: 819-425-2771 800-567-6767). Expensive.

Le St.-Jovite – An excellent service staff, a good dining room, and additional units have transformed the basic facilities here into a pleasurable place to stay. 1011 Rue Ouimet (phone: 819-425-2751). Moderate to inexpensive.

GATINEAU-LA VÉRENDRYE

Auberge Le Domaine – Being right in this vast park gives this inn a special air; and a good level of services takes it out of the realm of "camping on cots" into one of a true hostelry. Route 117 (phone: 819-435-2541). Expensive to moderate.

The Gaspé Peninsula

The southern shore of the St. Lawrence River ends at a peninsula of land that looks like a small child's fist thrown out against the Gulf of St. Lawrence. This is the Gaspé Peninsula. To the west is the ever-widening St. Lawrence River as it enters the gulf; to the north and east, the gulf itself and Anticosti Island; to the southeast, the Baie des Chaleurs (Bay of Warmth), which separates Gaspé from New Brunswick. The peninsula extends about 175 miles along the river, from the valley of the Matapédia River to its cape-edged shore on the gulf. The entire southern shoreline of the St. Lawrence is shaped something like a large, curved letter "P," and the Gaspé Peninsula forms the large loop at the letter's top.

The peninsula is considered one of the oldest landmasses on the planet, with life forms that have long since disappeared from other areas. The Chic-Chocs Mountains, called Sigsoon, or "rocky mountains," by the Micmac Indians, create a high-altitude sanctuary for the centuries-old alpine fir and the rangifer, or wood caribou, which is virtually extinct elsewhere. The heavily wooded valleys and highland regions rate among the world's best for moose, deer, and upland game-bird hunting, and the Chic-Chocs are the source of some of the finest Atlantic salmon rivers.

When Cartier first sailed through the Strait of Belle Isle and entered the Gulf of St. Lawrence, the lands of Labrador and Newfoundland were thought to be cold, barren, and forbidding — fit for fisheries and little else. After cruising the western shore of Newfoundland and discovering the Iles de la Madeleine, he entered the Baie des Chaleurs. The more tolerable climate and fertile lands prompted him to explore the peninsula, called Gespeg by the resident Micmac Indians. Before returning to France, he sailed in the summer of 1534 from the Baie des Chaleurs around the rugged shoreline of the Gespeg ("land's end" or "extremity") and across the mouth of the St. Lawrence River to Ile d'Anticosti. During his next voyage he explored the river, hoping it would provide the route to the spice lands of the East — the Northwest Passage. His reports of the beautiful and fertile lands of the *gaspé* (the European influence rapidly corrupted the language of the Indians) and visions of the wealth of resources yet undiscovered attracted settlers to New France.

The massive scale of this primitive area is illustrated by the unique Percé Rock; 1,420 feet long (plus a little extra for the piece that stands apart) and 288 feet tall, its weight is estimated at 400 million tons. It stands silent and alone just off the Gaspé coast. During his voyage, Cartier anchored his three ships in its protective shadow.

Given the accessibility of the Gaspé, it is surprising that the region remained so completely undeveloped. When Cartier arrived, the Micmac and Malecite tribes occupied the peninsula, but the Indians of the East Coast were restless peoples and rarely colonized areas they roamed. The land was crossed many times by the Abnaki, Montagnais, and Huron and war parties of the Iroquois. All these tribes contributed words, place names, and bits of history to its culture. Long before Cartier, the Basques had left their mark on the coast of this "tongue of land" and the seafaring Vikings had preceded them. But these groups were not colonists, and none built dwellings or bound themselves to any one place. They were explorers, hunters, sailors, travelers.

The coastal fishing settlements established by the French and other Europeans began as isolated, independent villages relatively oblivious to one another. In some sense this isolation is an abiding characteristic of Gaspé life. Few of the original inland villages have grown much, since most settlers arriving in successive waves followed the St. Lawrence farther inland, skipping the rugged peninsula in search of unexplored lands to the west. The extensive mountains of the peninsula — part of the Appalachian chain — may have seemed too difficult for settlers. In any case, growth in this part of the province always has been slow. The principal highway, Route 132, was completed in 1928 and runs through the Matapédia River Valley, following the rocky coastline and the shoreline of the St. Lawrence; commercial growth largely has been limited to tourist services. Because of competition from already developed areas of the province, industry has overlooked Gaspé. Visiting the Gaspé is like stepping backward in time. Most of the villagers continue to depend upon the sea for their livelihood, in many places still using the same methods and equipment as their grandparents. Sails and nets are still mended by hand, and salted fish, like cod and herring, are dried in open racks.

There is more to the Gaspé than the small fishing villages with their century-old dwellings, the handmade sails mounted on wooden fishing boats, and the stories of shipwrecks and ghosts. There is the unspoiled beauty of the forests; glimpses of moose, bear, and caribou in the underbrush; trout leaping from mountain streams; and the mountains themselves, which color the air with their ancient aura — the feeling of indomitable, massive power defying age. All this makes a most attractive vacation for hunters, anglers, naturalists, artists, and latter-day explorers.

The route originates across the river from Quebec City, and jumps quickly to Rivière du Loup, a distance of 123 miles (197 km) along the south bank of the St. Lawrence on Route 132. Route 20, the Trans-Canada Highway, can cut down on your travel time between the two cities, or take one of the many ferries from the north shore (see the *Beaupré/Charlevoix* route and *The North Shore* route). From Rivière du Loup the route follows the St. Lawrence on Route 132 and circles the peninsula. Since a large number of visitors drive this route (circling clockwise), we suggest you circle counterclockwise to avoid congestion. Rather than continue on Route 132 all the way up the south shore, turn right at Ste. Flavie and explore the Matapédia Valley to the Baie des Chaleurs, via Route 132, then follow the road as it traces the route of Cartier's exploration of the region — from south to north along the coast and up the St. Lawrence River. The journey covers some 220 miles (352 km), beginning at Quebec City and ending at the Ste.-Flavie–Mont Joli area. Rather than return to Quebec on a familiar route, combine this with the Beaupré/Charlevoix and North Shore routes and cover fresh ground.

QUEBEC CITY: This beautiful bit of history is more than a commercial hub and the travel center of eastern Canada: It embodies the soul of French Canada. Unless you have visited the city before, it is a necessary introduction to this unique province. For a detailed report, see *Quebec City,* THE CITIES.

    En Route from Quebec – The Pont de Québec (Quebec Bridge) leads to both Routes 20 and 132, so you can choose whether to take the newer highway, reaching Rivière du Loup in 2½ hours, or drive the more scenic Route 132. Either way, it is about 123 miles (197 km) and, although Route 20 does have rest areas, it is necessary to get off the Trans-Canada and onto Route 132 for food and gas.

LÉVIS: Shortly after leaving Quebec City (6 miles/10 km), Route 132 passes through Lévis. It was here, in 1648, that Father Pierre Bailloquet celebrated the south shore's first Mass. From terraces overlooking the river, the city of Quebec unfolds in a magnificent panorama. Pointe Lévis, directly opposite Quebec City, was used for a variety of purposes over the years, including the defense of the walled city. On April 18, 1793, Marie-Josephe Corriveau was hanged near the Plains of Abraham (outside Quebec) after being convicted of murdering her second husband with an ax. This may only have been the finale to a long string of murders she committed, and after being hanged, the body of La Corriveau, as she was nicknamed, was displayed in an iron cage on Pointe Lévis — in view of Quebec City — until May 25. The cage itself was recovered during the 1850s, and La Corriveau was immortalized as a female Jack the Ripper.

The *Alphonse-Desjardins House,* built in 1882–1884, (8 Mont-Marie St.; phone: 418-835-2090) is now a museum commemorating the founder of North America's first savings and loan institution, Les Caisses Populaires Desjardins, which began in 1901 in the kitchen.

En Route from Lévis – A little farther northeast is the city of Montmagny and the South Shore Archipelago — a group of seven small islands that are prime hunting ground for waterfowl. Each fall thousands of white geese and other migrating birds invade the shoreline flats of Ile aux Grues while hunters ferry from the mainland for the occasion. The mud flats also connect Ile aux Grues to Ile aux Oies. In 1655, this island was subjected to one of many Iroquois raids against French settlers, and the two daughters of farmer Jean-Baptiste Moyen were captured (the rest of the family was killed). Raphael Lambert Closse, acting governor of Montreal, saved both girls from the Indians and then married one. After his death (during a skirmish with Indians in 1662), the girls entered the Order of the Hospitalières de Québec, and part of the island was given as their dowry. Although the Order acquired the remainder of the island in 1713, a British regiment raided the island, killed the inhabitants and their stock, and burned all the buildings and farms in 1759. Only two nuns escaped the carnage. The island was sold to private interests in 1964.

ST.-JEAN PORT JOLI: Just 60 miles (96 km) from Quebec City, St. Jean Port Joli, known as the handicraft capital of the region, is well worth visiting. Just before entering the village, Route 132 passes a large group of wood sculpture and craft shops — the greatest concentration of handicrafts in the province. The Bourgault family, known through the region, provided the impetus for this loose association in 1936 by bringing their own shop and personal artistry in wood carving to the area. Soon they were joined by craftspeople working in an assortment of materials. An unrestored (1776) church, classified as an historic landmark, stands alongside the roadway at the edge of the village. Its sculptured wooden detail is exquisite. The *Musée des Anciens Canadiens* (332 Gaspé Avenue W.; phone: 418-598-3392) contains works of well-known woodcarvers. In town, try *Auberge du Faubourg* (280 Gaspé Avenue W.; phone: 418-598-6455 or 800-463-7045) for lunch.

RIVIÈRE DU LOUP: The town's name is derived from the *loups-marins* — seals — that at one time made frequent appearances in the St. Lawrence at its junction with the du Loup River. Although the seals are rarely seen nowadays, the town has kept the name — except for the period from 1850 to 1919, when it was called Fraserville. With its back to the northern slopes of the Notre Dame Mountains, this terraced town provides excellent views of the St. Lawrence River and three small islands. Each spring, a number of eider ducks nest on the easternmost isle of the group, Ile Blanche.

The town is a popular gathering spot for hunters and anglers preparing to enter the Gaspé. Guides point out the best nearby places to start. If you're hungry, stop at the dining room of the *Château Grandville* (94 Lafontaine St.; phone: 418-862-3551).

En Route from Rivière du Loup – It is possible to ferry across the St. Lawrence River from St.-Siméon on the north shore to join the route (or leave it during the return) at this point. The ferry runs from March to January (with some crossings from November to January) and usually makes several trips daily, depending upon demand (phone: 418-862-9545). It also is possible to take Route 185 southeast from Rivière du Loup toward New Brunswick and the northeast tip of Maine. The Gaspé region lies ahead on Route 132, 83 miles (133 km) away, at the town of

Ste.-Flavie. The newer highway, Route 20, has not been extended much past Ile Verte as yet, which increases the traffic on Route 132 into the Gaspé.

TROIS PISTOLES: A brief drive of 29 miles (46 km) beyond Rivière du Loup leads to the fishing village of Trois Pistoles. The town's name has been traced back to a legendary incident in 1621, when oarsmen crossing one of the many rivers in the area dropped a silver cup worth three "pistoles," the currency of the day, into the water. Their cry of "Voilà trois pistoles perdues!" ("There go three pistols!") gave rise to the town's name. Today, the town is known for its fish. The size and number of catches made by fishermen on the commercial craft available continue to draw anglers to the city. The town hosts the 10-day *Festival des Iles* (Island Festival) in mid-July, with 50 outdoor activities, entertainment, and games. Also worth a visit is a restored notary's house dating to 1842 (168 Rue Notre Dame E.; phone: 418-851-4849). It is a good example of the area's Kamouraska style of architecture and adjoins a handicraft shop and a bakery, all three of which are open year-round. One of its offshore islands bears the name Ile aux Basques, and three Basque whale oil furnaces have been reconstructed on the island. Along with the twin Iles Razades, these islands provide sanctuary for numbers of birds and are administered by the Provancher Society (a cousin of the Audubon Society). Check with the visitors' center for permission to visit the Basque furnaces (phone: 418-851-2959/3698). The islands also are visited each spring by schools of dolphins, easily seen from the shore, and whales visit from July to September when whale-watching cruises leave from Trois Pistoles' dock. (For more information call the *Association Touristique du Bas-St. Laurent;* phone: 418-867-1272).

Le Marmiton (70 Notre Dame St.; phone: 418-851-3202) is a good place to eat, whether you're waiting for a ferry or just passing through.

BIC: The small town of Bic, 25 miles (40 km) from Trois Pistoles, is a beautiful place to stop. The story told by most people around here is that during the creation of the earth, an overworked angel in charge of mountains and islands decided to end his day right there and unloaded everything at his disposal in and around Bic. They may be right, because the town is surrounded by heavenly hills and islands and 15 good walking and bicycle tours.

Bic also was blessed, perhaps by the same angelic gesture, with a deepwater harbor, making it a natural military port. During the British-French conflict, General Wolfe anchored his fleet here on his way toward Quebec, and during the American Civil War, fear of an American invasion prompted the British to dispatch the cutter *Persia* and a regiment of troops to the port city to prepare the defense of the Canada-Maine border. One of the offshore islands bears the gruesome name Ile du Massacre, and, beautiful as the island is, the name is accurate. In 1533 a band of about 200 Micmac Indians were driven from shelter in a cave and murdered by a party of Iroquois raiders.

There are two camping grounds in the area: *Bic* (phone: 418-736-4711) and *Delavoie* (phone: 418-736-4730), both directly off Route 132. Prices are reasonable. Route 132 leads to Bic Park and its nature center, inn, campground, and activities — clam-digging in summer, cross-country skiing in winter.

RIMOUSKI: Situated midway between Quebec City and Gaspé, this city, with a population of about 30,000, rates as one of the urban centers of the region. It is beginning to show signs of extraordinary development as a year-round shipping center. Almost 25% of the city was destroyed by fire in 1950, which provided space for the growth of many of the more modern facilities and subsequently attracted people and industry.

As the route enters the Gaspé, hunting and fishing improve, and the city of Rimouski is no exception. For river fishing, contact the *Association de Chasse et Pêche de Rivière-du-Loup* (phone: 418-862-5890), or the provincial fish and game office (phone: 418-722-3830); to arrange hunting, check the *Lechasseur Club* (phone: 418-775-3655) in nearby Mont Joli or make arrangements at the government-run Rimouski Reserve, which allows deer and small-game hunting. Although moose may not be hunted most of the year, bear in mind that the name Rimouski means land of moose, and these prize animals *can* be hunted (one per person) during late October, but check for the exact dates (phone: 418-722-3830). The season lasts only 1 or 2 weeks.

The city has a regional art museum, *Musée Regional de Remonski* (phone: 418-724-2272) open all year and an intriguing sea museum at Pointe-au-Père, (phone: 418-724-6214) 6 miles (10 km) from Rimouski (open mid-June to September) with displays on the area's maritime history. From late September to mid-October, the city stages a lively fall festival of arts and crafts displays, street fairs, concerts, and sporting events.

En Route from Rimouski – Rimouski and its suburbs spread along the coast, so it sometimes can be difficult to differentiate between localities. You'll have no trouble, however, in recognizing the sandy beaches of Ste. Luce, an old whaling village that has grown into a popular water sport resort. Go right over to the village wharf and charter a boat for deep-sea fishing. In the village of Ste. Luce sur Mer (a separate but indistinguishable entity) there is a French restaurant in the *Auberge Sainte-Luce* (phone: 418-739-4855) at Pointe-au-Père (see *Best en Route*), 6 miles (10 km) from Rimouski, which also provides the best accommodations in town (open in summer only). About 12 miles (19 km) from Rimouski, Route 132 splits and circles the peninsula in each direction. Since most traffic goes clockwise around the Gaspé, we've mapped a counterclockwise route to avoid crowds and aggravation.

The drive from Ste.-Flavie to Matapédia, at the Restigouche estuary on the Baie des Chaleurs, just under 100 miles (160 km), can be negotiated in about 2½ hours, but don't rush. The route follows an old Indian trail through the valley of the Matapédia River, which has some of the most beautiful scenery in the world. The valley is formed by the steep slopes of the central highlands paralleling the coast between Quebec and Ste. Flavie and the beginning of the Chic-Chocs Mountain Range. Between these two rocky masses, and fed by streams that run down their slopes, is the Matapédia River, aptly nicknamed "river of the 222 rapids."

Bypass the industrial town of Mont Joli and head inland through the farming and hunting villages of Ste. Angèle de Mérici and St. Moise to Sayabec, at the head of Matapédia Lake. In the village forestry museum is the trunk of a 700-year-old cedar tree and a fir tree growing *within* a cedar.

Val Brillant has the good fortune of sprawling along the western side of Matapédia Lake with a really fine beach. Take a few minutes to stop and relax. Amqui, at the confluence of the Matapédia and Humqui rivers, is the county seat. It's named after the Humqui River, which means "place of playful waters," but the spelling was altered in recent times. A secondary road from the town leads to the Matapédia wildlife reserve, a park encompassing 66 square miles of rivers, small lakes, and mountains.

Lac au Saumon, dominating a small lake formed by a widening of the Matapédia River, was originally settled by a group of Acadians from the Iles de la Madeleine. The area around it is filled with trout streams and small waterfalls, a favorite of many freshwater anglers. A few miles downstream is Causapscal, an industrial town by the standards of this region. With a population of 3,000, it is second by only a few hundred people to the county seat at Amqui. Built at the junction of the Matapédia and Causapscal rivers, it was once called Les Fourches ("the forks"). With two sets of riverbanks on which to draw, the scenery runs a close second to salmon fishing as favorite pastime. There are six fishing zones, four of which do not require reservations, so it's possible just to stop off and fish for a spell. Try your luck and skill because the Atlantic salmon that run in the river are considered one of the toughest fighting fish in the world. Those who prefer to watch can visit the Domaine Matamajaw (48 St.-Jacques St.; phone: 418-756-

3752), an interpretative center that recounts the history of salmon fishing. Observant visitors also may take in the sport along the Les Fourches Trail, where the Matapedia and Causapscal rivers meet. Local fishing guides can be hired for visiting anglers by calling Zec Casault (phone: 418-756-3670).

After you've taken your limit (check the fishing regulations for open season and limits), continue through the small farming village of Ste. Florence on to Routhierville. The only access to the village is across the old 259-foot covered bridge. The road to Routhierviell winds around the river, giving panoramic views of the rushing water below. There are a number of scenic rest areas en route. From here to Matapédia, 24 miles (38 km) south, there is little but farmland and river . . . and good fishing.

MATAPÉDIA: This small village is at the juncture of the Restigouche and Matapédia rivers; the Ristigouche flows on from here into the Baie des Chaleurs. The delta itself is a major salmon fishing area as well as a historical area. First settled by a group of Loyalists in 1808, the village was bolstered by the arrival of Irish immigrants in 1832 and Acadians in 1860. By 1872, population growth warranted the construction of a rail link with the northern and eastern regions of the peninsula.

On July 9, 1760, in a sea battle between the French and British, the ships *Machault* and *Bienfaisant* were scuttled in the north channel of the river delta, and a third French ship, the *Marquis de Malauze,* burned to its waterline. The hull of the *Marquis de Malauze* was refloated in 1939, and divers have recovered many artifacts from all three ships, including complete sets of dishes, kitchen utensils, and pieces of equipment.

En Route from Matapédia – If you are planning to visit New Brunswick or Prince Edward Island, this is an excellent approach. To see the Gaspé, however, stay on Route 132 as it bears east and begins to follow Cartier's route along the south coast of the peninsula. Restigouche, built on the site of a 17th-century Capuchin mission, is just a few miles away. The Bataille-de-la-Ristigouche National Historic Park (phone: 418-788-5676) at Pointe-a-la-Croix (open mid-June to early September), which commemorates the last naval battle between France and England in 1760, is where you can see the hull of the *Machault* and many of its recovered artifacts. The Historical Sites Commission is working to salvage as many artifacts as possible. A monument in front of the Church of St. Anne commemorates the conversion of a Micmac tribe to Christianity in 1610.

The parish of Notre Dame de la Garde, part of the village of Escuminac, is dedicated to a French officer, Donat de la Garde, who distinguished himself during the naval encounter in the Restigouche estuary in July 1760. Escuminac itself, a little farther east, lies on a high rise and dominates the roadstead of the estuary. Although the earliest settlers in the area were Loyalists, the parish of Notre Dame de la Garde was an outgrowth of a colony established in 1758 by Acadians who fled Nova Scotia to avoid deportation by the British.

A secondary road beyond Escuminac leads south onto a point occupied by the town of Miguasha, which is being transformed into a natural sciences park open from June to mid-October (phone: 418-794-2475). The cliffs supply specimens of plant and fish fossils to museums all over the world; fossils that have accumulated here date back 365 million years. The point, and the city of Dalhousie on the New Brunswick opposite shore, mark the beginning of the Baie de Chaleur and the end of the Restigouche estuary.

CARLETON: This city is an excellent example of the bicultural heritage of the Gaspé. Originally established in 1756 by Acadians forced from their homes by the British and named Petite-Tracadie, it was later renamed Carleton in honor of the British governor-general of the province by Loyalists who relocated here after the American Revolution. The city is still French-speaking, however, and the Notre Dame Oratory on Mont St. Joseph still dominates the town. From this point, almost 2,000 feet above the bay, you can see the mountains of the Gaspé to the east, north, and west and the shore of New Brunswick across the bay to the south. A minibus makes scheduled trips up the mountainside. The bus leaves from *Hotel Baie Bleue,* 1032 Perron Blvd. (phone: 418-364-3355).

When you come down from the mountain, check into the provincial campground if possible. It's on a ridge overlooking the sea, and the sunrise makes it worth getting up early to watch. Then go down to the water and swim. Cartier named this the Bay of Warmth for good reason; the water is warm enough for swimming even when it's chilly in surrounding areas. And if you are an early riser, look for reflections in the water from pieces of agate. The beach is loaded with them. Of course, the water here is loaded with other things, too, like mackerel, smelts, and flat fish that can be caught right from the wharf; charter boats are available for deep-sea fishing — sea trout, cod, and halibut. If you'd rather watch the animal life than mount it on your wall, just wander along the beaches and observe the sea terns, herons, and gannets that congregate here. Cultural offerings can be found along Perron Boulevard, site of a 120-year-old convent that has been converted to an art gallery, and the unusual *Penouil Ornithology Centre* (468 Perron Blvd.), which sells models of Gaspé birds made from fish bones and shells, open from June to September (phone: 418-364-3233).

If you fail to catch dinner or would rather not try, stop into the *Baie Bleue* hotel (482 Perron Boulevard; phone: 418-364-3355 or 800-463-9099) for an excellent French dinner (or lunch for that matter). See *Best en Route.*

MARIA: About 15 miles (24 km) east of Carleton on the area's only highway (Route 132), this city is the site of one of the two Micmac Indian reservations on the Baie des Chaleurs. A roadside cooperative operated by the Indians sells snowshoes and hand-woven baskets produced by the tribe. The Indian village, open to visitors, features a church in the shape of a teepee. Access is via a secondary road to the right of the crafts stand. Like many other communities in this area, Maria was originally settled by French-speaking people (who named the village Baie Ste.-Hélène) before the British conquest of Canada forced a name change. The newer name honors Maria Effingham, who became Lady Dorchester, wife of Governor-General (Sir Guy) Carleton, during his second term as British governor of the territory.

Stay on Route 132 across the Cascapédia River (and past Route 299, which cuts north across the peninsula) to Bonaventure, a distance of 25 miles (40 km). Casgapegiag was the Micmac name for the river — "large body of water."

BONAVENTURE: A popular resort on the south shore of the Gaspé, Bonaventure was named after one of the many ships that carried French nobles on tours of the region during the late 1500s. The village was a fishing port burned by the British after the battle of the Restigouche estuary. A group of Acadians rebuilt the village in the same year, following their forced exit at the hands of the British from the Nova Scotia colony. The *Acadian Museum,* in an original wooden structure contains many period pieces, including kitchen utensils, looms, furniture, and a fossil collection (97 Port-Royal Ave.; phone: 418-534-4000). Open mid-June to mid-September. The Gaspé Zoo (123 Route Des Vieux Ponts; phone: 418-534-3410) has some 65 animals, most native to the area. The zoo is open daily from 9 AM to 7 PM, June 1 to early September.

En Route from Bonaventure – Many of the villages on this part of the coast were settled by British Loyalists about the time of the American Revolution; others were established by Acadians fleeing the British in Nova Scotia. The fact that groups of such polarized individuals were able to settle within a few miles of each other and not fight is amazing — especially considering the frequency of conflicts between the two countries. Hope Town, just 21 miles east (34 km) of Bonaventure, is an example of British influence in the area. Established by Loyalists in 1786, and named for British Lieutenant-Governor Henry Hope, the village remains almost purely English in its outlook.

PORT DANIEL AND PORT DANIEL PARK: Port Daniel is at the end of the beach-lined, deepwater bay where Cartier anchored his ships for a week during his explorations. He called it Conche St. Martin (St. Martin Cove), but it was renamed for one of the many sea captains who later visited the area. Whether Cartier explored the Port Daniel River and the mountains from which it runs is unknown, but the river and surrounding peaks are some of the most splendid scenery in Gaspé. The park, 8 miles (13 km) north on a small secondary road, encompasses 18 separate trout lakes as well as the Port Daniel River, known for Atlantic salmon fishing (phone: 418-396-2789). The mountains in the north end of the park average 900 feet, and their wide range of climate, from cold and mountainous to almost temperate, supports an interesting variety of foliage.

En Route from Port Daniel – It is only about 52 miles (83 km) from Port Daniel to Percé, an active travel center and the entrance to the beautiful L'Ile Bonaventure Park, but allow time for a few stops on the way.

This part of the coast, facing east into the Gulf of St. Lawrence, has seen many shipwrecks, and the coastal villages are filled with tales of ghosts, phantom ships, and treasure. Anse aux Gascons, a few miles east of Port Daniel, for example, was the scene of the wreck of an English ship during the 19th century. The villagers were able to rescue a few survivors (burying the rest) and took the cargo of 40,000 gold louis for their pains. True to storybook fantasy, one of the sailors later married the daughter of the fisherman who saved him. Although it is unlikely that a search of the coastal rocks will turn up any of the treasure, the shore is filled with pieces of agate.

At the villages of Grande Rivière and Ste.-Thérèse de Gaspé, the villagers still hold pretty much with the ways of their ancestors, using open-air, cod drying racks to prepare their daily catches. Cap d'Espoir, 42 miles (67 km) from Port Daniel, is haunted, according to legend, by the ghost of a stray ship from Admiral Walker's fleet, which crashed into the rocks in 1711 and can sometimes be seen on summer nights, crashing onto the rocky cape. Try to arrive here around dusk and wait for it to reappear, then go on to Percé to watch the sun rise behind the immense rock that guards the town.

PERCÉ: With a population of over 5,500, this qualifies as a major town in the Gaspé, but it's just a small fishing village with many attractions for visitors. Primarily, there's Percé Rock, a natural wonder that defies accurate description. The rock rises 298 feet out of the sea, 1,420 feet long, and 300 feet wide with a natural arch, 50 feet high, in its eastern end. A few feet from this monolith stands a natural stone tower, all that is left of a second arch in the rock that collapsed in 1845. There is splendid silent power — a testament to obdurate, unyielding, inhuman endurance — in the rock, but at dawn, when the sun rises *through* the arch, the entire stone changes from something inorganic to a presence filled, if not with intelligence, at least with luminescence and the suggestion of intent. It certainly rates as one of the natural wonders of the world. There's a particularly good view of it from *Percé Natural History Centre* (phone: 418-782-2240) on the road to Petite Irlande. During low tide, you can walk out to the rock on a convenient sandbar at the foot of Mont Joli (be sure to check on when the tide will come *in*) to inspect the fossils (Devonian period, the fourth phase of the Paleozoic Era, just before trees began to appear on the east coast of North America) on the sides of the monolith.

The village is laid out in a semicircle surrounding two bays, with capes between and within a larger semicircle created by the slopes of the mountains that isolate it from the rest of the peninsula. The peak of Mont Ste.-Anne, used by the Micmac Indians in their sun-worshiping ceremonies, is accessible by walking up the dirt road near the church. The road is drivable only partway, but the weak of flesh can rent carts rather than make the 2½-to-3-hour hike. Not only is the peak historical (by virtue of the

Micmac ceremonies), but its 1,230-foot height makes an ideal viewpoint for planning your explorations. From here, you can see Percé Rock, Bonaventure Island, and the entire village at a glance. A trail behind the church leads to a small waterfall.

In the town itself, the *Percé Wildlife Interpretive Centre* (phone: 418-782-2240) can give a good idea, through dioramas and a filmstrip, of the stages of development that produced Percé Rock and the irregular coastline of the peninsula (it explains why the mouth of the Restigouche River is considered "drowned" in the Baie des Chaleurs). Open daily, June 24 to mid-October, 9AM to 5 PM. Admission charge.

Aside from its geography, Percé's other attraction is food. More than two dozen establishments serve excellent seafood and French dishes, and two of the best (both expensive) are the *La Normandie* hotel-motel (Route 132 at 221 Route des Failles; phone: 418-782-2112 or 800-463-0820) and *Restaurant de l'Auberge du Gargantua* (about a mile/1.6 km off Route 132 toward the mountains; phone: 418-782-2852). But don't limit yourself; the food here is half the trip.

From the wharf at Percé, take any of the many boat tours available to Bonaventure Island. Once the home of a community of fishermen-farmers, it now belongs exclusively to the birds. The dominant species — gannets — number about 50,000, although there also are kittiwakes, gulls, razor-billed auks, murres, and occasional sea pigeons and sea parrots. Most of the island's new residents have established nests along the cliffs that line the shore and can easily be photographed. The island is a sanctuary under the control of the Tourism, Fish, and Game Commission.

En Route from Percé – From Percé to Gaspé is a comfortable morning's drive — just under 50 miles (80 km) — through countryside that varies from cliffs to sandy beaches. The tiny village of Coin du Banc lies in a small pass that marks your exit from the guardian mountains of Percé and the entrance to the northern sectors of the peninsula. Its beach attracts avid windsurfers.

AUBERGE FORT PRÉVEL: The resort center of *Auberge Fort Prével,* (Route 132; phone: 418-368-2281) about 25 miles (40 km) from Percé, attracts diners and food fanatics from all over the world. The settlement began after a British sailor, George Prével, somehow floated onto a nearby shore — either swept overboard or shipwrecked — married a local girl, and set up housekeeping. During World War II, coastal guns were installed and barracks erected. These buildings, extensively redecorated, comprise the heart of the resort. The *Salle à Manger* (phone: 418-368-2281), inside the fort, is one of the top restaurants in the province — and with good cause. Besides drawing upon the waters of the gulf to supply the freshest fish possible, it also is a government training school from spring to early autumn catering to the hotel-restaurant trade. The inn also has a golf course, tennis court, and fitness center.

GASPÉ: This industrial hub of the peninsula is a deepwater port and the railhead of the region, linking the city with Montreal, Quebec City, and Matapédia. It fronts the Baie de Gaspé, which receives the waters of three of the region's major Atlantic salmon rivers — the Dartmouth, York, and St. Jean — all of which originate high in the mountains. Station Pisciculture de Gaspé, a fish hatchery near the mouth of the York River (5 miles/8 km on Route 198), provides almost 2 million salmon and trout to stock lakes and rivers all over the province. Open to the public daily, with guided tours offered during the summer (phone: 418-368-3395). You can go after the grown ones in all three rivers (within the limits set by law) as long as you make arrangements in advance with the lower Saint-Laurent and Gaspé government office (phone: 418-722-3830, or check limits in the current *Fishing, Hunting and Trapping Guide,* available at tourist offices); reservations are needed 48 hours ahead of time since the number of anglers is controlled. You may be able to get a space on only 24 hours' notice, but don't count on it.

The *Gaspé Museum* (Gaspé Blvd.; phone: 418-368-5710) holds periodic exhibitions during the summer, while the *Manoir Le Boutillier* (Anse-au-Griffon on Route; 132 phone: 418-892-5150) recalls the Gaspé's proud fishing heritage.

En Route from Gaspé – About 10 miles (16 km) outside Gaspé, Route 132 takes a sharp turn eastward, outlining the peninsula containing Forillon Park, while Route 197 cuts across the western end of the park, joining Route 132 on the other side. The park, encompassing some 92 square miles of the most varied landscape and vegetation, is a wonder in itself. It occupies almost all of the small peninsula; its low areas are almost marine (saltwater plants, sand dunes, grottoes, and occasional seals), while the mountains in the center nurture a variety of alpine vegetation, including species of plants which have survived since the Ice Age. Altogether, there are nine different levels of climatic variation and a spectacular array of wildlife — moose, black bear, whitetailed deer, fox, lynx, mink, otter, muskrat, and others. Scuba diving and nature walks are among the park's varied activities. The park's reception center in Penouille is open daily, 8 AM to 7 PM June to *Labor Day* (phone: 418-368-5505). Three private campgrounds in the park area provide most facilities.

On the south coast of this peninsula, along Route 132, is the village of Penouille. It is believed a Viking outpost may have been established here during the 11th century, and that Freydis (Eric the Red's illegitimate sister) may have visited the site — which would make her the first white female to set foot in Canada. The difficulty in proving this has been compounded by the destruction of the French settlements on this site by English troops on three separate occasions (1690, 1711, and 1759). The village of Cap aux Os, a few miles farther on, was named for the whale bones found here by the earliest settlers. While this does not prove that Vikings actually landed on this shore, it adds credence to the theory.

The Forillon Park draws its name from *pharillon,* or "little lighthouse," the name given to one of the tall towers of rock at the eastern tip of the peninsula, the site of signal fires to warn sailors off the rocky cape. The north side of the peninsula, Cap des Rosiers, is said to be the site of more shipwrecks than any other point on the Canadian coast. Its lighthouse, built in 1858, is a historic monument open 9 AM to 7 PM, from early June until late August (phone: 418-892-5613 or 368-5710).

Routes 132 and 197 reunite near Rivière au Renard, where descendants of a group of Irish sailors, shipwrecked at Cap des Rosiers, comprise a large part of the population. Route 132 continues along the north coast toward Grand Etang, 18 miles (29 km) west. Just past Grand Etang is tiny St. Yvon, where the remains of a German torpedo, which missed its target and exploded against the rocks, are kept in a shed. It is only 48 more miles (77 km) to Anse Pleureuse, where Route 198 leads to Gaspé Park, about 25 miles (40 km) inland.

Between Anse Pleureuse and Ste.-Anne des Monts are 42 miles (67 km) of irregular roadway, running so close to the water in places that spray splashes the cars, then climbing 1,200 feet over a rocky cape. Stop at the village of Mont St. Pierre, and take an hour to climb the mountain itself or drive up the jeep trail. From its peak, you can look out over the vast Gulf of St. Lawrence or face slightly westward and strain to see Pointe des Monts, at the base of the gulf on the north shore. Mont St.-Pierre with its glider launching pads is considered the glider capital of eastern Canada. The *Mont St.-Pierre* hotel-motel (60 Rue Prudent Cloutier; phone: 418-797-2850) serving good food at inexpensive prices, makes a timely stopping place (see *Best en Route*).

As you pass through the village of Tourelle, 37 miles (59 km) from Anse Pleureuse, keep an eye out for falling rocks as you approach from the east; the highway runs between the beach and the mountains, and in 1963, part of the village was wiped out by a landslide.

STE. ANNE DES MONTS: When you arrive at Ste. Anne des Monts, get off Route 132 and take the old road along the shore. Most of the older buildings were destroyed by fire in 1925, but the Theodore Lamontagne Residence now known as the *Auberge*

Château Lamontagne (170 1st Avenue E.; phone: 418-763-2524) still watches over the bay, and it's worth the 5-mile (8-km) drive to see the house and grounds and to try out its new restaurant. The road crosses the St. Anne River (where salmon fishing is allowed under government guidelines; see the current *Fishing, Hunting and Trapping Guide).* Between the hatchery upstream and the fish coming from the St. Lawrence, it is a good spot to land a salmon. If you're in the area for dinner, try *Auberge Gîte du Mont Albert* (phone: 418-763-2288 or 800-463-0860) in Gaspé Park. Route 299, through the middle of the park, runs right past it. The inn specializes in classic French cooking as well as regional dishes of the Gaspé and Quebec Province; it has been awarded high marks for service by gastronomes from all over the world. During the academic year, students from the Quebec Institute of Tourism and Hostelry show off their know-how for guests. Telephone for reservations and information before heading into the park (phone: 418-763-3039 or 392-5388). See *Best en Route.*

PARC DE LA GASPÉSIE: The park can be reached from Ste.-Anne des Monts via Route 299 (12 miles/19 km), from Anse Pleureuse via Routes 198 and 1000 (25 miles/40 km), or from New Richmond on the south shore of the Gaspé Peninsula (85 miles/136 km).

The Parc de la Gaspésie covers almost 500 square miles of magnificent mountainous land, preserving for all time a portion of the natural beauty that prompted Cartier's praise of the area called Gaspé in New France. This is one of the few places in the province where herds of caribou, moose, and deer still roam in the same area. The highest peaks of the Chic-Chocs Mountains preserve alpine vegetation that exists nowhere else at such a southern latitude.

The Chic-Chocs Mountains, an arm of the Appalachian chain, run the length of the park and most of the peninsula, from the Matapédia Valley to the eastern capes. They average 3,500 feet, and the highest peaks — like the McGerrigle — scrape the skies at 4,100 feet. It was the height of these slopes that kept the alpine flora from dying out during the last (Wisconsin) ice age, which lasted from about 15,000 to 5,000 BC. The alpine fir, representative of the period, rarely grows more than 8 feet tall. Mont Jacques Cartier has the largest concentration of these plants. Both Mont Jacques Cartier and the McGerrigle are frequented by herds of caribou most of the year. In the summer they remain in the cool of these peaks, venturing down to the lower region only during winter.

The vegetation of the park changes with the altitudes: Peat bogs on the valley floor give way to forested slopes, then to lichen, moss, and low shrubs on the windblown crests. Mont Albert is a naturalist's dream. Its base is lined with conifers (cone-bearing trees) such as firs and spruces, which gradually mix with subalpine forests of stubby alpine firs. Toward the peak, the trees thin out and are replaced by alpine tundra and Arctic vegetation — shrubs and moss — and in the barren areas, the intense cold and frost shatter massive chunks of exposed rock into gigantic boulders.

The park is crisscrossed by a network of hiking trails and drivable roads. Most conveniences are available in the park area. Trail guides and trained naturalists are on duty on an irregular basis, and many activities can be arranged with the help of the staff. Although hunting is strictly prohibited, the park's lakes and rivers yield speckled, sea, and Quebec red trout as well as hard-fighting Atlantic salmon. During the winter months, these slopes attract cross-country skiers from all over the world. This is still very much an untamed forest; the animals (including black bears) have rights to the area, and it does get dark quickly in the mountain forests. Be sure to *return to your campsite or car before dark* or you may get lost. The parks use a check-in, check-out system designed to keep track of all those wandering in the forest, but it might take a few hours to locate you.

This park is bordered by the Matane and Dunière parks, extensions of the Parc de la Gaspésie in geography and content but under a separate administration. The principal access to these areas is via Route 195 from Matane.

Continue eastbound on Route 132 along the south bank of the St. Lawrence River for 55 miles (88 km) to Matane.

MATANE: This industrial town was originally settled in 1795, but it remained basically a Micmac Indian village until 1845. During the mid-19th century, the town began to evolve into a river pilot station and grew with the lumber trade. Its name is based on the Indian word for "beaver pond." Ferries connect Matane with Godbout and Baie Comeau on the north shore of the St. Lawrence River (a good place to pick up the *North Shore* route for your return to Quebec). Atlantic salmon fishing in the Matane River is excellent. A stopover at Le Barrage Mathieu-D'Amours fish ladder, a short walk from the *Auberge des Gouverneurs* (250 Phares Ave. E.; 418-566-2651), is where the vicarious angler observes the salmon both above and below water as they struggle upstream in Des Iles Park.

JARDINS DE MÉTIS PARK: If you are returning toward Quebec on the south shore via Route 132, be sure to see Jardins de Métis Park. It is 32 miles (51 km) from Matane, and 6 miles (10 km) from Ste. Flavie, the turnoff for heading south across the Matapédia Valley through which the route passed much earlier. The park began as a private estate, one of many English-style manors established during the Victorian era. The formal gardens have been adapted to include approximately 4,000 species of plants of many different climates. There are alpine 500 species of shrubs, annuals and perennials, and experimental plantings of a group of aquatic plants. The success of these plantings is a tribute to Elsie Reford, who began the gardens in 1922. *Villa Reford* — her former home — is the centerpiece of the park and houses a museum, restaurant, and craft shop. Open daily, 8:30 AM to 8 PM, June to September (phone: 418-775-2221). Admission charge.

BEST EN ROUTE

The range of lodgings on the Gaspé Peninsula is especially wide, with inns that have kitchens of provincewide reputation in several parks and rustic, simple motel-hotel or even campground accommodations elsewhere. Expect to pay $65 or more for a double in the places listed as expensive; between $45 and $65 in those categorized as moderate; and under $45 in the inexpensive choices. These prices are valid for the summer season; off-season, rates are halved. All prices are quoted in US dollars.

RIVIÈRE DU LOUP

Auberge de la Pointe – A good spot at very reasonable prices. Fine dining and comfortable rooms with all services. Autoroute Jean LeSage, exit 507 (phone: 418-862-3514 or 800-463-1222). Expensive to moderate.

Lévesque – Not so plush, but comfortable, with 96 rooms and an excellent dining room. French and Canadian foods. 171 Fraser St. (phone: 418-862-6927 800-463-1236). Moderate.

Universel – A large 119-room motel in the center of town, offering all the facilities of most large hotels. The rooms are comfortable and the service excellent. Restaurant and a nice bar. 311 Hôtel de Ville Blvd. (phone: 418-862-9520 or 800-463-4495). Moderate.

Château Grandville – Small but cozy, it has 47 rooms and a fair restaurant. 94 Lafontaine St. (phone: 418-862-3551). Inexpensive.

RIMOUSKI

Hotel des Gouverneurs – Comfortable and modern, this 166-room property has excellent service and an average dining room. 155 René Lepage Blvd. E. (phone: 418-723-4422 or 800-463-2820). Expensive.

Auberge Universel – A small-scale version of a full-service establishment, with 63 rooms. 130 Rue St.-Barnabé (phone: 418-724-6944 or 800-463-4495). Moderate.

STE.-LUCE-SUR-MER

Auberge Ste. Luce – This small motel (29 rooms) is open in summer only. It is known mostly for its good restaurant. 52 Route du Fleuve Ouest (phone: 418-739-4955). Inexpensive.

MATAPÉDIA

Restigouche – Located along the banks of the Restigouche and Matapédia rivers, this 37-room motel is a popular spot among salmon fishermen. Comfortable, although not plush, with most rooms overlooking the bay; a good dining room. Rue du Saumon (phone: 418-865-2155). Moderate.

CARLETON

Baie Bleue – A 95-unit hotel-motel with a color TV set in each room. Guests have access to the heated pool and beach. *La Baie Bleue* restaurant is the best in the area, with fine French and Canadian dishes and seafood. 482 Perron Blvd. (phone: 418-364-3355 or 800-463-9099). Expensive to moderate.

Shick Shock – This 35-unit motel has comfortable rooms, a dining room, and a bar. 1746 Perron Blvd., East Carleton (phone: 418-364-3288). Inexpensive.

BONAVENTURE

Auberge Le Château – A decent 20-room hotel-motel with a restaurant. 98 Port Royal Ave. (phone: 418-534-3336). Moderate.

CHANDLER

Fraser – French and Canadian specialties and seafood are served in the restaurant at this 40-unit motel. Route 132 (phone: 418-689-2281 or 800-361-6162). Moderate.

St. Laurent – This is an older place with 65 comfortable rooms, good service, and a fair dining room. 499 Réhel St. (phone: 418-689-3355). Moderate to inexpensive.

PERCÉ

Le Bonaventure sur Mer – An 88-room, 36-unit hotel-motel offering comfortable accommodations, a bar, and a good restaurant. Route 132 (phone: 418-782-2166 or 800-463-4212). Expensive to moderate.

Pic de l'Aurore – Overlooking Percé Rock, this 18-unit motel has a fair dining room. Route 132 (phone: 418-782-2166). Expensive to moderate.

Auberge du Gargantua – A motel with 11 units overlooking Percé Rock, it is known for its fine restaurant, with French dishes and seafood. 222 Route des Failles (phone: 418-782-2852). Moderate to inexpensive.

Bleu-Blanc-Rouge – Here is a comfortable 13-room hotel-motel with a good dining room featuring seafood and French cooking. Route 132 (phone: 418-782-2142). Moderate to inexpensive.

Manoir Percé – A 38-unit establishment with a nice dining room. Route 132 (phone: 418-782-2022 or 800-463-0858). Moderate to inexpensive.

FORT PRÉVEL

Auberge Fort Prével – This is a comfortable 78-unit motel and resort area built from World War II army barracks. It features a 9-hole golf course and an excellent restaurant which capitalizes on fresh seafood and French recipes. Closed in winter. Route 132 (phone: 418-368-2281). Moderate.

GASPÉ

Auberge des Commandants – Certainly the best lodging spot on the Gaspé Peninsula, it has 44 rooms and overlooks the bay. 178 Rue de la Reine (phone: 418-368-3355). Expensive to moderate.

Adams – A 98-unit motel overlooking the ocean. Nice rooms, good service, and a dining room offering seafood and French dishes. Route 132, 2 Adam's St. (phone: 418-368-2244 or 800-463-4242). Moderate.

GRANDE VALLÉE

Frigault – This 21-unit motel has a pretty good French and seafood restaurant. Large rooms and good service. Route 132 (phone: 418-393-2720). Moderate.

MONT ST. PIERRE

Mont-St.-Pierre – Small motel on the ocean shore with a good restaurant. Prudent Cloutier St. (phone: 418-797-2202). Moderate to inexpensive.

STE. ANNE DES MONTS

Monaco des Monts – There are 46 rooms here and the dining facilities are good for the area. The guest services are average. 90 St.-Anne Blvd. W. (phone: 418-763-3321 or 800-361-6162). Moderate.

PARC DE LA GASPÉSIE

Gîte du Mont Albert – Besides 21 rustic rooms, this hotel-motel has a very famous restaurant. Open only during the summer. Route 299 (phone: 418-763-2288 or 800-463-0860). Expensive to moderate.

MATANE

Auberge des Gouverneurs – Here is an elegant establishment with 48 large, comfortable rooms. Good dining room and excellent service. 250 Phare Ave. E. (phone: 418-566-2651 or 800-463-2820). Expensive to moderate.

Iles de la Madeleine

The Iles de la Madeleine (Magdalen Islands) — anchored in the Gulf of St. Lawrence about 130 miles east by southeast of the Gaspé Peninsula, about 55 miles northeast of the tip of Nova Scotia's Cape Breton Island, and 60 miles east of Prince Edward Island — are an unusual and satisfyingly remote getaway spot.

Only seven of the dozen or so islands, islets, and reefs in this archipelago are inhabited, so that even as travelers discover them, it is easy to find a dune-lined beach where you can be alone with the sea. The major islands of the Madeleines cluster together and are connected by causeways, forming one long strip of islands and bays. They are Ile du Cap aux Meules, the centerpiece of this string, the largest of the Madeleines, and the starting point of most tours (at its community Cap aux Meules); Ile de Havre aux Maisons, Ile aux Loups, La Grosse Ile, and Ile de la Grande Entrée to the northeast; and Ile du Havre Aubert to the southeast. Accessible only by ferry is Ile d'Entrée. Because most of these islands are connected by causeways and are themselves divided into smaller sections also called islands, it only takes a quick glance at a map to make the geography of the islands perfectly comprehensible. Most of the coastal rocks are a soft grayish red, laced with sandstone and gypsum (hints of volcanic ancestry), stained ocher by the sea water and salt air, and carved for centuries into weird formations. Tall pillars overlook chasms and the crashing ocean. Atop overhanging ledges are picnic sites with panoramic views of neighboring islands and the sea; below are enchanting caves. These natural formations, the fine sandy beaches with their dunes and warm waters, make this quiet archipelago a summer destination of some romance and mystery.

The life-style of the Madelinot villagers reflects the quietude of the islands, affected most by the surrounding sea. Lobster, herring, mackerel, scallops, cod, and halibut are the mainstays of their economy, and most of the people belong to island-based cooperatives that freeze, can, smoke, and ship as well as market their catch. Until recently, the annual seal hunt (in March and April) was the second component of the economy, with most of the islanders taking part, but because of popular indignation and the depletion of the seal herds, attempts are under way to develop other resources to replace seal hides in the marketplace.

The Madelinots inherited the seal-hunting tradition from the Basque sailors who hunted and fished in these waters 4 centuries ago, although most of the islanders are of Acadian origin. The Acadian colony, based in Nova Scotia, was destroyed twice (in 1613 and in the 1750s), and each time many of the colonists resettled on these secluded islands. Of the 15,000 inhabitants occupying this 55,000-acre haven, about 1,000 are of Scottish ancestry; many others descend from shipwrecked sailors of all nationalities.

These attractive little islands have been prized ever since Cartier first explored them in June 1534. In his enthusiasm he named one isolated island Ile de Brion, after the grand admiral of France, Phillipe Chabot, Sieur de Brion (probably hoping the admiral would let him keep the rest for himself). The name Madeleine is derived from Madeleine Fontaine, wife of François Doublet, first seigneur of the islands. Doublet made the settling of the archipelago his life project. Sir Isaac Coffin, after being promoted to admiral of the British navy in 1814, was awarded the Iles de la Madeleine in 1815 as a reward for public service; on English maps Ile de la Grande Entrée is referred to as Coffin Island.

The relative isolation of the islands, even from each other, has allowed communities established by early settlers to retain their individuality — for example, Scottish communities concentrated on Grosse Ile and Ile d'Entrée. "Magdalen Islands" or "Grindstone" (English for Cap aux Meules) appears on many local fishing vessels, and even French maps of the islands are strewn with such names as Old Harry, Leslie, and Cap (Cape) Alright.

During the spring and fall migrations, the Iles de la Madeleine become a bird-watcher's haven. More than 50 species of waders, ducks, alcids (a family of diving birds), and other waterfowl, plus many varieties of land birds, take sanctuary here. In summer, the seas around are like fields for harvest. The deep-sea fishing for bluefin tuna is as good as anywhere in the world. The early days of summer are reserved for lobsters taken fresh from the gulf (you can buy them at wharves) and cooked on the beach. And the later summer months are perfect for swimming and long afternoons of basking on the dunes. Winters here are beautiful in their solitude, but few (except the seals) appreciate them.

Since the summer days are apt to attract many travelers, and since there are less than 200 hotel rooms — and about the same number of campsites — available, it is advisable to make arrangements far in advance. The best approach to Iles de la Madeleines is by air: *INTAIR* (phone: 418-969-2771, 418-692-1031 or 800-361-0200) flies from both Montreal and Quebec City to Havre aux Maisons, with stops at Mont Joli and Gaspé; *Air Atlantique* has daily service from Montreal (phone: 418-877-4283 or 800-361-4618) that connects with other flights to the island via Halifax Airport. Both *Inter-Canadian* (phone: 418-969-2760 or 800-361-0200) and *Canadian International* (phone: 418-692-0912) schedule daily flights during the summer. Many travelers prefer to drive to Cap Tormentine, New Brunswick, and take a ferry to Prince Edward Island. From the wharf at Borden, PEI, they drive across the island to Souris for the NM *Lucy Maud Montgomery* ferry to Cap aux Meules. Between Cap Tormentine and Borden, PEI, there is continuous service and little waiting time. The trip from Souris to the Madeleines takes 5 hours, with only one departure daily (at 2 PM, except Tuesdays when it leaves at 2 AM; in high season, a daily 2 AM ferry is added). Beginning in mid-March, reservations are taken for the round trip (phone: 418-986-3278). Check current schedules before you reserve. For information about the ferry, call 902-687-2181 (in Souris) or 418-986-6600 (in Cap aux Meules). Visitors also can travel by ship on the *CTMA Voyager,* which transports cargo and up to 15 passengers from Montreal to the Iles de la Madeleine. The ship departs on Fridays and returns on Sunday afternoons; return trips depart on Wednesdays and arrive in Montreal on Fridays. Round-trip fare, including meals and cabin accommodations, is approximately $630; cars are an additional $135. For more information, call 418-986-6600.

To get to Cap Tormentine from Montreal or Quebec, take Route 20 east along the south shore of the St. Lawrence River to Rivière du Loup, then pick up Route 185 across the Gaspé and into New Brunswick, where it encounters Route 2 to Moncton. Cap Tormentine is just a short distance away from here via local roadways. From New England, pick up US 1 from US 95 in Portland, Maine. It leads into Canadian Route 1, which goes through Saint John, New Brunswick, where it intersects Route 2 heading toward Moncton.

The relaxing atmosphere of the Madeleines permeates the air among those awaiting the ferry from Souris. The wharf is on the outskirts of the town, and many people, braced for the long wait for either the 8 PM or 8 AM run, set up their tents, explore the area, or start parties. With a restaurant and bar aboard the ferry, the 8 PM, 5-hour voyage often turns into an all-night international summer festival.

Whether you arrive at 8 in the morning or the evening, the first view of Ile d'Entrée (Entry Island) is astounding: a large grassy hillock protruding from the sea. Passing Cap Rouge and Pointe du Sud-Ouest, look for the hiking trails that lead along the cliffs and try to pick a spot among the red rock formations to visit later. The ferry docks at Cap aux Meules in a sheltered bay full of small fishing vessels and visiting sailing sloops. Local ferry service to Ile d'Entrée and Cap-Aux-Meules (phone: 418-985-2148) originates here. A tourist information booth is located at the exit for the ferry dock. To the left of the wharf is the formation known as Gros Cap. Ile du Cap aux Meules, the largest island in the archipelago, is the most heavily populated. Three municipalities are centered here: Cap aux Meules (a small district on the eastern shore of the island); Fatima (encompassing the north end of the island and a long beach and reef extending north from the perimeter), and Etang du Nord (occupying the southern end of the island).

Items made by the islanders are sold at reasonable rates on the islands. Cold, lonely winters provide many hours for exacting, detailed work. Carved pieces of whale bone and seal fur items are among the popular choices. The fishwells, where freshly caught fish and lobsters are kept ready for shipment, may be visited to see how these people pursue their arduous living from the sea (open to visitors Tuesdays and Fridays, all year). There is an excellent marina on the Gulf of St. Lawrence, with some interesting specimens on display. Check with the tourism office near the wharf (20 Route du Quai) for details on season and hours. Nine-meter sailboats with a captain can be rented, and fishing trips are scheduled daily, weather permitting. Check with *Fédération de Voile du Québec* (phone: 514-252-3097) about rentals and schools, and call the *Association Touristique des Iles* (phone: 418-986-2245) for information on sailing and fishing excursions.

Chemin du Gros Cap leads to the Gros Cap Scenic Area, which lies in the Etang du Nord district. A provincial campground with 38 sites is located just past Cap Rouge, about 4 miles (6 km) from the wharf. This point, like most of these exposed hills and cliffs, is subject to the 20-mph winds that created the rock carvings, so dress appropriately — wear a sweater and/or wind-breaker on the windier days. The same road, Chemin du Gros Cap, curves inland toward La Vernière, with a beautiful old wooden church near Butte du Vent, the highest point on the islands. The entire archipelago may be seen from this summit. And on a clear day you can see Cape Breton Island, almost 60 miles (96 km) away.

Route 199, the connecting highway that links most of the islands into a cohesive landmass, leads south from La Vernière through the Plage de la Martinique (Martinique Beach) and across a causeway to Ile du Havre Aubert. A similar connecting beach links the western sides of these two islands, creating a lagoon called Havre aux Basques (Basque Harbor). Along this western leg of Ile du Cap aux Meules, in the Etang du Nord district, you may see in the shallow offshore waters the remains of several wooden ships among the many wrecked here. The roadway bears east and follows the beach of Ile du Havre Aubert to the village of Havre Aubert. This busy harbor looks much like the bay at Cap aux Meules, populated by Madelinot fishers and fisheries. The *Musée de la Mer* (Marine Museum, phone: 418-937-5711) not only records the history of the archipelago, but also portrays the history of sailing and fishing.There is a reconstructed Madelinot village nearby. Two of the five campgrounds in the islands are located on the southern coast, near the village of Bassin. *Belle Plage* (phone: 418-937-5408) has 28 sites and *Plage du Golfe* (phone: 418-937-5224/5115) has 72 sites. Check the *Quebec Camping* booklet (available at the toursit office near the Prince Edward Island ferry terminal) for facilities available at each.

If you drove from Ile du Cap aux Meules on Route 199, then you should certainly return along the Plage de l'Ouest (West Beach). Try to keep an eye out for the shipwrecks in the gulf on your left and be sure to glance over at the waters of the lagoon to your right.

When you arrive at Ile du Cap aux Meules, take the road leading north through the village of Etang du Nord and toward Fatima. A private 32-site campground, *Le Barachois* (phone: 418-986-6055/5227), overlooks the northwest shore. This district on the northern end of the island extends along the Dune du Nord, a long, wide, sandy arm of dune-filled beach that connects with the outstretched southerly arm of Grosse Ile. At various points this elongated beach is called Plage de l'Hôpital and Plage de la Pointe au Loup. Here, too, a second arm paralleling the first (the northern extension of Ile du Havre aux Maisons) forms a lagoon between these two beaches.

Route 199, which runs along the east side of the lagoon south of Ile du Cap aux Meules and onto Havre aux Maisons, crosses this lagoon (north of Ile du Cap aux Meules) and runs along the west side on the Dune du Nord beach. The Grosse Ile district occupies two islands that form a severe V shape, pointing north. The western side is Grosse Ile; the other, obviously, is Ile de l'Est. Not so obvious is exactly where one island ends and the other begins. Route 199, traveling north along the west side of this question, passes through the village of Leslie, which was settled by Scots. To a large extent, their language has been lost in the French, but some of the customs of the families date back to early Scotland. Spend a little time in the village and try to get a taste of the Scottish-Madelinot atmosphere. The highway turns sharply south across the mouth of the bay (Baie Clarke) that forms the northern tip of the lagoon and continues in the direction of Old Harry on Ile de l'Est. The entire northern section, to your left if you're on Route 199 traveling clockwise, is comprised of two beach shorelines, the Plage de la Point l'Est (from Grosse Ile along the western side of the V) and the Plage de la Grande Echouerie — perhaps one of the most beautiful beaches in the world (along the eastern side of the island). The panorama of Ile de Brion to the north, over the dunes and the sea, is magnificent; and the southern view of the lagoon is equally so, especially at sunset.

Route 199 goes into the village of Old Harry, where the Anglican chapel is located, and on through to Ile de la Grande Entrée.

Ile de la Grande Entrée is a peninsula extending south from Ile de l'Est, helping to form the Lagune de la Grande Entrée, to a large bay, known as Havre de la Grande Entrée. Camping space on the island is limited to the 38-site *Grande Entrée Campground* (phone: 418-985-2833); *Base de Plein-Air "Les-Iles"* (phone: 418-985-2833) also is near Bassin Aux Huitres and offers accommodations.

Since the highway does not jump across the mouth of the lagoon, the Chenal de la Grande Entrée, to the northern extension of Ile du Havre aux Maisons, the Plage de la Dune du Sud, the return trip means retracing steps through Leslie and the Dune du Nord.

Halfway south on the Dune du Nord, take Route 199 across a causeway to Ile du Havre aux Maisons. This island comprises most of the eastern shoreline of the archipelago, so it's not so odd that the majority of the shipwrecks occurred on its shores as the boats sailed west to the New World. The northern section of the island is relatively barren, but the southern end is well settled. Be sure to visit the lighthouse at Cap Alright and the shipwreck at nearby Pointe Basse.

From here to Cap aux Meules is a quick ride west and south — across a short causeway and down the west coast of the island.

A short visit to Ile d'Entrée makes for a pleasant day — just rock formations, birds, and its own fishing port, of course.

For general information call the Iles de la Madeleine Tourist Board (phone: 418-986-2245).

BEST EN ROUTE

Although the islands are not exactly overflowing with hotel space, a few places can handle guests very nicely. Fluctuating exchange rates, inflation, and seasonal demand make prices difficult to predict, but most establishments are priced moderately; none can be called expensive. In those places listed as moderate, plan on spending $45 to $65 for two, and in places listed as inexpensive, rates are under $45 for double occupancy. Note that the provincial family vacations network also offers accommodations in private homes at Etang du Nord (phone: 418-658-0576, for information). All prices are quoted in US dollars.

HAVRE AUX MAISONS

Des Iles – Fairly large by island standards (28 rooms) and a relaxing place to stay.Route 199 (phone: 418-969-2931). Moderate.

Thériault – An excellent motel, with 20 units and a restaurant. Dune du Sud (phone: 418-969-2955). Moderate.

Au Vieux Couvent – A 9-unit hostelry in a convent. The rooms are spartan, but the bar gets a crowd almost every night; the restaurant specializes in serving island mussel dishes. Route 199 (phone: 418-969-2233). Inexpensive.

CAP AUX MEULES

Château Madelinot – Some of the 101 units in this motel have kitchenettes, and there's wheelchair access. Route 199 (phone: 418-986-3695). Expensive.

Bellevue – In the main village, atop a hill overlooking the sea, is this establishment with 35 comfortable rooms and a restaurant. 40 Rue Principale (phone: 418-986-4477). Moderate.

■**Note:** In addition to the campgrounds mentioned in the text, camping is allowed almost anywhere. Just follow basic rules of courtesy and ask permission before setting up; don't camp on anyone's front lawn.

Saskatchewan

Saskatchewan's southern grasslands and vast farmlands can be deceiving, giving the impression that it is completely a prairie province, but, in fact, trees cover much of the province's 251,700 square miles. In the northern areas the terrain changes, most noticeably at Prince Albert National Park, the forested entrance to Saskatchewan's wilds. And, once you've passed Prince Albert, traveling by air is a virtual necessity. Many roads have only gravel surfaces, and service stations are rare. Despite this inconvenience, campers, hikers, and fishermen make their way to the region's remote camps and lodges.

Although best known for its wilderness and prairies, Saskatchewan has been in the forefront of political innovation ever since it elected the first socialist government in North America in 1944. The socialists initiated a series of programs that changed many people's lives. They established government-owned businesses, modernized schools, and brought electricity to 99% of Saskatchewan's farms through the Saskatchewan Power Corporation.

These accomplishments have not altered the nature of life in the province, however. With a population of about 1 million pretty evenly divided between city and country, it still is sparsely populated. Farming and wheat production are the leading industries, followed by oil production. Longtime residents remain aware of their frontier heritage. Branches of the *Western Development Museum* dot the province, each focusing on a different historical perspective. The museum in North Battleford, for instance, emphasizes the 1800s pioneer life, complete with an outdoor village duplicating the look and feel of the era. Museums around the province also reflect the long-standing presence of the Royal Canadian Mounted Police, especially in the capital, Regina (pop. 179,-000), the group's original headquarters. Regina and Saskatoon are the province's two major urban centers. For a sense of rural life, farm vacations can be arranged through the *Saskatchewan Country Vacation Association,* Box 654, Gull Lake, Sask. S0N 1A0 (phone: 306-672-3970).

In the following pages we offer three itineraries across Saskatchewan: east to west on the Trans-Canada Highway, slicing through the heart of the rich prairie farmland in the province's southerly quarter; south to north, from the US North Dakota border at Estevan through Saskatoon to splendid Prince Albert National Park, poised on the edge of the vast wilderness stretching to the Northwest Territories; and east to west across the very center of the province on the Yellowhead Highway, Saskatchewan's richest historical area, where the memory of the early frontier is strongest. At several points these routes meet, cross, and can be combined for even longer tours. A map of Saskatchewan and a detailed guide may be obtained from Saskatchewan Tourism (address below). Both documents also may be obtained from the Canadian Government Office of Tourism in major US cities.

Information: *Tourism Saskatchewan,* 1919 Saskatchewan Drive, Regina, Saskatchewan S4P 3V7 (phone: 800-667-7191).

The Trans-Canada across Saskatchewan

The Trans-Canada Highway (Route 1), running 370 miles (592 km) through Saskatchewan's southern prairies and wheatfields, offers a good way to see much of the province. This road, passing through the cities of Regina and Swift Current, is best used as a principal east-west path from which to take side trips to the many other interesting sights on secondary roads to the north and south. Moose Mountain Provincial Park, near the eastern border, contradicts the notion that Saskatchewan can't be green and glamorous. Farther on, the Qu'Appelle Valley is rich in history and contains beautiful parkland. Regina offers the full range of urban pleasures and is the home of the Royal Canadian Mounted Police training center. Moose Jaw numbers among its attractions a wild animal park and an important historical museum. A side trip will take you to an ancient Indian settlement and to an important point in Canada's frontier history. Near the western border, Cypress Hills is a welcome stretch of pine-covered hills and high plateaus, and Fort Walsh Historical Park features a reconstruction of one of the earliest RCMP forts. And all along the way there are spots for swimming, fishing, and hunting. The Trans-Canada road is excellent, and most of the secondary roads are quite good. The roadbed frequently dips to break the tedium of driving through flat country.

En Route from Manitoba – Route 1 enters Saskatchewan from Manitoba in the east, passing through a series of small communities. At Whitewood, 41 miles (66 km) from the Manitoba border, turn south on Route 9 for Moose Mountain Provincial Park, one of the most popular of Saskatchewan's parks, a 38-mile (61-km) drive. In Whitewood, stop at *Old George Collectibles* (Route 1; phone: 306-735-2255) for prairie Victoriana.

MOOSE MOUNTAIN PROVINCIAL PARK: The park, with Kenosee Lake at its center, consists of rolling terrain covered with aspen, white birch, and spruce. The park's origins go back to 1906, when R. B. Clark established a resort beach along Lake Kenosee. The present park's chief building is a chalet-like, stonework field house. First built in 1930, the building was damaged by fire and reconstructed as a relief project by men thrown out of work by the Depression. Today, besides functioning as headquarters for park operations, it contains meeting rooms, a dining room, and a kitchen. Park accommodations range from cabins to a modern motel. In addition, there are about 329 campsites.

Recreational facilities include an 18-hole golf course, beaches for swimming, privately operated riding stables, biking and hiking trails, tennis courts, water slide, and supervised children's activities. In addition, there is good lake fishing for pike, pickerel, and perch. A 15-mile (24-km) gravel road stretches into the forest area, where one may see moose or elk grazing in the early morning or early evening. The park, which houses some 450 beaver lodges, also is a nesting place for geese and a wide variety of birds ranging from wood ducks to blue herons and vultures.

Adjoining Moose Mountain Park is Cannington Manor Historical Park, site of a 19th-century venture in community-building. In 1882, Captain Edward Mitchell Pierce and his son came here to establish a traditional English manor system in the New World. The middle class Pierce, hoping to lead the life of an aristocratic Victorian squire on this land, established five tenant homestead farms, a wagon shop, a paint business, and sawmills. The colony lasted 15 years. The inherent impracticality of the scheme, coupled with Pierce's costly indulgence in horse racing, caught up with the community and the effort was gradually abandoned. Today, visitors can see the original church and reconstructions of the blacksmith and carpenter shops. The original schoolhouse has been turned into a museum of memorabilia from the colony.

En Route from Moose Mountain – Go north on Route 9 to Whitewood, and rejoin Route 1 heading west through Saskatchewan's prairies and farming communities. After 68 miles (109 km) you will reach the town of Indian Head, where you can tour the Canada Agricultural Experimental Farm and examine its landscaping and its demonstration gardens of grain, vegetables, flowers, and trees. Turn north on Route 56 to tour the Qu'Appelle Valley area.

THE QU'APPELLE VALLEY: The valley, forming the shores of Qu'Appelle Lake, is another pocket of timberland in the Saskatchewan prairie. The valley's ready supply of wood for fuel and building made it attractive to the pioneers, and it thus became an early stop on the fur trade route and a haven for the area's first white settlers. It is significant in Indian history because a portion of the Sioux nation, fleeing north after the Battle of Little Big Horn, sought refuge here. In addition, Pauline Johnson, the popular Indian poet of the 1890s and early 1900s, commemorated the valley in several poems. The valley now is known for its parks and its arts and crafts.

Route 35 merges with Route 10 and leads to the town of Fort Qu'Appelle, 20 miles (32 km) north of the Trans-Canada. In Fort Qu'Appelle, *Qu'Appelle Crafts* and the *Hansen Ross Pottery Studio,* have local handicrafts and pottery. A short ride south on Route 56 takes you to Katepwa Provincial Park, whose name in Cree means "river that calls." Katepwa is a lakeside park designed primarily for day use and family activity. Traveling west from Fort Qu'Appelle, you will quickly reach Echo Valley Provincial Park, another lakeside park that specializes in swimming and fishing. Returning to the Trans-Canada, drive 21 miles (34 km) east to the town of Wolseley where, on Front Street, you'll find the *Banbury House Inn,* a restored Edwardian mansion (ca. 1906) that is now a small hotel with 9 guestrooms, a cozy bar, European fare, and moderate prices for accommodations (phone: 306-698-2239).

The simplest return route is to follow Route 10 southeast 30 miles (48 km), from Fort Qu'Appelle. Rejoin the Trans-Canada at Balgonie, 16 miles (26 km) from Regina.

REGINA: Saskatchewan's capital began in 1882 as a small frontier settlement near a spot named Pile of Bones for its large number of buffalo skeletons. Feeling the need for another name, the residents christened the new town Regina, in honor of Queen Victoria. Today, it is a modern city, with a full range of urban facilities — not exactly a mecca for vacationers, but visitors will find a number of entertaining attractions in town. Perhaps the most interesting is the *Royal Canadian Mounted Police Museum and Training Academy* (off Dewdney Ave. on the west side of the city), which offer one of the best opportunities to view the past and present of the RCMP. The nation's major display of Mountie history, its exhibits focus on the history of the Northwest Mounted Police in the Old West. The collection includes uniforms and weapons, models of forts, photographs, and pictorial representations of historical moments. In addition, there are more unusual exhibits: the crow's nest of the *St. Roch,* a ship instrumental in the establishment of a Northwest Passage; the tobacco pouch that Sitting Bull brought with him when he fled to Canada; and, since Saskatchewan was the center of the Riel Rebellion of the 1880s, the crucifix Louis Riel carried to his execution. The museum also devotes considerable space to the culture of the Plains Indians. And, with an appropriate touch of whimsy, a corner of the museum is given over to photographs of Jeannette MacDonald and Nelson Eddy.

The training academy, the RCMP's national center for basic training of recruits, is open to visitors, who may observe recruits exercising and drilling. Tours are largely do-it-yourself, although guided tours can be arranged. As you would expect, basic training is basic training, so there's little difference between the regimen here and that in armies and police forces elsewhere. More picturesque are the ceremonial drills, in which the Mounties march in their red-coated uniforms. The sergeant majors' parade is Mondays through Fridays at midday.

Many of the other places to visit are located in Wascana Centre, a 2,300-acre, manmade park built around Wascana Lake in the southern part of town. Here are the Legislative Buildings, the provincial seat of government, and the main campus of the University of Regina. On the center's north side, off College Avenue, are the *Museum of Natural History* (phone: 306-787-2815) and the *Norman Mackenzie Art Gallery* (phone: 306-779-4771). The museum concentrates on the flora and fauna of Saskatchewan largely through dioramas and paintings. Other sections are devoted to Native American life. The museum, enjoying a high reputation, sponsors a number of conservation and archaeological projects throughout the province, the results of which are on exhibit. The art gallery is a traditional museum featuring European art from the Renaissance onward and contemporary Canadian and US work. Also on the center's grounds is the Diefenbaker Homestead. Relocated here from Borden, Saskatchewan, this is the family home of John Diefenbaker, Canada's prime minister from 1957 to 1963. Even if you're not interested in Canadian politics, you may find a visit to the homestead interesting since it is furnished in an authentic pioneer manner. In the middle of Wascana Centre, the *Saskatchewan Centre of the Arts* houses a 2,000-seat theater that accommodates touring productions. Near the arts center, on the lakeshore, is a wild bird sanctuary. From an observation point on the opposite bank you have an excellent opportunity to view Canada geese, ducks, swans, and other shore birds.

The City Centre, in the middle of the city, is the headquarters of municipal government and services. In the public library (12th Ave. and Lorne St.), the Prairie History Room exhibits documents on local history and the Dunlop Art Gallery shows the work of local artists. On 11th Avenue, in the old City Hall, is the *Globe Theatre,* Regina's professional company. The historical drama *The Trial of Louis Riel* is staged each summer in Government House. Nearby on 11th Avenue and Scarth Street is the stylish *Cornwall Centre* shopping mall. Next door on Hamilton Street is the *Galleria,* an architecturally trendy collection of boutiques that opened in 1989. Also worth your attention are the *Queensbury Downs* a few blocks west of City Centre. *Buffalo Days,* the annual summer fair, is held here each August, and the *Agridome,* a multipurpose, 7,000-seat complex, may well be housing an attraction at any time. As for sports, there's horse racing at the *Queensbury Downs* track (Exhibition Pk. between Elphin St. and Dewdney Ave.); golf at nine courses encircling the city; and football at *Taylor Field* (at Albert St. and Dewdney Ave.) featuring the *Saskatchewan Roughriders.*

There are several interesting places to dine in Regina. *Bartleby's* (1920 Broad St.) creates an Old West atmosphere with a stand-up bar, player piano, and antique decorations. The food is reasonably good, too. The *Elephant & Castle* (11th Ave. at Scarth St.) is an English-style pub serving beer and good food. *Mieka's* (11th Ave. and Smith St.) has a contemporary decor, an ever-changing menu of continental and vegetarian fare, and moderate prices. *C.C. Lloyd's Dining Room* in the *Chelton Inn* (1907 11th Ave.) offers fine continental fare. There are two dinner-theaters — *Stage West* (in the *Regina Inn,* 1975 Braod St.) and *Celebrations* (669 Albert St.).

From Regina, it is only 44 miles (70 km) to Moose Jaw via Route 1. On the way, you can take an interesting side trip by turning north on Route 301 just before you reach Moose Jaw.

BUFFALO POUND PROVINCIAL PARK: A 13-mile (21-km) drive brings you to Buffalo Pound Provincial Park, where 260 acres of fenced-in land provide a grazing area for a herd of buffalo. The park is an excellent place to observe these animals in something close to a state of nature. Outside the buffalo pound, the park offers horse rentals and guided trail rides along old paths through some interesting scenery. Fishing is permitted in Buffalo Pound Lake, and there are tennis courts and a swimming pool. The park has a cafeteria, a grocery store, and 202 campsites. During the winter, the park operates the White Track Ski Resort and offers tobogganing, cross-country skiing, and ice fishing.

Upon leaving the park, you can return south on Route 301 and rejoin Route 1 heading west to Moose Jaw.

MOOSE JAW: This industrial city (pop. 35,000) is set in the heart of wheat country. Of greatest interest is the Moose Jaw Wild Animal Park, open year-round. This full-fledged zoo features animals from all over the world, perhaps a welcome change of pace from moose and buffalo. The children's section emphasizes Saskatchewan wildlife. At the junction of Routes 1 and 2, one of Saskatchewan's four Western Development museums provides a visual record of the area's growth of culture and technology from pioneer days onward. The Moose Jaw branch specializes in the history of transportation, the exhibits running from horse wagons and dogsleds through trains and airplanes.

Apart from the zoo and the museum, most of Moose Jaw's attractions are annual events: the summer fair the first week in July; the *Saskatchewan Air Show* in early July, which features demonstrations of both antique and modern planes; and the *International Band Festival,* a mid-May competition that draws marching bands from all around North America. The 80-room *Park Lodge Motor* hotel (on Highway 1 at the junction of Highway 2) has a dining room.

    En Route from Moose Jaw – If you're interested in history, you may want to make a somewhat lengthy side trip south to see the St. Victor petroglyphs and the reconstructed fort at Wood Mountain. Follow Route 2 south from Moose Jaw for 88 miles (141 km); a side road takes you a few miles farther to the park.

ST. VICTOR PETROGLYPHS HISTORIC PARK: The petroglyphs are carvings made in a sandstone rockface by Indians in prehistoric times. Pictured are animal and human figures and totemistic renderings of human faces. Getting to the carvings is a somewhat strenuous venture; you have to follow a path to the foot of the cliff, then climb a series of stairs to get to the ledge. Also, since the figures have faded through erosion, they are best seen when the sunlight is not directly on them.

Returning to Route 2, head south for a short distance to an unpaved road leading to Route 358, about 10 miles (16 km) west.

WOOD MOUNTAIN HISTORIC PARK: Following Route 358 south to the junction with Route 18 brings you to the entrance road to Wood Mountain Historic Park, with two reconstructed buildings from the Northwest Mounted Police post that existed here from 1874 to 1918. The buildings feature photographs and artifacts relating to the history of the fort, especially the fort's most memorable episode: Sitting Bull brought the Sioux Nation north from Montana following the Battle of Little Bighorn to settle for several years in the vicinity of Wood Mountain.

    En Route from Wood Mountain – From Wood Mountain follow Route 18 west to Valmarie in Grasslands National Park. Then take Route 4 north to Route 1 and the town of Swift Current.

SWIFT CURRENT: A town of 16,000, Swift Current preserves an Old West spirit, although you'll find all the modern amenities. Its pioneer tradition is particularly expressed in the *Frontier Days* celebration and rodeo, held annually around July 1, and the amateur fiddling contest in late September. Swift Current is convenient for an overnight stop since there are plenty of hotels. Major attractions are not plentiful, but there are interesting exhibits on pioneer history at the *Swift Current Museum* (phone: 306-778-2775) and artwork at the National Exhibition Centre, downtown.

En Route from Swift Current – Before heading west on Route 1, you may want to drive north on Route 4 to Saskatchewan Landing Provincial Park, 24 miles (38 km) away. A historical marker pinpoints the spot where generations of pioneers had to ford or ferry across the South Saskatchewan River to reach the Battlefords Trail and the route into northern Saskatchewan. Indian gravesites and teepee rings can be found in the hills throughout the park. And there is the Victorian Goodwin House mansion, built of fieldstone in 1900.

West from Swift Current on Route 1, you head deeper into ranching country. To the north of the highway are the Great Sand Hills, an open area of dunelike hills harboring an abundance of wildlife. You can get a closer look by turning north on Route 37 at Gull Lake, 34 miles (54 km) west of Swift Current.

Continuing west, Route 1 intersects Route 21 after another 46 miles (74 km). Turning south on Route 21 quickly brings you to Maple Creek, with a couple of small, local museums along the main route. The *Old-Timers Museum* concentrates on local history. About 22 miles (35 km) directly south of Maple Creek on Route 271 is Cypress Hills Provincial Park.

CYPRESS HILLS PROVINCIAL PARK: The Cypress Hills are a singular twist of nature — hilly, high-level plateaus covered with rich forests set in the midst of flat, dry, low-scrub prairie. Scientists believe that 30 million years ago, a river flowing eastward left a deposit of cobblestone in the area that was gradually lifted into prominence by the erosion of the surrounding strata. Later, when the Wisconsin glacier moved across Canada, it bypassed the 80 square miles that today form the summit of the hills.

Cypress Hills is a relief from monotonous prairies. It is filled with buttes, ridges, and plateaus, with huge areas of rolling ranchland in between. There's a manmade lake with a chalet, condominiums, and cabins on the shoreline. This main area has a 9-hole golf course, tennis courts, a swimming pool, and a beach. Hiking trails lead around the park; the trail to Bald Butte promontory is especially scenic. You can drive through cattle country and see curiously shaped rock formations and the impressive Conglomerate Cliffs. And the woodland is a good place to observe deer, moose, and other wildlife. During the winter, the park offers downhill and cross-country skiing, snowmobiling, skating, and tobogganing. In addition to cabins, the park has 200 camping spaces.

FORT WALSH NATIONAL HISTORIC PARK: Directly west of Cypress Hills, Fort Walsh can be reached from the park if you don't mind some rougher-than-usual driving. A road from Maple Creek also leads directly to Fort Walsh. Fort Walsh was the original headquarters of the Northwest Mounted Police. In May 1873, a battle took place in the Cypress Hills area between US and Canadian traders and the Assiniboine Indians. The traders lost badly, followed by a hue and cry resulting in the establishment of the Mounties. Fort Walsh, built in 1874, served as the main patrol center until 1882. The old fort has been duplicated at its original site, with original artifacts lending authenticity. Horses are kept at the fort, but there are no historical reenactments or Mounties in period uniforms. For the visitor, what distinguishes Fort Walsh from other Mountie reconstructions is the isolated setting evocative of a bygone age. Nearby is *Farwell's Trading Post,* restored to 1872 conditions, staffed with costumed guides.

En Route from Fort Walsh – The trip back to Maple Creek returns you to Route 21 and from there to Route 1. Heading west on Route 1 for 25 miles (40 km) takes you into the province of Alberta.

BEST EN ROUTE

Since the Trans-Canada is a principal highway, there is no trouble in finding adequate hotels, motels, or campgrounds. Some of the Regina inns are elaborate, with on premises entertainment and recreational facilities. Elsewhere, the motels tend to be functional, clean, and modern. Rates for hotels and motels are generally reasonable. Expect to pay $60 or more per night for a double room in the expensive range, $35 to $60 in the moderate range, and $20 to $35 in the inexpensive range. All prices are quoted in US dollars.

MOOSE MOUNTAIN PROVINCIAL PARK

Fish Creek Campground – This government-operated property has 333 campsites, 131 with electricity. Showers, flush toilets, firewood, laundry, and a grocery store are on the premises. Open mid-May to early September. Just 4 miles (6 km) west of the park entrance (phone: 306-577-2144). Inexpensive.

Moose Mountain Park Cabins – There are 30 cabins of deluxe, modern, and semi-modern style. Open mid-May to September. Inquiries to Park Superintendent. Box 100, Carlyle, Saskatchewan S0C 0R0 (phone: 306-577-2131). Inexpensive.

REGINA

Landmark – The inn's 188 units are distinctively furnished and have air conditioning. There is a heated indoor pool, a sauna, and a whirlpool bath, bar, and restaurant. 4150 Albert St. (phone: 306-586-5363 or 800-667-8191). Expensive.

Ramada Renaissance – In the new *Saskatchewan Trade and Convention Centre*, it has an indoor pool, waterslide, and extensive dining facilities. 1919 Saskatchewan Dr. (phone: 800-667-0400). Expensive.

Regina Inn – The best business hotel in the center of town. All 237 rooms, the convention floor, and main level have been renovated. An outdoor whirlpool bath, indoor pool with sauna, an exercise room, 2 restaurants, and a cocktail lounge round out the facilities. 1975 Broad St. (phone: 306-525-6767 or 800-667-8162). Expensive.

Sheraton Centre – All 251 units have air conditioning. Guests can enjoy a heated pool, an indoor waterslide, and a restaurant. Victoria Ave. and Broad St. (phone: 800-325-3535 or 306-569-1666). Expensive.

Imperial 400 – A motel with 200 rooms and dining, convention, and entertainment facilities, as well as a sauna, whirlpool bath, and indoor pool. 4255 Albert St. (phone: 800-667-0400 or 306-584-8800). Moderate.

Seven Oaks – Another motel, this one has 156 air conditioned rooms, a heated pool, a dining room, and a coffee shop. 777 Albert St. (phone: 800-667-8063 or 306-757-0121). Moderate.

Travelodge – The expanded inn now has 165 rooms. There also is a 3-story waterslide and a restaurant and bar complex on the mezzanine. 4177 Albert St. (phone: 306-586-3443 or 800-255-3050). Moderate.

Sandman Inn – This hostelry has 184 units with air conditioning and TV sets; also a dining room, cocktail lounge, indoor pool, and whirlpool bath. 4025 Albert St. (phone: 800-663-6900 or 306-586-2663). Moderate to inexpensive.

MOOSE JAW

Best Western Downtown – A lodge that has 28 units with an adjacent restaurant. 45 Athabasca St. E. (phone: 306-692-1884 or 800-528-1234). Moderate.

Best Western Heritage Inn – In addition to 90 units, facilities include an indoor pool, whirlpool bath, dining room, and a cocktail lounge. 1590 Main St. N. (phone: 306-693-7550 or 800-528-1234). Moderate.

Harwood Moose Jaw Inn – There are 89 rooms with air conditioning, a heated pool, wading pool, and a sauna. Also a coffee shop, dining room, and cocktail lounge with nightly entertainment. 24 Fairford St. E. (phone: 306-692-2366). Moderate to inexpensive.

SWIFT CURRENT

Horseshoe Lodge – Here are 49 units with a good view of the countryside. There is air conditioning, a heated pool, a dining room, and a cocktail lounge. Highway 1E on N. Service Rd. (phone: 306-773-4643). Moderate.

Imperial 400 – A motel with 142 air conditioned units, indoor pool, sauna, dining room, and lounge. 1150 Begg St. E. (phone: 800-667-0400 or 306-773-2033). Expensive to moderate.

MAPLE CREEK

Maple Grove – It's got 14 rooms and 6 serviced trailer sites, so one may be a guest or park a recreational vehicle. Highway 21 and 1st Ave W. (phone: 306-662-2658). Moderate to inexpensive.

Estevan to the Northern Lakes

A south-north trip through Saskatchewan is a long journey. The distance from Estevan, near the North Dakota border, to Prince Albert, the northern-most city, is 363 miles (581 km). And if you choose to head farther north or to make side trips in the southern part of the province, you could double that. The southern part of the journey can be arranged so that you pass through Regina and Saskatoon, Saskatchewan's two major cities, and so that you can see many of the province's most interesting attractions. The route can appeal to your sense of adventure, since it takes you partway into Saskatchewan's great northern wilderness. Less than half of Saskatchewan is populated; the entire northern portion is open forest country filled with lakes and dotted with only a few settlements. This north country offers some of the finest fishing anywhere; for others, it is a chance to observe open, undisturbed nature. While many sites are accessible only by airplane, roads do lead a fair distance into the wilderness. If you choose, you may end your northward trek at Prince Albert National Park, which gives you a taste of the wilderness close to civilization.

En Route from North Dakota – There are 13 points at which the border may be crossed from the US into Saskatchewan. North Dakota's Route 52 brings you to the border at North Portal. Once across, you can follow Route 39 to Estevan, 18 miles (29 km) to the northwest. Shortly after setting out on Route 39, you may want to stop at Roche Percée to view the badlands rock formations inscribed with Indian carvings and the signatures of early explorers.

ESTEVAN: A small city of 10,500, Estevan is a major center for oil and coal resources. Boundary Dam, just south of town on Route 47, is the largest lignite coalburning power station in Canada; it is open for tours. Southeast, Woodlawn Regional Park houses a reconstruction of a Northwest Mounted Police barracks from the 1870s. The Estevan Brick Wildlife Compound displays a collection of area animals.

En Route from Estevan – The entire southern edge of Saskatchewan has a lot of badlands territory, but if you want to see more spectacular badlands terrain, take a side trip west on Route 18 from Estevan for 73 miles (117 km) to the edge of the Big Muddy Badlands. You can then head north on Route 6 for 66 miles (106 km) to Regina.

If the prospect of more badlands does not excite you, leave Estevan, heading northwest on Route 39. You will find more than enough semi-arid terrain along this route. After 53 miles (85 km) you will arrive at the next major town, Weyburn. Here the *Soo Line Historical Society Museum* (411 Industrial La.; phone: 306-842-2922) is devoted to exhibits on local history, and there is a small art gallery in the town library. Forty-four miles (70 km) farther northwest, Route 39 joins Route 6 at the village of Corinne. Although you will want to take Route 6 north to Regina, staying on Route 39 a few miles past the intersection brings you to Wilcox, site of Notre Dame College, founded by Father Athol Murray. The Tower of God, a place of worship on campus, is open 24 hours a day. Backtracking to Corinne, head north on Route 6 to Regina, 28 miles (45 km) away.

REGINA: For a full account of Regina and its attractions, see *The Trans-Canada across Saskatchewan,* the preceding route.

En Route from Regina – The best route north from Regina is Route 11, a divided highway that continues most of the way to Saskatoon. The 154-mile (246-km) drive can be made quickly, but one lengthy side trip is recommended — to Gardiner Dam at Lake Diefenbaker. You can reach the dam by turning west on Route 44 at Davidson, about halfway between Saskatoon and Regina. After 31 miles (50 km), Route 44 crosses Route 19. Turn north on Route 19 and you will shortly see a turnoff heading west to the dam, 10 miles (16 km) away.

GARDINER DAM: The largest rolled-earth dam in Canada, Gardiner is an impressive sight. Over 3 miles long and 5,300 feet wide at its base, the dam rises to a height of 210 feet. It lies across the South Saskatchewan River, its backwash turning a 140-mile portion of the river into Lake Diefenbaker. Danielson Provincial Park, established around the dam, provides for camping, swimming, fishing, and boating. A visitors' pavilion shows the workings of the dam, and tours are available. Farther south along the lakeshore on Route 19 is Douglas Provincial Park, which also offers a full range of lake activities adjacent to the smaller Qu'Appelle Dam. Just north of Douglas on Route 19, the museum in the community of Elbow contains a pioneer sod house and a portion of a sacred Indian rock, Mistusinne. The original 400-ton glacial boulder was used by the Plains Indians for their offerings to the spirit Manitou. The museum is open during the summer months.

En Route from Gardiner Dam – Return to Route 19 and head north for 14 miles (22 km) until the road intersects Route 15. Turn west on Route 15, and another 14 miles (22 km) returns you to Route 11 at Kenaston. Continuing north on Route 11, another 25 miles (40 km) brings you to a turnoff for Blackstrap Provincial Park, which boasts a manmade mountain. When Saskatoon was asked to stage the *Canadian Winter Games* in 1970, a demand was made for a ski hill. An extra 150 feet was added to a hill overlooking the lake at Blackstrap, giving skiers a run of 300 feet onto the ice. In addition to this somewhat treacherous hill, Blackstrap has fishing, swimming, and a campground. From here, it is 20 miles (32 km) to Saskatoon.

SASKATOON: For a full account of Saskatoon and its attractions, see *The Yellowhead Route of the Trans-Canada Highway* route, which follows.

En Route from Saskatoon – Continuing north on Route 11 brings you to an area of considerable historical interest. Three historical sights lie off Route 11 about 40 miles (64 km) north. The first of these, Batoche National Historic Park, may be reached by turning east on Route 312 at Rosthern, traveling 10 miles (16 km), then turning north on Route 225 for 6 miles (10 km). At Batoche, a decisive battle took place in 1885 between Louis Riel and his Métis forces and General Middleton and his NWMP troops. The Métis were Canadians of European-Indian heritage who were largely neglected by the Canadian government, and their sense of injustice spilled into armed revolt. But the defeat of their leader, Riel, at Batoche marked the end of their war. Although one more battle took place at Steele Narrows, the Riel Rebellion was over. Most of the signs of the battle have disappeared, but you can still see some bullet scars on the walls of St.-Antoine de Padoue Church rectory. Inside the building, photographs and displays commemorate the battle, and the graves of slain Métis are nearby. By returning east on Route 312 a few miles, then heading south on an unpaved road for 11 miles (18 km), you can see the Fish Creek Battlefield, where the rebellion began.

Returning by Route 312 to Route 11, a brief drive north brings you to *Duck Lake Historical Museum*. The museum includes exhibits on the Riel Rebellion, a jail that once housed the Indian rebel Almighty Voice, and material relating to the Indian community at Duck Lake. From Duck Lake, a trip 18 miles (29 km) west on Route 212 takes you to Fort Carlton Historic Park. Fort Carlton, partially reconstructed, was an early Hudson's Bay Company outpost. Inside the fort is a replica of an early *Hudson's Bay* store, and several other buildings have been furnished in period decor.

Returning to Route 11, head north 35 miles (56 km) to Prince Albert.

PRINCE ALBERT: The city of Prince Albert is considered the gateway to the north, the point where the rolling prairies give way to the heavily treed, lake-dotted parklands. The *Prince Albert Historical Museum* in Bryant Park is housed in a log church built in 1866. Exhibits relate to area history and the inevitable artifacts from the NWMP. Adjacent to the church is a blockhouse dating from the Riel Rebellion. Lund's Wildlife Exhibit, on the shore of the North Saskatchewan downtown, contains an excellent collection of North American animals. Both are open only during the summer.

There also is some chance to sample art in Prince Albert. *The Little Gallery* presents art shows in a building that was once an opera house. The *Prince Albert Art Centre* presents work of local, national, and international artists. And the public library on 12th Street houses a small art and crafts gallery.

The most interesting annual event is the winter festival held in February, with dogsled races and king trapper competitions, in which contestants try to duplicate legendary pioneer acts of strength by lifting 600-pound loads onto their backs, cutting wood at great speed with different kinds of saws, and cooking traditional Indian dishes. The more conventional summer fair is usually held the first week in August.

As a jumping-off point for expeditions farther north, either by road or by air, Prince Albert offers a bewildering number of routes from which to choose. However, one trip not to be missed is the relatively short journey north to Prince Albert National Park. Head north from Prince Albert on Route 2. After 21 miles (34 km), a turnoff west onto Route 263 will shortly take you into the park; travel 26 miles (42 km) north through the park to the main townsite at Waskesiu Lake.

PRINCE ALBERT NATIONAL PARK: Here is an excellent introduction to Saskatchewan's northern wilderness. Characteristic of the north country, the 960,000-acre park is filled with lakes, ponds, and streams formed thousands of years ago by receding glaciers. The terrain is hilly and forested, with white spruce, black spruce, poplar, and birch prominent. Animals, including elk, moose, deer, and bear, are abundant. Waskesiu Lake, with the park's townsite on its shores, is the main center of water activity, but Crean and Kingsmere, two other large, neighboring lakes, also are popular, as are the smaller Namekus, Hanging Heart, and Sandy. There also are many less crowded lakes and streams and hiking trails.

The Waskesiu townsite has several motels, cabins, and hotels, and campgrounds in and around the park offer 500 camping sites. Most of the recreational facilities are based at Waskesiu Lake townsite: tennis courts, an 18-hole golf course, riding stables, lawn bowling greens; rentals of houseboats, motorboats, rowboats, and canoes; a boat launch, if you've brought your craft; and a paddlewheeler tour boat that makes excursions on the lake (phone: 306-663-5253). Most other lakes are accessible by road, but Crean and Kingsmere can be reached only by boat from Waskesiu. The fishing for lake trout is particularly good at Crean and Kingsmere. From the boat dock on the northwest shore of Kingsmere, a long hike leads to the home of Grey Owl, an Englishman adopted by the Ojibwas who became one of Canada's greatest naturalists.

Though the park is open year-round, many motels, campgrounds, and park facilities close in early October. The *Lakeview* hotel (phone: 306-663-5311), with 44 modern rooms, is one way to enjoy the off-season; another is to make use of the 16 winter campsites, all with electric hookups. Cross-country skiing, ice fishing, and skating are available, with more winter activities planned.

En Route from Prince Albert National Park – Prince Albert Park can mark the terminus of your northward journey. But if you want a further taste of the wilderness or if you are interested in serious fishing, head north to La Ronge. Leaving the park by the Waskesiu Lake gate, Route 2 north, after 92 miles (147 km) through unpopulated countryside, takes you to La Ronge.

LA RONGE and vicinity: The town sits on the southwest shore of Lac La Ronge, a large lake surrounded by a myriad of smaller lakes and streams. It is a good fishing spot in its own right and serves as a launching point for trips to resorts deeper into the wilderness, either by car on the Route 102 continuation of Route 2 or by plane from La Ronge's small airport. In town are a few motels, some resorts, and a small campground. And on the north shore of the lake, another 13 miles (21 km) on Route 2, is Lac La Ronge Provincial Park, where camping, more or less in the rough, is permitted.

Lac La Ronge is a good place to catch lake trout, and the Churchill River, just to the north, is plentiful in walleye and pike. While it is certainly possible to fish entirely on your own here, especially if you've brought your own boat, resorts in the area provide guides. *Kikinahk Friendship Centre* (phone: 306-425-2051), *Red's Camps* (phone: 306-425-2163), and *Camp Kinisoo* (phone: 306-425-2024) are resorts accessible by road and licensed as fishing outfitters. If you want to stay or use the facilities of a resort, it will be necessary to make reservations several months in advance. Even if you wish simply to rent a boat, you will do well to inquire ahead. The fishing season is short — from May to October — and resorts get booked up fast.

If you're not interested in fishing, Lac La Ronge and Churchill River are excellent for canoeing. The Saskatchewan Tourism Office, in a drive to promote canoeing, has worked out 56 canoe routes in northern Saskatchewan, several of them in the La Ronge area. A brochure detailing the routes is available on request from Tourism Saskatchewan (1919 Saskatchewan Dr., Regina). If nothing else, the La Ronge area is interesting as a place in which to get a stronger feel of the wilderness.

En Route from La Ronge – Fishermen can continue the eternal search for perch, pike, walleye, and lake trout farther north by road; wilderness buffs can use the same route to satisfy their sense of adventure. Just beyond the provincial park, Route 2, which became a gravel road several miles back, changes its designation to Route 102; the gravel road continues northeastward. For about 58 miles (93 km), it passes a series of smaller lakes, such as McLennan and Brabant, with a number of small, primitive campgrounds along the lakeshores. While roadside facilities are being developed and an occasional gas station can be found, it is wise to leave La Ronge with a full tank of gas and to keep your eye on the fuel gauge. Shortly past Brabant Lake, the road forks. Route 102 continues on for 27 miles (43 km) to the southern shore of large Reindeer Lake, where there is a small campground. Route 905 heads north for the long trip to Wollaston Lake. The Wollaston Lake camps all offer fly-in packages, and the most prominent, *Wollaston Lake Lodge* (phone: 306-633-2032), is almost exclusively a fly-in operation. Route 905 ends east of Collins Bay at Wollaston Lake. Be sure to have a full tank of gas, a good spare tire, and to drive very carefully on the gravel surface.

Saskatchewan maintains a list of fishing resorts and outfitters. The list, available from Tourism Saskatchewan (1919 Saskatchewan Dr., Regina) should be consulted by anyone seriously planning a fishing trip. You also can get further details on fishing by checking *Where They Bite,* DIVERSIONS. Again, reservations at fishing camps should be made months in advance.

An alternate fishing route from La Ronge is to backtrack south on Route 2 to the intersection with Route 165, 12 miles (19 km) south of town. Heading east on Route 165 through open country for 60 miles (96 km) to Route 106, then east for 18 miles (29 km) brings you to the shores of Deschambault Lake, a good spot for pike. Just before Deschambault, the road changes its designation to Route 106, and *Northern Lights Lodge* (mobile telephone: JP32028) and *Deschambault Lake* resort (phone: 306-632-2166) are both accessible from the highway. Route 106 turns northeast, and another 25 miles (40 km) brings you to the intersection with Route 135. Turning north on Route 135 quickly brings you to Jan Lake, famous for its pike fishing. There are five licensed outfitter lodges here, of which *Jan Lake Lodge* (phone: 306-632-4416) and *Martin's Cabins* (phone: 306-632-4400) are the most developed. Following Route 135 north for 25 miles (40 km) brings you to Pelican Narrows, another excellent fishing spot.

From the city of Prince Albert, it is possible to take a 155-mile (248 km) drive northeast via Routes 3, 55, and 924 to Dore Lake for fishing. And the city serves as a base for fly-ins to remote camps, such as Reindeer Lake, Cree Lake, and Wollaston Lake.

BEST EN ROUTE

Although only a few motels and campgrounds are listed here, you'll find a steady supply along this route. The greatest number — and most comfortable — are in Regina and Saskatoon, and these are discussed in the previous and following *Best en Route* sections. Otherwise, no accommodations along this route can be classified as expensive. Expect to pay $40 to $60 for two in the moderate range and under $40 in the inexpensive range. All prices quoted are in US dollars.

WEYBURN

Weyburn Inn – In addition to the 70 rooms, there is a coffee shop, dining room, and cocktail lounge. 5 Government Rd. (phone: 306-842-6543). Moderate.

REGINA

For a list of Regina's accommodations, see *The Trans-Canada across Saskatchewan,* the preceding route.

SASKATOON

For Saskatoon accommodations, see *The Yellowhead Route of the Trans-Canada Highway.*

PRINCE ALBERT

Imperial 400 – In addition to its 137 units, this motel has a heated pool and coffee shop. 3580 Second Ave. W. (phone: 306-764-6881). Moderate.

Marlboro Inn – A 112-unit hostelry with an indoor pool, a dining room specializing in smorgasbord, and a cocktail lounge. 67 13th St. E. (phone: 800-667-0400 or 306-763-2643). Moderate.

Coronet – There are 100 units, an indoor pool, whirlpool bath, sauna, dining room, and cocktail lounge with entertainment. 3551 Second Ave. W. (phone: 800-667-0400 or 306-764-6441). Moderate to inexpensive.

PRINCE ALBERT NATIONAL PARK

Northland – There are 13 units in this Waskesiu Lake townsite. Open April 15 to mid-October. Reservation deposit required. Box 57, Waskesiu (phone: 306-663-5377). Moderate.

Skyline – A 21-unit motel in Waskesiu. Reservation deposit required. Open April 1 to October 31. Box 22, Waskesiu (phone: 306-663-5461). Inexpensive.

Beaver Glen Campground – Here are 213 sites, showers, flush toilets, a dump station, and firewood. Operated by Parks Canada; open mid-May to late-September. Near the townsite (phone: 306-663-5322). Inexpensive.

The Yellowhead Highway

The Yellowhead Route of the Trans-Canada Highway describes a connected series of east-west routes through Canada's four western provinces. A promotional effort by the municipalities and businesses along the route, it calls attention to attractions that might otherwise be bypassed. The Yellowhead crosses central Saskatchewan, entering from Manitoba just east of Langenburg on Route 16, and heads northwest through Yorkton, Saskatoon, and North Battleford, entering Alberta at Lloydminster. The length of the Yellowhead in Saskatchewan is 433 miles (693 km). As a basic route, the Yellowhead gives you a fairly good view of Saskatchewan if you make side trips. The route is rich in reminders of the frontier of the late 1800s: three of Saskatchewan's Western Development museums, at Yorkton, Saskatoon, and North Battleford; fort sites at Fort Battleford Historic Park and Fort Pitt Historic Park; and battle sites at Cut Knife and Steel Narrows. Saskatoon is a large, modern city. Several provincial parks offer scenery, hiking, swimming, and fishing.

En Route from Manitoba – After entering Saskatchewan on Route 16, you pass quickly through the small communities of Marchwell and Langenburg. At Churchbridge, 18 miles (29 km) west of the border, you have your first opportunity for a side trip. Head north on Route 8 for 48 miles (77 km) to Kamsack, turn east for a few miles on Route 5 to Duck Mountain Provincial Park.

DUCK MOUNTAIN PROVINCIAL PARK: One of Saskatchewan's most picturesque parks, Duck Mountain is set in highlands formed over 10,000 years ago when glaciers halted their progress southward, melting where they stood. Tons of silt, sand, and gravel fell from the ice to form a hummocky moraine, "knob and kettle" topography. The center of the park is Madge Lake. Small and relatively shallow, it is a source of good perch, pickerel, and pike. Tall aspen cover the countryside. Whitetail deer and moose are abundant as are black bear and many fur-bearing animals; on occasion, golden and bald eagles can be seen. There are cabins and condominiums for rent. *Duck Mountain Lodge* (phone: 306-542-3466), in the park, handles all park accommodations. Recreational facilities include an 18-hole golf course and bicycle and hiking trails. Because of its higher elevation, the park is cooler and rainier than the surrounding plains.

En Route from Duck Mountain Park – Wend your way back to the Yellowhead through interesting countryside. If you head west on Route 5, you will find many signs of Ukrainian culture in this grain farming area. Most visible are the silver-domed Ukrainian Orthodox churches. At the village of Veregin, 13 miles (21 km) west of Duck Mountain Park, the *Museum of the Society of Doukhobors* (PO Box 99, Veregin; phone: 306-542-4441) is devoted to traditional Russian culture. At Canora, 28 miles (45 km) west of Duck Mountain, you can see the area's finest example of a Ukrainian church. Turn south onto Route 9 to rejoin the Yellowhead Highway at Yorkton.

GOOD SPIRIT LAKE PROVINCIAL PARK: Along the way, you will pass Good Spirit Lake Provincial Park, a translation of the Indian Kitchimanitou. A Hudson's Bay Company trading post in the 1880s, the site was established as a provincial park in 1931. It may be reached by unpaved roads from Canora or you can travel a few miles south on Route 5 and turn west on Route 229 for a short drive to the southeast entrance. Sand dunes stretching for 3 miles from the lakeshore reach heights of 18 feet. The shallow, sandy water makes for an easy swim. The park, heavily treed with poplar, offers 157 secluded, tree-lined campsites, each with its own fireplace and picnic table.

From the park, continue south on Route 5 to Yorkton, 31 miles (50 km) south of Canora.

YORKTON: A city of 16,000, Yorkton is a commercial center for the surrounding farming area. Its branch of the *Western Development Museum* (Western Development museums record daily life and industry in the late 19th and 20th centuries) focuses on Saskatchewan's ethnic groups and the development of agricultural technology. There are rooms furnished in the manner of the English, French, Ukrainian, and Swedish; the Plains Indians are represented by a tepee and bark canoe. The agricultural exhibits include a collection of old and new farm machinery. Most intriguing are the specimens of early tools. The museum, on the western portion of Route 16, is open all year.

The *Yorkton Art Council* (Smith St.) houses visiting art shows as well as a small permanent collection, and *Norinne Creative Hands* (on Broadway downtown), sells local handicrafts. A winter fair is held in February, a multicultural festival in June, and a summer fair in August. A *Pioneer Thresherman's* show is held in late summer. The *Yorkton Short Film & Video Festival,* which attracts entries from around the world, also is held every summer.

En Route from Yorkton – Go west on the Yellowhead, Route 16, through more farming country, to the town of Wynyard, 90 miles (144 km) northwest of Yorkton near the famous Quill Lakes. On one of the principal migration flyways for birds, the lakes provide 100 miles of shoreline for waterfowl nesting. A short drive north from Wynyard on an unpaved road will take you to the lakeshore, excellent for waterfowl hunting or a beautiful view. Continue west from Wynyard on Route 16 to Lanigan, another 37 miles (59 km). The area from here west toward Saskatoon contains a number of potash mines. Unfortunately, none offer public tours. From Lanigan it is 77 miles (123 km) to Saskatoon.

SASKATOON: A city of 177,600 on the banks of the South Saskatchewan River, Saskatoon is known as the City of Bridges. The riverfront and its many parks are a skillful blending of urban design with the work of nature. The *Bessborough* hotel (601 Spadina Crescent, Saskatoon; phone: 306-244-5521), built by the *Canadian National Railroad* in the 1930s, is a riverfront landmark downtown. On the opposite shore is the campus of the University of Saskatchewan.

Saskatoon's *Western Development Museum* (on Lorne Ave. in the southern part of the city) features Boomtown 1910, an indoor reconstruction of a frontier main street and stores a city block long. There are no false fronts; all the buildings are complete and fully furnished with material from the early 1900s. Footsteps echo on the wooden sidewalks as people roam the frame buildings. Cars and buggies are parked on the street, and a railway station is at one end of town. Some of the buildings include a barbershop, hotel, print shop, fire hall, town hall, dry goods store, drugstore, bank, school, and a church brought to the museum from a small village. The old-fashioned

Palace Theatre shows silent movies and historical films. The balcony on the *Saskatchewan* hotel is a good place from which to observe the Boomtown. Other exhibits include collections of vintage cars, farm machinery, and small planes. Some of the old farm machinery is used in threshing competitions during the fair at the nearby exhibition grounds during the third week of July.

The *University of Saskatchewan Museum of Anthropology and Archaeology*, in the Arts Building (phone: 306-966-4175), devotes much space to the life of Saskatchewan Indians before the coming of the white man. A small, privately operated Ukrainian museum is open during the summer. The *Ukrainian Museum of Canada* (910 Spadina Crescent, E.) houses exhibits of traditional clothing and handicrafts.

The *Mendel Art Gallery and Conservatory* (on Spadina Crescent on the riverfront) houses visiting exhibitions; its permanent collection includes Canadian, European, and Eskimo art. *Herold's Art Studio* (404 32nd St. W.) features native and local paintings. The *Photographer's Gallery* (236 Second Ave. S.) also emphasizes local work. Old time-keeping devices are available at *Wilkie's Antique Clocks* (Ave. L and 22nd St. W.), *Past and Present Antiques* (327 21st St. W.), *Prairie Pottery* (35-158 Second Ave. N.), and the *Trading Post* (226 Second Ave. S.). On the east side of town, off 115th Street, Forestry Farm Park exhibits 300 live animals from the Saskatchewan region and has picnic areas on the grounds.

Saskatoon's isolation hasn't hindered its residents' interest in food. Its restaurants include the *St. Tropez Bistro* (243 Third Ave. S.), which serves French fare; *Cousin Nik's* (1110 Grosvenor), a top-quality prairie steakhouse; and *Taunte Maria's* (2750 Faithfull Ave.) offers heavy Mennonite food.

The city's annual events include a Ukrainian festival in mid-May, *Louis Riel Day* and the annual exhibition in July, and a multicultural festival in August.

En Route from Saskatoon – If you want a day's run from Saskatoon, two small parks are within easy reach. Pike Lake Provincial Park, 19 miles (30 km) south, can be reached by taking Route 7 out of Saskatoon and going south on Route 60. Blackstrap Provincial Park lies 22 miles (35 km) to the south just off Route 11. Both have sandy beaches, boating, and fishing. From Saskatoon, the Yellowhead continues northwest 86 miles (138 km) through more farming country to North Battleford.

NORTH BATTLEFORD: This city and an adjacent smaller town, Battleford, are of interest for Fort Battleford National Historic Park and for the *Western Development Museum* (at the junction of Highways 16 and 40) featuring an outdoor reconstruction of a pioneer village. In contrast to Saskatoon's Boomtown, this village emphasizes home life, pioneer virtues, and the area's ethnic diversity. The village, comprised of 26 buildings, includes homes furnished in the manner of Ukrainian and French Canadian settlers, a railroad station, a barbershop, and a schoolhouse. The indoor exhibits concentrate on the history of agricultural technology and include examples of new and old machinery and tools. The museum is located at the junction of Routes 16 and 40.

Fort Battleford National Historic Park, across the North Saskatchewan River just off Central Avenue in Battleford, commemorates the Mountie post established here in 1876, which served as the capital of the Northwest Territories and played an important part in the Riel Rebellion. Five of the original buildings still stand; they are restorations, not reconstructions. Most impressive is the commanding officer's house, furnished with authentic Victorian furniture and rugged pioneer necessities like washbasins and wood stoves. The other buildings, including two barracks, a guardhouse, and the government house, display artifacts and other material.

In North Battleford, exhibits can be seen at the *North Battleford Arts Centre* (1301 104th St.) and at the *Western Development Museum* (junction of Highways 16 and 40). For handicrafts in Battleford, your best bet is the *Heritage Handcraft Society Spring Sale,* held each year in March.

Due west on Route 40, 25 miles (40 km) to the town of Cut Knife, is the Cut Knife Battlefield Historic Site, where plaques commemorate an 1885 battle between the Indians and the NWMP. In the west side of town, the *Clayton McLain Memorial Museum* (in Tomhawk Park) is a private operation with more exhibits on the battle and on pioneer and Indian life.

En Route from North Battleford – At this point you may follow Route 16 to the Alberta border, but if you still wish to see Saskatchewan scenery and historic sites, a trip north from the Yellowhead route will be rewarding. Taking Route 4 north from the Battlefords for 25 miles (40 km) brings you to Battlefords Provincial Park, geared for the camper with 380 camping sites, 168 of which have electricity. The golf course is the main attraction, and fishing is popular. Jackfish Lake is ideal for swimming. If you double back a short distance from the park, Route 4 will intersect Route 26 heading northwest. A drive up Route 26 will begin to introduce you to Saskatchewan's northern lake country, and after 100 miles (160 km) will bring you to the Steele Narrows Historic Park, the site of the 1885 battle that led to the final defeat of Louis Riel and the rebels. With the exception of some historic markers, the battlefield is the same as it was nearly a century ago.

Another 29 miles (46 km) north on Route 26 brings you to Meadow Lake Provincial Park.

MEADOW LAKE PROVINCIAL PARK: Meadow Lake, a large park centered around a series of lakes, sits on the edge of Saskatchewan's northern wilderness, yet it includes enough facilities so that the visitor never seems to be roughing it. The park offers a slight taste of wilderness free of commercialism, with no restaurants, bars, golf courses, tennis courts, or riding stables. But there are cabins for rent and 736 camping sites. Canoes can be rented, and fishing for pike and perch is good in all the lakes. Hunting is permitted in certain areas; check for signs. Cross-country skiing and power tobogganing are popular in the winter. The park is full of wildlife, with plenty of black bear and moose and pockets of elk, wolves, foxes, and coyotes.

En Route from Meadow Lake Park – Route 21 leads south from the western end of the park. But it is a rough road and you may find it easier to retrace your drive on Route 26. At St. Walburg, turn west on Route 3. After 17 miles (27 km) you will see a turnoff heading north; it's a short drive to the village of Frenchman Butts, where you can still see rifle pits left from the Riel. After returning to Route 3, another 10 miles (16 km) brings you to Fort Pitt Historic Park. An early Hudson's Bay Company post (1829) later figured in the Riel Rebellion. In the park, exhibits and reconstructions retrace this history. Fifteen miles (24 km) beyond Fort Pitt, Route 3 intersects Route 17, which runs along the Saskatchewan-Alberta boundary. Heading south on Route 17 for 16 miles (26 km) will bring you to Lloydminster and the Yellowhead portion of the Trans-Canada Highway.

LLOYDMINSTER: Straddling the Saskatchewan-Alberta border, Lloydminster was founded in 1903 by the British Barr colonists. Most of the interesting sights in town are located in the *Barr Colony Antique Museum* complex in Weaver Park. The museum's buildings contain exhibits on the Barr Colony, the RCMP, and area history. *Fuch's Wildlife Display,* in the complex, features preserved animals in settings duplicating their natural habitat. Also on the grounds is a gallery featuring more paintings by Berthold Imhoff. From Lloydminster, continue on the Yellowhead into Alberta.

BEST EN ROUTE

The best hotels and the widest range of accommodations are found in Saskatoon. But Yorkton and Lloydminster also offer a good selection of inns, and all along the route are motels for overnight stops. The best bets if you're camping are the government-operated Yellowhead Highway campgrounds and provincial parks campgrounds. Apart from Saskatoon, motel and hotel rates are not high. Expect to pay $60 to $90 per night for a double room in the expensive range, $40 to $60 in the moderate range, and under $40, inexpensive. All prices are quoted in US dollars.

YORKTON

Holiday Inn – This motor inn has 91 units, with a heated indoor pool, a wading pool, sauna, and a whirlpool bath. Also a restaurant specializing in Russian food and a nightclub. 110 E. Broadway (phone: 306-783-9781 or 800-667-1585). Expensive to moderate.

SASKATOON

Holiday Inn – Adjacent to a shopping mall and the *Centennial Auditorium,* this 187-unit motel has a heated indoor pool, a restaurant, and a cocktail lounge with entertainment. First Ave. and 22nd St. E. (phone: 306-244-2311 or 800-465-4329). Expensive.

Ramada Renaissance – This place has 291 rooms in an 18-story downtown tower. It has 14 luxury suites with extension phones and wet bars. There are 2 super waterslides in the recreation complex, which also has a sauna, whirlpool bath, and an indoor pool. Satellite TV and nightly entertainment also are available. 405 20th St. E. (phone: 800-667-0400). Expensive.

Saskatoon Inn – This establishment, 2 minutes from the airport, features a central courtyard with tropical plants. Each of its 257 rooms has a queen-size bed, and there is a sauna, whirlpool bath, indoor pool, nightly entertainment, a lounge, a coffee shop, and a licensed restaurant. 2002 Airport Dr. (phone: 306-242-1440 or 800-667-8789). Expensive.

Sheraton-Cavalier – The inn has 250 units, a pool, sauna, and a whirlpool bath. A restaurant-nightclub overlooks the river. 612 Spadina Crescent E. (phone: 306-652-6770 or 800-325-3535). Expensive.

Sands Motor Inn – Centrally located, with 171 modern rooms, convention facilities, free parking, nightly entertainment, an indoor pool, and a sauna. 806 Idylwyld Dr. N., on Yellowhead Highway 16 (phone: 306-665-6500). Expensive to moderate.

TraveLodge – Near the airport, with 221 units, an indoor pool with a waterslide, sauna, whirlpool bath, exercise room, and a dining room. 106 Circle Dr. W. (phone: 306-242-8881 or 800-255-3050). Expensive to moderate.

Parktown – This place has 109 units, with a heated indoor pool, sauna, whirlpool bath, restaurant, and disco. 924 Spadina Crescent E. (phone: 306-244-5564 or 800-667-3999). Moderate.

Holiday House – These 107 units are complemented by a heated outdoor pool, dining room, and cocktail lounge with entertainment. 2901 Eighth St. E. (phone: 306-374-9111). Moderate to inexpensive.

Relax Inn – Close to the airport, this motel has 192 rooms and special accommodations for the handicapped. Other amenities include a licensed restaurant, pool, and satellite TV. Corner of Airport and Circle Drs. (phone: 306-665-8121 or 800-661-9563). Moderate to inexpensive.

King George – Centrally located, it has 104 rooms and extensive indoor shopping in an underground arcade. 157 Second Ave. N. (phone: 306-244-6133). Moderate to inexpensive.

Patricia – A small, quiet, 45-room hostelry with a restaurant and a pub, near downtown shopping malls. 345 Second Ave. N. (phone: 306-242-8861). Inexpensive.

BORDEN

Borden Bridge Campground – Of 29 campsites, 12 have electricity. There are pit toilets, a dump station, and firewood. Government-operated; open mid-May to early September. Route 16 in Borden, between Saskatoon and North Battleford (phone: 306-933-6240). Inexpensive.

NORTH BATTLEFORD

Capri – There are 97 rooms (47 more in the adjacent sister motel of the same name), a dining room, and a nightclub. 992 101st St. (phone: 306-445-9425). Moderate.

Battlefords Provincial Park South Beach Campground – Of 380 sites, 168 have electricity. Showers, laundry, flush toilets, dump station, and firewood are available. Government-operated; open year-round. Off Route 4, northwest of the park gate (phone: 306-386-2212). Inexpensive.

MEADOW LAKE PROVINCIAL PARK

Kimball Lake Campground – Of the 14 campgrounds in the park, this one is government-operated and has 217 sites, 124 with electricity. Showers, laundry, flush toilets, a dump station, and firewood are available. There also is a grocery store, a beach, a playground, and a boat launch. Open late May to early September. Off Route 26, inside the park (phone: 306-236-3382). Inexpensive.

LLOYDMINSTER

Tropical Inn – This hostelry has an indoor pool with water slide, a children's play area, and 72 rooms. 5621 44th St. (phone: 403-875-7000). Expensive to moderate.

Imperial 400 – A property built with 100 rooms, it can accommodate guests in wheelchairs. 4320 44th St. (phone: 306-825-4400 or 800-667-0400). Moderate.

Wayside Flag Inn – Offered here are 99 rooms, a poolside restaurant, executive suites, and nightly entertainment. Highway 16, 2 blocks west of the Saskatchewan-Alberta border (phone: 403-875-4404). Moderate.

Capri – A 60-room inn with a restaurant and bar. 4615 50th Ave. (phone: 403-825-5591). Inexpensive.

Cedar Inn – This small (50 rooms) motel offers queen-size beds and complimentary coffee. 4526 44th St. (phone: 306-825-6155). Inexpensive.

Voyageur – A very basic economy motel with 31 rooms. 4724 44th St. (phone: 306-825-2248). Inexpensive.

The Yukon Territory

> There are strange things done in the midnight sun
> By the men who moil for gold;
> The Arctic trails have their secret tales
> That would make your blood run cold.
>
> — Robert Service,
> "The Cremation of Sam McGee"

For thousands of years only the native Indians lived in the Yukon; then, in the 19th century, as part of its constant search for fur, the Hudson's Bay Company began to push north and west. Under the auspices of the company, Robert Campbell and John Bell explored the upper watercourse of the Yukon River and the northern sections of the territory in the 1840s. Trappers and traders followed the trail of Hudson's Bay trading posts, and in 1869 the Alaska Commercial Company moved in, extending the system of trading posts. Prospectors began drifting into the area as early as 1863, encouraged by finds of gold traces along the course of the Yukon River.

The land, acquired from the Hudson's Bay Company in 1870, became a provisional district in 1895. At that time less than 1,000 Caucasians lived among the native Indians. By 1898, they had mushroomed to more than 60,000, nearly all living in decadent splendor and desperation in this vast, wild land 4,000 miles from the nearest city of any consequence.

An epic human drama, the Klondike Gold Rush of 1898 lasted less than 5 years and changed forever the face of Canada's virgin, 207,000-square-mile Yukon Territory.

Approximately 100,000 people, mostly Americans, scrambled madly in pursuit of a fortune in gold, enduring hardships for which they were ill prepared, driven by "Klondicitis" — gold fever. Their materialistic quest resembled a mass pilgrimage or a holy war, as they crept over treacherous mountain passes like a stream of ants, each hauling a ton or more of supplies. Less than half even reached the fabulous gold fields, and of these, perhaps 20,000 actually panned for gold. Only 4,000 found anything of value. Ironically, few of the successful seekers could call themselves wealthy; the richest claims had been staked long before the hordes reached the fabled creekbeds. And for most of those who did make small fortunes, their new wealth slipped through their fingers as quickly as it had appeared in their gold pans. This is the dominant thread in the Yukon's brief historical tapestry.

Miners' tales are like fish stories — there's always a big one that got away, a spot left barren where somebody else got a strike. The incident that caused the Klondike Gold Rush, created several millionaires, and ruined the lives of hundreds stands as one of the toughest hard-luck stories of all time.

A miner named Robert Henderson found a river of gold, or at least knew where it was, and told fellow prospector George Washington Carmack. Carmack, a white man whose wife was a Stick Indian, was a rare individual for that place in those days — a well-educated man. He maintained a library and kept an organ in his Yukon home. Henderson, who apparently didn't care for Indians, may have antagonized Carmack. After learning the location of the gold from Henderson, Carmack and his two Indian brothers-in-law began to work the juncture of the Klondike and Yukon rivers. On August 17, 1896, Carmack found the large nugget that sparked it all. Carmack, Skookum Jim, and Tagish Charley (his brothers-in-law) laid claim to the area once called Rabbit Creek where it met the Eldorado Creek, and later known as Bonanza Creek. Henderson was never told, losing the chance to stake a claim to one of the biggest strikes in the Klondike. He established a claim on another rich section, but failing health prevented him from working it himself. He sold it for $3,000 to another miner, who took an estimated half million in gold from the claim. In his later years, Henderson was awarded a government pension as co-discoverer of the Klondike gold fields, but he died a poor man in Vancouver.

Rather than trace this intriguing yarn down murky museum hallways, travel the "Trail of '98" yourself. Follow the actual path of the gold-crazed hordes — stampeders, as they were called. Take advantage of a unique opportunity to step back in time and retrace history where it happened, adding substance and a sense of adventure to a Yukon trip.

The Yukon Territory is shaped like a right-angle triangle — wide at the bottom and tapered at the top. Its base rests on the 60th Parallel, which also marks the northern boundary of British Columbia; the upright, western edge leans against Alaska. The northern end, lying within the Arctic Circle, opens on Beaufort Sea. The jagged eastern border of the Yukon is shared with the Northwest Territories.

When the gold rush started, most of the boundary lines between these states and nations hadn't even been conceived. The vast majority of the miners sailed from West Coast ports, cutting through the offshore islands to gain access to the Lynn Canal, which leads past Juneau to a point of land formed by the mouths of two rivers, the Skagway and the Taiya. Both these rivers arise in the southwest corner of the Territory from the St. Elias Mountains, a component of the chain of coastal mountains that extend along the Pacific from Alaska to the Baja.

They docked at one of two settlements, Dyea or Skagway, where they prepared for the overland trek to the headwaters of the Yukon River. The Yukon headwaters are just 30 miles from the Pacific Ocean, yet it flows north almost 500 miles (850 km) to Dawson, turns west into Alaska, and cuts completely across it before emptying into the Bering Sea, traveling a total of more than 2,000 miles.

The task of crossing the mountains in time to reach the Yukon River before freeze-up — when the river would ice over and curtail travel to the gold fields — drove the stampeders to desperation. Two passes were found through the mountains, the Chilkoot and the White. The Chilkoot, which parallels the Taiya River into the mountains, is 32 miles (51 km) long, and the White, which follows the Skagway River for a distance, is 41 miles (66 km) long. The two passes meet on the shores of Lake Bennett, at the headwaters of the

Yukon River. At this point, the stampeders could load their goods on boats and float to the fields. The camps they established and the trading posts they patronized grew into towns, forming a thin lifeline into the wilderness.

Although the 1898 gold rush, the building of the Alaska Highway in 1942, and other encroachments of civilization have taken a toll on Canada's last frontier, the Yukon remains largely untamed wilderness. Just 28,000 people live in this 207,000-square-mile area, and more than three-quarters of them are concentrated in the capital of Whitehorse (pop. 20,700), which sprawls over 12 square miles. Dawson City (pop. 1,800), Watson Lake (pop. 1,650), and Faro (pop. 1,600) are the next largest communities. The remaining inhabitants live in small, isolated communities.

An excellent transportation system allows them to share this bounty with the estimated 300,000 people who visit the Yukon each year.

For air travel: *Canadian Airlines International* (head office: Scotia Centre, Suite 2800, 700 Second St. SW, Calgary, AB T2P 2W2; phone: 403-294-2000); *Alkan Air* (Box 4008, Whitehorse, Yukon Y1A 3S9; phone: 403-668-6616); and *Air North* (Box 4998, Whitehorse International Airport, Yukon Y1A 4S2; phone: 403-668-2228). A number of smaller carriers provide charter service from the outside as well as between distant points within the territory.

For bus travel: *Gray Line of Alaska* (300 Elliott Ave. W, Seattle, WA 98119; phone: 206-281-0576 or 800-544-2206); *Atlas Tours Ltd.* (5th Fl., 609 W. Hastings St., Vancouver, BC V6B 4W4; phone: 604-669-1332); *Atlin Express* (Box 175, Atlin, BC V0W 1A0; phone: 604-651-7617); *Greyhound of Canada* (2191 Second Ave., Whitehorse, Yukon Y1A 3T8; phone: 403-667-2223); *Norline Coaches* (2191 Second Ave., Whitehorse, Yukon Y1A 3T8; phone: 403-668-3355); *Watson Lake Bus Lines* (Box 469, Watson Lake, Yukon Y1A 3S9; phone: 403-536-7381); *Westours, Ltd.* (2191 Second Ave., Whitehorse, Yukon Y1A 3S9; phone: 403-668-3225); and *Whitehorse Transit* (110 Tlingit St., Yukon Y1A 2Y6; phone: 403-668-2831) create a bus network linking most of the towns in the territory.

Package tours can be arranged through *Atlas Tours, Ltd.* (609 W. Hastings St., 5th Floor, Vancouver, BC V6B 4W4; phone: 604-669-1332), *Princess Tours* (2815 Second Ave., Suite 400, Seattle, WA 98121; phone: 206-728-4202), *Greyline Yukon/Westours* (300 Elliott Ave. W., Seattle, WA 98119; phone: 206-281-3535), and *Gold City Tours* in Dawson (PO Box 846, Dawson City, Yukon Y0B 1G0; phone: 403-993-5175).

For backcountry expeditions in the Yukon, 75 outfitters arrange wilderness encounters, outdoor adventures, and hunting and fishing trips. *Rainbow Tours* offers wilderness boating, camping, and backpacking trips (3089 Third Ave., Whitehorse Y1A 5B3; phone: 403-668-5598). Two others to try are the *Inconnu Lodge,* fishing and recreational resort on the east side of the Yukon, and *Kluane Wilderness Lodges* — by air to Welsley Lake and beyond for fishing expeditions (PO Box 1268, Station A, Kelowna, BC V1Y 7V8; phone: 604-764-2133).

Before making up your mind, ask the Department of Tourism (PO Box 2703, Whitehorse, Yukon Y1A 2C6; phone: 403-667-5340) for a complete list of services. Also request the latest copy of the hunting and fishing regulations and a list of outfitters. Careful wildlife management is needed to prevent depletion of herds, so the territory is divided into 20 active registered guiding areas; one outfitter has sole rights to guiding and outfitting in each. Any hunter from beyond the Yukon's borders must be accompanied by a licensed guide. Grizzly, black, and brown bear, Dall's and stone sheep, woodland and barren-ground caribou, moose, and mountain goat are abundant, and so are white-tailed ptarmigan, rock ptarmigan, four types of grouse, and various ducks and geese. Bag limits are more than generous.

Anglers who fish the waters of the Yukon Territory had better start thinking of new ways to describe "the one that got away," because no one's ever going to believe it. The fish up here, like the mountains, are big. The largest lake trout taken in recent years was 87 pounds, and catches of 20 to 30 pounds are common. With a daily limit of five each for northern pike (average 3 to 4 feet), Arctic grayling, Dolly Varden, rainbow trout, steelheads, and salmon (with a 2-day limit in your possession at any one time), you know the fish are striking. And there is no closed season. Guides are not required for fishing trips, but they're recommended.

Hunting season starts in early spring and extends into late fall, but the principal tourist season runs from mid-May to mid-September. Summer daytime temperatures often soar to the high 80s F (30s C), but average July temperatures are in the high 60s F (20s C). Yukon winters, with readings as low as −50F (−45C), are no time to tour. Some roads, like the Taylor or Top of the World Highway, are closed to winter travel. Travel arrangements, especially hotel reservations, should be made as far in advance as possible or you may find yourself shut out. Expect to book at least 90 days ahead. Even dining reservations at popular restaurants should be made in advance.

A few quick notes about traveling in the Yukon:

About 20% of the route is on gravel roads, and though these are generally well maintained, it's a good idea to put protective covers over your headlights and screens on windshields to protect them from flying rocks and stones.

Lengthen your following distances, especially behind large trucks or buses, because dust obscures your vision. If you require unleaded gas, it's available nearly everywhere in the Yukon. However, gas is quite a bit more expensive in the Yukon than in other parts of Canada. The roads are patrolled thoroughly, and services are spread along most highways, but spare tires and changing equipment are a must. First-aid kits and some dehydrated foods aren't a bad idea either, and if you must travel during winter, they're a necessity. The same is true of a camp stove, to provide heat in case of emergency.

If you're camping or just cooking on the side of the road, avoid foods that are highly aromatic since most animals are sensitive to smells. Caribou, moose, and grizzly, black, and brown bears abound. Do not be alarmed by them, but remember they are wild, and lives have been lost through unnecessary and (usually) foolish acts. *Do not try to corner a bear* or in any way force him to move against his will. Don't create a bad situation by feeding bears or any other animals, and be sure to burn all waste and foodstuffs when you're through. If you are confronted by a bear, the best policy is simply to back away slowly and quietly. Do not run, yell, or scream. Remember that the wilderness of the Yukon is not an inherently frightening place. Common sense and caution will carry you through almost anything new.

The Yukon is outdoor country and Yukoners usually dress casually. Caribou and grizzlies, after all, aren't impressed with the latest fashions. Nevertheless, it's a good idea to bring along a nice outfit for nights on the town. You won't need a heavy-duty parka during the summer, but a sweater or jacket will be useful.

Today, you can follow the footsteps of the stampeders of '98. In this chapter we trace two routes through the territory. The Dawson Circle Route, which explores the contemporary Yukon, begins and ends in the capital, Whitehorse, traveling the highways through the mining areas of the Yukon and crossing into nearby Alaska. The Trail of '98 actually follows the path used by most of those hopeful prospectors as they crossed the Chilkoot Pass through the St. Elias Mountains and then rafted 500 miles north on the Yukon River to the gold fields at Dawson. Today that same trip is no less difficult for any traveler who attempts to challenge the mighty river. Either way, exploring the Yukon Territory is an experience not soon forgotten.

Information: *Tourism Yukon,* Box 2703, Whitehorse, Yukon Territory Y1A 2C6 (phone: 403-667-5340).

The Dawson Circle Route

For a broader view of the Yukon Territory, travel the Dawson Circle Route, 333 miles (533 km) northwest from Whitehorse to Dawson via the Klondike Highway (Routes 1 and 2) and return to Whitehorse by way of Alaska. Hook up with the Alaska Highway (Routes 9 and 1) to Tetlin Junction, Alaska, a distance of 170 miles (272 km). The Circle Route, about 1,125 miles (1,800 km), provides an excellent overview of the area. Cameras and binoculars are a must.

Allow at least 6 days and 5 nights to travel the circle from Whitehorse past Dawson, through Alaska, swinging back to Whitehorse. If you dabble in fishing or would like to hike in Kluane, the trip may happily be extended.

WHITEHORSE: Between a 200-foot clay escarpment and the banks of the Yukon River lies Whitehorse. The Yukon's capital since 1953, this city had its origins in the Klondike Gold Rush. In the spring of '98 thousands of stampeders drifted down the Yukon River through Miles Canyon only to encounter the treacherous Squaw and White Horse Rapids, whose frothing white foam resembled white horses leaping through the air. After the first few boats were wrecked and men drowned, the stampeders constructed a wooden tramway system around the canyon and the rapids. A small settlement developed at the northern end of the tramway, where the stampeders stopped to get their second breath before continuing downriver. This settlement, on the opposite side of the river from the present city, was called White Horse.

The White Horse Rapids were tamed by the construction of a power dam. From June until mid-September, you can take a 2½-hour cruise through Miles Canyon aboard the MV *Schwatka.* A running commentary details the history of the canyon and the rapids.

Transportation to the dock on Schwatka Lake is available from all hotels and most RV parks. For tickets and additional information, contact *Atlas Travel Tours* (609 W. Hastings St., 5th Fl., Vancouver, BC V6B 4W4; phone: 604-669-1332) or *Yellow Cab* in Whitehorse (Second Ave.; phone: 668-4811).

Take the South Access Road from Whitehorse to Miles Canyon if you'd rather drive. Turn left just before the railroad tracks and follow the road around the west side of Schwatka Lake. The canyon also can be reached via an access road from Km. 1470 of the Alaska Highway. A suspension footbridge spans the canyon, leading from the parking area to a trail on the opposite side. The site of Canyon City, where the stampeders built the initial stage of a tramline above the rapids, is off to the right about 7 miles (11 km). Although little remains of Canyon City, the walk is a pleasant one and the path easy. Even if you don't feel up to walking the full distance, the area is excellent for picnics.

Between 1898 and 1900, construction of the White Pass and Yukon Railway was carried out simultaneously from Whitehorse and Skagway, Alaska, until the two lines met at Carcross in 1900. The northern terminus of the railroad was on the west bank of the Yukon River. The original town of White Horse moved across the river also. This new settlement was called Closeleigh, after English stockholders in the railway. However, people soon started calling the settlement Whitehorse again, and the name stuck.

During the gold rush years Whitehorse was a busy place. As the trains rolled into the station, sternwheelers docked along the riverbank and filled with people and cargo destined for Dawson. You can still see the old wooden pilings protruding from the river behind the White Pass station on First Avenue.

Ironically, the rail link from Skagway was completed about a year after the gold rush ceased. Subsequently, Whitehorse's population decreased drastically. Copper mining sustained the town for a while, but by the 1920s this proved unprofitable and the population dwindled to less than 400.

By the river, at the end of Second Avenue, rests the SS *Klondike,* a restored sternwheeler. Magnificent boats such as this were once a common sight as they plied their way downstream toward Dawson. Long after the gold rush, sternwheelers retained their position as a major means of transportation. The SS *Klondike,* built in 1936, carried ore concentrates from the silver mine at Mayo to freight cars at Whitehorse until 1955. Daily tours of the ship, in summer, are free.

You'll probably want to spend a day or two browsing around and shopping in Whitehorse. Since the downtown area is compact, you can walk to most of the stores. Typically northern items, such as gold nugget jewelry and Eskimo carvings and prints are available. *Northern Images* (Fourth Ave. and Jarvis St.) has a beautiful, if expensive, collection of soapstone carvings. *Murdoch's Gem Shop* (Main St.) is another good but fairly expensive place. Yukon items such as mukluks, parkas, and beaded jewelry can be purchased at the *Yukon Native Products* (4230 Fourth Ave.); *Yukon Gallery* (in the *Westmark* hotel on Steele St.); *Mac's Fireweed Books & Gifts* (305B Main St.); or *Books on Main* (203 Main St.).

Relics from the gold rush period can be seen at the *MacBride Museum* (First Ave. and Wood St.). Open daily May through September: admission charge. As well as containing the first telegraph key used in the Yukon during the gold rush and one of the original engines used on the *White Pass and Yukon Railway,* the museum has a collection of mounted Yukon wildlife, such as wolves, Dall's sheep, and grizzly bears.

You'll feel as though you're back in the gold rush days with the 1898 gaslight decor at *Charlie's* in the *Westmark Klondike Inn* (2288 Second Ave, see *Best en Route*). Other good bets for dinner include *Angelo's* (202 Strickland St.), which serves Italian dishes; *Golden Garter* (210 Main St.), which serves pricey but good European fare in a Klondike setting; or *the Parthenon* (204 Main St.), specializing in Greek and European cuisine. An outdoor barbecue at the *Westmark Whitehorse* hotel (Second Ave. and Wood St.) can be fun (see *Best en Route*).

The big evening show in Whitehorse is the "Frantic Follies" at the *Westmark Whitehorse* hotel (address above). It's a gold rush vaudeville stage show with whooping cancan dancers and honky-tonk piano music. There are two shows nightly, from mid-June until mid-September. Get your tickets during the day rather than take a chance in the evening.

En Route from Whitehorse – It is possible to drive directly to Dawson — 333 miles (534 km) — in 1 day, but if you wish to visit Faro, allow a full day just for this side trip. Carmacks is just over 100 miles (160 km) away and marks the Faro turnoff.

Take the Alaska Highway (Route 1) north out of Whitehorse for about 7 miles (11 km) to the Klondike Highway turnoff, and follow Route 2 toward Carmacks. A secondary roadway, the Takhini Hot Springs cutoff, is 3½ miles (5.6 km) north and leads to the Hot Springs area 6½ miles (10 km) off the main highway. A cement pool holding the naturally hot spring waters is open from 8 AM to 10 PM, for swimming. Swimwear can be rented at the springs, and the cost of swimming is nominal. There also are dining facilities available, featuring German food.

Return to the Klondike Highway and continue northward to *Braeburn Lodge* (phone: radio operator 2M3987), 55 miles (88 km) away. Here you get the largest servings of food anywhere in the Yukon — and at good prices. One of the most popular items on the menu is the Braeburn cinnamon bun, about a foot in diameter. On opposite sides of the highway, Twin Lakes is only 16 miles (26 km) from Braeburn. These two small lakes and the surrounding picnic sites are great places to stop. If the pike and grayling cooperate, you can catch lunch or dinner on the spot.

CARMACKS: Named after George Carmack, whose discovery of gold sparked the Klondike Gold Rush, Carmacks is a small, predominantly Indian settlement. About 400 people live at this one-time sternwheeler port. Stop for a cold beer or coffee at the *Carmacks* hotel (Klondike Highway, mailing address: PO Box 160, Carmacks, Yukon Y0B 1C0; phone: 403-863-5221), and gas up your vehicle.

En Route from Carmacks – From Carmacks it's only 2 miles (3 km) to the Robert Campbell Highway (Route 4) and the turnoff to Faro. The highway follows roughly the same route taken by Robert Campbell, the Hudson's Bay Company employee who explored the Territory in the mid-1800s. It's a 112-mile (179-km) trip east to Faro. One place to stop for gas, rest, or a bite to eat is 78 miles (125 km) along the road at *Little Salmon Lodge.* Dawson is 224 miles (358 km) north of Carmacks on the Klondike Highway.

FARO: This young town, named after the card game, is the fourth-largest settlement in the Yukon (pop. 1,600). Built in 1969, Faro is primarily a company town servicing the Curragh Resources lead-zinc mine.

If you turn off the Campbell Highway onto the access road to Faro and continue for 14 miles (22 km) past Faro, you'll come to the Anvil mine operated by Curragh Resources. The mine reopened in early 1986, and tours are available from mid-June through mid-September; call 403-994-2600.

While there are many more beautiful spots in the Yukon, the town of Faro and its mine represent an integral part of Yukon life. Perhaps you'll better appreciate the uncivilized and natural side of the Yukon all the more for having seen Faro.

En Route from Faro – You may camp overnight in one of the three government campgrounds along the way rather than drive back to Carmacks. There's a campground 26 miles (42 km) from Faro at Little Salmon Lake, where you might catch some pike, grayling, or trout to fry up for a good dinner. You can dine as fashionably late as you like during the long summer days. There's an average of

20 hours of daylight in the Yukon during July. (The days get longer the farther north you travel.)

If you want to put a few more miles behind you before bedding down, there's another campground 81 miles (130 km) from Faro and only 31 miles (50 km) from Carmacks. This is the *Frenchman Lake Campground,* 5 miles (8 km) off the main highway. You can fish here as well.

Unless you want to camp along the way, there's not much more to detain you en route to Dawson. But that's not to say the drive is uneventful, for, as on any Yukon highway, you'll find yourself absorbed in the beauty that surrounds you. You'll pass over dome-shaped mountains and wend your way along forested lakeshores.

From Carmacks to Stewart Crossing, your next food and gas stop, is 111 miles (178 km). Just 14 miles (22 km) north of Carmacks are the Five Fingers Rapids. Although not comparable to the dangerous White Horse Rapids, they posed some problems for the old sternwheelers. Ringbolts, through which heavy cables were threaded to pull the riverboats upstream, are still embedded in the rocks of Five Fingers. This is a good spot to pull over and gaze upon the Yukon River flowing steadily 500 feet below you.

In another 52 miles (83 km) you'll come to Pelly Crossing, a small native community of about 100. Facilities include the Ft. Selkirk Trading Post, a gas station, and a store with groceries and native handicrafts. *North Tuchone Tours & Outfitting* (mailing address: General Delivery, Pelly Crossing, Yukon; no phone) provides 1- to 7-day guided tours that explore historical sites in the Minto, Ft. Selkirk, and Pelly Crossing areas. Enjoy trophy fishing here or listen to native elders interpret and demonstrate traditional crafts and ways of life. Drive another 45 miles (72 km) to reach Stewart Crossing, where there is a lodge with a café and tavern as well as a service station. Leaving town, you'll cross the Stewart River Bridge, turn left, and continue toward Dawson. Just 15 miles (24 km) beyond Stewart Crossing is the *Moose Creek Lodge* (no phone), with 5 rustic cabins and a café featuring hearty, homemade food such as sourdough pancakes and mouth-watering pastries. The lodge is open from mid-May through mid-September. From this point, you have just 98 miles (157 km) to go before reaching Dawson.

Eighty-seven miles (139 km) from Stewart Crossing you'll come upon the *Klondike River Lodge* (phone: 403-993-6892) and the Dempster Highway turnoff. Once again you can gas up and get a bite to eat at the lodge. Then, if you want to see virgin wilderness rather than heading into Dawson, you can travel the Dempster Highway for 45 miles (72 km) due north until you come to *Tombstone Mountain* (no phone), a government campground near the north fork of the Klondike River. There are very few services along this newly constructed road, built to connect Yukon communities with Fort McPherson and Inuvik in the Northwest Territories.

From the Dempster Highway turnoff to Dawson City is only 28 miles (45 km). A mile before you reach Dawson, the Bonanza Creek Road on your left will take you to the historic creeks of the gold rush and George Carmack's Discovery Claim, which started it all. The road winds through 11 miles (18 km) of tailings left behind by the gigantic gold dredges that soon replaced the 1898 prospector with his pick, shovel, and gold pan. Some of the claims are private property, but if you wish to do a bit of gold panning, you can do so at Guggieville, about a mile (1.6 km) from the Dawson city center on the Bonanza Creek turnoff (phone: 403-993-5008).

After seeing the creeks, you've only a mile to go before reaching Dawson.

DAWSON: For one brief year this former moose pasture at the confluence of the Klondike and Yukon rivers was hailed as the San Francisco of the North. This transformation had been brewing for 2 years, ever since that August day in '96 when George

Carmack plucked from the bed of Bonanza Creek a gold nugget, reputedly the size of his thumb.

The first eager stampeders arrived in Dawson during the late fall of '97, many of them having slipped into the Yukon with inadequate supplies of food. Later, Canada insisted that each person bring a year's supply of food and clothing. There were already 3,500 people in Dawson at that time, many of them old-time prospectors who had been panning the creeks of the north for years. But there was no food to be bought in Dawson that fall. The supply ships didn't make it through before the water froze. Warnings were given — and fortunately heeded by some — to evacuate Dawson and head for the nearest outpost, 350 miles away. Only this evacuation prevented a full-fledged disaster. While those who remained did not die of starvation, scurvy was prevalent. Food was so scarce that, for a sack of flour, one man traded a mountain sheep.

Finally, in the spring, the stampeders arrived with all their goods. The law of supply and demand operated in a classic fashion. One man lugged 200 dozen eggs over the trail and sold them for $18 a dozen. Within an hour he'd dispensed of them all for a total of $3,600. By the week's end, with thousands arriving daily, the market was so saturated with eggs that the price dropped to $3 a dozen.

In the early summer of '98, the many thousands who had been waiting impatiently on the shores of Lindeman and Bennett lakes started arriving in Dawson only to discover that the richest claims they had so fanatically sought had been staked even before anybody outside had heard of the Klondike. Supplies these men had laboriously transported over the mountains were sold at any price to raise the fare home. The muddy streets of Dawson took on the appearance of a huge marketplace. While certainly not the streets of gold so many expected, an air of decadent extravagance permeated the city of 23,000. Dance hall queens bathed in champagne, and butlers were installed in a few of the gloomy, 1-room cabins of prospectors living along the hillsides and creeks.

Posh hotels complete with chandeliers, Persian carpets, and Turkish baths sprang up along Front Street. In their dining rooms, these establishments served such delicacies as lobster Newburg, cold tongue, and Bengal Club chutney prepared by San Francisco chefs. The luxuries were brought to Dawson because the Klondike Kings, the men who first staked the creekbeds in 1896 and 1897, invested their fabulous fortunes in hotels, dance halls, and numerous shipping companies. Thus, ships laden with Paris fashions and fresh oysters docked continuously at Dawson's shore during the summer of '98.

One of the wealthiest of the original prospectors was "Big Alex" McDonald. He owned many claims, and from one of his richest he panned $5,000 a day. Big Alex, who died penniless, was soon known throughout the world as the King of the Klondike. Such was his fame that while in Rome he was granted an audience with the Pope. Curiously, Big Alex exhibited a distinct contempt for gold. He left bowls full of nuggets on his sideboard and urged guests to help themselves, explaining he had no use for the things.

Big Alex's attitude was shared to some extent by the stampeders of '98. Few hoarded the precious metal they had sought; these men had their values tempered on the trail. They were no longer the naive young men who had set off in 1897, oblivious to the trials awaiting them. No, these men had been forced to struggle daily for their very existence. They had walked the fine line between life and death, never knowing from one minute to the next what hardship would befall them. But they had survived, and they came to Dawson wiser yet all the more foolish for that. They spent their days either frantically panning the creeks seeking their own bonanza or working for wages on the rich claims of men like Big Alex. Collecting a supply of nuggets and dust, they rushed down to Dawson's dance halls and frantically dispensed of their riches.

The dance halls lining Front Street were like fun houses at a carnival. There was a room for drinking, a room for gambling, and upstairs, numerous rooms where the dance hall queens entertained their guests in private. There also was a theater, complete with balconies, from which the Klondike Kings gazed down upon the plebeian masses who gathered to enjoy vaudeville and the plays. When the show was over, the theater turned into a large dance floor that shook with the stomping of feet until dawn. A man had to pay to dance with one of the women and some paid dearly.

But even more popular than the dance halls were the gaming rooms, for these were men who had gambled from the beginning. On the trail they'd learned to play for stakes that were higher than gold. Their experiences crossing the passes and shooting the rapids had imbued in them a deep understanding of the gambling maxim — winner takes all, loser gets nothing. So fortunes were won and lost in these dimly lit back rooms. The stakes were high, the pot in one poker game amounting to $150,000. And not only gold was laid on the line; the ownership of the dance halls themselves came up for bid, and as often as not the establishment changed hands with the flick of a card. So pervasive was gambling that two men are reported to have actually wagered $10,000 in a spitting duel. The city's brief life was a carnival gone mad, a grotesque ball unmasked during the summer of 1899.

Rumors of a new gold find near the mouth of the Yukon River were confirmed in August of '99. The fever set in once again. In 1 week alone, 8,000 people left Dawson for Nome, Alaska. Some, however, chose to remain in Dawson and make it their home. But the Dawson they created was a far cry from the San Francisco of the North. An air of respectability prevailed while Dawson served as the territory's capital until 1953. The digging for gold continued, but the individual prospector was quickly replaced by companies of men using massive dredges. The damage these huge machines did to the creekbeds and hillsides is still apparent (the dredging continues today).

Today, about 1,650 people live in Dawson through the long, cold, dark winters. Most residents are either government employees or involved in the summer tourism industry. The city has been designated a historical complex, and in the summer of 1977 the Canadian government announced that $20 million would be spent to restore some of the buildings and mining sites. Apart from these areas of employment, there are still many who live along the creeks, mining for gold.

Although the elaborate display of wealth is gone, the memory of those golden days remains. You can almost hear the carousing as you stroll down wooden sidewalks past old and empty buildings. Unfortunately, numerous fires during 1898 destroyed all but a few of the structures from that period, and the derelict buildings you see today date back to the 1900s. One 19th-century survivor is Arizona Charlie Meadows's *Palace Grand Theatre*. Meadows, a one-time American Indian fighter, built the theater from two steamboats he purchased and demolished for the purpose and opened it in July 1899. It sat in ruins until 1962, when it was rebuilt by the Canadian government. You may tour the theater during the day; at night you can enjoy an authentic 1898 vaudeville production, the *Gaslight Follies.* Performances are held nightly, except Tuesdays, from the end of May through early September. Advance tickets can be purchased at the Dawson City Visitor Reception Center (Front Street; 403-993-5566) or at the theater (King St. and Third Ave.).

A pleasant way to spend a few hours in the afternoon is to take the Yukon River Cruise aboard the *Yukon Lou.* The cruise departs at 1 PM daily, and coffee and muffins are served. Along the way, you may catch a glimpse of the sternwheeler graveyard ashore. The *Yukon Queen* also makes day trips from Dawson to Eagle, Alaska.

You also should try your luck at *Diamond Tooth Gertie's Gambling Hall* (Fourth Ave. near Queen St.), named for one of the dance hall queens of '98. This is the only full-time legalized gambling hall in Canada. The stakes may not be as high as before, but people have been known to walk out richer than when they arrived — and also poorer. There's a bar at *Gertie's* and three floor shows each evening featuring colorful cancan dancers and a singer-hostess — Gertie herself! *Gertie's* is open nightly except Sundays from 8 PM to 2 AM, mid-May through mid-September. Admission is about $2.50 at the door.

Another attraction in Dawson is the daily poetry reading by the "ghost" of Robert Service (the Yukon's gold rush bard). The free readings are held on the lawn or inside Service's log cabin (Eighth Ave. near Church St.) at 10 AM and 3 PM, June 1 through September 15.

Many visitors like to test their skill at gold panning. This can be done at Guggieville, at the Bonanza Creek turnoff (phone: 403-993-5008), which also is a campground with showers and hookups, a gift store, and car wash. You also can see George Carmack's original claim and the largest wooden-hulled gold dredge in the world. Transportation to the gold fields is available; contact the Tourist Information Centre (First Ave.) for a schedule.

You may want to plan your trip to coincide with Dawson's *Discovery Days* celebration, held the weekend of the third Monday in August. Raft races, handicrafts displays, and a parade are among the many activities. Dawson also is the site of its own *Labor Day* weekend craziness, with annual *Outhouse Races* in which contestants pull and push brightly colored outhouses (with one person sitting inside) through the city streets.

En Route from Dawson – It's a long drive from Dawson to Beaver Creek, 20 miles (32 km) inside the Yukon border near the southwestern corner of the territory, through a bit of Alaska and along one of the most impressive roads in the world — the Top of the World Highway. You'll climb up, winding your way on mountaintops from which you can gaze at the splendor around and below you. Snow hoods the distant peaks as the wind howls through the grass and mountain flowers bow to its passing. Then you'll descend to the lush valleys below.

Go 67 miles (107 km) west from Dawson to the US-Canadian border, where the crossing is open from 9 AM to 9 PM (Yukon time). There are no services between Dawson and the border, so plan accordingly. The village of Boundary, Alaska, is just 4 miles (6 km) into US territory, and services are available here. From Boundary, it's 112 miles (179 km) south to Tetlin Junction and another 100 miles (160 km) to Beaver Creek, Yukon. The border crossing here is open 24 hours a day.

BEAVER CREEK: This "town" has the distinction of being the most westerly community in all of Canada. With a population of about 100 people, it is a by-product of the Alaska Highway construction. It was created to provide highway services. Three motels with lounges and cafés do an admirable job. A KOA campground is located at the *Westmark Alas Kan Border Lodge* (phone: 403-778-5363), and a government campground with 20 sites (and great fishing) is at Snag Junction, 13 miles (21 km) beyond Beaver Creek.

En Route from Beaver Creek – Burwash Landing is a tiny, predominantly Indian village of about 80 people some 109 miles (174 km) from Beaver Creek. Virtually all the homes and cabins are heated by wood fires, and most look out over Kluane Lake. *Burwash Landing* resort, one of the nicest spots in the Yukon, is hidden on this shore (see *Best en Route*). While in Burwash, explore the *Kluane Museum of Natural History* (Alaska-Canada Highway, Mile 1093, Burwash Landing; phone: 403-841-5561), open from 9 AM to 9 PM from mid-May through mid-September, and handicrafts shop. Visitors should remember that this is home to the native residents and they may not appreciate being examined through the end of a camera lens. A bit of consideration can go a long way. Destruction Bay, another small community created by highway construction, lies 10 miles (16 km) from Burwash. Kluane Lake is 46 miles long, covers 153 square miles, and is filled with trout, grayling, steelfish, and pike. The trout can weigh up to 40 pounds, so be prepared.

After driving only 23 miles (37 km) from Destruction Bay, you'll probably want to stop at Slim's River Bridge. Crossing an ancient glacier moraine at the head of Kluane Lake, the bridge offers amazing views. Sheep Mountain borders the highway near this spot and, with an alert eye, you can often see the proud Dall's sheep on the hillside. There also is a new interpretive center at Sheep Mountain. Remember, Kluane is a national park; walking over spring vegetation could damage the animals' winter supply of food.

Drive another 6 miles (10 km) and take the short side road to the ghost town of Silver City. These old wooden buildings are the remains of a stopover point on the wagon road between Whitehorse and the Kluane gold fields.

The headquarters of Kluane National Park lie 35 miles (56 km) down the highway, only 3 miles (5 km) north of Haines Junction. Make a point of stopping here and finding out details about the hikes, slide shows, and overnight trips park personnel conduct for visitors. Kluane was set aside as a national park in 1972; many of the trails are marked, and maps are available. Experienced climbers who want to attempt the mountains and glaciers must first report to the park warden at headquarters.

KLUANE NATIONAL PARK: Most of the 186-mile (298-km) drive from Beaver Creek to Haines Junction will be within sight of the 8,500-square-mile Kluane National Park. This magnificent area is characterized by soaring snowcapped peaks that rise through the clear blue skies, piercing billowy white clouds as they tease the sun. The world's largest ice fields outside of the polar regions are within the park, and Canada's highest peak, Mt. Logan (19,520 ft.), rises majestically from these fields.

The 8,000-foot mountains that border the highway for 80 miles (128 km) are draped in white spruce, aspen, and balsam poplar until the treeline is reached at about 4,000 feet. Above, colorful Arctic and alpine flowers dot the mountainsides as do stunted species of shrubs. The jagged mountaintops are crowned in wreaths of snow. Check in with park authorities at park headquarters in Haines Junction.

HAINES JUNCTION: This community of about 575, in the shadow of the park, came into being with the construction of the Alaska Highway in 1942. Kluane National Park has a visitors' information center in town featuring an international award-winning audio-visual presentation on the park. Visitors probably will want to stay in one of the town's handful of hotels while you visit the park by day. If you prefer to camp, there is a government campground at Pine Creek, just 3 miles (5 km) east of Haines Junction.

En Route from Haines Junction – From here it's only a 98-mile (157-km) drive to complete the circle back to Whitehorse. Forty-one miles (66 km) from Haines Junction you'll pass through the almost deserted trading post of Champagne. At one time, this post serviced the Dalton Trail, which ran from Pyramid Harbor on the Lynn Canal to the Yukon's interior. Frontiersman Jack Dalton cut the trail, and 2,000 head of beef cattle were successfully driven across it in 1898. From the trading post, it's only 57 miles (91 km) to the lights of Whitehorse.

BEST EN ROUTE

So many travelers are attracted to the Yukon each year, it is necessary to reserve hotel rooms as far in advance as possible. Book your June vacation in January if you want to get first crack at top accommodations. Plan on spending over $50 for two at expensive accommodations, between $40 and $50 for a moderately priced double room, and a minimum of $30 for an inexpensive room. Reservations must be accompanied by a guaranteed deposit, usually the equivalent of one night's stay. Also try the *Yukon Bed and Breakfast Association* (102-302 Steele St., Whitehorse, Yukon; phone: 403-633-4609), which has accommodations in several communities. Private campground charges, based upon facilities, range from $4 to $8.50 per site, per night. Government campground rates are about $4, per site, per night, or about $20 annually, and are given out on a first-come, first-served basis. All prices are quoted in US dollars.

WHITEHORSE

Gold Rush Inn – Behind its chalet-like front are 87 units, with a gift shop, cable TV, a laundromat, lounge, and a dining room. 411 Main St. (phone: 403-668-4500). Expensive.

Westmark Klondike Inn – Here are 98 rooms, a coffee shop, restaurant and lounge, 2 saunas, and a hair salon. 2288 Second Ave. (phone: 403-668-7639). Expensive.

Westmark Whitehorse – This popular spot for businesspeople and tourists has 181 rooms, a café, dining room, lounge, gift shop, barbershop, art gallery, and a travel agency (*Atlas Travel Tours*). 201 Wood St., PO Box 4250 (phone: 403-668-4700). Expensive.

Regina – The lobby of this 53-room establishment is stocked with Yukon memorabilia. Amenities include cable TV and a dining room. 102 Wood St. (phone: 403-667-7801). Moderate.

Downtown Sourdough City RV Park – This campground features 104 fully serviced sites and 42 sites with electricity only, a laundromat, showers, gift shop, and dump. Open from May 1 to October 1. Second Ave. north of Ogilvie, at Second Ave. at Chevron (phone: 403-668-7938). Inexpensive.

MacKenzie's Campground – There are 54 serviced and 20 unserviced sites, free gold panning, a general store, video games, showers, and a laundromat. Open year-round. Km 1476 on the Alaska Highway, 6 miles (10 km) north of downtown Whitehorse (phone: 403-633-2337). Inexpensive.

Pioneer Trailer Park – There are 125 camping spaces; 73 full and 16 partial hookups, and 36 wooded areas; a laundromat, showers, restrooms, store, rec hall, and RV wash. Open May 1 to October 1. Km 1,465 of the Alaska Highway, 5 miles (8 km) south of Whitehorse. (phone: 403-668-5944). Inexpensive.

Robert Service Campground – A popular private campground on the banks of the Yukon River, it has 40 tents-only campsites as well as restrooms, picnic tables, a firepot, and nature trail. Open mid-May through mid-September. On the South Access Road, 1 mile (1.6 km) from downtown. Information: City of Whitehorse, Parks & Recreation Department, 2121 Second Ave. (phone: 403-668-3721). Inexpensive.

Wolf Creek Government Campground – If you don't want to pay for all the amenities, this is a good spot. It has 29 RV/tent sites, 11 tent-only sites, and free wood. Open mid-May to mid-October. 12 miles (19 km) south of Whitehorse on the Alaska Highway (km 1,459). No phone. Inexpensive.

DAWSON

Downtown – Features VIP suites, 60 rooms, Jacuzzi, conference room, and the *Jack London Grill.* Open year-round. PO Box 780, Dawson, Yukon YOB 1GO (phone: 403-993-5346). Expensive.

Eldorado – There are 53 rooms, VIP suites, and the *Bonanza* dining room. Open year-round. PO Box 338; Dawson, Yukon YOB 1GO (phone: 403-993-5451). Expensive.

Westmark Dawson City – A modern motel with 51 rooms, a gift shop, coin laundromat, travel agency and tour office (*Gold City Tours and Travel Limited*). PO Box 420; Dawson, Yukon YOB 1G0 (phone: 403-993-5542, June 1 through mid-September; 403-993-5542, other times). Expensive.

Yukon River Campground – A good government campground across the Yukon River from Dawson with 77 RV/tent sites, 20 for tents only. A ferry service is operated daily during the summer. Sites cost about $4.25 per night. For more information, call Parks and Outdoor Recreation, Government of the Yukon, at 403-667-5261 or 403-667-5648. Inexpensive.

Guggieville – Just about a mile (1.6 km) from downtown at the Bonanza Creek turnoff, this campground has showers and hook-ups along with a gift shop, car wash, and a gold panning operation; sites cost between $7 and $10 a night. PO Box 311, Dawson, Yukon Y0B 1G0 (phone: 403-993-5008). Inexpensive.

BEAVER CREEK

Westmark Inn – This is a good modern facility with 174 rooms, a dining room, gift shop, recreation area, and a lounge. To be safe, reservations should be made before you depart Whitehorse. Open May 15–September 28. Km 1934, Alaska Highway, Beaver Creek, Yukon (phone: 403-862-7501 or 800-544-0970 in the US, 206-281-0576, collect, in Canada). Expensive.

Customs Campground – Here are 69 serviced campsites, showers, laundromat, small store, and dump, with a lounge and restaurant nearby. Open June through mid-October. Write c/o General Delivery, Beaver Creek, Yukon Y0B 1A0 (phone: 403-862-7418). Expensive.

BURWASH LANDING

Burwash Landing – An old lodge on Kluane Lake, it has 34 units, a bar restaurant, wildlife museum, and 14 sites with hook-ups. Staff can arrange glacier flights and fishing and boating trips. Reservations necessary well in advance. Open year-round. Km 1759, Alaska Highway, Yukon Y1A 3V4 (phone: 403-841-4441). Moderate.

Kluane Wilderness Village – This place has 25 log cabins and 6 deluxe motel units, plus 72 campsites and a licensed restaurant. Facilities for the disabled are available. Km 1798 Alaska Highway, Yukon Y1A 3V4(phone: 403-841-4141). Moderate.

HAINES JUNCTION

Kluane Park Inn – Directly across from Kluane National Park, this popular spot, has 20 units with color, satellite TV, a cocktail lounge, and rec room. Reservations should be made prior to departure from Whitehorse. Open year-round. PO Box 5400, Haines Junction, Yukon Y0B 1L0 (phone: 403-634-2261). Moderate.

The Trail of '98

It is estimated that more than 100,000 people stormed the Yukon Territory during the boom years between 1896 and 1900. Perhaps 60,000 sailed up the Lynn Canal, cutting north across what is now the Alaskan panhandle, past Juneau, from the Pacific Ocean to the head of the canal, and docked at either Skagway or Dyea, Alaska. From there they struggled across the St. Elias Mountains of the Coast Mountain Range through the Chilkoot or White Pass to reach the settlement of Bennett, British Columbia, on the south shore of Lake Bennett just below the present Yukon boundary line. The tandem mountain lakes of Lindeman (which feeds north into its sister lake) and Bennett form the headwaters of the Yukon River. Here they built or boarded boats and rafts for the journey downriver, past Whitehorse, all the way to the gold fields at Dawson.

The 32-mile (51-km) Chilkoot Pass was the primary route of the earliest travelers into the region. It had been established by the Chilkat Indian tribe, who held a monopoly on trade between the seacoast and the Stick Indian tribe on the far side of the mountains. The Indians guarded their trade link violently, exacting a heavy toll from those who wished to cross the pass and occasionally killing a disagreeable traveler. A show of arms by a US gunboat convinced the tribe to make other arrangements. Thereafter, prospectors and explorers paid the Indians as guides and packers as a prerequisite for use of the trail; even an 1883 US Army expedition followed this practice.

During the pre-gold rush years, about 1,000 people took this route into the newly opened area, and interest in the unexplored lands began to grow. As more people flocked to the Yukon, the Indians lost control of the pass; soon only those affluent travelers who could afford their assistance paid the Chilkats as packers. Most of the stampeders carried their own goods along the well-worn trail. During the early stages of the rush, Canadian authorities required each stampeder to bring with him a year's supply of food, clothing, and equipment in an effort to stem deaths due to starvation and exposure. A Canadian surveying expedition discovered the White Pass, just a few miles east. Captain William Moore, a 74-year-old retired sea captain who was part of the expedition, felt that a rail line could be laid through this pass into the Yukon Territory; he also was sure that the trail of gold he had traced up from South America would lead to a massive strike in the North.

SKAGWAY AND DYEA: In 1887, Moore erected a cabin and a wharf on a point of land at the mouth of the Skagway River on the eastern side of the head of the Lynn Canal. On the west side of the canal stood the settlement of Dyea, at the mouth of the Taiya River, in a direct line with the Chilkoot Pass. Moore foresaw that with a railroad through White Pass, more facilities would be needed. He fully expected to found the town of Skagway as it grew around his homestead.

When news of the gold strike at Bonanza Creek reached the outside world, the flow of travelers that Moore had expected turned into a flood, forcing him to abandon his plans. The gold-crazed mob tore him from his cabin and took over his wharf. A city of tents and temporary buildings sprang up, obscuring Moore's claim. (His cabin still stands, just off Skagway's main thoroughfare, Broadway Street, behind *Kirme's* jewelry store.) Several years later, Moore took the matter to court and received some compensation for his losses. Eventually, his dream of a railroad through White Pass was realized, but by that time the Chilkoot Pass had become symbolic of the courage, determination, and recklessness of the stampeders.

An attempt to cross the White Pass during the late fall of 1897 was disastrous. Fully 5,000 people embarked on a 41-mile trek that became a continuous frozen hell. Men and horses died under the strain of their loads, and animals who could no longer walk were shot or abandoned as their owners trudged onward. It was a desperate fight for survival, a battle against time and the elements, and often against other men. Some were appalled by the horrors they had seen, others were hardened by the experience, but no one was untouched. Early rains and rocky trails created a morass that seemed to swallow men and horses whole, slowing the pace to a crawl and holding them captive until the winter snows caught them exposed in the mountains. Only a few of the hardiest made it through to the Yukon River before the winter freeze-up. Some returned to Skagway to await the spring thaw; many died on the path named Dead Horse Trail. Bits and pieces of their goods and equipment still line the trail in mute testimony.

Weary, frustrated men returned to Skagway. As tensions grew, the sound of gunfire became commonplace. With no laws to constrain them, mobs ruled the small town of tents and impromptu buildings. By midwinter, Skagway's population hovered around 5,000. Not all of them were bound for the Klondike: Their fortunes lay in providing entertainment for those en route to the gold fields. Saloons as well as gambling and dance halls crowded Skagway's already congested streets. The chaos of those early days was made to order for a particular type of businessman — the con artist.

Soapy Smith was an expert at his trade — the ultimate professional con artist. With a group of felons, thugs, and whores to back him, Soapy set out to dominate the town of Skagway. Card games were rigged, pokes stolen, greenhorns shot in the back, and outright robbery was the prevailing order as Smith penetrated every area of Skagway's vulnerable social fabric. Posing as a civic-minded member of the business community, he convinced the chamber of commerce of the righteousness of his activities, and the false-fronted buildings that lined the streets of Skagway camouflaged his numerous bogus business dealings. In fact, when an avalanche killed about 60 people on the Chilkoot, Smith, appointed coroner for the occasion, set up a tent into which the victims were brought for identification — and stripped of all valuables.

By February 1898, the people around Skagway decided that Soapy Smith had gotten out of hand and requested that US troops take charge of the town. Legend has it that in July of that year, Soapy robbed a prospector of over $2,000 in gold dust. The man refused to accept this as a matter of course, and word spread among the community that if the money wasn't returned, other prospectors would avoid the town. Faced with a loss of income, the citizens formed a vigilante committee to force Smith to return the money. Smith refused and, after getting drunk (remember, this is a legend), went out to face the mob. It seems that Smith had already fought with Frank Reid earlier that day and had challenged Reid to return "with a gun." The first man Smith encountered that night was Reid. Shots were fired and both men fell. Reid was taken to a doctor and lasted 2 weeks before dying; Soapy Smith was left dying in the street. Rumors persist that Reid couldn't have fired the fatal shot, but no one ever took credit for the deed. The two men lie buried, side by side, in the Gold Rush Cemetery. Soapy's former mistress was the only mourner at his funeral; the gang members had been rounded up and shipped out of town. Reid's funeral was the largest in Skagway's history.

Although Dyea was certainly not a quiet or conservative community, it never sank to the depths of squalor and degeneracy that permeated Skagway. Since the Chilkoot Pass was always open, the flow of traffic was steady. Prior to the summer of 1897, Dyea consisted of a trading post and village of about 125 Indian guides and packers. By the spring of '98, there were 4,000 people, several hotels, and even a newspaper. Shortly after the railroad construction began, the town started to evaporate, until only one resident remained in 1906.

En Route from Skagway – The most natural way to explore the Yukon is just to follow the route taken by the first travelers into the region: Sail up the Lynn Canal to Skagway, hike the Chilkoot Pass to Bennett, BC, then raft down the Yukon to Dawson. It's possible to cruise into Skagway aboard the *Alaska Marine Highway System* from Seattle. Ferries carry passengers and vehicles. Many travelers enjoy cruising one way and driving back the other (Pouch R, Juneau, AK 99811; phone: 907-465-3941).

The Skagway-Carcross road makes it possible to drive down from Whitehorse during the summer months, and airports in both Skagway and Whitehorse make travel into the Yukon easier than any trailhand ever expected. Unfortunately, the *White Pass and Yukon Railway,* completed in 1900 just after the gold rush, has closed down. It was a fascinating means of transportation here since the tracks follow closely the route of those stampeders who fought their way from Skagway to Bennett in the fall of 1897, then parallel the watercourse as far north as

Whitehorse. Now you can hike the Chilkoot as far as Bennett and then boat down the Yukon River to Whitehorse or Dawson, instead of taking the train. (Some bus service also is available at the trailhead in Dyea and near the trail's end; check schedules and pick-up points before starting out.)

CHILKOOT PASS: The most dramatic event in the history of the gold rush was the assault by thousands of stampeders upon the 3,739-foot summit of the Chilkoot Pass during the winter of 1897-98. Bent under the weight of their packs, sweat freezing upon their brows, these men trudged up a 40° slope for more than 6 hours while temperatures fell to −60F (−51C) to find themselves a mere 1,000 feet from where they had begun. Only a fanatical devotion to the gold they believed lay beyond enabled them to persevere. Finally reaching the summit and depositing their goods, often losing them in the 70 feet of snow that fell that winter, the weary men slid back down to strap on another pack and make the climb again. For the average stampeder, who could pack only 50 pounds at a time, it took 30 trips to bring his required ton of supplies to the peak.

During that winter, 1,500 steps were hacked out of the ice and snow by a few industrious stampeders. A rope, for balance, was strung beside these Golden Stairs that rose to the summit, providing some small assistance to the climbers. For the 22,000 people who crossed the Chilkoot Pass that winter, the experience invariably overshadowed all other memories of their gold rush days. Other trails lay ahead, but having conquered the pass, no longer were they *cheechakos* (naive newcomers to the North).

Necessity being the mother of invention, the first tramway was constructed from the base of the summit to the top in December 1897. Five such tramways were in operation by the spring of '98. The most effective one transported goods from Canyon City, 8 miles north of Dyea, to the summit, a distance of about 8 miles, at a rate of 9 tons per hour. But as was the case with the Indian carriers, not all the stampeders could afford the tramways. They trudged along while goods whisked by overhead. It took the average stampeder 3 months to lug his supplies 32 miles across the pass from Dyea to Lake Bennett.

Most hikers traveling the Chilkoot Pass now allow 4 days for the trip from Dyea to Bennett. The trail is well marked and patrolled daily by park rangers. They are stationed at Sheep Camp (Mile 13) on the American side and at Lindeman (Mile 25.5) on the Canadian side. Cabins at three points along the trail are open to hikers, but don't bet on finding a vacancy. Plan to sleep under canvas. While the trail is not too difficult, remember that it is not a Sunday stroll through the park. Don't even attempt it unless you're in good physical condition. Take the bus instead.

In addition to maps and information available from the Yukon Territory Department of Tourism and the Skagway, Alaska, Visitor Information Bureau on the pass, Archie Satterfield's *Chilkoot Pass* (Alaska Northwest Publishing Co., PO Box 4-EEE, Anchorage, AK 99509, 1973) is an excellent and entertaining guide. You'll find it a welcome traveling companion.

Your hike up the Chilkoot actually begins near Dyea, 8½ miles (14 km) west of Skagway. If you don't feel like walking to the starting point, it's possible to take a taxi from Skagway right to the trailhead at the south end of the Taiya River Bridge. A row of old pilings and a few rotten timbers about a mile away mark the old Dyea townsite. The nearby Slide Cemetery contains the graves of about 60 people killed in the Palm Sunday Avalanche of April 3, 1898. These stampeders were trapped under 30 feet of snow, and many of the bodies weren't recovered until months later.

The trek commences as you depart Dyea. Except for the initial one-quarter mile, which is very steep, the first 7 miles (11 km) are fairly easy, through level then gently rising and falling terrain. The trail cuts through thick timber, opening at times to enable you to peer out at the 5,000-foot (and higher) St. Elias and Coastal Mountain ranges ahead.

As you continue, the trail drops to the bank of the Taiya River. Across its banks can be seen the magnificent blue-green glaciers whose icy streams tumble noisily into the Taiya. Eventually the path rises over a trail of boulders and scrambles down to cross an old moss-and lichen-covered glacial moraine. Stunted conifer trees and wild flowers decorate the area. The Canyon City shelter, at Mile 7.75, will startle you with its sudden appearance. The one-room cabin has a wood-burning stove, a table, and benches. Forget about using the stove, and unless there's a storm brewing, you'll probably be more comfortable outside the cabin than in. A stream flows past the shelter, invigorated by a series of small waterfalls a short distance upriver. Many campers break at the Canyon City shelter area, so you may wish to go a little farther to secure some privacy.

About a half-mile up the trail, an old suspension bridge across the Taiya River leads to the original Canyon City site. At one time there were hotels, saloons, and stores here. Now it is rotting wood and rusting equipment. An old steam boiler, some rusty cooking utensils, half-rotten cabins, and a garbage dump are all that remain of the boom town.

Traveling north, the trail runs through some mildly hilly ground, as it crosses several streams that feed into the Taiya River. A handrail has been installed along the one steep climb about a mile beyond the bridge. Camp Pleasant, at Mile 10, is a beautiful place. Since the Sheep Camp Shelter is only 3 miles farther, not as many people stop here as at either Canyon City or Sheep Camp.

In its heyday, Sheep Camp had a population of about 1,500. It was then, and remains today, the last suitable place to camp before assaulting the summit. Park rangers stationed here enforce this dictum. A cabin, similar to the one at Canyon City, is open to hikers, and there are several campsites in the vicinity. The remains of Sheep Camp, in poor condition, are on the opposite bank of the Taiya, which can be crossed easily at this point since it is a small stream here. These slopes are the origin of the river.

In addition to the wagon wheels and other parts of their lives that the stampeders abandoned along this trail, glaciers and waterfalls abound. It's a rare moment when some antique object or glimpse of beauty doesn't catch your eye. Because of the altitude, snowstorms can occur at any time, even in the middle of summer, and winter snow often remains through June. Use extreme care in crossing any unbroken area of snow; you can't tell what's underneath.

The upward climb starts here, and the trail rises about 1,000 feet in the next 2 miles. You break through the treeline at about 1,900 feet, a mile outside of camp, so it's loose rock from here on up. Markers are placed daily along the safest path by rangers, but if they're down for any reason, just keep heading up. Ruins of a tramway tripod and an old building are on a flat bit of land near Mile 15.5. A short way from here, beyond an undulating progression of rocky ridges, is a deep depression. Cupped within its half-moon shape, formed by mountains on three sides, are the remains of cabins, machine parts, tools, equipment, and even bits of clothing. Here packs were retied, goods to be hauled by tram were weighed, and stampeders tightened their belts for the final ascent. This point, at Mile 16, is known as the Scales.

The half-mile from the Scales to the summit is virtually straight up, roughly 1,000 feet, to the notch in the peak that marks the Chilkoot Pass. The mountaintops resemble mounds of boulders and rocks piled higher and higher atop each other to form this barrier. Here, looking up at the crests, the Chilkoot lies between two such mounds, a shallow break in the ridgetop. As you climb toward the top, Chilkoot bears off slightly to the left. A second trail, which tends to be unsafe, leads to the right until it crosses the peak, then cuts back to the left. Avoid this route since the rocks may break loose. People can get hurt here. It can happen on the Chilkoot, too, but this trail is more dangerous. Climbers should allow extra space between each other while going through this area, since even small rocks can injure climbers too close below to avoid them. Also, remember to keep an eye on the hiker ahead of you at all times; unless you're the lead person, never turn your back on the slope. If you're in doubt about which trail to take, look for tramway cables on the ground — that's the Chilkoot.

When you reach the top, turn around for a spectacular view of the trail back to Alaska that you've just hiked. You'll have a satisfying sense of accomplishment as you gaze at these peaks. They are invariably covered with a coating of snow, which enhances their beauty. Then face north again and gaze off into Canada. If you're fortunate enough to make the crossing on a clear day, you'll be greeted by the sight of soaring mountains, immense glaciers, and unbelievably blue lakes.

The snow that blankets the peaks extends almost a mile down the reverse slope, right to the shores of Crater Lake at Mile 17.5. The lake is a volcanic crater, filled with icy glacial waters that tumble into the basin from the surrounding slopes. The lake was a major staging area for the stampeders; they hauled load after load of supplies to the crest of the pass, then brought the loads down to these shores, where they were ferried across the lake, then loaded again for the hike to Long Lake, about 4 miles away. Many stampeders set up camp here, and relics are lying about in several places. The trail from Crater Lake to Long Lake winds its way through mountain flowers, heather, and colorful varieties of moss and lichen. You'll pass another waterfall near the entrance to a canyon that opens on Long Lake. The waterfall, formed by Coltsfoot Creek, waters the first trees you see since breaking the treeline on the American side of the pass. This area, at Mile 21.5, is called Happy Camp. From here down to the lake is a rocky trail, but the land near Long Lake is a masterwork of natural gardening. The trail gently crosses back and forth to and from the bank of the lake, winding among a number of tarns and waterholes carved into the ground by glaciers and filled with freshly melted snow. Alpine firs and hemlocks, their growth stunted by the harsh weather, turn the wild expanse into a vast garden of Japanese miniatures.

A stream on the far shore drains the mountain waters of Long Lake into Deep Lake at Mile 23. Atop the cliffs overlooking Deep Lake are several beautiful campsites. More than one waterfall tumbles over the edge into the lake below. There are many islands in Deep Lake, and the north end, which feeds into Lake Lindeman, is a hazardous stretch of rapids. As the trail parallels the flow of water toward Lindeman, you cross back through the timberline into a well-forested area.

The trail emerges from the forest at the head of Lake Lindeman, at Mile 25.5. The Canadian ranger station and a cabin for hikers are both located here. The lake makes a good resting spot if you have the time; the stampeders who arrived too late to float down the river that winter set up a city here. The remains of several buildings can easily be seen, and there are rusty tools and pieces of equipment everywhere. A second cabin is located at Mile 26, along the side of the lake. The Chilkoot Trail ends at the head of Lake Bennett, at Mile 32.

BENNETT: Since the stream that connects Lindeman and Bennett lakes is large enough to be navigated and rocky enough to be dangerous, many of the stampeders built boats at Lindeman during the winter and tried to sail down to Lake Bennett after breakup. Some of them made it; others wrecked on the rocks. A larger camp was established at Bennett, and following breakup on May 29, 1898, over 7,000 small boats left for the gold fields at Dawson. Within a matter of days the camp was vacated.

    En Route from Bennett – If you really want to duplicate the Trail of '98 experience, you'll have to build a boat before continuing. It's more feasible, however, to arrange canoe rentals for the remainder of the journey. If you're an experienced canoeist, you already realize the importance of having the correct gear and accurate maps; if not, don't try it without a guide.

    The Carcross-Skagway road will provide car and bus access to Bennett.

    Be sure to make time to stop off in Carcross, at the north end of Lake Bennett.

CARCROSS: This quiet community of less than 350 lies in a mountain-rimmed valley with a sandy shore opening on the lake. Just 26 miles (42 km) from Bennett, it's not a difficult day's work if you're canoeing.

If you're staying in Whitehorse and choose not to take the Trail of '98, it's also easily reached by car via Route 2, a distance of about 45 miles (72 km). Driving south, on your left you'll pass the Carcross desert, reputed to be the smallest desert in the world. Emerald Lake, named for its shimmering green waters, also is along this roadway.

Prior to the gold rush, Carcross was known as Caribou Crossing; when the migrating herds of caribou came here to cross the narrows between Lake Bennett and Nares Lake, the Tagish Indians would camp in the area to hunt. It was here, in 1900, that the two sections of the railroad, one coming south from Whitehorse and the other north from Skagway, were linked with the traditional golden spike.

Stop at the Carcross Visitor Centre, (Klondike Highway, Km. 108; phone: 403-821-4591) where you can hear the history of the S.S. *Tutshi,* a 1917 sternwheeler that until 1955 plied the headwaters of the Yukon River. The boat, now docked beside the center, has been restored and is open to the public May 15 through September 20 (phone: 403-821-4431). Nearby sits the Duchess, an old *White Pass and Yukon Railway* engine, and next to her, a mail wagon from the early 1900s.

Another enjoyable diversion is the lively lunchtime show at the *Riverboat Warehouse Luncheon Theatre* (PO Box 144, Carcross, Yukon Y0B 1B0; phone: 403-821-4591). The site is a riverside warehouse that was once important to the British Yukon Navigation Company. Shows start at 11:30 AM daily, mid-May to mid-September (phone: 403-821-4591).

Watson's general store (Main St.; phone: 403-821-3501), built by Matthew Watson in 1911, also is an intriguing place. It is still heated by a wood-burning Yukon barrel stove, as is the *Caribou* hotel's tavern. Main St. (phone: 403-821-4501).

After stopping in Carcross, continue the journey to Whitehorse, or steer your canoe down the Yukon River to Whitehorse or all the way to Dawson.

YUKON RIVER: It's 500 miles (800 km) to the gold fields at Dawson, and there's no better way to tour the Yukon Territory than riding on the river that gives this wild land its name. The rapids, once greatly feared by the Klondikers, have been tamed by the construction of a power dam necessitating the only portage on the entire route.

Once past Whitehorse and Miles Canyon, you'll be hard pressed to find an experience comparable to the serenity that envelops you as your canoe floats lazily through the heart of this vast land. Perhaps you'll spot a cabin or two along the riverbank, but more likely the only signs of life you'll encounter will be an occasional moose or bear taking a swim or standing on the bank drinking the cool water. Set up camp on a deserted bank and watch as the summer days stretch into the night. If you stay awake long enough, you can detect subtle hues of pink permeating the night sky as the sun rolls over in its sleep at 1 or 2 in the morning. Eventually you'll turn a bend in the river and there, on the right bank, stands the tarnished ghost of Dawson, the city of gold.

BEST EN ROUTE

Again, so many travelers are attracted to the Yukon each year that it is necessary to make hotel reservations as far in advance as possible. Book your June vacation in January if you want to get first crack at the top accommodations. Plan on spending between $50 and $60 for a moderately priced room for two, a minimum of $40 for an inexpensive room, and more than $70 for expensive accommodations. Reservations must be accompanied by a guaranteed deposit, usually the equivalent of 1 night's stay. Charges at privately owned campgrounds range between about $6.50 and $10 per day, per site, depending upon facilities. Government-operated camping areas charge $4 per night, or $20 for an annual pass. Goverment campground sites are given out on a first-come, first-served basis. Since this is an outdoor route, you'll be sleeping under canvas or in cabins operated by your outfitter-guide. Detailed maps of the Yukon watercourse are available from the Alaska Northwest Publishing Company (PO Box

4-EEE, Anchorage, AK 99509). Even if you don't make the trip, the catalogue is worth reading. All prices are quoted in US dollars.

For information on Whitehorse and Dawson, see the relevant parts of *The Dawson Circle Route.*

SKAGWAY, ALASKA

Golden North – All of the 34 rooms in this lovely place are furnished with period antiques, each room dedicated to an 1890s character. There's an 1898 bar, a beauty shop, restaurant, and sightseeing services. PO Box 343 (phone: 907-983-2451). Moderate.

Sgt. Preston's – Bordering on Skagway's historic district, each of its 23 rooms has street-level access and cable TV. Sixth St. between Broadway and State. PO Box 473-AT (phone: 907-983-2521). Moderate.

Skagway Bed & Breakfast Inn – An intriguing and friendly guesthouse, the atmosphere here is totally 1898. In fact, the core of the building dates back to the gold rush, when this warm and respectable inn was, of all things, a home operated by "ladies of the night." With only 12 rooms it is small, but very popular. *Miss Emily's Tea Room,* for breakfast. PO Box 500 (phone: 907-983-2289). Moderate.

Irene's Inn – The 10 rooms in this gold-rush-era building have been remodeled. Some rooms share a bath. Sixth and Broadway. PO Box 5385-AT (phone: 907-983-2520). Moderate to inexpensive.

INDEX

Index